TUDOR ON
CHARITIES

AUSTRALIA
Law Book Co.—Sydney

CANADA and **USA**
Carswell—Toronto

HONG KONG
Sweet & Maxwell Asia

NEW ZEALAND
Brookers—Wellington

SINGAPORE and **MALAYSIA**
Sweet & Maxwell Asia
Singapore and Kuala Lumpur

TRUSTS, WILLS AND PROBATE LIBRARY

TUDOR ON
CHARITIES

NINTH EDITION

by

JEAN WARBURTON
LL.B., Solicitor,
Professor of Law,
University of Liverpool

assisted by

DEBRA MORRIS
LL.M.,
Lecturer in Law,
Cayman Islands Law School

N.F. RIDDLE
M.A. Cantab, Barrister

LONDON
SWEET & MAXWELL
2003

Published in 2003 by
Sweet & Maxwell Limited of
100 Avenue Road, London NW3 3PF,
http://www.sweetandmaxwell.co.uk
Typeset by J. & L. Composition, Filey, Yorks
Printed and bound in Great Britain by MPG Books Ltd,
Bodmin, Cornwall

No natural forests were destroyed to make this product:
only farmed timber was used and replanted

A CIP catalogue record for this book is available from the
British Library

ISBN 0 421 77450 9

ISBN 0-421-77450-9

9 780421 774506

PREFACE

There has been much activity in the field of charity law both in this country and abroad in the eight years since the last edition of Tudor. English courts have considered, amongst other matters, various aspects of charitable status and the extent to which the courts should interfere in the administration of charities. From abroad, New Zealand courts have provided guidance on *cy-près* and, together with Canadian courts, influenced the development of the definition of charity. Legislation having a major effect on charities has included the Trustee Act 2000, updating and enhancing the powers of charity trustees, and the Finance Act 2000 which increased and simplified tax reliefs for donors. As with every other area of law, charity law must now be interpreted in a way which is compatible with Convention rights. The result is that there are few areas of the text that have been free from amendment.

The last eight years have also seen a significant increase in the published contributions of the Charity Commissioners to the development of charity law and its administration. Important decisions on charitable status taken by the Commissioners now appear on the Charity Commissioners' website together with Review of the Register documents considering particular elements of charitable status and Operational Guidance setting out the internal procedures of the Commissioners. Charity Commissioners publications, including Operational Guidance, are referred to throughout the text where they assist in the interpretation of the present law or indicate possible future development.

Two recent government reports, the Cabinet Office, Strategy Unit report, *Private Action, Public Benefit. A Review of Charities and the Wider Not-For-Profit Sector* and H.M. Treasury Cross-Cutting Review, *The Role of the Voluntary Sector in Service Delivery*, have highlighted the increasingly important role of charities in society. One consequence of this has been the move of charity law out of the wings and into the limelight on the legal stage. Reform is in the air but legislation has yet to emerge. In the text, I have endeavoured to indicate where change might occur and to consider the potential effects of changes proposed in the Strategy Unit report and possible further effects of the Human Rights Act 1998.

This edition has benefited from contributions from the two assistant editors. Nick Riddle kindly undertook responsibility for Chapter 10 which has in large part been rewritten to take account of changes both in law and practice. I am also indebted to him for his helpful comments on other parts of the text. Debra Morris updated the chapter on fundraising. My thanks are also due to the past and present research assistants in the Charity Law Unit, Louise Platt and Karen Atkinson. I am grateful for the help I have received from the staff of the Charity Commissioners not only for challenging my views on charity law whilst I was a Commissioner but also then and subsequently for assistance on points of detail. Finally my thanks are due to the Publishers for their assistance in the preparation of this edition and for compiling the tables of statutes and cases and the index.

Jean Warburton
Charity Law Unit
Liverpool Law School
May 2003

CONTENTS

TABLE OF CASES

(References are to paragraph numbers)

TABLE OF STATUTES

(References are to paragraph numbers. The references in bold type are to paragraph numbers in the Appendix where the legislation is set out in full)

TABLE OF STATUTORY INSTRUMENTS

(References are to paragraph numbers. The references in heavy type are to paragraph numbers in the Appendix where the legislation is set out in full)

TABLE OF TREATIES AND CONVENTIONS

(References are to paragraph numbers)

TABLE OF CHURCH ASSEMBLY MEASURES

(References are to paragraph numbers)

CHAPTER 1

CHARITY AND CHARITABLE PURPOSES

THE MEANING OF "CHARITY" AND "CHARITABLE PURPOSES" IN THE LAW OF ENGLAND AND WALES

Introduction

Sir William Grant M.R., said of the word "charity" that in its widest **1–001** sense it denotes "all the good affections that men ought to bear towards each other; in its most restricted and common sense it denotes relief of the poor."[1] Lord Macnaghten said of "charity", "of all words in the English language bearing a popular as well as a legal signification I am not sure that there is one which more unmistakably has a technical meaning in the strictest sense of the term, that is a meaning clear and distinct, peculiar to the law as understood and administered in this country, and not depending upon or coterminous with the popular or vulgar use of the word."[2] It is a word which is "wide, elastic".[3] It "has a much wider meaning in law than it has in popular speech".[4]

For the purposes of the Charities Act 1993, "charity" means "any institution, corporate or not, which is established for charitable purposes and is subject to the control of the High Court[5] in the exercise of the court's jurisdiction[6] with respect to charities"[7]; "institution" includes any trust or undertaking, and "charitable purposes" means "purposes which are exclusively charitable according to the law of England and Wales.[8] To qualify for registration under s.3 of the Act[9] an institution must be a charity

---

[1] *Morice v Bishop of Durham* (1805) 9 Ves. 399 at 405: 10 Ves. 522.
[2] *Income Tax Special Purposes Commissioners v Pemsel* [1891] A.C. 531 at 581, 582.
[3] *Re Cranston* [1898] 1 I.R. 431 at 442, *per* Lord Ashbourne C.
[4] *Re Wedgwood* [1915] 1 Ch. 113 at 117, *per* Lord Cozens-Hardy, M.R.; and see *Incorporated Council of Law Reporting for England and Wales v Att-Gen* [1972] Ch. 73 at 90, *per* Sachs, L.J.
[5] *i.e.* not an institution established under the laws of another legal system, *Gaudiya Mission v Brahmachary* [1997] 4 All E.R. 957.
[6] The exercise of the court's jurisdiction does not necessarily require presence of the trustees within the jurisdiction, see *Re Carapiet's Trust* [2002] EWHC 1304, para.35, *per* Jacobs J.
[7] s.96(1). But not an ecclesiastical corporation, a Diocesan Board of Finance or any trust of property for purposes for which the property has been consecrated; s.96(2). *Construction Industry Training Board v Att-Gen* [1973] Ch. 173. In *Ashfield Municipal Corp. v Joyce* [1978] A.C. 122 it was held by the Privy Council that in the United Kingdom there was a strong presumption that the words "charity" and "charitable" appearing in a statute bore their technical legal meaning. See also (1993) 2 C.L.P.R. 149 (Hyams).
[8] s.97.
[9] See paras 1–027, *et seq.*, below.

within that meaning[10]; but at no time has there been a statutory definition
of those purposes which are charitable, save for the very limited definition
in s.1 of the Recreational Charities Act 1958.[11]

There have been various proposals over the years both in this country
and other common law jurisdictions for a new definition of charity. The
main proposals are considered below.[12] There has been a steady move in
favour of a statutory definition of charity and the present proposals from
the Strategy Unit[13] appear to manage to combine certainty with sufficient
flexibility for the definition of charity to continue to develop.

Essential elements of charitable status

1–002   Although there is no one definition of charity, it is generally accepted
that before any institution can be accepted as charitable three conditions
must be satisfied. First, the purposes of the institution must have charitable
character, that is, they must be within the spirit and intendment of the preamble to the Charitable Uses Act 1601. Secondly, the institution must exist
for the benefit of the public and, thirdly, it must be exclusively charitable.

Charitable character

1–003   Having regard to the history of the development of the law of charity
in England, it is perhaps not surprising that it was not deemed practicable
to delimit within the bounds of statute those purposes which are charitable. Historically the King as *parens patriae* took under his special care
charitable trusts as he took also infants and lunatics.[14] The jurisdiction of
the Court of Chancery and of its successor, the High Court of Justice, in
respect of charities and charitable trusts is a separate head of equity,[15] and
charity law is founded less upon statute than upon the principles evolved
by those courts and embodied in case law. It has, however, long been the
practice of the courts to look for guidance as to what purposes are
charitable to the preamble to the Charitable Uses Act 1601 (commonly
referred to as "the Statute of Elizabeth I"),[16] which lists as charitable:

---

[10] *Incorporated Council of Law Reporting for England and Wales v Att-Gen* [1972] Ch. 73 at
89, *per* Sachs L.J.
[11] See paras 2–098, *et seq.*, below.
[12] See para.1–014 below.
[13] Cabinet Office, Strategy Unit, *Private Action, Public Benefit. A Review of Charities and the
Wider Not-For-Profit Sector* (2002).
[14] For general historical surveys, see G.W. Keeton and L.A. Sheridan, *The Modern Law of
Charities* (4th ed.), Chap.1; M. Chesterman, *Charities, Trusts and Social Welfare*,
pp.11–108. For detailed surveys of particular periods, see G.H. Jones, *History of Charity
Law 1530–1827*; W.K. Jordan, *Philanthropy in England 1480–1660*; and see also by W.K.
Jordan, *The Charities of London 1480–1660* and *The Charities of Rural England
1480–1660*.
[15] *Income Tax Special Purposes Commissioners v Pemsel* [1891] A.C. 531 at 580, *per* Lord
Macnaghten; *National Anti-Vivisection Society v IRC* [1948] A.C. 31 at 68, *per* Lord
Simonds.
[16] See generally on the Statute, G.H. Jones, *op. cit.* pp.22–52; [1967] C.L.J. 224 (for Francis
Moore's Reading on the Statute of Charitable Uses); W.K. Jordan, *Philanthropy in England
1480–1660*, pp.112–115; G.W. Keeton and L.A. Sheridan, *op. cit.* pp.1–11.

"The relief of aged, impotent, and poor people; the maintenance of sick and maimed soldiers and mariners, schools of learning, free schools and scholars of universities; the repair of bridges, havens, causeways, churches, sea banks and highways; the education and preferment of orphans; the relief, stock or maintenance of houses of correction; marriages of poor maids; supportation, aid and help of young tradesmen, handicraftsmen and persons decayed; the relief or redemption of prisoners or captives and the aid or ease of any poor inhabitants concerning payments of fifteens, setting out of soldiers, and other taxes."[17]

The Statute of Elizabeth I was a reforming statute, itself long since repealed, directed not so much to the definition of charity as to the correction of abuses which had grown up in the administration of trusts of a charitable nature, and the preamble, preserved by s.13(2) of the Mortmain and Charitable Uses Act 1888, contained simply a catalogue of purposes which were, as long ago as 1601, considered to be charitable. Nevertheless, the preamble has had a limiting effect because the judges have not felt it open to them to hold purposes charitable unless they could fairly be said to be within the spirit and intendment of the preamble.[18] How limiting has depended on the circumstances in which the courts have been called upon to determine if a particular purpose was charitable. A desire to use the Mortmain and Charitable Uses Act 1736 to avoid devises of land to charity and restore the land to the heir lead to a number of cases adopting a generous interpretation of what amounted to a charitable purpose.[19] More recently, Lord Cross stated[20] that he considered judicial decisions as to charitable status were influenced by the automatic enjoyment of fiscal privileges by charities and subsequent cost to the taxpayer.

S.38 of the Charities Act 1960, repealed the law of mortmain: the Act **1–004** of 1888, and hence the provision therein which preserved the preamble to the Statute of Elizabeth I, was expressly repealed by s.39(1) and Sch.7, Pt II. On the other hand, s.38(4) provided that any reference in any enactment or document to a charity within the meaning, purview or interpretation of the Statute of Elizabeth I or the preamble to it shall be construed as a reference to a charity within the meaning which the word bears as a legal term according to the law of England and Wales. That is a clear reference to the developing body of case law built upon the foundation of

---

[17] The wording of the preamble resembles a passage in *The Vision of Piers Plowman* where rich merchants are counselled by Truth to use their fortunes for similar objects. For consideration of this resemblance, see W.K. Jordan, *op. cit.* p.112.

[18] See, *e.g. Morice v Bishop of Durham* (1804) 9 Ves. 399 at 405, *per* Sir William Grant, M.R.; *Williams' Trustees v IRC* [1947] A.C. 447 at 455, *per* Lord Simonds.

[19] See *Thornton v Howe* (1862) 31 Beav. 14; *Trustees of the British Museum v White* (1826) 2 Sim & St. 594; *Tatham v Drummond* (1864) 4 De G.F. & Sim 484. See also G.H. Jones, *History of the Law of Charity 1530–1827*, Chap. 9.

[20] See *Dingle v Turner* [1972] A.C. 601, 624–625. Lord Cross' fellow Law Lords specifically dissented from the view.

the preamble.[21] It follows that the Charities Act 1960 did nothing which changes the substantive law of charity.[22]

The preamble is still undoubtedly the accepted test, though only in a very wide and broad sense, whether a particular purpose is charitable.[23] From an early stage the purposes listed in the preamble were regarded merely as examples, and have through the centuries been regarded as examples[24] or guideposts for the courts in the differing circumstances of a developing civilisation and economy.[25]

Thus in *Scottish Burial Reform and Cremation Society v Glasgow Corporation*[26] Lord Wilberforce said[27]:

> "[I]t is now accepted that what must be regarded is not the wording of the preamble itself, but the effect of decisions given by the courts as to its scope, decisions which have endeavoured to keep the law as to charities moving according as new social needs arise or old ones become obsolete or satisfied."

1–005   What is regarded as charitable develops and changes as the needs of society change. As Lord Simonds pointed out in *National Anti-Vivisection Society v IRC*[28] a "purpose regarded in one age as charitable may in another be regarded differently". Thus charities for the advancement of education now cover physical as well as mental education[29] and a wide variety of purposes, for example, promotion of urban and rural regeneration[30] and the promotion of recycling,[31] have been recognised under the fourth head of charity. New legislation may indicate a change in society's views and lead to the acceptance of a purpose as charitable, for example, the promotion of human rights following the Human Rights Act 1998.[32] The fact that an earlier decision has determined that a particular purpose is not charitable is not a bar to the purpose becoming charitable later if there has been sufficient change in social and economic circumstances such that the purpose on the tests applied now is charitable.[33]

---

[21] In the repealed Charitable Trusts Act 1853, s.66, and the Charitable Trusts Amendment Act 1855, s.48, as amended by s.13(2) of the Mortmain and Charitable Uses Act 1888, "charity" meant every endowed foundation and institution taking or to take effect in England and Wales and coming within the meaning, purview, and interpretation of the Statute of Elizabeth I.

[22] The abolition of mortmain did, of course, change substantive law in that land devised for charitable uses no longer had to be sold.

[23] *Scottish Burial Reform and Cremation Society Ltd. v Glasgow Corporation* [1968] A.C. 138 at 151, *per* Lord Upjohn.

[24] Lord Macnaghten in *Income Tax Special Purposes Commissioners v Pemsel* [1891] A.C. 531 at 581, said that it had become the practice of the court to refer to the preamble as a sort of index or chart.

[25] *Incorporated Council of Law Reporting for England and Wales v Att-Gen* [1972] Ch. 73 at 87, *per* Russell L.J.

[26] [1968] A.C. 138.

[27] *ibid.*, 154.

[28] [1948] A.C. 31 at 74.

[29] See *IRC v McMullen* [1981] A.C. 1, and see para.(43) below.

[30] See para.2–076 below.

[31] See para.2–082 below.

[32] See para.2–106 below.

[33] See *National Anti-Vivisection Society v IRC* [1948] A.C. 31 at 74, *per* Lord Simonds; [2001] Ch. Com. Dec. April 2 (Decision that the General Medical Council charitable as circumstances changed sufficiently since *General Medical Council v IRC* [1928] All E.R. 252.)

It is clear that not every object beneficial to the community is necessarily charitable.[34] The question remains, therefore, as to the basis on which the courts use the preamble to determine whether a particular purpose is charitable. Within an overall broad approach to the preamble, three different routes to determining charitable status can be seen. The first assumes a new purpose beneficial to the community to be charitable unless reasons can be found to deny charitable status. This approach comes from the judgment of Russell L.J. in *Incorporated Council of Law Reporting for England and Wales v Att-Gen*[35] where he said:

> "In a case such as the present, in which in my view the object cannot be thought otherwise than beneficial to the community and of general public utility, I believe the proper question to ask is whether there are any grounds for holding it to be outside the equity of the Statute: and I think the answer to that is in the negative."

This approach has not been followed in subsequent cases, although Lord Browne-Wilkinson considered, obiter, in *Att-Gen of the Cayman Islands v Wahr-Hansen*[36] that the approach had much to commend it. It gives credence to the view that the broader and more liberal of the two following approaches should be taken.

The other two approaches require a new purpose to be analogous with purposes set out in the preamble or analogous to charitable purposes as decided by the courts but differ as to how specific the analogy must be. The narrower approach was set out by Dillon J. in *Barralet v Att-Gen*[37] when he said:

> "Therefore it seems to me that the approach to be adopted in considering whether something is within the fourth category is the approach of analogy from what is stated in the preamble to the Statute of Elizabeth or from what has already been held to be charitable within the fourth category."

The wider approach does not require a specific analogy but does require   **1–006**
a broader analogy with the kinds of purposes already accepted as charitable. Thus in *Re Strakosch*[38] Lord Greene M.R. said that the benefit which the court has to find does not, however, have to be in every way *ejusdem generis* with any of the purposes recited in the preamble, but only charitable in the same sense. Similarly, in *Incorporated Council of Law Reporting for England and Wales v Att-Gen* Sachs L.J. said[39]:

---

[34] *Re Macduff* [1896] 2 Ch. 451 at 466, *per* Lindley L.J.; *Att-Gen v National Provincial and Union Bank of England* [1924] A.C. 262 at 265, *per* Lord Cave L.C.; *Williams Trustees v IRC* [1947] A.C. 447 at 452, *per* Lord Simonds: and see *Dunne v Byrne* [1912] A.C. 407 at 411, *per* Lord Macnaghten; *Houston v Burns* [1918] A.C. 337, *Farley v Westminster Bank Ltd* [1939] A.C. 430; *Gilmour v Coates* [1949] A.C. 426 at 442, 443, *per* Lord Simonds.

[35] [1972] Ch. 73 at 88.

[36] [2000] 3 All E.R. 642 at 647; *cf. Brisbane City Council v Att-Gen for Queensland* [1979] A.C. 411 at 422, *per* Lord Wilberforce.

[37] [1980] 3 All E.R. 918 at 926.

[38] [1949] Ch. 529 at 538.

[39] [1972] Ch. 73 at 95.

"The answer being eminently a matter of first impression derived from an overall view of the preamble coupled with the general trend of some centuries of decision."

It is considered that the better view is that an analogy is required and that, in the absence of a specific analogy, a broader analogy can be taken. Any danger that this would result in too wide a category of charitable purposes is limited by the need to satisfy the requirement of public benefit which in the case of new purposes, certainly under the fourth head and possibly under all heads, must be proved positively.[40]

The development of the definition of charity is now essentially in the hands of the Charity Commissioners[41] in view of the very small number of cases on charitable status which reach the courts. The Commissioners have set out their approach to determining charitable status of novel purposes as follows[42]:

"The Commission will take a constructive approach in adapting the concept of charity to meet constantly evolving social needs and new ideas through which those needs can be met. Acting within the legal framework which governs the recognition of new charitable purposes, we would aim to act constructively and imaginatively.

In considering new purposes as charitable we will look closely at those purposes which have already been recognised as charitable either under the Preamble or in subsequent decision of the court or the Commission. We will also look at contemporary needs of society and relevant legislation passed by Parliament and, where Convention rights are in issue, to the European Convention on Human Rights and decisions of the European Court of Human Rights and the European Commission of Human Rights.

In identifying a new purpose as charitable we will, following the legal framework, need to be clear that there exists a sufficient correlation between those new purposes and purposes already accepted as charitable. While in most cases a sufficiently close analogy may be found, in others an analogy may be found by following the broad principles which may be derived from the scope of the Preamble or from decided cases of the court of the Commission.

In addition we will need to be clear that the purpose is not a political purpose as understood in charity law and that the purposes are expressed with clarity and certainty to facilitate monitoring by us and any subsequent control by the court should that be necessary."

1–007   The reference to the European Convention on Human Rights reflects the fact that the courts and the Charity Commissioners as public bodies must construe any precedents in a way which is compatible with Convention rights.[43] Thus, for example, any consideration of new pur-

[40] See para.1–009 below.
[41] See para.1–028 below.
[42] RR1a, *Recognising New Charitable Purposes* (2001), para.23.
[43] Human Rights Act 1998, s.6(1).

poses within the third head may need to have regard to Art.9, the right to freedom of thought, conscience and religion[44] and Art.2 of the First Protocol, the right to education, may be relevant to new purposes within the second head of charity. As charitable status gives rise to fiscal benefits, it can be argued that any consideration of new purposes must have regard to Art.1 of the First Protocol, protection of property, and that any rule which differentiates between purposes must pass the fair balance test.[45]

The requirement of public benefit

While it is not so stated in the preamble to the Statute of Elizabeth I, it **1–008** was established by the Court of Chancery that a trust, in order to be charitable, must be of a public character,[46] that is, it must be for the benefit of the community or an appreciably important section of the community. This requirement may involve the consideration of two questions which are closely related, first, whether the purposes of the trust confer a benefit on the public or a section of the public, and secondly, whether the class of persons eligible to benefit constitutes the public or a section of it.[47] So far as the first question is concerned, this is a matter to be determined by the court, not by the founder of the alleged charity.[48] The fact that the donor was moved by a desire to benefit the community, that he intended to benefit the community and that he believed that his gift would benefit the community is irrelevant.[49] Conversely, if the objects are charitable, the gift does not lose its charitable character because the donor's motives or intentions are not charitable. "The court cannot inquire into the motives of the donor if the gift is in its nature a charity."[50]

Where both benefit and harm flow from a particular purpose, the court will determine whether on balance there is public benefit. If the potential harm outweighs the benefits, the purpose will not be charitable. Thus a society having as its object the total suppression of vivisection was not charitable because any assumed public benefit in the advancement of morals was outweighed by the detriment to medical science and research and consequently to public health.[51] Similarly, if the court regards the

[44] See para.2–050 below.
[45] See *Sporrong and Lonnroth v Sweden* (A/52) (1982) 5 E.H.R.R. 35, para.69 and see S. Grosz, J. Beatson and P. Duffy, *Human Rights. The 1998 Act and the European Convention*, p.355.
[46] *Jones v Williams* (1767) Amb. 651 at 652; G.H. Jones, *History of Charity Law 1530–1827*, pp.22–52. The requirement of public benefit is considered in more detail under each of the four heads of charity in Chap.2.
[47] For surveys, see P.S. Atiyah (1958) 21 M.L.R. 138; G.H.L. Fridman (1953) 31 Can. Bar Rev. 357; S.G. Maurice (1951) 15 Conv.(N.S.) 328.
[48] *Re Hummeltenberg* [1923] 1 Ch. 237 at 242; *National Anti-Vivisection Society v IRC* [1948] A.C. 31 at 44, 66–67, disapproving *Re Foveaux* [1895] 2 Ch. 501 at 507; and see *Re Pinion* [1965] Ch. 85 at 106; *Re Wooton* [1968] 1 W.L.R. 680 at 685.
[49] *Re Hummeltenberg* [1923] 1 Ch. 237 at 241, 242; *National Anti-Vivisection Society v IRC* [1948] A.C. 31 at 66; *Re Shaw* [1957] 1 W.L.R. 729.
[50] *Hoare v Osborne* (1866) L.R. 1 Eq. 585 at 588, *per* Kindersley V.C. See also *Skegness UDC v Derbyshire Miners' Welfare Committee* [1959] A.C. 808 at 823, 824, *per* Viscount Simonds.
[51] *National Anti-Vivisection Society v IRC* [1948] A.C. 31.

benefit flowing from a particular purpose as incapable of proof it will decline to recognise the purpose as charitable.[52] Accordingly, in *Gilmour v Coates*[53] a gift for a community of cloistered nuns was held not to be charitable because the benefits of intercessory prayer and the example of pious lives to the public were too vague. The requirement of public benefit is usually satisfied by showing that tangible and objective benefits will flow from the particular purpose. If the benefits are intangible, the court will require some evidence that there is "approval by the common understanding of enlightened opinion"[54] or "general consensus of opinion or understanding"[55] before accepting such benefits as satisfying the requirement of public benefit. On this basis no trust can be charitable if it is illegal or contrary to public policy.[56]

Established English law provides that where the purpose appears to be for the relief of poverty or the advancement of education or the advancement of religion the court will assume it to be for the benefit of the community and, therefore, charitable[57] unless the contrary is shown. In such a case it is for those who dispute the validity of the gift or trust to satisfy the court that the community will not be benefited. So, for example, a trust for the advancement of education will not be charitable if it is shown that the particular education is not of public value.[58] In contrast, an organisation which claims to be charitable under the fourth head must prove that it is for the benefit of the community.

1–009   It can be argued that this approach to the requirement of public benefit is in breach of ECHR principles. Art.1 to Protocol 1 of the ECHR provides that every legal person is entitled to the peaceful enjoyment of his possessions. Charitable status gives rise to fiscal benefits. Thus to deny charitable status and, it follows, access to fiscal benefits could be said to be in breach of ECHR principles. Art.1 to Protocol 1 is qualified, however, by the right of the State to enforce such laws as it deems necessary to control the use of property in accordance with the general interest. In addition, for some organisations seeking charitable status Art.8, the right to respect for family life or Art.9,[59] the right to freedom of thought, conscience and religion, or Art.10, the right to freedom of expression[60] may be relevant. Further, Art.14 provides that ECHR rights should be enjoyed without discrimination. Accordingly, any rule which seeks to differentiate between organisations seeking charitable status must, in order to avoid breach of either Article 14 or Article 1 to Protocol 1, be prescribed by law, have a legitimate aim, be necessary in a democratic society[61] and not be discriminatory.[62]

---

[52] *McGovern v Att-Gen* [1981] 3 All E.R. 493 at 504, *per* Slade J.
[53] [1949] A.C. 426, see para.2–067 below.
[54] *National Anti-Vivisection Society v IRC* [1948] A.C. 31 at 49, *per* Lord Wright.
[55] *ibid.*, at 47, *per* Lord Wright.
[56] *ibid.*, at 65, *per* Lord Simonds.
[57] *ibid.*, at 65, *per* Lord Simonds.
[58] *ibid.*, at 42, *per* Lord Wright.
[59] See para.2–050 below.
[60] See para.2–040 below.
[61] See D.J. Harris, M. O'Boyle and C. Warbrick, *Law of the European Convention on Human Rights*, pp.285, *et seq.*
[62] See *Belgium Linguistic case* (1968) (No.2) 1 E.H.R.R. 252 paras 9–10 and D.J. Harris, M. O'Boyle and C. Warbrick, *Law of the European Convention on Human Rights*, pp.475,

There is settled English law that differentiates between those bodies and purposes which are entitled to the benefits which attach to charitable status and those which do not. In the absence of unlimited public resource, this is a legitimate aim. The test is based on the benefit to the public that flows from the bodies or purposes The test recognises that under the first three heads of charity public benefit is regarded as established and self-evident and that no further proof is required unless any doubt arises. So that, for example, the presumption of public benefit in the case of a religious purpose is rebutted if there is evidence that the purpose is subversive of morality,[63] or is a new belief system or public concern has been expressed about the organisation with that purpose.[64] A different test is taken under the fourth head where purposes are newer and public benefit must be shown to justify charitable status. The courts[65] and the Charity Commissioners,[66] however, do not insist on positive proof of public benefit for a fourth head purpose where the benefit is well accepted or self-evident. It is considered that the public benefit test as applied flexibly at present, is probably an objective and reasonable test consistent with ECHR principles to ensure that only purposes which benefit the public gain charitable status.[67] There is still potential for argument that the test is discriminatory and future decisions may hold that the public benefit test is only non-discriminatory if it abandons differentiation based on the four heads of charity and moves to a position where there is an assumption that existing charitable purposes are for the public benefit unless the contrary is shown and that all new purposes must prove public benefit.

The Strategy Unit report in its review of charitable status laid emphasis on the public character of charity and the provision of public benefit. The report proposed[68] that the public benefit test should be applied more consistently and that all charities should be required to demonstrate public benefit. In addition to removing the presumption of public benefit for certain purposes at the time of registration, the report proposed that the Charity Commissioners should undertake a rolling programme reviewing public character of exiting charities with particular reference to those charities which charge fees.[69]

With regard to the second question, whether the class of persons eligible **1–010** to benefit constitutes the public or a section thereof, it has long been established that in order to be charitable, the trust must not be merely for the benefit of particular private individuals, and, if it is, then (save in the

---

et seq. The same requirement in relation to Art.1 of Protocol 1 is expressed as the "fair balance" test—see *Sporrong and Lonnroth v Sweden* (A/52) (1982) 5 E.H.R.R., para.69.

[63] See *Re Watson* [1973] 1 W.L.R. 1472 at 1482, *per* Plowman J.
[64] See [1999] Ch. Com. Dec. November 17 (The Church of Scientology), pp.41–42.
[65] *McGovern v Att-Gen* [1981] 3 All E.R. 493 at 504, *per* Slade J.
[66] RR1a, *Recognising New Charitable Purposes* (2001), para.31.
[67] See RR1a, *Recognising New Charitable Purposes* (2001), para.34.
[68] Cabinet Office, Strategy Unit, *Private Action, Public Benefit. A Review of Charities and the Wider Not-For-Profit Sector* (2002), p.40. See also Cabinet Office, Strategy Unit, *Private Action, Public Benefit. Charitable Status* (2002). For a discussion of the proposed definition of charity see para.1–015 below.
[69] *ibid.*, p.41.

anomalous case of trusts for the relief of poverty),[70] it will not be in law a charity even though the benefit taken by those individuals is of the very character stated in the preamble.[71] The question often arises as to whether in a particular case a particular class of persons constitutes a sufficiently important section of the public to establish the validity of a trust alleged to be charitable, and it is difficult and perhaps impossible to formulate a satisfactory test in general terms: but a trust for a particular class of private individuals, such as the employees of a particular company, will not be charitable, no matter how large the class may be.[72] Whilst the distinction is not an easy one, its underlying rationale is to distinguish those organisations which look outward and seek to provide public benefits from those which are inward looking and self-serving. The public benefit requirement may be satisfied if, although there is a personal nexus between the beneficiaries, it is clear that a public class is intended and the class can be described otherwise than by reference to the personal nexus.[73] For example, beneficiaries can be described as residents of a particular geographical area although they all happen to be tenants of the same landlord.[74] At the other end of the scale the fact that the size of the beneficiary class is very small will not prevent the requirement of public benefit being satisfied if no arbitrary criterion, unrelated to the particular purpose, is used to delimit the class. A trust to relieve a need of members of a particular ethnic group in a geographical area is charitable even if the number of members of that ethnic group is small.[75]

The criteria are not applied equally to all heads of charity. Thus what is a sufficient section of the community to support a valid trust under one head will not necessarily be sufficient to support a trust under another head.[76] In respect of all heads of charity, the section of the community may not be defined by reference to colour[77] but it is permissible to restrict the benefits of a charity to persons of one sex.[78]

It is inherent in the public benefit requirement for charitable status that benefits must flow to the public and that any benefits to an individual must come either directly as a result of the carrying out of the charitable purpose, for example, receipt of a grant or an education, or be legitimately incidental to the pursuit of the charitable purpose. Determining whether

---

[70] See para.2–014 below.
[71] *Williams' Trustees v IRC* [1947] A.C. 337 at 457, *per* Lord Simonds.
[72] *Re Compton* [1945] Ch. 123; *Re Hobourn Aero Components Ltd.'s Air Raid Distress Fund* [1946] Ch. 194; *Oppenheim v Tobacco Securities Trust Co. Ltd.* [1951] A.C. 297; *IRC v Educational Grants Association Ltd.* [1968] Ch. 123, affirmed [1968] Ch. 998, C.A. See para.2–046 below.
[73] See RR8, *The Public Character of Charity* (2001), p.12. See also *Latimer v CIR* [2002] 3 N.Z.L.R. 195 at 208.
[74] See *Springhall Housing Action Committee v Commissioner of Valuation* [1983] N.I. 184.
[75] See RR8. *The Public Character of Charity* (2001), p.2.
[76] *Gilmour v Coates* [1949] A.C. 426 at 449, *per* Lord Simonds; *IRC v Baddeley* [1955] A.C. 572 at 615, *per* Lord Somervell; *Dingle v Turner* [1972] A.C. 601 at 624, *per* Lord Cross. See also *Re Dunlop* [1984] N.I. 408 and Dawson, *"Old Presbyterians Persons" – A Sufficient Section of the Public?* [1987] Conv. 114.
[77] Race Relations Act 1976, s.34. See [1976] Ch. Com. Rep., para.19.
[78] Sex Discrimination Act 1975, s.43. See *Hugh-Jones v St. John's College Cambridge* [1979] I.C.R. 848, and [1975] Ch. Com. Rep., para.25.

there is excessive private benefit which will prevent an organisation from attaining charitable status is particularly difficult for certain types of charity such as those for the relief of unemployment,[79] the promotion of urban and rural regeneration[80] or the promotion of professions.[81] A reasonable summation of the courts' approach to determining acceptable levels of private benefits is the test proposed by the Charity Commissioners in their Review of the Register paper, *The Public Character of Charity*[82];

> "a private benefit is legitimately incidental if it arises as a necessary but incidental consequence of a decision by the trustees which is directed only at furthering the organisation's charitable purposes (as opposed to a separate purpose of in effect providing private benefit), and the amount of the benefit is reasonable."[83]

The fact that a charity charges for its services does not prevent the requirement of public benefit being satisfied.[84] If charges, however, are set at a level which deters or excludes a substantial proportion of the beneficiary class, the public benefit requirement will not be met but charges may be set at a level which generates a surplus to assist the funding of a charity's other current or future activities.[85] The courts' approach to the determination of public benefit where a charity charges for its services can be seen from Lord Wilberforce's speech in *Re Resch's Will Trusts*[86] which involved a gift of income for the general purposes of St Vincent's Private Hospital:

1–011

> "In the present case, the element of public benefit is strongly present. It is not disputed that a need exists to provide accommodation and medical treatment in conditions of greater privacy and relaxation than would be possible in a general hospital and as a supplement to the facilities of a general hospital. This is what the private hospital does and it does so at, approximately, cost price. The service is needed by all, not only by the well-to-do. So far as its nature permits it is open to all: the charges are not low, but the evidence shows that it cannot be said that the poor are excluded: such exclusion as there is, is of some of the poor—namely those who have (a) not contributed sufficiently to a medical benefit scheme or (b) need to stay longer in the hospital than their benefit will cover or (c) cannot get a reduction

[79] See para.2–075 below.
[80] See para.2–076 below.
[81] See para.2–044 below.
[82] RR8, *The Public Character of Charity* (2001), p.4. A series of questions is set out by the Charity Commissioners to assist in determining if the test is satisfied.
[83] See *Midland Counties Institution of Engineers v IRC* (1928) 14 T.C. 285; *General Nursing Council for England and Wales v St Marylebone BC* [1959] A.C. 540; *Incorporated Council of Law Reporting for England and Wales v Att-Gen* [1972] Ch. 73; *New Zealand Society of Accountants v Commissioner of Inland Revenue* [1986] 1 N.Z.L.R. 147.
[84] *Joseph Rowntree Memorial Housing Association Ltd v Att-Gen* [1983] Ch. 159.
[85] *Re Resch's Will Trust, Le Cras v Perpetual Trustee Co Ltd* [1967] 3 All E.R. 915. See also RR8, *The Public Character of Charity* (2001), p.7.
[86] [1967] 3 All E.R. 915 at 923.

of or exemption from the charges. The general benefit to the community of such facilities results from the relief to the beds and medical staff of the general hospital, the availability of a particular type of nursing and treatment which supplements that provided by the general hospital and the benefit to the standard of medical care in the general hospital which arises from the juxtaposition of the two institutions."

It is well established that a trust for the relief of poverty,[87] or the advancement of education[88] or the advancement of religion[89] is no less charitable because it operates exclusively outside the UK. It was considered that a purpose under the fourth head could not be charitable unless the community or section of the community to be benefited was in the UK.[90] Jacob J. in *Re Carapiet's Trust*[91] has recently supported the approach of the Charity Commissioners[92] that, in determining the charitable status of an institution operating abroad, the first consideration should be whether it would be regarded as a charity if its operation were confined to the UK. If it would, then it should be presumed to be charitable, even though operating abroad, unless it would be contrary to public policy to recognise it. This approach to fourth head purposes based on public policy has its origin in Lord Evershed M.R.'s decision in *Camille and Henry Dreyfus Foundation Ltd. v IRC*.[93]

Exclusively charitable

1–012   A trust, in order to be charitable, must have objects which are exclusively charitable. If a trust has a main object which is not charitable it is not capable of being a charity, albeit benefit to the public flows from it.[94] Thus a body with charitable purposes but set up to carry out the wishes and policies of a government authority would not be exclusively charitable.[95] The fact that pursuit of the purposes of the trust may confer benefits on persons who are not themselves objects of charity will not deprive the trust of charitable status provided that all the purposes are charitable.[96]

---

[87] See *Re Geek* (1893) 69 L.T. 819; *Re Robinson* [1931] 2 Ch. 122; *Re Niyazi's Will Trusts* [1978] 1 W.L.R. 910.

[88] See *Att-Gen v Sturge* (1854) 19 Beav 597; *Whicker v Hume* (1858) 7 H.L.C. 124; *Re Marr's Will Trusts* [1936] Ch. 671; *Re Shaw's Will Trusts* [1952] Ch. 163.

[89] See *Income Tax Special Purposes Commissioner v Pemsel* [1891] A.C. 531; *Re Redish* (1909) 26 T.L.R. 42; *Re Norman* [1947] Ch. 349.

[90] See the 8th ed. of this work at p.6.

[91] [2002] E.W.H.C. 1304, para.17.

[92] See (1993) 1 Ch. Com. Dec. p.17.

[93] [1954] Ch. 672, 684. See also *Re Vagliano* [1905] 75 L.J. Ch. 119; *Armstrong v Reeves* [1890] L.R. 25 Ir. 325; *Re Jackson The Times*, June 11, 1910; *Mitford v Reynolds* [1854] 1 Ph. 185; *Re Jacobs* (1970) 114 Sol. J. 515; *Re Levy Estate* [1989] 58 D.L.R. (4th) 375; *Re Stone* [1970] 91 W.N. (N.S.W.) 704 and *Lander v Whitbread* [1982] 2 N.S.W.L.R. 530.

[94] *General Nursing Council for England and Wales v St. Marylebone BC* [1959] A.C. 540; *Att-Gen of the Cayman Islands v Wahr-Hansen* [2000] 3 All E.R. 642.

[95] See RR7, *The Independence of Charities from the State* (2001), para.7.

[96] *Royal College of Surgeons of England v National Provincial Bank Ltd* [1952] A.C. 631; *Royal College of Nursing v St. Marylebone BC* [1959] 1 W.L.R. 1077; *Incorporated Council of Law Reporting for England and Wales v Att-Gen* [1972] Ch. 73, 100 *per* Buckley J.

In four cases, the existence of a non-charitable purpose will not be fatal to charitable status for the relevant body. First, if the wording of the trust permits the property to be applied for both charitable and non-charitable purposes the court may apply the doctrine of severance, saving the charitable part of the fund.[97] Secondly a trust with some non-charitable purposes which came into operation before December 16, 1952 may be saved by the Charitable Trusts (Validation) Act 1954.[98] Thirdly, what is apparently a non-charitable purpose may be construed as a charitable purpose if conjunctive, as opposed to disjunctive, words have been used when listing the purposes of the trust.[99] Finally, if the main purpose of an organisation is charitable, power to carry on incidental, supplementary non-charitable activities will not bar that organisation from charitable status.[1] The non-charitable purpose must be entirely subsidiary to the main purposes and must not be too large a proportion of the organisation's activities in relation to its charitable purposes.[2] Thus, a trust which included provision of an annual dinner for the trustees did not fail as a charitable trust as the non-charitable purpose was considered to be ancillary to the better administration of the charity.[3]

Classification of charitable purposes

Looking to the preamble to the Statute of Elizabeth I, and not behind it, the courts have built up a great body of case law. "Often it may appear illogical and even capricious. It could hardly be otherwise when its guiding principle is so vaguely stated and is liable to be so differently interpreted in different ages."[4] For more than 200 years after the enactment of the Statute no attempt was made to classify the objects or purposes which had been held to be charitable as being within the letter or the spirit and intendment of the preamble. In 1805, however, Sir Samuel Romilly (then Mr. Romilly), arguing in *Morice v Bishop of Durham*[5] put forward a classification under four heads. Those heads were: first, relief of the indigent; secondly, the advancement of learning; thirdly, the advancement of religion; and, fourthly, "which is the most difficult, the advancement of objects of general public utility".

Lord Macnaghten in *Income Tax Special Purposes Commissioners v Pemsel*[6] substantially accepted Sir Samuel Romilly's classification with two significant variations. In a justly celebrated speech Lord Macnaghten classified charitable purposes under four heads:

1–013

---

[97] See, for example, *Salisbury v Denton* (1857) 3 K.&.J 529 and see para.3–009 below.
[98] See para.3–036 below.
[99] See paras 3–017 *et seq.*, below.
[1] *IRC v Glasgow (City) Police Athletic Association* [1953] A.C. 380, applied in *Att-Gen v Ross* [1986] 1 W.L.R. 252.
[2] Compare the first two cases cited in n.96, above and see para.1–010 above.
[3] *Re Charlesworth* (1910) 101 L.T. 908; *Re Coxen* [1948] Ch. 747.
[4] *Gilmour v Coats* [1949] A.C. 426 at 443, *per* Lord Simonds.
[5] (1805) 10 Ves. 522 at 531.
[6] [1891] A.C. 531 at 583.

(1)   The relief of poverty;
(2)   The advancement of education;
(3)   The advancement of religion;
(4)   Other purposes beneficial to the community not falling under any of the preceding heads.

The first significant variation is the substitution of the advancement of education for the advancement of learning. In this respect Lord Macnaghten's language was more accurate than the language used by Sir Samuel Romilly reflecting that some degree of dissemination is required.[7] The second significant variation is in Lord Macnaghten's fourth head, which is apparently wider than Sir Samuel Romilly's fourth head. As has been stated,[8] not every object of public general utility is necessarily charitable. On the other hand, Lord Macnaghten said[9] that trusts falling under the fourth head "are not the less charitable in the eye of the law, because incidentally they benefit the rich as well as the poor, as indeed every charity that deserves the name must do either directly or indirectly." The four heads of charity will be considered in detail in the following chapter.[10]

Development of the definition of charity

1–014   No statutory definition of charity was included in the Charities Act 1992. The White Paper, *Charities: A Framework for the Future*[11] took the view that any attempt to enact a statutory definition of charity was fraught with difficulty and put at risk the flexibility of the law which was its greatest and most valuable feature.[12] Debate continued, however, on the definition of charity and one of the proposals of the Deakin Commission[13] was that there should be a single overarching definition of charity to be drawn up by the Law Commission after consultation with the public.

The Government did not refer the matter to the Law Commission but the Charity Commissioners, in response, did start a Review of the Register. The aim of the Review was, within the present law, to clarify and to keep the definition of charity in accord, as far as possible, with present social thinking. The Commissioners identified a number of essential characteristics of a charity which they used as principles when conducting the Review.[14] A number of the Review papers sought to clarify general prin-

---

[7] See para.2–028, below.
[8] See para.1–005 above.
[9] [1891] A.C. 583. See also *Jones v Williams* (1767) Amb. 651; *Att-Gen v Haberdashers' Co.* (1834) 1 My. & K. 420. There are, on the other hand, weighty dicta to the effect that a trust for the exclusive benefit of the rich would not be charitable; see *Att-Gen v Duke of Northumberland* (1877) 7 Ch.D. 745 at 752 (correcting a dictum in *Gillam v Taylor* (1873) L.R. 16 Eq. 581); *Re Macduff* [1896] 2 Ch. 464 at 471; *Re White's Will Trusts* [1951] 1 All E.R. 528 at 530; *Re Resch's Will Trusts* [1969] 1 A.C. 514 at 544, PC.
[10] To Lord Macnaghten's catalogue should perhaps be added charities for the provision of recreation within the Recreational Charities Act 1958; see paras 2–098 *et seq.*, below.
[11] (1989) Cm. 694.
[12] *ibid.*, para.2.11.
[13] *The Report of the Commission on the Future of the Voluntary Sector*, National Council for Voluntary Organisations (1996).
[14] See RR1, *The Review of the Register of Charities* (2001), Pt.2.

ciples, for example Public Benefit,[15] and a number of new charitable purposes have been identified, for example, the promotion of urban and rural regeneration.[16]

There was also concern in other Commonwealth countries about the common law basis of the definition of charity and its accord with present social thinking. A number of countries have considered the definition of charity and the resultant reports show a steady move towards a statutory definition of charity. The first review was in Ontario where the Ontario Law Reform Commission produced a *Report on The Law of Charities* in 1996.[17] The Commission took a wide ranging and philosophical approach to the definition of charity and placed much emphasis on the concept of altruism. Whilst a true definition of charity with reference to Finnis' natural law theory was considered, the Commission did not recommend any fundamental change in the definition of charity. The Commission saw benefit in the flexibility of the common law system but recommended the introduction of an overall public benefit test. There was a similar concern with public benefit in Scotland where the Scottish Charity Law Review Commission reported in 2001 after reviewing the law relating to charities in Scotland. The Commission proposed that an organisation should be charitable if its overriding purpose is for the public benefit; it is non-profit distributing; it is independent and it is non-party political.[18]

Other countries, in particular Australia, have shown a preference for a statutory definition of charity. Australia had a number of different definitions of charity for different purposes, for example fiscal, and in 2000 set up a committee to review the state of charity law in Australia. *The Report of the Inquiry into the Definition of Charities and Related Organisations*[19] proposed a single statutory definition of charity. In response, the Australian government has set out a proposed legislative definition for consultation.[20] The proposed definition is that a charity is an entity (other than an expressly excluded entity) that is not for profit and has a dominant purpose or purposes that are charitable and, subject to express exceptions, for the public benefit. The charitable purposes, based on existing purposes, are listed under seven heads with the last being "other purposes beneficial to the community". Public benefit is also defined and emphasises that the organisation must be aimed at achieving a universal or common good; have practical utility; and be directed to the benefit of the general community or a sufficient section thereof. This statutory approach to the definition of charity, based on existing charitable purposes, has also been taken up by the Working Party on Registration, Reporting and Monitoring of Charities in New Zealand[21] and the Law Reform Committee of the Law Society of Ireland.[22]

1–015

---

[15] RR8, *The Public Character of Charities* (2001).

[16] RR2, *The Promotion of Urban and Rural Regeneration* (1999).

[17] *Report on the Law of Charities*, Ontario Law Reform Commission (1996).

[18] *Charity Scotland. The Report of the Scottish Charity Law Review Commission* (2001), *www.scotland.gov.uk/justice/charity law*.

[19] (2001), *www.cdi.gov.au*.

[20] Government Response to Charities Definition Inquiry. August 19, 2002.

[21] May (2002), *www.treasury.gov.nz/charities*.

[22] *Charity Law: The case for reform* (2002) and see H. Picarda, "Redefining 'Charity' in England and Wales, Eire and Australia" (2002) 8 C.L.P.R. 1.

In this country proposals for reform have come from the Strategy Unit of the Cabinet Office in their 2001 report.[23] The Strategy Unit sought to clarify what constitutes charity in the twenty-first century, to emphasise the public character of charity and to retain the flexibility of charity law to evolve as social and economic circumstances change.[24] The proposed definition is as follows:

"A charity should be defined as an organisation which provides public benefit and which has one or more of the following purposes[25]:

1. The prevention and relief of poverty.
2. The advancement of education.
3. The advancement of religion.
4. The advancement of health.[a]
5. Social and community advancement.[b]
6. The advancement of culture, arts and heritage.
7. The advancement of amateur sport.
8. The promotion of human rights, conflict resolution and reconciliation.
9. The advancement of environmental protection and improvement.
10. Other purposes beneficial to the community.

[a] including the prevention and relief of sickness, disease or of human suffering.
[b] including the care, support and protection of the aged, people with a disability, children and young people."

The purposes listed in the proposed definition are not exhaustive and are intended to be general wording around which the law can continue to develop. The 10th head, in particular, retains flexibility to develop the definition of charity. The 10 heads are clearly based on the existing types of purposes already recognised as charitable by case law and there is no intention to remove or make irrelevant existing case law.[26] The report suggests, however, that the preamble will become irrelevant.[27] The proposed definition gives greater emphasis to public benefit and all charities will have to demonstrate public benefit; there will be no presumption of public benefit.[28]

1–016   The majority of heads of the proposed definition simply reflect existing charitable purposes as established by case law but two of the heads repre-

[23] Cabinet Office, Strategy Unit, *Private Action, Public Benefit. A Review of Charities and the Wider Not-For Profit Sector* (2002), paras 36, *et seq., www.cabinet-office.gov.uk/innovation.*
[24] *ibid.,* p.38.
[25] *ibid.,* p.39. Reference is made to the proposed Australian definition and to the Barbados statutory definition, see Cabinet Office, Strategy Unit, *Private Action, Public Benefit. Charitable Status.*
[26] *ibid.,* p.41.
[27] *ibid.,* p.42 and see Cabinet Office, Strategy Unit, *Private Action, Public Benefit. Charitable Status* (2002).
[28] See para.1–008 above.

or for educational[69] or religious[70] purposes, or purposes synonymous therewith.[71] It is immaterial whether such intention is in favour of charity generally, or whether it is confined to a particular form of charity, such as the benefit of ministers belonging to a particular church,[72] or a particular kind of hospital,[73] provided only that the precise mode in which the intention is to be executed is not defined. In all these cases the law provides the mode in which the intention shall be carried out.

The case is the same where a testator gives property to such charitable uses as he shall name, and names none,[74] for the mere omission to make the particular nomination is not sufficient to revoke the charitable intention originally expressed.[75] So also where a testator directed a fund "to be applied to such charitable uses as he had by writing under his hand formerly directed," and no such writing was found.[76] The same applies where the names of the particular charities or some of them are left blank.[77] Thus in Re White,[78] a gift to "the following religious societies, namely—" was held to show an intention to devote the property in question to religious purposes, and to be therefore charitable.

If the nomination of the particular object is entrusted to an executor, the mere revocation of the appointment of the executor, without appointing another, will not affect the validity of the gift.[79] So also if the person charged with the duty of appointing the particular objects dies in the testator's lifetime,[80] as where there was a legacy to a person predeceasing the testator for the benefit of the clergy of a particular church,[81] or if,

---

[69] Whicker v Hume (1858) 7 H.L.C. 124; United States of America v Drummond (1838) cited ibid. 155; Re Macduff [1896] 2 Ch. 451 at 473. See also Bishop of Hereford v Adams (1802) 7 Ves. 324; Wilkinson v Malin (1832) 2 C. & J. 636; Att-Gen v Bovill (1840) 1 Ph. 672; Re Lambeth Charities (1853) 22 L.J.Ch. 959; School Board for London v Faulconer (1878) 8 Ch.D. 571; Re Campden Charities (1881) 18 Ch.D. 310; and see Re Richmond Parish Charity Lands (1965) 109 S.J. 755.

[70] Re White [1893] 2 Ch. 41; Re Macduff [1896] 2 Ch. 451; compare the Scottish case Grimond v Grimond [1905] A.C. 124.

[71] Morice v Bishop of Durham (1805) 10 Ves. 521 at 542; Re White [1893] 2 Ch. 41.

[72] Att-Gen v Hickman (1732) 2 Eq.Ca.Ab. 193; Att-Gen v Gladstone (1842) 13 Sim. 7.

[73] White v White (1778) 1 B.C.C. 12.

[74] Anon. (1690) Free.K.B. 331; 1 Mer. 59n.; Cook v Duckenfield (1743) 2 Atk. 562; Mills v Farmer (1815) 1 Mer. 55; Att-Gen v Fletcher (1835) 5 L.J.Ch. 75; Pocock v Att-Gen (1876) 3 Ch.D. 342; Re Pyne [1903] 1 Ch. 83.

[75] Mills v Farmer, above at para.1–019. Secus where the charitable intention is revoked: Wheeler v Sheer (1730) Mos. 288 at 301; 1 Mer. 72n.

[76] Att-Gen v Syderfen (1683) 1 Vern 224; 7 Ves. 43n. See also Moggridge v Thackwell (1802) 7 Ves. 36; Mills v Farmer (1815) 1 Mer. 55 at 95. In Commissioners of Charitable Donations v Sullivan (1841) 1 Dr. & W. 501, verbal directions had been given to the trustees.

[77] Pieschel v Paris (1825) 2 S. & S. 384. Where there is a blank in a will the instrument is construed according to the meaning of the words actually present: Re Macduff [1896] 2 Ch. 451 at 469.

[78] [1893] 2 Ch. 41. For a full discussion of this case, see para.2–053, above, Secus where blanks are left in a will for the amounts to be given to a charity: Ewen v Bannerman (1830) 2 Dow. & C. 74; Hartshorne v Nicholson (1858) 26 B. 58. See also Grimond v Grimond [1905] A.C. 124, a Scottish case somewhat similar to Re White, above, where the gift was held void for uncertainty, this decision being in accordance with Scots law.

[79] White v White (1778) 1 B.C.C. 12; and see Moggridge v Thackwell (1802) 7 Ves. 36 at 78; Mills v Farmer (1815) 1 Mer. 55 at 96.

[80] Moggridge v Thackwell (1802) 7 Ves. 36, see above, para.1–018; and see Ommanney v Butcher (1823) T. & R. 260, 270; Re Eades [1920] 1 Ch. 353; Re Willis [1921] 1 Ch. 44.

[81] Att-Gen v Hickman (1732) 2 Eq.Ca.Ab. 193, pl. 14; Att-Gen v Gladstone (1842) 13 Sim. 7.

being an executor, he renounces,[82] or if he neglects or refuses to appoint, the gift does not fail.[83] Thus, where there was a gift to such lying-in hospitals as another should appoint, and he died without appointing, the court determined to what hospitals the funds should be paid.[84] The same principles apply where a fund is directed to be divided among a particular class of persons at the discretion of a person who fails to deal with it.[85]

1–022   It makes no difference whether the person having the power of selection is a trustee or not, and whether or not he is obliged to make the selection within a definite period,[86] or that the name of the person to make the nomination has been left blank.[87]

Failure of trust machinery

1–023   The validity of a gift for charitable purposes does not depend upon the provision by the donor of machinery to carry his charitable purpose into effect. If the purposes of the gift are clearly charitable the law provides the machinery necessary to carry it into effect. As has been already stated, if no trust was intended, the Sovereign[88] becomes the trustee, and if a trust was intended, but no trustee has been appointed, the court supplies the omission.[89] Moreover, the breaking down of the particular trust machinery through which the donor intended the gift to be carried into effect will not defeat the gift. The only exception to this rule is where on the true construction of the instrument of gift it is clear that the donor only intends to give to charity if a particular person or institution will accept the gift.[90] Thus, the gift does not fail because the trustee named has died in the testator's lifetime,[91] as where there is a gift to the then president of a charitable institution by name for the benefit of that institution, and he predeceases the testator,[92] or where property is given for specified charitable purposes to an individual who predeceases the testator.[93]

Except where it is clear that the donor only intended the gift to take effect if the trustee chosen by him accepted the gift and agreed to perform

---

[82] *Att-Gen v Fletcher* (1835) 5 L.J.Ch. 75. Trustees subsequently appointed cannot, in the absence of an expressed intention to that effect, make the selection: *Hibbard v Lamb* (1756) Amb. 309.

[83] See *Att-Gen v Boultbee* (1796) 3 Ves. 220.

[84] *White v White* (1778) 1 Bro.C.C. 12.

[85] *Att-Gen v Wansay* (1808) 15 Ves. 231; *Att-Gen v Gladstone* (1842) 13 Sim. 7.

[86] *Re Willis* [1921] 1 Ch. 44.

[87] *Baylis v Att-Gen* (1741) 2 Atk. 239.

[88] See para.1–018, above. See *Re Bennett* [1960] Ch. 18.

[89] *Mills v Farmer* (1851) 1 Mer. 55 at 94, 95.

[90] See *Reeve v Att-Gen* (1843) 3 Ha. 191; *New v Bonaker* (1867) L.R. 4 Eq. 655. See also the cases cited para.11–017, below, as to the lapse of gifts to particular institutions which either dissolved before the death of the testator or disclaim; *cf. Re Lysaght* [1966] Ch. 191: see para.11–036, below.

[91] *Moggridge v Thackwell* (1802) 7 Ves. 36.

[92] *Walsh v Gladstone* (1843) 1 Ph. 209; *In the Goods of M'Auliffe* [1895] para.290; *In the Goods of Lalor* (1902) 85 L.T. 643.

[93] *Att-Gen v Hickman* (1732) 2 Eq.Ca.Ab.193, pl. 14; *Att-Gen v Gladstone* (1842) 13 Sim. 7; and see generally, para.1–021, above, as to persons entrusted with the nomination of the charitable objects dying in the donor's lifetime.

the trusts, the disclaimer of the trustees whether individuals,[94] or of a college,[95] or other charitable institution[96] (except where the gift is to the institution for its general purposes),[97] is immaterial. This is so even though the trustees were selected because of their peculiar fitness to accomplish the donor's purpose,[98] for "the testator's reliance on the individuals to the exclusion of the holders of the office for the time being must be expressed in clear and apt language."[99] Likewise, if a legatee upon a precatory trust for charity renounces the legacy, the trust will be effected by means of a scheme.[1]

However, where a legacy was given for a charitable purpose in a foreign country, and the government of the country refused it, it was held to have failed because the court had no power either to enforce the trust or to settle a scheme for the administration of the charity *cy-près*.[2]

On the same principle the incapacity of the trustee named will not defeat the trust, as where there is a devise to a corporation which, owing to the insufficiency of its corporate capacity,[3] or for some other reason,[4] cannot take. The position is the same where the devise is to a charitable corporation for its own purposes,[5] and a covenant to invest money for the benefit of a charity in the corporate names of persons who cannot hold the funds as a corporation will be enforced.[6]   **1–024**

Nor will the charitable intention be allowed to be defeated by negligence or default on the part of the trustees,[7] even though there may be a gift over,[8] unless it was the donor's clear intention that the default of the trustees should produce this effect.[9] It is not very easy to see the distinction between the two types of case.[10] Similarly, the charitable intention will be carried out where an instrument of appointment has been lost.[11]

---

[94] *Barclay v Maske-Lyne* (1858) 4 Jur.(N.S.) 1294, where the Colonial Secretary declined to act in the trusts of a charity for the assistance of emigrants; *Marsh v Att-Gen* (1861) 2 J. & H. 61.

[95] *Att-Gen v Andrew* (1798) 3 Ves. 633.

[96] *Denyer v Druce* (1829) Tam. 32; *Reeve v Att-Gen* (1843) 3 Ha. 191.

[97] See *Re Slevin* [1891] 2 Ch. 236 at 242.

[98] See *Reeve v Att-Gen* (1843) 3 Ha. 191; *Barclay v Maske-Lyne* (1858) 4 Jur.(N.S.) 1294.

[99] *Re Smith, Eastick v Smith* [1904] 1 Ch. 139 at 144.

[1] *Re Burley* [1910] 1 Ch. 215.

[2] *New v Bonaker* (1867) L.R. 4 Eq. 655.

[3] *Gravenor v Hallum* (1767) Amb. 643, where the devise was to churchwardens (not a corporation).

[4] *Sonley v Clockmakers' Co.* (1780) 1 B.C.C. 81; *Att-Gen v Brentwood School* (1833) 1 Myl. & K. 376 at 390.

[5] *Incorporated Society v Richards* (1841) 1 Dr. & W. 258 at 331, 332.

[6] *Tufnell v Constable* (1838) 7 A. & E. 798.

[7] *Att-Gen v Leigh* (1721) 3 P.Wms. 145n.; *Att-Gen v Boultbee* (1794) 2 Ves.J. 380; *Re Upton Warren* (1833) 1 Myl. & K. 410; *Att-Gen v Davis* (1870) 18 W.R. 1132 (Ireland).

[8] *Re Upton Warren* (1833) 1 Myl. & K. 410; *Re Hanbey's Will Trusts* [1956] Ch. 264.

[9] *Christ's Hospital v Grainger* (1849) 1 Mac. & G. 460.

[10] See *Re Hanbey's Will Trusts* [1956] Ch. 264 at 274, *per* Danckwerts J.

[11] *Att-Gen v Syderfen* (1683) 1 Vern. 224.

SPECIFIC CHARITIES

Exempt charities

1–025   Certain charities are termed "exempt charities" because, whilst they have charitable status, they are exempt from many of the provisions of the Charities Acts. The general law of charity declared in the Acts applies to them, and hence they are subject to the jurisdiction of the court at the relation of the Attorney General, but they are exempt from all the supervisory or restrictive powers of the Commissioners.[12] Their exclusion from supervision by the Commissioners is emphasised by the fact that they are not permitted to register.[13]

The basis of exemption is that Parliament, having been fully into the matter of their constitution, has been satisfied that there exist satisfactory arrangements for carrying out the objects of their trusts and safeguarding their property, and that in the circumstances it would be superfluous to submit them to the control of the Commissioners, or their constitution is such that supervision is unnecessary. Usually, Parliament has in fact provided for their supervision by other means, for example, by provision for a Visitor in the case of universities.

The categories of exempt charities are set out in Sch.2 to the Charities Act 1993[14] and include any institution which, if the Charities Act 1960 had not been passed, would be exempt under the Charitable Trusts Acts 1853 to 1939, universities, foundation schools, further education corporations, certain museums, the Church Commissioners, registered industrial and provident societies and registered friendly societies. Additional charities may become exempt by order.

Excepted charities

1–026   An excepted charity is one which is excepted by order or regulation from certain of the obligations imposed by the Charities Acts.[15] Such a charity is excepted from registration[16] and is not obliged to make an annual report to the Commissioners.[17] Otherwise, the extent of the exception for any particular charity from the obligations under the Acts depends upon the wording of the relevant order or regulation. In addition, a charity which has neither permanent endowment nor the use of land and whose income from all sources does not amount to more than £1,000 a year is excepted from registration,[18] and need not have its accounts independently examined, nor deliver an annual report to the Commissioners.[19]

---

[12] Charities Act 1993, s.8(1) proviso, s.46(1).
[13] *ibid.*, s.3(2).
[14] As extended by Charities Act 1993, ss.3(5A) and (5B).
[15] Charities Act 1993, s.3(13). Existing exceptions are continued until October 1, 2007 by the Charities (Exception from Registration)(Amendment) Regulations 2002 (SI 2002/1598).
[16] *ibid.*, s.3(5)(b).
[17] *ibid.*, s.46(4).
[18] *ibid.*, s.3(5)(c).
[19] *ibid.*, s.46(3).

The main categories of excepted charities are certain voluntary schools, Boy Scout and Girl Guide charities, certain charities for the advancement of religion, certain charities for the promotion of efficiency in the armed forces and universities which are not exempt charities.

The Strategy Unit proposed that the threshold for compulsory registration should be raised to £10,000 and that the two criteria relating to permanent endowment and use of land should no longer apply.[20] It was also proposed that excepted charities with income above £10,000 a year should be required to register.[21]

REGISTRATION

It is the duty of the trustees of any charity to apply for it to be registered **1–027** unless it has already been so registered[22] or it is an exempt charity.[23] The trustees of a charity which is excepted from registration[24] or which has neither permanent endowment, nor the use or occupation of land and whose income does not exceed £1,000 a year[25] may apply to be registered but are not obliged to do so.

Application

Application for registration is made to the Charity Commissioners and **1–028** must be accompanied by copies of the trusts of the charity together with such other documents or information as may be prescribed or as the Commissioners may require for the purposes of the application.[26] In practice, the Commissioners require every applicant to complete an application form.[27] If trustees fail to apply to register a charity which should be registered, they may be required by order to make good their default.[28] Failure to comply with such an order may be dealt with as a contempt of court.[29] The Charity Commissioners' function as keepers of the register means that they are now responsible at first instance for deciding what is, and what is not, a charity. The Commissioners' constructive and generous, as opposed to restrictive, approach has led to an increasingly wide variety of purposes being accepted as charitable.[30]

---

[20] Cabinet Office; Strategy Unit, *Private Action, Public Benefit. A Review of Charities and the Wider Not-For-Profit Sector* (2002), p.85.

[21] *ibid.*, p.87.

[22] Charities Act 1993, s.3(7)(a). See paras 9–010 *et seq.*, below.

[23] *ibid.*, ss.3(2), 3(5)(a); see para.1–025, above.

[24] *ibid.*, ss.3(2), 3(5)(b); see above.

[25] *ibid.*, ss.3(2), 3(5)(c).

[26] *ibid.*, s.3(6). There is no need to supply the Commissioners with copies of schemes or documents already in their possession, s.3(11).

[27] See App1, *Application for Registration as a Charity* and CC21, *Registering as a Charity* (2002).

[28] Charities Act 1993, s.87(1).

[29] *ibid.*, s.88(c).

[30] See para.1–006 above and RR1a, *Recognising New Charitable Purposes* (2002).

If an organisation is refused registration, the trustees may appeal to the Board of Charity Commissioners.[31] The Board considers written representations and cases of interest are reported by the Commissioners on the web site. If the appeal is unsuccessful the trustees may appeal to the High Court.[32] The Attorney General must be made a party to any appeal.[33]

Objection

1–029   Any person who is or may be affected by registration of an institution as a charity may, on the ground that it is not a charity, object to its being entered by the Commissioners in the register.[34] This allows next-of-kin whose financial interests may be affected by registration of a trust to whom a testator has left property to make objections to the Commissioners. The provision, however, is used mainly by the Inland Revenue Commissioners and rating authorities. In practice, if the Charity Commissioners are minded to register an institution they refer the case to the Inland Revenue to give them an opportunity to object.

If the Commissioners decide to register an institution as a charity an appeal[35] against that decision may be brought in the High Court by the Attorney General or by any person who has previously objected[36] to the proposed registration to the Commissioners. An appeal should be started in the Chancery Division. There is no time limit for an appeal although the usual time limits apply for any further appeal to the Court of Appeal or the House of Lords. Appeals concerning registration are not "charity proceedings"[37] and, accordingly, the usual restrictions on taking charity proceedings do not apply.

There is a similar right for any person affected to apply to the Charity Commissioners for a charity to be removed from the register on the grounds that it is not a charity.[38] Appeal against a refusal of the Commissioners to remove a charity lies to the High Court.[39]

1–030   If there is an appeal to the High Court against a decision of the Commissioners either to enter an institution on the register or to refuse to remove an institution from the register, the entry in the register is maintained pending the appeal but it is marked "in suspense".[40] The Commissioners are bound to take account of the fact that an appeal may be brought from the judge, and a further appeal from the Court of Appeal to the House of Lords: so long as there is a likelihood of further appeal the entry will remain in suspense.

---

[31] In practice, the Charity Commissioners' review procedure is followed with the Board being the final internal level of appeal, see OG 94, *Requests for a Decision Review*.

[32] Charities Act 1993, s.4(3). For appeals under this section see *Incorporated Council of Law Reporting for England and Wales v Att-Gen* [1971] Ch. 626, affirmed [1972] Ch. 73; *McGovern v Att-Gen* [1982] Ch. 321.

[33] R.S.C., Ord.108, r.5.

[34] Charities Act 1993, s.4(2).

[35] *ibid.*, s.4(3). For an appeal under this section see *IRC v McMullen* [1981] A.C. 1.

[36] *ibid.*, s.4(2).

[37] See Charities Act 1993, s.33(8) and paras 10–027, *et seq.*, below.

[38] Charities Act 1993, s.4(2).

[39] *ibid.*, s.4(3).

[40] *ibid.*, s.4(4).

Any question affecting the registration or removal from the register of an institution may, notwithstanding that it has been determined by a decision on appeal to the High Court, be considered afresh by the Commissioners.[41] Thus, the *res judicta* rule does not apply and the question of the status of an institution can be reopened.[42] The Commissioners are entitled to reconsider if it appears to them that there has been a change of circumstances or that the relevant decision is inconsistent with a later judicial decision.[43]

Effect of registration

An institution which is entered in the register is conclusively presumed for all purposes, other than rectification, to be a charity.[44] Thus relief from taxes and rates is available to any institution whilst it is in the register.[45] The fact that an institution is not in the register or, indeed, has been refused registration by the Commissioners is not presumptive that it does not have charitable status.[46] Once registered, a charity with a gross income of at least £10,000 in its last financial year must state that it is so registered on all its official documents.[47]

1–031

Removal

The Commissioners are obliged to remove from the register any institution which no longer appears to them to be a charity. They are also obliged to remove any charity which has ceased to exist or which does not operate.[48] Further, charity trustees are under a duty to notify the Commissioners if the charity ceases to exist or if there are any changes in the trusts.[49] An appeal against removal from the register lies to the High Court.[50]

1–032

An institution may cease to be charity in several ways. A charitable company may change its objects to non-charitable ones.[51] A trust may retain a power of revocation which, if exercised, will result in loss of charitable status. In both of these cases, the removal from the register will date back to the change.[52] A subsequent legal decision may show that a particular purpose until then thought to be charitable, not in fact to be so.[53] Change

---

[41] *ibid.*, s.4(5).
[42] See *National Anti-Vivisection Society v IRC* [1948] A.C. 31 and [2001] Ch. Com. Dec. 2 April (The General Medical Council).
[43] Charities Act 1993, s.4(5). Thus, the Commissioners refused to register the Burnley Rifle Club despite the previous decision in *Re Stephens* [1892] 8 T.L.R. 792, see (1993) 1 Ch. Com. Dec., p.4, *et seq.*
[44] Charities Act 1993, s.4(1).
[45] *Wynn v Skegness UDC* [1967] 1 W.L.R. 52, 56; *Finch v Poplar BC* (1967) 66 L.G.R. 324, 327.
[46] *Re Murawski's Will Trusts* [1971] 1 W.L.R. 707.
[47] Charities Act 1993, s.5.
[48] Charities Act 1993, s.3(4).
[49] *ibid.*, s.3(7)(b).
[50] *ibid.*, s.4(3).
[51] See para.12–006 below.
[52] Charities Act 1993, s.3(4).
[53] See *National Anti-Vivisection Society v IRC* [1948] A.C. 31.

in needs and values of society may lead to a particular purpose no longer being charitable.[54] In the latter two cases, loss of charitable status dates from removal from the register.

If an institution was entered on the register by mistake, whether of fact or law, the Charity Commissioners take the view that the institution should retain its property as it never was a charity.[55] In all other cases of loss of charitable status where the institution is a trust or unincorporated association the property will continue to be held for charitable purposes and the trustees will be obliged to apply for a *cy-près* scheme.[56] If the institution losing charitable status is a company, it is probable that a constructive trust would be imposed to ensure that the property of the institution remained available for charitable purposes.[57] In this way, loss of charitable status and potential removal of an institution from the register does not result in loss of the assets for charitable purposes.[58]

---

[54] See *National Anti-Vivisection Society v IRC* [1948] A.C. 31 at 74, *per* Lord Simonds and see para.1–005 above.
[55] See RR6, *Maintenance of an Accurate Register* (2000) pp.4 and 13 and see para.(429) below.
[56] See paras 13–005 and 13–008 below.
[57] See para.13–016 below.
[58] See RR6, *Maintenance of an Accurate Register* (2000), pp.5, *et seq.*

CHAPTER 2

THE FOUR HEADS OF CHARITY

THE RELIEF OF AGED, IMPOTENT AND POOR PEOPLE

Purposes to be construed disjunctively

The relief of aged, impotent and poor people is the first object set out **2–001** in the preamble to the Statute of Charitable Uses 1601. Formerly doubt existed as to whether the words "aged, impotent and poor" were capable of being construed disjunctively, or whether there must always be an element of poverty for a gift for aged or impotent people to be charitable,[1] but recent authorities have favoured a disjunctive construction, so that a gift for aged or impotent persons will be charitable, although such persons are not poor, provided that they are in need of relief[2]. While they should perhaps be considered to fall under the fourth head of charity since Lord Macnaghten in *Income Tax Special Purposes Commissioners v Pemsel*[3] did not refer to them under the first three heads, trusts for the relief of aged or impotent persons have long been considered by text-book writers in connection with trusts for the relief of poverty, and that practice is accordingly followed here.

The disjunctive construction in the case of a gift for the aged was adopted by Danckwerts J. in *Re Glyn*,[4] where, considering a bequest for building cottages for old women of the working classes of the age of 60 years or upwards, he said:

"I have not the slightest doubt that this is a good charitable bequest. The preamble to the Statute of Elizabeth refers to the relief of aged, impotent and poor people. The words, 'aged, impotent and poor' should be read disjunctively. It has never been suggested that poor people must also be aged to be objects of charity, and there is no reason for holding that aged people must also be poor to come within the meaning of the preamble to the Statute. A trust for the relief of aged

---

[1] *Att-Gen v Haberdashers' Company* (1834) 1 Myl. & K. 420, 428; *Re Lucas* [1922] 2 Ch. 52. Often, as in *Re Lucas*, poverty could be implied in a gift for the aged: see also *Att-Gen, v Comber* (1824) 2 Sim. & St. 93; *Thompson v Corby* (1860) 27 Beav. 649; *Re Wall* (1889) 42 Ch.D. 510; *Re Dudgeon* (1896) 74 L.T. 613; *Re Gosling* (1900) 48 W.R. 300; and see (1955) 71 L.Q.R. 16 (R.E.M.).

[2] *Joseph Rowntree Memorial Trust Housing Association Ltd. v Att-Gen* [1983] Ch. 159.

[3] [1891] A.C. 531 at 583.

[4] (1950) 66 T.L.R. (Pt. 2) 510 at 511.

persons would be charitable unless it was qualified in some way which would clearly render it not charitable."[5]

Re Glyn was followed by Vaisey J. in *Re Bradbury*,[6] where there was a gift for "an aged person in a nursing home", and in *Re Robinson*,[7] where there was a gift to "the old people over sixty-five years of Hazel Slade". In *Re Cottam*,[8] Danckwerts J. said of a trust to provide a flat or flats to be occupied by persons living within the boundaries of the County Borough of Huddersfield "being in every case over the age of sixty-five years" that it was for aged persons, and, therefore, prima facie a charitable trust, and he referred to *Re Robinson* as authority for that proposition. The fact that his Lordship went on to find that the trust was for the aged of small means does not, therefore, detract from *Re Cottam* as an authority for the disjunctive construction. In *Re Neal*,[9] where there was a gift for the founding of a home for old persons. Goff J. held that it was not necessary to find an intention to relieve poverty.

In *Re Lewis*,[10] where there were gifts "to 10 blind girls" and "to 10 blind boys", in each case "Tottenham residents if possible", and there was nothing in the will to import any element of poverty whatsoever, Roxburgh J. said: "There is no case which suggests that in the case of impotent persons, the Statute should not be read properly, that is to say disjunctively, so as to constitute impotent persons as a class *per se*."

2–002   In *Re Resch's Will Trusts*[11] there was a gift of income to be applied for the general purposes of a named private hospital which charged substantial fees but was not run for the profit of individuals, and it was objected that it was not carried on for purposes beneficial to the community because it provided only for persons of means capable of paying the fees required as a condition of admission. Delivering the judgment of the Judicial Committee of the Privy Council, Lord Wilberforce said[12]:

"In dealing with this objection, it is necessary first to dispose of a misapprehension. It is not a condition of validity of a trust for the

---

[5] In *Re Sanders' Will Trusts* [1954] Ch. 265 at 272 Harman J. said that the *ratio decidendi* in *Re Glyn* (1950) 66 T.L.R. (Pt. 2) 510 was that out of old age and working class it might be inferred that poverty was a necessary qualification. In the 6th edition of this book it was pointed out that this was not what Danckwerts J. said and that Harman J.'s views were not consistent with the application of *Re Glyn* in later cases. In *Joseph Rowntree Memorial Trust Housing Association Ltd. v Att-Gen* [1983] Ch. 159. 172, Peter Gibson J. said that he shared the editors' views.
[6] [1950] 2 All E.R. 1150, n.
[7] [1951] Ch. 198.
[8] [1955] 1 W.L.R. 1299.
[9] (1966) 110 S.J. 549.
[10] [1955] Ch. 104, 109. See also *Re Fraser* (1883) 22 Ch.D. 827; *Re Adams* [1968] Ch. 80 at 93; *cf. Re Elliott* (1910) 102 LT. 528, Parker J. considering a gift to train blind persons to earn their own living, inferred an intention to relieve poverty. So, too, in *Re Roadley* [1930] 1 Ch. 524, Bennett J. held that a trust to pay the income of a sum of £3,000 in paying the expenses of, and in maintaining patients from, certain parishes in either of two named hospitals was a trust for the relief of persons who were both impotent and poor, but see para.1–011 above in relation to the public benefit requirement.
[11] [1969] 1 A.C. 514, PC.
[12] *ibid.*, at 542.

relief of the sick that it should be limited to the poor sick. Whether one regards the charitable character of trusts for the relief of the sick as flowing from the word 'impotent' ('aged, impotent and poor people') in the preamble to 43 Eliz. c. 4 or more broadly as derived from the conception of benefit to the community, there is no warrant for adding to the condition of sickness that of poverty."

His Lordship pointed out that as early as *Income Tax Special Purposes Commissioners v Pemsel* Lord Herschell was able to say[13]:

"I am unable to agree with the view that the sense in which 'charities' and 'charitable purpose' are popularly used is so restricted as this. I certainly cannot think that they are limited to the relief of wants occasioned by lack of pecuniary means. Many examples may, I think, be given of endowments for the relief of human necessities, which would be as generally termed charities as hospitals or almshouses, where, nevertheless, the necessities to be relieved do not result from poverty in its limited sense of the lack of money."

Later Lord Wilberforce said[14]:

"To provide, in response to public need, medical treatment otherwise inaccessible but in its nature expensive, without any profit motive, might well be charitable: on the other hand to limit admission to a nursing home to the rich would not be so. The test is essentially one of public benefit, and indirect as well as direct benefit enters into the account. In the present case, the element of public benefit is strongly present. It is not disputed that a need exists to provide accommodation and medical treatment in conditions of greater privacy and relaxation than would be possible in a general hospital and as a supplement to the facilities of a general hospital. This is what the private hospital does and it does so at, approximately, cost price. The service is needed by all, not only by the well-to-do. So far as its nature permits it is open to all: the charges are not low, but the evidence shows that it cannot be said that the poor are excluded: . . . .".

The question of the construction of "aged, impotent and poor people" came before the Court in *Joseph Rowntree Memorial Trust Housing Association Ltd. v Att-Gen*[15] which was concerned with schemes to provide accommodation to meet the disabilities and requirements of the elderly. The question arose whether the schemes could be charitable in law having regard to the fact that they provided benefits by contract, not bounty, which were not capable of being withdrawn if a beneficiary ceased to qualify, and because they benefited private individuals, not a charitable class,

---

[13] [1891] 1 A.C. 531 at 571.
[14] [1969] 1 A.C. 544.
[15] [1983] Ch. 159. See also *D.V. Bryant Trust Board v Hamilton City Council* [1997] 3 N.Z.L.R. 342.

and were a commercial enterprise capable of producing profit for a beneficiary. Having considered the authorities in favour of the disjunctive construction. Peter Gibson J. said[16]: "These authorities convincingly confirm
the correctness of the proposition that the relief of the aged does not have
to be relief for the aged poor. In other words the phrase 'aged, impotent
and poor people' in the preamble must be read disjunctively."

The need for relief

2–003   While the aged and the impotent may be the subject of a charitable trust
without at the same time being poor, it is to be remembered that the
Statute of Charitable Uses refers to the "relief" of such persons. In *Joseph
Rowntree Memorial Trust Housing Association Ltd. v Att-Gen.*[17] Peter
Gibson J. pointed out that *Re Glyn,*[18] *Re Bradbury,*[19] *Re Robinson,*[20] *Re
Cottam*[21] and *Re Lewis,*[22] give support to the view that it is a sufficient
charitable purpose to benefit the aged, or the impotent, without more, and
appear to pay no regard to the word "relief." His Lordship said that he had
no hesitation in preferring the approach adopted in *Re Neal*[23] and *Re
Resch's Will Trusts*[24] that there must be a need which is to be relieved by
the charitable gift, such need being attributable to the aged or impotent
condition of the persons to be benefited. In the case of the schemes which
were before the Court in *Joseph Rowntree Memorial Trust Housing
Association Ltd v Att-Gen*[25] the plaintiff identified a particular need for
special housing to be provided for the elderly in the ways proposed in the
scheme and this was a charitable purpose.

Bounty or bargain

2–004   It has been said that to be charitable the relief of poverty must be given
by way of bounty and not by way of bargain. It has for some time been
apparent that that statement based on words of Rowlatt J. in *IRC v Society
of Widows and Orphans of Medical Men*[26] requires qualification, and that,
provided that there is relief, a trust for poor persons, and also for aged or
impotent persons, may be charitable although a financial contribution is
required from the beneficiary. Rowlatt J. said[27]:

---

[16] *Joseph Rowntree Memorial Trust Housing Association Ltd. v Att-Gen* [1983] Ch.159 at 174.
[17] *ibid.*
[18] (1950) 66 T.L.R. (Pt. 2) 510.
[19] [1950] 2 All E.R. 1150n.
[20] [1951] Ch. 198.
[21] [1955] 1 W.L.R. 1299.
[22] [1955] Ch. 104.
[23] [1966] 110 S.J. 549.
[24] [1969] 1 A.C. 514, PC.
[25] [1983] Ch. 159, 174.
[26] (1926) 136 L.T. 60 at 65.
[27] *ibid.*

"It seems to me that when it is said that the relief of poverty is a charity within the meaning of the rule which we are discussing that does mean the relief of poverty by way of bounty; it does not mean the relief of poverty by way of bargain. A purely mutual society among very poor people whose dependants would quite clearly always be very poor would not, I think, be a charity; it would be a business arrangement as has been said in one of the cases, whereby contractual benefits accrued to people whose poverty makes them very much in need of them. That would not be a charity. I think therefore, that the crux of this case is whether this is a case of that sort."

In *Joseph Rowntree Memorial Trust Housing Association Ltd v Att-Gen.*[28] Peter Gibson J. said that Rowlatt J.'s remarks must be understood in their limited context, and were entirely appropriate in determining whether a mutual society conferring rights on members was charitable. Peter Gibson continued:

"If a housing association were a co-operative under which the persons requiring the dwellings provided by the housing association had by the association's constitution contractual rights to the dwellings, that would no doubt not be charitable, but that is quite different from bodies set up like the trust and the association [now under consideration]. The applicants for dwellings under the schemes which I am considering would have no right to any dwelling when they apply. The fact that the benefit given to them is in the form of a contract is immaterial to the charitable purpose in making the benefit available."

Peter Gibson J. had already[29] referred to cases where beneficiaries only received benefits from a charity by way of bargain. The trust in *Re Cottam*[30] was for the provision of flats to be let at economic rents to persons over 65 years of age. The private hospital which benefited from *Re Resch's Will Trusts*[31] charged substantial fees. Trusts for fee-paying schools of which *Abbey Malvern Wells Ltd v Ministry of Local Government and Planning*[32] provides an example, are of a similar kind. In *Re Estlin*[33] there was a gift for the provision of homes of rest for lady teachers at a rent.[34] Peter Gibson J. pointed out that it was of course crucial in all those cases that the services provided by the gift were not provided for the private profit of the individuals providing them. It is also apparent that it is not the source from which the money is derived which

---

[28] [1983] Ch. 159 at 175.
[29] [1983] Ch. 159 at 174.
[30] [1955] 1 W.L.R. 1299.
[31] [1969] 1 A.C. 514, PC see para.2–002, above.
[32] [1951] Ch. 728.
[33] [1903] 89 L.T. 88.
[34] See also *Mary Clark Home (Trustees) v Anderson* [1904] 2 K.B. 645; *Re Gardom* [1914] 1 Ch. 662; *Shaw v Halifax Corporation* [1915] 2 K.B. 170; *Finch v Poplar Borough Council* (1967) 66 L.G.R. 324; *Scottish Burial Reform and Cremation Society Ltd. v Glasgow City Corporation* [1968] A.C. 138; *Abbeyfield (Harpenden) Society Ltd. v Woods* [1968] 1 W.L.R. 374; *Re Payling's Will Trusts* [1969] 1 W.L.R. 1595.

is material but the purpose to which it is devoted. Thus in *Spiller v Maude*[35] Sir George Jessel M.R. refused to draw any distinction between that part of the income of the York Theatrical Fund Society which was derived from voluntary subscriptions by the general public and that part of the income which was derived from members' contributions. Furthermore, it is clear that Rowlatt J. did himself mean that his words in *IRC v Society of Widows and Orphans of Medical Men*[36] should be given a limited context; although a small part of the income of the Society, the object of which was to relieve the distressed widows of medical men, was in fact derived from subscriptions which the medical men paid, his Lordship nevertheless held that the Society was a charity because the relief was given by way of bounty and not by way of bargain.

2–005   It would appear to follow from the approach taken in *Joseph Rowntree Memorial Trust Housing Association Ltd v Att-Gen*[37] that a charity may accept a transfer of money or property conditional on providing benefits for a particular beneficiary in the future. Clearly, such bargains for future benefits should only be made where the relevant person falls within the beneficiary class so that, for example, a charity which provides residential care for the disabled may enter into a bargain with the parents of a disabled child. There is a danger that if too many such arrangements are entered into by a charity it would become a mutual benefit society and cease to be a charity.[38]

It was also decided by *Joseph Rowntree Memorial Trust Housing Association Ltd v Att-Gen*[39] that a gift was not precluded from being charitable because there was no provision for withdrawing the benefit in the event of a beneficiary ceasing to qualify for relief, if benefits in that form were required to meet the particular need. Peter Gibson J. accepted that the inclusion in a lease granted by the plaintiff Association of a provision entitling it to terminate the lease in the event of a change in the financial circumstances of the tenant would have an unsettling effect on aged tenants, and that this was a valid reason for omitting any such provision. In holding that the trust was nonetheless charitable, his Lordship applied *Re Monk*[40] in which a testatrix set up a loan fund whereby loans for up to nine years were to be made available for the poor; this was held to be charitable, although the circumstances of a borrower might change while a loan was outstanding. Peter Gibson J. concluded[41] that if the grant of a long-term leasehold interest with the concomitant security of tenure which such an interest would give to the elderly was necessary to meet the identified needs of the elderly, then that was no objection to such a grant. The schemes were for the benefit of a charitable class, the aged having certain needs

---

[35] (1881) 32 Ch.D 158, n. See also *Skegness UDC v Derbyshire Miners' Welfare Committee* [1959] A.C. 807 at 824, *per* Viscount Simonds; *Waterson v Hendon BC* [1959] 1 W.L.R. 985 at 992, per Salmon J.
[36] (1926) 136 L.T. 60 at 65.
[37] [1983] Ch. 159.
[38] See (1993) 1 Ch. Com. Dec., para.18.
[39] [1983] Ch. 159 at 175.
[40] [1927] 2 Ch. 197, CA.
[41] [1983] Ch. 159 at 175, 176.

requiring relief therefrom, and it was not a valid objection to the schemes that an individual beneficiary might profit by an increase in the value of his equity; that was a matter incidental to the objective of the schemes and it was not a profit at the expense of the charity.

It has already been stated that where a body is established for charitable purposes, it will not be the less a charity because the pursuit of that purpose will or may confer benefits upon persons who are not themselves objects of charity.[42] It is submitted that it is entirely consistent with that principle that a trust for the relief of aged or impotent or poor people is not the less charitable because an object thereof reaps an incidental benefit from the manner in which it operates, over and above that specifically conferred upon him by the trustees. What matters is that the primary purpose of the trust is altruistic and not self-seeking.[43]

Meaning of aged

In *Re Wall*[44] Kay J. held that a gift to "men and women not under fifty years of age" was charitable. This may have been a reasonable view in 1889 when life for most people was hard and they often aged early; but it is thought that the Court would now take judicial notice of, or admit medical or other evidence of, the fact that most people do not nowadays fall victims to the disabilities of old age until they are at least 60, and that it would be imprudent for anyone who desired to establish a charitable trust for the benefit of aged persons to prescribe a lower age limit than 60. It follows that the trustees of a gift of property "as a home for aged persons", which is a good charitable gift,[45] probably ought not to accept as beneficiaries persons under 60 years of age. Retirement age is now flexible and "aged" has become a relative term. It is considered that the appropriate age would need to be assessed in the context of the particular purpose.

2–006

Meaning of impotent

The word "impotent" has never been defined by the Court, but it has been interpreted fairly liberally.[46] It is defined in the Oxford English Dictionary as meaning "physically weak; without bodily strength; unable to use one's limbs; helpless, decrepit", a definition sufficiently wide to cover not only those suffering from permanent disability, whether of body or mind, but those temporarily incapacitated by injury or illness, or in need of rest, and young children incapable of protecing themselves from the consequences of cruelty or neglect. The cases show that this definition,

2–007

---

[42] See para.1–021 above and the cases referred to in n.96.
[43] See CC4, *Charities for the Relief of the Poor* (2001) and CC6, *Charities for the Relief of Sickness* (2000).
[44] (1889) 42 Ch.D. 510.
[45] *Re Payling's Will Trusts* [1969] 1 W.L.R. 1595. The question as to the age of the intended occupants did not arise.
[46] See para.2–083, promotion and maintenance of health, para.2–085, resettlement and rehabilitation, para.2–087, care of children and para.2–098, Recreational Charities Act 1958.

or something like it, has guided the Courts. Thus gifts for the benefit of the blind,[47] the sick and wounded,[48] including former enemies who have been wounded,[49] the prevention of cruelty to children,[50] and faith-healing[51] have been held to be charitable.

Although in *Re Roadley*[52] a trust to apply income in payment of the expenses and maintenance of patients in a hospital was upheld on the grounds that it was for the relief of persons who were both impotent and poor, it is now clear[53] that (given always the necessary element of public benefit) gifts for the establishment or support of hospitals and nursing homes are charitable as being for the relief of impotent persons who need not necessarily be poor. Furthermore, a gift to provide accommodation for relations coming from a distance to visit patients critically ill in hospital is charitable.[54]

Gifts for the establishment or support of homes of rest are also charitable. The term "home of rest" connotes not primarily a home for persons who are old or worn out and so permanently in need of rest, but rather a convalescent home to which persons ordinarily actively employed in their various pursuits are enabled to retire.[55]

2–008   In *Re Estlin*[56] there was a gift for the support of a home of rest for lady teachers. There was no requirement that the beneficiaries should be poor, though no doubt they were in fact of small means. Kekewich J. held the gift to be charitable, but his reasons do not clearly appear from his judgment. In *Re James*[57] Farwell J. appears to have thought that the beneficiaries in *Re Estlin* were objects of charity as impotent persons. The testatrix in *Re James* gave her house upon trust to establish a home of rest for the sisters of a religious community, for the clergy of the Diocese of Truro, and such persons as the mother superior of the community should appoint, and also gave an endowment of £6,000 for the repair of the house and the maintenance and support of the inmates. There was no requirement of poverty, but the sisters were engaged in charitable work and their individual incomes were pooled, so that it is likely that they had taken

---

[47] *Re Fraser* (1883) 22 Ch.D. 827; *Re Lewis* [1955] Ch. 104; and see *Re Elliott* (1910) 102 L.T. 528, 530; *Barber v Chudley* (1922) 128 L.T. 766; see also *Re Spence* [1979] Ch. 483.

[48] *Re Hillier* [1944] All E.R. 480. The sick or wounded may be abroad, see [1990] Ch. Com. Rep., paras 2–087 (The Gdansk Hospice Fund).

[49] *Re Robinson* [1931] 2 Ch. 122 (Gift for disabled German Soldiers).

[50] *Commissioners for the Special Purposes of Income Tax v Pemsel* [1891] A.C. 531, 572. It may be that the prevention of cruelty to children is also charitable on another ground, namely, that such gifts are calculated to promote public morality by encouraging kindness, discouraging cruelty and stimulating humane sentiments for the benefit of mankind; see further paras 2–087 *et seq.*, below.

[51] *Re Kerin, The Times*, May 24, 1966: Goff J. held that faith-healing was for the relief of impotent persons or for the advancement of religion or for both purposes.

[52] [1930] 1 Ch. 524.

[53] See *Re Adams* [1968] Ch. 80, CA (reversing in part [1967] 1 W.L.R. 162); *Re Resch's Will Trusts* [1969] 1 A.C. 514, PC; see also *Liverpool and District Hospital for Diseases of the Heart v Att-Gen* [1981] Ch. 193 and para.2–002, above and para.2–083 below.

[54] *Re Dean's Will Trusts* [1950] 1 All E.R. 882.

[55] *Re White's Will Trusts* [1951] 1 All E.R. 528 at 529. See also *IRC v Roberts Marine Mansions (Trustees)* (1927) 11 T.C. 425.

[56] (1903) 72 L.J. Ch. 687.

[57] [1932] 2 Ch. 25.

vows of poverty. Farwell J. held that the gifts were charitable on the ground that the sisters and the clergy were good objects of a charity, and that if the mother superior did not appoint persons who were suitable objects of charity (though they themselves did not have to be engaged in charitable work) she would be in breach of trust. Although the word "impotent" is not used in Farwell J.'s judgment, the tenor of it is that admission to the home was not necessarily confined to persons who were poor but was open to those who were in need of rest (and so "impotent" within the meaning of the preamble). His Lordship said that the words "home of rest" indicated something in the nature of a hospital, providing the temporary inmates with the means and possibility of rest.

Re James was followed by Maugham J. in *Re Chaplin*[58] where the testator gave his house and its contents "to provide a home of rest that shall afford the means of physical and/or mental recuperation to persons in need of rest by reason of the stress and strain caused or partly caused by the conditions in which they ordinarily live and/or work." It was expressly provided that in considering the suitability of a candidate for admission to the home his financial position should not be taken into account, and he might be required to pay according to his means for board, lodging and other benefits and, where reasonably possible, for medical attendance and treatment. Maugham J. held that the trusts were charitable.

In *Re White's Will Trusts*[59] there was a gift "in trust for the Royal Infirmary, Sheffield, to be applied . . . for the purposes of a home of rest for nurses of that institution." Harman J.'s reasons for upholding the gift were that the work of the Infirmary was charitable, that the nurses were engaged in the charitable work of the Infirmary, and that the purpose of the gift was to increase the efficiency of the Infirmary as a hospital for the healing of the sick by providing a means for restoring the efficiency of the nurses for the performance of their duties. That suggests that his Lordship considered the true purpose of the gift to be the support of the Infirmary, and that he did not treat the nurses as the beneficiaries. On the other hand, he applied *Re Estlin*,[60] *Re James*[61] and *Re Chaplin*[62] which suggests that he also regarded the gift as being for the benefit of impotent persons, that is to say, the nurses who were in need of rest.

Meaning of poor

"Poor" is a relative term[63] and an individual need not be destitute in order to qualify as a poor person within the meaning of the preamble to   **2–009**

---

[58] [1933] Ch. 115.
[59] [1951] 1 All E.R. 528.
[60] (1903) 72 L.J. Ch. 687.
[61] [1932] 2 Ch. 25.
[62] [1933] Ch. 115.
[63] *Trustees of the Mary Clark Home v Anderson* [1904] 2 K.B. 645 at 655, *per* Channell J.; *Re Clarke* [1923] 2 Ch. 407 at 411, 412, *per* Romer J.

the Statute of Charitable Uses 1601.[64] The Courts have never defined
"poor": its meaning has to be ascertained from the reported cases, which
show that an individual is considered to be poor if he is in generally strait-
ened circumstances and unble to maintain a very modest standard of living for himself and the persons (if any) dependent upon him.[65] In *Re
Coulthurst*[66] Sir Raymond Evershed M.R. said:

> "It is quite clearly established that poverty does not mean destitution;
> it is a word of wide and somewhat indefinite import; it may not
> unfairly be paraphrased for present purposes as meaning persons who
> have to 'go short' in the ordinary acceptation of that term, due regard
> being had to their status in life and so forth."

The Court of Appeal was there considering a trust for the benefit of the
widows and orphaned children of deceased officers and ex-officers of a
bank. The trust was held to be charitable, and is thought that the decision
is clear authority for the proposition that a person who suffers hardship
from a reduction in his circumstances may be a proper object of charity,
so that, for example, trustees could in such a case meet the school fees of
a child who would otherwise have to be removed from a particular school
because of the premature death of his father. A person with insufficient
income to obtain a mortgage may be poor.[67]

Gifts for the relief of poverty

Inference of an intention to relieve poverty

2–010   Where the intention to relieve poverty is not expressed, but there is a
sufficient element of public benefit, the intention may be inferred from the
nature or amount of the gift being such as to show that only poor persons
would need it.[68] On the other hand, whereas a gift for a class of persons

---

[64] *Re De Carteret* [1933] Ch. 103 at 108 *per* Maugham J. See also "Some Recent
Developments in the Law of Charity" by Mr Geoffrey Cross Q.C. (as he then was), (1956)
72 L.Q.R. 182 at 206.

[65] *Trustees of the Mary Clark Home v Andersons* (1904) 2 K.B. 645; *Re Gardom* [1914] 1 Ch.
662 (reversed, but not on this point, [1914] 1 Ch. 674 (C.A.), affd. sub nom. *Le Page v
Gardom* (1915) 84 L.J. Ch. 749, HL; *Shaw v Halifax Corporation* [1915] 2 K.B. 170; *Re
Clarke* [1923] 2 Ch. 407; *Re De Carteret* [1933] Ch. 103.

[66] [1951] Ch. 661 at 665, 666 (affirming [1951] Ch. 193, Vaisey J.). See also *Re Niyazi's Will
Trusts* [1978] 1 W.L.R. 910, 913, *per* Sir Robert Megarry V.C.

[67] See (1995) 3 Ch. Com. Dec. pp.7–10 (Garfield Poverty Trust); (1994) 4 Ch. Com. Dec.
pp.13–16 (Habitat for Humanity Great Britain).

[68] *Att-Gen v Comber* (1824) 2 Sim. & St. 93 (widows and orphans); *Thompson v Corby* (1860)
27 Beav. 649 (aged widows and spinsters of a parish); *Re Wall* (1889) 42 Ch.D. 510 (annuities of £10 each to men and women not under 50 years of age who attended either of two
specified Unitarian chapels); *Re Dudgeon* (1896) 74 L.T. 613 (respectable single women of
good character above the age of 60 years, to be paid by monthly instalments, but so that
no recipient shall receive more than £10 per annum); *Verge v Somerville* [1924] A.C. 496 at
506 (repatriation fund for returned soldiers); *Re Coulthurst* [1951] Ch. 661 (widows and
orphaned children of deceased officers and deceased ex-officers of a bank considered by

whose nexus is not public but private may be upheld if it is expressly for the relief of poverty,[69] it seems that in the case of such a gift the intention to relieve poverty, where not expressed, will not be inferred.[70]

General and particular gifts

A charitable gift for the poor may be expressed in general and indefinite language,[71] or may be for the poor of a particular defined area (parish town or other place),[72] or poor persons of a particular religious denomination attending a specified chapel or chapels,[73] or the poor of a particular regiment,[74] or families of men or women (not being commissioned) in the armed forces,[75] or a particular class of poor people, such as poor gentle-women,[76] distressed gentlefolk,[77] or persons of moderate[78] or limited[79] means, who are not self-supporting,[80] or housekeepers,[81] or tradesmen of a particular kind,[82] or unsuccessful literary men,[83] or servants,[84] or "poor struggling youths of merit"[85] or poor pious persons,[86] or poor emigrants,[87] or persons descended from residents of a named borough in a

2–011

reason of financial circumstances most deserving), *Re Niyazi's Will Trusts* [1978] 1 W.L.R. 910; (a working men's hostel in Famagusta) but *cf. Re Sander's Will Trusts* [1954] Ch. 265.

[69] See para.2–014, below.
[70] See *Re Drummond* [1914] 2 Ch. 90 (gift towards the holiday expenses of low-paid workpeople of a particular firm).
[71] *Att-Gen v Peacock* (1676) Rep. t. Finch 245 (for the good of poor people for ever); *Att-Gen v Rance* (1728), cited in (1762) Amb. 422; *Nash v Morley* (1842) 5 Beav. 177; *Re Darling* [1896] 1 Ch. 50 (to the poor and the service of God, following *Powerscourt v Powerscourt* (1824) 1 Moll. 616).
[72] *Woodford (Inhabitants) v Parkhurst* (1639), Duke 70; *Att-Gen, v Pearce* (1740) 2 Atk. 87; *Att-Gen v Clarke* (1762) Amb. 422; *Att-Gen v Exeter Corporation* (1826) 2 Russ. 45; (1827) 3 Russ. 395; *Att-Gen v Wilkinson* (1839) 1 Beav. 370; *Att-Gen v Bovill* (1840) 1 Ph. 762; *Salter v Farey* (1843) 7 Jur. 831; *Re Lambeth Charities* (1853) 22 L.J. Ch. 959; *Att-Gen v Blizard* (1855) 21 Beav. 233; *Russell v Kellett* (1855) 3 Sm. & G. 264; *Re Lousada* (1887) 82 L.T.J. 358; *Re St. Alphage, London Wall* (1888) 59 L.T. 614; *Re Lucas* [1922] 2 Ch. 52; *Re Monk* [1927] 2 Ch. 197; *Re Roadley* [1930] 1 Ch. 524; *Guinness Trust (London Fund) Founded 1890 Registered 1902 v West Ham Borough Council* (1959) 1 W.L.R. 233; *Re Lepton's Charity* [1972] Ch. 276. The place may be abroad: *Re Niyazi's Will Trusts* [1978] 1 W.L.R. 910 (Famagusta).
[73] *Re Wall* (1889) 42 Ch.D. 510.
[74] *Re Donald* [1909] 2 Ch. 410.
[75] *Soldiers', Sailors' and Airmen's Families' Association v Att-Gen* [1968] 1 W.L.R. 313.
[76] *Att-Gen v Power* (1809) 1 Ball & B. 145; *Mary Clark Home (Trustees) v Anderson* [1904] 2 K.B. 645; *Re Gardom* [1914] 1 Ch. 662; *Shaw v Halifax Corporation* [1915] 2 K.B. 170.
[77] *Re Young* [1951] Ch. 344.
[78] *Re Clarke* [1923] 2 Ch. 407.
[79] *Re De Carteret* [1933] Ch. 103.
[80] *Re Central Employment Bureau for Women and Students' Career Association* [1942] 1 All E.R. 232.
[81] *Att-Gen v Pearce* (1740) 2 Atk. 87. "Housekeeper" is a word now used to denote someone who looks after the house of another, but in the case of old charities it sometimes means a person who is housebound and sometimes a householder.
[82] *Re White's Trusts* (1886) 33 Ch.D. 449.
[83] *Thompson v Thompson* (1844) 1 Coll. 381 at 395.
[84] *Reeve v Att-Gen* (1843) 3 Hare 191; *Loscombe v Wintringham* (1850) 13 Beav. 87.
[85] *Milne's Executors v Aberdeen University Court* (1905) 7 F. (Ct. of Sess.) 642.
[86] *Nash v Morley* (1942) 5 Beav. 177.
[87] *Barclay v Maske-Lyne* (1858) 32 L.T.(O.S.) 205. But a gift "for emigration uses" is not charitable: see *Re Sidney* [1908] 1 Ch. 488.

particular year needing assistance to improve their condition in life by emigrating,[88] or inmates of a workhouse,[89] or patients in a hospital,[90] or debtors,[91] or fifty needy and deserving old men and fifty deserving old women of a particular place,[92] or widows and orphans of poor clergymen,[93] or seamen of a particular port,[94] or victims of a particular disaster,[95] or widows and orphans of a particular parish,[96] or indigent bachelors and widowers "who have shown sympathy with science",[97] or the relief of domestic distress.[98]

Gifts for the relief of poor members of a particular church or religious denomination are charitable. Gifts of this kind which have been upheld were for the benefit of Jews,[99] Presbyterians,[1] Irvingites,[2] Moravians,[3] Unitarians,[4] and Methodists.[5] Such gifts have always been charitable in spite of the law avoiding gifts to superstitious uses (now practically obsolete).[6] The law was so tolerant as to enable the court to uphold a gift for ministers and others who had been reduced to poverty through upholding particular doctrines.[7] It does not seem to have been doubted in cases of this kind that the persons eligible to benefit constituted a sufficiently important section of the public.

---

[88] *Re Tree* [1945] Ch. 325. For the grounds on which Evershed J. distinguished *Re Compton* [1945] Ch. 123, see [1945] Ch. at 328–332; and see Cross, "Some Recent Developments in the Law of Charity" (1956) 72 L.Q.R. 182, 190, n.8, In *Re Tree* [1945] Ch. 325 the element of poverty was present. It is doubtful whether the decision could have been justified if that element had been absent: see *Davies v Perpetual Trustee Co.* [1959] A.C. 439 at 456.

[89] *Att-Gen v Vint* (1850) 3 De G. & Sm. 704.

[90] *Reading Corporation v Lane* (1601) Toth. 32; Duke 81; see also *Re Roadley* [1930] 1 Ch. 524.

[91] *Att-Gen v Painter-Stainers Co.* (1788) 2 Cox Eq.Cas. 51; *Att-Gen v Ironmongers Co.* (1834) 2 My. & K. 576.

[92] *Re Reed* (1893) 10 T.L.R. 87; and see also *Re Wall* (1889) 42 Ch.D. 510.

[93] *Waldo v Caley* (1809) 16 Ves. 206; an see *Re Friend of the Clergy's Charters* [1921] 1 Ch. 409, where this was assumed without argument.

[94] *Powell v Att-Gen* (1817) 3 Mer. 48.

[95] *Pease v Pattinson* (1886) 32 Ch.D. 154; *Re Hartley Colliery Accident Relief Fund* (1908) 102 L.T. 165n; *Cross v Lloyd-Greame* (1909) 102 L.T. 163 (where there were only six victims); *Re North Devon and West Somerset Relief Fund Trusts* [1953] 1 W.L.R. 1260 (flood disaster). It is suggested, however, that disaster relief funds fall more naturally under the fourth head of charities, as those relieved need not necessarily be poor. The emphasis of such a fund is need for relief". See para.2–086 below.

[96] *Att-Gen v Comber* (1824) 2 Sim. & St. 93; *Russell v Kellett* (1855) 3 Sm. & G. 264.

[97] *Weir v Crum-Brown* [1908] A.C. 162 (on appeal from the Court of Session).

[98] *Kendall v Granger* (1842) 5 Beav. 300 at 303.

[99] *Re Haendler The Times*, July 4, 1931, see also *Re Jewish Orphanage Charity Endowment Trusts* [1960] 1 W.L.R. 344.

[1] *Att-Gen v Wansay* (1808) 15 Ves. 231.

[2] *Att-Gen v Lawes* (1849) 8 Hare 32.

[3] *Income Tax Special Purposes Commissioners v Pemsel* [1891] A.C. 531.

[4] *Shore v Wilson* (1842) 9 Cl. & F. 355; *Att-Gen v Shore* (1843) 11 Sim. 592.

[5] *Dawson v Small* (1874) L.R. 18 Eq. 114.

[6] But in 1605, when the only religion recognised or tolerated was that taught and practised in the Church of England, it was held that a trust for the relief of poor recusants was void: *Lady Egerton's Case* (1605) Duke 8 at 127.

[7] *Att-Gen v Lawes* (1849) 8 Ha. 32.

Direct and indirect relief

Relief may be provided directly, as by the distribution of doles of money[8] or otherwise[9]; by apprenticing poor children[10]; by providing allotments or buying land to be let to the poor at a low rent[11]; by providing cheap flats to be let to aged persons of small means at rents which they can afford to pay[12]; and by providing small interest-free loans to poor and deserving inhabitants of a particular parish.[13]

2–012

Relief may also be provided by means of gifts for the establishment or support of institutions[14] for the benefit of particular classes of poor persons, such as hospitals, infirmaries or dispensaries,[15] almshouses,[16] orphan and other asylums,[17] orphanages for children of particular classes of persons, such as railway servants,[18] policemen,[19] or clergymen[20]; institutions for the support of decayed actors and actresses[21] or the distressed widows of medical men[22]; soup kitchens[23]; flats for needy ladies who were widows and dependants of deceased officers in the armed forces[24]; homes of various kinds.[25]

The Charity Commissioners have registered a number of charities which have adopted new methods of relieving poverty. The Fairtrade Foundation has general objects for the relief of poverty but operates by awarding the "fair trade mark" to particular brands of consumer products which benefit people in the third world employed in their production.[26] They have also recognised that it is charitable to provide loans to enable those who do not have sufficient means to afford a mortgage to purchase

---

[8] *Att-Gen v Bovill* (1840) 1 Ph. 762.

[9] *Att-Gen v Minshull* (1798) 4 Ves. 11; *Thompson v Thompson* (1844) 1 Coll. 395. (For the dislike of the court for dole charities in the latter half of the nineteenth century, see *Att-Gen v Marchant* (1866) L.R. 3 Eq., 424 at 431; *Re Campden Charities* (1883) 18 Ch.D. 310 at 327 where Jessel M.R. said: "We know that the extension of doles is simply the extension of mischief.") See also CC4, *Charities for the Relief of the Poor* (2001).

[10] *Att-Gen v Minshull* (1798) 4 Ves. 11; *Att-Gen v Winchelsea (Earl)* (1791) 3 Bro.C.C. 374; *Att-Gen v Wansay* (1808) 15 Ves. 231.

[11] *Crafton v Frith* (1851) 4 De G. & Sm. 237.

[12] *Re Cottam* [1955] 1 W.L.R. 1299.

[13] *Re Monk* [1927] 2 Ch. 197.

[14] See also Relief of unemployment, para.2–075 and Promotion of urban and rural regeneration, para.2–076 below.

[15] *Pelham v Anderson* (1764) 2 Eden 296; *Att-Gen v Kell* (1840) 2 Beav. 575; *Att-Gen v Gascoigne* (1833) 2 My & K. 647; *Biscoe v Jackson* (1887) 35 Ch.D. 460; *Re Cox* (1877) 7 Ch.D. 204; *Re Welsh Hospital (Netley) Fund* [1921] 1 Ch. 655.

[16] *Mayor of London's Case* (1640) Duke 83; *Re Whiteley* [1910] 1 Ch. 600.

[17] *Harbin v Masterman* (1871) L.R. 12 Eq. 559; *Harbin v Masterman* [1894] 2 Ch. 184 (affd. sub nom. *Wharton v Masterman* [1895] A.C. 186).

[18] *Hull v Derby Sanitary Authority* (1885) 16 Q.B.D. 163.

[19] *Re Douglas* (1887) 35 Ch.D. 472.

[20] *Re Clergy Society* (1856) 2 K. & J. 615.

[21] *Spiller v Maude* (1881) 32 Ch.D. 158, n.: *Re Lacy* [1899] 2 Ch. 149.

[22] *IRC v Society of Widows and Orphans of Medical Men* (1926) 136 L.T. 60.

[23] *Biscoe v Jackson* (1887) 35 Ch.D. 460.

[24] See *Soldiers', Sailors' and Airmen's Families' Association v Merton London Borough Council* [1966] 1 W.L.R. 736.

[25] *Rolls v Miller* (1884) 27 Ch.D. 71; *Re Sahal's Will Trusts* [1958] 1 W.L.R. 1243.

[26] (1995) 4 Ch. Com. Dec., pp.1–7.

accommodation.[27] A charity may decide that a form of social or programme related investment is a more effective way of relieving poverty
than a grant.[28]

2–013   Relief may also be provided indirectly, for example by providing accommodation for relatives coming from a distance to visit patients critically ill
in hospital,[29] and by providing a home of rest for the nurses at a particular hospital.[30] Other examples of gifts where the benefit given may be indirect are gifts to the sick and poor funds of a parish church,[31] gifts to a
religious community having as its objects the relief of the sick and poor,[32]
and gifts to friendly societies under whose rules relief may only be given to
members who are poor.[33]

The limit of the principle of indirect benefit appears to have been
reached in *Re Coxen*,[34] where it was held that a bequest to provide a dinner for the trustees of a charity (the Court of Aldermen of the City of
London) was charitable as tending to promote the efficient administration
of the charity.

Public benefit in the relief of poverty

2–014   It has already been stated[35] that, save in the case of trusts for the relief
of poverty, the class of persons eligible to benefit must, in order that a
trust may be charitable, be the public or an appreciable section thereof. It
is clear, however, that in the case of poor persons[36] and impotent persons[37]
and, it is thought, almost certainly aged persons (because it would be illogical for impotent persons and aged persons to be subject to different tests),
a very small number of persons described in general terms[38] may consti-

---

[27] (1995) 3 Ch. Com. Dec., pp.7–10 (Garfield Poverty Trust); (1995) 4 Ch. Com. Dec.,
   pp.13–16 (Habitat for Humanity Great Britain).
[28] See CC Guidance, *Charities and Social Investment*, (2002).
[29] *Re Dean's Will Trusts* [1950] 1 All E.R. 882.
[30] *Re White's Will Trusts* [1951] 1 All E.R. 528.
[31] *Re Garrard* [1907] 1 Ch. 382 (gift to sick and poor fund of Cheltenham parish church
   good).
[32] *Cocks v Manners* (1871) L.R. 12 Eq. 574: *Re Delaney* [1902] 2 Ch. 642.
[33] *Re Buck* [1896] 2 Ch. 727. See also *Re Lacy* [1899] 2 Ch. 149; *Spiller v Maude* (1881) 32
   Ch.D. 158, n.: *IRC v Society for Relief of Widows and Orphans of Medical Men* (1926) 136
   L.T. 60. Distinguish *Re Clark's Trust* (1875) 1 Ch.D. 497; *Cunnack v Edwards* [1896] 2 Ch.
   679; *Re Hobourn Aero Components, Ltd's Air Raid Distress Fund* [1946] Ch. 194. See *Re
   Forster* [1939] Ch. 22 and observations of Lord Greene M.R. thereon in [1946] Ch. at 205,
   206. *Re Tree* [1945] Ch. 325 ought probably to be treated as an example of the indirect
   relief of poverty. See *Davies v Perpetual Trustee Co.* [1959] A.C. 439 at 456, 357 *per* Lord
   Morton of Henryton delivering the judgment of the Privy Council.
[34] [1948] Ch. 747, following *Re Charlesworth* (1910) 101 L.T. 908.
[35] See para.1–010, above.
[36] *Att-Gen v Goulding* (1788) 2 Bro. C.C. 428; *Bristow v Bristow* (1842) 5 Beav. 289. In *Thomas
   v Howell* (1874) L.R. 18 Eq. a gift to "10 poor clergymen" was held not charitable, but the
   decision is of doubtful authority; see *Re Scarisbrick* [1951] Ch. 622 at 657, *per* Jenkins L.J.
[37] *Re Lewis* [1955] Ch. 104.
[38] As opposed to particular individuals named or designated: see *Rogers v Thomas* (1837) 2
   Keen 8 (persons living in a certain street); *Liley v Hey* (1842) 1 Hare 580 (24 named persons); *Stewart v Green* (1871) L.R. 5 Eq. 470 (the members of a convent or religious community at the date of the testator's death); *Brown v King* (1885) 17 L.R.Ir. 448 (children of
   donor's tenantry); *Laverty v Laverty* [1907] 1 I.R. 9 (persons bearing a certain surname);

tute a sufficiently important section of the public. A gift for poor persons will not necessarily fail to qualify as charitable because there is a personal nexus between them. There is, moreover, at least some suggestion in the judgment of Byrne J. in *Re Gosling*[39] that gifts for the relief of poverty are not the only ones which will not fail to be charitable because of a personal nexus. Dealing with a fund for "pensioning off" the old and worn-out clerks of a banking firm of which the testator had been a member, Byrne J. said:

> "The fact that the section of the public is limited to persons born or residing in a particular parish, district, or county, or belonging to or connected with any special sect, denomination, guild, institution, firm, name, or family, does not itself render that which would be otherwise charitable void for lack of a sufficient or satisfactory description or take it out of the category of charitable gifts. I therefore hold it to be a good charitable gift."

That passage was cited by Lord Cross of Chelsea in *Dingle v Turner*[40] and he added: "It is to be observed that [Byrne J.] does not confine what he says there to trusts for the relief of poverty as opposed to other forms of charitable trusts." Later Lord Cross said[41]:

> "In truth the question whether or not the potential beneficiaries of a trust can fairly be said to constitute a section of the public is a question of degree and cannot be by itself decisive of the question whether the trust is a charity. Much must depend on the purpose of the trust. It may well be that, on the one hand, a trust to promote some purpose, prima facie charitable, will constitute a charity even though the class of potential beneficaries might fairly be called a private class and that, on the other hand, a trust to promote another purpose, also prima facie charitable, will not constitute a charity even though the class of potential beneficiaries might seem to some people fairly describable as a section of the public."

Lord Cross' words were *obiter*, but they had the approval of the other Law Lords hearing the appeal. It is thought that they would have been prepared, had it been neccessary for them to do so, to decide that a gift for impotent people or for aged people having some personal nexus was charitable on the analogy of the poverty cases. Indeed, Lord Cross referred to the possibility of a trust for the advancement of religion amongst beneficiaries with a personal nexus being charitable.[42] Moreover, in *Oppenheim v*

and see *Cocks v Manners* (1871) L.R. 12 Eq. 574; *Re Delaney's Estate* (1881) 9 L.R.Ir. 226; *Re McEnery* [1941] I.R. 323. In Canada a gift to a single "needy displaced family of European origin (commonly known as 'D.P.s')" to be selected by the trustees was charitable: *Re Wedge* (1968) 67 D.L.R. (2d) 433, British Columbia C.A.

[39] (1900) 48 W.R. 300 at 301.
[40] [1972] A.C. 601 at 618.
[41] [1972] A.C. 601 at 624.
[42] [1972] A.C. 601 at 625.

Tobacco Securities Trust Co. Ltd.[43] Lord Simonds, in suggesting that the poverty cases might one day need to be reviewed by the House of Lords (though he indicated that it would be unwise to cast doubt on them), spoke of the law of charity having followed its own line so far as it related to aged, impotent and poor people. If his Lordship accepted the disjunctive construction, then, in saying that charity had followed its own line, he seems not to have distinguished between age, impotence and poverty. On the other hand it is clear from that case that even where the class is numerous a trust for the advancement of education will not be charitable if the beneficaries are united by a private nexus, such as employment by a particular company, and Lord Cross in *Dingle v Turner*[44] said that many "purpose" trusts falling under Lord Macnaghten's fourth head in *Income Tax Special Purposes Commissioners v Pemsel*[45] if confined to a class of employees would clearly be open to the same sort of objection as educational trusts. It should be noted, however, that in *Re Dunlop*[46] which concerned a gift to provide a home for "Old Presbyterian persons", Carswell J. took the view that the poverty exception to the usual rule of public benefit did not extend to trusts to relieve aged or impotent persons.[47]

2–015   The decision in *Dingle v Turner*[48] confirmed the charitable nature of trusts for the donor's relations and for the relief of poverty amongst other classes of persons having a private nexus, whether by reason of membership of a society or employment by a common employer. In the course of his speech, however, Lord Cross accepted the view that such "poor relations",[49] "poor members"[50] and "poor employees"[51] cases were anomolous.[52] It is suggested that such cases may be open to challenge as being in breach of ECHR principles in that the requirement of public benefit must be applied in a way which is non-discriminatory.[53] Provided that public benefit can be shown in such cases, as opposed to simply assumed, the rule may survive challenge as may application of the rule to trusts for the relief of the aged and the impotent.

Poor relations

2–016   The status of the "poor relations" trusts as valid charitable trusts had been recognised for more than two centuries.[54] It had been suggested that the reason for their anomalous position in the law of charity was "that the

---

[43] [1951] A.C. 297 at 308. See also *Re Cox* [1955] A.C. 627, PC.
[44] [1972] A.C. 601 at 625.
[45] [1891] A.C. 531 at 583.
[46] [1984] N.I. 408.
[47] See "'Old Presbyterian persons'—A Sufficient Section of the Public?", N. Dawson [1987] Conv. 114.
[48] [1972] A.C. 601.
[49] See para.2–016 below.
[50] See *Re Young's Will Trusts* [1955] 1 W.L.R. 1269.
[51] See para.2–018 below.
[52] *Dingle v Turner* [1972] A.C. 601 at 623.
[53] See para.1–009 above.
[54] [1972] A.C. 601, at 622, per Lord Cross of Chelsea.

relief of poverty is of so altruistic a character that the public benefit may necessarily be inferred."[55] In view of the need for the requirement of public benefit to be non-discriminatory,[56] it is suggested that this reference to the importance of altruism is relied upon.

A dictum of Sir William Grant M.R. in *Att-Gen v Price*[57] where he said of the gift he was considering: "It is to have perpetual continuance in favour of a particular description of poor; and is not like an immediate bequest of a sum to be distributed among poor relations" gave rise to a belief that a distinction was to be made between perpetual trusts of income for the benefit of poor relations, which were accepted as charitable, and gifts intended for immediate distribution. This dictum led Roxborough J. in *Re Scarisbrick*[58] to hold that a trust for "such relations of my . . . son and daughters as in the opinion of the survivor of my said son and daughters shall be in needy circumstances" was not charitable. The existence of such a distinction was, however, rejected by the Court of Appeal[59] which held that the distinction between a public or charitable trust and a private trust depended on whether as a matter of construction the gift was for the relief of poverty amongst a particular description of poor people or was merely a gift to particular poor persons, the relief of poverty among them being the motive of the gift.

Re Scarisbrick[60] was approved by the House of Lords in *Dingle v Turner*[61] so that the doubt which formerly existed as to whether gifts intended for immediate distribution could be charitable has been removed.

The rule now is that a gift for immediate distribution among poor relations, kindred, and so forth is charitable, except in cases where the intention of the donor, derived from the construction of the documents,[62] is to confine the benefit to the statutory next-of-kin. *Re Segelman (Deceased)*[63] concerned a trust for the benefit of poor and needy members of the testator's family. Chadwick J. considered *Re Scarisbrick*[64] and *Dingle v Turner*[65] and summarised the rule as follows:[66]

> "The basis for disqualification as a charitable gift must be that the restricted nature of the class leads to the conclusion that the gift is really a gift to the individual members of the class."

---

[55] *Re Scarisbrick* [1951] Ch. 622, 639, *per* Sir Raymond Evershed M.R.; see also *Re Compton* [1945] Ch. 123, 129; *Gibson v South American Stores (Gath & Chaves)*, Ltd. [1950] Ch. 177 at 197.

[56] See para.1–009 above.

[57] (1810) 17 Ves. 371 at 374.

[58] [1950] Ch. 226.

[59] [1951] Ch. 622. See also Re Cohen [1973] 1 W.L.R. 415.

[60] [1951] Ch. 622.

[61] [1972] A.C. 601.

[62] "Nearest relations" appears to mean statutory next of kin; *Edge v Salisbury* (1749) Amb. 70.

[63] [1995] 3 All E.R. 676.

[64] [1951] Ch. 622.

[65] [1972] A.C. 601.

[66] [1995] 3 All E.R. 676 at 692.

A trust for the benefit of the poor with a preference for poor relations is unquestionably charitable.[67]

2–017   Examples of charitable gifts or trusts for the poor relations of the donor or of some other person are bequests of a perpetual annuity for distribution among the poorest relations of the testator's wife[68]; or of a fund for apprenticing poor relations[69]; or to be distributed for ever among the testator's poor kinsmen and kinswomen and their issue dwelling in a certain county[70]; or for male descendants in want[71]; or a devise of real estate in trust "to such of my poor relations as my trustees shall think most deserving[72]; or upon trust for such relations of the son and daughters of the testatrix "as in the opinion of the survivor of my said son and daughters shall be in needy circumstances."[73]

While a friendly or other mutual benefit society which makes provision only for such of its members and dependants as are poor is a charity,[74] such a society is not a charity if poverty is not an essential qualification for the receipt of relief, for the object of such a society is not within the contemplation of the preamble to the Statute of Charitable Uses 1601.[75] Because the objects of such a society are not exclusively charitable, the fact that it receives donations and subscriptions cannot make it a charity.[76] Where on the other hand a society is charitable, because the necessary element of poverty is present, the whole of its income and property is applicable for charitable purposes. The source is immaterial, no distinction being drawn between voluntary subscriptions from the general public and the contributions of members.[77]

Poor employees

2–018   The first of the "poor employees" cases was *Re Gosling*[78] where Byrne J. accepted as charitable a fund for "pensioning off" the old and worn-out clerks of a banking firm of which the testator had been a member. In *Re Drummond*,[79] where there was a trust to pay income in contributing to the holiday expenses of the employees in the spinning department of a named company in Ilkley, Eve J. rejected an argument that the trust was for the relief of poverty. It was also submitted that the trust fell under the fourth

---

[67] *Waldo v Caley* (1809) 16 Ves. 206; *Att-Gen v Northumberland* (1877) 7 Ch. D. 745.
[68] *Isaac v Defriez* (1753) Amb. 595; 17 Ves. 373, n.
[69] *White v White* (1802) 7 Ves. 423.
[70] *Att-Gen v Price* (1810) 17 Ves. 371.
[71] *Bernal v Bernal* (1838) 3 My. & Cr. 559.
[72] *Hall v Att-Gen* (1829) cit. *Jarman on Wills*, 8th ed., Vol. I, p.242 n.m.
[73] *Re Scarisbrick* [1951] Ch. 622.
[74] *Spiller v Maude* (1886) 32 Ch.D 158n.; *Re Buck* [1896] 2 Ch. 727; Re Lacy [1899] 2 Ch. 149; *IRC v Society of Widows and Orphans of Medical Men* (1926) 136 L.T. 60.
[75] *Re Clark's Trust* (1875) 1 Ch.D. 497; *Cunnack v Edwards* [1896] 2 Ch. 679; and see *Re Gassiot* (1901) 70 L.J.Ch. 242.
[76] *Re Clark's Trust* (1875) 1 Ch.D. 497; *Re Buck* [1896] 2 Ch. 727.
[77] *Spiller v Maude* (1886) 32 Ch.D. 158n.; and see para.2–004, above.
[78] (1900) 48 W.R. 300.
[79] [1914] 2 Ch. 90.

head of charity in *Income Tax Special Purposes Commissioners v Pemsel*,[80] and it was argued that, as a trust to secure a holiday for a substantial number of the inhabitants of Ilkley, who though not poor might in many cases not otherwise be able to get a holiday, it promoted the general well-being of the community: but Eve J. held that it was not a trust for general public purposes, but a trust for a fluctuating body of private individuals and as such not charitable. The testator in *Re Sir Robert Laidlaw*[81] bequeathed a legacy of £2,000 upon certain trusts for the relief of poor members of the staff of a company, and the Court of Appeal held that this was a valid charity. The Court of Appeal followed that decison in *Gibson v South American Stores (Gath & Chaves) Ltd.*,[82] where there was a trust for a company's "necessitous" employees and ex-employees and for the dependants of such beneficaries living or dead, and held the trust to be charitable. That case was in turn followed by the Court of Appeal in *Re Coulthurst*,[83] where it was held that a trust to apply income to or for the benefit of the widows and orphaned children of deceased officers and ex-officers of the bank was charitable. The correctness of all these decisions on trusts for employees has been confirmed by *Dingle v Turner*.[84]

THE ADVANCEMENT OF EDUCATION

Trusts for the advancement of education have long been recognised as charitable trusts. The preamble to the Statute of Elizabeth I refers to "the maintenance of schools of learning, free schools and scholars in universities" and to "the education and preferment of orphans". Thus, there is no need for any element of poverty in a gift or trust for the advancement of education.[85]   **2–019**

For a trust for the advancement of education to be charitable it must be for an educational purpose which the law regards as charitable and fall within the letter or the spirit and intendments of the preamble to the Statute of Elizabeth I. Further, the education for which the donor intends to provide must be beneficial, *i.e.* of educational value to the community[86] and the benefits must be available to the public or to a sufficiently important section of the community.[87]

---

[80] [1891] A.C. 531 at 583.
[81] Unreported, January 11, 1935, CA.
[82] [1950] Ch. 177.
[83] [1951] Ch. 661.
[84] [1972] A.C. 601. See para.2–014, above.
[85] *R v Income Tax Special Commissioners* (1909) 78 L.J.K.B. 576 at 578.
[86] See para.2–030, below.
[87] See para.2–046, below.

Scope and meaning of "education" and "educational"

2–020   "Education" and "educational" bear, for the purposes of the law of charity, the meanings current in present day educated English speech.[88] The meaning of education evolves with changes in ideas about social values.[89] Care, therefore, has to be taken with any definition of education given in older cases. In 1972, the phrase "advancement of education" was said by the Court of Appeal to extend to "the improvement of a useful branch of human knowledge and its public dissemination".[90] More recently, the Canadian Supreme Court considered that education included the provision of information or training provided in a structured manner to advance the knowledge and abilities of the recipients.[91] Whilst "education" has consistently been given a wide meaning, a gift to increase the sum of knowledge available without provision for propagating it has been said not to be charitable.[92] A useful summary of the distinction was made by Iacobucci J. in *Vancouver Society of Immigrant and Visible Minority Women v Minister of National Revenue*[93]:

> "[T]he threshold criterion for an educational activity must be some legitimate targeted attempt at educating others, whether through formal or informal instruction, training, plans of self-study or otherwise. Simply providing an opportunity for people to educate themselves, such as by making available materials with which this might be accomplished but need not be, is not enough."

Thus gifts for the advancement of education generally are charitable, for example, "for the benefit, advancement and propagation of education and learning in every part of the world",[94] or for "the increase of knowledge among men".[95] A gift for "education purposes" without more, is prima facie charitable as it will be presumed, in the absence of any indication to the contrary, to be a gift for such educational purposes as are charitable.[96]

There are limits on the width of education in charity law. First, the purpose must have education value.[97] Secondly, the purpose must not be propagandist. The public must be presented with neutral information so that

---

[88] *IRC v McMullen* (1981] A.C. 1 at 15, *per* Lord Hailsham of St Marylebone. See para.1–025, above, for educational charities which are exempt, and para.1–026, above, for those which are excepted.

[89] *IRC v McMullen* [1981] A.C. 1 at 15 *per* Lord Hailsham of St. Marylebone.

[90] In *Incorporated Council of Law Reporting for England and Wales v Att-Gen* [1972] 1 Ch. 73 at 102, *per* Buckley L.J.

[91] *Vancouver Society of Immigrant And Visible Minority Women v Minister of National Revenue* (1999) 169 D.L.R. (4th) 34 at 113, *per* Iacobucci J.

[92] *Re Shaw* [1957] 1 W.L.R. 729. See also *Whicker v Hume* (1858) 7 H.L.C. 124 at 141, 155; *Re MacDuff* [1896] 2 Ch. 451 at 472; *cf. Re Hopkins Will Trust* [1965] Ch. 669 discussed at para.2–028 below.

[93] (1999) 169 D.L.R. (4th) 34 at 113.

[94] *Whicker v Hume* (1858) 7 H.L.C. 124.

[95] *United States President v Drummond* (1838) cited in *Whicker v Hume* above.

[96] *Re Ward* [1941] Ch. 308 at 317–318.

[97] See para.2–030 below.

they can choose for themselves[98] and not be presented with slanted and selective information in support of a pre-conceived point of view.[99] Thirdly, the purpose must not be political[1] and, fourthly, the usual requirement of public benefit must be complied with.[2] The necessary educational content of a charitable trust for the advancement of education can best be seen from a consideration of particular purposes. Particular gifts for schools and universities, in connection with aesthetic education and for research are set out below.

Schools and universities

Following the preamble,[3] gifts for the establishment or support of schools of learning generally are charitable[4] and also gifts for providing schoolmasters.[5] The establishment and support of colleges,[6] professorships,[7] fellowships,[8] lectureships,[9] scholarships,[10] and prizes[11] are all charitable purposes. A trust in favour of a student union is also charitable

2–021

---

[98] *Re Bushnell (Deceased)* [1975] 1 All E.R. 721 at 729, *per* Golding J. See also [1991] Ch. Com. Rep. App. D. (The Margaret Thatcher Foundation); (1993) 1 Ch. Com. Dec. pp.1–3 (Cult Information Centre).

[99] See (1994) 2 Ch. Com. Dec. pp.1–4 (Animal Abuse, Injustice and Defence Society).

[1] See para.2–031 below.

[2] See para.2–046 below.

[3] See para.1–003, above.

[4] *Gibbons v Maltyard* (1592) Poph. 6; *Case of Rugby School* (1626) Duke 80; *Att-Gen v Nash* (1792) 3 Bro.C.C. 588; *Kirbank v Hudson* (1819) 7 Price 212; *Att-Gen v Lonsdale* (1827) 1 Sim. 105, 109 (school for sons of gentlemen); *Hartshorne v Nicholson* (1858) 26 Beav. 58; *Re Sir Robert Peel's School at Tamworth* (1868) L.R. 3 Ch. 543; *Re Allsop* (1884) 1 T.L.R. 4 (a school of art); *Re Hawkins* (1906) 22 T.L.R. 521 (a school for religious teaching and elementary education); *Brighton College v Marriott* [1926] A.C. 204 (school for sons of noblemen and gentlemen). *The Abbey Malvern Wells Ltd. v Ministry of Local Government and Planning* [1951] Ch. 728 (girls' school carried on by private company but under a trust deed: all dividends applicable for the purposes of the school). See the observations of Danckwerts J. at 737 of the last case to the effect that all schools of learning are to be considered charities unless they exist purely as profit-making ventures. Distinguish *Re Girls' Public Day School Trust Ltd.* [1951] Ch. 400, where a similar school was held not to be a charity because the preference shareholders were entitled to substantial benefits.

[5] *Hynshaw v Morpeth Corp.* (1629) Duke 69; *Att-Gen v Winchelsea* (1791) 3 Bro.C.C. 374.

[6] *Porter's Case* (1592) 1 Co.Rep. 25b; *Plate v St. John's College* (1638) Duke 77, 110; *Att-Gen v Combe* (1679) 2 Ch.Ca. 18; *Att-Gen v Whorwood* (1750) 1 Ves. Sen. 534 at 536; *Case of Christ's College, Cambridge* (1757) 1 W.Bl. 90; *Walsh v Gladstone* (1843) 1 Ph. 290 (where the institution was a Roman Catholic college); *R. v Income Tax Special Commissioners, ex p. University College of North Wales* (1909) 78 L.J.K.B. 576.

[7] *Yates v University College of London* (1873) L.R. 8 Ch.App. 454; affirmed (1875) L.R. 7 J.L. 438; *Re Buckland* (1887) 22 L.J.N.C. 7.

[8] *Jesus College Case* (1616) Duke 78.

[9] *Att-Gen v Cambridge Margaret and Regius Professors* (1682) 1 Vern. 55.

[10] *R. v Newman* (1670) 1 Lev. 284; *Re Levitt* (1885) 1 T.L.R. 578; *Re Williams* (1908) 24 T.L.R. 716; *R. v Income Tax Special Commissioners, ex p. University College of North Wales* [1909] W.N. 57.

[11] *Thompson v Thompson* (1844) 1 Coll. 381, 398; *Farrer v St. Catherine's College, Cambridge* (1873) L.R. 16 Eq. 19; *Re Mariette* [1915] 2 Ch. 284; *Chesterman v Federal Commissioner of Taxation* [1926] A.C. 128.

provided that the union exists to support the college to which it is attached.[12]

A trust to buy books for a college and, it follows a school or other similar educational institution is charitable on the ground that a large well-assorted library tends to the promotion of education.[13]

"Education" is not restricted to education in academic subjects in a school, university or college, or in some other educational establishment[14]: it includes the promotion of education and the giving of instruction in a wide range of subjects. Thus the promotion of commercial education,[15] education in the Irish language,[16] Christian knowledge,[17] psychological healing,[18] ethical principles,[19] economic and sanitary science,[20] the arts of social intercourse,[21] archaeology[22] and the education of boys of all ages in the principles of discipline, loyalty and good citizenship[23] are charitable purposes.

2–022   Nor is "education" restricted to the development of the mind. It has been settled for many years that any gift or trust, the purpose of which is to promote and encourage the physical development of children or young persons at a particular school or other educational establishment is charitable. Thus in *Re Mariette*,[24] Eve J. upheld as charitable, a bequest of £1,000 to the Governing Body of Aldenham School for the purpose of building Eton fives courts or squash racket courts and another bequest to the headmaster for the time being of the school to provide a prize to be competed for in the school athletic sports in every year. In his judgment the value of organised games as an essential part of the education of boys was emphasised.

IRC v McMullen[25] extended the principle to the provision of facilities for the physical education of pupils of schools and universities generally. The case concerned the Football Association Youth Trust whose objects were, *inter alia*, "to organise or provide or assist in the organisation or pro-

---

[12] *Baldry v Feintuck* [1972] 1 W.L.R. 552; *London Hospital Medical College v Inland Revenue Commissioners* [1976] 1 W.L.R. 613; *Att-Gen v Ross.* [1986] 1 W.L.R. 252, but see para.2–032 below.

[13] *Att-Gen v Marchant* (1866) L.R. 3 Eq. 424 at 430. See also *Incorporated Council of Law Reporting for England and Wales v Att-Gen* [1972] Ch. 73.

[14] "Educational establishment" itself is capable of a wide meaning; the Charity Commissioners have registered the Training Workshops for (Young) Unemployed: [1980] Ch. Com. Rep., para.80. See also [1990] Ch. Com. Rep., para.39 (education on an organic farm).

[15] *Re Koettgen's Will Trusts* [1954] Ch. 252.

[16] *Att-Gen v Flood* (1861) Hayes Exch.R 611 (cited Hayes & J.App. XXI); *cf. Brownjohn v Gale* [1869] W.N. 133.

[17] *Att-Gen v Stepney* (1804) 10 Ves. 22 (trust for "the improvement of Christian knowledge and promoting religion"; the trust was both for the advancement of education and the advancement of religion).

[18] *Re Osmund* [1944] Ch. 206. See para.2–083 below for the advancement of alternative forms of medicine.

[19] *Re South Place Ethical Society* [1980] W.L.R. 565.

[20] *Re Berridge* (1890) 63 L.T. 470.

[21] *Re Shaw's Will Trusts* [1952] Ch. 163.

[22] *Yates v University of London* (1873) L.R. 8 Ch. 454; affd. (1875) L.R. 7 H.L. 438.

[23] *Re Webber* [1954] 1 W.L.R. 1500.

[24] [1915] 2 Ch. 284.

[25] [1981] A.C. 1.

vision of facilities which will enable and encourage pupils at schools and universities in any part of the United Kingdom to play association football or other games or sports and thereby to assist in ensuring that due attention is given to the physical education and development and occupation of their minds." The House of Lords, unanimously, held the trust to be charitable as being for the advancement of education.

The leading speech was given by Lord Hailsham of St. Marylebone L.C.[26] who emphasised that a liberal interpretation should be given to the meaning of the "education." In the course of his speech he said[27]:

> "What has to be remembered, however, is that, as Lord Wilberforce pointed out in *Re Hopkins' Will Trusts*,[28] and in *Scottish Burial Reform and Cremation Society Ltd. v Glasgow Corporation*,[29] both the legal conception of charity, and within it the educated man's ideas about education are not static, but moving and changing. Both change with changes in ideas about social values. Both have evolved with the years. In particular in applying the law to contemporary circumstances it is extremely dangerous to forget that thoughts concerning the scope and width of education differed in the past greatly from those which are now generally accepted."

After referring to ss.7 and 53 of the Education Act 1944[30] his Lordship continued:

> "There is no trace in these sections of an idea of education limited to the development of mental, vocational or practical skills, to grounds or facilities the special perquisite of particular schools, or of any schools or colleges, or term-time, or particular localities, and there is express recognition of the contribution which extra-curricular activities and voluntary societies or bodies can make even in the promotion of the purely statutory system envisaged by the Act. In the light of section 7 in particular I would be very reluctant to confine the meaning of education to formal instruction in the classroom or even the playground, and I consider it sufficiently wide to cover all the activities envisaged by the settlor in the present case."

The Charity Commissioners have stated that they will recognise as charitable the advancement of the physical education of young people not undergoing formal education.[31]

Trusts to provide for the care of schoolchildren in sickness are also charitable. Thus, the provision of a sanatorium at a boarding school was an educational purpose within the meaning of s.87 of the Education Act   **2–023**

---

[26] Minister of Education 1957, Minister of Higher Education 1963–1964, Secretary of State for Education and Science 1964.
[27] [1981] A.C. 1 at 15.
[28] [1965] Ch. 669 at 687.
[29] [1968] A.C. 138, especially at 154.
[30] [1981] A.C. 1 at 16.
[31] CC, *Charitable Status and Sport* (2002).

1944,[32] presumably because the boarders require care in sickness and the provision of a sanatorium conduces to the efficiency of the school.

Educational activities out of school hours can also be charitable.[33] Thus the purposes of the Boy Scouts are educational and so charitable. Therefore the Boy Scouts Association and the Boy Scouts Movement are charitable objects.[34] The purpose of the Association is the instruction of "boys of all ages in the principles of discipline, loyalty and good citizenship."

In *Re Dupree's Deed Trusts*,[35] Vaisey J. held that the game of chess had an educational value and that accordingly the organising of annual tournaments open to boys and young men under the age of 21 years resident in the city of Portsmouth and the award of prizes to the winners was a charitable purpose for the advancement of education. It appears from the report[36] that there was evidence before the court as to the educational value of the game which Vaisey J. accepted. It also appears from the report, that the learned judge would have been prepared, if necessary, to take judicial notice of the educational value of the game if no evidence had been filed. It is thought that the decision can be justified on the judge's finding of fact but that, in so far as the judge based his decision on the restriction of the gift to the inhabitants of a particular area or on the character of the trustees, his observations are not consistent with authority. It was not argued that the restriction of the area or the character of the trustees had any bearing on the question and the observations should be treated as *obiter*.[37]

2–024   By analogy to education in schools and universities various learned societies and institutions for the advancement of science,[38] though not within the letter of the preamble, are within its spirit and intendment and are charities; and gifts to such bodies for their general purposes are char-

---

[32] Which replaced s.117 of the Education Act 1921, and has itself now been repealed by s.48(2) and Sch.7 of the Charities Act 1960; see *Re Harrow School Governors and Murray's Contract* [1927] 1 Ch. 556.

[33] See *Re Mellody* [1918] 1 Ch. 228 (trust to apply the income of a trust fund in perpetuity for the provision of an annual school treat or field day for the school-children of T, held to be educational and so charitable); *Re Ward's Estate* (1937) 81 S.J. 397 (trust to provide an annual outing for the children of the members of a club for ex-servicemen held to be for an educational purpose and, therefore, charitable). The latter case seems doubtful. See *Re Pleasants* (1923) 39 T.L.R. 675, where a gift to provide a pennyworth of sweets for every child resident in a particular parish and not merely for the school-children of the parish was held not to be charitable. See also *IRC v McMullen* [1981] A.C. 1 (discussed at para.43, above).

[34] *Re Webber* [1954] 1 W.L.R. 1500, applying *Re Alexander, The Times*, June 30, 1932.

[35] [1945] Ch. 16.

[36] [1945] Ch. 16 at 18–19.

[37] The observations of Vaisey J. which are doubted are in [1945] Ch. at 20–21. The character of the trustees may be irrelevant: see *Dunne v Byrne* [1912] A.C. 407 and the many cases in which that case has been followed; and see generally *Re Rumball* [1956] Ch. 105. Moreover, if the trusts of the deed before the court had not been charitable, their localisation to a particular place would not have validated them; see *Williams' Trustees v IRC* [1947] A.C. 447; *Re Sanders' Will Trusts* [1954] Ch. 265 at 272, 273. For further discussion of these two points, see paras 2–060, *et seq.*, and paras 2–072, *et seq.*, below.

[38] In *Weir v Crum-Brown* [1908] A.C. 162 at 169, Lord Robertson said that the word "science" embraced a wide but perfectly ascertainable range of subjects.

itable.[39] Accordingly, gifts to or for the benefit of the Royal Society,[40] the Royal Geographical Society,[41] the Royal Literary Society,[42] the Royal College of Surgeons,[43] the Royal College of Nursing,[44] the British School of Egyptian Archaeology,[45] the Zoological Society of London[46] and the Institution of Civil Engineers[47] are charitable.

Aesthetic education

The word "aesthetic" is used here as meaning "of or pertaining to the appreciation or criticism of the beautiful," one of the definitions contained in the *Shorter Oxford Dictionary*. The cases hereinafter discussed or referred to illustrate the favour shown by the court, especially in recent years, to the advancement of "aesthetic education", an expression used by Lord Greene M.R. in *Royal Choral Society v IRC*.[48] **2–025**

Aesthetic education includes the provision for the public of opportunities to examine the work of craftsmen who lived long ago. Thus in *Re Cranstoun*,[49] a testator devised two ancient cottages to the Royal Society of Arts in order that the society might preserve them in their present condition; and he also gave a fund to the society for the maintenance of the cottages. It was proved that the testator knew at the date of his will that the society had opened a fund for the preservation of ancient cottages and that the objects of the fund were to preserve ancient cottages as specimens and models of English craftsmanship so as to teach the lessons of such craftsmanship. The cottages were Elizabethan and picturesque. Farwell J. may have based his decision primarily on the ground that the main object of the fund was for the good of the community at a large and within Lord Macnaghten's fourth class.[50] In *Re Verrall*,[51] which was followed in *Re Cranstoun*,[52] it had been held that the National Trust for Places of Historic Interest or Natural Beauty was a charity, and it appears from the judgment that it came within Lord Macnaghten's fourth class. Nevertheless, in

---

[39] (1963) 27 Conv.(N.S.) 469 (A. Samuels) but see paras 2–044, *et seq.*, below.
[40] *Beaumont v Oliviera* (1869) L.R. 4 Ch. 309; *Royal Society of London and Thompson* (1881) 17. Ch.D. 407.
[41] *Beaumont v Oliviera* (1869) L.R. 4 Ch. 309.
[42] *Thomas v Howell* (1874) L.R. 18 Eq. 198.
[43] *Royal College of Surgeons of England v National Provincial Bank Ltd.* [1952] A.C. 631.
[44] *Royal College of Nursing v St. Marylebone Borough Council* [1959] 1 W.L.R. 1077.
[45] *Re British School of Egyptian Archaeology* [1954] 1 W.L.R. 547. The "school" was a society the objects of which were (inter alia) to conduct excavations in Egypt and to publish works; *cf. Yates v University College, London* (1873) L.R. 8 Ch.App. 454; affirmed (1875) L.R. 7 H.L. 438, where a trust to found a professorship in archaeology was treated as charitable.
[46] *Re Lopes* [1931] 2 Ch. 130; applied by the Court of Appeal in *North of England Zoological Society v Chester RDC* [1959] 1 W.L.R. 773.
[47] *Institution of Civil Engineers v IRC* [1932] 1 K.B. 199.
[48] [1943] 2 All E.R. 101 at 105.
[49] [1932] 1 Ch. 537.
[50] *Income Tax Special Purposes Commissioners v Pemsel* [1891] A.C. 531 at 583.
[51] [1916] 1 Ch. 100. See also [1990] Ch. Com. Rep., para.42 (Settle and Carlisle Railway Trust).
[52] [1932] 1 Ch. 537 at 545.

the latter case it was said by Farwell J. that the preservation of ancient buildings was desirable for two main reasons: (1) because they were of interest, as being something historical, as it were visible examples of past history[53]; and (2) because they exhibited arts of craftsmanship which had been to some extent lost, the consideration and study of which might tend to teach and educate people at the present day in methods of building new cottages which had to be built to satisfy modern requirements. If the second ground of the decision may be regarded as, it is submitted, it ought to be regarded as an essential part of the *ratio decidendi*, the trust was a trust for the advancement of education, and the case is properly cited under this head.

Trusts to establish and support museums[54] and art galleries[55] are similarly charitable. For example, in *Re Spence*[56] there was a bequest to the corporation of Stockton-on-Tees of a collection of arms and antiques which were to be exhibited in a place accessible to the public. It was held that the object of the bequest was educational and so charitable. The Charity Commissioners[57] take a broad and inclusive view of art in the context of a trust to establish and maintain an art gallery but both museums and art galleries must satisfy a criterion of merit to be charitable.[58]

2–026   The promotion of artistic taste is a charitable purpose,[59] and so also are the encouragement of music,[60] the provision of a concert hall,[61] choral singing,[62] the encouragement of singing and the advancement of organ music,[63] the advancement of the works of a particular composer,[64] and the performance of the plays of an eminent playwright, the reviving of classical drama and the stimulating of the art of acting.[65]

The cases do not justify the general proposition that the fine arts are not an object of charity or that a gift to encourage artistic pursuits is never charitable.[66]

---

[53] For preservation of buildings as a fourth head purpose see para.2–081 below.

[54] *British Museum v White* (1826) 2 Sim. & St. 594; *Re Allsop* (1884) 1 T.L.R. 4; *Re Holburne* (1885) 53 L.T. 212.

[55] *Gwynn v Cardon* cited in (1805) 10 Ves. 522 at 533; *Abbott v Fraser* (1874) L.R. 6 P.C. 96; *Re Shaw's Will Trust* [1952] Ch. 163.

[56] [1938] Ch. 96.

[57] See RR10, *Museums and Art Galleries* (2002), para.8.

[58] See para.2–030 below.

[59] *Re Allsop* (1884) 1 T.L.R. 4.

[60] *Shillington v Portadown UDC* [1911] 1 I.R. 247, *IRC v Glasgow Musical Festival Association* [1926] S.C. 920 (society where objects were to stimulate public interest in music and encourage those members of the public who had musical gifts to cultivate them a charity).

[61] *Re Henry Wood National Memorial Trust* [1966] 1 W.L.R. 1601 (trust to establish a concert hall as a national music centre).

[62] *Royal Choral Society v IRC* [1942] 2 All E.R. 101.

[63] *Re Levien* [1955] 1 W.L.R. 964.

[64] *Re Delius* [1957] Ch. 299. In this case the court appears to have formed the aesthetic opinion that Delius was a great composer and that his music deserved to be made known to the public who would benefit from such knowledge.

[65] *Re Shakespeare Memorial Trust* [1923] 2 Ch. 398.

[66] *Royal Choral Society v IRC* [1943] 2 All E.R. 101 at 106, disapproving the statement in the 5th ed. of this work at p.39. See also *Perpetual Trustee Co. Ltd v Groth* (1985) 2 N.S.W.L.R. 278.

In *Re Ogden*[67] the testator desired that his executors, with the assistance of certain gentlemen and an art master and any persons they might call in to assist them, should expend his residuary estate in any manner they might think desirable to encourage artistic pursuits or assist needy students in art. The Court of Appeal held that the gift was not charitable. This case is inadequately reported and does not justify the general proposition mentioned above. The decision can be supported on the ground that a gift merely to encourage artistic pursuits might be expressed in a way that nobody would consider charitable; for instance, in merely providing for one or two individuals paint and paint brushes, or a grand piano on which the beneficiaries could play in their room.[68]

In *Re Town and County Planning Act 1947, Crystal Palace v Minister of* **2–027**
Town and County Planning[69] Danckwerts J. held that the promotion of art was a charitable purpose within the meaning of s.85 of the Town and County Planning Act 1947, and doubted the correctness of *Re Ogden*.[70]

It is considered that the decision of Danckwerts J. was clearly correct and is authority for the general proposition that the promotion of art is a charitable purpose, and that the decision ought not, as appears to have been suggested by Harman J. in *Re Shaw*,[71] to be treated only as a decision on s.85 of the Act of 1947. But it is submitted that it was not necessary for Danckwerts J. to cast doubt on the correctness of *Re Ogden*[72] and that he went further than was justified by anything said by Lord Greene M.R. in *Royal Choral Society v IRC*.[73] The word "artistic" is wide and vague, and, as pointed out by Lord Greene M.R. in that case, may include a number of purposes which are not charitable.

It is thought that the decision of Upjohn J. in *Associated Artists v IRC*[74] was not only correct in every particular but illuminated the whole question of gifts intended for the advancement of aesthetic education. The plaintiff company was a non-profit-making company limited by guarantee. Clause 3 of the memorandum of association (the objects clause) contained (*inter alia*) the following objects:

(a) To present classical, artistic, cultural and educational dramatic works in the United Kingdom of Great Britain and Northern Ireland;

(b) To foster, promote and increase the interest of the public in the dramatic art and in the correlated arts in the manner set out; and

(c) To encourage and promote the creation of, and to arrange for the presentation of new dramatic works and to foster and

---

[67] (1909) 25 T.L.R. 382.
[68] See *Royal Choral Society v IRC* [1943] 2 All E.R. 101 at 107 *per* Lord Greene M.R.
[69] [1951] Ch. 132, applied in *Construction Industry Training Board v Att-Gen* [1971] 1 W.L.R. 1303 (Pennycuick V.C.; affirmed. [1973] Ch. 173); see also IRC v White [1980] T.C. 155.
[70] (1909) 25 T.L.R. 382; see [1951] Ch. 132 at 140.
[71] [1957] 1 W.L.R. 729 at 737.
[72] (1909) 25 T.L.R. 382; see [1951] Ch. 132 at 140.
[73] [1943] 2 All E.R. 101 at 107.
[74] [1956] 1 W.L.R. 752. The advancement of aesthetic education abroad is charitable, see [1989] Ch. Com. Rep., para.33 (The European Script Fund).

enhance the art of affording advanced students facilities for training and for gaining practical stage experience.

The company's claim to be exempt from income tax under s.448(1)(c) of the Income Tax Act 1952,[75] as a body established for charitable purposes only, failed. One of the grounds of the decision was that object (a) had to be construed disjunctively as containing four separate objects, one of which was to present "artistic" plays which were not required to be classical, cultural or educational. The word "or" was in effect substituted for the word "and".[76] Having decided that the disjunctive construction was required, the learned judge held, and, it is submitted, rightly held, that the adjective "artistic" in the context in which it occurred was not a word to which any real charitable concept could be given and was too wide and vague to the charitable. The company was not a charity because under its memorandum it had power to engage solely in the production of "artistic" plays. Objects (b) and (c) were rightly held to be charitable on the authority of *Royal Choral Society v IRC*[77] and *Re Shakespeare Memorial Trusts*[78] respectively.[79]

Research

2–028   In *Re Hopkins' Will Trusts*,[80] the testatrix had given part of her residuary estate to the "Francis Bacon Society" to be applied towards finding the "Bacon-Shakespeare" manuscripts. One of the main objects of the Society was "to encourage the general study of the evidence of Francis Bacon's authorship of plays commonly ascribed to Shakespeare." The terms of the will were held to mean that the estate was to be used to search for manuscripts of plays commonly ascribed to Shakespeare but believed by the testatrix and the Society to have been written by Bacon. Wilberforce J. held that the purposes of search, or research, for original manuscripts of England's greatest dramatist were within the law's conception of a charitable purpose on two grounds, (i) as being for education and (ii) as being for other purposes beneficial to the community within the fourth head of Lord Macnaghten's classification, because it was a gift for the improvement of this country's literary heritage. Wilberforce J. commented on Harman J.'s dictum in *Re Shaw*[81] that if the object was merely the increase of knowledge that in itself was not a charitable object unless combined with "teaching or education." He was unwilling to treat these words as

---

[75] See now Income and Corporation Taxes Act 1988, s.505(1)(e).
[76] This substitution appears to have been justified: see para.3–017 *et seq.*, below.
[77] [1943] 2 All E.R. 101.
[78] [1923] 2 Ch. 398.
[79] The other ground of Upjohn J.'s decision was that clause 3(1) of the memorandum, which enabled the company to do all such other things as were incidental or which the company might think conducive to the attainment of its other objects, was itself a main object and prevented the company from qualifying as a charity. *Oxford Group v IRC* [1949] 2 All E.R. 537 was followed on this point, and rightly.
[80] [1965] Ch. 669.
[81] [1957] 1 W.L.R. 729.

meaning that the promotion of academic research was not a charitable purpose unless the researchers were engaged in teaching or education in the conventional sense. Wilberforce J.'s requirement for research to be charitable were considered by Slade J. in *Re Besterman's Will Trust*.[82] In that case Slade J. set out the principles governing the charitability of research as follows:

> "(1) A trust for research will ordinarily qualify as a charitable trust if, but only if (a) the subject-matter of the proposed research is a useful subject of study; and (b) it is contemplated that knowledge acquired as a result of the research will be disseminated to others; and (c) the trust is for the benefit of the public, or a sufficiently important section of the public. (2) In the absence of a contrary context, however, the court will be readily inclined to construe a trust for research as importing subsequent dissemination of the results thereof. (3) Furthermore, if a trust for research is to constitute a valid trust for the advancement of education, it is not necessary either (a) that a teacher/pupil relationship should be in contemplation or (b) that persons to benefit from the knowledge to be acquired be person who are already in the course of receiving 'education' in the conventional sense. (4) In any case where the court has to determine whether a bequest for the purposes of research is or is not of a charitable nature, it must pay due regard to any admissible extrinsic evidence which is available to explain the wording of the will in question or the circumstances in which it was made."

It is now clearly established that research is a charitable object and a number of trusts to further medical and scientific research have been registered by the Charity Commissioners.[83] An organisation will not be registered, however, if its research is directed towards confirming a pre-existing theory rather than challenging and validating the theory.[84]

Limits to "education" and "educational"

It has been seen that, generally speaking, education has been regarded as a conception of some breadth for the purposes of charity. However, there are limits beyond which the courts will not go. One of these is that the gift must be of some educational value. Another is that the trust must not be political or propagandist, and its purpose must not be to change the law. However, the presence of incidental non-charitable purposes does not affect the charitable status of a trust.

2–029

---

[82] January 21, 1980 unreported, referred to in *McGovern v Att-Gen* [1982] Ch. 327 at 352–353.
[83] See, for example, [1988] Ch. Com. Rep., para.24 (British Foundation for the Industrial Space University).
[84] (1994) 2 Ch. Com. Dec., p.4 (Animal Abuse, Injustice and Defence Society (1993)).

Educational value

2–030   Whether a trust has sufficient educational value is in the final analysis a question of degree for the courts. The court may receive evidence to assist it to decide whether or not a particular educational purpose is beneficial to the community,[85] and in the absence of any evidence or of any sufficient evidence the court may decide the question in the light of its own judicial knowledge.[86] There is no clear dividing line.[87]

The court's approach in determining whether a trust is of sufficient educational value can be seen from *Re Pinion*.[88] A testator gave his studio and pictures, one of which he attributed to Lely and some of which were painted by himself, his antique furniture, silver, china and other objects to be offered to the National Trust to be kept intact in the studio and maintained as a collection. If the National Trust declined the trust (as in fact it did) he authorized the appointment of trustees to carry out the trust. It was acknowledged that a gift to found a museum may be assumed to be charitable if no one questions it. But if the utility of the gift was brought into question, as it was here, it was essential to know something of the quality of the exhibits and for this purpose expert evidence was admissible to assist the court in judging the educational value of the gift. The evidence was to the effect that the collection was of low quality. The Lely was bogus and the testator's own paintings were bad. Among the furniture there were some genuine English and Continental pieces of the seventeenth and eighteenth centuries which might be acceptable as a gift to a minor provincial museum. But, according to the terms of the will, everything had to be exhibited together, and the good things would be stifled by the large number of absolutely valueless pictures and objects. Harman L.J. could conceive of no useful purpose in "foisting on the public this mass of junk".[89] The trust had neither public utility nor educational value and, therefore, failed as a charity.

The test of educational value in relation to museums and art galleries is, in practice, applied by the Charity Commissioners. If a collection is in a museum or art gallery which is registered with one of the recognised umbrella bodies it will usually be regarded as satisfying the criterion of merit. In other cases, expert evidence will be considered.[90]

---

[85] Expert evidence was admitted in *Re Pinion* [1965] Ch. 85, below. The evidence, which was adverse to the utility of the gift of paintings, etc., was accepted. In *Incorporated Council of Law Reporting for England and Wales v Att-Gen* [1972] 1 Ch. 73 at 87, 91, 101, an affidavit of Professor A.L. Goodhart on the need for reliable law reports was accepted.

[86] *Re Shaw* (1957) 1 W.L.R. 729.

[87] A trust to encourage children to play chess is charitable (*Re Dupree's Deed Trusts* [1945] Ch. 16), and so too is one to play football (*IRC v McMullen* [1981] A.C. 1). A trust to encourage the study of steam engines has been held not to be charitable (see [1965] Ch. Com. Rep., p.30 (Norfolk Steam Engine Club), a case in which there was a prevailing element of benefit to members; but the Charity Commissioners have registered railway preservation societies).

[88] [1965] Ch. 85.

[89] [1965] Ch. 85 at 107.

[90] See RR10, *Museums and Art Galleries* (2002), paras 9–10, Annex A, paras 2–17.

Political purposes

A trust for the education of the public in forms of government is for the   **2–031**
advancement of education and so charitable, and this is the case even if
the trustees are required to be persons holding specified political views.[91]
Where the purpose of a gift genuinely is to educate the public in political
matters, it is thought that education in the principles of the various political parties who are seeking the support of the electorate must be impliedly
authorised, and that the gift will not fail to be a charitable trust for the
advancement of education because express provision is made for instruction in the principles of a particular political party or movement, as the
dominant and overriding purpose of the gift would be charitable. If, however, a trust is predominantly political[92] or propagandist,[93] as where the
furtherance of the principles of one particular party is, on the true construction of the trust instrument, the main object of the trust, then though
it is worded in the terms of an educational trust, and there is provision for
lectures and/or discussion classes which are in themselves of an educational character, but subsidiary to the main object, the trust will fail to
qualify as a charitable trust for the advancement of education.[94]

A trust for the furtherance of the principles of a particular political
party has been held to be a valid charitable trust were it was combined
with other trusts which are charitable. Thus in *Re Scowcroft*[95] a gift for
"the furtherance of Conservative principles and mental and moral
improvement" was held charitable. The gift would not have been charitable if the word "or" had been substituted for the word "and" because in
that case the gift could have been applied exclusively for political purposes
without transgressing the terms of the gift.[96]

A case in which the trust was perhaps more obviously political was *Re
Bushnell*.[97] The testator created a fund to be used in the propagation of the
teaching of "Socialised Medicine" the income being used *inter alia* to
engage lecturers and publish information to demonstrate "that the full
advantage of Socialised Medicine can only be enjoyed in a Socialist State."
Goulding J. held that the dominant or essential objects were political and
not educational and that the trust was, therefore, not charitable.

This case should be contrasted with *Att-Gen v Ross*[98] which considered   **2–032**
the question whether the funds of a student's union at a polytechnic were
held upon charitable trusts. The union was formed and existed for the

---

[91] *Re The Trusts of the Arthur MacDougall Fund* [1957] 1 W.L.R. 81, applying *Dunne v Byrne*
[1912] 407. See *Att-Gen v Ross* [1986] 1 W.L.R. 252. (Students' Union).
[92] See *National Anti-Vivisection Society v IRC* [1948] A.C. 31 at 61, 76, 77; and see
para.2–035, below.
[93] *Report*, 1966, p.13.
[94] See *Bonar Law Memorial Trust v IRC* (1933) 17 T.C. 503 at 517; *Re Hopkinson* [1949] 1 All
E.R. 346, 348; *cf. Russel v Jackson* (1852) 10 Hare. 204.
[95] [1898] 2 Ch. 638.
[96] See and compare *Chichester Diocesan Board of Finance v Simpson* [1944] A.C. 341.
[97] [1975] 1 W.L.R. 1596.
[98] [1986] 1 W.L.R. 852, following *London Hospital Medical College v IRC* [1976] 1 W.L.R.
623. See also Warburton, "Student unions, charities and politics", (1986) 1 Trust L. & P.
47.

purpose of furthering the educational function of the polytechnic, and its funds, which were provided by the local educational authority, were intended to further the educational purposes for which that authority was responsible. The union was therefore established for charitable purposes and the fact that the polytechnic, in the furtherance of its educational function, encouraged its students, through the union, to develop political awareness and form views on political issues, was not inconsistent with that purpose.

Three trusts concerned with international relations were held not to be charitable, although an educational element was present in all of them. The object of the trust in *Anglo-Swedish Society v IRC*[99] was to promote a closer and more sympathetic understanding between the English and Swedish peoples, principally by affording opportunities for Swedish journalists to visit the United Kingdom in order to study British modes of thought and British national institutions. Had the trust been, for example, restricted to the education of Swedes in British history with an emphasis on philosophical thought in Britain and the establishment and development of national institutions, it would doubtless have been charitable: but Rowlatt J. found[1] that it was a trust "to promote an attitude of mind, the view of one nation by another," which did not fall within the preamble to the Statute of Elizabeth I and was, therefore, not charitable.

In *Re Strakosch*[2] the Court of Appeal found that a gift to trustees "for any purpose which in their opinion is designed to strengthen the bonds of unity between the Union of South Africa and the Mother Country and which incidentally will conduce to the appeasement of racial feeling between the Dutch and English speaking sections of the South African community" was not charitable. The very wide and vague scope of the gift and the unrestricted latitude of application which its language permitted made it impossible to find that it fell within the spirit and intendment of the preamble to the Statute. Lord Greene M.R. delivering the judgment of the court said[3] that it was unfortunate that the testator did not seek to constitute a trust which might well have been valid as an educational trust, but it was impossible to construe the trust as one confined to educational purposes: "[The] problem of appeasing racial feeling within the community is a political problem, perhaps primarily political."

2–033   In *Buxton v Public Trustee*[4] the purpose of the trust was to promote and aid the improvement of international relations and intercourse by various prescribed methods. Plowman J. held[5] that the trust was not charitable because its objects were "public utility or political," the element of education referred to the education for a political cause, by the creation of a "climate of opinion."

Both the courts and the Charity Commissioners now appear to be less inclined to hold trusts concerned with international and race relations

[99] (1931) 16 T.C. 34.
[1] (1931) 16 T.C. 34, 38.
[2] [1949] Ch. 529.
[3] [1949] Ch. 529 at 538.
[4] (1962) 41 T.C. 235.
[5] (1962) 41 T.C. 235 at 242.

non-charitable on political grounds. Since 1983,[6] the Commissioners have accepted as charitable trusts for the promotion of good race relations, for endeavouring to eliminate discrimination on the grounds of race and for encouraging equality between persons of different racial groups.

Re Koeppler's Will Trusts[7] concerned a gift to "the Warden and the Chairman of the Academic Advisory Council . . . of the institution known as Wilton Park . . . for the benefit at their discretion of the said institution as long as Wilton Park remains a British contribution to the formation of an informed international public opinion and to the promotion of greater co-operation in Europe and the West in general." "Wilton Park" was the name used to describe a series of conferences for a broad range of persons who were capable of influencing opinion in Member States of the Organisation for Economic Co-operation and Development (a grouping of most Western nations) and enabled participants from member nations of that and other major Western organisations to exchange views on political, economic and social issues of common interest. The conferences were private and unofficial.

The Court of Appeal, reversing the decision of Peter Gibson J.[8] found that the testator, in leaving part of his estate for the benefit of Wilton Park, was clearly doing so in order to enable the work which he had begun and carried on for 25 years under the name of Wilton Park to be carried on after his death. The trust was a purpose trust to be construed as one for the furtherance of the Wilton Park project. In providing that the gift should take effect only if Wilton Park remained a British contribution to the formation of an informed international public opinion and to the promotion of greater co-operation in Europe and the West in general, the testator was limiting his gift to take effect only if the work of Wilton Park still accorded with a specific description, and it was not correct to elevate that description to an exclusive, comprehensive statement of the purpose of the gift. On the evidence, there was no question of the conferences held at Wilton Park being intended to further the interests of a particular political party, nor of their being intended to procure changes in the laws or government policy of any other country; even when they touched on political matters they constituted no more than genuine attempts in an objective manner to ascertain and disseminate the truth. Accordingly, the purpose of the gift was charitable as being for the advancement of education. The Court of Appeal distinguished *Re Strakosch*[9] and *McGovern v Att-Gen.*[10]

2–034

---

[6] [1983] Ch. Com. Rep., para.15 *et seq.* See para.2–015 below.
[7] [1986] Ch. 423.
[8] [1984] 2 All E.R. 111.
[9] [1949] Ch. 529.
[10] [1982] Ch. 321. See para.2–036 below.

Trusts to change the law

2–035   Frequently the advancement of political purposes involves advocating changes in the law or in governmental policy. Trusts for such a purpose do not necessarily contain an educational element, but often do so, and it is therefore thought appropriate to consider the cases concerned with such trusts in the context of education.

In *Bowman v Secular Society Ltd.*[11] Lord Parker of Waddington stated the general principle as follows[12]:

> "[A] trust for the attainment of political objects has always been held invalid, not because it is illegal, for everyone is at liberty to advocate or promote by any lawful means a change in the law, but because the court has no means of judging whether a proposed change in the law will or will not be for the public benefit, and therefore cannot say that a gift to secure the change is a charitable gift."

This statement of principle was considered by the House of Lords in *National Anti-Vivisection Society v IRC*[13] where a society which had as its object the total suppression of vivisection was held not to be established for charitable purposes on two grounds: first, on the evidence, any assumed public benefit from its suppression would be far outweighed by the detriment to medical science and research and consequently to public health; and secondly, a main object of the society was the political object of the promotion of legislation to change the law. On this second ground for the decision Lord Simonds said[14]:

> "My Lords, I see no reason for supposing that Lord Parker in the cited passage used the expression 'political objects' in any narrow sense or was confining it to objects of acute political controversy. On the contrary he was, I think, propounding familiar doctrine, nowhere better stated than in a text-book, which has long been regarded as of high authority but appears not to have been cited for this purpose to the courts below (as it certainly was not to your Lordships), *Tyssen on Charitable Bequests*, 1st ed. The passage which is at p.176, is worth repeating at length: 'It is a common practice for a number of individuals amongst us to form an association for the purposes of promoting some change in the law and it is worth our while to consider the effect of a gift to such an association. It is clear that such an association is not of a charitable nature. However desirable the change may really be, the law could not stultify itself by holding that it was for the

---

[11] [1917] A.C. 406. See also *De Themmines v De Bonneval* (1828) 5 Russ. 288; a gift of stock upon trust to apply the dividends in printing and promoting the circulation of a treatise written in French and Latin which inculcated the doctrine of the absolute and inalienable supremacy of the Pope in ecclesiastical matters was held to be void as being contrary to the policy of the law.

[12] [1917] A.C. 406 at 442.

[13] [1948] A.C. 31.

[14] *ibid.,* at 62, 63.

public benefit that the law itself should be changed. Each court in deciding on the validity of a gift must decide on the principle that the law is right as it stands. On the other hand, such a gift could not be held void for illegality.' Lord Parker uses slightly different language but means the same thing, when he says that the court has no means of judging whether a proposed change in the law will or will not be for the public benefit. It is not for the court to judge and the court has no means of judging. The same question may be looked at from a slightly different angle. One of the tests, and a crucial test, whether a trust is charitable, lies in the competence of the court to control and reform it. I would remind your Lordships that it is the King as *parens patriae* who is the guardian of charity and that it is the right and duty of his Attorney-General to intervene and inform the court, if the trustees of a charitable trust fall short of their duty. So too it is his duty to assist the court, if need be, in the formulation of a scheme for the execution of a charitable trust. But, my Lords, is it for a moment to be supposed that it is the function of the Attorney-General on behalf of the Crown to intervene and demand that a trust shall be established and administered by the court, the object of which is to alter the law in a manner highly prejudicial, as he and His Majesty's Government may think, to the welfare of the state? This very case would serve as an example, if upon the footing that it was a charitable trust it became the duty of the Attorney-General on account of its maladministration to intervene."[15]

In *National Anti-Vivisection Society v IRC*[16] it was, as already stated, **2–036** held, as one of the two grounds for the decision, that the proposed change in the law was not for the public benefit, and accordingly the House of Lords considered that it had the means in that particular case of judging whether the proposed change in the law was or was not for the public benefit. The problem of reconciliation of this part of the decision with the statement of Lord Parker of Waddington in *Bowman v Secular Society Ltd.*,[17] that "the court has no means of judging whether a proposed change in the law will or will not be for the public benefit" was dealt with by Lord Wright in the *National Anti-Vivisection* case in the following passage[18]:

"While I was preparing this part of my opinion my noble and learned friend Lord Simonds was kind enough to draw to my attention the passage which, in due course, your Lordships will hear quoted by him

---

[15] See also *IRC v Temperance Council of The Christian Churches of England and Wales* (1926) 10 T.C. 748 (as the Council was instituted mainly with the direct purpose to effect changes in the law, it was not established for charitable purposes); *Animal Defence and Anti-Vivisection Society v IRC (No. 2)* (1950) 66 T.L.R. (Pt.1) 1091 (the objects of the Society included opposition to vivisection, which was not a charitable purpose).

[16] [1948] A.C. 31.

[17] [1917] A.C. 406 at 442.

[18] [1948] A.C. 31 at 50; and see *Animal Defence and Anti-Vivisection Society v IRC (No. 2)* (1950) 66 T.L.R. (Pt.1) 1091 at 1094.

from a work of authority. *Tyssen on Charitable Bequests*, 1st ed., p.177. It is, I think, a very important contribution to this question. It appears to me to go to explain and justify Lord Parker's opinion. I refer especially to Tyssen's words: 'the law could not stultify itself by holding that it was for the public benefit that the law itself should be changed' and again: 'each court . . . must decide on the principle that the law is right as it stands.' I am reminded of the words of a great common law judge who warned the courts against usurping the functions of the legislature. I do not regard the statements of Lord Parker and Tyssen as inconsistent but as complementary."

In *McGovern v Att-Gen*,[19] Slade J. analysed *Bowman v Secular Society Ltd.*[20] and *National Anti-Vivisection Society v IRC*[21] and extracted the principle that:

"the court will not regard as charitable a trust of which a main object is to procure an alteration of the law of the United Kingdom for one or both of two reasons: first, the court will ordinarily have no sufficient means of judging as a matter of evidence whether the proposed change will or will not be for the public benefit. Secondly, even if the evidence suffices to enable it to form a prima facie opinion that a change in the law is desirable, it must still decide the case on the principle that the law is right as it stands, since to do otherwise would usurp the functions of the legislature."

The first reason stated by Slade J. is of doubtful validity as the House of Lords in *National Anti-Vivisection Society v IRC*[22] had clearly indicated that a court could determine if a proposed change in the law was for the public benefit. The ground is even more doubtful after the coming into force of the Human Rights Act 1998; courts now have to balance the rights of individuals against the interests of the community as a whole in deciding whether a statutory provision or act of a public body infringes Convention rights.[23]

2–037 Slade J. summarised his conclusions in relation to trusts for political purposes as follows[24]:

"(1) Even if it otherwise appears to fall within the spirit and intendment of the preamble to the Statute of Elizabeth, a trust for political purposes falling within the spirit of Lord Parker's pronouncement in *Bowman's case*[25] can never be regarded as being for public benefit in the manner which the law regards as charitable.

---

[19] [1982] Ch. 321 at 336, 337.
[20] [1917] A.C. 406.
[21] [1948] A.C. 31.
[22] [1948] A.C. 31, see para.2–035 above.
[23] See G. Moffat, "Charity, Politics and the Human Rights Act 1998: Chasing a Red Herring?", (2001) Int. J. of Not for Profit Law, Vol. 4, Issue 1, 1, 6.
[24] [1982] Ch. 321 at 340.
[25] [1917] A.C. 406.

the freedom of any organisation to express whatever views it wants.[62] This argument ignores the fact that charitable status brings with it fiscal benefits which can assist an organisation to carry out its purposes, or, more to the point, the lack of which may prevent an organisation expressing its views. It is not, therefore, safe, to assume that a refusal to grant charitable status to an organisation because it has a political purpose is not a breach of Article 10. This is despite the view of the Canadian Supreme Court[63] that rules requiring an organisation to restrict itself to charitable purposes and activities, as those rules were settled in common law, did not breach the Canadian Charter of Rights and Freedoms as any organisation, by restricting itself to charitable purposes, could qualify for registration and the benefits which flow therefrom.

Can the principle that political purposes are not charitable be justified **2–042** under Article 10(2)? It is well accepted that any limitation on a freedom must be prescribed by law, be necessary in a democratic society, *i.e.* there must be a proportionate response to a pressing social need to protect the competing interest and it must be directed to a legitimate aim.[64] In addition, any rule which differentiates between persons and organisations must not discriminate within Article 14 and must, therefore, be objective and reasonable.[65] The rule that political purposes cannot be charitable is clearly set out in case law. The main reason given by the courts for the rule is that the courts should not usurp the function of the legislature[66] which co-incides with the purpose specified in Article 10(2) of "maintaining the authority and impartiality of the judiciary" and can, therefore, be considered to be a legitimate aim. The principle that the judiciary will not decide whether any particular changes should be made in the law can also be said to support the aim in Article 10(2) of protecting the right of others in their right to effective democracy.[67] The requirement of a pressing social need is met by the need to uphold the principle of separation of powers and impartiality of the judiciary. The only argument on proportionality would appear to be whether the excluded class of purposes based on politics could be more narrowly confined and yet still be effective to achieve the legitimate aim.[68] The rule does not appear to discriminate within Article 14 as the criterion for refusal of charitable status, *i.e.* political purpose is

---

[62] See CC, *Promotion of Human Rights* (2002), para.A2 and G. Moffat, "Charity, Politics and the Human Rights Act 1998; Chasing a Red Herring?", (2001) Int. J. of Not for Profit Law, Vol.4, Issue 1, 1, 15.

[63] *Vancouver Society of Immigrant and Visible Minority Women v M.N.R.* (1999) 169 D.L.R. (14th) 34, at 130, *per* Iacobucci J.

[64] See S. Grosz, J. Beatson, and P. Duffy, *Human Rights, The 1998 Act and the European Convention*, (2000), paras 5–08, *et seq.*

[65] See *op cit.*, paras C14–20, *et seq.*

[66] See *McGovern v Att-Gen* [1982] Ch. 321 at 336–337. The alternative ground for the rule that the court has no means of judging whether a proposed change in the law is for the public benefit is of doubtful validity—see para.2–036 above.

[67] See CC, *The Promotion of Human Rights*, (2002), paras A7–A14 and see G. Moffat, "Charity, Politics and the Human Rights Act 1998:Chasing a Red Herring?", (2001) Int. J. of Not for Profit Law, Vol.4, Issue 1, 1, 20.

[68] See para.2–039 above for a possible extension of charitable status to the advocacy of a change in the law.

that which is central to the achievement of the legitimate aims, impartiality of the judiciary and the maintenance of an effective democracy. The rule does not differentiate between different political purposes.

2–043   Although political purposes are not charitable, a charity can undertake activities of a political nature in pursuit of its charitable purposes provided it acts within its powers. The problem is determining the dividing line between political activities which are permissible in that they serve and are subordinate to a charity's purposes and those which become a political purpose in themselves and endanger charitable status. The Charity Commissioners have issued detailed guidance on the extent to which it considers charities may engage in political activities.[69] The emphasis of the guidance is on activity furthering the purposes of the charity and views being expressed that are based on a well-founded and reasonable case and expressed in a reasonable manner. For example, a charity should not seek to organise public opinion to support or oppose a political party, as opposed to a particular policy, but can seek to influence government and public opinion through well-founded, reasoned argument based on research and direct experience of issues.

Incidental non-charitable purposes

2–044   If the main objects of an institution or association are charitable, the mere fact that the members are benefited in the course of promoting the charitable purpose does not prevent the institution or assocation being estabished for charitable purposes only within the meaning of s.505 of the Income and Corporation Taxes Act 1988 or being an organisation whose main objects are charitable within the meaning of ss.43 and 45 of the Local Government Finance Act 1988.[70]

As Greer L.J. said[71]:

> "If you come to the conclusion, as you may in many cases, that one of the ways in which the public objects of an association can be served is be giving special advantages to the members of the association, then the association does not cease to be an association with a charitable object because incidentally and in order to carry out the charitable object it is both necessary and desirable to confer special benefits on the members."

Thus, in *Royal College of Surgeons of England v National Provincial Bank Ltd.*[72] the House of Lords held that the Royal College of Surgeons

---

[69] CC9, *Political Activities and Campaigning by Charities*, (1999). See also CC9a, *Political Activities and Campaigning by Local Community Charities*, (1997).

[70] ss.43 and 45 give relief from non-domestic rates.

[71] *Geologists Association v IRC* (1928) 14 T.C. 271 at 283. See also *Incorporated Council of Law Reporting for England and Wales v Att-Gen* [1972] Ch. 73 at 85, 94, 100; *London Hospital Medical College v IRC* [1976] 1 W.L.R. 613 at 620; [1978] Conv. 92 (N. P. Gravells).

[72] [1952] A.C. 631: see also [2001] Ch. Com. Dec. April 2 (The General Medical Council).

was a charity, because its main object, as set out in the recitals to the Royal Charter incorporating it, was "the due promotion and encouragement of the study and practice" of the art and science of surgery, and the professional protection of the College's members provided for in its by-laws was merely ancillary to that object. None of the learned lords cited the above-quoted observations of Greer L.J. but the principle was clearly in their minds and was the basis of their decision.

In *Royal College of Nursing v St. Marylebone Borough Council*[73] Romer L.J., delivering the considered judgment of the Court of Appeal, quoted and applied the observations of Greer L.J.[74] The case arose under s.8 of the Rating and Valuation (Miscellaneous Provisions) Act 1955. The Royal College of Nursing was incorporated by Royal Charter in 1928 and and claimed to be entitled under s.8(2) of the Act to rating relief in respect of premises occupied as a hall and offices as being an organisation "not established or conducted for profit and whose main objects are charitable or otherwise concerned with the advancement . . . of education or social welfare", within s.8(1). The objects set out in the charter were (a) to promote the science and art of nursing and the better education and training of nurses, and (b) to promote the advance of nursing as a profession in all or any of its branches. Object (a) was admitted to be charitable; but the Court of Appeal held, affirming the decision of the Divisional Court,[75] that (b) was also charitable as being directed to the advancement of nursing "for the relief of the sick". It was held that the fact that the advancement of nursing as a profession might advance the professional interests of nurses in a trade union sense was incidental, and that the college did not cease to be a charity because, incidentally, and in order to carry out the charitable object, it was both necessary and desirable to confer special benefits on the members.[76]

In *Incorporated Council of Law Reporting for England and Wales v Att-Gen*[77] the fact that the publication of law reports helps the lawyer to earn his livelihood is, according to Buckley L.J.,[78] "incidental to or consequential on the primary scholastic function of advancing and disseminating knowledge of the law, and does not detract from the exclusively charitable character of the Council's objects."

On the other hand an institution whose main object is in the protection and advantage of those practising a particular profession is not a charity even though the carrying out of the main object results in benefit to the community.[79] Because of this problem, several established charities have formed separate non-charitable bodies for negotiating purposes to preserve the charitable status of the original institution. For example, the

2–045

---

[73] [1959] 1 W.L.R. 1077 at 1085.
[74] (1928) 14 T.C. 271 at 283.
[75] [1958] 1 W.L.R. 95.
[76] See also *Institution of Civil Engineers v IRC* [1932] 1 K.B. 149; *Yorkshire Agricultural Society v IRC* [1928] 1 K.B. 611.
[77] [1972] 1 Ch. 73.
[78] *ibid.* at 103.
[79] *Geologists Association v IRC* (1928) 14 T.C. 271; *Chartered Insurance Institute v London Corporation* [1957] 1 W.L.R. 867; *General Nursing Council in England and Wales v St. Marylebone Borough Council* [1959] A.C. 540.

College of Radiographers is a charitable institution which promotes radiography and the Society of Radiographers is a non-charitable body which negotiates on behalf of its members.[80]

Public benefit[81]

2–046   Before a trust for the advancement of education can be charitable the court must be satisfied that the benefits are to be available to the community or to a sufficiently important section of the community. Limited classes of persons have been regarded as constituting a sufficiently important section of the community and gifts for their education have been upheld: namely, women and girls who are not self-supporting,[82] the daughters of missionaries,[83] and persons professing particular religious doctrines.[84] However, if there is a personal nexus between each of the beneficiaries and an individual or individuals or a company the trust will fail for lack of public benefit. Thus the relations or descendants of the donor or other named or designated persons,[85] the members of a friendly society or other mutual benefit society or organisation,[86] and the employees of an individual employer firm or limited company,[87] or their children,[88] do not constitute a section of the public.[89]

There are two quasi exceptions to the rule of public benefit in relation to educational trusts.

First, whilst a gift solely to educate "founder's kin" at a school or college is not charitable,[90] a trust where preference is directed to be given to the donor's descendants is charitable.[91] The reasoning is that a gift to a school or college is charitable because the maintenance of schools of learning, free schools and scholars of universities are objects specifically referred to in the preamble to the Statute of Elizabeth I, and that a gift to a school or college is none the less charitable if provision is made therein for the kinsmen of the donor to participate in the benefit conferred by the gift.

2–047   Secondly, it was held in *Re Koettgen's Will Trusts*[92] that, where the primary object of an educational trust is of a public nature, a direction to

---

[80] [1977] Ch. Com. Rep., paras 92–94.
[81] See para.1–008 above.
[82] *Re Central Employment Bureau for Women and Student's Careers Association (Incorporated)* [1942] 1 All E.R. 232.
[83] *German v Chapman* (1877) 7 Ch.D. 271.
[84] *Income Tax Special Purposes Commissioners v Pemsel* [1891] A.C. 531.
[85] *Re Compton* [1945] Ch. 123; *Davies v Perpetual Trustee Co.* [1959] A.C. 439; *cf. Laverty v Laverty* [1907] 1 I.R. 9 (education of "any boy or man" of a particular surname not charitable).
[86] *Re Hoburn Aero Components Ltd's Air Raid Distress Fund* [1946] Ch. 86.
[87] *Oppenheim v Tobacco Securities Trust Co. Ltd* [1951] A.C. 297. *Re Rayner* (1920) 89 L.J.Ch. 369 was doubted by the House of Lords and cannot be relied on. See also *IRC v Educational Grants Association* [1967] Ch. 123, affirmed. [1967] Ch. 993, CA.
[88] *Re Leverhulme* [1943] 2 All E.R. 173.
[89] See generally the speech of Lord Cross of Chelsea in *Dingle v Turner* [1972] A.C. 601.
[90] *Re Compton* [1945] Ch. 123 at 132–134 explaining *Att-Gen v Sidney Sussex College* (1869) L.R. 4 Ch. 722 and *Re Lavelle* [1914] 1 I.R. 194.
[91] *Spencer v All Souls College* (1762) Wilm. 163.
[92] [1954] Ch. 252.

prefer members of a limited class who would not by themselves constitute a section of the public does not invalidate the trust. In this case a trust was established for the furtherance of the commercial education of British-born persons, with a direction that preference should be given to employees of a particular firm. However, the essential question would seem to be whether or not there is a mere expression of preference. If it goes beyond that and amounts to a positive obligation the trust should not be regarded as charitable because the obligation will vitiate the public character of the trust. It is certainly possible to argue on this basis that *Re Koettgen's Will Trusts* is wrongly decided. Its correctness was indeed doubted by Lord Radcliffe in *Caffoor v Commissioners of Income Tax, Colombo*,[93] where it was held by the Privy Council that the trust in question was a family trust and not of a public character for charitable purposes. In essence the question will always be reduced to one of construction.[94] These cases may now be open to challenge on ECHR principles.[95]

Even if a trust directing that preference be given to certain individuals attains charitable status, it may not be given relief from income tax if too high a proportion of its income is paid to the preferred individuals as it cannot be said that its income is being applied for charitable purposes only.[96]

THE ADVANCEMENT OF RELIGION

A gift for religious purposes has to satisfy two conditions in order to come within the meaning of Lord Macnaghten's third head of charity.[97] First, the gift must contribute to the advancement of religion as that word is interpreted by the courts.[98] Secondly, the gift must promote the religious instruction or education of the public.[99] It is well settled, however, that, because the advancement of religion is within Lord Macnaghten's first three heads of charity, a gift for religious purposes is prima facia charitable, the necessary element of public benefit being presumed unless and until the contrary is shown.[1]

2–048

---

[93] [1961] A.C. 584.

[94] For the Charity Commissions' approach to the construction of such trusts, see [1978] Ch. Com. Rep., paras 86, *et seq.*

[95] See para.1–009 above.

[96] *IRC v Educational Grants Association Limited* [1967] Ch. 123 at 144, affirmed. [1967] Ch. 993, CA.

[97] *The Commissioners for Special Purposes of the Income Tax v Pemsel* [1879] A.C. 531 at 583.

[98] *Dunne v Byrne* [1912] A.C. 407. As to the meaning of religion, see below.

[99] *Cocks v Manners* (1871) L.R. 12 Eq. 574 at 585; *Yeap Cheah Neo v One Cheng Neo* (1875) L.R. 6 P.C. 381; *Re Joy* (1888) 60 L.T. 175; *Re Macduff* [1896] 2 Ch. 451; *Re Delaney* [1902] 2 Ch. 642 at 648; *Chesterman v Federal Commissioners of Income Tax* [1926] A.C. 128; *Gilmour v Coats* [1949] A.C. 426.

[1] *Re Ward* [1941] Ch. 308 at 311, 312; *Re Watson* [1973] 1 W.L.R. 1472 at 1482. This does not seem to be the case in Scotland: *Grimond v Grimond* [1905] A.C. 124. See para.1–008 above for consideration of the requirement of public benefit.

The meaning of "religion" and "religious"

2–049   "Religion" has been defined as meaning "A particular system of faith and worship" and "Recognition on the part of man of some higher unseen power as having control of his destiny, and as being entitled to obedience, reverence, and worship,"[2] and numerous cases concerned with gifts and trusts for the advancement of religion show that this is the meaning accepted by the court. Hence the advancement of promotion of religion means according to Lord Hanworth M.R. in *Keren Kayemeth Le Jisroel v IRC*,[3] the promotion of spiritual teaching in a wide sense, and the maintenance of the doctrines on which it rests, and the observances that serve to promote and manifest it." In *United Grand Lodge of Ancient Free and Accepted Masons of England v Holborn Borough Council*[4] Donovan J. said: To advance religion means to promote it, to spread the message ever wider among mankind; to take some positive steps to sustain and increase religious belief; and these things are done in a variety of ways which may be comprehensively described as pastoral and missionary." In *Re South Place Ethical Society*[5] Dillon J. said: "It seems to me that two of the essential attributes of religion are faith and worship; faith in a god and worship of that god," and he referred to the definition quoted above. Buckley L.J. in *R. v Registrar General Ex p. Segerdal*[6] considered religion to have the following characteristics: submission to the object worshipped; veneration of that object; thanksgiving, prayer and intercession.

The meaning of religion for the purpose of charity was considered most recently by the Charity Commissioners in their decision on the charitable status of The Church of Scientology (England and Wales).[7] In relation to the cases considered above, the Commissioners concluded that the definition of a religion in English charity law was characterised by a belief in a supreme being and an expression of that belief through worship.[8] The Commissioners, however, recognised that in most of the English cases the consideration of the meaning of religion was not directly for the purposes of charitable status but rather, for example, whether a building used by a particular organisation was a "place of meeting for religious worship" within the meaning of the Places of Worship Registration Act 1855.[9] In the absence of a clear and unambiguous definition of religion in English law, the Charity Commissioners took a positive and constructive approach conforming with ECHR principles[10] to identify what is a religion in charity law.[11]

---

[2] *The Oxford English Dictionary* 1979 (Compact) ed.
[3] [1931] 2 K.B. 465, 477, CA, affirmed. [1932] A.C. 650.
[4] [1957] 1 W.L.R. 1080 at 1090.
[5] [1980] 1 W.L.R. 1565 at 1572.
[6] [1970] 2 Q.B. 697 at 709.
[7] [1999] Ch. Comm. Dec. November 17.
[8] *ibid.*, p.14.
[9] *R. v Registrar General Ex p. Segerdal* [1970] 2 Q.B. 697.
[10] For a discussion of relevant ECHR Articles see para.2–050 below.
[11] [1999] Ch. Com. Dec. November 17, p.19.

The Commissioners considered decisions in other jurisdictions, in particular the decision of the High Court of Australia in *The Church of the New Faith v The Commissioners for Payroll Tax*[12] and the wider views of three of the judges in that case that belief in a supreme being was not necessary before a set of beliefs could be a religion. They also had regard to Indian[13] and Californian[14] decisions that concluded that religion is not necessarily theistic. Those cases also took a broad view of worship holding, for example, that "canons of conduct giving effect to the belief in question"[15] were sufficient.

The Charity Commissioners concluded[16] that belief in a supreme being remains a necessary characteristic of religion for the purposes of English charity law but that it would not be proper to specify the nature of that supreme being or to require it to be analogous to the deity or supreme being of a particular religion. They also concluded[17] that worship provided a clear criterion necessary to make the distinction in charity law between religious and non-religious belief systems. Worship in this context was taken to mean reverence and recognition of a supreme being. On this basis, the Commissioners decided[18] that the Church of Scientology was not a religion. Whilst the Church of Scientology professed belief in a supreme being, the core religious services, namely auditing and training, did not constitute worship.

2–050

The courts and the Charity Commissioners are public bodies and any definition of religion they adopt for the purposes of charity law must be compatible with the ECHR.[19] Relevant Articles are 9, the right to freedom of thought, conscience and religion; Article 14, the right to enjoyment of ECHR rights free from discrimination and Article 1 of the First Protocol, right to peaceful enjoyment of property. It can be argued that Article 9 is not relevant as charitable status does not prevent the ability to practice a particular religion or belief but the tax reliefs associated with charitable status may well affect the ability of an organisation to teach and pass on its beliefs. The tax reliefs similarly bring Article 1 of the First Protocol into play. Accordingly, any definition of "religion" which determines charitable status must be objective and have reasonable justification.[20] It is considered that the definition of religion adopted by the Charity Commissioners in the Church of Scientology case[21] of belief in a supreme being, broadly defined, and worship is consistent with ECHR

---

[12] (1983) 154 C.L.R. 120.
[13] *The Commissioner Hindu Religious Endowment Madras v Sri Lakshmindra Thirtha Swamiar of Sri Shirur Mutt* (1954)—Indian Supreme Court [1954] S.C.R. 1005.
[14] *Fellowship of Humanity v County of Alameda* 153 Cal. App. 2d 673 at 315P.2d 394 (1957).
[15] *The Church of the New Faith v The Commissioner for Payroll Tax* (1983) 154 C.L.R. 120 at 136, *per* Mason ACJ., Brennan J.
[16] [1999] Ch. Com. Dec. November 17, p.21.
[17] *ibid.,* p.24
[18] *ibid.,* p.25.
[19] Human Rights Act 1998, s.6.
[20] See *Tsirlis and Kouloumpas v Greece* (1997) 25 E.H.R.R. 198; *Belgian Linguistic Case* (1968) (No 2) 1 E.H.R.R. 252, paras 9–10.
[21] [1999] Ch. Com. Dec. November 17, see para.2–049.

principles.[22] However, any objective test of religion that seeks to exclude secular belief systems potentially excludes well accepted non-theistic religions such as Buddhism[23] and Jainism.[24]

The Strategy Unit proposed[25] that the current definition of religion should be widened to include faiths that are multi-deity, such as Hinduism, or non-deity, such as some types of Buddhism. Legislative clarification of the definition of religion was also proposed. Whilst clarification would be welcomed, it is questioned whether legislation is necessary in view of the wide liberal approach to the definition of religion now taken by the courts and the Charity Commissioners.

The law does not prefer one religion to another

2–051   In *Gilmour v Coats*[26] Lord Reid said:

"The law of England has always shown favour to gifts for religious purposes. It does not now in this matter prefer one religion to another. It assumes that it is good for man to have and to practise a religion but where a particular belief is accepted by one religion and rejected by another the law can neither accept nor reject it. The law must accept the position that it is right that different religions should each be supported irrespective of whether or not all its beliefs are true. A religion can be regarded as beneficial without it being necessary to assume that all its beliefs are true, and a religious service can be regarded as beneficial to all those who attend it without it being necessary to determine the spiritual efficacy of that service or to accept any particular belief about it."

It appears that only if the tenets of a particular sect inculcate doctrines adverse to the very foundations of all religion, and subversive of all morality,[27] will a gift for its advancement fail, and that it is not fatal to a gift that the opinions sought to be propagated are foolish or even devoid of foundation.[28]

In the 6th edition[29] of this work it was suggested that a religion must be monotheistic for the advancement of it to be charitable, this view being

---

[22] For a contrary view see P.W.Edge and J.M. Loughrey, "Religious Charities and the Jurisdiction of the Charity Commission", [2001] Legal Studies 36 at 61.
[23] See *R. v Registrar General Ex p. Segerdal* [1970] 2 Q.B. 697 at 707 for Lord Denning's acceptance of Buddhism as an exception to the need for a deity.
[24] See F. Quint and T. Spring, "Religion, Charity Law and Human Rights" (1999) 5 C.L.& P.R. 153 at 186.
[25] Cabinet Office, Strategy Unit, *Private Action, Public Benefit. A Review of Charities and the Wider Not-For-Profit Sector*, p.42.
[26] [1949] A.C. 426 at 458, 459. See also *Varsani v Jesani* [1999] Ch. 219 at 235, *per* Morritt L.J.
[27] See the discussion about the influence of certain religions and its effect on charitable status in *Charities: A Framework for the Future* (1989) Cm. 694., paras 2.22, *et seq.*
[28] *Thornton v Howe* (1862) 31 Beav. 14 at 20, *per* Sir John Romilly M.R. The case was followed in *Re Watson* [1973] 1 W.L.R. 1472 and *Holmes v Att-Gen*, *The Times*, February 12, 1981. See also *Re Caus* [1934] Ch. 162 at 168.
[29] At p.59.

based upon the speech of Lord Parker of Waddington in *Bowman v Secular Society Ltd.*,[30] but there is no direct authority to the effect that the advancement of a polytheistic religion is not charitable, and in the definition of "religion" cited above there is nothing to suggest that the "higher unseen power" must be a single god. Any argument today that the advancement of Christianity, Judaism or Islam was charitable, but that the advancement of a polytheistic religion like Hinduism was not, would be regarded as unacceptable.[31] Lord Denning M.R. in *R. v Registrar General, Ex p. Segerdal*[32] was apparently prepared to treat Buddhism as an exceptional case and as a religion in spite of the absence of a deity, and Dillon J. in *Re South Place Ethical Society*[33] thought that this might be the proper approach. In fact Dillon J. had before him the evidence of an eminent witness who did not accept the suggestion that "Buddhism denies a supreme being". Lord Denning[34] said that Buddhist temples were properly described as places of meeting for religious worship, and the regulations made under the Charities Act 1960[35] with regard to religious premises and the funds of religious bodies apply to non-Christian (as well as Christian) sects and make no distinction between monotheism and polytheism. The trust in *Yeap Cheah Neo v Ong Cheng Neo*[36] failed, not because of polytheism, but because the Privy Council found that the religious ceremonies involved, which related to ancestor worship, could lead to no public advantage and could benefit only the family itself.[37]

Consistently with the rule that one religion is not preferred to another, gifts for the promotion of the Roman Catholic[38] or the Jewish[39] religion or the study of the Jewish law and the repetition of Jewish prayers,[40] and the general benefit of dissenting denominations[41] are gifts for the advancement of religion and so charitable. So, too, are trusts for maintaining

---

[30] [1917] A.C. 406 at 409.

[31] See para.2–050 above for the relevance of ECHR principles.

[32] [1970] 2 Q.B. 697, 707, CA.

[33] [1980] 1 W.L.R. 1565 at 1573.

[34] [1970] 2 Q.B. 697, 707, CA.

[35] The Charities (Religious Premises) Regulations (SI 1962/1421); the Charities (Exception from Registration and Accounts) Regulations (SI 1963/2074).

[36] (1875) L.R. 6 P.C. 381.

[37] *ibid.*, at 396.

[38] *Bradshaw v Tasker* (1834) 2 My. & K. 221; *West v Shuttleworth* (1835) 2 My. & K. 684; *Walsh v Gladstone* (1843) 1 Phil. 290.

[39] *Straus v Goldsmit* (1837) 8 Sim. 614; *cf. Da Costa v De Paz* (1754) Amb. 228.

[40] *Re Michel's Trust* (1860) 28 Beav. 39.

[41] *Att-Gen v Wansay* (1808) 15 Ves. 231 (Presbyterians); *Shore v Wilson* (1843) 9 Cl. & F. 355; 11 Sim. 592 at 616; *Shrewsbury v Hornby* (1846) 5 Ha. 406 (Unitarians); *Thornton v Howe* (1862) 31 Beav. 14 (where a bequest for distributing the works of Joanna Southcote was held charitable); *Dawson v Small* (1874) L.R. 18 Eq. 114 (Methodists); *Re Brown* (1898) 1 I.R. 423 (Plymouth Brethren). The Holy Spirit Association for the Unification of World Christianity and the Sun Myung Moon Foundation (two institutions associated with the Unification Church, commonly known as the "Moonies") were registered as charities for the advancement of reglion; for comments on the legal status of the Moonies, see [1981] Ch.Com.Rep., paras 71, *et seq.*; [1982] Ch. Com. Rep., paras 36, *et seq.*

Dissenting[42] or Roman Catholic[43] chapels or meeting-houses or schools, or Jewish synagogues[44] or for the maintenance of Roman Catholic bishops,[45] or priests,[46] or Dissenting ministers,[47] or for a Roman Catholic college,[48] and the maintenance of Dissenting missionary establishments.[49] A trust for the purpose of promoting the faith of a particular Hindu sect was accepted as charitable without question by the Court of Appeal in *Varsani v Jesani*.[50]

The requirement of public benefit

2–052   Although a gift for the advancement of religion is prima facie charitable, the presumption can be rebutted and it remains a question for the court, and not the donor or testator, whether the gift in fact satisfies the requirement of public benefit.[51] It is considered that the presumption will be rebutted, and public benefit will have to be shown positively, if there is evidence that the purpose is subversive of all morality,[52] or it is a new belief system, or if there has been public concern expressed about the organisation carrying out the particular purpose,[53] or if it is focused too narrowly on its adherents.[54] It is on this basis that it has been decided that gifts to enclosed religious communities[55] and for private masses for the dead are not charitable.[56]

Gifts for religious purposes may be categorised as follows:

(a)   In general terms for religious purposes and to religious societies and institutions.

(b)   For the maintenance and promotion of public worship.

[42] *Att-Gen v Hickman* (1732) 2 Eq.Ca.Abr. 193, pl. 14; *Att-Gen v Fowler* (1808) 15 Ves. 85 (Baptist); *Att-Gen v Pearson* (1817) 3 Mer. 353; *Shore v Wilson* (1843) 9 Cl. & F. 355: *Shrewsbury v Hornby* (1846) 5 Ha. 406; *Att-Gen v Lawes* (1849) 8 Ha. 32 (Irvingite); *Re Barnett* (1860) 29 L.J.Ch. 871. See also *Holmes v Att-Gen, The Times*, February 12, 1981; [1981] Ch. Com. Rep., paras 22, *et seq.* (Exclusive Brethren); and see *Att-Gen v Guise* (1692) 2 Vern. 266 (Episcopalian in Scotland); *Bunting v Sargent* (1879) 13 Ch.D. 330 (Congregational); *Re Wall* (1889) 42 Ch.D. 510 (Unitarian); *Re Brown* [1898] 1 I.R. 423 (Plymouth Brethren); *Re St. John Street Chapel* [1893] 2 Ch. 629 (Wesleyan).
[43] *De Windt v De Windt* (1854) 23 L.J.Ch. 776.
[44] *Neville Estates Ltd. v Madden* [1962] Ch. 832.
[45] *Robb v Dorian* (1875) I.R. 11 Cl. 292. In *Att-Gen v Power* (1809) 1 Ball & B. 145 it was held that a bequest to Roman Catholic bishops and their successors was void, there being no such persons known to the law. This decision is no longer law.
[46] *Att-Gen v Gladstone* (1842) 13 Sim. 7; *Thornber v Wilson* (1855) 3 Drew 245, *Re Hetherington* [1990] Ch. 1. *Cf. Re Forster* [1939] Ch. 22.
[47] *Waller v Childs* (1765) Amb. 524; *Att-Gen v Lawes* (1849) 8 Ha. 32; *Lloyd v Spillett* (1740) 2 Atk. 148.
[48] *Walsh v Gladstone* (1843) 1 Ph. 290.
[49] *Commissioners for Special Purposes of Income Tax v Pemsel* [1891] A.C. 531.
[50] [1999] Ch. 219.
[51] *Re Hummeltenburg* [1923] 1 Ch. 237; *National Anti-Vivisection Society v IRC* [1948] A.C. 31 and see para.1–008 above.
[52] See *Re Watson* [1973] 1 W.L.R. 1472 at 1482, *per* Plowman J.
[53] See [1999] Ch. Com. Dec. November 17 (The Church of Scientology), pp.40, *et seq.*
[54] See *Re Hetherington* [1989] 2 All E.R. 129 at 134–135.
[55] See para.2–065 below.
[56] See para.2–069 below. Similarly if the core practices are conducted in private, see [1999] Ch. Com. Dec. November 17 (The Church of Scientology), p.47.

(c)   For the provision and maintenance of places of worship.
(d)   For the maintenance of churchyards and other burial places and particular tombs.
(e)   For the benefit of the clergy.
(f)   To the holders of religious offices.
(g)   To religious communities.
(h)   For masses.

An examination of the cases dealing with such gifts reveals how the necessary quality of public benefit is to be found.

(a) Gifts in general terms for religious purposes and to religious institutions and societies

As has already been stated,[57] a trust for "religious purposes" is prima facie charitable; the phrase must be taken to mean "purposes conducive to the advancement of religion.[58] So, too is a trust for "religious societies,[59] in the case of a gift for "charitable or religious" purposes,[60] or for "educational or charitable or religious purposes,[61] the court does not construe the phrase as indicating that there are included religious (or educational) purposes which are not necessarily charitable, a construction which would make the gift void for uncertainty.

2–053

In *Re White*[62] there was a bequest "to the following religious societies, *viz.*" followed by a blank in the will. The Court of Appeal construed the bequest as a bequest for "religious purposes". Having so construed the bequest, the court, being satisfied on the authorities that a bequest to a religious institution or for a religious purpose was prima facie charitable, filled in the blank space in the will by directing a scheme as to such part of the testator's personal estate as was pure personality at the date of his death. The court applied the general rule that a charitable trust does not fail for uncertainty.

A bequest to an institution or body which does not have any legal existence will not, however, be construed as a bequest for religious purposes[63]

---

[57] See para.2–048, above.
[58] *Re Ward* [1941] Ch. 308 at 311, 312, *per* Clauson L.J. See also *Baker v Sutton* (1836) 1 Keen 224; *Townsend v Carus* (1843) 2 Ha. 257; *Wilkinson v Lindgren* (1870) L.R. 5 Ch. 570; *Re Lloyd* (1893) 10 T.L.R. 66; *Arnott v Arnott* [1906] 1 I.R. 127; *Re Salter* [1911] 1 I.R. 289; *Rickerby v Nicholson* [1912] 1 I.R. 343.
[59] *Re White* [1893] 2 Ch. 41.
[60] *Re Salter* [1911] 1 I.R. 289.
[61] *Re Ward* [1941] Ch. 308.
[62] [1893] 2 Ch. 41; followed in *Re Ward* [1941] Ch. 308. It is not considered that the authority of *Re White* is affected by any comments in *Dunne v Byrne* [1912] A.C. 407 or *Grimond v Grimond* [1905] A.C. 124.
[63] *Re Thackrah* [1939] 2 All E.R. 4. (Bequest to "the Oxford Group" with a direction that the receipt of the secretary or other proper officer should be "full and sufficient discharge". No directions were given as to how the money was to be used. Bennett J. held that there could be no association unless the members were held together by some rules, either written or oral. The Oxford Group was not then incorporated and was not held together by any rules. The judge refused to construe the bequest as a bequest for a purpose, and on the

unless, on the construction of the whole of the will, it is possible to infer that the dominant intention of the testator was to promote a religious purpose and that the gift to the non-existent body was only the method whereby his intention was to be carried into effect.[64]

2–054   A gift to a particular church denomination or sect for its general purposes is construed as a gift which is applicable only for such of its purposes as are religious and at the same time satisfy the requirement of public benefit.[65] On the other hand, a gift "for Roman Catholic purposes" is not charitable, because not every Roman Catholic purpose is charitable,[66] and a gift to a vicar for the time being of a parish "for parochial institutions or purposes" is not charitable, because the words in question may include objects which are not charitable in the legal sense.[67] A gift to the respective vicars and churchwardens of two named parishes "for parish work" was held not to be charitable on the ground that those words in their ordinary meaning included objects which were not charitable in the legal sense.[68]

A gift in general terms to a particular church, *e.g.* "to the Church of England absolutely", prima facie imports the operative institution which ministers religion and gives spiritual edification to its members[69] and is charitable. So also is a gift to a particular church—*e.g.* the Roman Catholic Church—"for the use thereof".[70]

Examples of gifts for the advancement of religion in general terms, which have the necessary element of public benefit and are therefore, charitable, are gifts for "the increase and improvement of Christian knowledge and promoting religion,[71] to "such religious and charitable institutions as the trustees may think proper,"[72] or to be employed "in the service of my Lord and Master"[73] or for "the worship of God."[74]

2–055   Bequests for spreading Christianity among infidels,[75] for the maintenance of the missionary establishments of a particular Christian body among heathen nations,[76] for the distribution of Bibles and other religious

---

ground above mentioned (the first ground of his decision) he held that the bequest had failed). See also and compare *Re Goldschmidt* [1957] 1 W.L.R. 524.

[64] See *Re Davis* [1902] 1 Ch. 876; *Re Mann* [1903] 1 Ch. 232; *Re Webster* [1912] 1 Ch. 106.
[65] *Re Schoales* [1930] 2 Ch. 75; *Re Barnes* (1922) [1930] 2 Ch. 80, n.
[66] *MacLaughlin v Campbell* [1906] 1 I.R. 588.
[67] *Re Stratton* [1931] 1 Ch. 197.
[68] *Farley v Westminster Bank Ltd.* [1939] A.C. 430.
[69] *Re Barnes* (1922) reported in [1930] 2 Ch. 80 (n.) at 81, *per* Romer J. quoting *MacLaughlin v Campbell* [1906] 1 I.R. 588 at 597.
[70] *Re Schoales* [1930] 2 Ch. 75.
[71] *Att-Gen v Stepney* (1804) 10 Ves. 22 (the object was educational as well as religious).
[72] *Baker v Sutton* (1836) 1 Keen 224; *Wilkinson v Lindgren* (1870) L.R. 5 Ch. 570.
[73] *Powerscourt v Powerscourt* (1824) 1 Molloy 616, approved in *Re Darling* [1896] 1 Ch. 50; and see *Felan v Russell* (1842) 4 Ir.Eq.R. 701.
[74] *Att-Gen v Pearson* (1817) 3 Mer. 353, 409.
[75] *Att-Gen v City of London* (1790) 1 Ves. 243.
[76] *Commissioners of Income Tax v Pemsel* [1891] A.C. 531. The Christian body was the Moravian Church. As will appear, "missionary" is an ambiguous word; but in the context of the conveyance which was before the House of Lords it was clear that the work of the Moravian missions was the advancement of the Christian religion.

books[77] and for the spread of the Gospel,[78] are also charitable. So also are gifts to missionary bodies whose objects are the spread of Christianity, such as the Society for Promoting Christian Knowledge,[79] the Church Missionary Society,[80] the Society for the Propagation of the Gospel in Foreign Parts,[81] and the Sunday School Association.[82]

The expression "missionary purposes" is ambiguous and may comprise objects which are not charitable. Therefore, a gift for missionary purposes is not, like a gift for religious purposes, prima facie charitable, but is prima facie void for uncertainty.[83] However, a gift for missionary purposes is valid if there is sufficient context to show that religious purposes were meant,[84] and evidence of surrounding circumstances is admissible to prove that the donor or testator must have been using the expression in the narrower and more popular sense of Christian missionary work and thus to validate the gift.[85]

Gifts to bodies, such as the Protestant Alliance, having for their object the maintenance and defence of the doctrines of the Reformation, are charitable.[86]

(b) Gifts for the maintenance and promotion of public worship

Gifts having for their object the maintenance and promotion of public worship are charitable.[87] Specific gifts for such purposes, which have been held to be charitable, include gifts for the establishment of a bishopric,[88] or the benefit of ministers of religion in a particular town,[89] or the   **2–056**

---

[77] *Att-Gen v Stepney* (1804) 10 Ves. 22; *Thornton v Howe* (1862) 31 Beav. 14; *Re Watson* [1973] 1 W.L.R. 1472. *Browne v Yeall* (1790) 7 Ves. 50n., where it was held that a gift for purchasing and disposing of books tending to promote "the interests of religion and the happiness of mankind" was not charitable, would not be followed: see *Morice v Bishop of Durham* (1805) 10 Ves. 522 at 539; *Baker v Sutton* (1836) 1 Keen 224, 233; *Re Macduff* [1896] 2 Ch. 451 at 472, 473.
[78] *Re Lea* (1887) 34 Ch.D. 528.
[79] *Re Clergy Society* (1856) 2 K. & J. 615.
[80] *ibid.*
[81] *Re Maguire* (1870) L.R. 9 Eq. 632.
[82] *R. v Special Commissioners of Income Tax* [1911] 2 K.B. 434.
[83] *Scott v Brownrigg* (1881) 9 L.R.Ir. 246; *Commissioners for Special Purposes of Income Tax v Pemsel* [1891] A.C. 531.
[84] *Commissioners for Special Purposes of Income Tax v Pemsel* [1891] A.C. 531; *Dunne v Duignan* [1908] 1 I.R. 228; *Re Hall* (1915) 31 T.L.R. 396; *Jackson v Att-Gen* [1917] 1 I.R. 332; *Re Moon's Will Trusts* [1948] 1 All E.R. 300.
[85] *Re Kenny* (1907) 97 L.T. 130; *Re Redish* (1909) 26 T.L.R. 42; *Re Rees* [1920] 2 Ch. 59; *Re Moon's Will Trusts* [1948] 1 All E.R. 300.
[86] *Re Delmar Charitable Trust* [1897] 2 Ch. 163.
[87] *Att-Gen v Pearson* (1817) 3 Mer. 353, 409.
[88] *Att-Gen v Bishop of Chester* (1785) 1 Bro.C.C. 444; *Re Villiers-Wilkes* (1895) 72 L.T. 323. (But since the establishment of a new bishopric in England requires legislation, formerly an Act of Parliament, now, since the Church of England Assembly (Powers) Act 1919, a Measure of the General Synod (as successor of the Church Assembly: Synodical Government Measure 1969, s.2(1)), it might perhaps be argued that this is a political purpose and so not charitable: see *Bowman v Secular Society Ltd.* [1917] A.C. 406 at 442; *National Anti-Vivisection Society v IRC* [1948] A.C. 31 and para.2–035, above.
[89] *Magistrates of Dundee v Dundee Presbytery* (1861) 4 Macq. 228. This case would doubtless be followed in England.

unbeneficed curates of a particular deanery,[90] to maintain preaching ministers,[91] for increasing clergymen's stipends,[92] to provide or increase the stipend of the incumbent of a particular church,[93] even though subject to a condition that he shall teach a particular doctrine,[94] or preach a particular sermon,[95] to permit the sittings to be occupied free,[96] or in lieu of tithes,[97] to provide a pension for a perpetual curate,[98] and to assist education of candidates for holy orders in the Church of England.[99] Similarly, gifts to institutions such as the Additional Curates Society or the Church Pastoral Aid Society[1] are charitable.

Gifts to provide a stipend for a clerk or sexton,[2] or an organist[3] are charitable. So also is a gift to provide choristers for a parish church.[4] A gift to a vicar and churchwardens of a parish church "for the benefit of the choir" is charitable, because the object of the gift is the maintenance and improvement of the musical services of the church and that object is for the advancement of religion.[5]

A trust to appoint a suitably qualified clergyman to a benefice is not charitable because the owner of an advowson is under a legal duty to make such appointment.[6] A trust to expend the income or any portion of the capital of a trust fund in or towards the purchase of advowsons or presentations has never been a good charitable trust[7] unless the advowsons were to be made subject to charitable trusts which the court could execute or control.[8]

Gifts to provide a minister to preach on particular occasions,[9] or to preach to a particular class of persons, such as prisoners,[10] are charitable.

---

[90] *Pennington v Buckley* (1848) 6 Ha. 453.
[91] *Pember v Kington (Inhabitants)* (1639) Duke 82; *Pensterd v Pavier* (1639) *ibid.* 82.
[92] *Att-Gen v Brereton* (1752) 2 Ves.Sen. 426; *Middleton v Clitherow* (1798) 3 Ves. 734.
[93] *Durour v Motteux* (1749) 1 Ves.Sen. 320; *Att-Gen v Sparkes* (1753) Amb. 201; *Gibson v Representative Church Body* (1881) 9 L.R.Ir. 1.
[94] *Att-Gen v Molland* (1832) You. 562.
[95] *Re Parker's Charity* (1863) 32 Beav. 654.
[96] *Re Randell* (1888) 38 Ch.D. 213.
[97] *Millbank v Lambert* (1860) 28 Beav. 206. As to the extinguishment of the rentcharge (created by the Tithe Act 1836), see the Tithe Act 1936, s.1.
[98] *Att-Gen v Parker* (1747) 1 Ves.Sen. 43.
[99] *Re Williams* [1927] 2 Ch. 283.
[1] *Re Maguire* (1870) L.R. 9 Eq. 632.
[2] *Durour v Motteux* (1749) 1 Ves.Sen. 320.
[3] *Att-Gen v Oakaver* (1736) cit. *Att-Gen v Whorwood* (1750) 1 Ves.Sen. 534, 536; *Carbery v Cox* (1852) 3 I.R.Ch. 231.
[4] *Turner v Ogden* (1787) 1 Cox Eq.Cas. 316; *Re Hendry* (1887) 56 L.T. 908. *Att-Gen v Oakaver* (above) was supposed to have decided that such a gift was void because choristers never were allowed in parish churches. The last-mentioned case was always of doubtful authority; but it may now, so far as this point is concerned, be ignored; see *Re Royce* [1940] Ch. 514 at 518, 519, per Simonds J.
[5] *Re Royce* [1940] Ch. 514.
[6] *Re Church Patronage Trust* [1904] 2 Ch. 643.
[7] *Hunter v Att-Gen* [1899] A.C. 309.
[8] *Re St. Stephen, Coleman Street* (1888) 39 Ch.D. 492; *Re Hunter* [1897] 2 Ch. 105 (reversed *sub nom. Hunter v Att-Gen* [1899] A.C. 309 on the ground that there was no trust which the court could control).
[9] *Durour v Motteux* (1749) 1 Ves.Sen. 320; *Re Parker's Charity* (1863) 32 Beav. 654.
[10] *Re Hussey's Charities* (1861) 7 Jur.(N.S.) 325.

(c) Gifts for the provision and maintenance of places of worship

The repair of churches is the only specifically religious purpose **2–057** mentioned in the preamble to the Statute of Elizabeth I.

The law favours all gifts the purpose of which is to build endow, maintain or repair places of worship, to provide suitable furniture or ornaments, to facilitate the conduct of the services, and to promote the strictly religious work carried on in connection with the place of worship.

Thus a gift to provide or maintain a place of worship is charitable.[11] So also are gifts for the good of a parish church[12] for a named parish church[13]; for the reparation, furniture or ornaments[14] of a parish church, chapel or meeting house[15]; and for church expenses.[16] On the same principle the maintenance and repair of a building used as a Sunday school for religious teaching is a charitable purpose.[17] Gifts of this kind may be subject to a continuing condition, as for instance that the sittings in the church shall be free,[18] or that the services in the church shall be in "sound evangelical doctrine",[19] or that a black gown to be worn in the pulpit.[20]

Gifts for the provision or maintenance and repair of any part of the fabric or furniture of a church are charitable. On this ground gifts for the provision or repair of the chancel,[21] a gallery,[22] a monument in the church,[23]

---

[11] *Re Parker* (1859) 4 H. & N. 666; *Re Robinson* [1897] 1 Ch. 85. The law of Scotland is the same: see *Clephane v Magistrates of Edinburgh* (1864) 4 Macq. 603. See also *Re Beresford* (1966) 57 D.L.R. (2d) 380, British Columbia Supreme Court.

[12] *Wingfield's Case* (1629) Duke 80.

[13] *Re Gare* [1952] Ch. 80.

[14] *Att-Gen v Ruper* (1722) 2 P.Wms. 125; *Att-Gen v Vivian* (1826) 1 Russ. 226; *Att-Gen v Love* (1857) 23 Beav. 499; *Re Estate of Church of Donington-on-Baine* (1860) 6 Jur.(N.S.) 290; *Re Church Estate Charity* (1871) L.R. 6 Ch. 296; *Att-Gen v Dartmouth Corporation* (1883) 48 L.T. 933; *Re Palatine Estate Charity* (1888) 39 Ch.D. 54; *Re St. Alphage* (1888) 59 L.T. 614; *Re Manser* [1905] 1 Ch. 68; *Re Robertson* [1930] 2 Ch. 71; *Re Eighmie* [1935] Ch. 524.

[15] *Att-Gen v Cock* (1751) 2 Ves.Sen. 273; *Re Wall* (1889) 42 Ch.D. 510; *Re Brown* [1898] 1 I.T.R. 423; *Re Manser* [1905] 1 Ch. 68; *Re Williams* (1910) 26 T.L.R. 307; *Re Ramsay, The Times*, February 17, 1911.

[16] *Re Scowcroft* [1898] 2 Ch. 638 at 642.

[17] *R. v Special Commissioners of Income Tax* [1911] 2 K.B. 434; *Re Strickland's Will Trusts* [1936] 3 All E.R. 1027.

[18] *Re Randell* (1888) 38 Ch.D. 213. (In this case the income of a trust legacy was payable to the incumbent for the time being so long as he permitted the sittings to be occupied free.)

[19] This was one of the conditions prescribed by the testatrix whose will was before the Court of Appeal in *Re Robinson* [1897] 1 Ch. 85 and again before P.O. Lawrence J. in *Re Robinson* [1923] 2 Ch. 332. Its validity was not apparently questioned, and it seems to have been duly observed.

[20] *Re Robinson* [1897] 1 Ch. 85. If the condition subsequently becomes impracticable the property may be applied *cy-près*—see *Re Robinson* [1923] 2 Ch. 332 and para.11–046, below.

[21] *Hoare v Osborne* (1866) L.R. 1 Eq. 585. At common law the liability to repair the nave or body of the parish church rested on the parishioners, but on the parson to repair the chancel: *Representative Body of the Church in Wales v Tithe Redemption Commission* [1944] A.C. 228, 240, *per* Viscount Simon L.C. A trust providing that the churchwardens should apply income wholly about the parish church authorises the application of the income to general expenditure about the church including the chancel, and is a valid trust for a public purpose beneficial to the parish: *Att-Gen v Parr* [1920] 1 Ch. 339.

[22] *Att-Gen v Day* [1900] 1 Ch. 31.

[23] *Hoare v Osborne* (1866) L.R. 1 Eq. 585; *Re Rigley's Trusts* (1866) 36 L.J.Ch. 147; *Re Barker* (1909) 25 T.L.R. 753.

a stained-glass window,[24] bells,[25] a clock,[26] a spire,[27] an organ,[28] and seating accommodation,[29] are all charitable.

A gift for the upkeep of a church or chapel is a gift not merely for the purposes of repair but a gift in aid of all the expenses necessarily incurred in providing the services held therein.[30]

(d) Gifts for the maintenance of churchyards and other burial places and particular tombs

2–058 The maintenance of a churchyard or burial ground and of all the graves therein is a charitable purpose[31] even where the burial ground is restricted to members of a particular sect.[32] A gift of land for use as a cemetery is charitable.[33] By analogy a trust to encourage and provide facilities for cremation is charitable.[34]

A trust for the maintenance and upkeep of the tombs of a class of persons constituting a section of the public is also charitable. Thus in *Re Pardoe*[35] Kekewich J. held, with no apparent difficulty, that a gift by will of £700 to the vicar and churchwardens of the parish B, upon trust to apply the income thereof in or towards the erection of headstones to the graves in the churchyard of persons who when they died were residing as pensioners in certain almshouses within the parish was a gift upon a charitable trust. The learned judge seems to have considered that the *ratio decidendi* of the cases where it has been held that a trust to keep a churchyard in repair was charitable applied. It is not very easy to understand the expressed reasons for the decision. It had been argued that the gift, though not a gift for the general upkeep of the churchyard, was a gift to provide tombstones for the poor. This seems to imply that the gift was for the relief of poverty. No doubt the deceased pensioners were poor; but, since they were dead, it is not easy to see how the object of the gift could have been for the relief of poverty. The learned judge did not mention poverty in his judgment. It is submitted that the decision can be justified on the ground that the pensioners were a section of the public, that the purpose of the gift was to keep part of the churchyard in decent order and repair, and that

---

[24] *Re King* [1923] 1 Ch. 243; *Re Raine* [1956] Ch. 417.

[25] *Turner v Ogden* (1787) 1 Cox Eq.Cas. 316; *Re Palatine Estate Charity* (1888) 39 Ch.D. 54, 59.

[26] *Re Church Estate Charity, Wandsworth* (1871) L.R. 6 Ch. 296.

[27] *Re Palatine Estate Charity* (1888) 39 Ch.D. 54.

[28] *Att-Gen v Oakaver* (1736) cited in *Att-Gen v Whorwood* (1750) 1 Ves.Sen. 534, 536; *Carbery v Cox* (1852) 3 I.R.Ch. 231 (maintenance of an organ and organist for a Roman Catholic chapel a charitable purpose).

[29] *Re Raine* [1956] Ch. 417.

[30] *Re Strickland's Will Trusts* [1936] 3 All E.R. 1027. It is considered that a gift to a named church or chapel has the same effect. In *Re Gare* [1952] Ch. 80 Harman J. held that a gift to "St. Peter's Church, Staines" was a gift for church purposes, *i.e.* for purposes connected with the services of the church.

[31] *Re Vaughan* (1886) 33 Ch.D. 187; *Re Douglas* [1905] 1 Ch. 279; *Re Pardoe* [1906] 2 Ch. 184.

[32] *Re Manser* [1905] 1 Ch. 68, 73 (Quakers).

[33] *Att-Gen v Blizard* (1855) 21 Beav. 233.

[34] *Scottish Burial Reform and Cremation Society Ltd. v Glasgow Corp.* [1968] A.C. 138.

[35] [1906] 2 Ch. 184.

there was a sufficient element of public benefit to enable the gift to qualify as a charitable gift. It is thought that the case illustrates the general proposition that a trust for the repair and maintenance of part or parts of a churchyard or other bruial ground is charitable.

A bequest for building, maintaining, or keeping in repair the vaults or tombs (not being within a church) of the testator or members of his family is not for the benefit of the inhabitants of the parish generally and, therefore, is not charitable.[36] The public element is completely lacking.

(e) Gifts for the benefit of the clergy

A gift for the repair of the parsonage house is charitable,[37] no doubt **2–059** because it tends to increase the pastoral efficiency of the parson. On the same principle it can hardly be doubted that the repair of the residence of a curate, paid church worker, priest, minister or other religious leader is a charitable purpose; nor can it be doubted that the provision of a parsonage or such other residence as aforesaid is a charitable purpose. It was held, apparently without argument to the contrary, in *Re White's Will Trusts*,[38] that a devise of two houses as homes of rest for retired missionaries was charitable.

A gift of a fund upon trust to apply the income for the relief of infirm, sick or aged ministers of religion of a particular area is clearly charitable. The possible beneficiaries are either impotent or aged persons within the meaning of the preamble to the Statute of Elizabeth I,[39] and they constitute a sufficiently important section of the public. On this ground alone, therefore, the purpose of the gift is clearly charitable, even though the beneficiaries are not required to be poor. A gift of this kind may also be upheld as charitable as a gift tending indirectly to the advancement of religion. It makes the ministry more efficient by making it easy for the sick and old to retire and give place to the young and healthy; and it eases the minds of those actively engaged in the ministry to know that there is a fund to be used for their relief when they are overtaken by old age or struck down unexpectedly by sickness.[40]

---

[36] *Masters v Masters* (1718) 1 P.Wms. 421, 422, n.1; *Durour v Motteux* (1749) 1 Ves.Sen. 320; *Gravenor v Hallum* (1767) Amb. 643; *Doe v Pitcher* (1815) 3 M. & S. 407; *Mellick v Asylum (President and Guardians)* (1821) Jac. 180; *Willis v Brown* (1838) 2 Jur. 987; *Mitford v Reynolds* (1841) 1 Ph. 185, 198; *Adnam v Cole* (1843) 6 Beav. 353; *Lloyd v Lloyd* (1852) 2 Sim.(N.S.) 255; *Rickard v Robson* (1862) 31 Beav. 244; *Fowler v Fowler* (1864) 33 Beav. 616; *Hoare v Osborne* (1866) L.R. 1 Eq. 585; *Re Rigley's Trusts* (1866) 36 L.J.Ch. 147; *Fisk v Att-Gen* (1867) L.R. 4 Eq. 521; *Hunter v Bullock* (1872) L.R. 14 Eq. 45; *Dawson v Small* (1874) L.R. 18 Eq. 114; *Yeap Cheah Neo v Ong Cheng Neo* (1875) L.R. 6 P.C. 381; *Re Williams* (1877) 5 Ch.D. 735; *Re Birkett* (1878) 9 Ch.D. 576; *Re Vaughan* (1886) 33 Ch.D. 187; *Re Rogerson* [1901] 1 Ch. 715; *Re Dalziel* [1943] Ch. 277; and see *Toole v Hamilton* (1901) 1 I.R. 383; *Re Barker* (1909) 25 T.L.R. 753 for the various expedients whereby testators have with varying success attempted to provide for the upkeep of their tombs and those of their families. See para.3–011, below.

[37] *Att-Gen v Bishop of Chester* (1785) 1 Bro.C.C. 444.

[38] [1955] Ch. 188.

[39] See paras 2–001, *et seq.*, above.

[40] *Re James* [1932] 2 Ch. 25; *Re Forster* [1939] Ch. 22 at 25, per Bennett J. See also [1964] Ch. Com. Rep., 60 (App. E) and [1965] Ch. Com. Rep., 28 (App. C) for examples of funds

(f) Gifts to religious office holders

2–060   In the case of a gift to a person who holds an office the duties of which are charitable where the gift is made to him in his official name and by virtue of his office, two principles have to be borne in mind. These principles apply whether the recipient of the gift is the holder of a religious office or of an office related to a charity which is not for the advancement of religion, but nearly all the reported cases are concerned with gifts to persons holding some kind of religious office, so that it is convenient to consider the matter in the context of religious trusts.[41]

The principles in question are generally referred to as the *Re Garrard*[42] principle and the *Dunne v Byrne*[43] principle. They have been explained by Jenkins L.J. in *Re Spensley's Will Trusts*[44] and *Re Rumball*.[45] The *Re Garrard* principle is that when there is a gift to a person who holds an office the duties of which are charitable and the gift is made to him in his official name and by virtue of his office, then, if the purposes are not expressed in the gift itself, the gift is presumed to be for the charitable purposes inherent in that office. The *Dunne v Byrne*[46] principle is that if a trust is expressed in plain language, and it appears that on a true construction of the instrument declaring the trust the expressed purposes are not exclusively charitable, but that the trustee is given a discretion which would allow him to apply the fund, or any part of it, for purposes which may not be charitable, the mere fact that the trustee is the holder of an office the duties of which are charitable will not make the trust charitable. An examination of the reported cases shows that the principles are not easy to apply and that the decisions are not easy to reconcile with one another.

2–061   *Re Garrard*[47] and the many cases in which it has been followed or applied stem from *Thornber v Wilson*[48] and *Re Delany*.[49] In *Thornber v Wilson*[50] a gift to the Minister of a Roman Catholic chapel and his successors was held to be a gift to a minsiter as the holder of an office for the benefit of the chapel. Kindersley V.C. said that a gift to a minister as such was a charitable bequest, and this was and is clearly the law.[51] In *Re*

---

for the relief of sick and aged clergymen which have been registered by the Charity Commissioners.

[41] See generally (1960) 24 Conv.(N.S.) 306 "Gifts *Virtute Officii* to Donees of a Charitable Character", (V.T.H. Delany).
[42] [1907] 1 Ch. 382.
[43] [1912] A.C. 407.
[44] [1954] Ch. 233 at 243, 244.
[45] [1956] Ch. 105 at 121–124.
[46] See *Dunne v Byrne* [1912] A.C. 407 at 410, *per* Lord Macnaghten who, delivering the judgment of the Privy Council, said: "It is difficult to see on what principle a trust expressed in plain language, whether the words used be sufficient or insufficient to satisfy the requirements of the law, can be modified or limited in its scope by reference to the position or character of the trustee." The principle was not new when it was formulated by Lord Macnaghten, but owes its name to the fact that *Dunne v Byrne* immediately became a leading case.
[47] [1907] 1 Ch. 382.
[48] (1855) 3 Drew. 245; (1858) 4 Drew. 350.
[49] [1902] 2 Ch. 642.
[50] (1858) 4 Drew. 350 at 351.
[51] See *Att-Gen v Cock* (1751) 2 Ves.Sen. 273; *Att-Gen v Sparks* (1753) Amb. 201.

Delany[52] there were gifts to named members of a religious community "and their successors." The objects of the community were charitable. It was held that the gifts were to persons as the holders of offices in the community and were charitable. The *ratio decidendi* was the same as in *Thornber v Wilson*.[53]

In *Re Garrard*[54] a testatrix bequeathed £400 to the vicar and churchwardens for the time being of a named parish to be applied by them in such manner as they should in their sole discretion think fit. A gift to a private individual in such terms would not have created a trust, because he could have done what he liked with the money. But Joyce J. held that the bequest was a good charitable gift for ecclesiastical purposes in the parish, and by "ecclesiastical purposes" the learned judge obviously meant "religious purposes" or "church purposes".

In the course of a very short considered judgment Joyce J. referred only to *Thornber v Wilson*[55] and *Re Delany*,[56] on the authority of which he formulated three propositions, namely (1) that a legacy to the vicar for the time being of a parish was a charitable gift for the benefit of the parish for ecclesiastical purposes; (2) that a mere gift of a legacy to the vicar and churchwardens for the time being of a parish, without more, was also a gift or charitable legacy to them for ecclesiastical purposes in the parish, since the churchwardens were the officers of the parish in religious matters (a proposition which did not on any view of the law involve an extension of the principle upon which *Thornber v Wilson*[57] and *Re Delany*[58] had been decided): and (3) that the words directing that the legacy should be applied in such manner as the vicar and churchwardens should in their sole discretion think fit merely directed that the particular mode of application within the charitable purposes of the legacy was to be settled by those individuals, or rather that there was power to settle the mode of application subject always to the jurisdiction of the court. It was implicit in the judgment that the learned judge thought that the trusts were for the advancement of religion in the parish and that the vicar and churchwardens, as the minister and lay officials of the parish in ecclesiastical matters, took the legacy as trustees *virtute officii* and, though they had a power to determine how the legacy should be applied, had no power to apply it for any purpose which was not a religious purpose which satisfied the requirements of public benefit. If the vicar and churchwardens had applied the money for a purpose which was not both religious and for the benefit of

---

52 [1902] 2 Ch. 642.

53 (1855) 3 Drew. 245; (1858) 4 Drew. 350. Two much later cases, decided on the same principle, are *Re Barclay* [1929] 2 Ch. 173 (a legacy to the Superior of the Jesuit Church at Farm Street at the moment of the legacy falling due, held by the Court of Appeal to be a gift to the Superior upon trust for the benefit of the Church at Farm Street as he might at his discretion think fit); and *Re Ray's Will Trusts* [1936] Ch. 520 (a gift to the person who at the testatrix's death should be or should act as abbess of the convent where the testatrix was a nun, held to be a gift to the legatee *virtute officii* in trust for and as an addition to the funds of the community).

54 [1907] 1 Ch. 382.

55 (1855) 3 Drew. 245; (1858) 4 Drew. 350.

56 [1902] 2 Ch. 242.

57 (1855) 3 Drew. 245; (1858) 4 Drew. 350.

58 [1902] 2 Ch. 242.

the parish, the Attorney-General could have set the machinery of the court in motion to ensure that the money was not misapplied.

Re Garrard[59] has been followed and applied in many reported cases. Thus a gift to the vicar of a named parish church "for such objects connected with the church as he shall think fit", which was admittedly a gift to the vicar as the holder of an office upon trust, was held to be a charitable bequest on the ground that on the true construction of the words quoted the discretion vested in the vicar had to be exercised within the scope of church (*i.e.* religious) purposes and not parochial purposes.[60]

2–062   Other gifts to the holder of an office, with superadded words indicating how the gift is to be applied, which have been held charitable are a gift to the vicar and churchwardens of a named church "for any purposes in connection with the said church which they may select,"[61] a gift of residue "to His Eminence the Archbishop of Westminster Cathedral, London, for the time being to be used by him for such purposes as he shall in his absolute discretion think fit",[62] a gift of residue to the vicar of a named church "to be used for his work in the parish",[63] a gift of residue to the bishop for the time being of the Windward Islands to be used as he thinks fit in his diocese,[64] and a gift to the Bishop for the time being in Jerusalem for the general purposes of the diocese.[65]

Re Norman[66] seems to be the most extreme application of the *Re Garrard*[67] principle. Nevertheless the decision was applied by Jenkins J. in

---

[59] [1907] 1 Ch. 382.
[60] *Re Bain* [1930] 1 Ch. 224. In the court below Eve J. had held that the purposes of the gift were not charitable and in the Court of Appeal Russell L.J. agreed with him; but the views of Lord Hanworth M.R. and P.O. Lawrence L.J. prevailed. P.O. Lawrence L.J. expressly applied *Re Garrard* [1907] 1 Ch. 382. Lord Hanworth M.R. did not, but he was clearly applying the same principle. The difficulty of deciding which of the two principles, the *Re Garrard* (above) principle or the *Dunne v Byrne* [1912] A.C. 407 principle, applies in any given case is strikingly illustrated by the conflict of opinion between the four judges in *Re Bain* (above). The dissenting judgment of Russell L.J. is very cogent. Although Re Bain has since been followed or applied more than once (see *e.g. Re Eastes* [1948] Ch. 257) and is presumably unlikely to be overruled by the House of Lords, it is thought that it is a borderline case.
[61] *Re Eastes* [1948] Ch. 257. *Re Bain* [1930] 1 Ch. 224 was followed; but the gift bears a striking resemblance to the gift in *Re Garrard* [1907] 1 Ch. 382. The gift was to the vicar and churchwardens *virtute officii*. See also *Re Martley* (1931) 47 T.L.R. 392 (gift to Archbishop for benefit of the work of the cathedral).
[62] *Re Flinn* [1948] Ch. 241. The judgment of Jenkins J. contains a useful analysis of many of the relevant cases on the two principles.
[63] "The functions of the vicar of the church can be summed up in this, that he has the cure of souls in the particular district, parish or ecclesiastical district which is the locus of his benefice." The functions of the vicar of a church as so stated are charitable: see *Re Simson* [1946] Ch. 299 at 301, *per* Romer J., adopting the observations of Clauson L.J. in *Re Ashton* [1938] Ch. 482 at 501.
[64] *Re Rumball* [1956] Ch. 105. The Court of Appeal held, affirming the decision of Danckwerts J., that the gift was to the bishop virtute officii and that he took as trustee, and that the words following the description of the donee conferred on him a discretion limited by the charitable character of his office. The donor had not attempted to indicate or define the trusts on which the donee was to hold the property. The bishop could not in any event have used the trust property outside his diocese, and so the addition of the words "in his diocese" did not make any difference. They only expressed that which would otherwise have been implied
[65] *Re Money's Will Trusts* (1965) 109 S.J. 68.
[66] [1947] Ch. 349.
[67] [1907] 1 Ch. 382.

Re Flinn,[68] and it is not suggested that that case was wrongly decided. The facts in *Re Norman* were that a testatrix, who was a member of the religious body of Evangelical Christians known as "the Brethren" and had been a missionary overseas, by her will requested that the "residue of her moneys" (apparently held to include her residuary personalty) should be bequeathed to the editors of the missionary periodical called "Echoes of Service" to be applied by them or him (*sic*) for such objects as they might think fit. On the face of it the bequest was not a bequest to the holders of offices the duties of which were charitable, but a bequest to private individuals with no declaration of trust and, therefore, not charitable. Evidence was, however, admitted which showed that the editors were trustees and treasurers of the churches of "the Brethren" as regards the missionary activities of "the Brethren"; that, as trustees and treasurers, they received and dispensed contributions for the missions of "the Brethren"; and that "Echoes of Service" was the title of a magazine and the accepted designation of a charity recognised by the Inland Revenue authorities. The evidence was admitted and, it is considered, rightly admitted without argument as to its admissibility. In the light of this evidence Vaisey J. held that the gift to the editors was a gift to the trustees of a charitable organisation[69] who were obliged to apply it for such of the charitable purposes of the organisation as they thought fit. Although the learned judge did not expressly say so, it is obvious that he treated the gift as a gift to the holders of an office for the charitable purposes inherent in that office.

In *Dunne v Byrne*[70] a residuary bequest by a testator, who was a Roman Catholic priest, "to the Roman Catholic Archbishop of Brisbane and his successors to be used and expended wholly or in part as such Archbishop may judge most conducive to the good of religion in this diocese" was held by the Privy Council not to be a good charitable bequest but void. It appears from Lord Macnaghten's judgment that the bequest was void for uncertainty. The Privy Council held as a matter of construction that there was a trust expressed in plain language, but that it could not be assumed that every purpose which the Archbishop might judge most conducive to the good of religion in the diocese was charitable.[71] Their Lordships did not base their decision on the ground that the words "wholly or in part" left it uncertain how much of the subject-matter of the gift was impressed with the trust; they construed the words as merely giving to the trustee (the Archbishop) a discretionary authority to break in upon the capital of the trust fund.[72]

---

[68] [1948] Ch. 241.
[69] The reasons for the decision are stated in [1947] Ch. at 354, 355.
[70] [1912] A.C. 407.
[71] It was pointed out in *Dunne v Byrne* [1912] A.C. 407 at 410 that a devout Roman Catholic would consider that a trust for the benefit of an enclosed order was "conducive to the good of religion," but that such a gift was not charitable, and *Cocks v Manners* [1871] L.R. 12 Eq. 574 was referred to. See also *Gilmour v Coats* [1949] A.C. 426.
[72] [1912] A.C. 407 at 410, 411.

2–063   Other cases where the *Dunne v Byrne*[73] principle has been applied are *Re Davidson*[74] (gift to a Roman Catholic Archbishop for the time being to be distributed between charitable, religious or other societies; the testator had defined the trusts upon which the gift was to be held and they were not exclusively charitable); *Re Stratton*[75] (gift to vicar of named parish "for parochial institutions or purposes" not charitable); *Re Davies*[76] (gift to a Roman Catholic Archbishop for work connected with the archdiocese not charitable); and *Farley v Westminster Bank Ltd.*[77] (gift to vicars and churchwardens of named churches "for parish work" not charitable).

It is necessary to refer to two cases, which, if not correctly understood may lead to some confusion; one of them was inadequately reported and the other was not reported at all.

In the first of these cases, *Re Van Wart*,[78] Parker J. was at one time thought to have held that a gift to the Roman Catholic Archbishop of Westminster for diocesan purposes was charitable. If he had so decided, it would have been difficult, if not actually impossible, to reconcile his decision with such cases as *Re Stratton*[79] and *Farley v Westminster Bank Ltd.*,[80] unless it could have been said that "diocesan purposes" in the context meant purposes which were solely ecclesiastical and, therefore, charitable. However, in *Re Rumball*[81] Evershed M.R. sent for Parker J.'s order from the Public Record Office, and the material parts of the order are quoted in his Lordship's judgment.[82] As he points out,[83] on the face of the order it looks as though the view taken by Parker J. was that there was, as far as the relevant shares of residue were concerned, no effective trust at all; but that the Archbishop and his co-defendant gave an undertaking, which satisifed the Attorney-General, to apply the funds according to the trusts and purposes declared by the testator. The case only gives very slight support to the view that "diocesan purposes" were solely ecclesiastical. It is considered that no judge of first instance would be bound to hold that "diocesan purposes" are exclusively charitable and it is submitted that they are not.

---

[73] [1912] A.C. 407.
[74] [1909] 1 Ch. 567. In *Re Flinn* [1948] Ch. 241 (gift to Roman Catholic Archbishop for the time being to be used by him for such purposes as he should in his absolute discretion think fit held charitable), *Re Davidson* was distinguished for reasons admirably expressed by Jenkins J. at 246, 247.
[75] [1931] 1 Ch. 197. The word "parochial" does not mean "church," "religious" or "ecclesiastical." The vicar was authorised by the will to use the money for the benefit of institutions or purposes which were not necessarily charitable. For the distinction between "church purposes" and "parochial purposes" see *Re Bain* [1930] 1 Ch. 224 at 234, *per* P.O. Lawrence L.J.
[76] (1932) 49 T.L.R. 5.
[77] [1939] A.C. 430.
[78] *The Times*, February 17, 1911.
[79] [1931] 1 Ch. 197.
[80] [1939] A.C. 430.
[81] [1956] Ch. 105.
[82] *ibid.* at 119.
[83] *ibid.* at 119, 120. However, a gift "for diocesan purposes" was held charitable in New South Wales: see *Re Macgregor* (1932) 32 New South Wales Reports 483.

In *Re Warre's Will Trusts*[20] Harman J. held that a trust to apply income in perpetuity for the provision and upkeep of a diocesan retreat house in the diocese of Salisbury was not charitable because it lacked the necessary element of public benefit. A retreat house is a house devoted to a form of religious activity which is well known in the Church of England. Persons living in the world and accustomed to mix with their fellow citizens go into retreat for a few days for prayer, contemplation and cleansing of the soul. The learned judge did not doubt that a retreat was highly beneficial to the individual retreatant, but he considered that he was correctly applying *Cocks v Manners*[21] and *Gilmour v Coats*[22] in holding that the purposes of the trust in question were not charitable.

The decision in *Re Warre's Will Trusts* is open to criticism, and not the **2–068** less so, it is respectfully submitted, because it was approved by Goff J. in *Re Banfield*.[23] One essential difference between a convent of enclosed nuns and a retreat house seems to be that the convent is private property, held in trust for the members for the time being of the religious community who are not a section of the public but a fluctuating body of private individuals, whereas a diocesan retreat house is open to any member of the Church of England resident in the diocese, subject to accommodation being available. It cannot be denied that the members of the Church of England resident in a particular diocese constitute a sufficiently important section of the public in the case of a trust for religious purposes. Another essential and, perhaps, more obvious difference is that enclosed nuns do not emerge from their convent and mix with their fellow citizens, whereas retreatants after taking part in a form of religious observance which is well known in the Church of England leave the retreat house, associate with their fellow citizens and engage in mundane activities. Further in *Re Banfield*,[24] whilst approving the decision in *Re Warre's Will Trust*,[25] Goff J. held that the Pilsdon Community House was charitable as it opened out to reach the community. The difference would seem to be that the Pilsdon Community House did not restrict its guests to members of one religious community.

In *Neville Estates Ltd. v Madden*[26] Cross J. held (and, it is submitted rightly held) that although the Catford Synagogue was not open to the public as of right and although the members of the synagogue did not constitute a section of the public, there was an essential difference between the members of the synagogue and enclosed nuns, because the members of the synagogue spent their lives in the world while the nuns lived secluded from the world. The learned judge thought that the court was entitled to assume that some benefit accrued to the public from the attendance at

---

[20] [1953] 1 W.L.R. 725.
[21] (1871) L.R. 12 Eq. 574.
[22] [1949] A.C. 426.
[23] [1968] 1 W.L.R. 846.
[24] [1968] 1 W.L.R. 846. See also the discussion in (1995) 3 Ch. Com. Dec., pp.11, *et seq.*
[25] [1953] 1 W.L.R. 725.
[26] [1962] Ch. 832. *Re Warre's Will Trusts* [1953] 1 W.L.R. 725 was not cited. It is submitted that the views of Harman J. and Cross J. are not reconcilable and that the views of Cross J. are to be preferred.

places of worship of persons who lived in this world and mixed with their fellow citizens.[27]

The benefit to the public which Cross J. was able to find was an indirect benefit. It is submitted that, if an indirect benefit may be assumed to accrue to the public at large from the attendance of Jews at a synagogue for the purposes of religious observance, an indirect benefit may also be assumed to accrue to the public from the spiritual exercises of retreatants who return to the world and mix with their fellow citizens.[28] It has also been held that the Exclusive Brethren are not an enclosed type of organisation because, first, outsiders are allowed to attend meetings of the Brethren, other than the celebration of the Eucharist and business meetings; and secondly, the Brethren or some of them attempt to proselytise by conducting public campaigns.[29]

(h) Gifts for masses

2–069   In *Bourne v Keane*[30] the House of Lords held by a four to one majority, reversing the decision of the Court of Appeal,[31] that a bequest of personal estate for masses for the dead was not void as a gift to superstitious uses, thus overruling several longstanding authorities to the contrary.[32] Such gifts may still fail as charitable gifts, however, as the condition of public benefit may not be satisfied. The testator, and Irish Roman Catholic, died domiciled in England. He bequeathed certain sums of money "for masses foundation and other." The House of Lords decided that the gifts were not void as gifts for superstitious uses. It was not necessary to determine whether they were charitable, because they were immediate gifts and there was, therefore, no question of a perpetuity.

In *Re Caus*,[33] however, it was proved that a "foundation mass" was a mass the saying of which was to be paid for out of the income of an invested fund. Unless, therefore, the gift was charitable, it would have been void as infringing the rule against perpetuities. Luxmoore J. held that the gift was charitable, and in the course of his judgment said that there were many passages in the speeches of Lord Birkenhead, Lord Atkinson and Lord Parmoor in *Bourne v Keane*[34] which recognised and supported the view that such gifts were charitable; but, since he did not quote any passages from those

---

[27] [1962] Ch. at 852 at 853.
[28] See the views of the Goodman Committee Report (1976) on Charity Law and Voluntary Organisations, para.55.
[29] *Holmes v Att-Gen, The Times*, February 12, 1981; [1981] Ch. Com. Rep., paras 22 *et seq*. A meeting hall of the Exclusive Brethren was not, however, exempt for rating purposes under the General Rate Act 1967, s.39, as there was nothing about the building to indicate that it was a place of worship: *Broxtowe Borough Council v Birch* [1983] 1 W.L.R. 314. See para.8–042, below.
[30] [1919] A.C. 815.
[31] *Sub nom. Re Egan* [1918] 2 Ch. 350.
[32] The cases overruled were *West v Shuttleworth* (1835) 2 My. & K. 684; *Heath v Chapman* (1854) 2 Drew. 417; *Re Blundell's Trusts* (1861) 30 Beav. 360; *Re Fleetwood* (1880) 15 Ch.D. 594; *Re Elliott* (1891) 39 W.R. 297.
[33] [1934] Ch. 162.
[34] [1919] A.C. 815.

speeches, it is far from clear what passages were in his Lordships' mind. The expressed grounds of his Lordship's decision were that the gift was charitable (1) because it enabled a ritual act to be performed which was the central act of the religion of a larger proportion of Christian people, and (2) because it assisted in the endowment of priests whose duty it was to perform the act. The testator's will did not expressly require the foundation masses to be said in public, and in the judgment no distinction was made between masses said in pubic and masses said in private.

The question of the charitable status of gifts for the saying of masses came before the Vice-Chancellor, Sir Nicholas Browne-Wilkinson, in *Re Hetherington*.[35] The deceased's will contained two gifts for masses for her soul and the souls of members of her family. There was no stipulation as to whether the masses were to be said in public or private. After considering *Re Caus*[36] and *Gilmour v Coates*,[37] the Vice-Chancellor concluded that *Re Caus* is still good law. He held that the gifts for the saying of masses were charitable because they were for a religious purpose and contained the necessary element of public benefit, since in practice the masses would be celebrated in public and the provision of stipends for priests saying the masses relieved the Roman Catholic Church of the liability to provide such stipends to that extent.

In relation to the element of public benefit the Vice-Chancellor set out four propositions[38]: **2–070**

(1) A trust for the advancement of religion is prima facie charitable and assumed to be for the public benefit unless in can be shown that the particular trust in question cannot operate so as to confer a legally recognised benefit on the public as in *Gilmour v Coates*.[39]

(2) The celebration of a religious rite in public does confer a sufficient public benefit because of the edifying and improving effect of such celebration on the members of the public who attend.

(3) The celebration of a religious rite in private does not contain the necessary element of public benefit since any benefit by prayer or example is incapable of proof in the legal sense, and any element of edification is limited to a private, not public, class of those present at the celebration.

(4) Where there is a gift for a religious purpose which could be carried out in a way which is beneficial to the public (*i.e.* by public masses) but could also be carried out in a way which would not have sufficient element of public benefit (*i.e.* by private masses) the gift is to be construed as a gift to be carried out by the methods that are charitable, all non-charitable methods being excluded.[40]

---

[35] [1989] 2 All E.R. 129.
[36] [1934] Ch. 162.
[37] [1949] A.C. 426.
[38] [1989] 2 All E.R. 129 at 134–135.
[39] [1949] A.C. 426.
[40] See *Re White* [1893] 2 Ch. 41 at 52–53 and see para.2–053, above.

OTHER PURPOSES BENEFICIAL TO THE COMMUNITY, NOT FALLING
UNDER ANY OF THE PRECEDING THREE HEADS

Introduction

2–071   Reference has already been made[41] to the general proposition that not
every object beneficial to the community is necessarily charitable.[42] For a
purpose to be charitable under this head it is not enough that the purpose
is for the public benefit; it must be beneficial in a way in which the law
regards as charitable.[43] In other words, it must be within the spirit and
intendment of the preamble to the Charitable Uses Act 1601.

The courts no longer make any distinction[44] between Sir Samuel Romilly's
fourth category in *Morice v Bishop of Durham*[45] and Lord Macnaghten's
fourth category in *Income Tax Special Purposes Commissioners v Pemsel.*[46]
Thus, the fourth head now includes not only certain purposes of "general public utility" within the meaning of those words as used by Sir
Samuel Romilly but also purposes tending to promote mental or moral
improvement.

The courts' broad approach to determining which purposes are charitable has already been considered[47] but it has particular relevance under this
head. It remains the case that "beneficial to the community" means " for
the benefit of the community or of an appreciably important section of
the community".[48] It has already been stated[49] that where the purpose of
a gift appears to be for the relief of poverty or the advancement of education or the advancement of religion the court will assume it to be for the
benefit of the community and, therefore, charitable unless the contrary is
shown whereas the assumption does not apply under this head.[50] The
requirement of public benefit as it applies to identifying an eligible class
under this head of charity is considered in more detail below.[51] Finally, purposes which are accepted as falling within the fourth head are considered.[52]

Public benefit

2–072   It is not sufficient for a purpose to confer a benefit on the public in
a way which is accepted as being of charitable character, the class of

---

[41] See para.1–008, above.
[42] *Re Macduff* [1896] 2 Ch. 451; *Att-Gen v National Provincial and Union Bank of England*
[1924] A.C. 262 at 265; *William's Trustees v IRC* [1947] A.C. 447 at 453; *Re Strakosch*
[1949] Ch. 529.
[43] See *Peggs v Lamb* [1993] 2 All E.R. 15 at 33.
[44] See *Incorporated Council of Law Reporting for England and Wales v Att-Gen* [1972] Ch. 73
at 88, *per* Lord Russell.
[45] (1805) 10 Ves. 522 at 583.
[46] [1891] A.C. 531 at 583.
[47] See para.1–003 above.
[48] *Verge v Somerville* [1924] A.C. 496 at 499.
[49] See para.1–008 above.
[50] But see the arguments in relation to the application of ECHR principles to this rule at
para.1–009 above.
[51] See para.2–072 below.
[52] See para.2–073 below.

persons eligible to benefit must be the community or a sufficient section of the community.[53] In particular the section of the community intended to benefit must be identifiable.

The problem of identifying the community has arisen in at least two reported cases. In *Keren Kayemeth Le Jisroel Ltd. v IRC*[54] a company had been formed having as its main object the purchase of land in Palestine, Syria or other parts of Turkey in Asia and the peninsula of Sinai for the purpose of settling Jews in such lands. The company's memorandum contained numerous other powers which were to be exercised only in such a way as should in the opinion of the company be conducive to the attainment of the primary object, and no part of the company's income was distributed among its members. Since the House of Lords was unable to identify the community either as the community of all Jews throughout the world or as the community of the Jews in the region prescribed for settlement, the company's objects were held not to be charitable under Lord Macnaghten's fourth head. The difficulty of identifying the community of Welsh people who were to be eligible to enjoy the advantages of an institute for the moral, social and spiritual welfare of Welsh people in London was not the *ratio decidendi* in *Williams' Trustees v IRC*,[55] which was that, even if the objects of the trust were beneficial to the community, they were not charitable because they were not within the spirit and intendment of the preamble to the Statute of Elizabeth I, but Viscount Simonds observed in passing[56] that the definition of "Welsh people" in the first of the trust deeds under consideration was so comprehensive that the difficulty of finding the community of Welsh people was not less than the difficulty of finding the community of Jews in *Keren Kayemeth Le Jisroel Ltd v IRC*.[57]

When the reported cases in which gifts or trusts which have been held charitable under the fourth head are considered, it will be necessary also to consider what classes of the community and what number of persons constitute a sufficiently important section of the public. It will be submitted that, where a trust can be upheld if and only if it is for a purpose of general public utility, the requirement of benefit to the community will not be satisfied if any person physically capable of and desirous of enjoying the benefits of the trust is by the terms of the trust instrument excluded from those benefits because he is not engaged in a particular trade, business or calling, or because he is not the adherent of a particular religion or political party. In view of the large variety of purposes now comprised in the fourth head, no rigid definition of a section of the community can be given. As Lord Somervell of Harrow said:

> "I cannot accept the principle . . . that a section of the public sufficient to support a valid trust in one category must as a matter of law be sufficient to support a trust in any other category. I think that

---

[53] See para.1–008, above.
[54] [1932] A.C. 650. For public benefit and charities operating abroad, see para.1–011, above.
[55] [1947] A.C. 447.
[56] [1947] A.C. at 458.
[57] [1932] A.C. 650.

difficulties are apt to arise if one seeks to consider the class apart from the particular nature of the charitable purpose. They are, in my opinion, interdependent".[58]

Specific purposes falling within the fourth head

2–073   Within the general category of purposes of general public utility, provision for public works, the relief of unemployment, the promotion of urban and rural regeneration, the promotion of the effectiveness of charities, the protection of lives or property, the promotion and maintenance of health, the preservation of public order, resettlement and rehabilitation, the care of children, relief from rates or taxes, the promotion of industry, commerce and art, the benefit of a locality and public recreation are all accepted as being of charitable character. In addition purposes which promote the mental or moral improvement of the community, including the protection or benefit of animals, are charitable under this head. Trust for the benefit of aged or impotent people who are not required to be poor can be said to fall under this head but they have more conveniently been dealt with under the first head of charity.[59]

Public works and services

2–074   The preamble to the Statute of Charitable Uses 1601 refers to the repair of bridges, ports, havens, causeways and highways and many purposes involving public works and services have been held to be within the spirit and intendment of the preamble. Today the relevant public works, services or facilities are not usually paid for out of trust funds provided by public spirited donors or testators, but by some public authority out of public funds which the authority is bound or entitled to apply for the purpose in question.[60] Examples of such are trusts for the repair of highways[61]; to build bridges[62]; to provide a supply of pure water for the use of the inhabitants of a town[63]; to provide a town with lighting[64] for the improvement

---

[58] *IRC v Baddeley* [1955] A.C. 572 at 615. See also *Gilmour v Coats* [1949] A.C. 426 at 449, *per* Lord Simonds.

[59] See para.2–001, above.

[60] For the practice of the Charity Commissioners in making schemes for ancient charities for such purposes to apply the funds for more general purposes, see [1968] Ch. Com. Rep., paras 67–72; [1975] Ch. Com. Rep., paras 56–57; and see also *Re Richmond Parish Charity Lands* (1965) 109 S.J. 755, where the Court of Appeal held that the trusts in question were for the relief of the burdens of the parish of Richmond ratepayers in respect of the poor rate.

[61] *Att-Gen v Harrow School (Governors)* (1754) 2 Ves.Sen. 551; *Att-Gen v Day* [1900] 1 Ch. 31.

[62] *Forbes v Forbes* (1854) 18 Beav. 552.

[63] *Jones v Williams* (1767) Amb. 651.

[64] *Att-Gen v Heelis* (1824) 2 Sim. & St. 67 at 76, 77. (The dictum of Sir John Leach M.R. to the effect that funds supplied from the gift of the Crown or the legislature or from private gift for any legal, public or general purposes are charitable has sometimes been quoted out of context and when so quoted is misleading. In the next sentence the Master of the Rolls made it clear that he did not mean that any purpose was charitable if it was not either expressed in "the Statute" (*i.e.* the preamble) or within "the equity of the Statute".) See also *Att-Gen v Eastlake* (1853) 11 Hare 205.

of a town[65]; to build a courthouse[66]; to build a workhouse[67]; to provide a cemetery[68]; or a crematorium.[69] The provision of free community access to the Internet has been held charitable by analogy.[70]

Trusts for the provision of various public facilities in defined areas have been held charitable as being for objects of general public utility. Thus the provision of a library,[71] a museum,[72] a public hall,[73] a reading room,[74] and an observatory,[75] to which the public have access as of right, have all been held to be charitable purposes.

The question, what constitutes a sufficiently important section of the community to clothe a trust for the provision of public works, services or facilities with the necessary public character, has not been finally determined in any of the reported cases; but it is submitted that, as applied to trusts of this kind, "section of the community" means all the inhabitants of a sufficient area who can avail themselves of and wish to avail themselves of the benefits. It is considered that the primary test to apply for the purpose of deciding whether the trust has the necessary public character is not whether the number of persons who may be able and willing to avail themselves of the benefits is large or small, but whether or not any inhabitant of the area of the trust is excluded because he lacks some personal qualification. As Viscount Simonds indicated in *IRC v Baddley*,[76] the distinction is between a form of relief extended to the whole community yet by its very nature advantageous only to the few and a form of relief accorded to a selected few out of a large number willing and able to take advantage of it.

Relief of unemployment

It was for long considered that it was only charitable to relieve unemployment for those who were poor. However, in *IRC v Oldham Training and Enterprise Council*[77] Lightman J. found the relief of unemployment also to be charitable under the fourth head. He said[78]:

2–075

---

[65] *Howse v Chapman* (1799) 4 Ves. 542; *Att-Gen v Brown* (1818) 1 Swan. 265; *Att-Gen v Heelis* (1824) 2 Sim. & St. 67.

[66] *Duke on Charitable Uses*, 109 at 136.

[67] *Att-Gen v Blizard* (1855) 21 Beav. 233; *Re St. Botolph Without Bishopsgate (Parish Estates)* (1887) 35 Ch.D. 142; *Webster v Southey* (1887) 36 Ch.D. 9. The decision to the contrary effect in *Burnaby v Barsby* (1859) 4 H. & N. 690 was wrong.

[68] *Att-Gen v Blizard* (1855) 21 Beav. 233. If the cemetery had been for the burial of deceased members of a particular sect, the trust might not have been for an object of general public utility, but it would have been valid as a trust for the advancement of religion: *Re Manser* [1905] 1 Ch. 68.

[69] *Scottish Burial Reform and Cremation Society Ltd v Glasgow Corp.* [1968] A.C. 138.

[70] *Re Vancouver Regional Free Net Association and Minister of National Revenue* (1996) 137 D.L.R. (4th) 206 (Federal Court of Appeal).

[71] *Abbot v Fraser* (1874) L.R. 6 P.C. 96; *Re Scowcroft* [1898] 2 Ch. 638 at 642.

[72] *British Museum Trustees v White* (1826) 2 Sim. & St. 594; *Re Allsop* (1884) 1 T.L.R. 4; *Re Holburne* (1885) 53 L.T. 212.

[73] *Re Spence* [1938] Ch. 96.

[74] *Re Scowcroft* [1898] 2 Ch. 638.

[75] *Harrison v Southampton Corporation* (1854) 2 Sm. & G. 387.

[76] [1955] A.C. 572, 592.

[77] [1996] S.T.C. 1218.

[78] *ibid.*, at 1234.

"[I]f the object of setting up the unemployed in trade or business was not charitable as being for the relief of poverty, it would fall within the fourth head of charity. It is a matter of general public utility that the unemployed should be found gainful activity and that the state should be relieved of the burden of providing them with unemployment and social security benefits, and this object is within the spirit, if not the words, of the Statute of Elizabeth, which includes among its list of objects the 'supportation, aid and help of young tradesmen [and] handicraftsmen.'"

The particular organisation, Oldham Training and Enterprise Council, was not charitable because the objects conferred freedom to provide private benefit on individuals and businesses regardless of the likely consequences for employment.

The Charity Commissioners have issued guidance to organisations set up to relieve unemployment on the relevant criteria for charitable status.[79] A list of potential activities is set out including the payment by a grant-making charity to an existing commercial business to take on additional staff from among unemployed people.

Promotion of urban and rural regeneration

2–076   The Charity Commissioners have recognised[80] the promotion of urban and rural regeneration for public benefit in areas of social and economic deprivation as a charitable purpose. The references in the preamble to the 1601 Statute and subsequent cases on the provision of basic infrastructure such as bridges and lighting[81] and the recent decision on the charitable status of the relief of unemployment[82] provide a sound legal base for this recognition. The High Court of New Zealand has also held charitable the provision of a creamery to assist a small new rural community to become economically viable.[83]

The Charity Commissioners guidance[84] sets out possible activities for charitable regeneration organisations including the provision of housing for those in need, assistance and training to the unemployed, assistance to businesses and the provision of roads and public amenities. Any question of potential private, as opposed to public, benefit needs to be considered carefully in the context of the particular type of deprivation suffered by the area the organisation aims to regenerate.[85]

Linked with urban and rural regeneration is the decision of the Charity Commissioners that the promotion of community capacity building in relation to communities which are socially and economically (or in some

[79] RR3, *Charities for the Relief of Unemployment* (1999).
[80] RR2, *Promotion of Urban and Rural Regeneration* (1999).
[81] See para.2–074 above.
[82] *IRC v Oldham Training and Enterprise Council* [1996] S.T.C. 1218, see para.(92) above.
[83] *Re Tennant* [1996] 2 N.Z.L.R. 633.
[84] RR2, *Promotion of Urban and Rural Regeneration* (1999), para.7.
[85] *ibid.*, para.A7.

cases simply socially) disadvantaged is charitable.[86] Community capacity building here means developing the capacity and skills of members of a community in such a way that they are better able to identify and help meet their needs and to participate more in society. The relevant community may be geographical or may be a community of interest, for example, membership of a particular ethnic group.[87] As with the promotion of urban and rural regeneration, care is needed to ensure that any private benefit remains incidental.[88]

Promotion of the effectiveness of charities

It is well accepted that an organisation established to further an **2–077** accepted charitable purpose carried on by another is itself charitable.[89] On this basis it can be said that the promotion of the efficiency and effectiveness of charities by the provision of support and services is charitable.[90] By analogy, the Charity Commissioners have registered The Charity Bank Limited which is established to provide loans and guarantees on beneficial terms to charities by receiving donations and taking deposits on beneficial terms from the public and others in order to provide such loans and guarantees.[91] The Charity Commissioners are of the view that it is also charitable to promote the effective use of resources for charitable purposes by charities and non-charitable bodies.[92] By analogy with the promotion of industry and commerce[93] and the promotion of the mental and welfare and improvement of the community,[94] the Charity Commissioners regard the promotion of the voluntary sector for the benefit of the public as a charitable purpose.[95]

Protection of lives and property

The repair of sea-banks is one of the purposes recited in the preamble, **2–078** and the repair or construction of sea-banks prevents or greatly reduces the danger to the lives and property of the inhabitants of coastal areas.[96] It is

---

[86] RR5, *The Promotion of Community Capacity Building* (2000).
[87] *ibid.*, para.9, paras A7 to A10 give guidance as to possible indicators of economic and social disadvantage.
[88] *ibid.*, see para.A27 for a list of potential factors.
[89] *Re White's Will Trusts* [1951] 1 All E.R. 528 (a rest home for nurses); *London Hospital v IRC* [1976] 1 W.L.R. 613 (a students' union).
[90] For discussion for the types of services and support see CC Discussion Paper, *Promoting the Efficiency and Effectiveness of Charities and the Effective Use of Charitable Resources* (2001), Annex B.
[91] [2002] Ch. Com. Dec. November 1.
[92] See CC Discussion Paper, *Promoting the Efficiency and Effectiveness of Charities and the Effective Use of Charitable Resources* (2001), Annex C.
[93] See para.(103) below.
[94] See para.(115) below.
[95] CC Discussion Paper, *The Promotion of the Voluntary Sector for the Benefit of the Public* (2001); [2003] Ch. Com. Dec. March 7 (Guidestar UK).
[96] *Att-Gen v Brown* (1818) 1 Swan. 265; *Wilson v Barnes* (1886) 38 Ch.D. 507.

considered that a trust to repair or provide a sea wall may be regarded as
the preamble's example of a trust that includes among its objects the protection of human life as well as the protection of property; and that any
trust for the protection of human life is charitable in the same sense. Thus
a gift to provide a lifeboat at a particular town on the coast is charitable,[97]
for the crew of the lifeboat rescue shipwrecked mariners and voyagers
from the risk of drowning or death from exposure. On the same principle
gifts to the Royal National Lifeboat Institution[98] and the Royal Humane
Society for Saving Life[99] are charitable.

In *Re Wokingham Fire Brigade Trusts*[1] Danckwerts J. held that the provision and maintenance of a public fire brigade for the benefit of a defined
locality by means of voluntary donations and subscriptions and fees for
attending fires was a charitable purpose. The learned judge held (1) that
the fire brigade was a body of a non-profit making character; (2) that it
was formed to meet a public need for a means of fighting fires in the
Wokingham district, which was a public purpose; (3) that the brigade was
not formed for the benefit of the members, but for the benefit of the public, and that its purpose was to prevent damage and loss of life "in that
community" (in other words, among all members of the public residing in
the brigade's area of operation). Danckwerts J. made it abundantly clear
that, in his opinion, a trust for the prevention of damage to property and
loss of human life was a trust for a charitable purpose. By remarking that
the provision of a public fire brigade of that kind was as much a charitable purpose as the provision of a lifeboat the learned judge made it equally
clear that, in his opinion, the protection and preservation of human life
was in itself a charitable purpose.

Under this heading come trusts for national or local defence. The public interest requires that, so far as possible, the lives and property of all
members of the community or of all the inhabitants of a particular locality shall be protected not only from storm, tempest, fire or other catastro-
phe, but also from attacks by the Queen's enemies. It is considered that the
validity of trusts for the promotion of national or local defence can be justified on this general principle. It is not charitable under this head to promote the protection of the lives and property of a specific section of the
community defined other than by reference to geographical area.[2]

2–079   The preamble to the Statute of Elizabeth I includes "the aid or ease
of any poor inhabitants concerning payment of fifteens, setting out of

---

[97] *Johnston v Swann* (1818) 3 Madd. 457. This case is not very well reported. The *ratio decidendi* suggested in the text is not expressed in the brief report of the judgment of Leach
V.C. The comparison (at 465) with *Howse v Chapman* (1799) 4 Ves. 542 (improvement of the
city of Bath) seems rather far-fetched. The provision of a lifeboat is still left to voluntary
effort.

[98] *Thomas v Howell* (1874) L.R. 18 Eq. 198; *Re Richardson* (1887) 56 L.J.Ch. 784; *Re David*
(1889) 41 Ch.D. 168; affd. 43 Ch.D. 27, CA.

[99] *Beaumont v Oliveira* (1869) L.R. 4 Ch. 309. Likewise, a trust to promote road safety (see
The League of Highway Safety and Safe Drivers Ltd: Report, 1965, p.27) or to prevent
accidents generally is charitable.

[1] [1951] Ch. 373.

[2] See (1995) 4 Ch. Com. Dec. pp.8, *et seq.*, (Community Security Trust). For alternative
grounds for charitable status see para.2.104 below.

soldiers and other taxes." It would appear at first sight as if the preamble was referring to the relief of poor inhabitants from the burden of the taxes required for the setting out of soldiers; but, as Danckwerts J. observed in Re Sahal's Will Trusts,[3] the decisions have gone a long way from the interpretation in a number of cases in which what may be called "service charities" have been held to be objects of a charitable nature. Moreover, it is settled law that all gifts for the exclusive purpose of promoting efficiency of the armed forces are charitable.[4] All gifts to promote the efficiency of the armed forces, whether regular or auxiliary, are charitable in the same sense as trusts for the setting out of soldiers.[5] The increasing of the efficiency of the armed forces benefits the community at large and is within the spirit and intendment of the preamble.

Gifts that have been held charitable under this head include a gift for the benefit of a volunteer corps,[6] for teaching shooting,[7] to provide a prize to be competed for by cadets,[8] to maintain a library and plate for an officers' mess,[9] for an officers' mess generally[10] and to promote sport in a regiment.[11]

However gifts for the benefit of former members of the armed forces *simpliciter* and presumably former members of a police force *simpliciter* are not charitable on this principle[12] or any other principle.

The promotion of any form of defence is a charitable purpose and is **2–080** charitable in the same sense as the promotion of the efficiency of the armed forces. Thus a trust to provide a town with fortifications was held charitable[13]; and in *Re Driffill*[14] Danckwerts J. felt no difficulty in holding that a gift for promoting the defence of the United Kingdom from the attack of hostile aircraft was charitable. He considered that this was a case clearly falling within the well-known authorities in which gifts for the promotion of the efficiency of the armed forces of the Crown were held to be valid charitable bequests.[15]

[3] [1958] 1 W.L.R. 1243 at 1247. The cases that Danckwerts J. had in mind must have included *Re Good* [1905] 2 Ch. 60; *Re Donald* [1909] 2 Ch. 410 and *Re Gray* [1925] Ch. 362.
[4] *Re Driffill* [1950] Ch. 92; *IRC v City of Glasgow Police Athletic Association* [1953] A.C. 380 at 391.
[5] Similarly, trusts to encouarge the spirit of the army by holding parades etc. (*Old Contemptibles Association*, [1964] Ch. Com. Rep., App. E I A, or for the mixing together of serving officers and ex-officers to foster service traditions (*R.A.F.C. Co. Ltd. and Royal Air Force Club*, [1967] Ch. Com. Rep., App. D I A) are charitable. However, a trust to promote reunions and other social functions is not charitable (*Great Yarmouth Far East Prisoners of War Association*, [1966] Ch. Com. Rep., App. A II 2). See also *Re Chitty's Will Trusts* [1970] Ch. 254.
[6] *Re Stratheden and Campbell (Lord)* [1894] 3 Ch. 265.
[7] *Re Stephens* (1892) 8 T.L.R. 792. But see para.2–080, below.
[8] *Re Barker* (1909) 25 T.L.R. 753.
[9] *Re Good* [1905] 2 Ch. 60.
[10] *Re Donald* [1909] 2 Ch. 410.
[11] *Re Gray* [1925] 2 Ch. 362 but see the observations of Lord Normand and Lord Reid in *IRC v City of Glasgow Police Athletic Association* [1953] A.C. 380 at 391, 402.
[12] *Re Good* [1905] 2 Ch. 60; *Re Meyers* [1951] Ch. 534.
[13] *Att-Gen v Carlisle Corporation* (1828) 2 Sim. 437; *Att-Gen v Dartmouth Corporation* (1883) 48 L.T. 933 (where the trust was created in 1599, two years before the enactment of the Charitable Uses Act 1601).
[14] [1950] Ch. 92.
[15] *ibid*. at 95.

The Mercantile Marine does not form part of the armed forces of the Crown, but it is no less necessary for the defence and welfare of the realm than are efficient armed forces. It would have been surprising, therefore, if, in *Re Corbyn*[16] Morton J. had not held that a trust to invest the proceeds of the testator's estate to form a fund for the training of selected boys as officers in the Mercantile Marine was a valid charitable trust. Under the terms of the will the fund might have been applied in training potential officers either in the Royal Navy or in the Mercantile Marine. The former purpose was clearly charitable as being designed to promote the efficiency of part of the armed forces of the Crown. But the ground upon which the learned judge held that the latter purpose also was charitable was that the training of boys to become officers in the Mercantile Marine and the payment of money to them while being trained was a purpose beneficial to the community under Lord Macnaghten's fourth head. The Mercantile Marine was essential to the community not only in the then existing time of war but at all times and would remain essential unless and until this country could produce all the food and other essentials of life which it required, and it was of the greatest importance that boys should be suitably trained as officers.

Before a trust can be charitable under this heading it must be established that the activities of the particular trust promote the security of the nation and the defence of the realm, not merely that they are capable of doing so.[17] On this basis, the Charity Commissioners have taken the view that certain rifle clubs are not charitable as their primary purpose is providing members with facilities for the enjoyment of shooting as a recreation and the practice of shooting and that any promotion of the defence of the realm is incidental.[18]

2–081   This heading also includes trusts for the protection of property. The category extends beyond the preservation of particular buildings[19] and structures[20] to preservation of landscape. *Re Verrall*[21] decided that the National Trust established "for the purposes of promoting the permanent preservation for the benefit of the nation of lands and tenements (including buildings) of beauty or historic interest, and as regards land for the preservation (so far as practicable) of their natural aspect features and animal and plant life" was charitable. Gifts for the maintenance and protection of national parks[22] and particular geographical features[23] have been held to be charitable. A wide variety of purposes related to the protection of the environment for example, the preservation of the

---

[16] [1941] Ch. 400. The provision of a monthly allowance for boys who had qualified as Merchant Navy officers seems to have prevented the purposes of the trust from being purely educational. See also *The Royal British Legion Attendants Co. (Belfast) v Commissioner of Valuation* [1979] N.I. 138.

[17] See *IRC v City of Glasgow Police Athletic Association* [1953] A.C. 380 and para.2–084, below.

[18] (1993) 1 Ch. Com. Dec., paras 4, et seq.

[19] *Re Cranstoun* [1932] 1 Ch. 537 (a gift to the Royal Society of Arts of two Elizabethan cottages for their preservation).

[20] See [1989] Ch.Comm. Rep., App. A, The Settle and Carlisle Railway Trust.

[21] [1916] 1 Ch. 100. See para.2–025, above, for charitable status as a trust for the advance of education.

[22] *Re Bruce* [1918] N.Z.L.R. 16.

[23] *Re Spehr* [1965] V.R. 770; *Kaikoura County v Boyd* [1949] N.Z.L.R. 233.

flora and fauna in a particular area, have been registered by the Charity Commissioners.[24]

The Charity Commissioners have now issued guidance setting out their views on both organisations set up for the charitable purpose of the preservation of specific buildings of historical and architectural importance and those set up for the conservation of particular animals or birds or plant species or habitat and flora, fauna and the environment in general.[25] The charitable object of conversation, protection and improvement of the environment, in the view of the Charity Commissioners, extends to the promotion of biological diversity.[26] Both purposes, of preservation and conservation, require a criterion of merit to be satisfied so that, for example, a particular plant species must be worthy of conservation.[27]

The usual requirement of public benefit must be satisfied, which in this context means that there must be sufficient public access to the building or site in question. It is considered that the requirement set out in *Re Grove-Grady*[28] that there must be physical access to the relevant site before a trust to preserve wild birds and animals is charitable is no longer applicable in the light of advances of knowledge of conservation. Alternative means of access, such as video cameras, are acceptable if the site is fragile.[29]

Preservation of the environment as a charitable purpose has been held **2–082** by the Charity Commissioners to extend to cover the promotion of re-use and recycling.[30] Accordingly, they have held the promotion of sustainable waste management practices to be charitable.[31] Sustainable development is also a charitable purpose.[31a]

Promotion and maintenance of health

It has already been noted that the protection of human life is a well estab-   **2–083** lished charitable purpose within the preamble to the 1601 Act.[32] The relief of impotent people has also been seen to be a charitable purpose under the first head.[33] A number of purposes connected with health, beyond simply the relief of the sick, have been recognised as charitable and now probably fit together better as a sub-category under this head. A gift for the purposes of a hospital is charitable even if fees are charged.[34] The provision of a home for nurses is charitable.[35] The Charity Commissioners have recognised the purpose of the protection, promotion and maintenance of the health and safety of the community by ensuring proper standards in the

[24] See, for example, [1969] Ch. Com. Rep., para. 23; [1989] Ch. Com. Rep., para.29.
[25] RR9, *Preservation and Conservation* (2001).
[26] *ibid.*, para.A14.
[27] *ibid.*, paras 4, A5–A13.
[28] [1929] 1 Ch. 557.
[29] See RR9, *Preservation and Conservation* (2001), paras 4, A18–A27.
[30] [2002] Ch. Com. Dec. April (Recycling in Ottery).
[31] [2002] Ch. Com. Dec. April (Cylch).
[31a] See [2003] Ch. Com. Dec. January 24 (Environment Foundation).
[32] See para.2–078 above.
[33] See para.2–007 above.
[34] *Re Resch's Will Trusts* [1969] 1 A.C. 514, see para.2–002 above.
[35] *Re White's Will Trusts* [1951] 1 All E.R. 528, see para.2–008 above.

practice of medicine as a charitable purpose.[36] Accordingly, the General
Medical Council was registered as a charity. The Charity Commissioners
took the view[37] that circumstances had changed since 1928 when the
General Medical Council was held[38] non-charitable as a registration body
that benefited medical practitioners rather than the public.[39] In coming to
this conclusion, the Commissioners followed the earlier New Zealand
decision in *Commissioners of Inland Revenue v Medical Council of New
Zealand*.[40]

The Charity Commissioners have for some time accepted as charitable
the advancement of various forms of alternative medicine provided that
there is evidence of the effectiveness of the relevant treatment, although
such evidence is not required in the case of well know therapeutic activities
such as osteopathy.[41] In the case of complementary therapies which do not
purport to diagnose, lesser proof of efficacy is required.[42] The courts in
New Zealand have refused to differentiate between the provision of health
services in hospitals and other lawful institutions in determining charitable status[43] and have accepted the provision of psycho-therapy services as
charitable.[44] In this country, faith healing has been recognised as a charitable purpose without any religious element being included[45] and the promotion of public health by the promotion of spiritual healing has been
accepted by the Charity Commissioners as charitable.[46]

Preservation of public order

2–084   It is considered that the preservation of public order is a purpose which
is charitable in the same sense as the defence of the community against the
Queen's enemies. Without an efficient police force law and order could not
be maintained nor could the lives and property of the public be protected.
Therefore, a trust the main object of which is to promote the efficiency of
the police is obviously charitable: and this was the view of the House of
Lords in *IRC v City of Glasgow Police Athletic Association*.[47] It is charitable in the same sense as a trust to promote the efficiency of the armed
forces.[48] As Lord Cohen explained,[49] the question for decision was not
whether a gift for the promotion of efficiency in a police force was

---

[36] [2001] Ch. Com. Dec., April 2 (General Medical Council).
[37] *ibid.*, para.7.2.
[38] *General Medical Council v IRC* [1928] 1 All E.R. 252, affirmed in *General Nursing Council v St. Marylebone BC* [1959] A.C. 540.
[39] For the need for overall public benefit in professional bodies, see para.2–044 above.
[40] [1997] 2 N.Z.L.R. 297.
[41] [1975] Ch. Com. Rep., para.70.
[42] See [2002] Ch. Com. Dec. August 15 (NFSH Charitable Trust Limited).
[43] *Auckland Medical Aid Trust v Commissioner of Inland Revenue* [1979] 1 N.Z.L.R. 382 at 389, *per* Chilwell J.
[44] *Centrepoint Community Growth Trust v Commissioner of Inland Revenue* [1985] 1 N.Z.L.R. 673.
[45] *Re Le Cren Clarke* [1996] 1 All E.R. 715.
[46] [2002] Ch. Com. Dec. August 15 (NFSH Charitable Trust Limited).
[47] [1953] A.C. at 391, per Lord Normand.
[48] *ibid.,* at 401, 402, per Lord Reid. See para.2–079, above.
[49] *ibid.* at 404.

charitable but whether the City of Glasgow Police Athletic Association was formed for charitable purposes only. The House of Lords held by a majority[50] that the Association was a sports club formed for the purposes of providing recreation for the members, and that this was not a charitable purpose.

Resettlement and rehabilitation

Gifts for social rehabilitation and settlement have long been accepted as charitable.[51] The re-establishment in civilian life of demobilised soldiers, sailors or airmen is a charitable purpose[52] under this head, as is the relief of refugees[53] and the rehabilitation of those suffering from physical or mental illness, or a disability,[54] or from forms of abuse and deprivation.[55]   **2–085**

It is suggested that the reclamation of prostitutes, which in Ireland was held to be a charitable purpose,[56] and would presumably be held charitable in England may be regarded as a from of rehabilitation which justifies inclusion in this sub-division.

Thus in *Verge v Somerville*[57] the Privy Council held, affirming the judgment of the Supreme Court of New South Wales, that a bequest of residue for the benefit of New South Wales returned soldiers created a trust which was a valid charitable trust under Lord Macnaghten's fourth head, since it was for a purpose beneficial to the community and within the spirit and intendment of the preamble. The direct beneficiaries, the returned soldies, were held to be a sufficiently important section of the New South Wales community; and though the judgment of Lord Wrenbury is silent on the point, it is considered that the assisting of the returned soldiers conferred an indirect benefit on the entire population of the State of New South Wales.

Disaster funds within this category. If an appeal to the public for funds to provide relief for the victims of a disaster is so expressed as to make it clear that all moneys given or subscribed will be applied for the benefit of the victims and that no moneys will be applied for any non-charitable or vague and uncertain purposes, the court will readily conclude that the moneys are held on a charitable trust for purposes beneficial to the   **2–086**

---

[50] Lords Normand, Morton of Henryton, Reid and Cohen, Lord Oaksey dissenting. Gifts for recreational purposes are discussed at para.2–093, below.

[51] See also the discussion at paras 2–001—2–008, above, of "The Relief of Aged, Impotent and Poor People" and para.2–087, below, of "Care, upbringing and establishment in life of children and young persons."

[52] *Verge v Somerville* [1924] A.C. 496. See also [1990] Ch. Com. Rep., para.34 (The Gulf Trust).

[53] *Re Morrison*, The Times, July 8, 1967; *Vancouver Society of Immigrant and Visible Minority Women v Minister of National Revenue* (1999) 169 D.L.R. (4th) 34 (Supreme Court).

[54] See [1989] Ch. Com. Rep., para.31.

[55] See [1989] Ch. Com. Rep., para.32.

[56] *Mahoney v Duggan* (1880) 11 L.R.Ir. 260. A home of rescue for prostitutes would seem to be a charity in the same sense as the home which in *Re Sahal's Will Trusts* [1958] 1 W.L.R. 1243 was held to be a charity.

[57] [1924] A.C. 496. The soldiers had served in the war of 1914 to 1918. See also *The Royal British Legion Attendants Co. (Belfast) v Commissioner of Valuation* [1979] N.I. 138.

community or a section of the community (the victims of the disaster).[58] On the same principle the relief of air raid distress is a charitable purpose, if the relief fund is applicable for the relief of all the victims of air raids in a specified area.[59]

The question, what is a sufficiently important section of the community to validate a trust for purposes of rehabilitation, seems to be an open one. Thus, for example, it has not been judicially determined whether the requisite public element is present if the benefits of a "disaster fund" similar to the flood disaster fund in *Re North Devon and West Somerset Relief Fund*[60] or of an air raid distress fund[61] are available only to all the victims in a particular area who possess some personal qualification, such as membership of a particular religious denomination or profession or engagement in a particular trade, business or calling. It is thought, however, that, if any inhabitants of the trust's area of operation who would otherwise be capable of availing themselves of the benefits of the trusts related to the fund are excluded from benefit by reason of some personal disqualification, the trust would not be charitable.

Care, upbringing and establishment in life of children and young persons

2–087   The preamble refers to "the education and preferment of orphans". "the marriage of poor maids" and "the supportation, aid and help of young tradesmen, handicraftsmen and persons decayed", and a number of purposes involving the care, upbringing and establishment in life of children and young persons have been held to be charitable.

A gift for the benefit of orphans was held charitable in Ireland[62] and is clearly charitable in England. Gifts for orphanages are probably charitable under this sub-division, but some gifts of this kind may also be upheld as being for the relief of poverty.[63]

The provision and maintenance of a children's home is charitable.[64] In *Re Cole*[65] the Court of Appeal held that a gift of income for the general benefit and general welfare of the children in a home, the children including those with either no parents or beyond the control of their parents, was not charitable as, on the true construction of the gift, the income could be applied in providing amenities which did not come within the concept of charity as

---

[58] *Re North Devon and West Somerset Relief Fund Trusts* [1953] 1 W.L.R. 1260 (a fund raised by public subscription for victims of a flood disaster held to be a fund held on trust for charitable purposes). Distinguish *Re Gillingham Bus Disaster Fund* [1959] Ch. 62 where the language of the appeal was so vague that the trusts of the fund were void for uncertainty. See para.7–032 below, for the drafting of disaster appeals.

[59] *Re Hobourn Aero Components Ltd's Air Raid Distress Fund* [1946] Ch. 194 at 200, 201.

[60] [1953] 1 W.L.R. 1260.

[61] See *Re Hobourn Aero Components Ltd's Air Raid Distress Fund* [1946] Ch. 194.

[62] *Jackson v Att-Gen* [1917] 1 I.R. 332.

[63] *Re Clergy Society* (1856) 2 K. & J. 615; *Hall v Derby Sanitary Authority* (1885) 16 Q.B.D. 163; *Re Douglas* (1887) 35 Ch.D. 472; *Harbin v Masterman* [1894] 2 Ch. 184; affirmed *sub nom. Wharton v Masterman* [1895] A.C. 186.

[64] *Re Sahal's Will Trust* [1958] 1 W.L.R. 1234.

[65] [1958] Ch. 877.

found in the Preamble. Romer L.J. considered a television set and a grama-
phone and records to be the type of amenities that took the gift beyond the
charitable. This case is not followed. Lord Evershed M.R. dissented and
provided, it is considered, a correct view of the law when he said:[66]

> "[T]he care and upbringing of children, who for any reason have not
> got the advantage or opportunity of being looked after and brought
> up by competent persons, or who could, for these or other reasons
> properly be regarded as defenceless or 'deprived', are matters which
> prima facie qualify as charitable purposes."

This approach was taken by Jacobs J. in *Re Carapiet's Trusts*[67] when he held
that "the advancement in life of children" was a valid fourth head purpose.
A very wide variety of purposes relating to the welfare of children have now
been registered by the Charity Commissioners to support children whether
in residential accommodation or still with their families.[68]

A gift for the promotion of marriage is charitable within this head[69] and
the public benefit requirement is satisfied if the gift is restricted to members of a particular religion.[70] It is also charitable to assist young people
to emigrate.[71]

Relief of the community from rates and taxes

The purpose recited in the preamble which falls within this sub-division is   **2–088**
"the aid or ease of any poor inhabitants concerning payment of fifteens, the
setting-out of soldiers and other taxes". Therefore at first sight it looks as if
the purpose must be for the relief of poverty and so charitable under Lord
Macnaghten's first head of charity. But in the cases in which trusts have been
upheld as charitable under the present suggested sub-division of the fourth
class, it has not been laid down that any element of poverty is required; and
it is clear that it is not. Thus gifts for the relief of taxes,[72] or to reduce the
National Debt,[73] or in reduction or aid of the rates[74] are charitable.

It is considered that a gift to the Chancellor of the Exchequer to be
applied by him for the relief of the taxpayers would be a valid charitable
gift under this sub-division, but there is no reported case that so decides.[75]

---

[66] *ibid.*, at 892.
[67] [2002] E.W.H.C. 1304, para.27.
[68] See, for example, [2002] Ch. Com. Dec. September 12 (The Internet Content Rating
Association).
[69] The Preamble refers to the "marriage of poor maids".
[70] *Re Cohen* (1919) 36 T.L.R. 16. For a more detailed consideration of this case see the 8th
edition of this work at pp.101, *et seq.*
[71] *Re Tree* [1945] Ch. 325.
[72] *Att-Gen v Bushby* (1857) 24 Beav. 299.
[73] *Thellusson v Woodford* (1799) 4 Ves. 227; affirmed (1805) 11 Ves. 112 (H.L.); *Newland v
Att-Gen* (1809) 3 Mer. 684; *Ashton v Langdale (Lord)* (1851) 4 De G. & S. 402, 403; *Income
Tax Commissioners v Pemsel* [1891] A.C. 531 at 544.
[74] *Doe d. Preece v Howells* (1831) 2 B. & Ad. 744; *Att-Gen v Blizard* (1855) 21 Beav. 233; and
see *Gort and Limerick v Att-Gen* (1817) 6 Dowl. 136.
[75] In *Nightingale v Goulbourn* (1847) 5 Hare 484; (1848) 2 Ph. 594 there was a gift to "the
Queen's Chancellor of the Exchequer for the time being and to be by him appropriated to

It is also considered that all the council tax or ratepayers in the area of a particular rating authority constitute a section of the community for the purpose of trusts falling within this sub-division.

Promotion of industry, commerce and art

2–089   In *Crystal Palace Trustees v Minister of Town and Country Planning*,[76] which is the leading authority, the question for determination was whether the land owned by the plaintiffs, consisting of the site of the building formerly forming the site of the Crystal Palace and the park and other lands adjoining was land an interest in which was held "on charitable trusts or for ecclesiastical or other charitable purposes of any description", within the meaning of s.85 of the Town and Country Planning Act 1947. The answer to the question depended upon the true construction of s.14 of the Crystal Palace Act 1914.[77] In its opening words this section gave the control and management of the palace and park to the trustees "as a place for education and recreation and for the promotion of industry, commerce, and art". Danckwerts J. held that the words "promotion of industry, commerce, and art" did not in their context mean merely the promotion of the interests of those concerned in the manufacture and sale of their particular products,[78] but meant the promotion of industry, commerce and art,[79] for the benefit of the public and that all three purposes were charitable. Although the decision turned on the construction of s.14 of the Crystal Palace Act 1914, there seems to be no reason why it should not be regarded as authority for the general proposition that the promotion of industry, commerce and art are all charitable purposes.[80]

The promotion of industry includes not only the promotion of manufacturing industry, but also the promotion of horticulture[81] and agri-

---

the benefit and advantage of my beloved country, Great Britain." This was held by Wigram V.C. and Lord Cottenham to be a good charitable gift. Younger L.J. in *Re Tetley* [1923] 1 Ch. 258, 275 said that the foundation of that decision was that the gift was to the Chancellor of the Exchequer. In *Re Smith* [1932] 1 Ch. 153 at 173 P.O. Lawrence L.J. dissented from Younger L.J.'s observation and expressed the opinion that both the Vice-Chancellor and Lord Cottenham had been at pains to explain that the bequest was charitable in spite of the fact that the trustee was the Chancellor of the Exchequer. Romer L.J. agreed: see [1932] 1 Ch. at 174 at 175. For an ingenious reconciliation of *Re Tetley* (affirmed *sub nom. Att-Gen v National Provincial Bank* [1924] A.C. 262) see *Re Strakosch* [1948] Ch. 37. The whole judgment of Roxburgh J. is illuminating.

[76] [1951] Ch. 132.
[77] The section, which is very long, is printed in full in [1951] Ch. at 133 at 134.
[78] This would not have been a charitable purpose, since trusts for the benefit of persons engaged in a particular trade are not charitable unless the intention to relieve poverty can be read into the gift: *Re Gassiot* [1901] 70 L.J.Ch. 242; *Re Barnett* (1908) 24 T.L.R. 788. See also [1980] Ch. Com. Rep., para.97, WIRA formerly Wool Industries Research Association) not charitable because to a large degree the activities of WIRA were conducted for the benefit of its members and of the trade.
[79] The promotion of art may be charitable as being for the advancement of education, see para.2–027, above.
[80] See, however, *Re Shaw* [1957] 1 W.L.R. 729 at 737; *cf. Construction Industry Training Board v Att-Gen* [1971] 1 W.L.R. 1303, 1307; affirmed [1973] Ch. 173; and see *Council of Industrial Design*, [1973] Ch. Com. Rep., paras 68–70 (Council registered as a charity).
[81] *Re Pleasants* (1923) 39 T.L.R. 675 (Also the promotion of good housewifery).

culture.[82] Thus the promotion of agriculture generally, as opposed for benefiting those engaged in agriculture, was held to be charitable in *IRC v Yorkshire Agricultural Society*.[83] The preservation and improvement of fine craftsmanship is also charitable under this head.[84]

Other relevant charitable purposes are the relief of unemployment[85] and the promotion of urban and rural regeneration.[86]

Benefit of a locality

When no specific purpose is indicated, a gift in general terms for the benefit of a specified locality charitable. Gifts of this kind which have been held charitable include gifts for the benefit of a parish,[87] a ward in the City of London,[88] a county,[89] a borough or a town.[90]   **2–090**

Moreover, in *Re Smith*[91] the Court of Appeal held, that a bequest of the testator's residuary estate "unto my country England to and for—own use and benefit absolutely" was a valid gift for charitable purposes. The court followed *Nightingale v Goulbourn*,[92] where there was a gift "to the Queen's Chancellor of the Exchequer for the time being, and to be by him appropriated to the benefit and advantage of my beloved country, Great Britain." Romer L.J. considered that from the judgment of Lord Cottenham it was reasonably plain that a gift for the benefit of the country Great Britain was a good charitable gift, and that it did not cease to be a good charitable gift because the gift was to Great Britain through the Chancellor of the Exchequer.[93] The effect of *Re Smith*[94] is that a gift in

---

[82] *IRC v Yorkshire Agricultural Society* [1928] 1 K.B. 611; applied in *Brisbane City Council v Att-Gen for Queensland* [1979] A.C. 411, (P.C.) (showground); and see *Re Hadden* [1932] 1 Ch. 133. See also *Re Jacobs* (1970) 114 S.J. 515 (gifts for the planting of a grove of trees in Israel held to be charitable as promoting agriculture).

[83] [1928] 1 K.B. 611.

[84] See *IRC v White (Clerkenwell Green Association for Craftsmen)* [1980] T.R. 155.

[85] See para.2–075 above.

[86] See para.2–076 above.

[87] *West v Knight* (1669) 1 Ch.Cas. 134; *Att-Gen v Hotham (Lord)* (1823) Turn. & R. 209; *Att-Gen v Lonsdale (Earl)* (1827) 1 Sim. 105; *Att-Gen v Webster* (1875) L.R. 20 Eq. 483; *Re St. Bride's Fleet Street (Church or Parish Estate)* (1877) 35 Ch.D. 147n.; *Re St. Botolph Without Bishopsgate (Parish Estates)* (1887) 35 Ch.D. 142; *Re St. Alphage London Wall* (1888) 59 L.T. 614; *Re St. Stephen, Coleman Street* (1888) 39 Ch.D. 492; *Re St. Nicholas Acons (Parish)* (1889) 60 L.T. 532; *Re Norton's Will Trusts* [1948] 2 All E.R. 842.

[88] *Baylis v Att-Gen* (1741) 2 Atk. 239.

[89] *Att-Gen v Lonsdale (Earl)* (1827) 1 Sim. 105.

[90] *Wrexham Corporation v Tamplin* (1873) 21 W.R. 768; *Att-Gen v Dartmouth Corporation* (1883) 48 L.T. 933; *Re Baynes* [1944] 2 All E.R. 597 (gift to the Common Good Fund of the town council of Leven, Scotland); and see [1980] Ch. Com. Rep., para.92.

[91] [1932] 1 Ch. 153.

[92] (1847) 5 Hare 484; (1848) 2 Ph. 594.

[93] [1932] 1 Ch. at 174, 175. See also at 172, 173, *per* P.O. Lawrence L.J. It is submitted that the gift in *Nightingale v Goulbourn* (1847) 5 Hare 484; (1848) 2 Ph. 594 may now be supported on the further ground that, since no specific trust had been declared for the application thereof, the money had been given to the Chancellor of the Exchequer *virtute officii* and he was bound to apply it in aid of the revenue, thus relieving the taxpayer. This would have been within the spirit and intendment of the preamble; see, *e.g.* and compare *Re Garrard* [1907] 1 Ch. 382; *Re Flinn* [1948] Ch. 241; *Re Rumball* [1956] Ch. 105 (all gifts to holders of offices); and see para.2–060, above.

[94] [1932] 1 Ch. 153.

general terms for the benefit of a particular country differs in no essential respect from a similar gift for the benefit of a defined area within that country.

Where no specific purpose is indicated trusts for the benefit of all the inhabitants, or for the benefit of a particular class of the inhabitants, of a particular place are charitable. Examples of such trusts are a bequest for the native inhabitants of a town in India,[95] a trust for the freemen of a borough of the rents and profits of certain land,[96] or a trust for the free inhabitants of certain tenements in a borough.[97]

2–091   In *Goodman v Mayor of Saltash*[98] a right acquired by prescription to a several oyster fishery in a navigable tidal river was vested in the Corporation of Saltash, and this right was exercisable by the corporation and its lessees. From time immemorial the free inhabitants of ancient tenements in the borough (who were not necessarily poor) had, as of right, exercised the privilege of dredging for oysters in the river bed from February 2 until Easter Eve in each year. The free inhabitants could not claim the right by prescription as a *profit à prendre in alieno solo*, for they were a fluctuating body and were not separately incorporated, and so no grant could be presumed. The House of Lords, having sought a legal origin for the exercise of the right in question, found it by presuming that the original grant to the Corporation (which was itself a presumed grant) was subject to a trust or condition in favour of the free inhabitants of ancient tenements of the borough in accordance with the usage by them which had been proved. Lords Selborne, Cairns and Watson said that the rights vested in the free inhabitants arose under a charitable trust.[99] It seems that if the trust had not been a charitable trust it would have been void as infringing the rule against perpetuities, and that the claim of the free inhabitants would have failed.[1]

Lord Selborne said:

"A gift subject to a condition or trust for the benefit of the inhabitants of a parish or town, or of any particular class of such inhabitants, is (as I understand the law) a charitable trust: and no charitable trust can be void on the ground of perpetuity."[2]

Lord Cairns,[3] after saying that he found no difficulty in supposing a grant to the Corporation by the Crown before the time of legal memory with a condition that the free inhabitants of ancient tenements should

---

[95] *Mitford v Reynolds* (1841) 1 Ph. 185.
[96] *Re Norwich Town Charity* (1888) 40 Ch.D. 298.
[97] *Goodman v Mayor of Saltash* (1882) 7 App.Cas. 633.
[98] (1882) 7 App.Cas. 633.
[99] See (1882) 7 App.Cas. at 642 (*per* Lord Selborne), at 650 (*per* Lord Cairns) and at 665 (*per* Lord Watson).
[1] The decision was by a majority of four (Lords Selborne, Cairns, Watson and Fitzgerald) to one (Lord Blackburn).
[2] (1882) 7 App.Cas. at 642. Lord Selborne then proceeded to cite *Jones v Williams* (1767) Amb. 651, *Att-Gen v Mayor of Carlisle* (1828) 2 Sim. 437 and *Howse v Chapman* (1799) 4 Ves. 542 as his primary authorities and referred also to *Att-Gen v Heelis* (1824) 2 Sim. & St. 67 and *Att-Gen v Mayor, etc., of Dublin* (1827) 1 Bli.(N.S.) 347.
[3] (1882) 7 App.Cas. 633 at 650, 651.

enjoy the right which they had enjoyed from time immemorial continued as follows:

> "A grant of that kind . . . would be perfectly legal and perfectly intel-ligible, and there would be nothing in it which would infringe any principle of law. Such a condition would create that which in the very wide language of our courts is called a charitable, that is to say a pub-lic, trust or interest for the benefit of the free inhabitants of ancient tenements. A trust of that kind would not in any way infringe the law or rule against perpetuities, because we know very well that where you have a trust which, if it were for the benefit of private individuals or a fluctuating body of private individuals, would be void on the ground of perpetuity, yet if it creates a charitable, that is to say a pub-lic, interest, it will be free from any obnoxiousness to the rule with regard to perpetuities."[4]

It is obvious that Lord Cairns had in mind the rule that a trust for the ben-efit of private individuals or a fluctuating body of private individuals is not a charitable trust. It seems equally obvious that he and also Lord Selborne regarded the free inhabitants of the ancient tenements as a sufficiently important section of the community.

In *Peggs v Lamb*[5] two ancient trusts of rights over commons for the ben-efit of the freemen and widows of freemen of Huntingdon were upheld as charitable. In both cases it was inferred that there had been a grant to the ancient borough of Huntingdon subject to a trust in favour of the freemen and their widows. Following *Goodman v Mayor of Saltash*[6] Morritt J. considered that a lawful origin for the long usage and enjoyment by the freemen should, if reasonably possible, be presumed and such lawful origin could only be found in a charitable trust.

2–092

There are, however, problems of reconciliation, where there is a gift of rights over specified property in favour of a particular class of inhabitants in a particular area.[7] First, it is well settled that, if the trusts upon which a gift is to be held are specified and are not exclusively charitable, the gift is void, and there is a resulting trust in favour of the settlor or the testa-tor's or intestate's residuary legatee or next-of-kin, as the case may be.[8] Secondly, it is equally well settled that a trust, which would not be charitable if its area of operation extended over the whole world, does not

---

[4] The rule against perpetuities in relation to charitable trusts is considered at paras 3–019, *et seq.*, below.

[5] [1994] Ch. 172 at 186. See also *Re Christchurch Inclosure Act* (1888) 38 Ch.D. 20; *Re Norwich Town Close Estate Charity* (1888) 40 Ch.D. 298; *Att-Gen v Hyde* [2002] W.T.L.R. 1419.

[6] (1882) 7 App.Cas. 633.

[7] For a historical explanation as to how the old cases came to be decided as they were, see Geoffrey Cross, Q.C. (as he then was), "Some Recent Developments in the Law of Charity", (1956) 72 L.Q.R. 187, 200, 201. For a vigorous attack on the *Re Smith* [1932] Ch. 153 line of authority, see Albery, "Trusts for the Benefit of the Inhabitants of a Locality" (1940) 56 L.Q.R. 49.

[8] See, *e.g. Dunne v Byrne* [1912] A.C. 407; *Farley v Westminster Bank* [1939] A.C. 430; *Chichester Diocesan Fund and Board of Finance v Simpson* [1944] A.C. 341. See para.3–015, below.

become charitable merely because the area of operation is limited to a particular locality.[9]

In *Peggs v Lamb*[10] Morritt J. effected a reconciliation by determining that the trusts of the rights over the commons for the freemen in that case were not trusts for a specified charitable purpose but trusts for general purposes which were treated as being gifts for exclusively charitable purposes by being limited to the inhabitants of a particular area. He said[11]:

> "The inference[12] seem to be that whatever gives rise to the limitations on a gift for the benefit of a specified parish or town which renders it a gift for exclusively charitable purposes applies equally to a gift for the benefit of a particular class of such inhabitants."

Morritt J. stressed,[13] however, that the principle could not be applied where there is a specified purpose; in that situation the validity of the gift depends upon whether that purpose is charitable in law or not.[14] In the absence of specified purposes, the principle in *Re Smith*[15] applies and the property is applicable for charitable purposes for the benefit of the particular class of inhabitants in the specified locality.

Promotion of public recreation

2–093   Within this heading are included trusts for the encouragement of particular sports and those to provide facilities for recreational and leisure time activities, the latter purpose now largely governed by the Recreational Charities Act 1958.

2–094   **Sport**—Gifts or trusts for the encouragement or promotion of a particular game or sport in which the participants indulge for their own amusement

---

[9] *Houston v Burns* [1918] A.C. 337. The House of Lords held (in a Scottish appeal) that a bequest for public purposes to be selected by a third party would not have been charitable if it had not been limited to a particular locality, and was not rendered charitable by being limited to a particular locality. On this point English law and Scots law are the same: see *Williams' Trustees v IRC* [1947] A.C. 447 at 455, 456. See *Re Gwyon* [1930] 1 Ch. 255 (trust to apply income of a fund in clothing boys of F. and district who were not required to be at school or poor held not charitable); *Re Sanders' Will Trusts* [1954] Ch. 265 (the working classes are not poor and a gift to provide dwelling-houses for working classes in the area of P. is not charitable). See also *Re Davis* [1923] 1 Ch. 225 (residuary bequest of income in perpetuity for benefit of charitable or public institutions in Wales not charitable).

[10] [1994] Ch. 172.

[11] *ibid.*, at 195.

[12] From the speeches of Lord Selborne L.C. and Earl Cairns in *Goodman v Mayor of Saltash* (1882) 7 App.Cas. 633 and applying *Re Smith* [1932] 1 Ch. 153. Morritt J. rejected the suggested reconciliation at p.113 of the 7th ed. of this work that the particular purpose was in each case regarded as falling with the spirit and intendment of the preamble—[1994] 2 All E.R. 15 at 33–35.

[13] [1994] 2 All E.R. 15 at 35.

[14] The determination of whether the specified purposes are charitable often involves a question applying a conjunctive or a disjunctive method of construction to a list of purposes, see, for example, *Dolan v Macdermot* (1867) L.R. Eq 60; Re Allen [1905] 2 Ch. 400; *Houston v Burns* [1918] A.C. 337 and see para.3–017, below.

[15] [1932] 1 Ch. 153 at 169, *per* Lord Hanworth.

may be indirectly beneficial to the community to which they belong, but the purpose is not within the spirit and intendment of the preamble and, therefore, is not a charitable purpose. Thus, a gift to apply the income of a fund for ever in providing a prize for the encouragement of yacht racing was held not charitable but void as a perpetuity.[16] Similarly, trusts to promote the teaching of cricket,[17] or to promote angling[18] and foxhunting[19] have been held to be not charitable. Despite recent extensions of the circumstances in which the provision of sporting facilities can be charitable, the law remains that promotion of a particular sport for its own sake is not charitable.[20]

The encouragement of sport will be charitable, however, if it is part of a wider purpose which is itself charitable. Thus, a trust to promote sport in a specified regiment is charitable as tending to promote the physical efficiency of the armed forces.[21] It seems clear that the promotion of games and sports which are calculated to increase the efficiency of the police must be regarded as a purpose that is charitable in the same sense.[22] Similarly, a trust to encourage sport either in a particular school[23] or among young people at schools and universities generally[24] will be charitable as a trust for the advancement of education.[25] On the same reasoning, whilst the encouragement of chess as a game is not a charitable purpose,[26] a gift for the purpose of encouraging young people to play chess is educational and so charitable.[27]

There is now greater emphasis on the role of sport in promoting health and this caused the Charity Commissioners to re-examine charitable status in this area.[28] They concluded that the promotion of community participation in healthy recreation by providing facilities, including the organisation of sporting activity, for playing particular sports was charitable.[29] There is strong authority for this conclusion based on the cases which provide that the provision of facilities for the public for healthy recreation is charitable.[30] The comments of members of the Court of

---

[16] *Re Nottage* [1895] 2 Ch. 649. See [1989] Ch. Com. Rep., paras 48–55 (rejection of charitable status for the Birchfield Harriers).

[17] *Re Patten* [1929] 2 Ch. 276.

[18] *Re Clifford* (1911) 106 L.T. 14.

[19] *Peterborough Foxhound Show Society v IRC* [1936] 2 K.B. 497. *Re Thompson* [1934] Ch. 342 (where a legacy to a named person to be applied by him towards the promotion of fox hunting was ordered to be paid to the legatee upon his giving an undertaking to apply the legacy as directed by the will, and the residuary legatee was given liberty to apply to the court if the undertaking were broken) is not inconsistent with the case last cited.

[20] But see the separate tax relief for community amateur sports clubs, Finance Act 2002, s.59 and Sch.18.

[21] *Re Gray* [1925] Ch. 362. See para.2–079, above and (1993) 1 Ch. Com. Dec., p.4 (rifle clubs).

[22] IRC v City of Glasgow Police Athletic Association [1953] A.C. 380 at 391, 401, 402. See para.2–080, above.

[23] *Re Mariette* [1915] 2 Ch. 284 (a gift to build fives court and to provide a prize for athletic sports at a public school).

[24] *IRC v McMullen* [1981] A.C. 1 (the Football Association Youth Trust). See (1985) 1 Trust L. & P. 22 (D. Evans).

[25] See para.2–022, above.

[26] *Re Swann* (1908) 99 L.T. 604.

[27] *Re Dupree's Deed Trusts* [1945] Ch. 16. This case is very near the line.

[28] See CC Consultation paper, *The Promotion of Sport* (2001).

[29] See CC, *Charitable Status and Sport* (2002).

[30] *Re Hadden* [1932] 1 Ch. 133; *Re Morgan* [1955] 1 W.L.R. 738; *Shillington v Portadown UDC* [1911] 1 I.R. 247 and see para.2–096 below.

Appeal in *Re Nottage*[31] that they regarded the promotion of sport as non-charitable even though there were clear health benefits can be disregarded as obiter dicta as the case was concerned with whether the promotion of a particular sport, yacht racing, was charitable, not whether the promotion of sport was charitable where it advanced health. Clearly, the promotion of facilities for all sports will not be charitable within the wider charitable purposes of promotion of healthy recreation. Some sports such as walking and athletics obviously promote health but other such as billiards and motor sport do not and some dangerous sports can be adverse to health.[32] The usual rules as to public benefit apply in determining if a particular community amateur sports club is charitable. Thus the sports facilities should be available to the community; the cost of equipment and undue emphasis on competition should not be a bar to participation.[33] Similarly, restrictions on membership should be no more than is necessary to enable the sports club to operate effectively.[34]

2–095   The Strategy Unit report proposed that the advancement of amateur sport should be charitable and that "sport" should be defined as encompassing activities involving an element of physical skill which promote and maintain health.[35] Although sports clubs would have to show that they provided a public benefit before they were charitable, selection of members on the basis of ability or the presence of social members would not be an automatic bar to charitable status.[36]

2–096   **Public recreation**—A gift of land for the purposes of public recreation is charitable. Statute[37] had long impliedly recognised this before the decision of Clauson J. in *Re Hadden*.[38] Following *Re Hadden*, Harman J. in *Re Morgan*[39] upheld as charitable a bequest of a fund for the provision of a public recreation ground for the inhabitants of a particular parish. In Northern Ireland, it has been held that the purpose of providing the means of healthy recreation for the inhabitants of a particular town is

---

[31] [1895] 2 Ch. 649 at 655, *per* Lindley L.J., 656, *per* Lopes L.J.

[32] CC, *Charitable Status and Sport* (2002), paras 10–11, 22–25.

[33] *ibid.*, paras 26–28.

[34] *ibid.*, paras 15–21.

[35] Cabinet Office, Strategy Unit, *Private Action, Public Benefit. A Review of Charities and the Wider-Not-For Profit Sector* (2002). p.39.

[36] *ibid.*, p.43 and Cabinet Office, Strategy Unit, *Private Action, Public Benefit. Sport and Charitable Status.*

[37] Recreation Grounds Act 1859, The Mortmain and Charitable Uses Act 1888, ss.13(1) 4 and 6(4)(i), and the Open Spaces Act 1906, ss.3 and 5(1); see *IRC v Baddeley* [1955] A.C. 572 at 595 *per* Lord Reid. Whilst the Act of 1859 has been repealed by Charities Act 1960, s.39 and Sch.5, and the Act of 1888 has been repealed by s.48 and Sch.7 to the Act of 1960, this has not altered the substantive law. See also *Laverstoke Property Co. Ltd v Peterborough Corporation* [1972] 1 W.L.R. 1400 (conveyance of land under Open Spaces Act 1906, s.10, charitable).

[38] [1932] 1 Ch. 133 (provision of open air recreation for working people). See also *Re Foakes* (1933) February 21, unreported but cited in *IRC v Baddeley* [1955] A.C. 572 at 596 and *Re Chesters* (1936) July 25, unreported but edited *ibid.*

[39] [1955] 1 W.L.R. 738. See also [1984] Ch. Com. Rep, paras. 19–25 (provision of a public ice-rink) and *Bath and North East Somerset Council v Att-Gen* [2002] E.W.H.C. 1623 but *cf. Liverpool CC v Attorney General, The Times*, May 1, 1994 (recreation ground but no charitable intent).

charitable.[40] The provision of a recreation ground for the employees of a particular employer is clearly not charitable, however, as it lacks the necessary element of general public utility.[41]

The leading case is the decision of the House of Lords in *IRC v Baddeley*[42] which concerned two deeds of conveyance bearing the same duty by which certain trusts were declared of certain property thereby respectively conveyed. If the trusts so declared were charitable, stamp duty would have been smaller than if they were not charitable.[43] By the first of the deeds some land, on which were a mission church, lecture room and store, was conveyed to trustees upon trust to permit the premises to be used for the promotion of the religious, *social*[44] and physical well-being of persons resident in the boroughs of West Ham and Leyton by the provision of facilities for religious services and instruction and for the social and physical training and recreation of such aforementioned persons who were and were likely, in the opinion of specified persons, to become members of the Methodist Church and were of insufficient means otherwise to enjoy the advantages provided and by promoting and encouraging all forms of such activities as were calculated to contribute to the health and well-being of such persons. By the second deed four pieces of land were conveyed to the same trustees upon almost the same trusts; the only significant difference was that the trustees were to permit the pieces of land to be used for the moral (instead of religious) and physical well-being of the same class of persons, who may be shortly described as actual or potential Methodists resident in the specified areas.

The House of Lords[45] held that the trusts of the two conveyances were not charitable. The *ratio decidendi*, upon which Viscount Simonds, Lord Porter, Lord Tucker and Lord Somervell were all agreed[46] was that the trusts were not for the relief of poverty or for the advancement of education or religion,[47] and that the trusts did not fall within the fourth head of charity ("other purposes beneficial to the community") since the language

---

[40] *Shillington v Portadown UDC* [1911] 1 I.R. 247; and see the unreported cases of *Re Foakes and Re Chesters* (referred to by Lord Reid in *IRC v Baddeley* [1955] A.C. 572 at 596). See also *IRC v City of London* [1953] 1 W.L.R. 652 (the preservation of Epping Forest as an open space for the benefit of the public, under the Epping Forest Act 1878, is a charitable purpose); *Re Alexandra Park and Palace Acts, Alexandra Park Trustees v. Haringey London Borough Council* (1967) 111 S.J. 515 (a trust the main purpose of which was that Alexandra Park should be maintained as an open space for the free use and recreation of the public was charitable); *cf. Richmond-upon-Thames London BC v Att-Gen* (1983) L.G.R. 151 (gift of land to a vestry was not subject to charitable trusts; the land was transferred to the vestry in its capacity as an urban authority under the Public Health Act 1875).

[41] *Wernher's Charitable Trust (Trustees of) v IRC* [1937] 2 All E.R. 488. See also *Re Drummond* [1914] 2 Ch. 90; *Re Hobourn Aero Components Ltd's Air Raid Distress Fund* [1946] Ch. 194; *Oppenheim v Tobacco Securities Trusts Co. Ltd* [1951] A.C. 297; *Vernon v IRC* [1956] 1 W.L.R. 1169.

[42] [1955] A.C. 572.

[43] *ibid.* at 583, 584.

[44] Editors' italics.

[45] [1955] A.C. 572.

[46] Lord Reid dissenting.

[47] At no stage in the case's progress through the courts was it argued that the trusts were for the advancement of religion: see *Neville Estates Ltd. v Madden* [1962] Ch. 832 at 852, *per* Cross J.

in which they were expressed was so vague as to permit the property to be used for the purposes which the law did not regard as charitable.[48] It appears that the references to social well-being played an important and even a decisive part[49] in leading the majority of the House of Lords to the conclusion that the trusts as declared did not fall within the spirit and intendment of the preamble.[50] Viscount Simonds summed up his conclusion by describing the purpose of the trust as being "to establish a community centre in which social intercourse and discreet festivity may go hand in hand with religious observance and instruction." The majority of their Lordships regarded the objects of the trust as the establishment of a "community centre". All that they decided was that a centre of that kind was not a charity, and it is quite clear that their Lordships' decision would have been the same even if the centre had been open to all residents in the two boroughs who might wish to use it. The majority decision is no authority for the proposition that a trust to provide recreational facilities for the Methodists (or other limited classes of persons such as members of the Church of England, Roman Catholics, or Jews, or persons engaged in specified trades, businesses or callings) resident in a defined area is not charitable; and there seems to be no reported decision which establishes that proposition. It appears that the sole authority for that proposition must be found in the admittedly weighty dicta of Viscount Simonds[51] and Lord Somervell of Harrow.[52] It is submitted that Viscount Simonds' view is correct and that, apart from the Recreational Charities Act 1958, a trust for the provision of recreational facilities will not be valid if any special personal qualifications on the part of the beneficiaries is required, that is, if the requirement of public benefit is not satisfied.

2–097   The *ratio decidendi* in the *Baddeley* case is in line with the decision of the Court of Appeal in Nothern Ireland in *Londonderry Presbyterian Church House Trustees v IRC*[53] where the court declined to hold that a trust to permit certain premises to be used as a hall for meetings or for social or recreational purposes in connection with various Presbyterian churches in a specified area was charitable. It is also in line with the House of Lords' earlier decision in *Williams' Trustees v IRC*,[54] where an institute for Welsh people in London was held to be in the nature of a social club and not to be a charity.

2–098   **Recreational Charities Act 1958**—The decision in *IRC v Baddeley*[55] called in question the status of a very large number of institutions, including in particular a great number of village halls, the trusts of which contained language similar to that which was considerd by the House of Lords in

---

[48] It is clear that their Lordships had the preamble to the Charitable Uses Act 1601 in the forefront of their minds.

[49] See *Neville Estates Ltd. v Madden* [1962] Ch. 832 at 851, 852.

[50] See [1955] A.C. 572 at 586, *per* Viscount Simonds, at 613, *per* Lord Tucker and at 616, *per* Lord Somervell.

[51] [1955] A.C. at 589, 590.

[52] [1955] A.C. at 615.

[53] [1946] N.I. 178.

[54] [1947] A.C. 447.

[55] [1955] A.C. 572.

that case and which had long been considered to be charitable. Doubts were thus raised as to the charitable status of a large number of trusts and the situation was sufficiently serious for the Government to promote a Bill which, in the words of the explanatory memorandum accompanying it, had as its object the giving of "statutory recognition to the charitable nature of certain trusts and institutions which exist for the purposes of providing recreational or similar facilities, or whose purposes include the provision of such facilities in the interests of social welfare." That Bill became law as the Recreational Charities Act 1958,[56] on March 13, 1958.

S.1(1) of the Act declares that, subject to the provisions of that Act "it shall be and be deemed always to have been charitable to provide, or assist in the provision of, facilities for recreation or other leisure-time occupation, if the facilities are provided in the interests of social welfare."

The words "other leisure-time occupation" were intended to give a wide meaning to the word "recreation" and extend the application of the Act to recreation in its widest sense; not merely participation in sports, games or other forms of physical exercise. Debate on the Bill made reference to social intercourse and reading.[57]

The proviso, at the end of subs.(1), that nothing in s.1 shall be taken to derogate from the principle that a trust or institution to be charitable must be for the public benefit is the clearest possible declaration of the well-established and overriding principle that a trust is only charitable if it benefits the community or a sufficiently important section of the community.[58]   **2–099**

It is a condition precedent that the facilities should be provided "in the interests of social welfare". The words "social welfare"[59] are explained, though not defined,[60] in s.1(2). The requirement that the facilities must be provided in the interests of social welfare is not satisfied unless:

(a) the facilities are provided with the object of improving the conditions of life for the persons for whom the facilities are primarily intended; and

(b) either—

    (i) those persons have need of such facilities as aforesaid by reason of their youth, age, infirmity or disablement, poverty or social and economic circumstances; or

---

[56] (1959) 23 Conv(N.S.) 15 (S.G. Maurice); (1958) 21 M.L.R. 534 (L. Price); [1980] Conv. 173 (J. Warburton).

[57] See 582 H. of C. Off. Rep. 323, Mr Renton.

[58] Thus the trust in *IRC v Baddeley* [1955] A.C. 572 would probably still fail on the grounds that that class of beneficiaries is too limited to satisfy the conditions of public benefit; see para.2–072, above.

[59] The meaning of "social welfare" has been considered in a number of cases on s.8(1)(a) of the Rating and Valuation Act 1955 (repealed by s.29(2)(a) of the Rating and Valuation Act 1961, and now replaced by s.47 of the Local Government Finance Act 1988; see *National Deposit Friendly Society Trustees v Skegness UDC* [1959] A.C. 293; *Berry v St. Marylebone BC* [1958] Ch. 406; *Skegness UDC v Derbyshire Miners' Welfare Committee* [1959] A.C. 807; *General Nursing Council for England and Wales v St. Marylebone BC* [1959] A.C. 540. And see also (1959) 23 Conv.(N.S.) 365 (D.W.M. Waters).

[60] But see *IRC v McMullen* [1978] 1 W.L.R. 644 at 675, where Walton J. considered that "social welfare" was "in effect defined in section 1(2) of the 1958 Act".

(ii)   the facilities are to be available to the members or the female members[61] of the public at large.

Thus, before facilities may be said to be provided in the interests of social welfare they must satisfy three conditions:

(a)   be provided with the object of improving the conditions of the intended beneficiaries; and

(b)   be of a type capable of improving conditions of life; and

(c)   be provided for either the public at large or person falling within one of the specified categories.

The first condition requires that the facilities are supplied as a matter of social obligation to fulfil a social need. In addition, because the intended beneficiaries are defined in s.1(2)(b) as those in special need or the public at large, the facilities must be provided altruistically and not for the benefit of the founders.[62] Judicial interpretation of the phrase "social welfare" in other contexts has also highlighted the need for facilities to be provided to meet social needs[63] and as a matter of social obligation.[64]

2–100   With regard to the second condition, it is considered that the facilities must be of a type which are in themselves capable of improving the conditions of the recipients.[65] It is not sufficient that the trustees intend, subjectively, to improve conditions of life; the test is an objective one.[66] Facilities which are likely to meet such an objective test are those whose dominant feature is that they reduce social exclusion and encourage public participation or improve education or health where previously no, or no adequate, facilities existed.[67]

The persons for whom the facilities are primarily intended must be young,[68] old, infirm or disabled,[69] or be cut off from their homes or usual

---

[61] Inserted to protect womens' institutes. A club restricted to men only is not charitable: see [1965] Ch. Com. Rep., App.C (Wollerton Working Men's Club, Salop); *cf.* [1965] Ch. Com.Rep., App.C (Fowey Working Men's Institute; no restriction to men only).

[62] See RR4, *The Recreational Charities Act 1958* (2000), paras A14–A15.

[63] See *National Deposit Friendly Society Trustees v Skegness UDC* [1959] A.C. 293 at 314, *per* Lord MacDermott.

[64] See *General Nursing Council for England and Wales v St Marylebone BC* [1958] 1 Ch. 421 at 436, *per* Lord Evershed.

[65] Facilities capable of merely making life more enjoyable would not appear to be sufficient.

[66] See *Commissioners of Valuation for Northern Ireland v Lurgan Borough Council* [1968] N.I. 104 where the Court of Appeal for Northern Ireland considered not only the wording of the trust deed but also whether the work of the trust had in fact improved conditions of life in determining whether s.1(2)(a) of the Recreational Charities (Northern Ireland) 1958 had been satisfied. The Recreational Charities (Northern Ireland) Act 1958, s.1 is in precisely the same terms as the English Act. See also *Trustees of the Belfast Young Men's Christian Association v Commissioner of Valuation for Northern Ireland* [1969] N.I. 324, *per* Lord Curran. This objective approach would also seem to coincide with previous decisions as to the meaning of "social welfare" in cases on s.89(1)(a) of the Rating and Valuation Act 1955; see para.2–089 n.59 above.

[67] See RR4, *The Recreational Charities Act 1958* (2000), para.A8.

[68] See [1966] Ch. Com. Rep., App.A (Brockham Day Nursery registered as a charity, *inter alia*, under the 1958 Act).

[69] See [1965] Ch. Com. Rep., App.C (Manchester and District Social Club of the Blind registered as a charity) and [1990] Ch. Com. Rep., para.36 (British Paralympic Association).

social environment and unable by their unaided effort to provide themselves with adequate facilities for occupying themselves during their leisure-time.[70] If the facilities are provided for the young, old, etc., no further element of deprivation is required; the Act contemplates youth, age, etc, as a sufficient condition requiring relief.[71] The public benefit test, however, still has to be satisfied and this may be problematic if the particular restricted class is limited.[72]

By s.1(2)(b)(ii) the persons for whom the benefits are provided may be the members or the female members[73] of the public at large.[74]

No further element of deprivation is needed in such a case for the requirement of social welfare to be satisfied. Lord Keith of Kinkel in *Guild v IRC*[75] said, when considering a gift to the Sports Centre in North Berwick: **2–101**

> "I would reject the argument that the facilities are not provided in the interests of social welfare unless they are provided with the object of improving the conditions of life for persons who suffer from some form of social disadvantage. It suffices if they are provided with the object of improving the conditions of life for members of the community generally."

A community centre serving a housing estate was found to serve a sufficient section of the public in *Springhill Housing Action Committee v Commissioner of Valuation*.[76] The words "at large" make it clear that no person otherwise eligible to benefit may be excluded because he or she lacks some personal qualification.

The fact that the actual enjoyment of the facilities is restricted to persons identified by their membership of particular clubs or organisations does not mean automatic failure of the public benefit requirement.[77] However, if an organisation providing the facility of a sports centre, for example, operates a membership scheme, it will probably only satisfy the criterion of public benefit if the membership structure is adopted only as a matter of administrative convenience for the better delivery of benefits, rather than as a means of limiting them and the membership is in practice open to all who wish to join.[78] But community associations and

---

[70] Merchant seamen in foreign ports (*i.e.* foreign to them) and members of the armed forces of the Crown serving overseas would seem to come within the last five words of 1(2)(b)(i); and see *Wynn v Skegness UDC* [1967] 1 W.L.R. 52.

[71] *Guild v IRC* [1992] 2 All E.R. 10 at 17, *per* Lord Keith of Kinkel rejecting Walton J.'s remarks to the contrary in *IRC v McMullen* [1978] 1 W.L.R. 664 at 675 and upholding Bridge L.J.'s comments thereon in the Court of Appeal [1979] 1 W.L.R. 130 at 142.

[72] See RR4, *The Recreational Charities Act 1958* (2000), para.A29.

[73] There would appear to be a conflict between this limitation and ECHR principles.

[74] Any provision restricting benefits to club members must be purely for administrative convenience for the better delivery of benefits with membership in practice open to all who wish to join and not, in effect, creating a private group—see RR4, *The Recreational Charities Act 1958* (2000), paras A30, *et seq.*

[75] [1992] 2 All E.R. 10 at 18.

[76] [1983] N.I. 184.

[77] See *Bath and North East Somerset Council v Att-Gen* [2002] E.W.H.C. 1623, para.31, *per* Hart J.

[78] See RR4, *The Recreational Charities Act 1958* (2000), paras A30–A33.

recreational organisations established primarily for identifiable racial minority groups will be charitable if it can be shown that the group in question is in special need of those facilities.[79]

Subs.(3) gives examples of the type of trust covered by the section by providing that, subject to the requirement referred to, subs.(1):

> ". . . applies in particular to the provision of facilities at village halls, community centres and women's institutes, and to the provision and maintenance of grounds and buildings to be used for purposes of recreation or leisure-time occupation, and extends to the provision of facilities for those purposes by the organising of any activity."

The concluding words of the subsection, "and extends to the provision of facilities for those purposes by the organising of any activity" brings within the scope of the Act national organisations like The National Council of Voluntary Organisations which, while not themselves directly providing recreational facilities, provide the organisation and administration whereby they may be provided.

2–102   S.2 of the Recreational Charities Act is concerned with the rather specialised case of trusts declared before December 17, 1957 which required or purported to require property to be held for the purposes of activities which are social welfare activities within the meaning of the Miners' Welfare Act 1952. If at that date the whole or part of the property held on those trusts or of any property held with that property represented an application of moneys standing to the credit of the miners' welfare fund or moneys provided by the Coal Industry Social Welfare Organisation, those trusts are to be treated as if they were and always had been charitable (subs.(1)).[80] For the purposes of the section property held on the same trusts as other property is to be deemed to be held with it, though vested in different trustees (subs.(2)).

Promotion of mental or moral improvement

2–103   A number of purposes which have been held to be charitable can be grouped together as tending to promote mental or moral improvement. In some instances there is an element of temporal benefit to the community although the main purpose is mental or moral improvement.

In *Re Scowcroft*[81] Stirling J. held that a devise to the vicar for the time being of B. of a building used in the testator's lifetime as a village club and reading-room "to be maintained for the furtherance of Conservative principles and religious and mental improvement" was a good charitable gift. The furtherance of religious and mental improvement was an essential portion of the gift and the gift might, as the judge observed, be supported on the ground that it was for the public benefit just as the gift of a library

---

[79] See (1995) 4 Ch. Com. Dec., pp.17–21.
[80] See *Wynn v Skegness UDC* [1967] 1 W.L.R. 52.
[81] [1898] 2 Ch. 638.

or museum would have been held to be a good charitable gift. Thus the decision did not depend solely on the element of mental improvement, since there was also an element of general public utility. Similar considerations applied in *Re Hood*[82] to a gift for the promotion of temperance otherwise than by political means. Both elements were present.

In *Re Price*[83] the charitable character of the bequest depended exclusively on the element of moral improvement. A testatrix gave one-half of her residuary estate to an unincorporated association called the Anthroposophical Society of Great Britain to be used at the discretion of the Society's chairman and executive council for carrying on the teachings of the founder, Dr Rudolph Steiner. If Cohen J.'s first *ratio decidendi* was correct, it was not necessary for his Lordship to determine whether or not the trust was charitable, for he was satisfied that, although there was not an absolute gift to the Society, the Society was at liberty to spend capital as well as income in carrying out the trusts of the bequest. Therefore, no perpetuity was created and the bequest was valid.[84] However, the question whether the purposes of the gift were charitable was fully argued and the arguments were fully considered by Cohen J., who said that he would have been prepared to hold that the trusts were charitable.

Cohen J. considered,[85] first whether the gift would or might be operative   **2–104** for the public benefit and, secondly, whether the court could control the administration of the trust, and he answered both questions in the affirmative. The evidence before the court consisted of an affidavit of the teacher in the principal school conducted on Dr. Steiner's educational principles, in which those principles were formulated and explained, and in which the witness deposed as to the beneficial effect of those teachings on himself, and also of an affidavit by another gentleman who also deposed as to the beneficial effect on him of the teachings. On the evidence of the actual teachings apart from the evidence of benefit to individuals, Cohen J. was satisfied that the teachings were directed to the mental or moral improvement of man and that they were not *contra bonos mores*. He held as a matter of law that the court was not concerned to determine whether the carrying on of the teachings of Rudolph Steiner would in fact result in the mental or moral improvement of anyone, and he did not find as a fact that they would. His Lordship's only finding of fact was that the teachings might have that result, and his conclusion of law was that this was sufficient to satisfy the requirement of public benefit.

Although Cohen J. considered that the trusts of the residuary gift resembled trusts for the advancement of religion, he treated the gift as falling under Lord Macnaghten's fourth head of charity.

---

[82] [1931] 1 Ch. 240. See also *IRC v Falkirk Temperance Cafe Trust*, 1927, S.C. 261 at 269. The promotion of temperance by political action is not a charitable purpose; *IRC v Temperance Council of Christian Churches of England and Wales* (1926) 136 L.T. 27.

[83] [1943] Ch. 422.

[84] See *Leahy v Att-Gen for New South Wales* [1959] A.C. 457; *Neville Estates Ltd. v Madden* [1962] Ch. 832 at 849; see also *Re Recher's Will Trusts* [1972] Ch. 526. *Re Lipinski's Will Trusts* [1976] Ch. 235; *Re Grant's Will Trusts* [1980] 1 W.L.R. 360.

[85] See *Re Hummeltenberg* [1923] Ch. 237 at 240, 241.

In *Re South Place Ethical Society*,[86] Dillon J. held, as an alternative ground for his decision,[87] by analogy with *Re Scowcroft*,[88] *Re Hood*[89] and *Re Price*,[90] that the objects of the Society were charitable within the fourth head of Lord Macnaghten's classification as being for mental or moral improvement.

2–105   None of the cases considered provide a reasoned argument for the promotion of mental and moral improvement as a general charitable purpose, nor do they set any guidelines for the future application of this category of charity although the overall purpose is now fully acceptable as charitable. The Charity Commissioners have suggested[91] that *Re Price*[92] and *Re South Place Ethical Society*[93] provide authority for saying that an organisation that disseminates ideas which are broadly philosophical and which are generally accessible to and can be applied within the community and which can be adopted freely from time to time according to individual choice or judgment by member of the public should be charitable. Such a purpose is compatible with ECHR principles[94] if charitable status is not denied because the organisation is promoting a belief system which is not a religion in terms of English charity law or because membership or adherence to the organisation is not necessary.[95]

The Charity Commissioners have determined that the promotion of racial harmony is charitable by analogy to the promotion of moral or spiritual welfare or improvement.[96] In particular, the Community Security Trust was registered with one of its objects being the promotion of good race relations between the Jewish community and other members of society by working towards the elimination of racism in the form of anti-Semitism.[97] Similarly, trusts to support equal rights for women[98] and homosexuals[99] have been registered. By analogy, the Charity Commissioners have recognised that the promotion of religious harmony for the benefit of the public is a charitable purpose.[1]

The Charity Commissioners have also entered on the register a number of trusts within this category as promoting good citizenship.[2] In relation to the The Earl Mountbatten of Burma Statue Appeal Trust they considered that[3]:

---

[86] [1980] 1 W.L.R. 1565.
[87] See para.2–021, above.
[88] [1898] 2 Ch. 638.
[89] [1931] 1 Ch. 240.
[90] [1943] Ch. 422.
[91] [1999] Ch. Com. Dec. November 17 (The Church of Scientology), p.29.
[92] [1943] Ch. 422.
[93] [1980] 1 W.L.R. 1565.
[94] For the relevant ECHR Articles, see para.2–050 above.
[95] [1999] Ch. Com. Dec. November 17, p.35.
[96] [1983] Ch. Com. Rep., paras 15–20. See *Latimer v C.I.R.* [2002] 3 N.Z.L.R. 195 at 209.
[97] (1995) 4 Ch. Com. Dec., pp.8–12.
[98] See *Halpin v Seear* (1976) unreported, considered in [1977] Ch. Com. Rep., paras 34–36 (The Women's Service Trust)
[99] CC, *The Promotion of Human Rights* (2002), para.16 referring to The Gay Civil Liberties Trust.
[1] CC, *Promotion of Religious Harmony for the Benefit of the Public* (2002).
[2] See, for example, [1984] Ch. Comm. Rep., para.17 (provision of plaques commemorating police officers killed during the execution of their duties).
[3] [1981] Ch. Com. Rep., paras 68–70.

"the provision of a statue might be held to have a sufficient element of public benefit where the person being commemorated was nationally, and internationally, respected and could be said to be a figure of historical importance. In such a case the provision and maintenance of a statue can be held to be charitable as likely to foster patriotism and good citizenship, and to be an incentive to heroic and noble deeds."

The promotion of good citizenship can cover the promotion of public participation in the prevention of crime, particularly than which is racially motivated.[4]

The Commissioners have indicated that they regard the promotion of ethical standards of conduct by organisations as charitable within this category.[5] The promotion of the sound administration of the law can also be regarded as charitable as being for the promotion of moral improvement.[6]   **2–106**

By analogy with the promotion of moral improvement, the Charity Commissioners have concluded that the promotion of human rights is a charitable purpose.[7] Human rights are seen as fundamental to the proper functioning of society and respect for human rights is generally seen as a moral imperative.[8] Human rights may be promoted in a number of ways and some specific purposes, such as the relief of need of those suffering from human rights abuses and advancing education of human rights, are clearly charitable under other heads.[9] The acceptance of the wider purpose of the promotion of human rights as charitable does not mean, however, that the usual limitations can be ignored and, for example, any educational material must have educational value and not be propagandist.[10] Similarly, the limitation on political purposes[11] applies. Thus an organisation whose purposes include seeking to change the law or government policy to enforce human rights in a foreign country which does not have human rights enshrined in its domestic law will not be charitable. Human rights cover a very wide spectrum and it must not automatically be assumed that a trust for the promotion of human rights in any jurisdiction will satisfy the requirement of public benefit even if the purpose is not political. The advancement of education of human rights as understood and practised in this country, for example, may not be for the overall public benefit of people living in a completely different culture.[12]

The Strategy Unit report proposed that the promotion of human rights, conflict resolution and reconciliation should be a charitable purpose.[13] For

---

[4] See (1995) 4 Ch. Com. Dec., pp.8–12 (Community Security Trust).
[5] See (1994) 2 Ch. Com. Dec., pp.5, *et seq.* (Public Concern at Work).
[6] [1996] Ch. Com. Rep., paras 60–65 (JUSTICE).
[7] See CC, *The Promotion of Human Rights* (2002) and see *Public Trustee v Att-Gen of New South Wales* (1997) 42 N.S.W.L.R. 600.
[8] *ibid.*, para.17.
[9] See *McGovern v Att-Gen* [1982] Ch. 321.
[10] See paras 2–030—2–031 above.
[11] See paras (2–035 *et seq.*) above.
[12] See CC, *The Promotion of Human Rights* (2002), para.13.
[13] Cabinet Office, Strategy Unit, *Private Action, Public Benefit. A Review of Charities and the Wider Not-For-Profit Sector* (2002), p.39.

this purpose promotion of conflict resolution and reconciliation is distinguished from the promotion of pacifism.[14] The report does not propose
that charities with these purposes would be allowed to have political purposes but they would be allowed to carry out political activities subject to
the usual safeguards.[15]

Protection or benefit of animals

2–107   Gifts and trusts for the protection and benefit of animals[16] do not
appear to have been much considered by the court before the middle of the
nineteenth century. It seems probable that if they had been considered at
an earlier date the court would only have upheld as charitable gifts or
trusts for the protection and benefit of animals useful to man, on the
ground that the purposes were of general public utility.[17] It is now
accepted that a gift for the protection or benefit of animals, irrespective of
whether or not they are useful to man, is prima facie a charitable gift
because "it tends to promote and encourage kindness towards them, to
discourage cruelty, and to ameliorate the condition of the brute creation,
and thus to stimulate humane and generous sentiments in man towards
the lower animals, and by these means promote feelings of humanity and
morality generally, repress brutality, and thus elevate the human race."[18]
Thus the benefit to mankind is indirect.[19]

Thus in *London University v Yarrow*[20] Lord Cranworth L.C., with whose
judgment Knight Bruce and Turner L.JJ. concurred, was satisfied that the
establishment of a hospital in which animals useful to mankind should be
properly treated and cured and the nature of their diseases investigated,
with a view to public advantage, was a charity. In the judgment the emphasis was on the aspect of public utility. Again, some years after the court
had begun to apply the wider ground of moral improvement, it was
stated in *Re Douglas*[21] that the Home for Lost Dogs was a charity, and the
usefulness of dogs to mankind was emphasised.

Gifts to the Society for the Prevention of Cruelty to Animals,[22] the Home
for Lost Dogs,[23] the Dublin Home for Starving and Forsaken Cats,[24] the

---

[14] *ibid.*, p.43.
[15] See para.2–043 above.
[16] For trusts for conservation generally, including animals, see para.2–081 above.
[17] See *Att-Gen v Whorwood* (1750) I. Ves.Sen. 534 at 536.
[18] See *Re Wedgwood* [1915] 1 Ch. 113 at 122, *per* Swinfen Eady L.J.; *National Anti-Vivisection Society v IRC* [1948] A.C. 31 at 67, *per* Lord Simonds.
[19] See *IRC v Baddeley* [1955] A.C. 572 at 590.
[20] (1857) 1 De G. & J. 72.
[21] (1887) 35 Ch.D. 472 at 478, 479, *per* Kay J. and at 487, *per* Lindley L.J. Although the obser-
vations referred to were *obiter* they were obviously correct: see *Adamson v Melbourne and Metropolitan Board of Works* [1929] A.C. 142 at 148.
[22] *Tatham v Drummond* (1864) 4 De G.J. & Sm. 484. *Armstrong v Reeves* (1890) 25 L.R.Ir 325.
See also *Re Greens Will Trust* [1985] 3 All E.R. 455.
[23] *Re Douglas* (1887) 35 Ch.D. 472; *Adamson v Melbourne and Metropolitan Board of Works* [1929] A.C. 142; *Re Moss* [1949] 1 All E.R. 495 at 498.
[24] *Swifte v Att-Gen for Ireland (No. 2)* [1912] 1 I.R. 133.

CHAPTER 3

LEGAL STRUCTURES

INTRODUCTION

After the Statute of Uses in 1535,[1] general charitable uses became fre-   **3–001**
quent and the majority of charities are effected through the medium of a
charitable trust. The desire for limited liability led many charities, from the
late nineteenth century[2] onwards, to adopt the structure of a company; a
large number of charities are now registered in the form of a company limited by guarantee. The third common form of legal structure used by charities is an unincorporated association. In addition to the three structures
of common application, charities may also exist as friendly societies,
industrial and provident societies, or as a corporation, including eleemosynary corporations and substantial charities having a clear public purpose
may be established as charitable corporations by statute,[3] Church
Measure[4] or Royal Charter.[5]

The creation of a charity as a trust, company or unincorporated association is considered below together with an outline of the other forms of
legal structure.[5a] The construction of gifts for charitable purposes is
considered in the next chapter.

TRUSTS

The creation of a charity by dedication of property through the medium   **3–002**
of an express trust has been accepted since at least the sixteenth century.

> "The limitation of a use to the poor of the parish of Dale is good
> though no corporation; for though they are capable of no property at
> common law in the thing trusted, because . . . no indefinite multitude

---

[1] Repealed by the Law of Property Act, 1925, s.207 and Sch.7.
[2] After the Companies Act 1862.
[3] See, for example, *Construction Industry Training Board v Att-Gen* [1973] Ch. 173 (under the Industrial Training Act 1964).
[4] See, for example, Church Commissioners Measure 1947.
[5] See, for example, *Royal College of Surgeons of England v National Provincial Bank* [1952] A.C. 631.
[5a] For a consideration of the factors governing choice of structure, see (1994) 2 C.L.P.R. 131 (Hill).

without public allowance can take by a general name, yet they are capable of a trust."[6]

The trust does not have to be complete provided the overriding intention of the donor is charitable. The court will provide a mode by way of scheme if the objects or purposes have not been defined[7] and if no trustees are selected the Sovereign becomes the trustee by virtue of his or her prerogative as *parens patriae*.[8]

Statutory formalities

3–003   S.53(1)(b) of the Law of Property Act 1925 provides that a declaration of trust respecting any land or interest in land must be manifested and proved by some writing signed by some person who is able to declare such trust or by his will.[9] The usual form of writing is a declaration of trust or a conveyance or transfer to trustees which recites the trust. A subsequent memorandum of an earlier declaration will comply with the section if the settlor still holds the relevant property. In the absence of such writing, the trustee will obtain merely an estate at will.[10]

A charitable trust of personality may be created without writing.[11] If money is contributed, however, in response to an appeal for a charitable purpose before a trust deed has been drawn up, those who receive the money are under a responsibility to execute a trust deed declaring the precise trusts.[12]

The existence of writing is not always necessary, however, for a charitable trust of land or personalty because where rights have been enjoyed for a long time a legal origin will be presumed if possible and evidence of usage will be admissable.[13] Further, secret trusts in favour of charity have always been enforceable unless (before the commencement of the Charities Act 1960, s.38) they were made for the purposes of evading the provisions of the Mortmain Acts.[14] Evidence will be admitted to prove the existence and nature of the trust.[15]

---

[6] Gilb. Uses 44.

[7] See paras 1–017 *et seq.*, above.

[8] *Att-Gen v Matthews* (1677) 2 Lev. 167; *Att-Gen v Peacock* (1677) Finch 245; *Clifford v Francis* (1679) Freem.K.B. 330; *Att-Gen v Syderfen* (1683) 1 Vern. 224; *Att-Gen v Berryman* (1755) 1 Dick. 168; *Att-Gen v Herrick* (1772) Amb. 712; *Moggridge v Thackwell* (1802) 7 Ves. 83; *Morice v Bishop of Durham* (1805) 10 Ves. 541; *Paice v Archbishop of Canterbury* (1807) 14 Ves. 372; *Ommanney v Butcher* (1823) T. & R. 271; *Re Willis* [1921] 1 Ch. 44; *Re Bennett* [1960] Ch. 18. See para.1–019, above.

[9] Replacing the Statute of Frauds 1676. See *Adlington v Cann* (1744) 3 Atk. 141; see also *Boson v Statham* (1706) 1 Ed. 513. S.53(1)(b) does not affect the operation of resulting, implied or constructive trusts—s.53(2).

[10] Law of Property Act 1925, s.54.

[11] *Lyall v Kennedy* (1889) 14 App. Cas. 437 at 457.

[12] *Att-Gen v Mathieson* [1907] 2 Ch. 383. For public appeals, see para.7–032, below.

[13] See paras 4–009 *et seq.*, below.

[14] *O'Brien v Tyssen* (1885) 28 Ch.D. 372; *Re Wedgewood* [1915] 1 Ch. 113 (fully secret); *Re Huxtable* [1902] 2 Ch. 793; *Re Gardom* [1914] 1 Ch. 662 (half secret).

[15] *Re Fleetwood* (1880) 15 Ch.D. 594; *Re Gardom* [1914] 1 Ch. 662; *Re Wedgewood* [1915] 1 Ch. 113; *Blackwell v Blackwell* [1929] A.C. 318. See also *Re Colin Cooper* [1939] Ch. 811; *Re Young* [1951] Ch. 344; and distinguish *Re Keen* [1937] Ch. 236; *Re Jones* [1942] Ch. 328.

Subject-matter

Generally speaking, any kind of property, real[16] as well as personal, and **3–004** including incorporeal hereditaments, such as rent-charges,[17] advowsons and rights of presentation,[18] may be given to a charity. It has been stated however, that an easement, such as a right of way or passage, cannot be granted to a charitable use,[19] but this would not appear to represent the law and practice at the present time.

The Mortmain and Charitable Uses Act 1891[20] came into force on August 5, 1891, and applied to the wills of testators dying after that date. It provided that land[21] might be assured by will to or for the benefit of any charitable use; but the land had to be sold within one year from the testator's death unless retention for a longer period was authorised by the court or the Charity Commissioners.[22] Any personal estate by will directed to be laid out in the purchase of land was required to be applied or held to or for the benefit of the charitable uses as though there had been no such directon to lay it out in the purchase of land.[23] The Mortmain and Charitable Uses Act 1891 with the other Mortmain Acts was wholly repealed by the Charities Act 1960.[24] Therefore, if by the will of a testator dying after July 29, 1960, land is assured to or for the benefit of a charitable use, it may be retained unsold; and a testamentary direction to lay out personal estate in the purchase of land to be held to or for the benefit of a charitable use is valid and enforceable. The Charities Act 1960 operated retrospectively, so that land so assured by the will of a testator dying before the commencement of the Act and not sold by that date may be retained unsold.

In the case of ordinary legacies to individuals, a legatee having a vested interest may, on his attaining 18, call for payment of his legacy, notwithstanding any direction for accumulation.[25] At one time there was some

---

[16] A charitable use may be limited upon an estate tail (Duke, B. 134), but not upon an estate in frank marriage (*ibid.*) or in dower (*ibid.*) A jointure may, however, be made to a charitable use, because it may be upon condition (*Vernon's Case* (1572) 4 Co. 2; Duke B. 134), and, generally speaking, wherever a condition is limitable a charitable use is appointable (Duke B. 134). Lands held in frankalmoign could be subject to a charitable trust: *Att-Gen v Dean and Canons of Windsor* (1860) 8 H.L.C. 399.

[17] In *Att-Gen v West* (1858) 27 L.J.Ch. 789, the rent-charge was one varying according to the annual price of corn.

[18] *Att-Gen v Ward* (1829) 7 L.J.(o.s.) Ch. 114; *Att-Gen v Archbishop of York* (1854) 17 B. 495; *Att-Gen v Hospital of St. John* (1864) 10 Jur.(N.S.) 897; *Re St. Stephen, Coleman Street* (1888) 39 Ch.D. 492; *Re Hunter* [1897] 2 Ch. 105, *sub nom. Hunter v Att-Gen* [1889] A.C. 322; *Re Church Patronage Trust* [1904] 2 Ch. 643. It was formerly supposed that an advowson in gross could not be limited to a charitable use: Duke, B. 137.

[19] Duke, B. 137, 138.

[20] s.9.

[21] See the definition of "land" in s.3.

[22] s.5; and see also ss.6 and 8. See generally the notes to the Act in the 5th edition of this work.

[23] See s.7 of the Act of 1891 and the notes thereto in the 5th edition of this work; and see also s.8 and the notes thereto in the same edition.

[24] s.38, Sch.7, PtII.

[25] *Gosling v Gosling* (1859) John. 265; *Coventry v Coventry* (1865) 2 Dr. & Sm. 470; *Phillips v Phillips* [1877] W.N. 260; *Saunders v Vautier* (1841) 4 B. 115.

doubt whether this rule applied to charitable legacies,[26] but it is now settled law that the rule above stated, which is frequently referred to as the rule in *Saunders v Vautier*,[27] is applicable alike to charities if no one but the legatee has any interest in the accumulations.[28] Where there has been a bequest to a charity which has been unapplied and allowed to accumulate, the accumulations go to the charity along with the original bequest.[29]

Where there has been no admission of assets, or trust created, or sum set apart for the payment of a charitable legacy, the legacy is barred at the end of 12 years by the Limitation Act 1980.[30]

A charity established or supported[31] by voluntary contributions stands in the same position as any other charity so long as there is a fund or property impressed with a charitable trust. If there is, it is immaterial whether the source of it is the subscriptions of a number of people or the donation of a single individual.[32] Where a charity is established by subscriptions, the original subscribers alone are the founders: subsequent subscriptions do not constitute a new foundation, but are accretions to the original foundation.[33]

Certainty

3–005 In *Knight v Knight*,[34] Lord Langdale laid down the three essential requirements of a valid trust: (1) the words must be such that on the whole they ought to be construed as imperative; (2) the subject-matter of the trust must be certain; (3) the objects or persons intended to be benefited must be certain. It is proposed now to consider these "three certainties" in their application to charitable trusts.

Certainty of words

3–006 A trust may be created by any language sufficient to show the intention, and no technical words are necessary.[35] The use of such words as "intent"

---

[26] *Harbin v Masterman* (1871) L.R. 12 Eq. 559.

[27] (1841) 4 Beav. 115.

[28] *Wharton v Masterman* [1895] A.C. 186; *Re Knapp* [1929] 1 Ch. 341; *Re Green's Will Trust* [1985] 3 All E.R. 455, 459. See *Theobald on Wills* (15th ed.), p.636; *cf.* the rule that a charity entitled to income for an indefinite period is, unlike an individual, not entitled to call for the capital: *Re Levy* [1960] Ch. 346.

[29] *Forbes v Forbes* (1854) 18 B. 552.

[30] s.22; see *Cadbury v Smith* (1871) L.R. 9 Eq. 37.

[31] As to the meaning of "supported by voluntary subscriptions," see *Re Beard* [1904] 1 Ch. 270.

[32] See *Ex p. Pearson* (1818) 6 Price 214; *Att-Gen v Kell* (1840) 2 B. 575; *Att-Gen v Bishop of Manchester* (1867) L.R. 3 Eq. 436, 453; *Strickland v Weldon* (1885) 28 Ch.D. 426, 430. As to cases where there is no fund impressed with a charitable trust, see *Anon.* (1745) 3 Atk. 277; *Leslie v Birnie* (1826) R. Russ. 119.

[33] *Re St. Leonard, Shoreditch, Parochial Schools* (1884) 10 App. Cas. 304.

[34] (1840) 3 Beav. 148, 172. *Cf. Bowman v The Secular Society Ltd.* [1917] A.C. 406 at 436.

[35] *Salusbury v Denton* (1857) 3 K. & J. 529.

or "purpose,"[36] or a direction that a fund shall be applied by, or be at the disposal of, a person for the charitable purposes intended, may be as effectual as the use of the word "trust".[37] Even the words "authorise and empower" may be enough, upon the true construction of the instrument.[38] A mere promise to give to charity is, however, a *nudum pactum* and cannot be enforced. So also where a person deposited money at a bank in her own name, "as trustee for charitable purposes," without the trust having been communicated to anyone, it was held that no trust was intended to be created, and that the money formed part of her estate.[39]

A trust is also frequently held to be created by the use of words which are primarily words of condition.[40] "If I give an estate to A upon condition that he shall apply the rents for the benefit of B, that is a gift in trust to all intents and purposes".[41] A condition attached to a legacy to a charitable institution, requiring it to maintain two lifeboats, was construed as a trust.[42] Conditional words will, however, only create a trust where the requisites of a trust are present, namely, where there are purposes to which the subject-matter of the gift is required to be applied, and an obligation on the donee to satisfy those purposes.[43] Where words of condition create a trust it is of course enforceable as such[44] and the donees on condition of their being trustees are entitled to have the fund transferred to them,[45] and in a proper case the property may be applied *cy-près*.[46] The words used by the donor may, however, on a true construction be held to create only a charge, and not a trust, in favour of a charity or merely to impose a personal obligation. If, in a case in which specific charitable payments only are directed to be made out of an estate (the estate subject to the payments being the absolute property of the donees), no fiduciary obligation to make the payments is imposed on the donees, the result is to create a charge as distinguished from a trust.[47] If, however, a fiduciary obligation

---

[36] *Att-Gen v Leigh* (1721) 3 P.Wms. 145n.

[37] *Salusbury v Denton* (1857) 3 K. & J. 529.

[38] See the non-charitable case of *Brown v Higgs* (1799) 4 Ves. 707a; re-heard (1800) 5 Ves. 495; affd. (1803) 8 Ves. 561. The question, which is a question of construction, is whether the words in their context create a mere power or a trust power; see generally, in relation to non-charitable trusts and powers, *Underhill's and Hayton's Law of Trusts and Trustees* (15th ed.) pp.57–73, 108–111.

[39] *Sinnett v Herbert* (1872) 12 Eq. 201 at 206.

[40] *Att-Gen v Leigh* (1730) 3 P.Wms. 146n.; *Att-Gen v Christ's Hospital* (1790) 3 Bro.C.C. 165; *Poor v Miall* (1821) 6 Mad. 32; *Wright v Wilkin* (1860) 7 Jur.(N.S.) 441; *Att-Gen v Wax Chandler's Co.* (1873) L.R. 6 H.L. 1; *Goodman v Mayor of Saltash* (1882) 7 App. Cas. 633 at 642, per Lord Selborne; *Re Christchurch Enclosure Act* (1888) 38 Ch.D. 520, 531; *Re Niyazi's Will Trusts* [1978] 1 W.L.R. 910.

[41] *Att-Gen v Wax Chandler's Co.* (1873) L.R. 6 H.L. 1 at 21, per Lord Cairns.

[42] *Re Richardson* (1887) 56 L.J.Ch. 784; (1887) 57 L.T. 17. In this case there was a gift over in case the institution should decline to construct the lifeboats; and see *Re Conington's Will* (1860) 2 L.T. 525. See, para.3–025 below.

[43] See the non-charitable case of *Cunningham v Foot* (1878) 3 App. Cas. 987.

[44] *Re Richardson* (1887) 56 L.J.Ch. 784; 57 L.T. 17; *Re Niyazi's Will Trusts* [1978] 1 W.L.R. 910.

[45] *Re Richardson* (1887) 56 L.J.Ch. 784; (1887) 57 L.T. 17.

[46] *Re Richardson* (1888) 58 L.T. 45 and see, para.3–027 below.

[47] *cf. Commissioners of Charitable Donations v Wybrants* (1846) 2 J. & L. 182; and see the non-charitable cases of *Hodge v Churchward* (1847) 16 Sim. 71, and *Cunningham v Foot* (1878) 3 App. Cas. 974.

to see that the charitable purpose is carried out is imposed on the donees themselves, then they are bound by the obligation, except where other persons are expressly charged with this duty; for "by the ancient rule of equity no person could acquire an estate with notice of a charitable use without being liable to it".[48] A devisee of land subject to a charitable rent-charge was accordingly held to be a trustee of the rent-charge where no other person was appointed to carry out the charitable purpose.[49] The same conclusion was reached with regard to a devise (subject to and charged with annuities) to certain charitable institutions, and an annuity for the poor of a certain parish.[50] It appears that the same rule will apply to any gift subject to a charge in favour of charity.[51] On the other hand, if separate trustees were appointed of the sums directed to be applied to charity,[52] it appears that the devisees of the estates subject to the payments would not be charged with any fiduciary duties.[53]

3–007   It has been seen that in some cases a charitable trust may be created by the use of words which are primarily words of condition.[54] Charitable benefits may, however, also be conferred by means of conditions in the strict sense, that is, where there is a gift which imposes a personal obligation on the donee to fulfil certain charitable conditions without giving the charity any right against the subject-matter of the gift.[55] Thus in *Jack v Burnett*[56] a grant of land to a college, upon the condition of maintaining two bursars, was held to be a gift upon condition, and not a mere trust. So also where a gift was subject to a condition that the testator's tomb should be kept in repair, no part of the property being made applicable to that purpose,[57] and where an endowment for a church was made conditional on the minister wearing a black gown when preaching.[58]

---

[48] *Commissioners of Charitable Donations v Wybrants* (1846) 2 J. & L. 182. In the cases cited in this note there was no intention to devote the entire subject-matter of the gift to charity. If there had been such an intention the surplus income would have been applicable *cy-près* under a scheme: see *Re Raine* [1956] Ch. 417 and **Chap.** 11, below. If there had been no such intention and if on the true construction of the relevant wills the devisees had been intended to take only as trustees, they would have held the surplus income or the property in each case on a resulting trust for the testator's heir-at-law or residuary devisee: see *Re Stanford* [1924] 1 Ch. 73 and **Chap.** 11, below.

[49] *Commissioners of Charitable Donations v Wybrants* (1845) 2 J. & L. 182; and see *Att-Gen v Persse* (1842) 2 Dr. & W. 67.

[50] *Commissioners of Charitable Donations v Wybrants* (1845) 2 J. & L. 182; and see *Aylet v Dodd* (1741) 2 Atk. 238; *Att-Gen v West* (1858) 27 L.J.Ch. 789.

[51] See *Commissioners of Charitable Donations v Wybrants* (1845) 2 J. & L. 182; and *cf.* the non-charitable case of *Cunningham v Foot* (1878) 3 App. Cas. 995. See also *Mayor of Southmolton v Att-Gen* (1854) 6 H.L.C. 1.

[52] *Hodge v Churchward* (1847) 16 Sim. 71; *Cunningham v Foot* (1878) 3 App. Cas. 974.

[53] *Commissioners of Charitable Donations v Wybrants, supra.* The gift to existing charitable institutions in this case was in effect a gift to separate trustees, but the explanation probably is that no distinction could be drawn between them and the annuity to the poor.

[54] See para.3–006, above.

[55] *Att-Gen v Wax Chandler's Co.* (1873) L.R. 6 H.L. 1, 19, *per* Lord Cairns. See further as to conditions, paras 3–023 *et seq.*, below.

[56] (1846) 12 Cl. & F. 812. See also *Att-Gen v Cordwainers' Co.* (1833) 3 Myl. & K. 534; *Att-Gen v Christ's Hospital* (1830) 1 R. & M. 626.

[57] *Re Tyler* [1891] 3 Ch. 252; *Re Chardon* [1928] Ch. 464.

[58] *Millbank v Lambert* (1860) 28 B. 206; and see *Re Parker's Charity* (1863) 32 B. 654; *Re Robinson* [1892] 1 Ch. 99, CA; [1897] 1 Ch. 85; *Re Lysaght* [1966] Ch. 191.

A charitable trust may be made to attach to a part of the property only,[59] or it may be limited to particular payments directed to be made out of the income, as in the numerous cases where property was given to a college, or municipal corporation, or city guild, upon trust or to the intent that certain specified charitable payments should be made, or subject to or charged with certain charitable payments. In these cases, as will be seen,[60] the donees as a rule took beneficially, subject only to the specified charitable payments.

Certainty of subject-matter

It is essential to constitute a valid trust (whether charitable or not) that the subject-matter of the gift shall be capable of being ascertained.

3–008

Therefore, when blanks were left in a will for the amounts to be given to charity, the gift failed.[61] So also when a legacy of definite amount was given to increase till it amounted to—for building a hospital and supporting—boys.[62] However, if the object and scope of the gift are sufficiently defined by the donor or testator and the sum of money required to give effect to the gift can be ascertained, the gift is good. Thus in the Scottish case of *Magistrates of Dundee v Morris*[63] the House of Lords held, reversing the decision of the Court of Session, that a bequest to found a "hospital" (by which the testator meant a school) in Dundee for the education of 100 boys, to be conducted on the same lines as an existing institution, was valid. Their Lordships were satisfied that although the bequest was not of a specified sum, the sum of money required to establish the "hospital" was ascertainable. In the case last cited some guidance as to the amount necessary to establish the "hospital" was to be found in the will. But the general rule applicable to English trusts is considered to be well settled and to be that, where part of a fund is directed to be applied for charitable purposes, but the actual amount or the proportion to be so applied is not stated in the relevant instrument and no guidance is given as to how the amount or proportion is to be ascertained, the attempted charitable trust is void for uncertainty.[64] There is no uncertainty, however, in a gift to charity of a sum not exceeding a specified amount; it is a valid charitable gift of that sum.[65]

---

[59] *Poor v Miall* (1821) 6 Mad. 32, where, however, the trust was void under the Statute of Mortmain.

[60] See paras 11–059 *et seq.*, below.

[61] *Hartshorne v Nicholson* (1858) 26 B. 58.

[62] *Ewen v Bannerman* (1830) 2 Dow. & C. 74.

[63] (1858) 3 Macq. 131. See especially at 159, *per* Lord Chelmsford L.C. This case was considered in *Fisk v Att-Gen* (1867) L.R. 4 Eq. 521 and in *Re Birkett* (1878) 9 Ch.D. 576. It is clear that Lords Chelmsford and Cranworth would have reached the same conclusion had the bequest been contained in an English will, and the case is believed to be an authority binding on the English courts.

[64] *Chapman v Brown* (1801) 6 Ves. 410; *Re Porter* [1925] Ch. 746. The contrary Scottish case of *Macduff v Spences Trustees* [1909] S.C. 178 is of doubtful authority.

[65] *Thompson v Thompson* (1844) 1 Coll. 395; *cf. Cope v Wilmot* (1771) Amb. 704.

The requirement as to certainty is not satisfied if the sum of money or proportion of the fund applicable to charitable purposes can only be ascertained by entering into an unauthorised contract. Therefore, where a will contained a conditional direction to purchase a presentation to Chist's Hospital, and the condition was not satisfied, it was held that the amount to be applied to the charitable purpose was unascertainable, for it could only be determined by contracting to purchase the presentation, and the direction to enter into such a contract had not taken effect.[66]

3–009   The question as to whether a trust is void for uncertainty of the subject-matter has arisen most frequently in cases where gifts have been made partly for illegal or impossible objects and partly for charitable objects. It is clear that whether there is an enforceable trust for the charitable objects will depend upon whether the amount of the subject-matter to be devoted to them can be ascertained. This is a question of construction, and in deciding it the court will not regard previously decided cases as precedents, unless the words to be construed cannot be distinguished from words upon which an earlier decision has been given.[67]

The authorities as to gifts partly upon invalid and partly upon charitable trusts in undefined proportions fall into three groups. First, those in which the void and the charitable objects rank *pari passu*. Secondly, those in which the gift to charity is of the balance (if any) which would be left over after the void purpose had been satisfied. Third, those in which the whole fund is given to charity subject to payments for the void purpose.[68]

In the first situation, where a fund is given to be divided between charitable and illegal or impossible objects in such a way that neither part of the gift is residuary upon the other, the court will uphold the charitable part by apportioning the fund between the two groups of objects. This apportionment may be effected by means of an inquiry,[69] or, in a simple case, by an affidavit,[70] as to the amounts which would be required for the respective objects. If, however, it is impossible to ascertain what proportion shall be applied for each object, or the apportionment was intended to be a matter of discretion, the court will order an equal distribution among the named objects or classes of objects,[71] applying the maxim "equality is equity".

3–010   Accordingly, where the objects of the gift were poor relations and charitable purposes in unascertained proportions, the fund was equally divided.[72] The principle of equal division was also applied where a fund was given partly for educational purposes, and partly for the purchase of land

---

[66] *Cherry v Mott* (1883) 1 Myl. & Cr. 133 at 134; *cf. Mitford v Reynolds* (1848) 16 Sim. 105.

[67] *Re Taylor* (1888) 58 L.T. 538 at 542.

[68] See the classification of Eve J. in *Re Porter* [1925] Ch. 746 at 751.

[69] *Chapman v Brown* (1801) 6 Ves. 410; *Mitford v Reynolds* (1841) 1 Ph. 199; *Magistrates of Dundee v Morris* (1858) 3 Macq. 134; *Re Rigley's Trusts* (1866) 36 L.J.Ch. 147; *Hoare v Osborne* (1866) L.R. 1 Eq. 585; and see *Adnam v Cole* (1843) 6 Beav. 353; *Re Rogerson* [1901] 1 Ch. 715.

[70] *Re Vaughan* (1886) 33 Ch.D. 187.

[71] *Doyley v Att-Gen* (1735) 4 Vin.Abr. 485; *Salusbury v Denton* (1857) 3 K. & J. 529; *Re Rigley's Trusts* (1866) 36 L.J.Ch. 147; *Hoare v Osborne* (1866) L.R. 1 Eq. 585; *Hunter v Att-Gen* [1899] A.C. 309, 323, 324; *Re Gavacan* [1913] 1 Ir.R. 276; *Re Clarke* [1923] 2 Ch. 407.

[72] *Doyley v Att-Gen, Salusbury v Denton* (1857) 3 K. & J. 529.

to be let out to the poor, the second object being void under the old Mortmain Statute.[73] Where a fund was given partly for the repair of a tomb, and partly for valid charitable purposes, an equal division was directed,[74] but in other cases of the same kind the fund has been apportioned.[75]

Where a fund is directed to be divided among specified charitable objects in unascertained proportions, in cases where the duty of apportioning is entrusted to trustees or others who fail to make an apportionment, the rule of the court is to divide the fund among the different charitable objects equally.[76] Thus in *Att-Gen v Butler*[77] there was a bequest for the relief of the poor in such parishes and in such manner as the trustees should think fit, but a particular parish was to be one of those benefited. A scheme devoting a small part of the income to the parish named, and the rest to a parish at a distance, was held not conformable to the will, and an equal division between the two parishes was ordered.

Upon the increase of the income of a charity an apportionment is in some cases made among the objects.[78] Similar principals have been applied in cases where new objects have been admitted to participate. Accordingly, where there was a charitable gift to the inhabitants of a certain locality, such as the poor of a city, and other parishes were afterwards admitted within the citys precincts, an apportionment was made by the court in favour of such parishes.[79]

In the second situation where the gift to charity is residuary upon a void gift, the general rule is that it fails if the court, as it did in *Chapman v Brown*,[80] finds that the precedent gift is of an unascertainable amount. But the charitable gift is valid if the subject-matter needed for the precedent gift can be reduced to certainty by means of an inquiry.[81] The court will not direct an inquiry, and the gift to charity will fail, if it is manifestly impossible to determine the amount needed for the primary gift,[82] or if it is clear that there would be nothing left over after satisfying it.[83] Cases relating to gifts of the income of a fund for the upkeep of tombs followed by a gift of the particular residue to charity have received exceptional treatment and, although worded as though the charitable gift were residuary, are dealt with as examples of the class of gift next considered.

3–011

---

[73] *Crafton v Frith* (1851) 4 De G. & Sm. 237.
[74] *Hoare v Osborne* (1866) L.R. 1 Eq. 585; *Re Birkett* (1878) 9 Ch.D. 576.
[75] *Adnam v Cole* (1843) 6 B. 353; *Re Rigley's Trusts* (1866) 36 L.J.Ch. 147; *Re Vaughan* (1886) 33 Ch.D. 187. Distinguish *Re Rogerson* [1901] 1 Ch. 715. It is immaterial whether the non-charitable object is definite or indefinite: *Re Clarke* [1923] 2 Ch. 407 at 418.
[76] *Re Hall's Charity* (1851) 14 B. 115; *Hoare v Osborne* (1866) L.R. 1 Eq. 588 at 589; *Att-Gen v Marchant* (1866) 3 Eq. 424; *Re Douglas* (1887) 35 Ch.D. 485.
[77] (1822) Jac. 407.
[78] See further para.11–061 *et seq.*, below.
[79] *Att-Gen v Mayor of Rochester* (1674) Rep. t. Finch, 193; *ibid.* (1833) 6 Sim. 273 at 322; and see *Att-Gen v Grant* (1720) 1 P.Wms. 669.
[80] (1801) 6 Ves. 410. See also *Att-Gen v Hinxman* (1821) 2 J. & W. 270; *Fowler v Fowler* (1864) 33 Beav. 616; *Kirkman v Lewis* (1869) 38 L.J.Ch. 570; *Re Birkett* (1878) 9 Ch.D. 576; *Re Taylor* (1888) 58 L.T. 538; *Re Porter* [1925] Ch. 746.
[81] *Mitford v Reynolds* (1841) 1 Ph. 199. See *Re Dalziel* [1943] Ch. 277 at 282, *per* Cohen J. (approving this statement of the law); *cf. Magistrates of Dundee v Morris* (1858) 3 Macq. 134, see para.3–008, above.
[82] *Chapman v Brown* (1801) 6 Ves. 410; *Re Porter* [1925] Ch. 746.
[83] *Cramp v Playfoot* (1858) 4 K. & J. 479; Re Taylor (1888) 58 L.T. 538, at 541.

In the third situation where the gift is construed as devoting the whole fund to charitable objects subject to a payment for a void object, the failure of the latter will result in the whole fund becoming available for the charity. Therefore, where a capital sum was given to effect an impossible purpose and "the rest" (being what was not needed for the first object) was to be devoted to charity, the whole fund was directed to be paid to charitable objects: the court read the gift as a direction to pay all the fund to charity except what was needed for the impossible purpose.[84] Similarly, if a gift of a sum the income of which is to be applied primarily for an illegal purpose while the particular residue is given to charity can be read as a gift to charity subject to a charge for the illegal object, the charity will take the whole upon the failure of the charge.[85]

A number of cases,[86] in which there have been gifts upon trust to keep up tombs not forming part of the fabric of a church with a gift of the particular residue to charity, may be regarded as establishing a special rule of law. "Where a fund has been given to trustees upon trust to apply the income in keeping a tomb in repair, and as to the remainder of the income for valid charitable purposes, it has been held that the result of the failure of the trust for the repair of the tomb is that the whole of the income becomes applicable for the charitable purpose".[87] These cases are distinguished from *Chapman v Brown*[88] upon rather slender grounds, and in *Re Birkett*[89] Sir George Jessel M.R. followed them reluctantly. In *Re Dalziel*[90] Cohen J., after approving the above statement of the special doctrine in cases relating to tombs, expressed the opinion that the real foundation of the tomb cases was that the court felt itself able to construe the provision in the various wills as to the upkeep of tombs as imposing only a moral obligation; but the obligation to give all that is not applied for the upkeep of the tombs in favour of the valid charitable purpose is not honorary, but an enforceable trust which must be executed.[91] It seems that they will not be regarded as precedents for cases not involving trusts for the maintenance of tombs.[92]

3–012   Difficulties may also arise in cases of gifts of land and also of personalty for the maintenance of the land. Thus, where there was a legacy for "repairing, altering or adding to and improving" certain almshouses and their grounds, the court declared that all these objects (except adding to the grounds) were legal, and ordered the legacy to be paid.[93] Where, how-

---

[84] *Kelly v Att-Gen* [1917] 1 Ir.R. 183.
[85] See cases cited in the following note.
[86] *Fisk v Att-Gen* (1867) L.R. 4 Eq. 521; *Hunter v Bullock* (1872) L.R. 14 Eq. 45; *Dawson v Small* (1874) L.R. 18 Eq. 114; *Re Williams* (1877) 5 Ch.D. 735; *Re Birkett* (1878) 9 Ch.D. 576; *Re Vaughan* (1886) 33 Ch.D. 187; *Re Rogerson* [1901] 1 Ch. 715; *Secus, Fowler v Fowler* (1864) 33 Beav. 616.
[87] *Re Rogerson*, above, at 718, *per* Joyce J.
[88] (1801) 6 Ves. 404.
[89] (1878) 9 Ch.D. 576.
[90] [1943] Ch. 277 at 281; and see *Re Ryler* [1891] 3 Ch. 252.
[91] *Dawson v Small* (1874) 18 Eq. 114, 118; *Re Rogerson* [1901] 1 Ch. 715 at 719. See also *Fowler v Fowler* (1864) 33 Beav. 616; *Hunter v Bullock* (1872) 14 Eq. 45; *Re Williams* (1877) 5 Ch.D. 735; *Re Taylor* (1888) 58 L.T. 538.
[92] *Re Porter* [1925] Ch. 746 at 751.
[93] *Att-Gen v Parsons* (1803) 8 Ves. 186.

ever, void gifts have been made for establishing a building or institution, and by the same instrument bequests for its maintenance have also been made, the latter have generally been held void as being so dependent on the precedent gifts that they can only take effect if the precedent gifts are valid.[94]

Certainty of Objects

A charitable trust does not require certainty of objects but, rather, certainty that all potential objects are charitable. As Viscount Simon L.C. observed in *Chichester Diocesan Fund and Board of Finance (Incorporated) v Simpson*[95]:   **3–013**

> "The fundamental principle is that the testator must by the terms of his will himself dispose of the property with which the will proposes to deal. With one single exeption he cannot by his will direct executors or trustees to do the business for him. That exception arises when the testator is minded to make gifts for charitable purposes, and where he directs his executors or trustees, within such limitations as he chooses to lay down, to make the selection of charities to be benefited. This exception to the general principle that the testator has to decide in his will the specific destination of his property is allowed because of the special favour which the English law shows to charities, and the conception of what is charitable for such purposes has been elaborately worked out so that the courts are able to determine whether a gift is charitable or not. . . . ".

This principle applies to gifts and settlements inter vivos as well as to wills.[96] It is not infringed if the settlor or testator designates with sufficient certainty a class of persons or objects who are to be benefited but delegates to the trustees the selection of individual persons or objects within the ascertainable class.[97] But the principle is infringed if the class of persons or objects to be benefited is not indicated with sufficient certainty to enable them to be ascertained by inquiry.

---

[94] *Att-Gen v Goulding* (1788) 2 Bro.C.C. 428; *Att-Gen v Whitchurch* (1796) 3 Ves. 141; *Att-Gen v Davies* (1802) 9 Ves. 546; *Limbrey v Gurr* (1819) 6 Madd. 151; *Smith v Oliver* (1849) 11 Beav. 481; *Dunn v Bownas* (1854) 1 K. & J. 596; *Peek v Peek* (1869) 17 W.R. 1059; *Re Cox* (1877) 7 Ch.D. 204. These cases are instances of the failure of the primary gift under the Charitable Uses Act 1736. Since by s.38 of the Charities Act 1960, the law of mortmain has been repealed, these cases are only of historical interest, for under the present law all the primary gifts would be valid.

[95] [1944] A.C. 341 at 348. For other statements to the like effect see 349, *per* Lord Macmillan, and 371, *per* Lord Simonds; *Houston v Burns* [1918] A.C. 337 at 342, 343, *per* Viscount Haldane; *Att-Gen v National Provincial Bank* [1924] A.C. 262 at 268, *per* Viscount Haldane; *Re Tyler* [1967] 1 W.L.R. 1269 at 1277, *per* Pennycuick J.; see also *Re Wootton* [1968] 1 W.L.R. 681.

[96] *Re Astor's Settlement Trusts* [1952] Ch. 534.

[97] *Chichester Diocesan Fund and Board of Finance v Simpson* [1944] A.C. 341 at 349, *per* Lord Macmillan; *Houston v Burns* [1918] A.C. 337 at 342, 343, *per* Viscount Haldane. For consideration of the rules for certainty of objects in non-charitable trusts and powers, see *Underhill and Hayton, Law of Trusts and Trustees* (15th ed.) pp.64, *et seq.*

The basis of the rule that the objects of a trust which is not charitable must be certain is that equity will only recognise as valid a trust which can be carried into execution by the court. The court cannot act of its own motion; there must be somebody in whose favour the court can decree performance.[98] In the case of a non-charitable trust the court can only act on the application of an individual or individuals able to establish a claim to be beneficially interested in the subject-matter of the trust or by individuals who are trustees or the governing body of a defined or ascertainable institution which has a defined or ascertainable interest in the subject-matter of the trust. It was with the above considerations in mind that Lord Parker of Waddington, in *Bowman v Secular Society Ltd.*,[99] said that a trust to be valid must be for the benefit of individuals or must be charitable. Or, as Viscount Simonds said in *Leahy v Att-Gen (N.S.W.)*[1]:

> "A gift can be made to persons (including a corporation) but it cannot be made to a purpose or object; so also a trust may be created for the benefit of persons as *cestuis que trust* but not for a purpose or object unless the purpose or object be charitable. For a purpose or object cannot sue but, if it be charitable, the Attorney-General can sue to enforce it."

3-014   It is, therefore, clear that uncertainty as to the mode of application of the gift does not invalidate a charitable trust contrary to the general rule for non-charitable trusts stated above. Accordingly, if a trust is charitable the absence of an individual *cestui que trust* who can prove that he is interested in an ascertainable share of the trust fund or property does not matter. The court dispenses with the requirement that there must be a beneficiary because the Crown, as parens patriae taking all charities under its protection, is in a position to enforce the trust; and therefore, although there may be no specified charitable beneficiary who can come to the court and insist on having the trust performed, nevertheless the Attorney-General can apply and is entitled to insist on the trust being carried out, if necessary by a scheme *cy-près*.[2] Therefore, the trust is subject to control by the court.

Likewise, where the trust is for charitable purposes which are not clearly defined or are not defined at all, the trust never fails for uncertainty. A charitable gift whether *inter vivos* or by will can never fail for uncertainty of objects, because the Attorney-General, representing the Crown as *parens patriae*, can always intervene by way of propounding a scheme for the regulation of those trusts along channels which the law of the land

---

[98] *Morice v Bishop of Durham* (1804) 9 Ves. 399 at 405, *per* Sir William Grant M.R.; *Re Astor's Settlement Trusts* [1952] Ch. 534.

[99] [1917] A.C. 406 at 441. In this context the word "individual" includes not only a natural person but an incorporated or unincorporated body of persons. The Secular Society was a limited company incorporated under the Companies Act 1862.

[1] [1959] A.C. 457 at 478, 479.

[2] See *Re Diplock* [1941] Ch. 253 at 259, *per* Lord Greene M.R.; *Re Astor's Settlement Trusts* [1952] Ch. 534 at 541, *per* Roxburgh J., quoting *Att-Gen v Brown* (1818) 1 Swans. 265 at 290, *per* Lord Eldon L.C.; *Re Shaw* [1957] 1 W.L.R. 729 at 745, *per* Harman J.

regards as charitable.[3] Indeed, a settlor or testator who declares a charitable purpose can always leave it to his trustees to select the particular charities for whose benefit the fund is to be applied.[4] Or, to put the matter in another way, it may be said that there is no exception to the rule that there must be somebody in whose favour the court can decree performance and that the trusts must be of a kind that the court can execute, but that the court regards charity as an object sufficiently definite to make a trust enforceable. The following judicial observations illustrate the point:

> "When you get the idea of charity properly expressed in a will, you have a standard to go by, and one that has been adopted now for centuries—that is to say, a standard afforded by the preamble to the Statute of Elizabeth, which deals with certain things specifically as instances of existing charities, and from which by analogy you can deduce that certain other matters are also to be treated as charitable."[5]

> "The court knows what is charitable by reference to the preamble to the Statute of Elizabeth, to the objects therein enumerated and all others which 'by analogies are deemed within its spirit and intendment'."[6]

It is, however, required that, in order to be charitable, a trust must not only be declared in favour of objects of a charitable nature, but it must also be expressed that in its application it is confined to such objects. The question is not whether the trustee may apply the trust property upon purposes strictly charitable, but whether he is bound so to apply it.[7] The charitable application of the gift must, therefore, be compulsory,[8] otherwise it will fail, for if the gift is such that the trustee is not bound to apply it to purposes strictly charitable it is not in the eyes of the law a charitable gift at all. It follows that a gift of this kind is nonetheless invalid because the trustees have exercised their discretion by applying the fund for a charitable purpose if they were not obliged by the terms of the gift to do so:

> "The court is not to wait and see whether the executors will appoint to charitable objects or not, but to look at the will as at the date of

---

[3] See *Re Harpur's Will Trusts* [1962] Ch. 78 at 94, *per* Harman L.J., referring to *Morice v Bishop of Durham* (1804) 9 Ves. 399 at 404, *per* Sir William Grant M.R.; and see also *Houston v Burns* [1918] A.C. 337 at 342, 343, *per* Viscount Haldane. See para.1–019, above.

[4] *Att-Gen v National Provincial Bank* [1924] A.C. 262 at 264, *per* Viscount Cave L.C.

[5] *Re Macduff* [1896] 2 Ch. 451 at 469, per Rigby L.J.

[6] *Chichester Diocesan Fund and Board of Finance v Simpson* [1944] A.C. 341 at 371, *per* Lord Simonds.

[7] *Morice v Bishop of Durham* (1804) 9 Ves. 399 at 406, per Sir William Grant M.R.

[8] *ibid.*; affirmed. 10 Ves. 522; *James v Allen* (1817) 3 Mer. 19; *Ellis v Selby* (1836) 1 Myl. & Cr. 299; *Nash v Morley* (1842) 5 Beav. 182; *Re Macduff* [1896] 2 Ch. 465; *Houston v Burns* [1918] A.C. 337; *Re Davis* [1923] 1 Ch. 225; *Att-Gen v National Provincial Bank* [1924] A.C. 262; *Farley v Westminster Bank* [1939] A.C. 430; *Chichester Diocesan Fund and Board of Finance v Simpson* [1944] A.C. 341; *Oxford Group v IRC* [1949] 2 All E.R. 537; *Ellis v IRC* (1949) 31 T.C. 178; *Re Harpur's Will Trusts* [1962] Ch. 78.

the death of the testator, and at once say whether the gift is definite or indefinite, and, if the latter, that it is inoperative."[9]

3–015   The question which should be asked in all cases where there is an apparent vagueness as to the objects of a gift, and it is sought to uphold it as a gift to charity, is this: Is it clear that the only possible objects of the gift are charitable within the legal meaning of that word? If the answer is in the affirmative, the court will uphold the gift, if in the negative, the gift is void for uncertainty. Thus, in *Morice v Bishop of Durham*[10] the gift was to the Bishop upon trust to dispose of it to "such objects of benevolence and liberality" as he should most approve. The gift was held void for uncertainty. It was not denied that many "objects of benevolence and liberality" might be charitable in the legal sense of the word, but the gift was not on that account necessarily charitable, since the trustees were not obliged to devote the gift to those objects. As Sir William Grant M.R. said[11]: "The trusts may be completely exercised without bestowing any part . . . upon purposes strictly charitable."

Upon this principle and consistently with the decision in this case, gifts for the following purposes have been held void for uncertainty: benevolent,[12] philanthropic,[13] utilitarian,[14] emigration,[15] patriotic,[16] and public[17] purposes. Also gifts for "encouraging undertakings of general utility,[18] for hospitality,[19] for "pious purposes",[20] for "public institutions in Wales",[21] "religious, charitable, or educational institution or institutions or any organisations or institutions operating for the public good"[22] for such societies as should be, in the opinion of the trustees, "most in need of help,"[23] for such purposes, civil or religious, as a class of persons should appoint[24]; and, on the ground that they were not necessarily for religious purposes, a gift for missionary purposes,[25] and to the Pope to be

---

[9] *Re Jarman* (1878) 8 Ch.D. 584 at 587, *per* Hall V.C.; and see also *Chichester Diocesan Fund and Board of Finance v Simpson* [1944] A.C. 341 at 367, *per* Lord Simonds; *Ministry of Health v Simpson* [1951] A.C. 251.

[10] (1805) 9 Ves. 399; affirmed 10 Ves. 522.

[11] (1805) 9 Ves. 399 at 406.

[12] *James v Allen* (1817) 3 Mer. 17; *Re Barnett* (1908) 24 T.L.R. 788; *Att-Gen for New Zealand v Brown* [1917] A.C. 393; *Re Diplock* [1941] Ch. 253, affirmed sub nom. *Chichester Diocesan Fund and Board of Finance v Simpson* [1944] A.C. 341.

[13] *Re Macduff* [1896] 2 Ch. 451; *Re Eades* [1920] 2 Ch. 353.

[14] *Re Woodgate* (1886) 2 T.L.R. 674.

[15] *Re Sidney* [1908] 1 Ch. 488.

[16] *Att-Gen v National Provincial Bank* [1924] A.C. 262.

[17] *Vezey v Jamson* (1822) 1 S. & S. 69; *Blair v Duncan* [1902] A.C. 37; *Houston v Burns* [1918] A.C. 337.

[18] *Kendall v Granger* (1842) 5 B. 300; *Langham v Peterson* (1903) 87 L.T. 744.

[19] *Att-Gen v Whorwood* (1750) 1 Ves.Sen. 534; *Re Hewitt* (1833) 53 L.J.Ch. 132.

[20] *Heath v Chapman* (1854) 2 Dr. 417.

[21] *Re Davis* [1923] 1 Ch. 225.

[22] *Att-Gen of the Cayman Islands v Wahr-Hansen* [2001] A.C. 75.

[23] *Re Freeman* [1908] 1 Ch. 720.

[24] *Re Friends' Free School* [1909] 2 Ch. 675.

[25] *Scott v Brownrigg* (1882) 9 L.R.Ir. 246; *Jackson v Att-Gen* [1917] 1 Ir.R. 332; *Re Rees* [1920] 2 Ch. 59, where *Scott v Brownrigg* above was not questioned, but it was held, following *Re Kenny* (1907) 97 L.T. 130, that although the term "missionary purposes" was ambigu-

used "in the carrying out of his sacred office,"[26] have all been held invalid.

On the same principle the following gifts were also held void for uncertainty: to the Archbishop of Westminster for the time being to be distributed amongst such bodies as he should in his absolute discretion think fit,[27] to the Roman Catholic Archbishop of Brisbane to be used and expended wholly or in part as he might judge most conducive to the good of religion in his diocese,[28] to the Archbishop of Wales to be applied by him in or towards the general fund belonging to the Church in Wales,[29] to the Vicar of Mortlake to be applied among such parochial institutions or purposes as he should select,[30] to the Archbishop of Cardiff for work connected with the Roman Catholic Church in the said archdiocese,[31] to the churchwardens of an ecclesiastical parish "for parish work."[32]

A fortiori a trust is not charitable where it is merely for such persons,[33] **3–016** or purposes,[34] as the trustees may think fit or most deserving,[35] or as may seem "expedient"[36] or to "worthy" causes.[37] Nor will a power to make charitable payments, without a binding trust for the purpose, render a gift charitable.[38] And the court cannot validate an invalid trust by treating it as a valid power.[39] Where a legatee was merely empowered but not directed to devote the gift to a school "or whatever purpose he pleases", it was held that he took beneficially.[40]

Disjunctive and conjunctive construction—Where the trustees have an alter- **3–017** native power to apply the fund either to charitable purposes, or to indefinite purposes which are not charitable, the gift is void for uncertainty, unless validated by the Charitable Trusts (Validation) Act 1954.[41] Examples of such gifts are, for "such charitable or public purposes as the laws of the land would admit of or to any person or persons"[42]; "charity

---

ous it might be narrowed by evidence of surrounding circumstances tending to show that the testator used the expression in the popular sense of Christian missionary work.

[26] *Moore v The Pope* [1919] 1 Ir.R. 316.
[27] *Re Davidson* [1909] 2 Ch. 642.
[28] *Dunne v Byrne* [1912] A.C. 407.
[29] *Re Jackson* [1930] 2 Ch. 389.
[30] *Re Stratton* [1931] 1 Ch. 197.
[31] *Re Davies* (1932) 49 T.L.R. 5.
[32] *Re Ashton* [1938] Ch. 482, affirmed sub nom. *Farley v Westminster Bank Ltd.* [1939] A.C. 430.
[33] *Gibbs v Rumsey* (1813) 2 V. & B. 294.
[34] *Doe v Copestake* (1805) 6 East 328; *Fowler v Garlike* (1830) 1 R. & M. 232; *Buckle v Bristow* (1864) 13 W.R. 68.
[35] *Harris v Du Pasquier* (1872) 20 W.R. 668; *Yeap Cheah Neo v Ong Cheng Neo* (1875) 6 P.C. 381; *cf. Re Sutton* (1885) 28 Ch.D. 464; *Re Hurley* (1900) 17 T.L.R. 115.
[36] *Re Davies* [1915] 1 Ch. 543.
[37] *Re Atkinson's Will Trusts* [1978] 1 W.L.R. 586; and see *Re Gillingham Bus Disaster Fund* [1958] Ch. 300 at 305.
[38] *Coxe v Bassett* (1796) 3 Ves. 155; see also *Ommanney v Butcher* (1823) T. & R. 270.
[39] See *Re Shaw* [1957] 1 W.L.R. 729, applying *IRC v Broadway Cottages Trust* [1955] Ch. 20.
[40] *Re Harbison* [1902] 1 Ir.R. 103.
[41] See paras 3–036 *et seq.*, below.
[42] *Vezey v Jamson* (1822) 1 S. & S. 69.

or works of public utility"[43]; "charitable or public purposes"[44]; "charitable, religious or other [objects]"[45]; "public, benevolent or charitable purposes in connection with the parish of L."[46]; "charitable or benevolent purposes"[47]; "charitable uses or emigration purposes".[48] On the same principle, in the Scots case of *Grimond v Grimond*,[49] the House of Lords held void a gift for "such charitable or religious societies" as the testator's trustees might select, since by the law of Scotland "religious" purposes are not prima facie charitable.[50]

It will be observed that in all the above-mentioned cases the trustees had an alternative power to select between objects some of which were charitable and some not, and that the two groups of objects were separated by the word "or"; and that the court thus felt bound to employ what has been called "the disjunctive method" of construction. That is to say, the gift was interpreted to mean that the trust property might be applied for any one or more of the alternative objects specified by the donor. If the word "or" is replaced by "and", prima facie the words must be read conjunctively—that is, in such a way that the trust property can only be applied for objects to which all the qualifications mentioned by the donor apply. If any of the qualifications requires the object to be charitable, the gift can be supported as a gift to charity.

For the above reason the following gifts have been upheld: for "charitable and pious uses"[51]; for "charitable and benevolent" objects[52]; for "religious and benevolent societies or objects, chiefly the former"[53]; and for "charitable and deserving"[54] objects. And, in *Blair v Duncan*,[55] Lord Davey said that he thought that effect might be given to a gift for "charitable and public purposes". On the same principle a devise "for the furtherance of Conservative principles and religious and mental improvement" was held to be charitable.[56]

---

[43] *Langham v Peterson* (1903) 87 L.T. 744.

[44] *Blair v Duncan* [1902] A.C. 37.

[45] *Re Davidson* [1909] 1 Ch. 567.

[46] *Houston v Burns* [1918] A.C. 337.

[47] *Re Jarman* (1878) 8 Ch.D. 584; *Re Diplock* [1941] Ch. 253, affirmed sub nom. *Chichester Diocesan Fund and Board of Finance v Simpson* [1944] A.C. 341.

[48] *Re Sidney* [1908] 1 Ch. 488.

[49] [1905] A.C. 124.

[50] In England and Ireland "religious purposes" are prima facie charitable: *Baker v Sutton* (1836) 1 Keen 224; *Re White* [1893] 2 Ch. 41; *Re Lloyd Greame* (1893) 10 T.L.R. 66; *Rea v Crozier* [1911] 1 Ir.R. 289; *Rickerby v Nicholson* [1912] 1 Ir.R. 343; *Re Ward* [1941] Ch. 308.

[51] *Att-Gen v Herrick* (1772) Amb. 712.

[52] *Re Best* [1904] 2 Ch. 354; *Caldwell v Caldwell* (1921) 65 S.J. 765; see also *Jemmitt v Verril* (1826) Amb. 568n.; but see Lord Cottenham's observations on this case in *Ellis v Selby* (1836) 1 Myl. & Cr. 286, 292. See also *Hill v Burns* (1826) 2 Wils. & S. 80; *Crichton v Grierson* (1828) Wils. & S. 329; *Miller v Rowan* (1837) 5 Cl. & F. 99.

[53] *Re Lloyd-Greame* (1893) 10 T.L.R. 66. It is thought that a gift for "religious and benevolent" objects simpliciter ought to be construed conjunctively, but that the actual decision in this case may have been wrong as the last three words quoted seem to indicate a disjunctive use of "and." In this connection see also *Waldo v Caley* (1809) 18 Ves. 206 and *Johnston v Swann* (1818) 3 Mad. 457.

[54] *Re Sutton* (1885), 28 Ch.D. 464.

[55] [1902] A.C. 37 at 44.

[56] *Re Scowcroft* [1898] 2 Ch. 638.

Whether the language of a gift is to be read conjunctively or disjunc- **3–018**
tively does not, however, depend exclusively on which of the two words
"and" and "or" is used. Some gifts in which the second alternative class of
objects has been preceded by "and" have been read disjunctively, and
declared void for uncertainty. Such a case is *Williams v Kershaw*,[57] where
there was a bequest for such "benevolent, charitable and religious purposes" as the trustees should select, and Lord Langdale M.R. held that the
gift might be devoted to "benevolent purposes" and was therefore void.
This case was followed in *Re Eades*,[58] where the words of the gift were, "to
such religious, charitable and philanthropic objects" as three named persons might select. Sargant J. construed the word "and" disjunctively and
held that the trust was void for uncertainty. The learned judge expressed
the opinion that the greater the number of qualifications or characteristics
enumerated, the more probable it was that the disjunctive construction
was required.[59]

Attorney General of the Bahamas v Royal Trust Co.,[60] was concerned
with a bequest of residue to trustees to hold for "any purposes for and/or
connected with the education and welfare of Bahamian children and
young people." The words were construed disjunctively and the residuary
bequest failed. In giving the judgment of the Board, Lord Oliver stressed
that in this type of case, the question is one of constuction of the particular disposition and references to the construction placed on other dispositions, whilst useful as guidelines were, of necessity, of limited assistance.
He did, however, approve Sargant J.'s dicta in *Re Eades*[61] about the number of characteristics cited above. A further guideline in these cases is
that a gift may be saved by the *ejusdem generis* principle. Thus in *Re
Ludlow*[62] a gift to hospitals or convalescent homes, or other charitable or
benevolent institutions was held to be charitable applying that principle
of construction.

Perpetuity

Commencement

A charitable gift may be made to take effect at a future time, as upon **3–019**
the death of a tenant for life[63]; or the determination of other prior

---

[57] (1835) 5 L.J.Ch. 84.
[68] [1920] 2 Ch. 353.
[69] See also *Att-Gen for New Zealand v Brown* [1917] A.C. 393 (gift for such charitable, benevolent, religious and educational institutions, societies, associations and objects as trustees
should select construed disjunctively and held void for uncertainty): and see *Att-Gen v
National Provincial Bank* [1924] A.C. 262.
[60] [1986] 1 W.L.R. 1001.
[61] [1920] 2 Ch. 353 at 356, 357.
[62] (1923) 93 L.J.Ch. 30. See also *Dolan v Macdermot* (1868) L.R. 3 Ch. 676; *Re Allen* [1905]
2 Ch. 400; *Re Bennett* [1920] 1 Ch. 305 and see para.108, above.
[63] *Att-Gen v Craven* (1856) 21 B. 392; *Yates v University College* (1876) L.R. 7 H.L. 438.

limitations[64]; or upon a condition precedent,[65] such as that the testator's estate is sufficient for the purpose intended,[66] or amounts to a specified sum.[67] Where there is a condition precedent the gift fails if it is not satisfied.[68]

Unless the prior limitation is also charitable a future gift must be bound to take effect within the period allowed by the rule against perpetuities.[69] If the interest of the charity is so limited as to become effective upon a future event, which may be postponed beyond the limits of the period allowed by the rule against perpetuities, the limitation is void.[70] Thus a limitation over to charity on alienation,[71] or a trust in favour of charity after an indefinite failure of issue,[72] would be bad. In *Commissioners of Charitable Donations v De Clifford*,[73] a testator gave the surplus rents of real estate to the members of certain families, who should for the time being be lords or ladies of a particular manor, and in case they failed to satisfy certain conditions or became extinct, then to charity. It was held that the gift of the surplus rents was an equitable devise of a qualified fee, and that the limitation over after the determination of that estate was void for remoteness. Similarly, a charitable gift, subject to a condition precedent, which will not necessarily be satisfied within the permitted period, is too remote.[74] In *Re Lord Stratheden and Campbell*,[75] a charitable legacy, contingent on an appointment being made to a particular office, which might never take place, was held invalid.

Where, however, there is an immediate effectual gift to charity but the application is postponed, no question of remoteness can arise, although the particular object will not necessarily take effect within any assignable limit of time, and may never take effect at all.[76]

---

[64] *Re Roberts* (1882) 19 Ch.D. 520.

[65] *Chamberlayne v Brockett* (1872) L.R. 8 Ch. 206, 211; *Cherry v Mott* (1883) 1 Myl. & Cr. 132; *Re Swain, Monckton v Hands* [1905] 1 Ch. 669; see also *De Themmines v De Bonneval* (1828) 5 Russ. 289; *Re Tunno* [1886] W.N. 154.

[66] *Cherry v Mott* (1883) 1 Myl. & Cr. 132.

[67] *Thomas v Howell* (1874) 18 Eq. 198.

[68] *De Themmines v De Bonneval; Att-Gen v Craven; Chamberlayne v Brockett; Thomas v Howell; Cherry v Mott; Re Tunno*, above; *Re Emson* (1905) 21 T.L.R. 623; *Re University of London Medical Sciences Institute Fund* [1909] 2 Ch. 1. As to the cases in which, in bequests of personality, the condition may be rejected and the bequest upheld, see *Jarman on Wills* (8th ed.), Chap. XLI, s.II(viii); *Re Elliott* [1952] Ch. 217.

[69] *Society for the Propagation of the Gospel in Foreign Parts v Att-Gen* (1826) 3 Russ. 142; *Christ's Hospital v Grainger* (1848) 1 Mac. & G. 460; *Re Tyler* [1891] 3 Ch. 252; *Re Dalziel* [1943] Ch. 277.

[70] *Chamberlayne v Brockett* (1872) L.R. 8 Ch. 206 at 211; *Re White's Trusts* (1886) 33 Ch.D. 449 at 453; *Re Lord Stratheden and Campbell* [1894] 3 Ch. 265; *Worthing Corporation v Heather* [1906] 2 Ch. 532; *Re Dalziel* [1943] Ch. 277; *secus, Re Chardon* [1928] Ch. 464.

[71] *Pewterers' Co. v Christ's Hospital* (1683) 1 Vern. 161.

[72] *Re Johnson's Trusts* (1866) L.R. 2 Eq. 720.

[73] (1841) 1 Dr. & W. 245; *cf. Re Roberts*, above.

[74] *Chamberlayne v Brockett*, above; *Re Dalziel*, above; and see *Re White's Trusts*, above.

[75] [1894] 3 Ch. 265; and see *Re Wood* [1949] Ch. 498; *Re Mander* [1950] Ch. 547.

[76] *Edwards v Hall* (1855) 6 De G.M. & G. 74; *Thompson v Shakespear* (1860) 1 De G.F. & J. 399 at 407; *Chamberlayne v Brockett* (1872) 8 Ch. 211; *Re White's Trusts* (1883) 51 L.J.Ch. 830; *Re Gyde* (1898) 79 L.T. 261; *Wallis v Sol.-Gen. for New Zealand* [1903] A.C. 173; and see *Re Swain* [1905] 1 Ch. 669.

The Perpetuities and Accumulations Act 1964[77] introduced the "wait and see" principle, providing that a gift will fail only if and when it becomes established that the vesting must occur, if at all, after the end of the perpetuity period.[78]

Duration

A charitable trust may be made to endure for any period which the author of the trust may desire.[79] It may therefore be created for the application of the income in perpetuity to the charitable purpose, or it may be so framed as to require the immediate distribution of the capital, or the exhaustion of capital and income, during a limited or indefinite period.[80] This exception to the rule that a trust for the application of income for an indefinite period is void as tending to a perpetuity is well established.[81] It is founded upon grounds of public policy,[82] and is essential to the useful existence of charitable trusts.[83]

3–020

But to qualify for the benefit of the exemption from the rule against perpetuities, a trust must be charitable within the legal meaning of that word. Thus, a perpetual trust for the repair of a tomb, not forming part of the fabric of a church,[84] or for any other object or any institution or society not of a charitable character,[85] is void. Similarly, a gift in perpetuity of the income of a legacy, for the benefit of individuals answering a certain description, without any reference to age or poverty, is likewise void.[86] There is no escape from the dilemma that a perpetual trust must be either charitable, or void as tending to a perpetuity.[87]

---

[77] The Act applies to instruments taking effect after July 16, 1964: s.1.
[78] s.3.
[79] *Re Bowen* [1893] 2 Ch. 494 at 495.
[80] For examples, see *Att-Gen v Lawes* (1849) 8 Ha. 32; *Barclay v Maskelyne* (1859) 4 Jur.(N.S.) 1294; *Pease v Pattinson* (1886) 32 Ch.D. 154.
[81] *White v White* (1802) 7 Ves. 422; *Chamberlayne v Brockett*, above; *Att-Gen v Webster* (1875) 20 Eq. 483; *Goodman v Saltash* (1882) 7 A.C. 633 at 642, 650, 651, 662; *Re St. Stephen, Coleman Street* (1888) 39 Ch.D. 492 at 496, 501; *Re Norwich, etc., Charity* (1889) 40 Ch.D. 307; *Re Tyler* [1891] 3 Ch. 257; *Commissioners of Income Tax v Pemsel* [1891] A.C. 531 at 581; *Re Rymer* [1895] 1 Ch. 19, 25; and see *Re Bowen* [1893] 2 Ch. 491; *Re Swain* [1905] 1 Ch. 669.
[82] *Yeap Cheah Neo v Ong Cheng Neo* (1875) L.R. 6 P.C. 381 at 394.
[83] *Commissioners of Income Tax v Pemsel*, above; *Re Tyler*, above. A similar rule and the exception to it in the case of charitable uses are to be found in colonial law: *Yeap Cheah Neo v Ong Cheng Neo*, above.
[84] *Gravenor v Hallum* (1767) Amb. 643; *Doe v Pitcher* (1815) 3 M. & S. 407; *Lloyd v Lloyd* (1852) 2 Sim. (N.S.) 255; *Rickard v Robson* (1862) 31 B. 244; *Fowler v Fowler* (1864) 33 B. 616; *Hoare v Osborne* (1866) L.R. 1 Eq. 585; *Toole v Hamilton* [1901] Ir.R. 383.
[85] *Thomson v Shakespear* (1860) 1 De G.F. & J. 399; *Carne v Long* (1860) 2 De G.F. & J. 75; *Re Clark's Trust* (1875) 1 Ch.D. 497; *Yeap Cheah Neo v Ong Cheng Neo* (1875) L.R. 6 P.C. 381; *Re Dutton* (1878) 4 Ex.D. 54; *Hoare v Hoare* (1886) 56 L.T. 147; *Re Amos* [1891] 3 Ch. 159, 164; *Re Clarke* [1901] 2 Ch. 110; *Re Mann* [1903] 1 Ch. 232.
[86] *Re Gassiot* (1901) 70 L.J.Ch. 242.
[87] *Thomson v Shakespear* (1860) John. 617; *Carne v Long* (1860) 2 De G.F. & J. 75; *Rickard v Robson* (1862) 31 B. 244; *Att-Gen v Webster* (1875) 20 Eq. 491; *Re Dutton* (1878) 4 Ex.D. 54; *Goodman v Saltash* (1882) 7 A.C. 633 at 650; *Re St. Stephen, Coleman Street* (1888) 39 Ch.D. 492 at 503; *Re Norwich, etc., Charity* (1889) 40 Ch.D. 307; *Commissioners of Income Tax v Pemsel* [1891] A.C. 581. The doctrine above laid down was not apparently recognised

The rule against perpetual duration cannot be evaded by making a charity the trustee.[88] Thus a condition attached to a charitable gift, constituting a trust in favour of objects not charitable,[89] as, for instance, that the donor's tomb should be repaired for ever out of the trust funds,[90] or that the charity should grant a lease to private individuals 95 years hence,[91] or a lease for ever to the testator's relatives,[92] is void.

Accumulations

3–021   There is no exception from the statutory provisions restricting accumulations[93] in the case of charities.[94] If a charitable fund is directed to be accumulated beyond the limit allowed, a scheme may be settled by the court for the proper application of the fund.[95]

The rule in *Saunders v Vautier*[96] applies in the case of charities, so that if an accumulation is directed, and the capital and accumulations are given absolutely to a particular charitable institution, whether corporate or unincorporate, the institution has the same right as an individual would have under similar circumstances to stop the accumulations and call for the immediate payment of the gift.[97] The rules were applied in *Re Green's Will Trusts*[98] where the testatrix directed her trustees to invest the capital and accumulate the income of the residue of her estate and, if her missing son had not come forward by January 1, 2020, to establish a charitable foundation. Nourse J. directed that the income could be accumulated for 21 years from the testatrix's death and, if it became impossible for her son to come forward before the 21 years had expired, that charity was entitled to stop the accumulations and take capital and accumulations.

in certain anomalous cases in which it was held that a perpetual trust of an advowson was valid, but not charitable; or in *Att-Gen v Hewer* (1700) 2 Vern. 387, where a perpetual trust of a school for the inhabitants of a certain district was held not to be charitable. See as to these cases, *Re St. Stephen, Coleman Street*, above; and *Re Church Patronage Trust* [1904] 1 Ch. 41 at 50; 2 Ch. 643.

[88] *Re Tyler* [1891] 3 Ch. 258; and see *Re Bowen* [1893] 2 Ch. 491.
[89] As to conditions constituting trusts, see, paras 3–006, 3–007, above.
[90] *Re Tyler* above, at 259. *cf. Doe v Pitcher* (1815) 3 M. & S. 407; and as to trusts for repairing tombs, see para.3–011, above.
[91] (1855) 7 De G.M. & G. 647. Distinguish *Walsh v Secretary of State for India* (1863) 10 H.L.C. 367.
[92] *Att-Gen v Greenhill* (1863) 33 B. 193; *cf. Att-Gen v Catherine Hall* (1820) Jac. 381. A direction that the rents should not be raised during the lives of the existing tenants would be a valid gift for the benefit of those tenants: *Att-Gen v Catherine Hall*, above, at 395.
[93] Law of Property Act 1925, ss.164–166 (replacing the Thellusson Act 1800, thereby repealed); Perpetuities and Accumulations Act 1964, s.13. There is an exception in favour of funds given towards paying off the national debt: Superannuation and other Trust Funds (Validation) Act 1927, s.9.
[94] *Martin v Margham* (1844) 14 Sim 230; *Re Bradwell* [1952] Ch. 575; and see *Re Swain* [1905] 1 Ch. 669.
[95] *Re Monk* [1927] 2 Ch. 197.
[96] (1841) Cr. & Ph. 240.
[97] *Wharton v Masterman* [1895] A.C. 186; overruling the expression of opinion to the contrary contained in *Harbin v Masterman* (1871) L.R. 12 Eq. 559; and see *Re Travis* [1900] 2 Ch. 541.
[98] [1985] 3 All E.R. 455.

Determinable gifts

The interest of the charity may be limited to the enjoyment of the **3–022**
income, or to the usufruct of the property during a definite or indefinite
period. Thus, it may be limited to endure only during the continuance of
a particular state of circumstances, or until the happening of an uncertain
event,[99] as where freehold land was devised to a charity school with a
direction that the rents should be applied for the benefit of the school "so
long as it shall continue to be endowed with charity."[1] So also in the case
of a bequest for the benefit of the minister of a particular church, so long
as he teaches particular doctrines,[2] or conducts the services in a certain
way,[3] or permits the sittings to be occupied free.[4] Similarly, where there is
a gift over, or a direction that the fund shall fall into residue in the event
of the charitable purpose named becoming incapable of taking effect[5]; but
not where there is a mere gift of residue without a direction that the fund
in question shall fall into it.[6]

In these cases (differing in this respect from conditions in defeasance) the
interest of the charity terminates automatically on the cesser of the circumstances or the happening of the event in question. The burden of proving that a determinable interest has ceased is on those who allege it. Thus in
Re Hartshill Endowment[7] a trust for an incumbent so long as he "conducted
the service according to the rites and ceremonies of the Church of England,
in strict and literal accordance with the order of the Book of Common
Prayer" was held not to require a daily service.

The undisposed of interest remains with the donor,[8] or, in the case of a
will, falls into residue or else devolves upon the testator's legal personal
representatives, as the case may be,[9] and cannot under any circumstances
be appropriated for the benefit of the charity. The rule against perpetuities
had no application to an undisposed-of interest.[10] It made no difference
that the instrument creating the gift contained a direction that the property should go in the way in which it would, without such direction,

---

[99] As to the difference between a determinable limitation and a limitation on condition, see
para.3–026, n.26, below.

[1] *Att-Gen v Pyle* (1738) 1 Atk. 435.

[2] *Att-Gen v Molland* (1832) You. 562.

[3] *Re Hartshill Endowment* (1861) 30 B. 130.

[4] *Re Randell* (1888) 38 Ch.D. 213.

[5] See *Mayor of Lyons v Adv.-Gen. of Bengal* (1875) 1 App. Cas. 91; *Re Randell* (1888) 38
Ch.D. 213.

[6] See *Mayor of Lyons v Adv.-Gen. of Bengal* (1875) 1 App. Cas. at 115.

[7] (1861) 30 B. 160.

[8] *Re Randell* (1888) 38 Ch.D. 213; *Re Blunt's Trusts* [1904] 2 Ch. 767 at 773; *Re Stanford*
[1924] 1 Ch. 73. For the reconciliation of *Re Randell and Re Blunt's Trusts* with *Re Peel's
Release* [1921] 2 Ch. 218 and *Re Bowen* [1893] 2 Ch. 491, see *Re Talbot* [1933] Ch. 892 at
902 *per Maugham J.*, as explained in *Gibson v South American Stores (Gath and Chaves)*
[1950] Ch. 177; *Re Cooper's Conveyance* [1956] 1 W.L.R. 1096.

[9] *Att-Gen v Pyle* (1738) 1 Atk. 435; *Walsh v Secretary of State for India* (1863) 10 H.L.C.
367; *Re Randell* (1888) 38 Ch.D. 213.

[10] *Att-Gen v Pyle* (1738) 1 Atk. 435; *Re Randell* (1888) 38 Ch.D. 213; *Re Blunt's Trusts* [1904]
2 Ch. 267 at 772; see also *Re Bowen* [1893] 2 Ch. 195; and *cf. Walsh v Secretary of State for
India* (1863) 10 H.L.C. 367.

devolve according to the law.[11] For dispositions taking effect after July 15, 1964, a determinable gift will become absolute once it becomes established that the determining event must occur, if at all, outside the perpetuity period.[12]

Conditional gifts

3–023   A charitable gift may be subject to a condition precedent or a condition subsequent.

Conditions precedent

3–024   A charitable gift may be subject to a condition precedent, for example, that the testator's estate is sufficient for the purpose intended,[13] or amounts to a specified sum.[14] A condition may be implied, for example, that the particular purpose for which a legacy is given proves to be practicable,[15] or that other property is given for the same object.[16] If the condition precedent is not satisfied, the charitable gift fails to take effect.[17] The gift will also fail if the condition offends against the rule against perpetuities.[18]

Conditions subsequent

3–025   An example of a charitable gift subject to a condition subsequent is a devise to a charitable institution on condition of its maintaining certain children from a particular parish,[19] another is a gift to provide an income for the incumbent of a particular church on condition of his celebrating divine service at specified times, or in a particular way.[20] In *Re Tyler*,[21] the

---

[11] *Re Randell* (1888) 38 Ch.D. 213, at 218; *Re Blunt's Trusts* [1904] 2 Ch. 767 at 773; *cf. Mayor of Lyons v Adv.-Gen. of Bengal* (1876) 1 App. Cas. 91.

[12] Perpetuities and Accumulations Act 1964, s.12(1), s.3.

[13] *Cherry v Mott* (1836) 1 My. & Cr. 123.

[14] *Thomas v Howell* (1874) 18 Eq. 198.

[15] *Re London University Medical Sciences Fund* [1902] 2 Ch. 1.

[16] *McCormick v Queen's University of Belfast* [1958] N.I. 1.

[17] *De Themmines v De Bonneval* (1828) 5 Russ. 289; *Chamberlayne v Brockett* (1872) L.R. 8 Ch. 211; *Thomas v Howell* (1874) L.R. 18 Eq. 198; *Cherry v Mott* (1836) 1 My. & Cr. 123; *Re Tunno* [1886] W.N. 154; *Re Swain* [1905] 1 Ch. 669 at 676.

[18] See para.3–019, above.

[19] *Att-Gen v Christ's Hospital* (1790) 3 Br.C.C. 165. See also *Att-Gen v Christ's Hospital* (1830) 1 R. & M. 626.

[20] *Re Conington's Will* (1860) 8 W.R. 444; *Governors of Bethleham and Bridewell Hospital v Ironmongers' Co.* (1881), unreported, cited below, para.3–031 below. See also *Re Parker's Charity* (1863) 32 B. 654; *Re Robinson* [1892] 1 Ch. 95; [1897] 1 Ch. 85. In *Milbank v Lambert* (1860) 28 B. 206, the gift was in lieu of tithes.

[21] [1891] 3 Ch. 252; *cf. Doe v Pitcher* (1815) 3 M. & S. 407; *Re Davies* [1915] 1 Ch. 543. In *Re Welstead* (1858) 25 B. 612, a legacy to form an additional endowment for a district church, with a declaration that in consideration of the legacy the testator's nephew and his heirs should have every third nomination of the officiating clergyman, was construed as a bequest for the purchase of the right of nomination.

will not always give rise to a forfeiture. Thus, in *Re Upton Warren*[66] there was a trust for apprenticing poor boys from particular parishes, and a gift over of each year's income to Christ's Hospital in the event of no apprentice being maintained during that year. The trustees neglected to carry out the trusts for thirty-eight years, but it was held that Christ's Hospital was not entitled to the arrears of income, upon the ground that the primary objects of the trust were the inhabitants of the parishes named; and a scheme to apply the arrears for their benefit was directed.

Failure on the part of trustees to comply with the donor's directions will, however, occasion a forfeiture if the gift over is expressly directed to take effect in that event.[67]

It is, however, difficult to see what is the distinction between the cases where the default of the trustees to apply property in accordance with the directions of the donor or testator is nonetheless not allowed to defeat the gift[68] and the cases in which the default of the trustees does have the result of defeating the gift.[69] It is practically impossible to discover what is the dividing line.[70] It appears that where trustees hold a fund to apply the income in perpetuity for specified charitable purposes and there is a gift over of the fund to another charity in the event of the trustees at any time failing to distribute the income according to the directions of the settlor or testator, and the trustees subsequently find that they cannot comply strictly with the terms of the gift, the court has power in its discretion to direct a scheme continuing the original trusts in a different form, even though the effect of such scheme if directed would be to defeat the gift over; but that the court is not bound to direct a scheme and may by refusing such direction allow the gift over to take effect.[71] It would appear that the court will be unlikely to direct a scheme if the trustees have, though acting in complete good faith, misapplied the income for a long time and that the court will be more likely to direct a scheme if the trustees apply to the court as soon as practicable after it has become apparent that exact compliance with the terms of the gift has become impossible.[72]

3–031

Northumberland v Aylesford (1760) Amb. 540 at 657, a legacy was given on condition that the legatee should release certain claims, with a gift over if he refused. The legatee accepted the legacy but died without having executed a deed of release. It was held (at 658) that the acceptance of the legacy was "the release itself in equity and conscience", and the executors were ordered to execute a formal deed of release. In *Simpson v Vickers* (1807) 14 Ves. 341, this decision was said to have been shaken by *Beaulieu v Cardigan* (1766) Amb. 533, but in that case limitations of real estate were involved. In cases of this kind the gift over must be referred to the non-acceptance of the gift, not the breach of the condition.

[66] (1833) 1 Myl. & K. 410; *cf. Att-Gen v Boultbee* (1796) 2 Ves. 380.
[67] *Christ's Hospital v Grainger* (1849) 1 Mac. & G. 460.
[68] *Re Upton Warren* (1833) 1 Myl. & K. 410; *Re Richardson* (1888) 58 L.T. 45; *Re Trustees of Orchard Street School* [1878] W.N. 211.
[69] *Christ's Hospital v Grainger* (1849) 1 Mac. & G. 460.
[70] See *Re Hanbey's Will Trusts* [1956] Ch. 264 at 273, 274, *per* Danckwerts J.
[71] *Re Hanbey's Will Trusts* [1956] Ch. 264.
[72] *ibid.*, at 275, *per* Danckwerts J.

The burden of proving that a forfeiture has taken effect, is on those who allege it, and conditions involving a forfeiture are strictly construed.[73] The question is usually one of mixed construction and fact.[74]

In several old cases the question of what was sufficient to satisfy a condition requiring the performance of divine service arose. In *Re Conington's Will*[75] lands were demised to the use of a vicar of a parish on condition that he read prayers in the parish church at specified times, with a gift over of the rents and profits during the life of any vicar who neglected to comply with the condition, and it was held that neglect meant wilful neglect, and that omission to perform services in consequence of its having been found impossible to obtain a congregation was not wilful neglect. With the last-mentioned case may be compared an unreported case,[76] where a testator directed that the rents of certain land should be paid to some person to celebrate the divine service in the parish church every day in the week for ever; and in case of failure to perform service for more than three days together, the rents were directed to be paid to a hospital. Divine service not having been performed as required, the gift over was held to have taken effect. Jessel M.R. said:

> "It is no answer to say that there was no congregation. A congregation sufficient for saying the prayers is not limited by law to any number of persons. The minister and his clerk, and the sextoness, would have done very well, or the minister and his clerk would have done very well. There was no occasion to have any one else there. But what the testator required was that the service should be performed and anybody might have come and attended the church."

3–032   The compulsory purchase of the property under statutory powers will not apparently occasion a forfeiture.[77]

It should be observed that the right to claim the benefit of a gift over may be barred by lapse of time.[78] The old Statute of Limitations did not, and the Limitation Act 1980 does not, apply where the property remains in the hands of the trustees, and the question is only whether one or other of certain persons is the *cestui que trust*.[79]

If a gift over is valid, and the circumstances upon which it was to arise are shown to have happened, the property passes and cannot be recalled, and it makes no difference that the gift over is for the benefit of another charity.[80] For although equity can relieve against a forfeiture for breach of

---

[73] *Re Conington's Will* (1860) 8 W.R. 444; and *Re Beard's Trusts* [1904] 1 Ch. 270.

[74] The question seems to have been so treated in *Re Hanbey's Will Trusts* [1956] Ch. 264 at 275.

[75] (1860) 8 W.R. 444.

[76] *Bethlehem and Bridewell Hospitals v Ironmongers' Co.*, Jessel M.R. April 4, 1881. A transcript of the proceedings in this case is on the files of the Charity Commissioners.

[77] *Re Trustees of Orchard Street Schools* [1878] W.N. 211.

[78] See *Re Orchard Street Schools* [1878] W.N. 211; and as to laches, see *Re Upton Warren* (1833) 1 Myl. & K. 410.

[79] *Christ's Hospital v Grainger* (1849) 1 Mac. & G. 465. As to the application of the Statute of Limitations between trustee and *cestui que trust*, see Limitation Act 1980, s.21.

[80] *Christ's Hospital v Grainger* (1848) 1 Mac. & G. 460; *Re Orchard Street Schools* [1878] W.N. 211; *Bethlehem and Bridewell Hospitals v Ironmongers' Co.*, cited at n.76, above.

condition, where the condition can be subsequently satisfied, or where the breach admits of compensation,[81] it cannot do so where the property is given to another person on breach of the condition.[82] A gift over, in case the intended charitable dispositions should be invalid, is good.[83]

Patronage

It has already been noted that the rule of certainty of objects is satisfied if the selection of charitable objects is left to the trustees.[84] Patronage is the right of nominating who shall be a beneficiary of a charity. Patronage is, like visitation,[85] in that it is derived from the property which the founder has in the endowment of the charity,[86] and in the same way as visitation it belongs to the founder and his heirs or nominees.[87] Visitation, however, is generally confined to corporations,[88] and it accordingly follows that in such cases patronage and visitation are necessarily consequent upon each other.[89] The difference is that the right of patronage is not limited to corporations.[90]

3–033

The founder or his heirs will apparently forfeit the right of nomination by a corrupt or improper nomination. The same may also happen if they neglect to nominate, although here there can be no neglect in this sense until the founder or his heirs have had notice of the vacancy.[91]

The founder may confer the right of patronage upon others either expressly or by implication. Thus in *Att-Gen v Dean and Canons of Christ Church*[92] property was devised to the Dean and Canons of Christ Church, Oxford, in trust to constitute and support a grammar school at Portsmouth, to appoint a master and usher, and pay them a salary. The testator also ordered the Dean and Canons to direct the management of the school. Lord Eldon held that they also had the power to nominate free scholars. "The testator," observed his Lordship,[93] "has given the direction and management of the school to the Dean and Canons, and they are therefore the persons to nominate and appoint the scholars, and I do not know how any restriction on their power can be introduced. Is it not part of the management to nominate and send to the school the persons who are to be educated?"

---

[81] See the non-charitable cases of *Cage v Russel* (1682) 2 Ventris, 352; and *Hollinrake v Lister* (1826) 1 Russ. 508.

[82] See the non-charitable cases of *Cleaver v Spurling* (1729) 2 P.Wms. 528, and *Simpson v Vickers* (1807) 14 Ves. 341.

[83] See *De Themmines v De Bonneval* (1828) 5 Russ. 288; *Gilmour v Coats* [1949] A.C. 426; and see also *Carter v Green* (1857) 3 K. & J. 591; *Warren v Rudall* (1858) 4 K. & J. 618 at 619.

[84] See para.3–013, above.

[85] See para.10–063, below.

[86] *Green v Rutherforth* (1750) 1 Ves.Sen. 472; *Philips v Bury* (1788) 2 T.R. 352.

[87] *Philips v Bury*, above, at 352, 353; and see *Att-Gen v Leigh* (1721) 3 P.Wms. 145n.

[88] See para.10–063, below.

[89] *Philips v Bury*, above, at 352.

[90] *Att-Gen v Rigby* (1730) 3 P.Wms. 145.

[91] See *per* Lord Parker in *Att-Gen v Leigh*, above.

[92] (1821) Jac. 474. See also *Re Church Patronage Trust* [1904] 1 Ch. 41; 2 Ch. 643.

[93] (1821) Jac. 486.

3–034   The right of patronage, being in the nature of a freehold hereditament, is also capable of direct alienation. This was shown in *Att-Gen v Master of Brentwood School*.[94] In this case a grammar school was founded and endowed under letters patent which ordered that the school should be completely in the patronage and disposition of the founder and his heirs and that the schoolmasters and guardians should be nominated by them for ever. It was held that the right of patronage might be lawfully alienated. This case was followed in *Att-Gen v Boucherett*,[95] where a testator bequeathed a sum to a trustee upon trust to lay it out in lands for the endowment of a school and appointed that the trustee and his heirs "should be feoffees in trust and patrons and protectors of the said school for the electing a fit and sufficient schoolmaster." Romilly M.R. held that the right of patronage was alienable. "I am of opinion," said his Lordship, "that the case of *Att-Gen v Master of Brentwood School* governs this case, and that the right of patronage is quite as much within the power of alienation as it was in that case, and that no distinction arises from the fact that property here is given in trust, and that the feoffees take it in trust for the purposes of a school and that they are to be 'patrons and protectors of the school.' That gives them the power of appointment in the first instance, and it is impossible to say that it is more a trust in one case than in another. If the power is given, as it was in the case of *Brentwood School*, directly to appoint the schoolmaster, it is still a trust to be performed, for it is clear that the patron could not appoint a person manifestly unfit; he must appoint a person who is fit and proper for the purpose of carrying on the school, and to that extent, and no further, it is a trust in every such case."

Similarly, it has been held that where the owner of a manor has, as incident to it, the right of patronage in appointing the master and almspeople of a hospital, he may alienate the right of patronage without parting with the manor,[96] or, conversely, he can alienate the manor without parting with the right.[97] On the other hand, where the right of electing almsmen was, by the deed of foundation, vested in the minister, churchwardens, overseers and those of the parishioners who paid poor rates it was held that it did not pass to a vestry created by the Metropolis Management Act 1855.[98]

Subscribers to a charity who are entitled to votes in proportion to the amount of their subscriptions may vote for any candidate they please. Moreover, there is nothing illegal in an agreement between two such subscribers that if one will give certain votes at one election to an object favoured by the other, the latter will at a future election vote for the object favoured by the former.[99] The giving of the votes by the one is, in such a

---

[94] (1832) 3 B. & Ad. 59.
[95] (1858) 25 Beav. 116.
[96] *Att-Gen v Ewelme Hospital* (1854) 17 Beav. 366 at 384.
[97] *ibid.*
[98] *Att-Gen v Drapers' Co.* (1858) 4 Dr. 299.
[99] *Bolton v Madden* (1873) L.R. 9 Q.B. 55. See *Worthington v Hargood* (1873) 27 L.T. 786, where the question was with regard to the election of a medical officer of an infirmary by the votes of the governors. As to the election of a medical officer of an infirmary, see also

case, a legal consideration for the promise by the other, and the contract will be enforced accordingly.[1]

In selecting the charitable objects, regard must be had to any qualifications required by the instrument of foundation or scheme. Thus in *Re Storie's University Gift*,[2] where a scheme for a charity for the presentation of exhibitions to a university provided that two exhibitioners should be elected from boys who "shall have been" three years at a certain school, it was held that the three years must be those immediately preceding the election. Again, if the direction is that scholars are to be elected by competitive examination, with a preference, *ceteris paribus*, to a person possessing a certain qualification, it is only where the difference between two candidates is so slight that they are substantially equal that the direction as to preference can operate. Where the difference between two candidates is considerable, the competitive test alone can be taken into account.[3]

On the other hand, it is immaterial how the qualification has been acquired. The question is simply whether a proposed object possesses the qualification or not. If he does, it is of no consequence that he expressly and avowedly obtained it for the purpose of enabling him to partake in the charity.[4] Thus in *Etherington v Wilson*,[5] where the object of a charity was the election to Christ's Hospital of the sons of parishioners of a certain parish, it was held that the son of a person who answered the description of "parishioner" was a proper object, although he had become a parishioner temporarily in order to acquire the qualification. So also where compliance with certain religious directions is a necessary qualification any persons who comply with the directions are proper objects, and the trustees cannot proceed to inquire whether the compliance is sincere.[6]

3–035

Persons who have been elected in good faith but erroneously (*e.g.* under a mistaken interpretation of a scheme) will not be removed[7]: different considerations will apply to an election which is improper and this may be set aside.[8] Furthermore, payments to objects nominated by the wrong persons will also be allowed to stand. So in one case, where the heirs of the grantor, and not the grantees, were the persons to nominate the objects of the charity, but the grantees had for upwards of 60 years made the nominations, they were held not to be bound to account for the payments they had

---

Howard v Hill (1888) 37 W.R. 219. There is no right to vote by proxy unless given by statute or the rules of the society, and a proxy is only valid for the particular election for which it is given: *ibid*.

[1] *Bolton v Madden*, above.
[2] (1861) 2 De G.F. & J. 529; *cf. Re Rugby School* (1839) 1 Beav. 457.
[3] *Re Nettle's Charity* (1872) 14 Eq. 434. The examination for a close fellowship is merely to ascertain the fitness of the candidate, and no regard can be had to the comparative qualifications of others: *Ex p. Inge* (1831) 2 R. & M. 590.
[4] *Etherington v Wilson* (1875) 1 Ch.D. 160; *cf. Att-Gen v Calvert* (1857) 23 Beav. 248 at 261.
[5] (1875) 1 Ch.D. 160.
[6] *Att-Gen v Calvert* (1857) 23 Beav. 248 at 261.
[7] *Re Storie's University Gift* (1861) 2 De G.F. & J. 529; *cf. Att-Gen v Hartley* (1820) 2 J. & W. 353; *Att-Gen v Daugars* (1864) 33 Beav. 621.
[8] *Re Nettle's Charity* (1872) 14 Eq. 434; *Rooke v Dawson* [1895] 1 Ch. 480.

made and the court refused to disturb anything that had been already done.[9]

An application to the court in respect of an erroneous or improper election will require in the usual way[10] the consent of the Charity Commissioners.[11]

Validation

3–036 It has already been seen[12] that the inclusion of a non-charitable object will usually cause a gift for purportedly charitable purposes to fail. Three cases highlighted the problem in the 1940s: *Re Diplock*,[13] *Oxford Group v Inland Revenue Commissioners*[14] and *Ellis v Inland Revenue Commissioners*.[15] Other Commonwealth countries had already passed saving legislation for such gifts[16] and validating legislation was recommended by the Committee on the Law and Practice of Charitable Trusts.[17] The resultant legislation was the Charitable Trusts (Validation) Act 1954 which was retrospective and only validated certain trusts in existence before December 16, 1952. The Act was not well drafted, leading Harman J. to say that he had "been floored" by the terms of the statute on the two previous occasions he had to consider it.[18]

In view of the fact that the Act only applies to gifts contained in instruments taking effect over 40 years ago and its limited application to even those gifts,[19] the provisions are considered in outline only. Those requiring a more detailed examination of the Act are referred to earlier editions of this work.[20]

The 1954 Act applies to imperfect trust provisions which are defined[21] as "any provision declaring the objects for which property is to be held or applied and so describing those objects that, consistently with the terms of the provision, the property could be used exclusively for charitable purposes, but could nevertheless be used for purposes which are not charitable".[22] Any such provision which is contained in an instrument[23] taking

---

[9] *Att-Gen v Rigby* (1730) P.Wms. 145; *cf. Christ's Hospital v Charity Commissioners* (1889) 15 A.C. 172.

[10] See para.10–027, below.

[11] Charities Act 1993, s.33.

[12] See para.3–015, above.

[13] [1941] Ch. 253, (on appeal sub nom, *Chichester Diocesan Board of Finance (Incorporated) v Simpson* [1944] A.C. 341).

[14] [1949] 2 All E.R. 537.

[15] (1949) 31 T.C. 178.

[16] For example, in New South Wales, s.37D of the Conveyancing Act 1919 enacted in 1938. See (1967) 16 I.C.L.Q. 464 (M.C. Cullity); (1966) 17 N.I.L.Q. 235 (L.A. Sheridan).

[17] Report of the Committee on the Law and Practice relating to Charitable Trusts, Cmnd. 8710, Chap. 12.

[18] *Re Harpur's Will Trusts* [1962] Ch. 78 at 95.

[19] See, for example, *Vernon v Inland Revenue Commissioners* [1956] 1 W.L.R. 1169.

[20] See 7th ed., p.170, *et seq.*

[21] Charitable Trusts (Validation) Act 1954, s.1(1).

[22] See *Re Gillingham Bus Disaster Fund* [1959] Ch. 62; *Re Harpur's Will Trusts* [1962] Ch. 78; *Re Mead's Trust Deed* [1971] 1 W.L.R. 1244; *Re Saxone Co Ltd's Trust Deed* [1962] 1 W.L.R. 943; *Re South Place Ethical Society* [1980] 1 W.L.R. 1565.

[23] Includes a published appeal—*Re Gillingham Bus Disaster Fund* [1959] Ch. 62 at 70.

effect before December 16, 1952 is deemed to have effect in relation to any disposition or covenant to which the Act applies, before the commencement of the Act, as if the whole of the declared objects were charitable and, after the commencement, as if the provision had required the property to be held or applied for the declared objects only in so far as they authorised the use for charitable purposes.[24] The relevant dispositions and covenants are defined in s.2 of the 1954 Act and include donations to an appeal.[25]

UNINCORPORATED ASSOCIATIONS

The use of an unincorporated association as a legal structure for charities gained popularity in the eighteenth century with the rise of voluntary societies and reflected the change from individual to associated philanthropy.[26] The structure is now used mainly, although not exclusively, by smaller charities with multiple sources of funding for whom membership participation is important. It is not unusual for a charity to commence as an unincorporated association and then to change its legal structure to that of a company limited by guarantee as activities and potential liabilities to third parties increase.　　**3–037**

An unincorporated association is basically a contract between the members. The structure was defined by Slade L.J. in *Re Koeppler's Will Trusts*[27] as:

"an association of persons bound together by identifiable rules and having an identifiable membership."

A charity formed as an unincorporated association has no legal existence separate from its members. The rules of a charitable unincorporated association usually provide for the management of the charity to be the responsibility of a committee elected from amongst the members.[28]

Formalities

There are no statutory formalities to be complied with to found a charity as an unincorporated association. Indeed, there are no statutes specifically dealing with unincorporated associations. An unincorporated association is formed by the agreement between the members which is usually in the form of a written constitution or set of rules. Although it is preferable to have writing setting out the agreement between the members,　　**3–038**

---

[24] Charitable Trusts (Validation) Act 1954, s.1(2).
[25] *Re Gillingham Bus Disaster Fund* [1959] Ch. 62 at 70.
[26] See Owen, *English Philanthropy 1660–1960*, p.71.
[27] [1985] 2 All E.R. 869 at 874.
[28] See, for example, the Charity Commissioners' Model Constitution for a Charitable Unincorporated Association and the Charity Law Association's Constitution for a Charitable Unincorporated Association.

the fact that the agreement is oral will not prevent there being an unincorporated association. If a constitution has not been formally adopted, a set of rules which has been used consistently can be adopted as the constitution by long usage.[29]

The lack of separate legal status makes the holding of property by unincorporated associations problematic.[30] The difficulty is often solved by appointing separate trustees to hold the property for the charitable purposes of the association. Such a trust must comply with the usual rules for the formation of a charitable trusts.[31]

Effect of gifts

3–039   A gift to an unincorporated association, in general, can take effect in one of several ways. In *Neville Estates Ltd v Madden*[32] Cross J. specified[33] three: as a gift to the members of the association at the relevant date as joint tenants[34]; as a gift to the existing members subject to their respective contractual rights and liabilities to each other as members of the association[35]; or, to be held in trust for or applied for the purposes of the association as a quasi-corporate entity. To this list may be added a trust for the members of the association for the time being.[36]

A gift to a charitable unincorporated association tends to be construed by the courts as a gift on trust for the purposes of the association. Thus in *Re Vernon's Will Trusts*[37] Buckley J. said[38]:

> "Every bequest to an unincorporated association by name without more must take effect as a gift for a charitable purpose. No individual or aggregate of individuals could claim to take such a bequest beneficially. If the gift is to be permitted to take effect at all it must be as a bequest for a purpose, *viz.*, that charitable purpose which the named charity exists to serve."

Buckley J. had previously construed a gift to an unincorporated association, the World Refugee Year United Kingdom Committee, as a gift to be

---

[29] *John v Rees* [1970] Ch. 345 at 388 (not a charity case).
[30] See Warburton J. "The Holding of Property by Unincorporated Associations", [1985] Conv. 318.
[31] See paras 3–003 *et seq.*, above.
[32] [1962] Ch. 832.
[33] *ibid.*, at 849.
[34] See, for example, *Re St James Club* (1852) 2 De G.M. & G. 385; *Murray v Johnstone* (1896) 23 S.C. 981.
[35] For a more detailed consideration of this method of holding property see *Re Recher's Will Trusts* [1972] Ch. 526; *Re Grant's Will Trusts* [1980] 1 W.L.R. 360; Warburton, *Unincorporated Associations: Law and Practice* (2nd. ed.), pp.48, *et seq.*
[36] See, for example, *Cocks v Manners* (1871) 12 Eq. 574; *Re Clarke* [1901] 2 Ch. 110.
[37] [1972] Ch. 300n.
[38] *ibid.*, at 303. But *cf. Re Ogden* [1933] Ch. 678 at 681, 682 *per* Lord Tomlin to the effect that a gift to an unincorporated association for the attainment of its purposes "may . . . be upheld as a absolute gift to its members."

held on trust for charitable purposes.[39] The approach was followed by Goff J. in *Re Finger's Will Trusts*.[40]

Support for adopting the purpose trust basis of property holding for **3–040** gifts to charitable unincorporated associations can be seen in Cross J.'s judgment in *Neville Estates Ltd v Madden*[41] where he said:

> "If the gift is one of the second class, *i.e.* one which the members of the association for the time being are entitled to divide among themselves, then, even if the objects of the association are in themselves charitable, the gift would not, I think, be a charitable gift. If, for example, a number of persons formed themselves into an association with a charitable object—say the relief of poverty in some district—but it was part of the contract between them that, if a majority of members so desired, the association should be dissolved and its property divided between the members at the date of dissolution, a gift to the association as part of its general funds would not, I conceive, be a charitable gift."

COMPANIES

Charities have increasingly adopted the legal structure of a company **3–041** limited by guarantee[42] since the structure first appeared in the Companies Act 1862. The structure of a company limited by shares has rarely been used by charities and, after 1982, only a company limited by guarantee can apply to dispense with the word "limited" in its name. A charitable company will only be allowed to exclude "limited" from its name if by its memorandum and articles of association it is subject to four restrictions: first, that the income and property of the company be applied for the objects set out in the memorandum, such objects being exclusively charitable; secondly, that no dividend shall be payable to members; thirdly, that on dissolution any surplus assets are to be transferred to some other institution with similar charitable objects[43]; and, fourthly, that the company shall not alter its memorandum and articles of association to take it outside the exemption provisions.[44]

The definition[45] and other sections[46] of the Charities Act 1993 clearly indicate that the provisions of the Act are to apply to all charities, not

---

[39] *Re Morrison* (1967) 111 S.J. 758.
[40] [1972] Ch. 286 at 294.
[41] [1962] Ch. 832 at 849,850. For non-charitable unincorporated associations the courts seem to prefer to construe gifts as held by the members subject to the contract between them, *i.e.* beneficially and not on trust—see *Re Recher's Will Trust* [1972] Ch. 526 at 539 per Brightman J.
[42] For the general law on companies limited by guarantee, see West E., *Companies Limited by Guarantee* (2000).
[43] Companies Act 1985, s.30(3).
[44] *ibid.*, s.31(1). See, for example, the particular clauses in *Liverpool and District Hospital for Diseases of the Heart v Att-Gen* [1981] Ch. 193.
[45] ss.96, 97.
[46] ss.63–69.

merely those constituted in the form of a trust. Charitable companies are, in law, companies and therefore subject to company law and the control and supervision of the Registrar of Companies as well as charity law and the control and supervision of the Charity Commissioners and the Attorney General.[47]

3–042   The anomalous position of charitable companies was recently summarised by Neuberger J. in *Re ARMS (Multiple Sclerosis Research)*[48] as follows:

> "A company established for charitable purposes none the less has all the incidents of a company with limited liability, albeit that it has some other features (partly developed by the courts and partly contained in statute) as well."

Statutory formalities

3–043   A charitable company must comply with the usual statutory formalities for the formation of a company.[49] Thus, a memorandum[50] and articles of association[51] and the requisite forms and fees must be delivered to the Registrar of Companies for registration as a company. Thereafter, a charitable company is subject to the requirements of company law and must file accounts and annual returns with the Registrar of Companies[52] as well as the Charity Commissioners.

A charitable company which does not have the word "charity" or "charitable" in its name must state the fact that the company is a charity in legible characters in all the following documents: its bills of exchange, promissory notes, endorsements, cheques and orders for money or goods purporting to be signed on behalf of the company; conveyances purporting to be executed by the company and bills rendered by it and its invoices, receipts and letters of credit.[53] In addition, a charitable company must comply with the general requirement to publish its name on the same documents, save conveyances, even if it is exempted from using the word "limited".[54]

---

[47] For an example of the effect of dual law and supervision see the provisions relating to winding-up, para.13–011, below.

[48] [1997] 1 W.L.R. 877 at 881.

[49] See *Palmer's Company Law* (Vol. 1), paras 2.301, *et seq*.

[50] Companies Act 1985, s.10.

[51] *ibid.*, s.7. For a precedent for the memorandum and articles of association of a charitable company limited by guarantee see, the Charity Commissioners' Model Memorandum and Articles of Association for a Charitable Company and the Charity Law Association's Memorandum and Articles of Association for a Charitable Company.

[52] For the detailed provisions see *Palmer's Company Law* (Vol. 2), paras 9.001, *et seq*.

[53] Charities Act 1993, s.68. Failure to comply with the provision is a criminal offence—s.68(3).

[54] Companies Act 1985, s.349(1), Charities Act 1993, s.67. Failure to comply with the provisions is a criminal offence—s.349(2) to (4).

Capacity and powers

A charitable company has limited capacity—it only has power to carry **3–044** out the objects which are set out in its memorandum of association and anything else which is reasonably incidental to the carrying out of those objects. If a company is given specific powers in its memorandum they are usually stated to be subject to the charitable objects[55] and the courts are unlikely to imply powers to carry out non-charitable purposes.[56] A charitable company which attempts to carry out an *ultra vires* act can be restrained by injunction and the directors will be liable for funds expended on an *ultra vires* purpose.[57]

As regards third parties, companies in general have full capacity.[58] The doctrine of *ultra vires*, however, is retained to a limited extent for charitable companies in connection with transactions with third parties by s.65 of the Charities Act 1993. There are only three situations in which a transaction beyond the powers of a charitable company is binding; in all other cases such a transaction is void. First, a person who gives full consideration in money or money's worth and has no knowledge of the lack of capacity or authority can enforce a contract against a charitable company which is beyond the capacity of the company or its directors. Secondly, a person who did not know at the time the act was done that the company is a charity is protected,[59] and, thirdly, anyone who subsequently obtains title to property for full consideration without notice of the original invalidity cannot be required to return the property on the grounds that the original transfer was void. Thus, commercial transactions beyond the capacity of a charitable company or its directors are binding.[60] In an endeavour to ensure that property of a charitable company is retained for charitable purposes, s.65(4) of the 1993 Act provides that an *ultra vires* contract cannot be ratified under s.35(3) of the Companies Act 1985 without the written consent of the Charity Commissioners.

Transactions with third parties are generally not affected by any limitations on the powers of the directors of a company.[61] In relation to charitable companies, however, s.65 of the 1993 Act applies the same restrictions to transactions beyond the powers of the directors as those applying to *ultra vires* transactions. In addition to limiting the removal of restrictions on the powers of directors to essentially commercial contracts, s.65(4) provides that an act of the directors which is beyond their powers because of the objects of the company can only be ratified with the prior written consent of the Charity Commissioners.

---

[55] See, for example, the Charity Law Association's Memorandum and Articles of Association for a Charitable Company, cl.4.

[56] See *Rosemary Simmons Memorial Housing Association Ltd. v United Dominions Trust Ltd* [1987] 1 All E.R. 281. See also Warburton, "Charitable Companies and the Ultra Vires Rule", [1988] Conv. 275.

[57] See *Palmer's Company Law* (Vol. 2), paras 8541, *et seq.*

[58] Companies Act 1985, s.35.

[59] The fact that a company is a charity must appear on its documents—see para.3–043, above.

[60] See Warburton, "Charitable Companies and the Charities Act 1992" (1992) 1 C.L. & P.R. 203.

[61] Companies Act 1985, s.35A.

Effect of gifts

3–045   A charitable company is a separate legal entity capable of holding property. A gift to a charitable company is usually construed as a gift to the body beneficially. The courts' approach was set out by Buckley J. in *Re Vernon's Will Trusts*[62]:

> "There is no need in such a case to infer a trust for any particular purpose. The objects to which the corporate body can properly apply its funds may be restricted by its constitution, but this does not necessitate inferring as a matter of construction of the testator's will a direction that the bequest is to be held in trust for those purposes: the natural construction is that the bequest is made to the corporate body as part of its general funds, that is to say, beneficially, and without the imposition of a trust."

A charitable company may hold particular property, distinct from the general property of the company, on trust for specific charitable purposes. The context of a gift to a charitable company may lead the court to construe it as a gift on trust for the purposes of the company.[63] Clearly to misapply such property would be a breach of trust. It has been questioned whether a charitable company holds its general property on trust for the objects set out in the memorandum of association. The better view, however, would seem to be that such property is not subject to a trust in the strict sense but that it is held by the company subject to a binding legal obligation to apply it for charitable purposes only; the position of a charitable company in relation to its assets is, therefore, "analogous" to that of a trustee.[64]

The case law, however, is not perhaps wholly consistent. Corporate bodies have been held in some circumstances to be subject to the duties of trustees. In *Re Manchester Royal Infirmary*[65] a charitable corporation incorporated by special Act was held to be subject to the Trust Investment Act 1889 and in *Soldiers', Sailors' and Airmen's Family Association v Att-Gen*[66] a chartered corporation was held to be subject to the Trustee Investment Act 1961. In a similar way, directors of a chartered corporation have been refused remuneration on the ground that, although not technically trustees, they are in the same fiduciary position as trustees in respect of the affairs of the corporation.[67] In *Construction Industry Training Board v Att-Gen*[68] the Court of Appeal was concerned to see

[62] [1972] Ch. 300n at 303; see also *Bowman v Secular Society Ltd* [1917] A.C. 406 at 442; *Re Finger's Will Trusts* [1972] Ch. 286; *Rabin v Gerson Berger Association Limited* [1987] unreported but quoted in RR6, *Maintenance of an Accurate Register of Charities* (2000), p. 18.
[63] *Re Meyers* [1951] Ch. 534; *Re Finger's Will Trusts* [1972] Ch. 286 at 298.
[64] See *Liverpool and District Hospital for Diseases of the Heart v Att-Gen* [1981] Ch. 193 at 209.
[65] (1889) 43 Ch.D. 420.
[66] [1968] 1 W.L.R. 313.
[67] *Re French Protestant Hospital* [1951] Ch. 567.
[68] [1973] Ch. 173.

whether the Board was a charity within s.45(1) of the Charities Act 1960,[69] *i.e.* whether the Board was "subject to the control of the High Court in the exercise of the court's jurisdiction with respect to charities." The case was largely concerned with the construction and effect of particular statutory provisions affecting the Board and various provisions of the Charities Act 1960, but Buckley L.J. concluded that the funds from time to time in the hands of the Board were held "on a statutory trust for exclusively charitable purposes."[70] It has also been assumed that funds held by a charitable company limited by guarantee are held in trust for the purpose of applying those funds *cy-près*.[71]

Whilst the above cases may appear to be strong authority for the proposition that a charitable company holds all its assets on trust, in two of the cases[72] the presence of a trust was assumed and the question was considered only incidentally in another.[73]   **3–046**

In contrast, in *Re Vernon's Will Trusts*[74] Buckley L.J. had held earlier that a corporate body takes any gift beneficially, *i.e.* as part of its general funds unless a direction is given that the property be held on trust for the purposes of the corporation.[75] Moreover, in *Von Ernst et Cie SA v IRC*[76] Buckley L.J. was less emphatic than in *Construction Industry Training Board v Att-Gen*[77] in stating that "a company incorporated for exclusively charitable purposes is in the position of a trustee of its funds or at least in an analogous position.[78]

The question was considered most recently by Slade J. in *Liverpool and District Hospital for Diseases of the Heart v Att-Gen*[79] After reviewing the cases, Slade J. adverted to the fact that the concept of a company which was incapable of holding any assets beneficially and yet fully capable of incurring liabilities for itself in its own name was inconsistent with the general intention of the legislature as appearing from the Companies Act 1948. Slade J. said[80]:

---

[69] Now Charities Act 1993, s.96(1).

[70] [1973] Ch. 173 at 187.

[71] *Re Dominion Students Hall Trust* [1947] Ch. 183.

[72] *Re French Protestant Hospital* [1951] Ch. 567 and *Soldiers', Sailors', and Airmen's Families Association v Att-Gen* [1968] 1 W.L.R. 313. See also the assumption in *Harries v Church Commissioners for England* [1993] 2 All E.R. 300 at 303.

[73] *Construction Industry Training Board v Att-Gen* [1973] Ch. 173.

[74] [1972] Ch. 300, applied in *Re Finger's Will Trusts* [1972] Ch. 286.

[75] [1972] Ch. 300 at 303, *per* Buckley J.

[76] [1980] 1 W.L.R. 468 (not a charity case). Buckley L.J. said (at 490) that a corporation which was by its constitution debarred from using or acquiring assets for the purpose of making or obtaining any profit for itself or its corporators, and which served the purpose only of machinery for carrying on exclusively charitable activities, was not an object for the benefit of which settled property or income from it could be applied or which might become beneficially entitled to an interest in possession in settled property within the meaning of the Finance Act 1975, s.29 and Sch.7, para.3(2) (government securities free of capital transfer tax while in foreign ownership).

[77] [1973] Ch. 173.

[78] [1980] 1 W.L.R. 468 at 479.

[79] [1981] Ch. 193; see [1984] Conv. 112 (J. Warburton).

[80] *ibid.*, at 209.

"In a broad sense, a corporate body may no doubt aptly be said to hold its assets as a 'trustee' for charitable purposes in any case where the terms of its constitution place a legally binding restriction on it which obliges it to apply its assets for exclusively charitable purposes. In a broad sense it may even be said, in such a case, that the company is not the 'beneficial owner' of its assets. In my judgment, however, none of the authorities on which [counsel for the Attorney-General] has relied, (including the decision in *Construction Industry Training Board v Attorney-General*)[81] establish that a company formed under the Companies Act 1948 for charitable purposes is a trustee in the strict sense of its corporate assets, so that on a winding up these assets do not fall to be dealt with in accordance with the provisions of section 257 *et seq.* of that Act. They do, in my opinion, clearly establish that such a company is in position *analogous to that of a trustee* in relation to its corporate assets, such as ordinarily to give rise to the jurisdiction of the court to intervene in its affairs; but that is quite a different matter."

3–047   This rejection of the automatic imposition of a trust on assets given to a charitable company was followed by Neuberger J. in *Re ARMS (Multiple Sclerosis Research) Ltd.*[82] Accordingly, a charitable company in insolvent liquidation but not formally dissolved at the date of the testators' deaths took gifts by will. This was so even though it was not unlikely that had the testators known of the insolvent liquidation they would not have intended the gifts to go to the company. A charitable company in liquidation will not take a gift only if there are circumstances that show that the company was to take as a trustee. Neuberger J. did not go out of his way to find such circumstances[83]: all the gifts went to the insolvent company for the benefit of the creditors and, it follows, not for charitable purposes.

OTHER LEGAL STRUCTURES

3–048   Charities with particular objects may adopt the legal structure of an industrial and provident society or a friendly society. Charities may also exist as corporations and, in certain cases, the corporation may be established by statute, church measure or Royal Charter.

Industrial and provident societies

3–049   A charity may adopt the legal structure of an industrial and provident society[84] if it is established for the purpose of carrying on an industry, or

---

[81] [1973] Ch. 173.
[82] [1997] 1 W.L.R. 877.
[83] *ibid.*, at 882.
[84] See, Registrar of Friendly Societies, "Guide to the Law relating to Industrial and Provident Societies"; Snaith, *Handbook of Industrial and Provident Society Law.*

trade business intended to be conducted for the benefit of the community.[85] The structure is used mainly by charitable housing associations.[86]

An industrial and provident society is formed by registration with the Financial Services Authority Mutual Societies Section[87] after a minimum of seven members have submitted a set of rules containing the matters specified in section 1 of the Industrial and Provident Societies Act 1965. A registered society has corporate status with limited liability and can hold property and sue in its own name.[88] A transaction with a third party which is beyond the objects of a society is void and unenforceable.[89] A society is an exempt charity as it is under the supervision and control of the Financial Services Authority.

Friendly societies

A charitable mutual assurance association, *i.e.* one which restricts its members to those who are poor, may adopt the legal structure of a friendly society. Formation is by registration with the central office[90] after submission by at least seven members of a memorandum and rules which comply with the Friendly Societies Act 1992.[91] A registered friendly society has corporate status[92] and can hold property.[93] Transactions beyond the powers of a society are binding as against third parties[94] and third parties giving valuable consideration and in good faith are not affected by the rules of the society.[95] A registered friendly society is an exempt charity as it is subject to the supervision and control of the Financial Services Authority.

3–050

Corporations

A charity may be established as a corporation. Other corporations, whether municipal or sole, may hold property on charitable trusts[96] but they are not charitable corporations because their purposes are not exclusively charitable. An ecclesiastical corporation is not within the definition of "charity" in the Charities Act 1993.[97]

3–051

---

[85] Industrial and Provident Societies Act 1965, s.1.

[86] For the detailed law relating to housing associations see, Alder, *Housing associations: the law of social landlords* (1997).

[87] The Registry of Friendly Societies was abolished by the Financial Services and Markets Act 2000, s.335.

[88] Industrial and Provident Societies Act 1965, s.3.

[89] *Rosemary Simmons Memorial Housing Association Ltd v United Dominions Trust* [1987] 1 All E.R. 281.

[90] Friendly Societies Act 1992, s.5.

[91] *ibid.*, s.5 and Sch.3.

[92] *ibid.*, s.5(3). Older registered unincorporated friendly societies may be incorporated by registration under the 1992 Act—s.6.

[93] *ibid.*, ss.14, 15.

[94] *ibid.*, s.8(4)(5).

[95] *ibid.*, s.9(4)(5).

[96] See para.5–002, below. Individual trustees may also become incorporated, see para.5–019, below.

[97] Charities Act 1993, s.96(2).

A charitable corporation may be established directly by Royal Charter, or by Royal Charter granting the holder of an office the right to create corporations indefinitely[98] or by a private individual acting under Royal licence.[99] In addition, a corporation may be created by Act of Parliament.[1] It is possible for a corporation to exist by prescription.[2]

Provided there is a clear intention to incorporate, no particular form of words is required to create a charitable corporation either by charter or Act of Parliament.[3] In the case of a charitable corporation established directly by Royal Charter, the charity usually exists previously under another legal structure, for example, as an unincorporated association, which then petitions for a Royal Charter.[4] In the case of an eleemosynary corporation the founder has the right to make such provisions as he wishes for the government of the foundation,[5] including visitation.[6]

3–052   Eleemosynary corporations are those corporations constituted for the perpetual distribution of free alms and bounty of the founder to such persons as he has directed[7] and are generally hospitals or colleges.[8] Such corporations hold their corporate property upon charitable trusts.[9] Although other corporations have from time to time been regarded as trustees in relation to their general funds,[10] the better view is that non-eleemosynary corporations hold their general property beneficially and not on trust. Thus, in *Re Vernon's Will Trusts*[11] Buckley J. said:

> "A bequest to a corporate body, on the other hand, takes effect simply as a gift to that body beneficially, unless there are circumstances which show that the recipient is to take the gift as a trustee."

Such corporations can also hold, in addition to their general property, property for specific charitable purposes which is held on charitable trusts.

---

[98] For example, the Chancellor of Oxford University, Bl. Com. (16th ed.), 474.
[99] *Sutton's Hospital Case* (1613) 10 Co. Rep. 23a at 31a; *Ex p. Kirkby Ravensworth Hospital* (1808) 15 Ves. 305; *Att-Gen v Dulwich College* (1841) 4 Beav. 255.
[1] See, for example, *Construction Industry Training Board v Att-Gen* [1973] Ch. 173, Church Commissioners Measure 1947, s.2, 18 (Church Commissioners).
[2] *Birmingham School Case* (1725) Gilb. 178 at 180.
[3] *Sutton's Hospital Case* (1612) 10 Co. Rep. 23a at 28a.
[4] *Att-Gen v National Hospital for the Relief and Cure of the Paralysed and Epileptic* [1904] 2 Ch. 252 at 256.
[5] *Phillips v Bury* (1788) 2 T.R. 346 at 353; *Green v Rutherforth* (1750) 1 Ves. S. 462 at 472; *Spencer v All Souls College* (1762) Wilm. Notes 163.
[6] See p.374, below.
[7] 1 Bl. Com. (16th ed.), 459; Shelf, Mortmain 23.
[8] See para.10–064, below.
[9] *Thetford School Case* (1610) 8 Co. Rep. 130b at 131a; *Lydiatt v Foach* (1700) 2 Vern. 410 at 412; *Att-Gen v Whorwood* (1750) 1 Ves. 537; *Mayor of Colchester v Lowten* (1813) 1 V. & B. 226; *Ex p. Berkhampstead Free School* (1813) 2 V. & B. 134; *Att-Gen v Wyggeston's Hospital* (1852) 12 Beav. 113; *Att-Gen v St Cross Hospital* (1853) 17 Beav. 435 at 466; *Re Manchester Royal Infirmary* (1889) 43 Ch.D. 420 at 428 and see *Hume v Lopes* [1892] A.C. 112.
[10] See, for example, *Re Manchester Royal Infirmary* (1889) 43 Ch.D. 420 and the discussion at paras 3–045, *et seq*, above.
[11] [1972] 1 Ch. 300n. at 303. See also *Bowman v Secular Society Ltd* [1917] A.C. 406 at 447; *Re Ogden* [1933] Ch. 678 at 681, 682.

The capacity of a corporation established directly by Royal Charter and the means to control such a corporation was set out clearly by Browne-Wilkinson V.C. (as he then was) in *Pearce v University of Aston (No 2)* as follows[12]:

> "It is true that as against the outside world the university, being a body incorporated by royal charter, has the capacity of a natural person; as a result even acts done in contravention of a provision of its statutes are as against the outside world not ultra vires or void. But, as between those subject to the domestic law of the corporation, the members are entitled to insist on the lawful administration of the corporation."

In contrast a corporation established by statute has only those powers granted expressly or by implication by the statute.[13] In the hybrid case of case of a corporation established by Royal Charter pursuant to a statute, the extent of the powers exercisable by the corporation will depend on the construction and intent of the statute.[14]

Proposed new structure

It has long been recognised that none of the legal structures detailed above is ideal for charities.[15] All the legal structures require some adaptation for charities and some, such as trusts and unincorporated associations, impose what many regard as unacceptable levels of personal liability and others, such as companies limited by guarantee, impose the burden of dual registration. The Strategy Unit report proposed that there should be a new corporate structure specifically for charities, the Charitable Incorporated Organisation (CIO).[16]   **3–053**

The key features of the proposed structure are that it should be a body corporate, registered with the charity regulator,[17] with legal personality separate from that of its members, which can sue and be sued in its own registered name and that the liability of members be limited. It is proposed that the CIO should have both foundation and membership formats so that it is appropriate for charities with and without a membership structure. Legislation would set out the administrative powers, but in a flexible form to reflect the diversity of the sector in terms of size and purpose. It is intended that model constitutions will be prepared by co-ordinating

---

[12] [1991] 2 All E.R. 469 at 475.

[13] *Sutton's Hospital Case* (1612) 10 Co. Rep. 1a; *Hazell v Hammersmith and Fulham LBC* [1992] 2 A.C. 1, 39.

[14] *Bonanza v Creek Gold Mining Co Ltd* [1916] 1 A.C. 566, 577–578; *Hazell v Hammersmith and Fulham LBC* [1992] 2 A.C. 1 at 40.

[15] See *Meeting the challenge of change: voluntary action into the 21st century*, The Report of the Commission on the Future of the Voluntary Sector (1996), para.3.4.

[16] Cabinet Office, Strategy Unit, *Private Action, Public Benefit. A Review of Charities and the Wider Not-For-Profit Sector* (2002), p.58. See also, Department of Trade and Industry, *Modern Company Law for a Competitive Economy: Final Report* (2002), paras.4.63–4.67.

[17] *i.e.* the reformed Charity Commissioners, see para.9–004, below.

bodies, tailor-made for particular parts of the charity sector. Such constitutions would be complete and in plain English. The legislation would also
contain a default power for the constitution of a CIO to be amended by a
75 per cent majority of those present and voting at a meeting or by unanimous written resolution. Statutory provisions would set out the trustees'
duty of loyalty, trustees duty of care consistent with s.1 of the Trustee Act
2000 and the trustees and members duty to exercise their powers and discharge their duties in the interests of the CIO. There would be default
provisions to make it easy for existing charities to convert to a CIO.[18]

---

[18] See Cabinet Office, Strategy Unit, *Private Action, Public Benefit: Charitable Incorporated
Organisation* (2002). See also the report of the Charity Commissioners Advisory Group
which developed the proposals for a CIO on the Charity Commissioners' website.

CHAPTER 4

CONSTRUCTION

The overriding principle of construction in relation to gifts to charity is   **4–001**
that a benignant approach is taken. In certain circumstances, extrinsic evidence is admissible to assist in the construction of charitable gifts and the rules are discussed below. To a certain extent a distinction has to be made between construing documents relating to older established charities and those relating to new charities. The use of extrinsic evidence can be seen in relation to gifts to institutions. For new charities a particular problem is the extent to which it is possible to look at the activities pursued in addition to the terms of the governing instrument. Finally the construction of some more common gifts where problems arise in relation to objects and participants are examined.

BENIGNANT CONSTRUCTION

In regard to the construction of charitable gifts the rule of widest appli-   **4–002**
cation is that the court leans in favour of charity. "There is no better rule," said Lord Loreburn, "than that a benignant construction will be placed upon charitable bequests."[1]

Where a bequest is capable of two constructions, one of which would make it void, and the other would make it effectual, that latter will be adopted.[2] "It is better to effectuate than to destroy the intention".[3] The court's benignant approach can be seen in the not unusual construction of a gift to a charitable institution which has failed as a gift for the furtherance of the purposes carried by that institution.[4] The principle of benignant construction allows the court to presume that the trustees will only act in a lawful and proper manner where there is, for example, the possibility

---

[1] *Weir v Crum-Brown* [1908] A.C. 162 at 167. See *Magistrates of Dundee v Morris* (1858) 3 Macq. 134. This was a maxim of the civil law: "*Semper in dubiis benigniora praeferenda sunt*". There is a simpler maxim in English law: "*Ut res magis valeat quam pereat*". See *IRC v McMullen* [1981] C.A. 1 at 14, *per* Lord Hailsham of St Marylebone.

[2] *Att-Gen v Clarke* (1762) Amb. 422; *Bruce v Presbytery of Deer* (1867) L.R. 1 H.L. (Sc.) 96; *Houston v Burns* [1918] A.C. 337 at 342; *Re Bain* [1930] 1 Ch. 224 at 230; *Re Bradbury* [1951] 1 T.L.R. 130 at 131; *IRC v McMullen*, above.

[3] *Re Lloyd-Greame* (1893) 10 T.L.R. 66. The rule is the same in non-charitable cases: *Whicker v Hume* [1858] 7 H.L.C. 124, 153.

[4] See, for example, *Re Vernon's Will Trusts* [1972] Ch. 300; *Re Broadbent (Deceased)*, *The Times*, June 27, 2001 and see para.11–017.

of political activity within the terms of the trust.[5] On the other hand, the court "must not strain the will to gain money for the charity."[6]

When the governing instrument of an organisation is a statute that simply contains a list of functions for that organisation, the court may take a purposive approach to the construction of the statute. Such a focus on the wider purposes Parliament sought to discharge in enacting the legislation is more likely to determine a purpose for the organisation that is charitable.[7]

4–003   The same preferential treatment of charitable trusts which has led the court to effectuate by means of schemes the charitable intention underlying indefinite,[8] impracticable or illegal gifts[9] has induced it to remedy in favour of charity the defective execution of powers. It is now well settled that the defective execution of a power ought to be made good. Thus, where a testatrix, having a general power of appointment, exercised it in favour of charity without pursuing the formalities required by the power, it was nevertheless held to be a good appointment.[10]

Extrinsic evidence

4–004   In considering the extent to which extrinsic evidence is admissable to assist in the construction of gifts in favour of charity, a distinction has to be made between the wills of persons dying on or after January 1, 1983[11] and all other wills and written instruments. For documents other than post 1982 wills, the general rule remains that extrinsic evidence could only be received when a knowledge of extrinsic facts could be made ancillary to the right interpretation of a written instrument,[12] and evidence was not admissible to show that a testator or a party to an instrument *inter vivos* intended to write something which he had not written.[13] Again, where an ambiguity or mistake appeared upon the face of a will it was not permissible to tender evidence to prove what the testator meant to say; so that, for example, the amount of a legacy left blank was not allowed to be ascertained by means of parol evidence,[14] and evidence could not be given to prove that a gift of a sum of money was intended to be a gift only of the income of it.[15]

In relation to the construction of documents other than wills, the same distinction is made between admissible evidence of the "matrix of fact"

---

[5] *Re Koeppler's Will Trust* [1986] Ch. 423 at 437–438.
[6] Lord Cairns L.C., *Dolan v Macdermot* (1868) L.R. 3 Ch. 676 at 678; *cf. Re Sutton* (1885) 28 Ch.D. 464 at 465; and see *Re Koeppler's Will Trusts* [1984] 2 W.L.R. 973 at 982.
[7] See *CIR v Medical Council of New Zealand* [1997] 2 N.Z.L.R. 297 at 318, *per* Thomas J; [2001] Ch. Com. Dec. April 2 (The General Medical Council); *cf. General Medical Council v IRC* [1928] All E.R. 252 where a narrower approach to construction was taken.
[8] See para.1–017 above.
[9] See Chap.11, below.
[10] *Sayer v Sayer* (1848) 7 Ha. 377; *Innes v Sayer* (1851) 3 Mac. & G. 606.
[11] Administration of Justice Act 1982, s.76(11).
[12] See *Theobald on Wills* (15th ed.), pp.211, *et seq.*
[13] *Att-Gen v Calvert* (1857) 23 Beav. 248 at 263; *Att-Gen v Gould* (1860) 28 Beav. 485. See also *Shore v Wilson* (1842) 9 Cl. & F. 355.
[14] *Baylis v Att-Gen* (1741) 2 Atk. 239.
[15] *Re Huxtable* [1902] 2 Ch. 793.

against which the document was made and inadmissible evidence of the subjective intention of the parties to the document.[16] Thus where the relevant document purporting to establish the charity was a conveyance to a municipal corporation, the court refused to consider statements made by the corporation's officers as to the corporation's purposes in acquiring the property but did consider the statutory powers available to the corporation at the date of the conveyance.[17]

The rules in relation to the wills of persons dying on or after January 1, 1983 are examined below. The general rule is then considered as it applies to allow extrinsic evidence to be given in the case of latent ambiguity together with the extent to which contemporaneous evidence and evidence of usage is admissible. Finally, the particular problem of the correct indentification of the intended institution is considered.

Wills of persons dying on or after January 1, 1983

It remains the law that ordinarily evidence of a testator's intention may   **4-005**
not be given so as to contradict the words of a will. An exception to this rule is, however, made where there has been a clerical error or a failure to understand the testator's instructions: if the court is satisfied (necessarily by extrinsic evidence) that a will is so expressed that it fails to carry out the testator's intentions in consequence of such an error or such a failure, it may order that the will shall be rectified so as to carry out those intentions.[18] The power conferred upon the court is similar to and consistent with the power to rectify a document made *inter vivos*.[19]

Extrinsic evidence, including evidence of the testator's intention, may be admitted to assist in the interpretation of a will in so far as any part of it is meaningless or in so far as the language used in any part of it is ambiguous on the face of it (that is to say, there is a patent ambiguity): furthermore, in so far as evidence, other than (at this stage) evidence of the testator's intention,[20] shows that the language used in any part of the will is ambiguous in the light of surrounding circumstances (that is to say, there is a latent ambiguity), then again extrinsic evidence, including (at this stage) evidence of the testator's intentions, may be admitted to assist in the

---

[16] *Investors Compensation Scheme Ltd v West Bromwich Building Society* [1998] 1 W.L.R. 896 at 912, *per* Lord Hoffman.
[17] *Bath and North East Somerset Council v Att-Gen* [2002] E.W.H.C. 1623 at para.10, *per* Hart J. See also *Latimer v CIR* [2002] 3 N.Z.L.R. 195 at 207, *per* Blanchard J.
[18] Administration of Justice Act 1982, s.20(1). This accords with the recommendation of the Law Reform Committee on the Interpretation of Wills (1973, Cmnd. 5301) and prevents the frustration of the testator's intention in such circumstances as existed in, *e.g. Re Reynett-Jones* [1976] 1 W.L.R. 161.
[19] Such a power is, of course, dependent upon evidence of the grantor's intention being forthcoming and this may well be impossible if, for example, he is dead. Where, more than a century ago, a chapel was conveyed to trustees by a deed which gave them a power to appoint ministers, evidence was not admitted to show that such a power was incompatible with the intention of the founders: *Att-Gen v Clapham* (1854) 4 De G.M. & G.591.
[20] See *British Home and Hospital for Incurables v Royal Hospital for Incurables* (1903) 89 L.T. 495.

interpretation.[21] It is to be observed that by virtue of this rule it is not possible, when the words used are on the face of them plain and unambiguous, to adduce evidence of the testator's intention to show that the words do not represent his intention; unless, of course, there exist those limited conditions in which rectification is possible.[22]

Evidence admissible to explain latent ambiguity

4–006   In *Shore v Wilson*[23] Lord Lyndhurst said:

> "If . . . the terms which are made use of are obscure, doubtful, or equivocal, either in themselves or in the application of them, it then becomes the duty of the court to ascertain by evidence, as well as it is able, what was the intent of the founder of the charity, in what sense the particular expressions were used."

In that case there was an ancient trust for the benefit of "godly preachers of Christ's Holy Gospel" and other purposes and evidence of the existence of a religious party by whom that and other expressions in the deed were used, and the manner in which they were used, and that the settlor was a member of that party was admitted.

In *Drummond v Att-Gen*[24] an appeal to the House of Lords from the Court of Chancery in Ireland, their Lordships, while accepting that they were bound by the decree in *Shore v Wilson*,[25] took the view that evidence had in that case been admitted which ought to have been rejected. Of the evidence admissible in construing a trust deed Lord Brougham said[26]:

> "You admit it as you admit evidence in construing a will, not to modify the expressions of the will, not to affix a sense upon the will which it will not bear, nor to tell you what the meaning of the will is, but to tell you what were the circumstances in which the testator was when he used those expressions, for the purpose of enabling you to ascertian what meaning he affixed to the expressions that he used, and for no other purpose."

4–007   Lord Campbell said[27]:

> "You may look to the usage to see in what sense the words were used at that time; you may look to contemporaneous documents, as well as

---

[21] Administration of Justice Act 1882, s.21. See *Re Broadbent (Deceased)*, *The Times*, June 27, 2001, where the testatrix's knowledge that a church had closed was admitted confirming a construction that the gift was for the purposes of the church.

[22] Administration of Justice Act 1882, s.20: see para.4–005 above.

[23] (1842) 9 Cl. & F at 355, 390.

[24] (1850) 2 H.L.C. 837. See also *University of Aberdeen v Irvine* (1868) 1 H.L. (Sc.) 289.

[25] (1842) 9 Cl. & F. 355. For a case in which the Charity Commissioners relied upon *Shore v Wilson* when considering whether or not to accept an institution for registration under the Charities Act 1960, s.4, [1982] Ch. Com. Rep., paras 45–51.

[26] (1850) 2 H.L.C. 862.

[27] *ibid.* at 863.

to Acts of Parliament, to see in what sense the words were used in the age in which the deeds were executed[28]; but to admit evidence to shew the sense in which words were used by particular individuals, is contrary to sound principle."

In that case evidence was admitted to determine who were intended to have the benefit of a gift for "Protestant Dissenters".

In *Re Atkinson's Will Trusts*[29] Sir Robert Megarry V.C. pointed out that Lord Lyndhurst's statement in *Shore v Wilson*[30] was somewhat wide and general and did not appear to have received approval when the case was before the House of Lords. The learned Vice-Chancellor accepted[31] that evidence might be adduced of the surrounding circumstances in which a will was made, or of the habitual sense in which a testator used particular words: but he rejected a signed memorandum made by the solicitor who drew the will of the testatrix from which it was sought to show that she used the term "worthy causes" in a special sense, confining it to charities, or that she accepted the view of her solicitor that it held that special sense. His Lordship said that an accustomed meaning was one thing, and a special meaning for a particular occasion was another: the latter was inadmissible.[32]

A similar approach was taken by Slade J. in *McGovern v Att-Gen*[33] when construing the trust deed of Amnesty International. In order to construe ambiguous wording he referred to the statute of the predecessor association as it was part of the factual matrix accompanying the execution of the trust deed and showed how particular words were understood.[34]

Contemporaneous evidence

The contemporaneous acts and condition of a donor are of the greatest **4–008** possible importance for the purpose of construing a deed of gift executed by him,[35] as, for example, for the purpose of determining whether the whole of the property comprised therein is impressed with a charitable trust, or whether any surplus belongs to the donees in trust or beneficially.[36] So also the manner in which the donor of the fund, if he was the first trustee, conducted himself in distributing it,[37] the contemporaneous

---

[28] His Lordship referred to *Shore v Wilson* (1842) 9 Cl. & F. 355 at 413, *et seq.*

[29] [1978] 1 W.L.R. 586 at 589.

[30] (1842) 9 Cl. & F. 390.

[31] [1978] 1 W.L.R. 586, at 590.

[32] See also *Re How* [1930] 1 Ch. 66 in which Maugham J. rejected evidence of the sense in which the testator (a member of the "Brethren" or "Plymouth Brethren") used the words "good works." As to the importance of usage in construing an ancient trust instrument, see further at paras 4–009, below *et seq.*

[33] [1982] Ch.321.

[34] *ibid.* at 349 and see para.4–016 below.

[35] *Drummond v Att-Gen* (1850) 2 H.L.C. 837; *Att-Gen v Trinity College, Cambridge* (1856) 24 B. 383 at 399; *Att-Gen v Mayor of Dartmouth* (1883) 48 L.T. 933.

[36] *Att-Gen v Trinity College, Cambridge*, above; *Att-Gen v Dean and Canons of Windsor* (1860) 8 H.L.C. 369 at 402; *University of Aberdeen v Irvine* (1868) 1 H.L. (Sc.) 289.

[37] *Att-Gen v Brazen Nose College* (1834) 2 Cl. & F. 295.

application of the funds,[38] and contemporaneous deeds relating to the same charity,[39] are of importance.

The contemporanous acts of the donees are, however, usually of little value, as they only show their view in accepting the gift,[40] unless it appears that the trusts were not accepted *simpliciter*, but that at the time of acceptance modifications were bargained for.[41] An arrangement with regard to questions arising on the instrument of foundation, made at the time the trusts were accepted, and evidenced by contemporanous instruments, or even by constant subsequent usage only, will not be disturbed.[42]

Again, where the original subscribers were numerous, it was held that a declaration of trust executed by the persons in whom the property was vested at or about the time the funds were raised must be assumed to embody the intentions of the contributors.[43]

Evidence of usage

4-009   Where the trust instrument is lost, evidence of usage is admissible and relevant for the purpose of determining what the nature of the trusts is, as, for example, in whom the right to appoint new trustees is vested.[44] Any existing copies of the lost instrument are admissible in evidence. Thus, in *Att-Gen v Archbishop of York*,[45] the original charter was not in existence, but there were three copies of it. Two of the copies purported to be copies of the original charter in extenso, and the third omitted certain trusts found in the other two. It was held that the former must be acted upon, though it appeared that the property of the charity had been afterwards diminished, and it was alleged that in consequence thereof the visitor might, under the authority given by the original charter, have limited the trusts as shown in the third copy.

When an ancient trust instrument has to be construed extrinsic evidence of long-continued usage is of great weight. In *Att-Gen v Smythies*[46] Lord Brougham said:

"Is is impossible . . . to lay out of view the length of time during which a certain arrangement has subsisted, and a certain meaning has been given in practice to the instrument of foundation. If, indeed, the

---

[38] *Shore v Wilson* (1842) 9 Cl. & F. 355 at 569.
[39] *Att-Gen v Anderson* (1888) 57 L.J.Ch. 543. But not subsequent deeds: *Shore v Wilson*, above.
[40] *Att-Gen v Trinity College, Cambridge* (1856) 24 B. 383.
[41] *Att-Gen v Master of Catherine Hall* (1820) Jac. 381 at 391, 392; *Att-Gen v Drapers' Co.* (1844) 6 N. 382, 386; *Att-Gen v Caius College* (1838) 2 Keen, 150 at 163.
[42] *Att-Gen v Caius College*, above.
[43] *Att-Gen v Clapham* (1854) 4 De G.M. & G. 591.
[44] *Att-Gen v Dalton* (1851) 13 B. 141. In that case the court presumed that the legal estate was in the persons to whom it was purported to be conveyed, notwithstanding certain irregularities; *cf. Re Parish of St Nicholas Acons* (1889) 60 L.T. 532.
[45] (1854) 17 B. 495. See also *Att-Gen v Cashel* (1842) 3 Dr. & W. 294.
[46] (1831) 2 R. & M. 717, 749. See also *L. Schuler A.G. v Wickman Machine Tool Sales Ltd.* [1974] A.C. 235 at 261 *per* Lord Wilberforce (not a charity case); *cf. Att-Gen v Mayor of Bristol* (1820) 2 J. & W. 294 at 321, *per* Lord Eldon.

practice, though of centuries, has been a breach of trust, doubtless the lapse of time should be no bar. But long adverse enjoyment is not to be thrown out of view in seeking for the true construction of the provisions which both conflicting parties claim; and a principle of distribution under a known instrument of foundation, if long acquiesced in by all the objects of the bounty from whence the funds proceed, and to effectuate the purposes for which the instrument is framed, ought not without manifest reason to be disturbed".

Where an ancient instrument may bear two constructions, the court will lean towards that which has been supported by usage.[47] The reason for this is that, where the construction is doubtful, it will not be assumed that a long series of breaches of trust has been committed.[48]

Where rights have been enjoyed for a long time, the court will presume **4–010** that they had a legal origin if such an origin is possible in law,[49] but this presumption does not arise if the usage constitutes a breach of trust.[50] "If the court finds a clear trust expressed on a will, no length of time during which there has been a deviation from it can warrant this court, as I apprehend, in making a decree in contradiction to such a trust."[51] The presumption may also be rebutted by evidence of fact.[52]

No particular length of time is necessary to give rise to the presumption of a legal origin. It was presumed for a rent-charge which had been paid to charity for 30 years.[53] In one case,[54] 105, and in another[55] 350, years' continuous usage were considered sufficient to establish the existence of a charitable trust.[56] Where the subject-matter was consecrated ground, 300 years' user for parochial purposes was considered prima facie evidence of a charitable trust.[57] By the Roman Catholic Relief Act 1860, in cases to

---

[47] *Att-Gen v Smythies*, above; *Att-Gen v Mayor of Bristol*, above; *Att-Gen v Corporation of Rochester* (1854) 5 De G.M, & G. 797 at 822. See *Archbishop of York v Stapleton* (1740) 2 Atk. 136; *Att-Gen v Parker* (1747) 3 Atk. 576; *R. v Varlo* (1775) Cowp. 248; *R. v Osbourne* (1803) 4 East. 327 at 333; *Att-Gen v Brazen Nose College* (1834) 2 Cl. & F. 295 at 330; *Att-Gen v Drummond* (1842) 1 Dr. & W. 353.

[48] *Att-Gen v Sidney Sussex College* (1869) L.R. 4 Ch. 722 at 732.

[49] *Att-Gen v Fishmongers' Co.* (1841) 2 B. 588; *Att-Gen v Cashel* (1842) 3 Dr. & W. 294; *Att-Gen v Moor* (1855) 20 B. 119; *Att-Gen v West* (1858) 27 L.J.Ch. 789; *Goodman v Mayor of Saltash* (1882) 7 App. Cas. 633; *Stanley v Mayor of Norwich* (1887) 3 T.L.R. 506; *Haigh v West* [1893] 2 Q.B. 19. *Pegg v Lamb* [1994] 2 All E.R. 15.

[50] *Att-Gen v Mayor of Bristol* (1820) 2 J. & W. 294; *Att-Gen v Smythies* (1831) 2 R. & M. 717; *Drummond v Att-Gen* (1850) 2 H.L.C. 837; *Att-Gen v St. Cross Hospital* (1853) 17 B. 435; *Att-Gen v Clapham* (1854) 4 De G.M. & G. 591; *Att-Gen v Beverley* (1857) 6 De G.M. & G. 256; *Att-Gen v West* (1858) 27 L.J.Ch. 789; *Att-Gen v Gould* (1860) 28 B. 485; *Re Swansea Grammar School* [1894] A.C. 252.

[51] *per* Turner L.J., *Att-Gen v Mayor of Rochester* (1854) 5 De G.M. & G. 797 at 822.

[52] *Att-Gen v Ewelme Hospital* (1853) 17 B. 366; *Att-Gen v St. Cross Hospital* (1853) 17 B. 435.

[53] *Att-Gen v West* (1858) 27 L.J.Ch. 789.

[54] *Bunting v Sargent* (1879) 13 Ch.D. 335 at 336.

[55] *Att-Gen v Mercers' Co.* (1870) 18 W.R. 448.

[56] See also *Haigh v West* [1893] 2 Q.B. 19, and the non-charitable cases of *Cocks v Foley* (1685) 1 Vern. 359; *Steward v Bridger* (1705) 2 Vern. 516; *Holder v Chambury* (1734) 3 P. Wms. 256.

[57] *Re St. Alphage* (1888) 59 L.T. 614.

which the Act applied, 20 years' continuous usage was deemed sufficient evidence to establish the existence of a charitable trust.[58]

When the origin of a charitable trust of long standing is in dispute, the court will presume that everything was done to make the charity good.[59] Therefore the court was willing to go to extreme lengths in presuming that a charitable gift made 100 years previously complied with the Mortmain Act.[60] *A fortiori* when a lost grant was presumed, enrolment was presumed also.[61] Examples of various acts-in-the-law which have been presumed after a considerable lapse of time are: a conveyance to charitable trustees,[62] the repeal of the statutes governing a school,[63] a dispensation varying the statutes of a college of royal foundation,[64] the consent of the ordinary to the augmentation of a living,[65] and the consent of a college to an accession to its foundation.[66] Even an Act of Parliament may be presumed.[67]

4–011   The actual terms of the trust may be ascertained by evidence of long-continued usage.[68] Thus, where a fund had been devoted solely to one church since time immemorial, it was held that other churches had no right to participate in it.[69] Evidence of usage also may show that a school is a grammar school.[70] By the Nonconformist Chapels Act 1844,[71] it was provided that, where the trust instrument governing a place of worship to which the Act applied specified no particular doctrines which might be preached there, usage during the past 25 years should determine what doctrines might properly be preached.[72]

The ambiguity may not be sufficient, however, to admit evidence of usage. Where the trusts of a deed, executed in 1599, were "for and towards the repairing of the church and conduits of the town, the relief of the poor, the maintenance of the bulwarks and fortifications, and other charitable, needful, and necessary uses for the town," as to the trustees should seem meet, it was held that "charitable, needful, and necessary uses" meant purposes which were charitable within the meaning of the Statute of Elizabeth I and *ejusdem generis* with those previously enumerated,

---

[58] This Act was repealed by the Charities Act 1960, but without prejudice to the operation of s.5 as it applied to charities taking effect before the commencement of that Act: Charities Act 1960, s.39 and Sch.5.

[59] *Att-Gen v Moor* (1855) 20 B. 119 at 121.

[60] *ibid.*

[61] *Haigh v West* [1893] 2 Ch. 19.

[62] *Att-Gen v Dalton* (1851) 13 B. 141; *Re St. Nicholas Acons* (1889) 60 L.T. 532; *cf. Att-Gen v Stephens* (1854) 1 K. & J. 724.

[63] *Att-Gen v Middleton* (1751) 2 Ves.S. 330; *cf. Att-Gen v Scott* (1750) 1 Ves. S. 413; *Hull (Mayor) v Horner* (1774) 1 Cowp. 102.

[64] *Case of Queen's College* (1821) Jac. 1.

[65] *Re Parker's Charity* (1863) 32 B. 654.

[66] *Att-Gen v Drapers' Co.* (1844) 6 B. 382.

[67] *Att-Gen v Ewelme Hospital* (1853) 17 B. 366 at 390; *Re St. Paul's School* (1870) 18 W.R. 448 at 449.

[68] *Att-Gen v Ewelme Hospital* (1853) 17 B. 366; *Att-Gen v St. Cross Hospital* (1853) 17 B. 435.

[69] *Re Church Estate Charity, Wandsworth* (1870) L.R. 6 Ch. 296.

[70] *Att-Gen v Dalton* (1851) 13 B. 141; *Att-Gen v Bishop of Worcester* (1851) 9 Ha. 328 at 359.

[71] s.2. That Act was repealed by s.39 of and Sch.5 to the Charities Act 1960, but without prejudice to s.2 as it applied to charities taking effect before the commencement of the Act of 1960.

[72] See *Att-Gen v Bunce* (1868) L.R. 6 Eq. 563. See also *Att-Gen v Pearson* (1817) 3 Mer. 353, 400; *Att-Gen v Hutton* (1844) Dr. 480; *Att-Gen v Anderson* (1888) 57 L.J.Ch. 543.

and that there was not sufficient ambiguity to admit evidence of contemporaneous or subsequent usage to explain the meaning of the trusts.[73]

Intended institution

Where the identity of the object of a gift is in doubt, the first step taken **4–012** by the court is to direct an inquiry towards finding by extrinsic evidence whether there is an institution answering to the description given by the testator.[74] If there is only one institution corresponding to the description, the legacy will be paid to it, and extrinsic evidence as to whether it was the object intended by the testator will not be admissible.[75]

National Society for the Prevention of Cruelty to Children v Scottish National Society for the Prevention of Cruelty to Children,[76] is an example of a case in which the words were on the face of them plain and unambiguous. The testator gave a legacy to "The National Society for the Prevention of Cruelty to Children." The Society of that name was held entitled, and evidence to show that the testator intended to benefit The Scottish National Society for the Prevention of Cruelty to Children was excluded. Lord Loreburn said[77]:

> "My Lords, I think the true ground upon which to base a decision in this case is that the accurate use of a name in a will creates a strong presumption against any rival who is not the possessor of the name mentioned in the will. It is a very strong presumption and one which cannot be overcome except in exceptional circumstances. I use as a convenient method of expressing one's thought the term 'presumption.' What I mean is what a man has said ought to be acted upon unless it is clearly proved that he meant something different from what he said."

If a similar case came before the court today the result would be different only if it could be shown that there had been a clerical error or a misunderstanding of the testator's intentions.

Lord Loreburn's words were cited but the case distinguished by the Court of Appeal in *Re Satterthwaite's Will Trusts*,[78] where the testatrix by her will made in 1952 gave her residuary estate for division between a number of organisations connected with animal welfare including "the London Animal Hospital". This and some of the other organisations were listed in the 1951 ordinary London telephone directory to which reference

---

[73] *Att-Gen v Dartmouth* (1883) 48 L.T. 933.
[74] *Wilson v Squire* (1842) 1 Y. & C.C.C. 654; see also *Middleton v Clitherow* (1798) 3 Ves. 734. As to gifts to charities which have ceased to exist, see para.11–017, below.
[75] *Wilson v Squire* (1842) 1 Y. & C.C.C. 654; *Re Kilvert's Trusts* (1871) L.R. 7 Ch. 170 at 173; *Re Raven* [1915] 1 Ch. 673 at 681. See, however, *Re Beale* (1890) 6 T.L.R. 308 where evidence of this kind was admitted de bene esse, but considered by the Court of Appeal to be of doubtful admissibility.
[76] [1915] A.C. 207.
[77] *ibid.* at 212, 213.
[78] [1966] 1 W.L.R. 277; see also *Re Raven* [1915] Ch. 673.

may have been made in compiling a list of animal charities. "The London Animal Hospital" had from 1943 been carried on as a private business by R until July 1952 (six months before the testatrix made her will) when this name was removed from the telephone directory. R continued to carry on the same business under his own name. He claimed to be beneficially interested in the bequest. The Court of Appeal held that the gift showed an intention to benefit a purpose, namely, the welfare of animals, not to benefit a private individual, and as at the date of the will the business no longer bore the name used in the will, R was not entitled to take. Harman L.J. specifically held[79] that the fact that at the date of the will the business carried on by R no longer bore the name used in the will was just sufficient to displace the strong presumption that the testatrix intended to benefit the named organisation. The Blue Cross, which had under a former designation run an animal hospital in the area of London in which the testatrix lived, also claimed to be entitled to the gift, but evidence by two persons closely connected with the organisation to the effect that their hospital had been popularly known as "The London Animals' Hospital" (a similar but not precisely corresponding name) was insufficient to identify their organisation with the bequest, which in the event was directed to be applied *cy-près*.

4–013   A slight inaccuracy of description is immaterial, provided that it is plain what institution was intended.[80] Thus it is immaterial that a vicar is misdescribed as a rector,[81] or that an institution is described by a name which it formerly bore but has ceased to bear,[82] or that in the case of a legacy to an institution properly described there was added a direction that it should be laid out in completing the almshouses then in course of erection, the institution in question having no such almshouses.[83] In one case "the London Orphan Society in the City Road" was held to mean the Orphan Working School in the City Road[84]; in another case "the King's Cross Hospital" was held to mean the Great Northern Hospital, King's Cross.[85]

In considering whether an existing institution is to be identified with an inaccurate description in a will, the court will have regard to any directions as to the trusts upon which the property is to be held. The fact that the trusts declared do not correspond with the general purposes of the claimant is evidence against the claim.[86]

Where there is an institution which fits the description it cannot be rejected because there was formerly an institution which answered the

[79] [1966] 1 W.L.R. 283.
[80] *Re Kilvert's Trusts* (1871) L.R. 7 Ch. 170; *Re Pritt* (1916) 113 L.T. 136.
[81] *Hopkinson v Ellis* (1842) 5 B. 34.
[82] *Re Kilvert's Trusts* (1871) L.R. 7 Ch. 170 at 174; *cf. Re Satterthwaite's Will Trusts* [1966] 1 W.L.R. 277, discussed at para.4–012 above.
[83] *Smith v Ruger* (1859) 5 Jur.(N.S.) 905. See also as to what is a sufficient description: *Wallace v Att-Gen* (1864) 33 B. 384; *Makeown v Ardagh* (1876) Ir.R. 10 Eq. 445; *Re Adams* (1888) 4 T.L.R. 757.
[84] *Wilson v Squire* (1842) 1 Y. & C.C.C. 654.
[85] *Re Lycett* (1897) 13 T.L.R. 373; see also the Master's findings in *Re Glubb* (1897) 14 T.L.R. 66.
[86] *Verge v Somerville* [1924] A.C. 496 at 506.

description more exactly, but has since been dissolved.[87] If, however, the court is not satisfied that the inquiry has identified the named object with an existing charity with sufficient certainty, it may order a scheme to be settled for effecting the purposes which the testator apparently wished to benefit.[88]

Regard is paid to the context of the will. Thus in *Bradshaw v Thompson*[89] the Charing Cross Hospital was preferred to the Royal Westminster Ophthalmic Hospital because in other gifts in the same will, where a hospital other than a general hospital was intended, it was so described. There is, indeed, a presumption that "hospital" means a general hospital[90] and what before the National Health Service Act 1946, used to be called a "voluntary hospital".[91] It was therefore held, before the commencement of that Act, that an institution supported by voluntary contributions was to be preferred to one supported out of rates, unless the context showed an intention to benefit the latter class.[92]

4–014

It may also be important to determine which is the governing term in the testator's description of the institution.[93] For instance, where there is a reference to locality, the institution must prima facie satisfy that requirement. Thus where the gift was to "the Westminster Hospital, Charing Cross", the Charing Cross Hospital was held entitled in preference to the Westminster Hospital.[94] All and every the hospitals" was held to mean hospitals in the town in which the testatrix resided; and one standing a mile outside was excluded.[95]

Where the gift is "to the hospitals of London", London must be construed in a popular sense, and not confined to the City of London. Consequently no definite boundaries can be laid down; but it must be considered, as regards each institution suggested, whether it is within what the testator would have considered to be London.[96]

In cases of this kind, evidence of the testator having been acquainted with or having subscribed to, or otherwise taken an interest in, one of the institutions, is always received, and such evidence will usually turn the scale.[97]

4–015

[87] *Coldwell v Holme* (1854) 2 Sm. & G. 31; *Makeown v Ardagh* (1876) Ir.R. 10 Eq. 445; *Re Magrath* [1913] 2 Ch. 331.
[88] *Re Hill* (1909) 53 S.J. 228; and see *Re Satterthwaite's Will Trusts* [1966] 1 W.L.R. 277, discussed para.4–012, above.
[89] (1843) 2 Y. & C.C.C. 295.
[90] *Re Alchin's Trusts* (1872) L.R. 14 Eq. 230; *Re Smith* [1962] 1 W.L.R. 763.
[91] *Re Smith* [1962] 1 W.L.R. 763.
[92] *Lechmere v Cutler* (1855) 24 L.J.Ch. 647; *Re Davies's Trusts* (1871) 21 W.R. 154.
[93] *Bradshaw v Thompson* (1843) 2 Y. & C.C.C. 295; *Buxton v Blakiston* (1885) 2 T.L.R. 298.
[94] *Bradshaw v Thompson*, above. See also *Wilson v Squire* (1842) 1 Y. & C.C.C. 654; *Re Clergy Society* (1856) 2 K. & J. 615; *Re Kilvert's Trusts* (1871) L.R. 7 Ch. 170.
[95] *Masters v Masters* (1718) 1 P. Wms. 420.
[96] *Wallace v Att-Gen* (1864) 33 Beav. 384 and see *Ditcham v Chivis* (1828) 4 Bing. 706; *Beckford v Crutwell* (1832) 5 C. & P. 242; *Wilson v Squire* (1842) 1 Y. & C.C.C. 654 at 656. A hospital not in existence at the testator's death cannot take a share: *Wallace v Att-Gen*, above.
[97] *Att-Gen v Hudson* (1720) 1 P. Wms. 674; *Bunting v Marriott* (1854) 19 B. 163; *Re Kilvert's Trusts* (1871) L.R. 7 Ch. 170; *Re Briscoes's Trusts* (1872) 26 L.T. 149; *Re Fearn's Will* (1879) 27 W.R. 392; *Re Bradley* (1887) 3 T.L.R. 668. See also *Makeown v Ardagh* (1876) Ir.R. 10 Eq. 445.

So also will evidence that one institution had not existed when the testator lived in the neighbourhood.[98]

Where it cannot be ascertained which of two institutions the testator intended to benefit, the fund may be divided between them,[99] not necessarily in equal shares,[1] or if there is no opposition on the part of one institution the whole may be given to the other or others.[2]

A power given to trustees by the instrument of gift to determine questions of identity of the objects in case of doubt is ineffectual to oust the court's jurisdiction.[3]

Relevance of activities

4–016   A difficult question is the extent to which the activities a particular organisation is carrying out can be considered when determining whether that organisation is charitable. There is no doubt that the Charity Commissioners do ask for and, in certain circumstances, consider information about an organisation's activities when application is made for registration.[4] A proposal, however, to give the Charity Commissioners express statutory power to consider activities when determining charitable status was rejected in debate on the Bill which became the Charities Act 1992.[5] More recently, the Strategy Unit report proposed that the circumstances in which an "activities test" can be used as an aid to interpretating purposes should be clarified in statute.[6]

The problem remains which was neatly summarised by Scott J. in *Att-Gen v Ross*[7] when he said[8]:

> "The skill of Chancery draftsmen is well able to produce a constitution of charitable flavour intended to allow the pursuit of aims of a non-charitable or dubiously charitable flavour."

In other words, it is possible for the objects of an organisation to be drawn in such a way that, if read literally, they satisfy the requirement of being exclusively charitable, but are at the same time sufficiently wide and flexible to authorise the carrying on of non-charitable activities. The

---

[98] *King's College Hospital v Wheildon* (1854) 18 B. 30.
[99] *Simon v Barber* (1828) 5 Russ. 112, cited 3 Ha. 195n.; *Bennett v Hayter* (1839) 2 B. 81; *Gibson v Coleman* (1868) 18 L.T. 236; *Re Alchin's Trusts* (1872) L.R. 14 Eq. 230. See also *Wallen v Childs* (1765) Amb. 524; *Re Delmar Charitable Trust* [1897] 2 Ch. 163 at 167 and see further para.1–021, above.
[1] *Bennett v Hayter* (1839) 2 B. 81.
[2] *Bunting v Marriott* (1854) 19 B. 163.
[3] *Re Raven* [1915] 1 Ch. 673; *Re Wynn* [1952] Ch. 271.
[4] See Charity Commissioners, *Application for Registration as a Charity*, Pt 2; Cabinet Office, Strategy Unit, *Private Action, Public Benefit. A Review of Charities and the Wider Not-For-Profit Sector* (2002), p.78.
[5] *Hansard*, HL Vol. 532, col.837.
[6] Cabinet Office, Strategy Unit, *Private Action, Public Benefit. A Review of Charities and the Wider Not-For-Profit Sector* (2002), p.79.
[7] [1986] 1 W.L.R. 252.
[8] *ibid.* at 263.

related problem is where the governing instrument is prepared without the assistance of skilled draftsmen and is unclear.

When considering the relevance of activities, there are two separate questions to be addressed: What are the purposes of the organisation? Are those purposes charitable? In relation to the first question, the starting point is that if the objects are comprehensively set out in the governing instrument reference should be made to that document and that document alone.[9] If the words used are ambiguous, equivocal, doubtful or contradictory, the usual rules of construction apply and the court will look at the factual matrix accompanying the execution of the deed.[10] Thus in the *Amnesty International* case[11] the court looked at the Statute of Amnesty International to help to resolve ambiguities in the trust deed as the Statute was manifestly part of the factual matrix accompanying the execution of the trust.[12] The court may also admit evidence of the habitual sense in which particular words are used by the person setting up the charity in order to determine the meaning of words as used in the governing instrument.[13]

Even if the purposes as set out in the governing instrument are clear, it may not be clear that those purposes are charitable. In those circumstances, the court will look at the activities carried by the particular organisation provided that they are *intra vires* and are of probative value on the question of whether the main purpose of the organisation is charitable.[14] The basis on which and the extent to which extrinsic evidence is examined by the court in order to determine whether an organisation has charitable status has been variously expressed. An oft quoted approach is that of Sachs L.J. in *Incorporated Council of Law Reporting for England and Wales v Att-Gen*[15] where he said[16]: **4–017**

"Whilst appreciating what has been said as to the courts not being permitted, where plain language is used in a charter or memorandum, to admit extrinsic evidence as to its construction, it is yet plain from the course adopted by the courts in many cases that they are entitled to and do look at the circumstances in which the institution came into existence and the sphere in which it operates to enable a conclusion to be reached on whether its purposes are charitable."

An alternative approach focuses on the necessary element of public benefit for charitable status. Thus in *McGovern v Att-Gen*[17] Slade J. said[18]:

---

[9] *IRC v Oldham Training and Enterprise Council* [1996] S.T.C. 1218 at 1234.
[10] *McGovern v Att-Gen* [1982] 1 Ch. 321 at 349.
[11] *ibid.*
[12] *ibid.* at 349.
[13] *Shore v Wilson* (1842) 9 Cl. & F. 355.
[14] *Att-Gen v Ross* [1986] 1 W.L.R. 252 at 264.
[15] [1972] Ch. 73.
[16] *ibid.* at 91.
[17] [1982] Ch. 321.
[18] *ibid.* at 333. See also [2001] Ch. Com. Dec. August 24 (The Centre for Corporate Accountability).

"Save in the case of gifts to classes of poor persons, a trust must always be shown to promote a public benefit of a nature recognised by the courts as being such, if it is to qualify as being charitable. The question whether a purpose will or may operate for the public benefit is to be answered by the courts forming an opinion on the evidence before it: see *National Anti-Vivisection Society v Inland Revenue Commissioners* [1948] A.C. 31, 44 *per* Lord Wright. No doubt in some cases a purpose may be so manifestly beneficial to the public that it would be absurd to call evidence on this point. In many other instances, however, the element of public benefit may be much more debatable."

A number of circumstances can be identified where the court has looked at activities carried out by an organisation to assist in determining charitable status. If the objects are clearly set out in the governing instrument but there is doubt as to whether the particular objects are charitable, the court will look at the activities of the organisation in order to determine the consequences of pursing the objects.[19] This approach was taken by Lightman J. in *IRC v Oldham Training and Enterprise Council*[20] where evidence of the activities carried on showed that too great a degree of private benefit was conferred for the organisation to have charitable status. By comparison, examination of the factual background can show that, whilst an organisation has a number of potentially non-charitable objects, its overall predominant purpose is charitable. Thus in *Att-Gen v Ross*[21] a student union was held to be charitable as having a predominant purpose of furthering the educational function of the polytechnic of which it was a part although it had some objects allowing the pursuit of social and political activities.

4–018   The court will also look at activities where the objects contain an ambiguity. To a certain extent the court elides the questions of determining the objects and determining charitable status. *Southwood v Att-Gen*[22] concerned a trust for the advancement of the education of the public in the subjects of militarism and disarmament. In order to determine if the trust was charitable, the Charity Commissioners had looked at the surrounding facts including the activities of the promoters. In the light of the ambiguity as to the meaning of the trusts, Carnwath J. considered this a proper approach. The court also looked at the activities carried on before determining that the trust was political and not charitable. A similar approach was taken by the Court of Appeal[23] confirming that the trust was not charitable.

An additional circumstance in which the court may look at activities is where a governing document is a sham. There will be a sham where the document clearly sets out charitable purposes but hides the real objects of

---

[19] See *Incorporated Council of Law Reporting for England and Wales v Att-Gen* [1972] Ch. 73 at 99, *per* Buckley L.J. and [2001] Ch. Com. Dec. April 2 (The General Medical Council).
[20] [1996] S.T.C. 1218.
[21] [1986] 1 W.L.R. 252.
[22] *The Times*, October 26, 1998.
[23] [2000] W.T.L.R. 1199.

the organisation which are non-charitable and are immoral, fraudulent, dishonest or otherwise contrary to public policy. The potential for a sham deed to hide non-charitable purposes was recognised in *Re McDougal*.[24]

In all the circumstances in which activities may be considered to determine charitable status, with the exception of sham charities, the relevant activities are those which are permissible under the objects and powers as set out in the governing document. The fact that an organisation is, or is proposing, to carry out activities that are contrary to its objects is not relevant to the question of charitable status. Unauthorised activities are relevant to the question of whether there has been a breach of trust.[25]

PARTICULAR OBJECTS

Gifts for the poor

A trust for the poor[26] giving a preference to poor relations was held to mean, not that poor relations should be preferred to all other charitable purposes, but only that in the distribution to persons in distress poor relations should be preferred.[27] An inquiry may be directed as to who are poor relations.[28] **4–019**

If trustees who have a discretion to distribute a fund for the benefit of poor relations of the testator die without having exercised such discretion, or decline to exercise it, the court will direct an inquiry and distribute the fund.[29]

A gift "for the relief and use of the poorest of my kindred, such as are not able to work for their living, *viz.*, sick, aged, and impotent persons, and such as cannot maintain their own charge," was construed to be a gift for the kindred of the testator poor according to the definition of the will.[30]

The word "poor" was implied when there was a gift to "twenty aged widows and spinsters of a certain parish".[31] **4–020**

Where there is an indefinite gift for the poor, the Queen may appoint the charity[32] or the court may administer the gift by means of a scheme.[33] The jurisdiction of the court depends on the existence of a trust; and if there is no trust the gift is disposed of according to directions given by the Queen under the sign manual.[34]

The rule is that a charity intended to benefit the poor generally is not to be so applied as to relieve persons entitled to relief from public funds.

---

[24] [1957] 1 W.L.R. 81 at 91.
[25] *Re Cranstoun* [1932] 1 Ch. 537 at 547, *per* Farwell J.
[26] As to gifts for the poor, see generally Chap.2, paras 2–010 *et seq*, above.
[27] *Waldo v Caley* (1809) 16 Ves. 206. See also *Att-Gen v Northumberland* (1877) 7 Ch.D. 745.
[28] *Att-Gen v Price* (1810) 17 Ves. 371; and see *Att-Gen v Sidney Sussex College* (1865) 34 B. 654.
[29] *Doyley v Att-Gen* (1735) 7 Ves. 58n.; *Att-Gen v Bucknall* (1741) 2 Atk. 328.
[30] *Att-Gen v Northumberland* (1877) 7 Ch.D. 745.
[31] *Thompson v Corby* (1860) 27 B. 649; *Re Dudgeon* (1896) 74 L.T. 613. See also *Att-Gen v Comber* (1824) 2 Sim. & S. 93; *Collinson v Pater* (1831) 2 Russ. & My. 344; *Nash v Morley* (1842) 5 B. 177.
[32] *Att-Gen v Syderfen* (1683) 1 Vern.: 224; *Att-Gen v Rance* (1728) cited Amb. 422.
[33] *Nash v Morley* (1842) 5 B. 177; *Reeve v Att-Gen* (1843) 3 Ha. 191.
[34] *Re Bennett* [1960] Ch. 18. See para.1–019, above.

Thus before the poor law was abolished and its place was taken by national assistance[35] and subsequent social security benefits, persons in receipt of poor law relief were not entitled to share in the benefit of a charity intended for the poor[36] unless it was clear that the gift was to be applied in that manner.[37] This rule is well established, although it has sometimes been followed with reluctance.[38] The reason for the rule is that in such cases it was never intended that the charity should directly benefit the rich.[39]

4-021   The rule does not apply where the intention is that the gift shall be applied in aid of the rates, and such a gift is charitable[40]; and the income may properly be applied in or towards the relief of public financial burdens.[41]

Even where persons who are being maintained or supported out of public funds are not excluded from the benefits of a charity, the court will be slow to hold that the benefits are confined to such persons. Thus where an Act of Parliament[42] directed that the funds of a charity should be applied in maintaining and lodging 16 poor boys in a charity school, it was held that the trustees were not bound, in electing the poor boys, to confine themselves to those requiring parish relief[43]; and where a fund was bequeathed to trustees to pay the interest to the poor of a parish, it was held that the bequest was not within the meaning of a local Act which vested in the guardians of the poor all moneys held in trust for the poor of that parish.[44]

---

[35] National Assistance Act 1948, s.1.

[36] *Att-Gen v Exeter Corpn.* (1827) 3 Russ. 395; *Att-Gen v Wilkinson* (1839) 1 B. 370; *Att-Gen v Bovill* (1840) 1 Ph. 762; *Deptford (Churchwardens) v Sketchley* (1847) 8 Q.B. 394, 405; *Att-Gen v Leage* (1881), noted at p.1041 of the 4th ed. of this work. See also *Att-Gen v Price* (1744) 3 Atk. 108; *Att-Gen v Clarke* (1762) Amb. 422; *Hereford (Bishop) v Adams* (1802) 7 Ves. 324; *Att-Gen v Gutch* (1830), cited Shelford's Law of Mortmain, p.628; *Att-Gen v Rochester Corpn.* (1854) 5 De G.M. & G. 797; *Re Sekforde's Charity* (1861) 4 L.T. 321.

[37] *Att-Gen v Blizard* (1855) 21 B. 233. See also *Re Richmond Parish Charity Lands* (1965) 109 S.J. 755.

[38] *Att-Gen v Corporation of Exeter* (1827) 2 Russ. 45, 53; *Att-Gen v Bovill* (1840) 1 Ph. 762, 768; and see *Churchwardens of St. Nicholas, Deptford v Sketchley* (1847) 8 Q.B. 394 at 405. But see now Social Security Act 1986, s.33(9)(c).

[39] *Att-Gen v Wilkinson* (1839) 1 B. 370 at 373. See also *Att-Gen v Clarke* (1762) Amb. 422; *Re Prison Charities* (1873) L.R. 16 Eq. 129; *Att-Gen v Duke of Northumberland* (1889) 5 T.L.R. 237.

[40] *Att-Gen v Blizard* (1855) 21 B. 233; *Re Richmond Parish Charity Lands* (1965) 109 S.J. 755. See also *Att-Gen v Heelis* (1824) 2 S. & S. 67; *Att-Gen v Corporation of Berwick-upon-Tweed* (1829) Taml. 239.

[41] *Att-Gen v Blizard*, above; *Att-Gen v Corporation of Berwick-upon-Tweed*, above; *Re St. Botolph-without-Bishopsgate Parish Estates* (1887) 35 Ch.D. 142; *Re Richmond Parish Charity Lands* (1965) 109 S.J. 755.

[42] 1 Geo. 2, c.30 (an Act for the employment and maintenance of the poor in the City of Canterbury).

[43] *Guardians of Canterbury v Mayor, etc. of Canterbury* (1862) 31 L.J.Ch. 810.

[44] *Att-Gen v Freeman* (1818) 5 Price 425.

Gifts for religious objects

In many cases a charity is established for purposes purely religious.[45] **4–022** Dissenting chapels furnish a common instance of this.[46] Where this is the case two presumptions arise: the first is that the institution was intended for the inculcation or observance of some particular form of doctrine or worship; the second is that the form intended was that professed by the founder or founders.[47]

A charity for the "worship of God" is prima facie a charity for the benefit of the religion of the established church, *i.e.* the Church of England[48]; but, where the trust is expressed to be for the benefit of Protestant Dissenters generally, Dissenters of all denominations are prima facie included.[49]

Where the will establishing the charity was made before the Reformation, it must be construed as though it had been made after that date, and provisions as to the rites or doctrines of what was then the established religion must be read as referring to the Church of England as established after the Reformation.[50]

The founder's intention is a question of fact,[51] and if the founder's **4–023** intention is expressed in the instrument of foundation, whether a deed or will, no question as to the admission of extrinsic evidence arises; such evidence is neither relevant nor admissible. If the founder's intention is not expressed in the instrument, however, or if the intention is expressed in ambiguous language, extrinsic evidence is admitted. Such evidence may be of the known opinions of the founder, of the state of law existing at the date when the instrument took effect, or of contemporaneous usage, or the like, and the evidence is admitted to enable the court to determine the objects of the charity and the manner in which the trusts are to be performed.[52] In *Att-Gen v Pearson*[53] Lord Eldon L.C. said:

"Where a body of Protestant Dissenters have established a trust without any precise definition of the object or mode of worship, I know no means the court has of ascertaining it, except by looking to what

---

[45] As to what are religious charities, see paras 2–048, *et seq*, above.

[46] As to the right of Dissenters and others to have the trusts of their place of worship executed, see *Davis v Jenkins* (1814) 3 V. & B. 158, and para.2–051, above.

[47] *per* Romilly M.R., in *Att-Gen v Calvert* (1857) 23 B. 248 at 255, 256; see also *Craigdallie v Aikman* (1813) 1 Dow. 1; *Att-Gen v Pearson* (1817) 3 Mer. 353 at 410; *Dill v Watson* (1836) 2 Jones Ex.R. 48; *Free Church of Scotland v Overtoun* [1904] A.C. 515 at 613.

[48] *Att-Gen v Pearson* (1817) 3 Mer. 353 at 409.

[49] *Att-Gen v Murdoch* (1850) 7 Ha. 445. Dissenters could sue by information in the name of the Attorney-General. See *Att-Gen v Fowler* (1808) 15 Ves. 85; *Att-Gen v Dudley* (1815) G. Coop. 146.

[50] *Att-Gen v Calvert* (1857) 23 B. 248, 260; *cf. Glasgow College v Att-Gen* (1864) 1 H.L.C. 800.

[51] *per* Lord Lyndhurst in the Court of Chancery in *Shore v Wilson* (1842) 9 Cl. & F. 355 at 390. As to how far extrinsic evidence is admissible, see further, para.4–004, above.

[52] *Shore v Wilson* (1842) 9 Cl. & F. 355; *Drummond v Att-Gen* (1850) 2 H.L.C. 837; *Att-Gen v Molland* (1832) You. 562. With regard to Presbyterian Trusts, see *Westwood v McKie* (1869) 21 L.T. 165; *Free Church of Scotland v Overtoun* [1904] A.C. 515. The word "Presbyterian" does not define any particular doctrine: *Att-Gen v Bunce* (1868) L.R. 6 Eq. 563.

[53] (1817) 3 Mer. 353 at 410. See *Drummond v Att-Gen* (1850) 2 H.L.C. 837.

has passed, and thereby collecting what may, by fair inference, be presumed to have been the intention of the founders."

Where the trust is expressed to be for an existing congregation of Protestant Dissenters, the terms of the trust themselves open an inquiry into the character of the congregation.[54]

When the contributors are so numerous as to preclude the possibility of their all concurring in any instrument declaring the trust, a declaration of trust made by the person in whom the property is vested, at or about the time whens the sums were raised, may reasonably be taken as being prima facie a true exposition of the intention of the contributors.[55] Prima facie such person or persons has or have an implied authority to declare the trusts.[56] Contemporaneous deeds relating to the same chapel may be properly referred to.[57]

4–024   If the court can find no other means of ascertaining what form of religious worship was intended, it must investigate the usage of the congregation in respect to it, and if the usage turns out to be such as can be supported, it is the duty of the court to administer the trust in such a manner as best to establish the usage, treating the usage in question as a matter of implied contract between the members of the congregation.[58] It follows that the court may and will direct an inquiry for the purpose of ascertaining the objects for which the trusts were created and the usage of the congregation.[59] In such a case, as in all cases, extrinsic evidence is only relevant and admissible where the trusts have not been declared,[60] or where the language of the instrument of foundation is ambiguous.[61] Extrinsic evidence is never admissible to contradict the express provisions of a written instrument,[62] or to sanction a breach of trust.[63]

In consequence of the difficulties, which constantly arose, in determining which of several Dissenting sects was intended to have the benefit of a charity, and whether, in the execution of the trusts, the principles of the founders had been departed from, the Nonconformist Chapels Act 1844[64] was passed, s.2 of which provided that where in the case of a place of worship there was no express statement in the deed of foundation as to the particular doctrines for which it was to be employed, 25 years' usage was made conclusive.[65] In order to take a case out of the Act the particular

---

[54] *Att-Gen v Murdoch* (1850) 7 Ha. 445; *cf. Dill v Watson* (1836) 2 Jones Ex.R. 48.

[55] *Att-Gen v Clapham* (1855) 4 De G.M. & G. 591.

[56] *Att-Gen v Mathieson* [1907] 2 Ch. 383 at 394. As to the relevance of this case to disaster funds, see [1966] Ch. Com. Rep., pp.9, *et seq*; and see para.3–033, above.

[57] *Att-Gen v Anderson* (1888) 57 L.J.Ch. 543.

[58] *Att-Gen v Pearson* (1817) 3 Mer. 353 at 400; *Drummond v Att-Gen* (1850) 2 H.L.C. 837.

[59] *Att-Gen v Pearson* (1817) 3 Mer 353 at 420, where the form of order is given.

[60] *Att-Gen v Murdoch* (1850) 7 Ha. 445.

[61] *Att-Gen v Calvert* (1857) 23 B. 263; Att-Gen v Gould (1860) 28 B. 248 at 485.

[62] *Att-Gen v Clapham* (1855) 4 De G.M. & G. 591.

[63] *Drummond v Att-Gen* (1850) 2 H.L.C. 837.

[64] The Act was passed in consequence of the difficulties which arose in *Shore v Wilson* (1842) 9 Cl. & F. 355. See *Att-Gen v Bunce* (1868) L.R. 6 Eq. 571. The Act was repealed as obsolete by the Charities Act 1960, s.39, Sch.5, but without prejudice to the operation of s.2 as it applied to charities taking effect before the commencement of the Act of 1844.

[65] See *Att-Gen v Anderson* (1886) 56 L.J.Ch. 543 at 546, 547.

doctrines or mode of worship required or forbidden must be stated in express terms.[66] The use of a general description, as, for example, the Protestant dissenting congregation then of New Row,[67] or, having regard to the changes which have taken place in that sect, the use of the term "Presbyterian",[68] was not a sufficient requistion that any particular doctrines or mode of worship should be taught or observed. Where, however, under a deed of 1766, property was held in trust for a meeting-house "for Protestant Dissenters of the Presbyterian or independent denomination to worship in, as the same is now used, free of rent, so long as the laws of Great Britain shall tolerate Protestant Dissenters," it was held that the direction was sufficiently express to take the case out of the Act.[69] Moreover, a case in which the deed in which the direction expressed was void under the Charitable Uses Act (Mortmain Act) 1735[70] was taken out of the Act.[71]

A congregation of Unitarians, professing to be bound by no human authority, and to be at liberty to change their belief as often as their judgment satisfied them that they were in error, was held not to be deprived of the benefit of the Act by want of fixed doctrine, and to be capable of acquiring a right by 25 years' usage.[72]

A similar provision applicable to Roman Catholic charities was contained in the Roman Catholic Charities Act 1860.[73] By s.5 of that Act it was enacted, with regard to charities connected with the Roman Catholic religion, that, where the original trusts were not ascertained by means of a written instrument, consistent usage during 20 years was conclusive evidence of the trusts on which the property was settled.   **4–025**

The task of executing trusts of Dissenting chapels has often been found to be one of the greatest difficulty,[74] and it was said long ago that it is the duty of the founders of such trusts to declare their intentions clearly.[75] Many Dissenting sects endeavour to secure uniformity in the trusts of their chapels by means of "model deeds" or "forms" of deeds recommended for use. The model deed is an instrument prepared under the authority and with the approval of the lending members of the sect. It establishes and declares the trusts of a particular chapel, and is duly enrolled, and copies of it are printed and circulated. The trusts of any chapel requiring to be subsequently established can thus be declared by reference to the model deed. The use of the model deed or form in declaring the trusts of a chapel is, of course, voluntary, but is obviously advisable.

---

[66] *Att-Gen v Hutton* (1844) Dr.temp. Sug. 480; 7 Ir.Eq. 612.
[67] *ibid.*
[68] *Att-Gen v Bunce* (1868) 6 Eq. 563; *Att-Gen v Anderson* (1888) 57 L.J.Ch. 543.
[69] *Att-Gen v Anderson*, above.
[70] Replaced by the Mortmain and Charitable Uses Act 1888 (repealed by the Charities Act 1960, s.48, Sch.7, Pt II).
[71] *Att-Gen v Ward* (1848) 6 Ha. 477 at 483.
[72] *Att-Gen v Hutton* (1844) Dr.temp. Sug. 480; 7 Ir.Eq.R. 612.
[73] By the Charities Act 1960, s.39, Sch.5, this Act was repealed as obsolete, but without prejudice to the operation of s.5 as it applied to charities taking effect before the commencement of the Act of 1860.
[74] *Att-Gen v Pearson* (1817) 3 Mer. 353 at 397; *Foley v Wontner* (1820) 2 J. & W. 245.
[75] *Att-Gen v Pearson*, above, at 410.

The benefits of charities which have not been established primarily for religious purposes (as, for instance, eductional or eleemosynary charities) may be confined to perons holding a particular form of religious belief; and, where the founder's intention was that the benefits should be so confined, his intention must be carried out, unless the trusts are varied by the court or the Charity Commissioners.[76] There is, however, a presumption against such an intention, and the court accordingly assumes, in the absence of any expressed intention to the contrary, that the founder did not intend, in one case, that any particular religious doctrine should be combined with the secular education, and, in the other, that the benefit of the charity should be confined to persons professing one particular form of religious belief.[77]

4–026   In the case of an eleemosynary charity, the presumption against confining it to members of a particular church or sect is so strong that nothing short of an expression of unequivocal import will exclude any class of Dissenters from its benefits and evidence as to the particular tenents and opinions of the founder is not admissible as evidence of his intention.[78]

A gift for the endowment of a church means that the income only of the fund is to be applied for the benefit of the incumbent.[79] It is considered that a gift for the endowment of a Roman Catholic church or a Nonconformist chapel would be treated as a gift to apply the income for the priest or minister as the case may be.

A gift to the parish church of St Andrew, Holborn, was construed to be a gift to the parson and parishioners of that parish and their successors for ever.[80] But a gift in this form is now treated as a gift intended to be devoted to church purposes, namely, purposes connected with the services of the church. The fund is to be vested in the parochial church council and held by them as an appropriate trust suitably recorded.[81]

Gifts to holders of an office

4–027   If it is doubtful whether a gift is to persons in their corporate or their individual capacity,[82] the court will decide the point upon a reading of the

[76] *Craigdallie v Aikman* (1812) 1 Dow. 1, 16; *Broom v Summers* (1841) 11 Sim. 353; *Shore v Wilson* (1842) 9 Cl. & F. 353, 383; *Att-Gen v Welsh* (1846) 4 Ha. 572; *Att-Gen v Munro* (1848) 2 De G. & Sm. 122; *Att-Gen v Murdoch* (1850) 7 Ha. 445; *Att-Gen v Clapham* (1855) 4 De G.M. & G. 591; *Att-Gen v Calvert* (1857) 23 B. 248 at 254, 255. For a case where it was held upon the construction of a charter that the charity was for religious purposes, education, and relief of the poor exclusively, see *Att-Gen v Corporation of Boston* (1847) 1 De G. & Sm. 519.

[77] *Att-Gen v Calvert* (1857) 23 B. 248 at 256–258; *Att-Gen v Clifton* (1863) 32 B. 596. See *Re St. Leonard, Shoreditch, Parochial Schools* (1884) 10 Ap.Cas. 304.

[78] *Att-Gen v Calvert,* (1857) 23 B. 248. See also *Att-Gen v St. John's Hospital, Bath* (1876) 2 Ch.D. 554. For an instance of an eleemosynary charity for the benefit of dissenters, see *Shore v Wilson* (1842) 9 Cl. & F. 355.

[79] *Re Robinson* [1892] 1 Ch. 95 at 100.

[80] See *St Andrew's, Holborn Case,* cited in *Cheeseman v Partridge* (1739) 1 Atk. 436 at 437; and see *Att-Gen v Cock* (1751) 2 Ves.Sen. 273; *Re Parker's Charity* (1863) 32 B. 654.

[81] *Re Gare* [1952] Ch. 80.

[82] *Cheeseman v Partridge* (1739) 1 Atk. 436, a gift to the schoolmaster of a particular school by name of five pounds yearly, for teaching three boys, was held not to be a gift to the particular schoolmaster, but to the school itself, for teaching three boys in succession.

whole gift.[83] If there are no means of deciding the point, the gift may fail for uncertainty.[84]

Where a gift is made to a person described as the holder of a religious office, the court will decide whether an individual or a corporation sole is intended to benefit.[85] The fact that a person is described as the holder of such an office is not conclusive to show that he takes *ex officio*. Nor will the addition of the words "and his successor" necessarily show that a corporation is to take.[86]

Gifts for repair of a building

A trust for the "reparation" of a building will include restoring or rebuilding it if necessary.[87] A gift for the repair or ornament of a church will normally be held to include the chancel.[88] In *Re Palatine Estate Charity*,[89] the meaning of "reparations, ornaments, and other necessary occasions" of a parish church was discussed, and it was held that the erection of a spire came within those words. It was also held that the salaries of the sexton and verger, so far as their services related to the fabric of the church, might under those words continue to be paid, but not that of the organist or bell-ringer.[90]

4–028

Gifts to institutions

A gift generally[91] to an existing charitable institution or society, or for purposes identical with its general purposes[92] to the governors or treasurer of such an institution,[93] is applicable to the general purposes of the institution, and the governors or trustees or other officials responsible for the administration of the funds being trustees for that purpose. A similar approach was previously taken to general gifts to charitable corporations.[94] Thus a gift to or in trust for a college in general terms became

4–029

---

[83] *Re Delaney* [1902] 2 Ch. 642 at 647. See *Thornber v Wilson* (1855) 4 Dr. 350.

[84] *Att-Gen v Sibthorp* (1830) 2 R. & M. 107.

[85] *Doe d. Philips v Aldridge* (1791) 4 T.R. 264; *Grieves v Case* (1792) 4 B.C.C. 67 *Robb v Dorian* (1875) Ir.R. 9 C.L. 483; *Gibson v Representative Church Body* (1881) 9 L.R.Ir. 1; *Re Delany* [1902] 2 Ch. 642; *Re Garrard* [1907] 1 Ch. 382. See paras 2–060, *et seq.*, above.

[86] *Robb v Dorian* (1875) Ir.R. 9 C.L. 483.

[87] *Att-Gen v Wax Chandlers' Co*. (1873) 6 H.L. 1; *Re Palatine Estate Charity* (1888) 39 Ch.D. 54. See *Re Booth's Charities* (1866) 14 W.R. 761.

[88] *Att-Gen v Parr* [1920] 1 Ch. 344, and cases there cited.

[89] (1888) 39 Ch.D. 54.

[90] With regard to the meaning of "ornaments," see also *Westerton v Liddell* (1857), Moore's Rep. 156; *Phillimore's Ecclesiastical Law* (2nd ed.), Vol. I, p.716. See also *Woodward v Makepeace* (1689) 1 Salk. 164.

[91] *Incorporated Society v Richards* (1841) 1 Dr. & W. 258 at 294, 332; *Re White* [1893] 2 Ch. 41, 52; and see *Re Macduff* [1896] 2 Ch. 451, where the word "philanthropic" defeated an intention which, if the word has been omitted, would have been a general charitable intention.

[92] *Att-Gen v Sidney Sussex College* (1869) L.R. 4 Ch. 722 at 730.

[93] *Incorporated Society v Richards* (1841) 1 Dr. & W. 258 at 294; *Att-Gen v Sidney Sussex College* (1869) L.R. 4 Ch. 722.

[94] *Incorporated Society v Richards* (1841) 1 Dr. & W. 258, 332.

subject to its statutes and rules like the rest of its property.[95] A general gift to a charitable company will now probably be construed as a gift to the body beneficially.[96]

Where a gift is made to an institution, and the trusts are not stated, it will be presumed that it is to be held for the general purposes of the institution.[97] Where, however, the object of a gift is insufficiently defined, but the trusts upon which it was intended to be held are set out, an institution whose general purposes do not correspond with the trusts declared will be rejected in an inquiry to identify the object described with an existing institution.[98]

If there is a gift to a charitable corporation for the performance, to benefit particular individuals, of functions which it is itself established to perform, the intention prima facie is that the functions in question shall be performed by the corporation. Thus a gift to a college for the education of the testator's descendants will be contrued to mean their education at that college,[99] and, subject to the carrying out of the particular purposes directed, the property will usually be held to belong to the corporation for its general purposes.[1]

PARTICULAR PARTICIPANTS

Descendants or kindred

4–030   Unless the trust is one for the relief of poverty[2] or the special case of an educational endowment with preference for founder's kin[3] a gift to descendants or kindred will fail as a charitable gift. In the context of those two types of gift, however, questions have frequently arisen as to who are entitled to participate in a gift for the benefit of descendants or kindred. In *Ralph v Carrick*,[4] it was said that the word "descendants" included descendants of any degree and not just children. Prima facie, the expression "male descendants" means descendants claiming through males only,[5] but that prima facie meaning will readily yield to a very small indication to the contrary in the context of the instrument of gift.[6]

---

[95] *Green v Rutherforth* (1750) 1 Ves.Sen. 473.
[96] *Re Vernon's Will Trust* [1972] Ch. 300n at 303 and see para.3–045, above.
[97] See *Bowman v Secular Society Ltd.* [1917] A.C. 406, 442; and see *Neville Estates Ltd. v Madden* [1962] Ch. 832, 849.
[98] *Verge v Somerville* [1924] A.C. 496, 506.
[99] *Att-Gen v Sidney Sussex College* (1869) L.R. 4 Ch. 722 at 730, and as to "descendants" see below.
[1] *Att-Gen v Sidney Sussex College*, above. See also *Att-Gen v St. John's College* (1834) Coop. T. Brough. 394.
[2] See para.2–014, above.
[3] See para.2–046, above.
[4] (1879) 1 Ch.D. 873 at 883. See also *Carr v Bedford* (1679) 2 Rep. in Ch. 146; *Gillam v Taylor* (1873) L.R. 1 Eq. 581.
[5] *Bernal v Bernal* (1838) 3 Myl. & Cr. 559.
[6] See *Re Du Cros' Settlement Trusts* [1961] 1 W.L.R. 1252 at 1260; *Re Drake's Will Trust* [1971] Ch. 179. See the comments on the observations of Wickens V.C. in *Gillam v Taylor* (above) at 584 of Jessel M.R. in *Att-Gen v Northumberland* (1878) 7 Ch.D. 745 at 751, 752; and see the explanation and rationalisation of the "founder's kin" cases given by Lord Greene M.R. in *Re Compton* [1945] Ch. 123 at 132–135.

Gifts to poor relations are charitable.[7] The word "relations" is not construed restrictively and prima facie extends beyond statutory next of kin.[8]

Parishioners and inhabitants

The courts have frequently been called upon to determine the meaning of **4–031**
the words "inhabitant" and "parishioner." An analysis of the decisions may
still be useful notwithstanding that they may require to be reconsidered in
the light of the provisions of the Representation of the People Act 1949.

The cases have sometimes turned on the meaning of "inhabitant" or
"parishioner" alone. More frequently the words requiring to be interpreted have been "inhabitants and parishioners", this expression being
construed to mean "inhabitants who are also parishioners."[9]

"Inhabitant" prima facie includes every person dwelling in the parish or
place in reference to which the word is used, whether a householder or not.
Servants, lodgers and persons supported by parish relief were consequently
inhabitants, but not casual sojourners.[10] In *Rex v Hall*[11] Abbott C.J. said:

> "The inhabitants of any county, city, or other place, taking that word
> either in its strict or in its popular sense, are those persons only who
> have their dwelling therein; and all persons who have their dwelling
> therein are inhabitants thereof."

In *Att-Gen v Parker*[12] Lord Hardwicke said:

> "'Inhabitants' is still a larger word [than parishioners], takes in **4–032**
> housekeepers, though not rated to the poor; takes in also persons who
> are not housekeepers, as, for instance, such who have gained a settlement, and by that means become inhabitants."

If the qualification for participating in a charity is being a "parishioner", that word will be construed in its ordinary sense of a person occupying premises liable to be rated in a parish, whether he dwells there or
not.[13] Where the requisite qualification is in fact possessed, the object and
mode of its acquirement are immaterial.[14]

---

[7] See para.2–016 above.
[8] *Re Scarisbrick* [1951] Ch. 622.
[9] *Fearon v Webb* (1802) 14 Ves. 13.
[10] See Steer's *Parish Law* (6th ed.), p.12, citing *Holledge's Case* (1622) 2 Roll.Rep. 238; and
see Stroud's *Judicial Dictionary*. For a statutory definition of "inhabitant", see City of
London Burial Act 1857, s.8 (repealed).
[11] (1822) 1 B. & C. 123 at 136, 137. See also *Gateward's Case* (1607) 6 Co. 59 b; *Att-Gen v
Clarke* (1762) Amb. 422.
[12] (1747) 3 Atk. 576 at 577.
[13] *Jeffrey's Case* (1589) 5 Co. 66 b; *Att-Gen v Parker*, above; *Batten v Gedye* (1889) 41 Ch.D.
507; and see *Hansard v Parishioners of St Matthew, Bethnal Green* (1878) 4 P.D. 46. In
Etherington v Wilson (1876) 1 Ch.D. 160 it was held that a person who had contracted to
take a house and pay rent, and had caused his name to be entered on the ratebook, and
had paid a portion of the current rate, was a "parishioner." See also *Kensit v Rector, etc.,
of St. Ethelburga, Bishopsgate Within* [1900] P. 80.
[14] *Etherington v Wilson*, above.

Whether "parishioner" includes any persons except those who are council tax or rate-payers is a question upon which the authorities are not quite clear, but a casual sojourner is not a parishioner.[15] In *Att-Gen v Parker*[16] Lord Hardwicke said:

> "'Parishioner' is a very large word, takes in not only inhabitants of the parish, but persons who are occupiers of lands, that pay the several rates and duties, though they are not resiant, nor do contribute to the ornaments of the church."

He also said that it would not be unreasonable to confine the words "inhabitants and parishioners" to inhabitants paying scot and lot (*i.e.* church and poor rates). He, however, declined so to decide, and dismissed the information. Nor would he hold that the words must necessarily be confined to persons who would be entitled to attend a select vestry.

4–033   In each of the cases of *Att-Gen v Rutter*[17] and *Edenborough v Archbishop of Canterbury*[18] the question was who were entitled to vote at the election of a parson. In *Att-Gen v Rutter* the right of voting was vested in the "inhabitants and parishioners"; in *Edenborough v Archbishop of Canterbury* it was vested in the "parishioners". In the first of these cases there is nothing in the report to show that any evidence of usage was adduced; in the second of them such evidence was put forward, but the usage had not been uniform. Both cases must, therefore, be taken as decisions on the meaning of the words taken alone unassisted by any interpretation placed upon them by the conduct of the parties. In *Att-Gen v Rutter*, "inhabitants and parishioners" were confined to persons paying church and poor rates. A similar decision was arrived at in *Carter v Cropley*.[19]

In *Fearon v Webb*[20] the election of a person was vested in the inhabitants and parishioners "or the major part of the chiefest and discreetest of them." It was held that "chiefest" must be construed as meaning those who paid church and poor rates, and "discreetest" those who had attained the age of 21 years. The language used by Mellish L.J., in *Etherington v Wilson*[21] goes to show that in his opinion the observations of Lord Hardwicke in *Att-Gen v Parker*[22] as to the meaning of "parishioners", although in terms they amounted merely to a statement that all ratepayers are parishioners, not that all parishioners are ratepayers, were nevertheless intended to be a definition, and consequently that "parishioners" and "ratepayers" are convertible terms. That suggests that prima facie none but

---

[15] Steer's *Parish Law* (6th ed.), p.12. For statutory definitions of the word "parishioner", see City of London Burial Act 1857, s.8 (repealed); Public Worship Regulation Act 1874, s.6 (repealed).
[16] (1747) 3 Atk. 576 at 577.
[17] (1768) 2 Russ. 101n.
[18] (1826) 2 Russ. 93.
[19] (1856) 7 De G.M. & G. 681. See also *Faulkner v Elger* (1825) 4 B. & C. 449; *Att-Gen v Dalton* (1851) 13 B. 141.
[20] (1802) 14 Ves. 13.
[21] (1876) 1 Ch.D. 167.
[22] (1747) 3 Atk. 576 at 577.

ratepayers are parishioners, but in fact neither "parishioner" nor "inhabitant" has a fixed legal meaning. Each is construed *secundum subjectam materiam*.[23] Its signification varies according to the circumstances under which it is applied.[24]

In the case of "inhabitant" especially, the prima facie meaning is so wide that it would in almost all cases be quite impossible to construe the word according to the full extent of that meaning.[25] Thus, in cases of charitable gifts for the poor inhabitants of a place, the word "inhabitants" was restricted to persons not in receipt of relief from the rates or other public sources of relief.[26] In the Statute of Bridges 1530, "inhabitant" was construed on the one hand to include all occupiers of land in the county, although actually living in another county, and on the other hand not to include servants, lodgers or inmates, although actually dwelling in the county.[27]

The context and object of a charter giving a benefit to the "inhabitants" **4–034** of a place must be taken into consideration in determining the meaning which is to be placed upon the word.[28] In *Chilton v Corporation of London*,[29] Jessel M.R. was of opinion, although the case was not decided on that point, that a grant to the inhabitants of a parish meant the inhabitants of houses within the parish, and was restricted to houses lawfully erected, and did not apply to houses which had been illegally erected on common land and might be levelled at any moment.

Evidence of usage is admissible for the purpose of determining in what sense the word "inhabitant", or the word "parishioner", or the words "inhabitants and parishioners" are used.[30] Evidence of this kind, that is, evidence of a common consent among the persons entitled to vote,[31] has been put forward in most of the cases in which the question has been whether the right of voting at an election of a parson is restricted to ratepayers or not.[32] If there is evidence of uniform usage that is conclusive,[33] but not, of course, where the usage has varied.[34] In *Att-Gen v Davy*,[35] Lord Hardwicke held that "inhabitants" must be confined to persons paying church and poor rates.

So also, in the case of the words "inhabitants and parishioners". If, on the one hand, the usage has been to confine the right of voting to ratepayers, they alone can take part in the election.[36] If, on the other hand, the

---

[23] *Att-Gen v Forster* (1804) 10 Ves. 339.
[24] *R. v Mashiter* (1837) 6 A. & E. 153.
[25] See *Att-Gen v Parker* (1747) 3 Atk. 576 at 577; *Withnell v Gartham* (1795) 6 T.R. 398.
[26] *Att-Gen v Clarke* (1762) Amb. 422.
[27] *Att-Gen v Forster* (1804) 10 Ves. 339; *R. v Hall* (1822) 1 B. & C. 136 at 137. See also *Jeffrey's Case* (1589) 5 Co. 66 b, as to church rates.
[28] *R. v Mashiter* (1837) 6 A. & E. 165, *per* Littledale, J.; *R. v Dane* (1837) 6 A. & E. 374.
[29] (1878) 7 Ch.D. 735.
[30] *R. v Mashiter* (1837) 6 A. & E. 165.
[31] *Edenborough v Archbishop of Canterbury* (1826) 2 Russ. 100.
[32] See, further, paras 5–058 *et seq.*, below.
[33] *Att-Gen v Forster* (1804) 10 Ves. 338.
[34] *Edenborough v Archbishop of Canterbury*, above, 93 at 104, 107.
[35] (1741), cited 3 Atk. 577. See also *R. v Dane* (1837) 6 A. & E. 374.
[36] *Att-Gen v Newcombe* (1807) 14 Ves. 1; *Edenborough v Archbishop of Canterbury*, above.

usage has been to extend the right to persons who are not ratepayers, then such persons cannot be excluded.[37]

4-035   Assuming that "inhabitant", or "parishioner", or "inhabitants and parishioners", are confined to council tax and rate-payers, a further question arises whether it is necessary that a rate or tax should actually have been paid, or whether it is sufficient that a person is liable to be taxed or rated. It appears, although the position is far from clear, that where the qualification of being a council tax or rate-payer is required it is not attained until a tax or rate has been actually paid. In *Att-Gen v Forster*,[38] Lord Eldon L.C. said, "As to the word 'pay' there is no doubt, in a strict sense persons paying are those, who have paid. But in a popular sense persons paying to church and poor may be understood persons liable to pay; and if, in ordinary parlance persons liable to pay were excluded, the greater part would be excluded." And in *Edenborough v Archbishop of Canterbury*,[39] the same judge held that a person who came into the parish after a rate had been made had no right to vote as a "parishioner" before another rate had been made, unless the making of the rate had been postponed for an unfair purpose. On the other hand, in *Etherington v Wilson*,[40] although a payment in respect of rates had actually been made, Mellish L.J. nevertheless treated the question as depending on whether the person claiming to be a parishioner was *liable* to be rated. He said[41]: "The question whether he is actually rated or not is immaterial; but so far the fact of his being rated confirms the evidence that he was the occupier." It does, however, seem to be the position that a clearly established usage that the qualification shall be satisfied by assessment only, not followed by actualy payment, will be upheld.[42]

"Householders" is not so strict a word as "housekeepers", but it excludes servants, lodgers or inmates, who have no permanent interest in the place, but only a temporary residence.[43] Partners carrying on business, but not dwelling in a city, and paying rates in respect of their place of business, are householders.[44]

---

[37] *Att-Gen v Parker* (1747) 3 Atk. 577. See, further, paras 5–058, *et seq.*, below.
[38] (1804) 10 Ves. 335 at 339.
[39] (1826) 2 Russ. 110 at 111.
[40] (1876) 1 Ch.D. 160.
[41] *ibid.*, at 168.
[42] *Att-Gen v Newcombe* (1807) 14 Ves. 1.
[43] *R. v Hall* (1822) 1 B. & C. 137.
[44] *ibid.*, at 138. See also *Wescomb's Case* (1868) 4 Q.B. 110; *Dipstale's Case, ibid.*, at 114, for meaning of "inhabitant householder" and of "residence"; and see Stroud's *Judicial Dictionary*.

CHAPTER 5

APPOINTMENT AND REMOVAL OF TRUSTEES AND OFFICERS

This chapter is concerned with the appointment and removal of **5–001** "trustees" as defined in s.97(1) of the Charities Act 1993, *i.e.* the persons having the general control and management of the administration of a charity. Thus, in addition to trustees of a charitable trust, directors of charitable companies and members of the committee of charitable unincorporated associations are considered. It is not unusual to find directors of charitable companies called "trustees" and the members of a committee of an unincorporated association called "governors". Whatever the name used to designate those entrusted with the control of a charity, their appointment and removal will depend upon the particular legal structure adopted by the charity. The position of officers, such as members of colleges and holders of religious office, is also considered.

TRUSTEES OF A CHARITABLE TRUST

Capacity

Any individual who has the capacity to be a trustee of a private trust **5–002** may, in general, be a trustee of a charitable trust. A minor, therefore, cannot be a trustee of a charitable trust in England or Wales.[1] A corporation is capable of acting as a trustee of a charitable trust.[2] The common law rule that a corporation could not hold property on a joint tenancy has been amended by statute[3] and a corporation may now act as a trustee jointly with another corporation or individual. The fact that a person uses services provided by a charitable trust does not bar them from trusteeship but rules will be needed to deal with potential conflicts of interest.[4]

---

[1] Law of Property Act 1925, s.20.
[2] It was considered that a corporation could not be a trustee, 1 Kyd. Corp. 72, but the capacity of corporations to act as trustees was recognised in cases following the Statute of Elizabeth I which held that devises to corporations for charitable uses were within the relief intended by the Statute: *Flood's Case* (1616) Hob. 136; *Att-Gen v Tancred* (1757) 1 Eden 10, 14; *Att-Gen v Brentwood School* (1833) 1 Myl. & K. 376; *Att-Gen v Liverpool Corp.* (1835) 1 My & Cr. 171 at 201; *Incorporated Society v Richards* (1841) 1 Dr. & War. 258 at 302: *Bene't College v Bishop of London* (1788) 2 Wm. Bl. 1182 went further and held that such a devise was good at law but this has not been followed.
[3] Bodies Corporate (Joint Tenants) Act 1899; *Re Thompson's Settlement Trusts* [1905] 1 Ch. 229.
[4] See CC24, *Users on Board: Beneficiaries who become Trustees* (2000).

By s.72 of the Charities Act 1993 certain persons are disqualified from being a trustee and it is a criminal offence for any such person to act as a trustee.[5] A person is disqualified if he has been convicted of any offence involving dishonesty or deception,[6] if he has been adjudged bankrupt and not been discharged, if he has made a composition with his creditors and not been discharged, if he has been removed from office by the High Court or the Charity Commissioners,[7] or he has been disqualified as a company director. A person disqualified by court order[8] from working with children cannot be a trustee of a children's charity.[9] If a disqualified person does act as a charity trustee, any acts done for the charity are not invalid because of the disqualification[10] but he may be ordered by the Commissioners to pay back any sums received whilst so acting.[11]

The Commissioners have power to waive disqualification either generally or in relation to a particular charity or class of charities on application.[12] The Commissioners' starting point when considering whether to grant a waiver of disqualification is that any person who is disqualified as a trustee under one of the statutory provisions should remain disqualified until the relevant circumstances no longer prevail.[13] Following *Re Barings plc and others (No 3)*[14] the Commissioners take the guiding principle to be what is in the best interest of the charity. Relevant factors include the reason for and seriousness of the default, the risk to the charity, the objects of the charity, the importance to the charity of the particular individual and the views of the trustees.[15] Conditions may be imposed on a waiver, for example, that the particular trustee should not be a signatory on cheques or hold charity property.[16]

5–003   An eleemosynary corporation is entitled to hold property in trust for its general purposes.[17] It may also accept property as an accession to its foundation such as, in the case of a college, an additional fellowship.[18] In addition, it may accept property on special trusts connected with the objects of

---

[5] Charities Act 1993, s.73(1). The statutory provision does not cause automatic vacation of office. In the absence of a clause in the governing instrument providing that a disqualified trustee shall cease to hold office, the Charity Commissioners have power to remove under s.18(4) of the 1993 Act, see para.5–038 below.
[6] The disqualification is not limited to specific offences or conviction on indictment and is capable of being construed widely. It does not apply, however, to convictions spent for the purposes of the Rehabilitation of Offenders Act 1974, s.72(2)(a).
[7] The Charity Commissioners keep a register of those removed from office and the register is open to the public, s.72(6)(7).
[8] Criminal Justice and Court Services Act 2000, ss.28 and 29.
[9] *ibid.*, s.36(6)(c).
[10] Charities Act 1993, s.73(3).
[11] *ibid.*, s.73(4).
[12] *ibid.*, s.72(4).
[13] See OG 42 A1, *Waiver of Disqualification for Acting as a Charity Trustee. The Law*, s.5.
[14] [1999] 1 All E.R. 1017.
[15] See OG 42 B1, *Waiver of Disqualification for Acting as a Trustee. Processing Applications*, ss.4, 5 and 6.
[16] *ibid.*, s.6.
[17] *Lydiatt v Foach* (1700) 2 Vern. 410 at 412.
[18] *Att-Gen v Talbot* (1747) 3 Ark. 662; *Att-Gen v Whorwood* (1750) 1 Ves.S. 534, 537; *Att-Gen v Flood* (1816) Hayes & J.App.xxi, xxxv; *Re Catherine Hall, Ex p. Inge* (1831) 2 Russ. & M. 590, 596; *Att-Gen v Caius College* (1837) 2 Keen 150 at 163.

the foundation. Colleges have thus accepted trusts for scholarships[19] and for the maintenance of associated schools.[20] Provided that the accession is itself charitable there does not seem to be any rule requiring the trust to be consistent with the original foundation.[21] It has been doubted, however, whether a college can accept an accession to its foundation without the consent of the visitor.[22]

Corporations which are not eleemosynary, such as livery companies,[23] may hold property upon charitable trusts. Municipal corporations may also be trustees of charitable trusts[24] and local authorities may hold property on special trusts, for example, for the benefit of the borough freemen.[25] Corporations established by statute[26] or otherwise[27] for particular purposes which have no existence for any purposes outside those for which they were created cannot be trustees of charitable trusts for purposes other than those for which they were established. Local authorities cannot, by statute, act as trustees for ecclesiastical charities or charities for the relief of poverty.[28]

Corporations sole may be trustees for charities. They were originally ecclesiastical but not all religious officers are corporations sole. Only holders of certain offices in the Church of England are corporations sole and not, for instance, a Roman Catholic bishop[29] or a nonconformist minister.[30] If the person named is not a corporation sole, he himself can act as a trustee but the trusteeship will not pass to his successors.[31]

There are also lay corporations sole. For example, by the custom of **5–004** orphanage money in the City of London, the Chamberlain of the City is a corporation to make recognisances, obligations, etc., in trust for the portions of orphans.[32]

A corporation sole could not as a general rule hold chattels real or any other kind of personal property in succession[33] but could always hold

---

[19] *Att-Gen v Talbot*, above.
[20] *Att-Gen v Caius College*, above. As to the obligation to perform the trusts attached to property so accepted see *ibid.*, at 168, 169.
[21] *Att-Gen v Whorwood*, above, and *Att-Gen v Tancred* (1757) 1 Eden 10 are not authority for saying that the accession has to be consistent with the foundation. Different considerations will apply where a corporation has a limited capacity.
[22] *Att-Gen v Catherine Hall, Cambridge* (1820) Jac. at 381, 400.
[23] *Att-Gen v Grocer's Company* (1843) 6 Beav. 526.
[24] Municipal Corporations Act 1882, s.133. See *e.g.*, *Oldham MBC v Att-Gen* [1993] 2 All E.R. 432.
[25] *Goodman v Saltash Corp.* (1822) 7 App.Cas. 633 H.L.; *Prestney v Colchester Corp. and Att-Gen* (1882) 21 Ch.D. 111.
[26] *National Manure Co. v Donald* (1859) 28 L.J.Ex. 185 at 188; *Putney Overseers v L. & S.W. Ry. Co.* [1891] 1 Q.B. 440.
[27] See *Incorporated Society v Price* (1844) Jo. & Lat. 498.
[28] Local Government Act 1972, s.139(3). Some local authorities have special powers to permit them to hold on such trusts: see, *e.g.* Norwich Corporation Act 1933, and see also *Re Armitage* [1972] Ch. 438. The Commissioners have indicated that they have some concerns, based on conflict of interest, about appointing a local authority a sole trustee of a charity under s.139(3) of the 1972 Act- (1993) Ch. Com. Dec., p.29.
[29] *Att-Gen v Power* (1809) 1 Ball & B. 145 at 149.
[30] *Att-Gen v Lee* (1869) I.R. 4 Eq. 84.
[31] See the cases noted in nn.29 and 30 and compare *In the Goods of Lalor* (1901) 85 L.T. 643.
[32] *Fulwood's Case* (1591) 4 Co. 64b, 65a; Grant. 639; *Bird v Wilford* (1593) Cro.El. 464.
[33] *Grant on Corporations*, p.629; and see also *Fulwood's Case*, above.

realty on charitable trusts. A parson, for instance, could hold land in his corporate capacity on charitable trusts for the poor of the parish.[34] This difficulty was removed by the Law of Property Act 1925[35] which provides that any property vested in a corporation sole passes, and shall be deemed always to have passed, to his successors.

The Public Trustee, a corporation sole, may not act as trustee in religious or charitable trusts.[36] The Official Custodian for Charities, also a corporation sole, was constituted by the Charities Act 1960[37] to hold and transfer real and personal property but now has limited functions.

Acceptance of the trust

5–005   Neither an individual nor a corporated trustee is bound to act as trustee of a charitable trust. Thus, for example, a corporation is not bound to accept an accession to its foundation or property which is subject to a special trust or condition.[38] Whilst it is not bound to accept such property, if it does so, the trusts or conditions must be performed.[39] Where such a conditional gift is accepted, the obligation to comply with the conditions must be performed, whether the property given is adequate for the purpose or not.[40] The obligation cannot be discharged by a subsequent abandonment of the benefit of the gift.[41] The question what constitutes acceptance of a trust is one of fact. It has, however, been held that acts done during a preceding life estate for the purpose of preserving the property does not constitute acceptance.[42] For the avoidance of doubt, many trust instruments require that no one shall be entitled to act as a trustee until they have signed a declaration of acceptance and willingness to act in the trusts of the charity.[43]

Special types of trustees

Trustees of parochial and diocesan charities

5–006   There are several statutory provisions relating to trustees of parochial and diocesan charities. A "parochial charity" is defined as meaning, in relation to any parish or (in Wales) community, a charity the benefits of

---

[34] *Banister's Case* (1600) Duke 133; *Grant on Corporations*, p.648.
[35] s.180.
[36] Public Trustee Act 1906, s.2(5); *Re Hampton* (1918) 88 L.J.Ch. 103. The prohibition against the Public Trustee acting as a custodian trustee of charitable trusts does not apply to other corporations authorised to act as custodian trustees—*Re Cherry's Will Trust* [1914] 1 Ch. 83.
[37] The office of the Official Custodian of Charities is discussed para.5–018, below.
[38] *Att-Gen v Andrew* (1798) 3 Ves. 633; *Att-Gen v Caius College* (1837) 2 Keen 150 at 163.
[39] *Att-Gen v Andrew*, above; *Att-Gen v Caius College*, above; *Re Richardson* (1857) 57 L.T. 17; and see the cases cited in the next two notes.
[40] *Att-Gen v Christ's Hospital* (1790) 3 B.C.C. 165; *ibid.* (1830) 1 R. & M. 626; *Jack v Burnett* (1846) 12 Cl. & F. 812 at 828; *Att-Gen v Wax Chandlers Co.* (1873) 6 H.L. 1, 19; and *cf. Att-Gen v Merchants Venturers' Society* (1842) 5 Beav. 338.
[41] *Att-Gen v Christ's Hospital* (1830), above.
[42] *Att-Gen v Andrew*, (1798) 3 Ves. 633.
[43] See the Charity Commissioners' *Model Declaration of Trust for a Charity Trust*, cl.10.

which are, or the separate distribution of the benefits of which is, confined to the inhabitants of the parish or community, or of a single ancient ecclesiastical parish which included that parish or community or part of it, or of an area consisting of that parish or community with not more than four neighbouring parishes or communities.[44] Ecclesiastical charities are excluded from certain of the provisions in the Charities Act 1993 relating to parochial charities and are subject to special provisions under the Pastoral Measure 1983.[45] An "ecclesiastical charity" is defined[46] as having the same meaning as in the Local Government Act 1894 and, therefore, includes a charity the endowment of which is held for one or more of the following purposes: (1) for any spiritual purpose which is a legal purpose; (2) for the benefit of any spiritual person or ecclesiastical officer as such; (3) for use (if a building) as a church, chapel, mission room, or Sunday School or otherwise by any particular church or denomination, and any building which in the Charity Commissioners' opinion has been erected or provided within 40 years before March 5, 1894 mainly by or at the cost of members of any particular church or denomination; (4) for the maintenance, repair or improvement of any such building or for the maintenance of divine service therein; (5) otherwise for the benefit of any particular church or denomination, or for any members thereof as such.[47] Where any endowment of a charity, other than a building held for any of the above purposes, is held in part only for some of the above purposes, the charity is an ecclesiastical charity so far as that endowment is concerned. In such a case, the Charity Commissioners must, on application by any person interested, make such provision for the apportionment and management of that endowment as seems to them necessary or expedient for giving effect to the Act of 1894.[48] A charity may be an ecclesiastical charity, even if the benefit is not limited to religious benefit to the exclusion of mere temporal benefits, provided that the benefit is restricted to members of one particular church or denomination.[49]

Recreation grounds and allotments—Where trustees hold property for the purposes of a public recreation ground or of allotments for the benefit of the inhabitants of a parish[50] having a parish council or other charitable or public purposes connected with such a parish, except for an ecclesiastical charity,[51] they may transfer the property to the parish council or to persons appointed by the parish council provided that the Charity Commissioners approve and the parish council consents. The parish council or its appointees hold the property on the same trusts and subject to the

5-007

---

[44] Charities Act 1993, s.96(1).
[45] Consolidating with amendments the Pastoral Measure 1968 and the Pastoral (Amendment) Measure 1982.
[46] Charities Act 1993, s.96(1).
[47] Local Government Act 1894, s.75(2) (repealed in part by the Statute Law (Repeals) Act 1981, s.1 and Sch.1).
[48] ibid, proviso.
[49] Re Perry Almshouses, Re Ross' Charity [1899] 1 Ch. 21 at 37.
[50] In Wales, a community: Charities Act 1993, s.79 (7)(a).
[51] See text at n.46, above.

same conditions as the trustees did.[52] This provision does not affect the trusteeship, control or management of any foundation or voluntary school within the meaning of the School Standards and Framework Act 1998.[53]

5–008   **Local representatives as trustees**—Where the charity trustees of a parochial charity[54] in a parish,[55] other than an ecclesiastical charity,[56] or one founded less than 40 years previously, do not include persons elected by the local government electors, ratepayers or inhabitants of the parish or appointed by the parish council or parish meeting, the parish council or parish meeting may appoint additional charity trustees to such number as the Charity Commissioners may allow. If there is only a sole charity trustee of such a charity and he is not so elected or appointed, the Commissioners may approve the increase of the number of trustees to three, of whom one may be nominated by the person holding the office of sole trustee and one by the parish council or parish meeting.[57] An appointment of a charity trustee or a trustee for a charity under this provision will be for a term of four years, but a retiring trustee is eligible for reappointment.[58] However, if no previous appointment has been made under this provision or under the corresponding provision of the Local Government Act 1894 or the Charities Act 1960 and more than one trustee is appointed, half of those appointed (or as nearly as may be) must be appointed for a term of two years,[59] or if the appointment is to fill a casual vacancy the appointment must be for the remainder of the previous appointment.[60]

5–009   **Appointment of trustees by the parish council**—The inhabitants of a rural parish (whether or not in vestry) or a select vestry were sometimes entitled to appoint charity trustees for, or trustees or beneficiaries of, a charity before the passing of the Local Government Act 1894. Now, where under the trusts of a charity other than an ecclesiastical charity,[61] the parish[62] has a parish council, the appointment must be made by the parish council or in the case of beneficiaries, by persons appointed by the parish council, and where there is no parish council, the appointment must be made by the parish meeting.[63]

If, before the passing of the Local Government Act 1894, overseers or (except in the case of ecclesiastical charities)[64] churchwardens were charity trustees of or trustees for a parochial charity in a rural parish, either alone

---

[52] Charities Act 1993, s.79(1).
[53] *ibid.*, s.79(9).
[54] See Charities Act 1993, s.96(1) for the definition of "parochial charity".
[55] In Wales, a community; Charities Act 1993, s.79(7)(a).
[56] See text at n.46, above.
[57] Charities Act 1993, s.79(2) Trusteeship of voluntary or foundation schools is not affected, s.79(9).
[58] Charities Act 1993, s.79(8).
[59] *ibid.*, s.79(8)(a).
[60] *ibid.*, s.79(8)(b).
[61] See text at n.46, above.
[62] In Wales, a community; Charities Act 1993, s.79(7)(b).
[63] Charities Act 1993; s.79(3).
[64] See text at n.46, above.

or jointly with other persons, then the former overseer or churchwarden trustees are replaced by trustees appointed by the parish council, or if there is no parish council, by the parish meeting, to a number not greater than that of the former overseer or churchwarden trustees.[65]

Where, outside Greater London (other than the outer London boroughs), overseers of a parish were, immediately prior to April 1, 1927,[66] charity trustees of or trustees for any charity, alone or jointly, they are replaced by the trustees to a number not greater than the former overseer trustees, appointed in the case of a rural parish by the parish council or if there is no parish council by the parish meeting.[67] In the case of an urban parish which existed immediately before the passing of the Local Government Act 1972 but which after April 1, 1974 is not comprised in a parish, the appointment is made by the district council.[68] Charity trustees or trustees for a charity appointed under these provisions are to be appointed for a term of four years but a retiring trustee is eligible for re-appointment on retiring; an appointment to fill a casual vacancy, however, is for the remainder of the term.[69]

The above provisions do not affect the trusteeship, control or management of any foundation or voluntary school within the meaning of the School Standards and Framework Act 1998,[70] and do not extend to the Isles of Scilly.[71] In addition, they have effect subject to orders (including future orders) made under any enactment relating to local government.[72]

Incumbents and churchwardens—The Incumbents and Churchwardens (Trusts) Measure 1964 affects property held on charitable trusts by incumbents and churchwardens as such. It is concerned with interests in certain real property[73] held on charitable trusts for ecclesiastical purposes of the Church of England and personal property held on such trusts as permanent endowment, if it is vested in an incumbent or churchwardens or in an ecclesiastical corporation sole acting as joint trustee with an incumbent or churchwardens,[74] or if the presently acting trustee is the parochial church council but not validly appointed.[75] If such persons hold, acquire or administer any interest in such property they must inform the diocesan

5–010

---

[65] Charities Act 1993, s.79(4). In Wales the appointment is by the Community Council or council of the county or (as the case may be) county borough—s.79(7)(c).

[66] See the Overseers Order 1927, S.R. & O. 1927 No. 55; Charities Act 1993, s.79(11).

[67] Charities Act 1993, s.79(5). In Wales the appointment is by the Community Council or council of the county or (as the case may be) county borough—s.79(7)(c).

[68] Charities Act 1993, s.79(6).

[69] *ibid.*, s.79(8).

[70] *ibid.*, s.79(9).

[71] *ibid.*, s.79(10).

[72] *ibid.*

[73] Glebe and similar property, church moveables and ornaments, property vested in the Official Custodian for Charities, church educational endowments, land acquired as sites of proposed churches, parsonage houses, etc. under the New Parishes Measure 1943 (amended by the Church of England (Miscellaneous Provisions) Measure 1983), and land held under a yearly tenancy or term certain of a year or less is excepted: Incumbents and Churchwardens (Trusts) Measure 1964, s.2(2).

[74] Incumbents and Churchwardens (Trusts) Measure 1964, s.2(1)(a), (b).

[75] *ibid.*, s.2(1)(c).

authority[76] or the body appointed by the diocesan synod to act as trustee of diocesan trust property,[77] with a view to its being vested in the diocesan authority as custodian trustee. Upon becoming aware of the existence of property falling within the provisions, the diocesan authority must give notice[78] to persons interested, including the Charity Commissioners,[79] of the proposal as to vesting. Subject to objections and representations being received, the diocesan authority must make a vesting declaration[80] vesting the property in itself as custodian trustee. The authority must also establish a scheme for the management of the charity.[81]

Since 1964 incumbents and churchwardens have had no capacity to acquire interests in land or personal property to which the Incumbents and Churchwardens (Trusts) Measure 1964 applies, except an interest in personal property by gift or under a will, without the consent of the diocesan authority.[82]

Provision is made for the transfer of charity property held for ecclesiastical purposes of the Church of England from the incumbent of the old benefice to the incumbent of the new benefice, on a dissolution of a benefice, by a pastoral scheme under the Pastoral Measure 1983.[83]

5–011   **Bishops**—Where the limits of dioceses have been altered the Bishops Trusts Substitution Act 1858 empowers the Charity Commissioners, upon the application of the bishop concerned,[84] to make orders vesting charitable property held upon trust by the bishop of one diocese in the bishop of another diocese, and substituting one bishop for another as trustee.[85] No order may be made in relation to any advowson or right of patronage or presentation, part of the possessions of a see, which could be dealt with by scheme of the Church Commissioners, nor to any ecclesiastical patronage or power of nomination or appointment of a curate, chaplain or spiritual person without the consent of the Church Commissioners.[86] The powers conferred by the Act do not extend to trusts of a visitatorial or any other nature or character, exercised in or over colleges, halls or schools of the Universities of Oxford or Cambridge or the colleges or schools of Winchester, Eton or Westminster.[87] The Act does not extend to endowments of an eleemosynary or any other character governed by any specific Act of Parliament.[88]

---

[76] Incumbents and Churchwardens (Trusts) Measure 1964, s.1. (Diocesan authority is defined to mean the diocesan board of finance or any existing or future body appointed by the diocesan synod to act as trustee of diocesan trust property).
[77] *ibid.*, s.3(1).
[78] *ibid.*, Sched., para.2.
[79] For the Charity Commissioners' practice in these cases, see *Report*, 1967, pp.23–24.
[80] Such declaration has the effect prescribed by the Trustee Act 1925, s.40(1)(b): Incumbents and Churchwardens (Trusts) Measure 1964, s.3(3). Any person with an interest in the property must make or concur in the making of the transfer: s.3(4).
[81] Incumbents and Churchwardens (Trusts) Measure 1964, Sched., para.6.
[82] *ibid.*, s.4.
[83] Pastoral Measure 1983, s.17.
[84] Bishops Trusts Substitution Act 1858, s.2.
[85] *ibid.*, s.1.
[86] *ibid.*, s.2.
[87] *ibid.*, s.4.
[88] *ibid.*, s.5; for costs, see s.3.

Local authority charities

Local government in London was reorganised in 1963 and outside **5–012** London in 1972. There was also reorganisation in 1985 with the abolition of the Greater London Council and the Metropolitan Counties. Further reorganisation took place in 1992, in particular the creation of single tier authorities in non-metropolitan areas. A consequence of these reorganisations was that many local authorities ceased to exist and it became necessary to transfer any property held by them on charitable trusts, and any charitable functions exercised by them, to the new authorities.

Transfer outside London—The Local Government Act 1972 transfered **5–013** property held on charitable trusts by existing local authorities to the new authorities established by that Act.

On April 1, 1974 property held as sole trustee and exclusively for charitable purposes[89] by an existing authority vested in the new authority as set out below for the area which comprises the whole or the greater part of the area of the existing authority, unless the property was held for the benefit of, or the inhabitants of, or for any particular class or body of persons in, a specified area, in which case the property vested in the new authority for the whole or greater part of that area.[90]

Property held by an old authority vested as follows:

(a) by a county council (other than property held for the purposes of a registered educational charity),[91] in the new county council[92];

(b) by a borough or urban district council in England, in the parish council or, where there was no parish council, the district council[93];

(c) by a borough or urban council in Wales, in the community council or, where there was no community council, the district council[94];

(d) by a rural district council, in the parish council where the rural district was co-extensive with a new parish and, in any other case, in the district council[95];

(e) by a county or county borough council for the purposes of a registered educational charity,[96] in the new local education authority[97];

---

[89] See the Local Government Act 1972, s.210(1) and [1972] Ch. Com. Rep., paras 36, *et seq.*
[90] Local Government Act 1972, s.210(2), (3)(a).
[91] *i.e.* a charity registered under the Charities Act 1960, ss.2, 4; s.2 was repealed by the Education Act 1973, s.1(1)(a) as from February 1, 1974 and the reference to "registered educational charities" is to be taken as a reference to charities so registered immediately before that date.
[92] Local Government Act 1972, s.210(2)(a).
[93] *ibid.*, s.210(2)(b).
[94] *ibid.*, s.210(2)(c). Where necessary, now vested in the new county or county borough by Local Government (Wales) Act 1994, s.49. See The Local Government Reorganisation (Wales) (Charities) Order 1996 (SI 1996/183).
[95] *ibid.*, s.210(2)(d).
[96] See n.91, above.
[97] Local Government Act 1972, s.210(3)(b).

(f)   by the corporation of a borough included in a rural district, in the new parish council for the area of the borough.[98]

5–014   In Wales,[99] property held, as sole trustee, exclusively for charitable purposes:

(a)   by a parish council vested in the community council for the community or group of communities, the area or areas of which are co-extensive with the parish or parishes for which the parish council acts[1];

(b)   by a parish meeting or parish representative body vested in the community council if there is one[2] or in any other case, in the district council for the area of the existing rural parish.[3]

In every case the property vested in the new authority on the same trusts as those on which it was held by the existing authority.[4] These provisions did not apply to Greater London,[5] or to a parish council, parish meeting or parish representative body in England (all of which continue to exist), other than the corporation of a borough included in a rural district.[6]

Provision was also made[7] in respect of local authorities which were replaced by new authorities[8] for functions as charity trustees vested in those authorities or holders of offices with them, and powers in respect of charities vested in those authorities or holders of offices, to be transferred to the appropriate new authorities or office holders.[9] These provisions do not affect any power of the Crown, the court or any other person to alter the trusts of any charity.[10]

5–015   The metropolitan county councils were abolished on April 1, 1986,[11] and s.90(2) of the Local Government Act 1985 contains power for the Secretary of State to make such provision in relation to charities as

---

[98] Local Government Act 1972, s.210(1), (4).
[99] As to property held by a Welsh borough or urban district council, see the text to n.94, above.
[1] Local Government Act 1972, s.210(5)(a).
[2] *ibid.*, s.210(5)(b).
[3] *ibid.*, s.210(5)(c).
[4] *ibid.*, s.210(1).
[5] *ibid.* As to the transfer of powers on local government reorganisation in Greater London see below.
[6] Local Government Act 1972, s.210(1).
[7] *ibid.*, s.210(6), (7). This did not apply to charities incorporated under the Companies Acts or by charter: s.210(6).
[8] *i.e.* as set out above.
[9] The trustees became or the power vested in, as the case may be, the new local authority or the holder of the corresponding office of, or if there was no such office, the proper officer of, the new authority; Local Government Act 1972, s.210(6), (7). The powers in respect of charities which were transferred were those vested by statute or by the trusts of the charity (and did not include references to a power held by virtue of being a charity trustee), whereas the functions as charity trustees which were transferred were those arising out of the trusts of the charity: s.210(6), (7).
[10] Local Government Act 1972, s.210(10). Similarly, they did not apply in a case in which s.211 (Welsh Church funds) applies; s.210(10).
[11] Local Government Act 1985 (New Authorities) (Appointed Days) Order 1985 (SI 1989/1283).

appears to him necessary or expedient in consequence of the abolition of the councils including provision for transfer of property. No orders have been made under this section which does not affect the power of the court or the Commissioners to alter the trusts of any charity.

S.14 of the Local Government Act 1992 made provision for the creation of single tier local government authorities in non-metropolitan areas. Any property that was held by an abolished authority as sole trustee for charitable purposes vested in the successor authority for the area of benefit. If the property was held for charitable purposes not for a specified area or for the inhabitants of a particular area the property vested in the successor authority for the area of the abolished authority. In case of dispute, the successor authority is to be determined by the Charity Commissioners. In all cases, the property vested on the same trusts.[12]

S.9 of the Local Government and Rating Act 1997 permits a district or a unitary county council to conduct a review with a view to recommending the constitution of new parishes by establishment or by the aggregation, amalgamation or separation of existing parishes or recommending the abolition of parishes. Property held by an abolished or transferor parish held as sole trustee for charitable purposes vests in the transferee parish for the area of benefit. If property was held for charitable purposes not for a specified area or the inhabitants of such an area the property vests in the transferee parish for the area of the transferor or abolished parish. In case of dispute the transferee parish is to be determined by the Charity Commission. In all cases, the property vests on the same trusts.[13]

Transfer in London—The London Government Act 1963 transferred   **5–016**
property held on charitable trusts from the old to the new authorities in consequence of the reorganisation of local government in the Greater London area.[14]

Property held by an old authority as sole trustee for exclusively charitable purposes vested as follows:

  (a) by the London or Middlesex County Council (other than property held for the purposes of a registered educational charity), in the Greater London Council[15];

  (b) by a metropolitan or county borough, a county, district or parish council in the appropriate London borough[16];

  (c) by a county council for educational purposes, in the appropriate London borough[17] or the Inner London Education Authority if within the Inner London Education Area.[18]

---

[12] See The Local Government Changes for England (Property Transfer and Transitional Payments) Regulations 1995 (SI 1995/402).

[13] See Local Government (Parishes and Parish Councils) Regulations 1999 (SI 1999/545).

[14] See [1963] Ch. Com. Rep., pp.42–43.

[15] London Government Act 1963, s.81(1). As to registered educational charities see para.5–013, n.91, above.

[16] *ibid.*, s.81(2).

[17] *ibid.*, s.81(4)(a).

[18] *ibid.*, s.81(4)(b).

Provision is also made in respect of councils which are replaced by new authorities for functions as charity trustees and for powers in respect of charities to be transferred to the appropriate new authority or office holder.[19]

5–017   The Greater London Council was abolished on April 1, 1986,[20] and s.90(1) of the Local Government Act 1985 provided that any property held exclusively for charitable purposes by the Greater London Council and the Inner London Education Authority were the charity trustees of the charity to which the property relates, should vest in the new Inner London Education Authority. When the Inner London Education Authority was abolished, by s.192 of the Education Reform Act 1988 property held by the Inner London Education Authority for exclusively charitable purposes of a charity primarily for the benefit of a single inner London council was vested for the like purpose in that council. Where the charity did not have limited application, the property was vested in the London Residuary Body or such other person as the Charity Commissioners may appoint.[21] S.90(2) of the Local Government Act 1985 applies to any other charities affected by the abolition of the Greater London Council.[22]

S.14 of the Local Government Act 1992 made provision for the amalgamation and abolition of London Boroughs. Any property held for charitable purposes by an abolished authority was vested in the same way as charitable property held by an abolished non-metropolitan authority.[23]

Official custodian for charities

5–018   S.2 of the Charities Act 1993 makes provision for the continuation of the official custodian for charities, who is an officer of the Charity Commissioners and a corporation sole. The official custodian was originally established by s.3 of the 1960 Act and succeeded and combined the duties of The Official Trustee of Charity Lands and The Official Trustees of Charitable Funds. The official custodian's investment functions were drastically reduced by s.29 of the Charities Act 1992 and he now only holds land and property vested in him following an order previously made under s.20 of the 1960 Act or one made under s.18(1)(iii) of the 1993 Act.[24] Divestment gradually took place[25] with charities to whom the investments are returned being encouraged to use common investment funds.[26] In carrying out the functions of his office, the official custodian must perform his

---

[19] London Government Act 1963, s.81(3),(6),(7).
[20] Local Government Act 1985 (New Authorities) (Appointed Days) Order 1985 (SI 1985/1283).
[21] Trustees were sought when the London Residuary Body was dissolved during 1992—[1991] Ch. Com. Rep., para.29.
[22] See the text at para.5–015, above.
[23] See para.5–013 above.
[24] See para.9–044, below.
[25] For the official custodian's strategy for divestment see [1989] Ch. Com. Rep. para.107. For divestment in the case of land subject to the Reverter of Sites Act 1987, see Charities Act 1993, s.23.
[26] [1991] Ch. Com. Rep., para.57. For common investment funds. see paras 6–023, et seq., below.

duties in accordance with such general or specific directions as may be given by the Commissioners.[27]

S.21(1) of the 1993 Act gives the court and—by virtue of the concurrent jurisdiction which they possess under s.16[28]—the Commissioners unlimited jurisdiction by order to vest land held in trust for a charity in the official custodian for charities. S.21(2) provides for the discharge of the official custodian, and s.21(3) for the making of vesting orders and giving of directions consequential on his discharge, or on the trusts of property which he holds coming to an end. S.21(4) provides that no person shall be liable for any loss occasioned by his acting in conformity with an order made under the section or by his giving effect to anything done in pursuance of such an order, or be excused from so doing by reason of the order having been in any respect improperly obtained.

S.22 contains supplementary provisions as to property vested in the official custodian. S.22(1) emphasises the fact that he has no powers of management, and that his function is that of a holding trustee. This subsection declares that as trustee of any property vested in him he shall have the same powers, duties and liabilities and be entitled to the same rights and immunities as a corporation appointed custodian under s.4 of the Public Trustee Act 1906, except that he has no power to charge fees. In regard to land the function of the official custodian is a passive one because the charity trustees retain the power to execute conveyances,[29] leases or other deeds and the charity trustees can bind the charity property without his consent.[30] If the land has been vested in the official custodian following an order under s.18, no powers are exercisable in relation to the land without an order of the Court or the Commissioners.[31] In no case, however, must the charity trustees involve the official custodian in personal liability.[32]

Incorporation of trustees of charities

By s.50 of the Charities Act 1993, the Charity Commissioners are empowered to grant to the trustees of a charity a certificate of registration as a corporate body on application for incorporation being made in writing by the trustees. The advantage of incorporation is, of course, that it secures the perpetual succession of the trustees and obviates the need for conveyances of real property and the transfer of securities to new names whenever a change in the body of trustees occurs. This is particularly important following divestment by the official custodian.[33] The old procedure under the Charitable Trusts Incorporation Act 1872 was considerably amended by the Charities Act 1992 and the full provisions are now to be found in ss.50 to 62 of the 1993 Act.

5–019

---

[27] Charities Act 1993, s.2(3).
[28] See para.9–005, below.
[29] Charities Act 1993, s.22(2).
[30] *ibid.*, s.22(4).
[31] *ibid.*, s.22(3).
[32] *ibid.*, s.22(6).
[33] See para.5–018, above.

The effect of incorporation is to vest in the body corporate all property belonging to or held in trust for the charity, vested in the official custodian.[34] The liability of the trustees is not affected by their incorporation.[35] Gifts made to the charity before incorporation but not having actually taken effect, and gifts made subsequently to incorporation, have effect as if they had been made in favour of the incorporated body.[36]

The certificate granted by the Commissioners is conclusive evidence that all the preliminary requirements of incorporation have been complied with.[37] In granting their certificate the Commissioners may insert conditions or directions as they think fit[38] and may amend a certificate once granted.[39] Subject to any such conditions or directions, vacancies in the number of trustees are to be filled from time to time as required by the constitution of the charity by such legal means as would have been available if no certificate of incorporation had been granted.[40]

Appointment of trustees

5–020   It will normally be provided in the trust instrument who are to be the first trustees of a charitable trust. Charity property may be vested either in individual trustees or in corporations, either aggregate or sole. Where it is vested in individual trustees, the appointment of new trustees is required from time to time in accordance with the usual practice. A corporation endures for ever, being kept in being by a continual succession of members. However, it may be necessary, under special circumstances, to appoint new trustees in place of a corporation. Thus a corporation guilty of a breach of trust may be divested of its trust; new trustees will also be required if the corporate trustee becomes extinct.

There are a number of ways in which new trustees may subsequently be appointed. In addition to any express power of appointment in the trust instrument[41] the statutory powers in the Trustee Act 1925 may be used.[42] Trustees may also be appointed at meetings using the powers under the Trustees Appointment Acts[43] or s.83 of the Charities Act 1993.[44] Furthermore, the court[45] has an inherent as well as a statutory jurisdiction to appoint additional trustees of a charity and the Charity Commissioners[46] possess the like power and additional powers under s.18 of the 1993 Act.

[34] Charities Act 1993, s.51.
[35] *ibid.*, s.54.
[36] *ibid.*, s.59.
[37] *ibid.*, s.55.
[38] *ibid.*, s.50.
[39] *ibid.*, s.56.
[40] *ibid.*, s.53.
[41] See para.5–025, below.
[42] See para.5–027, below.
[43] See paras 5–028, *et seq.*, below.
[44] See para 5–031, *et seq.*, below.
[45] See para.5–033, below.
[46] See para.5–035, below.

Initial appointment

The donor will usually appoint the first trustees of a charity. It is a ques-   **5–021**
tion of construction as to who has actually been appointed.[47] A charitable
gift will not fail for want of a trustee. If money is given to charity generally without the intervention of trustees or specified objects the Crown is
trustee as *parens patriae*.[48] If, however, there is an intention to create a
charitable trust but no trustee is appointed the fund will be dealt with by
means of a scheme.[49]

Number of trustees

There are no restrictions on the number of charity trustees, either mini-   **5–022**
mum or maximum. The restrictions imposed by s.34 of the Trustee Act 1925
do not apply to charitable trusts and the recommendation in the White
Paper[50] that the Commissioners should be given a discretion to require that
a charity have at least three trustees was not enacted. There is no optimum
number of trustees; different types of charity require different numbers of
trustees.

There is no definite rule as to what number of vacancies will warrant[51]
an application to the court, but the court will not, generally speaking,
appoint new trustees merely to retain the original number so appointed.[52]
Normally, the court requires to be satisfied that the existing number of
trustees is insufficient.[53] However, it would appear that, by way of exception to this general practice, the court will, in the case of dissenting
chapels, fill up the full number of original trustees notwithstanding the
fact that a majority of the trustees may be competent to act in the trusts.[54]
The Charity Commissioners would act on the same principle.

The court is also entitled, when appointing new trustees of charitable
trusts, to provide for the future appointment of new trustees of charity
estates and for the trustees obtaining the directions of the court in other
specified contingencies (the application being made before a judge in
chambers),[55] and to empower the trustees themselves to appoint new
trustees in the future as occasion requires.[56] But in practice these matters
are usually dealt with by the Charity Commissioners.

[47] See, *e.g. Re Lavers, The Times*, November 7, 1908.
[48] *Att-Gen v Syderfen* (1683) 1 Vern. 224. See paras 1–023, *et seq.*, above.
[49] *Mills v Farmer* (1815) 1 Mer. 55 at 94–95; *Reeve v Att-Gen* (1843) 3 Hare 191 at 196, 197.
[50] "Charities: A Framework For The Future" (1989) Cm. 694, para.5.7.
[51] *Re Gloucester Charities* (1853) 10 Hare App. I, iii.
[52] *Re Gloucester Charities* (1853) 10 Hare App. I, iii: *Re Coventry Charities* (1845) 6 L.T.O.S. 42.
[53] *Re Hereford Charities* (1842) 6 Jur. 289; *Re Marlborough School* (1843) 13 L.J.Ch. 2: *Re Worcester Charities* (1847) 2 Ph.284; *Re Shrewsbury Municipal Charities* (1849) 1 Mac. & G. 84.
[54] *Davis v Jenkins* (1814) 3 Ves. & B. 151; *Att-Gen v Lawson* (1866) W.N. 343.
[55] *Re Conyers School* (1853) 10 Hare App. IV.
[56] See *Re Puckering's Charity* (1854) Seton (7th ed.), at 1264.

Selection of new trustees

5–023   The main criterion is that those selected as trustees should be those who are likely best to discharge the duties imposed on them by the trust.[57] If the instrument governing the charity contains directions as to the appointment of new trustees these must be observed.[58] Thus, for example, if the trustees are required by the instrument to be resident in a particular area, it is improper to appoint persons who do not satisfy the qualification, if eligible persons who satisfy it can be found.[59] However, in a proper case the area from which trustees may be selected will be enlarged.[60] Whilst a residence qualification has been held to be satisfied by a person who worked, but did not reside, within the area,[61] subsequent removal by a trustee to a distance so great as to make it impossible for him to attend to his duties will disqualify him from holding office.[62]

If there is no express provision to the contrary, residence at a short distance from the town where the charitable institution is situated is not a valid objection to a proposed new trustee.[63] In general, however, the best course is to appoint new trustees from within the neighbourhood of the charity.[64]

As a general rule, there is no objection to trustees being related to one another,[65] nor is temporary absence from the United Kingdom sufficient to justify removal from office.[66] It has also been held that it is not improper for two or three new trustees to be partisans of parties holding different views and for the third trustee to be an indifferent person.[67] However, suspicion of past abuses of power by trustees is sufficient to prevent their re-appointment.[68]

5–024   Where a charity is established for prescribed religious purposes or where the benefits of the charity are intended to be confined to persons holding prescribed religious views, the trustees should be persons professing the religious doctrines specified.[69] It has been held, therefore, in the case of a

---

[57] *Baker v Lee* (1860) 8 H.L.Cas. 495 at 513, *per* Lord Cranworth. For a review of best practice see the Charity Commissioners' Regulatory Report, RS1 *Trustee Recruitment, Selection and Induction* (2002).

[58] *Att-Gen v Stamford* (Earl) (1843) 12 L.J.Ch. (N.S.) 297, 300; *cf. Att-Gen v Pearson* (1817) 3 Mer. 353 at 402–403 (trust deed); *Foord v Baker* (1859) 27 Beav. 193 (scheme).

[59] *Att-Gen v Cowper* (1785) 1 Bro.C.C. 439; *Att-Gen v France* (1780) cited *ibid.*; *Att-Gen v Stamford* (Earl) (1843) 1 Ph. 737 at 748. See also *Att-Gen v Devon* (Earl) (1846) 16 L.J.Ch. 34, 35.

[60] *Re Sekforde's Charity* (1861) 4 L.T. 321; the sanction of the court or Charity Commissioners will be necessary for such enlargement.

[61] *Att-Gen v Stamford* (Earl) (1849) 16 Sim. 453.

[62] *Att-Gen v Clifton* (1863) 32 Beav. 596.

[63] *Re Lancaster Charities, Re Charitable Trusts Act 1853* (1860) 3 L.T. 582.

[64] *Att-Gen v Moises* (reported in the 4th ed. of this work, pp.1036, 1038).

[65] *Re Lancaster Charities* (1860) 3 L.T. 582.

[66] *Re Moravian Society* (1858) 26 Beav. 101.

[67] *Re Burnham National Schools* (1873) L.R. 17 Eq. 241 at 250.

[68] *Re Norwich Charities* (1837) 2 Myl. & Cr. 275 at 304.

[69] *Re Norwich Charities* (1837) 2 Myl. & Cr. 275 at 305; *Re Scarborough Corp.* (1837) 1 Jur. 36; *Att-Gen v Clifton* (1863) 32 Beav. 596; *Att-Gen v Bishop of Limerick* (1870) 18 W.R. 1192. The Charity Commissioners have taken the view that they have no power to appoint as trustees of the Unification Church controlling trustees unconnected with that church: see [1982] Ch. Com. Rep., para.6.

school founded in connection with the Church of England, that it is improper to appoint as trustees or governors persons who are not members of the Church of England.[70] The same principles have been held to apply to charities for the benefit of dissenting sects.[71] In the event of doubts as to the religious denomination for which the charity was founded, the court will have regard to the usage of the charity so far as necessary.[72] If a charity is established for purposes connected with a parish church the parson and churchwardens are considered proper trustees.[73] However, if the primary object of the charity is eleemosynary, no particular religious qualification is required in the trustees or governors.[74]

Whether, in regard to any trust, the appointors have a discretion to refuse to appoint a duly qualified person is a question of construction of the power or appointment.[75] If the court construes the instrument as not giving such a discretion, the appointment of a duly qualified person will in a proper case be enforced by mandamus if no other remedy is equally convenient and beneficial.[76]

Appointment under express power

A power to appoint new trustees in certain events is generally contained in the instrument of foundation of the charity or in the scheme by which it is regulated. It is a question of construction whether the power is in character a strict power or one which is merely directory. The same principles of construction apply whether the power is contained in trust instruments or in Acts of Parliament[77] or in orders of the court.[78]   **5–025**

Strict powers are those which can only be exercised in accordance with the exact circumstances laid down in the instrument governing the charity.[79] Thus, for example, if the power is determinable on the happening of a prescribed event, it ceases to be exercisable on the happening of that event.

---

[70] *Baker v Lee* (1860) 8 H.L.C. 495; *Re Stafford Charities* (1857) 25 Beav. 28; *Att-Gen v Clifton*, above; *Re Burnham National Schools* (1875) L.R.17 Eq. 241; *Re Hodgson's School* (1878) 3 App.Cas. 857.

[71] *Att-Gen v Pearson* (1817) 3 Mer. 353; *Shore v Wilson* (1842) 9 Cl. & F. 355; *Re Drogheda Charitable and Trust Estates* (1846) 2 Jo. & Lat. 422; *Att-Gen v Calvert* (1857) 23 Beav. 248; *Att-Gen v St. John's Hospital Bath* (1876) 2 Ch.D. 554 at 555–556.

[72] *ibid.*

[73] *Re Donnington Church Estate, Re Charitable Trusts Act 1853* (1860) 2 L.T. 10. In the case of a scheme relating to a parochial ecclesiastical charity, the Charity Commissioners usually include provisions making the diocesan board of finance custodian trustee and the parochial church council managing trustee.

[74] *Re Norwich Charities* (1837) 2 Myl. & Cr. 275; *Att-Gen v Calvert*, above; *Baker v Lee* (1860) 8 H.L.C. 495; *Att-Gen v Tottenham* (1870) 5 I.R.Eq. 241; *Att-Gen v St. John's Hospital, Bath*, above.

[75] *R. v Christ's Hospital Governors* [1917] 1 K.B. 19.

[76] *R. v Christ's Hospital Governors* [1917] 1 K.B. 19.

[77] *Doe d. Reed v Goodwin* (1822) 1 Dow. & Ry. K.B. 259. An Act of Parliament may also vary a power of appointment; thus appointment of trustees by successor authorities is authorised by the London Government Act 1963, s.81 and the Local Government Act 1972, s.210; see [1963] Ch. Com. rep., pp.42, 43; [1972] Ch. Com. Rep., paras 36, *et seq.*

[78] *Att-Gen v Scott* (1750) 1 Ves.Sen. 413 at 415.

[79] *Foley v Wontner* (1820) 2 Jac. & W. 245 at 247 may have been a case of this kind although the report is very obscure.

Outside the specified limits there is no power which can be exercised. However, lapse of time may preclude objections to an appointment made contrary to the provisions of a strict power.[80]

Directory powers are those where the power conferred is general, but there is an incidental direction that it shall be exercised at a prescribed time or within a prescribed period. Here the direction does not restrict the exercise of the power, but merely prescribes a certain occasion on which it is intended that at all events it shall be exercised. Although, therefore, it may be a wrongful omission on the part of the donees not to exercise the power in accordance with the direction, yet, notwithstanding their failure to do so, the power itself continues to subsist, the incidental direction being merely directory.[81] For example, a power to appoint a new trustee, coupled with a direction that it shall be exercised within four months after the death of a trustee, is a general power exercisable at any time, whether within or outside the period specified, the restrictions as to four months being merely a direction to the trustees as to the time within which it is desired that the power shall be exercised.

Appointment under a presumed power

5–026   Where the trust deed has been lost, the mode of appointing new trustees must be determined by the earliest evidence of usage. It is presumed that what such evidence shows to have been done was rightly done.[82] If necessary an inquiry will be directed as to who are entitled to appoint new trustees.[83]

Appointed under statutory powers

5–027   **Trustee Act 1925**—The usual power as to the appointment of new and additional trustees in the Trustee Act 1925[84] apply to charitable trusts.[85]

5–028   **Trustees Appointment Acts**—Under the Trustees Appointment Acts, 1850, 1869 and 1890, a convenient method was provided of appointing new trustees at a meeting for certain religious and educational charities without the necessity of applying to the court or the Charity Commissioners. Whilst these Acts were repealed by the Charities Act 1960, their effect was preserved for some charities.[86]

---

[80] *Att-Gen v Cuming* (1843) 2 Y. & C. Ch.Cas. 139.

[81] *Att-Gen v Floyer* (1716) 2 Vern. 748 at 750; *Att-Gen v Scott* (1750) 1 Ves.Sen. 413. *Att-Gen v Cowper* (1785) 1 Bro.C.C. 439; *Doe d. Dupliex v Roe* (1794) 1 Anst. 86 at 91; *Doe d. Reed v Goodwin* (1822) 1 Dow 8 Ry. K.B. 259.

[82] *Att-Gen v Dalton* (1851) 13 Beav. 141. As to evidence of usage see *Att-Gen v Pearson* (1817) 3 Mer. 353 at 402, 403; *Att-Gen v St. Cross Hospital* (1853) 17 Beav. 435; *Att-Gen v Ewelme Hospital* (1853) 17 Beav. 366.

[83] *Davis v Jenkins* (1814) 3 v & B. 151.

[84] Trustee Act 1925, ss.36, 37, 40–56.

[85] For the detailed law on the appointment of trustees under the 1925 Act, see Underhill and Hayton, *Law of Trusts and Trustees* (15th ed.), pp.729, *et seq.*

[86] Charities Act 1960, s.35(6) and see para.5–030, below.

The Trustees Appointment Acts provided that where any freehold or leasehold property in England or Wales was held for certain prescribed objects by trustees for any congregation, society or body of persons associated for religious or educational purposes and no mode of appointing new trustees had been prescribed, or the prescribed power had lapsed, the congregation, society or body was empowered to appoint new trustees at a meeting.[87] The objects for which the land was required to be held were a chapel or meeting house, a house and land for a minister, a schoolhouse with schoolmaster's house and garden or playground, a college or seminary and grounds, or rooms for meetings for the transaction of business,[88] or burial grounds.[89]

The above provisions were, by the Act of 1890, made applicable to land acquired by trustees in connection with any society or body of persons comprising several congregations or other sections or divisions or component parts associated together for any religious purpose,[90] when such land was held in trust for any of the following purposes: (1) a place of religious worship; (2) an endowment or provision for the maintenance of a place of religious worship or the minister thereof or provision for expenses connected therewith; (3) a burial ground; (4) a place for the education and training of students, whether for the ministry or any other purposes; (5) a schoolhouse for a Sunday school, day school, or other school; (6) a residence for a minister or schoolmaster, or for the caretaker of a place of religious worship, or of a schoolhouse, or a meeting house or offices or other buildings for or in connection with religious or educational purposes.[91]

Every such appointment, if made under these Acts, was required to be evidenced by deed under the hand and seal of the chairman for the time being of the meeting at which the appointment was made, and the deed had to be executed in the presence of the meeting and attested by two or more credible witnesses.[92] The resulting memorandum was conclusive evidence of the due constitution of the meeting and its proceedings.[93]   **5–029**

When such an appointment was made, the property vested without conveyance in the new trustees jointly with the continuing trustees, if any.[94] Furthermore, the provisions as to vesting contained in the Act of 1850 applied also to appointments under any statutory power which was exercisable with regard to trusts to which the Act of 1890 was applied.[95]

---

[87] Trustee Appointment Act 1850, s.1.
[88] *ibid.*, ss. 1, 3.
[89] Trustees Appointment Act 1869, s.7.
[90] The purpose of this provision was to resolve certain doubts arising out of *Re Hoghton Chapel* (1854) 2 W.R. 631. In this case it was held doubtful whether new trustees of a chapel vested in trustees on trusts in accordance with the Wesleyan constitution could be appointed under the Act of 1850, because the effect of the Wesleyan model deed, upon the trusts of which the chapel seems to have been held, was to vest the chapel in trustees, not for a particular congregation, but the whole of the Wesleyan connection, and an appointment by that body was impracticable.
[91] Trustees Appointment Act 1890, s.2.
[92] Trustee Appointment Act 1850, s.3.
[93] Trustees Appointment Act 1890, s.7.
[94] Trustee Appointment Act 1850, s.1.
[95] Trustees Appointment Act 1890, s.4.

One of the advantages of making appointments in accordance with the Trustees Appointment Acts, 1850 to 1890, was that, after the expiration of six months, unless proceedings were taken within that period to set aside the appointment, the memorandum of the appointment became conclusive evidence in favour of a purchaser or mortgagee that the persons purporting or appearing to have been appointed were the duly appointed trustees, and every conveyance or mortgage which such persons might make was valid and effectual in favour of a purchaser or mortgagee as if made by trustees duly appointed.[96] Indeed, under the settled conveyancing practice it was unnecessary to prove, for example, that trustees who were stated in the memorandum to have died were in fact dead.

5–030   S.35(6) of the Charities Act 1960 provided that the Trustees Appointment Acts of 1850, 1869 and 1890 were to cease to have effect; but where, on January 1, 1961, the provisions of those Acts as to appointments of trustees applied to any land, the provisions were to continue to have effect as if they were contained in the conveyance or other instrument declaring the trusts on which the land was held. Accordingly, if land was acquired before January 1, 1961, by any congregation, society, or body of persons for the purposes mentioned in those Acts, new trustees may continue to be appointed in accordance therewith. New provisions were introduced for charities which were not subject to the Trustees Appointment Acts prior to January 1, 1961.[97]

However, the extent to which s.35(6) had preserved the effect of the previous Acts appears to be questionable. In the first place, those Acts only apply as if their provisions were contained in the conveyance or other instrument declaring the trusts on which the land is held. A trustee cannot be divested of the legal estate without his concurrence in the absence of express statutory authority, and it is possible, therefore, that an appointment of a new trustee may be ineffectual if a trustee is stated erroneously in the memorandum to have died. Secondly, the provisions in the previous Acts as to vesting were not expressly retained or re-enacted by the Act of 1960. Retention, perhaps, of the above-mentioned provisions may be implied. But it seems reasonably clear that s.40 of the Trustee Act 1925, which enables a vesting declaration to be made or implied without the concurrence of trustees from whom the legal estate is divested, would not assist, because that section only applies where the actual appointment is made by deed, whereas a memorandum under the old Trustees Appointment Acts is only evidence of the appointment which was made at a meeting.

In view of these uncertainties the better course would appear to be for trustees to be appointed under the procedure now set out in s.83 of the Charities Act 1993 rather than under the Trustees Appointment Acts procedure, although these provisions themselves are not free from difficulty.

---

[96] Trustees Appointment Act 1890, s.6.
[97] See below.

S.83 of the Charities Act 1993—S.83 of the Charities Act 1993[98] provides   **5–031**
that where under the trusts of a charity trustees may be appointed or discharged by resolution of a meeting of the charity trustees, members or
other persons,[99] a memorandum declaring a trustee to have been so
appointed or discharged shall be sufficient evidence of that fact, if the
memorandum is signed either at the meeting by the person presiding or in
some other manner directed by the meeting, and is attested by two persons
present at the meeting.[1]

The above provisions are wider than those of the Trustees Appointment
Acts in that they apply to all charities[2] and not merely to the restricted
classes of charities to which the old Acts applied, and the memorandum
no longer has to be executed in the presence of the meeting.[3] The previous
Acts had a wider application in that they allowed an appointment where
no mode of appointing new trustees had been prescribed or the prescribed
mode had lapsed,[4] whereas the new provisions apply only where the trusts
of the charity permit appointment or discharge by resolution at a meeting.[5] Furthermore, the memorandum under s.83 is only "sufficient" evidence of the appointment or discharge, whereas under the previous Acts
the memorandum was conclusive evidence of the appointment.[6] The
provision as to "sufficiency" may in practice give rise to difficulties. Thus
if a purchaser has reason to suspect that the facts mentioned in the memorandum are incorrect, he is not entitled to rely on it. There may also be
difficulties where only an *appointment* of new trustees is made at a meeting. In this case a statement in the memorandum of, for example, the
deaths of previous trustees will not be sufficient evidence of their deaths,
from a conveyancing point of view, until 20 years from the execution of
the memorandum. Until the expiration of the 20 years period a purchaser
will require further evidence that the previous trustees have in fact died:
the memorandum is only "sufficient" evidence of the appointment or discharge itself, not of the facts on the basis of which the appointment or
discharge was made. This difficulty may be obviated but only in the case
of trusts which the discharge of trustees, by the meeting discharging all the
trustees save in so far as they have already ceased to be trustees, *e.g.* by
death (with the exception of those intended to continue) as well as
appointing new trustees. In this case the memorandum would be sufficient
evidence of the discharge itself and would apparently render it unnecessary
for a purchaser to require evidence that trustees have in fact died.

A memorandum made on or after January 1, 1961 evidencing the
appointment or discharge, if executed as a deed, has the like operation
under s.40 of the Trustees Act 1925, as if the appointment or discharge has

---

[98] Formerly Charities Act 1960, s.35.
[99] For example, the section will apply where a trustee of a charity for a recreation ground may
be appointed by a committee of a local sports club.
[1] Charities Act 1993, s.83(1).
[2] It also applies to institutions subject to the Literary and Scientific Institutions Act 1854;
Charities Act 1993, s.83(5).
[3] See para.5–029, above.
[4] See para.5–028, above.
[5] Charities Act 1993, s.83(1).
[6] See para.5–029, above.

been made by deed.[7] This means that it will operate to vest, by express or implied vesting declaration, all estates, interests and rights in the property in the persons who by virtue of the deed become or are the trustees for performing the trust.[8] It should be noted that the provisions of the Trustee Act 1925 as to vesting do not apply (a) to land conveyed by way of mortgage securing money subject to the trust, except land conveyed on trust for securing debentures or debenture stock; or (b) to land held under a lease which contains any covenant, condition or agreement against assignment or disposing of the land without licence or consent, unless prior to the execution of the deed containing expressly or impliedly the vesting declaration the requisite licence or consent has been obtained, or unless, by virtue of any statute or rule of law, the vesting declaration would not operate as a breach of covenant or give rise to a forfeiture; or (c) to any share, stock, annuity or property which is only transferable in books kept by a company or other body or in manner directed by an Act of Parliament.[9] Where a trustee, who actually retires from the trust, is discharged without an appointment of a new trustee the memorandum must be executed by both the retiring and the continuing trustees.[10] This should rarely happen in practice because an appointment of new trustees will normally be made.

5–032   It is further provided, for the purposes of s.83 of the Charities Act 1993, that where a document purports to have been signed and attested as mentioned above, then on proof (whether by evidence or as a matter of presumption) of the signature, the document is presumed to have been so signed and attested, unless the contrary is shown.[11] Where, therefore, a document is 20 years old it is presumed to have been duly signed, sealed and delivered according to its purport, if produced from the proper custody.[12]

Appointment by the court

5–033   In cases where no other method of appointing new trustees is available, recourse must be had to the court or the Charity Commissioners,[13] though as a general rule to the latter.

The High Court[14] has an inherent jurisdiction to appoint new trustees of charities,[15] even where there is no deficiency of trustees.[16] This jurisdiction is exercised by the Chancery Division.

---

[7] Charities Act 1993, s.83(2), (4).
[8] Trustee Act 1925, s.40(1), (2).
[9] *ibid.*, s.40(4).
[10] *ibid.*, ss.39, 40(2).
[11] Charities Act 1993, s.83(3).
[12] Evidence Act 1938, s.4.
[13] For the powers of the Commissioners, see para.5–035, below.
[14] The County Court has no jurisdiction to appoint charity trustees, Charities Act 1960, s.48 and Sch.7, Pt1.
[15] *Att-Gen v City of London Corp.* (1790) 3 Bro.C.C. 171; *Att-Gen v Stephens* (1834) 3 My. & K. 347.
[16] *Re Burnham National Schools* (1873) L.R. 17 Eq. 241 at 246; *Re Browne's Hospital v Stamford* (1889) 60 L.T. 288.

Whenever it is expedient to appoint a new trustee or new trustees, and it is inexpedient, difficult or impracticable to do so without an order of the court, the court has jurisdiction under the Trustee Act 1925 to make orders appointing a new trustee or new trustees, either in substitution for or in addition to any existing trustee or trustees, or although there is no existing trustee.[17] The court can also make an order vesting the property in the new trustees without the need for a conveyance.[18]

New trustees may be appointed by the court for the purpose of filling   **5–034** up vacancies[19] occasioned by death,[20] or where the appointment is rendered necessary by incapacity or bankruptcy[21] or misconduct[22] or unwillingness to act on the part of the old trustee or trustees.[23] The Trustee Act 1925 also makes express provision for the appointment by the court of a new trustee in place of one who is incapable by reason of mental disorder[24] or bankrupt or a corporation which is in liquidation or dissolved.[25] This statutory power is expressed to be without prejudice to the generality of the court's power to make appointments whenever it is inexpedient, difficult or impracticable to do so without an order of the court.[26]

Moreover, it appears that the court has an inherent jurisdiction to appoint new trustees even where there is a power of appointment in existence and there are persons capable of exercising it,[27] but, in general, it is improper in such cases to make an application to the court, except in cases of misconduct or refusal to exercise the power.

Applications to the court for the appointment of new trustees, unless made in a pending cause or matter, require the authorisation by order of the Charity Commissioners.[28]

The Judicial Trustees Act 1896 does not apply to charities.[29]

Appointment by the charity commissioners

S.16 of the Charities Act 1993 provides that, subject to the provisions of   **5–035** the Act, the Charity Commissioners may, by order, exercise the same jurisdiction and powers as are exercisable by the High Court in charity proceedings for (inter alia) appointing a charity trustee or trustees for a charity.[30]

---

[17] Trustee Act 1925, s.41(1). The Act applies to charities: *Re Coates to Parsons* (1886) 34 Ch.D. 370 (a case on the Conveyancing Act 1881, s.31, a statutory predecessor).

[18] *ibid.*, ss.44–52, 58.

[19] See para.5–022 above.

[20] *Drayson v Pocock* (1831) 4 Sim. 283; *Finlay v Howard* (1842) 2 Dr. & W. 490; *Re Nightingale's Charity* (1844) 3 Hare 336.

[21] *Bainbrigge v Blair* (1839) 1 Beav. 495; *Re Roche* (1842) Con. & L. 306.

[22] *Ex p. Greenhouse* (1818) 1 Madd. 92.

[23] *Re Beverley Charities* (1840) 9 L.J.Ch. 91.

[24] Mental Health Act 1959, Sch.7 (as amended by the Mental Health Act 1983, s.148 and Sch.6).

[25] Trustee Act 1925, s.41(1).

[26] *ibid.*

[27] See *Att-Gen v Clack* (1839) 1 Beav. 467.

[28] Charities Act 1993, s.33.

[29] Judicial Trustees Act 1896, s.6(2).

[30] s.16(1)(b).

They also have the same powers of vesting and transferring property and of requiring and entitling any person to call for or make any transfer of property or any payment.[31] Such an appointment may usually be made on the application of the charity or on an order of the court directing a scheme.[32] An appointment may be made without an application by all the charity trustees in the same circumstances in which the Commissioners can exercise their scheme-making powers.[33]

The foregoing provisions will apply notwithstanding the fact that there is in existence an express power of appointment in the trust instrument capable of being exercised. Appointments by the Commissioners are generally less expensive than appointments under a power. Before exercising their jurisdiction under the section however, otherwise than under an order of the court, the Commissioners are bound to give notice to all the charity trustees.[34]

An appeal against any order of the Commissioners may be brought in the High Court by the Attorney-General.[35] An appeal may also be brought, within three months of the publication of the order, by the charity or any of the charity trustees.[36] An appeal cannot be brought in the latter case, however, unless the Charity Commissioners certify that it is a proper case for appeal or the leave of the court is obtained.[37]

5–036   In the following cases the Commissioners may by order made of their own motion appoint a person to be a charity trustee: (a) in place of a charity trustee removed by them; (b) where there are no charity trustees, or where by reason of vacancies in their number or the absence or incapacity of any of their number the charity cannot apply for the appointment; (c) where there is a single charity trustee, not being a corporation aggregate, and the Commissioners are of opinion that it is necessary to increase the number for the proper administration of the charity; and (d) where the Commissioners are of opinion that it is necessary for the proper administration of the charity to have an additional charity trustee, because one of the existing charity trustees who ought nevertheless to remain a charity trustee either cannot be found or does not act or is outside England and Wales.[38] The Commissioners also have power under s.18(1)(ii) to appoint additional trustees as part of their temporary and protective powers after a s.8 inquiry.[39]

[31] s.16(1)(c).
[32] s.16(4).
[33] See s.16(5)(6)(7) and paras 9–005, et seq., below.
[34] s.16(9).
[35] s.16(11).
[36] s.16(12).
[37] s.16(13).
[38] Charities Act 1993, s.18(5).
[39] See para.9–043, below.

Removal and discharge of trustees

Removal by the court

The Court of Chancery always had an inherent jurisdiction to remove existing trustees and substitute new ones where this remedy was required.[40] This jurisdiction is now exercised by the Chancery Division.[41] Save where the proceedings are taken by the Attorney-General, and in the case of an exempt charity, the authority of the Charity Commissioners must be sought for an application to the court to remove trustees.[42]

5–037

In all cases where the trustees commit a wilful breach of trust, they may be removed. Cases where actions to remove trustees were successful included one in which the trustees of a dissenting meeting-house had converted it to the use of a sect for which it was not intended,[43] and another in which the trustees had procured themselves to be appointed with the object of converting a chapel to the use of a seceding section of a congregation of particular Baptists.[44] Again, where a trustee was lessee of a portion of charity lands regulated by a scheme, he was compelled to give up his lease or resign his office of trustee.[45] Moreover, if such trustees, by refusing to retire voluntarily, have rendered an action for their removal necessary, they will be liable for the costs.[46]

However, in cases where no wilful breach of trust has been committed, the position is different. Facts which would constitute a sufficient ground for not appointing a trustee are not necessarily a ground for removing him after he has been appointed.[47] Therefore, the court will not, in the absence of special circumstances, remove a trustee already appointed, because at the date of his appointment he was not a member of the religious sect with which the charity was connected, or because he subsequently ceased to belong to that sect[48]; nor will it do so if at the date of appointment he resided outside the prescribed district.[49] Even a misapplication of trust funds, if it was innocent, is not necessarily a ground for removal.[50] There is authority for the view that bankruptcy would not disqualify a testamentary trustee from administering a charitable trust if he is given a wide personal discretion,[51] together with a power to appoint a receiver of the rents of the trust estate, but, generally speaking, bankruptcy seems a

---

[40] *Letterstedt v Broers* (1844) 9 App.Cas. 371, 386 P.C. For a form of order removing a trustee, see *Att-Gen v Drummond* (1842) 3 Dr. & War. 162.

[41] The County Court has no jurisdiction to remove charity trustees or trustees for a charity, Charities Act 1960, s.48, Sch.7, Pt.1.

[42] Charities Act 1993, s.33. See para.10–027, below.

[43] *Att-Gen v Pearson* (1835) 7 Sim. 290 at 309; *Att-Gen v Shore, ibid.*, at 309, 317n.; and see *Att-Gen v Anderson* (1868) 57 L.J.Ch. 543 at 550.

[44] *Newsome v Flowers* (1861) 30 Beav. 461.

[45] *Foord v Baker* (1859) 27 Beav. 193.

[46] *Att-Gen v Murdoch* (1856) 2 K. & J. 571.

[47] *Att-Gen v Clapham* (1853) 10 Hare 540 at 613.

[48] *Baker v Lee* (1860) 8 H.L.C. 495 at 513; and see *Att-Gen v Dalton* (1851) 13 Beav. 141.

[49] *Att-Gen v Stamford* (1843) 1 Ph. 737 at 747–8; and see *Att-Gen v Clifton* (1863) 32 Beav. 596 at 601.

[50] *Att-Gen v Caius College* (1837) 2 Keen 150 at 166.

[51] *Archbold v Charitable Bequests Commissioners for Ireland* (1849) 2 H.L.C. 440.

sufficient ground for removal,[52] and furthermore the language of s.41 of the Trustee Act 1925 appears to give the court jurisdiction to appoint a new trustee in substitution for the bankrupt whether he is willing to retire or not.

Removal by the charity commissioners

5–038   The Charity Commissioners have the same jurisdiction and powers as the High Court to remove[53] or discharge[54] a charity trustee or a trustee for a charity. The jurisdiction is exercisable subject to the same conditions as the jurisdiction to appoint a new trustee.[55] However, before they make an order removing a trustee without his consent the Commissioners must, unless he cannot be found or has no known address in the United Kingdom, give him not less than one month's notice inviting representations to be made to them within a time specified in the notice.[56]

A person removed as a trustee or any person removed from any office or employment (unless he was removed with the concurrence of the charity trustees, or with the approval of the special visitor, if any, of the charity) may appeal against the order removing him, to the High Court, within three months of the publication of the order removing him.[57] Unless the removal is under section 18 of the Charities Act 1993 the certificate of the Commissioners or the leave of the court is required.[58]

The Charity Commissioners have power under section 18(2) of the Charities Act 1993, as part of their permanent and remedial powers after a section 8 inquiry, to remove trustees where it is necessary for the protection of the charity.[59] Secondly the Charity Commissioners may, by order of their own motion, remove a charity trustee who is bankrupt, or a corporation in liquidation, or who is incapable of acting by reason of mental disorder. In addition they may remove a trustee who has not acted and will not declare his willingness or unwillingness to act, or who is outside England and Wales or cannot be found or does not act, and his absence or failure to act impedes the proper administration of the charity.[60] Once removed by order, that person is disqualified from being a charity trustee in that or any other charity.[61]

---

[52] *Bainbrigge v Blair* (1839) 1 Beav. 495; *Re Roche* (1842) 1 Con. & L. 306; *Re Barker's Trusts* (1875) 1 Ch.D. 43.
[53] Charities Act 1993, s.16(1)(b).
[54] *ibid.*, s.16(8).
[55] See para.5–035, above. However the Commissioners need not give public notice if they consider it unnecessary and not in the interests of the trustee to be removed that publicity be given: s.20(2).
[56] Charities Act 1993, s.20(3).
[57] *ibid.*, s.16(12).
[58] *ibid.*, s.16(13).
[59] See para.9–046 below and OG 41 B1, *Disqualification for Acting as a Trustee. Vacation of Office of Trustee*, s.6.
[60] Charities Act 1993, s.18(4). This latter power can be used to remove a trustee disqualified under Charities Act 1993, s.72 as disqualification under that section does not lead to automatic vacation of office. See (1994) 2 Ch. Com. Dec., p.11, *et seq.* and para.5–002, above.
[61] Charities Act 1993, s.72, see para.5–002, above.

DIRECTORS OF CHARITABLE COMPANIES

The definition of charity trustee in the Charities Act 1993[62] is suffi- **5–039**
ciently wide to cover directors of a charitable company. Directors are,
therefore, subject to the jurisdiction of the Charity Commissioners who
may, for example, remove them.[63] The appointment and removal of
directors is, however, largely governed by the Companies Act 1985, the
Company Directors Disqualification Act 1986 and the terms of the
particular memorandum and articles of association; the reader is referred
to the standard texts on company law for the detailed provisions.

Capacity

Any person[64] or corporation has the capacity to be appointed a director **5–040**
of a charitable company, provided they do not come within one of the
statutory exceptions. In addition to the disqualifications in section 72 of
the Charities Act 1993,[65] s.302 of the Companies Act 1985 provides that
an undischarged bankrupt may only be appointed with the leave of the
court, a person over 70 only if approved by the company in general meeting or the articles provide otherwise and that no one prohibited by the
articles or who has been disqualified by the court from acting as a director may be appointed. The fact that a person uses services provided by a
charitable company does not bar them from being a director but rules will
be needed in articles of association to deal with potential conflicts of
interest.[66]

Appointment

Appointment of the first directors will be by the subscribers to the com- **5–041**
pany. Subsequent directors will be appointed in the way laid down in the
articles of association of the particular charitable company. For example,
the model articles for a charitable company produced by the Charity
Commissioners provides for the appointment of the directors at the
annual general meeting of the company with one third of the directors
retiring by rotation each year.

The court[67] probably has the same broad inherent jurisdiction to
appoint directors of charitable companies as it has to appoint charity
trustees.[68] The Charity Commissioners have similar powers by virtue of
s.16(1) of the Charities Act 1993. The Commissioners may also appoint

---

[62] s.97(1).
[63] See para.5–038, above.
[64] The Companies Acts set no minimum age for serving as a director but Companies House
guidance is that no one under 16 should be appointed.
[65] See para.5–002, above.
[66] See CC24, *Users on Board: Beneficiaries who become Trustees* (2000).
[67] The court has no specific statutory power to appoint company directors; reduction of the
number of members of a company below two is merely grounds for winding up, Insolvency
Act 1986, s.122.
[68] See para.5–003, above.

additional directors of a charitable company under s.18 of the 1993 Act in the same circumstances as they can appoint additional charity trustees.[69]

Removal

5–042   A director of a charitable company may be removed under the terms of the articles of association of the company, by the members, by the court or by the Charity Commissioners.

Articles of association

5–043   It is usual for the articles of association of a charitable company to set out the circumstances in which a director automatically vacates his office. For example, in the model articles of association produced by the Commissioners a person ceases to be a director if:

(a)   he ceases to be a director under the provisions of the Companies Act 1985 or becomes disqualified in law from being a director by virtue of s.72 of the 1993 Act;

(b)   he becomes incapable by reason of mental disorder, illness or injury of managing and administering his own affairs;

(c)   he resigns by notice to the company;

(d)   he is absent from meetings for more than six months without permission and the directors resolve that his office be vacated.

Members

5–044   By s.303 of the Companies Act 1985, the members of a company are given power to remove a director by ordinary resolution at a meeting and to replace him at the same meeting. The power exists despite any provision to the contrary in the articles but special notice must be given of the resolution and notice must be given to the director.[70]

The court

5–045   The court probably has the same broad inherent jurisdiction to remove directors of charitable companies as it has to remove charity trustees.[71] In relation to directors the court can also use the specific powers under the Company Directors Disqualification Act 1986. By ss.2 to 5 of the 1986 Act the court has power to make an order disqualifying a person from acting as a director of a company in the following circumstances:

---

[69] See para.5–036 above.
[70] For an express provision see the Charity Law Association's Memorandum and Articles of Association for a Charitable Company Limited by Guarantee, articles cl.3.6.6.
[71] See paras 5–037, *et seq.*, above.

(a) where he is convicted of an indictable offence in connection with the promotion, formation, management or liquidation of a company;

(b) where he appears to have been persistently in default in relation to the requirements of companies legislation for the filing and delivery of returns, accounts or documents or for the giving of any notices;

(c) where in the course of winding up a company it appears that he has been guilty of fraudulent trading or fraud;

(d) where he is convicted for contravention of any provision of the companies legislation requiring a return, account or document to be filed or notice given and has in the preceding five years been convicted of not less than three such offences.

In addition the court has power under ss.6 to 8 of the 1986 Act to make an order disqualifying a person as a director if he has been a director of a company which has gone into insolvent liquidation, in respect of which an administration order has been made or which has had a receiver appointed. The court must be satisfied that his conduct as a director makes him unfit to be concerned in the management of a company.[72]

The Charity Commissioners

By s.16(1) of the Charities Act 1993, the Charity Commissioners have **5–046** the same jurisdiction and powers as the court to remove the directors of a charitable company.[73] It would appear to follow that they can exercise not only the courts' usual jurisdiction in relation to charity trustees but also the statutory powers under the Company Directors Disqualification Act 1986.[74] The jurisdiction is only exercisable subject to the same restrictions as in the removal of charity trustees.[75]

The Charity Commissioners may also exercise their powers under s.18 of the 1993 Act to remove a director of a charitable company.[76]

MEMBERS OF THE COMMITTEE OF UNINCORPORATED ASSOCIATIONS

A charitable unincorporated association, because of the nature of the **5–047** legal structure,[77] will usually have both trustees who hold the property of the association and members of a management committee who will be concerned with the general running of the association. The appointment

---

[72] The Secretary of State may make a disqualification order under s.6 of the 1986 Act if it appears to him to be expedient after an inquiry under s.437 of the Companies Act 1985.
[73] Applying the extended definition of charity trustees in s.97(1) of the 1993 Act.
[74] See para.5–045, above.
[75] See para.5–038, above.
[76] See para.5–038, above.
[77] See para.3–037, above.

and removal of the property holding trustees will be subject to the usual rules for charity trustees.[78]

S.97(1) of the Charities Act 1993 defines "charity trustees" as "the persons having the general control and management of the administration of a charity". Members of the management committee of a charitable unincorporated association, as well as the property holding trustees, are thus subject to the jurisdiction of the Charity Commissioners.

Capacity

5–048   Any adult or corporation has the capacity to be a member of the committee of a charitable unincorporated association unless they are disqualified under s.72 of the 1993 Act.[79] Further limitations on who can be a member of a committee may flow from the constitution of the particular association. The constitution of a charitable unincorporated association will often provide that only a member of the association may be elected to the committee. In the absence of a rule that anyone agreeing with the aims of the association is eligible for membership,[80] the existing committee, or whoever is responsible for membership, can refuse to admit any person to membership; no-one has the right to be a member of an association and, thus, a member of the committee.[81]

It is not a breach of Article 11 of the European Convention on Human Rights, freedom of assembly and association, for a charity to have a membership policy which excludes those people whose reason for joining could render their membership contrary to the interests of the charity. As Lightman J. pointed out in *Royal Society for the Prevention of Cruelty to Animals v Att-Gen*,[82] such a policy needs to be implemented carefully with respect to individual applicants for membership and not arbitrarily if the important public image and reputation of the charity is not to be harmed. A person is not barred from being a member of the committee of a charitable unincorporated association if he uses services provided by the charity. The constitution, however, will require rules to deal with potential conflicts of interest.[83]

Appointment

5–049   The members of the first committee of a charitable unincorporated association will probably be the original proposers of the association. Thereafter, appointment of members of the committee will be governed entirely by the terms of the constitution of the particular association.[84]

---

[78] See paras 5–020, *et seq.*, above.
[79] See para.5–002, above.
[80] See *Woodford v Smith* [1970] 1 W.L.R. 806.
[81] See *Nagle v Feilden* [1966] 2 Q.B. 633 at 644, 653; *McInnes v Onslow Faine* [1978] 1 W.L.R. 1520 at 1529.
[82] [2001] 3 All E.R. 530 at 550–551.
[83] See CC24, *Users on Board: Beneficiaries who become Trustees* (2000).
[84] See generally, Warburton, *Unincorporated Associations: Law and Practice* (2nd ed., 1992), pp.19, *et seq.*

For example, the model constitution produced by the Charity Commissioners provides for the election of members of the committee at the annual general meeting of the association. In addition, provision is made for members of the committee to be nominated by outside bodies.

The court probably has the same broad inherent jurisdiction to appoint members of the committee of an unincorporated association as it has to apppoint charity trustees.[85] The same powers are available to the Charity Commissioners by virtue of s.16(1) of the Charities Act 1993. The Commissioners may also appoint additional members of the committee of a charitable unincorporated association under s.18 of the 1993 Act in the same circumstances that they can appoint additional charity trustees.[86]

Removal

The removal of a member of the committee of a charitable unincorporated association is governed by the constitution of the association. If there is no rule in the constitution for removal, removal is only possible by the court or the Charity Commissioners.[87]   **5–050**

The constitution

The constitution may set out the circumstances in which a member of   **5–051**
the committee automatically vacates his office. For example, the model constitution produced by the Charity Commissioners provides that a member of the committee ceases to hold office if:

(a) he is disqualified from acting as a member of the committee by virtue of s.72 of the 1993 Act;
(b) he becomes incapable by reason of mental disorder, illness or incapacity of managing and administering his affairs;
(c) he is absent without permission from all meetings for six months and the committee resolve that his office be vacated;
(d) he notifies to the committee a wish to resign.

It is, in fact, rare for a constitution to make specific provision for the removal of a member of the committee, as opposed to automatic vacation of office. It is more normal to rely on the rule for the expulsion of a member. A common clause is that a member may be expelled whose conduct is considered injurious to the association. If a charitable unincorporated association seeks to remove a member of the committee under such a rule, they must act bone fide, comply strictly with the rules in the constitution and satisfy the rules of natural justice.[88] Thus the committee

---

[85] See para.5–033, above.
[86] See para.5–036, above.
[87] *Dawkins v Antrobus* (1881) 17 Ch.D. 615.
[88] See generally, Warburton, *Unincorporated Associations: Law and Practice* (2nd ed., 1992), pp.69, *et seq.*

member should be given notice of the allegations against him, be heard by an unbiased tribunal and be given the right to be heard in answer to the allegations.[89]

The power to exclude from membership is a fiduciary one and members of the Committee must exercise that power for the purpose for which it is conferred in what they consider to be the best interests of the charity. When it is alleged that a number of members of a charity have acted contrary to the interests of the charity, each case should be considered individually.[90]

The court

5–052   The court probably has the same broad inherent jurisdiction to remove members of the committee of charitable unincorporated associations as it has to remove charity trustees.[91]

The charity commissioners

5–053   The Charity Commissioners are given the same powers as the court to remove members of the committee of a charitable unincorporated association by s.16(1) of the 1993 Act[92] but the jurisdiction is only exercisable subject to the same restrictions as in the removal of charity trustees.[93] The Commissioners may also exercise their powers under s.18 of the 1993 Act to remove a member of the committee of a charitable unincorporated association.[94]

OFFICERS

5–054   Many charities have officers in addition to the trustees or others, howsoever designated, who have the general control and management of the administration of the charity. Such officers are, for example, members of colleges and holders of religious office. The appointment and removal of such officers is subject to specific statutory provisions and the case law governing the interpretation of the statutes and instruments of the charitable institutions in question. In addition to the particular means available to remove each type of officer, any officer may be removed from office by the Charity Commissioners exercising their permanent and remedial powers under s.18(2) of the Charities Act 1993. It should also be remembered that by virtue of s.16(1) of the 1993 Act the Commissioners have the same powers of the court for removing an officer of a charity.

---

[89] *John v Rees* [1970] 1 Ch. 345.
[90] *Royal Society for the Prevention of Cruelty to Animals v Att-Gen* [2001] 3 All E.R. 530 at 546, 550, *per* Lightman J.
[91] See paras 5–037, *et seq.*, above.
[92] Applying the extended definition of charity trustee in s.97(1) of the 1933 Act.
[93] See para.5–038, above.
[94] See para.5–038, above.

Members of colleges

Questions as to the election and removal of members of colleges and **5–055** hospitals are generally decided by the visitors,[95] according to the statutes by which such institutions are regulated. In some respects, however these matters are controlled by statutes of general application.[96] Thus by the Simony Act 1588, elections of fellows, scholars and other persons, as members of colleges, schools, halls or societies, if made corruptly or for a money consideration, directly or indirectly, are void.[97] By the same Act, any fellow, officer or scholar taking money, reward or profit for resigning his place is liable to a fine on summary conviction and the person giving or agreeing to give or pay it is disqualified from the office at the next election.[98] Moreover, the Act, together with the orders and statutes of the college, school, hall or society, are to be read, under a penalty in default, publicly at every election.[99] The Universities Tests Act 1871 provides that no person in the Universities of Oxford, Cambridge and Durham shall be required before taking a degree (other than a degree in divinity[1]) or taking office (except in certain specified cases) to subscribe any article or formulary of faith, or to make any declaration or take any oath respecting his religious belief or profession.[2] The Act is confined to colleges subsisting before it was passed, and does not prevent the creation of fresh colleges, the endowments of which are confined to the members of a particular religious denomination.[3] The Universities of Oxford and Cambridge Act 1877, expressly provided that nothing therein should repeal the provisions of the Universities Tests Act 1871[4]; and where the Commissioners appointed by the Universities of Oxford and Cambridge Act 1877 by any statute made by them, erect or endow an office declared by them to require in the incumbent thereof the possession of the theological learning (which they are empowered to do save in the case of a headship or fellowship of a college), then the Universities Tests Act 1871 is with reference to that office to be read and have effect as if the statute had been made before and was in operation at the passing of that Act.[5] The Universities of Oxford and Cambridge, London and Durham, and their colleges and halls, together with certain other universities and colleges, are "exempt charities" within the meaning of the Charities Act 1993.[6]

---

[95] See para.10–063, *et seq.*, below.
[96] See, *e.g.* Simony Act 1588; Universities Tests Act 1871; Universities of Oxford and Cambridge Act 1877; Charities Act 1960; Education Reform Act 1988 and para.10–074 below.
[97] Simony Act 1588, s.1.
[98] s.2.
[99] s.3.
[1] By University statutes this restriction has been modified. By a statute passed by the Convocation of the University of Oxford (November 28, 1925) candidates for the degrees of B.D. and D.D. need not be ordained clergymen of the Church of England; and by Statute 42 of the University of Durham, no religious test is to be required of any student, except for a candidate for a licence in theology.
[2] Simony Act 1588, s.3.
[3] *R. v Hertford College* (1878) 3 Q.B.D. 693, where it was held that the Act did not apply to Hertford College.
[4] s.57.
[5] s.58.
[6] Charities Act 1993, s.96 and Sch.2.

Generally, however, elections are controlled by the statutes of the institution in question and most of the case law has been concerned with the interpretation of such statutes.

Appointment

5–056   Some of the cases have involved qualification for appointment. Accordingly, for example, where the college statutes required election to be made by the president and the majority of the fellows, it was held that the concurrent voice of the president was necessary in all such elections[7]; and where the election of fellows was to be "communi omnium assensu aut saltem ex consensu magistri et majoris partis communitatis", it was held that no election was valid in which the master did not concur.[8] A provision in the statutes that a fellow shall be "in sacerdotio constitutus" means that he must be in holy orders, but not necessarily in priest's orders.[9]

Where college statutes make the possession of property a disqualification for holding a fellowship, real property is in general the only property considered.[10] On the other hand, where real property is required as a qualification by the statutes, an interest in land which in equity is deemed personal property may be sufficient.[11] However, if possession of property of a certain amount is required as a qualification for the office of president of a college, it is not necessary for a candidate to show his qualification at the election itself.[12]

Unless the statutes of a college make the examination test conclusive, the college is not bound to elect the person who passes the examination, even though the statutes make an examination an indispensable preliminary to election to a fellowship.[13] Likewise, where only one of several candidates for a close fellowship fulfilled all the conditions required by the endowment, he was nevertheless held not exempt from the necessity of undergoing the usual college examination to prove his fitness for the office.[14] It has also been held that where a deed of endowment directed the election to the fellowship thereby created of a native of a particular town "if any such shall be found able within the university", if the persons qualified by birth are found of not sufficient ability, another candidate possessing the requisite ability, though without the requisite birth qualification, may be elected.[15]

---

[7] *Re Queen's College, Cambridge* (1828) 5 Russ. 64; but see *Case of Clare Hall* (1788) *ibid.*, 73n.; *Case of Gonville and Caius College* (1617) *ibid.*, 76n.

[8] *Case of St. Catherine's Hall* (1802) 5 Russ. 85n.

[9] *Re University College, Oxford* (1848) 2 Ph. 521; and see *Glasgow College v Att-Gen* (1848) 1 H.L.C. 800; *Re St. Catherine's Hall, Cambridge* (1849) Mac. & G. 473.

[10] *Case of Queens' College, Cambridge* (1821) Jac. 1 at 37.

[11] *ibid.* at 38.

[12] *ibid.* at 36.

[13] *R. v Hertford College* (1878) 3 Q.B.D. 693 at 698, 699. And as to the construction of college statutes with regard to examinations for fellowships, see *Re St. John's College* (1831) 2 R. & M. 603; *Re Downing College* (1837) 2 Myl. & Cr. 642; *Watson v All Souls' College, Oxford* (1864) 11 L.T. 166.

[14] *Re Catherine Hall* (1802) 5 Russ. 85n.

[15] *Re St. John's College, Cambridge* (1831) 2 R. & M. 603.

Where the qualification for a living to be granted to a fellow of a college was that he should not at such time "be presented, instituted, or inducted, into any other living", it was held that the condition was complied with by the previous resignation of another living. It was also held that a resignation of a former living sent by post to the bishop, who endorsed and signed a memorandum of his acceptance thereof, was sufficient without any public act.[16]

Forfeiture

Other cases have been concerned with the conditions for forfeiture of an appointment. Thus, for example, the words "a collegii emolumentis recedere" in college statutes have been held to import a forfeiture of the fellowship, and the word "discedere" was not to be confined to a vacancy by death.[17] On the other hand, in *Att-Gen v Stephens*[18] a fellow of a college, regularly elected, received his salary for five years, and then, instead of travelling beyond the seas for five years more, as he was required to do by the will under which the fellowship was created, upon a suggestion of ill-health resigned his fellowship. The trustees accepted the resignation, and it was held that they had dispensed with the condition and could not compel him to refund the salary which he had received. The case would have been otherwise if when he had offered to resign the fellowship the trustees had refused to accept the resignation unless he complied with the terms of the will or refunded the salary he had received.

5–057

Chaplains and curates

Appointment

According to the general ecclesiastical constitution of England, the right of presentation to a benefice in the established church is in general vested in the patron.[19]

5–058

Where a right of presentation is vested in trustees in trust for the inhabitants and parishioners of a place, the trustees must present the nominee of the majority of the electors.[20] Likewise, where the right of election is vested in the "inhabitants and parishioners" the electors must be persons satisfying both descriptions.[21] Thus, in *Fearon v Webb*,[22] the election was

---

[16] *Heyes v Exeter College, Oxford* (1806) 12 Ves. 336.
[17] *Re St. Catherine's Hall, Cambridge* (1849) 1 Mac. & G. 473. As to a fellowship being, under college statues, vacated by the acceptance of a professorship, see *Ex p. Edleston* (1854) 3 De G.M. & G. 742.
[18] (1737) 1 Atk. 358.
[19] *Att-Gen v Scott* (1750) 1 Ves.Sen. 413 at 414; *Herbert v Dean and Chapter of Westminster* (1721) 1 P.Wms. 773.
[20] For meaning of parishioners and inhabitants, see paras 4–031, *et seq.*, above.
[21] *Att-Gen v Rutter* (1768) 2 Russ. 101n.; *Fearon v Webb* (1802) 14 Ves. 13; *Edenborough v Archbishop of Canterbury* (1826) 2 Russ. 93; see *Att-Gen v Stafford* (1796) 3 Ves. 78; *Att-Gen v Webster* (1875) 20 Eq. 483.
[22] (1802) 14 Ves. 13.

to be made by the inhabitants and parishioners, "or the major part of the chiefest and discreetest of them," and it was held that the persons entitled to vote were confined to those who paid church and poor rate, as distinguished from those whom from poverty were supposed not to have a mind of their own, and to those who had attained 21, as distinguished from those who were under the disability of coverture or infancy. On the other hand, in *Edenborough v Archbishop of Canterbury*[23] Lord Eldon said[24] that "where the right of nominating a perpetual curate was given to the parishioners, a part of the parishioners could not, by their vote or declaration, so narrow the right of voting as to exclude those who did not pay church rates from sharing in the election," and this dictum appears to conflict with *Fearon v Webb*.

In every case, however, usage is regarded in determining the persons entitled to exercise the right of voting; indeed usage is often conclusive in determining whether the right of voting is confined to ratepayers or not.[25] If, on the one hand, the usage has been to confine the right of voting to ratepayers, they alone can take part in an election.[26] If, on the other hand, the usage has been not to confine it in that way, it cannot be limited.[27] Where the right of election is in the ratepayers, a person who comes into the parish after a rate has been made has no right to vote before another rate has been made, unless the making of the rate has been postponed for an unfair purpose.[28]

5–059   It was Lord Eldon's opinion that Jews, but not Roman Catholics, had a right to vote.[29]

Formerly, it was held that in elections by parishioners the voting must be by open polling,[30] but it has since been established that by a resolution of the parish the election may be by ballot.[31] The parishioners may also determine other matters with regard to the manner in which the election shall take place, such as the hours and times of polling.[32]

Irregular or even illegal conduct at a meeting held to determine the mode of election will not induce the court to disturb the election, unless it appears that a voter has been deprived of an opportunity of voting.[33] The court, in declining to interfere, acts upon the principle that the election is

---

[23] (1826) 2 Russ. 93.
[24] *ibid.* at 104.
[25] *Att-Gen v Forster* (1804) 10 Ves. 335 at 338.
[26] *Att-Gen v Newcombe* (1807) 14 Ves. 1; *Edenborough v Archbishop of Canterbury* (1826) 2 Russ. 93; *Att-Gen v Cuming* (1843) 2 Y. & C.C.C. 139.
[27] *Att-Gen v Parker* (1747) 3 Atk. 576 at 577.
[28] *per* Lord Eldon in *Edenborough v Archbishop of Canterbury*, above, at 110. It was said, in *Att-Gen v Forster* (1804) 10 Ves. 339, that persons paying to the church and poor rate were to be understood to mean persons liable to pay, not persons who had actually paid.
[29] *Edenborough v Archbishop of Canterbury*, above, at 111n. Lord Eldon gave no reason for expressing his opinion to this effect. Having regard to the Roman Catholic Relief Act 1926, s.3, it seems that if Lord Eldon's view was correct in 1826, it is still correct.
[30] *ibid.* at 109, and see *Faulkner v Elger* (1825) 4 B. & C. 449.
[31] *Shaw v Thompson* (1876) 3 Ch.D. 233.
[32] *Att-Gen v Forster* (1804) 10 Ves. 335; *Att-Gen v Newcombe* (1807) 14 Ves. 1, 9; *Davies v Banks* (1836) 5 L.J.Ch. 274; *Shaw v Thompson*, above.
[33] *Shaw v Thompson* (1876) 3 Ch.D. 233.

substantially fair, and the majority not likely to be disturbed by any change in the manner or form of voting.[34]

Notice of the meeting to elect a clerk must be given to all the trustees, **5–060** otherwise the election is void.[35] Where the right of election is vested in the trustees jointly with the parishioners, an election in which the majority of the trustees concur is valid.[36]

All the trustees having the right to present to a living, ought to join in signing the presentation, for if they do not, the ordinary cannot be compelled to admit the clerk therein named[37]; but where a valid election has taken place the majority may compel the dissenting minority to join in the presentation.[38]

An election by the trustees is not invalid merely because the full number of trustees has not been kept up.[39] A presentation by a sole surviving trustee has been supported[40]; and where, by neglect, the number of trustees in a trust to present to a living was not filled up at the time of an avoidance, the court refused, in the absence of special grounds, to stay by injunction the institution of a clerk presented under the legal title of the heir of the surviving trustee.[41] Furthermore, it has been held that an informality in the appointment of a trustee of a trust to elect to an advowson does not vitiate an election by the trustees.[42] Even a declaration that the trustees were to elect and present within a limited time after the death of the existing incumbent was construed as directory only, and an appointment made after the prescribed period was upheld.[43]

The court, however, takes care that the number of trustees shall be **5–061** properly filled up for the future[44]; and if an appointment is set aside and a new election consequently rendered necessary, the court will see that the number of trustees is filled up before the new election takes place.[45] Lord Eldon apparently went so far as to order the bishop to "institute and induct" the person whom the court considered properly elected.[46] Knight-Bruce V.C., however, observed that such an order, taken literally, would exclude the bishop from the right of deciding upon the fitness of the person presented. He thought, therefore, that Lord Eldon's attention could not have been directed to the particular words used in the decree.[47]

---

[34] *R. v St. Mary, Lambeth* (1838) 3 N. & p.416; *Ex p. Mawby* (1854) 3 E. & B. 718; *Davies v Banks* (1836) 5 L.J.Ch. 274. *Shaw v Thompson*, above.

[35] *Att-Gen v Scott* (1750) 1 Ves.Sen. 413. See also *Att-Gen v Cuming* (1843) 2 Y. & C.C.C. 139.

[36] *Att-Gen v Cuming*, above.

[37] *Att-Gen v Scott*, above; *Seymour v Bennett* (1742) 2 Atk. 482; *Wilson v Dennison* (1749) Amb. 82; and see Co.Litt. 186b.

[38] *Att-Gen v Cuming*, above. See *Att-Gen v Scott*, above. Trustees may sign the presentation by proxy; *Att-Gen v Scott*, above at 417; *Wilson v Dennison*, above, at 86.

[39] *Att-Gen v Scott*, above; *Att-Gen v Cuming*, above.

[40] *Att-Gen v Floyer* (1716) 2 Vern. 748.

[41] *Att-Gen v Bishop of Lichfield* (1801) 5 Ves. 825. See, however, *Davies v Jenkins* (1814) 3 V. & B. 151, 159.

[42] *Att-Gen, v Cuming* (1843) 2 Y & C.C.C. 139.

[43] *Att-Gen v Scott* (1750) 1 Ves. Sen. 413.

[44] See *Att-Gen v Scott*, above, at 419.

[45] See *Att-Gen v Scott*, above, at 419.

[46] *Edenborough v Archbishop of Canterbury* (1826) 2 Russ. 112, where the decree is given.

[47] *Att-Gen v Cuming* (1843) 2 Y. &. C.C.C. 139, at 155n.

All persons presented to ecclesiastical benefices are considered to be tenants for their own lives, unless the contrary is expressed in the form of donation.[48]

The Patronage (Benefices) Measure 1986 amended the law relating to the patronage of benefices. S.1 requires the compilation, in each diocese of the Church of England, of a register of patrons. A charity which owns an advowson and receives notice of a vacancy in the benefice must appoint an individual, who is able and willing to declare that he or she is an actual communicant member of the Church of England or is a clerk in Holy Orders, to act for the charity.[49] An advowson appendant to any land or manor became an advowson in gross, and, in the case of land belonging to a charity, now belongs to the charity.[50]

Remedies

5–062   Where a chaplain or vicar is improperly appointed the court will by injunction restrain him or any other person, except the one properly appointed, from performing divine service in the church or chapel, and the bishop from instituting or inducting him.[51]

In a case where an advowson was vested in trustees upon trust, upon every avoidance, to present to the ordinary the person nominated by the majority of the parishioners it was disputed, on the occurrence of a vacancy, as to which of two candidates had the majority of votes. The trustees refused to present and a mandamus was applied for. It was held that a mandamus would not lie, but that the remedy was either in equity or by *quaere impedit*.[52]

Ministers of dissenting chapels

Appointment

5–063   The ministers of dissenting meeting-houses, like trustees, should be appointed in the mode prescribed by the deed of trust,[53] the terms of which must, as in all other cases, be complied with.[54]

Where the trust deed of a dissenting meeting-house is silent as to the mode of appointment of the minister, regard may in a proper case be had to the usage which has prevailed,[55] although that is not necessarily con-

---

[48] 2 Bl.Comm. 123; *Att-Gen v Pearson* (1817) 3 Mer. 353 at 403.
[49] Patronage (Benefices) Measure 1986, s.8(2).
[50] *ibid.*, s.32(1). See [1987] Ch. Com. Rep., p.37.
[51] *Att-Gen v Earl of Powis* (1853) Kay 186; *Att-Gen v Cuming*, above; *Carter v Cropley* (1856) 8 De G.M. & G. 680. See also *Att-Gen v St. Cross Hospital* (1855) 18 Beav. 601, Affirmed on appeal, 8 De G.M. & G. 38 (after appointment of receiver, interference with chaplain restrained).
[52] *R. v Orton (Trustees)* (1849) 14 Q.B. 139.
[53] See para.5–023, above.
[54] *Att-Gen v Pearson* (1817) 3 Mer. 353 at 402, 403.
[55] *ibid.* at 403.

clusive.[56] Moreover, an inquiry may be directed as to who, according to the nature of the establishment, are the proper persons to elect the minister.[57] As a rule, however, where the trust deed contains no express provision, the election is by the majority of the congregation[58]; and where the trust deed itself provides that the minister shall be elected by the congregation, it seems that a majority of the congregation is presumed to be intended.[59]

Mere occupiers of seats or pews, although in one sense forming part of the congregation, are not necessarily so for the purpose of voting at the election of a minister. Thus, where a meeting-house of the Church of Scotland was held in trust for the congregation, it was held that persons who were merely seat-holders, but not members of the church in the sense of communicants, were properly excluded from voting at the election of a minister; and an application on their behalf for an injunction to restrain the individual elected from acting as minister was refused.[60]

In order that the election of a minister shall be valid, due notice must be given of the intention to hold the meeting; and persons who are not entitled to take part in the election, such as, for instance, persons who are not members of the congregation, must not interfere with the proceedings.[61]

Where the power of appointing the minister, or of approving his appointment, is vested in trustees, a majority of them may act.[62] Accordingly, an election by three survivors of a body of 12 has been held good.[63] But this power cannot be exercised by the representative of the last surviving trustee.[64]

Tenure

The principle of public policy which, in the case of the Established Church, gives the minister a life interest in his office does not extend to the case of dissenting ministers.[65] The minister may accordingly be elected for life, or for a shorter period, or merely during pleasure, and whichever plan is adopted the court is bound to carry it into effect.[66] The provisions of the

5–064

---

[56] *ibid.*
[57] *ibid.* at 420, where the form of order is given; *Davis v Jenkins* (1814) 3 v & B. 151, 159; *Leslie v Birnie* (1826) 2 Russ. 114.
[58] See *Davis v Jenkins*, above; *Att-Gen v Aked* (1835) 7 Sim. 321; *Cooper v Gordon* (1869) 8 Eq. 249.
[59] *Davis v Jenkins*, above, at 155. See *Fearon v Webb* (1802) 14 Ves. 13, 20.
[60] *Leslie v Birnie* (1826) 2 Russ. 11L.
[61] *R. v Trustees of Dagger Lane Chapel* (1804) 2 Smith 20; *Perry v Shipway* (1859) 4 De G. & J. 353 at 360.
[62] *Att-Gen v Lawson* (1866) 36 L.J.Ch. 130; *cf. Att-Gen v Cuming* (1843) 2 Y. & C.C.C. 139 and cases cited at para.5–060, above. It was held that a dissenting minister appointed by some of the trustees could not maintain an action for arrears of salary against all; *Cooper v Whitehouse* (1834) 6 C. & p.545.
[63] *Att-Gen v Lawson*, above.
[64] *Davis v Jenkins* (1814) 3 v & B. 151 at 159. *cf. Att-Gen v Bishop of Lichfield* (1801) 5 Ves. 825; *Att-Gen v Floyer* (1716) 2 Vern. 748.
[65] *Att-Gen v Pearson* (1817) 3 Mer. 353 at 403.
[66] *Att-Gen v Pearson* (1817) 3 Mer. 353 at 413.

trust deed with regard to the tenure of office and the mode of dismissal are binding.[67]

Difficulties may arise where the trust deed is silent with regard to the terms of office of the minister. In *Att-Gen v Pearson*,[68] Lord Eldon said: "Although a Court of Equity may not be disposed to struggle hard in support of such a plan (by which the minister is not appointed for life), yet were the court to find such a plan established, I know of no principle upon which the court would not be bound, if called upon for the purpose, to carry it into effect." This seems to suggest that the leaning of the court would be towards construing the tenure of office of the minister of a dissenting chapel to be for life. On the other hand, in *Porter v Clarke*[69] it was held that where the minister was entirely dependent on the voluntary contributions of his congregation, he was dismissible at will by the persons so voluntarily contributing. And in *Cooper v Gordon*[70] it was considered that the tenure of office of the minister of a dissenting meeting-house, unless an express provision was contained in the trust deed, was at the will of the congregation. It appears that, in the absence of an express provision in the trust deed, the usage of the congregation is important in determining the tenure of the minister's office.[71]

Removal

5–065   Where the minister holds his office at the will of the majority of the congregation, he can at any time be removed by such majority,[72] nor apparently need any specific ground for the removal be given.[73] But however arbitrary the power of dismissal may be, it must not be unjustly or oppressively exercised.[74] Thus in *Dean v Bennett*[75] the deed of settlement of a Baptist chapel provided that every minister should be liable to be dismissed by the decision of the church, made at one meeting and confirmed at a second meeting summoned by notice expressly stating the objects of the meeting. At the first meeting a resolution was passed that the minister, on the ground of alleged drunkenness and for other reasons, should be removed. The second meeting was convened by notice, which stated that it was for the purpose of confirming and ratifying the resolution passed at the previous meeting. The minister was not present at either meeting. It was held that he was not properly removed, and that it could not be said that a discretion had been exercised by a meeting which, on charges mentioned for the first time, the person charged not being present, came to a

---

[67] *Dean v Bennett* (1870) 6 Ch.App. 489. See *Perry v Shipway* (1859) 4 De G. & J. 353.
[68] (1817) 3 Mer. 353 at 403.
[69] (1829) 2 Sim. 520.
[70] (1869) L.R. 8 Eq. 249 at 258, 259.
[71] See *Att-Gen v Pearson* (1817) 3 Mer. 353 at 412, 413. *Att-Gen v Aked* (1835) 7 Sim. 321.
[72] *Cooper v Gordon* (1869) L.R. 8 Eq.249.
[73] *Dean v Bennett* (1871) L.R. 6 Ch. 489 at 494; *cf. R. v Governors of Darlington School* (1845) 6 Q.B. 682.
[74] See *Dean v Bennett*, above.
[75] (1871) L.R. 6 Ch. 489.

vague general finding that he had been guilty of falsehood and drunkenness. Moreover, as the notice of the second meeting did not specify the resolution to be confirmed, the meeting was unable effectually to confirm the resolution passed at the previous meeting.

Similarly, a minister in possession of a meeting-house vested in trustees is merely their tenant at will, and they may at any time determine his tenancy by a demand for possession, without previous notice.[76] The demand for possession puts an end to the legal right of the minister, but it leaves him whatever remedy to which he may be entitled against the trustees if they have improperly ejected him.[77]

Remedies

A minister who has been irregularly appointed may be restrained by injunction from disturbing the congregation in the use of the chapel and from officiating in it.[78] So also when a minister has been properly dismissed he may be restrained by injunction from preaching, officiating or collecting pew-rents.[79] On the other hand, where he has been improperly dismissed, an injunction may be granted to restrain any interference with him in the discharge of his duties.[80] Moreover, mandamus may be granted requiring the trustees of an endowed meeting-house to admit to the use of the pulpit as pastor, minister or preacher, a person duly elected.[81] However, an application for mandamus to restore a person to the office of minister of a congregation and to the use of the pulpit will not be successful unless the applicant makes out a prima facie title to such office and shows at least that he has complied with all the forms necessary to constitute his right.[82]

A minister who has ceased to hold the tenets of the congregation for which the chapel was founded will be removed,[83] and an injunction may be granted to restrain him from officiating,[84] or remaining in possession of the meeting-house,[85] for he cannot convert the chapel to the propagation of doctrines other than those for which it was established. In the case of a Presbyterian chapel, an injunction was granted to restrain the trustees

5–066

---

[76] *Doe v Jones* (1830) 10 B. & C. 718; *Doe v M'Kaeg, ibid.* at 721; *Browne v Dawson* (1841) 12 A. & E. 624; *Perry v Shipway* (1859) 4 De G. & J. 353; *Cooper v Gordon* (1869) L.R. 8 Eq. 249; *cf. Spurgin v White* (1861) 2 Giff. 473, at 487, as to the agent of a society.

[77] *Doe v Jones* (1859) 4 Del. & J. 353. See *Att-Gen v Aked* (1835) 7 Sim. 321.

[78] *Perry v Shipway*, above. See also *Porter v Clarke* (1829) 2 Sim. 520; and *Spurgin v White*, above, where the agent of a religious society who had been dismissed was restrained from disturbing the society in its possession of the agent's house.

[79] *Cooper v Gordon* (1869) 8 Eq. 249.

[80] *Daugars v Rivaz* (1859) 28 Beav. 233. See also *Att-Gen v Aked*, above; *Ward v Hipwell* (1862) 3 Giff. 547.

[81] *R. v Barker* (1762) 3 Burr. 1265; *cf. Davis v Jenkins* (1814) 3 v & B. 151 at 155.

[82] *R. v Jotham* (1790) 3 T.R. 575. See also *R. v Trustees of Dagger Lane Chapel* (1804) 2 Smith 20.

[83] *Att-Gen v Munro* (1848) 2 De G. & Sm. 122.

[84] *Att-Gen v Welsh* (1846) 4 Ha. 572. See also *Att-Gen v Munro*, above, 122 at 196; *Att-Gen v Murdoch* (1852) 1 De G.M. & G. 86.

[85] *Broom v Summers* (1841) 11 Sim. 353.

from electing as minister a person not duly licensed by the Church of Scotland.[86]

Pending a suit for the regulation of a dissenting meeting-house it has been held to be the practice of the court, if it finds a minister in possession, and ministering in the way in which he should minister, and preaching the doctrines which he ought to preach, to continue him in the meantime, whether he was duly appointed or not; for the first point is to have the service performed. The court will also pay him his salary.[87]

Masters of schools

5–067   This section is concerned with the equitable rules which govern the rights and remedies of masters of schools which are charitable foundations. Those rights and remedies will depend largely on the instrument of foundation or scheme of the relevant school. A master of such a school may have, in addition, rights and remedies as an employee at a school and the reader is referred to the standard texts on employment law and education law for the detailed provisions.

Appointment

5–068   Schoolmasters are appointed in various ways, but in all cases the mode of appointment or selection, if any, set forth in the instrument of foundation or scheme should be adhered to.[88] If the founder of a school gives no direction as to the appointment or selection of a schoolmaster, and appoints no visitor, he and his heirs, as patrons, are entitled to appoint the schoolmaster.[89]

Where the nomination of a schoolmaster is given to a number of persons, not constituting a corporation, an appointment by the majority is good.[90] Moreover, while the meeting of the electors continues the majority of them may rescind their resolution appointing a schoolmaster.[91] If it cannot be ascertained in whom the right of appointing a schoolmaster is vested, an application to the court may be necessary.[92]

The nomination of a schoolmaster does not lapse like the presentation to a living[93] and may be alienated.[94]

---

[86] *Milligan v Mitchell* (1833) 1 Myl. & K. 446.
[87] See *per* Lord Eldon, *Foley v Wontner* (1810) 2 J. & W. 245 at 247; *cf. Leslie v Birnie* (1826) 2 Russ. 114; *Milligan v Mitchell*, above. As to the jurisdiction of the court in the case of dissenting meeting-houses, see *Davis v Jenkins* (1814) 3 v & B. 151 at 155.
[88] *Att-Gen v Carrington* (1850) 4 De G. & Sm. 140. For a grant of the right to nominate the master of a hospital, see *Att-Gen v Ewelme Hospital* (1853) 17 Beav. 366.
[89] *Legh v Lewis* (1800) 1 East 391 at 395.
[90] *Withnell v Gartham* (1795) 6 T.R. 388; see also *Wilkinson v Malin* (1832) 2 C. & J. 636 at 655; *Re Butterwick Free Press* (1851) 15 Jur. 913.
[91] *Att-Gen v Matthew* (1827) Russ. 500.
[92] Possibly the Charity Commissioners could assist by giving their opinion and advice under the Charities Act 1993, s.29, but whether they could assist would depend upon the circumstances.
[93] *Att-Gen v Wycliffe* (1747) 1 Ves.Sen. 80.
[94] *Att-Gen v Brentwood School* (1832) 3 B. & Ad. 59; *Att-Gen v Boucherett* (1858) 25 Beav. 116; and see *Att-Gen v Ewelme Hospital* (1853) 22 L.J.Ch. 846.

Qualification

A person to be elected schoolmaster must possess the qualification **5–069** required by the statutes or instrument of foundation. Thus, where the schoolmaster was required by the statutes to be in priest's orders, it has been held that this requirement could not be dispensed with.[95] Similarly a schoolmaster of a Church of Scotland school ought, *ceteris paribus*, to be a member of that church, even though the instruction may be open to scholars of any religious demonination. But it is not absolutely necessary that the schoolmaster should belong to that church, and if the circumstances are sufficiently peculiar to justify it, the trustees do not commit a breach of trust by appointing a dissenter.[96]

A person who has a controlling power of assent to the election of a schoolmaster cannot himself hold the office and, if appointed, will be removed by the court.[97]

Tenure

The term of office of a schoolmaster depends upon the instrument of **5–070** foundation or scheme under which he is appointed.[98] He may, for example, if the terms of the instrument of foundation permit, be appointed for life, in which case he is said to have an estate of freehold in his office.[99] On the other hand, he may be appointed simply to hold office during pleasure.[1] Again, although his office may not be an estate of freehold, the power of removal may be fettered by various restrictions.[2]

In order to obtain greater power over schoolmasters, they have sometimes been required to give bonds of resignation on their appointment. The validity of such bonds has been questioned. In *Legh v Lewis*,[3] a schoolmaster of an ancient school, who, as it was alleged, had a freehold in his office, gave on his appointment a bond to his patron to resign when required by him or his heirs to do so. The Court of King's Bench held that the bond was good. The case later came before the Exchequer Chamber upon a writ of error,[4] but the court declined to give an opinion because it did not sufficiently appear on the record that the office was freehold. However, a different result was arrived at in *Re Royston Free Grammar*

---

[95] *Att-Gen v Wycliffe* (1747) 1 Ves.Sen. 80.

[96] *Att-Gen v Clifton* (1863) 32 Beav. 596; *cf. Baker v Lee* (1860) 8 H.L.C. 495.

[97] *Re Risley School* (1830) L.J.(o.s.)Ch. 129.

[98] *Att-Gen v Black* (1805) 11 Ves. 191; *R. v Governors of Darlington School* (1845) 6 Q.B. 682. See *Re Alleyn's College, Dulwich* (1875) 1 App.Cas. 68; *Re Phillips' Charities* (1845) 9 J.P.741.

[99] *Re Chipping Sodbury School* (1830); 8 L.J.(o.s.)Ch. 13. See *Legh v Lewis* (1800) 1 East 391; *Re Royston Free Grammar School* (1840) 2 Beav. 228; *Re Phillips' Charity* (1845) 9 Jur. 959; *Att-Gen v Warden of Louth Free Grammar School* (1851) 14 Beav. 201.

[1] *R. v Governors of Darlington School* (1845) 6 Q.B. 682.

[2] *Re Alleyn's College, Dulwich* (1875) 1 App.Cas.68; *cf. Benthall v Kilmorey* (1884) 25 Ch.D. 39; and see *Wilkinson v Malin* (1832) 2 C. & J. 636.

[3] (1800) 1 East 391.

[4] Sub nom. *Lewis v Legh* (1803) 3 Bos. & p.231.

School.[5] In this case the trustees of a free grammar school (the origin of which did not appear) held property "to the use of the school". Having elected a schoolmaster, they obliged him to enter into a bond and agreement, stipulating that he should not have or claim a freehold in the school or estates, and should quit at six months' notice, and should not intermeddle with the estates, and containing other stipulations as to the government and management of the school. Lord Langdale held that the regulations imposed by the trustees might be properly observed under their order and direction, yet it was not proper to enforce them by taking a bond from the schoolmaster; and that the trustees had exceeded their powers. A reference was accordingly directed to approve of a proper scheme for the management of the school. In this case, *Legh v Lewis*[6] does not appear to have been cited. The two cases are, however, to some extent distinguishable. In *Legh v Lewis* the bond was taken by the patron; in *Re Royston Free Grammar School* it was taken by the trustees. Moreover, the decision in the latter case was not that the bond itself was illegal, but that the trustees had not the power to impose it. In any case, if any corrupt use was intended to be made of such bond, the Attorney-General might *ex officio* be called upon to interfere, and upon application to the court the appointment would be taken out of the hands of the person who so exercised it corruptly.[7]

Removal

5–071   Where the master is appointed to hold office during pleasure, the trustees may at any time remove him at their discretion, provided they do not act from corrupt or improper motives[8] and it seems that no reason for his removal need be given.[9] But however arbitrary the power of removal may be, it must not be exercised oppressively or unjustly.[10] Moreover, where the instrument of foundation makes special provisions as to the mode in which a master is to be dismissed, he cannot be dismissed unless those provisions are observed.[11]

Even where a master is appointed to his office for life he is removable in case of misbehaviour[12] or the neglect of scholars.[13]

---

[5] (1840) 2 Beav. 228.
[6] (1803) 3 Bos. & p.231.
[7] *Legh v Lewis*, above.
[8] *R. v Governors of Darlington School* (1845) 6 Q.B. 682; *Re Buxton School* (1847) 11 Jur. 581; and see *Re Bedford Charity* (1833) 5 Sim. 578.
[9] *R. v Governors of Darlington School*, above; *Dean v Bennett* (1871) 6 Ch. 489 at 494.
[10] *Dean v Bennett* (1871) 6 Ch. 489; *Fisher v Jackson* [1891] 2 Ch. 84. See also *Re Phillips' Charity* (1845) 9 Jur. 959; *Ridge v Baldwin* [1964] A.C. 40.
[11] *Re Alleyn's College, Dulwich* (1875) 1 A.C. 68; *Lane v Norman* (1891) 66 L.T. 83. See *Willis v Childe* (1851) 13 Beav. 117; and *cf. Dean v Bennett*, above.
[12] A person appointed to an office *quamdiu se bene gesserit* has an estate for life; Cruise Dig. tit. XV. pl. 27. Conversely, if the office is granted for life, there is an implied condition that the grantee shall hold it only *quamdiu se bene gesserit*: *ibid.*, pl. 28; and see *Leeson v General Medical Council* (1890) 43 Ch.D. 366 at 383.
[13] *Doe v Cole* (1834) 6 C. & p.359.

However, before removing a schoolmaster for misconduct it is the duty of the trustees to reduce the charges which they made against him to writing and to cause them to be communicated to him and to give him a reasonable opportunity of meeting them.[14] But if that has been done, and the trustees have come to their conclusion upon evidence sufficient to satisfy a reasonable majority, their decision cannot be interfered with.[15]

Two cases may be contrasted in this connection. In *Ryan v Jenkinson*[16]   **5–072** it was held that a schoolmaster, whose contract of service was with trustees alone, could be dismissed independently of any consent of the parishioners, that the three months' notice specified in the contract was sufficient and that the master's claim for three-quarters' salary must be disallowed, he having, despite the service of notice of dismissal on him, remained on in office during that period. The facts were different in *Fisher v Jackson*.[17] In this case the power to dismiss the master of an endowed school was vested in three vicars. Two of them served him with a notice of dismissal containing charges of a vague character which were never reduced to a more precise form and which he was given no opportunity of meeting. It was held that the notice of dismissal was invalid.

In the latter case the trust deed made provision for meetings to be held, and directed that no act in the execution of the trust by a less number than two so meeting and agreeing should be valid. An opinion was expressed by the court (although it was not decided) that two of the persons could not exercise the power without a meeting of the three being summoned, although, if one declined to attend the meeting, the others could no doubt act without him.[18] A majority of the trustees have power to act, but they are bound to listen to the views of the minority if they choose to express any.[19]

The headmaster of any of the seven schools specified in the Public Schools Act 1868[20] is liable to be dismissed without notice and without reason being given as he is appointed and holds office at the pleasure of the respective governing body.[21]

Remedies

A schoolmaster who has been improperly appointed, or who has been   **5–073** properly removed, may be restrained by injunction from presenting himself at the school and teaching therein, and from remaining in occupation of the school-house.[22] Conversely, where a schoolmaster is improperly

---

[14] *Re Phillips' Charity* (1845) 9 Jur. 959; see *Dean v Bennett* (1871) 6 Ch. 489; *Fisher v Jackson* [1891] 2 Ch. 84. As to what is misconduct, see *Re Phillips' Charity*, above.

[15] *Re Fremington School* (1846) 11 Jur. 421.

[16] (1855) 25 L.J.Q.B. 11.

[17] [1891] 2 Ch. 84.

[18] *ibid.* at 101.

[19] *Fisher v Jackson* [1891] 2 Ch. 84 at 94. See also, as to the power of charity trustees to act by a majority, *Re Whiteley* [1910] 1 Ch. 600, 608.

[20] Eton, Winchester, Westminster, Charterhouse, Rugby, Harrow and Shrewsbury.

[21] Public Schools Act 1868, s.13 and see *Hayman v Rugby School Governors* (1874) L.R. 18 Eq. 28.

[22] *Holme v Guy* (1877) 5 Ch.D. 901.

removed, an injunction may be granted to restrain the trustees from enforcing his dismissal and ejecting him.[23] The consent and certificate of the Charity Commissioners[24] are not required in such proceedings.[25]

The court will also interfere, where a schoolmaster has been improperly appointed or removed, to declare such appointment or removal void[26]; and it will do so also in the case of a corporation as in the case of individual trustees.[27] Thus, where a schoolmaster has been deprived of his office from improper motives, as because he voted for a particular candidate at a parliamentary election,[28] or unjustly and oppressively,[29] however arbitrary the power of removal may be,[30] the court will declare such removal void; although it will not interfere where the trustees have arrived at their conclusion upon reasonably sufficient grounds.[31]

A master will be removed from a school if he insists upon holding an office inconsistent with the performance of his duties as schoolmaster, or which by the instrument of foundation it was intended he should not hold; but he may hold another office if it is not inconsistent with the performance of his duties as schoolmaster, and if it does not appear to have been intended that he should not hold such office. So in *Att-Gen v Hartley*[32] it was held that the offices of schoolmaster and vicar of the parish might be held together, and the court would only be justified in removing him if it were shown that he neglected his duties in the school.

5–074   The court will not remove a schoolmaster in consequence of a mere misunderstanding as to his duty. But where the duty is prescribed, the master cannot retain the situation without performing it.[33]

Where a person has acted as schoolmaster for a considerable time, although he was originally improperly appointed, the court will not remove him, or allow him to be removed unless he can be shown to have been guilty of misconduct which might have been made a ground for his discharge, if the appointment had originally been correct.[34]

Generally, where there is a visitor who has jurisdiction to act with regard to the amotion of a schoolmaster, the court declines to interfere,[35] and the same applies where visitatorial power is reserved to the Charity

---

[23] *Willis v Childe* (1851) 13 Beav. 117; *Lane v Norman* (1891) 66 L.T. 83; *Fisher v Jackson* [1891] 2 Ch. 84; *cf. Pottle v Sharp* (1896) 75 L.T. 265; and see *Bowers v Young* (1904) 48 S.J. 733 as to notice of dismissal. See also *Doe v Gartham* (1823) 8 Moo. 368.

[24] Under Charities Act 1993, s.33 replacing the Charities Act 1960, s.28 which replaced Charitable Trusts Act 1853, s.17.

[25] *Rendall v Blair* (1890) Ch.D. 139, 156 and see para.10–027, below.

[26] *Dummer v Corporation of Chippenham* (1808) 14 Ves. 245; *Att-Gen v Carrington* (1850) 4 De G. & Sm. 368.

[27] *Dummer v Corporation of Chippenham*, above.

[28] *ibid.*

[29] *Re Phillips' Charity* (1845) 9 Jur. 959.

[30] See *Dean v Bennett* (1871) 6 Ch. 489.

[31] *Re Fremington School* (1846) 11 Jur. 421.

[32] (1820) 2 J. & W. 353 at 360, 376.

[33] Lord Eldon in *Att-Gen v Coopers' Co.* (1813) 19 Ves. 187 at 192.

[34] See *per* Lord Eldon in *Att-Gen v Hartley* (1820) 2 J. & W. 353 at 375. See also *Att-Gen v Dixie* (1807) 13 Ves. 519 at 541; *Foley v Wontner* (1820) 2 J. & W. 245 at 247.

[35] See para.10–071, below. See also *Att-Gen v Magdalen College, Oxford* (1847) 10 Beav. 402; *Whiston v Dean and Chapter of Rochester* (1849) 7 Her. 532.

Commissioners.[36] But even though there is a visitor the court will interfere in the case of an express trust; for the existence of a visitor does not prevent the court from exercising its jurisdiction to see that trusts are properly executed.[37]

[36] See *R. v Wilson* [1888] W.N. 12.
[37] *Daugars v Rivaz* (1859) 28 Beav. 233.

CHAPTER 6

POWERS AND DUTIES OF CHARITY TRUSTEES

The powers and duties of charity trustees, as defined in s. 97 of the **6–001**
Charities Act 1993 as those persons having the general control and
management of the administration of a charity, are governed by the legal
structure adopted by the charity, the terms of the individual governing
instrument and the relevant statutory provisions. The detailed powers and
duties of trustees of a charitable trust are considered first followed by a
consideration of the position of directors of charitable companies and
members of committees of charitable unincorporated associations.

TRUSTEES OF A CHARITABLE TRUST

When considering the powers and duties of trustees of a charitable trust, **6–002**
it should be remembered that as a trust has no separate legal personality any
contracts entered into with third parties in pursuance of the exercise of such
powers and duties are entered into by the trustees in their personal capacity.
Although charity trustees have the usual right of indemnity from the trust
funds for liabilities properly incurred, this right is of little avail if the trust is
insolvent. Charitable trusts can and do contain trustee exemption clauses
but any exemption clause must recognise the irreducible core of obligations
owed by the trustees.[1]

Powers

Charity trustees have, in general, the same powers as ordinary trustees.[2] **6–003**
Thus, the position of charity trustees is, generally, the same as that of
other trustees under the Trustee Acts 1925 and 2000. Charity trustees do
not, however, have the power of other trustees to raise money by sale or
mortgage for purposes authorised by the trust instrument.[3] Further, the
restriction to four of the number of trustees who may hold land does not
apply to charity trustees.[4] In addition to the general powers of trustees

---

[1] See *Armitage v Nurse* [1998] Ch. 241; *Walker v Stones* [2001] Q.B. 902. This area of law is
   subject to review; see the Law Commission Consultation paper No. 171, *Trustee
   Exemption Clauses* (2003).
[2] See the general textbooks on the Law of Trusts, *e.g.* Underhill and Hayton, *Law of Trusts
   and Trustees* (15th ed.), pp.665 *et seq.*; Snell's *Equity* (30th ed.), pp.295, *et seq.*
[3] Trustee Act 1925, s.16 but see paras 6–008 and 6–012 below.
[4] *ibid.*, s.34(3).

derived from equity and statute, the trustees also have the powers given to them by the relevant trust instrument. Charity trustees are also given additional powers by the Charities Act 1993. These are the power to co-operate with local authorities and other charities[5] and the power to delegate, generally or specifically, the execution of documents to at least two of their number.[6] On the other hand, the Act restricts the circumstances in which charity trustees can exercise their power of sale or otherwise deal with charity property.[7]

Exercising the powers

6–004   It is necessary to construe the relevant instrument in order to determine who is entitled to exercise any given power.[8] If the power is given to trustees and even a testator's "said trustees" (who are named in the will) it is *prima facie* regarded as being attached to the office of trustee and exercisable by the trustees for the time being.[9] However, in an appropriate case the court may leave the selection of objects with the persons nominated by the testator as trustee, whilst appointing new trustees.[10] If the power is given to executors it is exercisable only by continuing[11] or surviving executors.[12] It is not exercisable by an executor who renounces[13] or by anyone subsequently appointed trustee.[14]

Where the power is exercisable by a person who is not a trustee of the property it cannot be exercised by anyone else.[15] If the person named does not exercise the power, the power or discretion is exercised by the court.[16]

When trustees exercise discretionary powers vested in them they must do so honestly[17] and with a fair consideration of the subject.[18] In *Scott v National Trust for Places of Historic Interest or Natural Beauty*,[19] Robert Walker J. set out the duty in more detail but also recognised the problems faced by trustees when he said[20]:

> "Certain points are clear beyond argument. Trustees must act in good faith, responsibly and reasonably. They must inform themselves, before making a decision, of matters which are relevant to the decision. These matters may not be limited to simple matters of fact but

---

[5] Charities Act 1993, s.78.
[6] *ibid.*, s.82.
[7] Charities Act 1993, ss.36–40. See para.6–014, below.
[8] *Re Mainwaring* [1891] 2 Ch. 261 at 267, 268.
[9] *Re Smith* [1904] 1 Ch. 139.
[10] *Re Taylor's Charity, Ex p. Blackburne* (1820) 1 Jac. & W. 297.
[11] *Re Mainwaring* [1891] 2 Ch. 261.
[12] *Att-Gen v Glegg* (1738) Amb. 584.
[13] *Att-Gen v Fletcher* (1835) 5 L.J.Ch. 75.
[14] *Hibbard v Lamb* (1759) Amb. 309.
[15] *In the Goods of M'Auliffe* (1895) P.290.
[16] *Moggridge v Thackwell* (1792) 1 Ves. 464 at 474, affirmed (1803) 7 Ves. 36 at 38.
[17] See *Armitage v Nurse* [1998] Ch. 241 at 251, *per* Millet L.J.
[18] *Re Beloved Wilkes Charity* (1851) 20 L.J.Ch. 588 at 597. See also *Turner v Turner* [1984] Ch. 100 (not a charity case).
[19] [1998] 2 All E.R. 705.
[20] *ibid.* at 717.

will, on occasion (indeed, quite often) include taking advice from appropriate experts, whether the experts are lawyers, accountants, actuaries, surveyors, scientists or whomsoever. It is however for advisers to advise and for trustees to decide: trustees may not (except in so far as they are authorised to do so) delegate the exercise of their discretions, even to experts. This sometimes creates real difficulties, especially when lay trustees have to digest and assess expert advice on a highly technical matter (to take merely one instant, the disposal of actuarial surplus in a superannuation fund)."

The public law rules of natural justice are not strictly applicable to char- **6–005**
ities. Charity trustees must inform themselves sufficiently so that they can make a sensible decision. Where their decision affects a particular beneficiary they are not obliged to give that beneficiary an opportunity to be heard if otherwise they have sufficient information.[21] Trustees do not have to give reasons for their decisions as a matter of course.[22] It is possible, however, that trustees may be compelled by discovery or subpoena to give the substance of the reasons for a decision if a particular decision is litigated.[23]

In the past, the courts have indicated that they are reluctant to interfere with trustees' decisions where the discretion arises by means of a scheme[24] although the courts have refused to dismiss an action seeking the interference of the court in order to maintain some control over trustees.[25] More recently, the courts have confirmed their general reluctance to interfere with the exercise of discretions by charity trustees but have also indicated the standard they expect trustees to comply with when exercising discretions.

Scott v National Trust for Places of Historic Interest or Natural Beauty[26] concerned a challenge to a decision by the council of the National Trust not to renew licenses to hunt deer on certain parts of its Devon and Somerset Estate. In determining the approach the court should take to the exercise of discretions by trustees Robert Walker J. started with the general principle set out by Lord Reed in *Dundee General Hospitals Board of Management v Walker*[27]:

> "If it can be shown that the trustees considered the wrong question, or that, although they purported to consider the right question they did not really apply their minds to it or perversely shut their minds to the facts or that they did not act honestly or in good faith, then there was no true decision and the court will intervene."

---

[21] *R. v Charity Commissioners for England and Wales Ex p. Baldwin* (2001) 2 W.T.L.R. 137.
[22] *Re Beloved Wilkes Charity* (1851) 20 L.J.Ch. 588 at 597.
[23] *Scott v National Trust for Places of Historic Interest or Natural Beauty* [1998] 2 All E.R. 705 at 719.
[24] *Powerscourt v Powerscourt* (1824) 1 Mol. 616; *Att-Gen v Gaskell* (1831) 9 L.J.O.S.Ch. 188; *Re Lea* (1887) 34 Ch. D. 528; *Re Hurley* (1900) 17 T.L.R. 115.
[25] *Att-Gen v Governors of Harrow School* (1754) 2 Ves. Sen. 551.
[26] [1998] 2 All E.R. 705.
[27] [1952] 1 All E.R. 896 at 905. See also *Re Hastings-Bass (Deceased)* [1975] 1 Ch. 25.

6–006   Later decisions in pension cases[28] have confirmed this approach of non-intervention unless the trustees have made a decision that no reasonable body of trustees would arrive at but as Robert Walker J. pointed out[29] the cases are not completely clear as to whether the test should be that the court should interfere if trustees properly advised and informed *would* have acted otherwise or whether it is that they *might* have acted otherwise.

It has been argued[30] that using the "reasonable trustee" test as a basis for determining the courts intervention in trustees' discretion is akin to importing public law *Wednesbury*[31] principles into private trust law and should not be extended. The test has already been used in relation to private trusts[32] and its continued use to test the decisions of trustees of charity trusts, which are public trusts, must be expected. Robert Walker J.'s warning in *Scott v National Trust for Places of Historic Interest or Natural Beauty*[33] should, however, be remembered:

> "To impose too stringent a test may impose intolerable burdens on trustees who often undertake heavy responsibilities for no financial reward; it may also lead to damaging uncertainty as to what has and has not been validly decided."

In determining whether the test has been met by particular charity trustees, the court may well have regard to guidance issued by the Charity Commissioners. For example, if the dispute concerns retention of income, Charity Commissioners' guidance[34] provides that charity trustees should have a policy covering the reasons why the charity needs reserves, the level of reserves required and how that level is to be achieved and maintained. Such guidance would seem relevant in determining whether a "reasonable trustee" test had been met.

6–007   Unless there is a power to delegate, either by statute[35] or in the trust instrument, powers must be exercised by the trustees themselves. It is possible, however, for trustees to enter into a contract by which they bind themselves as to the future exercise of their powers in a particular way if the arrangement as a whole is in the interests of the charity.[36] Thus charity trustees as part of a funding arrangement can agree, for example, that certain facilities will be provided for beneficiaries.[37]

---

[28] *Mettoy Pension Trustees Ltd v Evans* [1990] 1 W.L.R. 1587; *Stannard v Fisons Pensions Trust* [1992] I.R.L.R. 27; *Harris v Lord Shuttleworth* [1994] I.C.R. 991; *Edge v Pensions Ombudsman* [1999] 4 All E.R. 546 at 567.

[29] *Scott v National Trust for Places of Historic Interest or Natural Beauty* [1998] 2 All E.R. 705 at 718.

[30] See *e.g.*, Underhill and Hayton, *Law of Trusts and Trustees* (15th ed.), p.718.

[31] *Associated Provincial Picture Houses Ltd v Wednesbury Corp.* [1948] 1 K.B. 223.

[32] See *Wright v Olswang* [2001] C.P.Rep. 54; *Abacus Trust Company Isle of Man Ltd v National Society for the Prevention of Cruelty to Children* [2001] S.T.C. 1344; *Re Barr's Settlement Trusts* [2003] 1 All E.R. 763.

[33] [1998] 2 All E.R. 705 at 718.

[34] See CC19, *Charities' Reserves* (2002).

[35] See para.6–017 below.

[36] By analogy with the position of company directors, see *Fulham Football Club Ltd v Cabra Estates plc* [1994] 1 B.C.L.C. 363 at 392.

[37] See RR7, *The Independence of Charities from the State*, p.7.

In general, when exercising a discretion a majority of trustees of a charitable trust acting within the limits of the instrument of foundation[38] bind the minority.[39]

Particular powers

Power to borrow money

Charity trustees who hold land have power to borrow for a purpose in connection with the land they hold.[40] The trust instrument may contain an express power to borrow. It is debatable whether a general power to do "all such other lawful things as are necessary for the achievement of the objects" is sufficient to imply a power to borrow. Charity trustees may, however, seek an Order under s.26 of the 1993 Act from the Charity Commissioners conferring power to borrow.[41] Where charity trustees have power to borrow they may, subject to certain restrictions, charge the charity property to secure the loan.[42] The trustees, whilst entitled to be repaid out of the charity property if it is available and sufficient for that purpose, remain personally liable to repay the loan.

6–008

Power to insure

Charity trustees have the usual statutory power[43] to insure the charity property against risks of loss or damage due to any event and to pay the premiums out of the trust fund. The Charity Commissioners have, since 1991, taken the view that there is no objection in principle to a charity insuring against loss to its funds resulting from the acts and defaults of its trustees.[44] Indemnity insurance for trustees, however, is a trustee benefit and, unless there is express power to purchase such insurance in the trust instrument, application will have to be made to the Commissioners for authority to use charitable funds. The Charity Commissioners must be satisfied that the purchase of trustee indemnity insurance is in the interests of the charity.[45] The Charity Commissioners require any policy of insurance to exclude liability for loss arising from any act or omission that the trustee knew to be a breach of trust or duty or that was committed by the trustee in reckless disregard of whether it was a breach of trust or duty.[46]

6–009

The Charity Commissioners have now recognised that there is little risk to charity funds from the purchase of trustee indemnity insurance and,

---

[38] *Ward v Hipwell* (1862) 3 Giff. 547.
[39] *Re Whiteley* [1910] 1 Ch. 600 at 608.
[40] Trusts of Land and Appointment of Trustees Act 1996, s.6 and see OG 22 B1, *Borrowings and Mortgages. Power to Borrow.*
[41] See OG 22 B2, *Borrowings and Mortgages. How we confer authority.*
[42] Charities Act 1993, s.38. See para.6–015 below and CC33, *Acquiring Land* (2001).
[43] Trustee Act 1925, s.19 as substituted by Trustee Act 2000, s.19.
[44] [1991] Ch. Com. Rep., para.36.
[45] See CC49, *Charities and Insurance* (1996), para.20.
[46] CC49, *Charities and Insurance* (1996), para.21. This guidance is the subject of review.

having regard to the principle of proportionality, have introduced a simplified procedure by which they will authorise charity trustees to purchase such insurance.[47] The Commissioners will now grant authority by order under s.26 of the Charities Act 1993[48] if the trustees certify that they have identified the risks to which they are exposed and have decided that the purchase of trustee indemnity insurance is in the interests of the charity.

Power to make ex gratia payments

6–010   Charity trustees have, with the consent of the Charity Commissioners[49] or the Attorney-General, power to make *ex gratia* payments. The power was confirmed by Cross J. in *Re Snowden*.[50] In that case, the testator gave all his shares in three named companies to his three nearest relatives. He then gave pecuniary legacies, mostly to charities, and directed his residuary estate to be divided among the pecuniary legatees. Unfortunately, at his death the testator no longer held any of the stipulated shares. Thus, the relatives took nothing and the proceeds of the shares passed to the pecuniary legatees as part of the residuary estate. Most of the charities considered that they were under a moral obligation to make some payment to the relatives in order that the testator's obvious intention might be carried out. Cross J. emphasised that the power was not to be exercised lightly or on slender grounds but only in cases where it could be said that if the charity were an individual it would be morally wrong for him to refuse to make the payment.[51]

The Charity Commissioners' exercise of the power to consent to *ex gratia* payments is subject to the supervision and directions of the Attorney-General.[52] An application for consent to make an *ex gratia* payment should be made to the Commissioners by the charity trustees, not by the proposed recipient. The Commissioners require firm evidence that the making of an *ex gratia* payment is justified. A statement by someone who claims he is morally entitled to a payment is not sufficient. What is required is impartial evidence as to why, for example, a testator's real intention was frustrated.[53] The Charity Commissioners may refer an application to the Attorney-General where they consider it more appropriate that it should be dealt with by him, for example, because the application raises a point of principle on which the Attorney-General's guidance is needed.[54]

---

[47] See OG 100 A1, *Trustee Indemnity Insurance. Procedure for Authorising the Purchase of Trustee Indemnity Insurance.*

[48] See para.9.007 below.

[49] Charities Act 1993, s.27(1)(a) subject to the supervision and direction of the Attorney-General, s.27(2). For consideration of the Attorney-General's practice see para.10–023, below.

[50] [1970] Ch. 700. See also *Re Henderson, ibid.*

[51] *ibid.* at 710. By s.27(1)(ii) the Charity Commissioners can only consent if the charity trustees regard themselves as being under a moral obligation to make the payment.

[52] Charities Act 1993, s.27(2).

[53] For Charity Commissioners practice see CC7, *Ex Gratia Payment by Charities* (2001) and OG 11, *Ex Gratia Payments by Charities.*

[54] Charities Act 1993, s.27(3) and see CC7, *Ex Gratia Payments by Charities* (2001).

If the Charity Commissioners refuse to exercise the power, that does not preclude an application to the Attorney-General and his subsequent exercise of the power.[55] If no individual charity is concerned, the application should be made on behalf of the executors.[56]

Power to waive entitlement to property

The Charity Commissioners have the same power as the Attorney-General   **6–011**
to authorise charity trustees to waive a charity's entitlement to receive property[57] where the trustees regard themselves as being under a moral obligation to do so.[58] The power of the Commissioners is subject to the supervision and directions of the Attorney-General.[59] The only way in which a charity could be given power itself to refuse a legacy is by Act of Parliament as waiver amounts to an application of property for non-charitable purposes. Guidance as to when such a power of waiver should be given can be found in the *Alcoholics Anonymous* case[60] where the Commissioners gave the necessary permission to expend funds to obtain an Act of Parliament; the charity placed considerable emphasis on self-reliance and to accept a legacy would have been contrary to the whole ethos of the charity.

Power to deal with charity property

Sources of power—S.8(1) of the Trustee Act 2000 confers on all trustees a   **6–012**
statutory power to acquire freehold or leasehold land as an investment or for occupation by a beneficiary or for any other reason. The power to purchase land for occupation by a beneficiary has no application to charities as those receiving benefits from a charity do not have an interest in the property subject to the trust. It was confirmed during the debate on the Trustee Bill, however, that power to purchase "for any other reason" was wide enough to include the purchase of functional land by a charity.[61] The power conferred by s.8 is in addition to any other powers conferred on trustees but subject to any restrictions or exclusions in the trust instrument or imposed by any enactment or subordinate legislation.[62] The trust instrument could, for example, restrict charity trustees from purchasing commercial property as an investment. Where charity trustees are already trustees of land they may use their powers under s.6 of the Trusts of Land and Appointments of Trustees Act 1996 to acquire land and that power cannot be restricted by the trust instrument.[63] The statutory duty of

---

[55] Charities Act 1993, s.27(4).
[56] As in *Re Henderson* [1970] Ch. 700. For the practice to be followed, see para.342, below.
[57] Charities Act 1993, s.27(1)(b).
[58] *ibid.*, s.27(1)(ii).
[59] *ibid.*, s.27(2).
[60] [1986] Ch. Com. Rep., App.D.
[61] Committee Trustee Bill, HL (June 7, 2000). CWH, col. B.
[62] Trustee Act 2000, s.9.
[63] Trusts of Land and Appointment of Trustees Act 1996, s.8(1)(3). The power can be subject to an order of the court or the Charity Commissioners, s.6(6)(7).

care[64] applies to a trustee using the power to acquire land in s.8 of the 2000 Act or any other power.[65]

Charity trustees have always had a general power at law to sell, lease or mortgage charity land, whether expressly authorised by the instrument of foundation or not.[66] However, the transaction was liable to be set aside if the purchaser could not show that the transaction was beneficial to the charity,[67] unless lapse of time raised a presumption of power to sell.[68]

The trustees' power of sale has, since 1925, been regulated by statute and as there is some doubt as to whether the statutory powers have superseded the common law powers it is better to rely on the trustees' statutory powers to deal in charity land in the absence of any express powers in the governing instrument.[69]

6–013   Until January 1, 1997, a charity trustee's power to dispose or otherwise deal with land was to be found in s.29 of the Settled Land Act 1925. On that date land held on charitable, ecclesiastical or public trust ceased to be settled land and became held on a trust of land.[70] By s.6 of the Trusts of Land and Appointment of Trustees Act 1996, for the purpose of exercising their functions as trustees, trustees of land have in relation to the land subject to the trust all the powers of an absolute owner. This clearly confers wide powers of disposal over land on charity trustees and the power cannot be restricted or excluded by the trust instrument.[71] The power cannot, however, be exercised in contravention of an order of the court or the Charity Commissioners[72] or any rule of law or equity. Equity does not regard the giving of land for a specific charitable purpose as sufficient reason to prevent its subsequent sale, unless the property has particular qualities which themselves make the purpose of the gift charitable.[73]

If charity trustees have acquired land by using their powers under s.8 of the Trustee Act 2000[74] they are given similar powers to an absolute owner over that land.[75] These powers of disposal can be restricted by a provision in the trust instrument[76] unlike the powers under s.6 of the 1996 Act.

---

[64] For the statutory duty of care under Trustee Act 2000, s.1 see para.6–025 below.

[65] Trustee Act 2000, s.2 and Sch.1 para.2. For guidance on the exercise of the duty of care when acquiring land see CC33, *Acquiring Land* (2001), paras 9–11.

[66] *Re Manchester New College* (1853) 16 Beav. 610 at 628, 629; *Re Mason's Orphanage and London and North Western Railway Co.* [1896] 1 Ch. 596 at 604; *Re Howard Street Congregational Chapel, Sheffield* [1913] 2 Ch. 690 at 695; *Oldham Metropolitan BC v Att-Gen* [1993] Ch. 210.

[67] *Att-Gen v Warren* (1818) 2 Swan. 291 at 303; *Att-Gen v Hungerford* (1834) 2 Cl. & Fin. 357 at 374–375; *Att-Gen v Brettingham* (1840) 3 Beav. 91 at 95; *Att-Gen v South Sea Co.* (1841) 4 Beav. 453; *Att-Gen v Pilgrim* (1849) 12 Beav. 57 at 60; *Re Manchester New College*, above; *Att-Gen v Davey* (1854) 19 Beav. 521 at 525; *Re Clergy Orphan Corporation* [1894] 3 Ch. 145.

[68] *St. Mary Magdalen College, Oxford v Att-Gen* (1857) 6 H.L.Cas. 189 at 205.

[69] Express powers are not affected by the Settled Land Act 1925, s.29: *Re Booth and Southend-on-Sea Estate Co.'s Contract* [1927] 1 Ch. 579.

[70] Trusts of Land and Appointment of Trustees Act 1996, s.2(5).

[71] *ibid.*, s.8(1)(3). See generally CC28, *Disposing of Charity Land* (2000).

[72] For the power of the Charity Commissioners to prevent dealing in property, see Charities Act 1993, s.18(1)(iv) and para.9–043 below.

[73] *Oldham Metropolitan BC v Att-Gen* [1993] Ch. 210 at 222, *per* Dillon L.J. If the property is fundamental to the charitable purpose a cy-près scheme will be needed before sale can take place, see para.11–046 below.

[74] See para.6–012 above.

[75] Trustee Act 2000, s.8(3).

[76] *ibid.*, s.9(b).

Charity trustees also have power to deal with land for varying reasons deriving from a variety of statutes. Thus, they may grant land not exceeding one acre for the purposes of the School Sites Act 1841[77] and a similar area, with the consent of the Charity Commissioners, as a site for a literary or scientific institution.[78] If the trustees are liable to pay compensation for improvements to their tenants, they have power to grant a lease to relieve them from liability.[79]

Land held by them for charitable purposes may be disposed of in any manner they wish by county, district, London Borough, parish and community councils, and the parish trustees of a parish acting with the consent of the parish meeting.[80] The trustees cannot dispose of land in breach of any trust, covenant or agreement binding on them[81] and the usual restrictions under s.36 of the Charities Act 1993,[82] apply to the disposition of land.[83] Capital money received on a disposal must be applied in accordance with any directions given under the Charities Act 1993.[84] Charity trustees also have power to sell by agreement land subject to a compulsory purchase order.[85]

Restrictions on dealing—Whenever charity trustees sell, mortgage, lease or otherwise dispose of land they must have regard to the restrictions imposed by ss.36 to 40 of the Charities Act 1993.[86] The restrictions apply to dispositions of all land and not merely permanent endowment or functional land.[87] They do not apply if no interest in land is created, for example, if a licence only is granted.[88] **6–014**

By s.36 no land held in trust for a charity, other than an exempt charity, can be sold, leased or otherwise disposed of without an order of the Court or the Charity Commissioners unless the relevant conditions are complied with. The first condition is that the disposition must not be to a connected

---

[77] School Sites Act 1841, s.6.
[78] Literary and Scientific Institutions Act 1854, s.6.
[79] Landlord and Tenant Act 1927, s.14.
[80] Local Government Act 1972, ss. 123(1), 127(1) and 270(1). For the transfer property on the abolition of the Greater London Council and the Metropolitan Councils, see paras 5–013 *et seq.*, above.
[81] *ibid.*, s.131(1)(a).
[82] See below.
[83] Local Government Act 1972, s.131(3). The subsection also provides that the Act is not a statutory authority within the Charities Act 1993, s.36(9), enabling charitable property to be disposed of without an order.
[84] *ibid.*, ss.123(6) and 127(4).
[85] Compulsory Purchase Act 1965, ss.2, 3, Sch.1, para.2(2). This power is probably superfluous in view of the statutory power under the Trusts of Land and Appointment of Trustees Act 1996.
[86] Any provision in the trusts of a charity or an Act of Parliament or an order or scheme under the Education Act 1944 or 1973 which required the Commissioners to consent to any disposition of land of a charity ceased to have effect by s.36 of the Charities Act 1992. The restrictions only apply to the release by a charity of a rentcharge if less than 10 times the annual value of the rentcharge is received and to the release of a rentcharge which a charity is entitled to receive if it is not redeemed under ss.8 to 10 of the Rentcharges Act 1977, Charities Act 1993, s.40.
[87] Compare the former provision in Charities Act 1960, s.29. For the details of the former provisions see the 7th ed. of this work, p.419, *et seq.*
[88] See *Gray v Taylor* [1998] 1 W.L.R. 1093 (almshouse resident held to have a licence and not a lease).

person or a trustee or nominee for a connected person. Connected persons
are listed in Sch.5 to the 1993 Act and include a charity trustee, a close
relative of a trustee, an officer, agent or employee of the charity, an
institution or body corporate controlled by such person and a donor of
any land the charity, a close relative of or an institution or corporated
body controlled by him. The remaining conditions depend upon whether
the disposition is a sale or lease for more than seven years or a lease for
seven years or less. Further conditions are imposed if the land is held in
specie.

Sales and leases for more than seven years to unconnected person do
not require the consent of the Commissioners if three conditions are complied with before the agreement is entered into.[89] First the trustees must
have obtained and considered a written report on the proposed disposition
from a qualified surveyor, *i.e.* a fellow or a professional associate of the
Royal Institution of Chartered Surveyors or of the Incorporated Society
of Valuers and Auctioneers, or satisfy such other requirements as may be
specified in regulations.[90] The surveyor must have been instructed to act
exclusively for the charity and be reasonably believed by the trustees to be
of ability and experience in that particular type of land valuation. The
content of the surveyor's report must comply with the Charities (Qualified
Surveyors' Reports) Regulations 1992.[91] Secondly, the sale or lease must be
advertised in accordance with the surveyor's advice. Thirdly, the trustees
must decide that they are satisfied that the terms of the sale or lease are
the best that can reasonably be obtained for the charity. This condition
will probably be satisfied if all the trustees set the policy for disposals and
then delegate decisions as to particular sales or leases to a committee of
their number who report back at regular intervals.

6–015   The two conditions for the grant of a lease for seven years or less without the consent of the Charity Commissioners are to be found in section
36(5) of the 1993 Act. First, the trustees must consider the advice of a
person whom they reasonably believe to have the requisite ability and
experience to provide them with competent advice. Secondly, the trustees
must decide after considering the advice that the terms are the best that
can reasonably be obtained for the charity.

If the land is held on trusts which stipulate that it must be used for the
purposes of the charity, for example almshouses, no sale or lease is possible unless public notice has been given of the proposed disposition and
any representations made following such notice have been considered.[92]
This additional restriction does not apply if the disposition is with a view

---

[89] Charities Act 1993, s.36(2), (3).
[90] *ibid.*, s.36(4).
[91] (SI 1992/2980). The report should include a description of the land, whether it is leased by
or from the charity trustees, the easements or covenants to which the land is subject or the
benefit of which it enjoys, whether or not any buildings in it are in good repair, whether
alterations to any such buildings are desirable, advice as to the way the proposed disposition of the land is to be conducted, advice about VAT, the surveyor's opinion about the
value of the land and, where appropriate, his suggested alternative ways of disposing of
the land.
[92] Charities Act 1993, s.36(6).

to acquiring replacement property or it is the granting of a lease for two years or less[93] or the Commissioners have granted exemption.[94]

The charity trustees do not need to obtain the consent of the Commissioners or comply with the conditions in three situations set out in s.36(9): first, if there is general or special authority for the disposition by another statutory provision[95] or by a legally established scheme[96]; secondly if the disposition is to another charity for less than the best consideration and such a sale is within the authority of the charity trustees; and, thirdly, if it is a lease at less than the best rent with the intention that the property should be occupied for the purposes of the charity. A lease at a low rent by a charity for the relief of unemployment as part of a "business start up" is considered to come within the last exception.[97]

Charity trustees can mortgage charity land without the consent of the Charity Commissioners if they comply with the conditions laid down in s.38(2) of the 1993 Act or if they have other general or specific statutory authority.[98] To comply with s.38 the trustees must obtain and consider proper advice given in writing by a person whom the trustees reasonably believe is qualified by ability and practical experience in financial matters and who has no financial interest in making the loan in question; that person may be an officer or employee of the charity.[99] The advice must deal with three matters: first, whether the proposed loan is necessary in order for the charity to pursue the particular course of action for which the loan is sought; secondly, whether the terms are reasonable having regard to the fact that the borrower is a charity; and thirdly, the ability of the charity to repay the loan.[1]

There are several provisions to ensure that charity trustees comply with the relevant conditions when disposing of charity land. S.37(1) requires that any contract for sale or conveyance, lease or transfer of charity land must state[2] that the land is held by or in trust for a charity and that either restrictions on its disposition apply or that it is exempt. A similar statement[3] must be included where, as a result of the disposition, that land will become charity land.[4] Further, the charity trustees must certify in the instrument of disposition, if appropriate, that either the consent of the court of the Commissioners has been obtained or that they have power to effect the relevant disposition and the relevant conditions have been complied with, *i.e.* the conditions in ss.36(2) or (5).[5] If the charity land is

6–016

[93] *ibid.*, s.36(7).

[94] *ibid.*, s.36(8).

[95] For example, ss.8 to 10 of the Housing Associations Act 1985 as amended by s.78(1) of and Sch.6 to the Charities Act 1992 for housing associations.

[96] *i.e.* a scheme established by the court or the Commissioners; *Re Masons Orphanage and London and North Western Ry Co.* [1896] 1 Ch. 596. See also *Re Henry Smith's Charity Hartlepool* (1820) 20 Ch.D. 516 and *Att-Gen v National Hospital for Relief and Cure of the Paralysed and Epileptic* [1904] 2 Ch. 252.

[97] See RR3, *Charities for the Relief of Unemployment*, p.6.

[98] Charities Act 1993, s.38(1)(5) and see OG 22, *Borrowings and Mortgages*.

[99] *ibid.*, s.38(4).

[1] *ibid.*, s.38(3).

[2] For the form of statement, see Land Registry, *Charity Land Transactions*, Part B.

[3] For the form of statement, see Land Registry, *Charity Land Transactions*, Part B.

[4] Charities Act 1993, s.37(5).

[5] *ibid.*, s.37(2). For the relevant conditions see para.6–014 above.

registered, or the disposition is one which triggers registration, a restriction must be entered on the register either on the first disposition or on registration of title in the case of unregistered land.[6] A similar restriction must be entered if land becomes charity land as a result of a declaration of trust or a charity ceases to be exempt.[7] S.39 applies very similar provisions as to statements and certificates to mortgages of charity land.[8] The statements and certificates do not provide absolute protection for charity land because by ss.37(3) and 39(3) the facts stated in a certificate are conclusively presumed to be correct in favour of a person who acquires an interest in charity land for money or money's worth. Further, in favour of a purchaser in good faith acquiring an interest in charity land for money or money's worth, a disposition is valid whether or not the Commissioners have consented or whether or not the relevant conditions have been complied with.[9] This latter provision will only protect a person who is not aware that he is acquiring an interest in charity land.

Power to delegate

6–017 **Agents**—The difficulties encountered by charity trustees arising from a lack of any power to delegate anything other than administrative functions have been largely solved by s.11 of the Trustee Act 2000. The new power to employ agents is particularly important in enabling charity trustees to make maximum advantage of the wider powers of investment given by the same Act.[10]

Charity trustees can now delegate three functions to a person authorised as their agent. First, charity trustees can delegate any function consisting of carrying out a decision that the trustees have taken.[11] Secondly, any function relating to the investment of assets subject to the trust, including, in the case of land held as an investment, managing the land and creating or disposing of an interest in the land can be delegated by charity trustees.[12] This clearly covers discretionary investment management agreements. Thirdly, charity trustees can delegate any function relating to the raising of funds for the trust otherwise than by means of profits of the trade which is an integral part of carrying out the trust's charitable purposes.[13] To take account of future developments, the Secretary of State has power to prescribe further functions by order.[14]

---

[6] Charities Act 1993, s.37(8). For the form of restriction, see Land Registry, *Charity Land Transactions*, Part D.

[7] *ibid.*, s.37(10).

[8] See OG 22 C1, *Borrowings and Mortgages. Statements and Certificates in Mortgages Required by s.39.*

[9] Charities Act 1993, ss.37(4), 39(4). The subsections do not apply to a contract for sale— *Bayoumi v Women's Total Abstinence Educational Union Ltd* [2003] 1 All E.R. 864.

[10] See para.6–024 below and CC14, *Investment of Charitable Funds* (2003), paras 19, *et seq.*

[11] Trustee Act 2000, s.11(3)(a).

[12] *ibid.*, s.11(3)(b).

[13] *ibid.*, s.11(3)(c). A trade is "integral" if it is exercised in the course of carrying out a primary purpose of the charity or the work is mainly carried out by the beneficiaries and the profits are applied solely to the purposes of the charity, s.11(4).

[14] *ibid.*, s.11(3)(d).

The power to delegate to agents is not without limitation. The statutory duty of care[15] applies when delegating to an agent.[16] Whilst an agent may be paid,[17] trustees may not, unless it is reasonably necessary, authorise someone to act as their agent on terms which permit the agent to appoint a substitute, restrict the liability of the agent or his substitute or permit the agent to act in circumstances capable of giving rise to a conflict of interest.[18] The Charity Commissioners will accept that the test of reasonable necessity has been satisfied if charity trustees have good reason for wanting the services of a particular investment manager and that investment manager is insisting on one or more of the relevant terms.[19] In addition, any delegation of asset management functions by charity trustees must be in or evidenced in writing[20] and must be accompanied by a policy statement setting out how the function is to be exercised.[21] Any guidance in the policy statement must ensure that the agent will carry out his functions in the best interests of the charity.[22]

Nominees and Custodians—Charity trustees now have power to appoint a nominee to hold charity property.[23] They also have power to appoint a custodian to undertake safe custody of the assets of the trust.[24] The appointment of a nominee or custodian must be in or evidenced in writing[25] and the trustees must exercise the statutory duty of care when appointing.[26] A nominee or custodian may be paid[27] but only if it is reasonably necessary can the appointment include terms permitting the appointment of a substitute, or limiting liability of the nominee or custodian or allowing the nominee or custodian to act in circumstances capable of giving rise to conflict of interest.[28]

    6–018

Charity trustees can only appoint persons to be nominees or custodians who carry on business which consists of or includes acting as a nominee or custodian or who are a body corporate which is controlled by the trustees or recognised under s.9 of the Administration of Justice Act 1985.[29] In addition, charity trustees must act in accordance with the Guidance given by the Charity Commissioners when selecting a nominee or custodian.[30] The Guidance[31] requires charity trustees to ensure that the

---

[15] For the statutory duty of care see para.6–025 below.
[16] Trustee Act 2000, Sch.1, para.3(1)(a).
[17] *ibid.*, s.14(1).
[18] *ibid.*, s.14(2)(3).
[19] See OG 86 B3, *Power to employ agents and delegate functions to them*, section 3.
[20] Trustee Act 2000, s.15(1).
[21] *ibid.*, s.15(2)(4). For guidance as to the contents of a policy statement see, CC14, *Investment of Charitable Funds* (2003), paras 144, *et seq.*
[22] Trustee Act 2000, s.15(3).
[23] *ibid.*, s.16.
[24] *ibid.*, s.17.
[25] *ibid.*, s.16(2), 17(3).
[26] *ibid.*, Sch.1, para.3(b)(c), for the statutory duty of care see para.6–025 below.
[27] *ibid.*, s.20(1).
[28] *ibid.*, s.20(2)(3).
[29] *ibid.*, s.19. S.9 of the 1985 Act, covers solicitors' nominee companies.
[30] Trustee Act 2000, s.19(4).
[31] CC42, *Appointing Nominees and Custodians Guidance under s.19(4) of the Trustee Act 2000* (2001).

trust property held by the nominee or custodian remains in the beneficial ownership of the charity and that there is not merely a contractual arrangement with a nominee or custodian. Charity trustees are also directed to assess risk carefully before appointing a nominee or custodian in another jurisdiction or where there is possibility of conflict of interest. The Guidance is strengthened by a reminder to charity trustees to ensure that any nominee or custodian should agree to satisfactory reporting arrangements.

Charity trustees are required to keep under review the arrangements for the appointment of any agent, nominee or custodian and to consider if there is any need to intervene, for example, by giving directions or revoking the appointment. In the case of an agent appointed to manage assets, the policy statement should be reviewed both for applicability and compliance.[32] Provided that the trustees have complied with the statutory duty of care[33] when carrying out this duty of review and on the original appointment, they are not liable for the acts or defaults of any agent, nominee or custodian.[34] An appointment of an agent, nominee or custodian is not invalidated by any failure of the charity trustees to act within the limits of their powers to make such an appointment.[35]

Power of the Charity Commissioners to authorise dealings

6–019   If the trustees wish to deal with charity property in a way beneficial to the trust but have no power to carry out the particular transaction the Charity Commissioners may by order made under s.26 of the 1993 Act[36] sanction the action. The Commissioners may only sanction the proposed action by the trustees if it is expedient in the interests of the charity. If so sanctioned the action is deemed to be properly done in the exercise of the powers exercisable by the charity trustees in the administration of the charity.[37] Such an order may be made so as to authorise a particular transaction, compromise or the like, or a particular application of property, or so as to give a more general authority and (without prejudice to the generality of this provision) in particular may authorise a charity to use common premises, or to employ a common staff, or otherwise combine for any purpose of administration with any other charity.[38] The order may contain directions as to the meeting of expenditure.[39]

---

[32] Trustee Act 2000, s.22 and see CC14, *Investment of Charitable Funds* (2003), paras 153, *et seq.*
[33] Trustee Act 2002, Sch.1, para.3, for the statutory duty of care see para.6–025 below.
[34] *ibid.*, s.23(1).
[35] *ibid.*, s.24(1).
[36] See para.9–007 below.
[37] Charities Act 1993, s.26(1). Certain acts prohibited by Act of Parliament cannot be authorised s.26(5), (6); but see *Beaumont v The National Trust for Places of Historic Interest and Natural Beauty* [1984] Ch. Com. Rep., App.F.
[38] *ibid.*, s.26(2).
[39] *ibid.*, s.26(3), (4).

Duties

Charitable trusts do not, in general, differ from other trusts so far as **6–020** duties are concerned, and the reader is referred to books on equity where the matter is dealt with in full.[40] Thus, the usual duties of trustees, for example, of not delegating the trust and acting impartially between the beneficiaries apply to charity trustees.[41] The Charities Act 1993 imposes duties on charity trustees to register,[42] to keep accounts,[43] to have accounts audited or independently examined[44] and make an annual report[45] and an annual return to the charity Commissioners.[46] These duties also form part of the Charity Commissioners powers of monitoring and control and the detailed provisions are considered in Chapter 9. Certain of a charity trustee's duties are dealt with in detail below where they differ from an ordinary trustee's duties or are of particular concern to charity trustees. Cases of breach of charitable trusts have been selected which may prove useful as precedents.

Duty to comply with the terms of the trust

The main duty of charity trustees is to carry out the trust according to **6–021** the terms set out in the trust instrument;[47] charity trustees are not delegates of the body that appoints them.[48] Thus, it is a breach of trust for the trustees to conceal the existence of the trusts by not communicating them to the persons interested,[49] or to retain the charity funds in their hands without applying them for the purposes for which they should be applied,[50] for example, by failing to pay a rent to a charity in whose favour it was charged.[51]

It is similarly a breach of trust for trustees to divert a fund intended for one charitable object to another, for example, from the poor of one parish to the poor of another parish not designated by the donor,[52] or for general purposes of a town where specific purposes have been designated,[53] or for the repair of a different church from that directed to be benefited.[54]

---

[40] See, *e.g. Snell's Principles of Equity* (30th ed.), pp.245, *et seq*; Underhill and Hayton, *Law of Trusts and Trustees* (15th ed.), pp.465, *et seq*.
[41] A useful summary of a charity trustee's duties is to be found in the leaflet CC3(a), *Responsibilities of Charity Trustees* issued by the Charity Commissioners.
[42] Charities Act 1993, s.3(7); see para.1–027, above.
[43] *ibid.*, s.41; see para.9–020, below.
[44] *ibid.*, ss.42, 43; see para.9–028, below.
[45] *ibid.*, s.45; see para.9–032, below.
[46] *ibid.*, s.47; see para.9–010, below.
[47] *Duke of Charitable Uses*, at p.116.
[48] See RR7, *The Independence of Charities From the State* (2001), para.12.
[49] *Att-Gen v Alford* (1854) 4 De G.M. & G. 843 at 852.
[50] *ibid.*
[51] *Kennington Hastings Case* (1612) Duke 71.
[52] *Att-Gen v Brandreth* (1842) 1 Y. & C.Ch.Cas. 200.
[53] *Mann v Ballet* (1682) 1 Vern. 43.
[54] *Re St. John the Evangelist* (1889) 4 T.L.R. 69 and see also *Re Church Estate Charity Wandsworth* (1871) 6 Ch. App. 296.

Again, it is a breach of trust for trustees of several charities to apply the funds of one to the objects of another,[55] although this may not be the case where one fund is given for several institutions.[56] Nor may they treat as income a gift of a capital sum intended for investment.[57] Further, an interest in half of the income of an undivided fund is different from the whole income of a divided half of that fund, and if trustees make an improper division, they will be liable to account.[58]

6–022   In many of the above cases a *cy-près* scheme may be desirable, but it is not for the trustees to deal with the funds on their own authority,[59] even by the direction of the original subscribers of the charitable funds or (where the trust is for the benefit of a particular parish or place) of a meeting of the parishioners or inhabitants.[60]

Many examples of breach of the duty to observe the trust can be found in relation to religious trusts. Thus, where the benefit of a charity is restricted to persons holding a particular form of religious belief, it is a breach of trust to extend the benefit of the charity to persons not professing that belief.[61] Even if the charity is not established for a purely religious purpose but the intention is expressed that only persons professing a particular form of belief shall be the objects, that intention will be enforced.[62]

It is also a breach of trust to convert a chapel established for the observance of a particular form of religious belief to any other form of worship.[63] Nor can it be so converted even though the trustees and the entire congregation consent, and *a fortiori* if there are in fact dissentients.[64] Thus it was held that a chapel established for the doctrines of the Established Church of Scotland could not be converted to the use of members of the Free Church.[65] Similarly it was held that the Free Church, where property

---

[55] *Att-Gen v Corporation of Newbury* (1837) C.P.Coop. 72 at 77; *Andrews v M'Guffog* (1886) 11 A.C. 313.

[56] *Att-Gen v Geary* (1817) 3 Mer. 513.

[57] *Att-Gen v Belgrave Hospital* [1910] 1 Ch. 73.

[58] *Re Freeston's Charity* [1978] 1 W.L.R. 741, CA.

[59] *Att-Gen v Coopers Co.* (1813) 19 Ves. 187; *Att-Gen v Vivian* (1826) 1 Russ. 226 at 237; *Att-Gen v Bushby* (1857) 24 Beav 299; *Ward v Hipwell* (1862) 3 Giff. 547; *Re Campden Charities* (1881) 18 Ch.D. 310 at 328, 329. As to the duty to apply for a scheme, see para.6–033, below.

[60] *Att-Gen v Kell* (1840) 2 Beav. 575; and see *Att-Gen v Bovill* (1840) 1 Ph. 762.

[61] *Shore v Wilson* (1843) 9 Cl. & F. 355; *Drummond v Att-Gen for Ireland* (1850) 2 H.L.C. 837; *Att-Gen v Calvert* (1857) 23 Beav. 248; and see *Att-Gen v Pearson* (1817) 3 Mer. 353 at 409, 410, *Re Ilminster School* (1858) 2 De G. & F. 535; *Att-Gen v Anderson* (1888) 57 L.J.Ch. 543 at 550.

[62] *Att-Gen v Calvert* (1857) 23 Beav. 248 at 257.

[63] *Craigdallie v Aikman* (1812) 1 Dow 1; *Foley v Wontner* (1820) 2 J. & W. 245 at 247; *Dill v Watson* (1836) 2 Jones' Ex.R. 48 at 49; *Milligan v Mitchell* (1837) 3 My. & C. 72 at 73; *Broom v Summers* (1841) 11 Sim. 353; *Att-Gen v Welsh* (1846) 4 Ha. 572; *Att-Gen v Munro* (1848) 2 De G. & Sm. 122; *Att-Gen v Murdock* (1850) 7 Ha. 445; *Free Church of Scotland v Overtown* [1904] A.C. 515.

[64] *Broom v Summers*, above; *Att-Gen v Welsh*, above; *Att-Gen v Murdoch* (1850) 1 De G.M. & G. 86 at 114; *Att-Gen v Corporation of Rochester* (1854) 5 De G.M. & G. 797; *Ward v Hipwell* (1862) 3 Giff. 547; *Att-Gen v Aust* (1865) 13 L.T. 235; *Att-Gen v Anderson* (1888) 57 L.T.Ch. 543; *Re Hutchinson's Trusts* [1914] 1 Ir.R. 271.

[65] *Craigdallie v Aikman* (1812) 1 Dow 1; *Att-Gen v Welsh* (1846) 4 Ha. 572; *Att-Gen v Munro* (1848) 2 De G.& Sm. 122; *Att-Gen v Murdoch* (1850) 7 Ha. 455; *Free Church of Scotland v Overtoun* [1904] A.C. 515 at 613, *et seq.* See, however, *Westwood v McKie* (1849) 21 L.T. 165; and *cf. Att-Gen v Wilson* (1848) 16 Sim. 210; *Cairncross v Lorimer* (1861) 3 Mac. 827.

was concerned, had no power to alter or vary the doctrine of the church, or to unite with another body, namely, the United Free Church, which did not profess the doctrine of the church, and, accordingly, it was held to be a breach of trust to convert the property which originally belonged to the former body to the use of the latter.[66]

Moreover, even though power may be expressly given to the majority to make new laws or alter old ones, such a power does not extend to enable the majority to alter the fundamental trusts, but only to vary the laws and make new ones so far only as may be consistent with the primary trusts.[67] Similarly it is not for the trustees to determine whether the existing congregation hold the doctrines required to entitle them to the benefit of the charity or not, or to take steps to eject them on the ground that they do not hold the appropriate doctrines: that is a question for the court.[68] However, in all matters not involving an interference with the trusts there is nothing to prevent the congregation from effecting any changes they choose. If, therefore, it is no part of the essence of the trust that a particular doctrine should be inculcated, the majority of the members may alter the usage of the congregation with regard to it. Thus where the trusts of a chapel were for a congregation of Particular Baptists, and it appeared that among the Particular Baptists the doctrines of strict and free communion were both admitted, it was held that the majority of members might, notwithstanding long contrary usage, adopt strict or free communion, as they should from time to time determine, as it was not one of the fundamental doctrines of Particular Baptists.[69] So also the majority may make decisions as to the internal regulations of a chapel,[70] or new bye laws, provided that they are not inconsistent with the body of rules laid down by the governing instrument.[71]

6–023

If the trustees have for a long series of years recognised the title of their *cestuis que trust*, they cannot turn round on them and refuse to do so any longer.[72] In the same way, the dissentient minority of a congregation may be bound by acquiescence. Thus, where the majority of a congregation, including the minister, joined another dissenting body which was considered to hold the same doctrines, it was held that a small minority of the original congregation, who had raised no opposition at the time, could not, after the lapse or more than three years, maintain a suit to have it declared that the chapel was to be held for the use only of those who adhered to the original doctrine.[73] However, a "benignant" construction is

---

[66] *Free Church of Scotland v Overtoun*, above. See also *Att-Gen v Anderson* (1888) 57 L.J.Ch. 543 (Protestant dissenters). There may be a *cy-près* occasion, see *Varsani v Jesani* [1999] Ch. 219 and para.11–050 below.

[67] *Milligan v Mitchell* (1837) 3 My. & C. 72 at 83; see *Att-Gen v Murdoch* (1850) 1 De G.M. & G. 86 at 114.

[68] *Newsome v Flowers* (1861) 10 W.R. 26.

[69] *Att-Gen v Gould* (1860) 28 Beav. 485; *Att-Gen v Etheridge* (1863) 11 W.R. 199.

[70] *Att-Gen v Anderson* (1888) 57 L.J.Ch. 543 at 549.

[71] *Att-Gen v Smythies* (1833) 2 R. & M. 717 at 749. See also *Att-Gen v Smart* (1747) 1 Ves. Sen. 72.

[72] *Newsome v Flowers* (1861) 10 W.R. 26; and see *Neligan v Roche* (1874) 7 Ir.Eq. 332.

[73] *Cairncross v Lorimer* (1861) 3 Macq. 827.

placed upon charitable gifts.[74] Thus expenditure may be allowed, although it would not be permissible if the trust were read narrowly.[75]

Duty of investment

6–024   The powers and duties of trustees of a charity, in relation to investment of trust funds, are governed, in general, in the same manner as in the case of non-charitable trusts by the terms of the trust instrument (if any) and by the general law of trusts relating to investment.[76] Thus, for example, a corporation incorporated by royal charter cannot, by the making of rules or regulations confer upon itself powers wider than those conferred upon it by the general law or the royal charter.[77] Trustees were finally freed from the shackles of the Trustee Investment Act 1961 on February 1, 2001 with the coming into force of the Trustee Act 2000.[78] By s.3 of that Act trustees have power to make any kind of investment they could make if they were absolutely entitled to the assets of the trust. Charity trustees are enabled to take full advantage of this wide power by the inclusion in the Act of wider powers of delegation[79] and power to appoint nominees and custodians.[80] This general power of investment[81] does not give charity trustees[82] complete freedom in relation to investments. The power is subject to certain statutory safeguards in that the duty of care[83] and the standard investment criteria must be observed.[84] The general power of investment does not permit trustees to invest in land[85] and is subject to any restriction or exclusion[86] imposed by the trust instrument or by any enactment or any provision in any subordinate legislation,[87] unless the provision is in a trust instrument made before August 3, 1961.[88]

---

[74] See para.4–002, above.
[75] *Att-Gen v Stamford Corporation* (1747) 2 Swan. 591; *Att-Gen v Foyster* (1794) 1 Aust. 116, 122; *Wilkinson v Malin* (1832) 2 Tyr. HL 544 at 570; *Anderson v Wrights of Glasgow* (1865) 12 L.T. 805, HL.
[76] See generally *Lewin on Trusts* (17th ed.), pp.879, *et seq.*; Underhill and Hayton, *Law of Trusts and Trustees* (15th ed.), pp.563, *et seq.*
[77] *Soldiers', Sailors' and Airmen's Family Association v Att-Gen* [1968] 1 W.L.R. 313.
[78] Trustee Act 2000 (Commencement) Order 2001 (SI 2001/49).
[79] See para.6–017 above.
[80] See para.6–018 above.
[81] So defined by Trustee Act 2000, s.3(2).
[82] The power is not available to trustees of common investment funds and common deposit funds, s.38.
[83] See para.6–025 below. The restrictions do not apply to so-called "social investment" or "programme related investment" which is using charity property to assist beneficiaries, as opposed to producing an income, see CC Useful Guidelines, *Charities and Social Investment* (2002).
[84] See para.6–025 below.
[85] Trustee Act 2000, s.3(3) but there is power to acquire land in s.8, see para.6–012 above and CC 33, *Acquiring Land* (2001), paras 12, *et seq.*
[86] A provision will only be a "restriction or exclusion" if it is a specific direction to exclude certain types of investment, see Law Com. Rep. No. 260, "Trustees' Powers and Duties" (1999), p.99. See also CC14, *Investment of Charitable Funds* (2003), paras 26, *et seq.*
[87] Trustee Act 2000, s.6(1)(b).
[88] *ibid.*, s.7(2), *i.e.* before the coming into force of the Trustee Investment Act 1961.

Charity trustees only have power to purchase something which is in law an investment, *i.e.* something from which a return can be made. It is now accepted that earlier restrictions requiring an income return[89] no longer apply and that an income or capital return or both is permissible.[90] This wide approach to what is an investment was set out by Nicholls V.C. in *Harries v Church Commissioners for England*[91] when referring to the general principles applicable to the exercise of the power of the investment by charity trustees. He said[92]:

> "[T]he purposes of the trust will be best served by the trustees seeking to obtain therefrom maximum return, whether by way of income or capital growth; which is consistent with commercial prudence."

The Charity Commissioners take the view that the purchase of assets such as gold or works of art with a view to resale is not an investment. Nor do they regard the purchase of land with a view to development and sale as an investment.[93] The use of derivatives is regarded by the Commissioners as permissible if it is ancillary to the investment process but not otherwise.[94] Other types of investment, such as hedge funds and the underwriting of new shares, whilst within the wide definition of investment may well be rejected by charity trustees as too risky[95] after exercising their duty of care.[96]

When exercising the general power of investment, or any other power of investment, charity trustees must exercise the statutory duty of care.[97] The duty also applies when trustees are taking advice about investments or reviewing investments.[98] The duty of care is set out in s.1 of the Trustee Act 2000 and requires a trustee to exercise such care and skill as is reasonable in the circumstances having regard in particular to any special knowledge or experience that the trustee has or holds himself out as having. Accordingly, a higher duty of care in relation to investment decisions will be expected from a trustee who has investment analysis skills but not in relation to, say, employment decisions. If the trustee is acting in the course of a business or profession, what is reasonable care will be assessed against any special knowledge or experience that it is reasonable to expect of someone in that business or profession.[99] The duty of care can be restricted by the trust instrument.[1]

6–025

---

[89] See *Re Wragg* [1919] 2 Ch. 58 at 64, *per* P.O. Lawrence J.
[90] See Explanatory Notes to the Trustee Act 2000.
[91] [1992] 1 W.L.R. 1241.
[92] *ibid.* at 1246.
[93] See CC14, *Investment of Charitable Funds* (2003), para.12.
[94] *ibid.*, paras 15, *et seq.*
[95] *ibid.*, paras 98, *et seq.*
[96] See para.6–025 below.
[97] Trustee Act 2000, Sch.1(a).
[98] *ibid.*, Sch.1(b).
[99] This codifies the higher duty of care of professional trustees established by *Bartlett v Barclays Bank Trust Co Ltd* [1980] Ch. 515.
[1] Trustee Act 2000, s.6(1)(b).

Charity trustees must have regard to the standard investment criteria when both investing[2] and when carrying out their duty to review investments.[3] The modern portfolio theory of investment, *i.e.* evaluating investment decisions in the context of the trust portfolio as a whole, whilst endorsed by the Law Commission in the report leading to the Trustee Act 2000[4] was not specifically included in the 2000 Act. The standard investment criteria are consistent with the modern portfolio theory of investment and may well be interpreted with reference to the theory.[5] The standard investment criteria require trustees to consider the suitability to the trust of the investments proposed and the need for diversification of investments.[6] Charity trustees are required to consider not only the suitability of investments of the same kind as the particular investments proposed but also the suitability of that particular investment as an investment of that kind.[7] This requirement to consider suitability extends beyond pure investment criteria to considering the investments within the context of the objects of the trust and ethical investment considerations.[8]

The standard investment criterion in relation to diversification is to consider the need for diversification of investments for the trust in so far as it is appropriate in the circumstances of the trust.[9] This criterion has particular relevance if a charity is considering investment in a wholly or substantially owned trading company.[10] There may well be circumstances, however, in which it is appropriate for a charitable trust to have a far greater percentage of its portfolio in one investment, for example, where a charitable trust has been set up with a gift of a major shareholding in one company.[11] In considering diversification, charity trustees will need to have regard to a number of factors including, any terms of the trust deed or deed of gift prohibiting disposal of a holding without the consent of the donor or other third party, links between a holding and the objects of the charity, investment policy generally and the fact that the trust is charitable. The need for diversification in the case of smaller charities may be met by using a common investment fund[12] or, in the case of charities with common trusteeship, a pooling scheme.[13]

6–026   Charity trustees are under a duty to obtain and consider proper advice before exercising the general power of investment or any other power of

[2] Trustee Act 2000, s.4(1).
[3] *ibid.*, s.4(2).
[4] See Law Comm. Rep. No. 260 "Trustees' Powers and Duties" (1999), p.23.
[5] See Lord Nicholls, "Trustees and Their Broader Community: Where Duty, Morality and Ethics Converge", (1995) Tru. Law Int. 71.
[6] Trustee Act 2000, s.4(3).
[7] *ibid.*, s.4(3)(a).
[8] Explanatory Notes to the Trustee Act 2000 and see CC14, *Investment of Charitable Funds* (2003), para.56. For the extent to which ethical considerations can be taken into account see para.6–026 below.
[9] Trustee Act 2000, s.4(3)(b).
[10] See CC14, *Investment of Charitable Funds* (2003), para.72.
[11] See *Steel v Wellcome Trustees Ltd* [1988] 1 W.L.R. 167 at 173 where Hoffman J. accepted that 90 per cent of the charity's investment would remain in Wellcome plc for some time.
[12] See para.6–028 below.
[13] The general investment power in s.3 of the Trustee Act 2000 means that shared control investments are now possible. For the Charity Commissioners' practice in relation to pooling schemes see OG 49, *Pooling Schemes and Pool Charities*.

investment. The advice should have regard to the standard investment criteria.[14] Similarly, advice must be taken when reviewing investments.[15] To be proper advice, the advice must be obtained from a person who is reasonably believed by the trustees to be qualified to give it by his ability in and practical experience of financial and other matters relating to the proposed investment.[16] Charity trustees need not take advice, however, if they reasonably conclude that in all the circumstances it is unnecessary or inappropriate to do so. Relevant factors will clearly be the size of the fund and the type of the investment.[17]

The changes introduced by the Trustee Act 2000 do not affect the duty of charity trustees in formulating their investment policy to consider only the purposes of the trusts and not to do anything which conflicts with those purposes. They must generally invest in such a way as to provide the greatest financial benefits for the beneficiaries.[18] Similarly, in determining whether to sell an investment they should consider only investment criteria.[19] Charity trustees should not use charity funds as a means of making moral statements at the expense of the charity. They should not, however, invest in companies which are pursing activities directly contrary to the purposes and trusts of their charity even if the result is some financial detriment to the charity.[20] The appropriateness of charity trustees following an ethical investment policy was considered by Sir Donald Nicholls V.C. in *Harries v Church Commissioners for England*[21] where he concluded that the circumstances in which charity trustees are bound and entitled to make a financially disadvantageous investment decision for ethical reasons are extremely limited. He said this[22]:

> "There will also be some cases, again I suspect comparatively rare, when trustees' holdings of particular investments might hamper a charity's work either by making potential recipients of aid unwilling to be helped because of the source of the charity's money, or by alienating some of those who support the charity financially. In these cases the trustees will need to balance the difficulties they would encounter, or likely financial loss they would sustain, if they were to hold the investments against the risk of financial detriment if those investments were excluded from their portfolio. The greater the risk of financial detriment, the more certain the trustees should be of countervailing disadvantages to the charity before they incur that risk."

There is nothing to prevent charity trustees having a socially responsible investment policy provided that the overall duty to provide the best

---

[14] Trustee Act 2000, s.5(1).
[15] *ibid.*, s.5(2).
[16] *ibid.*, s.5(4).
[17] See CC14, *Investment of Charitable Funds* (2003), paras 52–53.
[18] *Cowan v Scargill* [1985] Ch. 270.
[19] See *Public Trustee v Cooper* (2000) 2 W.T.L.R. 901 (Effect of sale on employees of a company not relevant when deciding whether to sell a large holding of shares in that company).
[20] *Harries v Church Commissioners for England* [1993] 2 All E.R. 300 at 304.
[21] [1993] 2 All E.R. 300.
[22] *ibid.* at 304.

financial returns for the beneficiaries is complied with.[23] Charity trustees, however, cannot use their powers of investment to make, say, loans at low rates of interest to an organisation or individual which is carrying out a project that will aid the charity's beneficiaries. A charity may well be able to make this type of social- or programme-related investment to assist projects within its objects by using other powers, for example, that to make grants.[24]

6–027   Charity trustees are under the usual duty when exercising their powers of investment to have regard to the needs of present and future beneficiaries in an even-handed way.[25] The rules[26] for determining the treatment of investment returns from capital funds, designating particular returns as income and capital have, in recent years, caused trustees to be in breach of that duty unless they selected investments which gave a lower return than would otherwise be possible. Changes in the way companies make returns, for example, special dividends, also added to the difficulties in complying with the duty.[27] In the light of these developments, the Charity Commissioners will now give individual charities by order, under s.26 of the Charities Act 1993, power to allocate investment returns at their discretion from assets held on trust for investment. Charity trustees with such power will therefore be able to invest on a total return basis.[28] The power, if granted, is made subject to a number of safeguards. The statutory duty of care[29] applies to the exercise of the power to allocate an appropriate part of the unapplied total return to the trust for application (income), as does the duty of even-handedness between all beneficiaries. Proper advice must be taken and the use of the power must be disclosed by charity trustees in their annual report.[30] The form of order[31] giving power to adopt a total return approach to investment requires the trustees to establish a rational policy to periodically determine what part of the unapplied total return is from time to time to be applied to the trust for application (income) and to give consideration to the amount of total return which will remain unapplied after the allocation to the trust for application (income).[32] This recognises that it is possible for there to be a negative investment return in a particular year.

[23] See R. Meakin, "Socially Responsible Investment by Charities", (2001) 7 C.L.P.R. 137 and CC14, *Investment of Charitable Funds* (2003), paras 80, *et seq.*
[24] See CC Useful Guidelines, *Charities and Social Investment*. See also [2002] Ch. Com. Dec. November 1 (The Charity Bank Limited).
[25] See *Nestle v National Westminster Bank plc* [1994] 1 All ER 118 at 136, *per* Staughton LJ.
[26] For the detailed rules see Underhill and Hayton, *Law of Trust and Trustees* (15th ed.), pp.500, *et seq.*
[27] See Charity Commissioners Consultation Document, *Endowed Charities—A Fresh Approach to Investment Returns?* (2000).
[28] For the Charity Commissioners' detailed practice on the granting and exercise of this power see OG 83, *Endowed Charities: A Total Return Approach to Investments.* There is some dispute as to whether the Charity Commissioners have the power to make such a order. See Hill J. and Smith J., "Permanent Endowment and Total Return" (2001) 7 C.L.P.R. 125; Dutton J., "A Total Return Approach to Investment?" (2001) 7 C.L.P.R. 131.
[29] See para.6–025 above.
[30] See OG 83 B2, *Directions Relating to the Use of the Power.*
[31] See OG 83 C5, *Model Order Authorising Trustees' Adoption of a Total Return Approach to Investment.*
[32] See OG 83 B3, *Allocating the Unapplied Total Return.*

Common investment and deposit schemes—In order to make effective use of   **6–028**
the wide general powers of investment in the Trustee Act 2000 a substantial fund is necessary so that risk can be spread and management expenses
assimilated without difficulty. However, many charities have extremely
small trust funds and, if special provision had not previously been made,
a large number would not in practice be able to avail themselves effectually of the facilities provided by the Act and to diversify their funds.[33] The
Charities Act 1960[34] contained provision to establish common investment
schemes, for the joint administration of a number of charitable trust funds
for the purposes of investment. Common investment schemes had been
made before in particular cases by statute,[35] and the court,[36] and the Charity
Commissioners always had the power to make schemes of a similar nature,
but no general provisions were available until the passing of the Charities
Act 1960.

The provisions are now contained in section 24 of the Charities Act
1993 and enable the court and the Charity Commissioners' by order to
make schemes, known as "common investment schemes," for the establishment of common investment funds under trusts providing (a) for property transferred to the fund by or on behalf of a charity participating in
the scheme to be invested under the control of trustees appointed to manage the fund; and (b) for the participating charities to be entitled (subject
to the provisions of the scheme) to the capital and income of the fund in
shares determined by reference to the amount or value[37] of the property
transferred to it by or on behalf of each of them and to the value of the
fund at the time of the transfers.[38]

The court or the Commissioners may make a common investment
scheme on the application of two or more charities.[39] This was given a
wide interpretation in *Re University of London Charitable Trusts*[40] where
Wilberforce J. held that this provision, taken with the definition of "charity"
and "institution" in section 46(1) of the Charities Act 1960, enabled an
application to be made by the trustees of any two or more charitable trusts
for a pooling scheme, notwithstanding the fact that, as in that case, the
trustees of such trusts were the same.

---

[33] For the duty to have regard to diversification, see para.6–025 above.

[34] s.22.

[35] See the Universities and Colleges (Trusts) Act 1943 (6 & 7 Geo. 6, c.9), which enabled the
Universities of Oxford and Cambridge and the colleges in those universities, and
Winchester College, to make schemes providing for funds to be administered as a single
fund; the schemes are to be approved by Order in Council. The Act deals, however, only
with the capital of trust funds and does not permit an alteration of beneficial interests;
ibid. s.2(1); and see *Re Freeston's Charity* [1978] 1 W.L.R. 741 at 753 at 755, CA. Private
Acts have established common investment schemes for other universities; see, *e.g.*
Liverpool University Act 1931 (21 & 22 Geo. 5, c.xxx); Birmingham University Act 1948
(11 & 12 Geo. 6, c.x).

[36] See, *e.g. Re Royal Society's Charitable Trusts* [1956] Ch. 87; *Re University of London
Charitable Trusts* [1964] Ch. 282.

[37] Actual value, whether market value or assessed in some other way, not par value.

[38] s.24(1).

[39] s.24(2).

[40] [1964] Ch. 282.

6–029   It is likely that this power will be used less frequently in the future. One consequence of the wide general power of investment in s.3 of the Trustee Act 2000[41] is that charity trustees now have power to make investments jointly with others. Thus, trustees of two or more charities can create a common investment pool without reference to the court of the Charity Commissioners.[42]

A common investment scheme may be made in terms admitting any charity to participate, or, alternatively, the scheme may restrict the right to participate in it.[43]

A common investment scheme may provide for the establishment, investment, management and winding up of a common investment fund, including in particular (a) the remuneration of trustees holding or managing the fund; (b) restricting the size of the fund or regulating, as to time, amount or otherwise, the right to transfer property or withdraw from the fund, and enabling sums to be advanced from the fund on loan to a participating charity pending the withdrawal of property from the fund by the charity; (c) enabling income to be withheld from distribution with a view to avoiding fluctuations in the amounts distributed and, generally, for regulating distributions of income; (d) enabling money to be borrowed temporarily for the purpose of meeting payments to be made out of the funds; (e) for the determination by the trustees managing the fund of questions arising under the scheme as to the right of a charity to participate or as to the rights of participating charities or as to any other matter; and (f) regulating the accounts and information to be supplied to participating charities.[44]

The Charity Commissioners established the Charities Official Investment Fund, a common investment fund in which all charities may participate in 1962. The Charities Official Investment Fund contains power to invest in "any investments or property of any sort real or personal and whether or not being investment or property authorised by the general law for the investment or trust funds, or upon loan upon the security of any property of any description or without security."

There are now a number of schemes run by commercial providers, some of which have a restricted investment policy.[45] The restriction may be one justified by the objectives of the investing charities, for example, a common investment fund open to health charities which is permanently restricted from investing in tobacco shares. A common investment fund may be open to all charities but restricted to a particular type of investment, for example, land. The Charity Commissioners have issued model structures for common investment funds.[46] The model structures with the requirement for a common investment fund to be managed by a corporate trustee and a fund manager with an optional board of individuals was issued to take account of the removal of the status of exempt person

---

[41] See para.6–024 above.
[42] See CC14, *Investment of Charitable Funds* (2003), paras 38, *et seq.*
[43] s.24(3).
[44] s.24(4).
[45] See [1996] Ch. Com. Rep., para.54.
[46] See Ch. Com., "Common Investment Funds: Policy Statement" (1996).

under the Financial Services Act 1986 from a manager of a common investment fund.[47] A common investment fund is now subject to the supervision of the Financial Services Authority under the Financial Services and Markets Act 2000.

A scheme under s.24 may make provision for enabling sums to be deposited by or on behalf of a charity on the basis (though this is subject to the provisions of the scheme) that the charity will be entitled to repayment of the sums deposited together with interest at a rate determined by the scheme. The amount reasonably required for liabilities of the fund for repayment of deposits and interest, including amounts required by way of reserve, are to be excluded from the amount of capital and income to be shared between charities participating otherwise than by way of deposit,[48] though they will be entitled to any capital appreciation on such deposits as may accrue.

There is no power under s.24 to set up a common deposit fund uncon- **6–030** nected with a common investment fund.[49] A new power was introduced in the Charities Act 1992 and the relevant provision is now s.25 of the 1993 Act. By that section the court or the Commissioners have power by order to make schemes known as "common deposit schemes" to establish common deposit funds under trusts which provide (a) for sums to be deposited by or on behalf of a charity participating in the scheme and invested under the control of the trustees appointed to manage the fund; and (b) for any such charity to be entitled (subject to the provisions of the scheme) to repayment of any sums so deposited and to interest thereon at a rate determined under the scheme.[50] Common deposit schemes and funds are subject to the same provisions as common investment schemes and funds as far as participation and management are concerned.[51]

A number of miscellaneous provisions in ss.24 and 25 of the Charities **6–031** Act 1993 are also noteworthy:

(a) Except in so far as a common investment scheme or common deposit fund provides to the contrary, the rights under it of a participating charity are not capable of being assigned or charged.[52] Nor are the trustees required or entitled to take account of any trust or other equity affecting a participating charity or its property or rights.[53] The trustees of the fund deal only with the trustees of the charity.

(b) The investment powers of every charity include the power to participate in common investment schemes and common deposit funds unless this power is excluded by a provision specifically

---

[47] Financial Services Act 1986, s.45(1)(j) and Financial Services Act 1986 (Restriction of Exemption) Order 1999 (SI 1999/2999).
[48] Charities Act 1993, s.24(5).
[49] [1989] Ch. Com. Rep., para.121.
[50] s.25(1).
[51] By s.25(2)(a), s.24(2) and (4) apply see paras 6–028, 6–029, above; s.24(4)(b) and (c) are amended to reflect the fact of deposit rather than investment, s.25(3).
[52] Charities Act 1993, ss.24(6), 25(2)(5).
[53] ibid., s.24(6).

referring to common investment schemes in the trust of the charity.[54]

(c) A common investment scheme and a common deposit fund are deemed for all purposes to be charities.[55] It can accordingly be registered as such.[56] But if the scheme admits only exempt charities, the fund will likewise be an exempt charity.[57]

(d) The substance of paragraph (c) above is expressly made applicable not only to common investment funds and common deposit funds established under ss.24 and 25 of the Charities Act 1993, but also to any similar fund established for the exclusive benefit of charities by or under any enactment relating to any particular charity or class of charity.[58] The provision would therefore apply to those common investment funds established under the Universities and Colleges (Trusts) Act 1943, or, for example, under the Liverpool University Act 1931, and the Birmingham University Act 1948. But it would not apply to funds established by a scheme under the general jurisdiction of the court or the Commissioners, since it is limited to schemes established by or under statute.

Duty to conserve the trust property

6–032   A charity trustee is under the usual duty to conserve the trust property. Thus, it is an obvious breach of trust for trustees to occasion the destruction of the trust property,[59] to alienate it improperly[60] or negligently to permit others to misappropriate it.[61] Charity trustees should keep a careful check on the day-to-day running of the trust to avoid misappropriation of funds by staff.[62]

Duty to apply for a scheme

6–033   Where the case permits and requires the property or some part of it to be applied cy-près, a trust for charitable purposes places charity trustees under a duty to secure its effective use for charity by taking steps to enable

---

[54] Charities Act 1993, s.24(7), 25(2)(b).

[55] ibid., s.24(8), 25(2)(b).

[56] ibid., s.3. See para.9–010, below.

[57] ibid., s.24(8), 25(2)(b).

[58] ibid., s.24(9), 25(2)(b).

[59] Ex p. Greenhouse (1818) 1 Madd. 92, reversed on technical grounds, 1 Bli.(N.S.) 17, where trustees of a chapel had pulled down the chapel, sold the materials and converted a burying ground to other uses: "It is a breach of trust and such as could not be expected in a Christian country," per Plumer V.C. at 108.

[60] Att-Gen v East Retford Corporation (1838) 3 My. & Cr. 484; Att-Gen v Wisbech Corporation (1842) 11 L.J.Ch. 412. See para.7–039, below, for use of charity property in associated trading companies.

[61] Att-Gen v Leicester Corporation (1844) 7 Beav. 176.

[62] [1981] Ch. Com. Rep., para.107.

it to be applied *cy-près*.[63] Similarly, if there are administrative difficulties the trustees should apply to the Charity Commissioners for directions.[64] The Charity Commissioners have said that if trustees depart from their trust in the honest belief that what they are doing is better for the community they should have no fear in approaching the Commissioners for a scheme to alter the purposes of the charity. In their view failure to keep within the trusts may often be evidence of the need to alter the purposes of the charity rather than a dereliction of duty on the part of the trustees.[65]

Duty to act gratuitously

A charity trustree is under the usual duty not to derive a personal profit **6–034** from his trust unless specifically authorised in the trust instrument.[66] The Court of Appeal in *Re Duke of Norfolk's Settlement*,[67] relaxed somewhat the circumstances in which the court will exercise its inherent jurisdiction to authorise payment of remuneration to trustees. The courts, however, retain a restrictive approach to the payment of charity trustees. Thus in *Smallpiece v Att-Gen*[68] his Honour Judge Paul Baker Q.C. sitting as a deputy judge of the High Court sanctioned past payments which had been made to charity trustees because the charity had then been in considerable difficulty and drastic action was required to put its affairs in order; the persons receiving the payments had particular expertise in the field in which the charity operated and the amounts paid were reasonable in all the circumstances. He refused, however, to amend the governing instrument of the charity to allow the trustees to be paid in the future. The same judge took a similar restrictive approach in *Foster v Spencer*[69] limiting payment for past work by trustees to an annual fee rather than allowing payment on an hourly rate. The courts have also indicated that they are reluctant to relieve paid trustees of liability for breach of trust.[70]

A charity may be set up with a power in the trust deed for trustees to be paid. It must be remembered, however, that an organisation will not be a charity if it does not have exclusively charitable objects. Accordingly, if the power to remunerate can be exercised in such a way that a trustee becomes a beneficiary of the trust, the organisation will not be charitable. Standard charging clauses in model deeds are drafted with limitations to ensure that

---

[63] Charities Act 1993, s.13(5).
[64] See Charities Act 1993, ss.16 and 17 for the jurisdiction to make administrative schemes and s.29 for the power of the Charity Commissioners to advise charity trustees. An application to the court will not normally be needed and could in any case only be made (unless the charity is on exempt charity) after seeking the authority of an order of the Commissioners under *ibid.*, s.33(2).
[65] [1970] Ch. Com. Rep., paras 41, *et seq.*
[66] *Guinness plc v Saunders* [1990] 2 W.L.R. 324 at 332. For an example of specific authorisation see *Re Coren* [1948] 1 Ch. 747 (a bequest to provide a dinner for trustees of a charity).
[67] [1982] Ch. 61.
[68] [1990] Ch. Com. Rep., App.D.
[69] [1996] 2 All E.R. 672.
[70] *Steel v Wellcome Custodian Trustees Ltd* [1988] 1 W.L.R. 167 at 174.

charitable status is retained, for example, by limiting payment to usual professional charges for work in a professional capacity on behalf of the charity.[71] Such clauses also avoid problems of conflict of interest by limiting the number of trustees who may be paid and requiring a trustee whose remuneration is being considered to withdraw from the relevant meeting. Trustees exercising a power of remuneration need to remember the general duty to act in good faith, responsibly and reasonably[72] when deciding both whether to pay and when fixing the level of remuneration. Relevant considerations will be the need for the particular payment to be made and the reasonableness of the cost in comparison with alternative sources. A useful list of factors to be considered when making payment to trustees is set out in the Charity Commissioners' publication, *Payment of Charity Trustees*.[73]

If a charity does not have a remuneration clause in its trust instrument trustees may apply to the Charity Commissioners for an order under s.26 of the Charities Act 1993 to authorise payment to trustees. The Commissioners' starting point is that the office of trustee is unpaid but they will grant authorisation if the payment is necessary and reasonable for the proper administration of the charity. In determining whether to authorise remuneration in all cases the Commissioners will consider the size and type of charity, the reason for the payment, procedures proposed for managing the conflict of interest, the number of trustees to be paid, procedures for checking the level of payment and the budget of the charity. In the common situation of a charity seeking authorisation to pay a trustee for particular services, the Commissioners will also look to see if alternative quotes have been obtained and examine the tendering process. Where it is sought to pay a trustee for acting as a trustee, the Commissioners have indicated that they will expect trustees to show the steps they have taken to recruit unpaid trustees and that they have considered alternative ways of working rather than paying the trustee. In the more unusual case where charity trustees seek authority to pay one of their number as an employee of the charity, the Charity Commissioners expect the trustees to have advertised the post on the basis of open and fair competition, taken steps to recruit an unpaid trustee with the necessary skills and considered why the particular employee has to be a trustee and not merely advise the trustees before seeking power to remunerate.[74]

6–035   The power to allow trust corporations and professional trustees to be paid in s.29 of the Trustee Act 2000 does not extend to trustees of a charitable trust. Such a power may be introduced by way of regulation,[75] whether generally or in specific cases, but no such regulations have yet been made. The Strategy Unit report proposed that there should be a statutory power for trustees to pay any individual trustee to provide a service to a charity, outside their duties as a trustee, if they reasonably

---

[71] See Charity Commissioners, *Model Declaration of Trust for a Charitable Trust*, clause 25.
[72] See para.6–004 above.
[73] CC11 (2000).
[74] See CC11, *Payment of Charity Trustees* (2000).
[75] Trustee Act 2000, s.30.

believe it to be in the interests of the charity to do so.[76] It was considered that there should be no power to pay trustees for carrying out their duties as trustees.

MEMBERS OF THE COMMITTEE OF A CHARITABLE UNINCORPORATED ASSOCIATION

The property of a charitable unincorporated association will usually be **6–036** held by separate trustees. The duties and powers of those trustees in relation to the property will be the same as any other charity trustees.[77] Thus, for example, they will have power to sell charity land without the consent of the Charity Commissioners provided they satisfy the conditions in s.36 of the Charities Act 1993[78] and they will have the general power of investment under the Trustee Act 2000.[79]

Position of members of the committee

The members of the committee of a charitable unincorporated associa- **6–037** tion are the persons having the general control and management of the administration of the charity and come within the definition of "charity trustees" in the Charities Act 1993.[80] The members of the committee who are not holding property are not, in law, trustees. They are probably under a fiduciary duty although there is no direct authority on the point. In relation to a non-charitable unincorporated association, however, Megarry J. in *Woodford v Smith*[81] said:

> "The powers of the committee are powers to be exercised in the interests of the association as a whole, and not in the interests of a particular section of the committee."

Further, Danckwerts J. in *Re French Protestant Hospital*,[82] when holding that the directors of a charitable corporation were in the same fiduciary position as trustees, based his reasoning on the requirements of charity rather than the particular legal form taken by that charity. He said[83]:

> "It seems to me that in a case of this kind the court is bound to look at the real situation which exists in fact. It is obvious that the corporation

---

[76] Cabinet Office, Strategy Unit, *Private Action, Public Benefit. A Review of Charities and the Wider Not-For-Profit Sector* (2002), p.70. See also the Charity Commissioners' policy not to seek recovery of small sums paid to trustees for services to a charity, OG 205 B1, *Small Charities: Trustee Remuneration. De Minimis Payments.*
[77] See paras 6–008, *et seq.*, above.
[78] See para.6–014, above.
[79] See para.6–024, above.
[80] s.97(1).
[81] [1970] 1 W.L.R. 806.
[82] [1951] Ch. 567.
[83] *ibid.*, 570.

is completely controlled under the provisions of the charter by the governor, deputy governor and directors, and that those are the persons who in fact control the corporation and decide what shall be done. It is plain that those persons are as much in a fiduciary position as trustees in regard to any acts which are done respecting the corporation and its property."

Support for the proposition that members of the committee of a charitable unincorporated association are under a fiduciary duty can also be drawn from *Royal Society for the Prevention of Cruelty to Animals v Att-Gen*.[84] The case involved a challenge to the exercise by the council of the RSPCA of its power to exclude persons from membership. The RSPCA was originally an unincorporated association but was incorporated later by private Act of Parliament. In considering the powers of the council, Lightman J. said[85]:

"[T]he powers are fiduciary and, accordingly, the obligation is upon the council to exercise the powers for the purposes for which they are conferred in what they consider to be the best interests of the Society."

Lightman J. also considered that the council should have regard to the public image and reputation of the Society for fairness and justice when making its decision.[86]

Powers

6–038   The members of the committee, by virtue of coming within the definition of "charity trustees" in s.97 of the Charities Act 1993, have the powers to co-operate with local authorities and other charities, to delegate the execution of documents, to make *ex gratia* payments[87] and to waive entitlement to property.[88] The powers of the members of the committee beyond those conferred by the Charities Act 1993 will depend upon the terms of the constitution. The Charity Commissioners' model constitution, for example, provides that the members of the committee shall have power to raise funds, to buy and sell property, to borrow money, to employ staff, to co-operate with other bodies, to appoint advisory committee and to do all such other lawful things as are necessary for the achievement of the objects.

A charitable unincorporated association has no separate legal personality. Liability under any contracts entered into pursuant to the powers will fall on members of the committee, individual officers of the association or

---

[84] [2001] 3 All E.R. 530.
[85] *ibid.* at 546; see also *Gaiman v National Association for Mental Health* [1970] Ch. 317 at 330 *per* Megarry J.
[86] *ibid.* at 551.
[87] See para.6–010, above.
[88] See para.6–011, above.

individual members, personally according to the general law of agency.[89] A member of the committee may be entitled in law to an indemnity from the funds of the association for liabilities properly incurred[90] but they will certainly be so entitled if there is a clause to that effect in the constitution. The Charity Commissioners have indicated[91] that they will not normally confer a power for the funds of a charitable unincorporated association to be used to provide indemnity insurance for members of the committee unless there are special circumstances. The Commissioners take the view that if the activities of the association are so simple and uncomplicated that the possibility of loss either by deliberate wrong doing or by negligence could be dealt with by proper administrative controls, a power to insure is not necessary.

Duties

As "charity trustees", for the purposes of the Charities Act 1993, the members of the committee are under the duties to apply for a scheme, to register and to keep and submit accounts imposed by the 1993 Act.[92] As fiduciaries they are under the usual duties to exercise their powers for the benefit of the charitable association as a whole and not to profit from their office. By analogy with the higher duties placed on directors of charitable companies who are also fiduciaries,[93] they are also probably under a duty to act gratuitously.[94]

6–039

DIRECTORS OF A CHARITABLE COMPANY

Two matters must be borne in mind when considering the powers and duties of directors of a charitable company. First, a charitable company is a separate legal entity and any property will be held by the company and not the directors.[95] Secondly, a charitable company is registered under the Companies Act 1985 and the directors are subject to the provisions of the companies legislation in addition to obligations imposed by charity law.

6–040

Position of directors

The directors of a charitable company are the persons having the general control and management of the administration of a charity and come within the definition of "charity trustees" in the Charities Act 1993.[96] Company directors are not, in law, trustees but they are fiduciaries.[97]

6–041

---

[89] See Warburton, *Unincorporated Associations: Law and Practice* (2nd ed., 1992), pp.86, *et seq.*
[90] See the discussion in (1971) 34 M.L.R. 615 (Keeler).
[91] [1991] Ch. Com. Rep., para.39.
[92] See paras 6–020, *et seq.*, above.
[93] See below.
[94] To the extent that duty now applies to trustees—see paras 6–034, *et seq.*, above.
[95] See paras 3–045, *et seq.*, above.
[96] s.97(1).
[97] *Re City Equitable Fire Insurance Co.* Ltd [1925] Ch. 407 at 426, *per* Romer J.

Directors of charitable corporations have also been held to be in a fiduciary position.[98]

Powers

6–042   As directors of a charitable company come within the definition of "charity trustees" in the Charities Act 1993, they have the power to co-operate with local authorities and other charities, to make *ex gratia* payments[99] and to waive entitlement to property.[1] The powers of the directors, beyond those deriving from the 1993 Act, will depend upon the wording of the articles of association of the particular company. For example, the Charity Commissioners' model memorandum and articles of association for a charitable company provides that the business of the charity shall be managed by the directors who may exercise all the powers of the charity. The powers of the charity are set out in the memorandum and include, inter alia, the power to raise funds, to deal with property, to co-operate with other bodies and to do all such other lawful things as are necessary for the achievement of the objects. This last power is wide enough to imply a power to acquire land.[2]

The Charity Commissioners' model deed follows the common practice and limits the exercise of the powers to the furtherance of the objects. Thus, whilst the directors would appear to have wide powers to do "all such other lawful things", any implied powers will be limited to carrying out the charitable objects of the company. This limitation on the powers of the directors of a charitable company can be seen from the case of *Rosemary Simmons Memorial Housing Association Ltd v United Dominions Trust Ltd*.[3] The case concerned a charitable housing association registered under the Industrial and Provident Societies Act 1983 with corporate status; although not a charitable company the same principles apply. By its rules it had power to do "all things necessary or expedient for the fulfilment of its objects". The charitable housing association guaranteed the debts of a non-charitable company, closely linked with the charitable housing association in connection with the provision of housing by that company. Mervyn Davies J. held that the charitable housing association had no implied power to give away its assets to a non-charitable body.

Even if an act of the directors beyond their powers is binding in relation to a third party,[4] the directors will be liable to the charitable company for any loss occurring.[5] Under the Companies Act 1985 certain arrangements

---

[98] *Charitable Corporation v Sutton* (1742) 2 Atk. 400; *Re French Protestant Hospital* [1951] 1 Ch. 567.

[99] See para.6–010, above.

[1] See para.6–011, above.

[2] *Rosemary Simmons Memorial Housing Association Ltd v United Dominions Trust Ltd* [1987] 1 All E.R. 281.

[3] [1987] 1 All E.R. 281.

[4] See para.3–044, above.

[5] The Charity Commissioners will usually not object to an amendment to the memorandum of association giving power to the company to provide indemnity insurance for the directors, [1991] Ch. Com. Rep., para.38; (1994) 2 Ch. Com. Dec., p.27.

entered into by the directors in exercise of their powers require the approval of the company. By s.66 of the Charities Act 1993 such arrangements are ineffective without the prior written consent of the Charity Commissioners. The relevant provisions of the Companies Act 1985 are as follows:

(a) s.312, payment to a director in respect of loss of office or retirement;

(b) s.313(1), payment to a director in respect of loss of office or retirement made in connection with the transfer of undertaking or property of the company;

(c) s.319(3), incorporation in a director's service contract of a term whereby his employment will or may continue for a period of more than five years;

(d) s.320(1), an arrangement whereby assets are acquired by or from a director or a person connected with him;

(e) s.337(3)(a), provision of funds to meet certain expenses incurred by a director.[6]

In addition, by s.66 of the 1993 Act, any affirmation by the company of a voidable arrangement under which assets are acquired by or from a director or a person connected with him for the purposes of s.322(2)(c) of the 1985 Act is ineffective without the prior written consent of the Charity Commissioners.

Duties

Directors of charitable companies, by virtue of coming within the definition of "charity trustees" in the Charities Act 1993, are under the duties to apply for a scheme[7] and to register[8] imposed by the 1993 Act. The duties to keep and produce accounts in the 1993 Act do not apply to directors but they are placed under similar duties by Pt VII of the Companies Act 1985.[9] Directors are under the duty to provide an annual report to the Charity Commissioners but they are obliged to attach to the report the accounts and auditor's report prepared for the purposes of the Companies Act 1985.[10] They are under the duty to produce an annual return for the Commissioners.[11]

6–043

Directors of charitable companies are under the same statutory obligations imposed by the Companies Act 1985 as the directors of any other registered company. The reader is referred to the standard texts on company

---

[6] In view of the reluctance of the Commissioners and the courts to allow charity trustees to receive remuneration for their services, it is unlikely that the Commissioners will consent to directors of charitable companies receiving benefits in any of the above cases except in exceptional circumstances; see para.6–034, above and (1994) 2 Ch. Com. Dec., pp.17, et seq.

[7] See para.6–033, above.

[8] See para.1–027, above.

[9] For the detailed provisions, see *Palmer's Company Law*, Vol.2., pp.9013, et seq.

[10] Charities Act 1993, s.45(5).

[11] See para.9–011, below.

law for the detailed provisions. For example, the directors must make an annual return to the Registrar of Companies[12] and a director must not receive a loan from the company.[13]

As fiduciaries, the directors of a company are under a duty to exercise their powers for the purposes for which they were conferred and bona fide for the benefit of the company and not to put themselves in a position in which their duties to the company and their personal interests conflict.[14] For directors of a charitable company this must be interpreted to mean that they must exercise their powers in furtherance of the charitable objects of the company and not in the interests of some section of the company.[15] The courts have imposed higher duties on directors of charitable companies and they are obliged to act gratuitously.[16]

6–044   A director of a non-charitable company is not expected to show a greater degree of care than may be expected of the ordinary man and such degree of skill as may reasonably be expected from a person with his knowledge and experience.[17] This standard of duty of care is unlikely to be reduced by the courts on the grounds that a director is part-time or unpaid.[18] Indeed, whenever the courts have considered the position of those controlling charitable corporations they have regarded them as being in the position of trustees and subject to a correspondingly higher duty of care.[19] Thus, in *Re French Protestant Hospital*[20] Danckwerts J. said of the governors and directors of the hospital which was incorporated under Royal Charter:

> "[They] are in the position of trustees, and therefore so far as they exercise their powers at all, bound to exercise them in a fiduciary manner on behalf of the charitable trusts for which they act."

---

[12] Companies Act 1985, s.363.

[13] *ibid.*, s.330.

[14] See *Aberdeen Railway Co. v Blaikie Bros* (1854) 1 Macq. 461 at 471, *per* Viscount Finlay; *Bishopgate Investment Management (in Liquidation) v Maxwell* (No. 2) [1993] B.C.C. 120.

[15] See *Gaiman v National Association for Mental Health* [1971] Ch. 317 at 330.

[16] See *Re French Protestant Hospital* [1951] 1 Ch. 567; *Smallpiece v Att-Gen* [1990] Ch. Com. Rep., App.D. For the limited circumstances in which the Charity Commissioners will authorise remuneration either by an original clause in the Memorandum of Association or by consenting to an amendment of the Memorandum under the Charities Act 1993, s.64, see (1994) 2 Ch. Com. Dec., pp.17, *et seq.* and CC11, *Payment of Charity Trustees* (2000).

[17] *Re City Equitable Fire Insurance Co. Ltd* [1925] Ch. 407 at 428; *Dorchester Finance Co. Ltd v Stebbing* [1989] B.C.L.C. 498.

[18] See *Commonwealth Bank of Australia v Friedrich and Others* (1991) 9 A.C.L.C. 946.

[19] *Charitable Corporation v Sutton* (1742) 2 Atk. 400; *Re French Protestant Hospital* [1951] 1 Ch. 567.

[20] [1951] 1 Ch. 567 at 571. See also *Bray v Ford* [1896] A.C. 44; *Harries v Church Commissioners for England* [1992] 1 W.L.R. 1241 at 1245.

CHAPTER 7

FUND-RAISING

BACKGROUND

As the number of endowed charities has decreased, funds raised from **7–001** the public have become an important income source for many charities.

As far back as 1982[1] and 1983,[2] the Charity Commissioners were expressing their concern at complaints about dubious fund-raising techniques. The report in 1986 of a Working Party on the law governing charity fund-raising set up under the auspices of the National Council for Voluntary Organisations, recommended[3]: self-regulation by charities, increased public vigilance, and strengthening of statutory supervision. The Efficiency Scrutiny Report welcomed these findings.[4] In particular, it endorsed the Working Party's emphasis on "self-regulation" by the charitable sector. However, a number of the Working Party's suggestions for legislative change were also supported. The Efficiency Scrutiny Report also recommended that the Home Office and the Charity Commissioners should review the legislation relating to public collections in consultation with representatives of the local authorities and make recommendations to the Home Secretary.[5]

It was against this background that Pts II and III of the Charities Act 1992 were passed. Nevertheless, concerns that the public has a negative view of fund-raising continue. Whilst levels of trust in the charity sector may be generally high, concerns about fund-raising practice may be eroding public confidence.[6] Fund-raising is the public face of much of the charitable sector, and is therefore likely to have a marked influence on public attitudes. This has led to reforms being considered once more by the Strategy Unit Review.[7] The Strategy Unit report recommended reforms in

---

[1] [1982] Ch. Com. Rep., paras 17–23.
[2] [1983] Ch. Com. Rep., paras 1–9.
[3] Malpractice in Fund-raising for Charity, N.C.V.O., 1986.
[4] Efficiency Scrutiny of the Supervision of Charities (1987), paras 126–130.
[5] Efficiency Scrutiny of the Supervision of Charities (1987), para.132.
[6] Cabinet Office, Strategy Units *Private Action, Public Action. A Review of Charities and the Wider Not-For-Profit Sector* (2002), para.6.21.
[7] *ibid.*, paras 6.21–6.39.

four main areas related to fund-raising: self-regulation;[8] public collections;[9] commercial participators;[10] and charity trading.[11]

PROFESSIONAL FUND-RAISERS

7–002   Charity fund-raising has become increasingly specialised and charities
are beginning to turn to professionals who are growing in number as the
demand for assistance rises. The Institute of Charity Fund-raising
Managers (ICFM) was set up in 1984 to provide professional support to
fund-raisers. In 2002, the ICFM changed its name to the Institute of
Fund-raising. As well as providing opportunities for continuing professional education, a forum for discussion on issues of common concern,
and a source of information, the Institute has developed a code of conduct for fund-raisers, which all its members must abide by and support.[12] It has also established codes of practice for different areas of
fund-raising activity to which members and affiliated charities are committed. Existing codes are updated on a regular basis and new codes are
developed where a need for them is identified.
       Certain professional fund-raisers and their activities are subject to
control under Pt II of the Charities Act 1992.

Definition

7–003   For the purposes of Pt II of the Charities Act 1992, a professional fund-
raiser is defined[13] as any person (apart from a charitable institution[14] or a
connected company[15]) who carries on a fund-raising business, or any other
person who, for reward, solicits money or other property for the benefit of
a charitable institution, unless this is done in the capacity of an agent of a
person carrying on a fund-raising venture. The definition is aimed at
bringing within regulation those who run fund-raising businesses in relation to appeals and campaigns they organise for charitable institutions.[16]
It would not cover volunteers who receive only out-of-pocket expenses,
since they would not be acting for reward.[17] The definition is restricted by

---

[8] *ibid.*, paras 6.26–6.32. The report proposes a new independent fund-raising body to
  develop self–regulation, based on a new voluntary Code of Practice, and to oversee good
  practice. The report recommends that if this voluntary initiative fails, the Home Secretary
  should have a back-up power to introduce a compulsory system of regulation.
[9] See para.7–026 below.
[10] See para.7–011 below.
[11] See para.7–039 below.
[12] The Code of Conduct for Fund-raisers and all the Institute's Codes of Practice can be
  found on the Institute of Fund-raising's website: *www.institute-of-fundraising.org.uk*.
[13] Charities Act 1992, s.58(1).
[14] In this Act, the definition of a charitable institution is a charity *or* an institution (other
  than a charity) which is established for charitable, benevolent or philanthropic purposes.
  Charities Act 1992, s.58(1).
[15] See Charities Act 1992, s.58(5) for the definition of a company connected with a charitable institution.
[16] *Hansard*, HL Vol.535, col.1202 (1992).
[17] *Hansard*, HL PBC col.219 (1992).

s.58(2) which excludes a charitable institution and its associated trading company, employees and trustees of such an institution or company, a collector,[18] a person fronting a radio or television appeal, and a commercial participator. Volunteers who receive not more that £5 a day or £500 per year or £500 overall are also excluded.[19]

A "fund-raising business" is any business carried on for gain and wholly or primarily engaged in soliciting or otherwise procuring money or other property for charitable, benevolent or philanthropic purposes.[20]

The definition therefore covers those people who run their own fund-raising businesses in relation to appeals and campaigns that they organise for charitable institutions.

Legal basis for hiring professional fund-raisers

S.11 of the Trustee Act 2000 makes it clear that charities may employ agents in order to raise funds.[21] The functions that a trustee of a charitable trust may delegate are defined[22] to include income generating activities except in so far as the income is derived from profits of a "trade which is an integral part of carrying out the trust's charitable purpose".[23] Fund-raising activities which are an integral part of carrying out the trust's charitable purpose would therefore not be delegable. Examples of fund-raising activities which are not delegable would include the charging of fees by a school operating as a charitable trust.   7–004

Controls over the activities of professional fund-raisers

Before the introduction of statutory regulation in this area, fund-raisers may well have been able to retain as their remuneration an excessive proportion of the sums raised for charity. It was considered that it was perhaps lawful for a fund-raiser to enter into a contract with a charity under which commission as high as 80 or 90 per cent of receipts could be retained. Pt II of the Charities Act 1992 therefore introduced, for the first time in statute,[24] controls over the activities of professional fund-raisers in campaigns and promotional ventures connected with charitable institutions.   7–005

---

[18] Defined in Charities Act 1992, s.65(3)(b).

[19] Charities Act 1992, s.58(3). The definition of fund-raiser may be wide enough to bring within it "fulfilment houses"—companies employed specifically to handle responses to a promotion by a charity.

[20] Charities Act 1992, s.58(1).

[21] Although the directors of charitable companies do not, in relation to the corporate property of the company, directly acquire the wider powers contained in the Trustee Act 2000, their members may change their memoranda and articles of association so as to confer corresponding powers.

[22] Trustee Act 2000, s.11(3).

[23] The concept of a "trade which is an integral part of carrying out the trust's charitable purpose" is defined in Trustee Act 2000, s.11(4).

[24] See the dicta of Brightman J. in the *Sanctuary* Case. *Jones v Att-Gen, The Times*, November 10, 1976; [1976] Ch. Com. Rep., paras 25–29, (1993) 2 Ch. Com. Dec., p.33.

Requirement of an agreement in the prescribed form.

7–006   It is unlawful[25] for a professional fund-raiser to solicit funds on behalf of a charity without an agreement which satisfies the requirements prescribed by Regulations.[26]

The agreement must be in writing and signed on behalf of the charity and the professional fund-raiser. The agreement must contain the names and addresses of the parties to it, the date of signature and the period of time that it is to cover. If there are terms concerning variation of the agreement, or procedures relating to termination of the agreement before its date of expiry, these should also be included in the agreement. The agreement must also include a statement of its principal objectives and the methods to be used in pursuit of those objectives. Finally, it must contain provision as to the amount by way of remuneration or expenses which the professional fund-raiser is to be entitled to receive and the manner in which that amount is to be determined. The Regulations prescribe the minimum that a charity must agree, in writing, with a professional fund-raiser.

A charity may apply to the court without notice for an injunction to restrain any contravention of these requirements by a professional fund-raiser.[27]

Availability of books, documents or other records

7–007   A professional fund-raiser who is party to an agreement described above shall on request and at all reasonable times, make available in legible form to any charity which is a party to that agreement any books, documents or other records (however kept) which relate to the charity.[28] "Making available" may include giving the charitable institution the ability to copy documents if desired, though not necessarily the ability to remove them from the premises if the option to copy is available.

Breach of these requirements amounts to an offence punishable on summary conviction by a fine not exceeding the second level on the standard scale.[29]

Requirement of a statutory declaration

7–008   Each solicitation by professional fund-raisers must be accompanied by a statement disclosing information about the charity for which they are

---

[25] Charities Act 1992, s.59(1).
[26] *ibid.*, s.64 and The Charitable Institutions (Fund-Raising) Regulations 1994 (SI 1994/3024). See also, CC20, *Charities and Fund-Raising* (2002), Annex B for a checklist for agreements with a professional fund-raiser.
[27] Charities Act 1992, s.59(3).
[28] The Charitable Institutions (Fund-Raising) Regulations 1994 (SI 1994/3024), reg.5.
[29] *ibid.*, reg.8(2)(a). The standard levels of maximum fines on a summary conviction are to be found in Criminal Justice Act 1982, s.37(2).

raising funds and the method for determining their remuneration.[30] The disclosure concerning remuneration can be "in general terms". This means that it must be disclosed that there will be a payment and the general (rather than necessarily the specific) method by which that payment is to be determined. For example, it would be sufficient to state that payment would be as a percentage of the income from the appeal, as a fixed amount already decided, or as a fee for time and money spent. The statement should probably reflect what is said about disclosure in the agreement with the charity.

Where the professional fund-raiser is raising funds for "charitable, benevolent or philanthropic purposes" generally, then a statement to that effect must accompany the solicitation together with details of how the proceeds will be distributed between different charities, and a similar statement to that for a particular charitable institution.[31]

Breach of these requirements amounts to a criminal offence punishable on summary conviction by a fine not exceeding the fifth level on the standard scale.[32] It shall, however, be a defence for a person charged with such an offence to prove that all reasonable precautions were taken and all due diligence was exercised to avoid the commission of the offence.[33]

Transfer of money and other property to charity

There is a strict regime governing the transfer of money from the professional fund-raiser to the charity.[34] This regime must be followed irrespective of any inconsistent term in the agreement. Any money or cheques payable to the charity which are received by the professional fund-raiser, or any proceeds of sale, must be paid over to the charity as soon as is reasonably practicable and within 28 days of receipt or "such other period as may be agreed with the institution". It is suggested that, due to this provision, it may well be within the regulation for funds to be transferred outside the 28-day period, if some other time period has been mutually agreed. The money or cheques must be paid over to the trustees of the charity or paid into the charity's bank or building society account. Other property received must be securely held and must be dealt with in accordance with any instructions given by the charity.

7–009

Failure to comply with these requirements amounts to an offence punishable on summary conviction by a fine not exceeding the second level on the standard scale.[35]

---

[30] Charities Act 1992, s.60(1).
[31] *ibid.*, s.60(2).
[32] *ibid.*, s.60(7). The standard levels of maximum fines on a summary conviction are to be found in Criminal Justice Act 1982, s.37(2).
[33] Charities Act 1992, s.60(8).
[34] The Charitable Institutions (Fund-Raising) Regulations 1994 (SI 1994/3024), reg.6.
[35] *ibid.*, reg.8(2)(b). The standard levels of maximum fines on a summary conviction are to be found in Criminal Justice Act 1982, s.37(2).

Additional controls

7–010   A local authority may refuse to issue a permit to conduct a house–to–house collection because the applicant or any other person would be likely to receive an excessive amount by way of remuneration in connection with the collection.[36]

COMMERCIAL PARTCIPATORS

7–011   As well as using professional fund-raisers, charities are embarking increasingly upon joint promotions with commercial manufacturers and retailers in order to associate their charitable cause with products offered for sale.[37] Companies are aware that giving is good for business, and in this area self-interest and philanthropy are seen to conveniently coincide.[38] An example of such cause–related marketing is the emergence of the "affinity" credit card scheme, where banks and building societies give a donation to a particular charity for each new card-holder and sometimes after further transactions.[39] The Charity Commissioners advise that charities should research a proposed commercial partnership carefully and, if it proves to be appropriate and viable, establish a plan of how the partnership will be managed.[40] Also, all charities should consider taking advice from a professional or specialist prior to commencing a commercial partner agreement. The Charities Act 1992 introduced controls on the activities of certain commercial participators.[41]

Definition

7–012   For the purposes of Part II of the Charities Act 1992, a commercial participator is defined[42] as any person (apart from a company connected with the charity[43]) who carries on for gain a business other than a fund-raising business, but in the course of that business, engages in any promotional venture in the course of which it is represented that charitable contributions are to be given to or applied for the benefit of a charitable institution.[44]

---

[36] House to House Collections Act 1939, s.2(3). See para.7–027 below. See, also, Charities Act 1993, s.18(3).

[37] See RS2, *Charities and Commercial Partners* (2002).

[38] See Morris, "Corporate Support for Charity" [1990] J.B.L. 495.

[39] *Hansard*, HL PBC, cols. 223–224 (1992).

[40] RS2, *Charities and Commercial Partners* (2002), p.15.

[41] See Hill, "Enter the Commercial Participator" (1995) 3 C.L. & P.R. 17.

[42] In the USA, such a person is commonly called a "commercial co-venturer". See Luxton, *Charity Fund-raising and the Public Interest* (1990), p.62.

[43] See Charities Act 1992, s.58(5) for the definition of a company connected with a charitable institution.

[44] *ibid.*, s.58(1).

Controls over the activities of commercial participators

Requirement of an agreement in the prescribed form

It is unlawful[45] for a commercial participator to represent that charita-   **7–013**
ble contributions are to be given to or applied for the benefit of a charity
without an agreement with the charity which satisfies the requirements
prescribed by Regulations.[46]

The agreement must be in writing and signed on behalf of the charity
and the commercial participator. The agreement must contain the names
and addresses of the parties to it, the date of signature and the period of
time that it is to cover. If there are terms concerning variation of the agreement, or procedures relating to termination of the agreement before its
date of expiry, these should also be included in the agreement. The agreement must also include a statement of its principal objectives and the
methods to be used in pursuit of those objectives. In relation to each
method specified, there must be a description of the type of charitable
contributions which are to be given and of the circumstances in which they
are given. If there is more than one charity party to the agreement, the way
in which the proportion that each charity is to benefit is to be determined
must be stated. The way in which the proportion of the cost for goods or
services sold or supplied by the commercial participator, or of any other
proceeds of a promotional venture undertaken, which is to be given to
charity is to be determined, must be stated. Finally, the agreement must
state any amount by way of remuneration or expenses which the commercial participator is to receive and the manner in which any such amount is
to be determined. The Regulations prescribe the minimum that a charity
must agree, in writing, with a commercial participator.

A charity may apply to court without notice for an injunction to restrain
any contravention of these requirements by a commercial participator.[47]

The Charity Commissioners consider that these requirements should be
viewed as the minimum staring point for a charity drawing up an agreement with a commercial partner, and that charities should not simply
accept a commercial agreement drawn up by the other party.[48] A charity
should retain control over the process to ensure that the agreement is
appropriate and fulfills the best interests of the charity.

Availability of books, documents or other records

A commercial participator who is party to an agreement described   **7–014**
above shall on request and at all reasonable times, make available in legible form to any charity which is a party to that agreement any books,

---

[45] *ibid.*, s.59(2).
[46] *ibid.*, s.64 and The Charitable Institutions (Fund-raising) Regulations 1994 (SI 1994/3024).
   See also, CC20, *Charities and Fund-Raising* (2002), Annex B for a checklist for agreements
   with a commercial participator.
[47] Charities Act 1992, s.59(3).
[48] RS2, *Charities and Commercial Partners* (2002), p.19.

documents or other records (however kept) which relate to the charity.[49] The Charity Commissioners advise that charities should exercise their ability to request such documentation from commercial partners as part of an on-going monitoring and review process of any existing commercial partnerships.[50] "Making available" may include giving the charitable institution the ability to copy documents if desired, though not necessarily the ability to remove them from the premises if the option to copy is available.

Failure to comply with these requirements amounts to an offence punishable on summary conviction by a fine not exceeding the second level on the standard scale.[51]

Requirement of a statutory declaration

7–015   Each representation by a commercial participator must be accompanied by a statement clearly indicating the charity or charities concerned.[52] If there is more than one charity, the proportions in which they are to benefit must be disclosed. The statement must include the method by which the proportion of money from the sales that is to go to charity is to be determined or the method by which sums by way of donations are to be given. As for professional fund-raisers, this disclosure concerning funds can be "in general terms".[53]

Breach of these requirements amounts to an offence punishable on summary conviction by a fine not exceeding the fifth level on the standard scale.[54] It shall, however, be a defence for a person charged with such an offence to prove that all reasonable precautions were taken and all due diligence was exercised to avoid the commission of the offence.[55]

The Strategy Unit report identified two difficulties in relation to the statutory declaration to be made by commercial participators.[56] First, the declaration is insufficiently specific and does not achieve transparency. Secondly, there is a lack of enforcement of the requirement of a statutory declaration. The report recommended that the legislation be amended to require a specific statement of the return that will be made to charity from promotional ventures, and that these new measures should be appropriately publicised. It was also recommended that the Home Office should issue additional guidance setting out the form of statement appropriate to the particular type of promotion proposed.

---

[49] The Charitable Institutions (Fund-Raising) Regulations 1994 (SI 1994/3024), reg.5.
[50] RS2, *Charities and Commercial Partners* (2002), p.27.
[51] The Charitable Institutions (Fund-Raising) Regulations 1994 (SI 1994/3024), reg.8(2)(a). The standard levels of maximum fines on a summary conviction are to be found in Criminal Justice Act 1982, s.37(2).
[52] Charities Act 1992, s.60(3).
[53] See para.7–008 above.
[54] Charities Act 1992, s.60(7). The standard levels of maximum fines on a summary conviction are to be found in Criminal Justice Act 1982, s.37(2).
[55] Charities Act 1992, s.60(8).
[56] Cabinet Office, Strategy Unit, *Private Action, Public Benefit. A Review of Charities and the Wider Not-For-Profit Sector* (2002), para.6.33.

Transfer of money and other property to charity

There is a strict regime governing the transfer of money from the com- **7–016** mercial participator to the charity.[57] This regime must be followed irrespective of any inconsistent term in the agreement. Any money or cheques payable to the charity which are received by the commercial participator, or any proceeds of sale, must be paid over to the charity as soon as is reasonably practicable and within 28 days of receipt or as agreed. The money or cheques must be paid over to the trustees of the charity or paid into the charity's bank or building society account. Other property received must be securely held and must be dealt with in accordance with any instructions given by the charity.

Failure to comply with these requirements amounts to an offence punishable on summary conviction by a fine not exceeding the second level on the standard scale.[58]

Trading subsidiaries

Part II of the Charities Act 1992 and the 1994 Regulations do not apply **7–017** to commercial partnership agreements made between a charity's trading subsidiary[59] and a company. Nevertheless, the Charity Commissioners recommend that charities should use the legal requirements detailed therein to provide a framework for commercial partnership arrangements made between a charity's trading subsidiary and its commercial partner.[60] Enforcing these requirements will help the charity to control and monitor the trading subsidiary, ensuring that the best interests of the charity are protected.

CHARITABLE FUND-RAISING OTHERWISE THAN BY PROFESSIONAL FUND-RAISERS OR COMMERCIAL PARTICIPATORS

A person who carries on for gain a business which is *not* a fund-raising **7–018** business, but, in the course of that business, engages in any promotional venture during which it is represented that charitable contributions are to be applied for general (rather than specific) charitable, benevolent or philanthropic purposes, is also subject to legal regulation.[61] There must be a clear statement to the effect that the contributions are to be applied for general rather than specific charitable purposes. The statement must also reveal the method by which it is to be determined the donation or what proportion of the cost for goods or services sold or supplied, or any other proceeds of a promotional venture, is to be applied for charitable

---

[57] The Charitable Institutions (Fund-Raising) Regulations 1994 (SI 1994/3024), reg.6.
[58] *ibid.*, reg.8(2)(b). The standard levels of maximum fines on a summary conviction are to be found in Criminal Justice Act 1982, s.37(2).
[59] See para.7–039 below.
[60] RS2, *Charities and Commercial Partners* (2002), p.21.
[61] The Charitable Institutions (Fund-Raising) Regulations 1994 (SI 1994/3024), reg.7.

purposes. It must also be clear how the contributions will be distributed between different charitable institutions.

Failure to comply with these requirements amounts to an offence punishable on summary conviction by a fine not exceeding the second level on the standard scale.[62]

PROTECTION FOR DONORS

7–019   In certain circumstances, donors are given a right to cancel payments and agreements made in response to charitable appeals.[63] Payments made in response to a radio or television broadcast can be cancelled if made by credit or debit card.[64] It was considered that such payments were instant, whilst other forms of payment required some thought.[65] Payments or agreements made in response to a telephone appeal can be refunded or cancelled regardless of the form in which the payment was made.[66] In both cases repayments are restricted to donations over £50[67] and written notice must be given within seven days of the solicitation or representation.[68] In each case any refund to which a donor is entitled is subject to a deduction for reasonable costs incurred in making the refund, and is dependant on the restitution of any goods received in return for the payment.[69]

In addition to the general requirements for a statement outlined above, a professional fund-raiser or commercial participator must give relevant donors notice of their rights of repayment and cancellation.[70]

It is an offence[71] to solicit funds or other property for an institution with a representation that it is a registered charity when it is not.[72]

PROTECTION FOR CHARITIES

7–020   Before the Charities Act 1992, charities found it difficult, if not impossible, to prevent fund-raising being undertaken, allegedly on their behalf, by people of whose *bona fides* they were doubtful.[73] Now, in certain circumstances, a charity can prevent the misuse of its name by obtaining an injunction to prevent unauthorised fund-raising by persons other than

---

[62] *ibid.*, reg.8(2)(c). The standard levels of maximum fines on a summary conviction are to be found in Criminal Justice Act 1982, s.37(2).

[63] See, generally, Charities Act 1992, s.61.

[64] *ibid.*, s.61(1) and s.60(1)(2)(3).

[65] *Hansard*, HL PBC, col.236 (1992).

[66] Charities Act 1992, s.61(2)(3) and s.60(5).

[67] *ibid.*, s.61(1)(2)(3).

[68] *ibid.*

[69] *ibid.*, s.61(4).

[70] *ibid.*, s.60(4) and s.60(5).

[71] The offence is punishable on summary conviction by a fine not exceeding the fifth level on the standard scale. The standard levels of maximum fines on a summary conviction are to be found in Criminal Justice Act 1982, s.37(2).

[72] Charities Act 1992, s.63. There is a defence if the accused can prove a reasonable belief that the institution was registered.

[73] Malpractice in Fund-raising for Charity, N.C.V.O., 1986, para.5.32.

professional fund-raisers or commercial participators.[74] Where a person is soliciting funds for the benefit of a charity or representing that charitable contributions are to be given to a charity, the charity may apply to the court which may grant an injunction restraining such acts. The charity must show that one of three conditions is satisfied[75]: the person is using objectionable fund-raising methods; the person is not fit and proper to raise funds; or, if the person is making representations that money will be applied to a charity, the charity does not want to be associated with the venture. The injunction will not be granted unless the charity has served a written request on the person to stop the activity complained of.[76]

PARTICULAR FORMS OF FUND-RAISING

The term fund-raising covers many different activities.[77] At one end of **7–021** the scale it refers to the holding of lotteries,[78] fêtes, and jumble sales by charities. At the other end of the scale, it includes profit–sharing arrangements entered into by charities with large commercial organisations. Somewhere in the middle fall charitable appeals and the use of collection boxes. New forms of charity fund-raising are constantly being invented and some may well fall within the legal regulation of Pt II of the Charities Act 1992.

Telephone appeals

Telephone appeals have been a popular method of fund-raising in the **7–022** USA for some time,[79] and charities in the UK are now finding telemarketing an effective method of fund-raising. For example, universities are increasingly adopting this method of fund-raising, using students as callers. The use of the telephone in solicitation of support has been the subject of frequent criticism.[80] It was recommended[81] that the telephone be used for fund-raising only after careful training, under close supervision, and in accordance with a code of conduct which the Institute of Fund-raising should prepare.

The Institute of Fund-raising has since drawn up a code of practice on the use of telephones to solicit funds and support, which provides clear guidance to telemarketers and helps to ensure that supporters are not exploited.[82] The sort of issues covered include the question of the content

---

[74] See, generally, Charities Act 1992, s.62.
[75] *ibid.*, s.62(2).
[76] *ibid.*, s.62(3) and The Charitable Institutions (Fund-Raising) Regulations 1994 (SI 1994/3024), reg.4.
[77] The Charity Commissioners recommend that charities develop a fund-raising strategy, CC20, *Charities and Fund-Raising* (2002), para.5.
[78] See Luxton, "Charity Lotteries Past and Present" (1993) 2 C.L. & P.R. 17.
[79] See Luxton, *Charity Fund-raising and the Public Interest* (1990), pp.195–197.
[80] See, for example, Malpractice in Fund-raising for Charity, N.C.V.O., 1986, para.5.55.
[81] Malpractice in Fund-raising for Charity, N.C.V.O., 1986, para.5.56.
[82] Institute of Fund-raising, *Code Of Fund-raising Practice—Telephone Fund-raising*.

of the request for support, the need for advance written notice of a telephone call and the timing of the call.

Where employees of a fund-raising business are telephoning members of the public to encourage them to give donations to charity, the activity may well fall within professional fund-raising[83] and must therefore comply with the statutory requirements.[84] If this is the case, each solicitation must be accompanied by the necessary statement[85] which should be made during the telephone call. If a company simply receives incoming telephone calls and records credit card details from people who have already decided to make a donation following an appeal by a charity, and the donations are credited direct to the charity's bank account, the company *may* not be a professional fund-raiser. The distinction is a narrow one, and each particular case will need to be considered individually.

Advertising by charities[86]

7–023   Advertising has great potential as a fund-raising tool for charities. However, until 1988, the world's most powerful medium of persuasion was denied to charities. In September of that year the Home Office allowed the Independent Broadcasting Authority to lift the ban on television advertising.[87] The Independent Television Commission Advertising Standards Code contains guidelines in relation to content, tone and style which charities wishing to advertise must follow.[88] The guidelines are intended to prevent misrepresentation, in particular by individuals or organisations seeking to exploit public generosity for private or undisclosed ends, and more generally to ensure that the means of expression used in charity advertising reflect a broad sense of ethical responsibility.[89]

Chain letters

7–024   Chain letters are not illegal but their use is generally discouraged by the Charity Commissioners[90] and the Institute of Fund-raising[91] because they can be difficult to control. Once started they are difficult to stop and can

---

[83] See definition of "professional fund-raiser" and "fund-raising business" in Charities Act 1992, s.58. See para.7–003 above.

[84] See paras 7–006, *et seq.*, above.

[85] See Charities Act 1992, s.60(1). See para.7–008 above.

[86] See Morris, "The Media and the Message: An Evaluation of Advertising by Charities and an Examination of the Regulatory Frameworks" (1996) 3 C.L. & P.R. 157.

[87] See Morris, "Broadcast Advertising by Charities" [1990] Conv. 106.

[88] See s.11.3 of the ITC Advertising Standards Code, September 2002.

[89] For example, the notes to s.11.3.4 say that, *inter alia*, advertisements for charities should handle with care and discretion matters likely to arouse strong emotions in the audience, and they must not suggest that anyone will lack proper feeling or fail in any responsibility through not supporting a charity. See also the British Codes of Advertising, Sales Promotion and Direct Marketing (2003) which applies to non-broadcast advertisements and promotions. See particularly the Sales Promotion Rules, clause 37.1 which is concerned with charity-linked promotions.

[90] CC20, *Charities and Fund-Raising* (2002), para.22.

[91] Institute of Fund-raising, *Code Of Fund-raising Practice—Use of Chain Letters as a Fund-raising Technique.*

give rise, when the appeal target has been met, to claims that the charity is misleading the public.

A direct mail company sending out chain letters may be within the definition of a professional fund-raiser[92] and if that is the case, the statutory requirements[93] will apply. It may however be considered that the activities do not amount to soliciting if the direct mail company is doing no more than printing, filling envelopes and posting letters, without actually handling incoming donations.

Fund-raising in schools[94]

This is an area where fund-raising can be particularly sensitive. The **7–025** Institute of Fund-raising has drawn up a detailed code of practice relating to fund-raising in schools.[95] The stated policy is *inter alia* to offer children a positive opportunity for involvement in helping others by raising funds. It is recommended that trust should be at the heart of all fund-raising with school children and talks given should be both educational and non-political. The Head Teacher's views of the school's charity commitments should be accepted and school children should not be approached without his or her permission. It is also recognised that the use of incentives to encourage or reward individual efforts to raise money is a very delicate issue, and that the greatest care needs to be exercised in offering them to children.

Public charitable collections

The legislation governing public collections is outdated, restrictive and **7–026** inconsistent.[96] The current framework provides two different schemes for street collections[97] and door–to–door collections[98] respectively. Some newer forms of public collections, such as face to face fund-raising,[99] may not be covered by the legislation at all. Pt III of the Charities Act 1992 made provision for new Regulations to be made governing public charitable collections. The intention was to replace the separate existing legislation on street and house–to–house collections.[1] Pt III has not been brought into force, with difficulties involved in its implementation

---

[92] See definition of "professional fund-raiser" in Charities Act 1992, s.58. See para.(263) above.

[93] See paras 7–006, *et seq.*, above.

[94] See Morris, *Schools: An Education in Charity Law* (1996), Chap. 8.

[95] Institute of Fund-raising, *Code Of Fund-raising Practice—Fund-raising In Schools*. See also, Eastwood, Mountfield and Walker, *The Schools Funding Guide* (2001) and Mountfield and Eastwood, *School Fund-raising in England—A Directory of Social Change Research Report* (2000).

[96] Cabinet Office, Strategy Unit, *Private Action, Public Benefit. A Review of Charities and the Wider Not-For-Profit Sector* (2002), para.6.23.

[97] Police, Factories etc. (Miscellaneous Provisions) Act 1916, s.5 and regulations made thereunder.

[98] House to House Collections Act 1939 and regulations made thereunder.

[99] See para.7–030 below.

[1] For details see *Tudor on Charities* (8th ed.) pp.273–277.

identified after enactment. The Strategy Unit report recommended that a new updated and unified local authority licensing scheme for public collections[2] should be introduced, focussing on basic minimum requirements.[3] It should be geared towards encouraging legitimate collecting activity within the constraints imposed by competition for space and the avoidance of public nuisance.

House–to–house collections

7–027   The legislation regulates collections for "charitable purposes" which means any charitable, benevolent or philanthropic purpose, whether or not the purpose is charitable within the meaning of any rule of law.[4] The term "collection" includes visits house–to–house, and also visits to business premises to appeal for money, other property (for example, clothes) or to sell articles on the basis that part of the proceeds will go to a charity.[5]

It is an offence to conduct a house–to–house collection without a licence from the local authority (or if the collection is in London, the local police or the Common Council of the City of London).[6] Where a collection is conducted without a permit, both the promoter of that collection and the collector are guilty of an offence.[7] Local exemption certificates may be granted by the police where they are satisfied that the collection is local in character and will be completed in a short time.[8] Charities can be granted a Home Office exemption from the need to obtain a license if they are collecting over the whole or a substantial part of England and Wales.[9]

Licensing authorities may refuse or revoke a license for reasons set out in the Act.[10] These include where it is considered that the collection would not yield adequate amounts for charity in proportion to the value of the proceeds likely to be received, or where excessive remuneration is to be retained or received out of the proceeds.

7–028   Regulations govern the manner of making collections.[11] These regulations contain, for example, provisions as to certificates of authority and badges for collectors, collecting boxes or receipt books, and the furnishing of accounts.

A person under the age of 16 years may not act as a collector.[12]

---

[2] There are no proposals to extend regulation to private places such as shop premises, railway stations and other privately owned areas.

[3] Cabinet Office,Strategy Unit, *Private Action, Public Benefit. A Review of Charities and the Wider Not-For-Profit Sector* (2002), paras 6.23–6.24.

[4] House to House Collections Act 1939, s.11.

[5] *ibid.*

[6] *ibid.*, s.1(1).

[7] Penalties are detailed in *ibid.*, s.8.

[8] *ibid.*, s.1(4).

[9] *ibid.*, s.3.

[10] *ibid.*, s.2(3).

[11] House to House Collections Regulations 1947 (SR & O 1947/2662) as amended. See also, Institute of Fund-raising, *Code Of Fund-raising Practice—House To House Collections.*

[12] House to House Collections Regulations 1947 (SR & O 1947/2262)., reg.8.

Street collections

Raising money or selling articles for charity in streets or public places **7–029** usually requires a permit or licence from either the appropriate local authority or if the collection takes place in London, the local police or the Common Council of the City of London. Local authorities are given the power but not the duty to create licensing schemes by local regulations for street collections for charity or other purposes.[13] The model regulations for street collections[14] deal with such matters as the obstruction and hindrance caused to traffic by flag days, carnivals, rag weeks, etc. and the places where, and the conditions under which, persons may collect money or sell articles for charitable and other purposes. Each street collection must be separately licensed and a return should be made. This creates a heavy administrative burden for charities which collect frequently. Some local authorities do not ask for returns to be made. The relevant authority should be consulted before any attempt is made to raise funds in its area.

Under the model street collection regulations, a person under the age of 16 years may not act as a collector.[15]

Face–to–face fund-raising

Public (or face–to–face) fund-raising on high streets and house–to–house **7–030** is a fast growing and important technique for raising support from individuals for leading charities. In this way, many young donors are being introduced into a committed, long-term relationship with a charity (utilising covenants, standing orders and direct debits) often for the first time. In 2000, the Institute of Fund-raising produced a code of practice on "Personal Solicitation for Committed Gifts".[16] The code is concerned specifically with unsolicited personal approaches to members of the public for committed support to charities and other voluntary organisations that are undertaken as part of a structured fund-raising campaign, whether by house–to–house or within a place of general public access. The Code covers such issues as the manner, timing and location of the personal solicitation, and the recruitment, training and adequate supervision of all those making the personal solicitation. The Public Fund-raising Regulatory Association (PFRA) was formed in 2001 by over 60 charities, voluntary organisations and fund-raising agencies involved in this area of fund-raising, in co-operation with the Institute of Fund-raising, the Charity Commissioners and the Home Office. It aims to promote quality, integrity, and transparency in this new form of fund-raising, ensuring that charities and professional fund-raising organisations work together with other stakeholders to maintain an atmosphere of public confidence and regulatory satisfaction.

---

[13] Police, Factories etc. (Miscellaneous Provisions) Act 1916, s.5.
[14] Charitable Collections (Transitional Provisions) Order 1974 (SI 1974/140).
[15] *ibid.*, Sch., para.11.
[16] Institute of Fund-raising, *Code of Fund-raising Practice—Personal Solicitation for Committed Gifts on the Street and House to House.*

Where this sort of activity is undertaken by third–party agencies on behalf of charities, the agency would fall within the definition of a professional fund-raiser[17] and the statutory requirements[18] will apply.

The law is not entirely clear on the licensing requirements for this type of fund-raising activity. A local authority licence is probably required for house–to–house activity (unless the activity is covered by an existing Home Office exemption order[19]) but is not required for street activity. However, it is recommended that organisers check the licensing requirements with the relevant local authority before any attempt to raise funds by face–to–face fund-raising is made in an area.

Static collection boxes

7–031   The use of static collection boxes is not regulated by legislation. It is important that the authorities and the general public alike retain confidence in such a valuable source of charitable funds. The Institute of Fund-raising has developed a code of practice[20] designed to ensure the proper management and use of static collection boxes and to safeguard the public interest in their use. Where the management of static collection boxes is undertaken on behalf of charities by third parties who receive reward for this activity and who solicit in connection with it, they may well come within the definition of a professional fund-raiser[21] and the statutory requirements[22] will apply.

Labels placed on static collecting boxes together with literature that might be associated with the collection and all notices informing people of the collection are likely to be caught by s.5 of the Charities Act 1993.[23]

Appeals[24]

Drafting

7–032   As soon as an appeal is set up for funds from members of the public for particular purposes which are in law charitable, then a charitable trust is set up. Any funds donated must then be held on trust for the purposes which have already been referred to in the terms of the appeal. It is therefore crucial that the drafting of the appeal is given careful consideration, before the appeal is launched.

---

[17] See definition of "professional fund-raiser" in Charities Act 1992, s.58. See para.7–003 above.
[18] See paras 7–006, *et seq.*, above.
[19] See para.273 above.
[20] Institute of Fund-raising, *Code Of Fund-raising Practice—The Management Of Static Collection Boxes.*
[21] See definition of "professional fund-raiser" in Charities Act 1992, s.58. See para.7–003 above.
[22] See paras 7–006, *et seq.*, above.
[23] See para.1–031 above.
[24] See Suddards, *Administration of Appeal Funds* (Sweet & Maxwell, 1991).

Those organising the appeal should do all they can to make sure that the purpose of the appeal is clear and that donors know how their gifts will be used.[25]

Sometimes gifts may be sent before publication of the appeal. If there are more than can be acknowledged individually, the published appeal should indicate that gifts already made will be added to the appeal fund unless the donors notify the organisers within a reasonable time that this is not their wish.

Winding up

If the appeal fund is to be charitable, there should be a provision in the terms of the appeal which states that if and when the fund is wound up, any remaining funds will be applied to charitable purposes only.   **7–033**

Surplus funds

If the terms of the appeal refer to a specific purpose, there may be dif-   **7–034** ficulties if too much money is donated. For example, if the appeal is for money to buy a piece of hospital equipment, there is a possibility that the money donated might exceed the cost of the piece of equipment. If there is no provision in the terms of the appeal which cover this eventuality, then a scheme of the Charity Commissioners will be required to authorise the money to be used for a similar purpose. It is therefore important that the terms of the appeal include a provision for disposal of surplus funds, usu-ally for a similar charitable purpose, or such charitable purposes as the committee think fit.[26]

Failure

It may be the case that a charitable appeal will fail for some reason.   **7–035** Insufficient funds may be collected and it may not be possible to achieve the particular purpose. For example, if the appeal is for money to buy a piece of hospital equipment, there is a possibility that insufficient money to cover the cost of the piece of equipment might be raised. Again, the terms of the appeal should provide for this possibility and state how the funds will be distributed in this event. If there is no such provision, then the insufficient funds raised will usually be applied *cy-près* by the Charity Commissioners under ss.13 and 14 of the Charities Act 1993,[27] although individual donors may be able to reclaim their donations.[28]

[25] See Precedents in Suddards, *Administration of Appeal Funds* (Sweet & Maxwell, 1991), Chap.8.
[26] See para.11–056 below
[27] See para.11–038 below.
[28] See para.11–039 below.

Disaster appeals

7–036   Compassion for victims of wars, civil disturbances, natural disasters and accidents means that it is now predictable that the report of such a happening will be followed by the setting up of an appeal for those in need.

The Attorney General has noted that,

> "Action to set up a public appeal following some tragic accident or disaster, or an occasion on which some special misfortune is brought to the public eye, is generally taken with little time to prepare the ground. The community may well feel an urgent need to give practical expression to its sorrow and respect, and the response may well exceed expectations."[29]

It is not surprising that in these circumstances there may be doubt over the precise status of appeals after they have been set up. The appeal will only be considered charitable if it is for the relief of need. Where additional benefits are to be awarded to victims, over and above those appropriate to their needs, then a non–charitable fund will be established.

This problem was highlighted by the Penlee lifeboat disaster, and following that, in March 1982, the Attorney General published guidelines for those concerned with making disaster appeals. These have since been updated.[30] Complementary guidance on the tax treatment of appeals funds has been produced jointly by Inland Revenue and HM Customs and Excise.[31]

Sponsorship

Meaning

7–037   This is a form of fund-raising whereby the sponsor provides financial support to a charity in return for some benefit, such as publicity. Arrangements are as diverse as the imagination and include such activities as sponsorship of charity events and donations linked to sales of a particular product. Such corporate partners will usually fall within the category of "commercial participators"[32] and will therefore be bound by the provisions of Pt II of the Charities Act 1992.[33]

Charitable sponsorship by a company is not specifically tax deductible, but, companies can enjoy relief on payments made to sponsor a charitable activity or event, provided that the payment is not of a capital nature and that it is made wholly and exclusively for the purposes of the company's trade.[34]

---

[29] CC40, *Disaster Appeals* (2002), para.3.
[30] See now CC40, *Disaster Appeals* (2002). The guidelines are produced in full in App.3.
[31] Inland Revenue and Customs & Excise, "Guidelines On The Tax Treatment Of Appeal Funds", May 2001.
[32] See para.7–012 above.
[33] See paras 7–013 *et seq.*, above.
[34] Income and Corporation Taxes Act 1988, s.74(a).

Use of the charity name

A charity should not lend its name to a commercial product or serv- **7–038**
ice which is incompatible with the objective and image of the charity.
The Charity Commissioners are concerned to protect the name of a
charity which is considered to be a valuable asset. Consequently, charities are advised to take steps to protect and, where appropriate, take
professional advice on valuing, their name.[35] Before entering into an
agreement which allows the charity's name to be associated with a particular business or product the Charity Commissioners consider that the
charity needs to make sure that[36]: the relationship is appropriate for a
charity and will not damage either that particular charity or the good
name of charity as a whole; raising the same money in some other way
would be less efficient; the name will not be exploited for non-charitable
purposes; the terms are generally to the benefit of the charity; the terms
are precisely drafted in detail and kept under review so that the name is
not misused or improperly exploited; and, they have the right to prevent future use of the name if they are not satisfied about any of these
matters.

Trading[37]

There are two connected problems concerning trading by charities. The **7–039**
first, and most fundamental, is that trading is not, in itself, a charitable
purpose. Therefore, a charity itself cannot undertake permanent trading
activities of a substantial nature, since trading is not a charitable activity,
without expending charitable funds in breach of trust and endangering
charitable status. The second problem concerns any possible exemption
from income tax in respect of any profits resulting from trading which
charities do undertake.[38]

In order that charitable status will not be endangered, the most common method used to engage in substantial trading is for a charity to
undertake non-exempt trading activities through the medium of a separate limited company, whose shares are held by the charity.[39] The subsidiary trading company will then transfer back all its income–taxable
profits to the charity in each year in a tax effective way.[40]

In order for a charity to be able to take advantage of the separate
wholly–owned trading company option, its investment powers must permit such an investment in the trading company. Most charities will now
have such a power, either in their governing documents or as a result of

---

[35] See, RS2, *Charities and Commercial Partners* (2002), pp.5–6.
[36] CC20, *Charities and Fund-Raising* (2002), para.48.
[37] See CC35, *Charities and Trading* (2001) and Inland Revenue Leaflet IR 2001.
[38] See para.8–006 below.
[39] CC35, *Charities and Trading* (2001), paras 32–76.
[40] Under a new tax relief introduced in 2000, charities carrying out a small amount of
trading do not need to set up subsidiary trading companies. See para.8–006 below.

the Trustee Act 2000.[41] Before exercising such a power, trustees must have regard to the standard investment criteria.[42] These require trustees to consider whether a proposed investment in a subsidiary trading company is of a type which it is suitable for the charity to make, and whether the proposed investment is a suitable investment of that type. It must be considered whether or not a trading venture of this sort is too speculative for a charity. Trustees must also consider the need for diversity across the charity's investments as a whole. Trustees must normally also take professional investment advice.[43] When making and reviewing investments trustees must exercise such care and skill as is reasonable in the circumstances.[44]

7–040   Funds needed to sustain or expand the activities of the trading company should normally be borrowed from commercial sources. However, if the separate trading company is to receive a loan from the charity for this purpose, it should take the form of a secured loan on market terms.[45]

In order to minimise the potential for conflict of interest, the Charity Commissioners recommend there should be at least one person who is a trustee of the charity and not a director of the trading company, and at least one person who is a director of the trading company and not a trustee of the charity.[46]

Not all trading companies are profitable, and failed subsidiaries will cause problems for charity trustees, who may feel morally obliged to pay the company's creditors.[47] However, such a course of action should not normally be followed by the trustees as it would amount to a breach of trust.

7–041   Trading companies connected with charities generally do not come within the controls on fund-raising contained in the Charities Act 1992.[48] However, a trading company acting as a commercial participator in relation to a charitable institution *not* wholly controlling the company would fall within the definition.

The Strategy Unit report recommended that the legislation be amended to allow charities to undertake all trading within the charity, without the need for a trading company.[49] The power to undertake trade would be subject to a specific statutory duty of care.

---

[41] Trustee Act 2000, s.3, see para.6–024 above. The Act does not apply to the corporate property of charitable companies and other charities incorporated by or under legislation. A charity without such a power must apply to the Charity Commissioners for authority.
[42] Trustee Act 2000, s.4.
[43] *ibid.*, s.5.
[44] *ibid.*, s.1 and Sch.1.
[45] See Charity Commissioners, *War on Want Inquiry* (1991), para.2.20, where it was considered that advances to War on Want Trading without charging interest amounted to an application of charitable funds for non charitable purposes.
[46] CC35, *Charities and Trading* (2001), para.44.
[47] See [1988] Ch. Com. Rep., paras 45–48.
[48] See the definition of "professional fund-raiser" and "commercial participator" in Charities Act 1992, s.58.
[49] Cabinet Office, Strategy Unit, *Private Action, Public Benefit. A Review of Charities and the Wider Not-For-Profit Sector.* (2002), para.4.47.

Challenge events

Many charities are now raising funds from events based outdoors, **7–042** where participants are challenged to complete an activity that is sufficiently compelling to attract sponsorship. The participants might also receive a benefit, where they do not personally pay the whole cost of attending the event (which may include the costs of overseas travel), but use some of the sponsorship money for this purpose. As well as familiar issues, such as, should the activity be undertaken through a trading subsidiary,[50] there are considerable risks and responsibilities in organising these events, which have been the subject of media attention and some adverse publicity.

Such events have been commonly held in areas of attractive landscape which are under considerably increasing visitor pressure. There has thus been concern about the ecological effects of such fund-raising activities. The Institute of Fund-raising has issued a code of practice[51] which seeks to minimise the environmental impact of such activities. It also draws attention to the risks involved.

Where the challenge event is organised or promoted by a third party operating on behalf of the charity, it may well come within the definition of a professional fund-raiser[52] or commercial participator,[53] and the statutory requirements will apply.[54] Participants may also fall within the definition of professional fund-raiser if they receive a benefit worth more than £500. The organiser or promotor must also ensure that all printed documents and fund-raising material associated with the challenge event comply with the requirements of s.5 of the Charities Act 1993.[55]

The legal issues surrounding challenge events become more complex **7–043** when the events involve overseas travel.[56] Such overseas events are likely to bring charities within the remit of the rules on air travel. For example, generally anyone selling air travel must hold an Air Travel Organiser's Licence (ATOL) or be acting as an authorised agent of an ATOL holder.[57]

Events at home or abroad may be subject to regulation by the Package Travel, Package Holidays and Package Tours Regulations 1992.[58] To fall within the definition of "a package" the event must cover a period of more than 24 hours or include overnight accommodation, and at least two of the following three components must be present[59]: transport; accommodation;

---

[50] See para.7–039 above.
[51] Institute of Fund-raising, *Code of Fund-raising Practice—Outdoor Fund-raising Events in the UK*.
[52] See definition of "professional fund-raiser" in Charities Act 1992, s.58. See para.7–003 above.
[53] See definition of "commercial participator" in Charities Act 1992, s.58. See para.7–012 above.
[54] See paras 7–005, *et seq.*, and paras 7–013, *et seq.*, above respectively.
[55] See para.1–031 above.
[56] See Institute of Fund-raising, *Code of Fund-raising Practice—Charity Challenge Events*.
[57] Civil Aviation (Air Travel Organisers' Licensing) Regulations 1995 (SI 1995/1054). See also, Civil Aviation Authority, Consumer Protection Group, *Air Travel Organisers' Licensing Guidance Note Number 24—The ATOL Regulations: Advice for Charities and Organisations Offering Air Travel as Part of a Fund-raising Exercise*, April 2001.
[58] SI 1992/3288.
[59] *ibid.*, reg.2(1).

or other tourist service accounting for a significant proportion of the package. The Regulations govern the marketing, sale and performance of package holidays sold or offered for sale in the UK.

These events raise complex issues, largely due to the fact that they fall within several legislative regimes. However, they have proved to be a good way of both attracting funds from new sources which a traditional appeal will not reach, and raising a charity's profile. Despite the complexities, there are ways to structure the arrangements for such events so as to comply with the various legal obligations and to minimise liabilities.[60]

Fund-raising on the internet[61]

7–044   There are many different ways in which charities are using the internet for fund-raising.[62] One obvious use of the internet in fund-raising is through on-line credit card donations. Existing methods of fund-raising, such as sponsorship and cause–related marketing are also now being undertaken via the internet. A company may host a charity's website or there may be links between a charity's website and its corporate sponsor's website. Such corporate partners will usually fall within the category of "commercial participators"[63] and will therefore be bound by the provisions of Pt II of the Charities Act 1992.[64]

A number of areas of law need to be considered when fund-raising on the internet. These include: copyright of material on the website; security of credit card details; ownership of the domain name; potential liability for libellous comments made on a charity website that hosts a newsgroup or discussion forum; compliance with the Data Protection Act 1998 and the British Codes of Advertising and Sales Promotion.[65] In addition, charity websites and emails soliciting money should comply with s.5 of Charities Act 1993.[66]

---

[60] See Rigby, Alexander and Sayer, "Adventures in Fund-raising—rising to the legal challenges" April 1999 NGO Finance.
[61] See Lake, *Direct Connection's Guide to Fund-raising on the Internet* (1996).
[62] See Institute of Fund-raising, *Code of Fund-raising Practice—Fund-raising on the Internet.*
[63] See para.7–012 above.
[64] See paras 7–013, *et seq.*, above.
[65] See para.7–023 above.
[66] See para.1–031 above.

CHAPTER 8

TAXATION

Charities have enjoyed relief from taxation since the introduction of income tax by William Pitt.[1] The exemption survived Gladstone's fierce attack in his 1863 budget statement[2] and an attempt by the Inland Revenue in 1891 to restrict its scope to charities for the relief of poverty.[3] The various reliefs from taxation available to charities are now very valuable[4] and it has been suggested more than once[5] that "charity" should have a restricted definition for fiscal purposes. No such restriction, however, has been enacted, and all charities are equally entitled to relief from taxation, save for certain specific reliefs from Value Added Tax (VAT).

8–001

The courts are fully aware of the fiscal privileges attaching to charitable status and this factor can influence decisions as to the validity of charitable trusts.[6] The existence of tax exemptions can affect the granting of charitable status in two ways; first, cases on charitable status involving the Inland Revenue are far more likely to go to appeal than those between beneficiaries under a will,[7] and secondly, at the initial registration stage, there is close consultation between the Charity Commission and the Inland Revenue.[8]

Exemptions for charities occur across the whole spectrum of taxation; including income tax, corporation tax, capital gains tax, value added tax and stamp duty. It must be stressed that there is no general exemption from taxation for charities, but specific provisions relieving charities from liability for individual taxes. If all the conditions for a particular exemption are not complied with, tax will be payable. Similarly, tax will be payable if there is no specific exemption, for example, for income arising under Sch.E.

---

[1] Income Tax Act 1799, s.5.
[2] *Hansard* 170 at 200–247; see also Owen, *English Philanthropy 1660–1960* (1965), pp.331–332.
[3] *Income Tax Special Purpose Commissioners v Pemsel* [1891] A.C. 531.
[4] Estimated to be £1.2 billion from direct taxes alone, *Hansard*, vol.333 col.75 (June 15, 1999).
[5] Report of the Royal Commission on the Income Tax, Cmd. 615 (1920), paras 305–309; Final Report of the Royal Commission on the Taxation of Profits and Income (Radcliffe Commission) Cmd. 9474 (1955), paras 168–175. See also Warburton [2000] B.T.R. 144 at 146.
[6] *Dingle v Turner* [1972] A.C. 601 at 624, *per* Lord Cross of Chelsea; *cf.* Viscount Dilhorne, Lord MacDermott and Lord Hodson at 614.
[7] See, *e.g. IRC v McMullen* [1981] A.C. 1, which was funded to the House of Lords by the Inland Revenue as a test case.
[8] Charities Act 1993, s.10.

In addition to the fiscal privileges enjoyed by charities themselves, there are considerable tax incentives given to individuals and companies to make donations to charity. Taxation exemptions for donors have increased over the years. Changes to the exemptions were introduced in April 2000 with the specific intention of encouraging giving to charity. Relief is available from income tax, corporation tax, capital gains tax and inheritance tax.

EXEMPTION FOR CHARITIES

Income tax

8–002   The exemptions for charities from income tax are to be found in s.505(1) of the Taxes Act 1988. The specific provisions as they relate to particular sources of income are discussed below. The Inland Revenue have power to call for books, documents and other records to ensure that the relevant conditions for exemption have been complied with.[9] There is, however, one condition common to all the subsections; the income must be applied for charitable purposes. In the case of relief under s.501(a) and (c) relief is available if the income is paid for charitable purposes only which need not be the charitable purposes of the charity seeking relief.[10]

A charity satisfies the condition if all the income is distributed for charitable purposes, and, if this is the case, the court will not enquire as to the reason or motive for the distribution.[11] The condition is still satisfied if the income is reinvested and the accumulations held as part of the charity's funds. Similarly, tax will not be payable if the income is paid over to another charity, even if the second charity does not distribute the income.[12] The condition will not be satisfied, however, if part of the income is applied for non-charitable objects[13]; for example, when trustees of an educational trust made grants to children of employees of the founder of the trust, they were not exempt from income tax.[14] In the case of relief under s.505(1)(e) and (f) the profits must be applied for the purposes of the charity earning them.

Land

8–003   S.505(1)(a) provides an exemption from income tax under Schs.A and D in respect of any profits or gains arising in respect of rents and other receipts from an estate, interest or right in or over any land in the United Kingdom or elsewhere. The exemption is to the extent that the profits or

---

[9] Finance (No. 2) Act 1992, s.28.
[10] See *George Drexler Ofrex Foundation Trustees v IRC* [1966] Ch. 675 at 701.
[11] *Campbell v IRC* [1970] A.C. 77.
[12] *IRC v Slater (Helen) Charitable Trust Ltd.* [1982] Ch. 49. But see now Taxes Act 1988, s.505(2) at para.8–004, below.
[13] *Trade House of Glasgow v IRC* [1969] T.R. 529.
[14] *IRC v Educational Grants Association* [1967] Ch. 993.

gains arise in respect of rents or other receipts from an estate, interest or right vested in any person for charitable purposes and are applied for charitable purposes only.

Whether land is held for charitable purposes is usually determined by reference to the register of charities. The exemption in s.505(1)(a) extends only the profits and gains on rents or other receipts from land; it does not extend to any capital sum received on the disposal of land taxable under s.776 of the Taxes Act 1988.

Interest, annuities, dividends and annual payments

S.505(1)(c) provides exemption[15]:   **8–004**

> "(i) ....[16]
>
> (ii) from tax under Case III of Schedule D,
>
> > (iia) from tax under Case IV or V of Schedule D in respect of income equivalent to income chargeable under Case III of that Schedule but arising from securities or other possessions outside the United Kingdom,
> >
> > (iib) from tax under Case V of Schedule D in respect of income consisting in any such dividend or other distribution of a company not resident in the United Kingdom as would be chargeable to tax under Schedule F if the company were so resident, and
> >
> > (iic) from tax under Case VI of Schedule D in respect of non-trading gains on intangible fixed assets under Schedule 29 to the Finance Act 2002, and
>
> (iii) from tax under Schedule F in respect of any distribution,
>
> where the income in question forms part of the income of a charity, or is, according to rules and regulations established by Act of Parliament, charter, decree, deed of trust or will, applicable to charitable purposes only, and so far as it is applied to charitable purposes only;"

A variety of receipts are charged to income tax, or corporation tax as appropriate, by Case III of Sch.D. The most relevant of the receipts for charities are interest, annuities and other annual payments.[17] "Interest"[18] and "annuity" bear their usual meaning for income tax purposes. "Annual payments"[19] will only be exempt if they are income and not capital in the hands of the charity.[20] In order to determine whether a payment is capital

---

[15] The exemption does not apply to UK income of a charity established abroad; *Dreyfus (Camille and Henry) Foundation, Inc. v IRC* [1956] A.C. 39.

[16] s.505(1)(c)(i) was repealed by Finance Act 1996, s.79 and Sch.7, para.19, s.205 and Sch.41, PtV(2).

[17] See Taxes Act 1988, s.18.

[18] *Bennett v Ogston* (1930) 15 T.C. 374; *Riches v Westminster Bank Ltd.* [1947] A.C. 390; *Re Euro Hotel (Belgravia) Ltd.* [1975] 3 All E.R. 1075.

[19] *IRC v Whitworth Park Coal Co.* [1958] Ch. 792.

[20] *Campbell v IRC* [1970] A.C. 77.

or income the court will take an overall view of the agreement under which
the payment is made and, where necessary, will consider evidence of surrounding circumstances.[21] Annual payments were commonly made to a
charity under four-year covenants enabling charities to reclaim the tax
deducted by the donor.[22] The tax relief for payments under covenant
ceased to have effect in April 2000 and tax relief for donors is now given
under the Gift Aid regime.[23] A charity receiving a qualifying donation
under Gift Aid is treated as receiving an annual payment net of basic rate
tax[24] and can accordingly reclaim the tax from the Inland Revenue.

An anti-avoidance provision in s.505(2) of the Taxes Act 1988, deals
with the problems raised by *IRC v Slater (Helen) Charitable Trust*.[25] If a
payment is made by one charity to another, it is subject to tax under
Sch.D, Case III. The charge does not apply, however, if the payment is
made for full consideration in money or money's worth,[26] or would have
been liable to tax anyway,[27] or is eligible for relief under s.505(1).[28] A
payment caught by this charge is eligible for relief as an annual payment
under s.505(1)(c) if it is applied for charitable purposes only.

8–005   Charities are no longer able to claim payment of tax credits on company
distributions.[29] As compensation, charities are entitled to payments from
the Inland Revenue for five years from April 6, 1999.[30] The compensation
payments are on a sliding scale of 21 per cent to 4 per cent of the net
dividends received in the tax year.

There is a further tax exemption in s.505(1)(d) from tax under Sch.D in
respect of public revenue dividends[31] on securities which are in the names
of trustees to the extent that the dividends are applied for the repair of any
cathedral, college, church or chapel or any building used solely for the
purposes of divine worship.

Trading

8–006   If a charity undertakes any form of trade, the profits will be subject to
income tax under Sch.D, Case I, unless the charity can bring itself within
one of the limited exemptions in s.505(1)(e).[32] "Trade" bears its usual
meaning, and includes every trade, manufacture, adventure or concern in
the nature of trade,[33] as well as farming[34] and mining.[35] Charities have

---

[21] *IRC v Church Commissioners for England* [1976] 2 All E.R. 1037.
[22] For details of payment under deed of covenants see the 8th ed., pp.286 and 299.
[23] See para.8–031 below.
[24] Finance Act 1990, s.25(10).
[25] [1982] Ch. 49, see para.8–002, above.
[26] Taxes Act 1988, s.502(2)(b).
[27] *ibid.*, s.505(2)(c).
[28] *ibid.*, s.505(2)(d).
[29] Taxes Act 1988, s.231 as amended by Finance (No. 2) Act 1997, s.30.
[30] Finance (No. 2) Act 1997, s.35.
[31] "Public revenue dividends" are defined in Taxes Act 1988, s.505 (1A).
[32] See below.
[33] Taxes Act 1988, s.832(1).
[34] *ibid.*, s.53.
[35] *ibid.*, s.55.

been held to be trading when they have run a restaurant open to outsiders,[36] sold books[37] and let out rooms for public entertainment.[38] If the particular trade does not come within the exemptions, it is irrelevant that the profits were in fact applied for charitable purposes.[39]

Profits from trading will be exempt in three circumstances. The first is where the trade is exercised in the course of the actual carrying out of a primary purpose of the charity[40]; thus, for example, profits from courses run by an educational charity will not be taxable. The second is where the work in connection with the trade is mainly carried out by beneficiaries of the charity[41]; workshops for the blind are, therefore, exempt from income tax.

The third is where the charity can bring itself within the exemption for small trading in s.46 of the Finance Act 2000. Under that section a charity will be exempt from income tax on the profits from small trading or other fund-raising activities if its gross income does not exceed the requisite limit or there is reasonable expectation at the beginning of the chargeable period that the limit will not be exceeded.[42] The requisite limits are a gross income of £5,000 or, if greater, 25 per cent of the charity's incoming resources subject to an overall limit of £50,000.[43] In determining whether a charity has a reasonable expectation that the requisite limit will not be exceeded, the Inland Revenue will consider such matters as previous levels of income in the case of an established trade or forecasts in the case of a new trade.[44] The exemption is only available if the income is applied solely for the purposes of the charity[45] and is not available on certain income charged under Case VI of Sch.D, for example, gains on the development of land.[46]

By concession[47] charities are exempt from income tax on the profits of certain fund-raising events if the event is of a kind which falls within the exemption from VAT under Group 12 of Sch.9 to the Value Added Tax Act 1994 and the profits are transferred to charities or otherwise applied for charitable purposes only. The details of this concession are considered in the context of VAT.[48]   **8–007**

The fact that the income of a particular trade is exempt from income tax, either by right or by concession, does not necessarily mean that a charity has power carry out that trade. The power to trade depends on the

---

[36] *Grove v Young Men's Christian Association* (1903) 4 T.C. 613.
[37] *Religious Tract and Book Society of Scotland v Forbes* (1896) 3 T.C. 415; *Psalms and Hymns (Baptist) Trustees v Whitwell* (1890) 3 T.C. 7.
[38] *Coman v Rotunda Hospital Dublin (Governors)* [1921] 1 A.C. 1.
[39] *St Andrew's Hospital, Northampton v Shearsmith* (1887) 19 Q.B.D. 624.
[40] Taxes Act 1988, s.505(1)(e)(i); *IRC v Glasgow Musical Festival Association* (1926) 11 T.C. 154; *Dean Leigh Temperance Canteen (Trustees) v IRC* [1958] T.R. 385.
[41] *ibid.*, s.505(1)(e)(ii); *Brighton Convent of the Blessed Sacrament v IRC* (1933) 18 T.C. 76.
[42] Finance Act 2000, s.46(3).
[43] *ibid.*, s.46(4).
[44] See IR 2001, *Trading by Charities*.
[45] Finance Act 2000, s.46(3).
[46] *ibid.*, s.46(2).
[47] E.S.C. C4. See also IR 2001, *Trading by Charities*.
[48] See para.8–022 below.

usual interpretation of a charity's governing instrument. Nor does exemption from income tax absolve charity trustees from their obligation not to speculate with the assets of the charity. The Charity Commissioners have indicated that they will not normally question the carrying out of a trade which is within the statutory exemption from income tax unless the particular form of trade is high risk.[49]

If charity does wish to carry out a trade which is not within one of the exemptions, income tax can be avoided by using a separate trading company. The profits of such a company will be liable to corporation tax but that tax can be avoided if the company pays its profits to the charity by Gift Aid donation.[50] A donation made up to nine months after the end of an accounting period can be treated as made in that accounting period[51] which obviates the need for overpayment and reclaim to ensure maximum tax relief. The Inland Revenue has indicated[52] that it will not attack such a trading arrangement under the *Ramsay*[53] principle unless, for example, the trader effectively controls the charity using it as a tax free money box. Such an arrangement can also be used where the trade, although exempt from income tax, presents risks to the assets of the charity.

Lotteries

8–008   S.505(1)(f) excepts a charity from tax under Sch.D on profits accruing on certain types of lottery. The relevant lotteries are a small lottery incidental to exempt entertainment conducted in accordance with s.3 of the Lotteries and Amusements Act 1976 or a society's lottery conducted in accordance with s.5 of the 1976 Act.

Other income

8–009   Charities are exempt from tax on offshore income gains.[54] Trustees of a trust established for charitable purposes only are exempt from the additional rate of income tax payable on income which is accumulated or payable at their discretion.[55] Directors of companies established for charitable purposes are not "directors or higher paid employees" for the purposes of ss.153 to 168 of the Taxes Act 1988 by reason only of their directorship.[56] Directors of charitable companies, therefore, should not be charged income tax on any reimbursement of expenses. Nor is a director

---

[49] See CC35, *Charities and Trading* (2001), para.11.
[50] See para.8–030 below. For setting up a trading company, see para.7–039 above.
[51] Taxes Act 1988, s.339(7AA) inserted by Finance Act 2000, s.40.
[52] [1985] S.T.I. 572.
[53] *Ramsay (W.T.) v IRC* [1982] A.C. 300.
[54] Taxes Act 1988, s.761(6).
[55] Taxes Act 1988, s.686(2)(c).
[56] *ibid.*, s.167(5)(b).

of a charitable company chargeable to income tax in respect of living accommodation provided for the proper or better performance of his duties.[57]

Capital gains tax

By s.256(1) of the Taxation of Chargeable Gains Act 1992, a charity is **8–010** exempt from capital gains tax on gains accruing to the charity[58] and applied for charitable purposes. However, if charity property ceases to be subject to charitable trusts, the trustees are to be treated as if they had disposed of the property and immediately reacquired it for a consideration equal to its market value, and any gain on the disposal is not to be treated as accruing to the charity.[59] Also, if and so far as any of that property represents (directly or indirectly) the consideration for the disposal of assets by the trustees, any gain accruing on that disposal shall be treated as not accrued to a charity.[60] Any assessment under the latter provision can be made at any time not more than three years after the end of the year of assessment in which the property ceased to be subject to the charitable trusts. If all the unit holders in an authorised unit trust scheme are charities exempt from capital gains tax, the unit trust will also be exempt from capital gains tax.[61]

Corporation tax

Charitable corporations and unincorporated associations[62] have the **8–011** same exemptions from corporation tax in relation to income as charitable trusts have from income tax.[63] There is a similar exemption for chargeable gains.[64]

Restrictions on exemptions

The Finance Act 1986 introduced provisions to prevent certain misuse **8–012** of charitable status. The provisions are designed to restrict relief when funds are applied otherwise than for exclusively charitable purposes. Whilst the provisions do not normally apply to a charity with relevant income and gains of less than £10,000,[65] they will apply if it appears to the Inland Revenue that two or more charities are acting in concert with the

---

[57] *ibid.*, s.145(5).
[58] See *Prest v Bettison* (1982) 82 T.C. 437.
[59] Taxation of Chargeable Gains Act 1992, s.256(2)(a).
[60] *ibid.*, s.256(2)(b).
[61] *ibid.*, s.100(2).
[62] Taxes Act 1988, s.832(1); the definition of "company" includes unincorporated association.
[63] *ibid.*, s.9(4).
[64] *ibid.*, s.354(2).
[65] *ibid.*, s.505(3)(a); the £10,000 will be reduced proportionately if the chargeable period is less than 12 months: s.505(4).

aim of avoiding tax.[66] "Relevant income and gains" are the total of income which would not, apart from s.505(1), be exempt from tax, any other taxable income, gains which would, apart from s.145, be chargeable gains and any other chargeable gains.[67] Thus grants and donations are not included.

The provisions operate by designating expenditure incurred otherwise than for exclusively charitable purposes as "non-qualifying expenditure" and be deeming certain types of expenditure to be non-qualifying expenditure.[68] By comparison, "qualifying expenditure" is expenditure incurred for charitable purposes only.[69]

Tax exemptions to which a charity would otherwise be entitled are restricted if, in any chargeable period, the charity's relevant income and gains exceed its qualifying expenditure. The amount from which the exemptions are withdrawn, however, is restricted to the charity's non-qualifying expenditure in that chargeable period[70] and the charity may specify which items of its relevant income and gains are to become taxable as a result of the withdrawal of the relief. If the charity's total expenditure in the chargeable period exceeds its relevant income and gains, the excess non-qualifying expenditure may be attributed to earlier chargeable periods.[71]

8–013   "Non-qualifying expenditure" includes certain payments to overseas bodies, and loans and investments made by the charity. A payment made by a charity to a body outside the United Kingdom is treated as non-qualifying expenditure, unless the charity can show that it has taken reasonable steps to ensure that the payment will be used for charitable purposes only.[72]

The Inland Revenue will not usually challenge payments made by responsible charities that are clearly destined for charitable work abroad. Where appropriate, however, the Inland Revenue will ask for information about the activities and objectives of the overseas body and the arrangements for earmarking the payment for a particular purpose and checking on what it has been used for.[73]

Loans and investments are treated as non-qualifying expenditure unless they fall within one of the following categories of qualifying loans and investments.[74]
"Qualifying loans"[75]:

(a)   a loan made to another charity for charitable purposes only;
(b)   a loan to a beneficiary of the charity made in the course of its charitable activities;

---

[66] Taxes Act 1988, s.505(7).
[67] *ibid.*, s.505(5).
[68] *ibid.*, ss.505(3)(c), 506, Sch.20.
[69] *ibid.*, s.506(1).
[70] *ibid.*, s.505(3).
[71] *ibid.*, s.506(6), Sch.20, PtIII.
[72] *ibid.*, s.506(3).
[73] See HC Official Report, Standing Committee G, col.496 (June 17, 1986).
[74] Taxes Act 1988, s.506(4).
[75] Taxes Act 1988, Sch.20, PtII.

(c) money placed in a current account with a bank (unless this forms part of an arrangement under which the bank makes a loan to another person);

(d) any other loan made for the benefit of the charity and not for the avoidance of tax by the charity or any other person (the charity must make a claim to this effect[76]).

"Qualifying investments"[77]:   **8–014**

(a) authorised trustee investments including wider-range investments, but excluding mortgages of freehold and leashold property, listed in Schedule 1 to the Trustee Investments Act 1961[78];

(b) common investment funds[79] established under the provisions of s.22 of the Charities Act 1960 or s.24 of the Charities Act 1993 and similar funds;

(c) common deposit funds[80] established under s.22A of the Charities Act 1960 or s.25 of the Charities Act 1993 and similar funds;

(d) any interest in land, other than one held as security for a debt;

(e) shares or securities quoted on a recognised stock exchange, or dealt in on the Unlisted Securities Market;

(f) investments in unit trusts;

(g) certificates of deposit;

(h) bank deposits on which a commercial rate of interest is paid (unless this forms part of an arrangement under which the bank makes a loan to another person);

(i) any loan or other investment (including a mortgage) made for the benefit of the charity and not for the avoidance of tax by the charity or any other person. The charity must make a claim to this effect.

A special provision ensures that if a non-qualifying investment is made and realised, or a non-qualifying loan is made and repaid, during the same chargeable period, the reinvestment of the proceeds during that period is left out of account when determining the amount of the non-qualifying expenditure incurred by the charity. If the reinvestment exceeds the original amount, the excess is treated as non-qualifying expenditure.[81]

---

[76] *e.g.* a loan at a commercial rate of interest to a linked trading company. See *Nightingale v Price* [1996] S.T.C. (S.C.D.) 116 for the circumstances in which such loans will not be "non-qualifying expenditure".

[77] Taxes Act 1998, Sch.20, PtI.

[78] This restriction on qualifying investments remains despite the wide general power of investment given by s.3 of the Trustee Act 2000.

[79] See para.6–028, above.

[80] See para.6–030, above.

[81] Taxes Act 1988, s.506(5).

Value added tax

8–015   VAT is charged on any supply of goods or services made by a taxable person in the course or furtherance of any business carried on by him.[82] There is no general exemption for charities from VAT but there are five main ways in which charities may get some relief from VAT. Many charities do not pay VAT because they are not making supplies, or because they are not in business, or because their turnover is below the limit for registration. Even if a charity is in fact within the ambit of VAT, some of its supplies may be exempt from VAT, and others may be zero-rated.

Only zero-rating gives total relief from VAT. The other four ways provide only partial relief in that, whilst VAT is not chargeable by the charity on supplies it makes, input tax incurred on relevant supplies to the charity will not be recoverable.[83] Irrecoverable input tax now represents a major concern for charities.[84]

Legislation

8–016   The relevant legislation is now the Value Added Tax Act 1994 and the regulations and orders made thereunder. All the United Kingdom legislation, however, is subject to the relevant EU directives in particular the Sixth Council Directive on VAT.[85] The terms of the Directives, which are clear and unambiguous and do not contain conditions and discretions, are of direct effect.

The United Kingdom legislation must be construed in a way which is consistent with the Directive. This can operate to both widen and narrow the provisions of the 1994 Act. On the one hand, the exemption in Article 13A(1)(g) of the Sixth Directive for the supply of goods linked to welfare and social security work was held to be wider than the list of exempted goods and services then contained in Group 6 of Sch.6 to the Value Added Tax Act 1983.[86] On the other hand, the requirement to construe exemptions restrictively[87] led to the conclusion that an ordinary visit to the zoo was not educational and the supply not exempt with Group 6 of Sch.9 to the 1994 Act.[88] The court, or VAT and Duties Tribunal, may make a reference to the European Court of Justice for a preliminary ruling on the interpretation of the Directives under Article 177 of the EC Treaty.[89]

---

[82] Value Added Tax Act 1994, s.4.

[83] See below para.8–018 for non-business activities and para.8–020 for exempt supplies.

[84] Irrecoverable input tax for charities has been estimated at £460m. a year, HM Treasury, "Review of Charity Taxation" (1999), para.5.10.

[85] Dir. 77/388.

[86] *International Bible Students Association v Customs and Excise Commissioners, The Times,* December 23, 1987.

[87] *Stichting Vitvoering Financiele Acties v Staatssecretaris van Financien* [1989] E.C.R. 1737.

[88] *North of England Zoological Society v Customs and Excise Commissioners* [1999] S.T.C. 1027; cf. *North of England Zoological Society v Chester RDC* [1959] 1 W.L.R. 773, where the same organisation, Chester Zoo, was held entitled to relief from rates as a charity.

[89] See *e.g.*, *Customs and Excise Commissioners v Zoological Society of London* [1999] B.T.C. 5284.

VAT is administered by the Commissioners of Customs and Excise, who produce many explanatory leaflets, several of which are specifically relevant for charities.[90] The leaflets, which state the Commissioners' view of the law, are always subject to contrary decisions by the courts.

Registration

A charity will be required to register for VAT if, at the end of any month, its turnover in the past year has exceeded £56,000.[91] When determining the amount of turnover, any non-business activities[92] and exempt supplies[93] are excluded. There should be included, however, all the activities over which a charity has control; for example, branches run or controlled from head office. The turnover of independent local societies need not be included if they control their own affairs. Similarly, the turnover of separate fund-raising bodies who undertake financial responsibility for all their fund-raising activities need not be included.

8–017

Non-business activities

A charity will not be required to register for VAT if it does not carry on any business activities. If a charity is registered but also has some non-business activities, it will not be allowed to set off the input tax incurred in carrying out its non-business activities.[94]

8–018

"Business"[95] is defined in s.94(1) of the 1994 Act as including any trade, profession or vocation. S.94(2) provides specifically that the provision by a club, association or organisation, for a subscription or other consideration, of the facilities or advantages available to its members; and the admission for a consideration of persons to any premises are deemed to be the carrying on of a business. The scope of "business" for the purposes of VAT has been considered in several cases[96] from which a definition of "business" as "a serious undertaking earnestly pursued" emerges. A summary of the court's approach in the context of a charity was made by His Honour Stephen Oliver Q.C. in *The National Society for the Prevention of Cruelty to Children v Customs and Excise Commissioners*[97]:

---

[90] Charities 701/1/95; Clubs and Associations 701/5/02; other leaflets are referred to below.
[91] Value Added Tax Act 1994, Sch.1, para.1.
[92] See below.
[93] See para.8–020, below.
[94] Value Added Tax Act 1994, ss.25, 26; *Whitechapel Art Gallery v Customs and Excise Commissioners* [1986] 1 C.M.L.R. 79. If necessary, expenditure will be apportioned.
[95] The term used in the Sixth Directive is "economic activity"; Art.4(2) of Council Directive 77/388.
[96] See *Customs and Excise Commissioners v Morrison's Academy Boarding Houses Association* [1978] S.T.C. 1; *National Water Council v Customs and Excise Commissioners* [1979] S.T.C. 157; *Customs and Excise Commissioners v Lord Fisher* [1981] S.T.C. 238. See also Warburton, "Charities, Value Added Tax and Business" (1995) 3 C.L.P.R. 37.
[97] [1992] V.A.T.T.R. 417 at 422.

"The United Kingdom decisions establish that, for an activity to qualify as 'business' for VAT purposes it must amount to a continuing activity which is predominantly concerned with the making of supplies to others for a consideration. There are, in effect, two parts to the test. First, for there to be an 'activity' there must be sufficiency of scale to the supplies and they must be continued over a period of time. Second, the predominant concern of the person conducting the activity must be the making of supplies."

Before a charity can be said to be carrying on a business it must be making supplies, that is, supplies of goods and services in exchange for consideration.[98] There will not be any supplies if there is no direct link between the money received by a charity and any services provided.[99] Thus a charity may be carrying on many activities but if it relies totally on donations to cover its running costs it will not be regarded as carrying on a business for the purposes of VAT. A donation to a charity, even for a specific purpose of the charity, is not a supply for a consideration.[1]

8-019   Donations, legacies and other voluntary contributions are not the proceeds of a business activity.[2] The giving of a flag or other emblem in exchange for a donation will not turn it into a taxable supply. Similarly, grants are not regarded as the proceeds of business activity unless they are earmarked for a specific purpose.[3] Thus, the provision of a voluntary service[4] by a charity is a non-business activity outside the scope of VAT and the fact that some contribution is received towards administration costs will not make the provision of a voluntary service for the community a business activity.[5]

There will be business activity if a fee is charged for services provided by a charity. This will be so even if fees are less than market rate and no steps are taken to recover unpaid fees.[6] It is sufficient if facilities are provided in a regular business-like manner even if some users do not pay full rates and the balance of income is made up from donations.[7] If the basic conditions for business activity are satisfied a charity will be within the ambit of VAT even though it is non-profit making.[8] The fact that a body is pursuing a

---

[98] Value Added Tax Act 1994, s.5(2).

[99] *Staatssecretaris van Financien v Co-operatieve Aardappelenbewaarplaats GA* [1981] 3 C.M.L.R. 337; *Apple and Pear Development Council v Customs and Excise Commissioners* [1988] S.T.C. 221.

[1] *Customs and Excise Commissioners v Church Schools Foundation* [2001] S.T.C. 1661 at 1676, *per* Sir Andrew Morritt.

[2] *Tolsma v Inspecteur der Omzetbelasting Leeuwarden* [1994] S.T.C. 509.

[3] See *Hillingdon Legal Resources Centre Ltd. v Customs and Excise Commissioners* [1991] V.A.T.T.R. 39 (Hillingdon Legal Resources Centre providing free legal advice not a business as the grant support not earmarked).

[4] See *Whitechapel Art Gallery v Customs and Excise Commissioners* [1986] 1 C.M.L.R. 79 (provision of an art gallery with free admission).

[5] *Greater London Red Cross Blood Transfusion Service v Commissioners for Customs and Excise* [1983] V.A.T.T.R. 241; *cf. RSPCA v Customs and Excise Commissioners* [1991] V.A.T.T.R. 407.

[6] *RSPCA v Customs and Excise Commissioners* [1991] V.A.T.T.R. 407.

[7] *Yoga for Health Foundation v Customs and Excise Commissioners* [1985] 1 C.M.L.R. 340.

[8] *Customs and Excise Commissioners v Morrison's Academy Boarding Houses Association* [1978] S.T.C. 1.

charitable object is no reason for determining that it is not carrying on a business. Accordingly, the Royal Academy of Music[9] was held to be carrying on a business when it provided musical education in return for fees in accordance with its charitable objects.

Despite the wide definition of "business", there are some activities by charities which are not business activity for the purposes of VAT. These include making grants, including the advisory and administrative functions associated with those grants,[10] and the provision of places of worship.[11] Fund-raising, in itself, is not a business activity even if the charity can be described as "a serious undertaking earnestly pursued". Thus the Royal Exchange Theatre Trust which raised funds very effectively and efficiently to construct a theatre in Manchester was held not to be carrying on a business because it made a gift of the theatre to the Royal Exchange Theatre Trust.[12] To provide benefits in return for sponsorship, however, is likely to make the fund-raising a business acitivity.[13] The management by a charity of its investments is not a business activity, even on a large scale. Thus in *Wellcome Trust Ltd. v Customs and Excise Commissioners*[14] it was held that sales of shares raising over £2 billion was the mere exercise of rights of ownership and not economic activity within VAT.

Exempt supplies

Exempt supplies are listed in Sch.9 to the Value Added Tax Act 1994.   **8–020**
No VAT is chargeable on any exempt supplies but input tax incurred in respect of exempt supplies is not recoverable. In common with everyone else, a charity will not be subject to VAT on the provision of insurance[15] or financial services.[16] Betting, gaming and lotteries are generally exempt from VAT.[17] Thus no VAT is chargeable on a tombola or raffle held at a fund-raising event. Similarly, no VAT is chargeable on lottery tickets.[18]

The provision of education or vocational training by a school, university or college is exempt from VAT.[19] Education in this context is construed narrowly to mean a specific and structured form of training. It does not extend to education in the general sense of broadening the mind to cover such activities as a visit to the zoo.[20] Provision of education or vocational

---

[9] *Royal Academy of Music v Customs and Excise Commissioners* [1994] V.A.T.T.R. 105.

[10] *The Arts Council of Great Britain v Customs and Excise Commissioners* [1994] S.T.I. 713.

[11] *The Dean and Chapter of Hereford Cathedral v Customs and Excise Commissioners* [1994] S.T.I. 539.

[12] *Customs and Excise Commissioners v Royal Exchange Theatre* [1979] 3 All E.R. 797.

[13] See *Customs and Excise Commissioners v Tron Theatre Ltd* [1994] S.T.C. 177.

[14] [1996] S.T.C. 945. See also *The National Society for the Prevention of Cruelty to Children v Customs and Excise Commissioners* [1992] V.A.T.T.R. 417.

[15] Value Added Tax Act 1994, Sch.9, Group 2.

[16] *ibid.*, Group 5.

[17] *ibid.*, Group 4.

[18] See VAT leaflets 701/26/95, 701/27/00 and 701/28/97.

[19] Value Added Tax Act 1994, Sch.9, Group 6, Item 1.

[20] *North of England Zoological Society v Customs and Excise Commissioners* [1999] S.T.C. 1027; *cf.* the wide meaning of education for the purposes of charitable status, see *Re Lopes*

training by any other establishment is only exempt if it is provided other-wise than for profit[21]. A charity will be non-profit-making for these pur-poses even if it plans to make a surplus provided that the surplus income is applied to improve the educational services and not distributed.[22] The provision of research by any such bodies is also exempt but this exemption may be to wide.[23] Vocational training provided by any person is exempt if the consideration for the training is a charge on designated statutory funds.[24] The provision of goods and services or instruction supplemental to the provision of education is also exempt. For example, the provision of meals to students attending courses.[25]

Facilities provided by a youth club or an association of youth clubs to its members are exempt from VAT.[26] The Commissioners consider that for a youth club to be within the exemption, it must be non-profit-making, must cater mainly for people aged under 21 and must provide a regular programme of recreational, educational, social and/or cultural activities for its members.[27]

8–021   The provision of a right to enter a sports competition run by a non-profit making body is exempt.[28] The supply by a similar body of services closely linked with and essential to sport and physical education is also exempt. If the eligible body operates a membership scheme a supply to a non-member is not exempt.[29] An eligible body is one which is precluded from distributing profits other than to another non-profit making body, applies any profits for continuance or improvement of the services or the purposes of another non-profit making body and is not subject to com-mercial influence.[30] "Membership scheme" has been construed restric-tively to connote a scheme involving participation in the body in question. A scheme which provides a "membership card" giving benefits such as reduced rates to those using the sports facilities is not a "membership scheme" for these purposes.[31] Accordingly, those charities providing community sports facilities will usually be exempt from VAT.[32]

The supply by a charity, otherwise than for profit, of welfare services and connected goods is exempt from VAT.[33] Relevant services are those directly connected with the provision of care, treatment or instruction

---

[1931] 2 Ch. 130 and the text at para.2–024 above (Admission to a zoo is now potentially exempt under Group 13, see below para.8–023).

[21] Value Added Tax Act 1994, Sch.9, Group 6, Item 1.
[22] Value Added Tax Act 1994, Sch.9, Group 6, note 1(e).
[23] See *E.C. Commission v Federal Republic of Germany* [2002] S.T.C. 982.
[24] *ibid.*, Sch.9, Group 6, Items 5 and 5A.
[25] *ibid.*, Sch.9, Group 6, Items 4 and 5A.
[26] *ibid.*, Sch.9, Group 6, Item 6.
[27] See VAT leaflet 701/35/95.
[28] Value Added Tax Act 1994, Sch.9, Group 10, Item 2.
[29] *ibid.*, Item 3.
[30] *ibid.* Notes 2A–2C, see *Kennemer Golf and Country Club v Staatssecretaris van Financien* [2002] S.T.C. 502.
[31] *Basingstoke and District Sports Trust Ltd v Customs and Excise Commissioners* [1995] S.T.I. 1273 and see Warburton, "Members, Non-Members and VAT." (1996) 3 C.L.P.R. 133.
[32] See above para.2–094.
[33] Value Added Tax Act 1994, Sch.9, Group 7, Item 9.

which are designed to promote the physical or mental welfare of elderly, sick, distressed or disabled persons. Services connection with the protection of children and young person are also exempt.[34] The supply of accommodation or catering is not within the exemption, except where it is ancillary to the provision of care or treatment.[35] What amounts to care should be considered in the context of the person to whom help is being provided and care for the housebound elderly may extend to assistance with household tasks.[36]

Welfare services include services directly connected with the provision of spiritual welfare by a religious institution as part of a course of instruction or retreat, not being a course or retreat designed primarily to provide recreation or a holiday.[37]

Group 9 of Sch.9 to the 1994 Act exempts the subscriptions to a number of non-profit making bodies including associations for the advancement of a particular branch of knowledge or the fostering of professional expertise in connection with the profession or employment of its members; and bodies which have objects which are in the public domain and are of a political, religious, patriotic, philosophical, philanthropic or civic nature.[38] The exemption does not extend to any right of admission to premises, events or performances for which non-members have to pay.[39] **8–022**

Certain supplies by a charity[40], or its wholly owned non-charitable trading company which has agreed in writing to transfer its funds to charity, in connection with fund-raising events are exempt from VAT by Group 12 of Sch.9 to the 1994 Act.[41] The event must be organised and promoted with the primary purpose of raising funds for charity.[42] "Event" is given a very wide meaning and includes such things as balls, jumbles sales, art exhibitions and firework displays.[43] The definition extends to an event accessed by means of electronic communication.[44] There is no exemption if the event is likely to create distortion of competition such as to place a commercial enterprise carried on by a taxpayer at a disadvantage.[45] The

---

[34] *ibid.*, Sch.9, Group 7, Note 6.
[35] *ibid.*, Sch.9, Group 7, Note 7.
[36] *Watford District Old Peoples Housing Association Ltd. v Customs and Excise Commissioners* [1998] S.T.I. 529.
[37] Value Added Tax Act 1994, Sch.9, Group 7, Note 6.
[38] *ibid.*, Sch, Group 9, Item 1.
[39] *ibid.*, Note 1.
[40] The exemption extends to charity fund-raising events by a "qualifying body" which means (a) any non-profit making organisation mentioned in Item 1 of Group 9 (trade unions and certain professional and other public interest bodies); (b) any body that is an eligible body for the purposes of Group 10 and whose principal purpose is the provision of facilities for persons to take part in sport or physical recreation; or (c) any body that is an eligible body for the purposes of Item 2 of Group 13 (certain non-profit making museums, galleries, art exhibitions and zoos), Note 3.
[41] Substituted by The Value Added Tax (Fund-Raising Events by Charities and other Qualifying Bodies) Order 2000, (SI 2000/802).
[42] Value Added Tax Act 1994, Sch.9, Group 12, Items 1(b)(c), 2(b)(c), 3(c)(d).
[43] See Inland Revenue and HM Customs and Excise, CWL4, "Fund-raising events: Exemptions for Charities and Other Qualifying Bodies".
[44] Value Added Tax Act 1994, Sch.9, Group 12, Note 1.
[45] *ibid.*, Note 11.

exemption is lost completely if there are more than 15 events of the same kind in one year held at the same location.[46] "Location" will generally be taken to mean place, for example, concert hall or sports ground, and not town.[47] An event does not count towards the 15 if the weekly turnover from such events in that location does not exceed £1,000.[48] This is intended to preserve the exemption from VAT for small scale events such as jumble sales and coffee mornings held by charities.[49]

8–023   Group 13 of Sch.9 to the 1994 Act gives exemption to the supply by an eligible body of the right of admission to a museum, gallery, art exhibition or zoo, or a theatrical, musical or choreographic performance. A charity clearly satisfies the first two conditions of an eligible body[50] as being non-profit distributing and applying its profits for the continuance or improvement of its facilities. The third condition of being "managed and administered on a voluntary basis by persons who have no direct or indirect financial interest in its activities", however, proved problematic.[51] The European Court has now indicated that the condition is satisfied if those directing the body at the highest level and taking decisions of last resort in relation to policy are voluntary; the condition does not refer to those persons carrying out executive tasks.[52]

Zero-rated supplies

8–024   Charities benefit from zero-rating in two ways. First, if the particular supply is within the list of goods and services set out in Sch.8 to the Value Added Tax Act 1994, VAT will not be added to the cost to the charity. Secondly, if a registered charity makes zero-rated supplies, not only will no VAT be chargeable to the beneficiary, but the charity will also be able to recover input tax incurred in respect of that supply.

8–025   **Supply to a charity**—The supply to the Royal National Institute for the Blind (and similar charities) of specially adapted recording apparatus and magnetic tape for blind and severely handicapped people is zero-rated.[53] Supplies to charities of radios and cassette players for gratuitous loan to blind people are also zero-rated.[54] Because the zero-rating depends upon the use to which the goods are put, the supplier must be provided with an appropriate declaration of use.[55]

The supply to a charity of aids to be made available to handicapped (*i.e.* chronically sick or disabled) persons is zero-rated.[56] Specially designed and

---

[46] Value Added Tax Act 1994, Sch.9, Group 12, Note 4.
[47] See CWL4.
[48] Value Added Tax Act 1994, Sch.9, Group 12, Note 5.
[49] See the Explanantory Notes to SI 2000/802.
[50] Defined in Value Added Tax Act 1994, Sch.9, Group 13, Note 2.
[51] See *Glastonbury Abbey v Customs and Excise Commissioners* [1996] V.& D.R. 307.
[52] *Customs and Excise Commissioners v The Zoological Society of London* [2002] S.T.C. 521.
[53] Value Added Tax Act 1994, Sch.8, Group 4, Item 1.
[54] *ibid.*, Item 2.
[55] See VAT leaflet 701/1/95, Annex F.
[56] Value Added Tax Act 1994, Sch.8, Group 12, Item 2; see also VAT leaflet 701/7/94.

adapted vehicles and aids such as stair lifts are within this zero-rating, as is the provision of alarm systems.[57] The installation and adaption of goods for handicapped persons, and the repair and maintenance of such goods is also zero-rated[58]; similarly, no VAT is payable on supplies to charities of construction services to facilitate a handicapped person's entry or movement within a building.[59] The provision of bathroom facilities for handicapped persons in residential accommodation or day centres,[60] and buildings used principally by a charity for charitable purposes,[61] and of lifts[62] in residential homes and day-care centres for handicapped persons are zero-rated where the home or centre is run by a charity.

The supply of relevant goods for donation to a nominated, eligible body is zero-rated where the goods are purchased with funds provided by a charity.[63] Zero-rating will also apply if the supply is to an eligible body using funds supplied by a charity or is to an eligible body which is a charitable institution providing care[64] or medical or surgical treatment for handicapped persons.[65] "Relevant goods" includes such items as medical and computer equipment, parts and accessories,[66] and ambulances and vehicles adapted for use by handicapped persons in wheelchairs, but not general purpose goods, such as stationery supplies.[67] "Eligible body" includes such organisations as health authorities, non-profit-making hospitals or research institutions, charitable institutions providing care or medical or surgical treatment to handicapped persons, or rescue or first-aid services[68]. The repair and maintenance of relevant goods owned by an eligible body is also zero-rated.[69]

If a charity provides care or medical or surgical treatment for human beings or animals, or engages in medical research, its supplies of medicinal products will be zero-rated.[70] Supplies to a charity of a substance directly used for synthesis or testing in the course of medical research are also zero-rated.[71] **8–026**

The Royal National Lifeboat Institution does not pay VAT on the supply to it of lifeboats or other equipment such as winches and tractors.

---

[57] *ibid.*, Items 16 to 20.
[58] Value Added Tax Act 1994, Sch.8, Group 12, Items 4 to 7.
[59] *ibid.*, Item 8 to 9.
[60] *ibid.*, Item 11.
[61] *ibid.*, Item 12.
[62] *ibid.*, Items 17 and 18.
[63] Value Added Tax Act 1994, Sch.8, Group 15, Item 4; see also VAT leaflet 701/6/97.
[64] Providing financial assistance for purchase of equipment by disabled persons does not amount to providing "care"—*Medical Care Foundation v Customs and Excise Commissioners* [1991] V.A.T.T.R. 28.
[65] Value Added Tax Act 1994, Sch.8, Group 15, Item 5. For the appropriate certificate for the supplier, see VAT leaflet 701/6/97, supplement.
[66] "Accessories" is wide enough to cover an emergency generator to keep equipment running, *Royal Midland Counties Home for Disabled People v Customs and Excise Commissioners* [2001] S.T.I. 1967.
[67] Value Added Tax Act 1994, Sch.8, Group 15, Note 3.
[68] *ibid.*, Note 4.
[69] Value Added Tax Act 1994, Sch.8, Group 15, Items 6 and 7.
[70] *ibid.*, Item 9; see also VAT leaflet 701/1/95.
[71] Value Added Tax Act 1994, Sch.8, Group 15, Item 10. For the appropriate declaration for the supplier, see VAT leaflet 701/1/95, Annex I.

The modification, repair or maintenance of slipways used by the Royal National Lifeboat Institution is also zero-rated.[72]

The supply to a charity of advertising in any medium, including television, cinema, newspapers and the Internet, is zero-rated.[73] Zero-rating extends to the supply of design and production services in connection with such advertising.[74] Zero-rating does not apply if the intended recipients of the advertising are selected by or on behalf of the charity, for example, as in a direct mail campaign.[75] Nor does zero-rating extend to supplies received by a charity to produce its own advertising or website.[76]

8–027   **Supply by a charity**—Charities can take advantage of the general zero-rating provisions in relation to food, books and journals. Supplies of hot food and food in the course of catering, however, are at standard rate.[77] The zero-rating provision for books and journals extends to leaflets, pamphlets and newspapers, whether they are printed, photocopied or typed.[78]

The supply, by a charity, of goods which have been donated for sale, letting or export is zero-rated. The supply is also zero-rated where it is by an associated trading company which has agreed in writing to give its profits to the charity.[79] The sale or letting must be where the goods have been made available to the public or to those who are handicapped or receiving means tested benefits.[80] The donation of goods for sale, letting or export by charities or associated trading companies is also zero-rated.[81]

The export of goods by a charity to a place outside the EC is zero-rated and, accordingly, input tax relating to such goods may be recovered.[82] The supply of donated goods to a charity for export is also zero-rated.[83]

Buildings

8–028   The acquisition and occupation of buildings and land by a charity can involve both zero-rated and exempt supplies.

Supplies in connection with new buildings for charities may be zero-rated by Sch.8, Group 5 to the 1994 Act. Thus a charity will not be liable to pay VAT on the grant to it, by the builder, of the freehold or a lease for more than 21 years of a new building, provided the building is intended to be used for a relevant residential or a relevant charitable purpose[84] and the

---

[72] Value Added Tax Act 1994, Sch.8, Group 8, Item 3.
[73] *ibid.*, Sch.8, Group 15, Items 8, 8A; see also VAT Notice 701/58/02.
[74] *ibid.*, Item 8B.
[75] *ibid.*, Note 10A.
[76] *ibid.*, Note 10B, 10C.
[77] *ibid.*, Sch.8, Group 1; see also VAT leaflet 701/14/97.
[78] *ibid.*, Group 3; see also VAT leaflet 701/10/99.
[79] *ibid.*, Group 15 Item 1, 1A and Note 1E.
[80] *ibid.*, Note 1.
[81] *ibid.*, Item 2.
[82] *ibid.*, Item 3.
[83] *ibid.*, Item 2.
[84] Value Added Tax Act 1994, Sch.8, Group 5, Item 1(a); s.96(1).

relevant certificate has been given.[85] Zero-rating also applies on a grant by a person converting a non-residential building into dwellings or for a relevant residential purpose.[86] If a charity has a building constructed on its own land for a relevant residential or a relevant charitable purpose, zero-rating will apply to supplies to it of services, save those of an architect, surveyor or other person acting as consultant or in a supervisory capacity,[87] and building materials.[88] A "relevant residential purpose" includes such uses as a children's home, an old peoples' home and a hospice.[89] "A relevant charitable purpose" is the use of a building by a charity otherwise than in the course or furtherance of a business or use as a village hall or similarly in providing social or recreational facilities for a local community.[90] The meaning of "a relevant charitable purpose" was considered by the Court of Appeal in the conjoined appeals of *Jubilee Hall Recreation Centre v Customs and Excise Commissioners* and *Customs and Excise Commissioners v St Dunstan's Educational Foundation.*[91] Jubilee Hall, a recreational charity, ran a sports and fitness centre on a commercial basis in a listed building in Covent Garden. There were several categories of membership with discounts for senior citizens, residents, children and the unemployed but whilst many members worked in the area they lived elsewhere. In determining whether building works were zero-rated, the Court of Appeal stressed that the benefits of zero-rating were intended to apply where the local community was the final consumer and where the only economic activity was that which was an ordinary incident of the use the building by the local community for social, including recreational, purposes.[92] Zero-rating did not apply as the use of the building was not similar to the use of a village hall and it was doubtful if those who worked locally but lived elsewhere could be described as part of the local community. St Dunstan's constructed a sports centre for the use of the pupils of the fee-paying school which occupied its land and for use by organised groups recommended by the local authority. The Court of Appeal held that zero-rating depended on the intended use of the building. In this case it was primarily intended for the use of fee-paying pupils and only secondarily in providing social and recreational facilities for the community and so the construction work was not zero-rated.

If the building ceases to be used for a relevant residential or relevant charitable purpose within 10 years of the completion of the building a charge to VAT arises.[93] Supplies in connection with the reconstruction or approved alteration of listed buildings are also zero-rated if it is intended to use the building for a relevant residential or a relevant charitable purpose.[94]

---

[85] See VAT leaflet 708.
[86] Value Added Tax Act 1994, Sch.8, Group 5, Item 1(b).
[87] *ibid.*, Item 2. Housing associations may be entitled to zero-rating on conversion work, see Item 3.
[88] *ibid.*, Item 4.
[89] *ibid.*, Note 4.
[90] *ibid.*, Sch.8, Group 5, Note 6.
[91] [1999] S.T.C. 381.
[92] *ibid.* at 390, *per* Sir John Vinelott.
[93] Value Added Tax Act 1994, Sch.10, para.1.
[94] *ibid.*, Sch.8, Group 6.

A grant of any interest in land is generally an exempt supply and thus outside the charge to VAT.[95] A charity may, however, become liable to pay VAT on the rent of premises in certain circumstances. A landlord has an option to tax, *i.e.* to waive the exemption from VAT. If a landlord exercises the option, all subsequent leases or sales of the relevant land or buildings will be liable to VAT as standard rated supplies. An option to tax cannot be exercised to remove the exemption from the grant of an interest in a building intended for use solely for a relevant charitable purpose other than an office.[96] Thus, a charity may become liable to pay VAT on the rent of its office premises.

Stamp duty

8–029 No stamp duty is payable on conveyances or transfers on sale, voluntary dispositions or leases to bodies of persons, or trusts established for charitable purposes only.[97] The instrument must be adjudicated.[98]

EXEMPTIONS FOR DONORS

Income tax

8–030 Individual donors obtain relief from income tax on donations to charity in two main ways; by one-off gifts commonly called Gift Aid; or the payroll deduction scheme. The specific reliefs for payments under covenant ceased to have effect in April 2000 and such gifts now obtain relief under Gift Aid.[99] There are also reliefs available for gifts of shares and land. Individuals in business have certain additional reliefs for payments made in the course of their business.

Gift Aid

8–031 The Finance Act 1990 introduced tax relief for one-off gifts to charity, commonly known as Gift Aid. The scope of the relief was widened considerably by the Finance Act 2000 to make it the main way in which individuals gain relief from income tax on gifts to charity. A gift of any sum, without upper limit, is now capable of being a qualifying donation and entitling the donor to full tax relief.[1] A qualifying donation takes effect as if the amount paid by the donor was a net amount after deduction of basic rate income tax and the donor's basic rate limit is increased by the grossed amount of the gift.[2] It is sufficient if the donor has paid income

[95] Value Added Tax Act 1994, Sch.9, Group 1.
[96] *ibid.*, Sch.10, para.2.
[97] Finance Act 1982, s.129.
[98] *ibid.*, s.129(2).
[99] Finance Act 2000, s.1.
[1] Finance Act 1990, s.25(1)(2) as amended by Finance Act 2000, s.39.
[2] *ibid.*, s.25(6).

tax at any rate or capital gains tax equal to the basic rate tax on the gift.[3] A donor can elect for a payment made in one year to be treated as if it were a Gift Aid payment made in the previous year.[4]

A gift will only be a qualifying donation if the donor gives the charity an appropriate declaration.[5] The declaration is simple and can be given in writing, orally or by means of electronic communication.[6] A declaration must contain[7] the donor's name and address, the name of the charity, a description of the donations to which the declaration relates and a statement that the donations are to be treated as Gift Aid donations. Thus a declaration can cover earlier and future gifts if so desired. If the declaration is in writing it must contain a note explaining the requirement that the donor must pay an amount of income tax or capital gains tax equal to the amount of tax deducted from the donation. If the declaration is made orally, the donor must be sent a written record of the declaration. Such a donor has a right to cancel their declaration within 30 days of the sending of the written record.[8] The cancellation is retrospective.[9] Declarations can be cancelled prospectively at any time.[10]

A gift will not be a qualifying donation unless it is a sum of money[11] and only benefits within the permitted limits are received in return for the donation.[12] The permitted limits benefits are 25 per cent of the value of a gift not exceeding £100, £25 for a gift of between £101 and £1,000, 2.5 per cent of the value of the gift between £1001 and £10,000 and £250 for a gift of £10,001 or more.[13] These limits are adjusted if the benefits or gifts are by reference to a period of less than 12 months.[14] Charities for the preservation of property or the conservation of wild life are given special treatment by s.25(5E) of the Finance Act 1990. The benefit of any right of admission to view property or to observe wildlife is disregarded when calculating the value of benefits received in return for making a gift.

Payroll deduction schemes

The payroll deduction scheme for gifts to charity, also known as Give As You Earn (GAYE), introduced by the Finance Act 1986 was widened by the Finance Act 2000. An employee can direct his employer to deduct any amount from his pay as an expense before assessment of income tax

8–032

---

[3] *ibid.*, s.25(8).
[4] Finance Act 2002, s.98(1).
[5] Finance Act 1990, s.25(1)(c).
[6] The Donations to Charity by Individuals (Appropriate Declarations) Regulations 2000, (SI 2000/2074), reg.3.
[7] Finance Act 1990, s.25(3); The Donations to Charity by Individual (Appropriate Declarations) Regulations 2000, (SI 2000/2074), reg.4.
[8] The Donations to Charity by Individuals (Appropriate Declaration) Regulations 2000, (SI 2000/2074), reg.5.
[9] *ibid.*, reg.6.
[10] *ibid.*, reg.7.
[11] Finance Act 1990, s.25(2)(a).
[12] *ibid.*, s.25(2)(e), and see *St Dunstan's v Major* [1997] S.T.C. 212.
[13] *ibid.*, s.25(5A).
[14] *ibid.*, s.25(5B)–(5D).

under Sch.E.[15] Payments may, however, only be deducted in accordance with a scheme approved by the Inland Revenue[16] and must not include any sum due to a charity under a deed of covenant.[17]

Payroll deduction schemes operate by an employer entering into a contract with an approved agency.[18] The employees who wish to take part authorise their employer to deduct sums from their pay[19] and nominate the charities they wish to receive their gifts. The deducted sums are paid by the employer to the agency, who then distributes the gifts to the nominated charities after deducting any charges.[20] Payments must be made to charities by the agency within 60 days of receipt.[21]

To encourage donations to charity, for the period from April 6, 2000 to April 5, 2003, a 10 per cent supplement will be added by the Treasury to all payments made under the payroll deduction scheme. The payroll deduction agencies are required to add 10 per cent to all payments to charities and they can they reclaim the sum from the Inland Revenue.[22]

Gifts of shares and land

8–033   An individual disposing of a qualifying investment to a charity, otherwise than by way of bargain at arms length, is entitled to relief from income tax.[23] Relief is given by allowing the market value of the investment, less any consideration or value of benefits received, to be deducted from the donor's total income.[24] In the case of a gift, but not a disposal at an undervalue, the donor can also deduct the incidental costs of disposal. Qualifying investments are shares listed on a recognised stock exchange, authorised unit trusts, shares in an open-ended investment company and holdings in certain foreign collective investment schemes.[25] There is thus no income tax relief available to a donor on a gift of unlisted shares to a charity.

Similar relief from income tax is available on a gift of land in the UK.[26]

---

[15] Taxes Act 1988, s.202. The limit of £900 was repealed by Finance Act 2000, s.38(5).
[16] *ibid.*, s.202(3). See [1989] Conv. 175 (D. Morris) and [1991] 1 Trust Law Int. (D. Morris) for the operation of the scheme.
[17] Taxes Act 1988, s.202(6).
[18] *ibid.*, s.202(4).
[19] *ibid.*, s.202(5).
[20] *ibid.*, s.202(8), (9) and the Charitable Deductions (Approved Schemes) Regulations 1986 (SI 1986/2211).
[21] The Charitable Deductions (Approved Schemes) (Amendment) Regulations 2000 (SI 2000/759).
[22] Finance Act 2000, s.38; The Charitable Deductions (Approved Schemes) (Amendment No. 2) Regulations 2000 (SI 2000/2083).
[23] Taxes Act 1988, s.587B(1)(2), inserted by Finance Act 2000, s.43(1). See IR 178, "Giving Shares and Securities to Charity" for worked examples of how the relief operates.
[24] Taxes Act 1988, s.587B(4)(5).
[25] *ibid.*, s.587B(9).
[26] *ibid.*, s.587B(9) inserted by Finance Act 2002, s.97(1).

Other reliefs

Two additional reliefs were introduced by the Finance Act 2000 to **8–034** encourage donations to charities. The first applies where the beneficiaries of a UK resident trust include a charity. The settlor's charge to tax will be reduced by an amount equal to the income given to the charity by the trust.[27] The second applies in relation to loans to charities. A potential liability to tax has been removed by providing that the anti-avoidance provisions in Chapter 1A of Pt XV of the Taxes Act 1988, *i.e.* the settlement provisions, do not apply to an interest free or low interest loan made by an individual to a charity.[28]

Business expenses

Individuals taxed under Sch.D, Case I or II may be able to deduct as **8–035** expenses certain payments to charities which are wholly and exclusively incurred for business purposes. Thus, payments such as small annual subscriptions to trade-related charities and small donations to local charities which benefit the employees of a business will be deductible.[29] Similarly, sponsorship paid to support a charitable activity will be deductible if the sole purpose is to obtain publicity for the business. Whilst the cost of business gifts is not normally deductible,[30] the cost of a gift to a body established for charitable purposes only can be deducted as a business expense.[31] An individual who is an employer can deduct the costs of an employee who has been seconded on a temporary basis to a charity.[32]

An individual carrying on a trade, profession or vocation is now exempt from tax on a gift of trading stock or equipment to a charity. S.83A of the Taxes Act 1988[33] provides that no amount needs to be entered as a trading receipt in the business accounts when a gift is made and, further, that no disposal value needs to be brought into account for the purposes of the Capital Allowances Act 1990. The relief only applies to gifts of articles that the businessman manufactures or sells in the course of his business or has used to enable him to carry on his business.

Corporation tax

Companies are given relief from corporation tax on payments to char- **8–036** ity under Gift Aid, payments under covenant being brought within Gift Aid relief by the Finance Act 2000.[34] The exemption from income tax on

---

[27] Finance Act 2000, s.44.
[28] *ibid.*, s.45.
[29] See E.S.C. B7; but see also *Bourne and Hollingsworth v Ogden* (1929) 14 T.C. 349.
[30] Taxes Act 1988, s.577(8).
[31] *ibid.*, s.577(9); see also E.S.C. B7.
[32] *ibid.*, s.86.
[33] Inserted by Finance Act 1999, s.55. See also Taxes Act, s.84 in relation to gifts to designated educational establishments.
[34] Finance Act 2000, s.41.

a gift of qualifying investments also applies to companies[35] as does the relief on trading stock and equipment.[36]

Gift Aid

8–037   A company is entitled to tax relief on a qualifying donation to a charity of any amount.[37] Corporation tax relief is given by constituting a qualifying donation as a charge on income. As relief is now given by way of charge on income, there is no longer a requirement for companies to deduct income tax before making a donation to a charity; nor can a charity reclaim tax in respect of a donation from a company. There is no requirement for a company to complete a Gift Aid declaration. A donation by a close company will not attract tax relief, however, if any benefits received in return for the donation exceed the statutory limits.[38]

Capital gains tax

8–038   The disposal of an asset to a charity or to certain specified bodies,[39] otherwise than under a bargain at arm's length, is treated as being for such consideration that secures neither a gain nor a loss.[40] Thus, any unrealised gains pass to the charity where they will probably be exempt from tax on a later disposal.[41] This exemption applies to disposals by way of gift, including gifts in settlement and sales for a consideration not exceeding the expenditure available for capital gains tax purposes.[42] The exemption will also apply where there is a deemed disposal under s.71 of the Taxation of Chargeable Gains Act 1992, for example, where a charity becomes absolutely entitled under a trust on the termination of a life interest.[43] On any later disposal of the asset by the charity, the acquisition of the asset by the donor will be treated as the charity's acquisition.[44]

Inheritance tax

8–039   Gifts to charities without financial limit are exempt from Inheritance Tax.[45] A gift is within the exemption if it becomes the property of a charity or is held in trust for charitable purposes only.[46] The exemption will still

---

[35] Taxes Act 1988, s.587B, see para.8–033 above.
[36] *ibid.*, s.83A, see para.8–035 above.
[37] *ibid.*, s.339 as amended by Finance Act 2000, s.40.
[38] *ibid.*, s.339(3DA).The limits are the same as for Gift Aid donations by individuals, see above para.8–031.
[39] Listed in Inheritance Tax Act 1984, Sch.3.
[40] Taxation of Chargeable Gains Act 1992, s.257.
[41] See para.8–010, above.
[42] See Taxation of Chargeable Gains Act 1992, s.38.
[43] *ibid.*, s.257(3).
[44] *ibid.*, s.257(2)(6).
[45] Inheritance Tax Act 1984, s.23(1).
[46] *ibid.*, s.23(6).

be available even if the value transferred exceeds the value of the gift in the hands of the charity.[47] The exemption will not be available, however, if the gift is to take effect later, is defeasible,[48] is for an interest less than the donor's or is for a limited period.[49] Similarly, there will be no exemption if the donor reserves to himself an interest in the property for less than full consideration,[50] or if the property may be used for other than charitable purposes.[51]

In relation to settlements with no interest in possession, property held for charitable purposes only is excluded from the definition of "relevant property."[52] However, there is a charge to inheritance tax when property leaves a temporary charitable trust.[53] There is no charge on property ceasing to be relevant property if it becomes held for charitable purposes only.[54]

INTRODUCTION TO RATING

Considerable changes to local taxation were made by the Local Government Finance Act 1988; rating for domestic property was abolished and the community charge was introduced. Domestic property is now subject to council tax and the governing legislation is to be found in the Local Government Finance Act 1992. Non-domestic properties are subject to non-domestic rates under PtIII of the 1988 Act. Whilst there are reliefs available for charities from both council tax and non-domestic rates, they are not as wide as the previous relief from rates under s.40 of the General Rate Act 1967.[55] **8–040**

COUNCIL TAX

Council tax is payable in respect of dwellings[56] and a dwelling is a property which is not included in the non-domestic rating list or exempt from non-domestic rates under the Local Government Finance Act 1988.[57] S.66 of that Act defines domestic property as property used wholly for the purposes of living accommodation. Accordingly, almshouses, homes for the elderly or mentally ill and accommodation provided for employees of charities are all subject to council tax and not non-domestic rates.[58] **8–041**

---

[47] S.P.E.13.
[48] Inheritance Tax Act 1984, s.23(2). Any condition must be satisfied within 12 months.
[49] *ibid.*, s.23(3).
[50] *ibid.*, s.23(4).
[51] *ibid.*, s.23(5).
[52] *ibid.*, s.58(1)(a).
[53] *ibid.*, s.70.
[54] *ibid.*, s.76.
[55] For the previous reliefs see the 7th ed. of this work, pp.440, *et seq.*
[56] Local Government Finance Act 1992, s.1(1).
[57] *ibid.*, s.3.
[58] Compare the previous position under the rating legislation, see *Glasgow Corporation v Johnstone* [1965] A.C. 609.

Furthermore, it is the resident, and not the property owning charity, who is liable to pay the council tax even if that person is occupying under a licence. If there is more than one resident the liability is joint and several.[59]

There are no direct reliefs for charities although some reliefs are available in respect of some types of accommodation commonly provided by charities. Liability to council tax depends partly on the value of the premises and partly on the number and circumstances of the residents. It is in relation to the second half of the charge that reliefs are available. There is a discount of 25 per cent on the amount of council tax payable if there is only one resident and 50 per cent if there are no residents.[60] In determining the number of residents certain people are disregarded, for example, the severely mentally impaired, patients in residential care homes, nursing homes or mental nursing homes, care workers, those living in hostels and night shelters and members of religious communities.[61] Thus although accommodation owned and provided by a charity for its beneficiaries is subject to council tax, the result of the reliefs is that, in many cases, the actual amount paid by each beneficiary resident is not large.[62] In addition, property occupied by a disabled person which has been adapted to his needs is placed in a lower band, thus reducing the amount of council tax payable.[63]

Non-Domestic Rates

8-042   Properties other than dwellings occupied by a charity are subject to non-domestic rates.[64] Unlike council tax, direct reliefs are available for charities and certain premises are exempt from the charge. There is an automatic 80 per cent relief from non-domestic rates on premises which are occupied by a charity or trustees for a charity and used wholly or mainly for charitable purposes whether of that charity or of that and other charities.[65] In the case of unoccupied property which is owned by a charity similar relief is available if it appears that when next in use the property will be used wholly or mainly for charitable purposes.[66]

In determining whether the property is wholly or mainly used for charitable purposes the written constitution of the occupying charity should first be examined and only if there is any ambiguity in the objects expressed in the constitution should the actual activities of the charity be

---

[59] Local Government Finance Act 1992, s.6.
[60] *ibid.*, s.11(1).
[61] *ibid.*, s.11(5), Sch.1. See also The Council Tax (Discount Disregards) Order 1992 (SI 1992/548); The Council Tax (Additional Provisions for Discount Disregards) Regulations 1992 (SI 1992/552).
[62] Council tax benefit may also be available, see Local Government Finance Act 1992, s.103, Sch.9.
[63] Local Government Finance Act 1992, s.13; The Council Tax (Reductions for Disabilities) Regulations 1992 (SI 1992/554).
[64] Local Government Finance Act 1988, s.43 (occupied property), s.45 (unoccupied property).
[65] *ibid.*, s.43(5).
[66] *ibid.*, s.45(5).

looked at.[67] A property is treated as wholly or mainly used for charitable purposes if it is wholly or mainly used for the sale of goods donated to a charity and the proceeds of sale of the goods (after deduction of expenses) are applied for the purposes of a charity.[68] In determining if the first condition is satisfied a local authority will consider the percentage of sales space occupied by donated goods, the percentage of turnover and profit from donated goods and the percentage of individual items sold which are donated goods.[69]

Obviously, if a charity owns premises and does not occupy them—if in effect, they take the form of an income-producing endowment and are let accordingly—there is no possible ground for relief (unless, of course, the lessee happens to be an institution which is itself a charity, in which case relief will be available on account of the charitable status of that institution, not that of the lessor). Perhaps less obviously, if a charity remains in occupation of the premises, but either allows them to be used by others not being either charities or the beneficiaries of the charity, or uses the premises itself for purposes not directly related to the carrying out of its charitable objects, there will be no case for relief. In *Polish Historical Institution v Hove Corporation*,[70] the objects of the charity were the encouragement and promotion of research into the study of modern Polish history. The charity owned premises which it did not use for its purposes but as a source of income to be used in the pursuit of those purposes. This it did by letting the premises in furnished rooms or small apartments to persons who were not tenants but mere licensees, the charity remaining in actual occupation of the whole hereditament. The charity was entitled to use the premises as an investment, but could not say that it was in occupation for the purposes which were its declared objects, and its claim for relief failed.

8–043

A distinction was attempted by the Court of Appeal in *Aldous v Southwark LBC*.[71] Dulwich College was a charitable foundation with educational objects. Most of its income came from residential lettings of houses on the estate, which clearly did not qualify for relief. It was held, however, that the estate governors were entitled to relief in respect of workshops used for the maintenance and repair of the estate houses and cottages occupied by estate employees and of the estate offices from which the estate and funds were managed, because the management and administration were wholly and inseparably bound up with the carrying out of the main charitable purpose. Those activities made it possible to

---

[67] See *Victory (Ex-Services) Association Ltd v Paddington BC* [1960] 1 All E.R. 498 at 500, per Lord Parker C.J. See also *General Nursing Council for England and Wales v St Marylebone BC* [1959] A.C. 540 at 559; *Glasgow City Corp v Johnstone* [1965] A.C. 609.

[68] Local Government Finance Act 1988, s.64. The Rating (Charity Shops) Act 1976 was repealed by the Local Government Finance Act 1988, Sch.13.

[69] See HM Treasury, *Review of Charity Taxation* (1999), para.5.37.

[70] (1963) 61 L.G.R. 438, a decision on s.8(1)(a) of the Rating and Valuation (Miscellaneous Provisions) Act 1955; *cf. Soldiers', Sailors' and Airmens' Families Association v Merton LBC* [1967] 1 W.L.R. 127; *Ealing LBC v Ladyholme* [1975] J.P.L.32; *Forces Help Society and Lord Roberts' Workshops v Canterbury City Council* (1977) 77 L.G.R. 541.

[71] [1968] 1 W.L.R. 1671, CA, but see the comments on this case in *Oxfam v Birmingham City District Council* [1976] A.C. 126.

distinguish the case from one where a charity occupies premises to carry out a separate business for gain, or sets up a separate office in order to launch an appeal for funds which is excluded from relief.

8-044 A local authority has power to grant discretionary relief from non-domestic rates where the ratepayer is a charity.[72] Thus a charity may gain 100 per cent relief.

A place of public religious worship together with a church hall and associated office accommodation is exempt from non-domestic rates.[73] Specific exemption is also given for property used for the disabled as workshops, or for the provision of welfare services or for the provision of training or suitable occupation.[74]

---

[72] Local Government Finance Act 1988, s.47.
[73] *ibid.*, s.51, Sch.5, para.11 as amended by Local Government Finance Act 1992, Sch.10, para.3.
[74] *ibid.*, s.51, Sch.5, para.16.

CHAPTER 9

THE CHARITY COMMISSIONERS

THE CHARITY COMMISSIONERS

Introduction

The Charity Commissioners were first established by the Charitable   **9–001**
Trusts Act 1858[1] following Lord Brougham's investigations under the
Royal Commission of 1819.[2] The constitution of the Commissioners is
governed by the Charities Act 1993.[3] Although commonly known as the
Charity Commission, the Charity Commissioners are a non-Ministerial
government department which does not have corporate status. Their general function is the promotion of the effective use of charitable resources
by encouraging the development of better methods of administration by
giving charity trustees information or advice on any matter affecting the
charity and by investigating and checking abuses.[4] The general object of
the Commissioners is to act in the case of any charity (unless it is a matter of altering its purposes) as best to promote and make effective its work
in meeting the needs designated by its trusts.[5]

Following considerable concern about the administration of charities
and the effectiveness of the Charity Commissioners, a number of reports
suggested that the Commissioners should lay greater emphasis on the
monitoring and control of charities and that their powers should be
enhanced.[6] These reports led to the *White Paper, Charities: A Framework
For The Future*[7] and the Charities Act 1992. The Charity Commissioners'
powers are now to be found in the Charities Act 1993.

The Charity Commissioners are not permitted to act in the administration of a charity[8] but they have considerable monitoring and supervisory
powers. These powers include the keeping of the register,[9] the receipt of
annual accounts,[10] the powers to obtain information[11] and the temporary

---

[1] Repealed by the Charities Act 1960, Sch.7.
[2] See, Owen, *English Philanthropy 1660–1960* (1965), pp.183–197.
[3] s.1 and Sch.1, see para.9–002, below.
[4] Charities Act 1993, s.1(3).
[5] *ibid.*, s.1(4).
[6] Report of the Public Accounts Committee, "Monitoring and Control of Charities in
England and Wales" (1988); the National Audit Office Report, "Monitoring and Control
of Charities in England and Wales" (1987); Efficiency Scrutiny of the Supervision of
Charities" (the Woodfield report) (1987).
[7] Cm. 694 (1989).
[8] Charities Act 1993, s.1(4).
[9] Charities Act 1993, s.3; see para.9–010, below.
[10] *ibid.*, ss.41–49; see paras 9–013, *et seq.*, below.
[11] *ibid.*, ss.9 and 10; see paras 9–036, *et seq.*, below.

and protective and permanent and remedial powers exercisable following an inquiry.[12] Although other powers available to the Commissioners to enable them to carry out their general function and objects are not specifically intended for monitoring and supervisory purposes, in many instances exercise of such powers brings a charity under review by the Commissioners.[13] Such powers include the giving of advice to charities,[14] the making of schemes,[15] the sanctioning of acts beyond the powers of a charity[16] and the power to consent to charity proceedings.[17] The Charity Commissioners are assisted in carrying out their function and objects by having jurisdiction and powers concurrent with those of the High Court.[18]

Constitution

9–002   The constitution of the Charity Commissioners is governed by s.1 of and Sch.1 to the Charities Act 1993. This provides for a Chief Commissioner and two other Commissioners; at least two of them must be lawyers.[19] There is power to appoint additional Commissioners[20] and four part-time Commissioners have been appointed of whom two are lawyers. Whilst the Commissioners are appointed by the Home Secretary and are deemed to be civil servants,[21] the Home Secretary has no power to direct or guide them.[22] The Chief Commissioner has authority to appoint assistant Commissioners and other staff with the approval of the Treasury.[23]

The Commissioners act as a Board and, although not a body corporate, they may sue and be sued in the name of the Charity Commissioners for England and Wales.[24] They have power to regulate their own procedure.[25] Appeals from an exercise of the quasi-judicial powers of the Commissioners lies to the High Court.[26]

Governance

9–003   The responsibility for the strategy and future direction of the Charity Commissioners rests with the Board which consists of the Commissioners and executive directors. In addition to the Chief Commissioner and two part-time legal Commissioners, there are two other part-time Commission-

---

[12] *ibid.*, ss.18 and 19; see paras 9–042, *et seq.*, below.
[13] See [2001–2002] Ch. Com. Rep. p.9 for the Commissioners' regulatory approach.
[14] Charities Act 1993, s.29. See para.9–008, below.
[15] *ibid.*, s.16; see para.9–005, below.
[16] *ibid.*, ss.26 and 27; see para. 9–007.
[17] *ibid.*, s.33(2); see para.10–027, below.
[18] See para.9–005, below.
[19] Charities Act 1993, Sch.1, para.1(2).
[20] *ibid.*, Sch.1, para.1(5).
[21] *ibid.*, Sch.1, para.1(3). The Home Secretary represents the Commissioners and answers questions in Parliament.
[22] The statutory function given to the Commissioners by the Charities Act 1993, s.1(3) gives them independence.
[23] Charities Act 1993, Sch.1, para.2(1).
[24] *ibid.*, Sch.1, para.4.
[25] *ibid.*, Sch.1, para.3(3).
[26] *ibid.*, s.16(11)(12).

ers whose appointments reflect important aspects of the sector. There are directors of law, policy, resources and operations. Quasi-judicial decisions, remain exercisable by the Commissioners, not the full Board.[27]

Whilst the Commissioners are accountable to the courts for their quasi-judicial decisions[28] the Commissioners are accountable to Parliament for the proper use of funding agreed and provided by HM Treasury. The use of those funds has been considered by the Public Accounts Committee on several occasions. On the last occasion in 2002 the Committee noted considerable improvement in effectiveness and efficiency but made a number of recommendations for improvement.[29]

The Commissioners have adopted the aim of giving the public confidence in the integrity of charity. This is supported by three objectives: To ensure that charities are able to operate for their purposes within an effective legal, accounting and governance framework; to improve the governance, accountability, efficiency and effectiveness of charities; and to identify and deal with abuse and poor practice.[30]

Reform

The Strategy Unit report placed emphasis on the effective regulation of charities and made a number of proposals for reform of the Charity Commissioners.[31] It is proposed that the Charity Commissioners should become a statutory corporation called the Charity Regulation Authority whose relationship with Ministers is clearly defined in statute. The statute should set out the charity regulator's strategic objectives. It is also proposed that there should be four additional Commissioners with a separate Chair and Chief Executive and that there should be an open annual general meeting.

9–004

Concurrent jurisdiction

The Charity Commissioners have jurisdiction and powers concurrent with those of the High Court;

9–005

(a) to establish schemes for the administration of charities[32];

(b) to establish common investment schemes[33] and common deposit funds[34];

[27] See [2001–2002] Ch. Com. Rep., p.40.
[28] Charities Act 1993, s.16(11)(12).
[29] House of Commons, Committee of Public Accounts, *Giving Confidently: The Role of the Charity Commission in Regulating Charities* [2002] H.C. 412.
[30] See [2001–2002] Ch. Com. Rep., p.2.
[31] Cabinet Office, Strategy Unit, *Private Action, Public Benefit. A Review of Charities and the Wider Not-For-Profit Sector* (2002), pp.71, *et seq.*
[32] Charities Act 1993, s.16(1)(a). A scheme may be amended by further scheme, *Att-Gen v St John's Hospital, Bath* (1865) 1 Ch.App. 92 at 106 and the Commissioners have jurisdiction to alter schemes of the court, *Re Weir Hospital* [1910] 2 Ch. 124 at 131.
[33] *ibid.*, s.24; see para.6–028, above.
[34] *ibid.*, s.25; see para.6–030, above.

(c)   to appoint, discharge or remove any charity trustee, or trustee for a charity, or to remove officers and employees of charities[35];

(d)   to vest or transfer property, or to require or entitle any person to call for or make any transfer of property or any payment.[36]

Where the court directs a scheme, it may refer the matter to the Commissioners for them to settle the scheme and may provide for the scheme to be put into effect by order of the Commissioners without any further order of the court.[37] All questions of title to property arising between a charity and adverse claimants and any questions as to the existence of any charge or trust are expressly excluded from the jurisdiction of the Commissioners.[38] Nor may they exercise their jurisdiction if for any reason (including any special question of law or fact involved, or the contentious character of the case) they consider the case more fit to be adjudicated upon by the court.[39]

Ordinarily, the scheme making jurisdiction is only exercised on the application of a charity, or on reference by the court or, in the case of a charity other than an exempt charity, on the application of the Attorney General.[40] There are three situations, however, in which a scheme may be made by the Commissioners[41] even though all the charity trustees do not apply. First, in the case of a charity with an annual income of £500 or less which is not an exempt charity, the Commissioners may exercise their scheme making powers on the application of any one or more of the charity trustees, or any person interested in the charity or any two or more inhabitants of the area of the charity, if it is a local charity.[42] Secondly, where the commissioners are satisfied that the trustees of a charity (not being an exempt charity) ought in the interest of the charity to apply for a scheme but have unreasonably refused or neglected to do so, the Commissioners may proceed as if an application had been made for a scheme by the charity, provided that they have given the charity trustees an opportunity to make representations.[43] Thirdly, where a charity cannot apply for a scheme because of any vacancy among the trustees or the absence or incapacity of any of them, the Commissioners may proceed to make a scheme if an application is made by such number of the charity trustees as the Commissioners consider appropriate.[44]

The Commissioners have power to settle a scheme where it appears to them that one should be established for the administration of a charity but also that it is necessary or desirable for the scheme to alter the provision

---

[35] *ibid.*, s.16(1)(b).
[36] *ibid.*, s.16(1)(c).
[37] *ibid.*, s.16(2).
[38] *ibid.*, s.16(3).
[39] *ibid.*, s.16(10).
[40] *ibid.*, s.16(4).
[41] For the Charity Commissioners' practice on the making of schemes, see OGI, *Orders and Schemes*.
[42] Charities Act 1993, s.16(5).
[43] *ibid.*, s.16(6). The Commission do not have power, when acting under this subsection, to alter the purposes of a charity unless it has been established for 40 years.
[44] *ibid.*, s.16(7).

made by an Act of Parliament establishing or regulating the charity or otherwise goes beyond their general powers.[45] Effect is given to the scheme by an order of the Home Secretary made by statutory instrument, a draft of which is laid before Parliament.[46] If the scheme goes beyond the Commissioners' powers otherwise exercisable in altering a public general Act of Parliament the order must be approved by resolution of each House of Parliament.[47] The power has been used extensively by the Commissioners[48] and once a scheme has been made under s.17 of the 1993 Act, it may be altered as if it were a scheme made by the Commissioners under their general powers under s.16.[49]

Before exercising scheme making powers, other than on an order of the court, the Commissioners must give notice of their intention to do so to each of the charity trustees, except those which cannot be found, or have no known address in the United Kingdom or are part or privy to the application.[50] They must also give public notice of their proposal to establish a scheme inviting representations to be made to them within a specified period being not less than one month.[51]

9–006

In the light of these requirements, the Charity Commissioners have a policy of using their order making powers under s.26 of the 1993 Act[52] rather than a scheme wherever possible to effect alteration to the trusts of a charity.[53] The Strategy Unit went further and proposed that the whole formal scheme making procedure be speeded up and that advertisement be a matter of discretion for the Commissioners.[54]

It is not unusual for a scheme to contain a provision that any questions as to the construction of the scheme or validity of acts done under the scheme is a matter to be determined by the Commissioners. Any such determination by the Commissioners will not be subject to judicial review unless they have acted outside their jurisdiction.[55]

Orders

The Commissioners, by s.26 of the 1993 Act, have power by order to sanction an action not otherwise within the powers of a charity if they consider that the action proposed or contemplated is expedient in the interests of the charity. The power extends only to action in connection

9–007

[45] *ibid.*, s.17(1).
[46] *ibid.*, s.17(2). This method is also used where it is for any reason proper that a scheme should be subject to parliamentary review—s.17(1).
[47] *ibid.*, s.17(3).
[48] See, for example, the Charities (Bristol, Clifton and West of England Zoological Society) Order 2000 (SI 2000/1808).
[49] Charities Act 1993, s.17(4).
[50] *ibid.*, s.16(9), s.17(6).
[51] *ibid.*, s.20(1).
[52] See para.6–019 above and para.9–007 below.
[53] See OG1 A1, *Orders under section 26 of the Charities Act 1993*, s.2.
[54] Cabinet Office, Strategy Unit, *Private Action, Public Benefit. A Review of Charities and the Wider Not-For-Profit Sector* (2002), p. 47.
[55] *R. v The Charity Commissioners for England and Wales Ex p. Baldwin* (2002) 2 W.T.L.R. 137.

with the administration of the charity but can give a more general authority as well as giving specific authority, for example, to use common premises with another charity.[56] There is no power, however, to sanction acts
which are expressly prohibited by the trust of the charity or by Act of
Parliament unless it is one of the disabling Acts.[57]

An order is a much simpler way of giving additional powers to a charity than a scheme. A public notice of a proposal to make an order does not
have to be given. The Commissioners now use an order, as opposed to a
scheme, wherever possible and will now give a charity a general power to
amend its governing instrument by order.[58] To ensure that general authority is used properly by trustees, for example, a general power of amendment, the order will include directions relating to the use of the power.[59]
The directions will usually require the trustees to exercise the statutory
duty of care under s.1(1) of the Trustee Act 2000 when using the power.

Giving of advice

9–008   The Charity Commissioners have power under s.29 of the 1993 Act, on
the written application of any charity trustee, to give him their opinion or
advice on any matter affecting the performance of his duties. Advice may
be given, for example, as to whether a proposed action is within the objects
of the charity. When giving their advice the Commissioners must satisfy
themselves that the action proposed is within the powers of the trustee and
the trustee must supply the Commissioners with sufficient evidence to
allow them to make an informed decision.[60] The Commissioners will not,
however, advise on policy matters or on legal questions concerning rights
with those outside the charity. In the latter case the trustee will be told to
seek legal advice.[61]

A charity trustee who acts in accordance with the opinion or advice of
the Commissioners is deemed to have acted in accordance with the trust
unless either he knows or has reasonable cause to suspect that the opinion
or advice was given in ignorance of material facts or that the decision of
the court has been obtained on the matter or proceedings are pending to
obtain one.[62]

Any appeal against an opinion or advice of the Commissioners given
under s.29 must be brought before the court as charity proceedings under
s.33 of the 1993 Act. The existence of an effective right of appeal under
s.33, the disadvantages of a negligence action against the Commissioners
proceeding concurrently and the negative effect on the general good of
charities if the Commissioners' decision were open to attack by means of

---

[56] Charities Act 1993, s.26(2).
[57] *ibid.*, s.26(5). As to which are disabling Acts, see s.26(6).
[58] See OG1 B1, *Orders and Schemes Providing Trustees with a Power of Amendment*, s.3,
reversing previous policy set out in [1997] Ch. Com. Rep. paras 146, *et seq.*
[59] OG1 A1, *Orders under section 26 of the Charities Act 1993*, s.3.6.
[60] See [1991] Ch. Com. Rep., para.33 and *Marley v Mutual Security Merchant Bank & Trust
Co. Ltd* [1991] 3 All E.R. 198.
[61] See [1982] Ch. Com. Rep., paras 24–26.
[62] Charities Act 1993, s.29(2).

negligence actions by such a wide class as the potential objects of a charity have all been held to negative the existence of a duty of care owed by the Commissioners to the potential objects of a charity.[63] Thus in *Mills v Winchester Diocesan Board*[64] the claim by a number of inhabitants of a village against the Commissioners for damages arising from alleged negligent advice given under s.29 to the diocesan board of finance as trustees of the closed village school was struck out.

Proceedings by the Charity Commissioners

The Charity Commissioners have the same powers as are exercisable by   **9–009**
the Attorney General acting *ex officio* to take legal proceedings with reference to charities or the property or affairs of charities or to compromise claims with a view to avoiding or ending such proceedings.[65] The practice and procedure is the same as if the proceedings were being taken by the Attorney General.[66] The powers of the Commissioners in relations to legal proceedings may only be exercised, however, with the agreement of the Attorney General.[67] The power has been used to recover for a charity sums applied in breach of trust by or for the benefit of charity trustees.[68]

THE REGISTER

The Charity Commissioners continue to maintain the central register of   **9–010**
charities originally set up under the provisions of the Charities Act 1960.[69]
Entry on the register of an institution raises a conclusive presumption of charitable status.[70] Inclusion on the register is not, however, a "seal of approval", for example, implying that the trustees are competent or honest.[71] The register is regarded as an important tool in the Charity Commissioners' monitoring and supervision of charities. It also provides the public with access to basic information about charities.[72]

All charities are required to be entered on the register unless they fall within one of the four excepted categories.[73] Apart from exempt charities, all other excepted charities may apply for voluntary registration but, if registered, they will become subject to all the obligations of registered charities.[74] The Commissioners have power to remove from the register any institution which is no longer a charity, for example, because of

---

[63] *Mills v Winchester Diocesan Board* [1989] 2 All E.R. 317 at 332, *per* Knox J.
[64] [1989] 2 All E.R. 317.
[65] Charities Act 1993, s.32(1).
[66] *ibid.*, s.32(3); see paras 10–018 *et seq.*, below.
[67] *ibid.*, s.32(5).
[68] See [1999–2000] Ch. Com. Rep., p. 23 (Sherburn House Charity).
[69] Charities Act 1993, s.3(1).
[70] *ibid.*, s.4(1).
[71] [1992] Ch. Com. Rep., para.3.
[72] *Charities: A Framework For The Future*, Cm. 694 (1989), para.3.4.
[73] Charities Act 1993, s.3(2). See para.1–026, above.
[74] *ibid.*, s.3(2).

a change in its purposes, or because it has ceased to exist or does not operate.[75]

The first group of charities which are not required to register are exempt charities[76] which are listed in Sch.2 to the 1993 Act.[77] Secondly, charities which are excepted[78] by order or regulation are not required to register. Thirdly, a charity which has neither permanent endowment nor the use or occupation of land and whose income is not more than £1,000 a year need not be registered.[79] Finally, no charity is required to be registered in respect of a registered place of religious worship.[80]

9–011 The register is required to contain the name of every registered charity and such other particulars of, and information about, a charity as the Commissioners think fit.[81] The register is now computerised. The entry for a particular charity contains its name, classification, registration history, area of operation and contact details. The register also contains income and expenditure details, accounts information and annual return history.[82]

The Charity Commissioners have power to give a direction requiring the name of a charity to be changed if the name on the register is the same as, or too like, that of an existing charity. A change may also be directed if the name is likely to mislead the public as to the true purposes or activities of the charity, if the name contains any proscribed word[83] or expression and inclusion of such word or expression is in the opinion of the Commissioners likely to mislead the public as to the status of the charity, if the name gives an unfounded impression of government or other connections or if the name is offensive.[84] If the charity is a company, the name must be changed by resolution of the directors of the company and the new name entered on the register of companies.[85]

In order to ensure that the register remains up to date and accurate, every registered charity whose gross income or total expenditure in any financial year exceeds £10,000[86] is required to provide an annual return to the Commissioners within 10 months of the end of the financial year.[87] The return must include such information as is prescribed in regulations made by the Charity Commissioners.[88] It is a criminal offence for a per-

---

[75] *ibid.*, s.3(4). See para.1–032, above.

[76] See para.1–025, above.

[77] Charities Act 1993, s.3(5)(a).

[78] *ibid.*, s.3(5)(b). For excepted charities, see para.1–026, above.

[79] *ibid.*, s.3(5)(c). The £1,000 limit may be changed by the Secretary of State by statutory instrument under s.3(12).

[80] *ibid.*, s.3(5). A registered place of worship means any land or buildings falling within s.9 of the Places of Worship Registration Act 1855 as amended—s.3(14).

[81] *ibid.*, s.3(3).

[82] [2001–2002] Ch. Com. Rep., p. 26.

[83] For example, "British", "Official" and "School". See The Charities (Misleading Names) Regulations 1992 (SI 1992/1901).

[84] Charities Act 1993, s.6. For the practice of the Charity Commissioners on seeking a change of name and issuing a direction under s.6, see OG18, *Names of Charities*.

[85] *ibid.*, s.7.

[86] The £10,000 limit may be changed by the Secretary of State by statutory instrument under s.48(4).

[87] Charities Act 1993, s.48(1).

[88] These regulations are made by the Charity Commissioners annually and provide a form setting out the information required. See The Charities (Annual Return) Regulations 2002.

son, without reasonable excuse, to be persistently in default in failing to provide the Commissioners with an annual return.[89] The requirement for "persistent default" means that more than one return must be in default and reminders ignored before a criminal offence is committed.[90] The Commissioners have become more rigorous in enforcing the timely submission of annual returns and now name persistent defaulters on the website and have referred cases to the police for prosecution.[91] A charity's entry on the public register now sets out which annual returns have been made and the date of each return. Charities with income of less than £10,000 are asked annually to complete a Register Check form to advise of any changes to their registered particulars.[92]

The register must be open to public inspection at all reasonable times.[93] Computerisation of the register and placing it on the Charity Commissioners' website means that details of any one charity may be inspected by anyone with access to the internet. For those without such access, search facilities are provided at the London, Liverpool and Taunton offices of the Commissioners.[94] Any person is entitled to be furnished with copies of entries on the register.[95] There is power for the Commissioners to charge for both inspection of the register and the supply of copies of entries.[96]

9–012

ACCOUNTS AND ANNUAL REPORTS

A prerequisite for the effective supervision of charities by the Charity Commissioners is good financial information. The requirements under the Charities Act 1960 to both keep and submit accounts were limited; there was no provision for accounts to be audited and relatively few charities provided annual accounts for the Commissioners.[97] Accordingly, the Charities Act 1992 introduced far stricter provisions requiring charities to keep proper accounts, to have accounts audited or examined and to submit annual statements of accounts to the Commissioners. The provisions in relation to the annual reporting and accounting regime are now contained in Pt VI of the Charities Act 1993.

9–013

The position of the Charity Commissioners as a monitoring and supervisory body is considerably enhanced as annual reports and accounts sent to them are routinely monitored to identify those charities with legal and administrative difficulties.[98] The preparation by a charity of its annual report and accounts is regarded as discharging the charity trustees' duty of

---

[89] Charities Act 1993, s.49.
[90] See *Hansard* [1992] HL, PBC, cols 138, 143.
[91] See [2000–2001] Ch. Com. Rep., p.16.
[92] See [2001–2002] Ch. Com. Rep., p.26.
[93] Charities Act 1993, s.3(8).
[94] [2001–2002] Ch. Com. Rep., p.26.
[95] Charities Act 1993, s.84.
[96] *ibid.*, s.85 and see The Charity Commissioners Fees (Copies and Extracts) Regulations (SI 1992/2986).
[97] *Charities: A Framework For The Future*, Cm. 694 (1989), para.4.1.
[98] See [2000–2001] Ch. Com. Rep., p.15.

public accountability and stewardship.[99] The regime is directed to making it easier for the public to obtain information about charities and to compare one charity with another; the focus of accounts is on changes in resources rather than on profit and loss,[1] annual reports and accounts are available to the public[2] and accounts are in common form.

The legislation recognises that there is a balance to be struck between providing information and not placing undue burdens on charities. Thus charities with neither gross income or expenditure exceeding £10,000 are subject to a light touch regime and the full rigour of audit only applies to charities with gross income or total expenditure exceeding £250,000.[3] Although only about 33 per cent of the 160,000 main charities on the register have income over £10,000, they account for about 97 per cent of the gross income of all registered charities.[4] The Strategy Unit report has taken a risk based approach to regulation and recommended that the threshold for audit should be raised to £1 million income.[5] This reflects the fact that approximately 6 per cent of charities receive nearly 90 per cent of the total amount of income recorded.[6]

9–014   The structure of the regime is set out below together with an outline of the individual obligations placed on charities. The details of the various obligations are to be found in The Charities (Accounts and Reports) Regulations 1995[7] (the 1995 regulations), The Charities (Accounts and Reports) Regulations 2000[8] (the 2000 regulations) and the Statement of Recommended Practice on Accounting and Reporting by Charities[9] (the SORP). The main obligations imposed by the Regulations and the SORP are set out below and particular points of detail are highlighted where it is considered that there can be problems of interpretation or application. Charitable companies remain subject to the accounting and reporting regime imposed by the Companies Act 1985 but are also subject to certain provisions of Pt VI of the 1993 Act; they are considered separately. The accounting regime imposed by the Charities Act 1993 has generated a large amount of accompanying documentation which it is helpful to review before looking at the individual obligations imposed on charities.

---

[99] See the Statement of Recommended Practice on Accounting and Reporting by Charities, para.3.

[1] For the particular forms of account see para.9–023 below.

[2] See para.9–033 below.

[3] See Charities Act 1993, ss.42–45 as amended by the Deregulation and Contracting Out Act 1994, ss.28–30 and The Charities Act 1993 (Substitution of Sums) Order 1995 (SI 1995/2696).

[4] See [1999–2000] Ch. Com. Rep., pp.10–11.

[5] Cabinet Office, Strategy Unit, *Private Action, Public Benefit. A Review of Charities and the Wider Not-For-Profit Sector* (2002), p. 79.

[6] [2001–2002] Ch.Com. Rep., p.2.

[7] SI 1995/2724.

[8] SI 2000/2868.

[9] The original SORP, Statement of Recommended Practice for Accounting by Charities was revised and the present SORP was issued in October 2000.

BASIC STRUCTURE

A charity whose gross income or total expenditure does not exceed **9–015**
£10,000 may prepare a receipts and payments account rather than a full
statement of accounts[10] and may also prepare a simplified annual report.[11]
The accounts of such a charity need not be independently examined[12] and
the annual report only needs to be transmitted to the Charity Commissioners if they so request.[13] The obligation to furnish an annual return
does not apply[14] but the Charity Commissioners will request that the
Register Check form be returned to keep a charity's entry on the Central
Register of Charities up to date.[15]

If a charity's gross income or total expenditure is more than £10,000,
but its gross income is less than £100,000, it may still prepare a receipts
and payments account and a simplified annual report. The accounts, however, must be independently examined or audited[16] and the annual report
and accounts must be submitted to the Charity Commissioners.[17] An
annual return must also be made.[18]

A charity with gross income of more than £100,000, but with not more
than £250,000 gross income or total expenditure in the current or in either
of the preceding two years, must prepare a full statement of accounts[19] but
may provide a simplified annual report.[20] The accounts may still be independently examined.[21] The annual report and accounts[22] and the annual
return must be submitted to the Charity Commissioners.[23] A charity with
gross income or total expenditure in excess of £250,000 in the current or
either of the two preceding years must prepare a full statement of
accounts, a full annual report and its accounts must be audited.[24]

In the case of a conflict between the obligations imposed by Pt VI of the **9–016**
Charities Act 1993 and the provisions of the governing instrument of a
charity, generally the higher duty will apply. Thus if the constitution of a
charity with income less that £250,000 requires that the accounts be
audited, they must be audited. Similarly, if the governing instrument of a
charity with an income of over £250,000 directs that the accounts are to
be examined by an independent person, the accounts must still be audited.
Trustees of charities whose governing instrument imposes duties which are

---

[10] Charities Act 1993, s.42(3), see para.9–025, below.
[11] *ibid.*, s.45(1); The Charities (Accounts and Reports) Regulations 2000 (SI 2000/2868),
reg.7. See para.9–032, below.
[12] *ibid.*, s.43(3).
[13] *ibid.*, s.45(3A).
[14] *ibid.*, s.48(1A). See para.9–011 above.
[15] Charity trustees are under a duty to notify the Commissioners of any changes in the particulars of it entered on the register, Charities Act 1993, s.3(7)(b).
[16] Charities Act 1993, s.43(1)(3). See paras 9–028, *et seq.*, below.
[17] *ibid.*, s.45(1). See para.9–033, below.
[18] *ibid.*, s.48(1). See para.9–011 above.
[19] *ibid.*, s.42(1). See para.9–021, *et seq.*, below.
[20] *ibid.*, s.45; The Charities (Accounts and Reports) Regulations 2000 (SI 2000/2868), reg.7.
See paras 9–032, *et seq.*, below.
[21] *ibid.*, s.43(3).
[22] *ibid.*, s.45(1).
[23] *ibid.*, s.48(1)
[24] *ibid.*, s.43(1). See para.9–029, below.

more onerous than the statutory regime may wish to consider amending the governing instrument to impose the lesser duty where they have power to do so or asking the Charity Commissioners to amend the governing instrument by order or scheme.[25]

Gross income

9–017   A number of the provisions impose duties by reference to the gross income or total expenditure of a charity. S.97(1) states that gross income in relation to a charity means its gross income from all sources including special trusts. Thus a charity should include in its gross income the income of branches as defined in the SORP[26] and subsidiary charitable funds held for particular purposes but not the income of affiliated autonomous local groups.

The Charity Commissioners have issued definitions of "Gross income" and "Total expenditure".[27] In addition to the usual forms of income recognised for income tax purposes, gross income includes donations (other than capital donations), grants, gifts, legacies, subscriptions and gross proceeds from fund-raising. The proceeds of sale of investments and functional fixed assets and profits or gains on the disposal of such assets are not within the definition; nor are loans. The definition of total expenditure excludes loans and losses on the disposal of investments and functional assets but includes, when accounts are prepared on an accruals basis, depreciation or amortisation of assets. The purchase of functional fixed assets is excluded from expenditure to prevent a charity being subjected to more onerous obligations because a major asset is purchased in one year for which the charity has been fund-raising for a number of years. These definitions, being directed to the determination of when particular types of accounting obligation should apply, are narrower than the definitions of "income" and "expenditure" in the SORP[28] which are directed to ensuring that the accounts of a charity reflect changes in resources of that charity.

Exempt and excepted charities

9–018   The obligations of Pt VI of the 1993 Act do not apply to exempt charities.[29] A charity which is excepted from registration because its income does not exceed £1,000 a year and it has no permanent endowment or the use or occupation of property will only be under the duties to maintain proper accounting records, to prepare accounts and to make the accounts available to the public as long as it remains unregistered.[30] Any other

---

[25] See (1993) Ch. Com. Dec., p.29 for the Charity Commissioners' policy on amendment of governing instruments.
[26] See para.9–026, below.
[27] See CC63, *Independent Examination of Charity Accounts 2001. Directions and Guidance Notes*, App.3.
[28] See para.9–023, below.
[29] Charities Act 1993, s.46(1).
[30] *ibid.*, s.46(3).

excepted charity, whilst not registered, is subject to the same limited duties,[31] but the Commissioners may request such a charity to produce an annual report in respect of a specified financial year.[32]

DOCUMENTATION

A number of sections in Pt VI of the Charities Act 1993 leave the detail of the particular obligation imposed to be set out in regulations, for example, the method and principles to be observed in preparing the statement of accounts.[33] The relevant regulations are The Charities (Accounts and Reports) Regulations 1995[33a] and The Charities (Accounts and Reports) Regulations 2000.[34] There is also a Statement of Recommended Practice on Accounting and Reporting by Charities, the SORP.[35] Some parts of the SORP are incorporated into the Regulations and thus have the force of law. For example, the statement of accounts of a charity must be prepared in accordance with the methods and principles set out in the SORP.[36] Apart from those specific instances, the SORP does not have the force of law; it is a statement of recommended practice which is compatible with the law. The SORP itself requires that charity trustees should follow the standards laid down in the Statements of Standard Accounting Practice, Financial Reporting Standards and Urgent Issue Task Force abstracts issued or adopted by the Accounting Standards Board when preparing accounts. In relation to audit, Practice Note 11—the Audit of Charities, issued by the Auditing Practices Board is relevant.

9–019

The Charity Commissioner's objective in publishing a SORP for charities is to improve the quality of financial reporting by charities and to reduce the diversity in accounting practice and procedure.[37] Whilst some of the provisions of the SORP do not have the force of law, the Charity Commissioners nevertheless expect accounts of charities to comply fully with the SORP.[38] If a charity's accounts do diverge from the SORP in material respects an explanation should be given in the accounts. The Charity Commissioners regard divergence from the SORP as a matter to be taken into account when investigating a charity.[39] The SORP is of limited application to small charities, *i.e.* those with income of less than £100,000 a year. The Charity Commissioners have produced two guides for small charities—"CC64, Receipts and Payments Accounts Pack 2001" and "CC65, Accruals Accounts Pack"—which are based on the SORP. A standard form has been produced for a receipts and payments account and a statement of assets and liabilities.

---

[31] *ibid.*, s.46(4).
[32] *ibid.*, s.46(5).
[33] *ibid.*, s.42(2).
[33a] (SI 1995/2724).
[34] SI 2000/2868.
[35] The SORP is subject to annual review, see [2001–2002] Ch. Com. Rep., p.21.
[36] The Charities (Accounts and Reports) Regulations 2000 (SI 2000/2868) reg.3(6).
[37] SORP, para.12.
[38] Except where a more specialised SORP applies, for example Higher Education Institutions.
[39] See SORP, p.2.

The 1995 Regulations contain detailed provisions as to audit but auditors will also follow the Statements of Auditing Standards and the Practice Note 11, the Audit of Charities, issued by the Auditing Practices Board. The 1995 Regulations also contain provisions relating to the content of the report of an independent examiner. Under the authority of s.43(7)(b) of the 1993 Act the Charity Commissioners have issued CC63, *Independent Examination of Charity Accounts 2001. Directions and Guidance Notes.*

ACCOUNTING RECORDS

9–020   Charity trustees are under a duty to ensure that accounting records are kept for their charity, whatever its income, which are sufficient to show and explain all the charity's transactions.[40] In particular, the records should contain entries on a day to day basis[41] of details of all receipts and payments and a record of the assets and liabilities of the charity.[42] The records must be such as to disclose with reasonable accuracy at any time the financial position of the charity and to enable statements of account to be prepared which comply with regulations.[43] In order to satisfy the latter requirement, the records will need to distinguish unrestricted, restricted and endowment funds and to analyse income by reference to source and expenditure by reference to function or purpose. The accounting records of a charity must be kept for six years.[44] Exempt charities are outwith the obligations but they are still required to keep proper books of accounts.[45]

STATEMENT OF ACCOUNTS

9–021   Charity trustees are under a duty[46] in respect of each financial year of the charity, to prepare a statement of accounts which complies with The Charities (Accounts and Reports) Regulations 2000.[47] If the charity's gross income does not exceed £100,000 the trustees can elect to prepare, instead, a receipts and payments account and a statement of assets and liabilities.[48] The normal accounting period is 12 months but it must be no shorter than six months and no longer than 18 months.[49] An exempt charity, if not obliged under any other authority, must prepare a statement of accounts consisting of an income and expenditure account and a balance sheet relating to a period of not more than 15 months.[50] The statement of

[40] Charities Act 1993, s.41(1).
[41] Accounts need not, however, be accurate to the previous day, Hansard, (1992) HL, PBC, col.86.
[42] Charities Act 1993, s.41(2).
[43] *ibid.*, s.41(1).
[44] *ibid.*, s.41(3).
[45] *ibid.*, s.46(1).
[46] Charities Act 1993, s.42(1).
[47] SI 2000/2868.
[48] Charities Act 1993, s.42(3).
[49] The Charities (Accounts and Reports) Regulations 1995 (SI 1995/2724), reg.5.
[50] Charities Act 1993, s.46(1).

accounts consists of a statement of financial activities and a balance sheet which satisfy the requirements of the SORP.[51] The whole statement must be prepared in accordance with the methods and principles set out in the SORP, where possible, showing figures for the preceding accounting year[52] and providing such notes as are specified in the Schedule to the 2000 Regulations.[53] A cash flow statement is also required for large charities, *i.e.* a charity satisfying two of the following criteria:[54]

(a)   gross income in the year in excess of £2.8 million
(b)   a balance sheet total in excess of £1.4 million
(c)   more than 50 employees.

Accounting concepts and standards

Pt III of Sch.1 to the Regulations requires that the statement of finan-   **9–022**
cial activities should give a true and fair view of the incoming resources and application of the resources of the charity. Similarly, the balance sheet should give a true and fair view of the state of affairs of the charity at the end of the relevant financial year. The standards laid down in the Statements of Standard Accounting Practice, Financial Reporting Standards and Urgent Issue Task Force Abstracts issued or adopted by the Accounting Standards Board should be followed by charity trustees discharging their obligation to prepare accounts showing a true and fair view unless there are circumstances in which compliance with the requirements would be inconsistent with giving a true and fair view.[55] The notes to the accounts should, where necessary, contain additional information to ensure a true and fair view.[56]

Para.1(b) of the Schedule to the 2000 Regulations requires that the notes to the accounts should include a description of the accounting policies used and assumptions made in preparing the statement of accounts. The SORP[57] requires that accounts intending to show a true and fair view must be prepared on the going concern assumption and the accruals concept. The accounts should provide information that is relevant, reliable, comparable and understandable.

Statement of financial activities

The statement of financial activities is intended to show the total incom-   **9–023**
ing resources and application of the resources of a charity together with any

---

[51] The Charities (Accounts and Reports) Regulations 2000 (SI 2000/2868), reg.3(6)(a). The form of statement of accounts for Common Investment Funds and Common Deposit Funds is set out in Sch.2 to the 1995 Regulations.
[52] SI 2000/2868, reg.3(6)(b).
[53] *ibid.*, reg.3(10).
[54] SORP, App.2; The Charities (Accounts and Reports) Regulations 2000 (SI 2000/2868) reg.3(6)(a).
[55] The Charities (Accounts and Reports) Regulations 2000 (SI 2000/2868), reg.3(5)
[56] *ibid.*
[57] Para.33.

other movement in the total resources of the charity during the year.[58] It is considered that such a statement, which includes both capital and income resources, gives a far better explanation of a charity's activities than an income and expenditure account as net movement of funds, rather than simply profit or loss, in the financial year can be shown. If a charity holds endowment funds or other funds which are earmarked for particular purposes, *i.e.* restricted funds, the nature and purpose of such funds must be described in the notes to the accounts.[59] The charity trustees are under an obligation to account for the proper administration of the individual funds in accordance with their respective terms of trust.[60] To this end, para.57 of the SORP requires the information about resources to be analysed by reference to unrestricted income funds, income funds which are restricted in their use, and capital funds and provides a columnar form for the statement of financial activities.[61] As a result the statement shows a summary of the movements on the main types of funds as well as total movements.

The SORP requires incoming resources and expenditure to be analysed.[62] The categories of analysis are broadly donors, investment, operating activities and other. As far as possible incoming resources should be reported gross not net.[63] Expenditure is to be analysed into that relating to the cost of generating funds and charitable expenditure. The latter category should show separately grants payable, costs of activities in furtherance of the charity's objects, support costs for that expenditure and the resources expended on managing and administering the charity.[64]

The level of detail to be revealed in relation to grants made by a charity has caused considerable debate and the requirements were tightened when the SORP was re-issued. By notes to the accounts[65] charities should provide an appropriate analysis and explanation of the grants which it makes if grant making is material to the charity. Grant making will be regarded as material if in any accounting year more than 5 per cent of the charity's total expenditure is applied in making grants. The analysis should show for both individual and institutional grants the total number and total value of grants for different charitable purposes. In addition, for institutional grants the charity should give details of a sufficient number of grants to allow the reader to understand the charity's grant making activities; details include the names of recipients and the total grant received. In exceptional circumstances, where disclosure would seriously prejudice either the charity or the recipient in carrying out its purposes,

---

[58] The Charities (Accounts and Reports) Regulations 2000 (SI 2000/2868), reg.3(4)(a) and see SORP, para.56.

[59] The Charities (Accounts and Reports) Regulations 2000 (SI 2000/2868), Sch., Para.1(c).

[60] See SORP, para.38.

[61] SORP, para.69. For the detail of the analysis see SORP, paras 59, *et seq.* The notes to the accounts must disclose material movement of funds between type of funds—The Charities (Accounts and Reports) Regulations 2000 (SI 2000/2868) Sch.1, para.1(i).

[62] See SORP, paras 59, *et seq.* for the treatment of particular items of income and expenditure.

[63] SORP, para.76. For guidance on recognition of incoming resources see SORP, paras 75–84.

[64] SORP, para.60. A charity with income less than £250,000 but preparing accounts on an accruals basis can choose an alternative classification of expenditure, see SORP, para.348.

[65] The Charities (Accounts and Reports) Regulations 2000 (SI 2000/2868), Sch., para.1(o).

disclosure need not be made but details must still be given to the Charity Commissioners.[66]

In relation to particulars of expenditure it should be noted that the 2000 Regulations require[67] notes to the accounts to disclose particulars of related party transactions such as remuneration and other benefits paid to a trustee of a charity or purchase of property from a person connected with a charity trustee.[68] Notes to the accounts should also disclose particulars of the cost of indemnity insurance for trustees.[69]

Balance sheet

The balance sheet should show the state of the affairs of a charity at the end of the financial year in respect of which the statement of accounts is prepared.[70] The SORP[71] specifies the information to be included about the type of assets and liabilities of the charity and the breakdown required, for example, fixed assets should be divided into intangible assets, tangible assets for use by the charity and investments. Notes to the accounts should give more detail as to particular categories of asset and liability.[72] For example, in relation to tangible assets details should be given of freehold interests in land and buildings, any other interests in land or buildings, plant and machinery, fixtures, fittings and equipment and payments on account and assets in course of construction.[73]

9–024

Assets and liabilities are valued in accordance with the methods and principles set out in the SORP.[74] The basic principles adopted are that fixed assets,[75] other than investments, should be shown at cost (or valuation) less an appropriate provision for depreciation and investments should be shown at market value.[76] Current assets are to be shown at the lower of cost and net realisable value and liabilities at their settlement value.[77] The specific problems of some charities are recognised in that an inalienable or historic fixed asset need not be costed and appear on the balance sheet where it is difficult to cost but information about the asset should appear as a note.[78] Notes to the accounts should also give particulars of any outstanding loans[79] and guarantees.[80]

---

[66] SORP, paras 139–146.
[67] Sch., para.1(d) and see SORP, paras 157, *et seq.*
[68] The definition of "related parties" is wide, see SORP, App.1, para.26.
[69] The Charities (Accounts and Reports) Regulations 2000 (SI 2000/2868), Sch., para.1(g). For details of other items of expenditure to be revealed see paras 1(e), (f), (n) and (p).
[70] The Charities (Accounts and Reports) Regulations 2000 (SI 2000/2868), reg.3(4)(b)
[71] Paras 183, *et seq.*
[72] The Charities (Accounts and Reports) Regulations 2000 (SI 2000/2868), Sch., para.1(q)–(u).
[73] See also SORP, paras 203, *et seq.*
[74] The Charities (Accounts and Reports) Regulations 2000 (SI 2000/2868), reg.3(6).
[75] See SORP, paras 190, *et seq.*
[76] See SORP, paras 231, *et seq.*
[77] SORP, paras 242, *et seq.*
[78] See SORP, paras 208, *et seq.*
[79] The Charities (Accounts and Reports) Regulations 2000 (SI 2000/2868), Sch., para.1(l).
[80] *ibid.*, Sch., para.1(k).

Small charities

9–025   Charities with annual gross income of less than £100,000 may prepare a receipts and payments account and a statement of assets and liabilities rather than a full statement of accounts.[81] There are no provisions in the Regulations as to the content of this form of accounting. The Charity Commissioners have issued a guide, CC64, *Receipts and Payments Accounts Pack 2001* with pro forma accounts, but it does not have the force of law; it merely represents best practice.

A receipts and payments account is basically a factual record of money paid and received during the financial year. A statement of assets and liabilities is a list of significant possessions and outstanding financial obligations as at the end of the financial year. As this form of accounting is not intended to show a true and fair view, the only accountancy concept which applies is that of consistency.[82] To assist charities to account on a standard basis the Charity Commissioners have produced a standard accounts form.

Branches and subsidiary undertakings

9–026   Charities, particularly those which work across a wide geographical area, operate through a number of different structures both to carry out their purposes and to raise funds. Trustees need to establish the legal status of entities through which they operate in order to determine the form of accounts required.[83] "Branches", as defined in the SORP, must be accounted for in the accounts of the main charity. If a particular charitable organisation connected with a charity is a legal entity in its own right and falls outside the definition of "branch" because of its level of administrative autonomy, that charity should prepare its own accounts even if it is known as a branch of the main charity.[84] No special provision needs to be made for those groups or divisions of a charity which do not amount to a "branch", for example special interest groups.[85]

A "branch" for the purposes of accounting may be a separate legal entity or may simply be part of the administrative machinery of the main charity. The particular name used by the branch is irrelevant; what is important is whether it is administered by or on behalf of the main charity and whether its funds are held for specific purposes which are within the general purposes of the main charity. Characteristics of a branch are stated to be that it uses the name of the main charity within its own title, uses the main charity's registration number to receive tax relief and receives support from the main charity through advice, publicity and materials and, possibly, staff and funds. A branch will usually exclusively raise funds

---

[81] The Charities Act 1993, s.42(3).
[82] SORP, para.353.
[83] See SORP, para.51.
[84] SORP, para.52. The cost of preparing and having examined or audited a number of sets of accounts has and is causing some charities to move from a federal to a central structure.
[85] See SORP, App.1.

for the main charity and/or for its own local activities and be perceived by the public to be the main charity's local representative.[86]

A branch will exist where the Charity Commission direct that a charity established for any special purposes of, or in connection with, another charity shall be treated as forming part of that other charity.[87] There will also be a branch or branches where the Commission direct that two or more charities having the same charity trustees shall be treated as a single charity.[88]

There is no obligation to prepare individual accounts for a branch **9–027** which is an unincorporated charity.[89] All branch transactions should be accounted for gross in the main charity's own accounts. Similarly, all assets and liabilities of branches should be incorporated into the main charity's own balance sheet.[90]

The notes to the accounts of a charity should give information about any institution or body corporate connected with the main charity, in particular its name and the nature of the relationship.[91] If, by virtue of the control exercised by the main charity, a connected charity is a branch, it must be accounted for in the main charity's accounts. If a charity has one or more subsidiary undertakings[92] consolidated accounts must be prepared in addition to the main charity's own accounts unless the gross income of the group is £25,000 or less.[93] As an individual charity's accounts are required to be filed with the Charity Commissioners,[94] separate Statements of Financial Activities should be prepared and filed for the group and the parent company.[95]

AUDIT AND INDEPENDENT EXAMINATION

A charity whose gross income or total expenditure exceeds £250,000 in **9–028** the present or two preceding financial years must have its accounts audited.[96] If the gross income or total expenditure of a charity exceeds £10,000 but does not exceed £250,000 it may elect instead to have the accounts examined by an independent examiner.[97] The Charity Commissioners have power to order that a particular charity need not comply with the audit and examination requirements of s.43 of the 1993 Act.[98] The particular circumstances in which dispensation can be given are set out in

---

[86] SORP, App.1.
[87] Charities Act 1993, s.96(5).
[88] *ibid.*, s.96(6) inserted by Charities (Amendment) Act 1995.
[89] For charitable companies, see paras 9–034, *et seq.*, above.
[90] SORP, para.53.
[91] The Charities (Accounts and Reports) Regulations 2000 (SI 2000/2868) para.1(j)
[92] As defined in SORP, App.1.
[93] See SORP, paras 299, *et seq.* for the details of the form of consolidation required.
[94] Charities Act 1993, s.45(4).
[95] See SORP, para.304.
[96] Charities Act 1993, s.43(1).
[97] *ibid.*, s.43(3).
[98] *ibid.*, s.44(1)(f); The Charities (Accounts and Reports) Regulations 1995 (SI 1995/2724), reg.9.

reg.9 of the 1995 Regulations and are essentially cases where adequate alternative audit arrangements exist, although there is power, in exceptional circumstances, to allow independent examination rather than audit in a particular financial year.[99]

If a charity which is required to do so fails to have its accounts examined or audited within ten months of the end of the financial year, the Charity Commissioners have power to order that the accounts for that year are audited.[1] The auditor is appointed by the Commissioners[2] and the cost is recoverable from the charity trustees or, to the extent that that is impracticable, from the charity's funds.[3] The Commissioners also have power to order, where they consider it desirable, that accounts which have been independently examined should be audited.[4] In that case, the charity has the option to appoint its own auditor.[5]

Both auditors and independent examiners have a right of access to any books, documents and other records (however kept) which relate to the relevant charity.[6] Further, an auditor or independent examiner has a right to require of past or present trustees, officers and employees of the charity such information and explanations as he considers it necessary in order to carry out the audit or examination.[7] If a person refuses to co-operate with an auditor or independent examiner, the Charity Commissioners may order that person to give the auditor or independent examiner the relevant facility[8]; breach of such an order is a contempt of court.[9]

The court has power to grant whole or partial relief from liability to an auditor or independent examiner in respect of proceedings for negligence, default or breach of duty where it appears he has acted honestly and reasonably and that, having regard to all the circumstances, he ought fairly to be excused.[10]

Audit

9–029   The duty of an auditor is to ascertain that the statement of accounts complies with the Regulations as to form and content and that it gives a true and fair view of the state of affairs of the charity at the end of the financial year in question and of the incoming resources and application of the resources of the charity.[11] The audit must be carried out by a per-

[99] The Charities (Accounts and Reports) Regulations 1995 (SI 1995/2724), reg.9(2)(e).
[1] Charities Act 1993, s.43(4).
[2] ibid., s.43(5).
[3] ibid., s.43(6).
[4] ibid., s.43(4).
[5] ibid., s.43(5).
[6] ibid., s.44(1)(d); The Charities (Accounts and Reports) Regulations 1995 (SI 1995/2724), reg.8(1).
[7] Charities Act 1993, s.44(1)(e); The Charities (Accounts and Reports) Regulations 1995 (SI 1995/2724), reg.8(2).
[8] Charities Act 1993, s.44(2).
[9] ibid., s.88.
[10] ibid., s.44(3) applies Companies Act 1985, s.727 to charity auditors and independent examiners.
[11] ibid., s.44(1)(b); The Charities (Accounts and Reports) Regulations 1995 (SI 1995/2724), reg.6(2)(e). The duty is modified where a receipts and payments account and statement of assets and liabilities has been prepared—reg.6(3)(e).

son who is eligible to be appointed as an auditor of a company[12] or who is a member of a body specified in regulations and eligible under the rules of that body to be appointed to audit for charities.[13] The auditing standards applicable are the Statements of Auditing Standards produced by the Auditing Practices Board and Practice Note 11, the Audit of Charities.

The required contents of the auditor's report to the charity trustees are set out in the Regulations.[14] In particular, the auditor must include a statement of opinion and the grounds for that opinion if he considers that proper accounting records have not been maintained, or the accounts do not accord with the records, or the accounts are materially inconsistent with the trustees annual report, or he has not been supplied with relevant information or explanations.

The Regulations[15] impose a duty on the auditor to make a written report to the Charity Commissioners if he becomes aware of any matter in relation to the activities or affairs of the charity which he has reasonable cause to believe is, or is likely to be, of material significance to the Commissioners in relation to the exercise of their powers to institute inquiries[16] or to act for the protection of charities[17] in relation to that charity. This is sometimes known as "whistle blowing". Matters likely to be of material significance, and which should be reported, include lack of control over the charity by the trustees, for example, rubber stamping decisions taken by others, significant breach of legal or constitutional requirements, for example, trustee conflicts of interest, and abuse of property. The auditor is also under a duty to make a statement to the charity trustees on ceasing to hold office on any circumstances connected with his ceasing to hold office which he considers should be brought to their attention and a copy of that statement should go to the Commissioners unless there are no such circumstances.[18]

Independent examination

An independent examination is a less onerous form of scrutiny than audit; an examiner is not required to form an opinion as to whether the accounts show a true and fair view. The object is to enable the examiner to state whether or not any matters specified in reg.7(e)(f)(g)[19] of the Regulations have come to the examiner's attention. In carrying out his examination, an examiner must follow the Directions on the Carrying out of an Independent Examination issued by the Charity Commissioners under s.43(7)(b) of the 1993 Act.[20]

9–030

---

[12] See Companies Act 1989, s.25.
[13] Charities Act 1993, ss.43(2), 44(1). No regulations have yet been issued.
[14] The Charities (Accounts and Reports) Regulations 1995 (SI 1995/2724), reg.6(2) for statements of accounts and reg.6(3) for receipts and payments accounts.
[15] *ibid.*, reg.6(5).
[16] Charities Act 1993, s.8. See para.9–037 below.
[17] *ibid.*, s.18. See paras 9–042, *et seq.*, below.
[18] The Charities (Accounts and Reports) Regulations 1995 (SI 1995/2724), reg.6(6).
[19] See para.9–031, below.
[20] See CC63, *Independent Examination of Charity Accounts 2001. Directions and Guidance Notes.*

An independent examiner is a person who is reasonably believed by the trustees to have the requisite ability and practical experience to carry out a competent examination of the accounts.[21] The examiner, to be independent, should not have any connection with the trustees which might inhibit the impartial conduct of the examination so that, for example, a major donor or a business partner of a trustee should not be selected.[22] The type of person envisaged is a bank or building society manager, a local authority treasurer or a retired accountant. The Charity Commissioners recommend that a qualified accountant is the independent examiner if a charity has gross assets over £1,000,000 or the gross income over £100,000; a commensurate understanding of accountancy principles and accounting standards will be required where accounts are prepared on the accruals basis. The Commissioners also recommend that trustees check the knowledge and experience of a potential independent examiner and consider taking up references.

The Directions and Guidance Notes issued by the Commissioners[23] make it clear that an independent examination is not as detailed and onerous a review as an audit. For example, verification procedures only need to be carried out if material doubts or concerns arise on a review of the accounting records and accounts and no satisfactory explanation is received from the trustees. An examiner must, however, check that the election for examination, rather than audit, is valid, as is any election to prepare a receipts and payments account under s.42(3) of the 1993 Act. If accounts are prepared on an accruals basis the examiner should consider and review the accounting policies adopted and any significant estimate or judgment that had been made in preparing the accounts and see that the accounts comply with the Regulations. The examiner should also identify any major inconsistency between the accounts and the trustees' annual report.

9–031   The Directions place an obligation on an independent examiner to inform the Charity Commissioners in writing of any information or evidence which gives him reasonable cause to believe that one or more of the charity trustees has been responsible for deliberate or reckless misconduct in the administration of the charity. Thus, whilst an independent examiner is subject in the same way to a "whistle blowing" duty as an auditor,[24] the level of misconduct required is higher before the whistle has to be blown.

The required contents of the independent examiner's report to the charity trustees are set out in reg.7 of the 1995 Regulations. In particular, the examiner must state whether any matter has given him cause to believe that proper accounting records have not been kept properly, or that the accounts do not accord with the records or, where appropriate, that the statement of accounts does not comply with the Regulations.[25] He must

---

[21] Charities Act 1993, s.43(3)(a).
[22] For the guidance of the Charity Commissioners on the selection of an independent examiner issued under s.43(7)(a) of the 1993 Act, see CC63, *Independent Examination of Charity Accounts 2001. Directions and Guidance Notes*, p. 4 and App.1.
[23] See CC63, *Independent Examination of Charity Accounts 2001. Directions and Guidance Notes*.
[24] See para.9–029, above.
[25] The Charities (Accounts and Reports) Regulations 1995 (SI 1995/2724), reg.7(e).

also state whether or not any matter has arisen to which attention should be drawn to enable a proper understanding of the accounts to be reached.[26] Finally, his report should state if there has been material expenditure or action contrary to the trusts of the charity, or if information or explanation has not been provided to him and, in the case of accrual accounts, if the statement of accounts is inconsistent in any material respect with the trustees' annual report.[27]

ANNUAL REPORT

Charity trustees are under a duty to prepare an annual report, which complies with the Regulations, in respect of each financial year.[28] A charity may elect to produce a less detailed report if its gross income does not exceed £250,000 in any particular financial year.[29] The annual report, together with the accounts, is intended to provide timely and regular information on the charity and its funds. It is also intended to enable the reader to gain an understanding of the charity's objectives, structure, activities and achievements and to gain a full and proper appreciation of the charity's financial transactions during the year and the position of its funds at the end of the year.[30] **9–032**

Although the report need only be signed by one or more of the charity trustees authorised to do so,[31] it is the responsibility of all the trustees to prepare the report. The annual report and accounts should be approved by the charity trustees as a body. Any trustee who considers that the report and accounts should not be approved, and who cannot resolve his concerns with his fellow trustees or the auditor or independent examiner, should report those concerns to the Charity Commissioners.[32]

The report for a charity with a gross income not exceeding £250,000 should be a brief summary of the main activities and achievements of the charity during the year.[33] The report should also contain the basic legal and administrative information about the charity required by the Regulations, including the names of the trustees.[34] In addition the report should contain the trustees' policies, if any, in relation to reserves[35], selection of investments and for the selection of grant recipients.[36]

In the case of any other charity, the annual report should be a review of all activities of the charity, including material transactions and significant

---

[26] *ibid.*, reg.7(f).
[27] *ibid.*, reg.7(g).
[28] Charities Act 1993, s.45(1).
[29] The Charities (Accounts and Reports) Regulations 2000 (SI 2000/2868), reg.7(3)(a).
[30] See SORP, para.4.
[31] The Charities (Accounts and Reports) Regulations 2000 (SI 2000/2868), reg.7(3)(c).
[32] See SORP, para.28.
[33] The Charities (Accounts and Reports) Regulations 2000 (SI 2000/2868), reg.7(3)(a)
[34] *ibid.*, reg.7(4)(a)–(j). The names of the trustees need not be given if the Charity Commissioners accept that persons would be placed in personal danger and dispense with the requirement—reg.7(5).
[35] As to policy in relation to reserves see, CC19, *Charities' Reserves* (2002) and OG43, *Charity Income Reserves.*
[36] The Charities (Accounts and Reports) Regulations 2000 (SI 2000/2868), reg.7(4)(k).

developments during the year. Significant changes in the activities of the charity should be highlighted and any likely future developments considered and if the charity was in deficit at the beginning of the financial year, steps taken to eliminate the deficit.[37] In addition to the basic legal and administrative information, there should be included an explanation of the objects of the charity, a description of the organisational structure and how decisions are made and the relationship explained if the charity is part of a wider network.[38] The annual report should put the accounts of the charity in perspective and should help the reader to relate the accounts to the objects and activities of the charity. If relevant, the report should comment on the effectiveness of fundraising activities and the contribution of volunteers.[39] Where appropriate, the report should consider the relationship between the charity and related parties and other charities and organisations with which it co-operates in pursuing its charitable objects.[40]

The annual report of a charity whose gross income exceeds £250,000 should also include a statement as to whether the charity trustees have considered the major risks to which the charity is exposed and the systems designed to mitigate those risks.[41] In addition, the report should include a statement on the performance of any investments and a description of assets held whether for the charity itself or for any other charity.[42]

9–033   Where in any financial year of a charity its gross income or total expenditure exceeds £10,000 the annual report must be transmitted to the Charity Commissioners within 10 months of the end of the financial year,[43] otherwise an annual report need only be submitted if the Commissioners so request.[44] An annual report transmitted to the Commissioners must have attached to it the statement of accounts, or if appropriate, the account and statement[45] together with the auditor's or independent examiner's report.[46] If an annual report is not submitted to the Commissioners, it must be preserved by the trustees for at least six years.[47] It is a criminal offence for a person without reasonable excuse to be persistently in default in failing to provide the Commissioners with an annual report.[48]

Annual reports kept by the Charity Commissioners are open to public inspection[49] and the Commissioners must supply copies if requested.[50] A

---

[37] *ibid.*, reg.7(3)(b)(i). For guidance as to how this requirement should be fulfilled, see SORP, paras 26, *et seq.*

[38] *ibid.*, reg.7(4)(m) and SORP, para.31(a)(b).

[39] SORP, para.31(d).

[40] SORP, para.31(c).

[41] The Charities (Accounts and Reports) Regulations 2000 (SI 2000/2868), reg.7(3)(b)(ii). See also CC Guidance, *Charities and Risk* (2001).

[42] *ibid.*, reg.7(4)(l)(n).

[43] Charities Act 1993, s.45(3).

[44] *ibid.*, s.45(3A).

[45] *i.e.* that prepared under s.42(3).

[46] *ibid.*, s.45(4).

[47] *ibid.*, s.45(7).

[48] *ibid.*, s.49. The filing of annual reports and accounts is enforced by the Commissioners as part of the enforcement of the filing of annual returns, see para.9–011 above.

[49] *ibid.*, s.47(1).

[50] *ibid.*, s.84 and see The Charity Commissioner's Fees (Copies and Extracts) Regulations 1992 (SI 1992/2986).

person is also entitled to request, provided he pays any reasonable fee demanded, that charity trustees supply him with a copy of the charity's most recent accounts.[51] A trustee or other person who, without reasonable excuse, is persistently in default in failing to provide members of the public with charity accounts is guilty of a criminal offence.[52]

An exempt charity is not required to produce an annual report[53]; neither is a charity which is excepted from registration because its income does not exceed £1,000 and is not registered.[54] Other excepted charities are not required to produce an annual report unless requested to do so by the Charity Commissioners[55]; such a report must comply with the Regulations.[56]

CHARITABLE COMPANIES

The requirements of s.41 of the Charities Act 1993 to keep accounting records do not apply to charitable companies.[57] Similar requirements, however, are imposed on charitable companies by Pt VII of the Companies Act 1985. Similarly, charitable companies are not subject to the requirements under the 1993 Act to produce annual statements of account[58] but they must comply with the relevant requirements of Pt VII of the Companies Act 1985 in relation to annual accounts.[59] **9–034**

The SORP applies to charitable companies although, where necessary, it must be adapted to allow compliance with companies legislation.[60] A charity which is a small company for the purposes of the Companies Act 1985[61] can follow the Financial Reporting Standards for Smaller Entities except where it conflicts with the SORP.[62] In particular, a separate Summary Income and Expenditure Account may be needed in addition to the Statement of Financial Activities.[63] Separate accounts will have to be provided for branches if both the main charity and branches are incorporated.[64] If the charity has a subsidiary undertaking,[65] consolidated accounts should be prepared unless the gross income of the group is £250,000 or less.[66] The requirement for accounts to be audited or independently examined in

---

[51] Charities Act 1993, s.47(2).
[52] ibid., s.49.
[53] ibid., s.46(1).
[54] ibid., s.46(3).
[55] ibid., s.46(4)(5).
[56] ibid., s.46(6). The Charities (Accounts and Reports) Regulations 2000 (SI 2000/2868), reg.7(7).
[57] ibid., s.41(5).
[58] ibid., s.42(7).
[59] For the detailed provisions see *Palmer's Company Law*, paras 9.101, *et seq*.
[60] SORP, para.334.
[61] See Companies Act 1985, s.247(3). A small company must satisfy two of the three following conditions: Annual turnover of £2.8m or less; balance sheet total of £1.4m or less; and employees 50 or less.
[62] See SORP, paras 345–347.
[63] See SORP, paras 335–338
[64] SORP, para.47.
[65] As defined in SORP, App.1.
[66] SORP, paras 299, *et seq.*

the 1993 Act does not apply to charitable companies.[67] Companies legislation requires that the accounts of charitable companies which are not a small company as defined in the Companies Act 1985, with gross income over £250,000 or over £1.4 million balance sheet total must be audited. Small companies with gross income exceeding £90,000 but not £250,000 can opt for an audit exemption report from a reporting accountant.[68] If a charity is administering separate trusts, the trust accounts should be incorporated into the company's statutory accounts and audit will depend upon the aggregate income of the company and its trusts. In the case of subsidiary companies, whether charitable or trading, the accounts and audit regime in the companies legislation will apply in the usual way to each company.

The Charity Commissioners may order that the condition and accounts of a charitable company shall be investigated and audited by an auditor appointed by them. The auditor must be a person eligible for appointment as a company auditor under s.25 of the Companies Act 1985.[69] The auditor has wide powers to call for books and information.[70] Unlike an audit ordered by the Commissioners into an unincorporated charity,[71] the cost of an audit into a charitable company falls on the Commissioners.[72]

9–035   The obligation in s.45 of the 1993 Act to make an annual report applies to charitable companies. This is in addition to the requirement under the companies legislation for the directors to produce a report.[73] The annual report transmitted to the Charity Commissioners should have attached to it copies of the charity's annual accounts prepared for the financial year in question under Pt VII of the Companies Act 1985 together with a copy of any auditor's report or report from a reporting accountant.[74] A charitable company, thus, does not have to prepare a separate set of accounts complying with s.42 of the 1993 Act. Even though separate accounts may have been prepared for branches,[75] one annual report should be prepared to cover the main charity and its branches.[76]

Charitable companies are required to make an annual return to both the Charity Commissioners[77] and the Registrar of Companies.[78] The requirement to make accounts available to the public applies to charitable companies.[79] The accounts to be made available are those prepared under Pt VII of the Companies Act 1985.[80]

[67] Charities Act 1993, s.43(9).
[68] Companies Act 1985, ss.249A–249E. A charitable company with subsidiaries may still have audit exemption if it is part of a "small group" as defined by the 1985 Act.
[69] Charities Act 1993, s.69(1).
[70] ibid., s.69(2).
[71] ibid., s.43(6). See para.9–028, above.
[72] ibid., s.69(3).
[73] Companies Act 1985, s.234. For the detailed provisions, see Palmer's Company Law, paras 9.401, et seq. To save preparation of two separate documents, the Charity Commissioners are prepared to accept the directors' report if it contains the information required to comply with Pt VI of the 1993 Act—SORP, para.332.
[74] Charities Act 1993, s.45(5).
[75] See para.9–026, above.
[76] SORP, para.51.
[77] Charities Act 1993, s.48.
[78] Companies Act 1985, s.363.
[79] Charities Act 1993, s.47(2). See para.9–033, above.
[80] ibid., s.47(3)(c).

THE POWER TO OBTAIN INFORMATION

The Charity Commissioners can only carry out their monitoring and supervisory functions effectively if they have adequate information about charities. Several of the provisions originating in the 1992 Act were introduced to enhance the Commissioners' powers to obtain information. In addition to wide powers to require persons to provide information and documents and to institute inquiries, the Commissioners are also entitled to receive information from the Inland Revenue, Customs and Excise and other Government bodies. The Commissioners now also obtain much information about charities from the annual report and accounts.[81]

9–036

Inquiries

The Charity Commissioners have power to institute inquiries with regard to charities or any particular charity or class of charity (other than an exempt charity) generally or for a particular purpose.[82] They may conduct the inquiry themselves or appoint a person to conduct it and make a report to them.[83] A member of the Commissioners' own staff may be appointed or one or more outsiders, for example, an accountant.[84]

9–037

The person conducting the inquiry has considerable powers to obtain information. He may direct any person[85] to provide accounts and written statements and to furnish copies of documents in respect of any matter in question at the inquiry and to verify such accounts, statements and documents by statutory declaration.[86] The person conducting the inquiry may take evidence on oath[87] and can require persons to attend at a specified time and place to give evidence.[88]

Scargill v Att-Gen[89] concerned an appeal against removal from trusteeship. In the course of his judgment, in relation to the inquiry by the Charity Commissioners, Neuberger J. said:

> "Indeed, I would have thought that any self-respecting charitable trustee would, in the absence of very good reason to the contrary, co-operate with the reasonable requirements and requests of the Commissioners, even in the absence of any statutory obligation to do so."

[81] *ibid.*, s.48; see para.9–033, above.
[82] *ibid.*, s.8(1). An enquiry is only opened by the Commissioners after an evaluation process has been completed to ensure that inquiries are only opened where they have the most impact—see [2001–2002] Ch. Com. Rep., p. 21.
[83] *ibid.*, s.8(2).
[84] For example, the inquiry into War on Want was conducted by Mr David Spencer C.A. of Grant Thornton Accountants and Mr Charles Raines, a solicitor with the Commissioners, [1992] Ch. Com. Rep., para.62.
[85] The fact that a person is holding property adversely to a charity or freed or discharged from any charitable trust was removed as a reason not to provide information by s.6(4) of the Charities Act 1992.
[86] Charities Act 1993, s.8(3)(a)(b).
[87] *ibid.*, s.8(4).
[88] *ibid.*, s.8(3)(c).
[89] Unreported, September 4, 1998.

9–038   Once an inquiry has been completed, the Commissioners may cause the full report of the person conducting the inquiry to be published or some other statement of the results of the inquiry.[90] As a matter of practice the Commissioners publish brief reports on the results of an inquiry on the website drawing attention to any wider lessons for charities as a whole.[91] The Commissioners may order the report to be published even if they do not propose to take any action. A copy of the report of an inquiry, if certified by the Commissioners to be a true copy, is admissable in legal proceedings[92] as evidence of any fact stated in the report and of the opinion of the person conducting the inquiry.[93]

Documents and records

9–039   The Commissioners have power to order any person to provide them with any information in his possession which relates to any charity and is relevant to the discharge of their functions.[94] They also have power to order any person[95] to furnish them with copies or extracts of documents in his custody or under his control or to transmit the original for inspection.[96] If the documents are recorded otherwise than in legible form, for example, on computer, the Commissioners may require the information to be made available in legible form.[97] If a person fails to comply with an order of the Commissioners to give information, he may be treated as in contempt of court.[98]

These provisions are strengthened by s.11 of the 1993 Act which provides that any person knowingly or recklessly providing the Commissioners with false or misleading information is guilty of a criminal offence[99] if the information is supplied in purported compliance with a requirement of the 1993 Act, or he intends or could reasonably be expected to know that it would be used by the Commissioners for discharge of their functions under the Act. It is also an offence for a person to wilfully alter, suppress, conceal or destroy any document which is required to be produced to the Commissioners.[1] No prosecution in relation to information may be brought without the consent of the Director of Public Prosecutions.[2]

---

[90] Charities Act 1993, s.8(6).
[91] See [2001–2002] Ch. Com. Rep., p. 26.
[92] The legal proceedings must be instituted by the Commissioners under PtIV of the 1993 Act or be instituted by the Attorney-General, Charities Act 1993, s.34(2).
[93] Charities Act 1993, s.34(1).
[94] *ibid.*, s.9(1)(a).
[95] The fact that a person is holding property adversely to a charity or freed or discharged from any charitable trust was removed as a reason not to provide documents by the 1992 Act; see Charities Act 1992, s.7(3).
[96] Charities Act 1993, s.9(1)(b).
[97] *ibid.*, s.97(2).
[98] *ibid.*, s.88.
[99] See [1999–2000] Ch. Com. Rep., p.23 for details of a successful prosecution under this section.
[1] *ibid.*, s.11(2).
[2] *ibid.*, s.94. The penalty on summary conviction is a fine not exceeding the statutory maximum and on conviction on indictment, imprisonment for up to 2 years or a fine or both— s.11(3).

Disclosure of information

Since 1986,[3] the Commissioners of Inland Revenue have been permitted   **9–040**
to pass information to the Charity Commissioners where a charity
appears to be carrying on non-charitable activities or to be applying its
income for non-charitable purposes. The Charity Commissioners have
found this to be very useful in providing information to recover funds for
charity.[4] The Inland Revenue were already permitted to give the Charity
Commissioners the names and addresses of institutions which they treated
as charitable together with information as to the purposes of the institutions and the trusts under which they were established. The Charities
Act 1992 widened the sources of information available to the Charity
Commissioners by permitting the Commissioners of Customs and Excise
to reveal the same categories of information to the Commissioners.[5]

The Charities Act 1993 also provides that certain bodies are permitted
to disclose information received by them to the Charity Commissioners
if that disclosure is made for the purpose of enabling or assisting the
Commissioners to discharge any of their functions.[6] The relevant bodies
are any government department, any local authority, any constable and
any other body or person discharging functions of a public nature.[7]
The last category extends beyond public bodies and may include private
bodies exercising regulatory or supervisory functions in a particular area.[8]

Those with the most information about a charity and very often the first
to know when things are going wrong are charity workers. Such workers
are an important potential source of information. This is recognised by
the designation of the Charity Commissioners as a prescribed person
under the Public Interest Disclosure Act 1998.[9] A worker making a qualified disclosure, for example, about a breach of a legal obligation to the
Commissioners is protected from detrimental treatment.[10]

The Charity Commissioners themselves are permitted to disclose to   **9–041**
any of the bodies designated in s.10 of the 1993 Act[11] information which
they receive where disclosure is connected with the discharge of the Commissioners' functions or would assist that particular body to discharge its
functions.[12] Bodies which may be interested in receiving information from

---

[3] Charities Act 1960, s.9(3) inserted by Finance Act 1986.
[4] See [1987] Ch. Com. Rep., para.28.
[5] See now Charities Act 1993, s.10(2).
[6] *ibid.*, s.10(1).
[7] *ibid.*, s.10(6).
[8] Some guidance as to the bodies which may be regarded as discharging "functions of a public nature" may be obtained from judicial review cases; see *R. v Panel of Take-overs and
Mergers, Ex p. Datafin (Norton Opax intervening)* [1987] 1 Q.B. 815; *R. v Advertising
Standards Authority Ex p. The Insurance Service* [1990] 9 T.L.R. 169; *R. v Disciplinary
Committee of the Jockey Club, Ex p. Massingbred-Mundy* [1993] 2 All E.R. 207. Guidance
may also be obtained from cases involving the Human Rights Act 1998, see *R. (on the
application of Heather) v Leonard Cheshire Foundation* [2002] 2 All E.R. 936.
[9] The Public Interest Disclosure (Prescribed Persons) Order 1999 (SI 1999/1549).
[10] Employment Rights Act 1996, s.47B, inserted by the Public Interest Disclosure Act 1998,
s.2.
[11] This includes a body outside the UK discharging functions of a public nature; Charities
Act 1993, s.10(7).
[12] Charities Act 1993, s.10(4).

the Commissioners include the Serious Fraud Office and the Department of Trade and Industry.

The value of information given to the Charity Commissioners in the use of its investigatory powers would be reduced if all the information were automatically available to the public. Both the Data Protection Act 1998 and the Freedom of Information Act 2000 allow information received to be kept confidential in certain circumstances. There is exemption from the subject information provisions for the processing of personal data for certain regulatory functions of the Charity Commissioners. In particular, information need not be disclosed if it would be likely to prejudice the proper discharge of the Commissioners' functions of protecting charities against misconduct or mismanagement, protecting the property of charities or recovering the property of charities.[13] Similarly, information is exempt from disclosure under the Freedom of Information Act 2000 if its disclosure would be likely to prejudice the same regulatory functions.[14]

POWERS FOR THE PROTECTION OF CHARITIES

9–042   In addition to their powers to remove and appoint charity trustees,[15] the Charity Commissioners have a wide range of powers to act for the protection of a charity after an inquiry[16] has taken place.[17] The powers are divided into those which are essentially protective and temporary and those which are remedial and permanent.

Protective and temporary powers

9–043   None of the protective and temporary powers are exercisable by the Commissioners unless they have instituted an inquiry under s.8 of the 1993 Act and they are satisfied either[18] that there is or has been misconduct or mismanagement[19] in the administration of the charity or that action is desirable to protect and secure a proper application of the charity property.[20] Whether there has been misconduct or mismanagement is a question of fact but the condition is clearly satisfied by trustees who knowingly persevere in acting in breach of the terms of the charity's governing instrument.[21] In those circumstances, the Commissioners may take

---

[13] See Data Protection Act 1998, s.31(1)(2)(b)(c)(d).
[14] See Freedom of Information Act 2000, ss.31(1)(g), (2)(f)(g)(h).
[15] See paras 5–035, 5–038, above.
[16] i.e. an inquiry under Charities Act 1993, s.8. The recommendation in the White Paper, Cm. 694, para.5.14 that an inquiry should not be necessary before temporary powers are exercised by the Commissioners was not enacted in the 1992 Act.
[17] Charities Act 1993, s.18. The powers do not extend to exempt charities, s.18(16).
[18] The requirement for both misconduct and the need to act for the protection of charity property was removed by the Charities Act 1992, s.8.
[19] Misconduct or mismanagement includes the payment of excessive remuneration to persons acting on behalf of the charity, Charities Act 1993, s.18(3).
[20] Charities Act 1993, s.18(1).
[21] See Scargill v Att-Gen, unreported, September 4, 1998, Neuberger J. and [1998] Ch. Com. Rep., p. 22.

various steps in relation to the trustees and officers and property of a charity or they may appoint a receiver and manager.

To ensure the effectiveness of the Commissioners' protective and temporary powers they may be exercised without notice being given to the trustees of the charity.[22] In addition, breach of any order under s.18(1)(iv)(v) or (vi) of the 1993 Act[23] made by the Commissioners pursuant to such powers as a criminal offence.[24] An appeal against an order of the Commissioners lies to the High Court.[25]

The Commissioners have power to suspend any trustee, officer, agent or employee of a charity pending consideration being given to his removal.[26] Later removal may as an exercise of one of the Commissioners' remedial and permanent powers after an inquiry[27] or the Commissioners may elect to make an order removing a trustee under alternative powers.[28] The Commissioners may also appoint one or more additional trustees if they consider that it is necessary for the proper administration of the charity.[29]

The Commissioners may vest property of the charity in the official custodian for charities or require persons in whom charity property is vested to transfer it to him.[30] Any person who is holding property on behalf of the charity may be ordered not to part with it without the approval of the Commissioners.[31] Similarly, any debtor of the charity may be ordered not to make any payments to the charity without the Commissioners' approval.[32] The Commissioners may also by order restrict the transactions or payments which may be made by the charity without their approval.[33]   **9–044**

The Commissioners have power to appoint a receiver and manager in respect of the property and affairs of a charity.[34] The appointee must not be member of the staff of the Charity Commissioners.[35] The power is now one which is used regularly by the Commissioners particularly where the trustees are no longer in control of the charity, either because of disputes or lack of interest[36] or there is a need to preserve the assets of a charity.[37] To ensure a charity is placed on a firm footing, the power may be used in

---

[22] *ibid.*, s.18(12).
[23] See below.
[24] Charities Act 1993, s.18(14). The penalty on summary conviction is a fine not exceeding level 5 on the standard scale. The consent of the Director of Public Prosecutions is required before any criminal proceedings may be brought, s.94.
[25] *ibid.*, ss.18(8), 16(11)(12)(13). No certificate or leave is required to appeal against the appointment of a receiver, s.18(9)(a).
[26] *ibid.*, s.18(1)(i). Suspension should not be for more than 12 months, s.18(11). For an example of the use of this power see [1997] Ch. Com. Rep. paras 123–125.
[27] *ibid.*, s.18(2)(i).
[28] See para.5–038, above.
[29] Charities Act 1993, s.18(1)(ii). For an example of the use of this power see [1993] Ch. Com. Rep., para.65.
[30] *ibid.*, s.18(1)(iii).
[31] *ibid.*, s.18(1)(iv).
[32] *ibid.*, s.18(1)(v).
[33] *ibid.*, s.18(1)(vi).
[34] *ibid.*, s.18(1)(vii).
[35] Charities Act 1993, s.19(1).
[36] See [1993] Ch. Com. Rep., paras 61–64 (Fellowship Charitable Foundation); [1995] Ch. Com. Rep., paras 62–66 (Valley Books Trust); [1996] Ch. Com. Rep., paras 172–178 (CLIC).
[37] See [1997] Ch. Com. Rep., paras 116–122 (Destination Florida).

conjunction with other powers such as the appointment of new trustees.[38] In other circumstances, the receiver and manager may wind up the charity.[39] When appointing a receiver, the Commissioners may make provision with respect to the functions to be discharged by him, in particular, specifying which powers and duties of the trustees are to be exercisable by the receiver and not the trustees.[40] Provided he is acting within the powers specified, the receiver is entitled to possession of all the relevant charity property and to exercise the powers previously exercised by the trustees.[41] When discharging such functions, the receiver acts under the supervision of the Commissioners.[42] The receiver may apply to the Commissioners for advice and he will be protected if he acts in accordance with such advice.[43] The Commissioners themselves may apply to the High Court for directions in relation to the discharge of functions by a particular receiver.[44]

9–045   A person appointed as a receiver and manager must make a report to the Commissioners within three months of appointment setting out an estimate of the total value of the property of the charity, information about the property and affairs of the charity immediately before his appointment and his strategy for discharging his functions. Thereafter he must make annual reports to the Commissioners and a final report setting out how he has discharged his functions.[45] The report must be disclosed to a trustee of a charity who challenges the appointment of the receiver and manager and actions taken by the Commissioners consequent on the report.[46] The remuneration of a receiver and manager is determined by the Commissioners and is payable out of the income of the relevant charity.[47] Anyone appointed a receiver may be required to give security for the discharge of their functions within such time and in such form as the Commissioners may specify.[48]

Remedial and permanent powers

9–046   The Commissioners have power to take more permanent action if they are satisfied both that there is or has been misconduct or mismanagement[49] in the administration of the charity and that action is desirable to

---

[38] See [1996] Ch. Com. Rep., para.175.

[39] See [2001–2002] Ch. Com. Rep., p. 12 (CATCH!).

[40] Charities Act 1993, s.19(2)(3).

[41] See *Rezafard v Runacres*, unreported, November 4, 1998, Ferris J.

[42] Charities Act 1993, s.19(2). The Commissioners have power to disallow remuneration and to remove a receiver and manager after due notice, Charities Act 1993, s.19(6)(7), The Charities (Receiver and Manager) Regulations 1992 (SI 1992/2355), regs.3(3), 4(3).

[43] *ibid.*, ss.19(4)(a), 29.

[44] *ibid.*, s.19(4)(b), (5).

[45] The Charities (Receiver and Manager) Regulations 1992 (SI 1992/2355), reg.5.

[46] *Weth v Att-Gen* [1999] 1 W.L.R. 686 at 694, *per* Nourse L.J.

[47] The Charities (Receiver and Manager) Regulations 1992 (SI 1992/2355), reg.3. The fact that the remuneration of the receiver and manager comes from the assets of the charity makes such an appointment unsuitable in many cases, see [1996] Ch. Com. Rep., 169.

[48] Charities Act 1993, s.19(7), The Charities (Receiver and Manager) Regulations 1992 (SI 1992/2355), reg.2.

[49] Misconduct or mismanagement includes the payment of excessive remuneration to persons acting on behalf of the charity, Charities Act 1993, s.18(3).

protect and secure a proper application of the charity property.[50] In those circumstances, the Commissioners have power to remove a trustee,[51] officer, agent or employee of the charity who has been involved in the misconduct or mismanagement in question.[52] The Commissioners also have power to establish a scheme for the administration of the charity.[53] Before the Commissioners can exercise either of their remedial and permanent powers they must give notice of their intention to do so to each of the trustees of the charity except those who cannot be found or have no known address in the UK.[54] An appeal from an order of the Commissioners exercising powers under s.18 is to the High Court.[55] An appeal by a charity or a charity trustee against an order appointing a receiver and manager does not require leave; nor does an appeal by a charity trustee against removal.[56] The usual defendant is the Attorney General[57] but the Charity Commissioners can be represented if they so wish.[58] The appeal takes the form of a rehearing.[59]

---

[50] Charities Act 1993, s.18(2).
[51] For an example of the use of this power, see [1998] Ch. Com. Rep, p.22 (Yorkshire Miner's Welfare Trust Fund Scheme).
[52] Charities Act 1993, s.18(2)(i).
[53] *ibid.*, s.18(2)(ii). For an example of the use of this power, see the report of the inquiry into Iran Aid (2001) Charity Commissioners.
[54] *ibid.*, s.18(12).
[55] Charities Act 1993, ss.18(8), 16(11) to (13).
[56] *ibid.*, s.18(9).
[57] *Weth v Att-Gen* [1999] 1 W.L.R. 686 at 691, *per* Nourse L.J.
[58] See *Scargill v Att-Gen*, unreported, September 4, 1998, Neuberger J.
[59] *Weth v Att-Gen* [1999] 1 W.L.R. 686 at 692, *per* Nourse L.J.

CHAPTER 10

THE COURTS AND OTHER REGULATORY AUTHORITIES

Under the feudal system imposed following the Norman conquest the **10–001** Crown was liege lord to all citizens.[1] This quasi-parental relationship, which formerly imposed upon the Crown the duty of watching over the interests of wards[2] makes it the protector of charity in general.[3] Therefore, as Lord Eldon said:

> "Where money is given to charity generally and indefinitely, without trustees or objects selected, the King as *parens patriae* is the constitutional trustee."[4]

The duty of the Crown as *parens patriae* to protect charity property is executed by the Attorney-General.[5]

Other persons or bodies exercise a regulatory jurisdiction over charities, including:

(1) *The courts* From the earliest times of the Court of Chancery the courts have exercised an inherent jurisdiction over charities and have been the main authority for the monitoring and control of charitable trusts. Although in more recent times their functions have been to some extent taken over by the Charity Commissioners, the High Court continues to exercise an appellate jurisdiction over the Commissioners.[6]

(2) *The Charity Commissioners* These may now be regarded as the primary body controlling charities, with many powers concurrent with those of the High Court [7] and the Attorney-General.[8]

---

[1] *Calvin's Case* (1608) 7 Co. Rep. 1a at 5a.

[2] *Eyre v Countess of Shaftesbury* (1724) 2 P. Wms. 103.

[3] *Att-Gen v Gleg* (1736) 1 Atk. 356; *Att-Gen v Brown* (1818) 1 Sw. 265 at 291; *Wellbeloved v Jones* (1822) 1 S. & S. 43; *Att-Gen v Compton* (1842) 1 Y. & C.C.C. 417 at 427; *National Anti-Vivisection Society v IRC* [1947] A.C. 31 at 63; *Re Belling* [1967] Ch. 425; *Hauxwell v Barton-upon-Humber UDC* [1974] Ch. 432.

[4] *Moggridge v Thackwell* (1803) 7 Ves. 36 at 83. And see *Incorporated Society v Richards* (1841) 1 Dr. & W. 258 at 390.

[5] See para.10–018, below.

[6] Charities Act 1993, s.16; see para.9–005, above.

[7] See Charities Act 1993, s.63(2).

[8] Charities Act 1993, ss.16(11)(12), 18(8). See para.9–008, above for appeal against an opinion or advice of the Commissioners.

(3)   *Visitors* Some charitable corporations are subject to the supervision of an official known as a visitor.[9]

Charities are also subject to less direct monitoring and control, in a number of ways:

(1)   *Fiscal authorities* The increasing importance of tax concessions to charities means that fiscal authorities cannot be ignored as an instrument for the regulation of charities.[10]
(2)   *Funders* Grant-awarding bodies frequently insist on some ability to monitor the activities of the charities to whom they give grants.[11]
(3)   *Other authorities* Certain charities, by virtue of the legal structure that they have adopted, are subject to the control of other authorities, for example, the Registrar of Companies.[12]

THE CROWN: THE SIGN MANUAL

10–002   In cases where its powers have not been delegated to the Courts the Crown retains a primary jurisdiction over the application of charitable property. The jurisdiction of the court was founded on the existence of a trust; where there was no trust the application of the fund was beyond the jurisdiction of the court, and rests with the Crown alone.[13] Accordingly, it seems to have been established from very early times that where there is a gift for charity generally, as in the case of an assurance or devise to the use of charity,[14] or the poor,[15] or a devise or bequest "to charity",[16] or "to the poor",[17] without more, the nomination of the charitable objects devolves on the Crown.[18] The position is the same where the donor has intended to name objects but has not done so.[19] It was held, under the old law of superstitious uses, that a gift for a superstitious purpose, which was

---

[9] See paras 10–063, *et seq.*, below.
[10] See para.10–085, below.
[11] See para.10–086, below.
[12] See para.10–087, below.
[13] *Moggridge v Thackwell* (1803) 7 Ves. 36 at 83; *Cary v Abbot* (1803) 7 Ves. 490; *Morice v Bishop of Durham* (1805) 10 Ves. 522 at 541; *Ommanney v Butcher* (1823) T. & R. 260 at 271; *Construction Industry Training Board v Att-Gen* [1973] Ch. 173; see also para.1–018, above.
[14] *Clifford v Francis* (1679) Freem.K.B. 330; *Att-Gen v Bowyer* (1798) 3 Ves. 726; *Jones' Case* (1690), cited [1893] 2 Ch. 49n.
[15] *Att-Gen v Peacock* (1677) Finch 245.
[16] *Att-Gen v Syderfen* (1683) 1 Vern. 224; *Att-Gen v Herrick* (1722) Amb. 712; *Legge v Asgill* (1818) T. & R. 265n.; *Kane v Cosgrave* (1873) 10 Ir.R.Eq. 211.
[17] *Ware v Att-Gen* (1843) 3 Ha. 194n.
[18] *Moggridge v Thackwell* (1802) 7 Ves. 36 at 83; *Ommanney v Butcher* (1823) T. & R. 260 at 270, 271.
[19] *Att-Gen v Syderfen*, above; *Moggridge v Thackwell*, above at 36, 73, 74. The statement to the contrary in *Anon.* (1702) 3 Freem. 261 must be regarded as erroneous.

prompted by a charitable intention,[20] was disposable by the Crown,[21] on the ground that in such a case nothing remained except the general object of charity.[22] It was formerly doubtful whether a distinction ought to be drawn between gifts to charity generally without a trust and cases in which, although the gift was indefinite, the donor had intended the mode of application to be left to the discretion of a trustee, who failed to carry out his wishes.[23] This doubt was resolved by Lord Eldon in two cases. In the first, *Moggridge v Thackwell*,[24] there was a bequest of residue to an individual who predeceased the testatrix, "to dispose of the same in such charities as he shall think fit", with a recommendation in favour of a particular class of clergymen. In the second, *Paice v Archbishop of Canterbury*,[25] there was merely a gift in trust for charitable purposes generally. In both cases the donor had intended to create a trust and for this reason Lord Eldon held that the gifts ought to be applied under a scheme settled by the court. These two cases having settled the law on this subject,[26] the rule is that where the donor intended to create a trust the court has jurisdiction, if the circumstances so require, to direct the purposes to which the gift shall be applied, but that where no trust was intended this power belongs to the Crown.[27] So, where a testator, after bequeathing legacies and appointing executors, had "directed" that the residue should be applied to certain charitable purposes and other charitable purposes which he intended to name but did not name, it was held, in accordance with the rule, that the fund was disposable by the court.[28] On the same principle, a

---

[20] See para.11–008, below.

[21] *Att-Gen v Baxter* (1684) 1 Vern. 248; *Jones' Case* (1690), reported [1893] 2 Ch. 49n.; *R. v Portington* (1692) 1 Salk. 162; *Att-Gen v Whorwood* (1750) 1 Ves.S. 537; *Da Costa v De Pas* (1754) Amb. 228; *De Garcin v Lawson* (1798) 4 Ves. 433n.; *Moggridge v Thackwell* (1802) 7 Ves. 36 at 83; *Cary v Abbot* (1802) 490 at 495, 496; *Att-Gen v Power* (1809) 1 Ball & B. 145; *De Themmines v De Bonneval* (1828) 5 Russ. 292; *Att-Gen v Todd* (1837) 1 Keen 803.

[22] See *Att-Gen v Bowyer* (1798) 3 Ves. 729; *Moggridge v Thackwell* (1802) 7 Ves. 36 at 83.

[23] *Cook v Duckenfield* (1743) 2 Atk. 562 at 567; *Att-Gen v Berryman* (1755) 1 Dick. 168 in which the duty of nominating the objects was vested in the trustee; *Att-Gen v Herrick* (1772) Amb. 712; *Moggridge v Thackwell* (1802) 7 Ves. 36 at 83, *per* Lord Eldon. See also *Clifford v Francis* (1679) Freem. 330, where the commissioners under 43 Eliz. I, c. 10 were held to have jurisdiction where the purpose of the charity was expressed. *Cf. Grimond v Grimond* [1905] A.C. 124, a Scottish case, where, however, the trust was held void for uncertainty.

[24] (1802) 7 Ves. 36.

[25] (1807) 14 Ves. 364.

[26] *Ommanney v Butcher* (1823) T. & R. 260 at 270, 271; *Hayter v Trego* (1828) 5 Russ. 113; *Att-Gen v Ironmongers' Co.* (1833) 2 Myl. & K. 578; *Reeve v Att-Gen* (1843) 3 Ha. 197. See also *Copinger v Crehane* (1877) Ir.R. 11 Eq. 429; *Re Davis* [1902] 1 Ch. 876 at 888; *Re Pyne* [1903] 1 Ch. 83; *Re Bennett* [1960] Ch. 18.

[27] The following cases are inconsistent with *Moggridge v Thackwell*, and would presumably not now be followed: *Att-Gen v Marchioness of Londonderry* (1825) Shelf.Mort. 272 at 273, where land was vested in trustees in trust to apply the rents for certain charitable purposes and such other charitable purposes as the donors or the survivor of them should appoint, and the donors died without appointing: it was held that the power of appointment belonged to the Crown; *Att-Gen v Fletcher* (1835) 5 L.J.Ch. 75, where a gift to charitable purposes, according to the best judgment of an executor who renounced probate, was held to be disposable by the Crown; and *Felan v Russell* (1842) 4 Ir.Eq.R. 701, in which the disposition was held to devolve on the Crown, where the person entrusted with the nomination of the objects died after a scheme had been directed, but before it was settled. See also *Re Dickason* (1837) 3 Ha. 195n.

[28] *Mills v Farmer* (1815) 1 Mer. 55.

legacy to a charitable institution upon special trusts will, if disclaimed, be applicable by the court.[29] On the other hand, a legacy given by a will, which contained no trusts, to a non-existent charitable institution was held to be applicable in accordance with the directions of the Sovereign under the sign manual, since in the absence of any trust the court had prima facie no jurisdiction to direct a scheme.[30] In *Re White*[31] the same principle was held to apply in the case of a gift to religious societies of which the names were left blank. It does not appear from the report that there was any argument as to whether the personalty was applicable by the court under a scheme or by the Crown under the sign manual; but the testator's residuary estate was given to trustees upon trust for sale and the gifts to the unidentified religious societies were not to vest in possession until after the determination of two successive prior interests in income. It seems clear, therefore, that there was a trust and that the court had jurisdiction. It was held in *Re Slevin*[32] that a direct legacy to an institution which was in existence when the testator died, but was dissolved before payment, and which therefore fell into the assets of the defunct institution, was applicable by the Crown. In other cases,[33] however, the application was made by the court; thus in *Spiller v Maude*[34] the assets of a defunct institution, which were subject to a charitable trust, were applied by the court under a scheme.

Where the case falls within the jurisdiction of the Crown, the function of the court is limited to declaring that the property belongs to charity and protecting it until its application accordingly has been decreed on behalf of the Crown.[35] The old procedure by which administration by the sign manual was obtained involved the sovereign personally in signing a letter giving directions as to the administration.[36] The Attorney-General now signs in place of the sovereign.

---

[29] *Reeve v Att-Gen* (1843) 3 Ha. 191; *Re Lawton* [1936] 3 All E.R. 378; *contra, Denyer v Druce* (1829) Tam. 32.

[30] *Re Bennett* [1960] Ch. 18, applying *Moggridge v Thackwell* (1802) 7 Ves. 36 and *Paice v Archbishop of Canterbury* (1807) 14 Ves. 364. *Bennett v Hayter* (1839) 2 Beav. 81; *Re Clergy Society* (1856) 2 K. & J. 615 and *Re Maguire* (1870) L.R. 9 Eq. 632 are, it seems, out of line with the principle as stated by Lord Eldon and in none of them was it proper for the court to direct a scheme: see *Re Bennett* above at 24, 25, *per* Vaisey J.

[31] [1893] 2 Ch. 41.

[32] [1891] 2 Ch. 236.

[33] *Hayter v Trego* (1830) 5 Russ. 113; *Re Soley* (1900) 17 T.L.R. 118; *Re Moon's Will Trusts* [1948] 1 All E.R. 300.

[34] (1881) 32 Ch.D. 158n. *Cf. Cunnack v Edwards* [1896] 2 Ch. 679; and see *Re Buck* [1896] 2 Ch. 727.

[35] See *Da Costa v De Pas* (1754) Amb. 228; *Re Bennett* [1960] Ch. 18. In *Re Conroy* (1973) 35 D.L.R. (3d) 752 Macfarlane J., in the British Columbia Supreme Court, purporting to follow *Re Songest* [1956] 1 W.L.R. 897, assumed jurisdiction and avoided the sign manual procedure on the basis that the concurrence of the Attorney-General presumed the Crown's prerogative: but in fact *Re Songest* was decided on the basis that there was a trust.

[36] *Kane v Cosgrave* (1873) IR.R. 10 Eq. 211; and see also *Da Costa v De Pas*, above; *Att-Gen v Herrick* (1772) Amb. 712.

THE COURTS

Jurisdiction

The court's inherent jurisdiction over charitable trusts, stemming from **10–003** the original jurisdiction of the Court of Chancery, is now vested in the High Court of Justice and assigned to the Chancery Division.[37] Although the court's jurisdiction originally depended on the existence of a trust, the court's jurisdiction now extends to corporations and companies established for charitable purposes even though they may not, strictly, be trustees of their property.[38] Under its inherent jurisdiction the courts deal with both the validity of dispositions to charity and matters arising in the course of administration of a charity. The court also has inherent jurisdiction, extended by statute, to make schemes. An appeal against any decision of the Charity Commissioners to enter or not to an enter an institution in the register lies to the High Court[39] as does an appeal against any order of the Commissioners establishing a scheme for a charity or regulating a charity.[40]

Extensions of jurisdiction: schemes

The court's inherent jurisdiction to make schemes for charities has in **10–004** two instances been extended by statute: for charities founded by Royal Charter and for those completely regulated by statute.

The court had no inherent jurisdiction to establish a charity founded by Royal Charter,[41] for such a charity owes its establishment to a higher authority than that of the court.[42] The word "establish" in the present context means "re-found" or "re-establish".[43]

---

[37] Supreme Court Act 1981, s.61, Sch.1.

[38] See *Construction Industry Training Board v Att-Gen* [1973] Ch. 173. For the circumstances in which the existence of a trust is still important, see para.10–002, above.

[39] Charities Act 1993, s.4(3). For the procedure to be followed see CPR, PD 52–Appeals, para.23.8A.

[40] Charities Act 1993, ss.16(11), (12) and 18(8). For the procedure to be followed see CPR, PD 52–Appeals, para.23.8A.

[41] *Att-Gen v Smart* (1747) 1 Ves.Sen. 72; *Att-Gen v Middleton* (1751) 2 Ves.Sen. 327; *Att-Gen v Foundling Hospital* (1792) 2 Ves.Jun. 42 at 47; *Att-Gen v Dedham School* (1856) 23 Beav. 356. See also *Re Chertsey Market* (1819) 6 Price 261; *Att-Gen v Browne's Hospital, Stamford* (1889) 60 L.T. 288. Prior to the Statute of Charitable Uses 1601, the jurisdiction of the court to establish a charity on information was limited to the cases to which the procedure by commission under that statute became applicable, viz., charities "at large" not properly and regularly provided for by Royal Charter: *Att-Gen v Middleton* (1751) 2 Ves.Sen. 327 at 329; *Att-Gen v Governors of Harrow School* (1754) 2 Ves.Sen. 551. The statute expressly excepted "any college, hospital, or free school which have special visitors or governors or overseers appointed them by their founders." As this exception was held to extend to any college, hospital, or free school having a general visitor, whether specially appointed or constituted by opertion of law (*Att-Gen v Governors of Harrow School*, above), the result was to exclude all eleemosynary corporations from the operation of the statute.

[42] *Att-Gen v Smart* (1747) 1 Ves.Sen. 72; *Att-Gen v Governors of Christ's Hospital* [1896] 1 Ch. 879 at 888, *per* Chitty J. The court does have jurisdiction to resolve doubts as to the construction and effect of the charter; see *Soldiers', Sailors' and Airmen's Families Association v Att-Gen* [1968] 1 W.L.R. 313.

[43] *Re Whitworth Art Gallery Trusts* [1958] Ch. 461 at 467, *per* Vaisey J.

Where, however, a Royal Charter of incorporation is granted after the date of the original foundation of the charity, the charter is merely machinery for providing an incorporated trustee, armed with appropriate powers, to carry a pre-existing trust into effect. In that case, therefore, the grant of the charter does not affect the inherent powers of the court to establish and regulate the charity.[44] Furthermore, the inherent jurisdiction of the court enabled it to apply *cy-près* the funds of a charity founded by Royal Charter if the corporation became extinct,[45] or if it became impossible to carry out the purposes set out in the charter, as, for example, where the revenues had become insufficient,[46] or where through the exercise of compulsory powers the charity's property had been converted from land into money.[47]

10–005   By s.15 of the Charities Act 1993,[48] the court has power to make a scheme relating to a charity established by Royal Charter, or to the administration of property held by such a charity (including a scheme for the *cy-près* application of any such property), notwithstanding that the scheme cannot take effect without the alteration of the charter, but the scheme must be so framed that the whole or such part of it as cannot take effect without the alteration of the charter does not purport to come into effect unless or until Her Majesty thinks fit to amend the charter in such manner as will permit the scheme or such part of it to have effect. On the application of the charity Her Majesty may by Order in Council amend the charter in any way in which it could be amended by the grant and acceptance of a further charter, and any such order may be revoked or varied in like manner as the charter which it amends.[49] The statutory jurisdiction may be exercised by the Charity Commissioners.[50]

In the same way that the court has no inherent jurisdiction to alter a charter, it had no inherent jurisdiction to alter the trusts of a charity completely regulated by statute, for the court could not amend any Act of Parliament,[51] save only that the court sometimes had the necessary jurisdiction under and by virtue of the statute by which the charity was regulated.[52] When the statute did not completely regulate the charity the inherent jurisdiction of the court could be exercised in respect of all matters not dealt with by the statute.[53] *A fortiori* the inherent jurisdiction of the court was not excluded where the statute was no more than an enabling Act.

---

[44] *Att-Gen v Dedham School* (1856) 23 Beav. 350; see also *Att-Gen v Earl of Clarendon* (1810) 17 Ves. 491; *Att-Gen v St Olave's Grammar School* (1827) C.P. Cooper 267; *Att-Gen v Wyggeston's Hospital* (1849) 12 Beav. 113.

[45] *Att-Gen v Hicks* (1790) 3 Bro. C.C. 166n.; Highmore's Mortmain (2nd ed.) 336.

[46] *Berkhamstead School Case* (1866) L.R. 1 Eq. 102; *Re Whitworth Art Gallery Trusts* [1958] Ch. 461.

[47] *Clephane v Lord Provost of Edinburgh* (1869) 1 H.L.Sc. 417.

[48] Previously Charities Act 1960, s.15.

[49] Charities Act 1993 s.15(2).

[50] *ibid.*, s.16(1).

[51] *Re Shrewsbury Grammar School* (1849) 1 Mac. & G. 324 at 333.

[52] *ibid.*, at 331. See the Endowed Schools Act 1869, s.28 (now repealed); *Re Berkhamstead Grammar School* [1908] 2 Ch. 25; and see also *Re Sutton Coldfield Grammar School* (1881) 7 App.Cas. 93.

[53] *Re Shrewsbury Grammar School* (1849) 1 Mac. & G. 324 at 333.

Now the court is empowered in the case of certain charities to make schemes which modify or supersede in relation to those charities the provisions of certain statutes in the same way as if the statutory provisions had been made by a scheme of the court.[54] The statutes in question[55] provide for the administration of certain charities relating to seamen's funds, education, and allotments, charities established or regulated under certain statutes concerned with local government, certain regimental charities, and parochial charities. Some, though not all, of those statutes contain exhaustive provisions concerning the appointment of trustees and similar matters which could otherwise only be altered by statute. Thus the change may now be made without recourse to Parliament.[56]

Schemes

The court's jurisdiction to make schemes includes not only *cy-près* schemes but also schemes for the administration of charities. The court will also settle a scheme where the objects or the mode of carrying out the gift are uncertain[57] unless no trust was intended.[58] The court, however, will not settle a scheme if the charity is to be executed out of the jurisdiction.[59] **10–006**

Cy-près schemes

The general rule is that where a permanent charitable trust was intended the court[60] will not part with a fund over which it has once obtained control without first arranging for a proper trust to be established for the application of the fund.[61] This is the case whether the gift was to individual trustees or to an incorporated institution,[62] or its officers,[63] upon special trusts different from the trusts applicable to the general funds of the institution.[64] A scheme for the application of the fund has to be settled. The application of this rule is not excluded merely because the donor has conferred an unlimited discretion on the trustees.[65] **10–007**

---

[54] Charities Act 1993, s.15(3).
[55] See *ibid.*, Sch.4.
[56] For the power of the Charity Commissioners to settle schemes for charities established by Statute, see Charities Act 1993, s.17 and para.9–005, above.
[57] See para.1–018, above.
[58] The property will, in that case, be applied under the sign manual, see para.xx, above.
[59] See para.10–010, below.
[60] Or the charity Commissioners exercising their concurrent jurisdiction under the Charities Act 1993, s.16. See para.9–005, above.
[61] *Wellbeloved v Jones* (1822) 1 S. & S. 40. See para.11–066, below for the content of *cy-près* schemes.
[62] *Corporation of Sons of the Clergy v Mose* (1839) 9 Sim. 610.
[63] *Wellbeloved v Jones* (1822) 1 S. & S. 40.
[64] If the gift was not upon special trusts but for the general purposes of the institution, the only concern of the court is to ensure that the fund is paid or transferred to a person or persons who can give a valid receipt on behalf of the institution. See para.10–009, below.
[65] *Waldo v Caley* (1809) 16 Ves. 211; and see also *Barclay v Maskelyne* (1859) 4 Jur.(N.S.) 1294.

Thus the court sees to the execution of the trust whenever it is necessary to apply a charitable fund *cy-près* either because the expressed objects have become impracticable,[66] or by reason of the particular mode of executing the charitable intention having been left undefined.[67]

The same rule applies where it becomes necessary to modify the objects of a charitable trust to adapt them to changed circumstances,[68] or where the trust has been disputed, and the funds need to be reclaimed and applied to proper charitable objects,[69] or where deviations from the trust require to be corrected.[70]

Administrative schemes

10–008   Schemes may also be directed in various cases where it is not necessary to administer a fund *cy-près*,[71] as, for instance, where there has been misapplication on the part of the persons administering the charity,[72] or where increased income requires to be dealt with[73] or where, although there has been no misapplication, it is for any reason deemed advisable to regulate the administration of the charity.[74] So a scheme was directed for the division of funds between the two rival factions into which a religious sect had divided.[75] When a capital sum is given to be distributed for charitable purposes at the discretion of a particular person and no permanent trust is intended by the donor, the court[76] sometimes directs or authorises payment of the fund to that particular person and leaves him at liberty to exercise his discretion as to the mode of application,[77] though frequently

[66] *Att-Gen v City of London* (1790) 3 Bro. C.C. 171; *Att-Gen v Glyn* (1841) 12 Sim. 84; *Martin v Margham* (1844) 14 Sim. 230; *Incorporated Society v Price* (1844) 1 J. & Lat. 498; *Biscoe v Jackson* (1886) 35 Ch.D. 460; *Re Vernon's Will Trusts* [1972] Ch. 300n.; *Re Armitage* [1972] Ch. 438; and see Charities Act 1993, s.13, paras 11–046, *et seq.*, below.

[67] *Moggridge v Thackwell* (1802) 7 Ves. 36; *Mills v Farmer* (1815) 1 Mer. 55; *Att-Gen v Gladstone* (1842) 13 Sim. 7; *Reeve v Att-Gen* (1843) 3 Ha. 191; *Att-Gen v Lawes* (1849) 8 Ha. 32; *Re Stanes' Will* (1853) 21 L.T. (o.s.) 261; *Barclay v Maskelyne* (1859) 4 Jur.(N.S.) 1294; *Re Pyne* [1903] 1 Ch. 83.

[68] Charities Act 1993, s.13. See paras 11–046, *et seq.*, below, and *Att-Gen v Glasgow College* (1848) 2 Coll. 665; *Att-Gen v Dedham School* (1857) 23 Beav. 350; *Wallis v Sol-Gen for New Zealand* [1903] A.C. 173.

[69] *Att-Gen v Skinners' Co.* (1826) Jac. 629.

[70] *Att-Gen v Coopers' Co.* (1812) 19 Ves. 186; *Att-Gen v Louth Free School* (1851) 14 Beav. 201.

[71] *Att-Gen v St Olave's Grammar School* (1827) C.P.Coop. 267. See *Re Friends' Free School* [1909] 2 Ch. 675.

[72] *Att-Gen v Coopers' Co.* (1812) 19 Ves. 186.

[73] *Att-Gen v Earl of Winchelsea* (1791) 3 Bro.C.C. 373; *Att-Gen v Tonna* (1792) 2 Ves. 1; *Att-Gen v Barham* (1835) 4 L.J.Ch. 128; *Att-Gen v Solly* (1835) 5 L.J.Ch. 5; *Att-Gen v Caius College* (1837) 2 Keen 150; *Att-Gen v Ladyman* (1838) C.P.Coop. 180; *Re Kingsbridge School* (1819) 4 Madd. 479; *Re J.W. Laing* [1984] 1 All E.R. 50.

[74] *Att-Gen v Dedham School* (1857) 23 Beav. 350.

[75] *Varsani v Jesani* [1999] Ch. 219.

[76] Or the Charity Commissioners exercising their concurrent jurisdiction under the Charities Act 1993, s.16. See para.9–005, above.

[77] *Att-Gen v Gleg* (1738) Amb. 584; *Johnston v Swann* (1819) Amb. 585n.; *Re Barnett* (1860) 29 L.J.Ch. 871; *Re Lea* (1887) 34 Ch.D. 528.

even in cases of this kind a scheme is directed to be prepared for the execution of the trust.[78]

Thus in *Re Barnett*,[79] where there was a bequest to the minister or ministers of a Unitarian chapel, to be applied as he or they should think fit towards the support of Unitarians, it was held that there was no ground for the interference of the court, and the legacy was ordered to be paid to the ministers. On the other hand, in *Re Hurley*,[80] where there was a bequest for charitable purposes, including a payment to the vicar and churchwardens of a parish "for any purposes to which they think proper to apply it," a scheme was ordered.

Where income for a limited period, *e.g.* the lifetime of a particular person, is directed to be paid to a particular person to be applied at his discretion for general or special charitable purposes, the court does not take upon itself the execution of the trust.[81] Accordingly, in cases of this kind, no scheme is directed, and instead of directing a scheme the court gives liberty to any of the parties to apply as there may be occasion.[82] If the gift of income is accompanied by a gift of capital also to be distributed at discretion, and no intention is shown to draw any distinction between the two, the capital as well as the income will be paid to the person named in the instrument of gift.[83] The court may, however, compel the person charged with the application of a fund to account for its distribution even though it directs no scheme and does not interfere with his discretion.[84]

A legacy to an established charitable institution, whether corporate or **10–009** not, or to the treasurer, trustees, or other officers of the institution, as part of its general funds or upon trusts coinciding exactly with those on which its general funds are held, is paid without a scheme,[85] and if the trustee is the holder of an office of a permanent nature in a charitable organisation of a stable character, the fund will generally be paid over to him without

---

[78] *Doyley v Doyley* (1735) 7 Ves. 58n.; *Paice v Archbishop of Canterbury* (1807) 14 Ves. 364; *Baker v Sutton* (1836) 1 Keen 224; *Pocock v Att-Gen* (1876) 3 Ch.D. 342; *Att-Gen v Stepney* (1804) 10 Ves. 22; and see *Re Delmar Charitable Trust* [1897] 2 Ch. 163; *Warren v Clancy* [1898] 1 Ir.R. 127.

[79] (1860) 29 L.J.Ch. 871; *cf.* the Irish case, *Morris v Larkin* [1902] 1 Ir.R. 103, where there was a gift to a priest "for a Roman Catholic school, or for whatever other purpose he pleases," and it was held that the legatee took an absolute beneficial interest.

[80] (1900) 17 T.L.R. 115.

[81] *Waldo v Caley* (1809) 16 Ves. 206; *Powerscourt v Powerscourt* (1824) 1 Moll. 616; *Horde v Suffolk* (1833) 2 Myl. & K. 59; *Shrewsbury v Hornby* (1846) 5 Ha. 406; *Re Lea* (1887) 34 Ch.D. 528.

[82] *Waldo v Caley* (1809) 16 Ves. 206; *Horde v Suffolk* (1833) 2 Myl. & K. 59; *Re Lea* (1887) 34 Ch.D. 528.

[83] *Re Lea* (1887) 34 Ch.D. 528. See also *Horde v Suffolk* (1833) 2 Myl. & K. 59.

[84] *Att-Gen v Gleg* (1738) Amb. 584; *Att-Gen v Sherborne Grammar School* (1854) 18 Beav. 256.

[85] *Wellbeloved v Jones* (1822) 1 S. & S. 40, 43; *Emery v Hill* (1826) 1 Russ. 112; *Society for the Propagation of the Gospel v Att-Gen* (1826) 3 Russ. 142; *Walsh v Gladstone* (1843) 1 Ph. 290; *Carter v Green* (1857) 3 K & J. 591; *Makeown v Ardagh* (1876) Ir.R. 10 Eq. 445; *Re Richardson* (1887) 56 L.J.Ch. 784; *In the Goods of M'Auliffe* [1905] P. 292 where there was a gift of residue to one of the executors for the benefit of a Roman Catholic convent, and both the executors predeceased the testatrix, administration with the will annexed was granted to the reverend mother of the convent. *Secus* where the gift is not intended to become part of the general funds of the institution. See also *In the goods of Lalor* (1902) 84 L.T. 643.

a scheme.[86] Payment will also be made without a scheme where the bequest is to an existing charitable institution for its general purposes but subject to a particular condition or trust, as where there was a bequest to Christ's Hospital on condition of having certain rights of nomination to the hospital,[87] and where there was a bequest to the Royal National Lifeboat Institution on condition of it maintaining certain specified lifeboats.[88]

If a gift is to a charitable institution as part of its general funds and not on special trusts, it is paid to the institution or the proper officers.[89] Where, however, a bequest was to the municipal authorities of a city upon charitable trusts, it was ordered to be paid to such persons as they should nominate,[90] and where it was to an established institution upon special trusts, it was paid to the leading officials of the institution.[91]

Trusts to be executed abroad

10–010 Where a charitable trust is to be executed out of the jurisdiction, the court does not establish a scheme with regard to it, holding that the administration of a charitable fund in a foreign country must be left to the laws of that country.[92] In these cases if the donor has nominated satisfactory trustees in the foreign country to whom the fund can be paid, the court will usually direct payment of it to them,[93] appointing, if necessary, a new trustee for the purpose of receiving it.[94] Where, however, the fund and some of the trustees of a charity operating in a foreign country were in England, a scheme was directed.[95] In one case, where the original gift was for a school in a certain parish in America, which school had disappeared, it was paid to the governing body of another school in the same place.[96]

In other cases the fund has been retained in court, and the dividends paid to the persons charged with the distribution of them. In *Att-Gen v Lepine*,[97] for example, there was a bequest to the minister and church officers of a parish in Scotland to be applied for charitable purposes. In *Att-Gen v Sturge*,[98] a testatrix directed £1,000 to be paid to the consular chaplain at Genoa (naming him) for the support of a school. The chaplain

---

[86] *Walsh v Gladstone*, above; *In the Goods of M'Auliffe*, above.
[87] *Att-Gen v Christ's Hospital* (1830) 1 R. & M. 626.
[88] *Re Richardson* (1887) 56 L.J.Ch. 784.
[89] *Emery v Hill* (1826) 1 Russ. 112.
[90] *Provost of Edinburgh v Aubery* (1753) Amb. 236.
[91] *Minet v Vulliamy* (1819) 1 Russ. 113n.
[92] *Provost of Edinburgh v Aubery* (1753) Amb. 236; *Att-Gen v Lepine* (1818) 2 Swanst. 182; *Forbes v Forbes* (1854) 18 Beav. 552; *New v Bonaker* (1867) 4 Eq. 655; *Re Robinson* [1931] 2 Ch. 122. See also *Mayor of Lyons v Adv-Gen of Bengal* (1876) 1 A.C. 91, 110.
[93] *Martin v Paxton*, cited 1 Russ. 116; *Collyer v Burnett* (1829) Tam. 79; *Att-Gen v Stephens* (1834) 3 Myl. & K. 347; *Mitford v Reynolds* (1842) 1 Ph. 197.
[94] *Att-Gen v Stephens*, above.
[95] *Re Vagliano* [1905] W.N. 179.
[96] *Att-Gen v Fraunces* [1866] W.N. 280.
[97] (1818) 2 Swanst. 182.
[98] (1854) 19 Beav. 597.

being dead, the legacy was carried to a separate account, and the dividends paid to the consular chaplain for the time being, he rendering periodically to the Judge at Chambers and to the Attorney-General an account of its application.

In *Mayor of Lyons v East India Co.*,[99] where there was a bequest to executors for establishing a college in an independent Indian State, the court refused to hand it over to the Governor-General of India, on the ground that he was not a person whom the testator had pointed out as the hand to receive the fund, and that there was nothing to show that he could carry the testator's intention into effect.

In *Forbes v Forbes*,[1] where a testator made a bequest to his executors to   **10–011**
build a bridge in Scotland, an application was directed to the Court of Session to determine how the fund should be dealt with, and in the meantime it was retained in court. A similar course was adopted in *Re Fraser*,[2] where the sole surviving trustee and executor did not desire to act, and the Attorney-General was directed to make the application to the Scottish court.

Where a charitable bequest was directed to be applied at the discretion of the executors, and they appointed the income to be paid to a college in a British colony which afterwards became independent, a new scheme for the application of the income was ordered.[3]

The court will not allow an application of the funds of a charity to objects outside the jurisdiction, unless such application is expressly authorised by the trust instrument.[4]

The court will not exercise its charitable jurisdiction at all in relation to foreign charities, even if some of its charitable functions are performed in England and Wales.[5]

Practice on making schemes

Where the court undertakes the execution of charitable trusts, it does   **10–012**
not retain the funds under its own control and administer them from time to time as occasion may require; it gives the necessary directions to the trustees or governors and leaves it to them to carry the directions into effect.[6] Before the commencement of the Charities Act 1960, the directions of the court were nearly always given in the form of a scheme and the court directed a reference to chambers to settle the scheme.[7] A hearing

---

[99] (1836) 1 Moo.P.C.C. 176.
[1] (1854) 18 Beav. 552.
[2] (1883) 22 Ch.D. 827. See also *Att-Gen v Fraunces* [1866] W.N. 280.
[3] *Att-Gen v City of London* (1790) 1 Ves.J. 243.
[4] *Re Mirrlee's Charity* [1910] 1 Ch. 163.
[5] *Gaudiya Mission v Brahmachary* [1998] Ch. 341.
[6] *Att-Gen v Haberdashers' Co.* (1791) 1 Ves.J. 295; *Att-Gen v Solly* (1836) 5 L.J.Ch. 5; *Att-Gen v Haberdashers' Co.* (1852) 15 B. 397, 406.
[7] See, *e.g. Doyley v Doyley* (1735) 7 Ves. 58n.; *Baylis v Att-Gen* (1741) 2 Atk. 240n.; *Paice v Archbishop of Canterbury* (1807) 14 Ves. 360; *Waldo v Caley* (1809) 16 Ves. 211; *Wellbeloved v Jones* (1822) 1 S. & S. 40. This short list of old authorities does not pretend to be

in chambers was one to which the public generally had no right of access. Following the coming into force of the Civil Procedure Rules 1998 the expression "in chambers" is no longer officially used. The general rule is that hearings are to be in public, though provision is made for hearings to take place in private in certain limited circumstances.[8]

The court still can settle the scheme itself, at a special hearing arranged for that purpose; but more normally the court, in the exercise of the statutory power contained in the Charities Act 1993[9] refers the matter by order to the Charity Commissioners for them to settle a scheme in accordance with such directions (if any) as the court sees fit to give. Such an order will often provide for the scheme to be put into effect by order of the Commissioners without any further order of the court. This statutory procedure leads to a saving of costs which may be substantial.

In cases where the fund is small, or the directions required are simple, the scheme or mode of application may be made or determined by the court without either arranging a special hearing or referring the matter to the Charity Commissioners. Thus the court may itself deal with the matter immediately where it is merely necessary to decide a question of construction,[10] or to give a slight supplemental direction,[11] or to vary the existing trusts in a point of detail.[12]

10–013   Where the fund was small, and all that had to be done was to apportion it among certain specified charities, the court did not direct a scheme, but merely a reference to chambers to apportion the fund.[13] It is likely that in such a case a similar procedure would be followed today. It seems clear that a scheme will not be directed where it is only necessary to determine to which charitable institutions of a particular class a fund ought to be paid or transferred.[14] In all cases in which directions are required as to the administration of a charitable trust, the Attorney-General is a necessary party to the proceedings.[15]

Where a special hearing is arranged for the approval of a scheme, a draft of the scheme is submitted by the trustees, or, if the judge so directs, by the Attorney-General. If the trustees are responsible for the drafting of the scheme, a copy of the draft should be sent to the Treasury Solicitor for the Attorney-General's approval, and he is at liberty to raise

---

exhaustive. Other and more recent cases could have been cited; but the general rule is well settled and the citation of old cases demonstrates the antiquity.

[8] CPR, r.39.2.
[9] s.16(2)
[10] See *Re Randell* (1888) 38 Ch.D. 213.
[11] *White v White* (1778) 1 B.C.C. 12; *Gillan v Gillan* (1878) 1 L.R. Ir. 114; *Re Richardson* (1888) 58 L.T. 45.
[12] *Re Richardson*, above; *Re Murphy's Trusts* [1967] N.I. 36; *Re Lepton's Charity* [1972] Ch. 276.
[13] *Re Hyde's Trusts* (1873) 22 W.R. 69.
[14] *White v White* (1778) 1 B.C.C. 12; *Re Lousada* (1887) L.T.Jo., p.358. In that case there was a bequest of £50 "to the London poor". There being no charity of that name, it was held that the legacy was too small to direct a scheme, and discretion was given to the executors to distribute the fund among the poor boxes of the London magistrates.
[15] See paras 10–018, *et seq.*, below.

objections or make suggestions upon it.[16] In many cases the Treasury solicitor will consult with the Charity Commissioners.

Arrangements will then be made for the scheme to be settled by the Judge at a special hearing (which will be likely to be held in public), and the Attorney-General is served with notice to attend.[17] The Attorney-General may always, and as a rule must, be represented at the settlement of a scheme.[18] His attendance may, however, sometimes be dispensed with, for example, where the fund is small.[19] It may not be necessary for all persons interested to be represented at the hearing, the Attorney-General protecting their interests.[19a] In earlier times interested persons were sometimes prohibited from being represented, even at their own expense.[20] This practice is unlikely to be followed now, save in the most exceptional circumstances, and would arguably be inconsistent with Article 6 of the European Convention on Human Rights.[21] On the other hand, leave may be given to persons not parties to the action to be represented, only one set of costs being allowed.[22]

Any matters requiring to be argued will be dealt with at the hearing.[23] A **10–014** fair copy of the scheme as settled by the judge is signed by him and filed in the central office, and office copies of it can be obtained; and notice of the filing is sent to the Charity Commissioners from the central office. The order does not usually set out the scheme, but merely refers to the copy so filed.[24]

Where the donor's intention was that the mode of application should be left to the discretion of the trustees, the scheme is framed, so far as possible, in accordance with their views,[25] for in such a case the only object in directing a scheme is to ensure that the fund shall be applied to proper objects.[26]

---

[16] *Att-Gen v Stepney* (1804) 10 Ves. 29; *Jemmit v Verril* (1826) Amb. 585n.; *Re Wyersdale School* (1853) 10 Ha. App. ixxiv; *Re Lea* (1887) 34 Ch.D. 533, *arg.*; *Smith v Kerr* (No. 2) (1905) 74 L.J.Ch. 763.

[17] *Re Hanson's Trust* (1852) 9 Ha.App. liv.

[18] *Att-Gen v Goldsmiths' Co.* (1837) C.P. Cooper 292 at 312; *Att-Gen v Stamford* (1843) 1 Ph. 737, 749; *Re Wyersdale School*, (1853) 10 Ha.App., lxxiv; *Att-Gen v St Cross Hospital* (1855) 18 Beav. 475; *Re Clergy Society* (1856) 2 K. & J. 615: at *Re St Pancras Burial Ground* (1866) 3 Eq. 173; *Re Taylor* (1888) 58 L.T. 538. See *Re Stockport Ragged School* [1898] 2 Ch. 687.

[19] *Att-Gen v Haberdashers' Co.* (1834) 2 Myl. & K. 817.

[19a] *Re Shrewsbury Grammar School* (1850) 1 Mac. & G. 324 at 334; *Att-Gen v St Cross Hospital* (1853) 18 Beav 475; *Re Sekeford's Charity* (1861) 5 L.T. 488.

[20] *Att-Gen v St Cross Hospital,* above. For an attempt made by the Ecclesiastical Commissioners to attend the settlement of a scheme, see *Att-Gen v Wimbourne School* (1846) 10 Beav. 209.

[21] See Human Rights Act 1998, Sch.1.

[22] *Att-Gen v Shore* (1836) 1 Myl. & Cr. 394. As to the course to be pursued where a person is not served with the proceedings, and raises objections which were not brought forward when the scheme was being settled, see *Re Loppington Parish* (1849) 8 Ha. 198, and *Smith v Kerr* (1905) 74 L.J.Ch. 763. See also *Att-Gen v Ironmongers Co.* (1840) C.R. & P. 214.

[23] *Re Hanson's Trust* (1852) 9 Ha.App. liv.

[24] *Re Conyers' Free Grammar School* (1853) 10 Ha.App. v.

[25] *Att-Gen v Gleg* (1738) Amb. 584; *Johnson v Swann* (1818) Amb. 585n.; *Jemmit v Verril* (1826) Amb. 585n.; *Att-Gen v Gaskell* (1831) 9 L.J. (o.s.) Ch. 188; and see *Bennett v Honywood* (1772) Amb. 710; *Moggridge v Thackwell* (1802) 7 Ves. 84; and *cf. Re Delmar Charitable Trust* [1897] 2 Ch. 168.

[26] *Att-Gen v Stepney* (1804) 10 Ves. 22; *Waldo v Caley* (1809) 16 Ves. 211.

Alteration of schemes

10–015   No scheme whether made by the court, the Charity Commissioners,[27] the Board of Education[28] or its successors the Minister of Education and the Secretary of State for Education and Science,[29] or by the Crown,[30] is irrevocable, and a scheme may be altered in a proper case; for example, if through lapse of time or change of circumstances it has become clear that in the interests of the charity alteration is required.[31]

A proposed alteration of a scheme must be based on substantial grounds. It has been held that it is not enough to show that the existing scheme is not beneficial to the charity; it must also be shown that if the proposed alteration is made the scheme as amended will operate beneficially in a manner consistent with the objects of the foundation.[32]

A scheme providing for the application of income devoted to charity may well be regarded as a temporary measure which continues in force until further order or until a new scheme is settled.[33]

10–016   Schemes have been subsequently altered where they contained provisions which made an unfair division among the objects of the charity,[34] which imposed religious qualifications upon the master of a hospital which were not appropriate to an eleemosynary foundation,[35] which specified the number of governors,[36] which empowered the granting of building leases,[37] which fixed the maximum remuneration of the trustees' clerk at a level which became unrealistic[38] and which

---

[27] *Re Sutton Coldfield Grammar School* (1881) 7 App.Cas. 91.

[28] *Re Betton's Charity* [1908] 1 Ch. 205.

[29] The Secretary of State no longer has power to make schemes, but some powers of modification survive. Until 1973 the Secretary of State for Education and Science had jurisdiction concurrent with that of the Charity Commissioners, although it was exercised in practice only in relation to educational charities. His concurrent powers were terminated by the Education Act 1973, s.1(1) and Sch.1. He has, however, enlarged special powers relating to particular educational trusts. He may by statutory instrument modify the trust instruments of schools and other institutions affected by orders or regulations made under the Education Act 1944: Education Act 1973, s.1(2). He may also by statutory instrument make new provision as to the use of any endowment formerly held by a voluntary school wholly or partly for the provision of religious education: *ibid.*, s.2.

[30] *Att-Gen v Dedham School* (1857) 23 Beav. 350.

[31] *Glasgow College v Att-Gen* (1848) 1 H.L.C. 800; *Att-Gen v St John's Hospital Bath* (1865) L.R. 1 Ch. 92 at 106. See also *Att-Gen v Corporation of City of London* (1790) 3 Bro.C.C. 171; *Att-Gen v Bovill* (1840) 1 Ph. 762; *Att-Gen v Rochester Corporation* (1854) 5 De G.M. & G. 797; *Re Hussey's Charities* (1861) 7 Jur.(N.S.) 325; *Att-Gen v Hankey* (1867) L.R. 16 Eq. 140n.; *Re Murphy's Trusts* [1967] N.I. 36.

[32] *Att-Gen v Bishop of Worcester* (1851) 9 Hare 328 at 360. See also *Re Sekeford's Charity* (1861) 5 L.T. 488; *Att-Gen v Stewart* (1872) L.R. 14 Eq. 17.

[33] *Re Betton's Charity* [1908] 1 Ch. 205.

[34] *Att-Gen v Buller* (1822) Jac. 407.

[35] *Att-Gen v St John's Hospital Bath* (1876) 2 Ch.D. 554.

[36] *Re Browne's Hospital Stamford* (1889) 60 L.T. 288. See also *Re Yarm Free Grammar School* (1853) 10 Hare Appendix I, p.v.

[37] *Re Henry Smith's Charity, Hartlepool* (1882) 20 Ch.D. 516. (Express power to grant building leases contained in a scheme settled in 1856 ordered to be struck out, leaving granting of leases to be governed by the Charitable Trusts Act 1853. Now see the Settled Land Act 1925, s.29.)

[38] *Re Murphy's Trusts* [1967] N.I. 36.

conferred limited powers of investment that had become inadequate in more modern circumstances.[39]

If the testator has shown a charitable intention, whether general or special, and the court has *per incuriam* settled a scheme for the application of the gift which subsequently turns out to be invalid because not all the purposes therein set forth are charitable, the court can so amend the scheme as to make all the purposes charitable.[40]

Schemes settled by the court or by the Charity Commissioners or by the Secretary of State for Education and Science may be altered by the Commissioners to the same extent as the court may alter schemes settled by the court.[41]

The Attorney-General is a necessary party to any application to the court for the alteration of a scheme settled by the court, and he must either make the application himself or consent thereto.[42] There are cases in which it is the duty of the Attorney-General to make the necessary application.[43]

10–017

A scheme which the court has settled and to which the Attorney-General has not objected cannot be altered on the application of one of the interested parties.[44]

THE ATTORNEY-GENERAL

Functions and duties

The Attorney-General's function in relation to charities is to represent the Crown as *parens patriae*[45] and thus to act as the protector, both of charity in general and of particular charities. Historically, the Attorney-General's role in this respect has been unlimited in theory and wide-ranging in practice. Latterly, accompanying the strengthening of the legal powers of the Charity Commissioners, there has been an extension of their role which in two particular respects[46] overlaps with that of the Attorney-General. If this trend continues it is possible that, in practice, the Attorney-General's role in relation to charities will decrease further.

10–018

Apart from his function in relation to the sign manual,[47] there are currently three principal functions relating to charities which are proper to the Attorney-General: instituting legal proceedings to protect a charity, including proceedings against trustees who have failed in their duties;[48] representing the charitable interest in legal proceedings, for example,

---

[39] *Trustees of British Museum v Att-Gen* [1984] 1 W.L.R. 418.

[40] *Vernon v IRC* [1956] 1 W.L.R. 1169.

[41] *Re Betton's Charity* [1908] 1 Ch. 205 at 211, 212; *Re Weir Hospital* [1910] 2 Ch. 124 at 131.

[42] *Att-Gen v Stewart* (1872) L.R. 14 Eq. 17. See also *Att-Gen v Hall* (1875). Seton's Judgments and Orders (7th ed.) 1259.

[43] *Att-Gen v Bishop of Worcester* (1851) 9 Hare 328 at 360.

[44] *Att-Gen v Bishop of Worcester*, above; *Re Sekeford's Charity* (1861) 5 L.T. 488.

[45] See para.10–001, above.

[46] See the Charities Act 1993, ss.27, 32.

[47] See para.10–002, above.

[48] *Att-Gen v Brown* (1818) 1 Swan. 265 at 291, *per* Lord Eldon; *National Anti-Vivisection Society v IRC* [1948] A.C. 31 at 62 *per* Lord Simonds.

proceedings for a scheme or concerning the construction of a gift to charity,[49] brought by others; and exercising the power to approve *ex gratia* payments and the waiver of legal rights by individual charities on behalf of charity generally on purely moral grounds.[50]

Under s.1(1) of the Law Officers Act 1997, any function of the Attorney-General may be exercised by the Solicitor General.

Bringing proceedings

10–019   The function of instituting proceedings, with or without a relator,[51] for the protection of charities[52] exists because charitable trusts are matters which concern the public, not by virtue of any estate or interest of the Sovereign in the property concerned.[53] It is to be distinguished from the function of the Attorney-General where the Crown has a beneficial interest in the property sought to be recovered.[54] Thus where some private right of the Crown,[55] or the right to dispose of a surplus by sign manual,[56] comes in question,[57] it is necessary, although the action be commenced by the Attorney-General as the officer of the Crown, that the Solicitor-General should be made a defendant to support the private interests of the Crown. Conversely, where a claim is made by the Attorney-General on behalf of some private right of the Crown which is inconsistent with the claims of charity, the Solicitor-General should be joined as a defendant to safeguard the charitable interests.[58] The Solicitor General will also act in place of the Attorney-General in charity matters where the matter warrants personal attention and the Attorney-General is affected by some personal interest preventing him from so acting.[59]

The circumstances in which the Attorney-General is most likely to institute proceedings are those in which it is imperative that formal action should be taken to prevent or remedy damage to a charity, or to charity generally. Such proceedings are likely to be brought in the Chancery Division of the High Court and the relief sought may include, the restitu-

---

[49] *National Anti-Vivisection Society v IRC* [1948] A.C. 31 at 62; *Re Harpur's Will Trusts* [1962] Ch. 78 at 94, *per* Harman L.J. The function of the Attorney General in charity proceedings is fully discussed at paras 10–038, *et seq.*, below.

[50] *i.e.* under the principle in *Re Snowden* and *Re Henderson* [1970] Ch. 700; see para.10–023, below.

[51] See para.10–036 below.

[52] Expressly preserved by the Charities Act 1993, s.33(6).

[53] *Wellbeloved v Jones* (1822) Sim. & St. 40 at 43; *Att-Gen v Dean and Canons of Windsor* (1860) 8 H.L.C. 369. It is the duty of the officers of the Crown to protect and not to attack charities: *Wallis v Sol-Gen for New Zealand* [1903] A.C. 173 at 182.

[54] *Att-Gen v Magdalen Coll., Oxford* (1854) 18 Beav. 223 at 241; D.C.P., (8th ed.), 46, 49.

[55] *Att-Gen v Dean and Canons of Windsor* (1858) 24 Beav. 679 at 694; (1860) 8 H.L.C. 369.

[56] *Att-Gen v Mayor of Galway* (1828) 1 Mol. 95 at 106; and see *Att-Gen v Ironmongers' Co.* (1833) 2 Myl. & K. 578n.; also *Att-Gen v Mayor of Bristol* (1820) 2 J. & W. 294 at 309, 310; D.C.P., (8th ed.), 49.

[57] Also formerly where part of the property given to charitable uses was infected with a superstitious purpose; see para.11–008, below.

[58] *Att-Gen v Mayor of Bristol* (1820) 2 J. & W. 294 at 312; *Att-Gen v Ironmongers' Co.* (1833) 2 Myl. & K. 578n.; *Att-Gen v Dean and Canons of Windsor* (1860) 8 H.L.C. 7.

[59] *Att-Gen v Bristol Corporation* (1820) 2 Jac. & W. 294; *Att-Gen v Ironmongers' Co.* (1834) 2 My. & K. 576.

tion of charity property, the award of damages[60] and interest for breach of trust, injunctive relief[61] to prevent a breach of trust or its repetition, the appointment or removal of trustees or officers, the appointment of a receiver and manager,[62] the establishment of a scheme or the determination, by means of a declaration or otherwise, of questions arising in the administration of the charity or the application of its property.

Where the Attorney-General is exercising the Crown's power to act as protector of charity, and seeks an injunction, a cross-undertaking in damages will not be required from him as of course. On the other hand, where the Crown was asserting proprietary rights against a trustee and there were serious factual issues to be tried, it was held by Hoffmann J. in *Att-Gen v Wright*[63] that the interests of a defendant trustee should be protected by a cross-undertaking limited to the funds of the charity. It was not clear that the Attorney-General had the right by virtue of his office to resort to the charity funds for reimbursement of payments made in consequence of the cross-undertaking, but a receiver of the charity had been appointed by order of the court and would have had a such a right, so an injunction was granted conditional on a cross-undertaking by the receiver, limited to such amount as he was entitled to recover by ways of indemnity from the funds of the charity.

The extension to the Charity Commissioners of the Attorney-General's **10–020** power to take legal proceedings with reference to charities,[64] which has the effect that the Attorney-General himself is not required to be a party to proceedings brought by the Commissioners in his stead,[65] is subject to the requirement that the Attorney-General agrees to the Commissioners so acting on each occasion.[66] In the 8th edition of this work it was predicted that procedural arrangements would evolve as policy developed in this area. It appears that this prediction has not yet been fulfilled, though steps are being taken to develop such arrangements.[67] It is suggested that the Commissioners, rather than the Attorney-General, are more likely to take proceedings either where the proceedings follow a formal inquiry[68] and consequently the Commissioners are already apprised of the details of the matter, and it is therefore more convenient for them to act, or where the Attorney-General, or the Government, is directly or indirectly concerned with the matter in some other capacity and it would therefore be politically inconvenient for the Attorney-General to act.

---

[60] The word "damages" is sometimes used, but this is a misnomer and the remedy is more properly described as restitution, or equitable compensation: *Bartlett v Barclays Bank Trust Co. Ltd.* [1980] Ch. 515, *Hulbert v Avens, The Times*, February 7, 2003.

[61] *See Baldry v Feintuck* [1972] 1 W.L.R. 552.

[62] See *Att-Gen v Schonfeld* [1980] 1 W.L.R. 1182.

[63] [1988] 1 W.L.R. 164.

[64] Charities Act 1993, s.32(1)(a). See para.9–009, above.

[65] *ibid.*, s.32(4).

[66] *ibid.*, s.32(5).

[67] Charity Finance: Charity Law Association Supplement 2002, pp.12–13; [2000–2001] Ch. Com. Rep., 2001–2002, p.15, Cabinet Office, Strategy Unit, *Private Action, Public Benefit. A Review of Charities and the Wider Not-For-Profit Sector* (2002), p.89.

[68] *i.e.* under Charities Act 1993, s.8; see para.9–037, above. As in the case of Sherburn House Charity: see [1999–2000] Ch.Com. Rep., p.23.

In addition, it should be noted that the increased powers of the Charity Commissioners to deal with allegations of abuse,[69] coupled with the increased resources available to the Commissioners for those aspects of their work, may well result in a greater proportion of cases of maladministration being dealt with by the Commissioners under their statutory powers rather than by application to the court. It is not likely, for example, that in future the court will be asked to appoint a receiver and manager for a charity now that the Commissioners have power to make such an appointment themselves.[70]

Participating in other proceedings

10–021   Where legal proceedings concerning a charity[71] are brought by some other person, the Attorney-General is properly joined as a defendant to represent the beneficial interest in the charity, or may intervene in order to protect it. Charity in general, being established for a purpose rather than for persons, by definition has no individual beneficiaries, and even if those presently qualified to benefit from a specified charity can be sufficiently defined, they rarely have any enforceable rights in their capacity as beneficiaries.[72]

In practice, however, the Attorney-General will not consent to being made a party to proceedings where the charitable interest is already adequately represented, whether by the Charity Commissioners themselves or by trustees. It is unusual, for example, for the Attorney-General to be joined in an action by the trustees of a charity to recover property or enforce some other right belonging to the charity.[73] The cases in which his participation is most likely are where maladministration has allegedly occurred, the trustees are in dispute, a question as to the charitable status of a gift or trust[74] has been raised or a scheme is proposed.

The Attorney-General should take no part in the argument if he intends to be bound by the decree in any event. An appeal by a party who took no part in the argument in the court below is improper, but in the case of a charity the court will not on that ground refuse to entertain the appeal.[75] The Attorney-General may be permitted to appeal from the decision in proceedings to which he was not a party.[76]

---

[69] See Charities Act 1993, s.8, 9, 18 and 19; see para.9–042, above.
[70] Charities Act 1993, s.18(1)(vii); see para.9–044, above.
[71] *i.e.* either "charity proceedings" properly so called, see para.10–026, below, or, more rarely, "domestic" proceedings relating to charities, *e.g.* proceedings relating to property or to rights and duties under the general law.
[72] *Att-Gen v Cocke* [1988] Ch. 414.
[73] *c.p. Muman v Nagasena* [2000] 1 W.L.R. 299.
[74] *Hauxwell v Barton-upon-Humber UDC* [1974] Ch. 432.
[75] *Christ's Hospital v Grainger* (1849) 1 Mac. & G. 460 at 462.
[76] *Re Faraker* [1912] 2 Ch. 488.

Compromise[77]

In non-contentious matters of construction, typically where a charity **10–022**
has been misdescribed in a will, or, being correctly described, no longer
existed at the date of the testator's death, it is now very unusual for legal
proceedings to be instituted. Instead, the parties generally seek, through
the Treasury Solicitor, the view which the Attorney-General would have
taken had the matter come to court, and the Attorney-General had represented the charitable interest in the relevant proceedings. The solution is
then based upon that view. The result may be a scheme, made by the
Charity Commissioners, or a compromise of some kind to which the
Treasury Solicitor signifies in writing that the Attorney-General agrees or
has no objection. A scheme of the Commissioners is of course the
equivalent of an order of the High Court.[78]

In the case of such a compromise, where the Attorney-General has sig-
nified his approval or non-objection and the terms of the compromise
have been carried out in full, the executors or trustees of the will are
thereby protected from personal liability as respects any future claim from
beneficiaries or potential beneficiaries. It is submitted that, in practice, it
is unlikely that the Inland Revenue or any other official body, not being
party to the compromise, would be astute to look behind its terms.[79]

The Charity Commissioners are now entitled, with the agreement of the
Attorney-General, to exercise the same power with respect to compromise
as is exercisable by the Attorney-General himself.[80] It is likely that this
power will be widely exercised by the Commissioners in non-contentious
cases in order to avoid an application to the court, especially where the factual background is already known to the Commissioners, or where the
solution will involve the exercise of their scheme-making or other powers.

Moral claims

The third of the Attorney-General's principal functions is the consider- **10–023**
ation of applications, both from charity trustees and from executors or
trustees holding property which has been dedicated to charity by will, for
approval either to the waiver by the charitable interest of some legal right
or to the making of an *ex gratia* payment, where the failure to enforce the
right or the payment in question is morally justifiable but legally would
constitute a breach of trust. The Attorney-General's power to give or
withhold approval in such cases was considered fully in *Re Snowden*[81]
reported with *Re Henderson*. *Re Snowden* involved legacies to named charities whereas in *Re Henderson* the testatrix had left "Anything over to

---

[77] See para.10–043, below.
[78] See para.9–005, above.
[79] For example, by assessing an executor to income tax where the income in question was
received by a charity under a deed of variation.
[80] Charities Act 1993, s.32(1)(b).
[81] [1970] Ch. 700. See also *Att-Gen v Exeter Corp.* (1826) 2 Russ. 362; *Att-Gen v Brettingham*
(1840) 3 Beav. 91; *Att-Gen v Pretyman* (1841) 4 Beav. 462.

Charity". Cross J. held, contrary to what had been previously believed, that the court had jurisdiction to approve such a waiver or payment where it was satisfied that had the charity, or the charitable interest, been an individual it would have been morally wrong to refuse it. By extension, it was held that the same approval might be given by the Attorney-General, thus saving the cost of an application to the court, unless the Attorney-General considered in any particular case that the matter ought to be referred to the court.

Following the decision in *Re Snowden* the practice was established that any charity wishing to waive a right or make an *ex gratia* payment should approach the Charity Commissioners who after an initial investigation would report the facts to the Attorney-General's office direct for a decision. However in *Re Henderson* type cases the executors of a will faced with a similar problem in relation to a bequest to charity generally would approach the Treasury Solicitor who would similarly investigate and report.[82]

Under the Charities Act 1993[83] the Charity Commissioners are now empowered to exercise the same power as is exercisable by the Attorney-General in *Re Snowden* cases but directed to refer any particular application to the Attorney-General if they consider it desirable that he should consider it instead of them.[84] Thus, the Commissioners are evidently expected to refer exceptionally important or difficult cases to the Attorney-General rather than to the court. Further, *Re Henderson* cases, in which there are no identifiable charity trustees capable of making the initial application for approval, will still be a matter for the Treasury Solicitor and the Attorney-General, or the court, rather than the Commissioners.

10–024   It is clear from the statutory provisions[85] that control of the policy regarding *Re Snowden* cases will remain with the Attorney-General, who is empowered to give to the Commissioners directions as to the exercise of the jurisdiction and may require them to refrain from exercising it, or to consult him, in any case. Further, the charity may always re-apply to the Attorney-General if the Commissioners refuse the initial application.[86]

It is submitted that an application for approval under these principles is generally not appropriate, and should not be entertained, where there is a readily available alternative. Thus, it is not appropriate to invoke the jurisdiction where the person to whom the moral obligation is owed also has a viable legal claim against the charity or the estate, for example, under the Inheritance (Provision for Family and Dependents) Act 1975,[87] which is capable of being dealt with by compromise or otherwise. There are also cases where an *ex gratia* payment may be said to be beneficial to the char-

---

[82] See [1969] Ch. Com. Rep., para.30.
[83] Charities Act 1993, s.27(1).
[84] *ibid.*, s.27(3)(b).
[85] *ibid.*, s.27(2).
[86] *ibid.*, s.27(4).
[87] *i.e.* where a spouse, child or dependent of a deceased may claim reasonable financial provision from the estate of the deceased on proving that the deceased has failed to make reasonable provision for him or her. See [1977] Ch. Com. Rep., para.154.

ity, and thus justifiable without recourse to the *Re Snowden* principle, as where a retiring employee is rewarded for exceptional service by an additional payment, which benefits the charity by encouraging other employees to give comparable service.[88]

Despite the developments, since the decision of Sir Robert Megarry V.C., in the law relating to claims for professional negligence by those who do not receive the benefits they rightly expect under a testator's will,[89] it has not been the Attorney-General's usual practice to refuse an application under *Re Snowden* merely because a case in negligence might have been brought against the solicitor responsible for preparing the will, for example, where a technical defect in the drafting or execution of the will defeats the testator's clear intention to benefit a specified individual. It is submitted that this approach is justifiable on the ground that even if there were a viable claim against the solicitor, it would still be morally wrong for an individual in the charity's position to retain the unintended benefit.[90]

Questions nevertheless arise on the level of moral sensitivity to be expected of the hypothetical individual, and the degree of proof required to establish the facts on which the moral claim is based. To some extent, any doubt of this nature can be taken into account whilst setting the value of the benefit to be provided to the claimant: there is no presumption that the claim should be satisfied in full. Further, if the charity trustees or the executors or trustees of the will do not themselves consider that the claim is well founded they will be under no obligation to make an application to the Attorney-General or the Commissioners and are unlikely to be criticised for declining to do so.

10–025

PROCEEDINGS RELATING TO CHARITIES

The Civil Procedure Rules 1998

At the time of publication of the last edition of this work civil procedure in England and Wales was governed by the Rules of the Supreme Court 1965. Following Lord Woolf's Access to Justice Reports those rules were replaced by the Civil Procedure Rules 1998, which came into effect on April 26, 1999. It would not be appropriate for this work to contain a detailed exposition of the 1998 rules, for which reference should be had to the standard texts on practice and procedure. However, three points require specific mention.

10–026

(1) One of the fundamental principles underlying the 1998 rules is that litigation is to be regarded as a remedy of last resort.[91] This

---

[88] *i.e.* under the principle in *Parke v Daily News Ltd* [1962] Ch. 927. See now Companies Act 1985, s.719.

[89] *Ross v Caunters* [1980] Ch. 297; *White v Jones* [1995] 2 A.C. 207.

[90] Compare the attitude adopted by the court in *Walker v G.H. Medlicott & Son* [1999] 1 W.L.R. 727, where relief against the solicitors was refused when the claimant had an arguable case to have the defective will rectified.

[91] See *e.g.*, P.D.–Protocols, para.1.4(2).

principle is of particular importance in relation to charities: even before the coming into force of the rules it was recognised that it was undesirable for money that ought to be devoted to charitable purposes to be used to meet the costs of litigation.[92] The courts strongly encourage the use of alternative means of dispute resolution.[93]

(2)   Where litigation is unavoidable, it is the over-riding objective of the court to deal with the case justly, [94] and the parties are under a duty to help the court to achieve this overriding objective.[95]

(3)   The rules are not to be applied mechanistically but with close regard to the particular facts of each case. The view has been judicially expressed[96] that it would be undesirable for a body of satellite authority to be built up, such as developed under the 1965 rules, resulting in an undesirable re-writing of the rules through the medium of judicial decision.

One consequence of all these matters is that decided cases which were formerly regarded as authority for proper procedures under old rules of practice are now of only limited, if any, assistance.

Charity Proceedings

10–027   "Charity proceedings" as defined in s.33 of the Charities Act 1993 may only be brought by the persons specified in that section. Even if a person is within one of the permitted categories he may not proceed with a court action unless the taking of the proceedings is authorised by an order of the Charity Commissioners[97] or, in the event of their refusing permission, the High Court.[98] Permission is not readily given in cases where there is an internal dispute within the charity, for which litigation is not regarded as a satisfactory remedy; and the Charity Commissioners are prohibited from giving permission, without special reasons, if they can deal with the case themselves under their own powers.[99] Where permission is given to make a claim, the court will not permit the scope of the proceedings to be broadened beyond the extent of the permission.[1] There are no restrictions on bringing proceedings relating to a charity if they do not fall within the definition of "charity proceedings". However, charity trustees may need to

[92] Litigation between charities was described in *British Diabetic Association v Diabetic Society* [1995] 4 All E.R.812 at p.816 as "a deplorable, even scandalous thing to occur".
[93] See, the case of charities, *Muman v Nagasena* [2000] 1 W.L.R. 299, and para.10–029, below.
[94] C.P.R., r.1.1(1).
[95] C.P.R., r.1.3.
[96] *per* Jonathan Parker L.J. in *Audergon v La Baguette Ltd., The Times*, January 31, 2001.
[97] Charities Act 1993 s.33(2).
[98] *ibid.* s.33(5). For the procedure to be followed on an appeal against the Commissioners refusal to authorise charity proceedings see CPR, PD, 52–Appeals, para.23.8A.
[99] Charities Act 1993, s.33(3).
[1] *Singh v Sikka*, unreported December 2, 1998, CA.

seek the protection of the court or the Commissioners before expending charitable funds in bringing or defending a court action.[2]

Definition

"Charity proceedings" are defined as proceedings in any court in England or Wales brought under the court's jurisdiction with respect to charities, or brought under the court's jurisdiction with respect to trusts in relation to the administration of a trust for charitable purposes.[3] Thus in all cases in which administration of the charity property is sought or which necessarily involves either whole or partial administration or execution of the trusts of the charity an order of the Charity Commissioners must be sought.[4] Similarly, an action alleging a breach of trust is within the definition.

10–028

An action brought solely to enforce a common law right, whether arising out of contract or common law obligation or common law duty, does not fall within the definition of charity proceedings.[5] Thus an action on a contract of service or to recover rents does not need the consent of the Commissioners. However, an action that starts out as a simple common law claim may develop complexities that cause it to acquire the character of charity proceedings, as in one case in which a simple possession action developed into a struggle for control of the charity.[6] A body established elsewhere than in England and Wales is not a charity for the purposes of the Charities Act 1993, even if established for objects regarded as charitable by English law, and proceedings concerning the affairs of such a body are not charity proceedings for which consent is required.[7] Nor is an order of the Commissioners necessary to enable charity trustees to pay a charitable fund into court under s.63 of the Trustee Act 1925, although in all cases of doubt or difficulty as to the administration of the fund the trustees should apply to the Charity Commissioners before taking any legal proceedings with reference to the fund.[8] An order is not required authorising the taking of proceedings in any pending cause or matter[9] or for the bringing of any appeal.[10] Proceedings brought to determine a bona fide dispute as to whether or not a charitable trust exists are not within the definition of "charity proceedings".[11]

---

[2] Charity trustees may seek an order under s.26 or advice under s.29 of the 1993 Act. If the Commissioners decline to make an order, the trustees may seek a *Beddoe* order (see *Re Beddoe* [1893] 1 Ch. 547) from the court; but as a *Beddoe* summons is within the term "charity proceedings" it needs the authority of an order under s.33(2) or (5).

[3] Charities Act 1993, s.33(8).

[4] See *Rooke v Dawson* [1895] 1 Ch. 486 at 487, *per* Chitty J.

[5] *Holme v Guy* (1877) 5 Ch. D. 905; *Rendall v Blair* (1890) 45 Ch. D. 153.

[6] *Muman v Nagasena* [2000] 1 W.L.R. 299.

[7] *Gaudiya Mission v Brahmachary* [1998] Ch. 341.

[8] See *Re Poplar and Blackwell Free Schools* (1878) 8 Ch. D. 546.

[9] For an example of such proceedings see *Re Lister's Hospital* (1855) 6 De G.M.&G. 184.

[10] Charities Act 1993, s.33(4).

[11] See *Re Belling* [1967] Ch. 425; *Hauxwell v Barton-upon-Humber UDC* [1974] Ch. 432. and para.10–038, below.

Although the definition clearly covers proceedings in a County Court, and the indications are that, following the extension of the jurisdiction of the County Court[12] an increasing number of matters previously dealt with in the High Court are likely to be brought in the County Court, since the Charities Act 1960 charity proceedings have virtually always been commenced in the Chancery Division of the High Court, to which charity proceedings (other than those begun in the County Court) are assigned by the Civil Procedure Rules 1998.[13] The proceedings are begun by Claim Form.[14] Consistently with the spirit underlying the Civil Procedure Rules 1998 the courts will seek, if possible, to find some way of resolving the dispute otherwise than by contested litigation. For disputes concerning charities a special mediation service has been created by the Centre for Dispute Resolution jointly with the National Council for Voluntary Organisations, as described by Mummery L.J. in *Muman v Nagasena*.[15]

10–029   After referring to the healing effect of mediation Mummery L.J. went on to say, with reference to that particular case:

> "In this case very substantial sums of money have been spent on litigation without achieving a resolution. The spending of money on this kind of litigation does not promote the religious purposes of this charity. It is time for mediation. No more money should be spent from the assets of this charity until . . . all efforts have been made to secure a mediation of this dispute in the manner suggested."

Who may bring proceedings

10–030   Charity proceedings may be brought by the charity itself, one or more of the charity trustees, two or more inhabitants of the area of a charity if it is a local charity or by any person interested in the charity.[16] What amounts to sufficient interest for the last category of person is considered below. In addition such proceedings may be brought, without the requirement for prior leave or authority, by the Attorney-General, either *ex officio* or with a relator, although it must be observed that a relator action in a matter concerning a charity would now be very unusual.[17] S.32 of the Charities Act 1993 gives the Charity Commissioners the same powers with respect to the taking of legal proceedings with reference to charities or the property or affairs of charities as the Attorney-General acting *ex officio*.[18]

10–031   **A person interested**—The courts have refused to give a definition of "any person interested in the charity" for the purposes of s.33(1) of the 1993 Act. Thus in *Re Hampton Fuel Allotment Charity*[19] Nicholls L.J. said:

---

[12] High Court and County Court Jurisdiction Order 1991 (SI 1991/724).
[13] C.P.R., r.64.1(3).
[14] See para.10–045, below.
[15] [2000] 1 W.L.R. 299 at 305.
[16] Charities Act 1993, s.33(1).
[17] See paras 10–019, *et seq.*, above.
[18] See para.9–009, above.
[19] [1989] Ch. 484 at 494.

"Thus the interest which ordinary members of the public, whether or not subscribing to a charity and whether or not potential beneficiaries of a charity, have in seeing that a charity is properly administered is a matter in respect of which the Attorney-General remains charged with responsibilities. He can institute proceedings *ex officio* or *ex relatione*. This suggests, therefore, that to qualify as a plaintiff in his own right a person generally needs to have an interest materially greater than or different from that possessed by ordinary members of the public such as we have described.

In our view that may be as near as one can get to identifying what is the nature of the interest which a person needs to possess to qualify under this heading as a competent plaintiff. It is not a definition. But charitable trusts vary so widely that to seek a definition here is, we believe, to search for a will-o'-the-wisp. If a person has an interest in securing the due administration of a trust materially greater than, or different from, that possessed by ordinary members of the public as described above, that interest may, depending on the circumstances, qualify him as a 'person interested'."

It is, however, possible from the cases to gain some indication of the type of person who will be regarded as sufficiently interested to be permitted to bring charity proceedings. A person who funds or finances a charity[20] or whose donation gives him rights to participate in the running of a charity is a person interested.[21] By comparison a person who provides a modest financial contribution whether by paying under covenant or by making a one-off donation to an appeal is not.[22] The fact that a person is a potential beneficiary may not, on its own, be sufficient to make him a person interested.[23]

A contractual relationship with the trustees of a charity does not of itself make that person a person interested.[24] A person with a contract with a charity may be a person interested, however, if he is seeking to secure the due administration of the charity rather than to pursue an adverse claim against the trustees. Thus parents of children at a school run by a charity, who were neither beneficiaries or subscribers, were held to be persons interested for the purposes of an action arising from the manner of closure of the school.[25]

The executors of the will of a donor to a charity are not persons interested; they cannot in any circumstances be a beneficiary of the charity or take any interest under the trusts applicable to the property of the charity.[26] A local authority, however, may be a person interested in a charity operating in its area where there is an overlap between the statutory

10–032

---

[20] *Re Hampton Fuel Allotment Charity* [1989] Ch. 484 at 493.
[21] *Brooks v Richardson* [1986] 1 W.L.R. 385.
[22] *Re Hampton Fuel Allotment Charity* [1989] Ch. 484 at 493.
[23] *ibid.*
[24] *Haslemere Estates v Baker* [1982] 1 W.L.R. 1109, 1122.
[25] *Gunning v Buckfast Abbey Trustees Registered, The Times*, June 9, 1994.
[26] *Bradshaw v University College of Wales, Aberystwyth* [1988] 1 W.L.R. 190.

services provided by the council and the activities of the charity or where the local authority has power to appoint trustees.[27]

Huntsmen and tenant farmers co-operating with the National Trust in the management of the Trust's land had a sufficient interest to bring charity proceedings to challenge the Trust's decision not to renew licences to hunt on the land.[28] Existing members of a charitable unincorporated association had sufficient interest to enable them to take part in charitable proceedings concerning proposed changes in the rules of the association, but persons who were merely applicants for membership did not.[29]

Charities performing public functions – judicial review and human rights

10–033   Some charities perform statutory or public functions. Whether a charity falls into this category is relevant for two purposes: the availability of the remedy of judicial review, and the obligation not to act in a way incompatible with the rights embodied in the European Convention for the Protection of Human Rights and Fundamental Freedoms 1950.[30]

In an appropriate case an application for judicial review may lie against a charity that has a statutory or public law role.[31] It has been held to be proper for judicial review proceedings to be begun to establish whether or not the charity is is performing a public function,[32] though the Court of Appeal left undecided the question of whether the consent of the Charity Commissioners would be requisite under s.33(2) of the Charities Act 1993. As a general rule, however, proceedings of the nature of charity proceedings should be brought as charity proceedings and not by way of judicial review.[33] Judicial review is not in any circumstances available against a charity that has no public or statutory role.[34]

A charity that performs functions of a public nature is a "public authority"[35] for the purposes of the Human Rights Act 1998, s.6(1), and as such is prohibited from acting in a way which is incompatible with a Convention right. The actions of such a charity may therefore be challenged on the ground that they infringe this prohibition.

10–034   The question of whether a charity has a statutory or public law role, or performs public functions, is not entirely straightforward. It does not necessarily follow from the fact that a charity is performing a function that, if not performed by the charity, would have to be performed by a public

---

[27] *Re Hampton Fuel Allotment Charity* [1989] Ch. 484 at 493.
[28] *Scott v National Trust for Places of Historic Interest or Natural Beauty* [1998] 2 All E.R. 705.
[29] *Royal Society for the Prevention of Cruelty to Animals v Att-Gen* [2002] 1 W.L.R. 448.
[30] As set out in the Human Rights Act 1998, Sch.1.
[31] *Royal Society for the Prevention of Cruelty to Animals v Att-Gen* [2002] 1 W.L.R. 448 at 459.
[32] *R. v Leonard Cheshire Foundation* [2002] EWCA Civ 366, [2002] 2 All E.R. 936 at 948.
[33] *Scott v National Trust for Places of Historic Interest or Natural Beauty* [1998] 2 All E.R. 705; *Royal Society for the Prevention of Cruelty to Animals v Att-Gen* [2002] 1 W.L.R. 448.
[34] *R. v Leonard Cheshire Foundation* [2002] EWCA Civ 366 [2002] 2 All E.R. 936.
[35] Human Rights Act 1998, s.6(3)(b).

authority, that the charity itself is a public authority, and this is so even if the charity is funded by a public authority.[36] However, the activities of the charity may be so enmeshed with those of a public authority as to be public functions.[37] Each case turns on its own facts.[38] A charity that performs some functions that are public and others that are not is not susceptible to judicial review, or obliged to give effect to Convention rights, in the performance of those of its functions which are not public.[39]

Proceedings by the Attorney-General

The Attorney-General may commence and carry on proceedings of his own motion, and will normally do so if on an application to the Charity Commissioners for an order sanctioning charity proceedings by a plaintiff other than the Attorney-General the Commissioners inform the Attorney-General that it is desirable for him to take proceedings in the case of a charity which is not an exempt charity.[40]   **10–035**

Relator actions

A relator action is one in which, on the instigation and at the expense of some other person, the Attorney-General brings an action to assert a public right. Relator actions are rarely brought in practice,[41] and it would be most unusual for this procedure to be used in the case of a charity. It has therefore been thought unnecessary to repeat the description of the procedure which appeared at pp.347 to 350 of the 8th edition of this work, to which reference should be had if need arises.   **10–036**

Parties

The choice of parties to proceedings relating to charities is influenced by very similar considerations to those applying to proceedings involving private trusts. Two important differences, however, should be noted: first, charity proceedings may only be brought by specified persons[42]; and, secondly, the Attorney-General is usually a necessary party.   **10–037**

---

[36] *Poplar Housing and Regeneration Community Association Ltd. v Donoghue* [2001] EWCA Civ 595, [2002] Q.B. 49; *R. v Leonard Cheshire Foundation* [2002] EWCA Civ 366, [2002] 2 All E.R. 936.

[37] *ibid.*

[38] On this topic generally, see Warburton & Cartwright, "Human Rights, Public Authorities and Charities" (2000) 6 C.L. & P.R. 169, and Burton, "Mind the Gap" (2002) 152 N.L.J. 1933.

[39] See the cases referred to in n.36 above.

[40] Charities Act 1993, s.33(7). For the meaning of "exempt charity," see s.96(1). It is important to remember that all charity proceedings, except those relating to an exempt charity and those brought by the Attorney-General, require the Commissioners' order under s.33(2).

[41] The CPR contain no provision about relator actions.

[42] Charities Act 1993, s.33(1) and see para.10–030, above.

It should, however, be borne in mind that the rules as to joinder of parties are, in general, rules of practice rather than of substantive law.[43] Under the Civil Procedure Rules 1998 the court has wide powers of rectifying errors of procedure[44] and adding, removing or substituting parties,[45] and it is the duty of the court to exercise those powers for the purpose of giving effect to the overriding objective of dealing with cases justly.[46] This should be borne in mind when considering the decisions on procedure referred to below, which should not be regarded as laying down any immutable principles.

The Attorney-General as a party

10–038   By reason of his duty as the Sovereign's representative,[47] protecting all the persons interested in the charity funds,[48] the Attorney-General is as a general rule a necessary party to charity proceedings.[49] He represents the beneficial interest[50]; it follows that, in all proceedings in which the beneficial interest has to be before the court, he must be a party.[51] He represents all the objects of the charity, who are thus in effect parties through him.[52] It was accordingly held that, if all the subscribers to a charitable fund were plaintiffs, the action would still be defective for want of parties, unless the Attorney-General were also a party.[53]

In *Hauxwell v Barton-upon-Humber UDC*[54] local inhabitants had sought to establish that land was held by a local authority upon charitable trusts. Although the proceedings were not charity proceedings, because the existence of a charitable trust was in issue, the proceedings were defective for want of proper parties until the Attorney-General was substituted as plaintiff. Brightman J., said:

> "I am able to discern nothing in the cases which have been cited to me to indicate that anyone save the Attorney-General is entitled to maintain an action against supposed trustees to establish the existence of a charitable trust, or that anyone except the Attorney-General or the trustees of the charity can bring proceedings to recover charity property from a third person, or that persons are capable of maintaining

---

[43] See, *e.g. Dearman v Simpletest Ltd, The Times,* February 14, 2000.

[44] C.P.R., r.3.10.

[45] *ibid.,* r.19.2.

[46] *ibid.,* r.1.2.

[47] See para.10–018, above.

[48] *Re Sekeford's Charity* (1861) 5 L.T. 488; and see para.10–018, above.

[49] *Wellbeloved v Jones* (1822) 1 S. & S. 43; *National Anti-Vivisection Society v Inland Revenue Commissioners* [1948] A.C. 31, 62; Shelford, Mortm. 411.

[50] See *Ware v Cumberlege* (1855) 20 Beav. 503 at 511, *per* Romilly M.R.; *Re King* [1917] 2 Ch. 420.

[51] See *Strickland v Weldon* (1885) 28 Ch.D. 426 at 430.

[52] *Att-Gen v Brodie* (1846) 6 Moore, P.C.C. 12; *Att-Gen v Bishop of Worcester* (1852) 9 Ha. 361; *Re King* [1917] 2 Ch. 420.

[53] *Strickland v Weldon* (1885) 28 Ch.D. 426. As to right of subscribers, see para.10–042, below, and *Minn v Stant* (1851) 15 Beav. 49.

[54] [1974] Ch. 432.

such a suit on the ground that the charity is a local one and that they are persons of that locality who are thus potential recipients of benefits under the trust. The only case, as it seems to me, where the inhabitants of a locality can bring proceedings in respect of a local charity is where the proceedings are 'charity proceedings' within the meaning of section 28.[55] Such proceedings do not include proceedings which have as one of their objects the construction of a conveyance for the purpose of determining whether the conveyance was effective to create a charitable trust."[56]

However, in an earlier case before the same judge no point was taken that the Attorney-General was a necessary party to an application by a member of a student union for an interlocutory injunction restraining misapplication of the union's charitable funds.[57]

In *Ware v Cumberlege*,[58] Sir John Romilly M.R. laid down the following rules for the purpose of determining when the Attorney-General is or is not a necessary party to proceedings relative to the administration of the estates of testators who have given charitable legacies:

10–039

"The Attorney-General represents all absent charities, and it is sufficient to have him here to represent all absent charities. But absent charities may obviously be of two different characters: they may either be under gifts to specified individual charities, or to charity generally. In case the gift is for charity generally, no one can represent it but the Attorney-General, and he must be here to represent such general charities. When there are specified individual charities, then the Attorney-General's presence is not universally necessary; but it is required by the court upon various occasions, as, for instance, where any rules are required for the regulation of the internal conduct of the charity itself, such as the establishment of a scheme and the like; there the Attorney-General is necessary for the purpose of aiding and assisting the court in directing and sanctioning the general system and principle that ought to govern charities of those descriptions. But there are other cases where there is no question as to the conduct of management of the charities, but only whether the charity is entitled to a particular legacy or not. In those cases the Attorney-General is rather in the nature of a trustee for those charities, and the court prefers having before it the charities beneficially interested, for the purpose of putting their interests before the court in the light which they consider most favourable to them. In those cases I think it preferable that the charity itself should appear rather than that the Attorney-General should represent it."

---

[55] *i.e.* of the Charities Act 1960, now Charities Act 1993, s.33.
[56] [1974] Ch. 450.
[57] *Baldry v Feintuck* [1972] 1 W.L.R. 552.
[58] (1855) 20 Beav. 503 at 511.

Where it is desired to have a charitable gift declared invalid, the presence of the Attorney-General to represent the charity is required.[59] In a case where charity funds had been distributed for more than two centuries among certain parishes, it was held that an adverse claim by another parish to participate in the benefits of the charity was properly the subject of an information, and that the Attorney-General was a necessary party to the proceedings.[60] In a similar case today the Attorney-General would be a necessary party to the proceedings.

The Attorney-General is a necessary party to an appeal from an order of the Charity Commissioners,[61] and if his views on the appeal coincide with those of the Commissioners it is proper for him to represent their interest so that the Commissioners will not be necessary parties.[62] Nor will the Commissioners generally be necessary parties to an appeal against an order made by them in exercise of their powers under the Charities Act 1993.[63]

10–040 There are, however, cases where the Attorney-General's presence is not necessary. Most importantly the Attorney-General is not required to be a party where legal proceedings with reference to charities are taken by the Charity Commissioners.[64] The Attorney-General has been held by Lord Hardwicke, L.C., not to be a necessary party to a suit for the regulation of a voluntary society constituted to provide by weekly subscriptions for such of the members as should become necessitous and their widows: but Lord Hardwicke said it was in the nature of a private charity and not charitable in the legal sense at all.[65] Where a bill was filed for an account, the Attorney-General was held not to be a necessary party, merely because a legacy happened to be given to charity.[66]

If the bequest is to the treasurer or other officer of an established charitable institution as part of its general funds[67] or to specified persons as trustees and there is a question as to the validity of the trusts,[68] the Attorney-General need not be a party, but he must be a party where the legacy is to be held upon trusts differing from those on whichs the general funds of the institution are held.[69] The presence of the Attorney-General is not necessary where annual sums are given to be distributed in charity by specified trustees,[70] or where the fund, although a capital sum, is made

---

[59] *Kirkbank v Hudson* (1819) 7 Price 212; *Cook v Duckenfield* (1743) 2 Atk. 563.

[60] *Re Magdalen Land Charity* (1852) 9 Ha. 624.

[61] CPR P. D. 52—Appeals, para.23.8A(2).

[62] *Jones v Charity Commissioners* [1972] 1 W.L.R. 784 (varied on appeal on other grounds sub nom. *Jones v Att-Gen* [1974] Ch. 148).

[63] *Weth v Att-Gen* [1999] 1 W.L.R. 686.

[64] Charities Act 1993, s.32(4).

[65] *Anon.* (1745) 3 Atk. 277. *Semble*, however, the society would today be treated as charitable as being for the relief of poverty: see para.2–016, above.

[66] *Chitty v Parker* (1792) 4 Bro.C.C. 38; and see *Wellbeloved v Jones* (1822) 1 S. & S. 40.

[67] *Wellbeloved v Jones* (1822) 1 S. & S. 40; *In the goods of M'Auliffe* [1895] P. 290.

[68] See Practice Note [1945] W.N. 38.

[69] *ibid., Corporation of the Sons of the Clergy v Mose* (1840) 9 Sim. 610. But see *Monill v Lawson* (1719) Vin.Abr. tit. Char. Uses, H. pl. 11; *Att-Gen v Warren* (1818) 2 Swanst. 291.

[70] *Waldo v Caley* (1809) 16 Ves. 206; *M'Coll v Atherton* (1843) 12 Jur. 1042; and see *Re Randell* (1888) 38 Ch.D. 213. But see *Horde v Suffolk* (1833) 2 Myl. & K. 59.

immediately distributable.[71] Where a question arises whether a bequest can be applied *cy-près* or not, the Attorney-General must be a party.[72]

The Attorney-General is not a necessary party to an action by third persons against charity trustees for specific performance of an agreement.[73] In an action by some (on behalf of all) of the freemen of a borough to establish the right of all the individual freemen to share for their private benefit the net proceeds of certain properties vested in the corporation it was held that, whether the trust in question was in the nature of a charity or not, the parties claiming were entitled to sue under the Municipal Corporations Act 1835, without an information by the Attorney-General.[74] The presence of the Attorney-General was held to be unnecessary on the appointment of new trustees of a charity.[75] Since the Attorney-General is the only person who can represent the general body of beneficiaries under a charitable trust, it follows that no proceedings to which the Attorney-General is not a party are binding upon him as representing the charity, or upon the court in an action in the nature of an information instituted by the Attorney-General[76]; and the Attorney-General may be allowed to appeal from a decision in an action to which he was not a party.[77]

All the beneficiaries under a charitable trust are bound by proceedings to which the Attorney-General is a party.[78] If, therefore, the Attorney-General is a party to an action in which charities are cited but do not appear, the beneficial interest of the charities is bound by a compromise to which the Attorney-General has agreed.[79]

Other parties

Where proceedings are taken by or against trustees of a charity, all the trustees must be joined as parties, not only the acting trustees.[80] Where new trustees are appointed while an action is in progress but are not joined as parties before the hearing of the action, they are not bound by the decree, but may even put in a further defence to the suit.[81] Where the

10–041

---

[71] *Re Barnett* (1860) 29 L.J.Ch. 871. But see *Re Lea* (1887) 34 Ch.D. 528.
[72] *Re Taylor* (1888) 58 L.T. 538; *Re Unite* (1906) 75 L.J.Ch. 163.
[73] *Att-Gen v Warren* (1818) 2 Swanst. 291, 311; *Neville Estates Ltd. v Madden* [1962] Ch. 832.
[74] *Prestney v Mayor, etc., of Colchester* (1882) 21 Ch.D. 111 at 119, 120, but in cases not covered by statutory provisions similar to those in the Municipal Corporations Act, 1835, the Attorney-General must be joined as a party: see, *e.g. Re Christchurch Enclosure Act* (1888) 38 Ch.D. 520.
[75] *Att-Gen v Cooper* (1861) 8 Jur.(N.S.) 50.
[76] See *Att-Gen v Leage* [1881] W.N. 176; a note of this case will be found in the 4th edition of this book at p.1041. For a case in which the Attorney-General would not have been a proper party to the earlier proceedings, see *Att-Gen v Warren* (1818) 2 Swanst. 291 at 311, 312.
[77] *Re Faraker* [1912] 2 Ch. 488. It is thought that the Attorney-General, though not a party to the summons in *Re British Red Cross Balkan Fund* [1914] 2 Ch. 419, could have obtained leave to appeal and that his appeal might well have succeeded; see para.10–021, above.
[78] *Vince v Walsh* (1855) 3 W.R. 7.
[79] *Re King* [1917] 2 Ch. 420.
[80] CPR, r.64.4(1).
[81] *Att-Gen v Foster* (1842) 2 Ha. 81.

Attorney-General is representing a charity, the trustees are not as of right entitled to be heard in his support,[82] but in cases of information against the trustees where the Attorney-General appeared for the charity, and the trustees differed in good faith from the relators, the court heard the trustees.[83]

The general rule is that all persons having any interest in the subject-matter of an action relating to charities and within the jurisdiction of the court should be parties.[84] Persons (not being the general objects of the charity) having a beneficial or possible beneficial interest in the subject-matter of the action must be parties. Thus the heir-at-law had to be a party where the question was whether there was a resulting trust in his favour,[85] or whether or not he was entitled to the increased rent of charity estates.[86] Similarly, the master of a school was held to be a necessary party to an action to have surplus funds applied for his benefit.[87] As a rule, all the persons whose estates are liable must be parties to an action to establish a right to a rent-charge.[88] An exception is, however, established in the case of charities. In these cases the court determines the question whether the rent-charge is issuing out of the land of the persons actually before the court, although the other terre-tenants are not parties, and an inquiry is directed as to the other persons alleged to be liable.[89] In an action to set aside a lease of a charity estate, the lessee or his representative, as well as any assignees or underlessees of any part of the property, should be made parties,[90] and a lessee, even when not made a party, was given leave to attend.[91] In a case of a legacy to charity charged on lands, the executor is a necessary party to an action to ascertain the profits of the lands.[92] On an inquiry before a master, persons who are not parties to the action, but can show a prima facie right to intervene, will be allowed by the court to attend.[93]

---

[82] *Sol-Gen v Corporation of Bath* (1848) 18 L.J. Ch. 275; but see *Whicker v Hume* (1851) 14 Beav. 528. In both of these cases counsel for the trustees was allowed to be heard.

[83] *Sol-Gen v Corporation of Bath*, above.

[84] As to one or more of numerous parties having the same interest suing or defending as representative of them all, see CPR, r.19.6; D.C.P., (8th ed.), 1151; *Milligan v Mitchell* (1837) 3 Myl. & Cr. 72. Where a bill and information was filed by some of the trustees of a charity against the others only, it was considered that the individuals in respect of whose interest the suit was instituted ought to be parties either collectively or as suing for themselves and the others; *Att-Gen v Fowler* (1808) 15 Ves. 85 at 87. No doubt the position is the same under the modern practice.

[85] *Att-Gen v Green* (1789) 2 Bro.C.C. 492. Any other persons, *e.g.* the next-of-kin, who may be interested under a resulting trust are likewise necessary parties.

[86] *Att-Gen v Haberdashers' Co.* (1792) 4 Bro.C.C. 103 at 106; and see *Corporation of Ludlow v Greenhouse* (1827) 1 Bli.(N.S.) 17, 55.

[87] *Att-Gen v Smart* (1747) 1 Ves.S. 72.

[88] *Att-Gen v Jackson* (1805) 11 Ves. 365, 367.

[89] *ibid.*, at 367, 372; *Att-Gen v Naylor* (1863) 1 H. & M. 809. And see *Att-Gen v Shelley* (1712) 1 Salk. 163; *Att-Gen v Wyburgh* (1719) 1 P. Wms. 559; *Cooke v Smee* (1745) 2 Bro.P.C. 184. A tenant for years of land subject to a rent-charge is not liable in an action in the Chancery Division at the instance of the Attorney-General or the Charity Commissioners: *Re Herbage Rents* [1896] 2 Ch. 811.

[90] *Att-Gen v Backhouse* (1810) 17 Ves. 283 at 285. See also *Corporation of Ludlow v Greenhouse* (1827) 1 Bli.(N.S.) 17 at 73, 74; *Att-Gen v Greenhill* (1863) 33 Beav. 193.

[91] *Att-Gen v Pretyman* (1845) 8 Beav. 316.

[92] *Att-Gen v Twisden* (1678) Rep. t. Finch 336.

[93] *Att-Gen v Shore* (1836) 1 Myl. & Cr. 394. For the terms upon which the court makes the order, see *Re Shrewsbury Grammar School* (1850) 1 Mac. & G. 324; and see para.10–056, below.

Where a private founder of a charity subject to visitation had appointed no visitor, his heir-at-law, being in contemplation of law the visitor of the charity, was a necessary party to an action for the execution of the trusts.[94] The Court of Chancery, however, in a case of this kind, refused to dismiss an information because of the absence of the heir-at-law, but directed an inquiry to ascertain who he was.[95] Where an information was filed for the establishment of certain charities consisting of estates given for the endowment of a school, and of others given for the foundation of scholarships in a college for boys to be nominated by the master of the school, it was held to be defective for want of parties, because the Archbishop of York, who had the appointment of the schoolmaster in default of his being appointed within two months by the master and fellows of the college, was not a party.[96] Where an estate, charged with a fund in favour of a charity, is alleged to have been improperly sold, the purchasers must be made parties.[97]

In the event of a charity being a party it is necessary to determine whether the charity is incorporated or not. An incorporated charity is properly sued in its own name whereas an unincorporated charity is properly sued by suing its trustees, or, if none, its treasurer, secretary or other responsible officer on behalf of the charity.[98] An unincorporated charity cannot be sued in its name alone.[99]

Who are not necessary or proper parties

An agent who is employed by the trustees of a charity to manage its **10–042** affairs, who receives the income, and has the title-deeds in his possession, is not a proper party to an action for an account and scheme.[1] Where no charter of incorporation can be produced "the master, brethren, and sisters" of a charity ought not to be made parties as a corporation.[2]

Trustees entitled to a charitable legacy upon the happening of a contingency are not necessary parties to all charity proceedings. Thus where a testatrix had given a legacy in trust for the minister of a chapel, but had directed that upon a specified contingency it should go to the trustees of a college and the income of the legacy had for many years been paid to the

---

In *Att-Gen v Ironmongers' Co.* (1840) Cr. & Ph. 208 it was held that the master had no right to give leave to attend.

[94] *Att-Gen v Gaunt* (1790) 3 Swanst. 148n. See para.10–068, below. As to the question whether following the abolition of descent to the heir the visitatorial power has devolved on the Crown, see *ibid*.

[95] *ibid*. Under the present practice no cause or matter will be defeated merely by reason of the mis-joinder or non-joinder of parties: CPR, rr.3.10, 19.

[96] *Att-Gen v St. John's College* (1835) 7 Sim. 241.

[97] *Mayor of Southmolton v Att-Gen* (1854) 5 H.L.C. 1.

[98] See *Re Pritt* (1915) 85 L.J. Ch. 166.

[99] *Bloom v National Federation of Discharged and Demobilised Sailors and Soldiers* (1918) 35 T.L.R. 50.

[1] *Att-Gen v Chesterfield* (1854) 18 Beav. 596. The case would, of course, be different if a stranger had charity property in his possession and declined to deliver it up.

[2] *Att-Gen v Chester Corporation* (1849) 1 Hall & Tw. 46.

minister, it was held that the charity might be established in proceedings to which the trustees of the college were not parties.[3]

Persons who have no interest, as, for instance, the original subscribers to a charitable fund, are not required to be represented.[4] Where, however, the trustees of a chapel, who were authorised by the majority of the men subscribers to mortgage or sell, mortgaged the chapel and gave the mortgagee a power of sale, which he exercised, it was held that the men subscribers were necessary parties to a suit by the trustees praying a declaration that the purchaser should be considered merely as an assignee of the mortgagee. The ground of the decision was that if the purchaser succeeded in this action he would still be liable to an action by the subscribers.[5]

Compromise

10–043   A question relating to the interests of a charity may be compromised.[6] When the Attorney-General is a party to charity proceedings his consent is required to a compromise, and when that is obtained the compromise will be enforced.[7] A compromise in an action to which the Attorney-General has assented is binding upon charities who are cited in the action though they do not appear.[8]

Where consent to a compromise could otherwise be given by the Attorney-General it may instead be given by the Charity Commissioners, if the Attorney-General agrees to their exercising the power in his stead.[9] The separate, pre-existing power of the Charity Commissioners to sanction a compromise[10] is exercised, not in relation to charity proceedings, but in relation to claims made by someone outside the charity against the charity or vice versa.

The court, in the exercise of its discretion, may refer the case to the consideration of the Attorney-General,[11] and it is not always the duty of the Attorney-General to contend for his strict rights. In cases of hardship the court may sanction his acting with forbearance towards the parties, and postpone its decision to give the parties an opportunity of entering into an arrangement with him.[12]

---

[3] *Att-Gen v Goddard* (1824) T. & R. 348.
[4] *Att-Gen v Munro* (1848) 2 De G. & Sm. 122 at 161, 162; *Att-Gen v Gardner* (1847) 2 De G. & S. 102.
[5] *Minn v Stant* (1851) 15 Beav. 49.
[6] *Att-Gen v Landerfield* (1743) 9 Mod. 286; *Att-Gen v Bishop of Oxford* (1799) 4 Ves. 431; *Simpson's Case*, cited (1784) 5 Ves. 304; *Andrew v Merchant Taylors' Co.* (1802) 7 Ves. 223; *Andrew v Trinity Hall* (1804) 9 Ves. 532 at 533; *Att-Gen v Trevelyan* (1847) 16 L.J.Ch. 251.
[7] *Andrew v Merchant Taylors' Co.* above; *Andrew v Trinity Hall*, above; *Att-Gen v Mayor of Exeter* (1827) 2 Russ. 362; *Att-Gen v Fishmongers' Co.* (1837) C.P. Cooper 85; *Att-Gen v Corporation of Ludlow* (1842) 6 Jur. 1003; *Att-Gen v Trevelyan* (1847) 16 L.J.Ch. 521; *Att-Gen v Boucherett* (1855) 25 Beav. 116.
[8] *Re King* [1917] 2 Ch. 420.
[9] Charities Act 1993, s.32(1)(b), (5).
[10] Charities Act 1993, s.26. For examples of the exercise of the power see [1982] Ch. Com. Rep., paras 90, *et seq.*
[11] *Att-Gen v Green* (1819) 1 J. & W. 303; *Att-Gen v Pretyman* (1841) 4 Beav. 462 at 467.
[12] See *Att-Gen v Mayor of Exeter* (1827) 2 Russ. at 370, where Lord Eldon referred it to the Attorney-General to consider whether it would be proper for the charity to accept a less

In *Att-Gen v Brettingham*,[13] Lord Langdale expressed a hope that every   **10–044**
Attorney-General, whilst he acted in the vigorous discharge of his duty to
redress breaches of trust, would consider it his duty to act considerately
and with forbearance in proper cases. The law armed him with great
power, and enabled him to bring parties before the court without the peril
of costs. That power was intended for the benefit of the public, and ought
to be used, as it generally was, with forbearance and without oppression
to individuals. In a suitable case the court may actively encourage an *ex
gratia* payment from charity funds.[14]

The court will not normally act in accordance with an award in charity
cases without the consent of the Attorney-General[15] or presumably of the
Charity Commissioners if they have instituted the proceedings.[16] If, on the
other hand, the question to be determined depends upon the construction
of a will or document, the court will not refer the matter to the Attorney-
General.[17]

Procedure

Under the Civil Procedure Rules 1998 most types of proceeding are   **10–045**
commenced by Claim Form. Claim Forms are of two kinds: a Pt 7 Claim
Form (which has replaced the former Writ of Summons) and a Pt 8 Claim
Form (the equivalent of the former Originating Summons). Proceedings
for the administration of a trust,[18] and an application for permission to
begin charity proceedings,[19] must be begun by Pt 8 Claim Form. Except
where the application is made by the Attorney-General *ex officio*, the
order of the Charity Commissioners authorising the application, must be
left at the court office at the time the Claim Form is issued.

The Claim Form, when not taken out by the Attorney-General, must be
served upon the Treasury Solicitor, except where the Claim Form merely
asks for the appointment of trustees, or a vesting order, or an order for the
transfer of stock consequent on a vesting order,[20] and the Claim Form
must be served on all persons whose interests are affected.[21]

An appeal cannot be presented by a person (other than the Attorney-
General[22]) who did not appear in the court below, even though he is an

---

sum than that found due. The Attorney-General having certified that it was proper to
accept a less sum, his certificate was afterwards confirmed and acted on by the Lord
Chancellor. See also *Att-Gen v Corporation of Carlisle* (1830) 4 Sim. 275; *Att-Gen v
Pretyman* (1841) 4 Beav. 462; *Att-Gen v Tufnell* (1859) 12 Beav. 35.

[13] (1840) 3 Beav. 91 at 96.
[14] *National Provincial Bank Ltd. v Moore* (1967) 111 S.J. 357. As to *Re Snowden* [1970] Ch.
700 applications, see para.10–023, above.
[15] *Att-Gen v Hewitt* (1803) 9 Ves. 232.
[16] *i.e.* under Charities Act 1993, s.32(1)(a).
[17] *Att-Gen v Fea* (1819) 4 Madd. 274.
[18] CPR, r.64.3.
[19] *ibid.*, r.64.6(2).
[20] D.C.P. (8th ed.), 1738.
[21] *ibid.*
[22] See para.10–021, above.

interested party[23] unless the court gives permission for him to be added as a party.[24]

Costs

10–046   Although by statute the court has a discretion as to the costs of proceedings, that discretion is subject to (among other things) rules of court.[25] Concern at the increasing cost of litigation pervades the Civil Procedure Rules 1998. The saving of expense is an important part of the overriding objective.[26] The governing principles are to be found in Pt 44. Under r.44.3(1) the court has discretion as to whether costs are payable by one party to another, the amount of those costs; and when they are to be paid. The court is therefore not bound to make any order about costs. However, if it decides to do so r.44.3(2) lays down the general rule that the unsuccessful party should be ordered to pay the costs of the successful party, although the court retains the discretion to make some other order. In applying the general rule the court is bound to take into account all the circumstances, including some which are specified as of particular relevance (the first of which is the conduct of the parties),[27] and a range of possible orders is given.[28] The general rule is subject to any specific provisions as to the costs of particular parties such as trustees.[29] The discussion which follows, based on past cases, indicates the manner in which the court's discretion has been exercised in the past. In doing so it may give some guidance as to how the discretion will be exercised in the future. However, it must be emphasised that each case turns on its own facts, and reference to past cases cannot be relied upon as a substitute for the application of the detailed provisions of the rules to the precise facts of the particular case.

The Attorney-General

10–047   The rule established by the Administration of Justice (Miscellaneous Provisions) Act 1933,[30] is that in any civil proceedings[31] to which the Crown is a party the costs are in the discretion of the court, which must exercise its discretion in the same manner and on the same principles as in cases between subjects and may order the payment of costs by or to the Crown accordingly. Where, however, the Attorney-General as such is required to be made a party, the court must have regard to the nature of

---

[23] *Corporation of Ludlow v Greenhouse* (1827) 1 Bli.(N.S.) 17.
[24] As to the jurisdiction to add a party where justice requires this, see *Merrett v Babb* [2001] EWCA Civ 214, [2001] Q.B. 1174.
[25] Supreme Court Act 1981, s.1(1).
[26] CPR, r.1.1(2)(b).
[27] *ibid.*, r.44.3(4).
[28] *ibid.*, r.44.3(6).
[29] see paras 10–048, *et seq.*, below.
[30] s.7(1).
[31] Defined *ibid.*, s.7(2).

the proceedings and the character and circumstances in which the Attorney-General appears and may, in the exercise of its discretion, order any other party to the proceedings to pay the costs of the Attorney-General, whatever may be the result of the proceedings.[32]

As to when the Attorney-General receives costs, it has been said that in a court of first instance he is entitled to be put in the same position as any other claimant.[33] He may receive costs in cases in which, as a private individual, he would be entitled to them.[34] In one case,[35] where the question arose whether certain trusts were charitable, the Attorney-General, who appeared before the House of Lords in support of a judgment of the Court of Appeal, was allowed his costs out of the estate, although the judgment of the Court of Appeal was reversed. The Attorney-General, however, would not necessarily have received his costs, if the estate had not been a large one. Where a defendant who had been ordered to pay the costs of the Attorney-General and trustees became insolvent, the costs were ordered to be paid out of the charity estate.[36]

In the case of successful proceedings the Attorney-General is allowed costs on the standard basis.[37] He may also be allowed charges and expenses relating to the charity which are not costs in the matter, but must state the matter in respect of which payment of such charges and expenses is desired.[38]

Trustees

The rules applicable to the costs of charity trustees do not differ from those which apply in the case of private trustees.[39] As between themselves and other parties to the proceedings, trustees are in the same position as any other litigant. But as between themselves and the trust funds they are entitled to all costs, charges, and expenses properly incurred by them in connection with the trusts; such costs are a matter of contract, and are not, like the ordinary costs of an action, within the discretion of the court, and a trustee can only be deprived of them where he has been guilty of misconduct.[40] This principle receives recognition in the Civil Procedure Rules, under which trustees are normally entitled to be paid their costs on the indemnity basis out of the trust funds.[41] Therefore, trustees who have

10–048

---

[32] *ibid.* s.7(1), proviso (a).
[33] *Re Cardwell* [1912] 1 Ch. 779 at 793, *per* Warrington J.
[34] *Att-Gen v Ashburnham* (1823) 1 Sim. & St. 396; *Re Cardwell* [1912] 1 Ch. 779; Administration of Justice (Miscellaneous Provisions) Act 1933, s.7(1).
[35] *Hunter v Att-Gen* [1899] A.C. 309.
[36] *Att-Gen v Lewis* (1845) 8 Beav. 179.
[37] *Moggridge v Thackwell* (1802) 1 Ves. 464, 475; 7 Ves. 69 at 88; 13 Ves. 416; *Mills v Farmer* (1815) 19 Ves. 483 at 490; *Att-Gen v Stewart* (1872) L.R. 14 Eq. 17 at 25; *Re Cardwell*, above.
[38] *Re Dulwich College* (1873) L.R. 15 Eq. 294.
[39] Shelford, Mortm., pp.467, *et seq.*, but see *Att-Gen v Drummond* (1842) 3 Dr. & W. 164.
[40] See *Cotterell v Stratton* (1873) 8 Ch. 295 at 302; *Farrow v Austin* (1881) 18 Ch.D. 58; *Turner v Hancock* (1882) 20 Ch.D. 304; *Re Sarah Knight's Will* (1884) 26 Ch.D. 82; *Re Love* (1885) 29 Ch.D. 348; *Armitage v Nurse* [1998] Ch. 241.
[41] CPR, r.48.4.

not been guilty of misconduct are entitled to be recouped all costs of proceedings, including those which they do not recover from an opponent. Similarly, if the persons ordered to pay the costs cannot do so, the costs must come out of the charity funds.[42] Trustees have a right to reimburse themselves out of any funds in their hands in respect of all expenses properly incurred in performing the duties of their trust.[43] Further, in an appropriate case an application may be made for a prospective costs order, which is an order authorising, in advance, payment of the costs of the trustees, or of any other party, out of the trust fund.[44]

The case is different where the trustees have been guilty of a breach of trust. Thus, where they have, whether individuals or a corporation, mismanaged the charity funds or neglected its objects, they will be liable to costs.[45] Trustees were made liable for costs where they had suppressed and concealed evidence,[46] although such suppression was due merely to neglect to examine deeds and papers in their possession,[47] and where they had acted improperly in the appointment of a schoolmaster.[48]

Similarly, trustees may be fixed with costs where they have by their conduct given occasion to the suit,[49] or have acted vexatiously,[50] or where they set up a claim to continue a misapplication of the funds adversely to the charity,[51] or to be entitled to the property beneficially.[52]

10–049   A trustee, who had not been called upon by the body to whom he was liable to account, was nevertheless held liable to pay the costs of proceedings for an account.[53] In *Att-Gen v Webster*,[54] trustees who defended proceeding for a declaration that certain trusts were charitable, although they had been advised that they were charitable, were not allowed costs; but the Attorney-General did not press for costs against them personally. In *Re St Stephen's, Coleman Street*,[55] trustees who by petition under the City of London Parochial Charities Act 1883 instituted a test case as to whether the trust property was held for a charity or not, were deprived of costs. In *Att-Gen v Clack*,[56] where, pending proceedings for the appointment of new trustees, the surviving trustees of a charity had taken upon themselves to

---

[42] *Att-Gen v Lewis* (1845) 8 Beav. 179.

[43] *Att-Gen v Mayor of Norwich* (1837) 2 Myl. & Cr. 406 at 424.

[44] CPR P.D. to Pt 64—Estates, Trusts and Charities, para.6.

[45] *Haberdashers' Co. v Att-Gen* (1702) 2 Bro.P.C. 370, Toml. ed.; *East v Ryal* (1725) 2 P. Wms. 284. See also *Att-Gen v Mercers' Co.* (1833) 2 Myl. & K. 654, where the trustees were ordered to pay all the costs, except those which were incurred by the necessity of settling a scheme.

[46] *Borough of Hertford v Poor of Hertford* (1713) 2 Bro.P.C. 377, Toml. ed.

[47] *Att-Gen v Corporation of East Retford* (1833) 2 Myl. & K. 35.

[48] *Town of Salop v Att-Gen* (1726) 2 Bro.P.C. 402, Toml. ed.; *Att-Gen v Lord Carrington* (1850) 4 De G. & Sm. 140.

[49] *Att-Gen v Corporation of Stafford* (1740) Barnard 33; *Att-Gen v Murdoch* (1856) 2 K. & J. 571.

[50] *Att-Gen v Stroud* (1869) 19 L.T. 545.

[51] *Att-Gen v Drapers' Co.* (1841) 4 Beav. 67; *Att-Gen v Christ's Hospital, ibid.*, at 73.

[52] *Att-Gen v Webster* (1875) L.R. 20 Eq. 483 at 492. See also *Att-Gen v Mercers' Co.* (1870) 18 W.R. 448.

[53] *Att-Gen v Gibbs* (1846) 1 De G. & Sm. 156; 2 Ph. 327.

[54] (1875) L.R. 20 Eq. 483.

[55] (1888) 29 Ch.D. 492.

[56] (1839) 1 Beav. 467.

appoint new trustees without the sanction of the court, the appointment was set aside, and the trustees were ordered personally to pay all the extra costs that they had caused. Where trustees applied direct to the court for the administration of charity funds, instead of first applying to the Charity Commissioners, they were not allowed their costs.[57]

Charity trustees who have been removed for misconduct may be ordered to transfer the trust property to the new trustees at their own expense.[58]

If the court does not think it proper to allow charity trustees their costs, they are not entitled to charge those costs on the charity estate, and if they do so they will be ordered to restore to the charity funds the sums so misapplied.[59] Thus, in *Attorney-General v Daugars*,[60] trustees who had been ordered to pay costs personally but paid them out of the charity fund were ordered to refund the amount, with 4 per cent interest. But this principle applies only where the court expressly deprives the trustees of the right to take their costs out of the fund. A trustee who is refused his costs as against another party may still be able to recover them out of the fund.[61]

Where the court found that a lease was void as not sufficiently beneficial to the charity, the lessees were made to pay the costs of having it set aside.[62] Where a lease was made in pursuance of a direction which was void for perpetuity, the lessors were ordered to pay the lessees' costs.[63]

10–050

Even though the breach of trust has been beneficial to the charity, the trustees may be made liable for costs of an inquiry respecting it.[64] Trustees who had greatly exceeded the estimate for building authorised by the court were disallowed the costs of an inquiry whether the expenditure was for the benefit of the charity.[65] Where a corporation in granting building leases, etc., in breach of trust, had mixed up charity lands with their own, they were not allowed costs, notwithstanding that the property of the charity had been improved by the breaches of trust.[66] Similarly, where the balance of accounts when taken was found to be in favour of the trustees, they were, nevertheless, deprived of their costs because they had attempted to overcharge the charity funds by claiming a larger balance.[67]

When breaches of trust have been innocently committed by trustees and their predecessors for a long period, the existing trustees may at the discretion of the court be allowed their costs out of the charity funds. Thus, in *Att-Gen v Drummond*,[68] where Unitarians had wrongfully been allowed to participate in a charity. Sugden L.C. said:

---

[57] *Re Poplar and Blackwall Free School* (1878) 8 Ch.D. 547.
[58] *Mayor of Coventry v Att-Gen* (1720) 7 Bro.P.C. 235; *Ex p. Greenhouse* (1815) 1 Madd. 92, 102.
[59] *Re St Paul's School* (1870) 18 W.R. 448.
[60] (1863) 33 Beav. 621.
[61] *Armitage v Nurse* [1998] Ch. 241.
[62] *Att-Gen v Hotham* (1823) Turn. & R. 209; and see *Re Owen* (1805) 10 Ves. 555 at 562.
[63] *Att-Gen v Greenhill* (1863) 3 N.R. 236.
[64] *Sol-Gen v Corporation of Bath* (1849) 13 Jur. 866.
[65] *Att-Gen v Armitstead* (1854) 19 Beav. 584.
[66] *Sol-Gen v Corporation of Bath* (1849) 13 Jur. 866.
[67] *Att-Gen v Brewers' Co.* (1717) 1 P.Wms. 376; and see *Att-Gen v Gibbs* (1846) 1 De G. & Sm. 156.
[68] (1842) 3 Dr. & W. 163 at 164. See, however, *Shore v Wilson* (1842) 9 Cl. & F. 355, where the trustees were not allowed their costs.

"No doubt the general rule is, as it has been stated to be, that a trustee who acts wrongly, and against whom there has been a decision, is not entitled to costs. But it can hardly be said that the rule applies to a case of this nature, where for more than a century the funds have been applied in a manner in which the parties are now found fault with for having so applied them. I should treat the present trustees with great hardship if I were now to decide that they were not entitled to their costs when all their predecessors have escaped. The case is different from that of private trustees, where each must suffer for the consequences of his own mistake. Here there has been a succession of trustees, and were I to refuse the present trustees their costs, it would be, in fact, to visit upon them individually the error of their predecessors."

10–051   In *Att-Gen v Caius College*,[69] where the charitable funds had been misapplied by the trustees and their predecessors for two centuries without any improper motive, but, as a result of economy on their part, there had been considerable accumulations of charity property, the trustees were allowed costs out of the accumulated funds.

Where charity trustees have accidentally committed an error which they take the first opportunity to correct, the court might not make them pay costs.[70]

Charity trustees were not visited with costs in consequence of an error of the Charity Commissioners as to the construction of a public statute.[71]

A trustee or member of a corporation who severs his defence and supports a successful action by the Attorney-General may be allowed his costs.[72]

An unnecessary party who had been served with a petition in consequence of a claim set up by him had to bear his own costs.[73] Where, however, a solicitor made trustees plaintiffs to an action without their consent, the trustees were allowed to have their names struck out, and were given their costs.[74]

Other parties

10–052   Next-of-kin, where no improper point is raised on their behalf, were previously as a general rule allowed costs as between solicitor and client. They are not, however, entitled to them as of right, and such costs have

---

[69] (1838) 2 Keen 150.

[70] *Att-Gen v Drapers' Co.* (1842) 4 Beav. 67.

[71] *Moore v Clench* (1875) 1 Ch.D. 447 at 450, 451.

[72] *Att-Gen v Corporation of Chester* (1852) 14 Beav. 338; *Re St Paul's School* (1870) 18 W.R. 448.

[73] *Re Shrewsbury School* (1849) 1 Mac. & G. 85. Clearly the same principle applies to charity proceedings commenced by Claim Form.

[74] *Att-Gen v Maryatt* (1838) 2 Jur. 1060.

been refused to next-of-kin who unsuccessfully opposed a charitable bequest.[75] The heir-at-law was in the same position.[76]

The Official Custodian for Charities, if made a party to proceedings, must be indemnified against costs[77]; but in a case where there was no fund out of which to pay them, the plaintiffs would be ordered to do so.[78]

It should be noted that a party who would ordinarily be given his costs out of the fund many be deprived of them if he has acted otherwise than in accordance with the spirit of the Civil Procedure Rules 1998: thus, a beneficiary who, with a view to obtaining a tactical advantage, had insisted on starting proceedings even though the trustees were prepared to do so in the normal way was refused costs.[79]

Fund for payment

Prima facie costs should be paid out of the property recovered in the proceedings, but if justice to the relator or the interests of the charity render it necessary, they will be ordered to be paid out of the charity funds generally.[80] Thus where a defendant who had been ordered to pay the costs of the Attorney-General and the trustees became insolvent, the costs were ordered to be paid out of the charity estate.[81] **10–053**

The costs of proceedings to establish charitable legacies have accordingly often been allowed out of the testator's general assets.[82] Charities which make hopeless claims to a charitable bequest, or which make no attempt to prove that they are entitled but only attack the claim of other parties are likely to be deprived of all or part of their costs.[83]

Costs will, if necessary, be ordered to be raised by mortgage of part of the charity estates[84] and thus met from income. Similarly the costs of an application by a new master of a hospital for payment of the income of a fund in court were held to be payable out of income.[85]

Costs may be apportioned. Where one application had been made to settle a scheme for 20 charities, the costs were paid out of an existing available fund belonging to three of them, but it was ordered that they should **10–054**

---

[75] *Wilkinson v Barber* (1872) L.R. 14 Eq. 96 at 99. *Practice Direction (Costs)* [1960] 1 W.L.R. 114.

[76] *Att-Gen v Haberdashers' Co.* (1792) 4 Bro.C.C. 177; *Currie v Pye* (1811) 17 Ves. 462; *James v James* (1848) 11 Beav. 397. The heir was, it seems, not entitled as of right to solicitor and client costs: *Whicker v Hume* (1852) 14 Beav. 509 at 528. Sometimes the heir was allowed charges and expenses in addition to costs: *Att-Gen v Haberdashers' Co.*, above; *Att-Gen v Kerr* (1841) 4 Beav. 297 at 299.

[77] See Charities Act 1993, s.22(6).

[78] *Re Church Patronage Trust* [1904] 1 Ch. 41 at 51.

[79] See *D'Abo v Paget (No.2)*, *The Times*, August 10, 2000.

[80] *Att-Gen v Kerr* (1841) 4 Beav. 297 at 299.

[81] *Att-Gen v Lewis* (1845) 8 Beav. 179.

[82] *Kirkbank v Hudson* (1819) 7 Price 212 at 222; *Att-Gen v Hinxman* (1821) 2 J. & W. 270 at 278; *Daly v Att-Gen* (1860) 11 I.C.R. 41.

[83] *Re Daysh* (1951) 1 T.L.R. 257; *Re Preston's Estate* [1951] Ch. 878.

[84] *Att-Gen v Bishop of St. David's* (1849) Seton, (7th ed.), 1269; and see *Re Lambeth Charities* (1853) Seton, (7th ed.), 125; Shelf. Mortm. 478; *Att-Gen v Archbishop of York* (1854) 17 Beav. 495.

[85] *Att-Gen v Smythies* (1853) 16 Beav. 385.

be ultimately borne rateably by all the charities.[86] On the other hand where a testator has created several charities, and vested their respective properties in the same trustees but the charities are distinct, the costs of proceedings relating to one cannot be paid out of the property of the others.[87]

In the case of charity proceedings[88] the authority of an order of the Charity Commissioners or the court indicates that the proceedings are justified.[89] In other cases cost will be awarded if there are substantial grounds for the proceedings[90] and in one case the costs were allowed out of the charity estate even though the proceedings were dismissed as having been prompted by a "groundless apprehension".[91] However, the costs of proceedings which are vexatious[92] or abortive[93] may be disallowed.

In a charity case the court would grant the relief which should have been asked, whether it had in fact been asked or not, nevertheless it would take the frame of the suit into consideration in determining the question of costs.[94] Costs of particular proceedings which the court considers to have been improper may be excepted from the general costs of the action.[95]

Extent of award of costs

10–055   The courts have power[96] in matters of equitable jurisdiction to order an unsuccessful party to pay the costs of the action on the indemnity basis.[97]

Costs have been awarded on this basis[98] but in *Martin v Margham*,[99] where the court was endeavouring to carry out a testator's undefined intention by means of a scheme, it refused to give solicitor and client costs out of the estate except by consent.

10–056   If the court considers that proceedings have not been taken with a view to benefiting the charity or have been conducted with unnecessary expen-

---

[86] *Re Stafford Charities* (1859) 26 Beav. 567.
[87] *Att-Gen v Grainger* (1859) 7 W.R. 684, *per* Jessel M.R.
[88] Charities Act 1993, s.33(8).
[89] *ibid.*, s.33(2)(5).
[90] *Re Storie's University Gift* (1861) 2 De G.F. & J. 529. See also *Re St. Pancras Burial Ground* (1866) 3 Eq. 173 at 192. With regard to the costs of a petition under the Church Building Act 1845, see *Re Lambeth Charities* (1853) and *Att-Gen v Craven* (1860), both cited Seton (7th ed.), 1247.
[91] *Re Betton's Charity* [1908] 1 Ch. 205.
[92] *Chertsey Market Case* (1819) 6 Price 261.
[93] *Re Poplar and Blackwall Free School* (1878) 8 Ch.D. 543. See also *Att-Gen v Stewart* (1872) L.R. 14 Eq. 17.
[94] *Att-Gen v Hartley* (1821) 2 J. & W. 353 at 369, 370. This principle still applies.
[95] *Att-Gen v Ward* (1848) 11 Beav. 203 at 208; *Re St Paul's Schools, Finsbury* (1853) 52 L.J.Ch. 454. But see now CPR, r.44.3(7).
[96] *Andrew v Barnes* (1888) 39 Ch.D. 133.
[97] Formerly called common fund basis and prior to that solicitor and client basis. See now CPR, r.44.4(1)(b), *McPhilemy v Times Newspapers Ltd (No.2)* [2001] EWCA Civ 933; [2001] 4 All E.R. 861.
[98] *Edenborough v Archbishop of Canterbury* (1826) 2 Russ. 93 at 112; *Att-Gen v Cuming* (1843) 2 Y. & C.C.C. 139 at 155; *Andrews v Barnes*, above; and see *Att-Gen v Holland* (1837) 2 Y. & C. Ex. 683.
[99] (1844) 13 L.J.Ch. 392, 394.

diture, it may well award costs on the standard basis only to a successful claimant,[1] or even no costs at all.[2]

A party personally interested in a charity is entitled to his costs of attending the subsequent proceedings in chambers, but he will not be allowed out of the charity funds costs of attendances at chambers in regard to matters in which he is not interested, and where the charity is not likely to derive benefit from the attendance of parties at chambers, and they have no separate or individual interest, they will only be allowed to attend at their own expense.[3]

Taxation of costs

Costs ordered as between parties are subject to the process of assessment, to ensure that no more is recovered than is reasonable.[4] The costs may either be assessed summarily by the judge hearing the matter or referred to a costs officer for detailed assessment. As between a party and his legal representatives, s.31 of the Charities Act 1993 empowers the Charity Commissioners to order that a solicitor's bill of costs for business done for a charity, or for charity trustees, or for trustees for a charity, shall be taxed by the taxing officer of any division of the High Court or of any other court having jurisdiction to order taxation of the bill. It is considered that the Commissioners may order the taxation of a bill either at the request of the charity trustees or of their own motion.

10–057

Breach of trust

In the event of an actual or threatened breach of trust an action may be brought by the Attorney-General or the Charity Commissioners[5] or by the remaining trustees or any person interested in the charity. The remedies available to the court include granting an injunction, ordering the trustees to account and appointing a receiver and manager. In addition the court has power to remove trustees of a charity.[6]

10–058

Injunction

An injunction may be sought to restrain a threatened breach of a charitable trust. In *Baldry v Feintuck*,[7] for example, an injunction was granted on the application of a student restraining the University of Sussex Students' Union (which was conceded in argument to be an educational

10–059

---

[1] *Att-Gen v Fishmongers' Co.* (1837) 1 Keen 492 at 501.
[2] *Att-Gen v Cullum* (1837) 1 Keen 104.
[3] *Re Shrewsbury Grammar School* (1850) 1 Mac. & G. 324.
[4] CPR, r.44.7.
[5] Charities Act 1993, s.32(1)(a).
[6] See paras 5–037, *et seq.*, above.
[7] [1972] 1 W.L.R. 552. See also *Webb v O'Doherty, The Times*, February 11, 1991.

charity) from applying funds to a charitable (but non-educational) organisation and to a political campaign of protest against the Government's policy of ending the supply of free milk to schoolchildren. An example of the Attorney-General seeking an injunction to restrain an impending breach of trust is *Att-Gen v Wright*[8] where the trustees of an educational charity were intent on disposing of charity property for non-charitable purposes.

Personal action

10–060   Proceedings may be brought against the trustees personally. It appears that the rules as to limitation, laches and aquiescence do not apply, at least where the Attorney-General is the plaintiff.[9] The court, however, as a matter of general law, is entitled to relieve a trustee wholly or partially from personal liability if it appears that he has acted honestly and reasonably and ought fairly to be excused for the breach and for omitting to obtain the directions of the court.[10] The burden is on the trustee to prove that he has acted honestly and reasonably, which is a question of fact, depending on the circumstances of the case.[11]

If the trustee is liable the question arises as to the extent to which he is liable to account. In determining how far accounts against trustees of charitable trusts should be carried back, the court is guided by the particular circumstances of each case. In cases of wilful misapplication it would appear that the period from which trustees must account is the commencement of the misapplication of the funds.[12] However, if it can, for example, be shown that the trustees were acting under mistake or ignorance, the account will normally be confined to a more limited period; and provided that the trustees have acted honestly, but mistakenly or ignorantly, this will apply whether the funds have been employed in attaining the objects contemplated by the trust by unauthorised means, or whether they have been employed for the attainment of objects not within the trusts at all,[13] or whether they have been retained by the trustees for their own benefit, as in cases where there is a bona fide question whether surplus income belongs to the donees beneficially or is applicable to charity.[14] In cases of this kind accounts are not, as a rule, carried back before the commencement of the action,[15] although in some cases of innocent or

---

[8] [1988] 1 W.L.R. 164. See also *Att-Gen v Ross* [1986] 1 W.L.R. 252.
[9] *Att-Gen v Cocke* [1988] Ch. 414 and see [1988] Conv. 292 (Warburton).
[10] Trustee Act 1925, s.61.
[11] See *Re Turner* [1897] 1 Ch. 536; *Re Stuart* [1897] 2 Ch. 583; *National Trustee Co. of Australasia Ltd. v General Finance Co. of Australasia* [1905] A.C. 373, PC; *Re Paulings' Settlement Trusts* [1964] Ch. 303; *Re Rosenthal* [1972] 1 W.L.R. 1273.
[12] *Att-Gen v Cashel Corpn.* (1842) 3 Dr. & War. 294; *Att-Gen v Davey* (1854) 19 Beav. 521 at 527; see *Att-Gen v Exeter Corpn.* (1826) 2 Russ. 362.
[13] See *Andrews v M'Guffog* (1886) 11 A.C. 313 at 314.
[14] See *Att-Gen v Wax Chandlers' Co.* (1873) 6 H.L. 1.
[15] *Att-Gen v Winchester* (1825) 3 L.J.(o.s.) Ch. 64; *Att-Gen v Corporation of Exeter* (1826) 2 Russ. 45 at 54; (1827) 3 Russ. 395; *Att-Gen v Stationers' Co.* (1831) 9 L.J.(o.s.) Ch. 229; *Att-Gen v Caius College* (1837) 2 Keen 150; *Att-Gen v Drapers' Co.* (1841) 4 Beav. 67; *ibid.* 19

ignorant misapplication, depending on the circumstances, accounts have been directed from the time at which trustees first had notice that the propriety of their application of the funds was questioned,[16] or from the date of the decree declaring the application improper,[17] or from the date of the last appointment of a new trustee.[18] Every case depends on its own facts, so that the court may even decide that no action at all should be taken, for example, when litigation would be expensive and little benefit would accrue to the charity because of the sum involved.[19]

In *Re Freeston's Charity*,[20] Fox J. (at first instance) ordered an account from the first annual accounting period after the commencement of proceedings where University College, Oxford, as trustee, had innocently appropriated one moiety of the endowment of the charity into a scheme amalgamating many of the trusts of which the College was trustee. The terms of the charity were that one half of the net income was to be paid to the original foundation (the Charity of John Freeston for Normanton Grammar School) and the remaining half to be retained by the College beneficially. Fox J.[21] pointed out that the court had a considerable discretion when dealing with charitable corporations which have acted mistakenly but honestly. The facts of each particular case had to be considered and in the present case the College, after the appropriation in 1950, had supplied the foundation with annual accounts which showed that the income was not being divided into moieties and that the College was receiving a larger proportion of the total income than the foundation. Further, the foundation did not notify the College of any claim until 1967.

The fact that the trustee is a corporation appears to increase rather than **10–061** diminish the disposition to construe its proceedings leniently.[22] Although in contemplation of law the identity of a corporation is preserved through the ages, it has been held that to deal with it as an individual trustee and to take accounts during the whole period of its trusteeship would, in fact, be to visit the present members with the sins of their predecessors,[23] and "the ruin of half the corporations in the Kingdom."[24]

Beav. 558; *Att-Gen v Christ's Hospital* (1841) 4 Beav. 73; *Att-Gen v Wax Chandlers' Co.*, above.

[16] *Att-Gen v Corporation of Berwick-on-Tweed* (1829) Toml. 239; *Att-Gen v Burgesses of East Retford* (1833) 2 Myl. & K. 35 at 37.
[17] *Att-Gen v Drapers' Co.* (1847) 10 Beav. 558 at 559, 560; *Att-Gen v Tufnell* (1849) 12 Beav. 35.
[18] *Att-Gen v Mayor of Newbury* (1834) 3 Myl. & K. 647.
[19] *Att-Gen v Shearman* (1839) 2 Beav. 107.
[20] [1978] 1 W.L.R. 120; affirmed [1978] 1 W.L.R. 741, CA.
[21] *ibid.*, at 130.
[22] *cf.* the liability of a corporate non-charitable trustee, such as a bank: see *Re Pauling's Settlement Trusts* [1964] Ch. 303.
[23] See *per* Lord Brougham in *Att-Gen v Mayor of Newbury, ibid.*, at 651; *Att-Gen v Caius College* (1837) 2 Keen 150 at 169; see also *Att-Gen v Balliol College, Oxford* (1744) 9 Mod. 407 at 409, 410; *Lord Provost of Edinburgh v Lord Advocate* (1879) 4 A.C. 823.
[24] *per* Sir J. Leach in *Att-Gen v Burgesses of East Retford* (1833) 2 Myl. & Cr. 35 at 37.

Receiver

10–062   In some cases the court will appoint a receiver and manager for a charity. Thus, in *Att-Gen v Schonfield*,[25] where there was uncertainty over the trusteeship and trustees of the Jewish Secondary Schools Movement as well as disquiet at the way in which the schools for which it was responsible were being run, the court appointed a receiver and manager on the application of the Attorney-General to safeguard the assets of the charity and to protect the educational welfare of the children attending the schools.

VISITORS

Nature of visitation

10–063   Visitation is a form of supervision over the internal domestic affairs of an institution. It is most commonly associated with corporations, but the Inns of Court, which are voluntary societies, are subject to visitation by the judges,[26] and a constitution or trust deed constituting an unincorporated charity can appoint a visitor of the charity.[27] Although visitatorial jurisdiction is of ancient origin, in recent years it has been commended as providing a practical and expeditious means of resolving disputes.[28]

The basis of visitatorial jurisdiction was set out by Lord Griffiths in *Thomas v University of Bradford*[29] who said:

> "The jurisdiction stems from the power recognised by the common law in the founder of an eleemosynary corporation to provide the laws under which the object of his charity was to be governed and to be sole judge of the interpretation and application of those laws either by himself or by such person as he should appoint as a visitor."

Before examining the powers and duties of visitors it is necessary to consider how and by whom corporations are visitable. Corporations are divided into ecclesiastical and lay, and lay corporations are divided into eleemosynary and civil.[30] Ecclesiastical corporations are those which exist for the furtherance of religion and for perpetuating the rites of the

---

[25] [1980] 1 W.L.R. 1182. As to the power of the Charity Commissioners to appoint a receiver and manager, see Charities Act 1993, s.18(1)(vii) and paras 9–044–9–045, above.

[26] *Rex v Gray's Inn (Benchers)* (1780) 1 Doug. 353; *R. v Visitors to the Inns of Court Ex p. Calder* [1994] Q.B. 1.

[27] *Herring v Templeman* [1973] 2 All E.R. 581, [1973] 3 All E.R. 569. On the other hand, it is not the practice to appoint a visitor when a charitable company is incorporated under the Companies Act 1985. A charitable company is not a trustee in the strict sense: *Liverpool and District Hospitals for Diseases of the Heart v Att-Gen* [1981] Ch. 193; but see para.3–046, above.

[28] *Thomas v University of Bradford* [1987] A.C. 795 at 825, *per* Lord Griffiths; *R. v Lord President of the Privy Council Ex p. Page* [1993] A.C. 682 at 703.

[29] [1987] A.C. 795 at 814–815.

[30] Shelf. Mortmain 22 at 23.

Church.[31] The ordinary[32] is generally the visitor of ecclesiastical corporations,[33] being so constituted by canon law,[34] but Royal foundations, free chapels and donatives are subject only to the visitation of the patron, whether the patron is the Crown or a subject.[35] The right of visitation of some hospitals which was originally vested in the Pope was regulated by statute.[36]

It has been said incorrectly of civil corporations that they are subject to no visitation: strictly the Sovereign is constituted by law the visitor of all civil corporations, and for this reason they were visitable in the Court of Queen's Bench; so that today in the event of a dispute between the corporation and one of its members the court can intervene.[37] Civil corporations exist for various temporal purposes. They include the Sovereign herself, municipal and commercial corporations,[38] the Universities of Oxford and Cambridge, and, for example, learned societies such as The Royal Society, The Royal College of Physicians and The Royal College of Surgeons.[39]

10–064

The corporate property of ecclesiastical and civil corporations is not by its nature subject to any trust,[40] and the court has, therefore, no more jurisdiction over it than it has over the goods of private individuals.[41] Ecclesiastical and civil corporations may, however, and frequently do, accept and hold property, not for their own corporate purposes, but upon special charitable trusts connected with those purposes, and such property is as much subject to the jurisdiction of the court (and similarly of the Charity Commissioners[42]) as is any other property held upon charitable trusts. Moreover, ecclesiastical and civil corporations, in so far as their property is applied for charitable purposes (for example, the advancement of religion or education) enjoy the fiscal relief granted to charity.

Eleemosynary corporations are those established for the perpetual distribution of the free alms or bounty of the founder to such persons as he

---

[31] 1 Bl. Com. (16th ed.) 470; *Att-Gen v St Cross Hospital* (1853) 17 Beav. 435 at 465. Churchwardens are not a corporation, but they are a quasi-corporation for certain purposes; see *Cripps on Church and Clergy* (8th ed.) pp.158–160.

[32] *i.e.* a person, such as an archbishop or bishop, who has, in right of his own office and not by special deputation immediate jurisdiction in ecclesiastical cases.

[33] Roll. Abr. 229 *et seq.: Birmingham School Case* (1725) Gilb. 178 at 180; *Re Hartshill Endowment* (1861) 30 Beav. 180; and see Cathedrals Measure, 1963, s.6.

[34] 1 Bl. Com. (16th ed.), p.479; *Reg. v Dean of York* (1841) 2 Q.B. 1; *Reg. v Dean of Rochester* (1851) 17 Q.B. 1. See now Revised Canons Ecclesiastical, Canon C18, para.4.

[35] Co. Litt. 344a; *Fairchild v Gayre* (1604) Cro. Jac. 63; *Appleford's Case* (1670) 1 Mod. 85; *Anon* (1699) 12 Mod. 232; *Patel v Bradford University Senate* [1978] 1 W.L.R. 1488.

[36] Ecclesiastical Licences Act 1533; Suppression of Religious Houses Act 1539. See *Att-Gen v St Cross Hospital* (1853) 17 Beav. 435.

[37] 1 Bl. Com. (16th ed.) 480 at 481; Shelf. Mortmain 324 at 325; *Rex v University of Cambridge* (1723) 1 Str. 557 at 564, 566; *Patel v Bradford University Senate* [1978] 1 W.L.R. 1488 at 1495.

[38] 1 Bl. Com. (16th ed.) 470.

[39] *ibid.*, at 471; *Rex v Vice-Chancellor of Cambridge* (1765) 3 Burr. 1652 at 1656.

[40] *Att-Gen v Brereton* (1752) 2 Ves. s.435; *Mayor of Colchester v Lowten* (1813) 1 V. & B. 226; *Att-Gen v Wray* (1821) Jac. 307; *Att-Gen v Mayor of Liverpool* (1835) 1 Myl. & Cr. 171, 201; *Att-Gen v St. John's Hospital, Bedford* (1864) 2 De G.J. & S. 621 at 635.

[41] *Att-Gen v Mayor of Liverpool*, above; *Att-Gen v St John's Hospital, Bedford*, above; and see Charities Act 1993, s.96(2).

[42] Unless it is an institution within Sch.2 to the Charities Act 1993 (which lists exempt charities).

has directed.[43] They are generally hospitals[44] or colleges, the difference between such institutions being only one of degree[45] and depending upon the character of the persons benefited by the charity. They include the colleges and halls of Oxford and Cambridge universities (though not the Universities of Oxford and Cambridge themselves, since these are civil, not eleemosynary, corporations)[46] and corporate schools.[47] Unlike ecclesiastical and civil corporations, eleemosynary corporations hold their corporate property upon charitable trusts,[48] and they are therefore subject to the jurisdiction of the court like any other trustee, corporate or incorporate, lay or ecclesiastical.[49] The constitution of the visitor of an eleemosynary corporation is considered below.[50]

10–065   An eleemosynary corporation, established by charter from the Crown, is subject to no further control by the Crown than that reserved to it by the charter. The Crown cannot, therefore, without the consent of the corporation, alter the charter; nor can it add to or diminish the franchises of the corporation, or the number of its trustees or members, or control its administration.[51] For the same reason the prerogative power of the Sovereign as *parens patriae* does not extend to charities regulated by charter.[52] When, however, an integral part of the corporation is gone, and the corporation has no power of restoring it or of doing any corporate act, the corporation is so far dissolved that the Crown may grant a new charter.[53]

Where a corporate charity is founded under letters patent from the Crown, the founder cannot make any alteration in it, either by engrafting new members upon it, or by subjecting the corporate property to any trust for any other person or purpose.[54] The founder may make "statutes" and reserve the power of alteration; the reservation of "legislative power"

---

[43] 1 Bl. Com. (16th ed.) 459; Shelf. Mortmain 23. "The term 'eleemosynary charity' covers all charities directed to the relief of individual distress, whether due to poverty, age, sickness or other similar individual afflictions. Whether the term extends further it is not necessary for me to decide, and I express no opinion on the point": *Re Armitage* [1972] Ch. 438 at 445, *per* Goulding, J.

[44] "Hospital" formerly had a meaning considerable wider than that which it now bears. See *Dilworth v Commissioner for Stamps* [1899] A.C. 99 at 107; *Moses v Marsland* [1901] 1 K.B. 668 at 671.

[45] *Philips v Bury* (1788) 2 T.R. 346, 353; *Colchester v Kewney* (1866) 35 L.J. Ex. 206.

[46] *R. v Lord President of the Privy Council Ex p. Page* [1993] A.C. 682.

[47] *Eden v Foster* (1725) 2 P. Wms. 325; *Att-Gen v Price* (1744) 3 Atk. 108.

[48] *Thetford School Case* (1610) 8 Co. Rep. 130b at 131a; *Lydiatt v Foach* (1700) 2 Vern. 410 at 412; *Att-Gen v Whorwood* (1750) 1 Ves.S. 537; *Mayor of Colchester v Lowten* (1813) 1 V. & B. 226; *Ex p. Berkhampstead Free School* (1813) 2 V. & B. 134; *Att-Gen v Wyggeston's Hospital* (1852) 12 Beav. 113; *Att-Gen v St. Cross Hospital* (1853) 17 Beav. 435 at 466; *Re Manchester Royal Infirmary* (1889) 43 Ch.D. 420 at 428; and see *Hume v Lopes*, [1892] A.C. 112.

[49] *Att-Gen v St. John's Hospital, Bedford* (1864) 2 De G.J. & S. 621; *Baldry v Feintuck* [1972] 1 W.L.R. 552.

[50] See para.10–068, *et seq.*, below.

[51] *Rex v Pasmore* (1789) 3 T.R. 199.

[52] Spence Eq. 588, n. (h); 2 Fonbl. 208.

[53] *Rex v Pasmore*, above. In this case the court also has power to apply the revenues *cy-près*. See *Att-Gen v Hicks* (1790) 3 Bro. C.C. 166n.; Highmore's Mortmain (2nd ed.) 336.

[54] *Att-Gen v Dulwich College* (1841) 4 Beav. 255. See *Att-Gen v St. Cross Hospital* (1854) 18 Beav. 475.

would include such a power.[55] It would appear that in the case of a royal foundation without any such express reservation the Crown has power to dispense with the statutes either for a specific occasion or generally.[56] The statutes are clearly subordinate to the letters patent or charter. Thus a power to alter the statutes does not include power to change the character of the foundation.[57] Where the number of members is not defined the members of an eleemosynary corporation may incorporate new members, provided that they do not make an improper use of their power.[58]

Jurisdiction

It was at one time considered that the jurisdiction of the visitor was lim- **10–066** ited to questions between members of the foundation and to the question of admission to the foundation.[59] The jurisdiction over questions of admission is well established[60] but it is now recognised that this is but one example of the visitor's jurisdiction extending over the interpretation and application of the internal laws of the foundation. The position was set out by Lord Griffiths in *Thomas v University of Bradford*[61] when he said:

> "The explanation for the visitor's jurisdiction extending in cases of admission and removal from office (amotion) to those who are not corporators lies in the basis of his jurisdiction, namely, as the judge of the internal or domestic laws of the foundation. It is because those laws invariably provide for the conditions governing admission to and removal from membership of the foundation and sometimes of offices of the foundation short of membership that jurisdiction in such matters lies with the visitor.
>
> It is a mistake to consider that the visitor's jurisdiction derives from the status of membership . . . That is . . . putting the cart before the horse. The jurisdiction derives from the visitor's position as a judge of the internal laws of the foundation, and he has jurisdiction over question of status because it is upon those laws that status depends."

The extent of the visitors jurisdiction can be seen from *Oakes v Sidney Sussex College Cambridge*[62] where the Vice Chancellor, Sir Nicolas

---

[55] *St John's College v Todington* (1757) 1 Burr. 158. See also *Rex v Cambridge* (1765) 3 Burr. 1656.
[56] *Case of Queen's College* (1821) Jac. 1 at 20, 21, 34.
[57] *Ex p. Bolton School* (1789) 2 Bro. C.C. 662.
[58] *Att-Gen v Talbot* (1747) 3 Atk. 662 at 675.
[59] See *Patel v University of Bradford Senate* [1978] 1 W.L.R. 1488 at 1495, *per* Sir Robert Megarry V.C.
[60] *Rex v Warden of All Soul's College* (1682) T. Jo. 174; *St John's College v Todrington* (1757) 1 Burr. 158; *Rex v St Catherine's Hall* (1791) 4 T.R. 233; *Ex p. Wrangham* (1795) 2 Ves. 609; *R. v Hertford College* (1878) 3 Q.B.D. 693.
[61] [1987] A.C. 796 at 815–816; see also (1994) 2 C.L. & P.R. 103 (P.M. Smith).
[62] [1988] 1 W.L.R. 431.

Browne-Wilkinson declined to follow the previous view[63] that the visitor of an Oxford or Cambridge college has jurisdiction to determine a dispute with a scholar (*i.e.* a member of the college) but not an ordinary student. The Vice Chancellor said[64]:

> "Contrary to some of the earlier authorities, the jurisdiction of a visitor does not depend upon membership of the body as such, but on whether the rights being claimed arise under the domestic law. True it is that the vast majority of claims arising under domestic law will be claims put forward by people in virtue of their membership of that body. But the exact nature of their relationship to the body is not decisive. The crucial question is, "Are they claiming rights under the domestic law?" If so, they are subject to the exclusive jurisdiction of the visitor to determine those rights."

He further stated[65] after considering the speeches of Lord Griffiths and Lord Ackner in *Thomas v University of Bradford*[66]:

> "It does not matter whether the plaintiff was a corporator, a member or anything else. His claim is a claim to enforce rights which he enjoys under the internal law of the charity, Sydney Sussex College, Cambridge. The correct operation of that law is within the exclusive jurisdiction of the visitor."

10–067   Since *Thomas v University of Bradford*[67] it is no longer correct to say that a visitor can have no jurisdiction in any matter governed by contract. In that particular case, because the entire dispute centred upon the question of whether the statutes, ordinances and regulations of the University were correctly applied and fairly administered the dispute was held to fall within the jurisdiction of the visitor and not the courts of law, notwithstanding that its resolution would affect the plaintiff's contract of employment.[68] Although s.206 of the Education Reform Act 1988 has the effect of removing disputes as to university lecturers' contracts of employment from the jurisdiction of the visitor, the general statement of law is still sound.[69]

The visitor does not have jurisdiction, however, where the dispute between a corporation and a member turns upon the terms of a contract which involves no enforcement of or adjudication upon the domestic laws

---

[63] See *Ex p. Davidson*, unreported, July 25, 1772; *R. v Grundon* (1795) 1 Cowp. 315; *Herring v Templeman* [1973] 3 All E.R. 569; *Patel v University of Bradford Senate* [1978] 1 W.L.R. 1488.

[64] *Oakes v Sidney Sussex College, Cambridge* [1988] 1 W.L.R. 431 at 441. See also *R v Council of Legal Education Ex p. Halstead, The Independent*, August 9, 1994.

[65] *ibid.*

[66] [1987] A.C. 795 at 816–817, 828.

[67] *ibid.*, and see also *R. v Lord President of the Privy Council Ex p. Page* [1993] A.C. 682 at 695 per Lord Brown-Wilkinson; (1986) 136 N.L.J. 567 (P.M. Smith).

[68] See *Thomas v University of Bradford* [1987] A.C. 795 at 821, *per* Lord Griffiths.

[69] See para.10–074, below.

of the foundation.[70] Similarly, the visitor has no jurisdiction where there is a dispute between a corporation and a third party who was not a member of the corporation at the time the contract was entered into.[71] The courts maintain their jurisdiction over trusts and any question of construction of the terms of the trust is a matter for the courts and not the visitor whose jurisdiction extends only to those matters governed by the laws of the foundation.[72] In the case of an educational institution which has no visitor, the court has no jurisdiction to intervene in matters of academic judgment, but has power to adjudicate upon questions of contract.[73]

Constitution

Constitution of the visitor of an eleemosynary corporation

The founder of an eleemosynary corporation has full power to make "statutes", *i.e.* regulations for his creation.[74] Hence, in the absence of any express appointment, it was formerly the law that an eleemosynary corporation was visitable by the founder or his heirs.[75] Now that descent to the heir has been abolished,[76] it is not clear who is visitor in default of express appointment by the founder. It is to be observed, however, that if the founder's heirs became extinct,[77] or could not be found,[78] or the heir was a lunatic,[79] the visitatorial power devolved upon the Crown.[80] It is, therefore, thought that the effect of abolishing descent to the heir has been to vest the power of visitation in the Crown. At all events, where a corporation has been founded by letters patent or royal charter, then the Crown is the visitor, unless a power reserved in the charter to appoint a visitor has been exercised, and the visitatorial functions are exercised by the Lord Chancellor on behalf of the Crown.[81]

10–068

---

[70] *Thomas v University of Bradford* [1987] A.C. 795 at 821.

[71] *Casson v University of Aston in Birmingham* [1983] 1 All E.R. 88 as explained in *Thomas v University of Bradford* [1987] A.C. 795 at 822.

[72] *Green v Rutherforth* (1750) 1 Ves. Sen. 462; *Ex p. Berkhamsted Free School* (1813) 2 Ves. & Bea. 134; *Att-Gen v Magdalen College Oxford* (1847) 10 Beav. 402; *Thomas v University of Bradford* [1987] A.C. 795 at 823.

[73] *Clark v University of Lincolnshire and Humberside* [2000] 1 W.L.R. 1988.

[74] *Philips v Bury* (1788) 2 T.R. 346 at 353; *Green v Rutherforth* (1750) 1 Ves.S 462 at 472; *Spencer v All Souls' Coll., Wilm. Notes* 163.

[75] *Sutton Hosp. Case* (1613) 10 Co.Rep. 31a; *Parkinson's Case* (1689) Carth. 93; *Anon.* (1699) 12 Mod. 232; *Birmingham School Case* (1725) Gilb. 178 at 180; *Eden v Foster* (1725) 2 P.Wms. 326; *Att-Gen v Gaunt* (1790) 3 Swanst. 148; *Att-Gen v Dedham School* (1856) 23 Beav. 350.

[76] Administration of Estates Act 1925, s.45.

[77] *R. v St. Catherine's Hall* (1791) 4 T.R. 233.

[78] *Ex p. Wrangham* (1795) 2 Ves. 609; *Att-Gen v Black* (1805) 11 Ves. 191 at 192; *Att-Gen v Earl of Clarendon* (1811) 17 Ves. 498.

[79] *Att-Gen v Dixie* 13 Ves. 519 at 533.

[80] See also *Att-Gen v Ewelme Hospital* (1853) 17 Beav. 336 at 381.

[81] *Att-Gen v Clarendon* (1810) 17 Ves. 491 at 498; *Att-Gen v Dedham School* (1857) 23 Beav. 350 at 356; *Patel v Bradford University Senate* [1978] 1 W.L.R. 1488 at 1491, 1492. As Sir Robert Megarry, V.C., pointed out in the last-mentioned case (at 1492), the rule that the Crown is the visitor when a power to appoint a visitor reserved in the charter has not been exercised may not have been present to the minds of the court in *R v Aston University Senate* [1969] 2 Q.B. 538. Compare *Casson v University of Aston in Birmingham* [1983] 1

In ascertaining who is the founder it is relevant that, where eleemosy-nary corporations are endowed with lands, the law distinguishes two meanings of the term "foundation". First, there is the abstract act of founding the institution, the *fundatio incipiens*, or incorporation. The *fundatio incipiens* may be directly effected by letters patent or Royal Charter or Act of Parliament.[82] It may also be accomplished by private individu-als acting under Royal licence.[83] The Crown may also grant by charter the right to create corporations indefinitely.[84] A corporation may exist by prescription.[85]

Secondly, there is the tangible property which the founder provides, the *fundatio percipiens*, or endowment. In this second sense the first gift of rev-enues is the foundation, and he who gives them is the founder. It is in this sense that a man is generally called founder of a college or hospital.[86] If the Sovereign and a private individual join in endowing an eleemosynary corporation, the Sovereign alone is the founder.[87] With respect to monas-teries, however, it was said that if a private person were the founder, he would not cease to be so, if the Crown subsequently endowed the foundation with large possessions.[88]

10–069   Some of the colleges at Oxford have from time immemorial been sub-ject to the visitation of the Bishop of Lincoln, in whose diocese Oxford formerly was. This can only be ascribed to their having formerly been regarded as ecclesiastical corporations.[89]

The founder may delegate his power of visitation either generally or specially.[90] Special visitors may be appointed for a particular purpose,[91] the office of visitor may be divided among several persons,[92] and visitors may be subjected to the control of a superior visitor who has power to remove them.[93]

Unless the power of visitation is expressly qualified by the founder it will be deemed to be a general power.[94] In *Oakes v Sidney Sussex College*

All E.R. 88, where Lord Hailsham of St. Marylebone, L.C. heard a petition, sitting on the Sovereign's behalf. As to the position of the Lord Chancellor when acting as visitor, see further para.10–077, below.

[82] *Sutton's Hospital Case* (1613) 10 Co.Rep. 31a. The Hospitals for the Poor Act 1597, which enabled all persons (which included a corporation) to found corporate hospitals and houses of correction for the poor, was repealed as obsolete by the Charities Act 1960, s.39 and Sch.5.

[83] *Sutton's Hospital Case*, above; *Ex p. Kirkby Ravensworth Hospital* (1808) 15 Ves. 305; *Att-Gen v Dulwich College* (1841) 4 Beav. 255.

[84] The Chancellor of Oxford University has this power: Bl.Com. (16th ed.) 474.

[85] *Birmingham School Case* (1725) Gilb. 178 at 180.

[86] 10 Co. Rep. 33; Shelf. Mortm. 323 at 324.

[87] Co.Inst. pt. 2, 68.

[88] *ibid.*; *Att-Gen v Dedham School* (1856) 23 Beav. 350.

[89] 1 Bl.Com. (16th ed.) 483.

[90] *Eden v Foster* (1725) 2 P.Wms. 326.

[91] *St John's College v Todington*, (1757) 1 Burr 158; *Bishop of Ely v Bentley* (1732) 2 Bro.P.C. 220; *R. v Bishop of Ely* (1788) 2 T.R. 290 at 328; *R. v Bishop of Worcester*, (1815) 4 M.&S. 415.

[92] *Att-Gen v Middleton* (1751) 2 Ves.S. 327 at 329. See also *Att-Gen v Talbot* (1747) 3 Atk. 662.

[93] *Att-Gen v Middleton*, above.

[94] *St John's College v Todington* (1757) 1 Burr. 158 at 200; *R. v Bishop of Worcester* (1815) 4 M. & S. 415 at 420; *Oakes v Sidney Sussex College* [1988] W.L.R. 431 at 442.

Cambridge[95] it was argued that the visitor of the College was a special visitor. The presumption in favour of a general power of visitation was applied by the Vice-Chancellor, Sir Nicolas Browne-Wilkinson who said[96]:

> "The argument as it was originally put forward was that, by reason of the various limitations on the capacity of the visitor of the college in this case, he was in some sense a special visitor and not seised of all the powers which are inherent in the status of a visitor of a charity. That in my judgment is plainly wrong. Viscount De L'Isle and his descendants are appointed 'the visitor'. Having been so appointed, in the absence of clear words cutting down his position from that which is normal, he will have all the powers of a visitor: namely, the power to visit and to adjudicate on all disputes arising under the statutes. The mere fact that, in certain respects, his powers are limited in the way they can be exercised—for example by committing to some other body in the first instance the right to determine questions with an appeal to the visitor—does not cut him down from being a general visitor to a special visitor. He remains a general visitor, but bound to exercise his powers of general visitation in accordance with those limitations which are imposed expressly in the statutes."

No special form of words is necessary for the appointment of either a general or a special visitor.[97] Lord Eldon considered that a power to determine disputes arising on the statutes might be construed as giving visitatorial power.[98] Similarly, if governors of a corporate hospital are appointed, the founder is presumed to have intended them to be visitors.[99] But this is not the case if the governors of a hospital are incorporated and the poor (that is to say, the beneficiaries) are not.[1] So long as the governors do not receive the revenues, the fact that they are the owners of the legal estate is no reason why they should not be visitors[2]; but in the case of a school of Royal foundation, the Crown was held not to have parted with the right to visit by appointing governors by letters patent and vesting the legal estate in them.[3] **10–070**

Powers and duties of visitors

The powers normally vested in the visitor of a corporation may be summarised as follows: **10–071**

[95] [1988] 1 W.L.R. 431.
[96] *ibid.*, at 442.
[97] *Att-Gen v Talbot* (1747) 3 Atk. 662; *Att-Gen v Middleton* (1751) 2 Ves.S. 327 at 328; *St John's College v Todington* (1757) 1 Burr. 158 at 201.
[98] *Ex p. Kirkby Ravensworth Hosp.* (1808) 15 Ves. 305 at 315; and see *Patel v Bradford University, Senate* [1978] 1 W.L.R. 1488 at 1497.
[99] *Birmingham School Case* (1725) Gilb. 178 at 180; *Att-Gen v Middleton*, above.
[1] *Birmingham School Case* (1725) Gilb. 178.
[2] *Att-Gen v Middleton* (1751) 2 Ves.S. 327 at 329.
[3] *Eden v Foster* (1725) 2 P.Wms. 325.

1. To appoint and remove the members and officers of the corporation of which he is the visitor;
2. To regulate the management of the corporation's property;
3. To determine questions of construction arising under the statutes of the foundation; and
4. To hear and adjudicate upon all claims and complaints concerning the internal laws and procedures of the corporation.

The ordinary duties of a general visitor include the election and removal ("amotion") of corporators, such as the master[4] or fellows of a college, the pensioners of a hospital,[5] or the governors,[6] the regulation of and rectification of almonries, the internal management of the charity,[7] and the removal of officers.[8] In *Re Christ Church*[9] the application of part of the unappropriated income of the college to increasing the stipend of a university professorship, the endowment of which was one of the objects of the foundation of the college, received the sanction of the Crown as visitor.

The duties of a visitor also include that of construing the statutes of the foundation. Thus, the questions whether travelling fellows of Wadham must be members of the college,[10] or whether a fellow of a college had a right to let his chambers, were held to fall within the cognisance of the visitor.[11] Other questions held to fall within his cognisance were whether the master of a hospital was bound to reside there,[12] or perform divine service,[13] or how a university should conduct its examinations.[14]

10–072 In all cases the visitor is bound and must be guided by the statutes regulating the charity. If he exceeds or departs from them, he acts without jurisdiction, and his act is a nullity.[15]

---

[4] The circumstances that the electors of a master of a free school had made two elections, both of which were declared by the Lord Chancellor, as visitor on behalf of the Crown, to be void, did not authorise the visitor himself to appoint the master; *Att-Gen v Black* (1805) 11 Ves. 191.

[5] *Att-Gen v Talbot* (1747) 3 Atk. 662; *Bentley's Case*, cited *ibid.*, at 668; *Philips v Bury* (1788) 2 T.R. 346 at 357; *Ex p. Wrangham* (1795) 2 Ves. J. 609; *Att-Gen v Clarendon* (1811) 17 Ves. 491; *Att-Gen v Archbishop of York* (1831) 2 R. & M. 461; *Ex p. Inge* (1831) 2 R. & M. 590.

[6] *Att-Gen v Dixie* (1801) 13 Ves. 519; *Cases of Grantham School* and *Richmond School* (1811) cited 17 Ves. 499. It seems that no court or visitor would inquire into the original eligibility of a person who has held the office of governor for a long time: *Att-Gen v Clarendon* (1811) 17 Ves. 499.

[7] *Ex p. Berkhamstead Free School* (1813) 2 V. & B. 134; *Att-Gen v Dulwich College* (1841) 4 Beav. 255; *Att-Gen v Magdalen College* (1847) 10 Beav. 402.

[8] *Whiston v Dean and Chapter of Rochester* (1849) 7 Ha. 532.

[9] (1866) L.R. 1 Ch. 526.

[10] *Att-Gen v Stephens* (1737) 1 Atk. 360.

[11] *Att-Gen v Stephens*, above.

[12] *Ex p. Berkhamstead Free School* (1813) 2 V. & B. 134; *Att-Gen v Smythies* (1836) 2 My. & C. 142. As a rule it is the duty of the master to reside, in order that he may personally perform his duties, but in *Re Hospital of St. Mary Magdalen, Colchester* (1843) 12 L.J.Ch. 375, the Lord Chancellor as visitor exempted the master from living in the master's house on the ground of ill health.

[13] *Att-Gen v Crook* (1837) 1 Keen 121.

[14] *Thomson v University of London* (1864) 10 Jur.(N.S.) 669, where the question was whether two gold medals could be given at an examination for the degree of LL.D.

[15] *Green v Rutherforth* (1750) 1 Ves.S. 462 at 472; *Philips v Bury* (1788) 2 T.R. 346 at 357, 358.

A visitor may not alter the statutes unless such a power is expressly given to him.[16] It is possible, however, that where this power is reserved by the founder it attaches itself to the office of visitor.[17] Contumacy against the authority of the visitor is of itself a sufficient ground for the amotion of a corporator, whether the statutes so provide or not.[18]

The power of adjudicating and giving relief upon complaints and appeals is incident to the office of general visitor.[19] "Whatever relates to the internal arrangements of dealings with regard to the government and management of the house, of the domus, of the institution, is properly within the jurisdiction of the visitor."[20] "Subject to any restrictions imposed by the founder, the visitor has a general jurisdiction over all matters of dispute relating to the status of the foundation and the internal affairs and membership of the corporation."[21] A special visitor has the power which the founder has conferred upon him and no more; and he cannot lawfully exceed any qualification of or limitations on his power imposed by the founder.[22]

The powers of the visitor fall to be exercised in an almost infinite variety of situations, and the mode of their exercise must necessarily be left to the discretion of the visitor, provided that he acts judicially. In some cases, the exercise of a merely supervisory jurisdiction may be the only proper exercise of visitatorial powers.[23] It may be an abuse of the power for the visitor to enter upon matters which, by the statutes of the foundation, are expressly left in the discretion of specially designated officers or members; for example, the appointment of examiners. It follows that if the visitor declines to interfere with their decisions on matters which depend on academic or scientific or other technical judgment, then it is impossible to say that he has committed any error of law, unless the decisions are so plainly irrational or fraught with bias or some other obvious irregularity that they clearly cannot stand.[24] An appeal will thus lie to the visitor if a discretion has been exercised by the members of a corporation from wrong, illegal or corrupt motives.[25]

10–073

The powers of the visitor were considered by Simon Brown J. in *R. v Committee of the Lords of the Judicial Committee of the Privy Council acting for the Visitor of the University of London Ex p. Vijayatunga*[26] and the

---

[16] *St John's College v Todington* (1757) 1 Burr. 158 at 201.

[17] *ibid.* As to the power of the founder to alter or dispense with the statutes, see above, para.10–065; as to when a dispensation will be presumed, see *ibid.*

[18] *Philips v Bury* (1788) 2 T.R. 346 at 357, 358.

[19] *St John's College v Todington* (1757) 1 Burr. 158 at 202; and see *Att-Gen v Talbot* (1747) 1 Ves.S. 78.

[20] *Thomson v University of London* (1864) 33 L.J.Ch. 625 at 634, *per* Sir Richard Kindersley, V.C.

[21] *Patel v Bradford University Senate* [1978] 1 W.L.R. 1488 at 1493, *per* Sir Robert Megarry, V.C., citing the passage referred to in note 20, above.

[22] *Philips v Bury* (1788) 2 T.R. 346 at 358.

[23] See *Thomas v University of Bradford* (No. 2) [1992] 1 All E.R. 964.

[24] *R. v Her Majesty the Queen in Council Ex p. Vijayatunga* [1990] 2 Q.B. 444. See also *Ex p. Inge* (1831) 2 R. & M. 590; *Ex p. Wrangham* (1795) 2 Ves.J. 609 at 625; *R. v Hertford College* (1878) 3 Q.B.D. 693 at 698, 699; *Att-Gen v Clarendon* (1811) 17 Ves. 491 at 507.

[25] *R. v Hertford College* (1878) 3 Q.B.D. 693 at 701.

[26] [1988] Q.B. 322 at 344–345.

following passage from his judgment was approved by Bingham L.J. on appeal.[27]

"I conclude therefore that the visitor enjoys untrammelled jurisdiction to investigate and correct wrongs done in the administration of the internal law of the foundation to which he is appointed: a general power to right wrongs and redress grievances. And if that on occasion requires the visitor to act akin rather to an appeal court than to a review court, so be it. Indeed there may well be occasions when he could not properly act other than as an essentially appellate tribunal. The difference between visitatorial and this court's supervisory jurisdiction may be illustrated thus. It will often be inappropriate for this court in the exercise of its review jurisdiction to investigate the facts underlying the legal dispute before it. Equally this court must from time to time leave undisturbed a decision on the merits which it believes to be wrong because it recognises that there is properly room for two views upon the point. But in my judgment there are no such limitations upon the visitor's jurisdiction: he may, indeed should, investigate the basic facts to whatever depth he feels appropriate and he may interfere with any decision which he concludes to be wrong, even though he feels unable to categorise it as *Wednesbury*[28] unreasonable."

Since the decision of the House of Lords in *Thomas v University of Bradford*[29] it is no longer correct to say that a visitor has no power to order the payment of damages. A visitor has power to redress any grievance that has resulted from the misapplication of the domestic law of the foundation. Such redress can include the ordering of payment of arrears of salary or compensation where appropriate.[30]

Limitations on jurisdiction

10–074   An important limitation on the jurisdiction of a visitor is the existence of a statutory provision which overrides it, whether expressly or by necessary implication. If the visitor's jurisdiction is excluded by statute the court automatically has jurisdiction as it is only the existence of the visitor's jurisdiction which excludes the jurisdiction of the court.[31] An example of a statutory limitation on the jurisdiction of a visitor is s.206 of the Education Reform Act 1988 which provides that visitors of universities

---

[27] *R. v Her Majesty the Queen in Council Ex p. Vijayatunga* [1990] 2 Q.B. 444 at 457.
[28] *Associated Provincial Picture Houses Ltd v Wednesbury Corporation* [1948] 1 K.B. 223.
[29] [1987] A.C. 795.
[30] *ibid.* at 828, *per* Lord Ackner. See also *Murdoch University v Bloom and Kyle* [1980] W.A.R. 193 at 198.
[31] See *Pearce v University of Aston in Birmingham (No. 1)* [1992] 2 All E.R. 461 at 467, *per* Nourse L.J.

shall not have jurisdiction in respect of disputes relating to the appointment or employment or termination of employment of academic staff.[32]

A visitor must not be judge in his own cause, unless that power is expressly given to him by the founder. Thus, in *R. v Bishop of Ely*,[33] the question was whether the Bishop of Ely, as visitor of Peterhouse, Cambridge, had a right, under the statutes of the college, to appoint as master his own nominee, instead of one of two persons nominated by the college. It was held by the Court of Queen's Bench upon the principle "that the same person cannot be the visitor and visited", that the power of deciding the question on the construction of the statutes devolved on the court, and it granted a mandamus to appoint one of the two persons nominated by the college. The fact that a visitor of the collge has sanctioned the conditions of donation of a fellowship, however, presents no obstacle to his hearing an appeal challenging the legality of the conditions.[34]

Where the general visitatorial power is suspended, the jurisdiction vests in the Supreme Court. Thus, where the visitatorial power of a bishop over a college was suspended by his becoming warden (for he could not visit himself), the Court of King's Bench assumed jurisdiction and issued a mandamus to the bishop to admit a fellow of the college.[35]

It is doubtful whether a college can accept an accession to its foundation without the consent of the visitor.[36] On the other hand the visitor of an old foundation has no jurisdiction over a new foundation annexed to it unless it is expressly given to him by the creator of the new foundation. The visitatorial jurisdiction, being the private jurisdiction of the founder, "cannot extend further, unless some other person grafts upon it, and by express words or necessary implication subjects the estate or emolument given by him, to the same visitatorial power, and to be governed by the same rules; and then the former visitor is a visitor created by that subsequent founder or donor."[37] Accordingly, the visitor of the old foundation will be visitor of the new if the donor of the new foundation expressly so directs. The same result will ensue if the subsequent donor simply gives the new estate to the old foundation without either creating a distinct visitor or a special trust. In such a case it is considered that the donor intended that it should fall under the general statutes and rules of the college, and be regulated with the rest of its property.[38] Most of the old colleges of Oxford and Cambridge are made up (more or less) of fellowships

10–075

---

[32] This provision is not effective in relation to any particular university until the new appeal procedure for that university is in force, s.206(2). For the effect of the intervening provisions when the court and the visitor have concurrent jurisdiction see *Pearce v University of Aston in Birmingham (No. 1)* [1991] 2 All E.R. 461; *Hines v Birkbeck College (No. 2)* [1992] Ch. 33.

[33] (1738) 2 T.R. 290 and see *Att-Gen v Middleton* (1751) 2 Ves.S. 329; *R. v Bishop of Chester* (1791) 2 Str. 797.

[34] *R. v Hertford College* (1878) 3 Q.B.D. 693 at 703.

[35] *R. v Bishop of Chester*, above; and see *R. v Bishop of Ely* (1788) 2 T.R. 290.

[36] *Att-Gen v Catherine Hall* (1820) Jac. 381 at 400.

[37] *Green v Rutherforth* (1750) 1 Ves.S. 462 at 472, *per* Lord Hardwicke.

[38] *ibid.* 472, 473; *Att-Gen v Flood* (1816) Hayes & J.App.xxi: *Ex p. Inge* (1831) 2 R. & M. 590 at 596, *per* Lord Brougham.

engrafted by indenture, all of which are considered as part of the old body, and therefore subject to the same visitatorial power.[39]

It was said by Lord Eldon that if the Crown were a visitor of a college, and an accession were made to it by a founder, who said there should be no visitor at all, the Crown would still be the visitor of the new foundation.[40] Where, however, a special trust is declared with reference to property given to a college, the jurisdiction of the visitor is excluded.[41]

Procedure

10–076   A visitor is not bound to proceed according to the rules of common law[42]; but he must always observe the forms prescribed by the statutes.[43] Except when there is a general visitation, any question for the visitor's decision should come before him by way of appeal.[44] Both upon a general visitation and upon a particular appeal the visitor must proceed *summarie simpliciter, et de plano, sine strepitu aut figura judicii,* that is, summarily, simply and easily, without the clamour and ritual of a judicial trial, but according to law and right.[45] If an appeal is exhibited to the visitor, he must take it, and he must inhibit all proceedings against the appellant until the appeal is determined.

The exercise of visitatorial power is a judicial act, and, like a judge, a visitor cannot determine without hearing the parties concerned.[46]

In the case of charities that are to be regarded as public authorities for the purposes of the Human Rights Act 1998, visitors adjudicating upon questions involving the civil rights of the parties may need to satisfy the requirements of the European Convention on Human Rights and, in particular, Art.6 (embodying the right to a fair trial).[47] There is as yet no decided authority defining the extent to which the Convention will impinge on visitatorial jurisdiction, but common sense and good practice both suggest that visitors should respect and give effect to the parties' human rights whether or not strictly bound to do so. At any rate where issues of human rights do not arise a visitor is not bound to hear the appellants personally, or receive parol evidence, and it is sufficient if he gives his decision after receiving the grounds of the appeal and the answer

---

[39] *Att-Gen v Talbot* (1747) 3 Atk. 662.
[40] *Att-Gen v Catherine Hall* (1820) Jac. 381 at 400.
[41] *Green v Rutherforth* (1750) 1 Ves.S. 462; *Att-Gen v Flood* (1816) Hayes & J.App. xxi.
[42] *R. v Bishop of Ely* (1788) 2 T.R. 338; and see *Att-Gen v Atherstone Free School* (1834) 3 Myl. & K. 550; *Re Dean of York* (1841) 2 Q.B. 1.
[43] Com.Dig. Visitor, C.
[44] *ibid.*
[45] *ibid.*
[46] *R. v University of Cambridge* (1723) 8 Mod. 148; *R. v Bishop of Ely* (1738) 2 T.R. 290 at 336; *R. v Gaskin* (1799) 8 T.R. 209; *Doe v Gartham* (1823) 8 Moo. 368. See also *R. v Aston University Senate* [1969] 2 Q.B. 538, where the court held that examiners had failed to observe the rules of natural justice in exercising their discretion, but declined to interfere on other grounds. The court does not appear to have considered whether the appeal ought to have been heard by a visitor rather than by the court.
[47] See the illuminating discussion in *Education and the Law,* Vol. 11, No.3, 1999, at pp.165, *et seq.* (T. Kaye).

to it in writing.[48] Ordinarily, he should summon the parties interested to appear before him,[49] but he need not do so if the facts of the dispute appear sufficiently from the documents.[50] The visitor can administer an oath and require an answer upon oath, but he must give a convenient time for an answer and also for the examination of witnesses.

A visitation made contrary to the statutes of the corporation is of no **10–077** effect. Thus, if by the statutes of a college a visitor is, unless called at the request of the college, to make his visitation but once in five years, a visitation within the five years, which is not made in pursuance of a special summons, is void; and any sentence passed by the visitor is void, as having been made without jurisdiction.[51] A visitor has, however, a standing authority at all times to hear the complaints and redress the grievances of individual members of the body; for although the formal visitation can only be made at fixed times, the hearing of appeals and redressing of grievances is still the proper function of the visitor at any time.[52]

The visitatorial power of the Crown normally is exercised by the Lord Chancellor[53]; but the Crown may also visit by special commissioners.[54] The application to the Lord Chancellor as visitor on behalf of the Crown is by petition.[55] The Lord Chancellor, in the case of an appeal to him as visitor on behalf of the Crown, is not bound to observe any particular form of proceedings; and the parties may offer for his consideration as visitor anything which they may think pertinent and proper.[56] He will not, however, go into the merits of the petition until he is satisfied that the Crown is in fact visitor.[57] If the Crown has any direct interest, the Attorney-General must appear on its behalf.[58]

The Lord Chancellor has power to give costs upon petitions to him as visitor on behalf of the Crown. Thus in *Case of Queen's College*,[59] Lord Eldon directed the costs of petitions to him as visitor of the college,

---

[48] *R. v Bishop of Ely* (1794) 5 T.R. 477.

[49] *R. v University of Cambridge*, above; *R. v Bishop of Ely*, above. For cases of the hearing of appeal by visitors, see *Spencer v All Souls' College* (1762) Wilm. Notes. 163; *Watson v All Souls' College* (1864) 11 L.T. 166. And as to the effect of long possession in influencing the visitor's decision where the rights are doubtful, see *Re Downing College* (1837) 2 Myl. & C. 642.

[50] *Casson v University of Aston in Birmingham* [1983] 1 All E.R. 88.

[51] *Philips v Bury* (1788) 2 T.R. 346, 348.

[52] *Att-Gen v Price* (1744) 3 Atk. 108; *Philips v Bury*; ibid.; *Patel v Bradford University Senate* [1978] 1 W.L.R. 1488 at 1493.

[53] Co.Lit. 96a; *Eden v Foster* (1725) 2 P.Wms. 326; *R. v St. Catherine's Hall* (1791) 4 T.R. 244; *Att-Gen v Dixie* (1801) 13 Ves. 519; *Att-Gen v Clarendon* (1811) 17 Ves. 498; *Casson v University of Aston in Birmingham* [1983] 1 All E.R. 88.

[54] Com.Dig. Visitor A.; *Eden v Foster*, above. See *Anon.* (1699) 12 Mod. 233; Shelf. Mortm. 333. For an example of the appointment of a senior judge to act for the Crown as visitor; see *Thomas v University of Bradford (No. 2)* [1992] 1 All E.R. 964 (Lord Browne-Wilkinson).

[55] *Ex p. Wrangham* (1795) 2 Ves.J. 609; *Att-Gen v Black* (1805) 11 Ves. 191; *Ex p. Inge* (1831) 2 R. & M. 590; *Re Queen's College, Cambridge* (1837) 5 Russ. 64; *Re University College, Oxford* (1848) 2 Ph. 521; *Att-Gen v Dedham School* (1857) 23 Beav. 350 at 356; *Patel v Bradford University Senate* [1978] 1 W.L.R. 1488 at 1492.

[56] *Case of Queen's College* (1821) Jac. 1 at 19.

[57] *Re Garstang Church Town School* (1829) 7 L.J.(o.s.) Ch. 169 at 172.

[58] *Case of Queen's College* (1821) Jac. 1 at 19.

[59] Jac. 1 at 47. See *Ex p. Dann* (1804) 9 Ves. 547; *Att-Gen v Master of Catherine Hall, Cambridge* (1820) Jac. 401 at 402; *Re Bedford Charity* (1818) 2 Swanst. 532.

relative to the election of president, to be paid out of the college funds. The power of the Lord Chancellor does not, however, extend to altering the general constitution of the trust.[60]

Control over visitors

10–078   Historically, the court had very limited control over visitors. The basic principle of non-interference was confirmed by the House of Lords in *R. v Lord President of the Privy Council Ex p. Page*[61] in which Lord Browne-Wilkinson said[62]:

> "In my judgment this review of the authorities demonstrates that for over 300 years the law has been clearly established that the visitor of an eleemosynary charity has an exclusive jurisdiction to determine what are the internal laws of the charity and the proper application of those laws to those within his jurisdiction. The court's inability to determine those matters is not limited to the period pending the visitor's determination but extends so as to prohibit any subsequent review by the court of the correctness of a decision made by the visitor acting within his jurisdiction and in accordance with the rules of natural justice."

Thus in the absence of a breach of the rules of natural justice or, now, an interference with human rights, the court cannot control the discretion of a governing corporation,[63] or trustees,[64] or any other particular authority[65] in matters as to which a discretion is given to them. Accordingly, such authorities are not accountable for exercise of their discretion in matters relating to the internal management of the institution.[66]

Similarly, the court will refuse to interfere in matters relating to the election or amotion of corporators such as governors,[67] or masters,[68] or fel-

---

[60] *Ex p. Bolton School* (1789) 2 Bro.C.C. 662.

[61] [1993] A.C. 682. The court has no jurisdiction over ecclesiastical duties connected with a charity, *Att-Gen v Smithies* (1836) 1 Keen 289 and see para.10–064, above.

[62] *ibid.*, at 700. See also *Coveney's Case* (1561) 2 Dyer 209a; *Att-Gen v Harrow School Governors* (1754) 2 Ves.S. 551; *Att-Gen v Dulwich College* (1841) 4 Beav. 255; *Att-Gen v Magdalen College Oxford* (1847) 10 Beav. 402; *Thomson v University of London* (1864) 33 L.J.Ch. 625; *R. v Dunsheath Ex p. Meredith* [1951] 1 K.B. 127 at 132; *Thorne v University of London* [1966] 2 Q.B. 237 at 242; *Patel v University of Bradford Senate* [1978] 1 W.L.R. 1488 at 1493.

[63] *Eden v Foster* (1725) 2 P.Wms. 326.

[64] *Att-Gen v Harrow School* (1754) 2 Ves.S. 551.

[65] *Att-Gen v Bedford Corporation* (1754) 2 Ves.S. 505; see also *Costabadie v Costabadie* (1847) 6 Ha. 410; *Inderwick v Snell* (1850) 2 Mac. & G. 216; *Hayman v Rugby School* (1874) L.R. 18 Eq. 28.

[66] See *Eden v Foster* (1725) 2 P.Wms. 326; *Att-Gen v Lock* (1744) 3 Atk. 164 at 165; *Att-Gen v Foundling Hospital* (1792) 2 Ves.J. 42; *Ex p. Berkhamstead Free School* (1813) 2 V. & B. 134; *Ex p. Inge* (1831) 2 Russ. & M. 590; *Att-Gen v Mosely* (1848) 2 De G. & Sm. 398; *Re Wilkes* (1850) 3 Mac. & G. 440.

[67] *Att-Gen v Clarendon* (1811) 17 Ves. 598; *Re Bedford Charity* (1833) 5 Sim. 578; and see *Att-Gen v Lock* (1744) 3 Atk. 164, as to the removal of almsmen; *Chelmsford Poor v Milmay* (1649) Duke 83.

[68] *Doctor Patrick's Case* (1662) 1 Lev. 65.

lows,[69] or students[70]; or as to appointments to university committees[71]; or as to the internal regulation of a school, the erection of buildings, or the appointment or removal of university lecturers,[72] schoolmasters,[73] or other officers[74]; or whether the usher of a school,[75] or master of a hospital[76] should be in residence or not, or whether the master of a hospital should perform divine service or not.[77] Nor has the court any jurisdiction to interfere with the conduct by universities and other educational establishments of their examinations or other assessments of their students provided the rules of natural justice have been complied with.[78]

Visitors are not free from all control by the courts; they are subject to what has been described as a limited judicial review jurisdiction.[79] Thus judicial review will lie in cases where a visitor has acted outside his jurisdiction or where he has abused his power or where he has acted in breach of the rules of natural justice.[80] Judicial review will also lie if a visitor refuses to exercise his jurisdiction. It seems likely that in cases involving human rights the courts will have to adopt a more interventionist approach than they have previously been prepared to do. The courts are undoubtedly public authorities for the purposes of the Human Rights Act 1998 (s.6(3)(a)), and as such it would be unlawful for them to act in a way which did not give effect to the parties' human rights (in particular, the right to a fair trial).[81]

10–079

If a person assumes to act as visitor without having jurisdiction,[82] or, having jurisdiction, exceeds its limits,[83] or proceeds contrary to his citation, or to the statutes, for example, by inflicting penalties not warranted by them,[84] his decision will be subject to judicial review and a prohibition

---

[69] *Rex v New College, Oxford* (1670) 2 Lev. 14; *Reg. v Hertford College* (1878) 3 Q.B.D. 701 at 703.

[70] *Patel v Bradford University Senate* [1978] 1 W.L.R. 1488.

[71] *ibid.*

[72] *Rex v Dunsheath, Ex p. Meredith* [1951] 1 K.B. 127; and see *Bell v University of Auckland* [1969] N.Z.L.R. 1029.

[73] *Att-Gen v Bedford Corporation* (1754) 2 Ves.S. 505; *Att-Gen v Clarendon* (1811) 17 Ves. 507; *Att-Gen v Dulwich College* (1841) 4 Beav. 255; *Att-Gen v Magdalen College*, Oxford (1847) 10 Beav. 402; *Whiston v Dean, etc., of Rochester* (1849) 7 Ha. 532.

[74] *Att-Gen v Lock* (1744), 3 Atk. 164.

[75] *Ex p. Berkhamstead Free School* (1813) 2 V. & B. 134.

[76] *Att-Gen v Smythies* (1836) 2 Myl. & C. 135.

[77] *Att-Gen v Crook* (1837) 1 Keen 121.

[78] *Thomson v University of London* (1864) 33 L.J.Ch. 625; *Thorne v University of London* [1966] 2 Q.B. 237; *Patel v Bradford University Senate* [1978] 1 W.L.R. 1488; *cf. R. v Her Majesty the Queen in Council Ex p. Vijayatunga* [1990] 2 Q.B. 444 at 458 where Bingham L.J. stated that the court "could not properly interfere with any exercise of discretion or judgment by the Committee unless of opinion that it was *wrong in law*." This would appear to be too wide a view of the House of Lords decision in *R. v Lord President of the Privy Council Ex p. Page* [1993] A.C. 682, see para.10–081, below.

[79] *R. v Visitors to the Inns of Court Ex p. Calder* [1994] Q.B. 1 at 40, *per* Sir Donald Nicholls V.C.

[80] *R. v Lord President of the Privy Council Ex p. Page* [1993] A.C. 682 at 704.

[81] For a detailed discussion of this topic see T. Kaye, *Education and the Law*, Vol.11, No.3, 1999, at pp.165 *et seq.*

[82] *R. v Bishop of Chester* (1791) 1 W.Bl. 22 at 23; *Whiston v Dean and Chapter of Rochester* (1849) 7 Ha. 558.

[83] *Bishop of Chichester v Harward* (1787) 1 T.R. 650 at 651.

[84] *Bently v Bishop of Ely* (1729) 1 Barn.K.B. 192.

will lie against him, even though there has been a submission to his jurisdiction as visitor.[85]

If a visitor has jurisdiction, a want of procedural correctness is not a ground for judicial review. Thus if a visitor in his capacity of special visitor cites a person to appear before him when he ought in strictness to have cited that person in his capacity of general visitor, he may proceed upon that citation and prohibition will not lie, because he has equal jurisdiction in either character.[86]

10–080   If no person appears who claims the visitatorial power (except a person who has long exercised it), the court will not grant a prohibition on the motion of a single fellow of a college, who suggests that the power is vested in another.[87]

Although a visitor is the proper judge of the private laws of a college,[88] yet the courts will interfere where the general law is in issue. Thus in *R. v St John's College*[89] where several fellows did not take the oaths required by the Oaths of Allegiance and Supremacy Act 1688, the penalty for which was the avoidance of their fellowships, a mandamus was issued out of the Court of Queen's Bench to the head of the college and other fellows by which they were commanded to amove them. The court will intervene where the rules of natural justice have not been observed by the visitor.[90] An order of mandamus will also be granted where the visitor has seriously misapprehended his function, for example, by sitting as a reviewing tribunal and not as an appellate tribunal.[91]

Where a person is clearly entitled to act as visitor, but either acts improperly or declines to act at all, a mandamus will be issued to compel him to exercise his visitatorial powers.[92] Thus a mandamus will be granted to compel a visitor to receive or hear an appeal.[93] The court can compel the visitor to hear the parties and form some judgment. The court will not compel the visitor to go into the merits, for it is sufficient if the visitor decides that the appeal has come before him too late.[94]

10–081   An order of mandamus will not be granted unless it appears clearly that the person refusing to exercise a visitatorial power is in fact the visitor.[95] Nor will such an order be granted to compel an officer, according to the duty imposed on him by the statutes of the foundation, to execute the sen-

---

[85] *Green v Rutherforth* (1750) 1 Ves.S. 462 at 471; *Re Dean of York* (1841) 2 Q.B. 1.

[86] *Bishop of Ely v Bentley* (1732) 2 Bro.P.C. 220.

[87] *Martyn v Archbishop of Canterbury* (1738) Andr. 258.

[88] *R. v Lord President of the Privy Council Ex p. Page* [1993] A.C. 682, see para.10–081, below.

[89] (1694) 4 Mod. 368. See also *R. v Gower* (1694) 3 Salk. 230.

[90] *R. v Bishop of Ely* (1788) 2 T.R. 290 at 336.

[91] *R. v Visitors to the Inns of Court Ex p. Calder* [1994] Q.B. 1.

[92] *R. v University of Cambridge* (1723) 8 Mod. 148; *Gunston v Dare* (1738) 1 West's Rep. t. Hard. 576; *R. v Bishop of Ely* (1788) 2 T.R. 290; *R. v Bishop of Worcester* (1815) 4 M. & S. 415; *Whiston v Dean and Chapter of Rochester* (1849) 7 Ha. 558.

[93] *R. v Bishop of Lincoln* (1785) 2 T.R. 338n. At one time there had been a doubt on this point: *Usher's Case* (1700) 5 Mod. 452; *Dr. Walker's Case* (1736) Lee's Ca.t.Hard. 212 at 218.

[94] *R. v Bishop of Lincoln*, above; *R. v Bishop of Ely* (1794) 5 T.R. 475.

[95] *R. v Bishop of Ely* (1750) 1 W.Bl. 52 at 58; *Brideoak's Case* (1714), cited 1 W.Bl. 58.

tence of the visitor, for to make an order of mandamus in such a case would involve an interference with the privileges of the visitor.[96]

The object of mandamus is to put the visitatorial power in motion, but not to interfere with the visitor's exercise of his power, which if exercised in good faith cannot be reviewed by the court.[97] Therefore, it has been held that the court will not order the restoration of a fellow,[98] or chaplain of a college,[99] a sister of a hospital, or Charterhouse pupils, or Bluecoat or other almshouse residents.[1]

Although the decisions of visitors are subject to judicial review, with the possibility of an order of *certiorari*, the court has traditionally declined jurisdiction to review a decision of a visitor on the grounds of error of law made by the visitor within his jurisdiction. The reason for the restriction on the courts' usual powers of judicial review was set out by Lord Browne-Wilkinson in *R. v Lord President of the Privy Council Ex p. Page* as follows[2]:

> "As the authorities which I have cited demonstrate, the visitor is applying not the general law of the land but a peculiar, domestic law of which he is the sole arbiter and of which the courts have no cognisance. If the visitor has power under the regulating documents to enter into the adjudication of the dispute (*i.e.* is acting within his jurisdiction in the narrow sense) he cannot err in law in reaching this decision since the general law is not the applicable law. Therefore he cannot be acting *ultra vires* and unlawfully by applying his view of the domestic law in reaching his decision. The court has no jurisdiction either to say that he erred in his application of the general law (since the general law is not applicable to the decision) or to reach a contrary view as to the effect of the domestic law (since the visitor is the sole judge of such domestic law)."

The House of Lords was concerned to retain the visitor's jurisdiction as a speedy, cheap and final answer to internal disputes. The extent to which the courts will be able to sustain this policy of non-intervention in cases raising issues of human rights following the enactment of the Human Rights Act 1998 is questionable.   **10–082**

When a person is deprived by a visitor who has not exceeded the jurisdiction conferred on him by the statutes of the foundation but has only made a mistake in regard to something within his power, the person so deprived has no right of action against the visitor and no right of appeal to the court. If, however, in his sentence the visitor has exceeded the

---

[96] *R. v Bishop of Ely* (1738) Andr. 176; and see *Dr. Walker's Case* (1736) Lee t. Hard. 212.

[97] *Att-Gen v Archbishop of York* (1831) 2 R. & M. 461 at 469, *per* Lord Brougham.

[98] *Dr. Widdrington's Case* (1662) 1 Lev. 23; *Appleford's Case* (1670) 1 Mod. 82; *Case of Warden of All Souls' College* (1682) Sir T. Jones 174; *Parkinson's Case* (1689) 3 Mod. 265. See also *R. v Hertford College* (1878) 3 Q.B.D. 693. As to whether it is a good return to a mandamus that the office is full, see 3 Q.B.D. at 704, 705. See also *Att-Gen v Atherstone Free School* (1834) 3 Myl. & K. 550.

[99] *Prohurst's Case* (1691) Carth. 168.

[1] *R. v Wheeler* (1675) 3 Keb. 360.

[2] [1993] A.C. 682 at 702.

jurisdiction given to him by the statutes, the person so deprived can maintain an action against him.[3]

The court has in all cases, whether the trustee is an eleemosynary corporation or not,[4] and whether there is a visitor or not,[5] jurisdiction to enforce the performance of the trust of the charity property and to redress breaches of trust.[6] Accordingly, governors who are entrusted with the management and application of the charity property are accountable to the court in respect of their dealings with the estates and revenues, whether they are invested with any visitatorial authority or not.[7] Thus where a grammar school had been converted to a school of a different type, and the school chapel into a chapel of ease, the court interfered to rectify the breaches of trust[8]; so also where the charity property had been let to one of the governors,[9] and where a person was collusively appointed master of a school to receive the salary without performing the duties of the office,[10] and where application of charity funds to non-charitable purposes was threatened.[11]

10–083   S.23 of the Endowed Schools Act 1869,[12] empowered the Charity Commissioners to insert into a scheme made by them all powers and provisions which might be thought expedient for carrying its objects into effect. The practice of the court was to treat such powers and provisions as a species of visitatorial jurisdiction and not to interfere with the exercise of jurisdiction by the Commissioners.[13] In schemes made under the Charities Act 1960 and 1993, however, the Commissioners, recognising that the court's jurisdiction is valuable for the charity and should not be ousted, have never purported to retain exclusive jurisdiction.

---

[3] *Green v Rutherforth* (1750) 1 Ves.Sen. 472; *R. v Bishop of Chester* (1791) 1 Wils. 209.
[4] *Green v Rutherforth* (1750) 1 Ves.S. 462.
[5] *Re Chertsey Market* (1819) 6 Price 261; *Att-Gen v Bedford Corporation* (1754) 2 Ves.S. 505; *Att-Gen v Clarendon* (1811) 17 Ves. 491. *Att-Gen v Mansfield* (1827) 2 Russ. 501; *Att-Gen v Lubbock* (1837) C.P. Cooper 5.
[6] *Daugars v Rivaz* (1859) 28 Beav. 233; *Att-Gen v Dedham School* (1856) 23 Beav. 350; *Willis v Childe* (1851) 13 Beav. 117; *Att-Gen v St Cross Hospital* (1853) 17 Beav. 435; *Baldry v Feintuck* [1972] 1 W.L.R. 552.
[7] *Eden v Foster* (1725) 2 P.Wms. 235; *Att-Gen v Lock* (1744) 3 Atk. 164, 165; *Att-Gen v Foundling Hospital* (1792) 2 Ves.J. 42; *Kirkby Ravensworth Hospital* (1808) 15 Ves. 314. See also *Hynshaw v Morpeth Corporation* (1629) Duke 242, and *Sutton Coldfield Case* (1637) Duke 663, where it was held that a commission might be issued under the Charitable Uses Act 1601 in cases of this kind notwithstanding the exemption from that Act of colleges, hospitals, and free schools, having special visitors appointed by the founders. But if special visitors were appointed to see the trusts carried into execution no commission could be issued under that Act, even where the visitors or governors were trustees; *Sutton Coldfield Case*, above.
[8] *Att-Gen v Mansfield* (1827) 2 Russ. 501.
[9] *Att-Gen v Clarendon* (1811) 17 Ves. 491.
[10] *Att-Gen v Corporation of Bedford* (1754) 2 Ves.S. 505.
[11] *Baldry v Feintuck* [1972] 1 W.L.R. 552.
[12] Repealed by the Education Act 1973, s.1(4) and Sch.2, Pt II. In *R. v Charity Commissioners* (1897) 1 Q.B. 407 it was held that the Charity Commissioners could not be compelled to decide questions arising out of a scheme made under the Endowed Schools Act 1869, although the scheme contained a clause enabling them to do so.
[13] *R. v Wilson* [1888] W.N. 12; *Re Hodgson's School* (1878) 3 App.Cas. 857.

OTHER AUTHORITIES

Charities are subject to supervision and control by a number of other authorities in addition to the courts and the Charity Commissioners. The Inland Revenue is now a very important agent for the control of charities and the powers of the Commissioners for Customs and Excise must not be forgotten. The restrictions on tax relief for charities introduced by the Finance Act 1986[14] have had the effect of making grant awarding charities far more concerned to ensure that the charities to whom they give funds use them for charitable purposes only. Many charities are subject to additional controls by other authorities because of the legal structure they adopt.

10–084

The nature of a charity's activities may mean that they become subject to the control of other authorities. Thus, charitable housing associations are subject to the supervision of the Housing Corporation: its consent is required to land transactions and it also has specific powers of monitoring and investigation,[15] which, where appropriate, may be exercised alongside the investigatory powers of the Charity Commissioners. Charities who provide specific services under contract for local authorities or health authorities come under the supervision of those authorities who are concerned to enforce the terms of the relevant contracts.[16]

The philosophy behind the Charities Act 1992 was said to be that charities should be accountable to the public who have put their money in the public domain.[17] A number of provisions introduced by that Act can be seen to be directed to increasing the public's awareness of charities and their activities and the effectiveness of the public as an instrument of monitoring and control, for example, by requiring the status of a registered charity to appear on its documents[18] and by allowing members of the public to obtain copies of the accounts of charities.[19] The media not only give support to charities by publicising charitable events and achievements but also assist in the control of charities by reporting incidents of abuse.[20]

Fiscal authorities

The Inland Revenue acts as a controlling and supervisory body over charities by virtue of its work in connection with claims for tax relief by both charities and donors. When a charity makes a claim for exemption from tax under s.505(1) of the Income and Corporation Taxes Act 1988 the Inland Revenue have power to call for books, documents and other records of the charity which relate to the claim to be produced to a tax officer.[21] In addition to the routine work of the Financial Intermediaries

10–085

---

[14] Now Taxes Act 1988, ss. 505, 506; see para.8–012, above.
[15] See Housing Associations Act 1996, Pt I.
[16] See [1991] Conv. 419 (Morris and Warburton).
[17] *Hansard*, HL, PBC, col.93 (1991).
[18] See Charities Act 1993, s.5 and see para.1–031, above.
[19] See *ibid.*, s.47 and see para.9–033, above.
[20] See [1990] Ch. Com. Rep., para.73.
[21] Finance (No. 2) Act 1992, s.28.

and Claims office, for example, in ensuring that the rules for Gift Aid have been complied with,[22] the Investigation Branch deals with tax evasion and tax avoidance which involve charities and, where necessary, court proceedings will be taken.[23]

The Inland Revenue can pass to the Charity Commissioners any information they discover about a charity which indicates that the charity has been carrying on activities which are not charitable or that the charity has been applying its funds for purposes which are not charitable.[24] The Charity Commissioners in many cases then carry out their own investigations in an endeavour to ensure that any liability for tax arising from breach of trust falls on the defaulting trustees and not the charity.[25]

The Commissioners of Customs and Excise have wide powers to enter premises and to obtain information and documents in connection with the administration, collection and enforcement of value added tax.[26] A charity does not need to be registered for VAT to be subject to the control of the Commissioners of Customs and Excise; the powers are exercisable if the Commissioners consider that an unregistered charity should be paying VAT. The Commissioners of Customs and Excise have the same powers as the Commissioners of Inland Revenue to pass information to the Charity Commissioners.[27]

Funders

10–086   Grant-making bodies distributing money to charity frequently impose stringent conditions, and reserve powers of supervision. Examples are the Millennium Commission (in respect of money raised by the National Lottery) and The Foundation for Sport and the Arts.

Registration bodies

10–087   Charities which are limited liability companies are subject to the supervision of the Registrar of Companies. Thus charitable companies have to file annual reports with both the Charity Commissioners and the Registrar of Companies[28] and notify the Registrar of any alteration to the company's memorandum of association.[29]

Charities registered as friendly societies are exempt charities but they are subject to the supervision and control of the Financial Services Authority. Annual returns including accounts must be submitted to the Authority. An inspector may be appointed to investigate the affairs of a society.[30]

---

[22] See para.8–031, above.
[23] See, for example, *IRC v Plummer* [1980] A.C. 896.
[24] Charities Act 1993, s.10(2).
[25] See [1987] Ch. Com. Rep., para.28.
[26] Value Added Tax Act 1994, s.58 and Sch.11, paras 10–13.
[27] Charities Act 1993, s.10(2).
[28] *ibid.*, s.45(5); Companies Act 1985, s.242.
[29] Companies Act 1985, s.6(1).
[30] Friendly Societies Act 1974, s.87; Friendly Societies Act 1992, s.65.

Charities registered as industrial and provident societies are also exempt charities but subject to the supervision and control of the Financial Services Authority Mutual Societies Section to whom an annual return must be made.[31] The Authority has power to appoint an inspector to examine the affairs of a society.[32]

[31] Industrial and Provident Societies Act 1965, s.39.
[32] *ibid.*, s.49(1).

CHAPTER 11

THE DOCTRINE OF CY-PRÈS

INTRODUCTION

It is a fundamental principle of the law of charities that wherever a clear **11–001** intention to devote property to charity is shown, and that intention is not confined to a particular form of charity which is initially impracticable, or a purpose which is illegal, effect must be given to it. The law distinguishes between the charitable intention and the mode of executing it and makes provision for the charitable intention to be carried into effect *cy-près*, that is to say, by substituting for the mode indicated by the donor another mode as similar as possible to the mode indicated.

The doctrine of *cy-près* will only apply to a gift if the objects of the gift are exclusively charitable and if the subject matter of the gift is certain and validly assured. Further, the property will only be applied *cy-près* if a *cy-près* occasion has arisen. Formerly, the only *cy-près* occasions were where the purpose in question had become impossible or impracticable to perform. The narrow definitions of "impossibility" and "impracticability" adopted by the courts severely restricted the application of the doctrine of *cy-près*; inexpediency or uneconomic circumstances were not sufficient. Although s.13 of the Charities Act 1960 added further *cy-près* occasions, the application of the doctrine is still limited. If the original gift fails *ab initio*, a further condition has to be satisfied before the property can be applied *cy-près* – the donor must have shown a general, as opposed to a particular, charitable intention. In the case of subsequent failure, there must originally have been an outright gift to charity if the *cy-près* doctrine is to apply. Even if a *cy-près* occasion has arisen, the charity property may only be applied for new objects following a scheme by the courts or the Charity Commissioners and the new objects must be as near as possible to the original objects.

In many cases where it is not possible to carry out the specified charitable objects it may not be necessary to turn to the doctrine of *cy-près*. The law takes a benevolent view of charity and what is apparently a failed gift for charitable objects may on closer examination be found to be valid. The fact that the objects are uncertain or that no mode for carrying into effect the donor's charitable intention has been prescribed will not cause the gift to fail.[1] A gift to a charitable institution which has apparently ceased to

---

[1] See para.1–018, above.

exist is, in many cases, saved either by construing it as a gift for purposes or by finding that the institution still exists in another form.[2]

The origin of the special favour thus extended to charitable gifts can now only be conjectured.[3] It has been supposed to have arisen from the fact that the rules of construction applied by the civil law have been followed in the case of bequests to charity.[4] The doctrine was evolved from the practice of the ecclesiastical courts and later of the Courts of Chancery which became binding on the Charity Commissioners when the scheme-making powers of the Court of Chancery were conferred on them by the Charitable Trusts Act 1860.[5] Whatever the true explanation of its origin may be, it is clear that the principle in question came into existence at a time when the doctrine of resulting trusts was little understood; otherwise the rights of the heir-at-law would never in all probability have been ignored.[6]

INITIAL FAILURE

11–002   Before any property can be applied *cy-près* in the case of a gift for charitable purposes, it must be shown that it is impossible or impracticable to carry out that purpose. In the case of a gift to an institution, which is not construed as a gift for the purposes of that institution, the property will only be applicable *cy-près* if the institution has ceased to exist or has declined the gift.

Gifts for purposes

11–003   When considering a gift for charitable purposes it must first be ascertained whether failure has in fact occured. It is not possible to give a definition of "impossibility" or "impracticability" but examples of common forms of initial failure are considered. Particular problems occur where only part of the gift fails.

---

2 See paras 11–014, *et seq.*, below.
3 It was at one time even said that if a testament *ad pias causas* was found cancelled and it was not known whether the testator had willingly cancelled it, the law with reference to such legatee would presume it to have been cancelled unadvisedly and would give effect to it: Swinb. (7th ed.) p.67; *Mills v Farmer* (1815) 19 Ves. 483 at 486. See, generally, Sheridan and Delaney, *The Cy-près Doctrine* and G.H. Jones, *History of the Law of Charity*, pp.1532–1827.
4 See Domat, Book 4, tit.2, s.6.
5 See now the Charities Act 1993, s.16.
6 See Nathan Report, Cmd. 8710, para.300. *Att-Gen v Johnson* (1753) Amb. 190; *Att-Gen v Mayor of Bristol* (1820) 2 J.&W. 294 at 307; *Mayor of Beverley v Att-Gen* (1857) 6 H.L.C. 310 at 319. In *Att-Gen v Mayor of Bristol*, above, Lord Eldon strongly expressed his disapproval of the principle; see also *Mills v Farmer* (1815) 19 Ves. 485 at 486, where Lord Eldon referred to *Moggridge v Thackwell* (1802) 7 Ves. 69 as "a case that, bound by precedent I decided as much against my inclination as any act of my judicial life." See also *Mayor of Lyons v Adv. Gen. of Bengal* (1876) 1 App.Cas. 91 at 113.

Ascertainment of initial failure

The initial impossibility must be clearly established. If the court is not **11–004** satisfied that the avowed object of the gift can never be carried into effect but that it may be possible to carry it into effect at some future date, though not immediately, the court will not in the first instance direct a *cy-près* application.[7] Thus in *Attorney-General v Bishop of Chester*[8] Lord Thurlow L.C. refused to allow a fund given to establish a bishopric in America to be applied for other objects, notwithstanding that it was said that there was not the least likelihood of there ever being such a bishopric.[9] Likewise in *Re Villiers-Wilkes*[10] money was bequeathed as a contribution towards the cost of financing a bill before Parliament for establishing a new see at Birmingham. Owing to opposition that particular bill was abandoned. Stirling J. held that the object had not necessarily failed, since it might be accomplished at some future time, as in fact it was. However, the judge indicated that the money might be applied *cy-près*.[11]

However, although the court is prepared to allow money given for a particular charitable purpose to be held in abeyance and to remain in court for a time to see whether the purpose will become practicable, it seems that the money ought not to be allowed to remain in court indefinitely.[12] It is considered, therefore, that the trustees of the will or other instrument of gift or the Attorney-General ought to keep the position under review and that if, after a sufficient lapse of time, having regard to the circumstances of the case, it appears certain or virtually certain that the purpose will never become practicable, application should be made to the court for directions as to whether the money is now applicable *cy-près* under a scheme or is subject to a resulting trust.[13]

The relevant date for determining the possibility or impossibility of the gift is the date on which the gift vests indefeasibly either in possession[14] or in reversion or remainder expectant upon the determination of a prior interest or prior interests in the subject-matter of the gift.[15]

There is an initial impossibility in any case where the gift is an immediate gift for charitable purposes and the court is satisfied that the particular purpose cannot immediately take effect, that it is not bound to take effect within any ascertainable period, and that it may never take effect at

---

[7] *Att-Gen v Oglander* (1790) 3 Bro.C.C. 166.
[8] (1785) 1 Bro.C.C. 444; *Att-Gen v Bowyer* (1798) 3 Ves. 714; *Society for the Propagation of the Gospel in Foreign Parts v Att-Gen* (1826) 3 Russ. 142.
[9] The fund was ultimately applied for a bishop in Canada: see *Re White's Will Trusts* [1955] Ch. 188 at 193.
[10] (1895) 72 L.T. 323.
[11] See *Sinnett v Herbert* (1872) L.R. 7 Ch. 232 at 240, *per* Lord Hatherley L.C.; *Re White's Will Trusts* [1955] Ch. 188 at 193, *per* Upjohn J.
[12] *Sinnett v Herbert* (1872) L.R. 7 Ch. 232 at 240, *per* Lord Hatherley L.C.; *Re White's Wills Trusts* [1955] Ch. 188 at 193, *per* Upjohn J.
[13] See the Charities Act 1993, s.13(5).
[14] *Re Slevin* [1891] 2 Ch. 236; *Re Geikie* (1911) 27 T.L.R. 484.
[15] *Re Soley* (1900) 17 T.L.R. 118; *Re Moon's Will Trusts* [1948] 1 All E.R. 300; *Re Wright* [1954] Ch. 347; *Re White's Will Trusts* [1955] Ch. 188; *Re Tacon* [1958] Ch. 477; *Re Woodhams* [1981] 1 W.L.R. 493; see also *Re Martin, The Times*, November 17, 1977.

all.[16] It follows that if by the time that a vested testamentary gift in reversion or remainder falls into possession it has become impossible to carry it into effect, according to the testator's directions or wishes, the appropriate form of inquiry is "whether at the date of the death of the testator it was practicable to carry the intentions of the testator into effect or whether at the said date there was any reasonable prospect that it would be practicable so to do at any future time."[17]

Examples of initial failure

11–005   It is common for a charitable gift to fail initially where there are insufficient funds, where no suitable site is available and where the gift is illegal or contrary to public policy.

11–006   **Insufficiency of subject matter**—When the amount of the gift is too small the intention of the donor will be effected so far as possible.[18] If, however, the amount or value of the gift is so small that the donor's intentions cannot be carried out even to a limited extent, the gift fails. If it is a testamentary gift, it is held on a resulting trust for the testator's residuary legatees or next-of-kin,[19] unless the court can on the construction of the will impute a general charitable intention to the testator, in which case the gift is applied *cy-près* under a scheme.[20]

11–007   **No suitable site available**—It is only possible to effect many gifts for charitable purposes if a suitable site can be found from which to operate. Failure to acquire a site either because no available site is suitable or because of inadequacy of funds will cause the gift to fail. Thus in *Re White's Trusts*[21] the testator made a small gift, of £1,000 consols, to a City company upon trust as soon as conveniently might be, and when a proper site could be obtained, to erect almshouses for the benefit of certain defined classes of poor people. He evidently appreciated that his gift might well be too small for this purpose, for he proceeded to express the hope that some other person, actuated by the same charitable feelings, would endow the almshouses. The company could not obtain a site, there was no reasonable prospect of its ever doing so, and in any case the company had no funds available to endow and maintain the almshouses.

---

[16] *Re White's Will Trusts* [1955] Ch. 188 at 192, 193, *per* Upjohn J.; and see also *Att-Gen v Oglander* (1790) 3 Bro.C.C. 166.
[17] *Re White's Will Trusts* [1955] Ch. 188 at 193, *per* Upjohn J., disapproving the form of inquiry directed by Farwell J. in *Re James* [1932] 2 Ch. 25 and apparently followed by Wynn-Parry J. in *Re Wright* [1954] Ch. 347; see also *Re Payling's Will Trusts* [1969] 1 W.L.R. 1595.
[18] *Att-Gen v Pyle* (1738) 1 Atk. 435; *Re Reed* (1893) 10 T.L.R. 87; *Rodwell v Att-Gen* (1886) 2 T.L.R. 712.
[19] *Re Packe* [1918] 1 Ch. 437; *Re Whittaker* [1951] 2 T.L.R. 955; and see *Re White's Trusts* (1886) 33 Ch.D. 449. See also *Re Henry Wood National Memorial Trust* [1966] 1 W.L.R. 1601 (provision of concert hall where the funds contributed were insufficient).
[20] *Biscoe v Jackson* (1887) 35 Ch.D. 449. See para.11–036, below.
[21] (1886) 33 Ch.D. 449.

Bacon V.C. held that the gift could not be applied *cy-près* but fell into residue. There was no general charitable intention.[22] A gift will also fail if the premises which the testator has left as the site on which the charitable purposes are to be carried out are unsuitable.[23]

Gifts illegal or contrary to public policy—If the prescribed manner of effecting a general intention of charity cannot be adopted because it is illegal or contrary to public policy, it may be executed *cy-près*. Thus a legacy for providing the inmates of a workhouse with porter, which was proscribed by the Poor Law Amendment Act 1834, was applied for their benefit in other ways.[24] And if there is a trust for accumulation which is void as infringing section 164 of the Law of Property Act 1925, as amended by section 13 of the Perpetuities and Accumulations Act 1964, the income will be applied *cy-près* if there is a general charitable intention.[25] But if the general intention is illegal or contrary to public policy, the *cy-près* principle does not apply, because the gift is not charitable.[26]   **11–008**

Failure of part of the gift

In some cases a *cy-près* application is required by reason of the impracticability of part of the trust declared by the instrument of gift. Examples of such are gifts dependent upon void gifts, and gifts upon impossible conditions.   **11–009**

Gifts dependent on void gifts—If the main part of a charitable gift fails it does not necessarily involve the failure of a subservient part, provided that there is a general intention to benefit the objects of the gift. For instance, a testatrix left a house to a society to be used as a home for widows and orphans of the clergy, and an annuity for a long term to maintain the home. The house had to be sold within a year from the testatrix's death, pursuant to the Mortmain and Charitable Uses Act 1891; but it was held that the capital value of the annuity should be paid to the society on its undertaking to apply for a scheme.[27]   **11–010**

It more frequently happens that the court regards the dependent gift as so intimately connected with the main gift that if the main gift fails, the other fails with it. Thus where before the Mortmain and Charitable Uses

---

[22] Compare *Biscoe v Jackson* (1887) 35 Ch.D. 460, where there was found to be no site available in Shoreditch for the soup kitchen which the testator had wished to establish, but the court contrived to find a general charitable intention. For a discussion of this case, see para.11–036, below.

[23] *Att-Gen for New South Wales v Perpetual Trustee Co. Ltd* (1940) 63 C.L.R. 209.

[24] *Att-Gen v Vint* (1850) 3 De G. & Sm. 704.

[25] *Re Bradwell* [1952] Ch. 575; following *Martin v Margham* (1844) 14 Sim. 230. As to the right of a charity which is the only residuary legatee to stop an accumulation when its interest is vested and indefeasible, see *Wharton v Masterman* [1896] A.C. 186; distinguished in *Berry v Geen* [1938] A.C. 574, which was applied in *Re Robb* [1953] Ch. 459 and *Re Wragg* [1959] 1 W.L.R. 922. And see s.14 of the Perpetuities and Accumulations Act, 1964.

[26] *Thrupp v Collett* (No. 1) (1858) 26 B. 125; *Habershon v Vardon* (1851) 4 De G. & Sm. 467.

[27] *Re Cunningham* [1914] 1 Ch. 427.

Act 1891, there was an invalid gift by will for the establishment or erection of an almshouse. or some other charitable institution, a bequest for its endowment failed with the principal gift.[28] In *Chapman v Brown*,[29] where there was an invalid bequest for building or purchasing a chapel, followed by a direction that any overplus should "go towards the support of a faithful Gospel minister," it was held that the intention was to provide a minister to officiate at that particular chapel, not to support a ministry generally. The whole disposition was accordingly held void.

Similarly, where the gift is confined to the accomplishment of a charitable purpose in connection with property not itself dedicated to charity, as where there is a gift to found a school in a particular house which the testator has omitted to devote to that purpose,[30] or to provide a master for a school, and maintain the inmates of almshouses, where neither the school not the almshouses have been given to charity,[31] the dependent gift will fail. There was also failure where there was a bequest to form a museum at Shakespeare's house, which belonged to private individuals.[32]

11–011   Where, however, a void charitable trust is superadded to a private trust, the private trust may be effected although the charitable trust fails. Thus where there was a bequest to provide a school house for the children and grandchildren of certain of the testator's relations and other children, with directions which pointed to a permanent charitable trust, the trust was permitted to be carried out for the benefit of the children and grandchildren (so far as the objects were not too remote), although the charitable trust was obnoxious to the Statute of Mortmain then in force[33] and failed, and it was held that so long as the school was open for the children and grandchildren other children also might be admitted.[34]

On the other hand, effect cannot be given to a particular direction in favour of individuals where it forms part of a charitable trust which fails. In *Grieves v Case*,[35] where there was a bequest to be laid out in land, the rents to be paid in certain shares to the ministers of two chapels by name for their lives, and on their deaths for the persons succeeding them as ministers of the same chapels, it was held that the life interests to the existing ministers, being given to them as such ministers and as part of the general scheme for providing ministers for the chapels, failed with the rest of the trust.

[28] *Att-Gen v Goulding* (1788) 2 B.C.C. 428; *Att-Gen v Whitchurch* (1796) 3 Ves. 141; *Limbrey v Gurr* (1819) 6 Madd. 151; *Price v Hathaway* (1822) 6 Madd. 304; *Smith v Oliver* (1849) 11 B. 481; *Dunn v Bownas* (1854) 1 K. & J. 596; *Green v Britten* (1873) 42 L.J.Ch. 187; *Re Cox, Cox v Davie* (1877) 7 Ch.D. 204; *Re Taylor* (1888) 58 L.T. 538. The doubts as to the decision in *Att-Gen v Goulding*, above, expressed in *Att-Gen v Winchelsea* (1791) 3 B.C.C. 379 and *Att-Gen v Boultbee* (1794) 2 Ves.J. 388 were dispelled by *Att-Gen v Whitchurch*, above.
[29] (1801) 6 Ves. 404. See also *Att-Gen v Goulding* (1788) 2 B.C.C. 428; *Att-Gen v Hinxman* (1821) 2 J. & W. 270; *Cramp v Playfoot* (1858) 4 K. & J. 479; *Hoare v Hoare* (1887) 56 L.T. 147; *Att-Gen v Hodgson* (1864) 15 Sim. 146.
[30] *Att-Gen v Lonsdale* (1827) 1 Sim. 105.
[31] *Hoare v Hoare* (1887) 56 L.T. 167. This case must be distinguished from one like *Re Mann* [1903] 1 Ch. 232 (cited para.11–015, below), where there was an overriding charitable intention.
[32] *Thompson v Shakespear* (1860) 1 De G.F.&J. 399.
[33] 9 Geo. 2, c.36.
[34] *Blandford v Thackerell* (1793) 2 Ves.J. 238.
[35] (1791) 4 Br.C.C. 66.

Impossibility or impraticability of a subordinate part of the gift—The **11–012** impossibility of a subordinate part of a gift does not entail the failure of the whole. If the main purpose can be effected independently of that which fails, the court will allow the trustee to disregard the particular directions which cannot be carried out, and to give effect to the intention as far as possible. Thus in *Brantham v East Burgold*[36] there was a gift for the distribution of bread to poor persons attending divine service and chanting a particular version of the Psalms which could not be used. It was held that the distribution of bread was the main object and that it must be carried into effect notwithstanding that the subsidiary purpose could not be carried out. A similar question arose in *Attorney-General v Boultbee*,[37] where a trust was created for the benefit of the vicar of P. for the time being, "if he should be there settled by the nomination and appointment . . . of the trustees." On the death of a particular vicar the trustees neglected for some months to recommend a successor, and the Lord Chancellor (the presentation being in the Crown) presented to the vicarage a person not nominated by the trustees. It was held that this person was entitled to the benefit of the trust. The donor, it was said, had two objects in view; (1) to augment the vicarage and (2) to secure to himself or his trustees the recommendation of the person nominated; and the primary purpose could not be allowed to fail because by the neglect of the trustees the secondary purpose could not be effected.

In *Glasgow College v Attorney-General*[38] a fund was given to maintain at Oxford scholars born and educated in Scotland who should have spent a certain time as students at Glasgow College, each student executing a bond to take holy orders, and not to accept preferment in England or Wales. The charity was made the subject of a scheme under which students were admitted to Balliol College from Glasgow College, without regard to their destination for holy orders or their return to Scotland.

Impossible or impracticable conditions—If the donor attaches an impossi- **11–013** ble or impracticable condition to the gift, it will fail. Thus, where there was a bequest to the Royal National Lifeboat Institution on condition that the Institution should construct and keep two tubular lifeboats at specified places and there was evidence that one of the specified places did not require a lifeboat, the court substituted another lifeboat station and further directed that the boat should be self-righting and not tubular.[39] Similarly, if it is a condition of the gift that particular persons, and no-one

---

[36] (1794), cited 2 Ves. 388.
[37] (1794) 2 Ves. 379; 3 Ves. 220. See also *Att-Gen v Leigh* (1721), cited 2 Ves. 389. Followed in *Att-Gen v Davis* (1870) 18 W.R. 1132 (Ireland).
[38] (1864) 1 H.L.C. 800; S.C. sub nom. *Att-Gen v Glasgow College* (1864) 2 Coll. 665. This charity also came before the court in *Att-Gen v Guise* (1692) 2 Vern. 266 and *Att-Gen v Balliol College* (1744) 9 Mod. 407. See also *Andrew v Merchant Taylors' Co.* (1802) 7 Ves. 223, where a doubt was expressed whether an arrangement transferring funds from Cambridge to Oxford was an application *cy-près*.
[39] *Re Richardson's Will* (1887) 58 L.T. 45.

else, should be the trustees and those persons cannot or will not undertake the office the gift will fail.[40]

Once a gift has failed because either a specified condition of the gift is impossible or impracticable to perform or because the trustees refuse to accept the trust subject to the particular conditions, the property will be applied *cy-près* if the condition was not essential to the donor's main object, that is, if the donor has a paramount charitable intention.[41]

Gifts for institutions

11–014   In the case of a gift to a charitable institution two questions have to be asked in order to ascertain whether failure has occured. First, was the object of the gift the institution or the charitable purposes associated with it? Secondly, has the institution in fact ceased to exist? The two questions are considered below in the context of gifts to non-existent institutions, to misdescribed institutions, to closed institutions and to altered institutions.

Gifts to non-existent institutions

11–015   Gifts of this kind are usually made by will. Where the object of the gift is a non-existent institution but the charitable purposes which the gift was intended to promote can be inferred from the will as construed by the court, the gift is applicable for those purposes under a scheme. But if on the true construction of the will the court concludes that the gift was to the named non-existent institution as such and not a gift for purposes, the gift fails *ab initio* and cannot be applied under a scheme.[42]

If it appears that no such institution as the donor has indicated has ever existed but the court is able to judge what were the purposes which the donor wished to effect, the gift is applicable *cy-près*. The particular form of charity may be inferred from the name or description of the institution,[43] or, if and so far as this furnishes no guide, from indications drawn from other provisions in the same will.[44] Where the institution mentioned has never existed, the court feels justified in assuming that the donor's intention was not confined to it,[45] and will accept even a small indication of the donor's intention as showing that a purpose and not a person was intended.[46] In such circumstances the court has applied *cy-près* gifts to "the society instituted for the increase and encouragement of good servants",[47] "the Clergy Society",[48] "the home for the homeless, 27, Red Lion

---

[40] *Att-Gen v Andrew* (1798) 3 Ves. 633; *Denyer v Druce* (1829) Taml. 32; *Reeve v Att-Gen* (1843) 3 Hare 191; *Re Lysaght* [1966] Ch. 191.

[41] See paras 11–027, *et seq.*, below.

[42] *Re Tharp* [1942] 2 All E.R. 358 (reversed in part on the facts [1943] 1 All E.R. 257).

[43] *Re Maguire* (1870) L.R. 9 Eq. 633.

[44] *Re Clergy Society* (1856) 2 K. & J. 615; *Re Knox* [1937] Ch. 109.

[45] *Loscombe v Wintringham* (1850) 13 B. 87; *Re Clergy Society* (1856) 2 K. & J. 615; *Re Maguire* (1870) L.R. 9 Eq. 633.

[46] *Re Davis* [1902] 1 Ch. 876.

[47] *Loscombe v Wintringham* (1850) 13 B. 87.

[48] *Re Clergy Society* (1856) 2 K. & J. 615.

Square",[49] "the North American Institution"[50] and "the Newcastle-upon-Tyne Nursing Home".[51] There is usually no difficulty in inferring a paramount charitable intention where a donor has given property to a non-existent institution but if there is a bequest to a non-existent charitable institution followed by a gift of residue to charity, the court cannot find a general charitable intention and apply the gift *cy-près*.[52]

A useful illustration of the court finding a gift for charitable purposes where there was a gift to a non-existent institution is the case of *Re Mann*.[53] In that case the testatrix had during her lifetime purchased some land in the village of M. which was conveyed to her in her own name. On this land she had erected a building which she called and was known as "the Mann Institute" and the building was with her permission used for purposes beneficial to the inhabitants of M. The building was not conveyed to trustees, nor were any trusts declared. In effect the testatrix herself was "the Mann Institute". The testatrix bequeathed £3,000 to the trustees of her will to be applied by them at their discretion for the benefit of the Mann Institute. Although the Institute had no legal personality and no trusts had been declared, Farwell J. construed the bequest as a bequest for charitable purposes, the trusts being to apply the money for the purposes for which the Mann Institute was founded, namely, the benefit of the inhabitants of M.[54]

Gifts to misdescribed institutions

In some cases the testator would appear to have had a particular institution in mind, and to have described it wrongly: these gifts are accordingly devoted to the institutions which the testator appears to have intended. Thus a gift to "the Guernsey Hospital" was divided between the two hospitals which existed in Guernsey.[55] Where there was a legacy to the school of C., and there were to the testator's knowledge two schools at C., it was divided between them.[56]

11–016

In *Re Songest*[57] the testatrix gave her residuary estate upon trust for the Disabled Soldiers, Sailors and Airmen's Association absolutely. No association of that name existed either at the date of the will or the date of the testatrix's death. The Court of Appeal was satisfied that she had had a general charitable intention and directed that the residue should be

---

[49] *Re Davis* [1902] 1 Ch. 876.
[50] *Thorley v Byrne* (1830) 3 Ha. 195n.
[51] *Re Knox* [1937] Ch. 109. See also *Re Hill* (1909) 53 S.J. 228.
[52] *Re Goldschmidt* [1957] 1 W.L.R. 524.
[53] [1903] 1 Ch. 232.
[54] See *Re Webster* [1912] 1 Ch. 106, a very similar case. Distinguish *Re Joy* (1888) 60 L.T. 175, where there was a gift to a society for united prayer for the protection of animals from cruelty. The society never had any legal existence; in effect the testatrix herself was the society. The purpose of the society not being charitable, the gift lapsed.
[55] *Simon v Barber* (1828) 5 Russ. 112. See also *Bennett v Hayter* (1839) 2 B. 81; *Wilson v Squire* (1842) 1 Y. & C.Ch.C. 654; *Bunting v Marriott* (1854) 19 B. 163; *Re Maguire* (1870) L.R. 9 Eq. 632; *Re Alchin's Trusts* (1872) L.R. 14 Eq. 230; *Re Songest* [1956] 1 W.L.R. 897.
[56] *Gibson v Coleman* (1868) 16 W.R. 892.
[57] [1956] 1 W.L.R. 897.

divided equally between two charitable institutions whose claims were equally balanced. The jurisdiction of the court to direct a division by way of scheme, if the Attorney General does not object, instead of giving directions for a scheme to be settled,[58] rests upon the jurisdiction to apply the gift *cy-près* if the donor had a general charitable intention.[59]

Institutions which have closed down

11–017   It is not unusual to find that a testator has made a gift to a charitable institution which was in existence when he made his will but which ceased to exist before he died. It is first necessary to ascertain whether the institution has wholly ceased to exist. The fact that the charitable institution has ceased to carry on some activities since the testator's will was made will not cause the will to lapse,[60] nor will the fact that its continued existence is precarious.[61] Where an institution has power to dissolve itself, however, and does so the institution ceases to exist and any subsequent gift to the institution will lapse unless the donor can be shown to have had a paramount charitable intention.[62]

If the institution has ceased to exist it becomes necessary to determine whether the gift was to the institution itself or for the general or specific purposes of the institution. In the case of a gift to the institution itself, the gift will be applicable *cy-près* if the donor had a general or paramount charitable intention.[63] But if the gift is to a particular institution carried on in a particular place and it is not possible to impute a general charitable intention the gift will lapse.[64] Where a testator makes a bequest to a very particularly described charitable institution for a very particular purpose and the institution ceases to exist between the date of the will and the

---

[58] Either in chambers or by the Charity Commissioners under s.16(2) of the Charities Act 1993.

[59] See [1956] 1 W.L.R. 897 at 901, *per* Lord Evershed M.R. Before the order had been drawn up another charity having a stronger claim than the other two had, as a result of the publicity given to the proceedings, come forward, and with the consent of those charities and the approval of the Attorney-General a new order was made for payment of the legacy to the third charity by way of scheme: see [1956] 1 W.L.R. 1311.

[60] *Re Bradfield* (1892) 8 T.L.R. 696; *Re Waring* [1907] 1 Ch. 166.

[61] *Re Roberts* [1963] 1 W.L.R. 406.

[62] *Re Stemson's Will Trust* [1970] Ch. 16. The same principles apply to an unincorporated association which is dissolved under powers contained in its own constitution—*Re Finger's Will Trusts* [1972] Ch. 286. Moreover, if the institution is incorporated, it will not be restored to the register to receive a legacy on a death after dissolution—*Re Servers of the Blind League* [1960] 1 W.L.R. 564.

[63] *Marsh v Att-Gen* (1860) 2 J. & H. 61; *Re Hutchinson's Will Trusts* [1953] Ch. 387 at 393; and see also *Re Bradfield* (1892) 8 T.L.R. 696; *Re Morison, The Times,* July 8, 1967.

[64] *Fisk v Att-Gen* (1867) L.R. 4 Eq. 521; *Re Rymer* [1895] 1 Ch. 19; *Re Goldney* (1946) 115 L.J.Ch. 137; *Re Slatter's Will Trusts* [1964] Ch. 512; *Re Stemson's Will Trusts* [1970] Ch. 16; *Re Finger's Will Trusts* [1972] Ch. 286; *Re Spence* [1979] Ch. 483; *Re Rowell* (1982) 31 S.A.S.R. 361 and see *Att-Gen for New South Wales v The Perpetual Trustee Co. Ltd* (1940) 63 C.L.R. 209, 225. See also [1972] Conv. 198 (R.B.M. Cotterell); [1974] Conv. 187 (J. Martin); [1964] Ch. Com. Rep., p.43, 44; *Re Ovey* (1885) 29 Ch.D. 560, which has often been cited as one of the cases justifying the proposition in the text is of doubtful authority: see *Re Hutchinson's Will Trusts* [1953] Ch. 387 at 392, 393, *per* Upjohn J. and *Re Roberts* [1963] 1 W.L.R. 406 at 415, 416, *per* Wilberforce J.

date of death, it can be difficult for the court to find a paramount or general charitable intention.[65] If the testator's directions in relation to the use of the property by the institution are precatory, the court is more likely to conclude that it was a gift for the purposes of the institution.[66]

In determining whether the testator's gift was to the institution itself or for the purposes of that institution, it is necessary to consider the form of the institution. In *Re Vernon's Trust*[67] Buckley J. considered that a gift to an unincorporated body is *per se* a purpose trust and, provided that the work of the institution is still being carried on, the gift will be given effect to by a scheme, notwithstanding the disappearance of the donee during the lifetime of the testator unless there is something positive to show that the continued existence of the donee is essential to the gift. However, if the gift is to a corporation, then prima facie it takes effect as a beneficial gift and, therefore, there has to be something positive in the will to show that it was intended to create a valid purpose trust.[68] Gifts to both types of body occurred in *Re Finger's Will Trusts*.[69] There were gifts by will to an unincorporated association, the National Radium Commission, and to an incorporated body, the National Council for Maternity and Child Welfare. Both had been dissolved before the testator's death. Goff J. held that the gift to the Commission was a valid purpose trust for the work of the Commission which was not dependent on its continued existence, and the fund could be applied under a scheme. The gift to the Council, however, failed because the testator could not be taken as intending that the gift could be applied for its purposes. Nevertheless, Goff J. held that, although the gift to the Council failed, the share of the funds applicable to the Council could be applied *cy-près* because the will as a whole manifested a general charitable intention.[70] The distinction between incorporated and unincorporated institutions in this respect may give rise to difficulties[71] but it should be remembered that a gift to a charitable company can be made subject to a trust for charitable purposes.[72]

A charitable company does not cease to exist when it goes into insolvent liquidation; it only ceases to exist when it is formally dissolved. Accordingly, a gift by will to a charitable company which is in insolvent liquidation at the date of the testator's death does not fail. Neuberger J. in

11–018

---

[65] *Re Harwood* [1936] Ch. 285; *Re Roberts* [1963] 1 W.L.R. 406 at 416; *Re Spence* [1979] Ch. 483. See also *Re Rymer* [1895] 1 Ch. 19 as explained in *Re Lucas* [1948] Ch. 424 at 427, *per* Lord Green M.R.; *Re Roberts* above at 415, *per* Wilberforce J. and *Att-Gen for New South Wales v Public Trustee* (1987) 8 N.S.W.L.R. 550 at 554, *per* Hope J.A. See para.11–035, below.

[66] *Re Broadbent* (Deceased), *The Times*, June 27, 2001.

[67] [1972] Ch. 300n. applied in *Re Finger's Will Trusts* [1972] Ch. 286. See [1972] Conv. 198 (R.B.M. Cotterell) and [1974] Conv. 187 (J. Martin) for valuable discussion of the effect of the rules of construction on failure of corporated and unincorporated bodies.

[68] *ibid.*, at 303. However, gifts to a charitable company may be made subject to trusts for charitable purposes. See para.3–045, above.

[69] [1972] Ch. 286.

[70] See *Re Stemson's Will Trusts* [1970] Ch. 16; and see also *Re Rowell* [1982] 31 S.A.S.R. 361 (where a general charitable intention was found in respect of a gift to an unincorporated body which had been wound up and had ceased to exist).

[71] *Re Finger's Will Trusts* [1972] Ch. 286 at 294.

[72] See para.3–045, above.

Re ARMS (Multiple Sclerosis Research) Ltd[73] recognised that gifts by will in such circumstances would mainly benefit creditors of the charitable company but he did not consider that sufficient grounds to construe the gift as being for the charitable purposes of the company rather than a gift to the company itself.

Institutions amalgamated with or absorbed in other institutions or reorganised

11–019   A bequest may be made to a charitable institution which at the date of the will has a separate and independent existence but before the testator's death ceases to exist as a separate and independent entity. The change may be effected by a scheme settled by the Charity Commissioners, by statute or by the charity itself under the terms of its constitution. It is also not unknown for charitable institutions to informally amalgamate or reorganise.

Regardless of the manner in which the change has occurred to the charitable institution named in the will, the first question is always to determine the true nature of the gift. If on the true construction of the will the gift was not a gift for the purposes of the institution because it was so correlated with the physical premises where the institution was located at the date of the will, the gift will lapse unless the testator had a general or paramount charitable intention.[74] Thus if the gift is for the upkeep of a particular institution at a particular place and for no other purpose, and between the dates of the will and the testator's death the institution has been closed down and its assets dealt with under a scheme made by the Charity Commissioners the gift will lapse.[75] So also if the institution is closed down and without any scheme or order of the Commissioners its assets are transferred to another institution carried on for similar purposes elsewhere.[76] If the gift is construed as an augmentation of the funds of the charitable institution, the fact that the funds have been transferred elsewhere will not cause the gift to lapse; the gift will take effect in favour of the charitable body presently administering those funds even if the purposes of the holding charitable body are different from those of the original institution.[77] If the gift is construed as one for the general or specific purposes of the institution[78] the gift will not lapse and, in the absence of the original charitable institution, a scheme will be settled applying the gift for those purposes.

---

[73] [1997] 1 W.L.R. 877 applying *Re Vernon's Trust* [1972] Ch. 300n.
[74] *Re Lucas* [1948] Ch. 424 at 427; *Re Hutchinson's Will Trusts* [1953] Ch. 387 at 393.
[75] *Re Pochin* [1948] Ch. 183n.
[76] *Re Goldney* (1946) 115 L.J.Ch. 337. It is doubted whether Roxburgh J.'s construction of the will which was before him in this case was correct; see *Re Glass* [1950] Ch. 643 and *Re Meyers* [1951] Ch. 534 at 540. It is submitted that *Re Rymer* [1895] 1 Ch. 19 which Roxburgh J. purported to follow did not justify his construction; see *Re Watt* [1932] 2 Ch. 243n at 245n. and *Re Roberts* [1963] 1 W.L.R. 406 at 415.
[77] *Re Lucas* [1948] Ch. 175. This construction could be said to defeat the testator's intention, see [1974] Conv. 187 at 193 (J. Martin).
[78] See para.11–017, above.

A scheme made by the Charity Commissioners or the court—So long as   **11–020**
there are funds held in trust for the purposes of a charity the charity continues in existence and is not destroyed by any alteration in its constitution
or objects made in accordance with law, as, for example, by a scheme[79]
under the old Charitable Trusts Acts, or the Charities Acts 1960 or 1993.
A charity having funds held in trust for its purposes cannot die. Its objects
can be changed either by the court in exercise of its own jurisdiction or by
schemes established by the Charity Commissioners[80] to whom Parliament
has entrusted that particular duty.[81] Neither the Charity Commissioners
nor the court can take an existing charity and destroy it; they are obliged
to administer it.[82] Therefore, if the Charity Commissioners make a scheme
whereby the endowments of the charity named in or designated by the
will, together with the endowments of other charities, are consolidated
and trustees are appointed and charitable trusts are declared, a legacy
bequeathed to the charity by a will made before the settlement of the
scheme will be payable to the trustees of the scheme if, on the true construction of the will, the bequest is a bequest by way of an addition to the
endowments of the charity.[83]

Even if a trust for the particular purpose for which the gift was made
has been inadvertently omitted from the scheme, the gift nonetheless takes
effect; but application should be made to the Charity Commissioners to
amend the scheme.[84]

A change made under a charity's constitution—There is no distinction in   **11–021**
principle between the alteration of the objects and name of a charity
founded as a perpetual charity under a scheme and a like alteration of its
name and objects by the trustees themselves in exercise of an express
power given to them by the rules and the trust deed of the charity.
Therefore a legacy given to a charity whose name and objects have been
lawfully changed by the trustees after the date of the will and before the
testator's death will still be payable.[85] But if the trustees only have power

---

[79] *Re Lucas* [1948] Ch. 424 at 426.
[80] Charities Act 1993, s.16(1).
[81] *Re Faraker* [1912] 2 Ch. 488 at 493, *per* Cozens-Hardy M.R.
[82] *ibid.* at 495, *per* Farwell L.J.; and see *Re Stemson's Will Trusts* [1970] Ch. 16 at 26, *per* Plowman J.
[83] *Re Faraker* [1912] 2 Ch. 488; *Re Lucas* [1948] Ch. 424. In the former case it seems to have been assumed without argument that the bequest was intended as an augmentation of the endowments and for the purposes of the designated charity. In the latter case it was argued that on the true construction of the will the bequest was for the upkeep of a particular home in a particular place, and Roxburgh J. held that this was the true construction: see [1948] Ch. 175. The Court of Appeal [1948] Ch. 424, differing from Roxburgh J., construed the bequest as a bequest for purposes, as an addition to the funds of the home: *cf. Re Spence* [1979] Ch. 483 at 487–490, per Sir Robert Megarry V.C. See also [1969] Ch. Com. Rep., paras 14, 15.
[84] *Re Faraker* [1912] 2 Ch. 488. At 495, Farwell L.J. said that there was in that case no ques-
tion of a *cy-près* application. It is considered that his Lordship was right. The designated charity had been for the benefit of poor widows and, as Farwell L.J., observed, there could be no *cy-près* application until there was a failure of poor widows.
[85] *Re Bagshaw* [1954] 1 W.L.R. 238.

to terminate the existing trusts and have no power to declare new trusts, a scheme is necessary.[86]

11–022 **Statutory re-organisation**—The same principle applies where charities are by statute amalgamated with or absorbed in other charities or otherwise reorganised. The principal recorded examples are those afforded by the reorganisation of the auxiliary forces of the Crown by the Territorial and Reserve Forces Act 1907[87] and the nationalisation and reorganisation of hospitals by the National Health Service Act 1946.[88]

By s.29 of the Territorial and Reserve Forces Act 1907, and an Order in Council made thereunder, on March 19, 1908, the volunteer and yeomanry units were transferred to the new Territorial Force; and by s.34 of the same Act and an Order in Council made thereunder, on April 9, 1908, the militia units were transferred to the Army Reserve. Accordingly, in *Re Donald*[89] Warrington J. held that the Act had not destroyed but had only reorganised the several units named in the will of a testator who had died in 1902. His Lordship held that the legacies to two named volunteer units and to one named yeomanry unit were payable to the several county associations established under the Act of 1907 on behalf of the units of the Territorial Force which then represented those units, and that a legacy to the commanding officer of the Northamptonshire Militia, for a purpose which he held to be charitable, was payable to the officer commanding the unit of the Army Reserve which then represented the Northamptonshire Militia.[90]

The same principle has been applied to hospitals nationalised and reorganised under the provisions of the National Health Service Act 1946. Thus in *Re Morgan's Will Trusts*[91] the testatrix gave her residuary estate to her trustees for the benefit of the Liskeard Cottage Hospital. It was admitted that the Passmore Edwards Cottage Hospital at Liskeard was the hospital that she had in mind. That hospital at the date of the will had property, investments, trustees, a committee of management and rules and regulations. During the lifetime of the testatrix the hospital buildings and investments vested in the Minister of Health under the provisions of the

---

[86] *Re Roberts* [1963] 1 W.L.R. 406.

[87] Repealed by the Statute Law Revision Act 1966, s.1 and Sched. Amalgamations of armed forces charities following the 1991 White Paper "Options for Change" for review of the Armed Forces are by schemes by the Charity Commissioners and not by statute, see [1991] Ch. Com. Rep., para.28; [1992] Ch. Com. Rep., para.52.

[88] Repealed by the National Health Service Act 1977, s.129 and Sch.16. See now as to trusts in connection with the statutory health service *ibid.*, ss.90–96 as amended.

[89] *Re Donald* [1909] 2 Ch. 410.

[90] In *Re Magrath* [1913] 2 Ch. 331 the testatrix, who had made her will in 1913, bequeathed a pecuniary legacy to Queen's College, Belfast. That college had been dissolved by statute and replaced by the Queen's University, Belfast. The case has been cited as an illustration of the principle applied in *Re Donald* [1909] 2 Ch. 410 and *Re Faraker* [1912] 2 Ch. 488. But it was, as Warrington J. pointed out, a clear case of misdescription, as was *Caldwell v Holme* (1854) 2 Sm. & Giff. 31, which the learned judge followed. For instances of the above-mentioned citation of *Re Magrath*, above, which it is suggested are misleading, see *Tyssen's Charitable Bequests* (2nd ed.), p.134, and *Sheridan and Delany on The Cy-près Doctrine*, p.11, n.29.

[91] [1950] Ch. 637.

National Health Service Act 1946, free from trusts,[92] and the old commit-tee of management was dissolved.[93] Roxburgh J. held that the money was payable to the Plymouth, South Devon and East Cornwall Hospital Management Committee duly constituted in accordance with the provi-sions of the said Act[94] to be applied by that committee for the purposes of the Passmore Edwards Cottage Hospital.[95]

Roxburgh J. appears to have based his decision on the words "for the benefit of the Liskeard Cottage Hospital," for he observed that the gift was not a gift to anybody, but for the benefit of the hospital, and he regarded those words as showing that the gift was a gift for the purposes, namely, the work which at the date of the will and also at the date of the death, was being carried on on the premises described in the will.[96] However, it may presumably be taken as settled law that a gift "to" a named hospital should prima facie be construed as a gift for its work.[97] If the gift was for the purposes of a particular hospital, nationalised after the date of the testator's will but before his death, and the hospital was not designated as a teaching hospital before July 5, 1948, the legacy was payable either to the Hospital Management Committee or to the Regional Hospital Board.[98] If before July 5, 1948, the hospital had been designated as a teaching hospital, the legacy was payable to the new Board of Governors constituted under the Act of 1946.[99] The legacy was an endow-ment within the meaning of the Act.[1] This was the case even where the gift was to a hospital in aid of its invested funds and it had no such funds before July 5, 1948.[2]

11–023

A hospital which was nationalised by the National Health Service Act 1946,[3] did not cease to be a charity.[4] Accordingly, where a testator had bequeathed a pecuniary legacy to a named hospital and a further pecu-niary legacy to the same hospital to build a library, if still a voluntary hos-pital and not taken over by the state, and give his residuary estate to the same hospital unconditionally, the two legacies failed but the gift of residue was good.[5]

---

[92] s.6(1) and s.7(4).
[93] *ibid.*, s.78(1).
[94] *ibid.*, s.11(3).
[95] The new Hospital Management Committee had power to accept and administer the fund: National Health Service Act 1946, s.59(1).
[96] [1950] Ch. 637 at 642, 643.
[97] *Re Glass* [1950] Ch. 643n., where Vaisey J. followed *Re Morgan's Will Trusts* [1950] Ch. 637; and see *Re Hunter* [1951] Ch. 190; *cf. Re Lowry's Will Trusts* [1967] Ch. 638.
[98] National Health Service Act 1946, s.6(1).
[99] *ibid.*, s.7(1).
[1] *ibid.*, s.10.
[2] *Re Meyers* [1951] Ch. 534. There is no distinction between gifts to hospitals which before July 5, 1948, were incorporated and gifts to hospitals which were not incorporated before that date. For legacies of testators dying before July 5, 1948, see National Health Service Act 1946, s.60 and *Re Kellner's Will Trust* [1950] Ch. 46.
[3] ss.6 and 7.
[4] *ibid.*, s.59.
[5] s.59; see *Re Frere* [1951] Ch. 27. Gifts may still be made to hospitals upon special trusts for special purposes, *e.g.* to endow a bed. The gift may be of a fixed amount: *Re Ginger* [1951] Ch. 458; applying *Att-Gen v Belgrave Hospital* [1910] 1 Ch. 73. Or the gift may be of such sum as shall be sufficient for the purpose: *Re Mills* [1953] 1 W.L.R. 554. "Endow" has a flexible meaning: see *Re Adams* [1968] Ch. 80 at 94 (a gift for endowment of beds for

11–024   A major re-organisation of the health service took place following the setting up of NHS Trusts under the National Health Service and Community Care Act 1990. The Act made provision for trust funds held by health authorities and special trustees of teaching hospitals to be handed over to new NHS Trusts.[6] The funds may be held by separate trustees.[7] The same principles apply to allow NHS Trusts to take gifts[8] to hospitals reorganised under the 1990 Act. Many charitable trusts administered in connection with health authorities were not registered and the Charity Commissioners conducted a review of all National Health Service charities[9] including those which had been informally amalgamated.[10]

Re Trustees of Orchard Street Schools[11] affords a further instance of a charity which was first reorganised under a scheme and later reorganised by statute. The original trust, declared in 1811, was to use certain lands and a school-house thereon as a free school for boys, and there was a gift over to another charity if the scholars should be reduced below a specified number or the school should be discontinued or rendered incapable of taking effect for two years. In 1820 the trustees introduced small fees and under a scheme made by the Charity Commissioners in 1868 provision was made for small weekly payments. In 1877 the London School Board took over the school under the Elementary Education Acts and the purchase-money was paid into court. The charity entitled under the gift over claimed the money in court on the ground of forfeiture. It was held that the forfeiture occasioned in 1820 was barred by lapse of time and that the variation of payments under the scheme had not caused a fresh forfeiture. The taking of the school property by the Board under its statutory power did not destroy the charity or bring the gift over into operation. The gift over was to take effect only if it was found impossible to settle a scheme. This was a strong case.[12]

It is relevant to observe that in none of the cases relating to the statutory reorganisation of a charity did the decision of the court depend on the existence of a general charitable intention on the part of the donor or testator.

---

paying patients in two hospitals, one of which had no paying beds because of lack of accommodation, and the other of which had no need for more fee-paying beds); *cf. Re Mitchell's Will Trusts* (1966) 110 S.J. 291 where a gift for the provision of four beds in a hospital for colliery workers was held to fail, apparently because the hospital was unable to guarantee that there would always be four beds available.

[6] National Health Service and Community Care Act 1990, s.8 as amended by Health Act 1999, Sch.4, para.79 to deal with the property of primary care trusts.

[7] *ibid.*, s.11.

[8] NHS Trusts have specific power to accept gifts of money, land or other property for the specific purposes of the trust, NHS and Community Care Act 1990, Sch.2, para.16(1)(c).

[9] [1992] Ch. Com. Rep., para.68; [1994] Ch. Com. Rep., p.7; [1996] Ch. Com. Rep., paras 94, *et seq.* See Charity Commissioners, *NHS Charitable Funds: A Guide* (1996–97).

[10] See para.11–025, below.

[11] [1878] W.N. 211.

[12] See *Re Hanbey's Will Trusts* [1956] Ch. 264 at 273, *per* Danckwerts J. *Re Talbot* [1933] Ch. 895 (explained by Evershed M.R. in *Gibson v South American Stores (Gath & Chaves) Ltd.* [1950] Ch. 177 at 202) was a case in which the trusts declared by the will of a testator who belonged to the denomination known as "the United Methodists" were modified by statute, by s.18 of the Methodist Church Union Act 1929 (repealed and partly re-enacted by the Methodist Church Act 1976).

Informal amalgamation, absorption or reorganisation—In the absence of an express power the trustees or governing body of a charity which is in form perpetual cannot destroy the charity; and they ought never to deal with the funds and property of which they are trustees in any manner not authorised by the terms of their trust without the authority of a scheme. However, informal changes in the constitutions of charities do occur.

11–025

The underlying principle of the cases which will be referred to seems to be that if neither the court nor the Charity Commissioners can destroy a charity, neither can the trustees or the governing body.

It was held in *Re Joy*[13] that if a legacy is given to charity A and another legacy is given to charity B and the two charities, which had similar objects, have amalgamated informally after the date of the will but before the testator's death, the united charity will be entitled to both legacies.

Again, where a legacy was given to charity A, which, after the date of the last codicil confirming the will but before the testator's death, had amalgamated with charity B (having like objects) and the combined charity had assumed a new name, the combined charity was held to be entitled to a pecuniary legacy bequeathed to charity A.[14] There was evidence that the testatrix had subscribed to the combined charity.

In the cases referred to the gift was a gift for purposes which were still being carried out at the death of the testatrix though the trust machinery had been informally changed. This was also the state of affairs in *Re Watt*.[15] There the testator, a clergyman who died in 1929, had by his will made in 1925 bequeathed a share of residue to a charity which he described incorrectly but which was held to mean the Southwark Diocesan and South London Church Fund. A few months before the testator's death a new body had been incorporated for the purpose of taking over the assets of the fund from the existing trustees and for continuing the work of the fund, and the fund's property was transferred to the new body. Being satisfied that the gift was for purposes which were still being carried out, the Court of Appeal upheld it. No scheme was directed. There was clearly no question of a general charitable intention. Similarly, in *Re Withall*[16] the legatee was the Margate Cottage Hospital, the trustees of which after the date of the will but before the testatrix's death had closed the hospital and transferred its asset to a new hospital the Margate and District General Hospital. Clauson J. held this to be entitled to the gift. The purposes of both hospitals were the same and the gift was upheld as a trust for purposes.[17]

11–026

The facts in *Re Hutchinson's Will Trusts*[18] were very similar, but there the trustees, with the approval of the Minister of Health, had closed down

[13] (1888) 60 L.T. 175 (Chitty J.). The legatees which amalgamated were the Anti-Vivisection Society and the International Anti-Vivisection Society. In 1888 both societies were mistakenly believed to be charities: see *National Anti-Vivisection Society v Inland Revenue Commissioners* [1948] A.C. 31, overruling *Re Foveaux* [1895] 2 Ch. 501 (also decided by Chitty J.).

[14] *Re Pritt* (1915) 113 L.T. 136; and see also *Re Dawson's Will Trusts* [1957] 1 W.L.R. 391.

[15] [1932] 2 Ch. 243n.

[16] [1932] 2 Ch. 236.

[17] It is submitted that *Re Withall* should have been followed in *Re Goldney* [1946] 115 L.J. 337.

[18] [1953] Ch. 387.

the hospital designated in the will in anticipation of the enactment of the National Health Service Act, 1946, no scheme having been made. The Hospital Management Committee succeeded in its claim to the legacy; but Upjohn J., who applied *Re Faraker*,[19] *Re Lucas*[20] and *Re Withall*,[21] suggested that a scheme approved by the court or the Charity Commissioners might be necessary to enable the Committee to give a good receipt for the gift.[22]

It would appear that, as a rule, in cases where there has been an informal amalgamation or absorption or reorganisation a scheme is either necessary or desirable, even though in most of the cases so far referred to no scheme was required. This was the opinion of Wilberforce J. in *Re Roberts*,[23] where the assets of a charity which the trustees had discontinued under an express power to discontinue had been transferred by the trustees to another charity in purported exercise of a non-existent power to transfer the assets to the other charity. The judge upheld the bequest of residue as a bequest for the purposes of the discontinued institution and directed a scheme.[24]

It sometimes happens that a charitable institution which existed at the date of the will is divided into two before the testator's death. This is the converse of the cases which have just been considered. The divided institution does not cease to exist, but a legacy bequeathed to such institutions is divided between the two institutions, though not necessarily in equal shares.[25]

THE GENERAL OR PARAMOUNT CHARITABLE INTENTION

11–027   Where a gift fails *ab initio* whether by reason of the failure of the purpose itself[26] or of the institution to which the property is given,[27] the property can only be applied *cy-près* if the donor has shown a general or paramount charitable intention. The requirement of a general or paramount charitable intention is irrelevant in the case of a subsequent failure of a gift for charitable purposes—what is relevant then is whether there has been an outright gift of the property to charity.[28] The question of whether a donor had a general or paramount charitable intention is a question for the court of the construction of the relevant instrument. Whilst the courts have never laid down precise rules for the ascertainment of the donor's intention, it is now possible to differentiate two methods of

---

[19] [1912] 2 Ch. 488.
[20] [1948] Ch. 424.
[21] [1932] 2 Ch. 236.
[22] See [1953] Ch. 387 at 394.
[23] [1963] 1 W.L.R. 406.
[24] *Re Wedgwood* [1914] 2 Ch. 245 and *Re Dawson's Will Trusts* [1957] 1 W.L.R. 391 do not appear to have been cited. If they had been, they would have supported Wilberforce J.'s opinion that a scheme was required.
[25] *Re Wilson* (1909) 25 T.L.R. 465.
[26] See paras 11–002, *et seq*., above.
[27] See paras 11–014, *et seq*., above.
[28] See para.11–051, below.

approach. The older, or broader, approach seeks to find a general charitable intention beyond the particular mode or institution specified whereas the newer, or narrower, approach seeks to ascertain whether removal or modification of the conditions laid down by the donor would frustrate his plan or object. In view of the lack of clear guidance it is helpful to consider the history of general or paramount intention and the courts' approach in individual cases.

In the case of initial failure, if on the construction of the instrument of gift, it is possible to impute a general or paramount charitable intention, the property can be applied under a scheme. If, on the other hand, at the time of the gift the court is unable to infer a general or paramount charitable intention, it imputes to the donor the intention that, if his gift cannot be applied as he has directed, it shall wholly fail *ab initio* with all the legal consequences of such initial failure.[29] The legal consequences are that the property comprised in the gift which has failed *ab initio* is held on a resulting trust which arises by operation of law when the expectation of the donor, that the trust which he has created will absorb the whole fund, is for some reason cheated.[30] It is an inference of law based on after-knowledge of the event.[31]

Definition of general or paramount charitable intention

Although the doctrine of the general charitable intention had been evolved substantially in its modern form by the end of the eighteenth century,[32] the courts appear to have found it exceedingly difficult to frame a precise and accurate definition of the expression. It is certainly less difficult to indicate the characteristics of a general or paramount intention than to define it. Confusion can also arise because some cases refer to the necessity for the donor to have a general charitable intention whereas others refer to the need for a paramount charitable intention. What is certainly not required is an intention to benefit charity generally.[33] The courts often find a general, that is to say, a paramount or overriding, charitable intention in cases where the donor has given funds or property for a specific charitable purpose and has indicated with some degree of particularity the mode in which he desires his gift to be applied. It is perhaps,

11–028

---

[29] *Att-Gen v Bishop of Oxford* (1786) 1 Bro.C.C. 444n.; *Att-Gen v Goulding* (1788) 2 Bro.C.C. 427; *Att-Gen v Whitchurch* (1796) 3 Ves. 141; *Corbyn v French* (1799) 4 Ves. 418; *Cherry v Mott* (1835) 1 My. & Cr. 123; *Clark v Taylor* (1853) 1 Dr. 642; *Langford v Gowland* (1862) 3 Giff. 617; *Mackeown v Ardagh* (1876) L.R. 10 Eq. 445; *Re Rymer* [1895] 1 Ch. 19; *Re London University Medical Sciences Institute Fund* [1909] 2 Ch. 1; *Re Wilson* [1913] 1 Ch. 314; *Re Packe* [1918] 1 Ch. 437; *Re Goldney* (1946) 115 L.J. 337; *Re Good's Will Trusts* [1950] 2 All E.R. 653; *Re Slatter's Will Trusts* [1964] Ch. 512; *Re Stemson's Will Trusts* [1970] Ch. 16; *Re Spence* [1979] Ch. 483.
[30] *Re Gillingham Bus Disaster Fund* [1958] Ch. 300 at 310, *per* Harman J.; see also *Re Abbott* [1900] 2 Ch. 326; *Re Hobourn Aero Components Ltd's Air Raid Disaster Fund* [1946] Ch. 86 at 97, *per* Cohen J.; *Re Sayer* [1957] Ch. 423 at 437, *per* Upjohn J.
[31] *Re Gillingham Bus Disaster Fund* [1958] Ch. 300 at 310, *per* Harman J.
[32] See para.11–033, below.
[33] *Re Templemoyle School* (1869) I.R. 4 Eq. 295 at 301. See also *Governors of Erasmus Smith's Schools v Att-Gen* (1932) 66 I.L.T.R. 537; *Munster and Leinster Bank Ltd v Att-Gen* (1954) 91 I.L.T.R. 34.

therefore, more accurate to speak of the necessity for a paramount charitable intention, particularly when the more recent decisions of the courts
are born in mind.

A useful starting point is the judgment of Kay J. in *Re Taylor*[34] when he
said:

> "I take the line to be a very clear one: perhaps sometimes it is difficult
> to say on which side of the line a particular case comes; but the line,
> which we all very well understand, is one of this nature: if upon the
> whole scope and intent of the will you discern the paramount object
> of the testator was to benefit not a particular institution, but to effect
> a particular form of charity independently of any special institution
> or mode, then, although he may have indicated the mode in which he
> desires that to be carried out, you are to regard the primary para-
> mount intention chiefly, and if the mode for any reason fails, the
> court, if it sees a sufficient expression of a general intention of char-
> ity, will, to use the phrase familiar to us, execute that *cy-près*, that is,
> carry out the general paramount intention in some way as nearly as
> possible the same as that which the testator has particularly indicated
> without which his intention itself cannot be effectuated."

The question whether or not a general charitable intention can be found
was also considered in *Re Wilson*[35] by Parker J. who said:

> "First of all, we have a class of cases where, in form, the gift is given
> for a particular charitable purpose, but it is possible, taking the will as
> a whole, to say that, notwithstanding the form of the gift, the para-
> mount intention according to the true construction of the will is to
> give the property in the first instance for a general charitable purpose
> rather than a particular charitable purpose, and to graft onto the gen-
> eral gift a direction as to the desires or intentions of the donor as to
> the manner in which the general gift is to be carried into effect. In that
> case, though it is impossible to carry out the precise directions, on
> ordinary principles the gift for the general charitable purpose will
> remain and be perfectly good, and the court, by virtue of its admin-
> istrative jurisdiction, can direct a scheme as to how it is to be carried
> out. In fact the will will be read as though the particular direction had
> not been in the will at all, but there had been simply a general direc-
> tion as to the application of the fund for the general charitable pur-
> poses in question.
>   Then there is the second class of cases where, on the true construc-
> tion of the will, no such paramount intention can be inferred, and
> where the gift is held to fail."

---

[34] (1888) 58 L.T. 538 at 543.
[35] [1913] 1 Ch. 314, 320. To the same effect see *Clark v Taylor* (1853) 1 Dr. 642 at 644, *per*
Kindersley V.C.; *Re Monk* [1927] 2 Ch. 197, *per* Sargant L.J.

Both these cases show the courts considering the whole of the relevant document to seek, on the part of the donor, a paramount object beyond the terms of the particular gift. On this broad approach, the more detailed the donor's directions, the less likelihood there is of finding a general charitable intention.[36]

A different approach to the need for a general or paramount charitable intention can be seen from the joint judgment of Dixon and Evatt J.J. in *A.-G. for New South Wales v Perpetual Trustee Co. Ltd*[37] where they said that the distinction was:

11–029

> "between on the one hand, cases in which every element in the description of the trust is indispensable to the validity and operation of the disposition and, on the other hand, cases where a further and more general purpose is disclosed as the true and substantial object of the trust, which may therefore be carried into effect at the expense of some part of the particular direction given by the trust instrument."

A similar approach has been taken in this country[38] and in other jurisdictions.[39] Thus in *Re Woodhams deceased*[40] Vinelott J. said:

> "As I see it, one way of approaching the question whether a prescribed scheme or project which has proved impracticable is the only way of furthering a charitable purpose that the testator or settlor contemplated or intended, is to ask whether a modification of that scheme or project, which would enable it to be carried into effect at the relevant time, is one which would frustrate the intention of the testator or settlor as disclosed by the will or trust instrument in the light of any admissible evidence of surrounding circumstances."

On this narrower approach much greater attention is given to the nature of the gift itself rather than the wording of the whole document. The presence of detailed directions by the testator is no bar to the finding of a general or paramount intention; the question being whether the particular impossible direction is an indispensable part of the proposed charitable scheme.

Even on the narrower approach to a general or paramount charitable intention, there will still be some gifts which will not be applied *cy-près* because there is no wider purpose beyond the particular gift which has failed. A useful test was set out by Somers J. in *Alacoque v Roache*[41] were he said:

---

[36] See para.11–035, below.
[37] (1940) 63 C.L.R. 209 at 225.
[38] *Re Lysaght* [1966] Ch. 191; *Re Woodhams deceased* [1981] 1 W.L.R. 493.
[39] In *Re Steele* [1976] N.I. 66; *Shorthouse's Trustees v Aberdeen Medico-Chirugical Society* [1977] S.L.T. 148; *Re Rowell* (1982) 31 S.A.S.R. 361; *Re Stewart's Will Trusts* [1983] 11 N.I.J.B.
[40] [1981] 1 W.L.R. 493 at 503.
[41] [1998] 2 N.Z.L.R. 250 at 254.

"Adopting the test propounded by Dixon and Evatt JJ in *Att-Gen for New South Wales v Perpetual Trustee Co Ltd*[42] mentioned above, the question is whether the purposes expressed in the will were an indispensible part of the declared trust."

11–030   In the instant case the testatrix had left property to a particular convent which had closed before her death. The gift failed even though the nuns had moved to two nearby convents; benefit to the convent named was held to be the sole and indispensible purpose of the gift.

In the light of the authorities cited, the following definition is suggested: General or paramount charitable intention means either (a) an intention on the part of a donor that his gift shall be devoted to charity generally, that is to say, to the promotion of any object or purpose which is in law charitable or (b) an intention on the part of a donor to promote a particular form of charity falling under one of the four recognised heads of charity, if possible by carrying into effect the actual wishes expressed by the donor, as to the mode of application of the gift, but if full compliance with his wishes be impossible, by promoting the particular form of charity in some way which will give effect as nearly as possible to his expressed wishes as to the mode of application of the gift.

On the more recent narrower approach, the particular form of charity need be no more than the specific gift less one or more of the specified conditions.

History of general or paramount and particular charitable intention

11–031   The *cy-près* doctrine that a charitable gift may be saved from lapse by an application to another object "as near as may be" was evolved before the doctrine of resulting trusts had been worked out. Thus in *Attorney-General v Mayor of Bristol*[43] Lord Eldon observed that "in former times the court acted upon principles in the construction of deeds and wills, when charity was the object, which, if they could be reconsidered, would not now be adopted. If the doctrine of resulting trusts had then been understood, the right of the heir-at-law[44] would never, in all probability, have been got over." Even more emphatic was Lord Parker of Waddington, who, in *Bowman v Secular Society Ltd*,[45] remarked that the doctrine of the general charitable intention, however admirable in the interest of the public, had gone further than any rule or canon of construction in defeating the real intention of testators. However, as will be seen, the more modern doctrine of the particular charitable intention as applied in numerous reported cases has done much to reduce the element of legal fiction.

---

[42] (1940) 63 C.L.R. 209. See para.11–029, above.
[43] (1820) 2 J. & W. 294 at 307.
[44] Or, presumably, the rights of the next-of-kin.
[45] [1917] A.C. 405 at 442.

The origin of the conception of the "general intention of charity" is no doubt to be found in the bias in favour of pious and charitable dispositions of the ecclesiastical courts which formerly had jurisdiction over wills and intestacies.[46] Referring in *Moggridge v Thackwell*[47] to the history of the *cy-près* doctrine Lord Eldon observed:

> "In what the doctrine originated, whether, as supposed by Lord Thurlow in *White v White*,[48] in the principles of the civil law as applied to charities, or in the religious notions entertained formerly in this country, I know not; but we all know there was a period when in this country a portion of every man's estate was applied to charity, and the Ordinary thought himself obliged so to apply it, upon the ground that there was a general principle of piety in the testator. When the statute[49] compelled a distribution it is not impossible that the same favour should have been extended to charity in the construction of wills by their own force purporting to authorise such a distribution. I have no doubt that cases much older than those I shall cite may be found, all of which appears to prove that if the testator has manifested a general intention to give to charity, the failure of the particular mode in which the charity is to be effectuated shall not destroy the charity; but if the substantial intention is charity, the law will substitute another mode of devoting the property to charitable purposes, though the formal intention as to the mode cannot be accomplished."

The principle upon which the Ordinary acted was in accordance with the equitable rule that the intention of the donor must be observed; for in his view the donor's object was to benefit his own soul by charitable works, and therefore to allow the gift to be defeated by reason of the failure of a particular object of charity would have been to disappoint the donor's intention. The effecutation of indefinite gifts such as "for pious uses"[50] and to "the poor"[51] by the court or the sign manual may have furnished a precedent for the *cy-près* application of gifts where a mode was indicated by the donor but could not be adopted.

Among the earliest instances of gifts applied *cy-près* were those in which   **11–032**
the mode prescribed by the donor was contrary to public policy. The

---

[46] The ecclesiastical courts assumed jurisdiction over intestates' estates in the 12th or 13th century. Magna Carta, Chap. 27, provides: "If any freeman shall die intestate, his chattels shall be distributed by the hands of his nearest kinsfolk and friends, under the supervision of the Church, saving to everyone the debts which the deceased owed to him" (McKechnie, *Magna Carta*, p.382). Usually the personal estate was divided into three, the dead's part, the wife's part and the children's part, and the dead's part was given for pious and charitable works. In the case of wills, in the absence of express directions, it was understood that the residue should be similarly expended. (Pollock and Maitland, *History of English Law*, Vol.2, pp.39–363; Holdsworth, *History of English Law*, Vol.3, pp.534, 535; McKechnie, *op. cit.*)

[47] (1802) 7 Ves. 36 at 39.

[48] (1778) 1 Bro.C.C. 12.

[49] Statute of Distribution, 1670 (22 Car. 2, c.10); Statute of Frauds, 1677 (29 Car. 2, c.3).

[50] *Clifford v Francis* (1679) Freem. 390.

[51] *Att-Gen v Matthews* (1676) 2 Lev. 167.

underlying principle in these cases was said to be that whenever a testator was disposed to be charitable in his own way and upon his own principles the court was not to be content with disappointing his intention if disapproved by the court; but that it was for the court to make him charitable in the court's way and upon the court's principles.[52] Thus a gift for endowing a weekly sermon to be preached by a minister to be selected by the inhabitants of a place was, in 1679, applied by the court to one preached by a minister selected by the bishop of the diocese.[53] A gift for 60 pious ejected ministers was applied to a chaplain for Chelsea Hospital in 1684.[54] And in 1754 a bequest for holding a Jewish religious service was given to the Foundling Hospital.[55]

In all these cases it was held that there was an intention to benefit charity paramount to the particular trusts involved. In *Attorney-General v Baxter*[56] the point was put thus: "Then it was argued that if the charity was void the money ought to remain with the executor, but the court said there was a distinction between the charity and the use; and that the use was void and not the charity." The intention which was presumed to underlie a benefaction either to the Jewish religion or the Foundling Hospital was rightly regarded by Lord Eldon as something of a fiction: "The question is not so much what was the intention, as what, in the contemplation of law, must be presumed to have been the intention".[57]

The doctrine of the general charitable intention had achieved substantially its modern form by the beginning of the nineteenth century, as appears from the classic statements of Lord Eldon in *Moggridge v Thackwell*[58] and *Mills v Farmer*.[59] In the latter case Lord Eldon, referring to the former case, said: "In that case I took it to be firmly established, upon the authority of precedents too numerous to be mentioned, that, although in carrying into execution a bequest to an individual, the mode in which the legacy is to take effect must be of the substance of the legacy, yet where the testator has sufficiently indicated that charity is his legatee, the court will consider charity as the whole substance of the legacy; and, in such cases only, will provide a mode by which that legatee shall take, but by which no other than charitable legatees can take.[60]

11–033   In *Moggridge v Thackwell* Lord Eldon had said some thirteen years before:

> "If the testator has manifested a general intention to give to charity, the failure of the particular mode in which the charity is to be effectuated shall not destroy the charity; but if the general intention is charity, the law will substitute another mode of devoting the property

---

[52] See *Cary v Abbott* (1802) 7 Ves. 490.
[53] *Att-Gen v Combe* (1679) 2 Ca. in Ch. 18.
[54] *Att-Gen v Baxter* (1684) 1 Vern. 248.
[55] *Da Costa v De Pas* (1754) Amb. 228.
[56] (1684) 1 Vern. 248 at 251.
[57] *Mills v Farmer* (1815) 1 Mer. 55 at 79, 80; *cf. Moggridge v Thackwell* 7 Ves. 36 at 81.
[58] (1802) 7 Ves. 36.
[59] (1815) 1 Mer. 55; 19 Ves. 483.
[60] (1815) 1 Mer. 55 at 100; and see *Mayor of Lyons v Advocate-General of Bengal* (1876) 1 App.Cas. 91 at 113.

to charitable purposes, though the formal intention as to the mode cannot be accomplished."[61]

The great equity jurists of the end of the eighteenth century regarded with dislike the infringement of the rights of the heir consequent upon the *cy-près* application of charitable gifts, and they evolved the doctrine of "particular charitible intention" and began to distinguish between gifts made with a general charatable intention and gifts made with the intention of effecting a particular charitable purpose and none other. From and after the evolution of this more modern doctrine, the *cy-près* doctrine has, as a rule, been confined to gifts made with a general or paramount charitable intention. The doctrine that where there is no general charitable intention there will be a lapse upon the failure of the particular charitable object emerged for the first time in *Attorney-General v Bishop of Oxford*.[62] A testator had given the residue of his personal estate upon trust to build a church at Wheatley, which was in the parish of Cuddesden. The bishop was patron of the living and also the incumbent. The new church could not be built without his consent. He refused his consent and sought to have the money applied *cy-près* for other church purposes; but the next-of-kin insisted that a new church should be built and contended that any surplus belonged to them, thus in effect relying on the doctrine of the resulting trust. A compromise was reached, and by consent Lord Kenyon made an order that £3,000 should be devoted to building a church and forming a fund for its repair, that £1,000 should be donated to augmenting the minister's salary and that any residue should be paid to the next-of-kin.

There has since *Attorney-General v Bishop of Oxford* been a series of authorities in which the court, having found no general intention of charity, has decided that the property is held on a resulting trust for the next-of-kin or that gifts for charity have lapsed upon failure of the objects of the gift.[63]

Construction

It is a question of construction for the court as to whether a donor has shown a general or a particular charitable intention.[64] The donor may, of course, have specifically expressed his intention by stating a wider general purpose beyond the particular gift[65] or by declaring how his gift is to be disposed of if his express intention cannot be carried into effect.

11–034

When considering the donor's intention it is necessary to distinguish between, on the one hand, gifts made by an instrument in writing executed

---

[61] (1802) 7 Ves. 36 at 69.
[62] (1786) 1 Bro.C.C. 444n. In *Corbyn v French* (1799) 4 Ves. 418 at 432, *per* Lord Alvanley M.R. observed of that case that Lord Kenyon's decree was completely decisive, and that, the object not being capable of taking effect, the fund could not be applied to any other charitable purpose.
[63] See para.11–035, below.
[64] *Re Wilson* [1913] 1 Ch. 314 at 320.
[65] *Chamberlayne v Brockett* (1872) L.R. 8 Ch. 206 at 211; *Wallis v Sol. Gen. for New Zealand* [1903] A.C. 173; *Phillips v Roberts* (1975) 2 N.S.W.L.R. 207.

by the donor, such as a deed or other instrument *inter vivos* or a will; and on the other hand, gifts made by a donor in response to appeals for charitable purposes otherwise than by an instrument in writing executed by him.

Gifts made by instrument in writing

11–035   In the great majority of reported cases in which the donor or testator indicates or directs the mode of application of his gift he does not express any intention at all as to the mode of application of his gift if it cannot be applied precisely in accordance with his expressed indication or direction. When a man gives property for a specific purpose to be applied in a specific manner, he does so in the belief and expectation that his gift will be applied in this way and not in some other similar way approved by the court. Therefore, the responsibility of the court is to infer what would have been the wishes of the donor in the event, for which he has not provided, of exact compliance with his wishes proving to be initially impossible. The court does this by construing the relevant instrument in the light of any material and admissible evidence of the surrounding circumstances at the date of the instrument. It is submitted that if the courts finds only a particular intention that should be regarded as the primary intention imputed by law to the donor which the court is bound to observe, except of course where the donor has expressed an actual intention.

Most of the reported cases in which the court has had to determine whether or not a general charitable intention ought to be imputed to the donor have been cases upon the construction of wills. It is hardly surprising that no clear rules of construction for the purposes of determining this question can be deduced from the cases; a decision upon the construction of one will is seldom completely decisive upon the construction of another will containing different words. Indeed, it has been stressed that the question of the donor's intention is one of the proper interpretation of the will regard being had to the terms of the particular will and to the circumstances which may be taken into account rather than so called rules of construction.[66]

It was at one time considered that the more detailed the testator's directions as to the application of his gift, the more unlikely it was that the court would impute to him a general or paramount charitable intention. Thus, in *Re Wilson*[67] the testator gave all his property upon trust to apply the income towards the payment of the salary of a schoolmaster of a school which, the testator contemplated, would be erected by public subscription. He gave the most detailed directions as to the site of the school and the site of the master's house and as to the subjects to be taught in the School. Parker J. declined to find a general charitable intention. Again, in

---

[66] *Att-Gen for New South Wales v Public Trustee* (1987) 8 N.S.W.L.R. 550 (the fact that there was a gift to a named charity did not preclude a finding of a general charitable intention on the part of the donor).
[67] [1913] 1 Ch. 314.

Re Pack[68] where a testatrix had given her freehold cottage and £1,000 to the Poor Clergy Relief Corporation upon trust to use it as a holiday home or house of rest for Church of England clergymen and their wives, with an alternative trust for the benefit of ladies and gentlemen of limited means if the corporation should decline the gift of the cottage, and the corporation declined both gifts, Neville J. held that the gifts had been made for a particular purpose only and that, as it was impracticable, the property fell into residue, as there was no general charitable intention.

By comparison in *Biscoe v Jackson*[69] a testator had directed his trustees   **11–036** to set apart a sum of money out of such part of his personal estate as might by law be applied for charitable purposes, and to apply it in the establishment of a soup kitchen and cottage hospital for the parish of Shoreditch in such manner as not to violate the Mortmain Acts. The chief clerk having certified that it was impossible to apply the fund as directed by the will, it was held that the will showed a general charitable intention to benefit the poor of the said parish and that to carry this intention into effect the court would execute the trust *cy-près* by means of a scheme. The court, thus, regarded the particular direction as to a soup kitchen and cottage hospital as a means to an end and not as the end itself.

The Courts now take a more liberal approach to the search for a general charitable intention. A starting point for this approach may be said to the joint judgment of Dixon and Evatt J.J. in *Attorney-General for New South Wales v Perpetual Trustee Co. Ltd*[70] where it was said:

"For no definite presumption has been established in favour of a general charitable intention. At the same time the court leans, as it is said, in favour of charity and is ready to infer a general charitable intention. But little is therefore required as a ground for treating a wider purpose as the essential object of the trust."

A liberal approach was taken in *Re Lysaght*[71] where the testatrix by her will directed that moneys were to be applied to the Royal College of Surgeons to be held in trust for investment and application of income to establish and maintain medical studentships. There were detailed provisions including one which excluded Jews and Roman Catholics from the benefit of the testatrix's bounty. The trust was conditional on the College being able and willing to accept the office of trustee. The Council of the College informed the trustees of the will that it was unable to accept the bequest on the terms stated in the will because the specific exclusion of students of the Jewish or Roman Catholic faith was "so invidious and so alien to the spirit of the college's work as to make the gift inoperable in its present form," but was willing to accept the gift with that provision

---

[68] [1918] 1 Ch. 437.
[69] (1887) 35 Ch.D. 450. As to this case see *Re Wilson* [1913] 1 Ch. 314 at 320, 322; *Re Ulverston New Hospital Building Trusts* [1956] Ch. 622 at 631.
[70] (1940) 63 C.L.R. 209 at 227–228.
[71] [1966] Ch. 191; see also *Re Stewart's Will Trusts* [1983] 11 N.I.J.B.; and see *Shorthouse's Trustees v Aberdeen Medico-Chirurgical Society* 1977 S.L.T. 148; *Re Rowell* [1982] 31 S.A.S.R. 361; *cf. "Hay Memorial" Judicial Factor v Hay's Trustees* 1952 S.C., HL 29.

deleted. Buckley J. held that the primary and paramount intention of the testatrix was to found medical studentships and the detailed directions (including the direction excluding Jews and Roman Catholics) were not essential to that primary and paramount intention. They were concerned with the machinery of the trust to which the testatrix had given careful thought but which did not form essential parts of her intention.[72] Since the discriminatory provision was an inessential part of the testatrix's intention, and since insistence upon it would defeat her paramount intention because the College would disclaim the trusteeship, the court could and should enable the College to carry out the trust by the deletion of the offending provision and a scheme was directed to that effect.

11–037   A similar approach was taken in *Re Woodhams*,[73] where the testator gave the residue of his estate to two colleges of music to found scholarships which were to be restricted to boys who were absolute orphans from named children's homes. The colleges refused to accept on these conditions (partly because of the decrease in the number of orphans and partly because of the adequacy of public grants for education) but would accept if the restrictions were deleted. Vinelott J. held that the testator chose orphans from these homes as those most likely to need assistance, but it was not an essential part of the scheme that the scholarships should be thus restricted and accordingly the trust could be modified by a *cy-près* scheme without frustrating his intention. On this more liberal approach which concentrates on the terms of the gift itself rather than on the will as a whole, the fact that detailed provisions or conditions have been included by the donor is not fatal to the finding of a general or paramount charitable intention.

In some cases a general charitable intention may be found by reason of other charitable gifts contained in the same will. Thus, in *Re Satterthwaite's Will Trusts*[74] a gift of a share of residue had been made to the "London Animal Hospital". Although an individual had carried on business under that designation, he no longer did so at the date of the will, and this fact was held to preclude him from taking beneficially. However, from the nature of the other dispositions by the testatrix of the residue, which were in favour of various animal charities, a general charitable intention could be discerned in favour of charity through the medium of kindness to animals.[75] Accordingly the Court of Appeal directed the share of residue in question to be applied *cy-près*.

On the other hand the mere fact that one finds one gift for a non-charitable purpose among a number of gifts for charitable purposes will not enable the court to infer that the testator intended the non-charitable gift to take effect as a charitable gift when in its terms it is not charitable. This will be the position even though the non-charitable gift may have a

---

[72] [1966] Ch. 191, 205 at 206.
[73] [1981] 1 W.L.R. 493. See [1981] Conv. 231 (J. Warburton), *cf. Re Crowe* [1979] Ch. Com. Rep., para.40.
[74] [1966] 1 W.L.R. 277.
[75] *per* Russell L.J. at 286. An example of "charity by association": *per* Sir Robert Megarry V.C. in *Re Spence* [1979] Ch. 483 at 494.

close relation to the purposes for which the charitable gifts were made.[76] The principle of noscitur a sociis does not enable one to overlook self-evident facts.[77]

Gifts made by a donor in response to appeals for charitable purposes otherwise than by an instrument in writing

Gifts are commonly made in response to an appeal organised by individuals desirous of raising a fund for a charitable object or purpose.[78] If, after money has been subscribed, the avowed object of the appeal cannot be carried into effect, the court has to determine upon what trusts the money collected is held. Three possibilities have been considered in the cases: first, that there is a resulting trust in favour of the donors, arising by operation of law, which the court will execute by ordering the money to be restored to the donors; secondly, that the money is held in trust for the Crown as *bona vacantia*, freed and discharged from the trusts upon which it was originally intended to be held; and thirdly, that the money is held upon a charitable trust which the court will execute by applying the money *cy-près*.

11–038

If the avowed objects of the appeal are not exclusively charitable, there can be no question of applying the fund or any part thereof *cy-près*.[79] If the objects fail *ab initio* the money is held on a resulting trust for the donors and in execution of the trust the contributions of all donors who can be traced must be returned to them.[80] In *Re Gillingham Bus Disaster Fund*[81] Harman J. held that the contributions of unidentifiable donors were not held in trust for the Crown as *bona vacantia*; a resulting trust in their favour arose; and they must be paid into court under s.63 of the Trustee Act 1925. He said[82]: "I see no reason myself to suppose that the small giver who is anonymous has any wider intention than the large giver

---

[76] *Re Jenkins's Will Trusts* [1966] Ch. 249 at 256, *per* Buckley J.

[77] *ibid.*

[78] The Attorney-General has issued guidelines to be taken into account by persons making public appeals following accidents or disasters: see para.3C–001, *et seq.*, below. For gifts to health service bodies following an appeal see (1995) 3 Ch. Com. Dec. 35, *et seq.*

[79] Unless the appeal was made before December 16, 1952, and the terms of the appeal enable the court to treat it as an imperfect trust provision within the Charitable Trusts (Validation) Act 1954. See para.3–036, above.

[80] *Re Gillingham Bus Disaster Fund* [1958] Ch. 300 (Harman J.); affirmed on appeal [1959] Ch. 62. See Harman J.'s discussion, in [1958] Ch. at 311, 312, of *Cunnack v Edwards* [1896] 2 Ch. 679 and *Braithwaite v Att-Gen* [1909] 1 Ch. 510 when rejecting the Crown's claim to *bona vacantia*; and see also *Re Bucks Constabulary Widows' and Orphans' Fund Friendly Society (No. 2)* [1979] 1 W.L.R. 936; *cf. Re West Sussex Constabulary's Widows, Children and Benevolent (1930) Fund Trusts* [1971] Ch. 1.

[81] [1958] Ch. 300. There was no appeal by the Crown from this part of Harman J.'s decision; the trusts were held by Harman J. and by the majority of the Court of Appeal to be too vague to be charitable and not to constitute an imperfect trust provision which could be validated by the Charitable Trusts (Validation) Act 1954. The court was concerned with the disposition of a substantial surplus after carrying out the main purpose of the appeal. Thus there was no initial failure; but it is nonetheless considered that the decision justifies the propositions contained in the text. Clearly s.14 of the Charities Act 1993, does not apply to such a case: see paras 11–040, *et seq.*, below.

[82] *ibid.*, at 314.

who is named." On the other hand, in *Re West Sussex Constabulary's Widows, Children and Benevolent (1930) Fund Trusts*[83] Goff J. held that persons who put money into collecting boxes should be taken to intend to part with the money out and out in all circumstances and, therefore, the Crown was entitled to it as *bona vacantia* on a subsequent failure of the trusts.[84] It is thought that Harman J. applied the correct principle in *Re Gillingham Bus Disaster Fund*, although the inconvenience of this result is manifest.

In cases where the purposes are wholly charitable, it is necessary to consider separately the rights of identifiable donors, the rights of unidentifiable donors, and finally the question to what extent the rights of identifiable donors may be affected by reason of the fact that they contributed in circumstances showing that they must have foreseen that their donations would become mixed with the donations of anonymous and unidentifiable donors.

11–039   **Identifiable donors**—Where a fund has been raised for a particular charitable purpose by means of gifts received from donors who have given their names and addresses or who can be traced and the fund cannot be applied for the purpose for which it was collected, there is considered to be an initial failure of the purpose. Therefore, prima facie the trustees of the fund hold the money upon a resulting trust for the donors and must return the money to them in execution of the trust,[85] unless from the language of the appeal or the circumstances in which the money was given the court is able to conclude that the particular mode of application mentioned in the appeal was subsidiary to the promotion of a wider purpose, in which case the court will impute a general charitable intention to the donors and the fund will be applied *cy-près* under a scheme.[86]

On this principle it was held in *Re University of London Medical Sciences Institute Fund*[87] that if a testator bequeaths a legacy to a fund which is being raised by an appeal to the public and, before the avowed purpose of the fund has been abandoned as impossible, the executors of the will have paid the legacy they will be regarded in law as having paid the legacy conditionally upon the avowed purpose of the appeal being carried into effect. The trustees of the fund will be regarded as having accepted the legacy subject to the condition, and, pending the due performance thereof, as holding the legacy upon a resulting trust for the executors as part of the testator's

---

[83] [1971] Ch. 1. But see the discussion in *Davis v Richards & Wallington Industries Ltd* [1991] 2 All E.R. 563 at 589, *et seq.*

[84] It was held that same result followed in respect of the proceeds of entertainments, raffles and sweepstakes.

[85] *Re Ulverston and District New Hospital Building Trusts* [1956] Ch. 622 at 629, *per* Jenkins L.J. (approving *Re University of London Medical Sciences Institute Fund* [1909] 2 Ch. 1 at 8, *per* Farwell L.J.); *Re Henry Wood National Memorial Trust* (1965) 109 S.J. 876.

[86] See *Re Hillier's Trusts* [1954] 1 W.L.R. 700, as explained in *Re Ulverston and District New Hospital Building Trusts* [1956] Ch. 622. See also and compare *Re Welsh Hospital (Netley) Fund* [1921] 1 Ch. 655; *Re North Devon and West Somerset Relief Fund Trusts* [1953] 1 W.L.R. 1260 (in both of which cases the objects of the fund had been achieved and there was a surplus to be disposed of).

[87] [1909] 2 Ch. 1.

estate. If the condition becomes incapable of performance because the avowed purpose has been abandoned after the receipt of the legacy, the trustees will be bound to refund the legacy; and, if necessary, the court will execute the resulting trust by compelling the trustees to refund.

In *Re Ulverston and District New Hospital Building Trusts*[88] the terms of the appeal led to the clear conclusion that the money, collected over a period of some 14 years, had been subscribed with the sole object of building and maintaining a new hospital at Ulverston. On being satisfied that the proposed hospital could not be built, the Court of Appeal dismissed an appeal from the decision of Sir Leonard Stone V.C. that the subscriptions received from identified donors should be subject to a resulting trust for the persons by whom they were contributed.

Thus in most cases, an identifiable donor with a particular charitable **11–040** intention, is entitled to the return of his contribution in full. Where, however, a donor claims after property has been applied *cy-près* under s.14 of the Charities Act 1993[89] he will only be entitled to the return of his contribution if he claims within six months of the date on which the scheme was made.[90] Furthermore, the trustees will be entitled to deduct any expenses they have incurred after the date of the scheme in connection with his claim[91] and he will be paid only a proportion of his donation if the sum set aside by the charity trustees to meet such claims is insufficient.[92]

S.14 of the 1993 Act[93] has not abrogated the above rule. It has, however, made provision in certain specified cases for money given by named donors to be applied *cy-près* even though no general charitable intention can be imputed to them. Subs.(1) provides that property given for specific charitable purposes which fail[94] shall be applicable *cy-près* as if given for charitable purposes generally where it belongs:

(a) to a donor who after

    (i) the prescribed[95] advertisements and inquiries[96] have been published and made, and

    (ii) the prescribed period[97] beginning with the publication of those advertisements has expired

---

[88] [1956] Ch. 622.
[89] See below.
[90] Charities Act 1993, s.14(5)(b).
[91] *ibid.*, s.14(5)(b).
[92] *ibid.*, s.14(6).
[93] The section is retrospective, s.14(11).
[94] By s.14(7) charitable purposes are deemed to "fail" where any difficulty in applying property to those purposes makes that property or the part not applicable *cy-près* available to be returned to the donors.
[95] See The Charities (*Cy-près* Advertisements, Inquiries and Disclaimers) Regulations 1993. The advertisement must be published in English and the language of the appeal, if different, in a newspaper distributed in the area where the appeal was made and on two public notice boards in the case of a local appeal in the form set out in Sch.1 to the Regulations.
[96] Prior to January 1, 1993 reasonable advertisements and inquiries had to be made—*Re Henry Wood Memorial Trust* [1966] 1 W.L.R. 1601. Any inquiry must now be made in writing and contain the information specified in Sch.3 to the Charities (*Cy-près* Advertisements, Inquiries and Disclaimers) Regulations 1993.
[97] Three months—Charities (*Cy-près* Advertisements, Inquiries and Disclaimers) Regulations 1993, reg.5.

cannot be identified or cannot be found: or

(b)   to a donor who has executed a disclaimer in the prescribed[98] form of his right to have the property returned.

Before the Charities Act 1960 the money of names donors who could not be found would have had to be paid into court.

S.14(3) conclusively presumes certain property to belong to donors who cannot be identified thus allowing it to be applied *cy-près*. The relevant property is the proceeds of cash collections made by means of collecting boxes or other means not adapted for distinguishing one gift from another and the net proceeds of lotteries, competitions, entertainments, sales or similar money-raising activities. In addition, s.14(4) allows the court to direct that other property shall be treated as belonging to unidentified donors where it appears to the court either that it would be unreasonable, having regard to the amounts likely to be returned to the donor to incur expense with a view to returning the property or that it would be unreasonable, having regard to the nature, amounts and circumstances of the gifts, and to the lapse of time since the gifts were made, for the donors to expect the property to be returned.

11–041   **Unidentified donors**—Before the coming into force of the Charities Act 1960, the consensus of judicial opinion was that, unlike identifiable donors, anonymous donors to an appeal for a specific charitable purpose which failed *ab initio* must be presumed to have given their money out-and-out with no expectation of getting it back.[99] Any argument that the contributions became *bona vacantia* on the failure of the purpose for which they were contributed was dealt with by the Attorney General waiving the claim for *bona vacantia* and bringing in a scheme for the *cy-près* application of the part of the funds derived from anonymous sources.[1] There was judicial difference, however, on the question of whether on the initial failure of a gift, which was presumed to be an out-and-out gift, a general charitable intention ought to be imputed to the donor.[2]

S.14 of the 1960 Act, now s.14 of the 1993 Act, rendered the latter question academic in relation to anonymous donors. It has already been noted[3] that property given for specific charitable purposes which fail is applicable *cy-près* as if given for charitable purposes generally if a donor cannot be found after prescribed advertisements and inquiries.[4] In addition, the

---

[98] The disclaimer must be executed in English or Welsh in the form specified in Sch. 4 to the Charities (*Cy-près* Advertisements, Inquiries and Disclaimers) Regulations 1993.

[99] See *Re Ulverston and District New Hospital Building Trusts* [1956] Ch. 622 at 633, *per* Jenkins L.J. (who indicated that in certain circumstances the presumption might be rebutted); *Re Hillier's Trusts* [1954] 1 W.L.R. 700 at 707; *Re British School of Egyptian Archaeology* [1954] 1 W.L.R. 546 at 553.

[1] See *Re Ulverston and District New Hospital Building Trusts* [1954] 1 W.L.R. 622 at 633, 634.

[2] See *Re Hillier's Trusts* [1954] 1 W.L.R. 700 at 715 (the only case of initial failure); and see also *Re Welsh Hospital (Netley) Fund* [1921] 1 Ch. 655 at 659, 660; *Re Monk* [1927] 2 Ch. 197 at 211; *Re North Devon and West Somerset Relief Fund Trusts* [1953] 1 W.L.R. 1260 at 1266, 1267.

[3] See para.11–040, above.

[4] Charities Act 1993, s.14(1)(a).

proceeds of cash collections by means of collecting boxes and money raised by lotteries, competitions and similar money raising activities is exclusively presumed to belong to donors who cannot be identified and applicable *cy-près* as if given for charitable purposes generally.[5] There is thus, in effect, a statutory presumption that unidentified donors have a general charitable intention. Trustees of funds which fail should apply to the Charity Commissioners for a scheme under which the money will be applied *cy-près*.[6]

Donations to mixed funds—The expression "mixed fund" is used to denote   **11–042** a fund into which there are paid and mixed together the contributions of named or identifiable donors and contributions from unidentifiable donors.

It was unanimously held by the Court of Appeal in the *Ulverston* case[7] that, although the contributions received from named or identifiable donors had been paid into a mixed fund which included contributions received from unidentifiable donors who would not have expected to get their money back, no general charitable intention should merely for that reason be imputed to the identifiable donors in a case where it was clear that they had given their money only for the avowed object of the appeal. The money received from identifiable donors was held on resulting trusts for them and they were entitled to get it back. It was, however, in that case indicated[8] that where the circumstances in which a fund is raised (*e.g.* the language of the published appeal) leave it open to question whether named or identifiable donors did or did not contribute with a general as distinct from a particular charitable intention, the inclusion in the fund of contributions from anonymous sources would be a relevant factor in deciding that the gifts of the named or identifiable donors had been made with a general intention in favour of charity.

Following the Charities Act 1960 and the statutory presumption of a general charitable intention[9] it seems likely that the court will be inclined to impute a general charitable intention to the named and identifiable donors of a mixed fund which fails *ab initio* where the donors have not earmarked their gift for specific purposes and the terms of the appeal to the public were equivocal (though the purposes were charitable).

---

[5] *ibid.*, s.14(3).
[6] *ibid.*, s.16(1). See, for example, [1980] Ch. Com. Rep., para.135 (South Scarborough Pool Association).
[7] *Re Ulverston and District New Hospital Building Trusts* [1956] Ch. 622, explaining the majority decision of the Court of Appeal in *Re Hillier's Trusts* [1954] 1 W.L.R. 700, which must, it seems, be regarded as having been decided on its rather special facts. It was possible to construe the appeal as a general appeal in aid of hospital facilities in a particular area and not, as in the *Ulverston* case, an appeal to build and maintain a particular hospital in a particular place.
[8] [1956] Ch. 622 at 640, 641.
[9] Now Charities Act 1993, s.14, see para.11–040, above.

SUBSEQUENT FAILURE

11–043 As in the case of initial failure, property can only be applied *cy-près* if a *cy-près* occasion has arisen. Before 1960, it had to be shown that it was impossible or impracticable to carry out the purposes specified and some examples are given below. S.13 of the 1960 Act widened the circumstances which could amount to a *cy-près* occasion.

If a gift fails *ab initio*, the property may only be applied *cy-près* if the donor has shown a general or paramount charitable intention.[10] The courts have not always been clear in relation to the further conditions to be satisfied in the case of subsequent failure. The relevant question is whether there has been an outright gift of the property to charity.

Cy-près occasions

11–044 Prior to 1960, the insistence on impossibility or impracticability meant that a charity had to be virtually deprived of its objects before the property could be applied *cy-près*. This was so despite the occasional liberal interpretation of "impossibility" and "impracticability" by the courts.[11] The inability to apply *cy-près* funds which were still capable of being used for the original objects even though it was inexpedient, uneconomic and inefficient was to a certain extent remedied by s.13 of the Charities Act 1960, now s.13 of the Charities Act 1993.

General failure

11–045 There have been many cases where the funds of a defunct charity have been applied *cy-près*. Thus, where there was a trust for the redemption of British slaves in Barbary, and there ceased to be beneficiaries, the fund was applied *cy-près*.[12] Similarly, where there was a gift to convert infidels in America and the court was satisfied that there were no infidels left there, a scheme was directed to apply "the produce of the estates according to the intentions of the testator."[13] Again, trusts for the relief of prisoners for debt were applied for the benefit of other prisoners when this kind of imprisonment was abolished.[14]

The funds of a society for the mutual assistance of members of the theatrical profession, which was a charity, were applied *cy-près* when the society came to an end.[15] So also if there is a gift to support pupils at a particular school which is subsequently closed,[16] or the revenues of a charity become insufficient for the purpose of the charity,[17] or if the

---

[10] See para.11–027, above.
[11] See *Re Dominion Student Hall Trust* [1947] Ch. 183.
[12] *Ironmongers' Co v Att-Gen* (1844) 10 Cl. & F. 908.
[13] *Att-Gen v City of London* (1790) 3 Bro.C.C. 171.
[14] *Re Prison Charities* (1873) L.R. 16 Eq. 129; *Att-Gen v Hankey* (1873), cited *ibid.*, at 140n.
[15] *Spiller v Maude* (1881) 32 Ch.D. 158n; *cf. Dale v Powell* (1897) 13 T.L.R. 466.
[16] *Re Templemoyle School* (1869) Ir.R. 4 Eq. 295.
[17] *Berkhamstead School Case* (1865) L.R. 1 Eq. 102.

charity property is compulsorily purchased, a *cy-près* application will be ordered.[18] Again, where a school was founded for the education of the poor within a certain district, and the district was afterwards converted into a dock under a local Act of Parliament so that the objects of the charity failed, a scheme was directed for its administration *cy-près*.[19]

In certain cases a condition attached to a charitable gift has in course of time come to make the continuance of the charity impossible; and the court, acting upon the *cy-près* principle, has consented to the removal of the condition. Thus, in two cases, schools were founded and it was stipulated by the trust deeds that religious instruction according to the doctrines of the Church of England should be given. This condition disqualified the schools from receiving a grant from the Board of Education; and the court, finding that the schools could not exist without the grant, sanctioned an alteration in the trusts to satisfy the Board.[20] Likewise, where the objects of a trust have in fact changed, the court may vary the terms of the trust. For example, in *Attorney-General v Bunce*,[21] there was a bequest for the benefit of the Presbyterian congregation at a certain place. It was stated that there had been no Presbyterian congregation there for at least a hundred years, and their place had been taken by Baptists, who had enjoyed the bequest. The court found that the original objects had failed, and that the case was governed by the Nonconformist Chapels Act, 1844,[22] but that apart from that Act a case for *cy-près* had arisen, and the Baptists were the proper objects. In the circumstances of that case a scheme could now be made by the Charity Commissioners.[23]

Section 13

S.13 was necessary because of the pre-1960 principle that if a charity could be administered according to the directions of the founder, it must be so administered even though the original trusts had become largely outdated as a result of changing circumstances. The section sets out a series of specific circumstances in which property may be applied *cy-près*. It is no longer necessary to show that the original purposes have become impossible or impractible.[24] The section in part re-states the principles under the existing law but also extends those principles. It should be noted that the section does nothing further[25]; it does not enable trusts to be altered to entirely different purposes appearing to constitute a more urgent need, so long as it remains practicable to give effect to the original

11-046

---

[18] *Clephane v Lord Provost of Edinburgh* (1869) L.R. 1 H.L. Sc. 417.
[19] *Att-Gen v Glyn* (1841) 12 Sim. 84.
[20] *Re Queen's School, Chester* [1910] 1 Ch. 796; *Att-Gen v Price* [1912] 1 Ch. 667. See also *Re Robinson* [1923] 2 Ch. 332 and *Re Dominion Students' Hall Trust* [1947] Ch. 183 and the Charities Act, 1993, s.13(1)(a)(ii).
[21] (1868) L.R. Eq. 563.
[22] Repealed by the Charities Act 1960, s.39 and Sch.5.
[23] Charities Act 1993, s.13(1)(a)(ii).
[24] *Varsani v Jesani* [1999] Ch. 219.
[25] See Charities Act 1993, s.13(2). Nor does the section require a scheme where none was required before 1960, see *Oldham Borough Council v Att-Gen* [1993] 2 All E.R. 432.

trusts. Intervention is not possible unless the case falls within one of the paragraphs of s.13(1)[26] which can be categorised as circumstances in which the underlying purpose of the gift is being frustrated.[27] Whilst, however, the limitations on the section must be appreciated, it enables the Charity Commissioners to adopt the purposes of charities to present day conditions.

The section refers throughout to the "original purposes". "Original purposes" are to be construed as referring to the trusts as a whole and not generally in relation to its respective parts.[28] The phrase is also to be construed as referring to the purposes as amended by subsequent scheme, if relevant.[29] "Original purposes" does not encompass administrative provisions such as a stipulation as to distribution of capital. Thus, such an administrative provision cannot be altered under the *cy-près* doctrine but it can be altered under the courts' inherent jurisdiction.[30] The section also makes reference to "the spirit of the gift". This concept has been construed to mean the basic intention underlying the gift or the substance of the gift as opposed to the form of words used to express it or conditions imposed to effect it.[31] The intention should be ascertained from the terms of the relevant instrument read in the light of the admissible evidence.[32] If there is no founding document, the spirit of the gift has to be inferred.[33]

The first circumstance in which s.13 permits property to be applied *cy-près* is:

"where the original purposes, in whole or in part—

(i) have been as far as may be fulfilled; or
(ii) cannot be carried out, or not according to the directions given and to the spirit of the gift".[34]

This provision was used in *Re Lepton's Charity*[35] to order, in respect of a charity established in 1715, that moneys payable out of rents to the minister of a chapel should be raised from £3 to £100 a year. The reference to "directions" restates the courts' original jurisdiction[36] to remove impracticable conditions attached to charitable gifts.[37]

The second circumstance in s.13(1)(b) is:

"where the original purposes provided a use for part only of the property available by virtue of the gift."

---

[26] *Varsani v Jesani* [1999] Ch. 219 at 233, *per* Morritt L.J.
[27] See *Forest v Att-Gen for Victoria* [1986] V.R. 187 at 190.
[28] *Re Lepton's Charity* [1972] Ch. 276 at 285.
[29] Charities Act 1993, s.13(3).
[30] *Re J.W. Laing Trust* [1984] Ch. 143 at 153–155. See also [1985] Conv. 313 (P. Luxton).
[31] *Varsani v Jesani* [1999] Ch. 219 at 234, *per* Morritt L.J; and see Warburton, "The Spirit of the Gift" (1995) 3 C.L.P.R. 1.
[32] *Re Lepton's Charity* [1972] Ch. 276 at 285.
[33] *Peggs v Lamb* [1994] Ch. 172 at 197.
[34] Charities Act 1933, s.13(1)(a).
[35] [1972] Ch. 276. See also *Att-Gen v Hyde* [2002] W.T.L.R. 1419.
[36] See, for example, *Re Robinson* [1923] 2 Ch. 332; *Re Dominion Students' Hall Trust* [1947] Ch. 183.
[37] *Re J.W. Laing Trust* [1984] Ch. 143 at 152–153.

This restates the courts' original jurisdiction to apply surplus funds *cy-près*.[38]

A further circumstance is: **11–047**

"where the property available by virtue of the gift and other property applicable for similar purposes can be more effectively used in conjunction, and to that end can suitably, regard being had to the spirit of the gift, be made applicable to common purposes."[39]

A consolidation of charities was always possible prior to 1960 and it was not necessary to show impossibility.[40] There would appear to be an overlap with the general power to make schemes under s.16(1) of the 1993 Act. S.13(1)(d) provides:

"where the original purposes were laid down by reference to an area which then was but has since ceased to be a unit for some other purpose, or by reference to a class of persons or to an area which has for any reason ceased to be suitable, regard being had to the spirit of the gift, or to be practical in administering the gift."

This subsection allows a *cy-près* scheme to be made where it has become difficult to identify the area of benefit because of changes in local government boundaries. The area may also change where it has become unsuitable or impracticable, for example, the area of benefit may be enlarged if the funds of the charity are greatly increased.[41] There is a separate power to increase a charity's area of benefit under s.13(4) but the increase is limited to the areas specified in Sch.3.[42] S.13(1)(d) also permits the class of beneficiaries to be changed if it has become unsuitable or impracticable. This reference to unsuitability makes the provision wider than the previous law. For example, in *Peggs v Lamb*[43] the class of persons in two charitable trusts was enlarged from the freemen of the Ancient Borough of Huntingdon to the inhabitants as a whole when the number of freemen had decreased and the income had dramatically increased.

The major relaxation of the old *cy-près* occasions is provided by s.13(1)(e) which provides:

"where the original purposes, in whole or in part, have, since they were laid down,—

(i)   been adequately provided for by other means; or

(ii)   ceased, as being useless or harmful to the community or for other reasons, to be in law charitable; or

---

[38] See, *e.g. Re Douglas* [1905] 1 Ch. 279; *Re King* [1923] 1 Ch. 243.

[39] Charities Act 1993, s.13(1)(c). See also s.74 and para.12–008, below in relation to small charities. See also the power of the Charity Commissioners in s.28 to give directions to transfer amounts in dormant bank accounts of charities.

[40] *Re Faraker* [1912] 2 Ch. 488 at 495.

[41] See [1989] Ch. Com. Rep., para.80. The area of benefit of the Hampton Fuel Allotment Charity was extended to the London Borough of Richmond from the ancient town of Hampton on an increase of income from £13,000 a year to £48,000 a week.

[42] For the Charity Commissioners views on this power see [1984] Ch. Com. Rep., para.30.

[43] [1994] Ch. 72.

(iii) ceased in any other way to provide a suitable and effective method of using the property available by virtue of the gift, regard being had to the spirit of the gift."

This subsection has proved to be of practical use in enabling funds to be used for the benefit of the public. Sub-para.(i) may be illustrated by a *cy-près* scheme where the original benefits of the trust are now provided for by the statutory services of public or local authorities, for example, a charity for the upkeep of a road or bridge. The Charity Commissioners have made schemes under this sub-paragraph substituting for those purposes other general purposes for the benefit of the local inhabitants which may include, for instance, the promotion of the arts, the provision of seats or shelters, the preservation of old buildings or the improvement of local amenities.[44]

11–048   Sub-para.(ii) covers the rare case of purposes once considered charitable but which have ceased, as being useless or harmful to the community, or for other reasons, to be in law charitable. By s.4(1) of the 1993 Act an institution registered with the Charity Commissioners is conclusively presumed to be a charity whilst on the register for all purposes other than rectification of the register. If the statutory provisions alone are considered, there are strong arguments for saying that whenever a charity is removed from the register on the grounds that its purposes are no longer charitable[45] its property should be applied *cy-près*. A closer examination of the grounds for determining than institution is no longer charitable show that a *cy-près* occasion may not arise in all cases.

If an institution, which was never charitable, was entered originally on the register in error, the Charity Commissioners would have been acting *ultra vires* in carrying out the act of registration. Removal from the register of such a mistakenly registered institution merely restores the institution to its original non-charitable state. Accordingly, if the Charity Commissioners were given false or misleading information or themselves made an error at the time of registration, removal from the register will simply recognise the mistake and any property will remain with the institution in its confirmed non-charitable state.[46] The Charity Commissioners consider that this argument of retrospective nullity of the *ultra vires* acts of public authorities also applies where a widely held view of the law is revealed by a subsequent decision of the court to be wrong.[47] In view of the courts' present willingness to allow recovery of money paid on the basis of a settled understanding of the law which is later declared by the courts to be a mistake of law,[48] it is arguable that a *cy-près* occasion arises where a later judicial decision declares a particular purpose, once assumed to be charitable, not to be so.

---

[44] See [1968] Ch. Com. Rep., paras 67–72; [1975] Ch. Com. Rep., paras 54–57.
[45] Charities Act 1993, s.3(4).
[46] Money paid under a mistaken understanding that the institution was a charity may be the subject of restitutionary claims, for example, tax reliefs by the Inland Revenue.
[47] See RR6, *Maintenance of an Accurate Register of Charities* (2000), pp.4, 13.
[48] See *Kleinwort Benson Ltd v Lincoln City Council* [1999] 2 A.C. 349.

In determining whether the removal from the register of an institution registered in error amounts to a *cy-près* occasion, Art.1 of Protocol 1 of the European Convention on Human Rights will be relevant. Article 1 provides that a person should not be deprived of his possessions except in the public interest. The effect of determining that there is a *cy-près* occasion where there is an error, other than an error of law as to charitable status, is that property that was never dedicated intentionally to charitable purposes will be applied *cy-près* for charitable purposes and not the original non-charitable purposes. Thus a non-charitable institution could be deprived of its assets because it was registered in error as a charity. It may be countered that such an institution will have had the benefits of charitable status, including possible relief from taxation, whilst on the register.

If a particular charitable purpose is declared by statute to be no longer **11–049** charitable, any property held for that purpose will be applicable *cy-près* under s.13(1)(e)(ii). Similarly, where a purpose becomes no longer charitable because of a change in social circumstances[49] property held for that purpose will be applicable *cy-près* and the trustees will be under an obligation to apply for a scheme.[50]

It is considered that sub-para.(iii) provides the widest relaxation of all. The Charity Commissioners consider that they have jurisdiction to remove a limitation of the amount of any grant which may be made to relieve need, hardship or distress[51] and the jurisdiction can only arise under this sub-paragraph. However, although the wording of the sub-paragraph is wide, it is essential to establish that the mode of application that the donor selected has ceased to be suitable or effective. It is not sufficient that the original purpose selected by the donor is less effective than some other application.

An example of the use of sub-para.(iii) is *Re Lepton's Charity*.[52] In that case there was a gift in 1715 of land by will to be held on trust to pay out of the rents a sum of £3 a year to the minister of a chapel and the net overplus to the poor and aged of the town. The evidence was to the effect that at the date of the will the total income was £5 a year. The land had since been sold and was represented by investments yielding £791 a year. It was held that the basic intention of the gift was plainly defeated when, in the conditions of England today, the minister took a derisory £3 out of the total of £791 and an order was made by way of scheme to provide for the payment to the minister to be raised to £100 a year.

A further example of the use of s.13(1)(e)(iii) is *Varsani v Jesani*.[53] The **11–050** case involved a trust to promote the faith of a particular Hindu sect as practised in accordance with the teachings and tenets of its leader. Dispute arose between two groups with different beliefs who could no longer worship together in the same temple. The impasse between the groups could not be resolved as a matter of faith. The Court of Appeal held that it was

---

[49] See *National Anti-Vivisection Society v IRC* [1948] A.C. 31 at 74, *per* Lord Simonds.
[50] Charities Act 1993, s.13(5). See also RR6, *Maintenance of an Accurate Register of Charities* (2000), p.15.
[51] [1968] Ch. Com. Rep., para.18.
[52] [1972] Ch. 276. See also *Re Steele* [1976] N.I. 66 and *Att-Gen v Hyde* [2002] W.T.L.R. 1419.
[53] [1999] Ch. 219.

not necessary to ascertain the precise limits of the original purpose nor if that purpose had become impossible or impracticable. The original purposes had ceased to be a suitable and effective method of using the available property and it was held that a scheme should be made under s.13(1)(e)(iii). The spirit of the gift supported that conclusion.

There are few reported cases on the use of s.13; the majority of *cy-près* orders are made by the Charity Commissioners.[54] An indication of the shift in emphasis in the application of the doctrine of *cy-près* and the potential flexibility introduced by s.13 can be seen from the Australian case of *Forrest v Attorney General for Victoria*.[55] In that case the testator left the income of his residuary estate to be distributed, in effect, amongst those Victorian charities existing at the date of his death in 1965. The trustees applied to remove the qualifying condition of existence at the date of death for beneficiary charities. Nathan J. held that the fundamental purpose, or the spirit, of the gift was to benefit all Victorian charities and only 20 years after the testator's death made a *cy-près* scheme under the equivalent of s.13(1)(a)(ii) and (e)(iii) removing the condition.

Outright gift

11–051   Once a *cy-près* occasion has arisen, a *cy-près* scheme for the relevant property will be possible provided that there has been an outright, and not a limited, gift to charity. It is now clear that it is not necessary for the donor to have had a general or paramount charitable intention before an outright gift can be applied *cy-près* on a subsequent failure. When considering subsequent failure, it is necessary to distinguish absolute gifts, gifts for particular charitable purposes and limited gifts. The same principles apply where there is a surplus of capital after the purposes of the charity have been carried out. The question of the destination of surplus income is not necessarily a *cy-près* problem as there may not have been a failure of a charitable object but many judges have treated cases of surplus income as applications of the *cy-près* doctrine and it is convenient to deal with the situation at this point.

Absolute gifts

11–052   If property is given absolutely and free from any trust or condition to an incorporated or unincorporated charity which was in existence when the gift vested in possession or in interest but which has subsequently come to an end, the property is dealt with in the ordinary way as part of the assets of the charity.[56] If the gift was a direct gift, it will be applied in

---

[54] See, *e.g.* [1989] Ch. Com. Rep., paras 77–80; [1990] Ch. Com. Rep., paras 79–82; [1998] Ch. Com. Rep., p.7.

[55] [1986] V.R. 187. See also *Re Steele* [1976] N.I. 66.

[56] *Re Slevin* [1891] 2 Ch. 236; *Re Geikie* (1911) 27 T.L.R. 484; *Re Soley* (1900) 17 T.L.R. 118; *Re Moon's Will Trusts* [1948] 1 All E.R. 300; *Re Wright* [1954] Ch. 347; and see *Re Cooper's Conveyance Trusts* [1956] 1 W.L.R. 1096 at 1103; *Re Tacon* [1958] Ch. 447.

accordance with directions given by the Sovereign under the sign manual, now delegated to the Attorney-General.[57] If it was a gift by way of trust it will be applied *cy-près* under a scheme settled by the court,[58] or the Charity Commissioners.[59] It is irrelevant to consider whether the donor had a general charitable intention.[60]

Gifts for particular purposes

Although judges have devoted time in cases of subsequent failure to considering whether the donor had a general charitable intention,[61] it is now accepted that what is necessary is that the donor intended to give the property out-and-out for specific charitable purposes.[62] Thus, in *Re Wright*[63] Romer J. said:

11–053

> "Once money is effectually dedicated to charity, whether in pursuance of a general or a particular charitable intent, the testator's next of kin or residuary legatees are for ever excluded and no question of subsequent lapse, or anything analogous to lapse, between the date of the testator's death and the time when the money becomes available for actual application to the testator's purpose can affect the matter so far as they are concerned."

The principle is regarded as equally applicable to gifts inter vivos as to gifts by will.[64] *Re Wokingham Fire Brigade Trusts*[65] concerned a trust set up following a public appeal in 1876. In 1942, the National Fire Service took over the function of the Brigade and purchased its assets. In considering the trustees' application for a direction as to how the money should be dealt with Danckwerts J. said[66]:

> "I think that the subscribers intended to part with all interest in the subscriptions when they made them for the benefit of this public purpose. I do not believe that at that time they had any intention as to the future disposal of the money: and I do not think that was taken into account. The only thing which I think they took into account was the provision of the fire brigade, or the equipment for the fire brigade; and that being so, the funds were subscribed out-and-out for

---

[57] See [1989] Ch. Com. Rep., para.38.
[58] See *Re Bennett* [1960] Ch. 18 and paras 10–002, *et seq.*, above.
[59] Charities Act 1993, s.16(1).
[60] *Re Slevin* [1891] 2 Ch. 236 at 242, 243. See, generally, P. Luxton [1983] Conv. 107.
[61] See, *e.g. The Incorporated Society v Price* (1844) 1 J. & La T. 498; *Re Welsh Hospital (Netley) Fund* [1921] 1 Ch. 655; *Re Monk* [1927] 2 Ch. 197; *Re Royce* [1940] Ch. 514; *Re North Devon and West Somerset Relief Fund Trusts* [1953] 1 W.L.R. 1260.
[62] *Re Tacon* [1958] Ch. 447.
[63] [1954] Ch. 347 at 364.
[64] *Re Welsh Hospital (Netley) Fund* [1921] 1 Ch. 655; *Re North Devon and West Somerset Relief Fund Trusts* [1953] 1 W.L.R. 1260; *Re British School of Egyptian Archaeology* [1954] 1 W.L.R. 546.
[65] [1951] Ch. 373.
[66] *ibid.* at 377.

a charitable purpose. Though that purpose is no longer practicable by reason of the sale of the assets to a different body charged with the duties, the charitable trusts do not fail. It is not necessary to consider whether there was any general charitable intention, and the trusts should be modified by means of a *cy-près* scheme."

The courts have from time to time treated the intention to make an out-and-out gift and a general charitable intention as synonymous[67] but the two are not as *Re Wokingham Fire Brigade Trust*[68] well illustrates. Danckwerts J. in that case did not find that the subscribers had a general charitable intention. Accordingly, if the trust had failed *ab initio* the funds could not have been applied *cy-près*. The subscribers intention to make an outright gift, however, was sufficient to allow the funds to be applied *cy-près* on a subsequent failure.

Limited gifts

11–054   *Cy-près* will not be available on a subsequent failure if the property has not been the subject of an outright gift; the property may instead be held on resulting trust for the donor or his estate or as otherwise directed in the original gift. There are two separate situations which need to be distinguished. The first is where there is an absolute and perpetual gift to charity with a gift over and the second is where there is a gift to a charity for a limited period. In the first type of case, if the gift over fails for remoteness or some other reason, the original gift remains[69] and, in the event of subsequent failure, the property can be applied *cy-près* under a scheme, notwithstanding that the donor did not have a general charitable intention.[70] In the second type of case, *cy-près* is not available and the undisposed of interest results to the grantor.[71]

The type of gift, and consequences of subsequent failure, depends upon a true construction of the instrument of gift and the decisions are not easy to reconcile. When approaching the construction of a particular deed or will Upjohn J. in *Re Cooper's Conveyance Trusts*[72] said that it must be borne in mind that:

"whatever language is used, the whole question is what are the donor's intentions, to be ascertained on a true construction of the relevant documents in the light of the relevant surrounding circumstances.

---

[67] *Re Welsh Hospital (Netley) Fund* [1921] 1 Ch. 655 at 660–663, *per* P.O. Lawrence J; *Re Monk* [1927] 197 at 210, 211, *per* Sargant L.J.; *Re Hillier's Trusts* [1954] 1 W.L.R. 700 at 715, *per* Denning L.J. (who, it is submitted, misapprehended the meaning of Harman J.'s observations in *Re British School of Egyptian Archaeology* [1954] 1 W.L.R. 545, 553); *Re Raine* [1956] Ch. 417 at 423, *per* Vaisey J.

[68] [1951] Ch. 373.

[69] *Re Monk* [1927] 2 Ch. 197 at 211 applying the ruling in *Lassence v Tierney* (1849) 1 Mac. & G. 551 to charitable gifts.

[70] *Re Peel's Release* [1921] 2 Ch. 218; *Re Bowen* [1893] 2 Ch. 491.

[71] *Re Cooper's Conveyance Trusts* [1956] 1 W.L.R. 1096 at 1102.

[72] [1956] 1 W.L.R. 1096 at 1103.

Thus, even where the gift is unlimited in time but is followed by clauses of defeasance or powers of revocation, it is a question of construction whether a donor intended to devote his gift to charity out-and-out or in perpetuity or only for a limited purpose and period."

An example of a case falling into the first type is *Re Peel's Release*.[73] Land was conveyed to trustees upon trust "to permit and suffer the same to be for ever thereafter used as and for a place of instruction for seventy poor children" with a proviso, void for remoteness, that if the charitable purposes thereby intended should not take effect, or, having taken effect should afterwards cease or be defeated, the property should be held in trust for the grantor, his heirs and assigns. This proviso negatived the existence of any general charitable intention, but it was held that, the gift in terms being perpetual, there could be no reverter or resulting trusts for the grantor's heir or personal representatives, and a scheme was directed to be prepared.

Re Randall[74] provides a useful example of a case in the second category. In that case a testatrix left money on trust to pay the income to the successive incumbents of a church for so long as they permitted all sittings in the church to be free of claims for pew rents. She directed that the money was to fall into her residuary estate if pew rents were claimed. It was held that there was a charitable bequest which terminated automatically on pew rents being claimed and that on determination there would be a resulting trust for those entitled to the residue. The resulting trust expressed in the will only expressed what the law would otherwise have implied and thus did not transgress the rule against perpetuities.

The difficulty of construction can be seen from the case of *Re Cooper's*   **11–055**
Conveyance Trusts,[75] a case in the second category. On a first reading of the report it may seem difficult to reconcile the decision with that of *Re Peel's Release*.[76] Land was conveyed to trustees for ever upon trust for a specified purpose. The words "for ever" prima facie indicated an intention to give the property in perpetuity. But the proviso for cesser and the gift over were more emphatic than in *Re Peel's Release*, for it was provided that upon failure of the original trust at any time the land was to be held in

---

[73] [1921] 2 Ch. 218; followed in *Re Bawden's Settlement* [1954] 1 W.L.R. 33n and *Bath and Wells Diocesan Board of Finance v Jenkinson, The Times,* September 6, 2000.
[74] (1888) 38 Ch. D. 231. See also *Re Bowen* [1893] 2 Ch. 491; *Re Blunt's Trusts* [1904] 2 Ch. 767. Grants under the School Sites Act 1841, provide numerous examples of gifts, often expressed to be perpetual, for a limited particular charitable purpose. Where that purpose failed the gift used to revert to the grantor's estate by virtue of the third proviso to s.2. The effect of the proviso was to give statutory force to an event which would in any event occur through the operation of a resulting trust, as it did in *Bankes v Salisbury Diocesan Council of Education Incorporated* [1960] Ch. 631, a case under the School Sites Act 1836, which did not have the equivalent proviso. By the Reverter of Sites Act 1987 such land is now held on trust for sale for the person who, but for the 1987 Act, would be entitled by virtue of reverter but the trustees may apply to the Charity Commissioners for a scheme. For a detailed revue of the 1987 Act see [1987] Conv. 408 (D. Evans); (1994) 2 C.L. & P.R. 243 (D. Morris).
[75] [1956] 1 W.L.R. 1096.
[76] [1921] 2 Ch. 218.

trust for certain designated individuals and to be conveyed accordingly "and upon and for no other trust or purpose whatsoever". The proviso was void for remoteness but Upjohn J. held that as a matter of construction it negatived any general charitable intention and that it also negatived any intention to give the land out-and-out in perpetuity. In effect, the proviso deprived the words "for ever" of their prima facie meaning. Since there was no perpetual gift, but only a gift to take effect so long as the primary trust could be executed, and since the proviso was void for remoteness, there was an interest of the donor remaining undisposed of which was held on a resulting trust arising by operation of law.[77]

Surplus capital

11–056   It is clear that where a general charitable intention can be imputed to the donor, an initial as well as a subsequent surplus will always be applicable cy-près, for, as has been shown, there can be no resulting trust where there is a general charitable intention. It is submitted, however, that such an intention is not necessary if the court is satisfied that the donor's intention was to give the property out-and-out to charity. It is considered that such an intention is always sufficient in any case relating to the application of a surplus which arises after the fund or property has been transferred to a charity or to trustees for a charity or after the trustees of a will have appropriated the fund for the purposes of the charity. There may possibly be more doubt if before the transfer or appropriation it becomes certain that there will be a surplus, though it is questioned whether such doubt is justified.[78]

There are two situations to consider:

(1) Where the gift was made by an instrument in writing the court has to determine whether on the true construction of the instrument the donor either had a general charitable intention or, failing such intention, an intention for ever to deprive himself or his estate of any interest in the subject-matter of the gift.[79]

(2) Where the gift was made in response to an appeal for funds for a charitable purpose, the court has to ascertain from the published terms of the appeal and the circumstances in which it was made whether the donor had a general charitable intention or whether he gave his money out-and-out, reserving no interest to himself.

The second situation has already been discussed.[80]

11–057   **Gifts by instrument in writing**—In most of the reported cases the instrument was a will. If the subject-matter of a gift by will is the whole of the

---

[77] The decision in this case has been criticised but it can by justified by the reasoning of Maugham J. in *Re Talbot* [1933] Ch. 895 as explained in *Gibson v South American Stores (Gath & Chaves) Ltd* [1950] Ch. 177, 202 at 203.

[78] See para.11–057, below.

[79] *Re King* [1923] 1 Ch. 243; *Re Raine* [1956] Ch. 417; and see also *Re Douglas* [1905] 1 Ch. 274; *Re Monk* [1927] 2 Ch. 397; *Re Robertson* [1930] 2 Ch. 71; *Re Royce* [1940] Ch. 514.

[80] See paras 11–038, *et seq.*, above.

testator's residuary estate and the executors or trustees are directed to pay or transfer the residue to trustees for charity or to appropriate the whole residue for specified charitable purposes, the court will readily assume that the residue was intended to be dedicated to charity for ever and the court will, without necessarily finding a general charitable intention, direct a scheme for the application *cy-près* of property surplus to requirements. Thus in *Re King*[81] there was a testamentary gift of residue to provide a stained glass window in a church. There was a substantial surplus and the Court of Appeal directed a *cy-près* application of the surplus despite the absence of a general charitable intention.

Following *Re King* the courts in a number of cases concerning surplus funds directed their attention to the question of whether the testator had a general charitable intention rather than to determining whether there was an outright gift. In *Re Stamford*[82] a sum of £5,000 in consols was bequeathed on trust to the University of Cambridge for the purpose of publishing a particular dictionary. After publication of the dictionary, a surplus remained in the hands of the University. Eve J. held that the testator had not had a general charitable intention and that the surplus was to be held on resulting trust for the testator's estate. *Re King* was not cited in that case.

In *Re Monk*[83] the testator had given his residuary estate to charity trustees upon trust to make small loans of money to poor and deserving inhabitants of Foxton. It appears to have been proved or admitted that the amount of the residue was certain to considerably exceed the amount needed for the execution of the trust. The Court of Appeal found a general charitable intention to benefit the poor of Foxton and directed a scheme. Sargant L.J., however, evidently thought that the direction to transfer the residue to charity trustees out-and-out in itself enabled the court to direct a scheme. The final case in this group is *Re Royce*[84] where the testator had bequeathed a legacy and a large share of residue to the vicar and churchwardens of a parish church "for the benefit of the choir". Before the legacy and residue were paid or transferred to the vicar and churchwardens it had become clear that there would be a surplus. Simonds J. found a general charitable intention on the part of the testator. But, having observed that the gift was a perpetual gift given out-and-out to the vicar and churchwardens, he went on to say that in more than one case it had been held that a gift out-and-out to churchwardens or to any body of trustees was an indication that the testator intended the whole of the fund to be employed, if not in a particular mode, then according to a general intent.[85]

The most recent case is *Re Raine*[86] in which Vaisey J. followed *Re King*[87] **11–058** although the case is not free from difficulty. In that case the testatrix had

---

[81] [1923] 1 Ch. 243. see also *Re Robertson* [1930] 2 Ch. 71.
[82] [1924] 1 Ch. 73.
[83] [1927] 2 Ch. 197.
[84] [1940] Ch. 514.
[85] *ibid.*, at 521.
[86] [1956] Ch. 417.
[87] [1923] 1 Ch. 243.

by her will directed that the whole of her residuary estate should be sold and that the proceeds should be taken "for the continuation of the seating" of a specified church. A surplus of about £2,000 remained after the seating had been provided. Vaisey J. held that the testatrix had "a general and comprehensive intention" that the residuary gift was to be devoted to a charitable purpose but that she did not have a general charitable intention "in the wider and vaguer significance of the expression"[88] and ordered an application of the surplus *cy-près*.

There is clearly a difference of opinion about the intention required on the part of a testator before surplus funds can be applied *cy-près*. One possible distinction between the cases may be that where that which is given is a legacy of money or stock and the will contains a residuary gift, the court is less inclined to impute to the testator the intention to make an out-and-out gift, since there is no risk of a partial intestacy in the event of the whole sum of money or stock not being needed for the accomplishing of the declared purposes of the gift. But the court is disposed to assume that, when a testator makes a gift of residue or of a share of residue to charity, he intends to disinherit his next of kin and, in order to achieve that purpose, to give the residue or share therefore out-and-out for a charitable purpose.[89]

A second possible distinction is that when it is obvious from the beginning that the fund will exceed the amount which will be needed to effect the avowed purpose of the gift, and the fund has not yet been transferred or appropriated, the fund will be held by the personal representatives or will trustees on a resulting trust for the residuary legatees or next of kin. It can be argued that this situation is a case of initial, and not subsequent, failure and that a general charitable intention is required although there are doubts as to whether this argument is really tenable. It is considered that the better approach is to treat all cases of surplus funds as cases of subsequent failure for which an intention to make an outright gift is sufficient.

Surplus income

11–059   Where the property itself, or the entire income thereof, is not given to a charity simpliciter, but specific sums out of the income are directed to be paid to charity, it is a question of the construction of the particular instrument or gift whether or not the donor's intention was to give the entire income of the property to the charity.[90] If it was, then that is a dedication of the whole subject-matter of the gift to the charity, and the charity will

---

[88] It is assumed that this phrase meant the intention necessary to permit property to be applied *cy-près* in the case of initial failure.

[89] In *Re Robertson* [1930] 2 Ch. 71, Bennet J. went part of but not all the way towards formulating the view expressed in the text but it would appear that his efforts to support Eve J. were vitiated by an apparent tendency to confuse an out-and-out gift with a gift promoted by a general charitable intention. See also *Re Raine* [1956] Ch. 417 at 422.

[90] *Att-Gen v Mayor of Bristol* (1820) 2 J. & W. 294 at 318; *Att-Gen v Skinners' Co.* (1826) 2 Russ. 437; *Mayor of Beverley v Att-Gen* (1857) 6 H.L.C. 333.

become entitled to any subsequent increase in value; if it was not, then the rights of the charity are bounded by the limits of the charitable intention. "We must look at the instruments to be construed, and see whether, taking them altogether, we discover an intention on the part of the donors that the rent should be divided in certain proportions and given to the different objects of the bounty of the donors in those proportions, or whether the intention manifested is that specified sums should be permanently paid to particular objects of the bounty of the donors, and that they should be entitled to nothing more than the payment of these specified sums, without abatement and without augmentation."[91]

The cases may be classified under the following heads:

(1) those in which the specific payments directed to be made out of the income exhaust it at the time, and

(2) those in which they do not so exhaust it; the second class being subdivided into cases in which there is, and cases in which there is not, an overriding charitable intention.[92]

Where the income is exhausted—A gift to charity of a rentcharge equal to the annual value of the estate at the time carries any subsequent increase in the rents and profits.[93] So also if specific payments exhausting the income at the time are directed to be made to a number of different charitable objects. In the *Thetford School Case*,[94] which is the leading authority on this point, land of the then value of £35 per annum was devised for the maintenance of a preacher, a schoolmaster, and certain poor persons, specific sums amounting in the aggregate to £35 being given to each. The land having increased in value, it was held that the whole of the increased rents went to the charitable purposes. The *Thetford School Case* has been followed in many later cases,[95] and it is now a well-established rule of charity law that where specific charitable payments are directed to be made out of the income, which at the time exhaust it, an intention to give the whole

11–060

---

[91] *Att-Gen v Dean and Canons of Windsor* (1860) 8 H.L.C. 369 at 393, 394, 406, *per* Lord Campbell.

[92] As to the classification of the cases on this subject, see *Mayor of Southmolton v Att-Gen* (1854) 5 H.L.C. 32 at 33, *per* Lord St. Leonards; *Att-Gen v Wax Chandlers' Co.* (1870) L.R. 5 Ch. 503 at 509; (1873) L.R. 6 H.L. 1 at 9.

[93] Duke, Chap. VII, s.2, p.112; *Thetford School Case* (1610) 8 Co. 130b; *Inhabitants of Eltham v Warreyn* (1635) Duke 67; *Sutton Coldfield Case* (1637), *ibid.* 68; *Hynshaw v Mayor of Morpeth* (1629), *ibid.* 69; *Kennington Hastings Case* (1611), *ibid.* 71; *Att-Gen v Mayor of Bristol* (1820) 2 J. & W. 294 at 315–319.

[94] (1610) 8 Co. 130b. The case is also reported in Duke, p.71 (Duke, B. 588), but less accurately. See *Att-Gen v Smythies* (1833) 2 R. & M. 746 at 747; *Att-Gen v Brazen Nose College* (1834) 2 Cl. & F. 295 at 327, 328.

[95] *Arnold v Att-Gen* (1698) Show.P.C. 22; *Att-Gen v Mayor of Coventry* (1700) 2 Vern. 397; *Lad v London City* (1728) Moss. 99; *Att-Gen v Johnson* (1753) Amb. 190; *Att-Gen v Haberdashers' Co.* (1792) 4 Bro.C.C. 102; sub nom. *Att-Gen v Tonna*, 2 Ves. 1; *Att-Gen v Coopers' Co.* (1812) 19 Ves. 187; *Att-Gen v Barham* (1835) 4 L.J.Ch. 128; *Att-Gen v Christ's Hospital* (1841) 4 B. 73; *Att-Gen v Gilbert* (1847) 10 B. 517. See also *Att-Gen v Brazen Nose College* (1834) 2 Cl. & F. 295, 328; *Mayor of Southmolton v Att-Gen* (1854) 5 H.L.C. 1 at 32; *Mayor of Beverley v Att-Gen* (1857) 6 H.L.C. 310; *Att-Gen v Dean and Canons of Windsor* (1860) 8 H.L.C. 369; *Att-Gen v Marchant* (1866) L.R. 3 Eq. 424 (where the donor thought he was disposing of the whole income); *University of Aberdeen v Irvine* (1868) L.R. 1 H.L.Sc. 289.

to charity is thereby shown, and charity will accordingly have the benefit of any subsequent increase in value.[96] "The exhaustion of the fund indicates the founder's intention that the whole shall be charity fund, and none should be beneficiary to the trustees."[97] Similarly if the donor specifies certain charitable objects, and then disposes of the whole of the residue of the income for a charitable purpose.[98] So also where specific charitable payments are directed to be made out of the income which do not exhaust the income at the time, and the residue of the income is directed to be applied in the reparation of the devised property.[99] The case would, however, be different if the intention was that only so much of the surplus as was required for repairs was to be so expended.[1] Under the same head should also be classed gifts to colleges, or incorporated hospitals, for the maintenance of scholars or almsmen, in which case any accretion to the amount of the available income would go to providing increased maintenance for the scholars or almsmen.[2] In most cases of this kind, however, the gift is to the college or hospital simply, with a direction that each scholar or almsman shall receive a certain stipend, which brings them under a different rule.[3]

11–061   **Where the income is not exhausted**—If the charitable payments directed to be made out of the income do not originally exhaust it, the charities will only become entitled to a subsequent increase in the income of the property if a clear intention is expressed or implied to dedicate the whole to charity,[4] as, for instance, where the specific directions are preceded by a general gift of the whole property to charitable uses.[5] If a donor has manifested an intention that the whole income of his gift shall go to charity, the fact that he has specified the objects which are to benefit in the event of a surplus will not prevent anything that is left over after those objects

---

[96] *Sutton Coldfield Case* (1637) Duke 68; *Att-Gen v Townsend* (1670) Duke 34; *Att-Gen v Winchelsea* (1791) 3 B.C.C. 373; *Att-Gen v Mayor of Bristol* (1820) 2 J. & W. 294 at 317, 318, 322; *Mercers' Co. v Att-Gen* (1828) 2 Bli.(N.S.) 165; *Att-Gen v Wilson* (1834) 3 Myl. & K. 372; *Mayor of Southmolton v Att-Gen* (1854) 5 H.L.C. 32; *Mayor of Beverley v Att-Gen* (1857) 6 H.L.C. 310 at 320.

[97] *Att-Gen v Brazen Nose College* (1834) 2 Cl. & F. 295, 328.

[98] *Att-Gen v Winchelsea* (1791) 3 B.C.C. 373; *Att-Gen v Minshull* (1798) 4 Ves. 11; *Att-Gen v Coopers' Co.* (1812) 19 Ves. 187; *Att-Gen v Solly* (1836) 5 L.J.Ch. 5; *Att-Gen v Caius College* (1837) 2 Keen 150.

[99] *Mayor of Beverley v Att-Gen* (1857) 6 H.L.C. at 310, 324; *Merchant Taylors' Co. v Att-Gen* (1871) L.R. 6 Ch. 512; *Att-Gen v Wax Chandlers' Co.* (1873) L.R. 6 H.L. 1.

[1] See *Att-Gen v Wax Chandlers' Co.* (1873) L.R. 6 H.L. 1 at 10.

[2] *Att-Gen v Mayor of Bristol* (1820) 2 J. & W. 294 at 317; *Att-Gen v Smythies* (1833) 2 R. & M. 747. This would of course be subject to the power of the court to apply *cy-près* funds not required for the existing objects of the charity.

[3] See para.11–061, below.

[4] *Att-Gen v Sparks* (1753) Amb. 201; *Att-Gen v Painter-stainers' Co.* (1788) 2 Cox 51; *Att-Gen v Haberdashers' Co.* (1792) 4 B.C.C. 102; *Att-Gen v Wilson* (1834) 3 Myl. & K. 362; *Att-Gen v Grocers' Co.* (1843) 6 B. 546; *Att-Gen v Dean and Canons of Windsor* (1860) 8 H.L.C. 369. See *Mayor of Southmolton v Att-Gen* (1854) 5 H.L.C. 1 at 32, 33, *per* Lord St. Leonards.

[5] *Arnold v Att-Gen* (1698) Show.P.C. 22; *Att-Gen v Johnson* (1753) Amb. 190; *Att-Gen v Herrick* (1772) Amb. 712; *Att-Gen v Mayor of Bristol* (1820) 2 J. & W. 294 at 308, 320; *Att-Gen v Skinners' Co.* (1826) 2 Russ. 442; *Att-Gen v Wilson* (1834) 3 Myl. & K. 362; *Att-Gen v Drapers' Co.* (1840) 2 B. 508; *Mayor of Beverley v Att-Gen* (1857) 6 H.L.C. 310 at 318; *Re Waite* [1964] N.Z.L.R. 1034.

are satisfied from being applied for charitable purposes also; for the court will merely infer that he did not foresee that the surplus would extend to further payments. Thus in *Attorney-General v Earl of Winchelsea*[6] a testator gave the residue of his estate in trust to pay specified annual sums for certain charitable purposes, and to apply any surplus income in clothing and apprenticing three children. The surplus, beyond what was needed for this purpose, was ordered to be apportioned amongst all the charitable objects mentioned in the will. Moreover, where the surplus undisposed of was insignificant, and there was a direction that the particular payments should abate proportionately in the event of depreciation of the property, it was held that the inference was that they were in like manner to share proportionately in any increase.[7] But the difference between £66 13s. 4d. and £65 3s. 4d. was not considered to be insignificant, and, not being given to the charity, it was held to belong to the donees beneficially.[8]

However, where the specific charitable payments directed to be made out of the income do not exhaust it, and no intention is otherwise shown to devote the whole of the property to charity, no case has ever gone the length of deciding that the charities can claim the surplus. This was established by *Attorney-General v Mayor of Bristol*,[9] which has been followed in numerous decisions.[10] Furthermore, if there is any subsequent increase in the value of the property the charities cannot (except in the cases mentioned below) in the absence of an overriding charitable intention claim to participate in it, whether the interest given to the charities is only a portion of the income of, or is in the nature of a charge on, the estates[11] or whether it is the benefit of a condition.[12] It is immaterial that, by reason of the change in the value of money or otherwise, such payments have become inadequate to the charitable intentions of the founder.[13]

Under the head now under consideration must also be classified the cases in which it was held that where there is a gift to a college, or

---

[6] (1791) 3 B.C.C. 373; 4 Ves. 373.
[7] *Mercers' Co. v Att-Gen* (1828) 2 Bli.(N.S.) 165. In this case the surplus undisposed of was only 9s.
[8] *Att-Gen v Brazen Nose College* (1834) 2 Cl. & F. 295 at 327. See para.11–062, below.
[9] (1820) 2 . & W. 294.
[10] See *Att-Gen v Skinners' Co.* (1826) 2 Russ. 407 at 443; *Att-Gen v Cordwainers' Co.* (1833) 3 Myl. & K. 534; *Att-Gen v Brazen Nose College* (1834) 2 Cl. & F. 295; *Att-Gen v Fishmongers' Co.* (1841) 5 Myl. & Cr. 11; *Att-Gen v Grocers' Co.* (1843) 6 B. 526; *Mayor of Southmolton v Att-Gen* (1854) 5 H.L.C. 1, 34; *Att-Gen v Trinity College* (1856) 24 B. 383; *Mayor of Beverley v Att-Gen* (1857) 6 H.L.C. 310; *Att-Gen v Dean and Canons of Windsor* (1860) 8 H.L.C. 369; *Merchant Taylors' Co. v Att-Gen* (1871) L.R. 6 Ch. 519; *Att-Gen v Wax Chandlers' Co.* (1873) L.R. 6 H.L. 1 at 9, 10, 19; *Re Waite* [1964] N.Z.L.R. 1034.
[11] *Att-Gen v Mayor of Bristol* (1820) 2 J. & W. 294 at 318; *Att-Gen v Skinners' Co.* (1826) 2 Russ. 407; *Att-Gen v Smythies* (1833) 2 R. & M. 717 at 741; *Att-Gen v Brazen Nose College* (1834) 2 Cl. & F. 295; *Att-Gen v Fishmongers' Co.* (1841) 5 Myl. & Cr. 11; *Att-Gen v Grocers' Co.* (1843) 6 B. 526; *Mayor of Southmolton v Att-Gen* (1854) 5 H.L.C. 1; *Mayor of Beverley v Att-Gen* (1857) 6 H.L.C. 310; *Att-Gen v Dean and Canons of Windsor* (1860) 8 H.L.C. 369. See also *Att-Gen v Cordwainers' Co.* (1834) 3 Myl. & K. 534; *Jack v Burnett* (1846) 12 Cl. & F. 812. As to gifts subject to charges in favour of charity, see above, para.3–006.
[12] *Att-Gen v Cordwainers' Co.* (1834) 3 Myl. & K. 534; *Jack v Burnett* (1846) 12 Cl. & F. 812; *Att-Gen v Trinity College* (1856) 24 B. 383 at 395, 396; *Att-Gen v Wax Chandlers' Co.* (1873) L.R. 6 H.L. 1 at 9, 19. As to gifts on condition, see para.3–007, above.
[13] *Att-Gen v Gascoigne* (1832) 2 Myl. & K. 647; *Commissioners of Charitable Donations v De Clifford* (1841) 1 Dr. & W. 245.

incorporated hospital, for its maintenance, with a direction that each scholar or poor person shall receive a specified stipend, the scholars or poor persons cannot claim any share in a subsequent increase of income.[14] In the case of incorporated hospitals or almshouses this has led to the master being held entitled to the whole surplus income.[15] For example, in *Attorney-General v Smythies*[16] lands were granted to a charitable corporation consisting of a master and five poor persons, with a direction that 52s. yearly should be paid to each of the poor, and that the whole of the estate should go to the support of the master and poor persons and the maintaining and repairing of the houses and possessions of the charity. The rents having increased, it was held that the poor persons were not entitled to share in the surplus, but that the master was entitled to the whole of it, subject to the payments directed to be made thereout. If, however, the master is not intended to be a beneficiary under the charity, but merely to be recompensed for his services, he will not be permitted to receive more than a fair remuneration.[17] Nor will he be entitled to the whole surplus where the governors are empowered by the instrument of foundation to regulate his stipend.[18]

11–062   The only exception to the rule that in the cases now in question the charities are not entitled to share in any increase of income is where the proportion of the rents not given to charity is specifically disposed of as an aliquot share, and not as residue. Where this is the case the charity will become entitled to a proportionate part of any increased rents. Thus in *Attorney-General v Drapers' Co.*,[19] where there was a bequest to the Drapers' Company to be applied in purchasing lands of the annual value of £100, of which £96 was given to charity, and "the residue of the said sum of £100, being £4 yearly, to the company for their pains," it was held that all the objects were entitled to participate rateably in the increased rents. On the other hand, where a testator, after directing specific payments to be made out of the income, provided that "the overplus which the said" estates "do produce beyond and more than all these disbursements do amount unto (which I do find and compute to be about £60 per annum)" should be applied for other purposes, it was held that the gift of the "overplus" was residuary.[20]

---

14 *Att-Gen v Mayor of Bristol* (1820) 2 J. & W. 294 at 317; *Att-Gen v Smythies* (1833) 2 Russ. & M. 717 at 747, 748; *Mayor of Southmolton v Att-Gen* (1854) 5 H.L.C. 1 at 32, 33. See also *Ex p. Berkhamstead Free School* (1813) 2 V. & B. 134 at 144.

15 *Att-Gen v Smythies*, above; *Re Ashton's Charity* (1859) 27 B. 115; distinguishing *Att-Gen v Master of Brentwood School* (1833) 1 Myl. & K. 376; *Att-Gen v Governors of Atherstone School* (1834) 3 Myl. & K. 544, cases where the master was held not entitled to the surplus income.

16 (1833) 2 Russ & M. 717.

17 *Att-Gen v Brentwood School* (1833) 1 Myl. & K. 376.

18 *Att-Gen v Atherstone Free School* (1834) 3 Myl. & K. 544.

19 (1841) 4 Beav. 67. See also *Att-Gen v Coopers' Co.* (1840) 3 Beav. 29 and the observations thereon in *Mayor of Beverley v Att-Gen* (1857) 6 H.L.C. 310 at 324, 325; *Att-Gen v Jesus College* (1861) 29 B. 163.

20 *Mayor of Southmolton v Att-Gen* (1854) H.L.C. 1. See also *Mayor of Beverley v Att-Gen* (1857) 6 H.L.C. 310. See further, para.11–063, below, as to division of increased rents among charitable objects.

The question whether the gift of the balance is residuary or not is a question of intention the answer to which depends upon the construction of the whole instrument, and the use of the word "residue" or "surplus" is not conclusive.[21] The use of qualifying words, such as "or thereabouts," in the statement of the amount of the income may, however, indicate that the gift is residuary,[22] but the contrary may be inferred from an expressed intention that the charities are to suffer abatement if the income diminishes.[23] Where the charitable direction was to distribute yearly 138 quarters of coal, or money to buy the same, after the price of 8d. per quarter, "the sum total in money for all the foresaid 138 quarters of coals after the foresaid price of 8d. for every quarter amounteth to the sum yearly of £4 12s.", it was held that the charge was limited to £4 12s. per annum.[24]

The surplus income, and the benefit of any subsequent increase, which the charities do not take, may be specifically disposed of either by the donees being directed to retain it for their own benefit,[25] or by its being directed to be applied in other directions.[26] In these cases, of course, no difficulty arises. Where the surplus income is not specifically disposed of, it must either be held on a resulting trust or belong to the donees beneficially.[27] The general rule is that the donee takes the property for his own benefit, charged with the specific charitable payments,[28] or subject to the conditions imposed in favour of charity,[29] as the case may be. Indeed, "a surplus undisposed of is prima facie an indication of an intention to benefit the donee."[30] In accordance with this rule it was held that if a gift be made to a college upon trust to apply the whole income in the education of the donor's relatives, any income accruing while there are no objects of the trust belongs to the college for its general educational purposes.[31] The

---

[21] *Mayor of Southmolton v Att-Gen* (1854) 5 H.L.C. 1 at 25, 26. See also *Mayor of Beverley v Att-Gen* (1857) 6 H.L.C. 310 at 325, 326; *Att-Gen v Dean and Canons of Windsor* (1860) 8 H.L.C. 369, 406.

[22] *Att-Gen v Trinity College* (1856) 24 B. 383 at 393.

[23] *Att-Gen v Smythies* (1831) 2 R. & M. 717, 743; *Att-Gen v Trinity College*, above, at 394.

[24] *Re Jordeyn's Charity* (1833) 1 Myl. & K. 416.

[25] *Att-Gen v Gascoigne* (1823) 2 Myl. & K. 647, where surplus rents were given to the executors beneficially; *Att-Gen v Skinners' Co.* (1826) 2 Russ. 407; *Att-Gen v Drapers' Co.* (1841) 4 B. 67.

[26] *Re Jordeyn's Charity* (1833) 1 Myl. & K. 416; *Mayor of Southmolton v Att-Gen* (1854) 5 H.L.C. 1 See also *Commissioners of Charitable Donations v Clifford* (1841) 1 Dr. & W. 245, where there was a specific disposition of any subsequent increase in the rents.

[27] *Att-Gen v Mayor of Bristol* (1820) 2 J. & W. 294 at 307, 308.

[28] *Att-Gen v Catherine Hall, Cambridge* (1820) Jac. 381; *Att-Gen v Mayor of Bristol* (1820) 2 J. & W. 294; *Att-Gen v Smythies* (1833) 2 R. & M. 717 at 741; *Att-Gen v Cordwainers' Co.* (1833) 3 Myl. & K. 534; *Att-Gen v Brazen Nose College* (1834) 2 Cl. & F. 295; *Att-Gen v Fishmongers' Co.* (1841) 5 Myl. & Cr. 11; *Att-Gen v Grocers' Co.* (1843) 6 Beav. 526; *Jack v Burnett* (1846) 12 Cl. & F. 828; *Mayor of Southmolton v Att-Gen* (1854) 5 H.L.C. 1, 34; *Att-Gen v Trinity College* (1856) 24 Beav. 383; *Mayor of Beverley v Att-Gen* (1857) 6 H.L.C. 310; *Att-Gen v Dean and Canons of Windsor* (1860) 8 H.L.C. 369; *Att-Gen v Sidney Sussex College* (1869) L.R. 4 Ch. 722; *Merchant Taylors' Co. v Att-Gen* (1871) L.R. 6 Ch. 519; *Att-Gen v Wax Chandlers' Co.* (1873) L.R. 6 H.L. 1 at 9, 10, 19. As to charges in favour of charity and whether they are fiduciary or not, see para.3–006, above.

[29] *Att-Gen v Trinity College* (1856) 24 Beav. 383 at 395, 396; *Att-Gen v Wax Chandlers' Co.* (1873) L.R. 6 H.L. 1 at 19. "If the devise is accepted the conditions must be fulfilled, and the money must be paid whether the land devised is or is not adequate to make the payment", *per* Lord Cairns.

[30] *Att-Gen v Trinity College* (1856) 24 B. 383 at 392, *per* Lord Romilly, M.R.

[31] *Att-Gen v Sidney Sussex College* (1865) L.R. 4 Ch. 722; *Re Lavelle* [1914] 1 Ir.R. 194.

case is the same if the residue is appropriated to an object which may or may not exhaust the whole of it. Although (as already seen[32]), if specific charitable payments are directed to be made, and the residue is to be applied in repairing the devised property, the whole will be held to be dedicated to charity, yet the devisees will take the surplus beneficially if the intention is merely to charge the repairs upon it if and when repairs become necessary.[33]

11–063 The cases in which the donees have been held to take beneficially, subject to the particular charitable payments, have usually been cases of gifts to colleges, or municipal corporations, or city guilds, but the principle is not peculiar to gifts to such bodies.[34] In any case where the donees have undertaken obligations to make payments to charity, as where they have entered into covenants and subjected themselves to liabilities which remain binding whether the rents of the property increase or decrease, that is inconsistent with the notion of their taking the property merely as trustees.[35] Where, however, an intention to devote the whole property to charity is shown, the donees cannot take beneficially unless they are themselves a charity.[36] A power to frame statutes and ordinances for the regulation of the charity property implies that the donees of the power are not to take beneficially.[37] Moreover, usage for 350 years shows almost conclusively that property is held by a corporation upon a charitable trust, and not beneficially.[38]

CY-PRÈS SCHEMES

11–064 Once a *cy-près* occasion has arisen, the charity property may only be applied for new objects following a *cy-près* scheme. A scheme may be directed by the court or the Charity Commissioners. The new application of the property must be for a purpose which is *cy-près*, that is, as near as possible to the original purpose.

Schemes

11–065 Charity trustees cannot apply charity property *cy-près* on their own initiative however desirable it may appear[39]; a direction of the court or the

---

[32] para.11–061, above.
[33] *Att-Gen v Skinners' Co.* (1826) 2 Russ. 407; *Att-Gen v Coopers' Co.* (1840) 3 Beav. 29. See *Att-Gen v Wax Chandlers' Co.* (1873) L.R. 6 H.L. 1 at 10.
[34] *Merchant Taylors' Co. v Att-Gen* (1871) L.R. 6 Ch. 519.
[35] *Att-Gen v Mayor of Bristol* (1820) 2 J. & W. 294 at 303, arg.; *Jack v Burnett* (1846) 12 Cl. & F. 812 at 828; see *Att-Gen v Merchant Venturers' Society* (1842) 5 Beav. 338.
[36] *Att-Gen v Trinity College* (1856) 24 Beav. 383 at 399; and *cf. Att-Gen v Mayor of Bristol* (1820) 2 J. & W. 294 at 308.
[37] *Re St. Paul's School* (1870) 18 W.R. 448.
[38] *ibid.* The court will assume that long possession is founded on a good title: *Goodman v Mayor of Saltash* (1882) 7 App.Cas. 633; *Haigh v West* [1893] 2 Q.B. 19.
[39] As to the duty on charity trustees to apply for a scheme, see Charities Act 1993, s.13(5) and para.6–033, above.

Commissioners is required.[40] Similarly, a scheme is necessary to apply funds *cy-près* where the expressed objects are impracticable.[41]

Although the court has jurisdiction to make *cy-près* schemes,[42] the court will usually direct a scheme to be made by the Charity Commissioners under their concurrent jurisdiction,[43] save in cases which involve special complexities or difficult questions of law or fact.[44] By section 15(1) of the Charities Act 1993 the court and the Commissioners have jurisdiction to make *cy-près* schemes in relation to charities established or regulated by Royal Charter.[45] In addition, the court and the Commissioners have power to make *cy-près* schemes for certain property of ecclesiastical charities[46] and reserve force charities.[47]

The court has power to make *cy-près* schemes in relation to certain charities established or regulated by statute.[48] The relevant statutes include, for example, the Endowed Schools Act 1869 to 1948, and are listed in Schedule 4 to the 1993 Act. A number of statutes confer power on the Charity Commissioners[49] to make schemes under their ordinary powers in relation to specified charities, for example, the Commons Act 1899[50] in relation to allotments for recreation grounds. The Commissioners have power to make *cy-près* schemes for all charities established or regulated by statute under section 17 of the 1993 Act.[51]

The Commissioners have power to make a temporary order authorising charity trustees to apply accrued or accruing income for *cy-près* purposes.[52] Such an order may only be made if the Commissioners are satisfied that three conditions have been complied with: first, that the whole of the income cannot in existing circumstances be effectively applied for the purposes of the charity; secondly, that, if those circumstances continue, a scheme might be made for applying the surplus *cy-près* and, thirdly, that it is for any reason not yet desirable to make such a scheme.

---

[40] *Att-Gen v Coopers' Co.* (1812) 19 Ves. 187; *Att-Gen v Vivian* (1826) 1 Russ. 226; *Att-Gen v Kell* (1840) 2 Beav. 575; *Att-Gen v Bushby* (1857) 24 Beav. 299; *Ward v Hipwell* (1862) 3 Giff. 547; *Re Campden Charities* (1881) Ch. D. 310 at 328, 329.

[41] *Att-Gen v City of London* (1790) 3 Bro. C.C. 171; *Att-Gen v Glyn* (1841) 12 Sim. 84; *Martin v Margham* (1844) 14 Sim. 230; *Incorporated Society v Price* (1844) 1 J. & Lat. 498; *Biscoe v Jackson* (1886) 35 Ch. D. 460; *Re Vernon's Will Trusts* [1972] Ch. 300n. *Re Armitage* [1972] Ch. 438.

[42] For the courts' jurisdiction in relation to schemes see para.10–006, above.

[43] For the Charity Commissioners' jurisdiction in relation to schemes see para.9–005, above.

[44] See Charities Act 1993, s.16(10).

[45] See para.10–005, above.

[46] See Pastoral Measure 1983, s.55 and Redundant Churches and other Religious Buildings Act 1969, s.4.

[47] See Reserve Forces Act 1996, s.120 and Sch.5.

[48] See Charities Act 1993, s.15(3) and para.10–005, above.

[49] See, for example, *Trustees of the London Parochial Charities v Att-Gen* [1955] 1 All E.R. 1 (City of London Parochial Charities Act 1883).

[50] s.18.

[51] See para.9–005, above.

[52] See Charities Act 1993, s.19(8).

Cy-près purposes

11–066   The main principle to be observed in determining the new purposes for the charity property after a *cy-près* occasion has arisen is that the property can only be applied for purposes as near as possible to the original purposes.[53] The intention of the donor must be ascertained and the new purposes should be those which can most nearly give effect to that intention.[54] Purposes may be *cy-près* the original objects even if they seem to have no trace of resemblance to them if no purposes can be found which have a closer connection.[55] Generally, however, objects which are nearer to the donor's intention will be chosen in preference to those which are more remote.[56] Provided that the proposed new purposes under a *cy-près* scheme are substantially in accordance with the donor's intention the court will not be acute to discover discrepancies.[57] It is permissible to take into account the usefulness[58] of the proposed new purpose when considering a *cy-près* scheme together with its suitability and effectiveness.[59]

The application of the main principle means that generally the new purposes will be within the same head of charity as the original purposes.[60] Thus a gift for the advancement of education will not be applied *cy-près* for the relief of poverty. However in selecting the objects to which a charitable fund shall be applied, objects already fully provided for will be rejected. Thus a proposal to apply the funds of charities for the benefit of prisoners for debt towards a school for children of persons convicted of crime and undergoing sentence was refused, on the ground (among others) that the object was better provided for by the Industrial Schools Acts.[61]

In making a scheme under s.13(1)(e)(iii)[62] in relation to a religious charity which had developed two groups with different beliefs, the court held that it should take an agnostic role. Both groups should be treated as adherents to a branch of faith which required recognition and support. Striking a fair balance between both groups was consistent with Convention rights.[63]

11–067   A proposed object may also be rejected on the ground that it would merely have the effect of relieving the rates.[64] Thus, where a charity school

---

[53] *Cook v Duckenfield* (1743) 2 Atk. 562 at 569; *Att-Gen v City of London* (1790) 3 Bro. C.C. 171, 177; *Att-Gen v Boultbee* (1794) 2 Ves. 379 at 387; *Att-Gen v Whitchurch* (1896) 3 Ves. 114; *Mills v Farmer* (1815) 1 Mer. 55 at 102; *Att-Gen v Dixie* (1833) 2 Myl. & K. 342; *Att-Gen v Ironmongers' Co.* (1841) Cr. & Ph. 208, (1844) 10 Cl. & F. 908 at 922; *Glasgow College v Att-Gen* (1848) 1 H.L.C. 800; *Att-Gen v Hankey* (1873) L.R. 16 Eq. 140n.; *Re Prison Charities* (1873) L.R. 16 Eq. 129 at 148; *Re Avenon's Charity* [1913] 2 Ch. 261 (a case of surplus).
[54] See *Re Lambeth Charities* (1853) 22 L.J. Ch. 959.
[55] *Att-Gen v Ironmongers' Co.* (1841) Cr. & Ph. 208 at 227.
[56] *Re Bridewell Hospital* (1860) 2 L.T. 760; *Re Prison Charities* (1873) L.R. 16 Eq. 129; *Att-Gen v Duke of Northumberland* (1889) 5 T.L.R. 237.
[57] *Re De Noailles* (1916) 114 L.T. 1089 at 1094–1095.
[58] *Re Prison Charities* (1873) L.R. 16 Eq. 129.
[59] *Re Weir Hospital* [1910] 2 Ch. 124 at 132.
[60] *Clephane v Edinburgh Corporation* (1869) L.R. 1 H.L.Sc. 417 at 421.
[61] *Re Prison Charities* (1873) L.R. 16 Eq. 129. See also *Att-Gen v Duke of Northumberland* (1889) 5 T.L.R. 237.
[62] See para.11–048, above.
[63] *Varsani v Jesani* [2001] W.L. 825210, *per* Patten J.
[64] *Re Prison Charities* (1873) L.R. 16 Eq. 129; *Att-Gen v Duke of Northumberland* (1889) 5 T.L.R. 237.

had been transferred to the school board, it was held that a scheme for the application of the endowment ought to provide that the funds should be applied for the advancement of learning within the school, as by establishing exhibitions, etc. and not for the general purposes of the school.[65]

The Charity Commissioners, in 1988, reviewed the exercise of their powers to make *cy-près* schemes in the light of criticism that the existing law and its interpretation was hindering charitable activity.[66] The Commissioners confirmed the main principle that regard must be had first to the original trusts of the charity but stressed that it is essential not to erect artificial barriers to a flexible use of the doctrine.[67] Thus, in certain cases, for example, a charity whose purposes fall within one head of charity may be schemed so that its new purposes fall within another head of charity.

Proposed reforms

The Strategy Unit report[68] recognised that the *cy-près* doctrine could cause difficulties for charities who wished to change their objects either to develop themselves or to merge with other charities.[69] The report proposed that the Charity Commissioners should conduct a further review of the *cy-près* doctrine. Consideration should be given to relaxing the circumstances in which a *cy-près* occasion arises[70] either by amendment of s.13 or, in the case of merger, a more extensive use of s.13(1)(c).[71] There should also be consideration of the need for the new purpose to be as close as is reasonably practicable to the original one. In addition, the report proposed that the Charity Commissioners' review should consider a relaxation on restriction to changing the objects to allow a charity to enter into a contract which is in its best interests.[72]

11–068

---

[65] *Re Poplar and Blackwall Free School* (1878) 8 Ch.D. 543. The Charity Commissioners have prepared leaflets suggesting to trustees ways in which the income of charities for the relief of poverty and for the relief of sickness may be effectively applied: see Charity Commission Leaflets CC4 and CC6.

[66] [1988] Ch. Com. Rep., paras 50–55.

[67] [1989] Ch. Com. Rep., paras 72–77. For precedents for *cy-près* schemes see Atkins, *Court Forms* (2nd ed.), Vol.8, pp.400, *et seq.*

[68] Cabinet Office, Strategy Unit, *Private Action, Public Benefit. A Review of Charities and the Wider Not-For-Profit Sector* (2002), p.46.

[69] See para.12–010 above.

[70] See Cabinet Office, Strategy Unit, *Private Action, Public Benefit. Providing flexibility for charities to evolve and merge* (2002).

[71] See para.11–046 above.

[72] See Cabinet Office, Strategy Unit, *Private Action, Public Benefit. Providing flexibility for charities to evolve and merge* (2002).

CHAPTER 12

VARIATION AND MERGER

INTRODUCTION

Charities are under increasing pressure to operate effectively and effi- **12–001**
ciently.[1] The ways in which charities are expected to operate to achieve
their aims is also subject to change, for example, charities have seen a shift
in funding from grants to contracts.[2] Charities need the necessary powers
to enable them to operate effectively in a rapidly changing environment
and the extent to which charities can vary their governing instruments is
important. One form of response to the increasing pressures for effectiveness and efficiency is merger. It is in relation to merger of charities that
powers of variation have particular relevance. Other methods of joint
working[3] can also highlight the need for charities' governing instruments
to be varied.

VARIATION

The extent to which, and the way in which, a charity may be varied after **12–002**
it has been founded depends upon the legal structure of the charity and
the wording of the particular governing instrument. Charitable trusts,
unincorporated associations and companies limited by guarantee are,
therefore, considered separately. It should be remembered that the courts
and the Charity Commissioners have scheme making powers in relation to
charities, including those founded by Royal Charter[4] and those regulated
by statute.[5] Specific provisions in ss.74 and 75 of the Charities Act 1993
allow small charities to amend their objects or administrative provisions
or to spend capital by resolution of their trustees.

---

[1] See, *e.g.* Report of the Comptroller and Auditor General, *Giving confidently: The role of the Charity Commission in regulating charities* (2001) H.C. 234, p.7; Cabinet Office, Strategy Unit, *Private Action, Public Benefit. A Review of Charities and the Wider Not-For-Profit Sector* (2002), p.32.

[2] See J. Warburton and D. Morris, "Charities and the Contract Culture" [1991] Conv. 419; D. Morris, *Charities and the Contract Culture, Partners or Contractors? Law and Practice in Conflict* (The Charity Law Unit, University of Liverpool, 1999).

[3] For possible methods of joint working, see D. Leat and A. Passey, *Joint Working and Mergers in the Voluntary Sector* (National Council for Voluntary Organisations, 2000) and RS4, *Collaborative Working and Mergers* (2003).

[4] See para.10–005, above.

[5] See paras 9–005, 10–005, above.

Trusts

12–003   When a charity has been founded and trusts have been declared the founder has no power to revoke, vary or add to the trusts. This is so irrespective of whether the trusts have been declared by an individual,[6] or by a body of subscribers,[7] or by the trustees.[8]

Furthermore, a person who has conveyed land to a charity by way of gift cannot afterwards defeat that gift by selling the land for value. A voluntary conveyance of land for charitable purposes, if made in good faith, is not voidable at the instance of a subsequent purchaser under s.173 of the Law of Property Act 1925; for, when a charity has once been formed and endowed, the founder cannot by any act of his alter the endowment.[9]

The original and later trustees are similarly bound by the terms of the trust. Any attempt by the trustees to use the funds of the charitable trust for objects outside those specified in the trust instrument is liable to be restrained by injunction.[10] In the absence of any power of variation in the trust instrument,[11] the objects of a trust can only be altered by the court or the Charity Commissioners by means of a *cy-près* scheme.[12] There is much to be said, therefore, for drafting the objects of the trust as widely as possible, with specific activities merely indicated rather than comprising the main objects.

12–004   It is not unusual for a trust instrument to contain a power for the trustees to vary the administrative provisions of the trust[13] and this power can be used, for example, to alter the qualifications for trusteeship.[14] Any restrictions on the power of amendment, for example, no amendment permitting trustees to be paid without the written consent of the Charity Commissioners, must be observed as must any procedural requirements. In the absence of a power of amendment, the court has power to alter the administrative machinery of a charitable trust by scheme under its inherent jurisdiction.[15] The power is a wide one and can extend to altering conditions attached to gifts, for example, the date by which funds should be distributed, thus obviating the need for a *cy-près* scheme.[16] The test for the

---

[6] *Re Hartshill Endowment* (1861) 30 Beav. 130.

[7] *Att-Gen v Kell* (1840) 2 Beav. 575; *Att-Gen v Bovill* (1840) 1 Ph. 762.

[8] *Duke on Charitable Uses*, 116; *Andrews v McGuffog* (1886) 11 App. Cas. 313 at 329.

[9] *Corporation of Newcastle v Att-Gen* (1842) 12 Cl. & F. 412 (subnom. *Att-Gen v Corporation of Newcastle* (1842) 5 Beav. 312). See also *East Grinstead's Case* (1633) Duke 64; *Trye v Corporation of Gloucester* (1851) 14 Beav. 173 (where the point was mentioned but not decided).

[10] See, *e.g. Att-Gen v Ross* [1986] 1 W.L.R. 252; *Att-Gen v Wright* [1988] 1 W.L.R. 164 and see para.10–059, above.

[11] The Charity Commissioners usually refuse to register a charitable trust deed which contains a power which would allow a fundamental change of the objects clause.

[12] See paras 11–066, *et seq.*, above. The Secretary of State for Education has power by order to modify the trust instruments of foundation, voluntary and foundation special schools—School Standards and Framework Act 1998, s.82.

[13] See The Charity Law Associations Trust Deed for a Charitable Trust, clause 8, and the Charity Commissioners' Model Declaration of Trust for a Charitable Trust, clause 28.

[14] See, for example, *Re Holloway's Trusts* (1909) 26 T.L.R. 62.

[15] See para.10–008, above.

[16] *Re J W Laing Trust* [1984] Ch. 143.

making of an administrative scheme is whether it is expedient in the interest of the charity, taking into account all its circumstances.[17]

The Charity Commissioners have a similar power to provide a charity with a more appropriate administrative framework by virtue of s.16 of the Charities Act 1993.[18] A scheme may be a fully regulating one which deals with all aspects of a charity's purposes and administration. In that case the scheme becomes the governing document of the charity. Alternatively, the scheme may simply vary part of the trust deed.[19] Where only a variation of the trust instrument is required, the Commissioners will usually proceed by order under s.26 of the 1993 Act.[20] In addition, where trustees request a specific power, the Commissioners will usually offer a general power of amendment to enable the trust to adapt itself to changing conditions in the future.[21]

Unincorporated Associations

There is no implied power to alter the constitution, or rules, of a charitable unincorporated association; the constitution cannot be amended by a majority of members at a general meeting.[22] If the constitution does contain a power to alter the rules, clearly its terms must be followed.[23] A charitable unincorporated association is unlikely to be registered as a charity by the Charity Commissioners if the constitution contains an unfettered power to alter the objects of the association. The Commissioners' own model constitution for a charitable unincorporated association contains a clause permitting amendment but requires the written consent of the Commissioners before any alteration is made to the objects clause and forbids any alteration which would have the effect of making the association cease in law to be a charity.[24] The objects of an unincorporated association may be altered by a *cy-près* scheme made by the court or the Commissioners in the same way as a trust.[25]

The officers of a charitable unincorporated association will be prevented by injunction from applying the funds of the association for noncharitable purposes even if the association has altered its constitution in accordance with the rules to give power for the funds to be so applied. Thus, in *Baldry v Feintuck*[26] the students union of Sussex University was restrained by injunction from applying part of its funds to support "War on Want" and a separate political campaign even though the objects of the union had been changed to "The aims and objects of the union shall be

12–005

---

[17] *ibid.*, at 153.
[18] See para.9–005, above.
[19] See OG1 A2, *Orders and Schemes. An Overview*, s.2.
[20] See para.9–007, above.
[21] See OG1 A1, *Orders under Section 26 of the Charities Act 1993*, s.3 and see the Model Order in OG1 D2.
[22] *Re Tobacco Trade Benevolent Association Charitable Trusts* [1958] 1 W.L.R. 1113.
[23] See, Warburton, *Unincorporated Associations: Law and Practice* (2nd ed), pp.16–17.
[24] Clause U. See also The Charity Law Association's Constitution for a Charitable Unincorporated Association, clause 12.
[25] See above.
[26] [1972] 1 W.L.R. 552.

the promotion of any matter whatsoever of interest to its members". In the course of his judgment, Brightman J. said[27]:

"The union is, clearly, an education charity and the officers of the union who have power to dispose of the union's funds are, clearly, trustees of those funds for charitable educational purposes. It is not, therefore, open to the union, by a purported amendment to the union's constitution, to authorise the use of the union's funds for the purpose of promoting any object which may happen to interest the members of the union regardless of whether such object is charitable and educational or not."

Provided the constitution of a charitable unincorporated association contains a provision to alter the rules, there are no limitations in the way in which the administrative provisions of an association may be varied. If the constitution does not contain a power of alteration, the court or the Commissioners have similar powers to amend the administrative provisions of charitable unincorporated associations as they do charitable trusts.[28]

Companies

12-006   The objects of a company may be changed by the members of the company altering the memorandum by special resolution.[29] The purposes of a charitable trust may only be altered if all the conditions of *cy-près* are satisfied and the court or the Charity Commissioners make an appropriate scheme.[30] The question is, to what extent it is possible to alter the purposes for which a charitable company holds its funds and how any such alteration is to be carried out.

It is generally accepted that a charitable company can change its objects by the usual method of alteration of the memorandum[31] but there are restrictions on the changes that can be made. Where a charitable company alters its memorandum so that the company ceases to be charitable the alteration is ineffective as regards previously acquired property or the income of such property or property representing property so acquired, unless the property was acquired for full consideration in money or money's worth.[32] Thus, on a charitable company ceasing to be charitable, all the existing property remains subject to the original objects and only new property is applicable for the new objects.

By s.64(2) of the Charities Act 1993[33] a charitable company may not alter its objects clause, even to other charitable objects, without the writ-

---

[27] [1972] 1 W.L.R. 557.
[28] See para.12–003, above.
[29] Companies Act 1985, s.4, see *Palmer's Company Law*, para.2.617.
[30] See paras 9–001, *et seq.*, above.
[31] See Charities Act 1993, s.64 and [1971] Ch. Com. Rep., para.30.
[32] Charities Act 1993, s.64(1). This section applies to corporations generally.
[33] Originally, Companies Act 1989, s.111.

ten consent of the Charity Commissioners. The Commissioners are unlikely to consent to a proposed alteration which would alter the purposes of the company in a way that is so radical that it would not reasonably have been contemplated by those who supported the company.[34] The written consent of the Commissioners is also required to alter any other provisions in the memorandum or articles of association of a charitable company which direct or restrict the manner in which property of the company may be used or applied, for example, a clause in the memorandum requiring specific property to be used for specific purposes. In either case, a copy of the Charity Commissioners' written consent must be sent to the Registrar of Companies when notifying the alteration.[35]

Where a charitable company is holding funds on trust as well as general funds any change in the objects of the charity must be effected by both a change in the memorandum of the company and a *cy-près* scheme.[36] Thus, if there is any possibility of some of the funds of the charitable company being held on trust, either because of the terms of a particular gift or because the charity was initially founded as an unincorporated association, the Charity Commissioners must be approached for a scheme to be made *cy-près* at the same time as the company's memorandum is altered by the necessary resolution.

12–007

Small Charities

Small charities present particular difficulties in relation to the making of effective use of assets; governing instruments do not tend to have provisions permitting variation and the *cy-près* procedure is unduly complex for the size of the funds involved. The Charities Act 1985 was passed to make it easier for small charities to modernise their trusts and to dispose of funds. The Act, however, was not widely used[37] and the Charities Act 1992 extended the provisions to all small charities, not merely local charities for the relief of poverty, and increased the monetary limits. The provisions are now to be found in ss.74 and 75 of the Charities Act 1993.[38]

12–008

By s.74 of the 1993 Act, a charity whose gross income did not exceed £5,000 in the last financial year and which does not hold land on trusts which stipulate that the land is to be for the purposes, or any particular purposes, of the charity can resolve to transfer the charity property to one or more other charities, to modify the objects of the charity or to modify any of the administrative provisions of the trusts of the charity. By s.75 a charity which has a permanent endowment which does not consist of or comprise any land and whose gross income in the last financial year did not exceed £1,000 can resolve to spend the capital of the charity. The relevant conditions must be satisfied and the correct procedure followed for

---

[34] See OG47 B2, *Alterations to Governing Documents: Charitable Companies*, s.2.2.
[35] Charities Act 1993, s.46(3). Failure to submit the Charity Commissioners' consent is a criminal offence – s.64(4).
[36] [1971] Ch. Com. Rep., para.27.
[37] [1988] Ch. Com. Rep., para.49.
[38] See generally, CC44, *Small Charities* (2000).

any such resolution to be effective. The powers under ss.74 and 75 are not available to either exempt charities or charitable companies.[39]

Before charity trustees can resolve to transfer charity property to one or more other charities they must be satisfied that the existing purposes of the charity have ceased to be conducive to a suitable and effective application of the charity's resources and that the purposes of the charity or charities to which the property is to be transferred are as similar in character to the purposes of the transfer, or charity as is reasonably practicable[40] and the trustees of the receiving charity or charities must have given written confirmation that they are willing to accept the transfer of the property.[41] In order for charity trustees to resolve to modify all or any of the purposes of the charity, they must be satisfied that the existing purposes of the charity, or such of them as it is proposed to replace, have ceased to be conducive to a suitable and effective application of the charity's resources and that the purposes specified in the resolution are as similar in character to those existing purposes as is practical in the circumstances.[42]

12–009   Before charity trustees can resolve to spend the capital they must be of the opinion that the property of the charity is too small, in relation to its purpose, for any useful purpose to be achieved by the expenditure of income alone.[43] The trustees must also have considered whether any reasonable possibility exists of effecting a transfer of the charity's property to one or more charities under s.74.[44]

A resolution of charity trustees, whether to transfer property, to modify objects or administrative provisions or to spend capital must be passed by a majority of not less than two thirds of the trustees who voted on the resolution.[45] Once a resolution has been passed, the charity trustees must give public notice of it in such manner as they think reasonable in the circumstances[46] and send a copy of the resolution to the Charity Commissioners with a statement of their reasons for passing it.[47] The Commissioners may require the trustees to supply them with additional information about the passing of the resolution.[48] If the Commissioners notify their concurrence[49] with the resolution, the objects or administrative provisions stand modified or the trustees have power to spend capital, as appropriate, from the date specified in the notification.[50] In the case of

---

[39] For variation of charitable companies, see para.12–006, above.

[40] A transfer to a charity with wide objects, such as a Community Trust, is unlikely to satisfy the condition.

[41] Charities Act 1993, s.74(4). The charity to which the property is being transferred need not be registered – s.74(2). Thus, two small charities, both excepted from registration because their income is less than £1,000 a year, can merge without the need to register.

[42] *ibid.*, s.74(5). This condition would appear to be easier to satisfy than the normal *cy-près* conditions in s.13(1), see paras 11–046, *et seq.*, above.

[43] *ibid.*, s.75(2).

[44] *ibid.*, s.75(4).

[45] ibid., s.74(3), 75(3).

[46] The Commissioners must consider representations made within six weeks of their receiving the copy resolution – ss.74(7), 75(6).

[47] Charities Act 1993, ss.74(6), 75(5).

[48] *ibid.*, ss.74(7), 75(6).

[49] The Commissioners' decision must be made within three months of receipt of the copy resolution – see ss.74(8), 75(7).

[50] Charities Act 1993, ss.74(9)(b), 75(8).

a resolution to transfer property, once the Commissioners have notified their concurrence the trustees must arrange for the property to be transferred and, if necessary, the Commissioners, will make the appropriate vesting orders.[51]

The Strategy Unit report identified[52] the financial limits and detailed conditions in ss.74 and 75 of the Charities Act 1993 as barriers to charities wishing to develop as individual charities or to merge. The report proposes that the £5,000 limit on income[53] in s.74 for charities wishing to transfer property or modify objects should be raised to £10,000, the conditions broadened and simplified and the Charity Commissioners given discretion as to the requirement for publication of the resolution. Further, the income limit and the need for the Charity Commissioners' consent for making changes to administrative provisions should be removed.[54] The report also recommends easing the conditions in s.74 to be satisfied before a charity can spend its permanent endowment.[55] In particular, the report proposes that a charity itself should be able to resolve to spend capital up to the value of £10,000 and that the Charity Commissioners should be able to authorise conversion of permanent endowment above that figure if it is consistent with the spirit of the gift and will allow the charity to more effectively fulfil its purposes.[56]

MERGER

Charities seeking to merge can encounter a number of problems the **12–010** solution to which may involve exercising one or more of the powers of variation discussed above. There is no one method or form by which charities can merge; the method adopted will depend on the legal structures of the merging charities and a number of non-legal considerations, in particular the views of the trustees, staff, volunteers and members of the charities.[57] The more common forms of merger are the transfer of assets from one charity to another with subsequent dissolution of the first charity; the formation of a new charity with the subsequent dissolution of the merging charities and one charity taking control of another, for example, by becoming trustee.[58] The decision as to whether, and when, to dissolve an original charity will be largely dictated by the need to collect future

---

[51] *ibid.*, s.74(9)(a), (10). Property which was subject to restrictions on expenditure remains subject to those restrictions in the hands of the transferee charity.

[52] Cabinet Office, Strategy Unit, *Private Action, Public Benefit. A Review of Charities and the Wider Not-For-Profit Sector* (2002), p.46.

[53] See para.12–008, above.

[54] Cabinet Office, Strategy Unit, *Private Action, Public Benefit. Providing Flexibility for Charities to Evolve and Merge* (2002).

[55] See para.12–008, above.

[56] Cabinet Office, Strategy Unit, *Private Action, Public Benefit. A Review of Charities and the Wider Not-For-Profit Sector* (2002), pp.47–48.

[57] See D. Morris, *Legal Issues in Charity Mergers* (The Charity Law Unit, the University of Liverpool, 2001), pp.15, *et seq.*

[58] See J. Warburton, *Mergers: A Legal Good Practice Guide* (The Charity Law Unit, the University of Liverpool, 2001), p.2; Cabinet Office, Strategy Unit, *Private Action, Public Benefit. Providing Flexibility for Charities to Evolve and Merge* (2002).

legacies named for the original charity. Whilst the merged charity may be able to take a legacy in certain circumstances, for example, amalgamation by scheme of the Charity Commissioners[59] a gift specifically to a named charitable company, for example, will fail if that charity is dissolved.[60] If an original charity is retained as a "shell" charity it will have to comply with all the requirements of a registered charity in relation to accounts[61] and returns and is in danger of being removed from the register if it is inactive.[62]

All of the methods of merger give rise to questions as to whether the merging charities have the requisite powers to both actually merge and then to operate effectively in the future. These issues, and others relating to the use of charity property following merger, are discussed below. Mergers also raise problems in relation to the terms and conditions of staff[63] and readers are referred to the standard texts on employment law on these issues.[64]

Transfer of property

12–011   Where a merger involves the transfer of property from one charity to another, two questions arise. Does the first charity have power to transfer the property and, if so, can it transfer it to the second charity? If no power to transfer the relevant property for the purposes of merger exists, the governing instrument will need to be varied either by use of an existing power of amendment or by seeking an order from the Charity Commissioners. The precise procedure will depend on the legal structure of the charity seeking to transfer.[65] Even if a power to transfer the property exists, the trustees of the first charity will be acting in breach of trust if they transfer the property to a charity with objects wider than those of their own charity.[66] To enable a merger to proceed, charity trustees may need to seek a *cy-près* scheme to widen the objects of their charity to those proposed for the merged charity. If the charity is not able to operate effectively in its present form, a *cy-près* occasion may have arisen under s.13(1)(d) or s.13(1)(e)(iii) of the Charities Act 1993.[67]

Where a charity has a number of properties, the title to which it needs to transfer to another charity to effect a merger, it may be possible for the properties to be transferred by scheme made by the Charity Commissioners.[68] Whatever the method of transfer used, any restrictions

---

[59] See para.11–020 above.
[60] See para.11–017 above.
[61] See paras 9–013, *et seq.*, above.
[62] Charities Act 1993, s.3(4) and see para.1–032 above.
[63] See D. Morris, "The Employment Law Implications of Charity Mergers" (2001) 23 *Employee Relations* 271.
[64] See Harvey, *Industrial Relations and Employment Law*, Vol.1.
[65] See paras 12–001, *et seq.,* above.
[66] *Att-Gen v Brandreth* (1842) 1 Y. & c Ch.Cas. 200, see para.(245) above.
[67] See para.11–047, above.
[68] See [1999–2000] Ch. Com. Rep. 8.

on assignment will have to be observed, for example, any necessary landlord's consent to assign a lease will have to be obtained.[69]

Use of property

A charity which holds separate funds for particular purposes within its objects may be holding those funds on special trusts.[70] Whether funds are held on separate trusts or are merely held for designated purposes within the general property of the charity depends upon the intention of the donor.[71] In the course of merger, a merged charity may become trustee of the property of a merging charity which has narrower objects than those of the merged charity. The merged charity will then hold the property of the first charity on special trust and not as part of its general funds. In whatever way the special trusts have arisen, the funds can only be used for the restricted purposes of the special trusts and not the wider purposes of the charity. A merged charity with a number of special trusts, if it is incapable of operating without general use of the funds in those special trusts, may be able to establish that a *cy-près* occasion has arisen[72] and apply for a scheme to use all the funds for the general purposes of the merged charity. A merged charity can avoid any possible need to register special trusts separately by apply to the Charity Commissioners for a uniting direction under s.96(6) of the 1993 Act requiring that the special trusts be registered with the merged charity.[73]

12–012

If all the property of a charity cannot be expended without distinguishing between income and capital, the charity has permanent endowment.[74] Whether particular property is permanent endowment depends mainly on the intention of the donor in relation to the retention of the capital of his gift.[75] The trust obligation to retain the capital of permanent endowment is unaffected by merger which can present problems both as to the holding and use of permanent endowment.

The desire to avoid personal liability means that a merged charity is very often a company limited by guarantee. A charitable company, however, holds its general property beneficially and not on trust[76] and therefore cannot accept a transfer of any property which is permanent endowment from a merging charity. The solution is for the charitable company to become corporate trustee of the property that is permanent endowment. If a uniting direction under s.96(5) of the 1993 Act is made subsequently by the Charity Commissioners, the permanently endowed fund and the charitable company will be treated as a single charity for registration and accounting purposes.

---

[69] See J. Warburton and W. Barr, "Charity Mergers—Property Problems" [2002] Conv. 531.
[70] See Charities Act 1993, s.97(1).
[71] See *Re Church Army* (1906) 94 L.T. 559; *Neville Estates v Madden* [1962] 1 Ch. 832.
[72] See para.11–047, above.
[73] Separate accounts do not have to be produced, see Charities Act 1993, s.97(1).
[74] See Charities Act 1993, s.96(3).
[75] See *Re Clergy Orphan Corporation* (1894) 3 Ch. 145; *Re Church Army* (1906) 94 L.T. 559.
[76] See para.3–046, above.

12–013   A merger of charities may not be economically and practically possible
if the capital of funds which are permanent endowment cannot be used
for the general purposes of the merged charity. There are strong arguments that permanent endowment cannot be expended unless provision is
made for recoupment.[77] The courts themselves, however, have on occasion,
permitted expenditure of permanent endowment without a requirement
for recoupment.[78] It is considered that in the extreme case where one or
more charities cannot individually carry out their charitable objects effectively because of lack of income but could form an effective merged charity if capital of a permanently endowed fund could be spent, that the
Charity Commissioners would have power under s.26 of the 1993 Act to
make an order permitting expenditure of capital.[79]

Proposed reforms

12–014   Whilst the Strategy Unit was careful not to advocate merger of charities, it did recognise that charities seeking to merge faced barriers and the
report made a number of proposals to facilitate mergers.[80] The proposed
easing of the small charities provisions, in particular those permitting
charities to spend permanent endowment, have already been noted,[81] as
has the proposal for the Charity Commissioners to undertake a review of
the *cy-près* doctrine.[82] The report proposes statutory provision for the benefit of all future legacies and gifts to transfer automatically to the merged
charity thus obviating the need for shell charities. In addition, it is proposed that the Charity Commissioners should provide specific advice to
facilitate merger and, in particular, should draw up guidance on due
diligence which provides a light touch.[83]

---

[77] See para.13–001 above and *Andrews v McGuffog* (1886) 11 App. Cas. 313, HL.
[78] *Re Willenhall Chapel of Ease* (1865) 8 L.T. 854.
[79] See J. Warburton and W. Barr, "Charity Mergers—Property Problems" [2002] Conv. 531 at
537.
[80] Cabinet Office, Strategy Unit, *Private Action, Public Benefit. A Review of Charities and the
Wider Not-For-Profit Sector* (2002), p.46.
[81] See para.12–009.
[82] See para.11–068 above.
[83] Cabinet Office, Strategy Unit, *Private Action, Public Benefit. Providing flexibility for
charities to evolve and merge.*

CHAPTER 13

TERMINATION

INTRODUCTION

There is strong authority for the proposition that a charity cannot be **13–001** terminated. Thus in *National Anti-Vivisection Society v Inland Revenue*[1] Lord Simonds said[2]:

> "A charity once established does not die, though the nature may be changed."

Similarly, in *Re Faraker*[3] Farwell J. said[4]:

> "Suppose the Charity Commissioners or this court were to declare that a particular existing charitable trust was at an end and extinct, in my opinion they would go beyond their jurisdiction in so doing. They cannot take an existing charity and destroy it: they are obliged to administer it."

The proposition is certainly true to the extent that if the purposes of a charity become outdated the charity trustees are under a duty to apply for a *cy-près* scheme rather than to terminate the charity.[5]

It will become apparent, however, that the proposition has been diluted over the years but the emphasis on retention of permanent endowment for charity remains. A distinction has to be borne in mind between charity as a concept and the individual legal structure of a charity.

A charity is not terminated if it is altered in its constitution or objects **13–002** or amalgamated with another charity. This is so whether the alteration or amalgamation is done by way of scheme made by the Charity Commissioners or the court,[6] under a power in the charity's governing instrument,[7] by statute[8] or informally.[9] As Plowman J. said in *Re Stemson's*

---

[1] [1948] A.C. 31.
[2] *ibid.*, at 74.
[3] [1912] 2 Ch. 488.
[4] *ibid.*, at 495. See also *Att-Gen v Nethercoat* (1841) 10 L.J. Ch. 162 and *Darke v Williamson* (1858) 25 Beav. 623 on the courts' reluctance to destroy a charity by ordering a sale of charity property to reimburse trustees for expenses properly incurred.
[5] Charities Act 1993, s.13(5) and see para.6–033, above.
[6] *Re Lucas* [1948] Ch. 424; *Re Faraker* [1912] 2 Ch. 488. See para.11–020, above.
[7] *Re Bagshaw* [1954] 1 W.L.R. 238. See para.11–021, above.
[8] *Re Donald* [1909] 2 Ch. 410. See para.11–022, above.
[9] *Re Joy* (1888) 60 L.T. 175. See para.11–025, above.

Will Trusts[10] a charitable trust retains its existence despite such vicissitudes as schemes, amalgamations and changes of name so long as it has any funds.

It is not the case, however, that a charity can never be terminated. Wilberforce J. in *Re Roberts*[11] recognised one important limitation to the idea of perpetual existence when he said[12]:

> "Those words that it is not competent for the court or the charity commissioners to bring an endowed charity to an end, seem to me not necessarily to apply to a case where the trustees of the charity are given express powers to terminate the charity."

Thus where a charity is founded as an organisation liable to termination with a constitution which provides for the disposal of funds in that event, then if the organisation ceases to exist and its funds are disposed of, the charity or charitable trust itself ceases to exist.[13] For example, a charitable trust may require that all capital and income should be distributed within 10 years of its foundation.[14]

13–003   A charity will also terminate if it no longer has funds. For example, in *Re Withall*[15] Clauson J. said[16]:

> "... if the work of an institution such as the Margate Cottage Hospital is being carried on by those who are voluntarily administering its affairs, without funds, from day to day on such bounty as it can obtain, when those administrators cease for lack of means to carry on the work, the work ceases, there are no longer any persons associated for the purposes of the work, and there are no funds dedicated to the work which was therefore carried on: in such circumstances in a full and true sense that institution in my view has ceased to exist."

There is thus a distinction between a charity with a permanent endowment and a charity which has power to spend both income and capital. In the latter case, the charity trustees can terminate the charity by applying all its funds for the purposes set out in the governing instrument. Charity trustees of a small charity with a permanent endowment and an income of £1,000 or less a year can resolve, with the consent of the Charity Commissioners, to spend the capital and in that way terminate the trust.[17] In the case of a larger charity with a permanent endowment the only way in which the charity trustees would be able to expend all the funds of the charity is if the terms of the trust were varied by scheme by the Charity

---

[10] [1970] 1 Ch. 16 at 26.
[11] [1963] 1 W.L.R. 406.
[12] *ibid.*, at 413.
[13] *Re Stemson's Will Trusts* [1970] Ch. 16 at 26, *per* Plowman J. distinguishing *Re Vernon's Will Trusts* [1972] 1 Ch. 300n.
[14] See the trusts in *Re J. W. Laing's Trust* [1984] Ch. 143.
[15] [1932] 2 Ch. 236.
[16] *ibid.*, at 241.
[17] Charities Act 1993, s.75 and see para.12–008, above.

Commissioners. This is highly unlikely as the Commissioners probably do not have power to order such a variation if it is sought with a view to bringing the charity to an end; their general function is to promote the effective use of charitable resources[18] and not to destroy charities.[19] In such circumstances the Commissioners will probably seek another charity with similar purposes with which the original charity can amalgamate.[20]

There is a third situation in which the general proposition that a charity cannot die does not apply. A charity whose objects are dependent upon the existence of a particular institution or premises will terminate if the institution closes down or those premises are no longer available.[21] In the case of a charity linked to a particular institution, it does not matter that the failure of the institution has occurred because the need for that institution has gone or because of lack of funds.[22] The general proposition will apply, however, if the objects of the charity are purposes which can be carried on independently of the particular institution.[23]

Where termination of a charity is possible the procedure to be followed to dissolve the charity will depend upon the legal structure of the charity and the provisions of the particular governing instrument. The position in relation to charitable trusts, unincorporated associations and companies limited by guarantee is examined below. Once a charity has been dissolved the final trustees[24] are under a duty to notify the Charity Commissioners that the charity has ceased to exist.[25] The Commissioners are then obliged to remove the charity from the register.[26]

TRUSTS

It is in relation to charitable trusts that the general proposition that a charity cannot die is most powerful. Thus the model declaration of trust for a charitable trust produced by the Charity Commissioners provides no express power for the trustees to terminate the trust. Other precedents contain an optional power to dissolve and to distribute any surplus funds to similar charitable objects.[27]

While the Commissioners have power to dissolve an incorporated body of trustees, the property of the charity becomes vested in the trustees or such other persons as may be specified by the Commissioners and the

13–004

---

[18] Charities Act 1993, s.1(3) and see para.9–001, above.

[19] See the statement of Farwell J. in *Re Faraker* [1912] 2 Ch. 488 at 495 at para.13–001, above.

[20] For transfer of assets to another charity see para.13–004, below and see para.12–013 above for the use of permanent endowment in a merger of charities.

[21] *Re Rymer* [1895] 1 Ch. 19.

[22] *Re Slatter's Will Trust* [1964] 1 Ch. 512 at 527 *per* Plowman J.

[23] See *Re Finger's Will Trust* [1972] Ch. 286; [1974] Conv. 187 (J. E. Martin) and para.11–017, above.

[24] *i.e.* the persons having the general control and management of the administration of the charity–Charities Act 1993, s.97(1).

[25] Charities Act 1993, s.3(7)(b).

[26] *ibid.*, at s.3(4).

[27] See, *e.g.* the Charity Law Association's Trust Deed for a Charitable Trust, clause 10.

charity continues in being.[28] A small number of trusts are set up for a limited period of time and others, where the gift is subject to a condition subsequent, terminate on the failure of the specified conditions.[29] Most terminations of charitable trusts, however, occur because of lack of funds.

A termination because of lack of funds may be voluntarily in the sense that the charity trustees decide to distribute all the funds for the purposes of the charity[30] or to transfer the assets to another charity. Charity trustees can only transfer all the assets to another charity if there is specific power to do so in the trust instrument, otherwise there may be an unlawful delegation of the trustees' powers. The trustees of a charity with an income of £5,000 a year or less can, in certain circumstances, resolve with the concurrence of the Charity Commissioners, to transfer the property of the charity to another charity.[31] In any other case the Commissioners have power under s.26 of the Charities Act 1993 to sanction a transfer of assets to another charity.

The one situation in which the Commissioners are likely to sanction a transfer of assets is where the trustees wish to carry on the work of the charity but consider that it can be done more effectively through the structure of a charitable company. In that instance, there will be a transfer of assets to a new charitable company and the original charitable trust will terminate. As the charitable company will be carrying out the same purposes as the trust any legacies to the trust should be capable of being taken by the charitable company. What is relevant are the charitable purposes, not the legal structure through which they are being carried out.[32] The commissioners, however, are not prepared to transfer permanent endowment assets to a charitable company as those assets would then be held with the rest of the corporate property and be available to creditors.[33]

13–005   Where charity trustees intend to terminate a charitable trust voluntarily by distributing or transferring the assets of the trust they should only do so after all the debts and liabilities of the charity have been paid or settled. Trustees of a charitable trust are under personal liability in respect of all obligations entered into on behalf of the charity. Although trustees are entitled to an indemnity from the trust assets in respect of liabilities properly incurred,[34] that indemnity will cease to have any value once the assets of the charity are distributed or transferred. Charity trustees will, in any event, remain liable for any breaches of trust which occurred before the termination of the trust.[35]

The termination of a charitable trust will be involuntary where the trust has no funds because its liabilities exceed its assets. The trustees will remain personally liable to the extent that the charity's assets are not suf-

---

[28] Charities Act 1993, s.61. For incorporation of trustees, see para.5–019, above.

[29] See para.3–022, above.

[30] But only if there is no permanent endowment–see para.13–001, above.

[31] Charities Act 1993, s.74 and see para.12–008, above.

[32] See para.12–010 above for the obligation of charity trustees if the charitable trust is retained, out of caution, as a "shell" charity to receive legacies.

[33] See para.12–012 above for the mechanism of the charitable company becoming a corporate trustee.

[34] *Ex p. Garland* (1804) 10 Ves. 110.

[35] See para.10–058, above.

ficient to discharge all the debts. If the Charity Commissioners become concerned as to the way in which the insolvency situation has arisen, they may determine to conduct an inquiry under s.8 of the Charities Act 1993.[36] The Commissioners may then appoint additional trustees in exercise of their temporary and protective powers in s.18 of the 1993 Act[37] to take over the administration of the charity and to deal with the winding up of its affairs. In exceptional circumstances, the Official Solicitor may be appointed by the Commissioners as trustee to wind up a charitable trust.[38]

It is possible as a result of change in social habits and needs that a particular purpose once charitable is no longer so.[39] In those circumstances, trustees are obliged to apply for a *cy-près* scheme.[40] If the resultant *cy-près* scheme directs new purposes for the trust it will remain in existence as a charitable trust, albeit with new objects. If the *cy-près* scheme directs the assets of the trust to be transferred to another charitable institution, the trust will terminate once the assets have been transferred.[41]

Unincorporated Associations

When considering the termination of a charitable unincorporated association a distinction must be made beween the abstract concept of the charity and the institutional mechanism through which the funds of the charity are held and administered.[42] Although the chosen mechanism, the unincorporated association, may have been dissolved the charity will not terminate so long as the purpose of the charity are, or are capable of, being carried out.[43] This follows from the fact that gifts to charitable unincorporated associations are usually construed as gifts for the purposes of the association.[44] If the unincorporated association is essential to the charity, for example, because those purposes cannot be carried out by any other organisation, the termination of the charitable unincorporated association will also lead to the termination of the charity.[45] The charity will also terminate if the unincorporated association is terminated because of lack of funds.[46]

13–006

The dissolution of a charitable unincorporated association can be commenced either voluntarily by resolution of the members or by an order of the court. Spontaneous dissolution is also possible.

The rules of a charitable unincorporated association will usually contain a provision providing for dissolution by the members at a special general meeting. The model constitution produced by the Charity

---

[36] See para.9–037, above.
[37] See para.9–043, above.
[38] See [1984] Ch. Com. Rep., paras 51–53.
[39] *National Anti-Vivisection Society v IRC* [1948] A.C. 31 at 74, *per* Lord Simonds.
[40] Charities Act 1993, s.13(5), see para.6–033, above.
[41] See RR6, *Maintenance of an Accurate Register of Charities*, pp.6–7.
[42] See *Re Vernon's Will Trusts* [1972] 1 Ch. 300n at 304, *per* Buckley.
[43] See *Re Finger's Will Trusts* [1972] 1 Ch. 287, 297 *per* Goff J.
[44] See para.3–039, above.
[45] See *Re Vernon's Will Trusts* [1972] 1 Ch. 300n, 303.
[46] See para.13–003, above.

Commissioners, for example, provides for the Executive Committee to call a general meeting with not less than 21 days notice with the resolution to dissolve to be confirmed by a majority of two thirds of the members present and voting.[47]

13–007   In the absence of a provision in the constitution giving power to dissolve by resolution, it is not possible for a majority of members to dissolve a charitable unincorporated association.[48] As the basis of an unincorporated association is the contract between the members, it should be possible for all the members to effectively agree to dissolve the association even if there is no specific power to dissolve.[49] There must, however, be agreement to dissolve and not merely agreement not to collect subscriptions.[50] If a majority of members dissolve and dissentient members are inactive, the court may construe their inactivity as acquiescence to the dissolution.[51]

An order for the winding up of a charitable unincorporated association may be made by the High Court under its general equitable jurisdiction.[52] The court will not usually make an order unless either a clear majority of the members wish the association to be wound up or it is impracticable for the association to continue.[53] Further, the consent of the Charity Commissioners would have to be obtained before any application by the members could be made to the court for a winding up order as such an application would be charity proceedings within s.33 of the Charities Act 1993.[54]

A charitable unincorporated association can become dissolved by ceasing all of its activities.[55] This will only occur where the objects of the association are dependent upon a particular place or institution and not where the objects of the charity are wider purposes. If the particular institution which is the essence of the charity closes down or is destroyed or if a particular place becomes impracticable to use, the charitable unincorporated association will be dissolved without action by the members or the court.[56] Spontaneous dissolution will not occur if the charitable association merely becomes inactive[57] or if its objects are to carry out particular purposes for which the existence of a particular institution or place is not essential.

13–008   The dissolution clause of a charitable unincorporated association usually provides that any assets remaining after debts and liabilities have been

---

[47] For an example of dissolution by resolution of the members see [1978] Ch. Com. Rep., para.124 (Old Contemptibles Association).
[48] *Re Tean Friendly Society* (1914) 58 S.J. 234.
[49] See *Re William Denby & Sons* [1971] 1 W.L.R. 973 at 978; *Re Grant's Will Trusts* [1979] 3 All E.R. 359 at 366.
[50] See *Re William Denby & Sons* [1971] 1 W.L.R. 973 at 981.
[51] See *Abbatt v Treasury Solicitor* [1969] 1 W.L.R. 1575.
[52] *Re Lead Company's Workmen's Fund Society* [1904] 2 Ch. 196.
[53] *Blake v Smither* (1906) 22 T.L.R. 698.
[54] Charities Act 1993, s.33(2).
[55] See *Re William Denby & Sons* [1971] 1 W.L.R. 973; *Re GKN Bolts and Nuts Ltd (Automotive Division) Birmingham Works Sports and Social Club* [1982] 1 W.L.R. 774.
[56] See *Re Slater's Will Trusts* [1964] 1 Ch. 512 at 527 and [1974] Conv. 187, 191 (J. E. Martin).
[57] See *Re GKN Nuts and Bolts Ltd* [1982] 1 W.L.R. 774 at 860.

paid should be transferred to another charity with similar objects.[58] In the event of the dissolution of a charitable unincorporated association other than under a power in the constitution any surplus funds will be applied *cy-près* by the Charity Commissioners or the court.

If through change in social circumstances[59] the objects of an unincorporated association are no longer charitable, the trustees of the charity property[60] will be obliged to apply for a *cy-près* scheme.[61] If the unincorporated association amends its constitution so that it has exclusively charitable objects, the property will remain held for the charitable purposes of that charitable unincorporated association and no termination will occur. If the unincorporated association does not change its objects, the property will be held on trust for the charitable purposes settled by the *cy-près* scheme separately from the unincorporated association. The unincorporated association will be removed from the register by the Charity Commissioners as it will no longer appear to the Commissioners to be a charity.[62] The unincorporated association will then continue in existence as a non-charitable body unless it is dissolved in one of the ways set out above.

COMPANIES LIMITED BY GUARANTEE

Charitable companies limited by guarantee provide the major exception **13–009** to the rule that charities never die. Property of a charitable company is usually construed as being held beneficially rather than on trust for the purposes of the company.[63] Accordingly, the dissolution of the company will usually also cause the termination of the charity.[64] It is possible for a charitable company limited by guarantee to hold some or all of its property on trust for either general or specific purposes.[65] In that situation, the dissolution of the charitable company will not necessarily cause the termination of the charity.

A charitable company limited by guarantee is a company for the purposes of the Insolvency Act 1986 and the procedure for winding-up a charitable company, either voluntary or compulsory, is governed by that Act. The reader is accordingly referred to the standard works on company law and insolvency for the detailed rules.[66] There are, however, a number of differences to the normal procedure which should be noted, in particular, as to who may present a winding-up petition and the ultimate

---

[58] See, *e.g.* The Charity Law Association's Constitution for a Charitable Unincorporated Association, clause 14.

[59] See para.13–005, above.

[60] For the holding of property for charitable unincorporated associations, see para.3–039 above.

[61] Charities Act 1993, s.13(5), see para.(254) above.

[62] *ibid.*, s.3(4) and see RR6, *Maintenance of an Accurate Register of Charities,* p.7.

[63] *Re Vernon's Will Trusts* [1972] 1 Ch. 300n at 303 and see para.3–045, above.

[64] *Re Stemson's Will Trusts* [1970] 1 Ch. 16 at 26.

[65] *Re Meyers* [1951] Ch. 534 and see para.3–045, above.

[66] See *Palmer's Company Law,* Vol.2, paras 15.001, *et seq.*; Bailey, Groves and Smith, *Corporate Insolvency: Law and Practice* (2nd ed.).

distribution of assets. In addition, the liabilities of directors of charitable companies in relation to winding-up require consideration. A member, however, will only be liable to pay the amount he or she has guaranteed to contribute in the event to dissolution under the terms of the memorandum of association.[67]

Presentation of a winding-up petition

13–010   A winding-up petition may be presented in the usual way by the charitable company itself, the members or creditors. By s.63(1) of the Charities Act 1993 the Attorney General is given power to present a petition. He may do so where a charitable company has failed to file annual returns for a considerable period, is inactive and difficulties have arisen over dealings with property.[68]

The Charity Commissioners are also empowered to present a winding-up petition[69] but only if they have instituted a formal inquiry under s.8 of the 1993 Act. Before presenting the petition the Commissioners must be satisfied either that there is or has been misconduct or mismanagement in the administration of the charity or that it is necessary or desirable to act for the purpose of protecting the property of the charity.[70]

Distribution of property

13–011   Any assets remaining after creditors have been paid are dealt with in accordance with s.154 of the Insolvency Act 1986.[71] The memorandum of association of most charitable companies, however, usually provides that on winding-up surplus property should not be distributed amongst the members but should be transferred to another charity with similar objects.[72] Such a clause overrides any provisions in the 1986 Act that surplus assets are to be divided amongst the members. The position was made clear by Slade J. in *Liverpool & District Hospital for Diseases of the Heart v Attorney General*[73] when he said:

> "The association has been incorporated, with all the privileges attached to incorporation, on the footing expressly stated in its memorandum of association that on a dissolution the surplus assets are to be transferred not to members but to other charitable institutions to be selected in the manner specified in clause 9. The provisions of

---

[67] Usually a small amount; £10 in the Charity Commissioner's Model Memorandum of Association for a Charitable Company.

[68] See *Liverpool & District Hospital for Diseases of the Heart v Att-Gen* [1981] 1 Ch. 193 at 200.

[69] Charities Act 1993, s.63(2).

[70] *i.e.* the conditions laid down in s.18(1)(a) or (b) of the 1993 Act.

[71] *Liverpool & District Hospital for Diseases of the Heart v Att-Gen* [1981] 1 Ch. 193 at 211.

[72] See, *e.g.* clause 8 of the Model Memorandum of Association for a Charitable Company produced by the Charity Commissioners.

[73] [1981] 1 Ch. 193 at 213.

clause 9 are, in my judgment, binding both on the liquidator and the court and are not capable of being overridden by section 265 or section 302".[74]

If no recipient charity for the surplus assets has been specified by the members, for example, because no members of the company can be traced at the date of dissolution, the court will order a *cy-près* scheme.[75]

Liabilities of directors

Although directors of charitable companies will not be personally liable for the obligations of the company in the event of a shortfall of assets on dissolution, the winding-up of a charitable company does not free the directors from all potential liabilities. A director will remain liable on any contract entered into in a personal capacity in connection with the activities of the charity, for example, a personal guarantee of a loan to the charity. Similarly, a director who has been in breach of his fiduciary duties will remain liable to make good any loss arising therefrom after the dissolution of the charitable company.[76]

13–012

A director of a charitable company has always been subject to potential personal liability for fraudulent trading[77] but as liability requires proof of intent to defraud creditors the liability is theoretical rather than real. The introduction of the concept of wrongful trading, however, in the Insolvency Act 1986 does present real problems for directors of charitable companies.

Wrongful trading

Wrongful trading occurs where a company goes into insolvent liquidation[78] and prior to the liquidation a director knew or ought to have concluded that there was no reasonable prospect that the company could avoid going into insolvent liquidation and took insufficient steps in the circumstances to minimise the potential loss to the company's creditors.[79] If wrongful trading is established, the director may, on the application of the liquidator, be required by the court to make a contribution to the company's assets.[80] Thus there is a danger of liability for wrongful trading for the directors of any charitable company involved in service provision. For example, if a funding contract or grant is not renewed, the only steps the directors may be able to take to minimise the potential loss to the charity's

13–013

---

[74] Of the Companies Act 1948, now ss.154 and 107 of the Insolvency Act 1986.

[75] *Liverpool & District Hospital for Diseases of the Heart v Att-Gen* [1981] 1 Ch. 193 at 214.

[76] See para.6–043, above.

[77] Now under Insolvency Act 1986, s.213.

[78] For the circumstances in which a company is deemed to be unable to pay its debts, see Insolvency Act 1986, s.122.

[79] Insolvency Act 1986, s.214(2)(3).

[80] *ibid.*, s.214(1).

creditors, and hence liability for wrongful trading, is to apply for an administration order[81] or present a winding-up petition.

In determining whether a director ought to have concluded that an insolvent liquidation was unavoidable, the court must ask whether that would have been the conclusion of a reasonably diligent person having both the general knowledge, skill and experience that might reasonably be expected of a person carrying out that particular director's duties with the company and the general knowledge, skill and experience actually possessed by that director.[82] A similar test is applied when considering the steps which ought to have been taken to minimise potential loss. Thus although the test is an objective one, the standard of knowledge, skill and experience will vary. It has been held that the expertise expected of a director of a small company is less than that expected of a director of a large company with more complex accounting procedures.[83] Directors of a charitable company will usually be unpaid and acting part-time. Those are clearly factors that the court can take into account when considering whether to impose liability for wrongful trading but those factors alone will not be sufficient to avoid liability; directors of charitable companies are under the same obligations as the directors of commercial companies.[84]

The Charity Commissioners consider that directors of charitable companies may use company funds to insure against liability for wrongful trading provided that there is an exclusion clause in the cover if the directors continued to trade knowing that the charitable company was insolvent or in reckless disregard and whether it was insolvent or not.[85] Thus the extent to which insurance may be obtained against liability to wrongful trading at the expense of the charity is severely limited.

Restoration to the register

13–014   In the normal course of events a charitable company will be automatically dissolved three months after the completion of the winding-up and the company will be removed from the register of companies.[86] The court has power under s.651 of the Companies Act 1985 to make an order declaring a dissolution void. An application for such an order may be made by the liquidator, any other person who appears to the court to be interested[87] or the Charity Commissioners.[88] The court has refused to make an order for restoration to the register to allow a charitable company to take a legacy under the will of a testator who died after the date of dis-

---

[81] Insolvency Act 1986, s.9.
[82] *ibid.*, s.214(4)(5).
[83] *Re Produce Marketing Consortium (No. 2)* [1989] B.C.L.C. 520 at 550, *per* Knox J.
[84] See *Commonwealth Bank of Australia v Friedrich* (1991) 9 A.C.L.C. 946.
[85] See Companies Act 1985, s.310(3)(a); [1991] Ch. Com. Rep., para.38 and (1994) 2 Ch. Com. Dec., p.27.
[86] Insolvency Act 1986, s.201.
[87] Companies Act 1985, s.651.
[88] Charities Act 1993, s.63(3).

solution.[89] The Commissioners may apply for an order where it becomes apparent that assets of a former charitable company are in the hands of third parties and have not been included in the winding-up. In such circumstances, the court may make an order restoring the company to the register to allow proceedings to be taken to recover the assets for charity.

The Companies Registrar has power to strike a company off the register if he has reasonable cause to believe that it is not in operation.[90] The Charity Commissioners may to apply to the court under s.653(2) of the Companies Act 1985 for an order that such a company be restored to the register.[91] By the exercise of this power, a charitable company can be restored to the register to enable it to take proceedings to recover property rightly due to it before deregistration.

Objects no longer charitable

There can be no question of a charitable company terminating if it changes its objects to non-charitable ones by amending its memorandum of association. Any previously acquired property is subject to a statutory charitable trust and must continue to be held for the original charitable objects.[92]

13–015

The position is less clear where the objects of a charitable company cease to be charitable because of a change in social circumstances.[93] There are arguments, on the basis that a charitable company does not hold its property on trust,[94] for saying that the company should simply continue to hold the property for the original objects which are now no longer charitable.[95] On this argument, the company must be removed from the register of charities as no longer charitable[96] but it would continue in existence as a non-charitable company.

The alternative argument, which it is suggested the court would adopt, is that a constructive charitable trust would be imposed on the assets of the company to ensure that the property remained applicable for charitable purposes. The reasons for suggesting that a constructive charitable trust would be imposed are twofold. First, whilst the courts have not regarded the property of a charitable company as held on trust, they have regarded the property as irrevocably dedicated to charitable purposes. Thus in *Liverpool and District Hospital for Diseases of the Heart v Att-Gen*[97] Slade J[98] applied the surplus of the charitable company *cy-près*, rather than allowing the funds to be distributed among the members of the company. The position was set out by Buckley J. in *Re Vernon's Will Trusts*[99]:

[89] *Re Servers of the Blind League* [1960] 1 W.L.R. 564.
[90] Companies Act 1985, s.652.
[91] Charities Act 1993, s.63(4).
[92] Charities Act 1993, s.64(1); see para.12–006 above.
[93] See *National Anti-Vivisection Society v IRC* [1948] A.C. 31 at 74, *per* Lord Simonds.
[94] See para.3–046 above.
[95] See J. Dutton, "Charitable Companies Ceasing to be Charitable" (2001) 7 C.L.P.R. 31.
[96] Charities Act 1993, s.3(4).
[97] [1981] 1 Ch. 193.
[98] *ibid.*, at 214 and see para.13–011 above.
[99] [1972] Ch. 300.

"Whether and how far it would be right to regard the funds of the incorporated Guild as subject to a charitable trust, I do not pause to consider beyond pointing out that any assets which it took over from the unincorporated Guild would appear to have been subject to such a trust. Trust or no trust, however, it is true to say that the assets of the incorporated Guild were all effectively dedicated to charity. In no circumstances—at least without the intervention of Parliament—could any of those funds have been used otherwise than for charitable purposes the kind for which the Guild existed so long as those purposes remained practicable. Even if those purposes cease to be practical, the charity would not cease to exist, although its funds would be applied *cy-près*. Such a charity, considered as a charity and apart from the mechanism provided for the time being and from time to time for holding its property and managing its affairs, could never cease to exist except by exhaustion of all its assets and cessation of its activities. A change merely in its mechanical aspect could not involve the charity ceasing to exist. The principle of the decision in *Re Faraker* [1912] 2 Ch. 488 and *In re Lucas* [1948] Ch. 424 is, in my judgment, equally applicable to an incorporated charity of this kind as to a charity constituted by means of a trust. In such cases the law regards the charity, an abstract conception distinct from the institutional mechanism provided for holding and administering the fund of the charity".

13–016   Secondly, the imposition of a constructive charitable trust on a charitable company in the situation of its objects ceasing to be charitable because of a change in social circumstances, would establish a consistency of approach regardless of the legal structure used by a charity.[1] It would be unfortunate if the retention of assets for charitable purposes depended on the legal structure by which those assets were held, particularly as in some cases the choice of legal structure is a matter of accident rather than design.

If the conclusion is reached that a charitable constructive trust is imposed where a charitable company's objects cease to be charitable as a result of a change in social circumstances, the trust would have to be enforced by the Charity Commissioners, where necessary by a *cy-près* scheme. The Commissioners take the view that in those circumstances, the company may argue that it would be inequitable to impose a trust and that the property ought to continue to be held by the company for the stated, now non-charitable, objects.[2]

---

[1] For the treatment of charitable trusts and unincorporated associations, see paras 13–005 and 13–008 above.
[2] See RR6, *Maintenance of an Accurate Register of Charities*, Annex E.

HOUSE TO HOUSE COLLECTIONS ACT 1939

NOTES
An Act to provide for the regulation of house to house collections for charitable purposes; and for matters connected therewith.
[July 28, 1939]

1. Charitable collections from house to house to be licensed

(1) Subject to the provisions of this Act, no collection for a charitable purpose shall be made unless the requirements of this Act as to a licence for the promotion thereof are satisfied.

1A–001

(2) If a person promotes a collection for a charitable purpose, and a collection for that purpose is made in any locality pursuant to his promotion, then, unless there is in force, throughout the period during which the collection is made in that locality, a licence authorising him, or authorising another under whose authority he acts, to promote a collection therein for that purpose, he shall be guilty of an offence.

(3) If a person acts as a collector in any locality for the purposes of a collection for a charitable purpose, then, unless there is in force, at all times when he so acts, a licence authorising a promoter under whose authority he acts, or authorising the collector himself, to promote a collection therein for that purpose, he shall be guilty of an offence.

(4) If the chief officer of police for the police area comprising a locality in which a collection for a charitable purpose is being, or is proposed to be, made is satisfied that that purpose is local in character and that the collection is likely to be completed within a short period of time, he may grant to the person who appears to him to be principally concerned in the promotion of the collection a certificate in the prescribed form, and, where a certificate is so granted, the provisions of this Act, except the provisions of sections five and six thereof and the provisions of section eight thereof in so far as they relate to those sections, shall not apply, in relation to a collection made for that purpose within such locality and within such period as may be specified in the certificate, to the person to whom the certificate is granted or to any person authorised by him to promote the collection or to act as a collector for the purposes thereof.[. . .[1]][2]

Notes: S.1(4) applied by War Charities Act 1940 (c. 31), s.7(2), s.7(2), repealed (Scotland) by Civic Government (Scotland) Act 1982 (c.45), ss.119(15), 137, Sch.4.

2. Licences

1A–002   (1) Where a person who is promoting, or proposes to promote, a collection in any locality for a charitable purpose makes to the [licensing]¹ authority for the [. . .]² area comprising that locality an application in the prescribed manner specifying the purpose of the collection and the locality (whether being the whole of the area of the authority or a part thereof) within which the collection is to be made, and furnishes them with the prescribed information, the authority shall, subject to the following provisions of this section, grant to him a licence authorising him to promote a collection within that locality for that purpose.

[(1A) In this section "licensing authority" means—

    (a)   in relation to the City of London, the Common Council;

    (b)   in relation to the Metropolitan Police District, the Commissioner of Police for the Metropolis; and

    (c)   in relation to a district exclusive of any part thereof within the Metropolitan Police District, the district council]³

(2) A licence shall be granted for such period, not being longer than twelve months, as may be specified in the application, and shall, unless it is previously revoked, remain in force for the period so specified:

Provided that, if it appears to a licensing⁴ authority to be expedient to provide for the simultaneous expiration of licences to be granted by them in respect of collections which in their opinion are likely to be proposed to be made annually or continuously over a long period, they may, on the grant of such a licence, grant it for a period shorter or longer than that specified in the application therefor, or for a period longer than twelve months (but not exceeding eighteen months), as may be requisite for that purpose.

(3) A licensing⁵ authority may refuse to grant a licence, or, where a licence has been granted, may revoke it, if it appears to the authority—

    (a)   that the total amount likely to be applied for charitable purposes as the result of the collection (including any amount already so applied) is inadequate in proportion to the value of the proceeds likely to be received (including any proceeds already received);

    (b)   that remuneration which is excessive in relation to the total amount aforesaid is likely to be, or has been, retained or received out of the proceeds of the collection by any person;

    (c)   that the grant of a licence would be likely to facilitate the commission of an offence under section three of the Vagrancy Act 1824, or that an offence under that section has been committed in connection with the collection;

    (d)   that the applicant or the holder of the licence is not a fit and proper person to hold a licence by reason of the fact that he has been convicted in the United Kingdom of any of the offences specified in the Schedule to this Act, or has been convicted in any part of His Majesty's dominions of any offence conviction for which necessarily involved a finding that he acted fraudulently or dishonestly, or of an offence of a kind the commission of which would be likely to be facilitated by the grant of a licence;

(e)   that the applicant or the holder of the licence, in promoting a collection in respect of which a licence has been granted to him, has failed to exercise due diligence to secure that persons authorised by him to act as collectors for the purposes of the collection were fit and proper persons, to secure compliance on the part of persons so authorised with the provisions of regulations made under this Act, or to prevent prescribed badges or prescribed certificates of authority being obtained by persons other than persons so authorised; or

(f)   that the applicant or holder of the licence has refused or neglected to furnish to the authority such information as they may have reasonably required for the purpose of informing themselves as to any of the matters specified in the foregoing paragraphs.

(4) When a licensing[6] authority refuse to grant a licence or revoke a licence which has been granted, they shall forthwith give written notice to the applicant or holder of the licence stating upon which one or more of the grounds set out in subsection (3) of this section the licence has been refused or revoked and informing him of the right of appeal given by this section, and the applicant or holder of the licence may thereupon appeal to the Secretary of State against the refusal or revocation of the licence as the case may be and the decision of the Secretary of State shall be final.

(5) The time within which any such appeal may be brought shall be fourteen days from the date on which notice is given under subsection (4) of this section.

(6) If the Secretary of State decides that the appeal shall be allowed, the licensing[7] authority shall forthwith issue a licence or cancel the revocation as the case may be in accordance with the decision of the Secretary of State.[. . .[8]][9]

Notes: S.2(3) amended by War Charities Act 1940 (c. 31), s.7(1), by reason of the amendment (Scotland) of War Charities Act 1940 (c.31), s.7(1) by Civic Government (Scotland) Act 1982 (c.45), s.119(15) the reference to s.7(1) is no longer applicable (Scotland).
[1] Word substituted by Local Government Act 1972 (c. 70), Sch.29, para.23(1).
[2] Word repealed by Local Government Act 1972 (c. 70), Sch.30.
[3] S.2(1A) inserted by Local Government Act 1972 (c.70), Sch.29, para.23(2).
[4] Word substituted by Local Government Act 1972 (c. 70), Sch.29, para.23(3).
[5] Word substituted by Local Government Act 1972 (c. 70), Sch.29, para.23(3).
[6] Word substituted by Local Government Act 1972 (c. 70), Sch.29, para.23(3).
[7] Word substituted by Local Government Act 1972 (c. 70), Sch.29, para.23(3).
[8] In relation to Scotland: s.2 is repealed.
[9] Repealed by Civic Government (Scotland) Act 1982 (c.45), ss.119(15), 137, Sch.4.

3. Exemptions in the case of collections over wide areas

(1) Where the Secretary of State is satisfied that a person pursues a charitable purpose throughout the whole of England or a substantial part thereof and is desirous of promoting collections for that purpose, the Secretary of State may by order direct that he shall be exempt from the provisions of subsection (2) of section one of this Act as respects all collections for that purpose in such localities as may be described in the order,

                                                           1A–003

and whilst an order so made in the case of any person is in force as respects collections in any locality, the provisions of this Act shall have effect in relation to the person exempted, to a promoter of a collection in that locality for that purpose who acts under the authority of the person exempted, and to a person who so acts as a collector for the purposes of any such collection, as if a licence authorising the person exempted to promote a collection in that locality for that purpose had been in force.

(2) Any order made under this section may be revoked or varied by a subsequent order made by the Secretary of State.[. . . [1]][2]

[1] In relation to Scotland: s.3 is repealed.
[2] Repealed by Civic Government (Scotland) Act 1982 (c.45), ss.119(15), 137, Sch.4.

4. Regulations

1A–004   (1) The Secretary of State may make regulations for prescribing anything which by this Act is required to be prescribed, and for regulating the manner in which collections, in respect of which licences have been granted or orders have been made under the last foregoing section, may be carried out and the conduct of promoters and collectors in relation to such collections.

(2) Without prejudice to the generality of the powers conferred by the foregoing subsection, regulations made thereunder may make provision for all or any of the following matters, that is to say:—

(a)   for requiring and regulating the use by collectors, of prescribed badges and prescribed certificates of authority, and the issue, custody, production and return thereof, and, in particular, for requiring collectors on demand by a police constable or by any occupant of a house visited to produce their certificates of authority;

(b)   in the case of collections in respect of which licences have been granted, for requiring that the prescribed certificates of authority of the collectors shall be authenticated in a manner approved by the chief officer of police for the area in respect of which the licence was granted, and that their prescribed badges shall have inserted therein or annexed thereto in a manner and form so approved a general indication of the purpose of the collection;

(c)   for prohibiting persons below a prescribed age from acting, and others from causing them to act, as collectors;

(d)   for preventing annoyance to the occupants of houses visited by collectors;

(e)   for requiring the prescribed information with respect to the expenses, proceeds and application of the proceeds of collections to be furnished, in the case of collections in respect of which licences have been granted, by the person to whom the licence was granted to the [. . .][1] authority by whom it was granted, and, in the case of collections in respect of which an order has been made, by the person thereby exempted from the provisions of subsection (2) of section one of this Act to the Secretary of State, and for requiring the information furnished to be vouched and authenticated in such manner as may be prescribed.

(3) Any person who contravenes or fails to comply with the provisions of a regulation made under this Act shall be guilty of an offence.

(4) Any regulations made under this Act shall be laid before Parliament as soon as may be after they are made, and if either House of Parliament, within the period of forty days beginning with the date on which the regulations are laid before it, resolves that the regulations be annulled, the regulations shall thereupon become void, without prejudice, however, to anything previously done thereunder or to the making of new regulations.

In reckoning any such period of forty days as aforesaid, no account shall be taken of any time during which Parliament is dissolved or prorogued or during which both Houses are adjourned for more than four days.[. . .²]³

¹ Word repealed by Local Government Act 1972 (c. 70), Sch.30.
² In relation to Scotland: s.4 is repealed.
³ Repealed by Civic Government (Scotland) Act 1982 (c.45), ss.119(15), 137, Sch.4.

5. Unauthorised use of badges, etc.

If any person, in connection with any appeal made by him to the public in association with a representation that the appeal is for a charitable purpose, displays or uses—   1A–005

   (a)   a prescribed badge or a prescribed certificate of authority, not being a badge or certificate for the time being held by him for the purposes of the appeal pursuant to regulations made under this Act, or

   (b)   any badge or device, or any certificate or other document, so nearly resembling a prescribed badge or, as the case may be, a prescribed certificate of authority as to be calculated to deceive,

he shall be guilty of an offence.[. . . ¹]²

¹ In relation to Scotland: s.5 is repealed.
² Repealed by Civic Government (Scotland) Act 1982 (c.45), ss.119(15), 137, Sch.4.

6. Collector to give name, etc. to police on demand

A police constable may require any person whom he believes to be acting as a collector for the purposes of a collection for a charitable purpose to declare to him immediately his name and address and to sign his name, and if any person fails to comply with a requirement duly made to him under this section, he shall be guilty of an offence.[. . .¹]²   1A–006

¹ In relation to Scotland: s.6 is repealed.
² Repealed by Civic Government (Scotland) Act 1982 (c.45), ss.119(15), 137, Sch.4.

7. Delegation of functions

(1) [. . .]¹   1A–007

(2) The functions conferred on a chief officer of police by this Act or regulations made thereunder may be delegated by him to any police officer not below the rank of inspector.[. . .²]³

¹ Repealed by Local Government Act 1972 (c. 70), Sch.30 and Local Government (Scotland) Act 1973 (c. 65), Sch.29.
² In relation to Scotland: s.7 is repealed.
³ Repealed by Civic Government (Scotland) Act 1982 (c.45), ss.119(15), 137, Sch.4.

8. Penalties

(1) Any promoter guilty of an offence under subsection (2) of section one of this Act shall be liable, on summary conviction, to imprisonment   1A–008

for a term not exceeding six months or to a fine not exceeding [level 3 on the standard scale][1] , or to both such imprisonment and such fine.

(2) Any collector guilty of an offence under subsection (3) of section one of this Act shall be liable, on summary conviction, in the case of a first conviction, to a fine not exceeding [£25],[2] or in the case of a second or subsequent conviction, to imprisonment for a term not exceeding three months or to a fine not exceeding [£50],[3] or to both such imprisonment and such fine.

(3) Any person guilty of an offence under subsection (3) of section four of this Act shall be liable on summary conviction, to a fine not exceeding level 1 on the standard scale.[4]

(4) Any person guilty of an offence under section five of this Act shall be liable, on summary conviction, to imprisonment for a term not exceeding six months or to a fine not exceeding level 3 on the standard scale,[5] or to both such imprisonment and such fine.

(5) Any person guilty of an offence under section six of this Act shall be liable, on summary conviction, to a fine not exceeding level one on the standard scale.[6]

(6) If any person in furnishing any information for the purposes of this Act knowingly or recklessly makes a statement false in a material particular, he shall be guilty of an offence, and shall be liable, on summary conviction, to imprisonment for a term not exceeding six months or to a fine not exceeding level 3 on the standard scale,[7] or to both such imprisonment and such fine.

(7) Where an offence under this Act committed by a corporation is proved to have been committed with the consent or connivance of, or to be attributable to any culpable neglect of duty on the part of, any director, manager, secretary, or other officer of the corporation, he, as well as the corporation, shall be deemed to be guilty of that offence and shall be liable to be proceeded against and punished accordingly.[. . .[8]][9]

[1] Words substituted by Criminal Justice Act 1982 (c.48), ss.38, 46.
[2] Words substituted by Criminal Justice Act 1982 (c.48), ss.35 (in relation to liability on first and subsequent convictions) and 46 (substitution of references to levels on the standard scale) apply.
[3] Words substituted by Criminal Justice Act 1982 (c.48), ss.35 (inrelation to liability on first and subsequent convictions) and 46 (substitutionof references to levels on the standard scale) apply.
[4] Words substituted by Criminal Justice Act 1982 (c.48), s.46.
[5] Words substituted by Criminal Justice Act 1982 (c.48), ss.38, 46.
[6] Words substituted by Criminal Justice Act 1982 (c.48), s.46.
[7] Words substituted by Criminal Justice Act 1982 (c.48), ss.38, 46.
[8] In relation to Scotland: s.8 is repealed.
[9] Repealed by Civic Government (Scotland) Act 1982 (c.45), ss.119(15), 137, Sch.4.

9. Application to metropolitan police district

1A–009   (1) [. . .][1]

(2) The functions which may be delegated by a chief officer of police by virtue of subsection (2) of section seven of this Act shall not include any functions conferred on the Commissioner of Police for the Metropolis by virtue of his being a licensing authority within the meaning of section 2 of this Act.[2] [. . .[3]][4]

[1] Repealed by Local Government Act 1972 (c. 70), Sch.30.
[2] Words substituted by Local Government Act 1972 (c. 70), Sch.29, para.23(5).
[3] In relation to Scotland: s.9 is repealed.
[4] Repealed by Civic Government (Scotland) Act 1982 (c.45), ss.119(15), 137, Sch.4.

10. Application to Scotland

This Act shall apply to Scotland subject to the following modifica-   1A–010
tions—

[(a) sections 1 , 2 and 4 shall apply as if for references to the police
authority for the police area comprising a locality and to the
chief officer of police of such an area there were substituted
respectively references to the islands or district council for the
area comprising a locality and to the proper officer of such a
council;][1]

(b) in paragraph (c) of subsection (3) of section two for references
to section three of the Vagrancy Act 1824 there shall be substituted references to sections four hundred and eight or four hundred and ten of the Burgh Police (Scotland) Act 1892 or to the
corresponding provisions of any local Act;

(c) in subsection (1) of section three of the word "England," there
shall be substituted the word "Scotland";

(d) any offence against this Act for which the maximum penalty that
may be imposed does not exceed ten pounds may be prosecuted
in any court of summary jurisdiction within the meaning of the
Summary Jurisdiction (Scotland) Act 1908, having jurisdiction
in the place where the offence was committed; [. . .][2]][3]

(e) [. . .][4]

[1] s.10(a) substituted by Local Government (Scotland) Act 1973 (c. 65), s.188, Sch.24, para.37.
[2] In relation to Scotland: s.10 is repealed.
[3] Repealed by Civic Government (Scotland) Act 1982 (c.45), ss.119(15), 137, Sch.4.
[4] Repealed by Local Government (Scotland) Act 1973 (c. 65), s.188, Sch.24, para.37, Sch.29.

11. Interpretation

(1) In this Act the following expressions have the meanings hereby   1A–011
respectively assigned to them, that is to say—

"charitable purpose" means any charitable, benevolent or philanthropic purpose, whether or not the purpose is charitable within the
meaning of any rule of law;
"collection"means an appeal to the public, made by means of visits
from house to house, to give, whether for consideration or not,
money or other property; and "collector" means, in relation to a collection, a person who makes the appeal in the course of such visits as
aforesaid;
"house" includes a place of business;
"licence" means a licence under this Act;

[. . .][1]

"prescribed" means prescribed by regulations made under this Act;
"proceeds" means, in relation to a collection, all money and all other
property given, whether for consideration or not, in response to the
appeal made;
"promoter"means, in relation to a collection, a person who causes
others to act, whether for remuneration or otherwise, as collectors for

the purposes of the collection; and "promote" and "promotion"have corresponding meanings.

(2) For the purposes of this Act, a collection shall be deemed to be made for a particular purpose where the appeal is made in association with a representation that the money or other property appealed for, or part thereof, will be applied for that purpose.[. . .²]³

¹ Definitions of "police area", "police authority" and "chief officer of police" repealed by Police Act 1964 (c. 48), Sch.10, Pt I and Local Government (Scotland) Act 1973 (c. 65), Sch.29.
² In relation to Scotland: s.11 is repealed.
³ Repealed by Civic Government (Scotland) Act 1982 (c.45), ss.119(15), 137, Sch.4.

12. Short title, commencement, interpretation and extent

1A–012

(1) This Act may be cited as the House to House Collections Act 1939.
(2) [. . .]¹
(3) References in this Act to any enactment shall be construed as references to that enactment as amended by any subsequent enactment.
(4) This Act shall not extend to Northern Ireland.[. . .²]³

Notes: Title is not a reliable guide to the current text.
¹ Repealed by Statute Law Revision Act 1950 (c. 6).
² In relation to Scotland: s.12 is repealed.
³ Repealed by Civic Government (Scotland) Act 1982 (c.45), ss.119(15), 137, Sch.4

SCHEDULE 1

Offences to which Paragraph (D) of Subsection (3) of Section Two Applies

1A–013

1. Offences under sections forty-seven to fifty-six of the Offences against the Person Act 1861.
Robbery, burglary, and blackmail¹
Offences in Scotland involving personal violence or lewd, indecent, or libidinous conduct, or dishonest appropriation of property.
Offences under the Street Collections Regulation (Scotland) Act 1915.
Offences under section five of the Police, Factories &c. (Miscellaneous Provisions) Act 1916.[. . .²]³

¹ Words substituted by Theft Act 1968 (c. 60), Sch., Pt III.
² In relation to Scotland: schedule is repealed.
³ Repealed by Civic Government (Scotland) Act 1982 (c.45), ss.119(15), 137, Sch.4.

RECREATIONAL CHARITIES ACT 1958

NOTES
An Act to declare charitable under the law of England and Wales the provision in the interests of social welfare of facilities for recreation or other leisure-time occupation, to make similar provision as to certain trusts heretofore established for carrying out social welfare activities within the meaning of the Miners' Welfare Act 1952, to enable laws for corresponding purposes to be passed by the Parliament of Northern Ireland, and for purposes connected therewith.
[March 13, 1958]

1. General provisions to recreational and similar trusts, etc.

(1) Subject to the provisions of this Act, it shall be and be deemed always to have been charitable to provide, or assist in the provision of, facilities for recreation or other leisure-time occupation, if the facilities are provided in the interests of social welfare: **1B–001**

Provided that nothing in this section shall be taken to derogate from the principle that a trust or institution to be charitable must be for the public benefit.

(2) The requirement of the foregoing subsection that the facilities are provided in the interests of social welfare shall not be treated as satisfied unless—

    (a)   the facilities are provided with the object of improving the conditions of life for the persons for whom the facilities are primarily intended; and

    (b)   either—

        (i)   those persons have need of such facilities as aforesaid by reason of their youth, age, infirmity or disablement, poverty or social and economic circumstances; or

        (ii)   the facilities are to be available to the members or female members of the public at large.

(3) Subject to the said requirement, subsection (1) of this section applies in particular to the provision of facilities at village halls, community centres and women's institutes, and to the provision and maintenance of grounds and buildings to be used for purposes of recreation or leisure-time occupation, and extends to the provision of facilities for those purposes by the organising of any activity.

2. Miners' welfare trusts

1B–002   (1) Where trusts declared before the seventeenth day of December, nineteen hundred and fifty-seven, required or purported to require property to be held for the purpose of activities which are social welfare activities within the meaning of the Miners' Welfare Act 1952 and at that date the whole or part of the property held on those trusts or of any property held with that property represented an application of moneys standing to the credit of the miners' welfare fund or moneys provided by the Coal Industry Social Welfare Organisation, those trusts shall be treated as if they were and always had been charitable.

(2) For the purposes of this section property held on the same trusts as other property shall be deemed to be held with it, though vested in different trustees.

3. Savings and other provisions as to past transactions

1B–003   (1) Nothing on this Act shall be taken to restrict the purposes which are to be regarded as charitable independently of this Act.

(2) Nothing in this Act—

(a)   shall apply to make charitable any trust, or validate any disposition, of property if before the seventeenth day of December, nineteen hundred and fifty-seven, that property or any property representing or forming part of it, or any income arising from any such property, has been paid or conveyed to, or applied for the benefit of, the persons entitled by reason of the invalidity of the trust or disposition; or

(b)   shall affect any order or judgment made or given (whether before or after the passing of this Act) in legal proceedings begun before that day; or

(c)   shall require anything properly done before that day, or anything done or to be done in pursuance of a contract entered into before that day, to be treated for any purpose as wrongful or ineffectual.

(3) Except as provided by subsections (4) and (5) of this section, nothing in this Act shall require anything to be treated for the purposes of any enactment as having been charitable at a time before the date of the passing of this Act, so as to invalidate anything done or any determination given before that date.

(4) For the purposes of income tax, this Act shall not require anything to be treated as having been charitable at a time before the date of the passing of this Act unless it would have been so treated in accordance with the practice applied by the Commissioners of Inland Revenue immediately before the eighteenth day of December, nineteen hundred and fifty-two; but, subject to that and to paragraphs (a) and (b) of subsection (2) of this section, there shall be made all such adjustments, whether by way of repayment of tax, additional assessment or otherwise, as are made necessary in relation to income tax by the retrospective operation of sections one and two of this Act, and nothing in the Income Tax Act 1952 shall preclude the repayment by virtue of this Act of tax for the year 1946–47 or a subsequent year of assessment if a claim is made in that behalf to the

Commissioners of Inland Revenue within two years from the date of the passing of this Act.

(5) As respects stamp duty on any instrument executed before the date of the passing of this Act, this Act shall not require anything to be treated as having been charitable for the purposes of subsection (1) of section fifty- four of the Finance Act 1947 (which excepted instruments in favour of charities from certain increases of stamp duty under that Act), unless it would have been so treated in accordance with the practice applied by the Commissioners of Inland Revenue immediately before the eighteenth day of December, nineteen hundred and fifty-two; but subject to that and to paragraphs (a) and (b) of subsection (2) of this section, where more stamp duty has been paid on an instrument executed on or after the said eighteenth day of December and before the date of the passing of this Act than ought to have been paid having regard to sections one and two of this Act, the provisions of sections ten and eleven of the Stamp Duties Management Act 1891 shall apply as if a stamp of greater value than was necessary had been inadvertently used for the instrument, and relief may be given accordingly, and may be so given notwithstanding that, in accordance with the provisions of section twelve of the Stamp Act 1891, the instrument had been stamped before the passing of this Act with a particular stamp denoting that it was duly stamped.

An application for relief under the said section ten as applied by this subsection may be made at any time within two years from the date of the passing of this Act, notwithstanding that it is made outside the time limited by that section.

4. [. . .]¹   1B–004

¹ Repealed by Northern Ireland Constitution Act 1973 (c. 36), Sch.6, Pt I.

5. Application to Crown

This Act, and (except in so far as the contrary intention appears) any   1B–005
enactment of the Parliament of Northern Ireland passed for purposes similar to section one of this Act, shall bind the Crown.

6. Short title and extent

(1) This Act may be cited as the Recreational Charities Act 1958.   1B–006

(2) Sections one and two of this Act shall affect the law of Scotland and Northern Ireland only in so far as they affect the operation of the Income Tax Acts or of other enactments in which references to charity are to be construed in accordance with the law of England and Wales or, without prejudice to the foregoing generality, of the Local Government (Financial Provisions etc.) (Scotland) Act 1962.¹

¹ Words added by Local Government (Financial Provisions etc.) (Scotland) Act 1962 (c. 9), s.12(1), Sch.2.

CHARITIES ACT 1992

PART II

CONTROL OF FUND-RAISING FOR CHARITABLE INSTITUTIONS

PRELIMINARY

1C–001   **58. Interpretation of Part II**

(1) In this Part—
"charitable contributions", in relation to any representation made by any commercial participator or other person, means —

    (a)   the whole or part of—
        (i)   the consideration given for goods or services sold or supplied by him, or
        (ii) any proceeds (other than such consideration) of a promotional venture undertaken by him, or
    (b)   sums given by him by way of donation in connection with the sale or supply of any such goods or services (whether the amount of such sums is determined by reference to the value of any such goods or services or otherwise);

"charitable institution" means a charity or an institution (other than a charity) which is established for charitable, benevolent or philanthropic purposes;
"charity" means a charity within the meaning of [the Charities Act 1993][1];
"commercial participator", in relation to any charitable institution, means any person [(apart from a company connected with the institution)][2] who—

    (a)   carries on for gain a business other than a fund-raising business, but
    (b)   in the course of that business, engages in any promotional venture in the course of which it is represented that charitable contributions are to be given to or applied for the benefit of the institution;

"company" has the meaning given by section [97 of the Charities Act 1993][3];

"the court" means the High Court or a county court;

"credit card" means a card which is a credit-token within the meaning of the Consumer Credit Act 1974;

"debit card" means a card the use of which by its holder to make a payment results in a current account of his at a bank, or at any other institution providing banking services, being debited with the payment;

"fund-raising business" means any business carried on for gain and wholly or primarily engaged in soliciting or otherwise procuring money or other property for charitable, benevolent or philanthropic purposes;

"institution" includes any trust or undertaking;

"professional fund-raiser" means —

    (a)   any person (apart from a charitable institution [or a company connected with such an institution][4]) who carries on a fund-raising business, or

    (b)   any other person (apart from a person excluded by virtue of subsection (2) or (3)) who for reward solicits money or other property for the benefit of a charitable institution, if he does so otherwise than in the course of any fund-raising venture undertaken by a person falling within paragraph (a) above;

"promotional venture" means any advertising or sales campaign or any other venture undertaken for promotional purposes;

"radio or television programme" includes any item included in a programme service within the meaning of the Broadcasting Act 1990.

(2) In subsection (1), paragraph (b) of the definition of "professional fund-raiser" does not apply to any of the following, namely—

    (a)   any charitable institution or any company connected with any such institution;

    (b)   any officer or employee of any such institution or company, or any trustee of any such institution, acting (in each case) in his capacity as such;

    (c)   any person acting as a collector in respect of a public charitable collection (apart from a person who is to be treated as a promoter of such a collection by virtue of section 65(3));

    (d)   any person who in the course of a relevant programme, that is to say a radio or television programme in the course of which a fund-raising venture is undertaken by—

        (i)   a charitable institution, or

        (ii) a company connected with such an institution,

           makes any solicitation at the instance of that institution or company; or

    (e)   any commercial participator;

and for this purpose "collector" and "public charitable collection" have the same meaning as in Part III of this Act.

(3) In addition, paragraph (b) of the definition of "professional fund-raiser" does not apply to a person if he does not receive—

(a) more than—
   (i)   £5 per day, or
   (ii) £500 per year,
   by way of remuneration in connection with soliciting money or other property for the benefit of the charitable institution referred to in that paragraph; or
(b) more than £500 by way of remuneration in connection with any fund-raising venture in the course of which he solicits money or other property for the benefit of that institution.

(4) In this Part any reference to charitable purposes, where occurring in the context of a reference to charitable, benevolent or philanthropic purposes, is a reference to charitable purposes whether or not the purposes are charitable within the meaning of any rule of law.

(5) For the purposes of this Part a company is connected with a charitable institution if—

(a) the institution, or
(b) the institution and one or more other charitable institutions, taken together,

is or are entitled (whether directly or through one or more nominees) to exercise, or control the exercise of, the whole of the voting power at any general meeting of the company.

(6) In this Part—

(a) "represent" and "solicit" mean respectively represent and solicit in any manner whatever, whether expressly or impliedly and whether done—
   (i)   by speaking directly to the person or persons to whom the representation or solicitation is addressed (whether when in his or their presence or not), or
   (ii) by means of a statement published in any newspaper, film or radio or television programme,
   or otherwise, and references to a representation or solicitation shall be construed accordingly; and
(b) any reference to soliciting or otherwise procuring money or other property is a reference to soliciting or otherwise procuring money or other property whether any consideration is, or is to be, given in return for the money or other property or not.

(7) Where—

(a) any solicitation of money or other property for the benefit of a charitable institution is made in accordance with arrangements between any person and that institution, and
(b) under those arrangements that person will be responsible for receiving on behalf of the institution money or other property given in response to the solicitation,

then (if he would not be so regarded apart from this subsection) that person shall be regarded for the purposes of this Part as soliciting money or other property for the benefit of the institution.

(8) Where any fund-raising venture is undertaken by a professional fund-raiser in the course of a radio or television programme, any solicitation which is made by a person in the course of the programme at the instance of the fund-raiser shall be regarded for the purposes of this Part as made by the fund-raiser and not by that person (and shall be so regarded whether or not the solicitation is made by that person for any reward).

(9) In this Part "services" includes facilities, and in particular—

(a) access to any premises or event;
(b) membership of any organisation;
(c) the provision of advertising space; and
(d) the provision of any financial facilities;

and references to the supply of services shall be construed accordingly.

(10) The Secretary of State may by order amend subsection (3) by substituting a different sum for any sum for the time being specified there.

[1] Substituted by Charities Act 1993, s.98 (1), Sch.6, Para.29(1), (5).
[2] Inserted by Deregulation and Contracting Out Act 1994, s.25(2).
[3] Substituted by Charities Act 1993, s.98 (1), Sch.6, Para.29(1), (5).
[4] Inserted by Deregulation and Contracting Out Act 1994, s.25(3).

59. Prohibition on professional fund-raiser etc. raising funds for charitable institution without an agreement in prescribed form

(1) It shall be unlawful for a professional fund-raiser to solicit money or other property for the benefit of a charitable institution unless he does so in accordance with an agreement with the institution satisfying the prescribed requirements.

(2) It shall be unlawful for a commercial participator to represent that charitable contributions are to be given to or applied for the benefit of a charitable institution unless he does so in accordance with an agreement with the institution satisfying the prescribed requirements.

(3) Where on the application of a charitable institution the court is satisfied—

(a) that any person has contravened or is contravening subsection (1) or (2) in relation to the institution, and
(b) that, unless restrained, any such contravention is likely to continue or be repeated,

the court may grant an injunction restraining the contravention; and compliance with subsection (1) or (2) shall not be enforceable otherwise than in accordance with this subsection.

(4) Where—

(a) a charitable institution makes any agreement with a professional fund-raiser or a commercial participator by virtue of which—
   (i) the professional fund-raiser is authorised to solicit money or other property for the benefit of the institution, or
   (ii) the commercial participator is authorised to represent that charitable contributions are to be given to or applied for the benefit of the institution,
as the case may be, but

1C–002

(b)   the agreement does not satisfy the prescribed requirements in any respect,

the agreement shall not be enforceable against the institution except to such extent (if any) as may be provided by an order of the court.

(5) A professional fund-raiser or commercial participator who is a party to such an agreement as is mentioned in subsection (4)(a) shall not be entitled to receive any amount by way of remuneration or expenses in respect of anything done by him in pursuance of the agreement unless—

(a)   he is so entitled under any provision of the agreement, and
(b)   either—
    (i)   the agreement satisfies the prescribed requirements, or
    (ii)   any such provision has effect by virtue of an order of the court under subsection (4).

(6) In this section "the prescribed requirements" means such requirements as are prescribed by regulations made by virtue of section 64(2)(a).

60. Professional fund-raisers etc. required to indicate institutions benefiting and arrangements for remuneration

1C–003   (1) Where a professional fund-raiser solicits money or other property for the benefit of one or more particular charitable institutions, the solicitation shall be accompanied by a statement clearly indicating—

(a)   the name or names of the institution or institutions concerned;
(b)   if there is more than one institution concerned, the proportions in which the institutions are respectively to benefit; and
(c)   (in general terms) the method by which the fund-raiser's remuneration in connection with the appeal is to be determined.

(2) Where a professional fund-raiser solicits money or other property for charitable, benevolent or philanthropic purposes of any description (rather than for the benefit of one or more particular charitable institutions), the solicitation shall be accompanied by a statement clearly indicating—

(a)   the fact that he is soliciting money or other property for those purposes and not for the benefit of any particular charitable institution or institutions;
(b)   the method by which it is to be determined how the proceeds of the appeal are to be distributed between different charitable institutions; and
(c)   (in general terms) the method by which his remuneration in connection with the appeal is to be determined.

(3) Where any representation is made by a commercial participator to the effect that charitable contributions are to be given to or applied for the benefit of one or more particular charitable institutions, the representation shall be accompanied by a statement clearly indicating—

(a) the name or names of the institution or institutions concerned;
(b) if there is more than one institution concerned, the proportions in which the institutions are respectively to benefit; and
(c) (in general terms) the method by which it is to be determined—

    (i) what proportion of the consideration given for goods or services sold or supplied by him, or of any other proceeds of a promotional venture undertaken by him, is to be given to or applied for the benefit of the institution or institutions concerned, or

    (ii) what sums by way of donations by him in connection with the sale or supply of any such goods or services are to be so given or applied,

as the case may require.

(4) If any such solicitation or representation as is mentioned in any of subsections (1) to (3) is made—

(a) in the course of a radio or television programme, and
(b) in association with an announcement to the effect that payment may be made, in response to the solicitation or representation, by means of a credit or debit card,

the statement required by virtue of subsection (1), (2) or (3) (as the case may be) shall include full details of the right to have refunded under section 61(1) any payment of £50 or more which is so made.

(5) If any such solicitation or representation as is mentioned in any of subsections (1) to (3) is made orally but is not made—

(a) by speaking directly to the particular person or persons to whom it is addressed and in his or their presence, or
(b) in the course of any radio or television programme,

the professional fund-raiser or commercial participator concerned shall, within seven days of any payment of £50 or more being made to him in response to the solicitation or representation, give to the person making the payment a written statement—

    (i) of the matters specified in paragraphs (a) to (c) of that subsection; and

    (ii) including full details of the right to cancel under section 61(2) an agreement made in response to the solicitation or representation, and the right to have refunded under section 61(2) or (3) any payment of £50 or more made in response thereto.

(6) In subsection (5) above the reference to the making of a payment is a reference to the making of a payment of whatever nature and by whatever means, including a payment made by means of a credit card or a debit card; and for the purposes of that subsection—

(a) where the person making any such payment makes it in person, it shall be regarded as made at the time when it is so made;
(b) where the person making any such payment sends it by post, it shall be regarded as made at the time when it is posted; and

(c)   where the person making any such payment makes it by giving, by telephone or by means of any other telecommunication apparatus, authority for an account to be debited with the payment, it shall be regarded as made at the time when any such authority is given.

(7) Where any requirement of subsections (1) to (5) is not complied with in relation to any solicitation or representation, the professional fundraiser or commercial participator concerned shall be guilty of an offence and liable on summary conviction to a fine not exceeding the fifth level on the standard scale.

(8) It shall be a defence for a person charged with any such offence to prove that he took all reasonable precautions and exercised all due diligence to avoid the commission of the offence.

(9) Where the commission by any person of an offence under subsection (7) is due to the act or default of some other person, that other person shall be guilty of the offence; and a person may be charged with and convicted of the offence by virtue of this subsection whether or not proceedings are taken against the first-mentioned person.

(10) In this section—

"the appeal", in relation to any solicitation by a professional fundraiser, means the campaign or other fund-raising venture in the course of which the solicitation is made;

"telecommunication apparatus" has the same meaning as in the Telecommunications Act 1984.

61. Cancellation of payments and agreements made in response to appeals

1C–004   (1) Where—

(a)   a person ("the donor"), in response to any such solicitation or representation as is mentioned in any of subsections (1) to (3) of section 60 which is made in the course of a radio or television programme, makes any payment of £50 or more to the relevant fund-raiser by means of a credit card or a debit card, but

(b)   before the end of the period of seven days beginning with the date of the solicitation or representation, the donor serves on the relevant fund-raiser a notice in writing which, however expressed, indicates the donor's intention to cancel the payment,

the donor shall (subject to subsection (4) below) be entitled to have the payment refunded to him forthwith by the relevant fund-raiser.

(2) Where—

(a)   a person ("the donor"), in response to any solicitation or representation falling within subsection (5) of section 60 , enters into an agreement with the relevant fund-raiser under which the donor is, or may be, liable to make any payment or payments to the relevant fund-raiser, and the amount or aggregate amount which the donor is, or may be, liable to pay to him under the agreement is £50 or more, but

(b)   before the end of the period of seven days beginning with the date when he is given any such written statement as is referred to

(a)   a charitable institution has served on any person a notice under
       subsection (3) ("the relevant notice") and that person has
       complied with the notice, but

(b)   that person has subsequently begun to carry on activities which
       are the same, or substantially the same, as those in respect of
       which the relevant notice was served,

the institution shall not, in connection with an application made by it
under this section in respect of the activities carried on by that person, be
required by virtue of that subsection to serve a further notice on him, if
the application is made not more than 12 months after the date of service
of the relevant notice.

(5) This section shall not have the effect of authorising a charitable institution to make an application under this section in respect of anything
done by a professional fund-raiser or commercial participator in relation
to the institution.

63. False statements relating to institutions which are not registered charities

(1) Where—   1C–006

(a)   a person solicits money or other property for the benefit of
       an institution in association with a representation that the
       institution is a registered charity, and

(b)   the institution is not such a charity,

he shall be guilty of an offence and liable on summary conviction to a fine
not exceeding the fifth level on the standard scale.

[(1A) In any proceedings for an offence under subsection (1), it shall be
a defence for the accused to prove that he believed on reasonable grounds
that the institution was a registered charity.][1]

(2) In [this section][2] "registered charity" means a charity which is for the
time being registered in the register of charities kept under [section 3 of
the Charities Act 1993.][3]

[1] Inserted by Deregulation and Contracting Out Act 1994, s.26(2).
[2] Substituted by Deregulation and Contracting Out Act 1994, s.26(3).
[3] Words substituted by Charities Act 1993 (c.10), Sch.6, Para.29(6).

SUPPLEMENTARY

64. Regulations about fund-raising   1C–007

(1) The Secretary of State may make such regulations as appear to him
to be necessary or desirable for any purposes connected with any of the
preceding provisions of this Part.

(2) Without prejudice to the generality of subsection (1), any such
regulations may—

(a)   prescribe the form and content of—
       (i)   agreements made for the purposes of section 59 , and
       (ii)   notices served under section 62(3) ;

(b)   require professional fund-raisers or commercial participators who are parties to such agreements with charitable institutions to make available to the institutions books, documents or other records (however kept) which relate to the institutions;

(c)   specify the manner in which money or other property acquired by professional fund-raisers or commercial participators for the benefit of, or otherwise falling to be given to or applied by such persons for the benefit of, charitable institutions is to be transmitted to such institutions;

(d)   provide for any provisions of section 60 or 61 having effect in relation to solicitations or representations made in the course of radio or television programmes to have effect, subject to any modifications specified in the regulations, in relation to solicitations or representations made in the course of such programmes—

(i)   by charitable institutions, or

(ii)   by companies connected with such institutions,

and, in that connection, provide for any other provisions of this Part to have effect for the purposes of the regulations subject to any modifications so specified;

(e)   make other provision regulating the raising of funds for charitable, benevolent or philanthropic purposes (whether by professional fund-raisers or commercial participators or otherwise).

(3) In subsection (2)(c) the reference to such money or other property as is there mentioned includes a reference to money or other property which, in the case of a professional fund-raiser or commercial participator—

(a)   has been acquired by him otherwise than in accordance with an agreement with a charitable institution, but

(b)   by reason of any solicitation or representation in consequence of which it has been acquired, is held by him on trust for such an institution.

(4) Regulations under this section may provide that any failure to comply with a specified provision of the regulations shall be an offence punishable on summary conviction by a fine not exceeding the second level on the standard scale.

CHARITIES ACT 1993

NOTES
An Act to consolidate the Charitable Trustees Incorporation Act 1872 and, except for certain spent or transitional provisions, the Charities Act 1960 and Part I of the Charities Act 1992.

PART I

THE CHARITY COMMISSIONERS AND THE OFFICIAL CUSTODIAN FOR CHARITIES

1. The Charity Commissioners

(1) There shall continue to be a body of Charity Commissioners for England and Wales, and they shall have such functions as are conferred on them by this Act in addition to any functions under any other enactment for the time being in force.

1D–001

(2) The provisions of Schedule 1 to this Act shall have effect with respect to the constitution and proceedings of the Commissioners and other matters relating to the Commissioners and their officers and employees.

(3) The Commissioners shall (without prejudice to their specific powers and duties under other enactments) have the general function of promoting the effective use of charitable resources by encouraging the development of better methods of administration, by giving charity trustees information or advice on any matter affecting the charity and by investigating and checking abuses.

(4) It shall be the general object of the Commissioners so to act in the case of any charity (unless it is a matter of altering its purposes) as best to promote and make effective the work of the charity in meeting the needs designated by its trusts; but the Commissioners shall not themselves have power to act in the administration of a charity.

(5) The Commissioners shall, as soon as possible after the end of every year, make to the Secretary of State a report on their operations during that year, and he shall lay a copy of the report before each House of Parliament.

2. The official custodian for charities

1D–002 (1) There shall continue to be an officer known as the official custodian for charities (in this Act referred to as "the official custodian") whose function it shall be to act as trustee for charities in the cases provided for by this Act; and the official custodian shall be by that name a corporation sole having perpetual succession and using an official seal which shall be officially and judicially noticed.

(2) Such officer of the Commissioners as they may from time to time designate shall be the official custodian.

(3) The official custodian shall perform his duties in accordance with such general or special directions as may be given him by the Commissioners, and his expenses (except those re-imbursed to him or recovered by him as trustee for any charity) shall be defrayed by the Commissioners.

(4) Anything which is required to or may be done by, to or before the official custodian may be done by, to or before any officer of the Commissioners generally or specially authorised by them to act for him during a vacancy in his office or otherwise.

(5) The official custodian shall not be liable as trustee for any charity in respect of any loss or of the mis-application of any property unless it is occasioned by or through the wilful neglect or default of the custodian or of any person acting for him; but the Consolidated Fund shall be liable to make good to a charity any sums for which the custodian may be liable by reason of any such neglect or default.

(6) The official custodian shall keep such books of account and such records in relation thereto as may be directed by the Treasury and shall prepare accounts in such form, in such manner and at such times as may be so directed.

(7) The accounts so prepared shall be examined and certified by the Comptroller and Auditor General, and the report to be made by the Commissioners to the Secretary of State for any year shall include a copy of the accounts so prepared for any period ending in or with the year and of the certificate and report of the Comptroller and Auditor General with respect to those accounts.

PART II

REGISTRATION AND NAMES OF CHARITIES

REGISTRATION OF CHARITIES

3. The register of charities

1D–003 (1) The Commissioners shall continue to keep a register of charities, which shall be kept by them in such manner as they think fit.

(2) There shall be entered in the register every charity not excepted by subsection (5) below; and a charity so excepted (other than one excepted by paragraph (a) of that subsection) may be entered in the register at the request of the charity, but (whether or not it was excepted at the time of

registration) may at any time, and shall at the request of the charity, be removed from the register.

(3) The register shall contain—

    (a)   the name of every registered charity; and

    (b)   such other particulars of, and such other information relating to, every such charity as the Commissioners think fit.

(4) Any institution which no longer appears to the Commissioners to be a charity shall be removed from the register, with effect, where the removal is due to any change in its purposes or trusts, from the date of that change; and there shall also be removed from the register any charity which ceases to exist or does not operate.

(5) The following charities are not required to be registered—

    (a)   any charity comprised in Schedule 2 to this Act (in this Act referred to as an "exempt charity");

    (b)   any charity which is excepted by order or regulations;

    (c)   any charity which has neither—

        (i)   any permanent endowment, nor

        (ii) the use or occupation of any land,

        and whose income from all sources does not in aggregate amount to more than £ 1,000 a year;

and no charity is required to be registered in respect of any registered place of worship.

[(5A) In subsection (5) above, paragraph (a) shall be read as referring also to—

    (a)   any higher education corporation within the meaning of the Education Reform Act 1988, and

    (b)   any further education corporation within the meaning of the Further and Higher Education Act 1992.][1]

[(5B) In addition, in subsection (5) above—

    (a)   paragraph (a) shall be read as referring also to—

        (i)   any body to which section 23(1)(a) or (b) of the School Standards and Framework Act 1998 applies, and

        (ii) any Education Action Forum established by virtue of section 10(1) of that Act; and

    (b)   paragraph (b) shall be read as referring also to any foundation to which section 23(3) of that Act applies;

but an order of the Commissioners, or regulations made by the Secretary of State, may provide that section 23(3) of that Act shall cease to apply to any such foundation as is mentioned in that provision or to any such foundation of a description specified in the order or regulations.][2]

(6) With any application for a charity to be registered there shall be supplied to the Commissioners copies of its trusts (or, if they are not set out in any extant document, particulars of them), and such other documents or information as may be prescribed by regulations made by the Secretary

of State or as the Commissioners may require for the purpose of the application.

(7) It shall be the duty—

    (a)   of the charity trustees of any charity which is not registered nor excepted from registration to apply for it to be registered, and to supply the documents and information required by subsection (6) above; and

    (b)   of the charity trustees (or last charity trustees) of any institution which is for the time being registered to notify the Commissioners if it ceases to exist, or if there is any change in its trusts or in the particulars of it entered in the register, and to supply to the Commissioners particulars of any such change and copies of any new trusts or alterations of the trusts.

(8) The register (including the entries cancelled when institutions are removed from the register) shall be open to public inspection at all reasonable times; and copies (or particulars) of the trusts of any registered charity as supplied to the Commissioners under this section shall, so long as it remains on the register, be kept by them and be open to public inspection at all reasonable times, except in so far as regulations made by the Secretary of State otherwise provide.

(9) Where any information contained in the register is not in documentary form, subsection (8) above shall be construed as requiring the information to be available for public inspection in legible form at all reasonable times.

(10) If the Commissioners so determine, subsection (8) above shall not apply to any particular information contained in the register and specified in their determination.

(11) Nothing in the foregoing subsections shall require any person to supply the Commissioners with copies of schemes for the administration of a charity made otherwise than by the court, or to notify the Commissioners of any change made with respect to a registered charity by such a scheme, or require a person, if he refers the Commissioners to a document or copy already in the possession of the Commissioners, to supply a further copy of the document; but where by virtue of this subsection a copy of any document need not be supplied to the Commissioners, a copy of it, if it relates to a registered charity, shall be open to inspection under subsection (8) above as if supplied to the Commissioners under this section.

(12) If the Secretary of State thinks it expedient to do so—

    (a)   in consequence of changes in the value of money, or

    (b)   with a view to extending the scope of the exception provided for by subsection (5)(c) above,

he may by order amend subsection (5)(c) by substituting a different sum for the sum for the time being specified there.

(13) The reference in subsection (5)(b) above to a charity which is excepted by order or regulations is to a charity which—

    (a)   is for the time being permanently or temporarily excepted by order of the Commissioners; or (b)　is of a description permanently or temporarily excepted by regulations made by the Secretary of State,

and which complies with any conditions of the exception.

(14) In this section "registered place of worship" means any land or building falling within section 9 of the Places of Worship Registration Act 1855 (that is to say, the land and buildings which if the Charities Act 1960 had not been passed, would by virtue of that section as amended by subsequent enactments be partially exempted from the operation of the Charitable Trusts Act 1853), and for the purposes of this subsection "building"includes part of a building.

[1]　Added by Teaching and Higher Education Act 1998, s.44(1) Sch.3, Para.9.

[2]　Added by School Standards and Framework Act 1998 (c.31), Sch.30, para.48.

4. Effect of, and claims and objections to, registration

(1) An institution shall for all purposes other than rectification of the register be conclusively presumed to be or to have been a charity at any time when it is or was on the register of charities.　　　　　　**1D–004**

(2) Any person who is or may be affected by the registration of an institution as a charity may, on the ground that it is not a charity, object to its being entered by the Commissioners in the register, or apply to them for it to be removed from the register; and provision may be made by regulations made by the Secretary of State as to the manner in which any such objection or application is to be made, prosecuted or dealt with.

(3) An appeal against any decision of the Commissioners to enter or not to enter an institution in the register of charities, or to remove or not to remove an institution from the register, may be brought in the High Court by the Attorney General, or by the persons who are or claim to be the charity trustees of the institution, or by any person whose objection or application under subsection (2) above is disallowed by the decision.

(4) If there is an appeal to the High Court against any decision of the Commissioners to enter an institution in the register, or not to remove an institution from the register, then until the Commissioners are satisfied whether the decision of the Commissioners is or is not to stand, the entry in the register shall be maintained, but shall be in suspense and marked to indicate that it is in suspense; and for the purposes of subsection (1) above an institution shall be deemed not to be on the register during any period when the entry relating to it in suspense under this subsection.

(5) Any question affecting the registration or removal from the register of an institution may, notwithstanding that it has been determined by a decision on appeal under subsection (3) above, be considered afresh by the Commissioners and shall not be concluded by that decision, if it appears to the Commissioners that there has been a change of circumstances or that the decision is inconsistent with a later judicial decision, whether given on such an appeal or not.

5. Status of registered charity (other than small charity) to appear on official publications etc.

(1) This section applies to a registered charity if its gross income in its last financial year exceeded [£10,000][1].　　　　　　**1D–005**

(2) Where this section applies to a registered charity, the fact that it is a registered charity shall be stated [. . . .][2] in legible characters—

(a)   in all notices, advertisements and other documents issued by or on behalf of the charity and soliciting money or other property for the benefit of the charity;

(b)   in all bills of exchange, promissory notes, endorsements, cheques and orders for money or goods purporting to be signed on behalf of the charity; and

(c)   in all bills rendered by it and in all its invoices, receipts and letters of credit.

[(2A) The statement required by subsection (2) above shall be in English, except that, in the case of a document which is otherwise wholly in Welsh, the statement may be in Welsh if it consists of or includes the words "elusen cofrestredig" (the Welsh equivalent of "registered charity").][3]

(3) Subsection (2)(a) above has effect whether the solicitation is express or implied, and whether the money or other property is to be given for any consideration or not.

(4) If, in the case of a registered charity to which this section applies, any person issues or authorises the issue of any document falling within paragraph (a) or (c) of subsection (2) above [which does not contain the statement][4] required by that subsection, he shall be guilty of an offence and liable on summary conviction to a fine not exceeding level 3 on the standard scale.

(5) If, in the case of any such registered charity, any person signs any document falling within paragraph (b) of subsection (2) above [which does not contain the statement][5] required by that subsection, he shall be guilty of an offence and liable on summary conviction to a fine not exceeding level 3 on the standard scale.

(6) The Secretary of State may by order amend subsection (1) above by substituting a different sum for the sum for the time being specified there.

[1]   Words substituted by Charities Act 1993 (Substitution of Sums) Order, SI 1995/2696 art.2(2).
[2]   Repealed by Welsh Language Act 1993, ss.32, 35(1), Sch.2.
[3]   Inserted by Welsh Language Act 1993, s.32.
[4]   Substituted by Welsh Language Act 1993, s.32.
[5]   Inserted by Welsh Language Act 1993, s.32.

CHARITY NAMES

6. Power of Commissioners to require charity's name to be changed

1D–006   (1) Where this subsection applies to a charity, the Commissioners may give a direction requiring the name of the charity to be changed, within such period as is specified in the direction, to such other name as the charity trustees may determine with the approval of the Commissioners.

(2) Subsection (1) above applies to a charity if—

(a)   it is a registered charity and its name ("the registered name")—
(i)   is the same as, or
(ii)   is in the opinion of the Commissioners too like,
the name, at the time when the registered name was entered in the register in respect of the charity, of any other charity (whether registered or not);

(b) the name of the charity is in the opinion of the Commissioners likely to mislead the public as to the true nature—
    (i) of the purposes of the charity as set out in its trusts, or
    (ii) of the activities which the charity carries on under its trusts in pursuit of those purposes;

(c) the name of the charity includes any word or expression for the time being specified in regulations made by the Secretary of State and the inclusion in its name of that word or expression is in the opinion of the Commissioners likely to mislead the public in any respect as to the status of the charity;

(d) the name of the charity is in the opinion of the Commissioners likely to give the impression that the charity is connected in some way with Her Majesty's Government or any local authority, or with any other body of persons or any individual, when it is not so connected; or

(e) the name of the charity is in the opinion of the Commissioners offensive;

and in this subsection any reference to the name of a charity is, in relation to a registered charity, a reference to the name by which it is registered.

(3) Any direction given by virtue of subsection (2)(a) above must be given within twelve months of the time when the registered name was entered in the register in respect of the charity.

(4) Any direction given under this section with respect to a charity shall be given to the charity trustees; and on receiving any such direction the charity trustees shall give effect to it notwithstanding anything in the trusts of the charity.

(5) Where the name of any charity is changed under this section, then (without prejudice to section 3(7)(b) above) it shall be the duty of the charity trustees forthwith to notify the Commissioners of the charity's new name and of the date on which the change occurred.

(6) A change of name by a charity under this section does not affect any rights or obligations of the charity; and any legal proceedings that might have been continued or commenced by or against it in its former name may be continued or commenced by or against it in its new name.

(7) Section 26(3) of the Companies Act 1985 (minor variations in names to be disregarded) shall apply for the purposes of this section as if the reference to section 26(1)(c) of that Act were a reference to subsection (2)(a) above.

(8) Any reference in this section to the charity trustees of a charity shall, in relation to a charity which is a company, be read as a reference to the directors of the company.

(9) Nothing in this section applies to an exempt charity.

7. Effect of direction under s.6 where charity is a company

(1) Where any direction is given under section 6 above with respect to a charity which is a company, the direction shall be taken to require the name of the charity to be changed by resolution of the directors of the company.   **1D–007**

(2) Section 380 of the Companies Act 1985 (registration etc. of resolution and agreements) shall apply to any resolution passed by the directors in compliance with any such direction.

(3) Where the name of such a charity is changed in compliance with any such direction, the registrar of companies—

    (a)   shall, subject to section 26 of the Companies Act 1985 (prohibition on registration of certain names), enter the new name on the register of companies in place of the former name, and

    (b)   shall issue a certificate of incorporation altered to meet the circumstances of the case;

and the change of name has effect from the date on which the altered certificate is issued.

<h2 style="text-align:center">PART III</h2>

<h3 style="text-align:center">COMMISSIONERS' INFORMATION POWERS</h3>

8. General power to institute inquiries

1D–008   (1) The Commissioners may from time to time institute inquiries with regard to charities or a particular charity or class of charities, either generally or for particular purposes, but no such inquiry shall extend to any exempt charity.

(2) The Commissioners may either conduct such an inquiry themselves or appoint a person to conduct it and make a report to them.

(3) For the purposes of any such inquiry the Commissioners, or a person appointed by them to conduct it, may direct any person (subject to the provisions of this section)—

    (a)   to furnish accounts and statements in writing with respect to any matter in question at the inquiry, being a matter on which he has or can reasonably obtain information, or to return answers in writing to any questions or inquiries addressed to him on any such matter, and to verify any such accounts, statements or answers by statutory declaration;

    (b)   to furnish copies of documents in his custody or under his control which relate to any matter in question at the inquiry, and to verify and such copies by statutory declaration;

    (c)   to attend at a specified time and place and give evidence or produce any such documents.

(4) For the purposes of any such inquiry evidence may be taken on oath, and the person conducting the inquiry may for that purpose administer oaths, or may instead of administering an oath require the person examined to make and subscribe a declaration of the truth of the matters about which he is examined.

(5) The Commissioners may pay to any person the necessary expenses of his attendance to give evidence or produce documents for the purpose of an inquiry under this section, and a person shall not be required in obedience to a direction under paragraph (c) of subsection (3) above to go more than ten miles from his place of residence unless those expenses are paid or tendered to him.

(6) Where an inquiry has been held under this section, the Commissioners may either—

    (a)   cause the report of the person conducting the inquiry, or such other statement of the results of the inquiry as they think fit, to be printed and published, or

    (b)   publish any such report or statement in some other way which is calculated in their opinion to bring it to the attention of persons who may wish to make representations to them about the action to be taken.

(7) The council of a county or district, the Common Council of the City of London and the council of a London borough may contribute to the expenses of the Commissioners in connection with inquiries under this section into local charities in the council's area.

9. Power to call for documents and search records

(1) The Commissioners may by order—   **1D–009**

    (a)   require any person to furnish them with any information in his possession which relates to any charity and is relevant to the discharge of their functions or of the functions of the official custodian;

    (b)   require any person who has in his custody or under his control any document which relates to any charity and is relevant to the discharge of their functions or of the functions of the official custodian—

        (i)   to furnish them with a copy of or extract from the document, or

        (ii)   (unless the document forms part of the records or other documents of a court or of a public or local authority) to transmit the document itself to them for their inspection.

(2) Any officer of the Commissioners, if so authorised by them, shall be entitled without payment to inspect and take copies of or extracts from the records or other documents of any court, or of any public registry or office of records, for any purpose connected with the discharge of the functions of the Commissioners or of the official custodian.

(3) The Commissioners shall be entitled without payment to keep any copy or extract furnished to them under subsection (1) above; and where a document transmitted to them under that subsection for their inspection relates only to one or more charities and is not held by any person entitled as trustee or otherwise to the custody of it, the Commissioners may keep it or may deliver it to the charity trustees or to any other person who may be so entitled.

(4) No person properly having the custody of documents relating only to an exempt charity shall be required under subsection (1) above to transmit to the Commissioners any of those documents, or to furnish any copy of or extract from any of them.

(5) The rights conferred by subsection (2) above shall, in relation to information recorded otherwise than in legible form, include the right to require the information to be made available in legible form for inspection or for a copy or extract to be made of or from it.

10. Disclosure of information to and by Commissioners

1D–010   (1) Subject to subsection (2) below and to any express restriction imposed by or under any other enactment, a body or person to whom this section applies may disclose to the Charity Commissioners any information received by that body or person under or for the purposes of any enactment, where the disclosure is made by the body or person for the purpose of enabling or assisting the Commissioners to discharge any of their functions.

(2) Subsection (1) above shall not have effect in relation to the Commissioners of Customs and Excise or the Commissioners of Inland Revenue; but either of those bodies of Commissioners ("the relevant body") may disclose to the Charity Commissioners the following information—

   (a)   the name and address of any institution which has for any purpose been treated by the relevant body as established for charitable purposes;

   (b)   information as to the purposes of an institution and the trusts under which it is established or regulated, where the disclosure is made by the relevant body in order to give or obtain assistance in determining whether the institution ought for any purpose to be treated as established for charitable purposes; and

   (c)   information with respect to an institution which has for any purpose been treated as so established but which appears to the relevant body—

      (i)   to be, or to have been, carrying on activities which are not charitable, or

      (ii)   to be, or to have been, applying any of its funds for purposes which are not charitable.

(3) In subsection (2) above, any reference to an institution shall, in relation to the Commissioners of Inland Revenue, be construed as a reference to an institution in England and Wales.

(4) Subject to subsection (5) below, the Charity Commissioners may disclose to a body or person to whom this section applies any information received by them under or for the purposes of any enactment, where the disclosure is made by the Commissioners—

   (a)   for any purpose connected with the discharge of their functions, and

   (b)   for the purpose of enabling or assisting that body or person to discharge any of its or his functions.

(5) Where any information disclosed to the Charity Commissioners under subsection (1) or (2) above is so disclosed subject to any express restriction on the disclosure of the information by the Commissioners, the Commissioners' power of disclosure under subsection (4) above shall, in relation to the information, be exercisable by them subject to any such restriction.

(6) This section applies to the following bodies and persons—

   (a)   any government department (including a Northern Ireland department);

(b)   any local authority;
(c)   any constable; and
(d)   any other body or person discharging functions of a public nature (including a body or person discharging regulatory functions in relation to any description of activities).

(7) In subsection (6)(d) above the reference to any such body or person as is there mentioned shall, in relation to a disclosure by the Charity Commissioners under subsection (4) above, be construed as including a reference to any such body or person in a country or territory outside the United Kingdom.

(8) Nothing in this section shall be construed as affecting any power of disclosure exercisable apart from this section.

(9) In this section "enactment" includes an enactment comprised in subordinate legislation (within the meaning of the Interpretation Act 1978).

11. Supply of false or misleading information to Commissioners, etc.

(1) Any person who knowingly or recklessly provides the Commissioners with information which is false or misleading in a material particular shall be guilty of an offence if the information—

(a)   is provided in purported compliance with a requirement imposed by or under this Act; or   **1D–011**
(b)   is provided otherwise than as mentioned in paragraph (a) above but in circumstances in which the person providing the information intends, or could reasonably be expected to know, that it would be used by the Commissioners for the purpose of discharging their functions under this Act.

(2) Any person who wilfully alters, suppresses, conceals or destroys any document which he is or is liable to be required, by or under this Act, to produce to the Commissioners shall be guilty of an offence.

(3) Any person guilty of an offence under this section shall be liable—

(a)   on summary conviction, to a fine not exceeding the statutory maximum;
(b)   on conviction on indictment, to imprisonment for a term not exceeding two years or to a fine, or both.

(4) In this section references to the Commissioners include references to any person conducting an inquiry under section 8 above.

[12. Data protection

An order under section 30 of the Data Protection Act 1984 (exemption from subject access provisions of data held for the purpose of discharging designated functions in connection with the regulation of financial services etc.) may designate for the purposes of that section, as if they were functions conferred by or under such an enactment as is there mentioned, any functions of the Commissioners appearing to the Secretary of State to be—

(a)   connected with the protection of charities against misconduct or mismanagement (whether by trustees or other persons) in their administration; or

(b)   connected with the protection of the property of charities from loss or misapplication or with the recovery of such property][1]

[1] Repealed by Data Protection Act 1998, s.74(2), Sch.16, Pt I.

PART IV

APPLICATION OF PROPERTY CY-PRÈS AND ASSISTANCE AND SUPERVISION OF CHARITIES BY COURT AND COMMISSIONERS

EXTENDED POWERS OF COURT AND VARIATION OF CHARTERS

13. Occasions for applying property cy-près

1D–012   (1) Subject to subsection (2) below, the circumstances in which the original purposes of a charitable gift can be altered to allow the property given or part of it to be applied cy-près shall be as follows—

(a)   where the original purposes, in whole or in part—
  (i)   have been as far as may be fulfilled; or
  (ii)   cannot be carried out, or not according to the directions given and to the spirit of the gift; or

(b)   where the original purposes provide a use for part only of the property available by virtue of the gift; or

(c)   where the property available by virtue of the gift and other property applicable for similar purposes can be more effectively used in conjunction, and to that end can suitably, regard being had to the spirit of the gift, be made applicable to common purposes; or

(d)   where the original purposes were laid down by reference to an area which then was but has since ceased to be a unit for some other purpose, or by reference to a class of persons or to an area which has for any reason since ceased to be suitable, regard being had to the spirit of the gift, or to be practical in administering the gift; or

(e)   where the original purposes, in whole or in part, have, since they were laid down,—
  (i)   been adequately provided for by other means; or
  (ii)   ceased, as being useless or harmful to the community or for other reasons, to be in law charitable; or
  (iii)   ceased in any other way to provide a suitable and effective method of using the property available by virtue of the gift, regard being had to the spirit of the gift.

(2) Subsection (1) above shall not affect the conditions which must be satisfied in order that property given for charitable purposes may be applied cy-près except in so far as those conditions require a failure of the original purposes.

(3) References in the foregoing subsections to the original purposes of a gift shall be construed, where the application of the property given has been altered or regulated by a scheme or otherwise, as referring to the purposes for which the property is for the time being applicable.

(4) Without prejudice to the power to make schemes in circumstances falling within subsection (1) above, the court may by scheme made under the court's jurisdiction with respect to charities, in any case where the purposes for which the property is held are laid down by reference to any such area as is mentioned in the first column in Schedule 3 to this Act, provide for enlarging the area to any such area as is mentioned in the second column in the same entry in that Schedule.

(5) It is hereby declared that a trust for charitable purposes places a trustee under a duty, where the case permits and requires the property or some part of it to be applied cy-près, to secure its effective use for charity by taking steps to enable it to be so applied.

14. Application cy-près of gifts of donors unknown or disclaiming

(1) Property given for specific charitable purposes which fail shall be applicable cy-près as if given for charitable purposes generally, where it belongs—   **1D–013**

   (a) to a donor who after—
     (i) the prescribed advertisements and inquiries have been published and made, and
     (ii) the prescribed period beginning with the publication of those advertisements has expired,
    cannot be identified or cannot be found; or
   (b) to a donor who has executed a disclaimer in the prescribed form of his right to have the property returned.

(2) Where the prescribed advertisements and inquiries have been published and made by or on behalf of trustees with respect to any such property, the trustees shall not be liable to any person in respect of the property if no claim by him to be interested in it is received by them before the expiry of the period mentioned in subsection (1)(a)(ii) above.

(3) For the purposes of this section property shall be conclusively presumed (without any advertisement or inquiry) to belong to donors who cannot be identified, in so far as it consists—

   (a) of the proceeds of cash collections made by means of collecting boxes or by other means not adapted for distinguishing one gift from another; or
   (b) of the proceeds of any lottery, competition, entertainment, sale or similar money-raising activity, after allowing for property given to provide prizes or articles for sale or otherwise to enable the activity to be undertaken.

(4) The court may by order direct that property not falling within subsection (3) above shall for the purposes of this section be treated (without any advertisement or inquiry) as belonging to donors who cannot be identified where it appears to the court either—

(a)   that it would be unreasonable, having regard to the amounts likely to be returned to the donors, to incur expense with a view to returning the property; or

(b)   that it would be unreasonable, having regard to the nature, circumstances and amounts of the gifts, and to the lapse of time since the gifts were made, for the donors to expect the property to be returned.

(5) Where property is applied cy-près by virtue of this section, the donor shall be deemed to have parted with all his interest at the time when the gift was made; but where property is so applied as belonging to donors who cannot be identified or cannot be found, and is not so applied by virtue of subsection (3) or (4) above—

(a)   the scheme shall specify the total amount of that property; and

(b)   the donor of any part of that amount shall be entitled, if he makes a claim not later than six months after the date on which the scheme is made, to recover from the charity for which the property is applied a sum equal to that part, less any expenses properly incurred by the charity trustees after that date in connection with claims relating to his gift; and

(c)   the scheme may include directions as to the provision to be made for meeting any such claim.

(6) Where—

(a)   any sum is, in accordance with any such directions, set aside for meeting any such claims, but

(b)   the aggregate amount of any such claims actually made exceeds the relevant amount,

then, if the Commissioners so direct, each of the donors in question shall be entitled only to such proportion of the relevant amount as the amount of his claim bears to the aggregate amount referred to in paragraph (b) above; and for this purpose "the relevant amount" means the amount of the sum so set aside after deduction of any expenses properly incurred by the charity trustees in connection with claims relating to the donors' gifts.

(7) For the purposes of this section, charitable purposes shall be deemed to "fail" where any difficulty in applying property to those purposes makes that property or the part not applicable cy-près available to be returned to the donors.

(8) In this section "prescribed" means prescribed by regulations made by the Commissioners; and such regulations may, as respects the advertisements which are to be published for the purposes of subsection (1)(a) above, make provision as to the form and content of such advertisements as well as the manner in which they are to be published.

(9) Any regulations made by the Commissioners under this section shall be published by the Commissioners in such manner as they think fit.

(10) In this section, except in so far as the context otherwise requires, references to a donor include persons claiming through or under the original donor, and references to property given include the property for the time being representing the property originally given or property derived from it.

(11) This section shall apply to property given for charitable purposes, notwithstanding that it was so given before the commencement of this Act.

15. Charities governed by charter, or by or under statute

(1) Where a Royal charter establishing or regulating a body corporate is amendable by the grant and acceptance of a further charter, a scheme relating to the body corporate or to the administration of property held by the body (including a scheme for the cy-près application of any such property) may be made by the court under the court's jurisdiction with respect to charities notwithstanding that the scheme cannot take effect without the alteration of the charter, but shall be so framed that the scheme, or such part of it as cannot take effect without the alteration of the charter, does not purport to come into operation unless or until Her Majesty thinks fit to amend the charter in such manner as will permit the scheme or that part of it to have effect.

1D–014

(2) Where under the court's jurisdiction with respect to charities or the corresponding jurisdiction of a court in Northern Ireland, or under powers conferred by this Act or by any Northern Ireland legislation relating to charities, a scheme is made with respect to a body corporate, and it appears to Her Majesty expedient, having regard to the scheme, to amend any Royal charter relating to that body, Her Majesty may, on the application of that body, amend the charter accordingly by Order in Council in any way in which the charter could be amended by the grant and acceptance of a further charter; and any such Order in Council may be revoked or varied in like manner as the charter it amends.

(3) The jurisdiction of the court with respect to charities shall not be excluded or restricted in the case of a charity of any description mentioned in Schedule 4 to this Act by the operation of the enactments or instruments there mentioned in relation to that description, and a scheme established for any such charity may modify or supersede in relation to it the provision made by any such enactment or instrument as if made by a scheme of the court, and may also make any such provision as is authorised by that Schedule.

POWERS OF COMMISSIONERS TO MAKE SCHEMES AND ACT FOR PROTECTION OF CHARITIES ETC

16. Concurrent jurisdiction with High Court for certain purposes

(1) Subject to the provisions of this Act, the Commissioners may by order exercise the same jurisdiction and powers as are exercisable by the High Court in charity proceedings for the following purposes—

1D–015

    (a)   establishing a scheme for the administration of a charity;

    (b)   appointing, discharging or removing a charity trustee or trustee for a charity, or removing an officer or employee;

    (c)   vesting or transferring property, or requiring or entitling any person to call for or make any transfer of property or any payment.

(2) Where the court directs a scheme for the administration of a charity to be established, the court may by order refer the matter to the Commissioners for them to prepare or settle a scheme in accordance with such directions (if any) as the court sees fit to give, and any such order may provide for the scheme to be put into effect by order of the Commissioners as if prepared under subsection (1) above and without any further order of the court.

(3) The Commissioners shall not have jurisdiction under this section to try or determine the title at law or in equity to any property as between a charity or trustee for a charity and a person holding or claiming the property or an interest in it adversely to the charity, or to try or determine any question as to the existence or extent of any charge or trust.

(4) Subject to the following subsections, the Commissioners shall not exercise their jurisdiction under this section as respects any charity, except—

    (a)   on the application of the charity; or
    (b)   on an order of the court under subsection (2) above; or
    (c)   in the case of a charity other than an exempt charity, on the application of the Attorney General.

(5) In the case of a charity which is not an exempt charity and whose income from all sources does not in aggregate exceed £500 a year, the Commissioners may exercise their jurisdiction under this section on the application—

    (a)   of any one or more of the charity trustees; or
    (b)   of any person interested in the charity; or
    (c)   of any two or more inhabitants of the area of the charity if it is a local charity.

(6) Where in the case of a charity, other than an exempt charity, the Commissioners are satisfied that the charity trustees ought in the interests of the charity to apply for a scheme, but have unreasonably refused or neglected to do so and the Commissioners have given the charity trustees an opportunity to make representations to them, the Commissioners may proceed as if an application for a scheme had been made by the charity but the Commissioners shall not have power in a case where they act by virtue of this subsection to alter the purposes of a charity, unless forty years have elapsed from the date of its foundation.

(7) Where—

    (a)   a charity cannot apply to the Commissioners for a scheme by reason of any vacancy among the charity trustees or the absence or incapacity of any of them, but
    (b)   such an application is made by such number of the charity trustees as the Commissioners consider appropriate in the circumstances of the case,

the Commissioners may nevertheless proceed as if the application were an application made by the charity.

(8) The Commissioners may on the application of any charity trustee or trustee for a charity exercise their jurisdiction under this section for the purpose of discharging him from his trusteeship.

(9) Before exercising any jurisdiction under this section otherwise than on an order of the court, the Commissioners shall give notice of their intention to do so to each of the charity trustees, except any that cannot be found or has no known address in the United Kingdom or who is party or privy to an application for the exercise of the jurisdiction; and any such notice may be given by post, and, if given by post, may be addressed to the recipient's last known address in the United Kingdom.

(10) The Commissioners shall not exercise their jurisdiction under this section in any case (not referred to them by order of the court) which, by reason of its contentious character, or of any special question of law or of fact which it may involve, or for other reasons, the Commissioners may consider more fit to be adjudicated on by the court.

(11) An appeal against any order of the Commissioners under this section may be brought in the High Court by the Attorney General.

(12) An appeal against any order of the Commissioners under this section may also, at any time within the three months beginning with the day following that on which the order is published, be brought in the High Court by the charity or any of the charity trustees, or by any person removed from any office or employment by the order (unless he is removed with the concurrence of the charity trustees or with the approval of the special visitor, if any, of the charity).

(13) No appeal shall be brought under subsection (12) above except with a certificate of the Commissioners that it is a proper case for an appeal or with the leave of one of the judges of the High Court attached to the Chancery Division.

(14) Where an order of the Commissioners under this section establishes a scheme for the administration of a charity, any person interested in the charity shall have the like right of appeal under subsection (12) above as a charity trustee, and so also, in the case of a charity which is a local charity in any area, shall any two or more inhabitants of the area and the council of any parish or (in Wales) any community comprising the area or any part of it.

(15) If the Secretary of State thinks it expedient to do so—

    (a)   in consequence of changes in the value of money, or
    (b)   with a view to increasing the number of charities in respect of which the Commissioners may exercise their jurisdiction under this section in accordance with subsection (5) above,

he may by order amend that subsection by substituting a different sum for the sum for the time being specified there.

17. Further powers to make schemes or alter application of charitable property

1D–016

(1) Where it appears to the Commissioners that a scheme should be established for the administration of a charity, but also that it is necessary or desirable for the scheme to alter the provision made by an Act of Parliament establishing or regulating the charity or to make any other provision which goes or might go beyond the powers exercisable by them

apart from this section, or that it is for any reason proper for the scheme to be subject to parliamentary review, then (subject to subsection (6) below) the Commissioners may settle a scheme accordingly with a view to its being given effect under this section.

(2) A scheme settled by the Commissioners under this section may be given effect by order of the Secretary of State, and a draft of the order shall be laid before Parliament.

(3) Without prejudice to the operation of section 6 of the Statutory Instruments Act 1946 in other cases, in the case of a scheme which goes beyond the powers exercisable apart from this section in altering a statutory provision contained in or having effect under any public general Act of Parliament, the order shall not be made unless the draft has been approved by resolution of each House of Parliament.

(4) Subject to subsection (5) below, any provision of a scheme brought into effect under this section may be modified or superseded by the court or the Commissioners as if it were a scheme brought into effect by order of the Commissioners under section 16 above.

(5) Where subsection (3) above applies to a scheme, the order giving effect to it may direct that the scheme shall not be modified or superseded by a scheme brought into effect otherwise than under this section, and may also direct that that subsection shall apply to any scheme modifying or superseding the scheme to which the order gives effect.

(6) The Commissioners shall not proceed under this section without the like application and the like notice to the charity trustees, as would be required if they were proceeding (without an order of the court) under section 16 above; but on any application for a scheme, or in a case where they act by virtue of subsection (6) or (7) of that section, the Commissioners may proceed under this section or that section as appears to them appropriate.

(7) Notwithstanding anything in the trusts of a charity, no expenditure incurred in preparing or promoting a Bill in Parliament shall without the consent of the court or the Commissioners be defrayed out of any moneys applicable for the purposes of a charity but this subsection shall not apply in the case of an exempt charity.

(8) Where the Commissioners are satisfied—

(a)   that the whole of the income of a charity cannot in existing circumstances be effectively applied for the purposes of the charity; and

(b)   that, if those circumstances continue, a scheme might be made for applying the surplus cy-près; and

(c)   that it is for any reason not yet desirable to make such a scheme;

then the Commissioners may by order authorise the charity trustees at their discretion (but subject to any conditions imposed by the order) to apply any accrued or accruing income for any purposes for which it might be made applicable by such a scheme, and any application authorised by the order shall be deemed to be within the purposes of the charity.

(9) An order under subsection (8) above shall not extend to more than £300 out of income accrued before the date of the order, nor to income accruing more than three years after that date, nor to more than £100 out of the income accruing in any of those three years.

18. Power to act for protection of charities

(1) Where, at any time after they have instituted an inquiry under section 8 above with respect to any charity, the Commissioners are satisfied—

(a) that there is or has been any misconduct or mismanagement in the administration of the charity; or

(b) that it is necessary or desirable to act for the purpose of protecting the property of the charity or securing a proper application for the purposes of the charity of that property or of property coming to the charity,

the Commissioners may of their own motion do one or more of the following things—

(i) by order suspend any trustee, charity trustee, officer, agent or employee of the charity from the exercise of his office or employment pending consideration being given to his removal (whether under this section or otherwise);

(ii) by order appoint such number of additional charity trustees as they consider necessary for the proper administration of the charity;

(iii) by order vest any property held by or in trust for the charity in the official custodian, or require the persons in whom any such property is vested to transfer it to him, or appoint any person to transfer any such property to him;

(iv) order any person who holds any property on behalf of the charity, or of any trustee for it, not to part with the property without the approval of the Commissioners;

(v) order any debtor of the charity not to make any payment in or towards the discharge of his liability to the charity without the approval of the Commissioners;

(vi) by order restrict (notwithstanding anything in the trusts of the charity) the transactions which may be entered into, or the nature or amount of the payments which may be made, in the administration of the charity without the approval of the Commissioners;

(vii) by order appoint (in accordance with section 19 below) a receiver and manager in respect of the property and affairs of the charity.

(2) Where, at any time after they have instituted an inquiry under section 8 above with respect to any charity, the Commissioners are satisfied—

(a) that there is or has been any misconduct or mismanagement in the administration of the charity; and

(b) that it is necessary or desirable to act for the purpose of protecting the property of the charity or securing a proper application for the purposes of the charity of that property or of property coming to the charity,

the Commissioners may of their own motion do either or both of the following things—

(i) by order remove any trustee, charity trustee, officer, agent or employee of the charity who has been responsible for or privy to the misconduct or mismanagement or has by his conduct contributed to it or facilitated it;

    (ii)   by order establish a scheme for the administration of the charity.

(3) The references in subsection (1) or (2) above to misconduct or mismanagement shall (notwithstanding anything in the trusts of the charity) extend to the employment for the remuneration or reward of persons acting in the affairs of the charity, or for other administrative purposes, of sums which are excessive in relation to the property which is or is likely to be applied or applicable for the purposes of the charity.

(4) The Commissioners may also remove a charity trustee by order made of their own motion—

  (a) where, within the last five years, the trustee—
    (i)   having previously been adjudged bankrupt or had his estate sequestrated, has been discharged, or
    (ii)   having previously made a composition or arrangement with, or granted a trust deed for, his creditors, has been discharged in respect of it;
  (b) where the trustee is a corporation in liquidation;
  (c) where the trustee is incapable of acting by reason of mental disorder within the meaning of the Mental Health Act 1983;
  (d) where the trustee has not acted, and will not declare his willingness or unwillingness to act;
  (e) where the trustee is outside England and Wales or cannot be found or does not act, and his absence or failure to act impedes the proper administration of the charity.

(5) The Commissioners may by order made of their own motion appoint a person to be a charity trustee—

  (a) in place of a charity trustee removed by them under this section or otherwise;
  (b) where there are no charity trustees, or where by reason of vacancies in their number or the absence or incapacity of any of their number the charity cannot apply for the appointment;
  (c) where there is a single charity trustee, not being a corporation aggregate, and the Commissioners are of opinion that it is necessary to increase the number for the proper administration of the charity;
  (d) where the Commissioners are of opinion that it is necessary for the proper administration of the charity to have an additional charity trustee because one of the existing charity trustees who ought nevertheless to remain a charity trustee either cannot be found or does not act or is outside England and Wales.

(6) The powers of the Commissioners under this section to remove or appoint charity trustees of their own motion shall include power to make any such order with respect to the vesting in or transfer to the charity trustees of any property as the Commissioners could make on the removal or appointment of a charity trustee by them under section 16 above.

(7) Any order under this section for the removal or appointment of a charity trustee or trustee for a charity, or for the vesting or transfer of any property, shall be of the like effect as an order made under section 16 above.

(8) Subject to subsection (9) below, subsections (11) to (13) of section 16 above shall apply to orders under this section as they apply to orders under that section.

(9) The requirement to obtain any such certificate or leave as is mentioned in section 16(13) above shall not apply to—

    (a)   an appeal by a charity or any of the charity trustees of a charity against an order under subsection (1)(vii) above appointing a receiver and manager in respect of the charity's property and affairs, or

    (b)   an appeal by a person against an order under subsection (2)(i) or (4)(a) above removing him from his office or employment.

(10) Subsection (14) of section 16 above shall apply to an order under this section which establishes a scheme for the administration of a charity as it applies to such an order under that section.

(11) The power of the Commissioners to make an order under subsection (1)(i) above shall not be exercisable so as to suspend any person from the exercise of his office or employment for a period of more than twelve months; but (without prejudice to the generality of section 89(1) below), any such order made in the case of any person may make provision as respects the period of his suspension for matters arising out of it, and in particular for enabling any person to execute any instrument in his name or otherwise act for him and, in the case of a charity trustee, for adjusting any rules governing the proceedings of the charity trustees to take account of the reduction in the number capable of acting.

(12) Before exercising any jurisdiction under this section otherwise than by virtue of subsection (1) above, the Commissioners shall give notice of their intention to do so to each of the charity trustees, except any that cannot be found or has no known address in the United Kingdom; and any such notice may be given by post and, if given by post, may be addressed to the recipient's last known address in the United Kingdom.

(13) The Commissioners shall, at such intervals as they think fit, review any order made by them under paragraph (i), or any of paragraphs (iii) to (vii), of subsection (1) above; and, if on any such review it appears to them that it would be appropriate to discharge the order in whole or in part, they shall so discharge it (whether subject to any savings or other transitional provisions or not).

(14) If any person contravenes an order under subsection (1)(iv), (v) or (vi) above, he shall be guilty of an offence and liable on summary conviction to a fine not exceeding level 5 on the standard scale.

(15) Subsection (14) above shall not be taken to preclude the bringing of proceedings for breach of trust against any charity trustee or trustee for a charity in respect of a contravention of an order under subsection (1)(iv) or (vi) above (whether proceedings in respect of the contravention are brought against him under subsection (14) above or not).

(16) This section shall not apply to an exempt charity.

19. Supplementary provisions relating to receiver and manager appointed for a charity

(1) The Commissioners may under section 18(1)(vii) above appoint to be receiver and manager in respect of the property and affairs of a   **1D–018**

charity such person (other than an officer or employee of theirs) as they think fit.

(2) Without prejudice to the generality of section 89(1) below, any order made by the Commissioners under section 18(1)(vii) above may make provision with respect to the functions to be discharged by the receiver and manager appointed by the order; and those functions shall be discharged by him under the supervision of the Commissioners.

(3) In connection with the discharge of those functions any such order may provide—

(a) for the receiver and manager appointed by the order to have such powers and duties of the charity trustees of the charity concerned (whether arising under this Act or otherwise) as are specified in the order;

(b) for any powers or duties exercisable or falling to be performed by the receiver and manager by virtue of paragraph (a) above to be exercisable or performed by him to the exclusion of those trustees.

(4) Where a person has been appointed receiver and manager by any such order—

(a) section 29 below shall apply to him and to his functions as a person so appointed as it applies to a charity trustee of the charity concerned and to his duties as such; and

(b) the Commissioners may apply to the High Court for directions in relation to any particular matter arising in connection with the discharge of those functions.

(5) The High Court may on an application under subsection (4)(b) above—

(a) give such directions, or

(b) make such orders declaring the rights of any persons (whether before the court or not),

as it thinks just; and the costs of any such application shall be paid by the charity concerned.

(6) Regulations made by the Secretary of State may make provision with respect to—

(a) the appointment and removal of persons appointed in accordance with this section;

(b) the remuneration of such persons out of the income of the charities concerned;

(c) the making of reports to the Commissioners by such persons.

(7) Regulations under subsection (6) above may, in particular, authorise the Commissioners—

(a) to require security for the due discharge of his functions to be given by a person so appointed;

(b) to determine the amount of such a person's remuneration;

(c) to disallow any amount of remuneration in such circumstances as are prescribed by the regulations.

20. Publicity for proceedings under ss.16 to 18

(1) The Commissioners shall not make any order under this Act to establish a scheme for the administration of a charity, or submit such a scheme to the court or the Secretary of State for an order giving it effect, unless not less than one month previously there has been given public notice of their proposals, inviting representations to be made to them within a time specified in the notice, being not less than one month from the date of such notice, and, in the case of a scheme relating to a local charity, other than on ecclesiastical charity, in a parish or (in Wales) a community, a draft of the scheme has been communicated to the parish or community council or, in the case of a parish not having a council, to the chairman of the parish meeting.

(2) The Commissioners shall not make any order under this Act to appoint, discharge or remove a charity trustee or trustee for a charity (other than the official custodian), unless not less than one month previously there has been given the like public notice as is required by subsection (1) above for an order establishinga scheme but this subsection shall not apply in the case of—

(a) an order under section 18(1)(ii) above; or

(b) an order discharging or removing a trustee if the Commissioners are of opinion that it is unnecessary and not in his interest to give publicity to the proposal to discharge or remove him.

(3) Before the Commissioners make an order under this Act to remove without his consent a charity trustee or trustee for a charity, or an officer, agent or employee of a charity, the Commissioners shall, unless he cannot be found or has no known address in the United Kingdom, give him not less than one month's notice of their proposal, inviting representations to be made to them within a time specified in the notice.

(4) Where notice is given of any proposals as required by subsections (1) to (3) above, the Commissioners shall take into consideration any representations made to them about the proposals within the time specified in the notice, and may (without further notice) proceed with the proposals either without modification or with such modifications as appear to them to be desirable.

(5) Where the Commissioners make an order which is subject to appeal under subsection (12) of section 16 above the order shall be published either by giving public notice of it or by giving notice of it to all persons entitled to appeal against it under that subsection, as the Commissioners think fit.

(6) Where the Commissioners make an order under this Act to establish a scheme for the administration of a charity, a copy of the order shall, for not less than one month after the order is published, be available for public inspection at all reasonable times at the Commissioners' office and also at some convenient place in the area of the charity, if it is a local charity.

(7) Any notice to be given under this section of any proposals or order shall give such particulars of the proposals or order, or such directions for obtaining information about them, as the Commissioners think sufficient

and appropriate, and any public notice shall be given in such manner as they think sufficient and appropriate.

(8) Any notice to be given under this section, other than a public notice, may be given by post and, if given by post, may be addressed to the recipient's last known address in the United Kingdom.

PROPERTY VESTED IN OFFICIAL CUSTODIAN

21. Entrusting charity property to official custodian, and termination of trust

1D–020   (1) The court may by order—

(a)   vest in the official custodian any land held by or in trust for a charity;
(b)   authorise or require the persons in whom any such land is vested to transfer it to him; or
(c)   appoint any person to transfer any such land to him;

but this subsection does not apply to any interest in land by way of mortgage or other security.

(2) Where property is vested in the official custodian in trust for a charity, the court may make an order discharging him from the trusteeship as respects all or any of that property.

(3) Where the official custodian is discharged from his trusteeship of any property, or the trusts on which he holds any property come to an end, the court may make such vesting orders and give such directions as may seem to the court to be necessary or expedient in consequence.

(4) No person shall be liable for any loss occasioned by his acting in conformity with an order under this section or by his giving effect to anything done in pursuance of such an order, or be excused from so doing by reason of the order having been in any respect improperly obtained.

22. Supplementary provisions as to property vested in official custodian

1D–021   (1) Subject to the provisions of this Act, where property is vested in the official custodian in trust for a charity, he shall not exercise any powers of management, but he shall as trustee of any property have all the same powers, duties and liabilities, and be entitled to the same rights and immunities, and be subject to the control and orders of the court, as a corporation appointed custodian trustee under section 4 of the Public Trustee Act 1906 except that he shall have no power to charge fees.

(2) Subject to subsection (3) below, where any land is vested in the official custodian in trust for a charity, the charity trustees shall have power in his name and on his behalf to execute and do all assurances and things which they could properly execute or do in their own name and on their own behalf if the land were vested in them.

(3) If any land is so vested in the official custodian by virtue of an order under section 18 above, the power conferred on the charity trustees by subsection (2) above shall not be exercisable by them in relation to any trans-

action affecting the land, unless the transaction is authorised by order of the court or of the Commissioners.

(4) Where any land is vested in the official custodian in trust for a charity, the charity trustees shall have the like power to make obligations entered into by them binding on the land as if it were vested in them; and any covenant, agreement or condition which is enforceable by or against the custodian by reason of the land being vested in him shall be enforceable by or against the charity trustees as if the land were vested in them.

(5) In relation to a corporate charity, subsections (2), (3) and (4) above shall apply with the substitution of references to the charity for references to the charity trustees.

(6) Subsections (2), (3) and (4) above shall not authorise any charity trustees or charity to impose any personal liability on the official custodian.

(7) Where the official custodian is entitled as trustee for a charity to the custody of securitiesor documents of title relating to the trust property, he may permit them to be in the possession or under the control of the charity trustees without thereby incurring any liability.

23. Divestment in the case of land subject to Reverter of Sites Act 1987

(1) Where—   1D–022

(a) any land is vested in the official custodian in trust for a charity, and

(b) it appears to the Commissioners that section 1 of the Reverter of Sites Act 1987 (right of reverter replaced by [trust][1]) will, or is likely to, operate in relation to the land at a particular time or in particular circumstances,

the jurisdiction which, under section 16 above, is exercisable by the Commissioners for the purpose of discharging a trustee for a charity may, at any time before section 1 of that Act ("the 1987 Act") operates in relation to the land, be exercised by them of their own motion for the purpose of—

(i)   making an order discharging the official custodian from his trusteeship of the land, and

(ii) making such vesting orders and giving such directions as appear to them to be necessary or expedient in consequence.

(2) Where—

(a) section 1 of the 1987 Act has operated in relation to any land which, immediately before the time when that section so operated, was vested in the official custodian in trust for a charity, and

(b) the land remains vested in him but on the trust arising under that section,

the court or the Commissioners (of their own motion) may—

(i)   make an order discharging the official custodian from his trusteeship of the land, and

(ii)   (subject to the following provisions of this section) make
       such vesting orders and give such directions as appear to it
       or them to be necessary or expedient in consequence.

(3) Where any order discharging the official custodian from his trusteeship of any land—

(a)   is made by the court under section 21(2) above, or by the
      Commissioners under section 16 above, on the grounds that sec-
      tion 1 of the 1987 Act will, or is likely to, operate in relation to
      the land, or
(b)   is made by the court or the Commissioners under subsection (2)
      above,

the persons in whom the land is to be vested on the discharge of the official custodian shall be the relevant charity trustees (as defined in subsection (4) below), unless the court or (as the case may be) the Commissioners
is or are satisfied that it would be appropriate for it to be vested in some
other persons.
    (4) In subsection (3) above "the relevant charity trustees" means—

(a)   in relation to an order made as mentioned in paragraph (a) of
      that subsection, the charity trustees of the charity in trust for
      which the land is vested in the official custodian immediately
      before the time when the order takes effect, or
(b)   in relation to an order made under subsection (2) above, the
      charity trustees of the charity in trust for which the land was
      vested in the official custodian immediately before the time
      when section 1 of the 1987 Act operated in relation to the land.

    (5) Where—

(a)   section 1 of the 1987 Act has operated in relation to any such
      land as is mentioned in subsection (2)(a) above, and
(b)   the land remains vested in the official custodian as mentioned in
      subsection (2)(b) above,

then (subject to subsection (6) below), all the powers, duties and liabilities
that would, apart from this section, be those of the official custodian as
trustee of the land shall instead be those of the charity trustees of the
charity concerned; and those trustees shall have power in his name and on
his behalf to execute and do all assurances and things which they could
properly execute or do in their own name and on their own behalf if the
land were vested in them.
    (6) Subsection (5) above shall not be taken to require or authorise those
trustees to sell the land at a time when it remains vested in the official
custodian.
    (7) Where—

(a)   the official custodian has been discharged from his trusteeship
      of any land by an order under subsection (2) above, and
(b)   the land has, in accordance with subsection (3) above, been
      vested in the charity trustees concerned or (as the case may be)
      in any persons other than those trustees,

the land shall be held by those trustees, or (as the case may be) by those persons, as [trustees][2] on the terms of the trust arising under section 1 of the 1987 Act.

(8) The official custodian shall not be liable to any person in respect of any loss or misapplication of any land vested in him in accordance with that section unless it is occasioned by or through any wilful neglect or default of his or of any person acting for him; but the Consolidated Fund shall be liable to make good to any person any sums for which the official custodian may be liable by reason of any such neglect or default.

(9) In this section any reference to section 1 of the 1987 Act operating in relation to any land is a reference to a [trust][3] arising in relation to the land under that section.

[1] Words substituted by Trusts of Land and Appointment of Trustees Act 1996 (c.47), Sch.3, Para.26 (d).
[2] Words substituted by Trusts of Land and Appointment of Trustees Act 1996 (c.47), Sch.3, Para.26 (d).
[3] Words substituted by Trusts of Land and Appointment of Trustees Act 1996 (c.47), Sch.3, Para.26 (d).

ESTABLISHMENT OF COMMON INVESTMENT OR DEPOSIT FUNDS

24. Schemes to establish common investment funds

(1) The court or the Commissioners may by order make and bring into effect schemes (in this section referred to as "common investment schemes") for the establishment of common investment funds under trusts which provide—   1D–023

- (a) for property transferred to the fund by or on behalf of a charity participating in the scheme to be invested under the control of trustees appointed to manage the fund; and
- (b) for the participating charities to be entitled (subject to the provisions of the scheme) to the capital and income of the fund in shares determined by reference to the amount or value of the property transferred to it by or on behalf of each of them and to the value of the fund at the time of the transfers.

(2) The court or the Commissioners may make a common investment scheme on the application of any two or more charities.

(3) A common investment scheme may be made in terms admitting any charity to participate, or the scheme may restrict the right to participate in any manner.

(4) A common investment scheme may make provision for, and for all matters connected with, the establishment, investment, management and winding up of the common investment fund, and may in particular include provision—

- (a) for remunerating persons appointed trustees to hold or manage the fund or any part of it, with or without provision authorising a person to receive the remuneration notwithstanding that he is also a charity trustees of or trustee for a participating charity;

(b)   for restricting the size of the fund, and for regulating as to time, amount or otherwise the right to transfer property to or withdraw it from the fund, and for enabling sums to be advanced out of the fund by way of loan to a participating charity pending the withdrawal of property from the fund by the charity;

(c)   for enabling income to be withheld from distribution with a view to avoiding fluctuations in the amounts distributed, and generally for regulating distributions of income;

(d)   for enabling money to be borrowed temporarily for the purpose of meeting payments to be made out of the funds;

(e)   for enabling questions arising under the scheme as to the right of a charity to participate, or as to the rights of participating charities, or as to any other matter, to be conclusively determined by the decision of the trustees managing the fund or in any other manner;

(f)   for regulating the accounts and information to be supplied to participating charities.

(5) A common investment scheme, in addition to the provision for property to be transferred to the fund on the basis that the charity shall be entitled to a share in the capital and income of the fund, may include provision for enabling sums to be deposited by or on behalf of a charity on the basis that (subject to the provisions of the scheme) the charity shall be entitled to repayment of the sums deposited and to interest thereon at a rate determined by or under the scheme; and where a scheme makes any such provision it shall also provide for excluding from the amount of capital and income to be shared between charities participating otherwise than by way of deposit such amounts (not exceeding the amounts properly attributable to the making of deposits) as are from time to time reasonably required in respect of the liabilities of the fund for the repayment of deposits and for the interest on deposits, including amounts required by way of reserve.

(6) Except in so far as a common investment scheme provides to the contrary, the rights under it of a participating charity shall not be capable of being assigned or charged, nor shall any trustee or other person concerned in the management of the common investment fund be required or entitled to take account of any trust or other equity affecting a participating charity or its property or rights.

(7) The powers of investment of every charity shall include power to participate in common investment schemes unless the power is excluded by a provision specifically referring to common investment schemes in the trusts of the charity.

(8) A common investment fund shall be deemed for all purposes to be a charity; and if the scheme admits only exempt charities, the fund shall be an exempt charity for the purposes of this Act.

(9) Subsection (8) above shall apply not only to common investment funds established under the powers of this section, but also to any similar fund established for the exclusive benefit of charities by or under any enactment relating to any particular charities or class of charity.

25. Schemes to establish common deposit funds

1D–024   (1) The court or the Commissioners may by order make and bring into effect schemes (in this section referred to as "common deposit schemes") for the establishment of common deposit funds under trusts which provide—

(a)   for sums to be deposited by or on behalf of a charity partici-
      pating in the scheme and invested under the control of trustees
      appointed to manage the fund; and
(b)   for any such charity to be entitled (subject to the provisions of
      the scheme) to repayment of any sums so deposited and to
      interest thereon at a rate determined under the scheme.

(2) Subject to subsection (3) below, the following provisions of section
24 above, namely—

(a)   subsections (2) to (4), and
(b)   subsections (6) to (9),

shall have effect in relation to common deposit schemes and common
deposit funds as they have effect in relation to common investment
schemes and common investment funds.

(3) In its application in accordance with subsection (2) above, subsection (4) of that section shall have effect with the substitution for
paragraphs (b) and (c) of the following paragraphs—

"(b) for regulating as to time, amount or otherwise the right to
repayment of sums deposited in the fund;

(c) for authorising a part of the income for any year to be credited to
a reserve account maintained for the purpose of counteracting any
losses accruing to the fund, and generally for regulating the manner
in which the rate of interest on deposits is to be determined from time
to time;".

ADDITIONAL POWERS OF COMMISSIONERS

26. Power to authorise dealings with charity property etc

(1) Subject to the provisions of this section, where it appears to the   **1D–025**
Commissioners that any action proposed or contemplated in the administration of a charity is expedient in the interests of the charity, they may by
order sanction that action, whether or not it would otherwise be within the
powers exercisable by the charity trustees in the administration of the
charity; and anything done under the authority of such an order shall be
deemed to be properly done in the exercise of those powers.

(2) An order under this section may be made so as to authorise a particular transaction, compromise or the like, or a particular application of
property, or so as to give a more general authority, and (without prejudice
to the generality of subsection (1) above) may authorise a charity to use
common premises, or employ a common staff, or otherwise combine for
any purpose of administration, with any other charity.

(3) An order under this section may give directions as to the manner in
which any expenditure is to be borne and as to other matters connected
with or arising out of the action thereby authorised; and where anything
is done in pursuance of an authority given by any such order, any directions given in connection therewith shall be binding on the charity trustees

for the time being as if contained in the trusts of the charity; but any such directions may on the application of the charity be modified or superseded by a further order.

(4) Without prejudice to the generality of subsection (3) above, the directions which may be given by an order under this section shall in particular include directions for meeting any expenditure out of a specified fund, for charging any expenditure to capital or to income, for requiring expenditure charged to capital to be recouped out of income within a specified period, for restricting the costs to be incurred at the expense of the charity, or for the investment of moneys arising from any transaction.

(5) An order under this section may authorise any act notwithstanding that it is prohibited by any of the disabling Acts mentioned in subsection (6) below or that the trusts of the charity provide for the act to be done by or under the authority of the court; but no such order shall authorise the doing of any act expressly prohibited by Act of Parliament other than the disabling Acts or by the trusts of the charity or shall extend or alter the purposes of the charity.

(6) The Acts referred to in subsection (5) above as the disabling Acts are the Ecclesiastical Leases Act 1571, the Ecclesiastical Leases Act 1572, the Ecclesiastical Leases Act 1575 and the Ecclesiastical Leases Act 1836.

(7) An order under this section shall not confer any authority in relation to a building which has been consecrated and of which the use or disposal is regulated, and can be further regulated, by a scheme having effect under the Union of Benefices Measures 1923 to 1952, the Reorganisation Areas Measures 1944 and 1954, the Pastoral Measure 1968 or the Pastoral Measure 1983, the reference to a building being taken to include part of a building and any land which under such a scheme is to be used or disposed of with a building to which the scheme applies.

27. Power to authorise ex gratia payments etc

1D–026   (1) Subject to subsection (3) below, the Commissioners may by order exercise the same power as is exercisable by the Attorney General to authorise the charity trustees of a charity—

   (a)   to make any application of property of the charity, or
   (b)   to waive to any extent, on behalf of the charity, its entitlement to receive any property,

in a case where the charity trustees—

   (i)   (apart from this section) have no power to do so, but
   (ii)   in all the circumstances regard themselves as being under a moral obligation to do so.

(2) The power conferred on the Commissioners by subsection (1) above shall be exercisable by them under the supervision of, and in accordance with such directions as may be given by, the Attorney General; and any such directions may in particular require the Commissioners, in such circumstances as are specified in the directions—

   (a)   to refrain from exercising that power; or
   (b)   to consult the Attorney General before exercising it.

(3) Where—

(a) an application is made to the Commissioners for them to exercise that power in a case where they are not precluded from doing so by any such directions, but

(b) they consider that it would nevertheless be desirable for the application to be entertained by the Attorney General rather than by them,

they shall refer the application to the Attorney General.

(4) It is hereby declared that where, in the case of any application made to them as mentioned in subsection (3)(a) above, the Commissioners determine the application by refusing to authorise charity trustees to take any action falling within subsection (1)(a) or (b) above, that refusal shall not preclude the Attorney General, on an application subsequently made to him by the trustees, from authorising the trustees to take that action.

28. Power to give directions about dormant bank accounts of charities

1D–027

(1) Where the Commissioners—

(a) are informed by a relevant institution—

(i) that it holds one or more accounts in the name of or on behalf of a particular charity ("the relevant charity"), and

(ii) that the account, or (if it so holds two or more accounts) each of the accounts, is dormant, and

(b) are unable, after making reasonable inquiries, to locate that charity or any of its trustees,

they may give a direction under subsection (2) below.

(2) A direction under this subsection is a direction which—

(a) requires the institution concerned to transfer the amount, or (as the case may be) the aggregate amount, standing to the credit of the relevant charity in the account or accounts in question to such other charity as is specified in the direction in accordance with subsection (3) below; or

(b) requires the institution concerned to transfer to each of two or more other charities so specified in the direction such part of that amount or aggregate amount as is there specified in relation to that charity.

(3) The Commissioners may specify in a direction under subsection (2) above such other charity or charities as they consider appropriate, having regard, in a case where the purposes of the relevant charity are known to them, to those purposes and to the purposes of the other charity or charities; but the Commissioners shall not so specify any charity unless they have received from the charity trustees written confirmation that those trustees are willing to accept the amount proposed to be transferred to the charity.

(4) Any amount received by a charity by virtue of this section shall be received by the charity on terms that—

(a) it shall be held and applied by the charity for the purposes of the charity, but

(b)   it shall, as property of the charity, nevertheless be subject to any restrictions on expenditure to which it was subject as property of the relevant charity.

(5) Where—

(a)   the Commissioners have been informed as mentioned in subsection (1)(a) above by any relevant institution, and

(b)   before any transfer is made by the institution in pursuance of a direction under subsection (2) above, the institution has, by reason of any circumstances, cause to believe that the account, or (as the case may be) any of the accounts, held by it in the name of or on behalf of the relevant charity is no longer dormant,

the institution shall forthwith notify those circumstances in writing to the Commissioners; and, if it appears to the Commissioners that the account or accounts in question is or are no longer dormant, they shall revoke any direction under subsection (2) above which has previously been given by them to the institution with respect to the relevant charity.

(6) The receipt of any charity trustees or trustee for a charity in respect of any amount received from a relevant institution by virtue of this section shall be a complete discharge of the institution in respect of that amount.

(7) No obligation as to secrecy or other restriction on disclosure (however imposed) shall preclude a relevant institution from disclosing any information to the Commissioners for the purpose of enabling them to discharge their functions under this section.

(8) For the purposes of this section—

(a)   an account is dormant if no transaction, other than—
(i)   a transaction consisting in a payment into the account,

or

(ii)   a transaction which the institution holding the account has itself caused to be effected,

has been effected in relation to the account within the period of five years immediately preceding the date when the Commissioners are informed as mentioned in paragraph (a) of subsection (1) above;

(b)   a "relevant institution" means —
(i)   the Bank of England;
(ii)   a person who has permission under Part 4 of the Financial Services and Markets Act 2000 to accept deposits;
(iii) an EEA firm of the kind mentioned in paragraph 5(b) of Schedule 3 to that Act which has permission under paragraph 15 of that Schedule (as a result of qualifying for authorisation under paragraph 12(1) of that Schedule) to accept deposits; or
(iv)   such other person who may lawfully accept deposits in the United Kingdom as may be prescribed by the Secretary of State.]
(v)   such other institution mentioned in Schedule 2 to the Banking Act 1987 as the Secretary of State may prescribe by regulations; and

(c) references to the transfer of any amount to a charity are references to its transfer—
  (i)   to the charity trustees, or
  (ii) to any trustee for the charity,
  as the charity trustees may determine (and any reference to any amount received by a charity shall be construed accordingly).

[(8A) Sub-paragraphs (ii) to (iv) of the definition of "relevant institution" in subsection (8)(b) must be read with—

(a) section 22 of the Financial Services and Markets Act 2000;
(b) any relevant order under that section; and
(c) Schedule 2 to that Act.][1]

(9) For the purpose of determining the matters in respect of which any of the powers conferred by section 8 or 9 above may be exercised it shall be assumed that the Commissioners have no functions under this section in relation to accounts to which this subsection applies (with the result that, for example, a relevant institution shall not, in connection with the functions of the Commissioners under this section, be required under section 8(3)(a) above to furnish any statements, or answer any questions or inquiries, with respect to any such accounts held by the institution).
  This subsection applies to accounts which are dormant accounts by virtue of subsection (8)(a) above but would not be such accounts if sub-paragraph (i) of that provision were omitted.
  (10) Subsection (1) above shall not apply to any account held in the name of or on behalf of an exempt charity.
[1] Added by Financial Services and Markets Act 2000 (Consequential Amendments and Repeals) Order (SI 2001/3649), Pt 8, art.339(3).

29. Power to advise charity trustees

(1) The Commissioners may on the written application of any charity trustee give him their opinion or advice on any matter affecting the performance of his duties as such.   **1D–028**

(2) A charity trustee or trustee for a charity acting in accordance with the opinion or advice of the Commissioners given under this section with respect to the charity shall be deemed, as regards his responsibility for so acting, to have acted in accordance with his trust, unless, when he does so, either—

(a) he knows or has reasonable cause to suspect that the opinion or advice was given in ignorance of material facts; or
(b) the decision of the court has been obtained on the matter or proceedings are pending to obtain one.

30. Powers for preservation of charity documents

(1) The Commissioners may provide books in which any deed, will or other document relating to a charity may be enrolled.   **1D–029**

(2) The Commissioners may accept for safe keeping any document of or relating to a charity, and the charity trustees or other persons having the custody of documents of or relating to a charity (including a charity which has ceased to exist) may with the consent of the Commissioners

deposit them with the Commissioners for safe keeping, except in the case of documents required by some other enactment to be kept elsewhere.

(3) Where a document is enrolled by the Commissioners or is for the time being deposited with them under this section, evidence of its contents may be given by means of a copy certified by any officer of the Commissioners generally or specially authorised by them to act for this purpose; and a document purporting to be such a copy shall be received in evidence without proof of the official position, authority or handwriting of the person certifying it or of the original document being enrolled or deposited as aforesaid.

(4) Regulations made by the Secretary of State may make provision for such documents deposited with the Commissioners under this section as may be prescribed by the regulations to be destroyed or otherwise disposed of after such period or in such circumstances as may be so prescribed.

(5) Subsections (3) and (4) above shall apply to any document transmitted to the Commissioners under section 9 above and kept by them under subsection (3) of that section, as if the document had been deposited with them for safe keeping under this section.

31. Power to order taxation of solicitor's bill

1D–030   (1) The Commissioners may order that a solicitor's bill of costs for business done for a charity, or for charity trustees or trustees for a charity, shall be taxed, together with the costs of the taxation, by a taxing officer in such division of the High Court as may be specified in the order, or by the taxing officer of any other court having jurisdiction to order the taxation of the bill.

(2) On any order under this section for the taxation of a solicitor's bill the taxation shall proceed, and the taxing officer shall have the same powers and duties, and the costs of the taxation shall be borne, as if the order had been made, on the application of the person chargeable with the bill, by the court in which the costs are taxed.

(3) No order under this section for the taxation of a solicitor's bill shall be made after payment of the bill unless the Commissioners are of opinion that it contains exorbitant charges; and no such order shall in any case be made where the solicitor's costs are not subject to taxation on an order of the High Court by reason either of an agreement as to his remuneration or the lapse of time since payment of the bill.

LEGAL PROCEEDINGS RELATING TO CHARITIES

32. Proceedings by Commissioners

1D–031   (1) Subject to subsection (2) below, the Commissioners may exercise the same powers with respect to—

     (a)   the taking of legal proceedings with reference to charities or the property or affairs of charities, or

     (b)   the compromise of claims with a view to avoiding or ending such proceedings,

as are exercisable by the Attorney General acting ex officio.

(2) Subsection (1) above does not apply to the power of the Attorney General under section 63(1) below to present a petition for the winding up of a charity.

(3) The practice and procedure to be followed in relation to any proceedings taken by the Commissioners under subsection (1) above shall be the same in all respects (and in particular as regards costs) as if they were proceedings taken by the Attorney General acting ex officio.

(4) No rule of law or practice shall be taken to require the Attorney General to be a party to any such proceedings.

(5) The powers exercisable by the Commissioners by virtue of this section shall be exercisable by them of their own motion, but shall be exercisable only with the agreement of the Attorney General on each occasion.

33. Proceedings by other persons

(1) Charity proceedings may be taken with reference to a charity either   **1D–032**
by the charity, or by any of the charity trustees, or by any person interested in the charity, or by any two or more inhabitants of the area of the charity if it is a local charity, but not by any other person.

(2) Subject to the following provisions of this section, no charity proceedings relating to a charity (other than an exempt charity) shall be entertained or proceeded with in any court unless the taking of the proceedings is authorised by order of the Commissioners.

(3) The Commissioners shall not, without special reasons, authorise the taking of charity proceedings where in their opinion the case can be dealt with by them under the powers of this Act other than those conferred by section 32 above.

(4) This section shall not require any order for the taking of proceedings in a pending cause or matter or for the bringing of any appeal.

(5) Where the foregoing provisions of this section require the taking of charity proceedings to be authorised by an order of the Commissioners, the proceedings may nevertheless be entertained or proceeded with if, after the order had been applied for and refused, leave to take the proceedings was obtained from one of the judges of the High Court attached to the Chancery Division.

(6) Nothing in the foregoing subsections shall apply to the taking of proceedings by the Attorney General, with or without a relator, or to the taking of proceedings by the Commissioners in accordance with section 32 above.

(7) Where it appears to the Commissioners, on an application for an order under this section or otherwise, that it is desirable for legal proceedings to be taken with reference to any charity (other than an exempt charity) or its property or affairs, and for the proceedings to be taken by the Attorney General, the Commissioners shall so inform the Attorney General, and send him such statements and particulars as they think necessary to explain the matter.

(8) In this section "charity proceedings" means proceedings in any court in England or Wales brought under the court's jurisdiction with respect to charities, or brought under the court's jurisdiction with respect to trusts in relation to the administration of a trust for charitable purposes.

34. Report of s.8 inquiry to be evidence in certain proceedings

1D–033   (1) A copy of the report of the person conducting an inquiry under section 8 above shall, if certified by the Commissioners to be a true copy, be admissible in any proceedings to which this section applies—

(a)   as evidence of any fact stated in the report; and
(b)   as evidence of the opinion of that person as to any matter referred to in it.

(2) This section applies to—

(a)   any legal proceedings instituted by the Commissioners under this Part of this Act; and
(b)   any legal proceedings instituted by the Attorney General in respect of a charity.

(3) A document purporting to be a certificate issued for the purposes of subsection (1) above shall be received in evidence and be deemed to be such a certificate, unless the contrary is proved.

MEANING OF "TRUST CORPORATION"

35. Application of provisions to trust corporations appointed under s.16 or 18

1D–034   (1) In the definition of "trust corporation" contained in the following provisions—

(a)   section 117(xxx) of the Settled Land Act 1925,
(b)   section 68(18) of the Trustee Act 1925,
(c)   section 205(xxviii) of the Law of Property Act 1925,
(d)   section 55(xxvi) of the Administration of Estates Act 1925, and
(e)   section 128 of the Supreme Court Act 1981,

the reference to a corporation appointed by the court in any particular case to be a trustee includes a reference to a corporation appointed by the Commissioners under this Act to be a trustee.

(2) This section shall be deemed always to have had effect; but the reference to section 128 of the Supreme Court Act 1981 shall, in relation to any time before 1st January 1982, be construed as a reference to section 175(1) of the Supreme Court of Judicature (Consolidation) Act 1925.

PART V

CHARITY LAND

36. Restrictions on dispositions

(1) Subject to the following provisions of this section and section 40 **1D–035**
below, no land held by or in trust for a charity shall be sold, leased or otherwise disposed of without an order of the court or of the Commissioners.

(2) Subsection (1) above shall not apply to a disposition of such land
if—

    (a)   the disposition is made to a person who is not—
        (i)   a connected person (as defined in Schedule 5 to this Act),
           or
        (ii)   a trustee for, or nominee of, a connected person; and
    (b)   the requirements of subsection (3) or (5) below have been
        complied with in relation to it.

(3) Except where the proposed disposition is the granting of such a lease
as is mentioned in subsection (5) below, the charity trustees must, before
entering into an agreement for the sale, or (as the case may be) for a lease
or other disposition, of the land—

    (a)   obtain and consider a written report on the proposed disposi-
        tion from a qualified surveyor instructed by the trustees and
        acting exclusively for the charity;
    (b)   advertise the proposed disposition for such period and in such
        manner as the surveyor has advised in his report (unless he has
        there advised that it would not be in the best interests of the
        charity to advertise the proposed disposition); and
    (c)   decide that they are satisfied, having considered the surveyor's
        report, that the terms on which the disposition is proposed to
        be made are the best that can reasonably be obtained for the
        charity.

(4) For the purposes of subsection (3) above a person is a qualified
surveyor if—

    (a)   he is a fellow or professional associate of the Royal Institution
        of Chartered Surveyors or of the Incorporated Society of
        Valuers and Auctioneers or satisfies such other requirement or
        requirements as may be prescribed by regulations made by the
        Secretary of State; and
    (b)   he is reasonably believed by the charity trustees to have ability
        in, and experience of, the valuation of land of the particular
        kind, and in the particular area, in question;

and any report prepared for the purposes of that subsection shall contain
such information, and deal with such matters, as may be prescribed by regulations so made.

(5) Where the proposed disposition is the granting of a lease for a term ending not more than seven years after it is granted (other than one granted wholly or partly in consideration of a fine), the charity trustees must, before entering into an agreement for the lease—

    (a)   obtain and consider the advice on the proposed disposition of a person who is reasonably believed by the trustees to have the requisite ability and practical experience to provide them with competent advice on the proposed disposition; and

    (b)   decide that they are satisfied, having considered that person's advice, that the terms on which the disposition is proposed to be made are the best that can reasonably be obtained for the charity.

(6) Where—

    (a)   any land is held by or in trust for a charity, and

    (b)   the trusts on which it is so held stipulate that it is to be used for the purposes, or any particular purposes, of the charity,

then (subject to subsections (7) and (8) below and without prejudice to the operation of the preceding provisions of this section) the land shall not be sold, leased or otherwise disposed of unless the charity trustees have previously—

    (i)   given public notice of the proposed disposition, inviting representations to be made to them within a time specified in the notice, being not less than one month from the date of the notice; and

    (ii)   taken into consideration any representations made to them within that time about the proposed disposition.

(7) Subsection (6) above shall not apply to any such disposition of land as is there mentioned if—

    (a)   the disposition is to be effected with a view to acquiring by way of replacement other property which is to be held on the trusts referred to in paragraph (b) of that subsection; or

    (b)   the disposition is the granting of a lease for a term ending not more than two years after it is granted (other than one granted wholly or partly in consideration of a fine).

(8) The Commissioners may direct—

    (a)   that subsection (6) above shall not apply to dispositions of land held by or in trust for a charity or class of charities (whether generally or only in the case of a specified class of dispositions or land, or otherwise as may be provided in the direction), or

    (b)   that that subsection shall not apply to a particular disposition of land held by or in trust for a charity,

if, on an application made to them in writing by or on behalf of the charity or charities in question, the Commissioners are satisfied that it would be in the interests of the charity or charities for them to give the direction.

(9) The restrictions on disposition imposed by this section apply notwithstanding anything in the trusts of a charity; but nothing in this section applies—

    (a)   to any disposition for which general or special authority is expressly given (without the authority being made subject to the sanction of an order of the court) by any statutory provision contained in or having effect under an Act of Parliament or by any scheme legally established; or

    (b)   to any disposition of land held by or in trust for a charity which—

        (i)   is made to another charity otherwise than for the best price that can reasonably be obtained, and

        (ii)   is authorised to be so made by the trusts of the first-mentioned charity; or

    (c)   to the granting, by or on behalf of a charity and in accordance with its trusts, of a lease to any beneficiary under those trusts where the lease—

        (i)   is granted otherwise than for the best rent that can reasonably be obtained; and

        (ii)   is intended to enable the demised premises to be occupied for the purposes, or any particular purposes, of the charity.

(10) Nothing in this section applies—

    (a)   to any disposition of land held by or in trust for an exempt charity;

    (b)   to any disposition of land by way of mortgage or other security; or

    (c)   to any disposition of an advowson.

(11) In this section "land" means land in England or Wales.

37. Supplementary provisions relating to dispositions

(1) Any of the following instruments, namely—   **1D–036**

    (a)   any contract for the sale, or for a lease or other disposition, of land which is held by or in trust for a charity, and

    (b)   any conveyance, transfer, lease or other instrument effecting a disposition of such land,

shall state—

    (i)   that the land is held by or in trust for a charity,

    (ii)   whether the charity is an exempt charity and whether the disposition is one falling within paragraph (a), (b) or (c) of subsection (9) of section 36 above, and

    (iii)   if it is not an exempt charity and the disposition is not one falling within any of those paragraphs, that the land is land to which the restrictions on disposition imposed by that section apply.

(2) Where any land held by or in trust for a charity is sold, leased or otherwise disposed of by a disposition to which subsection (1) or (2) of section 36 above applies, the charity trustees shall certify in the instrument by which the disposition is effected—

    (a)   (where subsection (1) of that section applies) that the disposition has been sanctioned by an order of the court or of the Commissioners (as the case may be), or

    (b)   (where subsection (2) of that section applies) that the charity trustees have power under the trusts of the charity to effect the disposition, and that they have complied with the provisions of that section so far as applicable to it.

(3) Where subsection (2) above has been complied with in relation to any disposition of land, then in favour of a person who (whether under the disposition or afterwards) acquires an interest in the land for money or money's worth, it shall be conclusively presumed that the facts were as stated in the certificate.

(4) Where—

    (a)   any land held by or in trust for a charity is sold, leased or otherwise disposed of by a disposition to which subsection (1) or (2) of section 36 above applies, but

    (b)   subsection (2) above has not been complied with in relation to the disposition,

then in favour of a person who (whether under the disposition or afterwards) in good faith acquires an interest in the land for money or money's worth, the disposition shall be valid whether or not—

    (i)   the disposition has been sanctioned by an order of the court or of the Commissioners, or

    (ii)   the charity trustees have power under the trusts of the charity to effect the disposition and have complied with the provisions of that section so far as applicable to it.

(5) Any of the following instruments, namely—

    (a)   any contract for the sale, or for a lease or other disposition, of land which will, as a result of the disposition, be held by or in trust for a charity, and

    (b)   any conveyance, transfer, lease or other instrument effecting a disposition of such land,

shall state—

    (i)   that the land will, as a result of the disposition, be held by or in trust for a charity,

    (ii)   whether the charity is an exempt charity, and

    (iii)   if it is not an exempt charity, that the restrictions on disposition imposed by section 36 above will apply to the land (subject to subsection (9) of that section).

(6) [. . .][1]

(7) Where—

(a) the disposition to be effected by any such instrument as is mentioned in subsection (1)(b) or (5)(b) above will be a registered disposition, or

(b) any such instrument will on taking effect be an instrument [in relation to which section 123A][2] of the Land Registration Act 1925 (compulsory registration of title) applies,

the statement which, by virtue of subsection (1) or (5) above, is to be contained in the instrument shall be in such form as may be prescribed.

(8) Where—

(a) an application is duly made—
  (i)   for registration of a disposition of registered land, or
  (ii) for registration of a person's title under a disposition of unregistered land, and

(b) the instrument by which the disposition is effected contains a statement complying with subsections (5) and (7) above, and

(c) the charity by or in trust for which the land is held as a result of the disposition is not an exempt charity,

the registrar shall enter in the register, in respect of the land, a restriction in such form as may be prescribed.

(9) Where—

(a) any such restriction is entered in the register in respect of any land, and

(b) the charity by or in trust for which the land is held becomes an exempt charity,

the charity trustees shall apply to the registrar for the restriction to be withdrawn; and on receiving any application duly made under this subsection the registrar shall withdraw the restriction.

(10) Where—

(a) any registered land is held by or in trust for an exempt charity and the charity ceases to be an exempt charity, or

(b) any registered land becomes, as a result of a declaration of trust by the registered proprietor, land held in trust for a charity (other than an exempt charity),

the charity trustees shall apply to the registrar for such a restriction as is mentioned in subsection (8) above to be entered in the register in respect of the land; and on receiving any application duly made under this subsection the registrar shall enter such a restriction in the register in respect of the land.

(11) In this section—

(a) references to a disposition of land do not include references to—
  (i)   a disposition of land by way of mortgage or other security,
  (ii)   any disposition of an advowson, or
  (iii) any release of a rentcharge falling within section 40(1) below; and

(b) "land" means land in England or Wales;

and subsections (7) to (10) above shall be construed as one with the Land Registration Act 1925.

¹ Repealed by Trusts of Land and Appointment of Trustees Act 1996, s.25(2), Sch.4.
² Words substituted by Land Registration Act 1997 (c.2), Sch.1, Pt I, Para.6(1).

38. Restrictions on mortgaging

1D–037   (1) Subject to subsection (2) below, no mortgage of land held by or in trust for a charity shall be granted without an order of the court or of the Commissioners.

(2) Subsection (1) above shall not apply to a mortgage of any such land by way of security for the repayment of a loan where the charity trustees have, before executing the mortgage, obtained and considered proper advice, given to them in writing, on the matters mentioned in subsection (3) below.

(3) Those matters are—

    (a)   whether the proposed loan is necessary in order for the charity trustees to be able to pursue the particular course of action in connection with which the loan is sought by them;

    (b)   whether the terms of the proposed loan are reasonable having regard to the status of the charity as a prospective borrower; and

    (c)   the ability of the charity to repay on those terms the sum proposed to be borrowed.

(4) For the purposes of subsection (2) above proper advice is the advice of a person—

    (a)   who is reasonably believed by the charity trustees to be qualified by his ability in and practical experience of financial matters; and

    (b)   who has no financial interest in the making of the loan in question;

and such advice may constitute proper advice for those purposes notwithstanding that the person giving it does so in the course of his employment as an officer or employee of the charity or of the charity trustees.

(5) This section applies notwithstanding anything in the trusts of a charity; but nothing in this section applies to any mortgage for which general or special authority is given as mentioned in section 36(9)(a) above.

(6) In this section—

"land" means land in England or Wales;

"mortgage" includes a charge.

(7) Nothing in this section applies to an exempt charity.

39. Supplementary provisions relating to mortgaging

1D–038   (1) Any mortgage of land held by or in trust for a charity shall state—

    (a)   that the land is held by or in trust for a charity,

    (b)   whether the charity is an exempt charity and whether the mortgage is one falling within subsection (5) of section 38 above, and

(c)   if it is not an exempt charity and the mortgage is not one falling within that subsection, that the mortgage is one to which the restrictions imposed by that section apply;

and where the mortgage will be a registered disposition any such statement shall be in such form as may be prescribed.

[(1A) Where any such mortgage will be one falling within section 123(2) of the Land Registration Act 1925—

(a)   the statement required by subsection (1) above shall be in such form as may be prescribed; and
(b)   if the charity is not an exempt charity, the mortgage shall also contain a statement, in such form as may be prescribed, that the restrictions on disposition imposed by section 36 above apply to the land (subject to subsection (9) of that section).

(1B) Where—

(a)   an application is duly made for registration of a person's title to land in connection with such a mortgage as is mentioned in subsection (1A) above, and
(b)   the mortgage contains statements complying with subsections (1) and (1A) above, and
(c)   the charity is not an exempt charity,

the registrar shall enter in the register, in respect of the land, a restriction in such form as may be prescribed; and section 37(9) above shall apply in relation to any such restriction as it applies in relation to one entered in pursuance of section 37(8).][1]

(2) Where subsection (1) or (2) of section 38 above applies to any mortgage of land held by or in trust for a charity, the charity trustees shall certify in the mortgage—

(a)   (where subsection (1) of that section applies) that the mortgage has been sanctioned by an order of the court or of the Commissioners (as the case may be), or
(b)   (where subsection (2) of that section applies) that the charity trustees have power under the trusts of the charity to grant the mortgage, and that they have obtained and considered such advice as is mentioned in that subsection.

(3) Where subsection (2) above has been complied with in relation to any mortgage, then in favour of a person who (whether under the mortgage or afterwards) acquires an interest in the land in question for money or money's worth, it shall be conclusively presumed that the facts were as stated in the certificate.

(4) Where—

(a)   subsection (1) or (2) of section 38 above applies to any mortgage of land held by or in trust for a charity, but
(b)   subsection (2) above has not been complied with in relation to the mortgage,

then in favour of a person who (whether under the mortgage or after-wards) in good faith acquires an interest in the land for money or money's worth, the mortgage shall be valid whether or not—

  (i)   the mortgage has been sanctioned by an order of the court or of the Commissioners, or

  (ii) the charity trustees have power under the trusts of the charity to grant the mortgage and have obtained and considered such advice as is mentioned in subsection (2) of that section.

(5) [. . .][2]

(6) In this section—

"mortgage" includes a charge, and "mortgagee" shall be construed accordingly;

"land" means land in England or Wales;

"prescribed" [and subsections (1) to (1B) above shall be construed as one with the Land Registration Act 1925.][3]

[1] Inserted by Land Registration Act 1997, s.4(1), Sch.1, Pt 1, Para.6(2) from a day to be appointed.

[2] Repealed by Trusts of Land and Appointment of Trustees Act 1996, s.25(2), Sch.4.

[3] Words substituted by Land Registration Act 1997 (c.2), Sch.1, Pt I, Para.6(3).

40. Release of charity rentcharges

1D–039   (1) Section 36(1) above shall not apply to the release by a charity of a rentcharge which it is entitled to receive if the release is given in consideration of the payment of an amount which is not less than ten times the annual amount of the rentcharge.

(2) Where a charity which is entitled to receive a rentcharge releases it in consideration of the payment of an amount not exceeding £500, any costs incurred by the charity in connection with proving its title to the rentcharge shall be recoverable by the charity from the person or persons in whose favour the rentcharge is being released.

(3) Neither section 36(1) nor subsection (2) above applies where a rentcharge which a charity is entitled to receive is redeemed under sections 8 to 10 of the Rentcharges Act 1977.

(4) The Secretary of State may by order amend subsection (2) above by substituting a different sum for the sum for the time being specified there.

PART VI

CHARITY ACCOUNTS, REPORTS AND RETURNS

41. Duty to keep accounting records

1D–040   (1) The charity trustees of a charity shall ensure that accounting records are kept in respect of the charity which are sufficient to show and explain all the charity's transactions, and which are such as to—

  (a)   disclose at any time, with reasonable accuracy, the financial position of the charity at that time, and

(b) enable the trustees to ensure that, where any statements of accounts are prepared by them under section 42(1) below, those statements of accounts comply with the requirements of regulations under that provision.

(2) The accounting records shall in particular contain—

(a) entries showing from day to day all sums of money received and expended by the charity, and the matters in respect of which the receipt and expenditure takes place; and

(b) a record of the assets and liabilities of the charity.

(3) The charity trustees of a charity shall preserve any accounting records made for the purposes of this section in respect of the charity for at least six years from the end of the financial year of the charity in which they are made.

(4) Where a charity ceases to exist within the period of six years mentioned in subsection (3) above as it applies to any accounting records, the obligation to preserve those records in accordance with that subsection shall continue to be discharged by the last charity trustees of the charity, unless the Commissioners consent in writing to the records being destroyed or otherwise disposed of.

(5) Nothing in this section applies to a charity which is a company.

42. Annual statements of accounts

(1) The charity trustees of a charity shall (subject to subsection (3) below) prepare in respect of each financial year of the charity a statement of accounts complying with such requirements as to its form and contents as may be prescribed by regulations made by the Secretary of State.   **1D–041**

(2) Without prejudice to the generality of subsection (1) above, regulations under that subsection may make provision—

(a) for any such statement to be prepared in accordance with such methods and principles as are specified or referred to in the regulations;

(b) as to any information to be provided by way of notes to the accounts;

and regulations under that subsection may also make provision for determining the financial years of a charity for the purposes of this Act and any regulations made under it.

(3) Where a charity's gross income in any financial year does not exceed [£100,000],[1] the charity trustees may, in respect of that year, elect to prepare the following, namely—

(a) a receipts and payments account, and

(b) a statement of assets and liabilities,

instead of a statement of accounts under subsection (1) above.

(4) The charity trustees of a charity shall preserve—

(a) any statement of accounts prepared by them under subsection (1) above, or

(b)   any account and statement prepared by them under subsection (3) above,

for at least six years from the end of the financial year to which any such statement relates or (as the case may be) to which any such account and statement relate.

(5) Subsection (4) of section 41 above shall apply in relation to the preservation of any such statement or account and statement as it applies in relation to the preservation of any accounting records (the references to subsection (3) of that section being read as references to subsection (4) above).

(6) The Secretary of State may by order amend subsection (3) above by substituting a different sum for the sum for the time being specified there.

(7) Nothing in this section applies to a charity which is a company.

[1] Words substituted by Charities Act 1993 (Substitution of Sums) Order (SI 1995/2696), art.2(3).

43. Annual audit or examination of charity accounts

1D–042   (1) Subsection (2) below applies to a financial year of a charity ("the relevant year") if the charity's gross income or total expenditure in any of the following, namely—

(a)   the relevant year,
(b)   the financial year of the charity immediately preceding the relevant year (if any), and
(c)   the financial year of the charity immediately preceding the year specified in paragraph (b) above (if any),

exceeds [£250,000].[1]

(2) If this subsection applies to a financial year of a charity, the accounts of the charity for that year shall be audited by a person who—

(a)   is, in accordance with section 25 of the Companies Act 1989 (eligibility for appointment), eligible for appointment as a company auditor, or
(b)   is a member of a body for the time being specified in regulations under section 44 below and is under the rules of that body eligible for appointment as auditor of the charity.

(3) If subsection (2) above does not apply to a financial year of a charity [and its gross income or total expenditure in that year exceeds £10,000][2], then (subject to subsection (4) below) the accounts of the charity for that year shall, at the election of the charity trustees, either—

(a)   be examined by an independent examiner, that is to say an independent person who is reasonably believed by the trustees to have the requisite ability and practical experience to carry out a competent examination of the accounts, or
(b)   be audited by such a person as is mentioned in subsection (2) above.

(4) Where it appears to the Commissioners—

  (a) that subsection (2), or (as the case may be) subsection (3) above, has not been complied with in relation to a financial year of a charity within ten months from the end of that year, or

  (b) that, although subsection (2) above does not apply to a financial year of a charity, it would nevertheless be desirable for the accounts of the charity for that year to be audited by such a person as is mentioned in that subsection,

the Commissioners may by order require the accounts of the charity for that year to be audited by such a person as is mentioned in that subsection.

(5) If the Commissioners make an order under subsection (4) above with respect to a charity, then unless—

  (a) the order is made by virtue of paragraph (b) of that subsection, and

  (b) the charity trustees themselves appoint an auditor in accordance with the order,

the auditor shall be a person appointed by the Commissioners.

(6) The expenses of any audit carried out by an auditor appointed by the Commissioners under subsection (5) above, including the auditor's remuneration, shall be recoverable by the Commissioners—

  (a) from the charity trustees of the charity concerned, who shall be personally liable, jointly and severally, for those expenses; or

  (b) to the extent that it appears to the Commissioners not to be practical to seek recovery of those expenses in accordance with paragraph (a) above, from the funds of the charity.

(7) The Commissioners may—

  (a) give guidance to charity trustees in connection with the selection of a person for appointment as an independent examiner;

  (b) give such directions as they think appropriate with respect to the carrying out of an examination in pursuance of subsection (3)(a) above;

and any such guidance or directions may either be of general application or apply to a particular charity only.

(8) The Secretary of State may by order amend subsection (1) [or (3)][3] above by substituting a different sum for the sum for the time being specified there.

(9) Nothing in this section applies to a charity which is a company.

[1] Words substituted by Charities Act 1993 (Substitution of Sums) Order (SI 1995/2696), art.2(4).

[2] Inserted by Deregulation and Contracting Out Act 1994, s.28(2).

[3] Inserted by Deregulation and Contracting Out Act 1994, s.28(3).

44. Supplementary provisions relating to audits etc

1D–043   (1) The Secretary of State may by regulations make provision—

    (a)   specifying one or more bodies for the purposes of section 43(2)(b) above;

    (b)   with respect to the duties of an auditor carrying out an audit under section 43 above, including provision with respect to the making by him of a report on—

        (i)   the statement of accounts prepared for the financial year in question under section 42(1) above, or

        (ii)   the account and statement so prepared under section 42(3) above,

        as the case may be;

    (c)   with respect to the making by an independent examiner of a report in respect of an examination carried out by him under section 43 above;

    (d)   conferring on such an auditor or on an independent examiner a right of access with respect to books, documents and other records (however kept) which relate to the charity concerned;

    (e)   entitling such an auditor or an independent examiner to require, in the case of a charity, information and explanations from past or present charity trustees or trustees for the charity, or from past or present officers or employees of the charity;

    (f)   enabling the Commissioners, in circumstances specified in the regulations, to dispense with the requirements of section 43(2) or (3) above in the case of a particular charity or in the case of any particular financial year of a charity.

(2) If any person fails to afford an auditor or an independent examiner any facility to which he is entitled by virtue of subsection (1)(d) or (e) above, the Commissioners may by order give—

    (a)   to that person, or

    (b)   to the charity trustees for the time being of the charity concerned,

such directions as the Commissioners think appropriate for securing that the default is made good.

(3) Section 727 of the Companies Act 1985 (power of court to grant relief in certain cases) shall have effect in relation to an auditor or independent examiner appointed by a charity in pursuance of section 43 above as it has effect in relation to a person employed as auditor by a company within the meaning of that Act.

45. Annual reports

1D–044   (1) The charity trustees of a charity shall prepare in respect of each financial year of the charity an annual report containing—

    (a)   such a report by the trustees on the activities of the charity during that year, and

    (b)   such other information relating to the charity or to its trustees or officers,

as may be prescribed by regulations made by the Secretary of State.

(2) Without prejudice to the generality of subsection (1) above, regulations under that subsection may make provision—

    (a)   for any such report as is mentioned in paragraph (a) of that sub-section to be prepared in accordance with such principles as are specified or referred to in the regulations;

    (b)   enabling the Commissioners to dispense with any requirement prescribed by virtue of subsection (1)(b) above in the case of a particular charity or a particular class of charities, or in the case of a particular financial year of a charity or of any class of charities.

(3) [Where in any financial year of a charity its gross income or total expenditure exceeds £10,000, the annual report required to be prepared under this section in respect of that year][1] shall be transmitted to the Commissioners by the charity trustees—

    (a)   within ten months from the end of that year, or

    (b)   within such longer period as the Commissioners may for any special reason allow in the case of that report.

[(3A) Where in any financial year of a charity neither its gross income nor its total expenditure exceeds £10,000, the annual report required to be prepared under this section in respect of that year shall, if the Commissioners so request, be transmitted to them by the charity trustees—

    (a)   in the case of a request made before the end of seven months from the end of the financial year to which the report relates, within ten months from the end of that year, and

    (b)   in the case of a request not so made, within three months from the date of the request,

or, in either case, within such longer period as the Commissioners may for any special reason allow in the case of that report.][2]

(4) Subject to subsection (5) below, [any annual report transmitted to the Commissioners under this section][3] shall have attached to it the statement of accounts prepared for the financial year in question under section 42(1) above or (as the case may be) the account and statement so prepared under section 42(3) above, together with—

    (a)   where the accounts of the charity for that year have been audited under section 43 above, a copy of the report made by the auditor on that statement of accounts or (as the case may be) on that account and statement;

    (b)   where the accounts of the charity for that year have been examined under section 43 above, a copy of the report made by the independent examiner in respect of the examination carried out by him under that section.

(5) Subsection (4) above does not apply to a charity which is a company, and any annual report transmitted by the charity trustees of such a charity under [this section][4] shall instead have attached to it a copy of [the charity's annual accounts prepared for the financial year in question under

Part VII of the Companies Act 1985, together with a copy of [any auditors' report or report made for the purposes of section 249A(2) of that Act][5] on those accounts.

(6) Any annual report transmitted to the Commissioners under [this section][6] above, together with the documents attached to it, shall be kept by the Commissioners for such period as they think fit.

[(7) The charity trustees of a charity shall preserve, for at least six years from the end of the financial year to which it relates, any annual report prepared by them under subsection (1) above which they have not been required to transmit to the Commissioners.

(8) Subsection (4) of section 41 above shall apply in relation to the preservation of any such annual report as it applies in relation to the preservation of any accounting records (the references in subsection (3) of that section being read as references to subsection (7) above).

(9) The Secretary of State may by order amend subsection (3) or (3A) above by substituting a different sum for the sum for the time being specified there.][7]

[1] Substituted by Deregulation and Contracting Out Act 1994, s.29(1).
[2] Inserted by Deregulation and Contracting Out Act 1994, s.29(2).
[3] Substituted by Deregulation and Contracting Out Act 1994, s.29(3).
[4] Substituted by Deregulation and Contracting Out Act 1994, s.29(4).
[5] Substituted by Companies Act 1995 (Audit Exemption) Regulations 1994, reg.6.
[6] Substituted by Deregulation and Contracting Out Act 1994, s.29(5).
[7] Added by Deregulation and Contracting Out Act 1994 (c.40), Pt I, c II, s.29(2)(6).

46. Special provision as respects accounts and annual reports of exempt and other excepted charities

1D–045   (1) Nothing in sections 41 to 45 above applies to any exempt charity; but the charity trustees of an exempt charity shall keep proper books of account with respect to the affairs of the charity, and if not required by or under the authority of any other Act to prepare periodical statements of account shall prepare consecutive statements of account consisting on each occasion of an income and expenditure account relating to a period of not more than fifteen months and a balance sheet relating to the end of that period.

(2) The books of accounts and statements of account relating to an exempt charity shall be preserved for a period of six years at least unless the charity ceases to exist and the Commissioners consent in writing to their being destroyed or otherwise disposed of.

(3) Nothing in sections 43 to 45 above applies to any charity which—

(a)   falls within section 3(5)(c) above, and
(b)   is not registered.

(4) Except in accordance with subsection (7) below, nothing in section 45 above applies to any charity (other than an exempt charity or a charity which falls within section 3(5)(c) above) which—

(a)   is excepted by section 3(5) above, and
(b)   is not registered.

(5) If requested to do so by the Commissioners, the charity trustees of any such charity as is mentioned in subsection (4) above shall prepare an

annual report in respect of such financial year of the charity as is specified in the Commissioners' request.

(6) Any report prepared under subsection (5) above shall contain—

    (a)   such a report by the charity trustees on the activities of the charity during the year in question, and

    (b)   such other information relating to the charity or to its trustees or officers,

as may be prescribed by regulations made under section 45(1) above in relation to annual reports prepared under that provision.

(7) Subsections (3) to (6) of section 45 [(as originally enacted)][1] above shall apply to any report required to be prepared under subsection (5) above as if it were an annual report required to be prepared under subsection (1) of that section.

(8) Any reference in this section to a charity which falls within section 3(5)(c) above includes a reference to a charity which falls within that provision but is also excepted from registration by section 3(5)(b) above.
[1] Words inserted by Deregulation and Contracting Out Act 1994 (c.40), PtI, c II, s.29 (7).

47. Public inspection of annual reports, etc.

(1) Any annual report or other document kept by the Commissioners in pursuance of section 45(6) above shall be open to public inspection at all reasonable times—						1D–046

    (a)   during the period for which it is so kept; or

    (b)   if the Commissioners so determine, during such lesser period as they may specify.

(2) Where any person—

    (a)   requests the charity trustees of a charity in writing to provide him with a copy of the charity's most recent accounts, and

    (b)   pays them such reasonable fee (if any) as they may require in respect of the costs of complying with the request,

those trustees shall comply with the request within the period of two months beginning with the date on which it is made.

(3) In subsection (2) above the reference to a charity's most recent accounts is—

    (a)   [. . .][1]

    (b)   in the case of [a charity other than one falling within paragraph (c) or (d) below][2], a reference to the statement of accounts or account and statement prepared in pursuance of section 42(1) or (3) above in respect of the last financial year of the charity in respect of which a statement of accounts or account and statement has or have been so prepared;

    [(c)   in the case of a charity which is a company, a reference to the most recent annual accounts of the company prepared under Part VII of the Companies Act 1985 in relation to which any of the following conditions is satisfied—

    (i)   they have been audited;

    (ii)   a report required for the purposes of section 249A(2) of that Act has been made in respect of them; or

    (iii) they relate to a year in respect of which the company is exempt from audit by virtue of section 249A(1) of that Act; and][3]

   (d)   in the case of an exempt charity, a reference to the accounts of the charity most recently audited in pursuance of any statutory or other requirement or, if its accounts are not required to be audited, the accounts most recently prepared in respect of the charity.

[1] Repealed by Deregulation and Contracting Out Act 1994, Sch.17.
[2] Words substituted by Deregulation and Contracting Out Act 1994 (c.40), Sch.11, Para.12(b).
[3] Substituted by Companies Act 1995 (Audit Exemption) Regulations 1994, reg.7.

48. Annual returns by registered charities

1D–047   (1) [Subject to subsection (1A) below][1], Every registered charity shall prepare in respect of each of its financial years an annual return in such form, and containing such information, as may be prescribed by regulations made by the Commissioners.

[(1A) Subsection (1) above shall not apply in relation to any financial year of a charity in which neither the gross income nor the total expenditure of the charity exceeds £10,000.][2]

(2) Any such return shall be transmitted to the Commissioners by the date by which the charity trustees are, by virtue of section 45(3) above, required to transmit to them the annual report required to be prepared in respect of the financial year in question.

(3) The Commissioners may dispense with the requirements of subsection (1) above in the case of a particular charity or a particular class of charities, or in the case of a particular financial year of a charity or of any class of charities.

[(4) The Secretary of State may by order amend subsection (1A) above by substituting a different sum for the sum for the time being specified there.][3]

[1] Inserted by Deregulation and Contracting Out Act 1994, s.30(2).
[2] Inserted by Deregulation and Contracting Out Act 1994, s.30(3).
[3] Added by Deregulation and Contracting Out Act 1994 (c.40), PtI, c II, s.30(2),(3),(4).

49. Offences

1D–048   Any person who, without reasonable excuse, is persistently in default in relation to any requirement imposed—

   (a)   by section 45(3) [or (3A)][1] above (taken with section 45(4) or (5), as the case may require), or

   (b)   by section 47(2) or 48(2) above,

shall be guilty of an offence and liable on summary conviction to a fine not exceeding level 4 on the standard scale.

[1] Words inserted by Deregulation and Contracting Out Act 1994 (c.40), PtI, c II, s.29(8).

PART VII

INCORPORATION OF CHARITY TRUSTEES

50. Incorporation of trustees of a charity

(1) Where—   1D–049

- (a) the trustees of a charity, in accordance with section 52 below, apply to the Commissioners for a certificate of incorporation of the trustees as a body corporate, and
- (b) the Commissioners consider that the incorporation of the trustees would be in the interests of the charity,

the Commissioners may grant such a certificate, subject to such conditions or directions as they think fit to insert in it.

(2) The Commissioners shall not, however, grant such a certificate in a case where the charity appears to them to be required to be registered under section 3 above but is not so registered.

(3) On the grant of such a certificate—

- (a) the trustees of the charity shall become a body corporate by such name as is specified in the certificate; and
- (b) (without prejudice to the operation of section 54 below) any relevant rights or liabilities of those trustees shall become rights or liabilities of that body.

(4) After their incorporation the trustees—

- (a) may sue and be sued in their corporate name; and
- (b) shall have the same powers, and be subject to the same restrictions and limitations, as respects the holding, acquisition and disposal of property for or in connection with the purposes of the charity as they had or were subject to while unincorporated;

and any relevant legal proceedings that might have been continued or commenced by or against the trustees may be continued or commenced by or against them in their corporate name.

(5) A body incorporated under this section need not have a common seal.

(6) In this section—

"relevant rights or liabilities" means rights or liabilities in connection with any property vesting in the body in question under section 51 below; and

"relevant legal proceedings" means legal proceedings in connection with any such property.

51. Estate to vest in body corporate

The certificate of incorporation shall vest in the body corporate all real   1D–050
and personal estate, of whatever nature or tenure, belonging to or held by
any person or persons in trust for the charity, and thereupon any person
or persons in whose name or names any stocks, funds or securities are

standing in trust for the charity, shall transfer them into the name of the body corporate, except that the foregoing provisions shall not apply to property vested in the official custodian.

52. Applications for incorporation

1D–051   (1) Every application to the Commissioners for a certificate of incorporation under this Part of this Act shall—

    (a) be in writing and signed by the trustees of the charity concerned; and
    (b) be accompanied by such documents or information as the Commissioners may require for the purpose of the application.

    (2) The Commissioners may require—

    (a) any statement contained in any such application, or
    (b) any document or information supplied under subsection (1)(b) above,

to be verified in such manner as they may specify.

53. Nomination of trustees, and filling up vacancies

1D–052   (1) Before a certificate of incorporation is granted under this Part of this Act, trustees of the charity must have been effectually appointed to the satisfaction of the Commissioners.
    (2) Where a certificate of incorporation is granted vacancies in the number of the trustees of the charity shall from time to time be filled up so far as required by the constitution or settlement of the charity, or by any conditions or directions in the certificate, by such legal means as would have been available for the appointment of new trustees of the charity if no certificate of incorporation had been granted, or otherwise as required by such conditions or directions.

54. Liability of trustees and others, notwithstanding incorporation

1D–053   After a certificate of incorporation has been granted under this Part of this Act all trustees of the charity, notwithstanding their incorporation, shall be chargeable for such property as shall come into their hands, and shall be answerable and accountable for their own acts, receipts, neglects, and defaults, and for the due administration of the charity and its property, in the same manner and to the same extent as if no such incorporation had been effected.

55. Certificate to be evidence of compliance with requirements for incorporation

1D–054   A certificate of incorporation granted under this Part of this Act shall be conclusive evidence that all the preliminary requirements for incorporation under this Part of this Act have been complied with, and the date of incorporation mentioned in the certificate shall be deemed to be the date at which incorporation has taken place.

56. Power of Commissioners to amend certificate of incorporation

(1) The Commissioners may amend a certificate of incorporation either   **1D–055**
on the application of the incorporated body to which it relates or of their
own motion.

(2) Before making any such amendment of their own motion, the
Commissioners shall by notice in writing—

   (a)   inform the trustees of the relevant charity of their proposals, and
   (b)   invite those trustees to make representations to them within a
       time specified in the notice, being not less than one month from
       the date of the notice.

(3) The Commissioners shall take into consideration any representations made by those trustees within the time so specified, and may then
(without further notice) proceed with their proposals either without
modification or with such modifications as appear to them to be desirable.

(4) The Commissioners may amend a certificate of incorporation
either—

   (a)   by making an order specifying the amendment; or
   (b)   by issuing a new certificate of incorporation taking account of
       the amendment.

57. Records of applications and certificates

(1) The Commissioners shall keep a record of all applications for, and   **1D–056**
certificates of, incorporation under this Part of this Act and shall preserve
all documents sent to them under this Part of this Act.

(2) Any person may inspect such documents, under the direction of the
Commissioners, and any person may require a copy or extract of any such
document to be certified by a certificate signed by the secretary of the
Commissioners.

58. Enforcement of orders and directions

All conditions and directions inserted in any certificate of incorporation   **1D–057**
shall be binding upon and performed or observed by the trustees as trusts
of the charity, and section 88 below shall apply to any trustee who fails to
perform or observe any such condition or direction as it applies to a person guilty of disobedience to any such order of the Commissioners as is
mentioned in that section.

59. Gifts to charity before incorporation to have same effect afterwards

After the incorporation of the trustees of any charity under this Part of   **1D–058**
this Act every donation, gift and disposition of property, real or personal,
lawfully made before the incorporation but not having actually taken
effect, or thereafter lawfully made, by deed, will or otherwise to or in
favour of the charity, or the trustees of the charity, or otherwise for the
purposes of the charity, shall take effect as if made to or in favour of the
incorporated body or otherwise for the like purposes.

60. Execution of documents by incorporated body

1D–059   (1) This section has effect as respects the execution of documents by an incorporated body.

(2) If an incorporated body has a common seal, a document may be executed by the body by the affixing of its common seal.

(3) Whether or not it has a common seal, a document may be executed by an incorporated body either—

(a) by being signed by a majority of the trustees of the relevant charity and expressed (in whatever form of words) to be executed by the body; or

(b) by being executed in pursuance of an authority given under subsection (4) below.

(4) For the purposes of subsection (3)(b) above the trustees of the relevant charity in the case of an incorporated body may, subject to the trusts of the charity, confer on any two or more of their number—

(a) a general authority, or

(b) an authority limited in such manner as the trustees think fit,

to execute in the name and on behalf of the body documents for giving effect to transactions to which the body is a party.

(5) An authority under subsection (4) above—

(a) shall suffice for any document if it is given in writing or by resolution of a meeting of the trustees of the relevant charity, notwithstanding the want of any formality that would be required in giving an authority apart from that subsection;

(b) may be given so as to make the powers conferred exercisable by any of the trustees, or may be restricted to named persons or in any other way;

(c) subject to any such restriction, and until it is revoked, shall, notwithstanding any change in the trustees of the relevant charity, have effect as a continuing authority given by the trustees from time to time of the charity and exercisable by such trustees.

(6) In any authority under subsection (4) above to execute a document in the name and on behalf of an incorporated body there shall, unless the contrary intention appears, be implied authority also to execute it for the body in the name and on behalf of the official custodian or of any other person, in any case in which the trustees could do so.

(7) A document duly executed by an incorporated body which makes it clear on its face that it is intended by the person or persons making it to be a deed has effect, upon delivery, as a deed; and it shall be presumed, unless a contrary intention is proved, to be delivered upon its being so executed.

(8) In favour of a purchaser a document shall be deemed to have been duly executed by such a body if it purports to be signed—

(a) by a majority of the trustees of the relevant charity, or

(b) by such of the trustees of the relevant charity as are authorised by the trustees of that charity to execute it in the name and on behalf of the body, and, where the document makes it clear on its face that it is intended by the person or persons making it to be a deed, it shall be deemed to have been delivered upon its being executed.

For this purpose "purchaser" means a purchaser in good faith for valuable consideration and includes a lessee, mortgagee or other person who for valuable consideration acquires an interest in property.

61. Power of Commissioners to dissolve incorporated body

(1) Where the Commissioners are satisfied—

1D–060

(a) that an incorporated body has no assets or does not operate, or
(b) that the relevant charity in the case of an incorporated body has ceased to exist, or
(c) that the institution previously constituting, or treated by them as constituting, any such charity has ceased to be, or (as the case may be) was not at the time of the body's incorporation, a charity, or
(d) that the purposes of the relevant charity in the case of an incorporated body have been achieved so far as is possible or are in practice incapable of being achieved,

they may of their own motion make an order dissolving the body as from such date as is specified in the order.

(2) Where the Commissioners are satisfied, on the application of the trustees of the relevant charity in the case of an incorporated body, that it would be in the interests of the charity for that body to be dissolved, the Commissioners may make an order dissolving the body as from such date as is specified in the order.

(3) Subject to subsection (4) below, an order made under this section with respect to an incorporated body shall have the effect of vesting in the trustees of the relevant charity, in trust for that charity, all property for the time being vested—

(a) in the body, or
(b) in any other person (apart from the official custodian),

in trust for that charity.

(4) If the Commissioners so direct in the order—

(a) all or any specified part of that property shall, instead of vesting in the trustees of the relevant charity, vest—
  (i) in a specified person as trustee for, or nominee of, that charity, or
  (ii) in such persons (other than the trustees of the relevant charity) as may be specified;
(b) any specified investments, or any specified class or description of investments, held by any person in trust for the relevant charity shall be transferred—
  (i) to the trustees of that charity, or
  (ii) to any such person or persons as is or are mentioned in paragraph (a)(i) or (ii) above;

and for this purpose "specified" means specified by the Commissioners in the order.

(5) Where an order to which this subsection applies is made with respect to an incorporated body—

(a) any rights or liabilities of the body shall become rights or liabilities of the trustees of the relevant charity; and

(b) any legal proceedings that might have been continued or commenced by or against the body may be continued or commenced by or against those trustees.

(6) Subsection (5) above applies to any order under this section by virtue of which—

(a) any property vested as mentioned in subsection (3) above is vested—
(i) in the trustees of the relevant charity, or
(ii) in any person as trustee for, or nominee of, that charity; or

(b) any investments held by any person in trust for the relevant charity are required to be transferred—
(i) to the trustees of that charity, or
(ii) to any person as trustee for, or nominee of, that charity.

(7) Any order made by the Commissioners under this section may be varied or revoked by a further order so made.

62. Interpretation of Part VII

1D–061   In this Part of this Act—
"incorporated body" means a body incorporated under section 50 above;
"the relevant charity", in relation to an incorporated body, means the charity the trustees of which have been incorporated as that body;
"the trustees", in relation to a charity, means the charity trustees.

PART VIII

CHARITABLE COMPANIES

63. Winding up

1D–062   (1) Where a charity may be wound up by the High Court under the Insolvency Act 1986, a petition for it to be wound up under that Act by any court in England or Wales having jurisdiction may be presented by the Attorney General, as well as by any person authorised by that Act.

(2) Where a charity may be so wound up by the High Court, such a petition may also be presented by the Commissioners if, at any time after they have instituted an inquiry under section 8 above with respect to the charity, they are satisfied as mentioned in section 18(1)(a) or (b) above.

(3) Where a charitable company is dissolved, the Commissioners may make an application under section 651 of the Companies Act 1985 (power

of court to declare dissolution of company void) for an order to be made under that section with respect to the company; and for this purpose subsection (1) of that section shall have effect in relation to a charitable company as if the reference to the liquidator of the company included a reference to the Commissioners.

(4) Where a charitable company's name has been struck off the register of companies under section 652 of the Companies Act 1985 (power of registrar to strike defunct company off register), the Commissioners may make an application under section 653(2) of that Act (objection to striking off by person aggrieved) for an order restoring the company's name to that register; and for this purpose section 653(2) shall have effect in relation to a charitable company as if the reference to any such person aggrieved as is there mentioned included a reference to the Commissioners.

(5) The powers exercisable by the Commissioners by virtue of this section shall be exercisable by them of their own motion, but shall be exercisable only with the agreement of the Attorney General on each occasion.

(6) In this section "charitable company" means a company which is a charity.

64. Alteration of objects clause

(1) Where a charity is a company or other body corporate having power **1D–063** to alter the instruments establishing or regulating it as a body corporate, no exercise of that power which has the effect of the body ceasing to be a charity shall be valid so as to affect the application of—

    (a)   any property acquired under any disposition or agreement previously made otherwise than for full consideration in money or money's worth, or any property representing property so acquired,

    (b)   any property representing income which has accrued before the alteration is made, or

    (c)   the income from any such property as aforesaid.

(2) Where a charity is a company, any alteration by it—

    (a)   of the objects clause in its memorandum of association, or

    (b)   of any other provision in its memorandum of association, or any provision in its articles of association, which is a provision directing or restricting the manner in which property of the company may be used or applied,

is ineffective without the prior written consent of the Commissioners.

(3) Where a company has made any such alteration in accordance with subsection (2) above and—

    (a)   in connection with the alteration is required by virtue of—

        (i)   section 6(1) of the Companies Act 1985 (delivery of documents following alteration of objects), or

        (ii)   that provision as applied by section 17(3) of that Act (alteration of condition in memorandum which could have been contained in articles),

    to deliver to the registrar of companies a printed copy of its memorandum, as altered, or

(b) is required by virtue of section 380(1) of that Act (registration etc. of resolutions and agreements) to forward to the registrar a printed or other copy of the special resolution effecting the alteration,

the copy so delivered or forwarded by the company shall be accompanied by a copy of the Commissioner's consent.

(4) Section 6(3) of that Act (offences) shall apply to any default by a company in complying with subsection (3) above as it applies to any such default as is mentioned in that provision.

65. Invalidity of certain transactions

1D–064   (1) Sections 35 and 35A of the Companies Act 1985 (capacity of company not limited by its memorandum; power of directors to bind company) do not apply to the acts of a company which is a charity except in favour of a person who—

(a) gives full consideration in money or money's worth in relation to the act in question, and

(b) does not know that the act is not permitted by the company's memorandum or, as the case may be, is beyond the powers of the directors,

or who does not know at the time the act is done that the company is a charity.

(2) However, where such a company purports to transfer or grant an interest in property, the fact that the act was not permitted by the company's memorandum or, as the case may be, that the directors in connection with the act exceeded any limitation on their powers under the company's constitution, does not affect the title of a person who subsequently acquires the property or any interest in it for full consideration without actual notice of any such circumstances affecting the validity of the company's act.

(3) In any proceedings arising out of subsection (1) above the burden of proving—

(a) that a person knew that an act was not permitted by the company's memorandum or was beyond the powers of the directors, or

(b) that a person knew that the company was a charity,

lies on the person making that allegation.

(4) Where a company is a charity, the ratification of an act under section 35(3) of the Companies Act 1985, or the ratification of a transaction to which section 322A of that Act applies (invalidity of certain transactions to which directors or their associates are parties), is ineffective without the prior written consent of the Commissioners.

66. Requirement of consent of Commissioners to certain acts

(1) Where a company is a charity—   **1D–065**

    (a) any approval given by the company for the purposes of any of the provisions of the Companies Act 1985 specified in subsection (2) below, and

    (b) any affirmation by it for the purposes of section 322(2)(c) of that Act (affirmation of voidable arrangements under which assets are acquired by or from a director or person connected with him),

is ineffective without the prior written consent of the Commissioners.

(2) The provisions of the Companies Act 1985 referred to in subsection (1)(a) above are—

    (a) section 312 (payment to director in respect of loss of office or retirement);

    (b) section 313(1) (payment to director in respect of loss of office or retirement made in connection with transfer of undertaking or property of company);

    (c) section 319(3) (incorporation in director's service contract of term whereby his employment will or may continue for a period of more than five years);

    (d) section 320(1) (arrangement whereby assets are acquired by or from director or person connected with him);

    (e) section 337(3)(a) (provision of funds to meet certain expenses incurred by director).

67. Name to appear on correspondence etc

Section 30(7) of the Companies Act 1985 (exemption from require-   **1D–066**
ments relating to publication of name etc.) shall not, in its application to any company which is a charity, have the effect of exempting the company from the requirements of section 349(1) of that Act (company's name to appear in its correspondence etc.)

68. Status to appear on correspondence etc

(1) Where a company is a charity and its name does not include the   **1D–067**
word "charity" or the word "charitable" then [subject to subsection (1A)]¹, the fact that the company is a charity shall be stated [. . .]² in legible characters—

    (a) in all business letters of the company,

    (b) in all its notices and other official publications,

    (c) in all bills of exchange, promissory notes, endorsements, cheques and orders for money or goods purporting to be signed on behalf of the company,

    (d) in all conveyances purporting to be executed by the company, and

    (e) in all bills rendered by it and in all its invoices, receipts, and letters of credit.

[(1A) Where a company's name includes the word "elusen" or the word "elusennol" (the Welsh equivalents of the words "charity" and "charitable"), subsection (1) above shall not apply in relation to any document which is wholly in Welsh.

(1B) The statement required by subsection (1) above shall be in English, except that, in the case of a document which is otherwise wholly in Welsh, the statement may be in Welsh if it consists of or includes the word "elusen" or the word "elusennol".][3]

(2) In subsection (1)(d) above "conveyance" means any instrument creating, transferring, varying or extinguishing an interest in land.

(3) Subsections (2) to (4) of section 349 of the Companies Act 1985 (offences in connection with failure to include required particulars in business letters etc.) shall apply in relation to a contravention of subsection (1) above, taking the reference in subsection (3)(b) of that section to a bill of parcels as a reference to any such bill as is mentioned in subsection (1)(e) above.

[1] Repealed by Welsh Language Act 1993, ss.33, 35(1), Sch.2.
[2] Repealed by Welsh Language Act 1993, ss.33, 35(1), Sch.2.
[3] Added by Welsh Language Act 1993 (c.38), PtIII, s.33(3).

69. Investigation of accounts

1D–068

(1) In the case of a charity which is a company the Commissioners may by order require that the condition and accounts of the charity for such period as they think fit shall be investigated and audited by an auditor appointed by them, being a person eligible for appointment as a company auditor under section 25 of the Companies Act 1989.

(2) An auditor acting under subsection (1) above—

(a) shall have a right of access to all books, accounts and documents relating to the charity which are in the possession or control of the charity trustees or to which the charity trustees have access;

(b) shall be entitled to require from any charity trustee, past or present, and from any past or present officer or employee of the charity such information and explanation as he thinks necessary for the performance of his duties;

(c) shall at the conclusion or during the progress of the audit make such reports to the Commissioners about the audit or about the accounts or affairs of the charity as he thinks the case requires, and shall send a copy of any such report to the charity trustees.

(3) The expenses of any audit under subsection (1) above, including the remuneration of the auditor, shall be paid by the Commissioners.

(4) If any person fails to afford an auditor any facility to which he is entitled under subsection (2) above the Commissioners may by order give to that person or to the charity trustees for the time being such directions as the Commissioners think appropriate for securing that the default is made good.

PART IX

MISCELLANEOUS

POWERS OF INVESTMENT

70. [. . .]¹   1D–069

¹ Repealed by Trustee Act 2000 (c.29), Sch.4, PtI, Para.1.

71. [. . .]¹   1D–070

¹ Repealed by Trustee Act 2000 (c.29), Sch.4, PtI, Para.1.

DISQUALIFICATION FOR ACTING AS CHARITY TRUSTEE

72. Persons disqualified for being trustees of a charity

(1) Subject to the following provisions of this section, a person shall be   1D–071
disqualified for being a charity trustee or trustee for a charity if—

   (a)   he has been convicted of any offence involving dishonesty or
         deception;
   (b)   he has been adjudged bankrupt or sequestration of his estate has
         been awarded and (in either case) he has not been discharged;
   (c)   he has made a composition or arrangement with, or granted a
         trust deed for, his creditors and has not been discharged in
         respect of it;
   (d)   he has been removed from the office of charity trustee or trustee
         for a charity by an order made—
         (i)   by the Commissioners under section 18(2)(i) above, or
         (ii)   by the Commissioners under section 20(1A)(i) of the
                Charities Act 1960 (power to act for protection of charities)
                or under section 20(1)(i) of that Act (as in force before the
                commencement of section 8 of the Charities Act 1992), or
         (iii) by the High Court,
   on the grounds of any misconduct or mismanagement in the administration of the charity for which he was responsible or to which he
   was privy, or which he by his conduct contributed to or facilitated;
   (e)   he has been removed, under section 7 of the Law Reform
         (Miscellaneous Provisions) (Scotland) Act 1990 (powers of
         Court of Session to deal with management of charities), from
         being concerned in the management or control of any body;
   (f)   he is subject to a disqualification order or disqualification
         undertaking under the Company Directors Disqualification Act
         1986 to a disqualification order under Part II of the Companies
         (Northern Ireland) Order 1989or to an order made under sec-
         tion 429(2)(b) of the Insolvency Act 1986 (failure to pay under
         county court administration order).

(2) In subsection (1) above—

   (a)   paragraph (a) applies whether the conviction occurred before or
         after the commencement of that subsection, but does not apply
         in relation to any conviction which is a spent conviction for the
         purposes of the Rehabilitation of Offenders Act 1974;
   (b)   paragraph (b) applies whether the adjudication of bankruptcy
         or the sequestration occurred before or after the commencement
         of that subsection;
   (c)   paragraph (c) applies whether the composition or arrangement
         was made, or the trust deed was granted, before or after the
         commencement of that subsection; and
   (d)   paragraphs (d) to (f) apply in relation to orders made and
         removals effected before or after the commencement of that
         subsection.

   (3) Where (apart from this subsection) a person is disqualified under
subsection (1)(b) above for being a charity trustee or trustee for any charity which is a company, he shall not be so disqualified if leave has been
granted under section 11 of the Company Directors Disqualification Act
1986 (undischarged bankrupts) for him to act as director of the charity;
and similarly a person shall not be disqualified under subsection (1)(f)
above for being a charity trustee or trustee for such a charity if—

   [(a) in the case of a person subject to a disqualification order or
         disqualification undertaking under the Company Directors
         Disqualification Act 1986, leave for the purposes of section
         1(1)(a) or 1A(1)(a) of that Act has been granted for him to act
         as director of the charity,
   (aa) in the case of a person subject to a disqualification order under
         Part II of the Companies (Northern Ireland) Order 1989, leave
         has been granted by the High Court in Northern Ireland for him
         to act as director of the charity][1],
   (b)   in the case of a person subject to an order under section
         429(2)(b) of the Insolvency Act 1986, leave has been granted by
         the court which made the order for him to so act.

   (4) The Commissioners may, on the application of any person disqualified under subsection (1) above, waive his disqualification either
generally or in relation to a particular charity or a particular class of
charities; but no such waiver may be granted in relation to any charity
which is a company if—

   (a)   the person concerned is for the time being prohibited, by virtue
         of—
         (i)   a disqualification order [or disqualification undertaking][2]
               under the Company Directors Disqualification Act 1986,
               or
         (ii) section 11(1), [12(2) or 12A][3] of that Act (undischarged
               bankrupts; failure to pay under county court administration
               order [Northern Irish disqualification orders][4]),
         from acting as director of the charity; and

   (b)   leave has not been granted for him to act as director of any other company.

(5) Any waiver under subsection (4) above shall be notified in writing to the person concerned.

(6) For the purposes of this section the Commissioners shall keep, in such manner as they think fit, a register of all persons who have been removed from office as mentioned in subsection (1)(d) above either—

   (a)   by an order of the Commissioners made before or after the commencement of subsection (1) above, or

   (b)   by an order of the High Court made after the commencement of section 45(1) of the Charities Act 1992;

and, where any person is so removed from office by an order of the High Court, the court shall notify the Commissioners of his removal.

(7) The entries in the register kept under subsection (6) above shall be available for public inspection in legible form at all reasonable times.

[1] Words inserted by Insolvency Act 2000 (c.39), Sch.4, PtII, Para.18.
[2] Words inserted by Insolvency Act 2000 (c.39), Sch.4, PtII, Para.18.
[3] Words inserted by Insolvency Act 2000 (c.39), Sch.4, PtII, Para.18(c)(ii).
[4] Words inserted by Insolvency Act 2000 (c.39), Sch.4, PtII, Para.18(c)(ii).

73. Person acting as charity trustee while disqualified

(1) Subject to subsection (2) below, any person who acts as a charity   **1D–072** trustee or trustee for a charity while he is disqualified for being such a trustee by virtue of section 72 above shall be guilty of an offence and liable—

   (a)   on summary conviction, to imprisonment for a term not exceeding six months or to a fine not exceeding the statutory maximum, or both;

   (b)   on conviction on indictment, to imprisonment for a term not exceeding two years or to a fine, or both.

(2) Subsection (1) above shall not apply where—

   (a)   the charity concerned is a company; and

   (b)   the disqualified person is disqualified by virtue only of paragraph (b) or (f) of section 72(1) above.

(3) Any acts done as charity trustee or trustee for a charity by a person disqualified for being such a trustee by virtue of section 72 above shall not be invalid by reason only of that disqualification.

(4) Where the Commissioners are satisfied—

   (a)   that any person has acted as charity trustee or trustee for a charity (other than an exempt charity) while disqualified for being such a trustee by virtue of section 72 above, and

   (b)   that, while so acting, he has received from the charity any sums by way of remuneration or expenses, or any benefit in kind, in connection with his acting as charity trustee or trustee for the charity, they may by order direct him to repay to the charity the whole or part of any such sums, or (as the case may be) to pay to the charity the whole or part of the monetary value (as determined by them) of any such benefit.

(5) Subsection (4) above does not apply to any sums received by way of remuneration or expenses in respect of any time when the person concerned was not disqualified for being a charity trustee or trustee for the charity.

SMALL CHARITIES

74. Power to transfer all property, modify objects etc

1D–073   (1) This section applies to a charity if—

    (a)   its gross income in its last financial year did not exceed £5,000, and

    (b)   it does not hold any land on trusts which stipulate that the land is to be used for the purposes, or any particular purposes, of the charity,

and it is neither an exempt charity nor a charitable company.

(2) Subject to the following provisions of this section, the charity trustees of a charity to which this section applies may resolve for the purposes of this section—

    (a)   that all the property of the charity should be transferred to such other charity as is specified in the resolution, being either a registered charity or a charity which is not required to be registered;

    (b)   that all the property of the charity should be divided, in such manner as is specified in the resolution, between such two or more other charities as are so specified, being in each case either a registered charity or a charity which is not required to be registered;

    (c)   that the trusts of the charity should be modified by replacing all or any of the purposes of the charity with such other purposes, being in law charitable, as are specified in the resolution;

    (d)   that any provision of the trusts of the charity—

        (i)   relating to any of the powers exercisable by the charity trustees in the administration of the charity, or

        (ii)   regulating the procedure to be followed in any respect in connection with its administration,

should be modified in such manner as is specified in the resolution.

(3) Any resolution passed under subsection (2) above must be passed by a majority of not less than two-thirds of such charity trustees as vote on the resolution.

(4) The charity trustees of a charity to which this section applies ("the transferor charity") shall not have power to pass a resolution under subsection (2)(a) or (b) above unless they are satisfied—

(a)   that the existing purposes of the transferor charity have ceased to be conducive to a suitable and effective application of the charity's resources; and

(b)   that the purposes of the charity or charities specified in the resolution are as similar in character to the purposes of the transferor charity as is reasonably practicable;

and before passing the resolution they must have received from the charity trustees of the charity, or (as the case may be) of each of the charities, specified in the resolution written confirmation that those trustees are willing to accept a transfer of property under this section.

(5) The charity trustees of any such charity shall not have power to pass a resolution under subsection (2)(c) above unless they are satisfied—

(a)   that the existing purposes of the charity (or, as the case may be, such of them as it is proposed to replace) have ceased to be conducive to a suitable and effective application of the charity's resources; and

(b)   that the purposes specified in the resolution are as similar in character to those existing purposes as is practical in the circumstances.

(6) Where charity trustees have passed a resolution under subsection (2) above, they shall—

(a)   give public notice of the resolution in such manner as they think reasonable in the circumstances; and

(b)   send a copy of the resolution to the Commissioners, together with a statement of their reasons for passing it.

(7) The Commissioners may, when considering the resolution, require the charity trustees to provide additional information or explanation—

(a)   as to the circumstances in and by reference to which they have determined to act under this section, or

(b)   relating to their compliance with this section in connection with the resolution;

and the Commissioners shall take into account any representations made to them by persons appearing to them to be interested in the charity where those representations are made within the period of six weeks beginning with the date when the Commissioners receive a copy of the resolution by virtue of subsection (6)(b) above.

(8) Where the Commissioners have so received a copy of a resolution from any charity trustees and it appears to them that the trustees have complied with this section in connection with the resolution, the Commissioners shall, within the period of three months beginning with the date when they receive the copy of the resolution, notify the trustees in writing either—

(a)   that the Commissioners concur with the resolution; or

(b)   that they do not concur with it.

(9) Where the Commissioners so notify their concurrence with the resolution, then—

    (a) if the resolution was passed under subsection (2)(a) or (b) above, the charity trustees shall arrange for all the property of the transferor charity to be transferred in accordance with the resolution and on terms that any property so transferred—

        (i) shall be held and applied by the charity to which it is transferred ("the transferee charity") for the purposes of that charity, but

        (ii) shall, as property of the transferee charity, nevertheless be subject to any restrictions on expenditure to which it is subject as property of the transferor charity,

and those trustees shall arrange for it to be so transferred by such date as may be specified in the notification; and

    (b) if the resolution was passed under subsection (2)(c) or (d) above, the trusts of the charity shall be deemed, as from such date as may be specified in the notification, to have been modified in accordance with the terms of the resolution.

(10) For the purpose of enabling any property to be transferred to a charity under this section, the Commissioners shall have power, at the request of the charity trustees of that charity, to make orders vesting any property of the transferor charity—

    (a) in the charity trustees of the first-mentioned charity or in any trustee for that charity, or

    (b) in any other person nominated by those charity trustees to hold the property in trust for that charity.

(11) The Secretary of State may by order amend subsection (1) above by substituting a different sum for the sum for the time being specified there.

(12) In this section—

    (a) "charitable company" means a charity which is a company or other body corporate; and

    (b) references to the transfer of property to a charity are references to its transfer—

        (i) to the charity trustees, or

        (ii) to any trustee for the charity, or

        (iii) to a person nominated by the charity trustees to hold it in trust for the charity,

as the charity trustees may determine.

75. Power to spend capital

1D–074   (1) This section applies to a charity if—

    (a) it has a permanent endowment which does not consist of or comprise any land, and

    (b) its gross income in its last financial year did not exceed £1,000,

and it is neither an exempt charity nor a charitable company.

(2) Where the charity trustees of a charity to which this section applies are of the opinion that the property of the charity is too small, in relation to its purposes, for any useful purpose to be achieved by the expenditure of income alone, they may resolve for the purposes of this section that the charity ought to be freed from the restrictions with respect to expenditure of capital to which its permanent endowment is subject.

(3) Any resolution passed under subsection (2) above must be passed by a majority of not less than two-thirds of such charity trustees as vote on the resolution.

(4) Before passing such a resolution the charity trustees must consider whether any reasonable possibility exists of effecting a transfer or division of all the charity's property under section 74 above (disregarding any such transfer or division as would, in their opinion, impose on the charity an unacceptable burden of costs).

(5) Where charity trustees have passed a resolution under subsection (2) above, they shall—

(a)   give public notice of the resolution in such manner as they think reasonable in the circumstances; and

(b)   send a copy of the resolution to the Commissioners, together with a statement of their reasons for passing it.

(6) The Commissioners may, when considering the resolution, require the charity trustees to provide additional information or explanation—

(a)   as to the circumstances in and by reference to which they have determined to act under this section, or

(b)   relating to their compliance with this section in connection with the resolution;

and the Commissioners shall take into account any representations made to them by persons appearing to them to be interested in the charity where those representations are made within the period of six weeks beginning with the date when the Commissioners receive a copy of the resolution by virtue of subsection (5)(b) above.

(7) Where the Commissioners have so received a copy of a resolution from any charity trustees and it appears to them that the trustees have complied with this section in connection with the resolution, the Commissioners shall, within the period of three months beginning with the date when they receive the copy of the resolution, notify the trustees in writing either—

(a)   that the Commissioners concur with the resolution; or

(b)   that they do not concur with it.

(8) Where the Commissioners so notify their concurrence with the resolution, the charity trustees shall have, as from such date as may be specified in the notification, power by virtue of this section to expend any property of the charity without regard to any such restrictions as are mentioned in subsection (2) above.

(9) The Secretary of State may by order amend subsection (1) above by substituting a different sum for the sum for the time being specified there.

(10) In this section "charitable company" means a charity which is a company or other body corporate.

LOCAL CHARITIES

76. Local authority's index of local charities

1D–075   (1) The council of a county [or county borough][1] or of a district or London borough and the Common Council of the City of London may maintain an index of local charities or of any class of local charities in the council's area, and may publish information contained in the index, or summaries or extracts taken from it.

(2) A council proposing to establish or maintaining under this section an index of local charities or of any class of local charities shall, on request, be supplied by the Commissioners free of charge with copies of such entries in the register of charities as are relevant to the index or with particulars of any changes in the entries of which copies have been supplied before; and the Commissioners may arrange that they will without further request supply a council with particulars of any such changes.

(3) An index maintained under this section shall be open to public inspection at all reasonable times.

(4) A council may employ any voluntary organisation as their agent for the purposes of this section, on such terms and within such limits (if any) or in such cases as they may agree; and for this purpose "voluntary organisation" means any body of which the activities are carried on otherwise than for profit, not being a public or local authority.

(5) A joint board discharging any of a council's functions shall have the same powers under this section as the council as respects local charities in the council's area which are established for purposes similar or complementary to any services provided by the board.

[1] Words inserted by Local Government (Wales) Act (1994 c.19), s.66(6), Sch.16, Para.101 (1).

77. Reviews of local charities by local authority

1D–076   (1) The council of a county [or county borough][1] or of a district or London borough and the Common Council of the City of London may, subject to the following provisions of this section, initiate, and carry out in co-operation with the charity trustees, a review of the working of any group of local charities with the same or similar purposes in the council's area, and may make to the Commissioners such report on the review and such recommendations arising from it as the council after consultation with the trustees think fit.

(2) A council having power to initiate reviews under this section may co-operate with other persons in any review by them of the working of local charities in the council's area (with or without other charities), or may join with other persons in initiating and carrying out such a review.

(3) No review initiated by a council under this section shall extend to any charity without the consent of the charity trustees, nor to any ecclesiastical charity.

(4) No review initiated under this section by the council of a district shall extend to the working in any county of a local charity established for purposes similar or complementary to any services provided by county councils unless the review so extends with the consent of the council of that county.

[(4A) Subsection (4) above does not apply in relation to Wales.][2]

(5) Subsections (4) and (5) of section 76 above shall apply for the purposes of this section as they apply for the purposes of that section.
[1] Added by Local Government (Wales) Act 1994 (c.19), s.66(6), Sch.16, Para.101(2).
[2] Added by Local Government (Wales) Act 1994 (c.19), s.66(6), Sch.16, Para.101(2).

78. Co-operation between charities, and between charities and local authorities

(1) Any local council and any joint board discharging any functions of such a council—   **1D–077**

- (a) may make, with any charity established for purposes similar or complementary to services provided by the council or board, arrangements for co-ordinating the activities of the council or board and those of the charity in the interests of persons who may benefit from those services or from the charity; and
- (b) shall be at liberty to disclose to any such charity in the interests of those persons any information obtained in connection with the services provided by the council or board, whether or not arrangements have been made with the charity under this subsection.

In this subsection "local council" means[, in relation to England,][1] the council of a county, or of a district, London borough, [or parish],[2] and includes also the Common Council of the City of London and the Council of the Isles of Scilly [and, in relation to Wales, the council of a county, county borough or community.][3]

(2) Charity trustees shall, notwithstanding anything in the trusts of the charity, have power by virtue of this subsection to do all or any of the following things, where it appears to them likely to promote or make more effective the work of the charity, and may defray the expense of so doing out of any income or money applicable as income of the charity, that is to say—

- (a) they may co-operate in any review undertaken under section 77 above or otherwise of the working of charities or any class of charities;
- (b) they may make arrangements with an authority acting under subsection (1) above or with another charity for co-ordinating their activities and those of the authority or of the other charity;
- (c) they may publish information of other charities with a view to bringing them to the notice of those for whose benefit they are intended.

[1] Inserted, or as amended by, Local Government (Wales) Act 1994 (c.19), s.66(6), Sch.16, Para.101(3)(b).
[2] Inserted, or as amended by, Local Government (Wales) Act 1994 (c.19), s.66(6), Sch.16, Para.10(3)(b).
[3] Inserted, or as amended by, Local Government (Wales) Act 1994 (c.19), s.66(6), Sch.16, Para.10(3)(b).

79. Parochial charities

(1) Where trustees hold any property for the purposes of a public recreation ground, or of allotments (whether under inclosure Acts or otherwise),   **1D–078**

for the benefit of inhabitants of a parish having a parish council, or for other charitable purposes connected with such a parish, except for an ecclesiastical charity, they may with the approval of the Commissioners and with the consent of the parish council transfer the property to the parish council or to persons appointed by the parish council; and the council or their appointees shall hold the property on the same trusts and subject to the same conditions as the trustees did.

This subsection shall apply to property held for any public purposes as it applies to property held for charitable purposes.

(2) Where the charity trustees of a parochial charity in a parish, not being an ecclesiastical charity nor a charity founded within the preceding forty years, do not include persons elected by the local government electors, ratepayers or inhabitants of the parish or appointed by the parish council or parish meeting, the parish council or parish meeting may appoint additional charity trustees, to such number as the Commissioners may allow; and if there is a sole charity trustee not elected or appointed as aforesaid of any such charity, the number of the charity trustees may, with the approval of the Commissioners, be increased to three of whom one may be nominated by the person holding the office of the sole trustee and one by the parish council or parish meeting.

(3) Where, under the trusts of a charity other than an ecclesiastical charity, the inhabitants of a rural parish (whether in vestry or not) or a select vestry were formerly (in 1894) entitled to appoint charity trustees for, or trustees or beneficiaries of, the charity, then—

    (a)   in a parish having a parish council, the appointment shall be made by the parish council or, in the case of beneficiaries, by persons appointed by the parish council; and

    (b)   in a parish not having a parish council, the appointment shall be made by the parish meeting.

(4) Where overseers as such or, except in the case of an ecclesiastical charity, churchwardens as such were formerly (in 1894) charity trustees of or trustees for a parochial charity in a rural parish, either alone or jointly with other persons, then instead of the former overseer or church warden trustees there shall be trustees (to a number not greater than that of the former overseer or churchwarden trustees) appointed by the parish council or, if there is no parish council, by the parish meeting.

(5) Where, outside Greater London (other than the outer London boroughs), overseers of a parish as such were formerly (in 1927) charity trustees of or trustees for any charity, either alone or jointly with other persons, then instead of the former overseer trustees there shall be trustees (to a number not greater than that of the former overseer trustees) appointed by the parish council or, if there is no parish council, by the parish meeting.

(6) In the case of an urban parish existing immediately before the passing of the Local Government Act 1972 which after 1st April 1974 is not comprised in a parish, the power of appointment under subsection (5) above shall be exercisable by the district council.

(7) In the application of the foregoing provisions of this section to Wales—

    (a) for references in subsections (1) and (2) to a parish or a parish council there shall be substituted respectively references to a community or a community council;

    (b) for references in subsections (3)(a) and (b) to a parish, a parish council or a parish meeting there shall be substituted respectively references to a community, a community council [or the council of the county or (as the case may be) county borough][1];

    (c) for references in subsections (4) and (5) to a parish council or a parish meeting there shall be substituted respectively references to a community council or the [council of the county or (as the case may be) county borough][2].

(8) Any appointment of a charity trustee or trustee for a charity which is made by virtue of this section shall be for a term of four years, and a retiring trustee shall be eligible for re-appointment but—

    (a) on an appointment under subsection (2) above, where no previous appointments have been made by virtue of that subsection or of the corresponding provision of the Local Government Act 1894 or the Charities Act 1960, and more than one trustee is appointed, half of those appointed (or as nearly as may be) shall be appointed for a term of two years; and

    (b) an appointment made to fill a casual vacancy shall be for the remainder of the term of the previous appointment.

[(9) This section shall not affect the trusteeship, control or management of any [foundation or voluntary school within the meaning of the School Standards and Framework Act 1998][3].][4]

(10) The provisions of this section shall not extend to the Isles of Scilly, and shall have effect subject to any order (including any future order) made under any enactment relating to local government with respect to local government areas or the powers of local authorities.

(11) In this section the expression "formerly (in 1894)" relates to the period immediately before the passing of the Local Government Act 1894, and the expression "formerly (in 1927)" to the period immediately before 1st April 1927; and the word "former" shall be construed accordingly.

[1] Words substituted by Local Government (Wales) Act 1994, s.66(6), Sch.16, Para.101(4).
[2] Words substituted by Local Government (Wales) Act 1994, s.66(6), Sch.16, Para.101(4).
[3] Words substituted by School Standards and Framework Act 1998 (c.31), s.140(1), Sch.30, Para.49.
[4] Words substituted by Education Act 1996, s.582(1), Sch.37, PtI, Para.119.

SCOTTISH CHARITIES

80. Supervision by Commissioners of certain Scottish charities

1D–079

(1) The following provisions of this Act, namely—

(a) sections 8 and 9,

(b) section 18 (except subsection (2)(ii)), and

(c) section 19,

shall have effect in relation to any recognised body which is managed or controlled wholly or mainly in or from England or Wales as they have effect in relation to a charity.

(2) Where—

(a) a recognised body is managed or controlled wholly or mainly in or from Scotland, but

(b) any person in England and Wales holds any property on behalf of the body or of any person concerned in its management or control,

then, if the Commissioners are satisfied as to the matters mentioned in subsection (3) below, they may make an order requiring the person holding the property not to part with it without their approval.

(3) The matters referred to in subsection (2) above are—

(a) that there has been any misconduct or mismanagement in the administration of the body; and

(b) that it is necessary or desirable to make an order under that subsection for the purpose of protecting the property of the body or securing a proper application of such property for the purposes of the body;

and the reference in that subsection to the Commissioners being satisfied as to those matters is a reference to their being so satisfied on the basis of such information as may be supplied to them by the Lord Advocate.[1]

(4) Where—

(a) any person in England and Wales holds any property on behalf of a recognised body or of any person concerned in the management or control of such a body, and

(b) the Commissioners are satisfied (whether on the basis of such information as may be supplied to them by the Lord Advocate or otherwise)—

(i) that there has been any misconduct or mismanagement in the administration of the body, and

(ii) that it is necessary or desirable to make an order under this subsection for the purpose of protecting the property of the body or securing a proper application of such property for the purposes of the body, the Commissioners may by order vest the property in such recognised body or charity as is specified in the order in accordance with subsection (5) below, or require any persons in whom the property is vested to transfer it to any such body or charity, or appoint any person to transfer the property to any such body or charity.

(5) The Commissioners may specify in an order under subsection (4) above such other recognised body or such charity as they consider appropriate, being a body or charity whose purposes are, in the opinion of the Commissioners, as similar in character to those of the body referred to in paragraph (a) of that subsection as is reasonably practicable; but the Commissioners shall not so specify any body or charity unless they have received—

(a) from the persons concerned in the management or control of the body, or

(b) from the charity trustees of the charity,

as the case may be, written confirmation that they are willing to accept the property.

(6) In this section "recognised body" has the same meaning as in Part I of the Law Reform (Miscellaneous Provisions) (Scotland) Act 1990 (Scottish charities).

¹ Now the Secretary of State: see the Transfer of Functions (Lord Advocate and Secretary of State Order 1999 (SI 1999/678), art.2(1)., Sch.

81. Manner of giving notice of charity meetings, etc

(1) All notices which are required or authorised by the trusts of a char- **1D–080**
ity to be given to a charity trustee, member or subscriber may be sent by post, and, if sent by post, may be addressed to any address given as his in the list of charity trustees, members or subscribers for the time being in use at the office or principal office of the charity.

(2) Where any such notice required to be given as aforesaid is given by post, it shall be deemed to have been given by the time at which the letter containing it would be delivered in the ordinary course of post.

(3) No notice required to be given as aforesaid of any meeting or election need be given to any charity trustee, member or subscriber, if in the list above mentioned he has no address in the United Kingdom.

82. Manner of executing instruments

(1) Charity trustees may, subject to the trusts of the charity, confer on **1D–081**
any of their body (not being less than two in number) a general authority, or an authority limited in such manner as the trustees think fit, to execute in the names and on behalf of the trustees assurances or other deeds or instruments for giving effect to transactions to which the trustees are a party; and any deed or instrument executed in pursuance of an authority so given shall be of the same effect as if executed by the whole body.

(2) An authority under subsection (1) above—

(a) shall suffice for any deed or instrument if it is given in writing or by resolution of a meeting of the trustees, notwithstanding the want of any formality that would be required in giving an authority apart from that subsection;

(b)   may be given so as to make the powers conferred exercisable by any of the trustees, or may be restricted to named persons or in any other way;

(c)   subject to any such restriction, and until it is revoked, shall, notwithstanding any change in the charity trustees, have effect as a continuing authority given by the charity trustees from time to time of the charity and exercisable by such trustees.

(3) In any authority under this section to execute a deed or instrument in the names and on behalf of charity trustees there shall, unless the contrary intention appears, be implied authority also to execute it for them in the name and on behalf of the official custodian or of any other person, in any case in which the charity trustees could do so.

(4) Where a deed or instrument purports to be executed in pursuance of this section, then in favour of a person who (then or afterwards) in good faith acquires for money or money's worth an interest in or charge on property or the benefit of any covenant or agreement expressed to be entered into by the charity trustees, it shall be conclusively presumed to have been duly executed by virtue of this section.

(5) The powers conferred by this section shall be in addition to and not in derogation of any other powers.

83. Transfer and evidence of title to property vested in trustees

1D–082   (1) Where, under the trusts of a charity, trustees of property held for the purposes of the charity may be appointed or discharged by resolution of a meeting of the charity trustees, members or other persons, a memorandum declaring a trustee to have been so appointed or discharged shall be sufficient evidence of that fact if the memorandum is signed either at the meeting by the person presiding or in some other manner directed by the meeting and is attested by two persons present at the meeting.

(2) A memorandum evidencing the appointment or discharge of a trustee under subsection (1) above, if executed as a deed, shall have the like operation under section 40 of the Trustee Act 1925 (which relates to vesting declarations as respects trust property in deeds appointing or discharging trustees) as if the appointment or discharge were effected by the deed.

(3) For the purposes of this section, where a document purports to have been signed and attested as mentioned in subsection (1) above, then on proof (whether by evidence or as a matter of presumption) of the signature the document shall be presumed to have been so signed and attested, unless the contrary is shown.

(4) This section shall apply to a memorandum made at any time, except that subsection (2) shall apply only to those made after the commencement of the Charities Act 1960.

(5) This section shall apply in relation to any institution to which the Literary and Scientific Institutions Act 1854 applies as it applies in relation to a charity.

PART X

SUPPLEMENTARY

84. Supply by Commissioners of copies of documents open to public inspection

The Commissioners shall, at the request of any person, furnish him with copies of, or extracts from, any document in their possession which is for the time being open to inspection under Parts II to VI of this Act.

1D–083

85. Fees and other amounts payable to Commissioners

(1) The Secretary of State may by regulations require the payment to the Commissioners of such fees as may be prescribed by the regulations in respect of—

1D–084

(a) the discharge by the Commissioners of such functions under the enactments relating to charities as may be so prescribed;
(b) the inspection of the register of charities or of other material kept by them under those enactments, or the furnishing of copies of or extracts from documents so kept.

(2) Regulations under this section may—

(a) confer, or provide for the conferring of, exemptions from liability to pay a prescribed fee;
(b) provide for the remission or refunding of a prescribed fee (in whole or in part) in circumstances prescribed by the regulations.

(3) Any regulations under this section which require the payment of a fee in respect of any matter for which no fee was previously payable shall not be made unless a draft of the regulations has been laid before and approved by a resolution of each House of Parliament.

(4) The Commissioners may impose charges of such amounts as they consider reasonable in respect of the supply of any publications produced by them.

(5) Any fees and other payments received by the Commissioners by virtue of this section shall be paid into the Consolidated Fund.

86. Regulations and orders

(1) Any regulations or order of the Secretary of State under this Act—

1D–085

(a) shall be made by statutory instrument; and
(b) (subject to subsection (2) below) shall be subject to annulment in pursuance of a resolution of either House of Parliament.

(2) Subsection (1)(b) above does not apply—

    (a)   to an order under section 17(2), [. . .]¹ or 99(2); [or]²
        [. . .]³

    (c)   to any regulations to which section 85(3) applies.

(3) Any regulations of the Secretary of State or the Commissioners and any order of the Secretary of State under this Act may make—

    (a)   different provision for different cases; and
    (b)   such supplemental, incidental, consequential or transitional provision or savings as the Secretary of State or, as the case may be, the Commissioners consider appropriate.

(4) Before making any regulations under section 42, 44 or 45 above the Secretary of State shall consult such persons or bodies of persons as he considers appropriate.

¹ Repealed by Trustees Act 2000 (c.29), Sch.2, PtI, Para.2(2)(a), 3.
² Inserted by Trustees Act 2000 (c.29), Sch.2, PtI, Para.2(2)(b).
³ Repealed by Trustee Act 2000 (c.29), Sch.2, PtI, Para.2(2)(a).

87. Enforcement of requirements by order of Commissioners

1D–086   (1) If a person fails to comply with any requirement imposed by or under this Act then (subject to subsection (2) below) the Commissioners may by order give him such directions as they consider appropriate for securing that the default is made good.

(2) Subsection (1) above does not apply to any such requirement if—

    (a)   a person who fails to comply with, or is persistently in default in relation to, the requirement is liable to any criminal penalty; or
    (b)   the requirement is imposed—
        (i)   by an order of the Commissioners to which section 88 below applies, or
        (ii) by a direction of the Commissioners to which that section applies by virtue of section 90(2) below.

88. Enforcement of orders of Commissioners

1D–087   A person guilty of disobedience—

    (a)   to an order of the Commissioners under section 9(1), 44(2), 61, 73 or 80 above; or
    (b)   to an order of the Commissioners under section 16 or 18 above requiring a transfer of property or payment to be called for or made; or
    (c)   to an order of the Commissioners requiring a default under this Act to be made good;

may on the application of the Commissioners to the High Court be dealt with as for disobedience to an order of the High Court.

89. Other provisions as to orders of Commissioners

(1) Any order made by the Commissioners under this Act may include   **1D–088**
such incidental or supplementary provisions as the Commissioners think
expedient for carrying into effect the objects of the order, and where the
Commissioners exercise any jurisdiction to make such an order on an
application or reference to them, they may insert any such provisions in
the order notwithstanding that the application or reference does not
propose their insertion.

(2) Where the Commissioners make an order under this Act, then (without prejudice to the requirements of this Act where the order is subject to
appeal) they may themselves give such public notice as they think fit of the
making or contents of the order, or may require it to be given by any person on whose application the order is made or by any charity affected by
the order.

(3) The Commissioners at any time within twelve months after they
have made an order under any provision of this Act other than section
61 if they are satisfied that the order was made by mistake or on misrepresentation or otherwise than in conformity with this Act, may with
or without any application or reference to them discharge the order in
whole or in part, and subject or not to any savings or other transitional
provisions.

(4) Except for the purposes of subsection (3) above or of an appeal
under this Act, an order made by the Commissioners under this Act shall
be deemed to have been duly and formally made and not be called in question on the ground only of irregularity or informality, but (subject to any
further order) have effect according to its tenor.

90. Directions of the Commissioners

(1) Any direction given by the Commissioners under any provision   **1D–089**
contained in this Act—

    (a)   may be varied or revoked by a further direction given under that
           provision; and
    (b)   shall be given in writing.

(2) Sections 88 and 89(1), (2) and (4) above shall apply to any such
directions as they apply to an order of the Commissioners.

(3) In subsection (1) above the reference to the Commissioners
includes, in relation to a direction under subsection (3) of section 8
above, a reference to any person conducting an inquiry under that
section.

(4) Nothing in this section shall be read as applying to any directions
contained in an order made by the Commissioners under section 87(1)
above.

91. Service of orders and directions

(1) This section applies to any order or direction made or given by the   **1D–090**
Commissioners under this Act.

(2) An order or direction to which this section applies may be served on
a person (other than a body corporate)—

(a) by delivering it to that person;

(b) by leaving it at his last known address in the United Kingdom; or

(c) by sending it by post to him at that address.

(3) An order or direction to which this section applies may be served on a body corporate by delivering it or sending it by post—

(a) to the registered or principal office of the body in the United Kingdom, or

(b) if it has no such office in the United Kingdom, to any place in the United Kingdom where it carries on business or conducts its activities (as the case may be).

(4) Any such order or direction may also be served on a person (including a body corporate) by sending it by post to that person at an address notified by that person to the Commissioners for the purposes of this subsection.

(5) In this section any reference to the Commissioners includes, in relation to a direction given under subsection (3) of section 8 above, a reference to any person conducting an inquiry under that section.

92. Appeals from Commissioners

1D–091

(1) Provision shall be made by rules of court for regulating appeals to the High Court under this Act against orders or decisions of the Commissioners.

(2) On such an appeal the Attorney General shall be entitled to appear and be heard, and such other persons as the rules allow or as the court may direct.

93. Miscellaneous provisions as to evidence

1D–092

(1) Where, in any proceedings to recover or compel payment of any rentcharge or other periodical payment claimed by or on behalf of a charity out of land or of the rents, profits or other income of land, otherwise than as rent incident to a reversion, it is shown that the rentcharge or other periodical payment has at any time been paid for twelve consecutive years to or for the benefit of the charity, that shall be prima facie evidence of the perpetual liability to it of the land or income, and no proof of its origin shall be necessary.

(2) In any proceedings, the following documents, that is to say,—

(a) the printed copies of the reports of the Commissioners for enquiring concerning charities, 1818 to 1837, who were appointed under the Act 58 Geo. 3. c. 91 and subsequent Acts; and

(b) the printed copies of the reports which were made for various counties and county boroughs to the Charity Commissioners by their assistant commissioners and presented to the House of Commons as returns to orders of various dates beginning with 8th December 1890, and ending with 9th September 1909,

shall be admissible as evidence of the documents and facts stated in them.

(3) Evidence of any order, certificate or other document issued by the Commissioners may be given by means of a copy retained by them, or taken from a copy so retained, and certified to be a true copy by any officer of the Commissioners generally or specially authorised by them to act for this purpose; and a document purporting to be such a copy shall be received in evidence without proof of the official position, authority or handwriting of the person certifying it.

94. Restriction on institution of proceedings for certain offences

(1) No proceedings for an offence under this Act to which this section applies shall be instituted except by or with the consent of the Director of Public Prosecutions.

1D–093

(2) This section applies to any offence under—

   (a)   section 5;
   (b)   section 11;
   (c)   section 18(14);
   (d)   section 49; or
   (e)   section 73(1).

95. Offences by bodies corporate

Where any offence under this Act is committed by a body corporate and is proved to have been committed with the consent or connivance of, or to be attributable to any neglect on the part of, any director, manager, secretary or other similar officer of the body corporate, or any person who was purporting to act in any such capacity, he as well as the body corporate shall be guilty of that offence and shall be liable to be proceeded against and punished accordingly.

1D–094

In relation to a body corporate whose affairs are managed by its members, "director" means a member of the body corporate.

96. Construction of references to a "charity" or to particular classes of charity

(1) In this Act, except in so far as the context otherwise requires—
"charity" means any institution, corporate or not, which is established for charitable purposes and is subject to the control of the High Court in the exercise of the court's jurisdiction with respect to charities;
"ecclesiastical charity" has the same meaning as in the Local Government Act 1894;
"exempt charity" means (subject to section 24(8) above) a charity comprised in Schedule 2 to this Act;
"local charity" means, in relation to any area, a charity established for purposes which are by their nature or by the trusts of the charity directed wholly or mainly to the benefit of that area or of part of it;
"parochial charity" means, in relation to any parish or (in Wales) community, a charity the benefits of which are, or the separate distribution of the benefits of which is, confined to inhabitants of the parish or community, or of a single ancient ecclesiastical parish which included that parish or community or part of it, or of an area consisting of that

1D–095

parish or community with not more than four neighbouring parishes or communities.

(2) The expression "charity" is not in this Act applicable—

(a) to any ecclesiastical corporation (that is to say, any corporation in the Church of England, whether sole or aggregate, which is established for spiritual purposes) in respect of the corporate property of the corporation, except to a corporation aggregate having some purposes which are not ecclesiastical in respect of its corporate property held for those purposes; or

(b) to any Diocesan Board of Finance [or any subsidiary thereof][1] within the meaning of the Endowments and Glebe Measure 1976 for any diocese in respect of the diocesan glebe land of that diocese within the meaning of that Measure; or

(c) to any trust of property for purposes for which the property has been consecrated.

(3) A charity shall be deemed for the purposes of this Act to have a permanent endowment unless all property held for the purposes of the charity may be expended for those purposes without distinction between capital and income, and in this Act "permanent endowment" means, in relation to any charity, property held subject to a restriction on its being expended for the purposes of the charity.

(4) References in this Act to a charity whose income from all sources does not in aggregate amount to more than a specified amount shall be construed—

(a) by reference to the gross revenues of the charity, or

(b) if the Commissioners so determine, by reference to the amount which they estimate to be the likely amount of those revenues,

but without (in either case) bringing into account anything for the yearly value of land occupied by the charity apart from the pecuniary income (if any) received from that land; and any question as to the application of any such reference to a charity shall be determined by the Commissioners, whose decision shall be final.

(5) The Commissioners may direct that for all or any of the purposes of this Act an institution established for any special purposes of or in connection with a charity (being charitable purposes) shall be treated as forming part of that charity or as forming a distinct charity.

[(6) The Commissioners may direct that for all or any of the purposes of this Act two or more charities having the same charity trustees shall be treated as a single charity.][2]

[1] Substituted by the Church of England (Miscellaneous Provisions) Measure 2000, s.11.
[2] Substituted by Charities (Amendment) Act (1995 c.48), s.1.

97. General interpretation

1D–096   (1) In this Act, except in so far as the context otherwise requires—

"charitable purposes" means purposes which are exclusively charitable according to the law of England and Wales;

"charity trustees" means the persons having the general control and management of the administration of a charity;

"the Commissioners" means the Charity Commissioners for England and Wales;

"company" means a company formed and registered under the Companies Act 1985 or to which the provisions of that Act apply as they apply to such a company;

"the court" means the High Court and, within the limits of its jurisdiction, any other court in England and Wales having a jurisdiction in respect of charities concurrent (within any limit of area or amount) with that of the High Court, and includes any judge or officer of the court exercising the jurisdiction of the court;

"financial year" —

    (a)   in relation to a charity which is a company, shall be construed in accordance with section 223 of the Companies Act 1985; and

    (b)   in relation to any other charity, shall be construed in accordance with regulations made by virtue of section 42(2) above;

but this definition is subject to the transitional provisions in section 99(4) below and Part II of Schedule 8 to this Act;

"gross income", in relation to charity, means its gross recorded income from all sources including special trusts;

"independent examiner", in relation to a charity, means such a person as is mentioned in section 43(3)(a) above;

"institution" includes any trust or undertaking;

"the official custodian" means the official custodian for charities;

"permanent endowment" shall be construed in accordance with section 96(3) above;

"the register" means the register of charities kept under section 3 above and "registered"shall be construed accordingly;

"special trust" means property which is held and administered by or on behalf of a charity for any special purposes of the charity, and is so held and administered on separate trusts relating only to that property but a special trust shall not, by itself, constitute a charity for the purposes of Part VI of this Act;

"trusts" in relation to a charity, means the provisions establishing it as a charity and regulating its purposes and administration, whether those provisions take effect by way of trust or not, and in relation to other institutions has a corresponding meaning.

(2) In this Act, except in so far as the context otherwise requires, "document" includes information recorded in any form, and, in relation to information recorded otherwise than in legible form—

    (a)   any reference to its production shall be construed as a reference to the furnishing of a copy of it in legible form; and

    (b)   any reference to the furnishing of a copy of, or extract from, it shall accordingly be construed as a reference to the furnishing of a copy of, or extract from, it in legible form.

(3) No vesting or transfer of any property in pursuance of any provision of Part IV or IX of this Act shall operate as a breach of a covenant or condition against alienation or give rise to a forfeiture.

98. Consequential amendments and repeals

1D–097
(1) The enactments mentioned in Schedule 6 to this Act shall be amended as provided in that Schedule.

(2) The enactments mentioned in Schedule 7 to this Act are hereby repealed to the extent specified in the third column of the Schedule.

99. Commencement and transitional provisions

1D–098
(1) Subject to subsection (2) below this Act shall come into force on 1st August 1993.

(2) Part VI, section 69 and paragraph 21(3) of Schedule 6 shall not come into force until such day as the Secretary of State may by order appoint; and different days may be appointed for different provisions or different purposes.

(3) Until the coming into force of all the provisions mentioned in subsection (2) above the provisions mentioned in Part I of Schedule 8 to this Act shall continue in force notwithstanding their repeal.

(4) Part II of Schedule 8 to this Act shall have effect until the coming into force of the first regulations made by virtue of section 42(2) above for determining the financial year of a charity for the purposes of the provisions mentioned in that Part.

100. Short title and extent

1D–099
(1) This Act may be cited as the Charities Act 1993.

(2) Subject to subsection (3) to (6) below, this Act extends only to England and Wales.

(3) Section 10 above and this section extend to the whole of the United Kingdom.

(4) Section 15(2) extends also to Northern Ireland.

(5) Sections 70 and 71 and so much of section 86 as relates to those sections extend also to Scotland.

(6) The amendments in Schedule 6 and the repeals in Schedule 7 have the same extent as the enactments to which they refer and section 98 above extends accordingly.

SCHEDULE 1

Constitution etc. of Charity Commisioners

Para 1

1D–100
(1) There shall be a Chief Charity Commissioner and two other commissioners.

(2) Two at least of the commissioners shall be persons who have a seven year general qualification within the meaning of section 71 of the Courts and Legal Services Act 1990.

(3) The chief commissioner and the other commissioners shall be appointed by the Secretary of State, and shall be deemed for all purposes to be employed in the civil service of the Crown.

(4) There may be paid to each of the commissioners such salary and allowances as the Secretary of State may with the approval of the Treasury determine.

(5) If at any time it appears to the Secretary of State that there should be more than three commissioners, he may with the approval of the Treasury appoint not more than two additional commissioners.

Para 2

(1) The chief commissioner may, with the approval of the Treasury as to number and conditions of service, appoint such assistant commissioners and other officers and such employees as he thinks necessary for the proper discharge of the functions of the Commissioners and of the official custodian.   **1D–101**

(2) There may be paid to officers and employees so appointed such salaries or remuneration as the Treasury may determine.

Para 3

(1) The Commissioners may use an official seal for the authentication of documents, and their seal shall be officially and judicially noticed.   **1D–102**

(2) The Documentary Evidence Act 1868, as amended by the Documentary Evidence Act 1882, shall have effect as if in the Schedule to the Act of 1868 the Commissioners were included in the first column and any commissioner or assistant commissioner and any officer authorised to act on behalf of the Commissioners were mentioned in the second column.

(3) The Commissioners shall have power to regulate their own procedure and, subject to any such regulations and to any directions of the chief commissioner, any one commissioner or any assistant commissioner may act for and in the name of the Commissioners.

(4) Where the Commissioners act as a board, then—

(a)   if not more than four commissioners hold office for the time being, the quorum shall be two commissioners (of whom at least one must be a person having a qualification such as is mentioned in paragraph 1(2) above); and

(b)   if five commissioners so hold office, the quorum shall be three commissioners (of whom at least one must be a person having such a qualification);

and in the case of an equality of votes the chief commissioner or in his absence the commissioner presiding shall have a second or casting vote.

(5) The Commissioners shall have power to act notwithstanding any vacancy in their number.

(6) It is hereby declared that the power of a commissioner or assistant commissioner to act for and in the name of the Commissioners in accordance with sub-paragraph (3) above may, in particular, be exercised in relation to functions of the Commissioners under sections 8, 18, 19 and 63 of this Act, including functions under sections 8, 18 and 19 as applied by section 80(1).

Para 4

Legal proceedings may be instituted by or against the Commissioners by the name of the Charity Commissioners for England and Wales, and shall not abate or be affected by any change in the persons who are the commissioners.   **1D–103**

SCHEDULE 2

Exempt Charities

Para 1

1D–104   The following institutions, so far as they are charities, are exempt charities within the meaning of this Act, that is to say—

   (a)   any institution which, if the Charities Act 1960 had not been passed, would be exempted from the powers and jurisdiction, under the Charitable Trusts Acts 1853 to 1939, of the Commissioners or Minister of Education (apart from any power of the Commissioners or Minister to apply those Acts in whole or in part to charities otherwise exempt) by the terms of any enactment not contained in those Acts other than section 9 of the Places of Worship Registration Act 1855;

   (b)   the universities of Oxford, Cambridge, London, Durham and Newcastle, the colleges and halls in the universities of Oxford, Cambridge, Durham and Newcastle, Queen Mary and Westfield College in the University of London and the colleges of Winchester and Eton;

   (c)   any university, university college, or institution connected with a university or university college, which Her Majesty declares by Order in Council to be an exempt charity for the purposes of this Act;

   (d)   [. . .][1];

   [(da) the Qualifications and Curriculum Authority;][2]

   (e)   [. . .][3];

   [(f)   the Qualifications, Curriculum and Assessment Authority for Wales;][4]

   (g)   [. . .][5];

   (h)   [. . .][6];

   (i)   a successor company to a higher education corporation (within the meaning of section 129(5) of the Education Reform Act 1988) at a time when an institution conducted by the company is for the time being designated under that section;

   (j)   [. . .][7];

   (k)   the Board of Trustees of the Victoria and Albert Museum;

   (l)   the Board of Trustees of the Science Museum;

   (m)   the Board of Trustees of the Armouries;

   (n)   the Board of Trustees of the Royal Botanic Gardens, Kew;

   (o)   the Board of Trustees of the National Museums and Galleries on Merseyside;

   (p)   the trustees of the British Museum and the trustees of the Natural History Museum;

   (q)   the Board of Trustees of the National Gallery;

   (r)   the Board of Trustees of the Tate Gallery;

   (s)   the Board of Trustees of the National Portrait Gallery;

   (t)   the Board of Trustees of the Wallace Collection;

   (u)   the Trustees of the Imperial War Museum;

   (v)   the Trustees of the National Maritime Museum;

   (w)   any institution which is administered by or on behalf of an institution included above and is established for the general purposes of, or for any special purpose of or in connection with, the last-mentioned institution;

   (x)   the Church Commissioners and any institution which is administered by them;

   (y)   any registered society within the meaning of the Industrial and Provident Societies Act 1965 and any registered society or branch within the meaning of the Friendly Societies Act 1974;

   (z)   the Board of Governors of the Museum of London;

   (za)   the British Library Board.

   [(zb) the National Lottery Charities Board.][8]

[1] Paragraph (d) repealed by School Standards and Framework Act (1998 c.31), Sch.31, Para.1.
[2] Substituted by Education Act 1997, s.57(1), Sch.7, Para.7(a).
[3] Repealed by Education Act 1996, s.582(2), Sch.38, Pt 1.
[4] Substituted by Education Act 1997, s.57(1), Sch.7, Para.7(b).
[5] Repealed by Education Act 1996, s.582(2), Sch.38, Pt 1.
[6] Repealed by Teaching and Higher Education Act 1998, s.140(3), Sch.31.
[7] Repealed by Teaching and Higher Education Act 1998, s.140(3), Sch.31.
[8] Added by National Lottery etc Act 1993, s.37(2), Sch.5, Para.12.

SCHEDULE 3

Enlargement of Areas of Local Charities

Para 1

Existing area	Permissible enlargement	
1. Greater London	Any area comprising Greater London.	**1D–105**
2. Any area in Greater London and not in, or partly in, the City of London.	(i) Any area in Greater London and not in, or partly in, the City of London; (ii) the area of Greater London exclusive of the City of London; (iii) any area comprising the area of Greater London, exclusive of the City of London; (iv) any area partly in Greater London and partly in any adjacent parish or parishes (civil or ecclesiastical), and not partly in the City of London.	
3. A district	Any area comprising the district	
[3A. A Welsh county or county borough	Any area comprising that county or county borough.][1]	
4. Any area in a district	(i) Any area in the district; (ii) the district; (iii) any area comprising the district;(iv) any area partly in the district and partly in any adjacent district or in any adjacent Welsh county or county borough.	
[4A. Any area in a Welsh county or county borough	(i) Any area in the county or county borough (ii) the county or county borough; (iii) any area comprising the county or county borough; (iv) any area partly in the county or county borough and partly in any adjacent Welsh county or county borough or in any adjacent district.][2]	
5. A parish (civil or ecclesiastical), or two or more parishes, or an area in a parish, or partly in each of two or more parishes.	Any area not extending beyond the parish or or parishes comprising or adjacent to the area in column 1.	
6. In Wales, a community, or two or more communities, or an area in a community, or partly in each of two or more communities.	Any area not extending beyond the community or communities comprising or adjacent to the area in column 1.	

[1] Entry inserted by Local Government (Wales) Act 1994, s.66(6), Sch.16, Para.101 (5).
[2] Entry inserted by Local Government (Wales) Act (1994 c.19), s.66(6), Sch.16, Para.101 (5).

SCHEDULE 4

Court's Jurisdiction Over Certain Charities Governed by or Under Statute

Para 1

1D–106   The court may by virtue of section 15(3) of this Act exercise its jurisdiction with respect to charities—

(a) in relation to charities established or regulated by any provision of the Seamen's Fund Winding-up Act 1851 which is repealed by the Charities Act 1960;

(b) in relation to charities established or regulated by schemes under the Endowed Schools Act 1869 to 1948, or section 75 of the Elementary Education Act 1870 or by schemes given effect under section 2 of the Education Act 1973[or section 554 of the Education Act 1996][1];

(c) [. . .][2]

(d) in relation to fuel allotments, that is to say, land which, by any enactment relating to inclosure or any instrument having effect under such an enactment, is vested in trustees upon trust that the land or the rents and profits of the land shall be used for the purpose of providing poor persons with fuel;

(e) in relation to charities established or regulated by any provision of the Municipal Corporations Act 1883 which is repealed by the Charities Act 1960 or by any scheme having effect under any such provision;

(f) in relation to charities regulated by schemes under the London Government Act 1899;

(g) in relation to charities established or regulated by orders or regulations under section 2 of the Regimental Charitable Funds Act 1935;

(h) in relation to charities regulated by section 79 of this Act, or by any such order as is mentioned in that section.

Para 2

1D–107   Notwithstanding anything in section 19 of the Commons Act 1876 a scheme for the administration of a fuel allotment (within the meaning of the foregoing paragraph) may provide—

(a) for the sale or letting of the allotment or any part thereof, for the discharge of the land sold or let from any restrictions as to the use thereof imposed by or under any enactment relating to inclosure and for the application of the sums payable to the trustees of the allotment in respect of the sale or lease; or

(b) for the exchange of the allotment or any part thereof for other land, for the discharge as aforesaid of the land given in exchange by the said trustees, and for the application of any money payable to the said trustees for equality of exchange; or

(c) for the use of the allotment or any part thereof for any purposes specified in the scheme.

[1] Words inserted by Education Act 1996, Sch.37, Pt I.

[2] Repealed by Statute Law (Repeals) Act 1993, s.1(1), Sch.1.

SCHEDULE 5

Meaning of "Connected Person" for Purposes of Section 36(2)

Para 1

In section 36(2) of this Act "connected person", in relation to a charity, means —   **1D–108**

    (a)   a charity trustee or trustee for the charity;

    (b)   a person who is the donor of any land to the charity (whether the gift was made on or after the establishment of the charity);

    (c)   a child, parent, grandchild, grandparent, brother or sister of any such trustee or donor;

    (d)   an officer, agent or employee of the charity;

    (e)   the spouse of any person falling within any of sub-paragraphs (a) to (d) above;

    (f)   an institution which is controlled—

        (i)   by any person falling within any of sub-paragraphs (a) to (e) above, or

        (ii)   by two or more such persons taken together; or

    (g)   a body corporate in which—

        (i)   any connected person falling within any of sub-paragraphs (a) to (f) above has a substantial interest, or

        (ii)   two or more such persons, taken together, have a substantial interest.

Para 2

(1) In paragraph 1(c) above "child" includes a stepchild and an illegitimate child.

(2) For the purposes of paragraph 1(e) above a person living with another as that person's husband or wife shall be treated as that person's spouse.

Para 3

For the purposes of paragraph 1(f) above a person controls an institution if he is able to secure that the affairs of the institution are conducted in accordance with his wishes.

Para 4

(1) For the purposes of paragraph 1(g) above any such connected person as is there mentioned has a substantial interest in a body corporate if the person or institution in question—

    (a)   is interested in shares comprised in the equity share capital of that body of a nominal value of more than one-fifth of that share capital, or

    (b)   is entitled to exercise, or control the exercise of, more than one-fifth of the voting power at any general meeting of that body.

(2) The rules set out in Part I of Schedule 13 to the Companies Act 1985 (rules for interpretation of certain provisions of that Act) shall apply for the purposes of sub-paragraph (1) above as they apply for the purposes of section 346(4) of that Act ("connected persons" etc).

(3) In this paragraph "equity share capital" and "share"have the same meaning as in that Act.

SCHEDULE 6

Consequential Amendments the Places of Worship Registration Act 1855 (C.81)

Para 1

1D–109   (1) Section 9 of the Places of Worship Registration Act 1855 shall be amended as follows.

(2) For "subsection (4) of section four of the Charities Act 1960" there shall be substituted "subsection (5) of section 3 of the Charities Act 1993".

(3) At the end there shall be added—

"(2) Section 89 of the said Act of 1993 (provisions as to orders under that Act) shall apply to any order under paragraph (b) above as it applies to orders under that Act."

The Open Spaces Act 1906 (C.25)

Para 2

1D–110   At the end of section 4 of the Open Spaces Act 1906 there shall be added—

"(4) Section 89 of the Charities Act 1993 (provisions as to orders under that Act) shall apply to any order of the Charity Commissioners under this section as it applies to orders made by them under that Act."

The New Parishes Measure 1943 (No. 1)

Para 3

1D–111   (1) The New Parishes Measure 1943 shall be amended as follows.

(2) In subsection (1)(b) of section 14 for "the Charities Act 1960" there shall be substituted "the Charities Act 1993".

(3) At the end of that section there shall be added—

"(4) Section 89 of the Charities Act 1993 (provisions as to orders under that Act) shall apply to any order under section (1)(b) above as it applies to orders under that Act."

(4) In section 31 for "the Charities Act 1960" there shall be substituted "the Charities Act 1993".

The Clergy Pensions Measure 1961 (No. 3)

Para 4

1D–112   In section 33 of the Clergy Pensions Measure 1961 for "section 32 of the Charities Act 1992" and "the Charities Act 1960" there shall be substituted respectively "section 36 of the Charities Act 1993" and "that Act".

The Finance Act 1963 (C.25)

Para 5

1D–113   [. . .]¹
¹ Repealed by Finance Act (1999 c.16), Sch.20 (V) (5), Para.1.

The Cathedrals Measure 1963 (No. 2)

Para 6

1D–114   (1) The Cathedrals Measure 1963 shall be amended as follows.

(2) In section 20(2)(iii) for "section 32 of the Charities Act 1992" there shall be substituted "section 36 of the Charities Act 1993".

(3) In section 51 for "the Charities Act 1960" there shall be substituted "the Charities Act 1993".

The Incumbents and Churchwardens (Trusts) Measure 1964 (No.2)

Para 7

In section 1 of the Incumbents and Churchwardens (Trusts) Measure 1964 for "subsection (3) of section forty-five of the Charities Act 1960" there shall be substituted "section 96(3) of the Charities Act 1993".   **1D–115**

The Leasehold Reform Act 1967 (C.88)

Para 8

In section 23(4) of the Leasehold Reform Act 1967 for "section 32 of the Charities Act 1992" there shall be substituted "section 36 of the Charities Act 1993".   **1D–116**

The Greater London Council (General Powers) Act 1968 (C.XXXIX)

Para 9

In section 43 of the Greater London Council (General Powers) Act 1968, in the definition of "night café", for "section 4 of the Charities Act 1960" and "subsection (4) thereof" there shall be substituted respectively "section 3 of the Charities Act 1993" and "subsection (5) thereof".   **1D–117**

The Reduntant Churches and Other Religious Buildings Act 1969 (C.22)

Para 10

(1) The Redundant Churches and other Religious Buildings Act 1969 shall be amended as follows.   **1D–118**

(2) In subsection (6) of section 4 for "section 18 of the Charities Act 1960" there shall be substituted "section 16 of the Charities Act 1993".

(3) In subsection (7) of that section for "subsection (4) of section 18 of that Act" there shall be substituted "subsection (4) of section 16 of that Act".

(4) In subsection (8) of that section for "section 18 of the Charities Act 1960" and (where next occurring) "section 18" there shall be substituted respectively "section 16 of the Charities Act 1993" and "section 16" and for "section 21" there shall be substituted "section 20".

(5) In subsection (13) of that section for "sections 45 and 46 of the Charities Act 1960" there shall be substituted "sections 96 and 97 of the Charities Act 1993".

(6) In section 7(2) for "the Charities Act 1960" and "section 23" there shall be substituted respectively "the Charities Act 1993" and "section 26".

The Sharing of Church Buildings Act 1969 (C.38)

Para 11

(1) The Sharing of Church Buildings Act 1969 shall be amended as follows.   **1D–119**

(2) In section 2(4) for "the Charities Act 1960" there shall be substituted "the Charities Act 1993".

(3) In subsection (1) of section 8 for "the Charities Act 1960" there shall be substituted "the Charities Act 1993".

(4) In subsection (2) of that section for "section 45(2) of the Charities Act 1960" there shall be substituted "section 96(2) of the Charities Act 1993".

(5) In subsection (3) of that section for " Section 32 of the Charities Act 1992" there shall be substituted "Section 36 of the Charities Act 1993".

The Local Government Act 1972 (C.70)

Para 12

1D–120

(1) The Local Government Act 1972 shall be amended as follows.

(2) In sections 11(3)(c) and 29(3)(c) for "section 37 of the Charities Act 1960" there shall be substituted "section 79 of the Charities Act 1993".

(3) In sections 123(6) and 127(4) for "the Charities Act 1960" there shall be substituted "the Charities Act 1993".

(4) In section 131(3) for "section 32 of the Charities Act 1992" and "section 32(9)(a) of that Act" there shall be substituted respectively "section 36 of the Charities Act 1993" and "section 36(9)(a) of that Act".

The Fire Precautions (Loans) Act 1973 (C.11)

Para 13

1D–121

In section 1(7) of the Fire Precautions (Loans) Act 1973 for "Section 34 of the Charities Act 1992" there shall be substituted "Section 38 of the Charities Act 1993".

The Theatres Trust Act 1976 (C.27)

Para 14

In section 2(2)(d) of the Theatres Trust Act 1976 for "sections 32 and 34 of the Charities Act 1992" there shall be substituted "sections 36 and 38 of the Charities Act 1993".

The Interpretation Act 1978 (C.30)

Para 15

1D–122

In Schedule 1 to the Interpretation Act 1978, in the definition of "Charity Commissioners" for "section 1 of the Charities Act 1960" there shall be substituted "section 1 of the Charities Act 1993".

The Reserve Forces Act 1980 (C.9)

Para 16

1D–123

[. . .] [1]

[1] Repealed by Reserve Forces Act (1996 c.14), Sch.11, Para.1.

The Disused Burial Grounds (Amendment) Act 1981 (C.18)

Para 17

1D–124

In section 6 of the Disused Burial Grounds (Amendment) Act 1981 for "section 13(5) of the Charities Act 1960" there shall be substituted "section 13(5) of the Charities Act 1993".

The Pastoral Measure 1983 (No. 1)

Para 18

(1) The Pastoral Measure 1983 shall be amended as follows.   **1D–125**

(2) In section 55(1) for "the Charities Act 1960" and "section 45(2)(b)" there shall be substituted "the Charities Act 1993" and "section 96(2)(c)".

(3) In section 63(3) for "the Charities Act 1960" there shall be substituted "the Charities Act 1993".

(4) In section 87(1) for "section 45 of the Charities Act 1960" there shall be substituted "section 96 of the Charities Act 1993".

(5) In paragraphs 11(6) and 16(1)(e) of Schedule 3 for "section 18 of the Charities Act 1960" there shall be substituted "section 16 of the Charities Act 1993".

The Rates Act 1984 (C.33)

Para 19

In section 3(9) of the Rates Act 1984 for "section 4 of the Charities Act 1960"   **1D–122** there shall be substituted "section 3 of the Charities Act 1993".

The Companies Act 1985 (C.6)

(1) The Companies Act 1985 shall be amended as follows.   **1D–123**

(2) In sections 35(4) and 35A(6) for "section 30B(1) of the Charities Act 1960" there shall be substituted "section 65(1) of the Charities Act 1993".

(3) In section 209(1)(c) and paragraph 11(b) of Schedule 13 after "the Charities Act 1960" there shall be inserted "or section 24 or 25 of the Charities Act 1993".

The Housing Associations Act 1985 (C.69)

(1) The Housing Associations Act 1985 shall be amended as follows.   **1D–124**

(2) In section 10(1) for "sections 32 and 34 of the Charities Act 1992" there shall be substituted "sections 36 and 38 of the Charities Act 1993".

(4) In section 35(2)(c) for "section 32 of the Charities Act 1992" there shall be substituted "section 36 of the Charities Act 1993".

(5) In section 38—

(a) in paragraph (a) for "the Charities Act 1960" there shall be substituted "the Charities Act 1993";

[. . .]¹

¹ Repealed by SI 1996/2325 (Housing Act 1996 (Consequential Provisions) Order), Sch.1 (1), Para.1.

The Financial Services Act 1986 (C.60)

Para 22

In section 45(1)(j) of the Financial Services Act 1986 after "the Charities Act   **1D–125** 1960" there shall be inserted ", section 24 or 25 of the Charities Act 1993".

The Coal Industry Act 1987 (C.3)

Para 23

(1) In section 5 of the Coal Industry Act 1987 for subsection (8) there shall be   **1D–126** substituted—

"(8) Sections 16(3), (9), (11) to (14), 17(1) to (5) and (7) and 20 of the Charities Act 1993 shall apply in relation to the powers of the Charity Commissioners and the making of schemes under this section as they apply in relation to their powers and the making of schemes under that Act and sections 89, 91 and 92 of that Act shall apply to orders and decisions under this section as they apply to orders and decisions under that Act."

(2) In subsection (8A) of that section for "section 29" (in both places) there shall be substituted "section 17".

The Reverter of Sites Act 1987 (C.15)

1D–127

Para 24

In section 4(4) of the Reverter of Sites Act 1987 for "sections 40, 40A and 42 of the Charities Act 1960" there shall be substituted "sections 89, 91 and 92 of the Charities Act 1993".

The Income and Corporation Taxes Act 1988 (C.1)

1D–128

Para 25

In Schedule 20 to the Income and Corporation Taxes Act 1988—

(a) in paragraph 3 after "the Charities Act 1960" there shall be inserted ", section 24 of the Charities Act 1993";

(b) in paragraph 3A after "the Charities Act 1960" there shall be inserted "or section 25 of the Charities Act 1993".

The Courts and Legal Services Act 1990 (C.41)

1D–129

Para 26

In Schedule 11 to the Courts and Legal Services Act 1990, in the reference to a Charity Commissioner, for "under the First Schedule to the Charities Act 1960" there shall be substituted "as provided in Schedule 1 to the Charities Act 1993".

The London Local Authorities Act 1990 (C.VII)

1D–130

Para 27

In section 4 of the London Local Authorities Act 1990, in the definition of "night café", for "section 4 of the Charities Act 1960" and "subsection (4) thereof" there shall be substituted respectively "section 3 of the Charities Act 1993" and "subsection (5) thereof".

The London Local Authorities Act 1991 (C.XIII)

1D–131

Para 28

In section 4 of the London Local Authorities Act 1991, in the definition of "establishment for special treatment", for "section 4 of the Charities Act 1960" and "subsection (4) of that section" there shall be substituted respectively "section 3 of the Charities Act 1993" and "subsection (5) of that section".

The Charities Act 1992 (C.41)

1D–132

Para 29

(1) The Charities Act 1992 shall be amended as follows.

(2) In section 29(2)(b) after "Act" there shall be inserted "or section 18 of the Charities Act 1993".

(3) In section 30(1)(b) after "Act" there shall be inserted "or section 22(1) of the Charities Act 1993".

(4) In section 30(3)(a) after "Act" there shall be inserted "or section 18 of the Charities Act 1993".

(5) In section 58(1), in the definition of "charity" for "the Charities Act 1960" there shall be substituted "the Charities Act 1993" and in the definition of "company" for the words after "section" there shall be substituted "97 of the Charities Act 1993".

(6) In section 63(2) for "section 4 of the Charities Act 1960" there shall be substituted "section 3 of the Charities Act 1993".

(7) In section 72 for subsection (5) there shall be substituted—

"(5) Section 89(1), (2) and (4) of the Charities Act 1993 (provisions as to orders made by the Commissioners) shall apply to an order made by them under this section as it applies to an order made by them under that Act.

(6) In this section "charity" and "charitable purposes" have the same meaning as in that Act."

(8) In section 74 after subsection (3) there shall be inserted—

"(3A) Any person who knowingly or recklessly provides the Commissioners with information which is false or misleading in a material particular shall be guilty of an offence if the information is provided in circumstances in which he intends, or could reasonably be expected to know, that it would be used by them for the purpose of discharging their functions under section 72.

(3B) A person guilty of an offence under subsection (3A) shall be liable—

    (a)   on summary conviction, to a fine not exceeding the statutory maximum;
    (b)   on conviction or indictment, to imprisonment for a term not exceeding two years or to a fine, or both."

Other Amendments

Para 30

In the following provisions for "the Charities Act 1960" there shall be substituted   **1D–133**
"the Charities Act 1993"—

The National Health Service Reorganisation Act 1973 section 30(5).
The Consumer Credit Act 1974 section 189(1).
The Rent (Agriculture) Act 1976 section 5(3)(f).
The Rent Act 1977 section 15(2)(b).
The National Health Service Act 1977 section 96(2).
The Dioceses Measure 1978 section 19(4).
The Ancient Monuments and Archaeological Areas Act 1979 section 49(3).
The Greater London Council (General Powers) Act 1984 section 10(2)(n).
The Local Government Act 1985 section 90(4).
The Housing Act 1985 sections 525 and 622.
The Landlord and Tenant Act 1987 section 60(1).
The Education Reform Act 1988 sections 128(5) and 192(11).
The Copyright, Designs and Patents Act 1988 Schedule 6 paragraph 7.
The Housing Act 1988 Schedule 2 Part I Ground 6.
The University of Wales College of Cardiff Act 1988 section 9.
The Imperial College Act 1988 section 10.
[. . .][1]

[1] Words repealed by Housing Grants, Construction and Regeneration Act (1996 c.53), Sch.3 (I), Para.1.

SCHEDULE 7

Repeals

Section 98(2)

1D–134

Chapter	Short title	Extent of repeal
35 & 36 Vic. c.24.	The Charitable Trustees Incorporation Act 1872.	The whole Act so far as unrepealed.
10 & 11 Geo.5. c.16.	The Imperial War Museum Act 1920.	Section 5.
24 & 25 Geo.5. c.43.	The National Maritime Museum Act 1934.	Section 7.
8 & 9 Eliz.2 c.58.	The Charities Act 1960	The whole Act so far as unrepealed except— section 28(9) section 35(6) section 38(3) to (5) section 39(2) sections 48 and 49 Schedule 6.
1963 c.33.	The London Government Act 1963.	Section 81(9)(b) and (c).
1963 c.xi.	The Universities of Durham and Newcastle-upon-Tyne Act 1963.	Section 10.
1965 c.17.	The Museum of London Act 1965.	Section 11.
1972 c.54.	The British Library Act 1972.	Section 4(2).
1972 c.70.	The Local Government Act 1972.	Section 210(9).
1973 c.16.	The Education Act 1973.	In section 2(7) the words from "but" onwards. In Schedule 1, paragraph 1(1) and (3).
1976 No.4.	The Endowments and Glebe Measure 1976.	Section 44.
1983 c.47.	The National Heritage Act 1983.	In Schedule 5, paragraph 4.
1985 c.9.	The Companies Consolidation (Consequential Provisions) Act 1985.	In Schedule 2 the entry relating to the Charities Act 1960.
1985 c.20.	The Charities Act 1985.	Section 1.
1986 c.60.	The Financial Services Act 1986.	In Schedule 16, paragraph 1.
1988 c.40.	The Education Reform Act 1988.	In Schedule 12, paragraphs 9, 10, 63 and 64.
1989 c.40.	The Companies Act 1989.	Section 111.
1989 c.xiii.	The Queen Mary and Westfield College Act 1989.	Section 10.

1990 c.41.	The Courts and Legal Services Act 1990.	In Schedule 10, paragraph 14.
1992 c.13.	The Further and Higher Education Act 1992.	In Schedule 8, paragraph 69.
1992 c.41.	The Charities Act 1992.	The whole of Part I except—section 1(1) and (4) sections 29 and 30 section 36 sections 49 and 50 Section 75(b). Section 76(1)(a). In section 77, subsections (2)(a), (b) and (c) and in subsection (4) the figures 20, 22 and 23. Section 79(4) and (5). Schedules 1 to 4. In Schedule 6, paragraph 13(2). In Schedule 7, the entries relating to section 8 of the Charities Act 1960 and (so far as not in force at the date specified in section 99(1) of this Act) the Charities Act 1985.
1992 c.44.	The Museums and Galleries Act 1992.	In Schedule 8, paragraphs 4 and 10. In Schedule 9, the entry relating to the Charities Act 1960.

SCHEDULE 8

Transitional Provisions

Part I

Provisions Applying Pending Coming Into Force of Part VI etc.

Para 1
In the Charities Act 1960—
section 8
section 32
Part V so far as relevant to those sections.

Para 2
In the Charities Act 1985
section 1
sections 6 and 7 so far as relevant to section 1.

Part II

Provisions Applying Pending Coming Into Force of Financial Year Regulations

Section 5
In section 5(1) of this Act "financial year"—

(a) in relation to a charity which is a company, shall be construed in accordance with section 223 of the Companies Act 1985;
(b) in relation to any other charity, means any period in respect of which an income and expenditure account is required to be prepared whether under section 32 of the Charities Act 1960 or by or under the authority of any other Act, whether that period is a year or not.

Sections 74 and 75

In sections 74(1)(a) and 75(1)(b) of this Act "financial year" means any period in respect of which an income and expenditure account is required to be prepared whether under section 32 of the Charities Act 1960 or by or under the authority of any other Act, whether that period is a year or not.

APPENDIX TWO

STATUTORY INSTRUMENTS

Charities (Qualified Surveyors' Reports) Regulations (SI 1992/ 2980)

(In force from January 1, 1993)

In exercise of the powers conferred upon me by sections 32(4) and 77(3) of the Charities Act 1992, I hereby make the following Regulations:

1—(1) These Regulations may be cited as the Charities (Qualified Surveyors' Reports) Regulations 1992 and shall come into force on 1st January 1993.

    2A–001

(2) In these Regulations—

"relevant land" means the land in respect of which a report is being obtained for the purposes of section 32(3) of the Charities Act 1992; and

"the surveyor" means the qualified surveyor from whom such a report is being obtained.

2—A report prepared for the purposes of section 32(3) of the Charities Act 1992 (requirements to be complied with in respect of the disposition of land held by or in trust for a charity otherwise than with an order of the court or of the Charity Commissioners or where section 32(5) of that Act applies) shall contain such information and deal with such matters as are prescribed by the Schedule to these Regulations (together with such other information and such other matters as the surveyor believes should be drawn to the attention of the charity trustees).

    2A–002

Kenneth Clarke

One of Her Majesty's Principal Secretaries of State

Home Office

29th November 1992

SCHEDULE 1 INFORMATION TO BE CONTAINED IN, AND MATTERS TO BE DEALT WITH BY,

Para 1

(1) A description of the relevant land and its location, to include—

(a) the measurements of the relevant land;
(b) its current use;
(c) the number of buildings (if any) included in the relevant land;
(d) the measurements of any such buildings; and
(e) the number of rooms in any such buildings and the measurements of those rooms.

(2) Where any information required by sub-paragraph (1) above may be clearly given by means of a plan, it may be so given and any such plan need not be drawn to scale.

Para 2

Whether the relevant land, or any part of it, is leased by or from the charity trustees and, if it is, details of—

(a) the length of the lease and the period of it which is outstanding;
(b) the rent payable under the lease;
(c) any service charge which is so payable;
(d) the provisions in the lease for any review of the rent payable under it or any service charge so payable;
(e) the liability under the lease for repairs and dilapidations; and
(f) any other provision in the lease which, in the opinion of the surveyor, affects the value of the relevant land.

Para 3

Whether the relevant land is subject to the burden of, or enjoys the benefit of, any easement or restrictive covenant or is subject to any annual or other periodic sum charged on or issuing out of the land except rent reserved by a lease or tenancy.

Para 4

Whether any buildings included in the relevant land are in good repair and, if not, the surveyor's advice—

(a) as to whether or not it would be in the best interests of the charity for repairs to be carried out prior to the proposed disposition;
(b) as to what those repairs, if any, should be; and
(c) as to the estimated cost of any repairs he advises.

Para 5

Where, in the opinion of the surveyor, it would be in the best interests of the charity to alter any buildings included in the relevant land prior to disposition (because, for example, adaptations to the buildings for their current use are not such as to command the best market price on the proposed disposition), that opinion and an estimate of the outlay required for any alterations which he suggests.

Para 6

Advice as to the manner of disposing of the relevant land so that the terms on which it is disposed of are the best that can reasonably be obtained for the charity, including—

    (a)   where appropriate, a recommendation that the land should be divided for the purposes of the disposition;

    (b)   unless the surveyor's advice is that it would not be in the best interests of the charity to advertise the proposed disposition, the period for which and the manner in which the proposed disposition should be advertised;

    (c)   where the surveyor's advice is that it would not be in the best interests of the charity to advertise the proposed disposition, his reasons for that advice (for example, that the proposed disposition is the renewal of a lease to someone who enjoys statutory protection or that he believes someone with a special interest in acquiring the relevant land will pay considerably more than the market price for it); and

    (d)   any view the surveyor may have on the desirability or otherwise of delaying the proposed disposition and, if he believes such delay is desirable, what the period of that delay should be.

Para 7

(1) Where the surveyor feels able to give such advice and where such advice is relevant, advice as to the chargeability or otherwise of value added tax on the proposed disposition and the effect of such advice on the valuations given under paragraph 8 below.

(2) Where either the surveyor does not feel able to give such advice or such advice is not in his opinion relevant, a statement to that effect.

Para 8

The surveyor's opinion as to—

    (a)   the current value of the relevant land having regard to its current state of repair and current circumstances (such as the presence of a tenant who enjoys statutory protection) or, where the proposed disposition is a lease, the rent which could be obtained under it having regard to such matters;

    (b)   what the value of the relevant land or what the rent under the proposed disposition would be-

        (i)   where he has given advice under paragraph 4 above, if that advice is followed; or

        (ii) where he has expressed an opinion under paragraph 5 above, if that opinion is acted upon; or

        (iii) if both that advice is followed and that opinion is acted upon;

    (c)   where he has made a recommendation under paragraph 6(a) above, the increase in the value of the relevant land or rent in respect of it if the recommendation were followed;

    (d)   where his advice is that it would not be in the best interests of the charity to advertise the proposed disposition because he believes a higher price can be obtained by not doing so, the

amount by which that price exceeds the price that could be obtained if the proposed disposition were advertised; and

(e) where he has advised a delay in the proposed disposition under paragraph 6(d) above, the amount by which he believes the price which could be obtained consequent on such a delay exceeds the price that could be obtained without it.

Para 9

Where the surveyor is of the opinion that the proposed disposition is not in the best interests of the charity because it is not a disposition that makes the best use of the relevant land, that opinion and the reasons for it, together with his advice as to the type of disposition which would constitute the best use of the land (including such advice as may be relevant as to the prospects of buying out any sitting tenant or of succeeding in an application for change of use of the land under the laws relating to town and country planning etc.)

Charities (Misleading Names) Regulations 1992
(SI 1992/1901)

(In force from September 1, 1992)

In exercise of the powers conferred upon me by section 4(2)(c) of the Charities act 1992,[1] I hereby make the following Regulations:

1. These Regulations may be cited as the Charities (Misleading Names) Regulations 1992 and shall come into force on September 1, 1992.

2. The words and expressions set out in the Schedule to these Regulations, together (where appropriate) with the plural and possessive forms of those words and expressions and any abbreviation of them, are hereby specified for the purposes of section 4(2)(c) of the Charities Act 1992.

Home Office

Kenneth Clarke

July 28, 1992

One of Her Majesty's Principal Secretaries of State

SCHEDULE

Regulation 2

2B–001

SPECIFICATION OF WORDS AND EXPRESSIONS FOR THE PURPOSES OF SECTION 4(2)(C) OF THE CHARITIES ACT 1992

Assurance	National
Authority	Nationwide
Bank	Northern Ireland
Benevolent	Northern Irish
British	Official
Building Society	Polytechnic
Church	Prince
Co-operative	Princess
England	Queen
English	Registered
Europe	Royal
European	Royale
Friendly Society	Royalty
Grant-Maintained	School
Great Britain	Scotland
Great British	Scottish
Her Majesty	Trade Union
His Majesty	United Kingdom
Industrial & Provident Society	University
International	Wales
Ireland	Welsh
Irish	Windsor
King	

[1] 1992, c.41.

Charities (Receiver and Manager)
Regulations 1992/2355

(In force from November 1, 1992)

In exercise of the powers conferred upon me by sections 20A(6) and (7) and 43 of the Charities Act 1960[1], I hereby make the following Regulations:

[1] section 20A was inserted by section 9 of the Charities Act 1992 (c. 41) and section 43 was amended by the Education Act 1973 (c. 16) Schedule 1 paragraph 1 ,and the Charities Act 1992, Schedule 3, paragraph 17.

1—Citation, commencement and interpretation

2C–001

(1) These Regulations may be cited as the Charities (Receiver and Manager) Regulations 1992 and shall come into force on 1st November 1992.

(2) In these Regulations—

"the 1960 Act" means the Charities Act 1960;

"the appointed person" means a person appointed by order under section 20(1)(vii) of the 1960 Act[1] to be receiver and manager in respect of the property and affairs of a charity;

"the relevant charity" means the charity in respect of which that person was appointed; and

"the relevant order" means the order by which that person was appointed.

[1] Section 20(1) was substituted by section 8 of the Charities Act 1992.

GENERAL MATERIALS

2—Security by appointed person

2C–002

The Commissioners[1] are hereby authorised to require the appointed person to give security to them for the due discharge of his functions within such time and in such form as they may specify.

[1] By virtue of section 11 of the Interpretation Act 1978 (c. 30) this expression has the same meaning as in section 46 of the 1960 Act.

3—Remuneration of appointed person

2C–003

(1) The Commissioners are hereby authorised to determine the amount of an appointed person's remuneration.

(2) The remuneration of an appointed person shall be payable out of the income of the relevant charity.

(3) The Commissioners are hereby authorised to disallow any amount of remuneration of an appointed person where, on the expiry of the time specified in the notice referred to in regulation 4(2) below and after consideration of such representations, if any, as are duly made in response to such a notice, they are satisfied that he has failed in such manner as is set

out in paragraph (a) or (b) of regulation 4(1) below and specified in such a notice.

4—Notice of failure to, and removal of, appointed person

(1) Where it appears to the Commissioners that an appointed person has failed— 2C–004

(a) to give security within such time or in such form as they have specified, or

(b) satisfactorily to discharge any function imposed on him by or by virtue of the relevant order or by regulation 5 below,

and they wish to consider exercising their powers under regulation 3(3) above or paragraph (3) below, they shall give him, whether in person or by post, a written notice complying with paragraph (2) below.

(2) A notice given to an appointed person under paragraph (1) above shall inform him of—

(a) any failure under paragraph (1)(a) or (b) above in respect of which the notice is issued;

(b) of the Commissioners' power under regulation 3(3) above to authorise the disallowance of any amount of remuneration if satisfied as to any such failure;

(c) of their power under paragraph (3) below to remove him if satisfied as to any such failure; and

(d) of his right to make representations to them in respect of any such alleged failure within such reasonable time as is specified in the notice.

(3) On the expiry of the time specified in the notice referred to in paragraph (2) above and after consideration of such representations, if any, as are duly made in response to such a notice, the Commissioners may remove an appointed person where they are satisfied that he has failed in such manner as is set out in paragraph (1)(a) or (b) above and specified in such notice (whether or not they also exercise the power conferred by regulation 3(3) above).

5—Reports by appointed person

(1) This regulation makes provision in respect of the reports which are to be made by an appointed person to the Commissioners (and which, in addition to the matters which are required to be included by virtue of paragraphs (2) to (4) below, may also include particulars of any matter which, in his opinion, should be brought to their attention). 2C–005

(2) An appointed person shall make a report to the Commissioners not later than three months after the date of his appointment setting out—

(a) an estimate by him of the total value of the property of the relevant charity on, or shortly after, the date of his appointment;

(b) such information about the property and affairs of the relevant charity immediately prior to his appointment as he believes should be included in the report, notwithstanding that it may also be eventually included in a report under section 6 of the 1960 Act[1] ; and

(c) his strategy for discharging the functions conferred on him by or by virtue of the relevant order.

(3) For as long as an appointed person holds office as such, he shall make a report to the Commissioners not later than one month after each anniversary of his appointment setting out—

(a) an estimate by him of the total value of the property of the relevant charity on that anniversary of his appointment in respect of which the report is required to be made;

(b) a summary of the discharge by him of the functions conferred on him by or by virtue of the relevant order during the twelve months ending with that anniversary; and

(c) where there are changes to his strategy as last set out in a report in accordance with paragraph (2)(c) above or, as the case may be, this sub- paragraph, those changes.

(4) Subject to paragraph (5) below, an appointed person shall make a report to the Commissioners not later than three months after the date when he ceased to hold office as such setting out—

(a) an estimate by him of the total value of the property of the relevant charity on that date; and

(b) a summary of the discharge by him of the functions conferred on him by or by virtue of the relevant order during the period ending with that date and beginning with either—

(i) the date of his appointment; or

(ii) if that date is more than twelve months before the date when he ceased to hold office as an appointed person, the day immediately after the last anniversary of his appointment.

(5) Paragraph (4) above does not apply where an appointed person ceased to hold office one month or less after an anniversary of his appointment and a report had been made to the Commissioners in accordance0 with paragraph (3) above in respect of that anniversary.

[1] Section 6 has been amended by section 6 of the Charities Act 1992 (c. 41).

Kenneth Clarke

One of Her Majesty's Principal Secretaries of State

Home Office

1st October 1992

Charity Commissioners' Fees (Copies and Extracts) Regulations 1992/ 2986

(SI 1992/2986)

(In force from: January 1, 1993)

In exercise of the powers conferred upon me by sections 51(1) and (2) and 77(3) of the Charities Act 1992, I hereby make the following Regulations:

1—(1) These Regulations may be cited as the Charity Commissioners' Fees (Copies and Extracts) Regulations 1992 and shall come into force on 1st January 1993.

2D–001

(2) In these Regulations"relevant document" means any document[1] which is kept by the Commissioners[2] under the enactments relating to charities and of or from which section 9 of the Charities Act 1960[3] or section 7 of the Charitable Trustees Incorporation Act 1872[4] requires the Commissioners to furnish copies or extracts at the request of any person.

[1] By virtue of section 11 of the Interpretation Act 1978 (c. 30) and section 1(2) of the Charities Act 1992, section 46(2) of the Charities Act 1960 (c. 58). as inserted by paragraph 19(b) of Schedule 3 to the Charities Act 1992, applies for the interpretation of the expression "document".

[2] By virtue of section 11 of the Interpretation Act 1978 and section 1(2) of the Charities Act 1992, this expression has the same meaning as in section 46(1) of the Charities Act 1960.

[3] Section 9 was substituted by paragraph 3 of Schedule 3 to the Charities Act 1992.

[4] Section 7 was repealed in part by paragraph 7 of Schedule 4 to the Charities Act 1992.

2—Where a photocopier is used in response to a request to furnish a copy of, or extract from, a relevant document, there shall, subject to regulation 6 below, be payable to the Commissioners for such a copy or extract—

2D–002

(a) where there are not more than six sheets of photocopied material, a fee of £1.80; and

(b) where there are more than six sheets of photocopied material, a fee of £ 1.80 and an additional 30p for each such sheet in excess of the first six.

3—(1) Where a request is made for a copy of, or extract from, a relevant document and the information contained in that document is recorded otherwise than in legible form, there shall, subject to paragraph (2) and regulation 6 below, be payable to the Commissioners for such a copy or extract (which, by virtue of section 46(2) of the Charities Act 1960[1], must be furnished in legible form) a fee of 60p for each sheet of paper on which such a copy or extract is printed.

2D–003

(2) Paragraph (1) above shall not apply for the purposes of the calculation of the fee payable on the furnishing of extracts from a relevant document where—

   (a)   the extracts requested are such that the request is capable of being dealt with as a request under regulation 4 below, and
   (b)   the fee payable under that regulation for such extracts is lower than the fee which would otherwise be payableunder paragraph (1) above.

[1] As to section 46(2) , see the second footnote to these Regulations.

2D–004   **4**—(1) This regulation applies to a request for an extract (or extracts) from the register of charities (which is a relevant document because section 9 of the Charities Act 1960 applies to it by virtue of the requirement in section 4(7) of that Act that the register be kept open to public inspection) where—

   (a)   the information contained in that register is recorded otherwise than in legible form, and
   (b)   the request is in respect of any registered charity (or charities) identified by either its name (or their names) or the number under which it is registered (or the numbers under which they are registered).

(2) Subject to regulation 6 below, where a request of the kind described in paragraph (1) above is for a short extract (or extracts) from the register of charities, there shall be payable to the Commissioners in respect of furnishing it (or them) a fee of £2 with an additional 15p for each charity in respect of which a short extract is so furnished.

(3) Subject to regulation 6 below, where a request of the kind described in paragraph (1) above is for a standard extract (or extracts) from the register of charities, there shall be payable to the Commissioners in respect of furnishing it (or them) a fee of £2 with an additional 20p for each charity in respect of which a standard extract is so furnished.

(4) Subject to regulation 6 below, where a request of the kind described in paragraph (1) above is for a detailed extract (or extracts) from the register of charities, there shall be payable to the Commissioners in respect of furnishing it (or them) a fee of £2 with an additional 25p for each charity in respect of which a detailed extract is so furnished or, where it is not possible to furnish such an extract (because the criterion which distinguishes a detailed extract from a standard extract and is referred to in paragraph (5) below is not satisfied) 20p for each charity in respect of which a standard extract is so furnished.

(5) In this regulation and regulation 5 below—

"a short extract" means an extract (not being a standard or detailed extract) which includes the name and registration number of the charity in question;

"a standard extract" means an extract (not being a detailed extract) which, in addition to the information about the charity in question included in a short extract, also includes the purposes of that charity and an address for correspondence with the charity trustees; and "a detailed extract" means an extract which, in addition to the information about the charity in question included in a standard extract, also includes the names of any other (subsidiary) charity registered in the register of charities under the same number as that charity.

5—(1) This regulation applies to a request for an extract (or extracts) from the register of charities where—   **2D–005**

    (a) the information contained in that register is recorded otherwise than in legible form, and

    (b) the request is framed by reference to criteria other than the name of any registered charity (or charities) or the number under which it is registered (or the numbers under which they are registered).

(2) Subject to regulation 6 below, there shall be payable to the Commissioners in respect of the furnishing of an extract (or extracts) from the register of charities in response to a request of the kind described in paragraph (1) above a fee of £2 with an additional £40 for each criterion by reference to which the extracts are to be identified, and an additional—

    (a) 15p for each extract which is a short extract;

    (b) 20p for each extract which is a standard extract; or

    (c) 25p for each extract which is a detailed extract.

6—Where it appears to the Commissioners appropriate to do so, they may confer such exemption as they see fit from the liability to pay a fee prescribed by regulations 2 to 5 above.   **2D–006**

Signatures

Kenneth Clarke

One of Her Majesty's Principal Secretaries of State

Home Office

29th November 1992

The Charities (Cy-près Advertisements, Inquiries and Disclaimer) Regulations 1993

(In force from June 24, 1993)

In exercise of the powers conferred on them by section 14(1) and (5A) of the Charities Act 1960[1] the Charity Commissioners for England and Wales hereby make the following Regulations:

2E–001   1.—(1) These regulations may be cited as the Charity (Cy-Près Advertisements, Inquiries and Disclaimer) Regulations 1993 and shall come into force on the date on which they are made.

(2) In these Regulations:

"the Act" means the Charities Act 1960;

"advertisement" means an advertisement published in pursuance of section 14(1)(a)(i) of the Act;

"appeal" means an invitation to the public or a section of the public whether in writing, by means of television or radio or otherwise;

"property" means property given for specific charitable purposes which have failed.

2E–002   2.—(1) Advertisements shall be in the form specified in Schedule 1 to these Regulations or in a form equivalent to that form in any other language required or permitted by paragraph (2) of this Regulation.

(2) Advertisements shall be published:

(a)   in English in every case; and

(b)   where the appeal was published in another language, in that language;

and may, in addition, be published in Welsh in any case where the appeal was not made in Welsh.

2E–003   3—Any advertisement published in pursuance of section 14(1)(a)(i) of the Act shall be published in the manner specified in Schedule 2 to these Regulations.

2E–004   4—Any inquiry made in pursuance of section 14(1)(a)(i) of the Act shall:

(a)   be made in writing;

(b)   be sent by post to the address of each donor recorded in the records of the trustees of the property; and

(c)   contain at least the information specified in Schedule 3 to these Regulations.

---

[1] [1960, c. 58. Section 14(1) was amended by, and subsection (5A) was inserted by, the Charities Act 1992 (c. 41)]

5—The period prescribed for the purposes of section 14(1)(a)(ii) of the Act shall be three months.

2E–005

6—Any disclaimer executed in pursuance of section 14(1)(b) of the Act shall either:

2E–006

(a) be executed in English in the form specified in Schedule 4 to these Regulations; or

(b) be executed in Welsh in the form equivalent in that language to the form specified in Schedule 4 to these Regulations.

SCHEDULE 1—Regulation 2

Form of Advertisement prescribed for the purposes of section 14(1)(a)(i) of the Charities Act 1960

"**ADVERTISEMENT**

Name of charity (if applicable):

Registered charity number (if applicable):

Purpose for which money or other property was given:

NOTICE is given that money and other property given for this purpose cannot be used for that purpose because [state reasons].

2.   If you gave money or other property for that purpose you are entitled to claim it back. If you wish to do so you must tell [insert name] of [insert address] within 3 months of [specify date: see note below]. If you wish the moeny or other property to go to a similar charitable purpose and to disclaim your right to the return of the money or other property, you must ask the person named above for a form of disclaimer.

3.   If you do not either make a claim within the 3 months or sign a disclaimer, the Charity Commissioners may make a Scheme applying the property to other charitable purposes. You will still be able to claim the return of your money or other property (less expenses), but **only if you do so within six months from the date of any Scheme made by the Commissioners**.

4.   Date of this notice: **[specify date: see note below]**"

[Note: [This Note does not form part of the prescribed advertisement] If this advertisement is to be published in a newspaper or other periodical, the words "the date of this publication" should be inserted in paragraphs 2 and 4 above.

If this advertisement is to be published on a public notice board, the date inserted here should be the date on which the advertisement was fixed to the public notice board.]

SCHEDULE 2—Regulation 3

Manner of publishing advertisements in pursuance of section 14(1)(a)(i) of the Act

1. Every advertisement shall be published in a newspaper or other periodical which is:

    (a) written in the same language as the advertisement; and

    (b) is sold or distributed throughout the area in which the appeal was made.

2. Where the purposes of the appeal were directed towards the benefit of an area contained wholly or mainly within a local authority district or a London Borough or the City of London, a copy of every advertisement published under paragraph 1 shall also be published by fixing copies of it to two public notice boards in the relevant area.

SCHEDULE 3—Regulation 4

**Information to be contained in inquiries to be made in pursuance of
section 14(10)(a)(i) of the Act**

1. The name and address of the charity to which the property was given by
    the donor;

2. A description of the specific charitable purpose for which the property
    was given by the donor;

3. The reasons why that purpose has failed;

4. A description of the property (including the amount of any money)
    given for that purpose by the donor;

5. A statement of the donor's right to have the property returned;

6. A statement that the donor may disclaim the right to have the property
    described in paragraph 4 above returned by executing a disclaimer in the
    prescribed form;

7. A statement that, where the donor disclaims his right in respect of such
    property, the property may be applied for other charitable purposes
    similar to those for which it was given by a Scheme established by the
    Commissioners or by the court; and

8. A statement that, where the donor has not replied in writing to the
    inquiry within three months from the date of service of the inquiry, he
    will be treated for the purposes fo section 14(1)(a) as a donor who can-
    not be identified or found, but that he will be able to claim the property,
    less expenses, within six months from the date of any Scheme made by
    the Commissioners or the court.

SCHEDULE 4—Regulation 6

Form of disclaimer prescribed for the purposes of section 14(1)(a)(ii) of the Charities Act 1960

"DISCLAIMER I HEREBY DISCLAIM my right to the return of the sum of £...../the property consisting of (insert description of property)* given by me for (insert name of charity to which, or description or purposes for which, the money or property was given).

Signed	....
Name in capitals	....
Address	....
Date	....

Signed#	....
Name in capitals	....
Address	....
Date	....

*Delete as appropriate
#This paragraph may be repeated if further signatures are required.

The Seal of the Charity Commissioners for England and Wales was affixed hereto by order ot the Commissioners.

24 June 1993

Charitable Institutions (Fund-Raising) Regulations
(SI 1994/ 3024)

(In force from March 1, 1995)

The Secretary of State, in exercise of the powers conferred upon him by sections 64 and 77(3) of the Charities Act 1992[1] and, having regard to the definition of "the prescribed requirements" in section 59(6) , section 59 of that Act, and after such consultation as is mentioned in section 77(4) of that Act, hereby makes the following Regulations:

[1] section 77 was repealed in part by Schedule 7 to the Charities Act 1993 (c.10).

1—Citation, commencement and interpretation

2F–001　　(1) These Regulations may be cited as the Charitable Institutions (Fund-Raising) Regulations 1994 and shall come into force on 1st March 1995.

(2) In these Regulations, "authorised deposit taker" means—

 (a) the Bank of England;

 (b) a person who has permission under Part 4 of the Financial Services and Markets Act 2000 to accept deposits; or

 (c) an EEA firm of the kind mentioned in paragraph 5(b) of Schedule 3 to that Act, which has permission under paragraph 15 of that Schedule (as a result of qualifying for authorisation under paragraph 12(1) of that Schedule) to accept deposits.

[(2A) Paragraph (2) must be read with—

 (a) section 22 of the Financial Services and Markets Act 2000;

 (b) any relevant order under that section; and

 (c) Schedule 2 to that Act.[1]]

(3) In these Regulations, any reference, in relation to an agreement made for the purposes of section 59 of the Charities Act 1992, to a charitable institution, commercial participator or professional fund-raiser[2], shall, unless the contrary intention appears, be construed as a reference to any charitable institution, commercial participator or professional fund-raiser, respectively, which is or who is a party to the agreement.

[1] added by SI 2001/3649 (Financial Services and Markets Act 2000 (Consequential Amendments and Repeals) Order), Pt 9 Art 480 (3)

[2] These expressions have, by virtue of section 11 of the Interpretation Act 1978 (c.30) the meanings assigned to them in section 58 of the Charities Act 1992 as amended by section 25 of the Deregulation and Contracting Out Act 1994 (c.40).

GENERAL MATERIALS

2—Agreements between charitable institutions and professional fund-raisers

(1) The requirements as to form and content of an agreement made for   **2F–002**
the purposes of section 59(1) of the Charities Act 1992 are those set out
in the following provisions of this regulation.

(2) Such an agreement (hereafter in this regulation referred to as "the
agreement") shall be in writing and shall be signed by or on behalf of the
charitable institution and the professional fund-raiser.

(3) The agreement shall specify—

(a)   the name and address of each of the parties to the agreement;
(b)   the date on which the agreement was signed by or on behalf of
      each of those parties;
(c)   the period for which the agreement is to subsist;
(d)   any terms relating to the termination of the agreement prior to
      the date on which that period expires; and
(e)   any terms relating to the variation of the agreement during that
      period.

(4) The agreement shall also contain—

(a)   a statement of its principal objectives and the methods to be
      used in pursuit of those objectives;
(b)   if there is more than one charitable institution party to the
      agreement, provision as to the manner in which the proportion
      in which the institutions which are so party are respectively to
      benefit under the agreement is to be determined; and
(c)   provision as to the amount by way of remuneration or expenses
      which the professional fund-raiser is to be entitled to receive in
      respect of things done by him in pursuance of the agreement
      and the manner in which that amount is to be determined.

3—Agreements between charitable institutions and commercial participators

(1) The requirements as to form and content of an agreement made for   **2F–003**
the purposes of section 59(2) of the Charities Act 1992 are those set out
in the following provisions of this regulation.

(2) Such an agreement (hereafter in this regulation referred to as "the
agreement") shall be in writing and shall be signed by or on behalf of the
charitable institution and the commercial participator.

(3) The agreement shall specify-

(a)   the name and address of each of the parties to the agreement;
(b)   the date on which the agreement was signed by or on behalf of
      each of those parties;
(c)   he period for which the agreement is to subsist;
(d)   any terms relating to the termination of the agreement prior to
      the date on which that period expires; and
(e)   any terms relating to the variation of the agreement during that
      period.

(4) The agreement shall also contain-

    (a)   a statement of its principal objectives and the methods to be used in pursuit of those objectives;

    (b)   provision as to the manner in which are to be determined—

        (i)   if there is more than one charitable institution party to the agreement, the proportion in which the institutions which are so party are respectively to benefit under the agreement; and

        (ii)   the proportion of the consideration given for goods or services sold or supplied by the commercial participator, or of any other proceeds of a promotional venture undertaken by him, which is to be given to or applied for the benefit of the charitable institution, or

        (iii)   the sums by way of donations by the commercial participator in connection with the sale or supply of any goods or services sold or supplied by him which are to be so given or applied,

    as the case may require; and

    (c)   provision as to any amount by way of remuneration or expenses which the commercial participator is to be entitled to receive in respect of things done by him in pursuance of the agreement and the manner in which any such amount is to be determined.

(5) The statement of methods referred to in paragraph (4)(a) above shall include, in relation to each method specified, a description of the type of charitable contributions which are to be given to or applied for the benefit of the charitable institution and of the circumstances in which they are to be so given or applied.

4—Notice prior to injunction to prevent unauthorised fund-raising

2F–004   A notice served under subsection (3) of section 62 of the Charities Act 1992 shall, in addition to satisfying the requirements of that subsection, specify the circumstances which gave rise to the serving of the notice and the grounds on which an application under that section is to be made.

5—Availability of books, documents or other records

2F–005   (1) A professional fund-raiser or commercial participator who is a party to an agreement made for the purposes of section 59 of the Charities Act 1992 shall, on request and at all reasonable times, make available to any charitable institution which is a party to that agreement any books, documents or other records (however kept) which relate to that institution and are kept for the purposes of the agreement.

(2) In the case of any record which is kept otherwise than in legible form, the reference in paragraph (1) above to making that record available shall be construed as a reference to making it available in legible form.

6—Transmission of money and other property to charitable institutions

(1) Any money or other property acquired by a professional fund-raiser or commercial participator for the benefit of, or otherwise falling to be given to or applied by such a person for the benefit of, a charitable institution (including such money or other property as is referred to in section 64(3) of the Charities Act 1992) shall, notwithstanding any inconsistent term in an agreement made for the purposes of section 59 of that Act, be transmitted to that institution in accordance with thefollowing provisions of this regulation.

2F–006

(2) A professional fund-raiser or commercial participator holding any such money or property as is referred to in paragraph (1) above shall, unless he has a reasonable excuse—

(a) in the case of any money, and any negotiable instrument which is payable to or to the account of the charitable institution, as soon as is reasonably practicable after its receipt and in any event not later than the expiration of 28 days after that receipt or such other period as may be agreed with the institution—
  (i) pay it to the person or persons having the general control and management of the administration of the institution; or
  (ii) pay it into an account held by [an authorised deposit taker]¹ in the name of or on behalf of the institution which is under the control of the person, or any of the persons, specified in sub-paragraph (i) above; and
(b) in the case of any other property, deal with it in accordance with any instructions given for that purpose, either generally or in a particular case, by the charitable institution:

Provided that—

(i) any property in the possession of the professional fund-raiser or commercial participator either pending the obtaining of such instructions as are referred to above or in accordance with such instructions shall be securely held by him;
(ii) the proceeds of the sale or other disposal of any property shall, from the time of their receipt by the professional fund-raiser or commercial participator, be subject to the requirements of sub-paragraph (a) above.

¹ possible drafting error – words purportedly substituted in reg.6:(2): (iii) which does not exist; words substituted in reg.6:(2):(ii) instead by SI 2001/3649 (Financial Services and Markets Act 2000 (Consequential Amendments and Repeals) Order), Pt 9 Art 480 (4)

7—Fund-raising for charitable etc. purposes otherwise than by professional fund-raisers or commercial participators

(1) This regulation applies to any person who carries on for gain a business other than a fund-raising business but, in the course of that business, engages in any promotional venture in the course of which it is represented that charitable contributions are to be applied for charitable, benevolent or philanthropic purposes of any description (rather than for the benefit of one or more particular charitable institutions).

2F–007

(2) Where any person to whom this regulation applies makes a representation to the effect that charitable contributions are to be applied for such charitable, benevolent or philanthropic purposes as are mentioned in paragraph (1) above he shall, unless he has a reasonable excuse, ensure that the representation is accompanied by a statement clearly indicating—

(a)   the fact that the charitable contributions referred to in the representation are to be applied for those purposes and not for the benefit of any particular charitable institution or institutions;

(b)   (in general terms) the method by which it is to be determined—

  (i)   what proportion of the consideration given for goods or services sold or supplied by him, or of any other proceeds of a promotional venture undertaken by him, is to be applied for those purposes, or

  (ii)   what sums by way of donations by him in connection with the sale or supply of any such goods or services are to be so applied,

  as the case may require; and

(c)   the method by which it is to be determined how the charitable contributions referred to in the representation are to be distributed between different charitable institutions.

8—Offences and penalties

2F–008   (1) Failure to comply with any of the provisions of these Regulations specified in paragraph (2) below shall be an offence punishable on summary conviction by a fine not exceeding the second level on the standard scale.

(2) The provisions referred to in paragraph (1) above are—

(a)   regulation 5(1) ;
(b)   regulation 6(2) ; and
(c)   regulation 7(2) .

Signatures

Blatch

Minister of State

Home Office

28th November 1994

Charities (Accounts and Reports) Regulations

(SI 1995/2724)

(In force from March 1, 1996)

The Secretary of State, in exercise of the powers conferred upon him by sections 42, 44, 45 and 86(3) of the Charities Act 1993[1], and after such consultation as is mentioned in section 86(4) of that Act, hereby makes the following Regulations:

[1] Section 42 was amended by the Charities Act 1993 (Substitution o sums) Order 1995 S.I. 1995/2696) and section 45 was amended by section 29 of the Deregulation and Contracting Out Act 1994 (c.40) and by Part II of Schedule 1 to the Companies At 1985 (Audit Exemption) Regulations 1994 (S.I. 1994/1935).

1—Citation and commencement

These Regulations may be cited as the Charities (Accounts and Reports) Regulations 1995 and shall come into force on 1st March 1996.

2G–001

2—Interpretation

(1) In these Regulations, the expression—

2G–002

"common deposit fund" means a common deposit fund established by a scheme [under section 22A of the Charities Act 1960[1] or[2]] under section 25 of the 1993 Act;

"common investment fund" means a common investment fund established by a scheme under section 22 of the Charities Act 1960 or under section 24 of the 1993 Act, other than a fund the trusts of which provide for property to be transferred to the fund only by or on behalf of a participating charity of which the charity trustees are the trustees appointed to manage the fund;

"financial year" shall be construed in accordance with regulation 5 below;

"institution or body corporate connected with the charity", in relation to a charity, means an institution or body corporate which—

(a) in the case of an institution, is controlled by,
(b) in the case of a body corporate, in which a substantial interest is held by, the charity or any one or more of the charity trustees acting in his or their capacity as such;

"recognised stock exchange" has the meaning assigned to it by section 841 of the Income and Corporation Taxes Act 1988; and

"the 1993 Act" means the Charities Act 1993.

(2) For the purposes of these Regulations, a person is connected with a charity trustee if—

(a) he is the child, parent, grandchild, grandparent, brother or sister of the charity trustee;

(b) he is the spouse of the charity trustee or of any person connected with him by virtue of sub-paragraph (a) above;

(c) he is a trustee of any trust, not being a charity, the beneficiaries or potential beneficiaries of which include the charity trustee or any person connected with him by virtue of sub-paragraph (a) or (b) above and is acting in his capacity as such;

(d) he is a partner of the charity trustee or of any person connected with him by virtue of sub-paragraph (a), (b) or (c) above and is acting in his capacity as such; or

(e) the person is a body corporate, not being a company which is connected with a charitable institution within the meaning of section 58(5) of the Charities Act 1992, in which the charity trustee has, or the charity trustee and any other charity trustee or trustees or person or persons connected with him by virtue of sub-paragraph (a), (b), (c) or (d) above, taken together, have, a substantial interest.

(3) Any expression in this regulation which also appears in Schedule 5 shall be construed in accordance with paragraphs 2 to 4 of that Schedule.

[1] Section 22A was inserted by the Charities Act 1992 (c.41).

[2] Words inserted by SI 2000/288 (Charities (Accounts and Reports) Regulations), reg.8(1)(a).

3—Form and content of statements of accounts

2G–003 (1) Subject to regulation 4 below, the requirements as to form and contents of a statement o accounts prepared in accordance with section 42(1) of the 1993 Act are those set out in the following provisions of this regulation.

(2) The statement shall consist of the following, that is to say—

(a) a statement of financial activities which satisfies the requirements set out in Part I of Schedule 1 to these Regulations; and

(b) a balance sheet which satisfies the requirements set out in Part II of that Schedule.

(3) The statement shall be prepared in accordance with the methods and principles specified and referred to in Part III of Schedule 1 to these Regulations.

(4) There shall be provided by way of notes to the accounts the information specified in Part IV of Schedule 1 to these Regulations.

(5) Part V of Schedule 1 to these Regulations shall have effect for the purposes of defining expressions used in that Schedule.

(6) The balance sheet shall be signed by one or more of the charity trustees of the charity, each of whom has been authorised to do so, and shall specify the date on which the accounts to which the statement relates were approved by the charity trustees.

4—Form and contents: special cases

2G–004 (1) In the case of a common investment fund or a common deposit fund which is deemed to be a charity by virtue of section 24(8), including that subsection as applied by section 25(2), of the 1993 Act, the requirements as to form and contents of a statement of accounts prepared in accordance with section 42(1) of the 1993 Act are those set out in paragraphs (2) to (6) below.

(2) Subject to paragraph (8) below, the statement shall consist of the following, that is to say—

(a) a statement of total return which satisfies the requirements set out in Part I of Schedule 2 to these Regulations; and

(b) a statement of movement in funds which satisfies the requirements set out in Part II of Schedule 2 to these Regulations; and

(c) a balance sheet which satisfies the requirements set out in Part III of Schedule 2 of these Regulations.

(3) The statement shall be prepared in accordance with the methods and principles specified and referred to in Part IV of Schedule 2 to these Regulations.

(4) There shall be provided by way of notes to the accounts the information specified in Part V of Schedule 2 to these Regulations.

(5) Part VI of Schedule 2 to these Regulations shall have effect for the purpose of defining expressions used in that Schedule.

(6) The balance sheet shall be signed by one or more of the trustees appointed to manage the fund, each of whom has been authorised to do so, and shall specify the date on which the accounts to which the statement relates were approved by the trustees appointed to manage the fund in accordance with the scheme by which the fund was established.

(7) In the case of a charity which—

[(a) is a registered social landlord within the meaning of the Housing Act 1996 and whose registration has been recorded under section 3(3) of that Act; or][1]

(b) has during the financial year in question—

(i) conducted an institution in relation to which a designation made, or having effect as if made, under section 129 of the education Reform Act 1988[2] or Section 28 of the further and Higher Education Act 1992 has effect;

(ii) received financial support from funds administered by a higher education funding council or further education funding council within the meaning of that Act of 1992 in respect of expenditure incurred or to be incurred by the charity in connection with what institution; and

(iii) incurred no expenditure for charitable purposes other than the purposes of that institution or any other such institution,

the requirements as to form and contents of a statement of accounts prepared in pursuance of section 42(1) of the 1993 Act are that the statement shall consist of a balance sheet as at the end of the financial year in respect of which the statement of accounts is prepared and an income and expenditure account.

(8) In the case of any financial year of a common deposit fund in which there are no gains or losses on disposal or revaluation of assets, paragraph (2) above shall have effect as if sub-paragraph (b) were omitted.

[1] Substituted by SI 2000/2868 (Charities (Accounts and Reports) Regulations), reg.8(2).

[2] Section 129 was amended by section 72(1) of the Further and Higher Education Act 1992.

5—Financial Year

2G–005   (1) The financial year of a charity shall, for the purposes of the 1993 Act and regulations made thereunder, be determined in accordance with the following provisions of this regulation.

(2) The first financial year of a charity shall be—

(a)   in the case of a charity which is established before the date on which these Regulations come into force, the period beginning with the day immediately following the end of the period in respect of which a statement of accounts was required to be prepared under any statutory provision contained in or having effect under an Act of Parliament applicable to that charity before the coming into force of section 42 of the 1993 Act and ending with the accounting reference date of the charity or such other date, not more than seven days before or after the accounting reference date, as the charity trustees may determine;

(b)   in the case of a charity which is established on or after the date on which these Regulations come into force, the period beginning with the day on which the charity is established and ending with the accounting reference date of the charity or such other date, not more than seven days before or after the accounting reference date, as the charity trustees may determine.

(3) Subsequent financial years of a charity begin with the day immediately following the end of the charity's previous financial year and end with its accounting reference date or such other date, not more than seven days before or after the accounting reference date, as the charity trustees may determine.

(4) The accounting reference date of a charity shall, for the purposes of this regulation, be—

(a)   in the first financial year of a charity which is established before the date on which these Regulations come into force, such date, not less than 6 months nor more than 18 months after the date on which that financial year began, as the charity trustees may determine;

(b)   in the first financial year of a charity which is established on or after the date on which these Regulations come into force, such date, not less than 6 months nor more than 18 months after the date on which the charity was established, as the charity trustees may determined;

(c)   in any subsequent financial year of a charity, the date 12 months after the previous accounting reference date of the charity or such other date, not less than 6 months nor more than 18 months after the previous accounting reference date of the charity as the trustees may determine:

Provided that—

(i)   the charity trustees shall not exercise their powers under sub-paragraph (c) of this paragraph so as to determine an accounting reference date in respect of any financial year which is consecutive, or follows immediately after a financial year which is consecutive, to a previous financial year in respect of which that power was exercised; and

(ii)   the charity trustees shall exercise their powers under sub-paragraph (a) or (c) of this paragraph so as to determine a date earlier or later than 12 months from the beginning of the financial year only where satisfied that there are exceptional reasons to do so (which reasons shall, in the case of a charity subject to the requirements of regulation 3(4) or 4(4) above, be disclosed in a note to the accounts).

6—Annual audit of charity accounts

(1) The duties of an auditor carrying out an audit of the accounts of a charity under section 43 of the 1993 Act[1] shall be those specified in the following provisions of this regulation.

2G–006

(2) Where a statement of accounts has been prepared under section 42(1) of the 1993 Act for the financial year in question the auditor shall make a report on that statement to the charity trustees which—

(a)   states the name and address of the auditor and the name of the charity concerned;

(b)   is signed by him or, where the office of auditor is held by a body corporate or partnership, in its name by a person authorised to sign on its behalf and states that the auditor is a person falling with paragraph (a) or, as the case may be, (b) of section 43(2) of the 1993 Act;

(c)   is dated and specified the financial year in respect of which the accounts to which it relates have been prepared;

(d)   specifies that it is a report in respect of an audit carried out under section 43 of the 1993 Act and in accordance with regulations made under section 44 of that Act;

(e)   states whether the auditor's opinion the statement of accounts complies with the requirements of regulation 3 or, as the case may be, [regulation 5][2], above and gives a true and fair view of the state of affairs of the charity at the end of the financial year in question and of the [income and expenditure][3] of the charity in that year;

(f)   where the auditor has formed the opinion—

(i)   that accounting records have not been kept in respect of the charity in accordance with section 41 of the 1993 Act; or

(ii)   that the statement of accounts does not accord with those records, or

(iii)   that any information contained in the statement of accounts is inconsistent in any material respect with any report of the charity trustees prepared under section 45 of the 1993 Act in respect of the financial year in question; or

(iv)   that any information or explanation to which he is entitled under regulation 8 below has not been afforded to him,

contains a statement of that opinion and of his grounds for forming it.

(3) Where a receipts and payments account and statement of assets and liabilities have been prepared under section 42(3) of the 1993 Act for the financial year in question the auditor shall make a report on that account and statement to the charity trustees which—

(a) states the name and address of the auditor and the name of the charity concerned;

(b) is signed by him or, where the office of auditor is held by a body corporate or partnership, in its name by a person authorised to sign on its behalf and states that the auditor is a person falling within paragraph (a) or, as the case may be, (b) of section 43(2) of the 1993 Act;

(c) is dated and specifies the financial year in respect of which the accounts to which it relates have been prepared;

(d) specifies that it is a report in respect of an audit carried out under section 43 of the 1993 act and in accordance with regulations made under section 44 of that Act;

(e) states whether in the auditor's opinion—

    (i) the account and statement properly present the receipts and payments of the charity for the financial year in question and its assets and liabilities as at the end of that year; and

    (ii) the account and statement adequately distinguish any material special trust or other restricted fund of the charity;

(f) where the auditor has formed the opinion—

    (i) that accounting records have not been kept in respect of the charity in accordance with section 41 of the 1993 Act; or

    (ii) that the account and statement do not accord with those records; or

    (iii) that any information or explanation to which he is entitled under regulation 8 below has not been afforded to him,

contains a statement of that opinion and of his grounds for forming it.

(4) The auditor shall, in preparing his report for the purposes of paragraph (2) or, as the case may be, (3) above, carry out such investigations as will enable him to form an opinion as to the matters specified in sub-paragraph (e) and (f) of that paragraph.

(5) The auditor shall communicate to the Commissioners, in writing, any matter of which the auditor becomes aware in his capacity as such which relates to the activities or affairs of the charity or of any institution or body corporate connected with the charity and which the auditor has reasonable cause to believe is, or is likely to be, of material significance for the exercise, in relation to the charity of the Commissioners' functions under section 8 (general power to institute inquiries) or 18 (power to act for protection of charities) of the 1993 Act.

(6) Where an auditor appointed by charity trustees ceases for any reason to hold office he shall send to the charity trustees a statement of any circumstances connected with his ceasing to hold office which he considers should be brought to their attention or, if he considers that there are no such circumstances, a statement that there are none; and the auditor shall send a copy of any statement sent to the charity trustees under this paragraph (except a statement that there are no such circumstances) to the Commissioners.

(7) In the case of an auditor appointed by the Commissioners, the report required by paragraph (2) or, as the case may be, (3) above shall be made to the Commissioners instead of to the charity trustees.

[1] Section 43 was amended by section 28 of the Deregulation and Contracting Out Act 1994.
[2] words substituted by SI 2000/2868 (Charities (Accounts and Reports) Regulations), reg 6.(a).
[3] words substituted by SI 2000/2868 (Charities (Accounts and Reports) Regulations), reg.6(a).

7—Independent examination of charity accounts

An independent examiner who has carried out an examination of the accounts of a charity under section 43 of the 1993 Act shall make a report to the charity trustees which—   **2G–007**

(a)   states his name and address and the name of the charity concerned;

(b)   is signed by him and specifies any relevant professional qualifications or professional body of which he is a member;

(c)   is dated and specifies the financial year in respect of which the accounts to which it relates have been prepared;

(d)   specifies that it is a report in respect of an examination carried out under section 43 of the 1993 Act and in accordance with any directions given by the Commissioners under subsection (7)(b) of that section which are applicable;

(e)   states whether or not any matter has come to the examiner's attention in connection with the examination which gives him reasonable cause to believe that in any material respect—

(i)   accounting records have not been kept in respect of the charity in accordance with section 41 of the 1993 Act; or

(ii)   the accounts do not accord with those records; or

(iii) in the case of an examination of accounts a statement of which has been prepared under section 42(1) of the 1993 Act, the statement of accounts does not comply with any of the requirements of regulation 3 or, as the case may be, 4 above except the requirements specified in paragraph 1 of Part III of Schedule 1 to these Regulations;

(f)   states whether or not any matter has come to the examiner's attention in connection with the examination to which, in his opinion, attention should be drawn in the report in order to enable a proper understanding of the accounts to be reached;

(g)   where any of the following matters has become apparent to the examiner during the course of the examination, namely, that—

(i)   there has been any material expenditure or action which appears not to be in accordance with the trusts of the charity; or

(ii)   any information or explanation to which he is entitled under regulation 8 below has not been afforded to him; or

(iii) in the case of an examination of accounts a statement of which has been prepared under section 42(1) of the 1993 Act, any information contained in the statement of accounts is inconsistent on any material respect with any report of the charity trustees prepared under section 45 of the 1993 Act in respect of the financial year in question,

contains a statement to that effect.

8—Audit and independent examination: supplementary provisions

(1) An auditor or independent examiner carrying out an audit or   **2G–008**

examination of the accounts of a charity under section 43 of the 1993 Act shall have a right of access to any books, documents and other records (however kept) which relate to the charity concerned and which the auditor or examiner in question considers it necessary to inspect for the purposes of carrying out the audit or, as the case may be, examination.

(2) Such an auditor or independent examiner shall be entitled to require, in the case of the charity concerned, such information and explanations from past or present charity trustees or trustees for the charity, or from past or present officers or employees of the charity, as he considers it necessary to obtain for the purposes of carrying out the audit or, as the case may be, examination.

9—Dispensations from audit or examination requirements

2G–009   (1) The Commissioners may, in the circumstances specified in paragraph (2) below, dispense with the requirements of section 43(2) or (3) of the 1993 Act in the case of a particular charity or of a particular financial year of a charity.

(2) The circumstances referred to in paragraph (1) above are where the Commissioners:

(a)   are satisfied that the accounts of the charity concerned are required to be audited in accordance with any statutory provision contained in or having effect under an Act of Parliament which, in the opinion of the Commissioners, imposes requirements which are sufficiently similar to the requirements of section 43(2) for those requirements to be dispensed with;

(b)   are satisfied that the accounts of the charity concerned have been audited by the or by the Auditor General for Wales;

(c)   are satisfied that the accounts of the charity concerned for the financial year in question have been [or will be][1] audited or, as the case may be, examined in accordance with requirements or arrangements which, in the opinion of the Commissioners, are sufficiently similar to the relevant requirements of section 43 of the 1993 Act applicable to that financial year of that charity for those requirements to be dispensed with;

(d)   are satisfied that there has in the financial year in question been no transaction on the part of the charity concerned which would be required to be shown and explained in the accounting records kept in pursuance of section 41 of the 1993 Act;

(e)   consider that, although the financial year in question of the charity concerned is one to which subsection (2) of section 43 of the 1993 Act applies, there are exceptional circumstances which justify the examination of the accounts by an independent examiner instead of their audit in accordance with that subsection, and the accounts have been so examined,

and where the charity trustees of the charity concerned have supplied the Commissioners any report made to them with respect to the accounts of that charity for the financial year in question which the Commissioners have requested.

[1] Words inserted by SI 2000/2868 (Charities (Accounts and Reports) Regulations), reg.8(3)(b).

10—Annual reports

(1) Subject to paragraph (4) below, the report on the activities of a char-   **2G–010**
ity during the year which is required to be contained in the annual report
in respect of each financial year of the charity prepared under section 45
of the 1993 Act shall specify the financial year to which it relates and
shall—

   (a)   in the case of any financial year of a charity in which its gross
income does not exceed £100,000 be a brief summary of the
main activities and achievements of the charity during the year
in relation to its objects;

   (b)   in the case of any financial year of a charity in which its gross
income exceeds £100,000, be a review of all activities, including
material transactions, significant developments, and achievements, of the charity during the year in relation to its objects,
any significant changes in those activities during the year, any
important events affecting those activities which have occurred
since the end of the year and any likely future developments in
those activities; and

   (c)   in either case, be dated and be signed by one or more of the
charity trustees, each of whom has been authorised to do so.

(2) Subject to paragraphs (4), (5) and (6) below, the information relating
to a charity and to its trustees and officers which is required to be
contained in that annual report shall be—

   (a)   the name of the charity as it appears in the register and any
other name by which unit makes itself known;

   (b)   the number assigned to it in the register and, in the case of a
charitable company, the number with which it is registered as a
company;

   (c)   the principal address of the charity and, in the case of a
charitable company, the address of its registered office;

   (d)   a description of the trusts of the charity;

   (e)   the names of the charity trustees or, in the case of a charity having more than 50 charity trustees, the names of 50 of those
trustees including any charity trustee who is also an officer of
the charity and the name of any person who has at any time during the financial year in question been a charity trustee and of any
person or body entitled to appoint a charity trustee of the charity;

   (f)   a description of the organisational structure of the charity; and

   (g)   a description of any assets held by the charity, or on behalf of
the charity by any trustee of the charity, for another charity, and
particulars of any special arrangements made with respect to the
safe custody of such assets and their segregation from assets of
the charity not so held and of the objects of the charity on
whose behalf the assets are held.

(3) The Commissioners may, where they are satisfied that, in the case of
a particular charity or class of charities, or of a particular financial year
of a charity or class of charities,—

(a) the disclosure of the name of any person whose name is required by paragraph (2)(e) above to be contained in the annual report of a charity could lead to that person being placed in any personal danger; or

(b) the disclosure of the principal address of the charity in accordance with paragraph (2)(c) above could lead to any such person being placed in any personal danger,

dispense with the requirement—

(i) in sub-paragraph (e) of that paragraph so far as it applies to the name of any such person;

or

(ii) in sub-paragraph (c) of that paragraph so far as it applies to the principal address of the charity,

as the case may require.

(4) In the case of a common investment fund or a common deposit fund which is deemed to be a charity by virtue of section 24(8), including that section as applied by using 25(2), of the 1993 Act, this regulation shall have effect as if—

(a) for sub-paragraphs (a) to (c) of paragraph (1) above there were substituted the following sub-paragraphs:

"(a) be a review of the investment activities and policies of the trustees during that year;

(b) contain particulars of any significant alteration in the terms of the scheme by which the fund was established or in the investment policies of the trustees during that year;

(c) specify any material events affecting the fund which have occurred since the end of the year;

(d) contain a statement as to whether the trustees have examined whether any person to whom they have delegated their functions in respect of the management of the fund has complied with the terms of the scheme by which the fund was established and with any agreement between the trustees and that person;

(e) be dated and signed by one or more of the trustees appointed to manage the fund, each of whom has been authorised to do so.";

(b) for sub-paragraph (e) of paragraph (2) above there were substituted the following sub-paragraph:

"(e) the names and any professional qualifications of the trustees appointed to manage the fund and any other person who has been a trustee of the fund during the financial year in question and of any person or body entitled to appoint such a trustee;";

(c) for sub-paragraph (g) of paragraph (2) above there were substituted the following sub-paragraphs:

"(g) the name and address of any person to whom the trustees have delegated their functions in respect of the management of the fund or the holding of property transferred to, or sums deposited in, the fund or whom they have appointed to advise them on investment matters;

(h) the name of any regulatory body of which any person referred to in sub-paragraph (g) above is a member; and

(i) a description of any powers delegated by the trustees and of the procedures adopted to ensure that those powers are exercised consistently with the scheme by which the fund was established and the investment policies of the trustees."

and

(d) paragraph (3) were omitted.

(5) In the case of a report prepared under section 46(5) of the 1993 Act (excepted charities which are not registered), paragraph (2) above shall effect as if,

(a) in sub-paragraph (a) the words from "as it appears in the register" to the end, and

(b) in sub-paragraph (b) the words "the number assigned to it in the register and,", were omitted.

(6) In the case of a report in respect of a financial year of a charity in which its gross income does not exceed £100,000, paragraph (2) above shall have effect as if sub-paragraphs (f) and (g) were omitted.

Signatures

Blatch

Minister of State

Home Office

17th October 1995

SCHEDULE 1 FORM AND CONTENTS OF STATEMENTS OF ACCOUNTS

PART I

STATEMENT OF FINANCIAL ACTIVITIES

Para 1

The statement of financial activities shall show the total incoming resources and application of the resources, together with any other movements in the total resources, of the charity during the financial year in respect of which the statement of accounts is prepared.

2G–011

Para 2

The information required by paragraph 1 above shall be analysed by reference to—

(a) the nature of the incoming resources or application of or movements in resources concerned, in accordance with paragraph 3 below; and

(b) the type of fund to which it relates, in accordance with paragraph 4 below.

Para 3

Subject to paragraph 5 below, the analysis required by paragraph 2(a) above is as follows:

(a) all incoming resources other than those required to be entered by sub-paragraph (e) below, divided into—

        (i)   incoming resources from donors;

        (ii)   income from investment;

        (iii) income from trading activities—

            (A)   which are in furtherance of the object of charity, and

            (B)   which are for commercial or fund-raising purposes; and

        (iv) any other incoming resources;

    (b)   all resources expended, divided into—

        (i)   expenditure directly relating to the objects of the charity;

        (ii)   expenditure on fund-raising and publicity; and

        (iii) expenditure on the cost of managing and administering the charity;

    (c)   gross transfers between the funds of the charity;

    (d)   net incoming or outgoing resources for the financial year before calculation of gains or losses on disposal of fixed assets intended for investment or on revaluation of fixed assets intended for use or investment (that is to say, the aggregate of all amounts entered in pursuance of sub-paragraphs (a), (b) and (c) above);

    (e)   any gains or losses on disposal of fixed assets intended for investment or on revaluation of fixed assets intended for use or investment, divided into—

        (i)   gains or losses on disposal of assets intended for investment;

        (ii)   unrealised gains or losses on revaluation of assets intended for investment; and;

        (iii) unrealised gains or losses on revaluation of assets intended for use;

    (f)   net movement in funds in the financial year (that is to say, the total of all entries made in pursuance of sub-paragraphs (d) and (e) above);

    (g)   the total funds brought forward from the previous financial year; and

    (h)   the total of funds carried forward to the next financial year (that is to say, the amount entered in pursuance of sub-paragraph (f) above plus the amount entered in pursuance of sub-paragraph (g) above).

Para 4

The analysis required by paragraph 2(b) above is as follows:

    (a)   unrestricted income funds;

    (b)   income funds which are restricted as to their use;

    (c)   capital funds; and

    (d)   the total for all funds of the charity (that is to say, the total of the amounts entered in pursuance of sub-paragraphs (a), (b) and (c) above).

Para 5

In the case of any financial year of a charity in which the gross income of the charity does not exceed £100,000 but in respect of which the charity trustees have made no election in pursuance of section 42(3) of the 1993 Act, paragraph 3(b) above shall have effect as if for the words from "divided into" to the end there were substituted the words "divided into such categories as reasonably enable the user to gain an appreciation of the expenditure of the charity during the year".

Part II

Balance Sheet

Para 1

2G–012   The balance sheet shall show, by reference to the information specified in paragraph 2 below, the state of affairs of the charity as at the end of the financial year in respect of which the statement of accounts is prepared.

Para 2

The information referred to in paragraph 1 above is as follows:

(a) fixed assets, divided into—
    (i) intangible assets;
    (ii) tangible assets for use by the charity; and
    (iii) investments; and
(b) current assets, divided into—
    (i) stock and work in progress;
    (ii) debtors;
    (iii) investments; and
    (iv) cash at bank and in hand;
(c) short-term creditors;
(d) net current assets or liabilities (that is to say, the difference between the total amount entered in pursuance of sub-paragraph (b) above and the total amount entered in pursuance of sub-paragraph (c) above);
(e) total assets after deduction of current liabilities (that is to say, the total amount entered in pursuance of sub-paragraph (a) above plus the amount entered in pursuance of sub-paragraph (d) above);
(f) long term creditors;
(g) provisions for liabilities or charges;
(h) net assets (that is to say, the amount entered in pursuance of sub-paragraph (e) above less the total amounts entered in pursuance of sub-paragraphs (f) and (g) above); and
(i) funds of the charity, divided into—
    (i) unrestricted income funds;
    (ii) income funds which are are restricted as to their use; and
    (iii) capital funds.

PART III

METHOD AND PRINCIPLES

Para 1

(1) The statement of financial activities shall give a true and fair view of the incoming resources and application of the resources of the charity in, and the balance sheet shall give a true and fair view of the state of affairs of the charity at the end of, the financial year in respect of which the statement of accounts is prepared.   **2G–013**

(2) Where compliance with Part I, or, as the case may be, Part II and Part IV of this Schedule would not be sufficient to give a true and fair view, the necessary additional information shall be given in the accounts or a note to them.

(3) If in special circumstances compliance with any of those provisions is inconsistent with the requirement to give a true and fair view, the charity trustees shall depart from that provision to the extent necessary to give a true and fair view; particulars of any such departure, the reasons for it and its effect shall be given in a note to the accounts.

Para 2

(1) In respect of every amount required by paragraph 3 or 4(d) of Part I of this Schedule to be shown in the statement of financial activities or b Part II of this Schedule to be shown in the balance sheet, the corresponding amount for the financial year immediately preceding that to which the statement or balance sheet relates shall also be shown.

(2) Where that corresponding amount is not comparable with the amount to be shown for the item in question in respect of the financial year to which the statement of financial activities or balance sheet relates, the former amount shall be adjusted; particular of any material adjustment under this sub-paragraph shall be disclosed in a note to the accounts.

(3) Where in the financial year to which the statement of accounts relates there is nothing required to be shown by one of more of the provisions specified in sub-paragraph (1) above but an amount was required to be shown by that provision in

the immediately preceding financial year, this paragraph shall have effect as if such an amount were required to be shown in the financial year to which the statement of accounts relates and that amount were nil.

Para 3

The values of assets and liabilities of the charity shall, for the purposes of entry in the accounts, be determined in accordance with the methods and principles for inclusion of assets and liabilities in the balance sheet set out in the Statement of Recommended Practice for Accounting by Charities issued in October 1995.

PART IV

NOTES TO THE ACCOUNTS

Para 1

2G–014 Subject to paragraph 2 below, the information to be provided by way of notes to the accounts shall, insofar as not provided in the statement of accounts, be as follows:

(a) a description of the accounting policies of, and assumptions made for the purposes of preparing the statement of accounts by, the charity trustees, including any material change in these, the reason for such change and its effect (if material) on the accounts;

(b) a description of the nature and purpose of all significant funds of the charity;

(c) a statement as to whether any remuneration or other benefits (together with the amount of such remuneration or, as the case may be, the monetary value of such benefits) has been paid or is payable to any charity trustee or person connected with such a trustee directly or indirectly from the funds of the charity or from the property of any institution or body corporate connected with the charity and the name of that person;

(d) particulars of the cost to the charity of—

   (i) any policies of insurance against loss arising from the neglect or default of any of the charity trustees or trustees for the charity; of

   (ii) indemnifying the charity trustees, or any of the trustees, for the charity in respect of the consequences of any such loss;

(e) particulars of any transaction undertaken in the name of or on behalf of the charity in which any charity trustee or person connected with such a trustee has a material interest;

(f) a description of any incoming resources which represent capital, according to whether or not that capital is permanent endowment;

(g) an itemised analysis of any material movement between any of the restricted funds of the charity, or between a restricted and an unrestricted fund of the charity, together with an explanation of the nature and purpose of each of those funds;

(h) the name of any institution or body corporate connected with the charity, together with a description of the nature of the charity's relationship with that institution or body corporate and of its activities, including, where material, its turnover and net profit or loss for the corresponding financial year of the institution or body corporate and any qualification expressed in an auditor's report on its accounts;

(i) particulars of any loan or guarantee secured against any of the assets of the charity;

(j) particulars of any remuneration paid to an auditor or independent examiner in respect of auditing or examining the accounts of the charity and particulars of any remuneration paid to him in respect of any other services rendered to the charity;

(k) such particulars of any grant made by the charity to another institution of which the Statement of Recommended Practice for Accounting by

Charities issued in October 1995 requires disclosure as may be required by that Statement;

(l) an analysis of any entry in the balance sheet relation to fixed assets—

   (i) in the case of tangible assets for use by the charity, according to the following categories—

      (A) freehold interests in land and buildings;

      (B) any other interest in land or buildings;

      (C) plant and machinery;

      (D) fixtures, fittings and equipment; and

      (E) payments on account and assets in course of construction;

   (ii) in the case of investments, according to the following categories—

      (A) investment properties;

      (B) investments listed on a recognised stock exchange;

      (C) investments in a common deposit fund, a common investment fund or any other collective investment scheme within the meaning of [section 235 of the Financial Services and Markets Act 2000][1]

      (D) investments in an institution or body corporate connected with the charity;

      (E) securities which are not listed on a recognised stock exchange;

      (F) cash; and

      (G) other investments,

   (iii) in the case of any such entry, which records—

      (A) the aggregate value of assets specified in each of paragraphs (i) to (iii) of paragraph 2(a) of Part II of this Schedule at the beginning of the financial year to which the balance sheet relates and at the date of the balance sheet, determined in accordance with the methods and principles specified in paragraph 3 of Part III of this Schedule but without making provision for depreciation or diminution in value;

      (B) the effect on the entry in the balance sheet made in pursuance of each of those paragraphs of any acquisitions, disposals or transfers of assets, or revisions in their recorded value, made during that financial year; and

      (C) the cumulative amount of provisions for depreciation or diminution in value of assets specified in each of those paragraphs as at each of the dates referred to in sub-paragraph (A) above, the amount of any such provisions made in respect of that financial year, the amount of any adjustments made in respect of any such provisions during that year in consequence of the disposal of any assets and the amount of any other adjustments made in respect of any such provisions during that year;

(m) an analysis of any entry in the balance sheet relating to debtors, according to the following categories—

   (i) trade debtors;

   (ii) amounts owed by any institution or body corporate connected with the charity;

   (iii) other debtors; and

   (iv) prepayments and accrued income;

(n) an analysis of any entry in the balance sheet relating to creditors (whether short-term or long-term creditors), according to the following categories—

   (i) loans and overdrafts;

   (ii) trade creditors;

   (iii) amounts owed to any institution or body corporate connected with the charity;

      (iv)   other creditors; and

      (v)   accruals and deferred income;

  (o)   the following particulars of any contingent liability, that is to say, its amount or estimated amount, its legal nature and whether any valuable security has been provided by the charity in connection with that liability and, if so, what;

  (p)   particulars of any other financial commitments which have not been provided for and are relevant to assessment of the state of affairs of the charity;

  (q)   in the case of any amount required by any of the preceding sub-paragraphs (other than sub-paragraph (g), (k) or (l)(iii)) to be disclosed, the corresponding amount for the financial year immediately preceding that to which the accounts relate;

  (r)   a statement as to whether or not the accounts have been prepared in accordance with any applicable accounting standards and statements of recommended practice and particulars of any material departure from those standards and practices and the reasons for such departure;

  (s)   where the charity trustees have exercised their powers under regulation 5(4)(a) or (c) above, a statement of their reasons for doing so; and

  (t)   any other information which is required by these Regulations to be disclosed in a note to the accounts or which may reasonably assist the user to understand the statement of accounts.

[1] Words substituted by SI 2001/3649 (Financial Services and Markets Act 2000 (Consequential Amendments and Repeals) Order), Pt 9, art.516.

Para 2

Sub-paragraphs (d) and (r) of paragraph 1 above shall not apply in the case of any financial year of a charity in which the gross income of the charity does not exceed £100,000 but in respect of which the charity trustees have made no election in pursuance of section 42(3) of the 1993 Act.

PART V

INTERPRETATION

Para 1

2G–015   In this Schedule the following expressions have the meanings hereafter assigned to them—

"fixed assets" means the assets of a charity which are intended for use or investment on a continuing basis;

"long-term creditor" means an amount falling due after more than one year from the end of the financial year;

"provisions for liabilities or charges" means any amount retained as reasonably necessary for the purpose of providing for any liability or loss which is either likely to be incurred, or certain to be incurred but uncertain as to amount or as to the date on which it will arise;

"resources expended" means all charges relating to the financial year in respect of which the statement of accounts is prepared, including provision for depreciation and permanent diminution in value of fixed assets, calculated on the basis that the charity is carrying on its activities as a going concern; and

"short-term creditor" means an amount falling due within one year.

Para 2

For the purposes of paragraph 1 above, an amount shall be treated as falling due on the earliest date on which payment of any part of it may be required by the person entitled to payment, if he exercised all options and rights available to him.

SCHEDULE 2—FORM AND CONTENTS OF STATEMENTS OF ACCOUNTS: COMMON INVESTMENT FUNDS AND COMMON DEPOSIT FUNDS

PART I

STATEMENT OF TOTAL RETURN

Para 1

The statement of total return shall show the net gain or loss on investments, **2G–016** gross income, total expenditure and total return of the fund, and the total amount distributed or due, including interest paid or payable, to participating charities out of the fund, during the financial year in respect of which the statement of accounts is prepared.

Para 2

The information required by paragraph 1 above shall be analysed by reference to—

- (a) net gains or losses on investments, indicated by—
    - (i) gains or losses on investments sold during the financial year in question, based on the historical cost of the investment sold;
    - (ii) any net appreciation or depreciation of such investments recognised in earlier accounting periods;
    - (iii) the gains or losses on such investments based on their value as shown in the accounts (that is to say, the difference between or, as the case may be, the sum of the amounts entered in pursuance of paragraphs (i) and (ii) above); and
    - (iv) net unrealised appreciation or depreciation of investments during the financial year in question;
- (b) gains or losses on other assets;
- (c) gross income, divided into—
    - (i) dividends in respect of shares;
    - (ii) scrip dividends;
    - (iii) interest on securities;
    - (iv) interest on deposits at banks and building societies;
    - (v) underwriting commission; and
    - (vi) other income;
- (d) expenditure incurred in the administration of the scheme under which the fund was established, divided into—
    - (i) amounts payable directly or indirectly by way of remuneration, reimbursement of expenses or otherwise to any trustee appointed to manage the fund or person connected with such a trustee;
    - (ii) amounts payable directly or indirectly by way of remuneration, reimbursement of expenses or otherwise to any person to whom the trustees have delegated their functions in relation to management of the fund or to any person connected with that person;
    - (iii) fees payable in respect of any audit carried out by an auditor under section 43 of the 1993 Act;
    - (iv) any fees payable to the person carrying out such an audit in respect of other services for the fund provided by him;
    - (v) any fees payable in respect of the safe custody of assets; and
    - (vi) other expenditure divided into such categories as reasonably enable the use to gain an appreciation of the expenditure incurred;
- (e) tax borne by the fund in respect of income, profits or gains during the financial year in question, divided into—

(i)   income tax or capital gains tax to which the fund is liable in the United Kingdom; and

(ii)   overseas tax;

(f)   net income (that is to say, the total amount entered in pursuance of sub-paragraph (c) above less the total of the amounts entered in pursuance of sub-paragraphs (d) and (e) above);

(g)   total return (that is to say, the total of the amounts entered in pursuance of sub-paragraphs (a), (b) and (f) above);

(h)   the amount distributed or due in respect of income and accumulation shares, and interest paid or payable to charities who have deposited sums, during the financial year in question; and

(i)   net increase or decrease in the value of the fund resulting from its activities (that is to say, the difference between the amounts entered in pursuance of sub-paragraphs (g) and (h) above).

Para 3

In the case of a common investment fund established by a scheme which, in pursuance of section 24(5) of the 1993 Act, includes provision for enabling sums to be deposited by or on behalf of a charity on the basis that (subject to the provisions of the scheme) the charity shall be entitled to repayment of the sums deposited and to interest thereon at a rate determined by or under the scheme, the analysis required by paragraph 2 above shall distinguish between the amount of capital and income to be shared between charities participating otherwise than by way of deposit and the amounts excluded from such amount under provision made in pursuance of section 24(5) of the 1993 Act (that is, such amounts as are from time to time reasonably required in respect of the liabilities of the fund for the repayment of deposits and for the interest on deposits, including amounts required by way of reserve).

Para 4

In respect of any information required by a sub-paragraph of paragraph 2 above to be divided into separate categories denoted by paragraphs of that sub-paragraph, the division of that information into such separate categories may, if the trustees appointed to manage the fund so elect, be effected by means of a note to the accounts made in pursuance of Part V of this Schedule rather than by division in pursuance of that sub-paragraph.

PART II

STATEMENT OF MOVEMENT IN FUNDS

Para 1

2G–017   The statement of movement in funds shall provide a reconciliation between the net assets of the fund at the beginning of the financial year in respect of which the statement of accounts is prepared and the net assets of the fund at the end of that year.

Para 2

The reconciliation referred to in paragraph 1 above shall show—

(a)   the value of the net assets at the beginning of the financial year in question;

(b)   in the case of a common investment fund, the amount or value of any property transferred to or withdrawn from the fund during that year by participating charities;

(c)   the net increase or decrease in the value of the fund resulting from its activities during that year (that is to say, the amount entered in pursuance of sub-paragraph (i) of paragraph 2 of Part I of this Schedule).

(d) in the case of a common investment fund, the amount of any distribution of income due in respect of accumulation shares; and

(e) the value of the net assets at the end of the financial year in question.

Para 3

In the case of a common investment fund such as is described in paragraph 3 of Part I of this Schedule, the analysis required by paragraph 2 above shall distinguish between the amount of capital and income to be shared between charities participating otherwise than by way of deposit and the amounts excluded from such amount under provision made in pursuance of section 24(5) of the 1993 Act.

PART III

BALANCE SHEET

Para 1

The balance sheet shall show, by reference to the information specified in paragraph 2 or, as the case may be, 3 below, the state of affairs of the fund as at the end of the financial year.

2G–018

Para 2

Subject to paragraph 4 below, in the case of a common investment fund, the information referred to in paragraph 1 above is as follows:

(a) tangible fixed assets for use by the fund;
(b) investments;
(c) current assets, divided into—
  (i) debtors;
  (ii) deposits and loans;
  (iii) cash at bank and in hand; and
  (iv) others;
(d) liabilities, divided into—
  (i) creditors
  (ii) bank overdrafts;
  (iii) other loans; and
  (iv) distributions payable to participating charities;
(e) net current assets less liabilities (that is to say, the difference between the total amount entered in pursuance of sub-paragraph (c) above and the total amount entered in pursuance of sub-paragraph (d) above); and
(f) net assets (that is to say, the total of the amounts entered in pursuance of sub-paragraphs (a), (b) and (e) above); and
(g) total funds of the common investment fund.

Para 3

In the case of a common deposit fund, the information referred to in paragraph 1 above is as follows:

(a) cash at bank and in hand;
(b) debtors;
(c) deposits and investments, divided into—
  [(i) deposits at the Bank of England;
  (ii) deposits with a person who has permission under Part 4 of the Financial Services and Markets Act 2000 to accept deposits;]¹
  (iii) other bank deposits;
  (iv) other deposits; and
  (v) other investments;
(d) current assets not included in any of paragraphs (a) to (c) above;
(e) tangible fixed assets for use by the fund;

(f) gross assets (that is to say, the total of the amounts entered in pursuance of sub-paragraphs (a) to (e) above);

(g) sums deposited by participating charities;

(h) other liabilities, divided into—

    (i)   creditors;

    (ii) bank overdrafts;

    (iii) other loans; and

    (iv) interest accrued or payable to participating charities;

(i) total liabilities (that is to say, the total of the amounts entered in pursuance of sub-paragraphs (g) and (h) above); and

(j) total funds of the common deposit fund (that is to say the amount entered in pursuance of sub-paragraph (f) above less the amount entered in pursuance of sub-paragraph (i) above).

¹ substituted by SI 2001/3649 (Financial services and Markets Act 2000 (Consequential Amendments Repeals) Order), Pt 9 Art 517 (2)

Para 4

In the case of a common investment fund such as is described in paragraph 3 of Part I of this Schedule, the information referred to in paragraph 1 above is—

(a) in relation to the amount of capital and income to be shared between charities participating otherwise than by way of deposit, the information specified in paragraph 2 above; and

(b) in relation to the amounts excluded from such amount under provision made in pursuance of section 24(5) of the 1993 Act, the information specified in paragraph 3 above.

Para 5

In respect of any information required by sub-paragraph (c) of paragraph 3 above to be divided into separate categories denoted by paragraphs of that sub-paragraph, the division of that information into such separate categories may, if the trustees appointed by manage the fund so elect, be effected by means of a note to the accounts made in pursuance of Part V of this Schedule rather than by division in pursuance of that sub-paragraph.

PART IV

METHODS AND PRINCIPLES

Para 1

2G–019   The methods and principles specified and referred to in Part III of Schedule 1 to these Regulations shall apply for the purposes of the preparation of the statement of accounts of a common investment fund or common deposit fund as the do for the purposes of the preparation of the statement of accounts of a charity to which that Schedule applies, subject to the following modifications.

Para 2

(1) For any reference to "the charity" or "charity trustees" there is substituted a reference to the fund or, as the case may be, the trustees appointed to manage the fund.

(2) In paragraph 1(1), for "statement of financial activities" there is substituted "statement of total return".

(3) After paragraph 1(1), there is inserted the following sub-paragraph:

"(1A) The statement of movement in funds shall give a true and fair view of the movements in the net assets of the fund between their position at the beginning of that year and their position at the end of that year".

(4) In their paragraph 1(2), for "Part I or, as the case may be, Part II and Part IV of this Schedule" there is substituted "Part I, II or, as the case may be, III and Part V of Schedule 2 to these Regulations".

(5) For paragraph 2(1), there is substituted the following sub-paragraph:

"(1) In respect of every amount required by paragraph 2 of Part 1 of Schedule 2 to these Regulations to be shown in the statement of total return, or by paragraph 2 of Part II of that Schedule to be shown in the statement of movement in funds, or by paragraph 2 or, as the case may be, 3 of Part III of that Schedule to be shown in the balance sheet, the corresponding amount for the financial year immediately preceding that to which the statement or balance sheet relates shall also be shown.".

(6) In paragraph 2(2), for "statement of financial activities" there is substituted "statement of total return, statement of movement in funds".

(7) In paragraph 3, for "Statement of Recommended Practice for Accounting by Charities issued in October 1995" there is substituted "Statement of Recommended Practice for Authorised Unit Trust Schemes issued in April 1991".

PART V

NOTES TO THE ACCOUNTS

Para 1

The information to be provided by way of notes to the accounts of a common investment fund or common deposit fund is the information specified Part IV of Schedule 1 to these Regulations in relation to the accounts of charities to which that Schedule applies, modified in accordance with the following provisions of this Part.

2G–020

Para 2 (1)

For any reference to "the charity" there is substituted a reference to the fund and for any reference to "the charity trustees" or "trustees for the charity" or to any of them there is substituted a reference to the trustees appointed to manage the fund or to any of them, as the case may required.

(2) For paragraph 1(a) and (b) there are substituted the following sub-paragraphs:

"(a) a description of the accounting policies of the trustees, particularly regarding the basis of valuation of investments, the recognition of dividend income or interest and the conversion of any amounts expressed in currency other than pounds sterling, and of the accounting assumptions made by them, including any material change in these, the reason for such change and its effect (if material) on the accounts;

(b) where the trustees appointed to manage the fund have during during the financial year in question entered into any transaction, agreement or arrangement made for the purpose of minimising the risk of loss to the fund in consequence of fluctuations in interest rates or in the market value of securities or in the rates of foreign exchange, or entered into any other transaction in financial futures or options relating to shares, securities, foreign currency or other financial instrument which is a trading transaction in its own right, the nature of and reason for entering that transaction, agreement or arrangement and the total value of, and the maximum extent of financial exposure as at the date of the balance sheet resulting from, that transaction, agreement or arrangement;".

(3) In paragraph 1(c), (d)(i) and (ii) and (e), after "trustees appointed to manage the fund" there is inserted "or any person to whom they have delegated their functions in relation to management of the fund".

(4) For paragraph 1(f) and (g) there are substituted the following sub-paragraphs:

"(f) an analysis of the amount and date of any distribution in respect of income and accumulation shares or payment of interest to participating charities;

(g) a note of any adjustments made in the statement of total return to reflect the amount of income included in the creation or cancellation price of a unit or share in the fund;".

(5) For paragraph 1(j) to (n) there are substituted the following sub-paragraphs—

"(j) an explanation of any amount entered in pursuance of paragraph 2(e)(i) of Part I of this Schedule (United Kingdom tax);

(k) an analysis of any entry in the balance sheet relating to:
  (i) tangible fixed assets for use by the fund, according to the following categories:
    (A) freehold interests in land and buildings;
    (B) any other interest in land or buildings;
    (C) payments on account and assets in course of construction; and
    (D) plant, machinery, fixtures, fittings and equipment;
  (ii) debtors, according to the following categories—
    (A) in the case of a common investment fund, amounts receivable in respect of property transferred to the fund;
    (B) amounts receivable in respect of securities sold;
    (C) accrued income; and
    (D) other debtors;
  (iii) creditors, according to the following categories—
    (A) in the case of a common investment fund, amounts payable in respect of property withdrawn from the fund;
    (B) amounts payable in respect of securities purchased;
    (C) accrued expenses; and
    (D) other creditors;

(l) in the case of a common investment fund, the following statements, made up to the date of the balance sheet, that is to say—
  (i) a portfolio statement, specifying—
    (A) details of each investment held by or on behalf of the fund, including its market value at that date;
    (B) the category of each such investment according to its geographical area or industrial sector;
    (C) the percentage of net assets represented by each investment so held and by each category of investment specified under paragraph (B) above; and
    (D) whether or not the investment in question is listed on a recognised stock exchange;
  (ii) a statement of major changes in the portfolio, specifying—
    (A) where the aggregate value of purchases or sales of a particular investment during the financial year in question exceeds 2 per cent of net assets at the beginning of that year, that value;
    (B) unless disclosed in pursuance of paragraph (A) above, the value of the 20 largest purchases and sales of a particular investment during the financial year in question; and
    (C) the total cost of purchase and net proceeds from sales of investments during the financial year in question;
  (iii) a statement of the number of shares issued as at the beginning of the year and as at the date of the balance sheet and the value of each income or accumulation share as at each of those dates, calculated by reference to the net asset value of the fund; and

> (iv)   a statement of the amount, if any, in the dividend equalisation reserve;
>
> (m)   in the case of a common deposit fund, details of sums deposited by participating charities as at the date of the balance sheet, divided into—
>> (i)   sums repayable on demand; and
>> (ii)   deposits with agreed maturity dates or periods of notice, divided into—
>>> (A)   those repayable in not more than three months;
>>> (B)   those repayable in more than three months but not more than one year;
>>> (C)   those repayable in more than one year but not more than five years; and
>>> (D)   those repayable in more than five years;
>
> (n)   in the case of a common deposit fund, details as at the date of the balance sheet of—
>> (i)   sums placed on deposit, divided into—
>>> (A)   sums repayable on demand; and
>>> (B)   other deposits, indication whether they are repayable in not more than 3 months, more than 3 months but not more than 1 year, more than 1 year but not more than 5 years or more than 5 years; and
>> (ii)   investments other than deposits, analysed in accordance with sub-paragraph (m) above;".

(6) For paragraph 1(q) there shall be substituted the following sub-paragraph:

"(q) in the case of any amount required by any of the preceding sub-paragraphs (other than sub-paragraph (1)(i) and (ii)) to be disclosed, or the percentage of net assets represented by each category of investment required by sub-paragraph (1)(i)(C) above to be disclosed, the corresponding amount or percentage for the financial year immediately preceding that to which the accounts relate;".

PART VI

INTERPRETATION

Para 1

In this Schedule, "dividend equalisation reserve" means income withheld from distribution with a view to avoiding fluctuations in the amounts distributed.   **2G–021**

Para 2

For the purposes of this Schedule, a person is connected with a trustee appointed to manage the fund or a person to whom the trustees appointed to manage the fund have delegated their functions in relation to management of the fund (in this paragraph referred to as "the manager") if—

> (a)   he is the child, parent, grandchild, grandparent, brother or sister of the manager;
> (b)   he is the spouse of the manager or of any person connected with him by virtue of sub-paragraph (a) above;
> (c)   he is the trustee of any trust, not being a charity, the beneficiaries or potential beneficiaries of which include the manager or any person connected with him by virtue of sub-paragraph (a) or (b) above and is acting in his capacity as such;
> (d)   he is a partner of the manager or of any person connected with him by virtue of sub-paragraph (a), (b) or (c) or above and is acting in his capacity as such, or

(e)   the person is a body corporate, not being a company which is connected with a charitable institution without the meaning of section 58(5) of the Charities Act 1992, in which the manager has, or the manager and any other manager or managers or person or persons connected with him by virtue of sub-paragraph (a), (b), (c) or (d) above, taken together, have, a substantial interest.

Para 3

Any expression in paragraph 2 above which also appears in Schedule 5 to the 1993 Act shall be construed in accordance with paragraphs 2 to 4 of that Schedule.

Para 4

[In Part III of this Schedule, paragraph (3)(c)(ii) must be read with—

(a)   section 22 o the Financial Services and Markets Act 2000;
(b)   any relevant order under that section; and
(c)   Schedule 2 to that Act.]

[1] Added by SI 2001/3649 (Financial Services and Markets Act 2000 (Consequential Amendments and Repeals) Order), Pt 9, art. 517(3).

Charities (Accounts and Reports) Regulations

(SI 2000/2868)

(In force from November 15, 2000)

The Secretary of State, in exercise of the powers conferred upon him by sections 42 , 44, 45 and 86(3) of the Charities Act 1993[1] and after such consultation as is mentioned in section 86(4) of that Act, hereby makes the following Regulations:

[1] Section 42 was amended by the Charities Act 1993 (Substitution of Sums) Order 1995 (SI 1995/2696) and section 45 was amended by section 29 of the Deregulation and Contracting Out Act 1994 (c. 40) and by Pt II of Sch 1 to the Companies Act 1985 (Audit Exemption) Regulations 1994 (SI 1994/1935).

1—Citation and commencement

These Regulations may be cited as the Charities (Accounts and Reports) Regulations 2000 and shall come into force on 15th November 2000.

2H–001

GENERAL MATERIALS
2—Interpretation

In these Regulations—

"director" includes any person occupying the position of a director, by whatever name called, and in relation to a body corporate whose affairs are managed by its members means a member of the body corporate;

2H–002

"ex gratia payment" means any such application of the property of a charity, or any such waiver by a charity of any entitlement to receive any property, as may be authorised under section 27(1) of the 1993 Act;

"the 1993 Act" means the Charities Act 1993;

"the 1995 Regulations" means the Charities (Accounts and Reports) Regulations 1995;

"financial year" shall be construed in accordance with regulation 5 of the 1995 Regulations;

"fixed assets" means the assets of a charity which are intended for use or investment on a continuing basis;

"fund" means particular assets of a charity held on trusts which, as respects the purposes for which those assets are held, or as respects the powers of the charity trustees to use or apply those assets, are not identical with those on which other assets of the charity are held;

"income reserves" means those assets in the unrestricted fund of a charity which the charity trustees have, or can make, available to apply for all or any of its purposes, once they have provided for the commitments of the charity and its other planned expenditure;

"institution or body corporate connected with the charity" has the same meaning as in the 1995 Regulations;

"the SORP" means the Statement of Recommended Practice for Accounting and Reporting by Charities, issued by the Charity Commissioners on 17th October 2000;

"special case charity" means a charity which is either—

   (a) a registered social landlord within the meaning of the Housing Act 1996 and whose registration has been recorded under section 3(3) of that Act; or
   (b) has during the financial year in question—
        (i)   conducted an institution in relation to which a designation made, or having effect as if made, under section 129 of the Education Reform Act 1988[1] or section 28 of the Further and Higher Education Act 1992[2] has effect;
        (ii) received financial support from funds administered by a higher education funding council or further education funding council within the meaning of the said Act of 1992 in respect of expenditure incurred or to be incurred by the charity in connection with that institution; and
        (iii) incurred no expenditure for charitable purposes other than the purposes of that institution or any other such institution;

"trustee for a charity" includes a custodian trustee and a nominee;

"unrestricted fund" means a fund which is to be used or applied in any way determined by the charity trustees for the furtherance of the objects of a charity, and "restricted fund" means any other fund of a charity.

[1] Section 129 was amended by section 72(1) of the Further and Higher Education Act 1992.
[2] Section 28 was amended by para.109 of Sch.37 to the Education Act 1996 (c. 56) and by paras 33 and 38 of Sch.30 to the School Standards and Framework Act 1998 (c. 31).

3—Form and content of statements of accounts

2H–003   (1) This regulation applies to a statement of accounts prepared by the charity trustees of a charity (other than a charity specified or referred to in regulation 4 of the 1995 Regulations) in accordance with section 42(1) of the 1993 Act in respect of a financial year—

   (a) which begins on or after 1st January 2001; or
   (b) which begins before that date if—
        (i)   the charity trustees determine that this regulation, rather than regulation 3 of the 1995 Regulations, shall apply to the statement of accounts; and
        (ii) the charity trustees have not, before the date when these regulations come into force, either approved the accounts of the charity in respect of that financial year, or authorised the signature of an annual report in respect of that financial year in accordance with regulation 10(1)(c) of the 1995 Regulations.

(2) If the charity trustees make a determination under sub-paragraph (b) above, they shall also make a determination under regulation 7(1)(b) below, if they are required to prepare an annual report in respect of the financial year in question.

(3) The requirements as to form and content of a statement of accounts

to which this regulation applies are those set out in the following provisions of this regulation.

(4) The statement shall consist of—

(a) a statement of financial activities which shall show the total incoming resources and application of the resources, together with any other movements in the total resources, of the charity during the financial year in respect of which the statement is prepared; and

(b) a balance sheet which shall show the state of affairs of the charity as at the end of the financial year in respect of which the statement is prepared.

(5) The statement shall be prepared in accordance with the following principles, namely that—

(a) the statement of financial activities shall give a true and fair view of the incoming resources and application of the resources of the charity in the financial year in respect of which the statement is prepared;

(b) the balance sheet shall give a true and fair view of the state of affairs of the charity at the end of that year;

(c) where compliance with the following requirements of this regulation would not be sufficient to give a true and fair view, the necessary additional information shall be given in the statement of accounts or in notes to the accounts;

(d) if in special circumstances compliance with any of those requirements would be inconsistent with giving a true and fair view, the charity trustees shall depart from the requirement to the extent necessary to give a true and fair view.

(6) The statement—

(a) shall be prepared in accordance with the methods and principles set out in the SORP; and

(b) subject to the following three paragraphs of this regulation, shall, with respect to any amount required to be shown in the statement of financial activities or in the balance sheet, also show the corresponding amount for the financial year immediately preceding that to which the statement or balance sheet relates.

(7) Where that corresponding amount is not comparable with the amount to be shown for the item in question in respect of the financial year to which the statement of financial activities or balance sheet relates, the former amount shall be adjusted.

(8) Where in the financial year to which the statement of accounts relates the effect of paragraph (5) and paragraph (6)(a) above is that there is nothing required to be shown in respect of a particular item, but an amount was required to be shown in respect of that item in the statement of accounts for the immediately preceding financial year, those provisions shall have effect as if such an amount were required to be shown in the statement of accounts in the financial year to which the statement relates, and that amount were nil.

(9) Where a charity has more than one fund, only amounts corresponding to the entries in the statement of financial activities relating to the totals of both or all of the funds of the charity need be shown.

(10) There shall be provided by way of notes to the accounts the information specified in the Schedule to these Regulations, and proviso (ii) to regulation 5(4) of the 1995 Regulations shall have effect as if for the reference to regulation 3(4) of those Regulations there were substituted a reference to this paragraph of this regulation.

(11) The balance sheet shall be signed by one or more of the charity trustees of the charity, each of whom has been authorised to do so, and shall specify the date on which the statement of accounts of which the balance sheet forms part was approved by the charity trustees.

4—Audit and independent examination

2H–004   In relation to a statement of accounts to which regulation 3 applies—

(a)   regulation 6(2)(e) of the 1995 Regulations shall have effect as if, for the reference to regulation 3 of those Regulations, there were substituted a reference to regulation 3 above; and

(b)   regulation 7(e)(iii) of the 1995 Regulations shall have effect as if, for the reference to regulation 3 of those Regulations, there were substituted a reference to regulation 3 above, and as if, for the reference to paragraph 1 of Part III of Schedule 1 to the 1995 Regulations, there were substituted a reference to sub-paragraphs (a) and (b) of paragraph (5) of regulation 3 above.

5—Form and content: special cases

2H–005   (1) This regulation applies to a statement of accounts prepared by the charity trustees of a special case charity in accordance with section 42(1) of the 1993 Act in respect of a financial year which begins on or after 1st January 2001.

(2) The requirements as to form and content of a statement of accounts to which this regulation applies are those set out in the following provisions of this regulation.

(3) The statement shall consist of an income and expenditure account and a balance sheet as at the end of the financial year in respect of which the statement of accounts is prepared.

(4) The statement shall be prepared in accordance with the following principles, namely that—

(a)   the income and expenditure account shall give a true and fair view of the income and expenditure of the charity for the financial year in respect of which the statement of accounts is prepared; and

(b)   the balance sheet shall give a true and fair view of the state of affairs of the charity at the end of that year.

6—Audit and independent examination

2H–006   In relation to a statement of accounts to which regulation 5 applies—

(a)   regulation 6(2)(e) of the 1995 Regulations shall have effect as if, for the reference to regulation 4 of those Regulations, there were substituted a reference to regulation 5 above and as if for the words "incoming resources and application of the resources" there were substituted the words "income and expenditure"; and

(b) regulation 7(e)(iii) ofthe 1995 Regulations shall have effect as if, for the reference to regulation 4 of those Regulations, there were substituted a reference to regulation 5 above, and as if for the reference to paragraph 1 of Part III of Schedule 1 to those Regulations, there were substituted a reference to regulation 5(4) above.

7—Annual reports

(1) This regulation applies to an annual report prepared by the charity trustees of a charity (other than a charity specified in regulation 10(4) of the 1995 Regulations) in accordance with section 45(1) of the 1993 Act in respect of a financial year—   **2H–007**

(a) which begins on or after 1st January 2001; or
(b) which begins before that date if—
    (i) the charity trustees determine that this regulation, rather than regulation 10 of the 1995 Regulations, shall apply to the annual report; and
    (ii) the charity trustees have not, before the date when these Regulations come into force, either authorised the signature of an annual report in respect of that financial year in accordance with regulation 10(1)(c) of the 1995 Regulations or approved a statement of accounts which has been prepared for the charity in respect of that financial year under regulation 3 of those Regulations.

(2) If the charity trustees make a determination under sub-paragraph (b) above, they shall also make a determination under regulation 3(1)(b) above, if they prepare a statement of accounts under section 42(1) of the 1993 Act in respect of the financial year in question and the charity is one to which regulation 3 above may apply.

(3) The report on the activities of a charity during the year which is required to be contained in the annual report in respect of each financial year of the charity prepared under section 45 of the 1993 Act shall specify the financial year to which it relates and shall—

(a) in the case of any financial year of a charity in which its gross income does not exceed £250,000, be a brief summary of the main activities and achievements of the charity during the year in relation to its objects;
(b) in the case of any financial year of a charity in which its gross income exceeds £250,000—
    (i) be a review of all activities, including—
        (aa) material transactions, significant developments and achievements of the charity during the year in relation to its objects;
        (bb) any significant changes in those activities during the year;
        (cc) any important events affecting those activities which have occurred since the end of the year and any likely future developments in those activities; and

(dd) where any fund of the charity was in deficit at the beginning of the financial year, the steps taken by the charity trustees to eliminate that deficit; and

(ii) contain a statement as to whether the charity trustees have given consideration to—

(aa) the major risks to which the charity is exposed; and

(bb) systems designed to mitigate those risks; and

(c) in either case, be dated and be signed by one or more of the charity trustees, each of whom has been authorised to do so.

(4) Subject to paragraphs (5) to (8) below, the information relating to a charity and to its trustees and officers which is required to be contained in that annual report shall be—

(a) the name of the charity as it appears in the register of charities and any other name by which it makes itself known;

(b) the number assigned to it in the register and, in the case of a charitable company, the number with which it is registered as a company;

(c) the principal address of the charity and, in the case of a charitable company, the address of its registered office;

(d) particulars, including the date if known, of any deed or other document containing provisions which regulate the purposes and administration of the charity;

(e) a description of the objects of the charity;

(f) the name of any person or body of persons entitled by the trusts of the charity to appoint one or more new charity trustees, and a description of the method provided by those trusts for such appointment;

(g) the name of any person who is a charity trustee of the charity on the date when the authority referred to in paragraph (3)(c) above is given, and, where any charity trustee on that date is a body corporate, the name of any person who is a director of the body corporate on that date;

(h) the name of any other person who has, at any time during the financial year in question, been a charity trustee of the charity;

(i) the name of any person who is a trustee for the charity on the date referred to in sub-paragraph (g) above;

(j) the name of any other person who has, at any time during the financial year in question, been a trustee for the charity;

(k) a description of the policies (if any) which have been adopted by the charity trustees—

(i) for the purpose of determining the level of income reserves which it is appropriate for the charity to maintain in order to meet effectively the needs designated by its trusts;

(ii) for the selection of investments for the charity; and

(iii) for the selection of individuals and institutions who are to receive grants out of the assets of the charity;

(l) a statement regarding the performance during the financial year of the investments belonging to the charity (if any);

(m) a description of the organisational structure of the charity; and

(n) a description of any assets held by the charity or by any charity trustee of, or trustee for, the charity, on behalf of another charity, and particulars of any special arrangements made with respect to the safe custody of such assets and their segregation from assets of the charity not so held and a description of the objects of the charity on whose behalf the assets are held.

(5) The Commissioners may, where they are satisfied that, in the case of a particular charity or class of charities, or in the case of a particular financial year of a charity or class of charities—

    (a)   the disclosure of the name of any person whose name is required by any of sub-paragraphs (f) to (j) of paragraph (4) above to be contained in the annual report of a charity could lead to that person being placed in any personal danger; or

    (b)   the disclosure of the principal address of the charity in accordance with paragraph (4)(c) above could lead to any such person being placed in any personal danger,

dispense with the requirement—

    (i)   in any of sub-paragraphs (f) to (j) of that paragraph, so far as it applies to the name of any such person; or

    (ii)   in sub-paragraph (c) of that paragraph, so far as it applies to the principal address of the charity,

as the case may require.

(6) In the case of a charity having more than 50 charity trustees on the date referred to in paragraph (4)(g) above—

    (a)   that sub-paragraph shall have effect as if for the words "name of any person who is a charity trustee of the charity" there were substituted the words "names of not less than 50 of the charity trustees of the charity, including any charity trustee who is also an officer of the charity"; and

    (b)   paragraph (4)(h) shall have effect as if, at the end of the sub-paragraph, there were inserted the words "other than the name of any charity trustee whose name has been excluded from the report in pursuance of sub- paragraph (g) above".

(7) In the case of a report prepared under section 46(5) of the 1993 Act (excepted charities which are not registered), paragraph (4) above shall have effect as if—

    (a)   in sub-paragraph (a) the words from "as it appears in the register of charities" to the end, and

    (b)   in sub-paragraph (b) the words "the number assigned to it in the register and,", were omitted.

(8) In the case of a report in respect of a financial year of a charity in which its gross income does not exceed £250,000, paragraph (4) above shall have effect as if sub-paragraphs (l) to (n) were omitted.

8—Minor amendments to the 1995 Regulations

  (1) In regulation 2(1) —

(a)   after the words "deposit fund established by a scheme" there shall be inserted the words "under section 22A of the Charities Act 1960[1] or"; and

(b)   after the words "investment fund established by a scheme" there shall be inserted the words "under section 22 of the Charities Act 1960 or".

(2) For regulation 4(7)(a) there shall be substituted the following—

"(a) is a registered social landlord within the meaning of the Housing Act 1996 and whose registration has been recorded under section 3(3) of that Act; or".

(3) In regulation 9(2) —

(a)   in sub-paragraph (b) , after the words "Comptroller and Auditor General" there shall be inserted the words "or by the Auditor General for Wales"; and

(b)   in sub-paragraph (c) , after the words "have been" there shall be inserted the words "or will be".

[1]   Section 22A was inserted by the Charities Act 1992 (c. 41).

Signatures

Paul Boateng

Minister of State

Home Office

19th October 2000

SCHEDULE 1—NOTES TO THE ACCOUNTS

2H–009   Para 1 Subject to paragraph 2 below, the information to be provided by way of notes to the accounts shall, insofar as not provided in the statement of financial activities or in the balance sheet, be as follows:

(a)   particulars of any material adjustment made pursuant to regulation 3(7) above;

(b)   a description of the accounting policies of, and assumptions made for the purposes of preparing the statement of accounts by, the charity trustees, including any material change in these, the reason for such change and its effect (if material) on the accounts, in accordance with the methods and principles set out in the SORP;

(c)   a description of the nature and purpose of all material funds of the charity in accordance with the methods and principles set out in the SORP;

(d)   such particulars of the related party transactions of the charity, or of any institution or body corporate connected with the charity, as may be required by the SORP to be disclosed;

(e)   such particulars of the cost to the charity of employing staff as may be required by the SORP to be disclosed;

(f)   such particulars of the emoluments of staff employed by the charity as may be required by the SORP to be disclosed;

(g)   particulars of the cost to the charity of—

(i)   any policies of insurance against loss arising from the neglect or default of any of the charity trustees or trustees for the charity; or

(ii) indemnifying the charity trustees, or trustees for the charity, or any of them, in respect of the consequences of any such loss;

(h) a description of any incoming resources which represent capital, according to whether or not that capital is permanent endowment;

(i) an itemised analysis of any material movement between any of the restricted funds of the charity, or between a restricted and an unrestricted fund of the charity, together with an explanation of the nature and purpose of each of those funds;

(j) the name of any institution or body corporate connected with the charity, together with a description of the nature of the charity's relationship with that institution or body corporate and of its activities, including, where material, its turnover and net profit or loss for the corresponding financial year of the institution or body corporate and any qualification expressed in an auditor's report on its accounts;

(k) particulars of any guarantee given by the charity, where any potential liability under the guarantee is outstanding at the date of the balance sheet;

(l) particulars of any loan outstanding at the date of the balance sheet—
  (i) which was made to the charity, and which is secured by an express charge on any of the assets of the charity; or
  (ii) which was made by the charity to any institution or body corporate connected with the charity;

(m) particulars of any fund of the charity which is in deficit at the date of the balance sheet;

(n) particulars of any remuneration paid to an auditor or independent examiner in respect of auditing or examining the accounts of the charity and particulars of any remuneration paid to him in respect of any other services rendered to the charity;

(o) such particulars of any grant made by the charity as may be required by the SORP to be disclosed;

(p) particulars of any ex gratia payment made by the charity;

(q) an analysis of any entry in the balance sheet relating to fixed assets, debtors and creditors, according to the categories set out in the SORP;

(r) an analysis of all material changes during the financial year in question in the values of fixed assets, in accordance with the methods and principles set out in the SORP;

(s) the following particulars of any contingent liability existing at the date of the balance sheet, that is to say, its amount or estimated amount, its legal nature and whether any valuable security has been provided by the charity in connection with that liability and, if so, what;

(t) particulars of any other financial commitments which are outstanding at the date of the balance sheet, and which have not been provided for and are relevant to assessment of the state of affairs of the charity;

(u) if the market value (as at the date of the balance sheet) of any land forming part of the property of the charity differs substantially from the amount at which that land is included in the balance sheet, and the difference is, in the opinion of the charity trustees, of such significance as to require that attention be drawn to it, particulars of that difference;

(v) in the case of any amount required by any of the preceding sub-paragraphs (other than sub-paragraph (i), (o) or (r) to be disclosed), the corresponding amount for the financial year immediately preceding that to which the accounts relate;

(w) a statement as to whether or not the accounts have been prepared in accordance with any applicable accounting standards and statements of recommended practice and particulars of any material departure from those standards and statements of practice and the reasons for such departure;

(x) where the charity trustees have exercised their powers under sub- para-graph (a) or (c) of regulation 5(4) of the 1995 Regulations so as to deter-mine an accounting reference date earlier or later than 12 months from the beginning of thefinancial year, a statement of their reasons for doing so;

(y) if, in accordance with regulation 3(5)(d) above, the charity trustees have departed from any requirement of that regulation, particulars of any such departure, the reasons for it, and its effect; and

(z) any additional information—

   (i) which is required to ensure that the statement of accounts com-plies with the requirements of regulations 3 above; or

   (ii) which may reasonably assist the user to understand the statement of accounts.

Para 2 Sub-paragraphs (g) and (w) of paragraph 1 above shall not apply in the case of any financial year of a charity in which the gross income of the charity does not exceed £250,000.

Charities (Exception from Registration) (Amendment) Regulation (SI 2002/1598)

(In force from August 1, 2002)

The Secretary of State, in exercise of the powers conferred upon him by section 3(5) and (13) of the Charities Act 1993, hereby makes the following Regulations:

1—Citation and commencement

These Regulations may be cited as the Charities (Exception from Registration) (Amendment) Regulations 2002 and shall come into force on 1st August 2002.

2I–001

2—Amendment of the Charities (Exception from Registration) Regulations 1996

(1) The Charities (Exception from Registration) (Amendment) Regulations 1996[1] are amended as follows.

2I–002

(2) In regulation 4(1) (temporary exception of certain religious charities connected with certain bodies) for the words "until 1st October 2002" substitute "until 1st October 2007".

[1] As amended by the Charities (Exception from Registration) (Amendment) Regulations 2001 (SI 2001/260).

3—Revocation of 2001 Regulations

The Charities (Exception from Registration) (Amendment) Regulations 2001 are hereby revoked.

2I–003

Signatures

Filkin

Parliamentary Under-Secretary of State

Home Office

18th June 2002

Appendix Three

ACCOUNTING AND REPORTING BY CHARITIES
STATEMENT OF RECOMMENDED PRACTICE
(REVISED 2000)

Accounting and Reporting by Charities

This Statement of Recommended Practice ("SORP") sets out recommendations on the way in which a charity should report annually on the resources entrusted to it and the activities it undertakes. It supersedes the previous SORP issued in October 1995 and follows initial consultation in September 1998 and consultation on the exposure draft in December 1999.

3A–00A

These recommendations need not be applied to immaterial items, that is items that are not significant in the context of the charity. A definition of what is "material" is included in the Glossary.

The Glossary is intended to help charity trustees and their staff, as well as their legal and financial advisers, auditors and independent examiners, to understand the terms and words used in this SORP.

The attention of charities in Scotland, Northern Ireland and the Republic of Ireland is drawn to paragraphs 19, 20 and 21 respectively.

The attention of smaller charities is drawn to paragraphs 344–358.

A book of examples is separately available.

Statement by the Accounting Standards Board

The aims of the Accounting Standards Board (the ASB) are to establish and improve standards of financial accounting and reporting, for the benefit of users, preparers, and auditors of financial information. To this end, the ASB issues accounting standards that are primarily applicable to general purpose company financial statements. In particular industries or sectors, further guidance may be required in order to implement accounting standards effectively. This guidance is issued, in the form of Statements of Recommended Practice (SORPs), by bodies recognised for the purpose by the ASB.

3A–00B

The Charity Commission has confirmed that it shares the ASB's aim of advancing and maintaining standards of financial reporting in the public interest and has been recognised by the ASB for the purpose of issuing SORPs. As a condition of recognition, the Commission has agreed to follow the ASB's code of practice for bodies recognised for issuing SORPs.

The code of practice sets out procedures to be followed in the development of SORPs. These procedures do not include a comprehensive review of the proposed SORP by the ASB, but a review of limited scope is performed.

On the basis of its review, the ASB has concluded that the SORP has been developed in accordance with the ASB's code of practice and does not appear to contain any fundamental points of principle that are unacceptable in the context of present accounting practice or to conflict with an accounting standard or the ASB's plans for future standards.

Statement by the Charity Commissioners for England and Wales

3A–00C   The Trustees of all charities are under a duty to keep proper accounting records for their charity which are sufficient to show and explain all the charity's transactions. This revised Statement of Recommended Practice (SORP) sets out how a charity should report annually on resources entrusted to it and the activities it undertakes.

This SORP applies to all charities regardless of their size, constitution or complexity – except where a more specialised SORP applies (eg Higher Educational Institutions, Registered Social Landlords). The impact of the SORP will, however, depend upon the size and complexity of a charity's operation. To help smaller charities in particular, the Charity Commission produces a range of simplified guidance.

The Commission expects charities to comply fully with this or any other applicable SORP. In so far as a charity diverges from the SORP in material respects, the charity's accounts should identify any divergence clearly and provide a full explanation. If no explanation is given or the explanation is unsatisfactory, the Commission may raise the matter with the charity and, if circumstances warrant it, institute an inquiry.

Where, the Commission finds that difficulties have arisen as a result of any divergence from this or any other applicable SORP, the Commission will take such divergence and any explanation the Trustees have given into account. The failure of Trustees without good reason to apply the appropriate SORP principles may be relevant to their responsibility for the difficulties arising.

INTRODUCTION

Effective Date of Commencement

3A–001   1. This Charities Statement of Recommended Practice (SORP) is applicable to all accounting periods beginning on or after **1 January 2001**. Early adoption is encouraged.

The Objective

3A–002   2. The objective in publishing these recommendations is to improve the quality of financial reporting by charities and to assist those who are responsible for the preparation of the charity's Annual Report and Accounts. The intention is that these recommendations will reduce diversity in accounting practice and presentation. In all but exceptional circumstances charities preparing accruals accounts should follow this SORP in order for their accounts to give a true and fair view.

Purpose of Charity's Annual Report and Accounts

3A–003   3. The purpose of preparing a charity's Annual Report and Accounts is to discharge the charity trustees' duty of public accountability and stewardship. This SORP sets out recommended practice for this purpose but charity trustees should consider providing such additional information as to give donors, beneficiaries and the general public a greater insight into the charity's activities and achievements. Accounts prepared on the basis of this SORP are not a substitute for management accounts required to run the charity on a daily basis.

4. The report and accounts should therefore:

(a) provide timely and regular information on the charity and its funds;
(b) enable the reader to understand the charity's objectives, structure, activities and achievements; and
(c) enable the reader to gain a full and proper appreciation of the charity's financial transactions during the year and of the position of its funds at the end of the year.

5. The SORP is principally a guide for those who prepare and audit charity accounts. It is necessarily written in the language of accounting principles and standards and may not readily be understood by people who have no or little knowledge of accounting. Trustees are, however, ultimately responsible for the charity's resources and finances as reflected in the accounts and those who have no or little knowledge of accounting will need to reassure themselves on such matters with the help of colleagues, staff or professional advisers.

How to Use the SORP

6. **There will be few, if any, charities to which all parts of this SORP apply since it caters for a wide variety of charity activities and transactions. Charities should ignore those sections which do not apply to them.** For instance advice on how to account for gifts in kind and the proceeds of trading activities will not apply to all charities. Readers whose charity does not have receipts from those sources may safely pass over the passages dealing with them and any other passages which do not apply to their charity's own activities. **However, there are several passages which will apply to all or nearly all charities.**   3A–004

7. **The main test of the SORP deals with the normal accounting practice for those charities producing full accruals accounts.** Some charities will have to meet additional requirements and others may have the option of preparing briefer reports and accounts. The following sections have therefore been provided to explain the additional or optional requirements for:

(a) Consolidation of subsidiary undertakings—paragraphs 229–319.
(b) Accounting for Associates, Joint Ventures and Joint Arrangements— paragraphs 320–330.
(c) Charitable Companies—paragraphs 331–343.
(d) Accounting for Small Charities—paragraphs 344–358.

8. The disclosure requirements have been separately identified throughout the SORP. **Those disclosure paragraphs which are applicable to all charities have been marked as AA and should be included in the accounts or the annual report as required.** Other disclosure requirements have not been marked with **AA** since they will not be relevant to the circumstances of every charity but, where they are relevant, they should be included in the notes to the accounts.

9. The main obligation of the trustees in preparing accruals accounts (but not receipts and payments accounts) is to give a true and fair view of the charity's incoming resources and application of resources during the year and of its state of affairs at the end of the year. To achieve this, the trustee's judgement may dictate the disclosure of more information than specifically recommended in this SORP. Similarly trustees may occasionally find that following a recommendation is incompatible with the obligation to give a true and fair view. They should then use the alternative accounting treatment which gives a true and fair view and provide particulars (in accordance with paragraph 280) of any material departure from the recommendations in this SORP, in the Annual Report and the notes to the accounts. **A departure is not justified simply because it gives the reader a more appealing picture of the financial position or results of the charity.**   3A–005

Interpretation of Accounts

3A–006   10. Charities are highly disparate in character, so any comparison of the financial information they produce must be undertaken with care, even if the charities involved seem to be similar. Essentially the accounts should include all the money and other assets entrusted to the charity for whatever purpose, and show how they have been expended during the year and how the balance of each fund is deployed at the end of the accounting period.

11. The Statement of Financial Activities of a charity is not intended to demonstrate a charity's efficiency nor to provide any indication of the charity's future needs but shows how a charity receives and applies its resources to meet its objectives. Similarly, the balance sheet is not necessarily a measure of the wealth of the charity but does show the resources available, what form those resources take, and how they are held in the different funds.

Scope

3A–007   12. This SORP is intended to apply to all charities in the United Kingdom and the Republic of Ireland regardless of their size, constitution or complexity. It provides the basis for the preparation of accruals accounts to give a true and fair view and also provides recommendations in other cases *e.g.* on the preparation of receipts and payments accounts. However, where a separate SORP exists for a particular class of charities, the trustees of charities in that class should adhere to that Statement of Recommended Practice.

13. **Each recommendation should be considered in the context of what is material** (see Appendix 1: Glossary) **to the particular charity.**

14. Where necessary these recommendations should be adapted to meet:

    (a)   any statutory requirements relating to the form and content of accounts, such as are contained in companies legislation, the Industrial and provident Societies acts 1965 and 1978, in determinations made by the Housing Corporation under the provisions of the Housing Act 1996 or regulations made under the Law Reform (Miscellaneous Provision) (Scotland) Act 1990; and

    (b)   any requirements imposed by the charity's own governing document to the extent that these exceed statutory requirements.

3A–008   15. The trustees of Common Investment Funds (CIFs) in England and Wales, other than pooling scheme funds (see Appendix 1: Glossary) should, in the preparation of their accounts and the notes to them, follow the Statement of Recommended Practice (currently January 1997) for authorised unit trust schemes which has been published by the Investment Management Regulatory Organisation (IMRO) and the appropriate part of the Regulations set out in the Charity (Accounts and Reports) Regulations 1995 and the Charity (Accounts and Reports) Regulations 2000 and any subsequent regulations which may be made. The trustees of Common Deposit Funds (CDFs) should meet the requirements of those regulations.

16. Several guides are produced for different segments of the charity sector and within different parts of the United Kingdom. These guides do not replace the SORP or, where applicable, the Regulations. They should be regarded as supplementary, recommending a way in which the Charities SORP and the Regulations can be applied to specific situations. If a charity uses one of these guides it should ensure that there is proper compliance with the SORP against which the Charity Commission monitors accounts of charities in England and Wales.

The SORP and the Law applicable in the UK

17. The SORP is compatible with the requirements of the law. The purpose of **3A–009** the SORP is to show how to prepare a charity's annual report and accounts so that the conform with the legal requirements and that the accounts (except for receipts and payments accounts) give a true and fair view of the charity's financial activities and position. Preparing the accounts and report in accordance with this SORP will not only ensure that they are in accordance with the law but also help the reader to gain a clearer understanding of the nature and extent of the charity's work.

The SORP and the Law applicable in England and Wales

18. Different types of charity must follow legislation in relation to their accounts **3A–010** (see paragraph 14). For non-company charities in England and Wales, the legislation relating to the form and content of charity reports and accounts is PART VI Charities Act 1993, and the Charities (Accounts and Reports) Regulations 1995, and the Charities (Accounts and Reports) Regulations 2000, both made under Part VI (referred to together as "the Regulations"). (Charitable companies see paragraphs 331–343). The Regulations cover the legal requirements in a number of areas, including:

(a) the form and content of accruals accounts;
(b) the form and content of annual reports
(c) the accounting methods and principles which must be followed in preparing accruals accounts;
(d) the further information which must be provided in the notes to the accounts.

The SORP and the Law applicable in Scotland

19. Whilst the remit of the Charity Commission does not extend to Scotland the **3A–011** content of this SORP is intended to apply except where it would be inappropriate to do so. The legislation in Scotland relating to the form and content of non-company charities' report and accounts is the Law Reform (Miscellaneous Provisions) (Scotland) Act 1990 and regulations made thereunder. In particular, this legislation requires Scottish non-company charities to prepare, as a primary statement, an Income and Expenditure Account; this statement should be provided in addition to those statements requires under this SORP. In a small number of cases the disclosure requirements may be more onerous that those set out in the SORP and in such cases the legislative requirement must be followed.

The SORP and the Law applicable in Northern Ireland

20. In Northern Ireland, charities are governed by the Charities Act (Northern **3A–012** Ireland) 1964 and the Charities (Northern Ireland) Order 1987. There is no Charity Commission for Northern Ireland: the charity authority is the Department for Social Development. There is no register of charities for Northern Ireland, and no requirement for accounts to be filed with the Department, except where this is specifically directed by the High Court of Justice in Northern Ireland or the Department acting under specific statutory powers. Section 27 of the Charities Act (Northern Ireland) 1964 requires the trustees of a charity to keep proper accounts and to preserve them for at least 7 years.

The SORP and the Law applicable in the Republic Of Ireland

3A–013   21. In the Republic of Ireland, charities are governed by the Charities Acts 1961 and 1973. Neither of these Acts requires charities to register or to prepare and submit accounts.

Accounts Structure

3A–014   22. The accounts are a report in financial terms on the activities and resources of the charity. Where accruals accounts are prepared they should comprise:

    (a)   a **Statement of Financial Activities** for the year that shows all incoming resources and all resources expended by it and reconciles all changes in its funds. The statement should consist of a single set of accounting statements and be presented in columnar form if the charity operates more than one class of fund;

    (b)   a separate **summary income and expenditure account** only in the case of certain charitable companies. Paragraphs 335–338 fully describe the circumstances in which a summary income and expenditure account is necessary in addition to the Statement of Financial Activities;

    (c)   a **balance sheet** that shows the recognised assets, the liabilities and the different types of fund of the charity;

    (d)   a **cash-flow statement**, where required, in accordance with accounting and reporting standards;

    (e)   **notes** explaining the accounting policies adopted (as set out in paragraphs 277–291) and other note which explain or expand upon the information contained in the accounting statements referred to above or which provide further useful information. This will include notes analysing the figures in the accounts and explaining the relationships between them. Notes which are applicable to all charities have been clearly marked as such with **AA**.

23. The corresponding figures for the previous accounting period should be provided in the accounts in accordance with generally accepted accounting practice. The duration of the current and previous accounting periods should also be shown.

24. The Statement of Financial Activities, the summary income and expenditure account (in the case of certain charitable companies only per paragraphs (335–338) the balance sheet and the cash-flow statement (where required), are all considered to be "primary statements", and should therefore be given equal prominence in the accounts and should not be relegated to the notes to the accounts.

Summary Financial Information

3A–015   25. Where summary financial information of any kind is prepared, trustees are reminded that these accounts should always be fair and accurate. This is dealt with in paragraphs 292 to 297.

TRUSTEES' ANNUAL REPORT

AA Duty to Prepare Annual Report and Accounts

3A–016   26. All of a charity's trustees are jointly responsible for the preparation of the Annual Report and the Accounts and should prepare in respect of each financial year:

(a) a report describing what the charity is trying to do and how it is going about it in accordance with paragraph 31. As part of the report, or attached to it, there should also be a statement containing the legal and administrative details of the charity as described in paragraph 30;

(b) accounts and notes thereto in accordance with this SORP.

Whilst the report is legally a separate document from the accounts they are normally presented together in the same publication.

27. Trustees should include any additional information which they are required by law to report and confirm that the accounts comply with current statutory requirements, the requirements of the charity's governing document and the requirements of this SORP.

28. The annual report and accounts should be approved by the trustees as a body in accordance with their usual procedures (drafts being given to the trustees a reasonable time in advance) and both documents should be signed on behalf of the trustees by one of their number authorised so to do. The date of approval should be stated. The usual procedure of the charity trustees will not require the unanimous approval of the report and accounts. But any trustees who consider that the report and/or accounts should not be approved, or should not have been approved, should report to the Charity Commission (in the case of charities in England and Wales) or other regulator, any of their concerns which they are unable to resolve with their fellow trustees and/or with the auditors or examiners of the accounts.

29. The Trustees' Annual Report should be attached to the accounts whenever a full set of accounts is distributed. Any audit, independent examination or other statutory report on the accounts should also be attached. **3A–017**

Legal and Administrative Information

30. The legal and administrative information provided in the Trustees' Annual Report should include: **3A–018**

(a) **AA** the name of the charity, which in the case of a registered charity means the name by which it is registered. A registered charity should also give any other name by which it makes itself known;

(b) **AA** an indication of the nature of the governing document (*e.g.* trust deed; memorandum and articles of association; Charity Commission Scheme; Royal Charter; etc) and how the charity is (or its trustees are) constituted (*e.g.* limited company; unincorporated association; trustees incorporated as a body; etc). The charity registration number (in Scotland the charity recognition number) and the company registration number as applicable should also be provided;

(c) (i) **AA** the names of all of the charity's trustees on the date the report was approved or the names of at least 50 trustees (including all the officers of the charity, *e.g.* chair, treasurer etc and custodian trustees) where there are more than 50 trustees; where the charity trustees are incorporated this should include the name of the corporate body;

(ii) **AA** the name of other persons who served as charity trustees or custodian trustees (Appendix 1: Glossary) in the financial year in question;

(iii) **AA** the method of appointment or election of trustees;

(iv) **AA** the name of any other person or body entitled to appoint one or more of the charity trustees; and

(v)   where the charity trustee is a company; the names of its current directors or other persons managing it.

Where disclosure of the names of any charity trustees and persons with power of appointment—and likewise the charity's principal address (see (d) below)—could lead to that person being placed in personal danger (*e.g.* in the case of a women's refuge) the trustees may dispense with the disclosure provided that (for charities in England and Wales) the Charity Commission has given the trustees the authority to do so. It is recommended that the reasons for such non-disclosure should be given in the report. The directors of charitable companies should note that there is no corresponding dispensation in relation to the disclosure requirements for the statutory directors' report;

(d)   **AA** the address of the principal office of the charity, which may be omitted as described in (c) above except in the case of a charitable company where it is the same as the address of its registered office and must always be given;

(e)   **AA** the names and addresses of any other relevant organisations or persons. This should include the names and addresses of those acting as bankers, solicitors, auditor (or independent examiner or reporting accountant) and investment or other principal advisers;

(f)   where applicable, details of any specific restrictions imposed by the governing document concerning the way in which the charity can operate;

(g)   **AA** a summary of any specific investment powers and their authority (*e.g.* the governing document; Charity Commission Order; etc).

Narrative Information

3A–019   31. The Trustees' Annual Report should explain what the charity is trying to do and how it is going about it. It should show whether the charity has achieved its objectives during the year and explain its plans for the future. It should also help the reader of the report and accounts understand how the numerical part of the accounts relates to the organisational structure and activities of the charity. Each charity should adapt the narrative according to its own particular circumstances but should cover all of the following:

(a)   **AA** an explanation of the objects of the charity. This should be by reference to the governing document but may also include the mission statement of the charity;

(b)   **AA** a description of the organisation structure of the charity and how decisions are made. Where the charity is part of a wider network than the relationship involved should also be explained;

(c)   **AA** a statement regarding the relationships between the charity and related parties (paragraphs 157–165 and Appendix 1: Glossary) and with any other charities and organisations with which it co-operates in the pursuit of its charitable objectives;

(d)   **AA** a review of the activities of the charity (including its subsidiary undertakings if applicable) in the context of its strategy, including significant changes, developments and achievements in the past year, events affecting those activities since the year end and plans for the future. Where applicable comments should be made on the contribution of volunteers and the effectiveness of fundraising activities;

(e)   **AA** a statement of the charity's policies, in particular:
       AA the charity's policy on reserves (Appendix 1: Glossary) stating the level of reserves held and why they are held;
       where applicable, the investment policy and performance against policy; and

where applicable, grant making policies (where grants have not been disclosed in accordance with paragraph 146 the annual report should include a statement as to whether or not those details have been given to the regulatory body);

(f) **AA** where funds are in deficit an explanation of why they are in deficit and what action is to be taken on them;

(g) **AA** a statement confirming that the major risks to which the charity is exposed, as identified by the trustees, have been reviewed and systems have been established to mitigate those risks.

Funds Held as Custodian Trustee on Behalf of Others

32. Responsibility for preparing the Annual Report and Accounts rests with the trustees rather than with those who may hold charity property as custodian trustees (Appendix 1; Glossary) on behalf of a charity. Such custodian trustees should, therefore, make available to the trustees copies of their records relating to the administration of the charity's funds. In addition, where any charity is, or its trustees are, acting as custodian trustees, they should not include the funds in their balance sheet but disclose them by way of note and in their Annual Report as follows:

    3A–020

(a) give a description of the assets which they hold in this capacity;

(b) state the objects of the charity on whose behalf the assets are held and how this activity falls within their own objects;

(c) give details of the arrangements for safe custody and segregation of such assets from the charity's own assets.

GENERAL PRINCIPLES

Fundamental Accounting Concepts

33. Accounts intending to show a true and fair view must be prepared on the going concern assumption and the accruals concept and provide information that is relevant, reliable, comparable and understandable (Appendix 2: SSAP2/FRED 21). In the case of those charities which choose to prepare receipts and payments accounts the information must be comparable which is normally achieved through the application of consistent policies. (see paragraphs 350–356).

    3A–021

Accounting Standards

34. In meeting the obligation to prepare accounts showing a true and fair view (see paragraph 9) the accounts should follow the standards laid down in Statements of Standard Accounting Practice (SSAPs), Financial Reporting Standards (FRSs) and Urgent Issues Task Force abstracts (UITFs) issued or adopted by the Accounting Standards Board or its predecessors or successors which are relevant to the charity's circumstances and accounts. This SORP provides guidance and interpretation of the most suitable application of accounting standards for charities, but it is supplementary to those standards and, as with the law, does not seek to repeat all of their requirements (see Appendix 2).

    3A–022

35. The section on smaller charities (paragraphs 344–358) explains who the Financial Reporting Standards for Smaller Entities (FRSSE) can be applied by charities (whether or not they are companies) which are under the thresholds for small companies as described in the Companies Acts (Appendix 5).

Accounting for Separate Funds

36.   Fig 1 – The funds of a charity

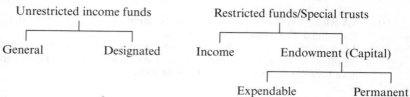

3A–023

37. The main purpose of the accounts is to give an overall view of the total incoming resources during the year and how they have been expended, with a balance sheet to show the overall financial position at the year-end. There are additional requirements for charities that have to account for more than one fund under their control. The accounts should provide a summary of the main funds, differentiating in particular between the unrestricted income funds, restricted income funds and endowment funds. The columnar format of the Statement of Financial Activities is designed to achieve this. Depending on the materiality (Appendix 1: Glossary) of each, the notes to the accounts should group the restricted funds under one or more heads.

38. Charities need to account for the proper administration of the individual funds in accordance with their respective terms of trust and accounting records must be kept in a way which will adequately separate transactions between different funds. Some charities may hold one or more restricted funds, some of which may be permanent or expendable endowment funds. Appendix 3 explains in detail the legal position as regards transactions involving these various funds. The position is summarised in the following paragraphs:

Unrestricted Income Funds (Including Designated Funds)

3A–024

39. Nearly all charities have a fund which is available to the trustees to apply for the general purposes of the charity as set out in its governing document. This is the charity's "unrestricted" fund (sometimes called a "general" fund) because the trustees are free to use it for any of the charity's purposes. Income generated from assets held in an unrestricted fund will be unrestricted income.

40. The trustees may set aside part of the charity's unrestricted funds to be used for particular purposes in the future. Such sums are described as "designated funds" and should be accounted for as part of the charity's unrestricted funds. The trustees have the power to reallocate such funds within unrestricted funds unless and until expended.

Restricted Funds

3A–025

41. Many charities hold funds that can only be applied for particular purposes within their objects. These are restricted funds and have to be separately accounted for. The restriction may apply to the use of income or capital or both. Income generated from assets held in a restricted fund will be subject to the same restriction unless either the terms of the original restriction specifically say otherwise (for example the expressed wishes of a donor or the terms of an appeal) or the restricted fund is an endowment fund, the income of which is expendable at the discretion of the trustees.

Endowment Funds

42. Another form of restricted fund is an "endowment", which is held on trust   **3A–026**
to be retained for the benefit of the charity as a capital fund. Where the trustees
must permanently maintain the whole of the fund it is known as permanent
endowment. Such a fund cannot normally be spent as if it were income. Any
expenses incurred in the administration, or protection of that fund should be
charged to it (*i.e.* against the capital of the investments in the fund). For example,
the fees of someone who manages the investments in a permanently endowed fund,
or the cost of improvements to investment land in a permanently endowed fund.
Only where the trusts of the charity provide to the contrary or there are insufficient funds in the endowment to meet such costs can they be charged against the
other funds held by the charity. In some instances the trustees may have a power
of discretion to convert endowed capital into income in which case the fund is
known as expendable endowment.

43. The initial give and subsequent increases and decreases in the amount of any
endowment funds should be shown in the Statement of Financial Activities as part
of those funds.

44. All incoming resources derived from assets held in an endowment fund should
be included in the Statement of Financial Activities. Normally the income forms
part of the unrestricted funds but if the application of the income is restricted by a
particular purpose the income and corresponding expenditure should be appropriately identified in the restricted funds. Any income not spent at the year end should
be carried forward in the appropriate unrestricted or restricted fund.

Gains and Losses

45. Realised and unrealised gains and losses on assets held in a particular fund   **3A–027**
form part of that fund. Similarly, provisions for depreciation, or for a permanent
fall in value, form part of the fund in which the asset is held.

Overhead Costs

46. Unless specifically forbidden by the donor or the terms of the trust a rea-   **3A–028**
sonable allocation of overhead expenses (*e.g.* management and administration;
costs of generating funds) can be set against restricted funds.

Movement of Funds

47. The treatment of movements of funds should not be affected by the type of   **3A–029**
fund involved. This means, for example, that restricted and unrestricted incoming
resources receivable at the same time should be accounted for in the Statement of
Financial Activities at the same time.

Reconciliation of Funds

48. The Statement of Financial Activities should reflect the principal move-   **3A–030**
ments between the opening and closing balances on all the funds of the charity. It
should be analysed between unrestricted income funds, restricted income funds
and endowment funds (permanent and expendable combined).

AA Particulars of Individual Funds and Notes to the Accounts

3A–031   49. The notes to the accounts should provide information on the structure of the charity's funds so as to disclose the fund balances and the reasons for them differentiating between unrestricted income funds (both general and designated), restricted income funds, permanent endowment and expendable endowment as well as identifying any material individual funds among them in particular:

  (a)   **AA** The assets and liabilities representing each type of fund of the charity should be clearly summarised and analysed (*e.g.* investments, fixed assets, net current assets) between those funds.

  (b)   **AA** Disclosure of how each of the funds has arisen (including designated funds), the restrictions imposed and the purpose of each fund. An indication should be given as to whether or not sufficient resources are held in an appropriate form to enable each fund to be applied in accordance with any restrictions. For example, if a charity has a fund which is to be spend in the near future, it should be made clear in the notes whether or not the assets held (or expected to be received) in the fund are liquid assets.

  (c)   **AA** Any funds in deficit should always be separately disclosed. An explanation should be given in the Trustees' Annual Report (see paragraph 31(f)). Designated funds should never be in deficit.

  (d)   **AA** Explanations should be provided for material movements in the funds. In disclosing details of movements on funds, material transfers between different funds and allocations to designated funds should be separately disclosed, without netting off, and should be accompanied by an explanation of the nature of the transfers or allocations and the reasons for them.

50. Separate sets of statements may be produced for each major fund and linked to a total summary. The trustees should decide on the most suitable form of presentation, bearing in mind the complexity of the fund structure and the need to avoid confusion between the movements on the various funds.

Branches

3A–032   51. Before preparing accounts, trustees must be quite clear as to the legal structure of the charity. A charity may operate through branches to raise funds and/or carry out its charitable purposes. Branches as defined in the glossary (see Appendix 1) will be accounted for as part of the whole charity. But if both reporting charity and the branches are companies, company law requires each entity to prepare its own accounts. In such a case, one annual report should normally be prepared to cover both the reporting charity and its branch(es) and consolidated accounts should be prepared in accordance with paragraph 299 to 319.

52. Separate legal entities which may be known as branches but do not fall within the definition of a branch in the Glossary should prepare their own Annual Report and Accounts and, if they are connected charities the relationship should be explained in the trustees report (see paragraph 31 (c)).

53. All branch transactions should be accounted for gross in the reporting charity's own accounts excluding those transactions which net off *e.g.* branch to branch transactions or those between the branches and the head office. Similarly all assets and liabilities of the branch including, for example, funds raised but not remitted to the reporting charity at the year end should be incorporated into the reporting charity's own balance sheet. This provision need not apply where the transactions

and balances of the branches in aggregate are not material to the charity's accounts.

54. Funds raised by a branch for the general purpose of the reporting charity will be accounted for as unrestricted funds in the accounts of the main charity. Funds raised by a branch for specific purposes of the reporting charity will need to be accounted for as restricted funds in the accounts of the main charity. Funds held for the general purposes of a branch which is a separate charity should usually be accounted for as restricted funds in the accounts of the reporting charity. **3A–033**

55. Where a branch is not a separate legal entity, its accounts must form part of the accounts of the reporting charity but it may be in the interests of local supporters and beneficiaries for additional accounts to be prepared covering only the branch.

STATEMENT OF FINANCIAL ACTIVITIES

Introduction

56. The Statement of Financial Activities is a single accounting statement with the objective of showing all incoming resources and resources expended by the charity in the year on all its funds. It is designed to show how the charity has used its resources in furtherance of its objects for the provision of benefit to its beneficiaries. It shows whether there has been a net inflow or outflow of resources, including capital gains and losses on assets, and provides a reconciliation of all movements in the charity's funds. **3A–034**

Presentation of Information

Structure of the Statement

57. In the Statement of Financial Activities the charity's incoming resources and resources expended must be analysed so that the reader can see where its resources came from and what it spent its resources on during the year. As a minimum it must also distinguish between unrestricted income funds, restricted income funds and the endowment funds of the charity. All of the charity's incoming resources and resources expended can be categorised between these funds, but a charity will not necessarily have funds of all three types. **3A–035**

58. If it has more than one type of fund, the statement should show, in columns, the movements in the different types of funds as well as the total movements of all the funds. Comparative figures for the previous financial year, given on the face of the statement will normally only be given for the line totals (*e.g.* donations, investment income etc) rather than for the split of each line across the various types of funds.

59. The various categories of incoming resources should be analysed as appropriate to the charity and should be shown separately where material as recommended below:

Incoming Resources:

(i)   donations, legacies and similar incoming resources (paragraphs 87–94);
(ii) incoming resources from operating activities of the charity distinguishing between (paragraphs 101–108);
    (a)   activities in furtherance of the charity's objects; and
    (b)   activities for generating funds;
(iii) investment income (paragraphs 112–113);

       (iv) other incoming resources (*e.g.* net gains on disposals of fixed assets for use by the charity) (paragraph 118);

       (v) the total by column of the above resources arising in the year.

3A–036   60. In the next section of the statement all resources expended for the year should be summarised, totalled and analysed as shown below.

Resources Expended:

      (i)   Costs of generating funds (paragraphs 132–135);

      (ii) Charitable expenditure showing separately;

          (a) grants payable in furtherance of the charity's objects (paragraphs 138–146);

          (b) costs of activities in furtherance of the charity's objects (paragraphs 147–150);

          (c) support costs for (a) and (b) (where material) (paragraphs 147–150); and

          (d) resources expended on managing and administering the charity (paragraphs 151–152);

      (iii) the total by column of the above resources expended in the year.

61. Each column should be totalled to show the net incoming/outgoing resources before transfers.

62. All material transfers between the different classes of funds should then be shown separately. These should not be netted off but should be shown gross.

3A–037   63. Each column should be totalled to show the net incoming/outgoing resources before revaluations and investment asset disposals.

64. The next section records separately (see also paragraphs 155–156):

      (i)   gains and losses on revaluation of fixed assets for the charity's own use; and

      (ii) gains and losses on revaluation and disposal of investment assets.

65. Each column of the Statement of Financial Activities will be totalled to show the net movement in the charity's funds for the year.

3A–038   66. The net movement in total charity funds should be reconciled to the total funds as shown in the balance sheet as follows:

      (i)   net movement in funds for the year;

      (ii) total funds brought forward;

      (iii) total funds carried forward.

67. In order to comply with Financial Reporting Standard 3 (FRS 3) where a charity has discontinued any of its operations or acquired new ones, the Statement of Financial Activities should distinguish between continuing, discontinued and acquired operations. This will normally apply to the whole of a distinctive type of activity of a charity but not to the development or cessation of new projects within that activity.

68. The following table shows how the Statement of Financial Activities is constructed.

69. Table 1.

3A–039

Description	Unrestricted Funds	Restricted Funds	Endowment Funds	Total Funds	Prior Year Total Funds
Incoming resources analysed per paragraph 59					
Total incoming resources	A	A	A	A	A
Resources expended analysed per paragraph 60					
Total resources expended	B	B	B	B	B
Net incoming resources before transfers = A–B	C	C	C	C	C
Gross transfers between funds	D	D	D	D	D
Net incoming resources before revaluations and investment asset disposals = C+D	E	E	E	E	E
Gains and losses on revaluations of fixed assets for the charities own use	F	F	F	F	F
Gains and losses on revaluations and disposals of investment assets	G	G	G	G	G
Net movement in funds = E+F+G	H	H	H	H	H
Total funds brought forward	I	I	I	I	I
Total funds carried forward = H+I	J	J	J	J	J

Adaptation of Formats

70. The Statement of Financial Activities should be prepared following the structure described in paragraphs 57 to 69. However, individual charities should expand it where necessary in order to present a true and fair view and convey a proper understanding of the nature of all their activities. It is recommended that the charity's aim is to have a clear link between the incoming and outgoing resources and in particular the functional split of activities. Two examples of this are:

3A–040

    (a)   a charity running a care home could use the sub-heading "Residential Care Income" within 59(ii)(a) (activities in furtherance of the charity's objects) and "Residential Care Costs" 60(ii)(b) (cost of activities in furtherance of the charity's objects);

(b)   a charity fundraising through a shop could use the sub-heading "shops" within 59(ii)(b) (activities for generating funds) and 60(i) (costs of generating funds).

Thus incoming resources expended can be linked together by using similar or identical headings in different parts of the Statement of Financial Activities. A charity may also find it helpful to show extra columns, for instance, to highlight the financial impact of a particular activity.

71. Some charities may find it informative to their readers to insert an additional subtotal after 60(i) (the costs of generating funds). Where this is done the subtotal should be called "net incoming resources available for charitable application" and a further subtotal may be inserted for the costs in 60(ii) (charitable expenditure).

3A–041   72. Whilst the Statement of Financial Activities may be adapted to give a true and fair view disclosure requirements must always be met and the underlying structure should not be changed. Trustees should balance the provision of information with clarity.

73. Headings should be omitted where there is nothing to report in both the current and preceding periods.

Disclosure

3A–042   74. The notes to the accounts should give a description of the sources of any material incoming resources.

Recognition of Incoming Resources

3A–043   75. The value of all resources—both for income and endowment funds—accruing to the charity should be recorded in the Statement of Financial Activities as soon as it is prudent and practicable to do so. In all cases incoming resources should not be recognised until the conditions for receipt have been met and there is reasonable assurance of receipt. This will be dependent on the following three factors being met:

(a)   entitlement—normally arises when a particular resources is receivable or the charity's right to it becomes legally enforceable'

(b)   certainty—when there is reasonable certainty that the incoming resource will be received;

(c)   measurement—when the monetary value of the incoming resource can be measured with sufficient reliability.

76. All incoming resources should be reported gross whether raised by the charity or its agents. Netting off expenditure against income is only allowable for small fundraising events where it will not materially understate the gross incoming resources and gross resources expended for the event. However, in no case should the charity's own staff costs be netted off against the proceeds of any such events when reported in the accounts.

77. Some receipts can be regarded as reimbursements and can be offset against the related expenditure charged in the statement of financial activities (though a separate asset must be shown in the balance sheet see paragraph 254). FRS 12 explains when this is possible, for instance, the receipt of an insurance payment will meet this criteria. However, the receipt of a grant to meet resources expended already paid or accrued as a liability will not be regarded as a reimbursement and cannot be netted off against the accrued liability.

3A–044   78. Some charities earn income by charging for goods and services as part of their charitable activities. Where such unrestricted incoming resources are received in advance then a charity may not have entitlement to these resources until the goods or services are provided. In this situation incoming resources received in advance should be deferred until the charity becomes entitled to the resources.

79. In addition charities often receive incoming resources by way of grant or donation to fund general or specific activities. Charities are normally entitled to these incoming resources when they are receivable. This is the case even if the resources are received in advance of the performance of the activity and they should not be deferred. Incoming resources may be deferred only when the donor has imposed restrictions on the expenditure of resources which amount to preconditions for use (*e.g.* the receipt in advance of a grant for expenditure in a future accounting period). However, when the conditions for receipt have been met then the charity is entitled to the incoming resources and must recognise them in the Statement of Financial Activities. Incoming resources cannot be deferred simply because the related expenditure has not been incurred.

80. When either incoming resources are given specifically to provide a fixed asset or a fixed asset is donated (a gift of kind), the charity will normally have entitlement to the incoming resources when they are receivable. At this point, all of the incoming resources should be recognised in the Statement of Financial Activities and not deferred over the life of the asset. As explained in paragraph 79 the possibility of having to repay the incoming resources does not affect their recognition in the first instance. Once acquired, the use of the asset will either be restricted or unrestricted (see paragraph 86). If its use is unrestricted the trustees should consider creating a designated fund reflecting the book value of the asset. The relevant fund will then be reduced over the useful economic life of the asset in line with its depreciation. This treatment accords with the requirements under accounting standards for the recognition of assets and liabilities and provides the most appropriate interpretation of SSAP 4 for charities.

81. Some incoming resources do not belong to the charity, for instance where it receives the resources in circumstances where the trustees acting as agents (and not as custodian trustees) are legally bound to pay them over to a third party and have no responsibility for their ultimate application. In these circumstances the transaction is legally a transfer of resources from the original payer (who remains the principal) to the specified third party. If the original payer retains the legal responsibility for ensuring the charitable application of the funds, the intermediary charity should not recognise the resources in the Statement of Financial Activities or the balance sheet (see paragraph 248). **3A–045**

82. However, in some cases an intermediary charity may own the resources prior to transfer to the third party and its trustees will act as principal and have responsibility for their charitable application. For instance, where the trustees of the intermediary charity may have applied for the grant of the resources or are able to direct how the grant should be used by the third party or both. Other forms of funding arrangements involving intermediary charities may need their trustees to accept the legal responsibility for the transfer of the grant to the third party (and for its charitable application, where the third party is not a charity). In all of these circumstances the resources should then be included in the intermediary charity's Statement of Financial Activities and balance sheet (see paragraph 249).

Disclosure

83. Where any incoming resources have been deferred the notes to the accounts should analyse the movement on the deferred account between incoming resources deferred in the current year and amounts realised from previous years. Incoming resources of a similar nature can be grouped together in the notes as appropriate. **3A–046**

84. Where a charity has held resources for a third party which have not been included in the Statement of Financial Activities, the notes to the accounts should

analyse the movement of these resources during the year relating to each party or type of party where material. Where resources have been held for related parties the required disclosure of paragraphs 163 to 164 should be given.

Incoming Resources Subject to Restrictions

3A–047   85. The fact that an incoming resources if for a restricted purpose does not affect whether or not it is recognised in the Statement Financial Activities. There is an important difference for accounting purposes between restrictions on the purposes for which a particular resource may be used and conditions which must be fulfilled prior to its receipt or use by the charity. If receipt is dependent upon pre-conditions which cannot be or have not been met, then the incoming resource should not be recognised in the Statement of Financial Activities or the balance sheet. A similar treatment should continue to be applied where the charity is unable to meet, even at a later stage, any pre-conditions for its use. A contingent asset may exist (see paragraph 262).

86. Funds received for the restricted purpose of providing fixed assets should be accounted for immediately as restricted funds. The treatment of the fixed assets provided with those funds will depend on the basis on which they are held. The terms on which the funds were received may either require the fixed asset acquired to be held in a restricted fund or the fixed assets' acquisition may discharge the restriction and treatment will depend upon the circumstance of each individual case. (See Appendix 3.) Where assets move from one fund to another this should be reflected as a transfer between the relevant funds.

Donations, Legacies and Similar Incoming Resources

3A–048   87. This section of the Statement of Financial Activities is intended to show incoming resources of a voluntary nature usually given by the founders, patrons, supporters and the general public, government and non-statutory bodies such as businesses and charitable foundations. It will include grants which provide core funding or are of a general nature but will not include those which are specifically for the performance of a service or production of charitable goods, for instance a service agreement with a local authority. In addition it may include incoming resources from membership subscriptions, gifts in kind, intangible income and sponsorships where these are regarded as donations rather than payment for goods or services.

Disclosure

3A–049   88. The material components of donations legacies and similar incoming resources should be shown separately on the face of the Statement of Financial Activities or in the notes to the accounts.

Legacies

3A–050   89. It is good practice to monitor a legacy from the time when notification is received to its final receipt. A charity should not, however, regard a legacy as receivable simply because it has been told about it. It should only do so when the legacy has been received or if, before receipt, it becomes reasonably certain that the legacy will be received and the value of the incoming resources can be measured with sufficient reliability (see paragraph 75).

90. There will normally be reasonable certainty of receipt for example, as soon as a charity receives a letter from the personal representatives of the estate advising that payment of the legacy will be made or that the property bequeathed will

be transferred. It is likely that the value of the resource will also be measurable from this time. However, legacies which are not immediately payable should not be treated as receivable until the conditions associated with payment have been fulfilled (*e.g.* the death of a life tenant).

91. It is unlikely in practice that the entitlement, certainty of receipt and measurability conditions will be satisfied before the receipt of a letter from the personal representatives advising of an intended payment or transfer. The amount which is available in the estate for distribution to the beneficiaries may not have been finalised and, even if it has, there may still be outstanding matters relating to the precise division of the amount. In these circumstances entitlement may be in doubt or it may not be possible to provide a reasonable estimate of the legacy receivable, in which case it should not be included in the Statement of Financial Activities.

92. Where a charity receives a payment on account of its interest in an estate or a letter advising that such a payment will be made, the payment, or intended payment, on account should be treated as receivable. **3A–051**

93. Similarly, where a payment is received or notified as receivable (by the personal representatives) after the accounting year end, but it is clear that it had been agreed by the personal representatives prior to the year end (hence providing evidence of a condition that existed at the balance sheet date), then it should be accrued in the Statement of Financial Activities and the balance sheet.

Disclosure

94. Where the charity has been notified of material legacies which have not been included in the Statement of Financial Activities (because the conditions for recognition have not been met), this fact and an estimate, where possible, of the amounts receivable should be disclosed in the notes to the accounts. **3A–052**

Gifts in Kind

95. Incoming resources in the form of gifts in kind should be included in the Statement of Financial Activities in the following ways: **3A–053**

(a) Assets given for distribution by the charity should be recognised as incoming resources for the year within "donations legacies and similar incoming resources" only when distributed.

(b) Assets given for use by the charity (*e.g.* property for its own occupation) should be recognised as incoming resources when receivable. Where the donor intended the assets to be used on a continuing basis then they should be accounted for in accordance with paragraph 80.

(c) Where a gift has been made in kind but on trust for conversion into cash and subsequent application by the charity, the incoming resource should normally be recognised in the accounting period when receivable. However in certain cases this will not be practicable and the incoming resources should be included in the accounting period in which the gift is sold. The most common example is that of second-hand goods donated for resale, which, whilst regarded as a donation in legal terms, is in economic terms similar to trading and should be included within "activities for generating funds" (see paragraph 106).

96. In all cases the amount at which gifts in kind are brought into account should be either a reasonable estimate of their gross value to the charity or the amount actually realised.

Disclosure

3A–054   97. The basis of any valuation should be disclosed. Where material, an adjustment should be made to the original valuation upon subsequent realisation of the gift.

98. Referring to 95(a) above, where there are undistributed assets at the year end, a general description of the items involved and an estimate of their value should be given by way of a note to the accounts provided such value is material.

Intangible Income

3A–055   99. A charity may receive assistance in the form of donated facilities, beneficial loan arrangements, donated services or services from volunteers. Such assistance is generally referred to as "intangible income". Such intangible incoming resources should be included in the Statement of Financial Activities where another party is bearing the financial cost of the resources supplied and the benefit is quantifiable and measurable. (This will not normally apply to commercial discounts where they are clearly intended as a donation). Where there is no financial cost borne by another party for the provision of the assistance (*e.g.* in the case of volunteers), the intangible income should not be included in the Statement of Financial Activities. The value placed on resources included in the Statement of Financial Activities should be the financial cost to the third party of providing them. However, where this information is not available or if the charity considers the value to be less than the costs borne by the third party, a reasonable estimate of their gross value to the charity should be given. An equivalent amount should be included as expenditure under the appropriate heading in the Statement of Financial Activities.

Disclosure

3A–056   100. The notes to the accounts should give an analysis of intangible incoming resources included in the Statement of Financial Activities distinguishing appropriately between the different major items *e.g.* seconded staff, loaned assets etc. Material intangible incoming resources which are not included in the Statement of Financial Activities (*e.g.* volunteers) should be commented on in the Trustees Annual Report (see paragraph 31 (d)).

Incoming Resources from Operating Activities

3A–057   101. For the purpose of analysing incoming resources from operating activities, such as activities fall into two principal categories:

    (a)   activities in furtherance of the charity's objects;
    (b)   activities for generating funds.

102. A charity should expand these broad headings appropriately to reflect the activities which it carries out. Activities may be aggregated at a suitable level with the possibility of further subdivisions being given in the notes to the accounts (see paragraph 108).

103. All incoming resources received for activities which are in the nature of a payment for the provision of goods or services should be combined together under the relevant activity. This will include trading income and those grants (although legally donations) (See Appendix 1: Glossary) which have conditions which make them similar in economic terms to trading income, such as service agreements with local authorities. However, grants which are for core funding or do not have particular service requirements or are in response to an appeal are donations and

should be included in the section for "donations, legacies and similar incoming resource".

104. **Activities in furtherance of the charity's objects** may include: 3A–058

(a) the sale of goods or services as part of the directly charitable activities of the charity (known as primary purpose trading) or the letting of a non-investment property in furtherance of the objects:

(b) the sale of goods or services made or provided by the beneficiaries of the charity;

(c) incoming resources from government or public authorities where these are received in the normal course of trading under (a) or (b) *e.g.* fees for respite care;

(d) grants in specifically for the provision of goods and services as part of the directly charitable activities or provided by the beneficiaries;

(e) ancillary trades connected to a primary purpose in (a) and (b) where the principal aim is to provide a service to the charity's beneficiaries.

105. **Activities for generating funds** have the principal features that they are not part of the directly charitable activities but are carried out in order to generate incoming resources to support those activities. This will include fundraising events such as jumble sales, firework displays and concerts (which are legally considered to be trading activities) and those sponsorships and social lotteries which cannot be considered as pure donations.

106. Activities for generating funds can include selling donated goods and bought in goods, providing services to other than the charity's beneficiaries, licensing arrangements, the letting of non investment property and many others. Whilst selling donated goods is legally considered to be the realisation of a donation in kind (see paragraph 95 (c)), in economic terms it is similar to a trading activity and should be included in this section. Ancillary trades where the principal aim (whilst still providing a service to the beneficiaries) is to generate incoming resources to support or contribute to the the charitable activities, should also be included in this section. Sometimes all these activities are carried on separately and other times mixed together in a single enterprise.

107. It may be possible to segregate the incoming resources and resources 3A–059 expended for each different type of activity (this may have to be done for tax purposes) but an enterprise carrying on a mix of activities will often be viewed as a single economic unit. Charity trustees should consider the balance of the activities being undertaken to determine the most appropriate place to include the incoming resources from such enterprises but having done this the mix of incoming resources need not be segregated further. For example a shop may mainly sell donated and bought in goods, but it may also sell a small amount of goods made by its beneficiaries and incidentally provide information about the charity. It would be acceptable to class all the incoming resources from the ship as "shop income" under "activities for generating funds".

Disclosure

108. An analysis of activities should be given in the notes to the accounts to sup- 3A–060 plement the analysis on the face of the Statement of Financial Activities. It should be sufficiently detailed so that the reader of the accounts understands the main activities carried out by the charity and the main components of the gross incoming resources receivable for each activity.

Subsidiary Undertakings

3A–061   109. All payments to the charity by its subsidiary undertakings and all dividend entitlements from them should be separately recognised and appropriately described in the charity's Statement of Financial Activities. The operating results of the subsidiary undertakings themselves will only be accounted for by the charity in its consolidated Statement of Financial Activities of the group (see paragraphs 299–319).

110. Where trading activities of any kind are being carried out for the benefit of a charity by a subsidiary undertaking (but not acting as an agent), the subsidiary undertaking should account for the results in its own accounts in accordance with the normal accounting rules.

Disclosure

3A–062   111. Where a charity presents its own accounts in a separate publication from the consolidated accounts it should give the disclosure required by paragraph 315.

Investment Income

3A–063   112. Incoming resources from investment assets, including dividends, interest and rents but excluding capital returns, should be included as investment income in the Statement of Financial Activities.

Disclosure

3A–064   113. The notes to the accounts should show the gross investment income arising from each category of investment in accordance with paragraph 238.

Incoming Resources from Government and Other Public Authorities

3A–065   114. Incoming resources from the government and other public authorities arise in many and varied ways such as grants, contracts and service agreements. They include resources from the European Union and other EU bodies and incoming resources from the National Lottery.

115. These resources should be treated in a similar manner to other incoming resources and included under the relevant headings of the Statement of Financial Activities which will normally be "donations legacies and similar incoming resources" or "activities in furtherance of the charity's objects" (see paragraphs 87 and 101–104).

116. These resources should also be dealt with in accordance with any conditional terms which create a special trust and therefore a restricted fund, though this can be difficult to determine in practice. Sometimes the conditions may represent the authority's expectations of service provision without imposing a restriction but each case must be judged on its own merits. However, where the incoming resources are for a services (or goods) and, upon full performance of the service, any surplus funds can be retained and used for greater purposes, this most likely indicates that the incoming resources and related expenditure will be unrestricted. Whereas, if upon full performance any surplus is retrievable by the authority then the resources are most likely to be restricted.

Disclosure

117. The notes to the accounts should give a description of the sources of any material incoming resources, by category. For example this could distinguish between type of authority and resources such as fees, grants and service agreements.

3A–066

Other Incoming Resources

118. Other incoming resources will include the receipt of any resources which the charity has not been able to categories. This will be a minority of incoming resources and many charities will not need to use this category. The most common example is the gain on the disposal of a fixed asset for the charity's own use (paragraph 156(b)).

3A–067

Expenditure and Costs

Recognition of Liabilities

119. All expenditure should be included in the Statement of Financial Activities in accordance with the accruals concept. (Appendix. 2: SSAP 2). A liability arises as soon as there is a legal or constructive obligation committing the charity to the expenditure as described in Financial Reporting Standards (FRS's) 5 and 12.

3A–068

120. Expenditure, with the exception of grants payable, is not usually incurred until consideration for the expenditure has passed *i.e.* until something is received in exchange for the expenditure.

121. In the case of grants and certain other expenditure relating directly to charitable activities an exchange for consideration does not normally arise. Nevertheless, the charity may still have a liability (Appendix 1: Glossary) which needs to be recognised.

122. A liability will arise when a charity is under obligation to make a transfer of value to a third party. The liability and related expenditure should be recognised in full in the charity's accounts as soon as the obligation arises.

3A–069

123. Liabilities may arise from a constructive (Appendix 1: Glossary) rather than a legal obligation. This is a matter of judgement but an important factor in determining whether a constructive obligation exists is whether a valid expectation has been created in the mind of the recipient or possibly another third party in accordance with FRS 12. This will be influenced by, amongst other things, the policies of the charity, both its current and past practice in making the payments and specific communications including public pronouncements made by the charity.

124. A charity may enter into commitments which are dependent upon explicit conditions being met by itself or the recipient before payment is made or upon future reviews. Such conditions may prevent a grant from being a liability until they are met. Where a liability is not accrued, because conditions have not been met, such a commitment should normally be treated as a contingent liability. The balance sheet treatment for both outstanding commitments and contingent liabilities is given in paragraphs 250 to 269.

125. Some of these commitments may give rise to liabilities payable over several years *e.g.* the funding of a research fellowship over three years payable by instalments. In reaching the best estimate of the amount to be included in the Statement of Financial Activities for such expenditure the value of the liability must be assessed. Consideration should be given to the terms on which the grant has been made and the uncertainties and risks surrounding the settlement of the obligation and, where appropriate, discount rates reflecting the effect of time on its value (see paragraphs 251–252 for balance sheet treatment).

3A–070

126. The trustees may wish to designate some of the charity's unrestricted funds to represent contingent liabilities and other planned expenditure which may not have created a liability.

127. Where later events make the recognition of a liability no longer appropriate, the provision should be cancelled by credit against the relevant expenditure heading in the Statement of Financial Activities. The credit should mirror the treatment originally used to recognise the expenditure for the liability and should be disclosed separately.

Disclosure

3A–071 128. **AA** The accounting policies for the recognition of different categories of liabilities should be disclosed in the notes to the accounts (see paragraph 284).

129. If the trustees set up a designated fund the notes to the accounts should explain why the trustees have set up such a fund.

130. Where material provisions have been cancelled the notes to the accounts should give a clear explanation of the reversed amounts and the reasons for them.

Resources Expended

3A–072 131. Resources expended are split into two main categories being the costs of generating funds and the actual costs of charitable activities. The principles involved in each cost category are detailed in the following paragraphs.

Costs of Generating Funds

3A–073 132. These are the costs which are associated with raising funds from all the possible sources of incoming resources. This will mainly be fundraising costs (Appendix 1: Glossary) in attracting donations, legacies and similar incoming resources and the costs of activities for income generation. In addition it may include costs associated with raising funds for the provision of goods and services in the furtherance of the charity's objects, but it should not include any of the costs of performing or supporting those activities. For instance the costs of negotiating a contract or applying for a grant for a charitable activity could be regarded as a cost of generating funds. The costs of carrying out the activity will be costs in furtherance of the charity's objects and the costs of monitoring performance in line with the contract or grant could be support costs.

133. Expenditure on fundraising should be all the costs incurred in raising the fundraising proceeds (see paragraph 60(i)) shown in the accounts, including agents' costs where used. This should include publicity costs associated with fundraising or raising the profile of the charity but not those which are used in an educational manner in furtherance of the charity's objects. Such distinctions should be drawn in line with the particular nature and circumstance of each charity and its publicity material. Policies for drawing these distinctions should be disclosed to meet the requirements of paragraph 284.

134. The costs of generating funds should also include investment management costs for both income generation and capital maintenance (also see paragraph 42).

Disclosure

3A–074 135. **AA** Where material, the difference categories of the costs of generating funds should be shown on the face of the Statement of Financial Activities or in the notes to the accounts. An analysis of the major items of expenditure should be given in the notes to the accounts. This should, where possible, be linked to the incoming resource categories reflecting the funds raised.

Charitable Expenditure

136. Charitable expenditure comprises all the expenditure incurred by the charity in meeting its charitable objectives as opposed to the cost of raising the funds to finance these activities and should be analysed between the following subheadings.   **3A–075**

(a) grants payable in furtherance of the charity's objects (paragraphs 138–146);
(b) costs of activities in furtherance of the charity's objects (paragraphs 147–150);
(c) support costs of (a) and (b) where material (paragraphs 147–150);
(d) costs of management and administration of the charity (paragraphs 151–152).

137. Costs such as depreciation, amortisation or losses on disposal of fixed assets used wholly or mainly for charitable activities, including where the assets are written off as project expenditure, should be allocated within this section in accordance with the principles in paragraph 153.

Grants Payable in Furtherance of the Charity's Objects

138. A grant is any payment which, in order to further its objects, a charity makes voluntarily to another institution or to an individual. A grant may or may not be repayable to the charity in certain circumstances. However, a payment which a charity must make in return for the supply of goods or services is not a grant.   **3A–076**

Disclosure

139. If grant-making is material to a charity, the charity should provide an appropriate analysis and explanation of the grants which it makes. Whether grant-making is material will to some extent depend on the size of the charity and the importance of grant-making to its overall operation. If in any accounting year a charity makes grants totalling at least 5% of its total resources expended in that year the charity should regard its grant-making as material. However there may be circumstances where the value of grants to an institution in an accounting year is material compared to the total institutional grants in that year and information regarding such grants could be useful to the users of the accounts and should be disclosed.   **3A–077**

140. When analysis and explanation is required, its purpose is to help the reader of the accounts understand how the grants made relate to the objects of the charity and the policy adopted by the trustees in pursuing these objects. The charity may give the analysis and explanation in the notes to the accounts, as part of the trustees' report or by means of a separate publication. Whichever means is chosen, the required information should be disclosed in accordance with paragraphs 141 to 144 below. The notes to the accounts should include a reconciliation between the grant expenditure as stated in the Statement of Financial Activities and the details shown in the analysis and make reference to the analysis if it is in the trustees report or separate publication. When the analysis is contained in a separate publication, it should be made available to the public in the same way as the accounts. The notes to the accounts should identify the publication and state how copies of it can be obtained.

141. The analysis should clearly indicate whether grants are individual or institutional. An individual grant is one which is made for the direct benefit of the individual who receives it, for example to relieve financial hardship. All other grants

should be regarded as institutional. For example, a grant which is made to an individual to carry out some research project should be regarded as a grant to the institution with which the individual is connected rather than as a grant to the individual.

3A–078

142. For both individual and institutional grants, an analysis should be given which discloses the total number and the total value of the grants given for different charitable purposes. The charity should decide upon classifications which are appropriate for an understanding of its policy. For example, institutional grants may be grouped into categories covering social welfare, medical research, the performing arts, etc. Similarly, grants to individuals may be grouped in categories covering, for example, the welfare of people in financial need or help to people seeking to further their education. Some charities may decide that it is appropriate to provide further levels of analysis, for example, showing a geographical analysis of the number and value of grants made.

143. In addition, **in the case of institutional grants**, and subject to paragraph, 146, the trustees should disclose details, as specified in paragraph 144, of a sufficient number of institutional grants to convey a proper understanding of the charity's grant-making activities. The number of grants which is sufficient will vary with circumstances. Where a charity has made fewer than 50 material institutional grants in a year all the grants should be disclosed. Otherwise, the disclosure should cover at least the 50 largest institutional grants or any larger number which is necessary for the proper understanding of the charity's grant-making activity. There is no requirement to disclose any grants which are below £1,000 in total.

144. The disclosure for institutional grants should include the name of the recipient institution and the number and total value of grants made to that institution in the accounting year. where grants have been made to a particular institution for different charitable purposes, the number and total value of the grants made for each purpose should be disclosed. For example, a charity may have made grants to different officers of a particular university for different projects. As has already been explained (paragraph 141), the grants should all be treated as having been made to the institution but an analysis should be given of the number and total of grants made for each purpose.

3A–079

145. The analysis required by paragraphs 140–144 should be clearly reconciled to the amount for grants in the Statement of Financial Activities. In order to demonstrate this reconciliation, it may be necessary to include in lists of grants a summary of the value and total of the institutional grants of which full details have not been disclosed, or to indicate how some grant commitments have been discounted in line with the requirements of paragraph 125 or treated as contingent liabilities in accordance with paragraph 124.

146. Exceptionally, even though the grants to a particular institution are material, it is possible that the disclosure of the details of those grants could seriously prejudice the furtherance of the purposes either of the recipient institution or of the charity itself. In these circumstances a charity may withhold details of each grant concerned but should:

(a)   disclose in the notes to the accounts the total number, value and general purpose of those grants the details of which have not been disclosed;

(b)   before the trustees sign the accounts, give the full details of such grants in writing to the Charity Commission (English and Welsh charities only) or other appropriate regulatory body, fully explaining the reasons why those details have not been disclosed in the accounts;

(c)   state in the Trustees' Report whether or not those details have been given to the regulatory body (see paragraph 31 (e)).

It is unlikely in practice that all the material institutional grants of a charity would fall within this exception.

Costs of Activities in Furtherance of the Charity's
Objects and Support Costs

147. Expenditure on activities in furtherance of the charity's objects (*i.e.* on the   **3A–080**
provision of services or of goods) should be appropriately analysed by the activities of the charity (functional classification) to assist the reader of the accounts in
understanding how the charity spends its resources. This should mirror the operational activities in furtherance of the charity's objects in the incoming resources
section but may have additional activities which do not generate incoming
resources.

148. Where applicable, and where the amount is material, it is recommended
that support costs (*e.g.* salaries, office, communications and other costs) identifiable as an integral part of grants payable and/or the costs of activities in furtherance of the charity's objects are shown separately in the Statement of Financial
Activities (see Appendix 1: Glossary—"Support Costs").

Disclosure

149. The major items of expenditure within each type of charitable activity   **3A–081**
should be appropriately analysed in the notes to the accounts. The activities disclosed should be consistent with those disclosed for incoming resources.

150. **AA** An analysis of all the major items included in support costs should be
given in the notes to the accounts.

Management and Administration

151. Expenditure on the management and administration of the charity will   **3A–082**
normally include both direct and indirect costs under this heading. Direct costs
will include such items as internal and external audit, legal advice for trustees and
costs associated with constitutional and statutory requirements *e.g.* the cost of
trustee meetings and preparing statutory accounts. There should also be an apportionment of indirect costs involved in managing and administering the charity, (as
distinct from directly pursuing its charitable activities). This will include a proportion of management (and other staff) time and the overhead costs connected with
it, *e.g.* office and communications costs.

Disclosure

152. **AA** There should be a clear analysis of all the main items of expenditure on   **3A–083**
management and administration in the notes to the accounts.

Allocations of Costs

153. It is not practicable to define precisely what should be included under   **3A–084**
each expenditure heading as each charity's circumstances will be different.
Furthermore, charities will often group expenditure under different headings for
internal reporting purposes from those which should be disclosed in the annual
accounts. In attributing costs the following principles should be applied:

    (a)   No part of expenditure incurred on activities falling directly within one
          cost category should be allocated to any other cost category.

    (b)   Items of expenditure which involve more than one cost category, for
          example the cost of running an office which houses both fundraising and

charitable project support functions, should be apportioned on a reasonable, justifiable and consistent basis to the cost categories involved.

(c)   Where costs should not be allocated to the categories in paragraph 60(i) (costs of generating funds) and 60 (ii) (a–c) (grants payable, costs of operating activities, and support costs) they should be included within 60(ii)(d) management and administration of the charity.

Disclosure

3A–085   154. **AA** The basis and principles used for the allocation of all costs should be disclosed clearly in the accounting policies (see paragraph 284 (c)).

Gains and Losses on Fixed Assets

3A–086   155. Gains and losses arising on disposal, revaluation or impairment of fixed assets—whether held for the charity's own use or for investment purposes—will form part of the particular fund in which the investment or other asset concerned is or was held at the time of disposal, revaluation or impairment.

156. Such gains and losses should be recognised as follows:

(a)   Impairment losses of assets held for the charity's own use (*i.e.* not investments) should be regarded as additional depreciation of the impaired asset and included appropriately in the resources expended section of the statement of financial activities.

(b)   Gains on the disposal of fixed assets for the charity's own use should be included under the heading "other incoming resources". Losses on disposal should be treated as additional depreciation and included appropriately in the resources expended section of the Statement of Financial Activities.

(c)   Revaluation gains or losses (which are not considered to be impairment losses (see paragraphs 224–230)) on assets held for the charity's own use should be included in the section on gains and losses on revaluations of fixed assets for the charity's own use.

(d)   Any gains and losses on investment assets (including property investments) should be included under the gains and losses on the revaluation and disposal of investment assets. Realised and unrealised gains and losses may be included in a single line.

Other Matters to be Covered in the Notes to the Accounts

Related Party Transactions

3A–087   157. Subject to paragraphs 160 and 165 below, disclosure in a note to the accounts is required where the reporting charity (which for these purposes includes any institution connected with it; Appendix 1: Glossary) enters into a related party transaction. A related party transaction is one where the charity has a relationship with another party or parties (the related party) which might inhibit it from pursing its own separate interests. Related parties include:

(a)   a charity trustee or someone else who is related to the charity (Appendix 1; Glossary): and

(b)   someone who is either connected with a charity trustee or to a person who is related to the charity (Appendix 1: Glossary).

158. A charity can be a related party of another charity (Appendix 1: Glossary), for example, if one is the trustee of the other, or if one has the power to appoint

or remove a significant proportion of the charity trustees of the other, or if the two charities are subject to common control (for instance a majority of trustees in common). However, they are not necessarily related simply because a particular person happens to be a trustee of both (though if one charity subordinates its interests to the other charity in any transaction because of this relationship then the charities will be related).

159. Any decision by a charity to enter into a transaction ought to be influenced only by the consideration of the charity's own interests. This requirement is reinforced by legal rules which, in certain circumstances, can invalidate transactions where the charity trustees have a conflict of interest. This does not necessarily mean that all transactions with related persons are influenced by the consideration of interests other than the charity's nor that they are liable to invalidation.

160. However, transparency is particularly important where the relationship **3A–088** between the charity and the other party or parties to a transaction suggests that the transaction could possibly have been influenced by interests other than the charity's. It is possible that the reported financial position and results may have been affected by such transactions and information about these transactions is therefore necessary for the users of the charity's accounts.

161. Related party transactions potentially include (exceptions in paragraph 165):

(a) purchases, sales, leases and donations (including donations which are made in furtherance of the charity's objects) of goods, property, money and other assets such as intellectual property rights to or from the related party;

(b) the supply of services by the related party to the charity, and the supply of services by the charity to the related party. Supplying services includes providing the use of goods, property and other assets and finance arrangements such as making loans and giving guarantees and indemnities;

(c) any other payments and other benefits which are made to trustees under express provisions of the governing document of a charity or in fulfilment of its charitable objectives.

162. Only material transactions need to be disclosed in the notes to the accounts subject to paragraph 166(a). Transactions should be disclosed whether or not they are at arms length.

163. The required disclosure is as follows (also see paragraph 238(c) re **3A–089** investments):

(a) the name(s) of the transacting related party or parties;

(b) a description of the relationship between the parties (including the interest of the related party of parties in the transaction);

(c) a description of the transaction;

(d) the amounts involved;

(e) outstanding balances with related parties at the balance sheet date and any provisions for doubtful debts from such persons;

(f) any amounts written off from such balances during the accounting year; and

(g) any other elements of the transactions which are necessary for the understanding of the financial statements.

164. Subject to paragraph 166(b) the disclosure can be given in aggregate for similar transactions and type of related party, unless disclosure of an individual transaction or connected transactions is necessary for an understanding of the impact of the transactions on the accounts of the charity or is a legal requirement.

165. Some related party transactions are such that they are unlikely to influence the pursuance of the separate independent interests of the charity. These need not be disclosed unless there is evidence to the contrary. Examples are:

(a)   donations received by the reporting charity from a related party, so long as the donor has not attached conditions which would, or might, require the charity to alter materially the nature of its existing activities if it were to accept the donation (but any material grant by the reporting charity to a charity which is a related party should be disclosed);

(b)   minor or routine unremunerated services provided to a charity by people related to it;

(c)   contracts of employment between a charity and its employees (except where the employees are the charity trustees or people connected with them);

(d)   contributions by a charity to a pension fund for the benefit of employees; (also see paragraph 172);

(e)   the purchase from a charity by a related party of minor articles which are offered for sale to the general public on the same terms as are offered to the general public.

(f)   the provision of services to a related party (including a charity trustee or person connected with a charity trustee), where the related party receives the services as part of a wider beneficiary class of which he is a member, and on the same terms as other members of the class (for example, the use of a village hall by members of its committee of management, as inhabitants of the area of benefit); and

(g)   the payment or reimbursement of out-of-pocket expenses to a related party (including a charity trustee or person connected with a charity trustee—but see paragraphs 167 to 169).

AA Trustee Remuneration

3A–090   166. Unlike in the case of the directors of commercial companies, it is not the normal practice for charity trustees, or people connected with them, to receive remuneration, or other benefits, from the charities for which they are responsible, or from institutions connected with those charities. Detailed disclosures are, therefore, required, where the related party is a charity trustee, or a person connected with a charity trustee. The following points should be borne in mind when reporting on related party transactions, where the related party is a charity trustee or a person connected with a charity:

(a)   (See paragraph 162.) The transaction should always be regarded as material, and should, therefore, be disclosed regardless of its size, unless one of the exceptions in paragraph 165 applies.

(b)   (Paragraph 164). Each type of related party transaction must be separately disclosed. This means, for example, that particulars of remuneration paid to each charity trustee or person connected with a charity trustee, should be given individually in the notes. Where the charity has made any pension arrangements for charity trustees or persons connected with them, the amount of contributions paid and the benefits accruing must be disclosed in the notes for each related party.

(c)   Where remuneration has been paid to a charity trustee or a person connected with a charity trustee, the legal authority under which the payment was made (*e.g.* provision in the governing document of the charity, order of the Court or Charity Commission) should also be given, as should the reason for such remuneration.

(d)   Where neither the trustees nor any persons connected with them have received any such remuneration, this fact should be stated.

AA Trustee Expenses

167. Where a charity has met individual expenses incurred by trustees for services provided to the charity, either by reimbursement of the trustee or by providing the trustee with an allowance or by direct payment to a third party, the aggregate amount of those expenses should be disclosed in a note to the accounts. The note should also indicate the nature of the expenses (*e.g.* travel, subsistence, entertainment etc.) and the number of trustees involved. **3A–091**

168. Sometimes trustees act as agents for the charity and make purchases on its behalf and are reimbursed for this expenditure, *e.g.* payment for stationery or office equipment. Such expenditure is not related to the services provided by a trustee and there is no need to disclose it. Likewise there is no need to disclose routine expenditure which is attributable collectively to the services provided by the trustees, such as the hire of a room for meetings or providing reasonable refreshment at the meeting.

169. Where the trustees have received no such expenses, this fact should be stated.

Indemnity Insurance

170. If funds belonging to the charity have been used for the purchase of insurance: **3A–092**

(a) to protect the charity from loss arising from the neglect or defaults of its trustees, employees or agents; or

(b) to indemnify the trustees or other officers against the consequences of any neglect or default on their part;

these facts and the cost involved in providing such insurance should be disclosed in detail in the notes to the accounts.

AA Staff Costs and Emoluments

171. It is important that the accounts disclose the costs of employing staff who work for the charity whether or not the charity itself has incurred those costs. This includes seconded and agency staff and staff employed by connected or independent companies. For instance, staff working for a charity may have contracts with and be paid by a connected company. Payments may also be made to independent third parties for the provision of staff. Where such arrangements are in place and the costs involved are material (in relation to the charity's own expenditure) there should be disclosure by way of note which outlines the arrangement in place, the reasons for them and the amounts involved. **3A–093**

172. The total staff costs should be shown in the notes to the accounts giving the split between gross wages and salaries, employer's national insurance costs and pension contributions for the year. An estimate of the average number of full time equivalent employees for the year should be disclosed in the notes to the accounts providing sub-categories according to the manner in which the charity's activities are organised.

173. The notes should also show the number of employees whose emoluments for the year (including taxable benefits in kind but not employer pension contributions) fell within each band of £10,000 from £50,000 upwards. Bands in which no employee's emoluments fell should not be listed.

174. In addition pension details must be disclosed in total for higher paid staff in paragraph 173 as follows: **3A–094**

(a) contributions in the year for the provision of money purchase benefits (normally money purchase schemes); and

(b) the number of staff to whom retirement benefits are accruing under money purchase and defined benefit schemes respectively.
(Pension schemes are defined in Appendix 1: Glossary)

175. If there are no employees with emoluments above £50,000 this fact should be stated.

Cost of Audit, Independent Examination or Reporting Accountant Services and other Financial Services

3A–095   176. **AA** The notes to the accounts should disclose separately the amounts payable to the auditor, independent examiner or reporting accountant in respect of:

(a) the costs of their respective external scrutiny; and
(b) other financial services such as taxation advice, consultancy, financial advice and accountancy.

177. In addition, where a charity has incurred other non-statutory costs of external scrutiny, such as a branch audit, the total of these costs should be identified and disclosed separately.

Ex-Gratia Payments

3A–096   178. The total amount or value of any:

(a) payment; or
(b) non-monetary benefit; or
(c) other expenditure of any kind; or
(d) waiver of rights to property to which a charity is entitled.

which is made not as an application of funds or property for charitable purposes but in fulfilment of a compelling moral obligation should be disclosed in the notes to the accounts. Where trustees require and obtain the authority of the Court, the Attorney General or the Charity Commission, the nature and date of the authority for each such payment should also be disclosed.

179. Payments which the trustees reasonably consider to be in the interests of the charity (more than a moral obligation) should not be treated as ex-gratia, even though there is no legal obligation to make them. For example, the trustees may think that it will motivate retained staff and hence benefit the charity if they make redundancy payments over and above the minimum legally required.

Note of Changes in Resources Applied for Fixed Assets for Charity Use

3A–097   180. Where resources expended during the year on the acquisition of functional fixed assets is material, this fact should be explained in a note to the accounts to help the reader understand the impact on the more liquid funds of the charity. It may be useful for this note to follow on immediately after the reconciliation of funds at the bottom of the Statement of Financial Activities. The format should, where necessary, show:

(a) net movement in funds for the year (from the Statement of Financial Activities);
(b) resources used for net acquisitions (or obtained from net disposals) of fixed assets for charity use (*i.e.* the increase or decrease in the net book value of functional fixed assets);

(c)   net movement in funds available for future activities (*i.e.* those not held in functional fixed assets).

BALANCE SHEET

Introduction

181. The balance sheet provides a snapshot of the charity's assets and liabilities   **3A–098** at the end of its accounting year and how the net asset position is split between the different types of funds. The balance sheet will not always include all of the assets and liabilities of a charity, nor attach an up to date valuation for all assets. Some inalienable and historic assets (see paragraphs 208–217), or contingent liabilities (see paragraphs 261–269) may be omitted. Where such assets and liabilities exist and are not included in the balance sheet, details must be provided in the notes to the accounts.

182. The objective of the balance sheet is to show the resources available to the charity and whether these are freely available or have to be used for specific purposes because of legal restrictions on their use. It may also show which of the resources the trustees have designated for specific future use. It will normally be necessary to read the reserves policy in the trustees report (see paragraph 31(e)) to gain a full understanding of the availability and planned use of the charity's funds.

Presentation

Structure of the Balance Sheet

183. The funds of a charity should be grouped together in the balance sheet   **3A–099** according to their kind. It should distinguish, as a minimum, between, unrestricted income funds, restricted income funds and endowments. Distinctions between permanent and expendable endowment and designated funds can also be made.

184. The balance sheet should show assets and liabilities under the following headings:

(i)   Fixed assets, sub-divided between:
  (a)   intangible assets;
  (b)   tangible assets;
  (c)   inalienable and historic assets;
  (d)   investments.
(ii)   Current assets sub-divided between:
  (a)   stocks and work-in-progress;
  (b)   debtors;
  (c)   investments; and
  (d)   cash at bank and in hand
  (sub totals should be given for (i) and (ii) above).
(iii)   Creditors: amounts falling due within one year.
(iv)   Net current assets or liabilities (*i.e.* the amount in (ii) less the amount in (iii)).
(v)   Total assets less current liabilities (*i.e.* the amount in (i) plus (or minus) the amount in (iv)).
(vi)   Creditors: amounts falling due after more than one year.
(vii)   Provisions for liabilities and charges.
(viii)   Net assets (*i.e.* the amount in (v) less the amounts in (vi) and (vii)).
(ix)   The funds of the charity divided between:
  (a)   unrestricted income funds;
  (b)   restricted income funds; and
  (c)   endowment funds.

185. The balance sheet can be presented in one continuous vertical format or it can be presented in columns appropriately divided between the three types of fund.

3A–100   186. In addition, the assets and liabilities should be analysed in a way that enables the reader to gain a proper appreciation of their spread and character. For example, long-term debtors should, where the total is material, be separately stated in the balance sheet—otherwise their total amounts by category (see paragraph 245) should be disclosed in the notes to the accounts.

187. If there are no amounts for the current and prior year then no entries need to be made on the balance sheet and the headings can be omitted.

188. As explained in paragraph 5 of Appendix 3 expenditure may be incurred in anticipation of the receipt of restricted income, possibly leading to a negative balance on a specific fund. Where such balances are material they should not simply be netted off against balances on the fund category in the balance sheet. This means that the balance sheet may need to separately identify positive and negative balances on restricted funds.

The Principles for the Inclusion of Assets and Liabilities in the Balance Sheet

Intangible Fixes Assets

3A–101   189. Intangible fixed assets should be included in the balance sheet in accordance with Financial Reporting Standard 10 (FRS 10) "Goodwill and Intangible Assets".

Tangible Fixed Assets (Other than Investments)

3A–102   190. Financial Reporting Standard 15 (FRS 15) "Tangible Fixed Assets" requires that all fixed assets should be capitalised on initial acquisition and included in the balance sheet at cost or valuation. They may then be periodically revalued. Subsequent expenditure which enhances (rather than maintains) the performance of fixed assets should also be capitalised.

191. Within charities, tangible fixed assets (other than investments) fall into two categories, those held for charity use (including those used for the running and administration of the charity) and those classed as inalienable and historic assets. There may be some overlap in that some inalienable and historic assets may also be used in the functional activities (Appendix 1: Glossary) of the charity. the following paragraphs 192 to 207 describe the general rules for inclusion of tangible fixed assets in the balance sheet. However there are some special considerations for inalienable and historic assets which are described in paragraphs 208 to 217.

192. Subject to the circumstance in paragraphs 193 to 195 below, tangible fixed assets should initially be included at their cost of acquisition including costs that are directly attributable to bringing the assets into working condition for their intended use. This can include costs of interest on loans to finance the construction of such assets but only where the charity has adopted this as a policy for all tangible fixed assets and capitalisation should cease when the asset is ready for use. This applies whether assets are bought outright or through hire purchase or finance leasing.

3A–103   193. If a fixed asset is acquired in full or in part from the proceeds of a grant it should be included at its full acquisition cost (or in the case of a joint arrangement at the gross value of the charity's share in the asset) without netting off the grant proceeds (see paragraph 328).

194. Where functional fixed assets have been donated they should be valued at the amount of the gift included in the Statement of Financial Activities (see paragraphs 95–96).

195. Similarly where such assets are capitalised some time after being acquired, for example as a result of a change in accounting policy, they should be included

at original cost or at the value at which the gift was included in the Statement of Financial Activities less an amount for depreciation. However, if neither of these amounts is ascertainable, a reasonable estimate of the asset's cost or current value to the charity should be used. Such a valuation will be regarded as the asset's initial carrying amount and will not be regarded as a revaluation (see paragraphs 218–223).

196. Where the net book value of a fixed asset is higher than its recoverable amount, it will be impaired and should be written down to its recoverable amount. This is covered in more detail in paragraphs 224 to 230. **3A–104**

Mixed Use of Fixed Assets (Functional and Investment)

197. Where land and buildings are held for mixed purposes, *i.e.* partly as functional property and partly as investment, the way in which they are capitalised depends upon the primary purpose for holding the asset and the extent to which they are separable. In general the following rules should be followed: **3A–105**

(a) Assets held primarily for charity use of which a part is leased at a commercial rent can be regarded as functional fixed assets if:
(i)   only a small part of the asset is leased; or
(ii) the lease is for a short period of time.
(b) Assets held primarily for investment purposes (Appendix 1: Glossary) where a small part is used for functional purposes should be classed as investment assets.
(c) Assets which contain clearly distinguishable parts which are held for different purposes *i.e.* partly functional and partly investment and do not fall under (a) and (b) above should be split in the balance sheet between functional and investment assets.

Depreciation of Tangible Fixed Assets (Other than Investments)

198. Most tangible fixed assets depreciate; that is they wear out, are consumed or otherwise suffer a reduction in their useful life through use, the passing of time or obsolescence. Their value is thus gradually expended over their useful economic life. This expenditure should be recognised by means of annual depreciation charged in the Statement of Financial Activities and shown in the balance sheet as accumulated depreciation deducted from the value of the relevant fixed assets. **3A–106**

199. Fixed assets held for use by the charity which are included in the balance sheet should be depreciated at rates appropriate to their useful economic life in each case.

200. Exceptions to charging depreciation may only arise if any of the following conditions apply:

(a) the asset is freehold land which is considered to have an indefinitely long useful life;
(b) the depreciation charge and accumulated depreciation are not material because:
(i)   the asset has a very long useful life; or
(ii) the residual value (based on prices at the time of acquisition or subsequent revaluation) of the asset is not materially different from the carrying amount of the asset;
provided the stringent conditions of paragraphs 89–91 of FRS 15 are met and the asset is subject to an annual impairment review (except for charities under the threshold for following the FRSSE);
(c) the assets are inalienable or historic and have not been included in the balance sheet (see paragraphs 208–217).

3A–107   201. Where a fixed asset for charity use comprises two or more major components with substantially different useful lives, each component should be accounted for as a separate asset and depreciated over its individual useful life.

202. The useful economic lives and residual values of fixed assets should be reviewed at the end of the accounting period and, where there is a material change, the value of the asset should be depreciated over its remaining useful life.

Disclosure

3A–108   203. Tangible fixed assets for use by the charity should be analysed in the notes to the accounts within the following categories:

    (a)   freehold interest in land and buildings;
    (b)   leasehold and other interests in land and buildings;
    (c)   plant and machinery including motor vehicles;
    (d)   fixtures, fittings and equipment; and
    (e)   payments on account and assets in the course of construction.

These are broad categories and any charity may, within reason, split the headings or adopt other narrower classes that meet the definition of a class of tangible fixed assets and are appropriate to its operations.

204. The notes should summarise all material changes in the values of each class of functional fixed assets and reconcile the opening and closing balances. This should include, separately stated:

at the beginning and end of the period:

    (a)   cost, valuation or revalued amount;
    (b)   accumulated depreciation and impairment provisions;
    movements on both carrying amount and depreciation during the period:
    (c)   additions;
    (d)   disposals;
    (e)   revaluations;
    (f)   transfers;
    (g)   impairment losses (or reversals).

205. Totals should be given for all classes of assets (including a combined total) separately identifying the depreciation charged for the period.

3A–109   206. The methods of depreciation used and useful economic lives or depreciation rates should be disclosed in the accounting policy notes (see paragraph 285).

207. There is often a considerable difference between the carrying value and market value of interests in land and buildings not held as investments. Where the trustees consider this to be so significant that it needs to be drawn to the attention of the users of the accounts then the difference should be included, with such precision as is practicable, in the notes to the accounts. If it is not practicable to quantify the difference a written explanation will suffice.

Inalienable and Historic Fixed Assets

3A–110   208. FRS 15 requires that all fixed assets should be capitalised in the balance sheet (see paragraph 190). In principle this includes fixed assets which are inalienable (Appendix 1: Glossary) or historic (Appendix 1: Glossary) such as ancient monuments, historic buildings or a collection of artistic or scientific works. They should be included in a separate line in the balance sheet and can be further sub-divided into classes appropriate to each charity *e.g.* churches, collections, historic houses, artefacts. An appropriate depreciation policy should be applied in accordance with paragraphs 198 to 202. However, charities will not need to capitalise or value inalienable and historic assets when the circumstances in paragraph 211 apply.

209. In addition to assets which are legally inalienable there are some assets which can be clearly identified as historic, artistic or scientific. They are often unique and form part of the heritage of the nation, for instance ancient churches and works of art. Other assets such as war memorials or nature reserves are also preserved as part of the heritage of the nation. They can be considered as historic where they are held as the objects of the charity (rather than as a means of achieving the objects) and the charity has a policy of long term retention. Inalienable and historic assets do not normally represent a store of financial resources for the charity, and public access to them, (whether free or otherwise) is often essential to demonstrate the public benefit of holding such assets. In the case of buildings this may be achieved by using them for the charitable purposes for which they were intended.

210. Where an inalienable or historic asset is used for administrative or fund generating purposes, such as a visitor centre or a shop, or is held as an investment, it should not be regarded as inalienable or historic and should be capitalised within the appropriate category of fixed assets. Similarly if a decision has been made to sell an asset it should be included at its net realisable value within fixed assets or as a current asset investment.

211. It may be difficult or costly to attribute a cost or value to inalienable and historic assets. In such cases these assets may be excluded from the balance sheet if:

      3A–111

   (a)   reliable cost information is not available and conventional valuation approaches lack sufficient reliability; or

   (b)   significant costs are involved which may be onerous compared with the additional benefit derived by users of the accounts in assessing the trustees stewardship of the assets.

212. It may also be difficult or costly to attribute a cost or valuation to inalienable and historic fixed assets which are donated. Where assets are purchased by the charity or by another party who then shortly afterwards donates the asset to the charity, the purchase price should be considered as reliable cost information and could be used as a reference point for the fair value of donations of similar assets. Where an asset is partly purchased and partly donated a reasonable estimate of the cost or value to the charity should be made.

213. The value of inalienable and historic assets in cultural, environmental, educational and historic terms is unlikely to be full reflected in a financial value derived from a market mechanism or the price of such assets. It is, therefore, essential that the disclosure requirements in paragraphs 215–217 are met.

214. Using the criteria set out in paragraph 211 charities should evaluate whether or not to attribute a cost or value to any of their inalienable and historic assets, paying particular attention to the comparison of costs against benefits of such an exercise and taking into account valuation fees, the cost of researching past records etc. In this context, examples of inalienable and historic assets for which a cost or valuation may not be attributed are:

      3A–112

   (a)   museum and gallery collections and other collections including the national archives;

   (b)   archaeological sites, burial mounds, ruins, monuments and statues.

Disclosure

3A–113   215. Information on alienable or historic assets (whether or not they have been capitalised) should be given in the notes to the accounts or in another publication which is referred to in the notes to the accounts and is available to the public in the same way as the accounts. This should specify why the assets are considered to be inalienable or historic and be sufficient to enable the reader to appreciate the age and scale of these assets and what use is made of them. This can be done in aggregate for similar types of assets. These details can only be omitted if the publication of the information would prejudice the efficient working of the charity (*e.g.* by materially increasing the risk of theft or vandalism of the assets in question). If any inalienable and historic assets have not been capitalised or valued, a statement to this effect should be included in the notes to the accounts.

216. The amount spent on acquiring inalienable and historic assets during the year should be disclosed in the notes to the accounts.

217. The accounting policy notes should include the acquisition and disposal policy for inalienable and historic assets (see paragraph 285(c)).

Revaluation of Tangible Fixed Assets (Other than Investments)

3A–114   218. In accordance with FRS 15, tangible fixed assets (other than investment assets) do not need to be revalued unless the charity adopts a policy of revaluation. Where such a policy is adopted, whilst it need not be applied to all fixed assets it must be applied to entire classes of fixed assets. Therefore if an individual fixed asset is revalued all other assets in that class must also be revalued. Classes of assets can be narrowly defined, within reason, according to the operations of the charity (see paragraph 203).

219. The initial valuation of an asset when it is donated or where it is capitalised as a result of the change in an accounting policy will not be regarded as a revaluation and hence will not require the entire class of such assets to be revalued.

220. Similarly where a charity is holding assets at a revalued amount at the date of commencement of this SORP this will not be regarded as a revaluation unless the trustees so choose.

3A–115   221. Where there is a policy to revalue such fixed assets their value must be updated on a regular basis. The trustees may use any reasonable approach to valuation at least every five years subject only to obtaining advice as to the possibility of any material movements between individual valuations. Where a charity has a number of such assets it will be acceptable for valuations to be carried out on a rolling basis over a five year period. Independent formal professional valuations are not mandatory in the case of a charity, which instead can rely on the option of a suitably qualified person who could be a trustee or employee for this purpose.

222. In the case of assets other than properties, such as motor vehicles, there may be an active second-hand market for the asset, or appropriate indices may exist allowing a valuation to be made with reasonable certainty by an appropriate person (but not necessarily a qualified valuer) either internal or external to the charity. Where this method of valuation is used the assets' values must be updated annually. As an alternative to market value such assets can be recorded at depreciated replacement cost.

Disclosure

3A–116   223. Where any class of functional fixed assets of a charity has been revalued the notes to the accounts should give:

   (a)   the name and qualification of the valuer and whether they are a member of staff or a trustee or external to the charity;

(b) the basis or bases of valuation;
(c) where records are available, the historical cost less depreciation;
(d) date of the previous full valuation;
(e) if the value has not been updated in the reporting period, a statement by the trustees that they are not aware of any material changes since the last valuation.

Impairment of Fixed Assets for Use by the Charity

224. On rare occasions a functional fixed asset may become impaired. This **3A–117** occurs if its net book value (at cost or valuation) is higher than its recoverable amount. In such a case Financial Reporting Standard 11 (FRS 11) would require it to be written down to its recoverable amount.

225. The recoverable amount is the higher of the net realisable value and the value in use. Value in use is normally the present value of the future cash flows obtainable as a result of an asset's continued use. If a fixed asset is not held for the main purpose of generating surplus cash flows either by itself or in conjunction with other assets, it is not appropriate to measure the value in use of the asset at an amount based on expected future cash flows. In such cases an alternative measure of its service potential may be more relevant, such as the intrinsic worth of the service delivery or the replacement cost of the asset. Each charity can determine its own measure of service delivery but this must be reasonable, justifiable and consistently operated.

226. Impairment reviews should only be carried out where this is some indication that the recoverable amount of a functional fixed asset is below its net book value. Such a review should as far as possible be carried out on individual assets or where this is not possible then certain categories of assets can be grouped. Events or changes which may indicate an impairment are:

(a) physical deterioration, change or obsolescence of the fixed asset;
(b) social, demographic or environmental changes resulting in a reduction of beneficiaries for a charity;
(c) changes in the law, other regulations or standards which adversely affect the activities of a charity;
(d) management commitments to undertake a significant reorganisation;
(e) a major loss of key employees associated with particular activities of a charity;
(f) operating losses on activities using fixed assets primarily to generate incoming resources.

227. Where an impairment review is required the charity should first determine **3A–118** the net realisable value of the asset. If this is lower than the net book value the value in use will need to be considered. If the value in use is considered to be above the net book value the asset should be valued at the net book value. If a decision is made to sell the asset it should be valued at its expected net realisable value.

228. Value in use calculations should not be used to manipulate the write down of fixed assets. For instance when a new specialised asset is purchased, although it may have a low net realisable value, it is unlikely that it will suffer an impairment in service delivery within the first years after acquisition.

229. Where there is an impairment loss that needs to be recognised, charities should determine this in accordance with the requirements of FRS 11 (whilst being able to use alternative valuation methods for some assets). The loss should be treated as additional depreciation and included in the Statement of Financial Activities in accordance with paragraph 198. The revised carrying amount of the asset should be depreciated over its remaining useful economic life.

Disclosure

3A–119   230. The methods used in the impairment review to determine net realisable value and value in use should be disclosed in the notes to the accounts. This should include details required in paragraph 223.

Investment Assets

3A–120   231. Investment assets (including investments and investment properties (Appendix 1: Glossary) and cash held for investment purposes) should be classified as a separate category within fixed assets except where the intention is to realise the asset without reinvestment of the sale proceeds. In such a case, it should be reclassified as a current asset. The reason for this is that investment assets are generally held with the overall intention of retaining them long-term (*i.e.* as fixed assets) for the continuing benefit of the charity in the form of income and capital appreciation.

Valuation of Investment Assets

3A–121   232. All investment assets should be shown in the balance sheet at market value or at the trustees' best estimate of market value as described below. Market value best represents a true and fair view of the value of these assets to the charity, given the duty of the trustees to administer the portfolio of investment assets so as to obtain the best investment performance without undue risk. Investment assets should not be depreciated. All changes in value in the year, whether or not realised, should be reported in the "gains and losses on revaluations and disposals of investment assets" section of the Statement of Financial Activities (see paragraphs 155–156).

233. Most freely tradable investments will have a readily available market price *e.g.* shares on a recognised stock exchange. For investment assets for which there is no readily identifiable market price the trustees should adopt a reasonable approach: for instance, valuing shares in unlisted companies by reference to underlying net assets or earnings or the dividend record, as appropriate. Sometimes, where there is no readily available market value for an investment asset (such as a trading subsidiary), the cost of obtaining a valuation outweighs the benefit to the users of the accounts. In such a situation the asset may be included in the accounts at cost.

234. For investment assets other than shares or securities, the trustees may use any reasonable approach to valuation which must be done at least every five years subject only to obtaining advice as to the possibility of any material movements between individual valuations. If there is a material movement the assets must be revalued. Where a charity has a number of such assets it will be acceptable for valuations to be carried out on a rolling basis over a five year period.

Disclosure

3A–122   235. Where values are determined other than by reference to readily available market prices, (Appendix 1: Glossary) the notes to the accounts should disclose who has made the valuation giving their name, qualification and position (*e.g.* trustee, employee, external valuer) and how the valuation has been carried out.

236. In the rare case where the size or nature of a holding of securities is such that the market is thought by the trustees not to be capable of absorbing the sale of the shareholding without a material effect on the quoted price, the trustees should summarise the position in the notes to the accounts. If they are able to do so, the trustees should give an opinion on how much the market price should be adjusted to take this fact into consideration.

237. The notes to the accounts should show all changes in values of investment assets and reconcile the opening and closing book values.

238. The notes should also show the total value of investment assets divided between distinct types. As a minimum this would normally include: **3A–123**

    (a)   investment properties:
    (b)   investments listed on a recognised stock exchange or ones valued by reference to such investments, such as unit trusts and common investment funds;
    (c)   investments in subsidiary or associated undertakings or in companies which are connected persons (Appendix 1: Glossary);
    (d)   other unlisted securities;
    (e)   cash and settlements pending held as part of the investment portfolio;
    (f)   any other investments.
Items in categories (a) to (f) above should be further analysed between;
    (i)   investment assets in the UK;
    (ii) investment assets outside the UK.

239. The total value of shares or investment schemes (including unit trusts) relating to companies listed on a UK stock exchange or incorporated in the UK are treated as investment assets in the UK and no further analysis is required of whether such entities invest their funds in the UK or outside the UK.

240. Further details should be given in the notes to the accounts to show how the portfolio is structured. This should indicate direct and indirect investment in listed securities (including unit trusts), details of any material investments (any over 5% by value of the portfolio) and any material restrictions which might apply on the realisation of any such assets.

241. The notes to the accounts should indicate the value of investments held in each type of fund. This may be included in the overall analysis of assets held in the different types of funds (see paragraph 49(a)). **3A–124**

Current Assets, Liabilities and Long-term Creditors

242. Current assets (other than investments, see paragraph 232) should normally be recognised at the lower of their cost and net realisable value. **3A–125**

243. Liabilities should normally be recognised at their settlement value. In the case of provisions this will be the amount that an entity would rationally pay to settle the obligation at the balance sheet date or to transfer it to a third party at that time and may therefore involve discounting (see paragraph 252).

Disclosure

244. Where there are debtors or creditors which do not fit into any of the following categories the headings may be added to or adapted as appropriate to the type of debtor or creditor and nature of the charity. **3A–126**

245. Debtors should be analysed in the notes to the accounts between short term and long term (above one year) giving amounts for the following:

    (a)   trade debtors;
    (b)   amounts due from subsidiary and associated undertakings;
    (c)   other debtors;
    (d)   prepayments; and
    (e)   accrued income.

246. Where investments are held as current assets the same disclosure is required as for fixed asset investments (see paragraph 238).

3A–127   247. The totals for both short-term and long-term creditors should each be separately analysed in the notes giving amounts for the following:

    (a)   loans and overdrafts;
    (b)   trade creditors;
    (c)   amounts due to subsidiary and undertakings;
    (d)   other creditors;
    (e)   accruals; and
    (f)   deferred income.

248. Where a charity is acting as an intermediary agent (as opposed to a custodian trustee, paragraph 32) for another organisation as described in paragraph 81 any assets held and the associated liabilities should be separately identified in the notes to the accounts but not included in the balance sheet. The notes to the accounts should provide sufficient detail so that the reader of the accounts understands the relationship and nature of the transactions between the charity, the funding organisation and the recipient of the funds.

249. The details in paragraph 248 should also be provided when the charity is acting as an intermediary but is the principal as described in paragraph 82. However in this case the assets and liabilities will be included in the balance sheet.

Provisions for Commitments

3A–128   250. Expenditure resulting from provisions that arise due to a legal or constructive obligation (as per FRS 12) should be accounted for in the Statement of Financial Activities in accordance with paragraphs 119 to 130. Such provisions should be appropriately split in the balance sheet between liabilities due within one year and those falling due after one year.

251. The amount recognised as a liability should be the best estimate of the expenditure required to settle the present obligation at the balance sheet date or to transfer it to a third party at that time. When calculating this amount consideration should be given to:

    (a)   the timing of cash flows;
    (b)   future events and uncertainties which may affect the amount required to settle the obligation.

252. Where provisions are accrued in the current financial year but are to be paid over several years then future payments may have a reduced value in today's terms (current value). Where the effect is material the outflow of resources required to settle the obligation at the balance sheet date should be discounted to their present value. The discount rate used should reflect the current assessments of the time value of money and the risks specific to the provision. The interest rate either for the cost of borrowing or investment could be an appropriate discount rate.

3A–129   253. The best estimate of the liability should be reviewed and the balance sheet date and adjusted appropriately. If a transfer of resources is no longer needed to settle the obligation then the amount of the liability no longer representing an obligation should be deducted from the expenditure category where it was originally charged in the Statement of Financial Activities.

254. In some instances charities may receive funding for the obligations from a third party which may be regarded as reimbursements and can be netted off against the liability accrued in the statement of financial activities (see paragraph 77). But if they exist at the balance sheet date such resources must be shown as a separate asset in the balance sheet.

255. Some expressions of financial support are not binding upon the trustees or do not meet the definition of a constructive obligation. If they cannot be enforced and the trustees retain the option to discontinue future instalments, they should

not be treated as liabilities but disclosed as an "intention". Where the trustees have decided to incur the expenditure out of existing unrestricted funds, they should account for such intentions by transfer to an appropriate designated fund.

Disclosure

256. Particulars of all material provisions for commitments accrued in the balance sheet as liabilities should be disclosed in the notes. Similarly particulars of all material commitments in respect of specific charitable projects should be disclosed if they have not been charged in the accounts.   **3A–130**

257. These particulars should include the amounts involved, when the commitments are likely to be met and the movements on commitments previously reported. Particulars of all other material binding commitments should also be disclosed (*e.g.* operating leases).

258. The notes should distinguish between those commitments included on the balance sheet as liabilities and those that are intentions to spend and are not included but in both cases should detail:

(a) the reason for the commitments, giving separate disclosure for material objects;

(b) the total amount of the commitments, including amounts already charged in the accounts;

(c) the amount of commitments outstanding at the start of the year;

(d) any amounts charged in the Statement of Financial Activities for the year;

(e) any amounts released during the year due to a change in the value in the commitments;

(f) the amount of commitments outstanding at the end of the year and an indication as to how much is payable within one year and over one year.

259. Any designated funds should be separately disclosed as part of the unrestricted funds of the charity and appropriately described in the notes. The purpose of the disclosure is to identify that portion of the unrestricted funds that has been set aside to meet the commitments. Activities that are to be wholly financed from future income would not form part of such designation.   **3A–131**

Guarantees

260. All material guarantees given by the charity, and the conditions under which liabilities might arise as a result of such guarantees, should be disclosed in a note to the accounts.   **3A–132**

Contingent Assets and Liabilities

261. A charity may have contingent assets and liabilities as defined in Financial Reporting Standard 12 (FRS 12) (Appendix 1: Glossary) (Appendix 2: FRS 12).   **3A–133**

262. A charity should not recognise incoming or outgoing resources or gains and losses arising respectively from contingent assets or contingent liabilities in the Statement of Financial Activities or the balance sheet.

263. Contingent assets are not recognised because it could result in the recognition of incoming resources that may never be realised. However, when the realisation of the incoming resources is virtually certain, then the asset is not a contingent asset and the resource/gain arising should be included in the Statement of Financial Activities as an incoming resource and in the balance sheet as a debtor.

3A–134   264. Where it becomes probable that there will be a future outflow of resources to settle an item previously regarded as a contingent liability it should cease to be contingent and should be accrued in the accounts. The amount of the liability should (except in extremely rare circumstances where no reliable estimate can be made) be capable of being estimated with reasonable accuracy at the date on which the accounts are approved.

265. The probability of a contingent asset or liability resulting in a future transfer of resources (to or from the charity) should be continually assessed and the recognition of the asset or liability should be reviewed as appropriate.

Disclosure

3A–135   266. Material contingent assets and liabilities should be disclosed in the notes to the accounts unless the probability of a future transfer of resources (to or from the charity) is extremely remote—in which case no disclosure is necessary.

267. The accounts should disclose the nature of each contingency, the uncertainties that are expected to affect the outcome, and a prudent estimate of the financial effect where an amount has not been accrued. If such an estimate cannot be made, the accounts should explain why it is not practicable to make such an estimate.

268. Where there is more than one contingent asset or liability they may be sufficiently similar in nature for them to be grouped together as one class and be disclosed in a single statement.

3A–136   269. Where a liability has been accrued but there is still a contingent liability arising from the same set of circumstances then the notes to the accounts should link the provision and the contingent liability.

Loan Liabilities

3A–137   270. If any specific assets (whether land or other property) of the charity are subject to a mortgage or charge given as security for a loan or other liability, a note to the accounts should disclose:

(a)   particulars of the assets which are subject to the mortgage or charge;
(b)   the amount of the loan or liability and its proportion to the value of the assets mortgaged or charged.

271. The amounts and interest and repayment terms of all inter-fund loans (summarised, if necessary) should be disclosed in the notes to the accounts. Loans made to trading subsidiaries, the security provided, the interest payable and the repayment terms should be disclosed as a separate item in the notes to the accounts.

Cash-flow Statement

Application

3A–138   272. The preparation of a cash-flow statement is a requirement of Financial Reporting Standard 1 (Revised 1996) for all charities above the thresholds (specified in Appendix 2: FRS 1). (The limits regarding the production of cash flow statements by Scottish charities are set down in regulations made under the Law Reform (Miscellaneous Provisions) (Scotland) Act 1990.) The object is to show the cash received and used by the charity in the accounting period.

273. Wherever a Cash-flow Statement is prepared it should comply with the requirements of FRS 1 (Revised 1996) subject to the following paragraphs.

274. The analysis of the cash movements should accord with the charity's operations as reported in its Statement of Financial Activities, and be given in appropriate detail. The starting point will normally be "net incoming/outgoing resources before revaluations and investment asset disposals".

275. Movements in endowment should not be included in cash flows from "operating activities" but should be treated as increases or decreases in the financing section. This is achieved as follows: **3A–139**

(a) cash donations to endowment should be treated as additions to endowment in the "financing" section,;

(b) the receipts and payments from the acquisition and disposal of investments should be shown gross in the "capital expenditure and financial investment" section of the cash-flow statement. A single line should then be included in this section showing the net movement in cash-flows attributable to endowment investments. A corresponding line should be included in the "financing" section for the same amount. The line in the "financing" section should reflect the cash into/(cash out of) the endowment fund whereas it will be the opposite direction in the "capital expenditure and financial investment" section;

(c) on the rare occasion when payments are made out of permanent endowment this should be shown as a decrease in the "financing" section;

(d) transactions which do not result in cash flows should not be reported in the Cash-flow Statement (*e.g.* depreciation, revaluations, accruals,) but may need to be disclosed (see paragraph 276).

Disclosure

276. The disclosure requirements of FRS 1 (Revised 1996) will depend upon the exact basis of preparation and content of the cash-flow statement for each charity but the following are some of the more common disclosures: **3A–140**

(a) major transactions not resulting in cash movements should be disclosed in the notes if necessary for an understanding of the underlying transactions. For instance the release of expendable endowment;

(b) cash (and any financing) movements should be reconciled to the appropriate opening and closing balance sheet amounts; and

(c) a reconciliation of cash-flows from "operating activities" within the cashflow statement to the net incoming resources/expenditure line of the statement of financial activities.

DISCLOSURE OF ACCOUNTING POLICIES

AA The Basis of the Preparation of the Accounts

277. Charity accounts should include notes on the accounting policies chosen which should be the most appropriate in the particular circumstances of each charity for the purpose of the giving a true and fair view. The policies should be consistent with this SORP, Accounting Standards and relevant legislation. FRED 21 explains how accounting policies should be determined. **3A–141**

278. Accounting policies are the principles, bases, conventions and rules by which transactions are recognised, measured and presented in the accounts. They are supplemented by estimation techniques where judgement is required in recording the value of incoming and outgoing resources and of assets and liabilities. It is essential that the accounts are accompanied by an explanation of the basis and estimation techniques on which they have been prepared. Accounts are normally

prepared on the basis that the charity is a going concern and must include relevant, reliable, comparable and understandable information.

279. **AA** The notes regarding the basis of preparation of the accounts should state that the accounts have been prepared in accordance with:

(a) this SORP and accounting standards or with this SORP and FRSSE (see paragraphs 345–347);

(b) the Charities Act or the Companies Act or other legislative requirements; and

(c) the historic cost basis of accounting except for investments (and if applicable, fixed assets) which have been included at revalued amounts.

3A–142   280. **AA** If the accounts depart from accounting standards in any material respect, this should be stated in the accounting policies and Annual Report giving the reason and justification for the departure and the financial impact. Similarly the following details should be given for any material departure from this SORP:

(a) a brief description of how the treatment adopted departs from this SORP;

(b) the reasons why the trustees judge that the treatment adopted is more appropriate to the charity's particular circumstances; and

(c) an estimate of the financial effect on the accounts where this is needed for the accounts to give a true and fair view.

A departure is not justified simply because it gives the reader a more appealing picture of the financial position or results of the charity

3A–143   281. If any branches (Appendix 1: Glossary) have been omitted from the accounts the reason for omission must be given although the individual branches do not need to be named. Reference should also be made to any potentially linked organisations (such as supporters associations or subsidiaries not consolidated) explaining the accounting treatment adopted.

Specific Policies

3A–144   282. Trustees should explain in the notes to the accounts the accounting policies they have adopted to deal with material items. Explanations need only be brief but they must be clear, fair and accurate. Significant changes to any of the policies from the preceding year must be disclosed in detail. The following are some examples of matters on which the accounting policies should be explained where the amounts involved are material. Trustees should only include those notes which are relevant to their charity.

AA Incoming Resources Policy Notes

3A–145   283. **AA** The policy for including each type of material incoming resource should be given. This will normally be on a receivable basis but may need further details in some cases, for instance:

(a) a description of when a legacy is receivable;

(b) the basis of recognition of gifts and intangible income, specifically covering when such items are not included in the Statement of Financial Activities and the methods of valuation;

(c) the basis of recognition of all grants receivable, including those for fixed assets, and how the grants are split between the different types of incoming resources;

(d) whether any incoming resources are deferred and the basis for any deferrals (this will normally only apply to contractual incoming resources received or invoiced in advance);
(e) the basis for including subscriptions for live membership;
(f) whether the incoming resources from endowment funds are unrestricted or restricted;
(g) whether any incoming resources have been included in the Statement Financial Activities net of expenditure and the reason for this.

AA Resources Expended Policy Notes

284. (a) **AA** The policy for the recognition of liabilities including constructive obligations should be given. Where the liabilities are included as provisions, the point at which the provision is considered to become binding and the basis of any discount factors used in current value calculations for long term commitments should be given. This is particularly applicable to grants, the policy for which must be separately identified.   **3A–146**

(b) **AA** The policy for including items within types of resources expended should be given. In particular the policy for including items within:
   (i) costs of generating funds;
   (ii) grants payable in furtherance of the charity's objects, activities in furtherance of the charity's objects and support costs;
   (iii) management and administration costs;
   and in addition,

(c) **AA** The methods and principles for the allocation and apportionment of all costs between the different categories of expenditure in (b). This disclosure should include the underlying principle *i.e.* whether based on staff time, staff salaries, space occupied or other. Where the costs apportioned are significant, then further clarification on the method of apportionment used is necessary, including the proportions used to undertake the calculations.

Assets Policy Notes

285. The policy for capitalisation of fixed assets for charity use should be stated including: **3A–147**

(a) whether each class of asset is included at cost, valuation or revaluation and the method of valuation where applicable;
(b) the value below which fixed assets are not capitalised;
(c) whether or not inalienable and historic assets are capitalised and if not, the reason why (*e.g.* lack of reliable information, cost/benefit reason etc.: see paragraph 211), specifying the acquisition and disposal policies for such assets;
(d) the rates of depreciation applying to each class of fixed asset; and
(e) the policy with respect to impairment reviews of fixed assets.

286. The policy for including investments in the accounts should be given. This should be at market value but may need to be modified for the valuation of:

(a) investments not listed on a recognised stock exchange;
(b) investment properties; and
(c) investments in subsidiary undertakings.

287. The basis of inclusion in the Statement of Financial Activities of unrealised and realised gains and losses on investments should be stated.

3A–148   288. The basis for inclusion of stocks and work in progress (where relevant the amount of unsold or unused goods and materials should be given).

AA Funds Structure Policy Notes

3A–149   289. **AA** A brief description should be given of the different types of fund held by the charity, including the policy for any transfers between funds and allocations to or from designated funds. Transfers may arise for example where there is a release of restricted or endowed funds to unrestricted funds or charges are made from the unrestricted to other funds.

290. The policy for determining each designated fund should be stated.

Other Policy Notes

3A–150   291. These could include policies for the recognition of the following:

    (a) pension contributions;
    (b) foreign exchange gains and losses;
    (c) treatment of exceptional items;
    (d) treatment of finance and operating leases;
    (e) treatment of irrecoverable VAT.

SUMMERY FINANCIAL INFORMATION AND STATEMENTS

General Principles

3A–151   292. Some charities produce statements which summarise financial information based on the full financial statements in their publications. They do this to communicate key financial information without providing the greater detail required in the full accounts. Charitable companies must follow the provisions of the Companies Act 1985 concerning non-statutory financial statements but there are no legal provisions for other charities.

293. As the form of such publications will vary considerably, depending on the purpose for which they have been prepared, it is not practicable to give detailed recommendations on the content of summary financial information. Some general principles which ought to be followed are set out below.

294. Regardless of the intended circulation of any summary financial information, the full annual report and accounts should always be produced. Such summary information should contain information on both the Statement of Financial Activities and the balance sheet, must be consistent with the full accounts and should not be misleading either by omission or amalgamation of details.

3A–152   295. Summarised financial statements are to be accompanied by a statement, signed on behalf of the trustees, indicating:

    (a) that they are not the statutory accounts but a summary of information relating to both the Statement of Financial Activities and the balance sheet;

    (b) whether or not the full financial statements from which the summary is derived have as yet been externally examined (whether audit, independent examination, or reporting accountants report); and

    (c) where they have been externally examined whether there was an unqualified report;

    (d) where the report is qualified, contains an explanatory paragraph or emphasis of matter, sufficient details should be provided in the summary financial information to enable the reader to appreciate the significance of the report;

(e) where branch accounts are produced it must be clearly stated that the summary is for the branch only and has been extracted from the full accounts of the main charity (giving its name);

(f) details of how the full annual accounts, the external examiners report (as applicable) and the trustees report can be obtained;

(g) the date on which the annual accounts were approved; and

(h) for charities registered in England and Wales, say whether or not the annual report and accounts have been submitted to the Charity Commission.

296. If the full accounts have been externally examined (either audited, independently examined or subject to a reporting accountants report) the external examiner should attach a statement giving an opinion as to whether or not the summary financial information is consistent with the full annual accounts.

297. Any other summary financial information in whatever form which does not include information on the Statement of Financial Activities and the balance sheet must be accompanied by a statement signed on behalf of the trustees as to:

(a) the purpose of the information;

(b) whether or not it is from the full annual accounts;

(c) whether or not these accounts have been audited, independently examined or subject to a reporting accountants report;

(d) details of how the full annual accounts, trustees report and external examiners report (as appropriate) can be obtained.

Special Sections

298. The main text of the SORP deals with the normal accounting practice for those charities producing full accruals accounts. Some charities will have to meet additional requirements and others may have an option of preparing briefer reports and accounts. The following sections have therefore been provided to explain the additional or optional requirements for: **3A–153**

(a) Consolidation of Subsidiary Undertakings—paragraphs 299–319.

(b) Accounting for Associates, Joint Ventures and Joint Arrangements—paragraphs 320–330.

(c) Charitable Companies—paragraphs 331–343.

(d) Accounting for Smaller Charities—paragraphs 344–358.

Consolidation Of Subsidiary Undertakings

Purpose and Scope

299. The purpose of consolidated accounts is to present a true and fair view of the state of financial affairs of all the group interests of the reporting charity including its subsidiary undertakings. The principles and methods of consolidation are covered by Financial Reporting Standard 2 (FRS 2). **3A–154**

300. A parent charity (Appendix 1: Glossary) should prepare consolidated accounts including all its subsidiary undertakings (Appendix 1: Glossary) except where:

(a) the gross income of the group in the accounting period is no more than the audit threshold (Appendix 5) under the Charities Act 1993 which can be revised by Ministerial Order;

(b) the subsidiary undertakings or undertakings results are not material to the group;

(c)   the accounts have to be aggregated under charity legislation in England and Wales.

301. FRS 2 allows subsidiaries to be excluded from consolidation in certain limited circumstances. It is unlikely that these exclusions will apply to a charitable group except on rare occasions. The difference between profit and not for profit undertakings is not sufficient of itself to justify non-consolidation. However, where a subsidiary undertaking is a registered company, is insolvent and being wound up then the subsidiary undertaking can be excluded from consolidation.

3A–155   302. Consolidated accounts should be prepared for the reporting charity and its charitable subsidiary undertakings whether or not the subsidiaries are also companies. However, where the subsidiary undertaking is a non-company charity it will normally be accounted for in the consolidated accounts in the same manner as a branch in accordance with paragraphs 51 to 55. Similarly, charities—whether companies or not—which use non-charitable subsidiary undertakings to carry out their charitable purposes should prepare consolidated accounts for the charity and such subsidiary undertakings.

303. Accounts for each member of the group, *i.e.* parent and subsidiary undertakings, should be prepared for approval by the respective boards of trustees and/or directors. The consolidated group accounts should then be prepared by the parent charity.

304. Consolidated accounts must be prepared under accounting standards in order to give a true and fair view of the group. However, in England and Wales, the Charities Act 1993 require the individual charity's accounts to be filed with the Charity Commission. To meet these requirements, where the group and parent charity's accounts are included in the same set of consolidated accounts, as well as two balance sheet there should be two Statements of Financial Activities (one for the group and one for the parent). However consolidated accounts are often filed with the Commission omitting the Statement of Financial Activities for the parent charity. The Commission is prepared to accept these accounts as long as the assets and liabilities of the charity can be distinguished from those of its subsidiary/ies and that the turnover and results of the subsidiary/ies are clearly stated. However, the Commission retains the power to require the production and filing of any individual charity Statement of Financial Activities and similarly members of the public have a legal right to request this statement.

Subsidiary Undertakings

3A–156   305. Subsidiary undertakings can be identified by the measure of control (Appendix 1: Glossary) exercised by the parent charity. FRS 2 outlines how such control can be determined in the context of voting rights (mainly stemming from share ownership) and dominant influence over the board or activities of the subsidiary. This embodies the requirements of the Companies Act 1985 which should be followed by those undertakings registered under this Act.

306. A non-company charity can only be regarded as a subsidiary undertaking where the parent charity can be shown to be exercising dominant influence over the subsidiary. This can arise in any of the following situations:

(a)   the charity trustees and/or members and or employees of the parent charity are, or have the right to appoint or remove, a majority of the charity trustees of the subsidiary charity;

(b)   the governing document of the subsidiary charity reserves to the parent charity's trustees and/or members the right to direct, or to give consent to, the exercise of significant discretions by the trustees of the subsidiary charity;

(c)   the objects of the subsidiary charity are substantially or exclusively confined to the benefit of the parent charity.

307. The basis for treating a non-company charity as a subsidiary is that the connection between it and some other charity is such that the operating and financial policies of the former are likely to be set in accordance with the wishes of the latter. This is likely to be the case where one of the relationships described in the previous paragraph exists, but trustees may, in a particular case, be able to produce evidence to the contrary.

308. A further instance where the relationship is similar to that of a parent and subsidiary undertaking may arise where the parent charity transacts with another undertaking in such a way that all the risks and rewards of the transactions remain with the parent undertaking. For instance transfers of assets to another entity whilst retaining exclusive use of those assets and the costs of maintaining them. Such undertakings are regarded as quasi subsidiaries and should be accounted for in accordance with Financial Reporting Standard 5 (FRS 5).

3A–157

Method of Consolidation

309. The normal rules will apply regarding the method of consolidation, which should be carried out on a line by line basis as set out in FRS 2.

3A–158

310. All items of incoming resources and resources expended should be shown gross after the removal of intra-group transactions. Clearly it is desirable that similar items are treated in the same way. For instance operating activities for generating funds in the charity should be combined with similar activities in the subsidiary, and charitable activities within the charity should be combined with charitable activities in the subsidiary. Similarly costs of generating funds and or administration costs in the subsidiary should be aggregated with those of the charity.

311. Each charity should choose appropriate line headings within the permissible format of the Statement of Financial Activities and suitable amalgamations of activities. The headings should be expanded and changed to reflect the underlying activities of the group. In practice it may not be possible to find exactly matching items between the subsidiary undertaking and the parent charity in which case segmental information should be provided so that the results of the parent charity and each subsidiary undertaking are transparent (see paragraph 318).

Disclosure

312. There should be a separate comment in the Trustees' Annual Report concerning the performance of the charity's subsidiary undertakings (see paragraph 31(d).

3A–159

313. Where consolidated accounts are prepared the method of consolidation should be stated in the policy notes and which subsidiaries or associated companies are included and excluded from the consolidation.

314. In general the notes to the consolidated accounts should give the position of the group as well as the parent undertaking.

315. The notes to the accounts should state the aggregate amount of the total investment of the charity in its subsidiary undertakings and, unless the subsidiary is not material, in relation to each one:

3A–160

- (a) its name;
- (b) particulars of the charity's shareholding or other means of control;
- (c) how its activities relate to those of the charity;
- (d) the aggregate amount of its assets, liabilities and funds;
- (e) a summary of its turnover and expenditure and its profit or loss for the year (or equivalent categories for charitable subsidiary undertakings).

Similar details should be provided relating to any minority interest external to the charity held in the subsidiary undertakings including any restrictions that may be placed on the groups' activities.

316. If a charity has a large number of subsidiary undertakings such that the disclosure in paragraph 315 would result in information of excessive length being given, the information need only be given in respect of those undertakings whose results or financial position materially affected the figures shown in the charity's annual accounts. The full disclosure must be made available (in the same way as the accounts) to any member of the public upon request.

317. In addition, if subsidiary undertakings are excluded or consolidated accounts are not prepared then following paragraphs 300 to 301, the trustees should explain the reasons in a note to the charity's accounts with reference to each excluded subsidiary undertaking.

3A–161

318. As stated in paragraph 311 segmental information may need to be provided where the aggregation and adjustments required to consolidate financial information may obscure information about the different undertakings and the activities included in the consolidated accounts. It is important that the presentation adopted and disclosure in the notes is sufficiently detailed to distinguish the key results of the charity from those of its subsidiary undertakings. Examples of those items that should be separately disclosed include the costs of generating funds, management and administration and the costs of charitable activities.

319. In consolidated accounts, funds or reserves retained by subsidiary undertakings other than funds used in carrying out the charity's objects should be included under an appropriate separate fund heading in the balance sheet (*e.g.* "non-charitable trading funds").

ASSOCIATES, JOINT VENTURES AND JOINT ARRANGEMENTS

Introduction

3A–162

320. This section explains the additional accounting requirements in consolidated accounts where a charity has associates, joint ventures or joint arrangements.

Identification

3A–163

321. Financial reporting Standard 9 (FRS 9) covers the accounting for associates, joint ventures and joint arrangements and provides detailed guidance on how to determine the relationship between the entities involved. Where these exist consolidated accounts should be prepared subject to the exemptions in paragraph 300.

322. Where a charity has a long term participating interest in another undertaking and exercises significant influence over its operating and financial policy then this is likely to be an associate undertaking. Where a charity beneficially holds 20% or more of the voting rights in any undertaking, it will be presumed to have a participating interest and significant influence over its operating and financial policy, unless the contrary is shown.

323. In a joint venture situation, a separate entity is jointly controlled by two or more undertakings, all of which have a say in the operations of the joint venture, so that no one investing undertaking controls the joint venture but all together can do so. It is possible for a charity to beneficially hold 20% or more of the voting rights in an undertaking but for the management arrangements to be such that control is clearly shared with the other partners and hence the undertaking is a joint venture as opposed to an associate.

3A–164

324. Often charities also undertake joint arrangements where they may carry out activities in partnership with other bodies but without establishing a separate legal entity.

Methods of Accounting for Associates, Joint Ventures and Joint Arrangements

325. Associates should be included in the accounts based on the net equity **3A–165** method. The consolidated Statement of Financial Activities should show the net interest in the results for the year in the associates as a separate line after the "net incoming/(resources expended)" line. In the balance sheet the net interest in associates should be shown as a separate line within fixed asset investments.

326. Joint ventures should be accounted for on a gross equity method. This requires the reporting entity to present its share of the gross incoming resources of joint ventures on the face of the consolidated profit and loss account. However, this does not form part of the group incoming resources and must be clearly distinguished. For charities this can be achieved by including gross incoming resources from joint ventures in the Statement of Financial Activities on a line by line basis with an additional line showing the total share of gross incoming resources from joint ventures as a reduction in total incoming resources. In addition a line showing the net interest in the results for the year in the joint ventures as a separate line after the "net incoming/(resources expended)" line must be included (this may be combined with that of the associates). In the balance sheet the share of the gross assets and the gross liabilities should be shown in a linked presentation within fixed assets investments.

327. Where there are gains and loses on investments and unrealised gains on other fixed assets, the net share relating to associates should be shown on a separate line, with the gross share relating to joint ventures being shown either on a separate line or combined with the appropriate lines on the statement of financial activities.

328. Where there is a joint arrangement the charity's gross share of the incom- **3A–166** ing resources and resources expended and the assets and liabilities should be included in the accounts in the same way as for a branch per paragraphs 51 to 55. If under the arrangement the charity is jointly and severally liable for an obligation, it should accrue the part of the obligation for which it is responsible and treat the part of the obligation which is expected to be met by the other parties as a contingent liability.

Disclosure

329. The following disclosure should be given in respect of each associate and **3A–167** joint venture and this will normally be compliant with FRS 9:

(a) its name;
(b) the charity's shareholding and other interests in it;
(c) the nature of the activities of the associate or join venture;
(d) the charity's interest in the results showing separately its share in:
    (i) gross incoming resources by type;
    (ii) costs of generating funds;
    (iii) expenditure on charitable activities;
    (iv) expenditure on management and administration;
    (v) the net results (where tax is payable the share of the results pre and post tax and the share in the tax should be shown);
    (vi) gains or losses on investments and the share in unrealised gains on other fixed assets;
    (vii) fixed assets;
    (viii) current assets;
    (ix) liabilities under one year;
    (x) liabilities over one year;
    (xi) the different funds of the charity;
    (xii) contingent liabilities and other commitments;

(xiii) particulars of any qualifications contained in any audit or other statutory report on its accounts, and any note or reservation in those accounts to call attention to a matter which, apart from the note or reservation, would properly have been referred to in such a qualification.

330. For joint arrangements the notes to the accounts should provide appropriate details of the charity's commitments in the arrangement.

THE SORP IN RELATION TO CHARITABLE COMPANIES IN THE UK

Introduction

3A–168   331. This section explains the position of this SORP with respect to charitable companies. In following this SORP charitable companies will normally meet most of the reporting requirements under the Companies Act. However the SORP does not reproduce these requirements in full and a charity must have regard to its own circumstances when considering the application of the Companies Act. In addition to following the main section of this SORP and the other special sections as applicable, there are certain further requirements which must be met by charitable companies. Ways of meeting the most common of these requirements are suggested below. But these too must be considered in the light of the company's individual circumstances.

Accounts and Reports

3A–169   332. Charitable companies must comply with the Companies Act 1985 with respect to the form and content of their accounts. This Act also stipulates the contents of the annual (directors') report. Strictly, the directors of charitable companies, in England and Wales, have to prepare both that report, and the annual (trustees) report under Part VI of the Charities Act 1993, but the Charity Commission is prepared to accept the directors' report for filing under Part VI if it also contains the information required under Part VI. Charitable companies (unlike non company charities) do not have an exemption to leave out the names of the directors from the annual report.

333. The Companies Act 1985 requires a company to prepare annual financial statements which give a true and fair view of its state of affairs at the end of the year and of its profit and loss for that year. In addition, Paragraph 3. (3) of Part 1, section A of Schedule 4 to this Act requires the directors to adapt the headings and subheadings of the balance sheet and profit and loss account in any case where the special nature of the company's business requires such adaptation.

334. The requirement to show a true and fair view and to adapt the accounts for the special nature of charity means that there is a strong presumption that charitable companies will in all but exceptional circumstances have to comply with this SORP in order to meet the requirements of company law. Particulars of any material departures from this SORP are required to be disclosed in accordance with paragraph 280. **A departure is not justified simply because it gives the reader a more appealing picture of the financial position or results of the charity.**

The statement of Financial Activities and the Summary Income and Expenditure Account

3A–170   335. All charitable companies registered under the Companies Act 1985 must include an income and expenditure account in their financial statements. The Statement of Financial Activities is designed to include all the gains and losses of a charity which would be found in the income and expenditure account and the statement of total recognised gains and losses as required by FRS 3. A separate income and expenditure account is therefore not necessarily required. Circumstances where it will probably be required may arise where the income and expenditure account cannot be separately identified within the Statement of Financial Activities and there are items which may be open to challenge if they are included in an Income and Expenditure Account, such as:

(a) movement on endowment (capital) funds during the year; and
(b) unrealised gains and losses arising during the year.

Whilst unrealised gains and losses are not allowed in the income and expenditure account most of these are included in the Statement of Financial Activities below the point at which a conventional income and expenditure account would end as explained in paragraph 336.

336. Where the Statement of Financial Activities of a charitable company does not include any of the items in paragraph 335 it may not need to produce a separate summary income and expenditure account but the headings in the Statement of Financial Activities must be changed so that:

(a) the title clearly indicates that it includes an income and expenditure account and statement of total recognised gains and loses (if required); and
(b) there is a prominent sub total entitled "net income/(expenditure) for the year" which replaces or is in addition to the heading of "net incoming/(outgoing) resources for the year".

Care must also be taken to ensure that all realised gains and losses are included in the Statement of Financial Activities in such a way that they fall within the bounds of the headings for (a) and (b) within the income and expenditure account. Particular attention may need to be given to impairment losses and reversals which, in accordance with the guidance in FRS 11 are realised in some circumstances and unrealised in others.

337. Where a summary income and expenditure account is required, it should be derived from and cross-referenced to the corresponding figures in the Statement of Financial Activities. It need not distinguish between unrestricted and restricted income funds but the accounting basis on which items are included must be the same as in the Statement of Financial Activities. It should show separately in respect of continuing operations, acquisitions and discontinued operations:

(a) gross income from all sources;
(b) net gains/losses from disposals of all fixed assets belonging to the charity's income funds;
(c) transfers from endowment funds of amounts previously received as capital resources and now converted into income funds for expending;
(d) total income (this will be the total of all incoming resources—other than revaluation gains—of all the income funds but not for any endowment funds);
(e) total expenditure out of the charity's income funds;
(f) net income or expenditure for the year.

In practice, the format may need to be modified to comply with specific statutory requirements or those of the charity's own governing document.

338. Where consolidated accounts are prepared a summary income and expenditure account should be included for the group (when it is required).

3A–171

The Balance Sheet Format

3A–172   339. If a columnar format is chosen (see paragraph 185) then charitable companies will still have to show the funds of the charity as a single line or split between
the various different types of fund in order to comply with the Companies Act
requirements.

Revaluation Reserve

3A–173   340. Where fixed assets are revalued upwards a revaluation reserve will arise
being the difference between the original depreciated cost or valuation of the asset
and the revalued amount. Separate reporting of the reserve is not significant for
charities as they do not distribute profits, but a revaluation reserve will, nevertheless, arise. This will form part of the funds in which the revalued assets are held. In
certain circumstances (as described in FRSs 11 and 15) impairment losses or other
downward revaluations can be offset against the revaluation reserve.

341. To comply with the Companies Act 1985 charitable companies must separately disclose the revaluation reserve within the funds section on the face of the
balance sheet but may change the heading as appropriate. This may be best
effected by use of a prominent inset.

Summary Financial Information

3A–174   342. Charitable companies should follow the recommendations in paragraphs
292 to 297 but their summary financial information must also include a statement
indicating whether or not the statutory accounts for the relevant year(s) have been
delivered to the Registrar of Companies.

343. Any summary financial information prepared by a charitable company will
almost all be non-statutory (the statutory option for the publication of summary
financial statements only applies to listed companies) and the auditor's report cannot be published with them without the statutory accounts to which it relates. This
mans in effect that companies can produce summarised accounts without the
backing of an audit report.

ACCOUNTING FOR SMALLER CHARITIES

Introduction

3A–175   344. In the context of this SORP a smaller charity is one which due to its size
does not have to adopt all the requirements of this SORP. However this encom-
passes charities of various sizes. This section explains the alternatives available to
small charities starting with the larger ones.

The Application of the Financial Reporting Standard for Smaller Entities (FRSSE)

3A–176   345. Any charity (whether or not it is a company) which is under the thresholds
for small companies as described in the Companies Act (Appendix 5) can follow
the Financial Reporting Standard for smaller Entities (FRSSE) in preparing its
financial accounts except where it conflicts with this SORP in which case this
SORP should be followed. Where consolidated accounts or receipts and payments
accounts are produced smaller entities cannot follow the FRSSE in preparation of
their accounts.

346. In following the FRSSE the accounts will meet most of the requirements of
the SORP for such entities. They will, however, have to include a Statement of
Financial Activities in place of a profit and loss account and statement of total

recognised gains and losses, and adopt the principles of fund accounting through-out the accounts. This will include appropriate descriptions of the funds and notes showing the composition of the funds and the differentiation of funds on the balance sheet. Charities which follow another SORP or have to prepare additional accounts in a format required by other bodies, such as HM Treasury, may find that they cannot follow the FRSSE for these purposes.

347. In addition the following specific points must be followed:

(a) All investments including investment properties must be shown at market value.
(b) Those foreign exchange gains and losses which may be allowed to be taken to reserves (as prescribed in the FRSSE) must be shown in the bottom of the Statement of Financial Activities.
(c) Those exceptional items which are required to be shown after operating profit must be shown in an appropriate place on the Statement of Financial Activities.

Charities with Gross Income not Exceeding £250,000 (England and Wales)

348. Charities with gross income not exceeding £250,000 preparing accounts on the accruals basis do not have to use the expenditure headings and sub-headings in paragraph 60. They may choose expenditure classifications to suit their circumstances (*e.g.* salaries and wages, office costs, repairs and maintenance, etc.). **3A–177**

Departures from the SORP

349. Non-company charities in England and Wales which prepare accounts on the accruals basis are required to make disclosures of particulars of any material departure from the recommendations in this SORP in accordance with paragraph 280. **A departure is not justified simply because it gives the reader a more appealing picture of the financial position or results of the charity.** **3A–178**

Receipts and Payments Accounts

350. There are many relatively small charities with very simple structures and no control of other organisations. The vast majority of them will have cash and deposit accounts but few other assets. Apart from charitable companies (which must always prepare accruals accounts) these charities will often find that receipts and payments accounts meet both their needs and those of others who read their accounts. This form of accounts contains a summary of money received and money spent during the year and a list of assets. **3A–179**

351. Part VI of the Charities Act 1993, which regulates the form and content of the accounts of most charities in England and Wales recognises this and allows charities with gross income below a threshold set by Ministerial Order to choose between accruals accounts and receipts and payments accounts. There are similar alternatives for Scottish Charities (under regulations made under the Law Reform (Miscellaneous Provisions) (Scotland) Act 1990. Details of the current thresholds are given in Appendix 5 but can be subject to alteration. Small charitable companies must always prepare accruals accounts and are not covered by these concessions.

352. Before deciding which form of accounts to prepare trustees should make sure they are not required to prepare accruals accounts (for example by virtue of size, the charity's governing document, a regulatory framework or donor imposed conditions).

353. Receipts and payments accounts have the following general features: **3A–180**

(a) The accounting statements showing what happened during the financial year summarise only cash movements (compared with resource movements in accruals accounts).

(b) A statement listing assets and liabilities is required (in place of a balance sheet required by accruals accounts).

(c) No asset valuations are required, unless an evaluation is essential to a meaningful description of the asset (they may be provided if trustees' wish).

(d) Notes to the accounts are not often necessary, although it is recommended that these are prepared where doing so would increase the user's understanding of the accounts. The regulations made under the Law Reform (Miscellaneous Provisions) (Scotland) Act 1990 requires notes on certain matters to be provided where applicable. It is recommended that notes on related party transactions, trustee remuneration in accordance with paragraph 166, should always be given, as well as information on significant non monetary resources.

(e) They do not claim to show a true and fair view of the charity's financial activities and state of affairs. Accounting standards, which are primarily concerned with the presentation of a true and fair view, will therefore not generally apply to such accounts.

(f) The only accounting convention always applicable to receipts and payments accounts is comparability through consistency, that is they are prepared in a consistent way from year to year. Where valuations are provided the estimates should also be relevant, reliable and understandable and normally the going concern concept will also apply.

354. Receipts and payments accounts and statements of assets and liabilities may be organised in any way that the trustees feel appropriate. There is also flexibility in extending the titles as long as they include "Receipts and Payments" and "Statement of Assets and Liabilities" (Statement of Balances in Scotland) However there are some general principles that trustees should be aware of:

(a) In this context "cash" includes near cash (bank and building society current and deposit accounts) where the amount deposited (the "capital" sum) is not at risk and is not subject to withdrawal term conditions.

(b) Bank balances must be reconciled for unpaid cheques and deposits before the receipts and payments accounts are drawn up. Cheques paid out but not cleared through the bank must not be counted as creditors. Cash received but not yet banked is still cash in the hands of the charity and must accounted for.

(c) Trust law requires that trustees should be able to account separately for each trust fund they manage. It will therefore be important for trustees to account separately for cash belonging to unrestricted funds, restricted funds and endowment funds. This may be achieved by using a columnar receipts and payments account (similar to the Statement of Financial Activities) or by having three (or more) separate accounts. As with accruals accounts it is acceptable to add together all restricted funds in one statement and all endowment funds in another, though the bookkeeping records must enable accounts to be drawn up for each separate trust fund.

(d) Receipts and Payments accounts will normally summarise the cash movements in that all payments for similar purposes (*e.g.* wages) and receipts for similar purposes (*e.g.* donations) should be grouped together and not shown separately. Two forms of grouping of expenditure are normally used: by nature (wages, rent, electricity, etc.) or by function (charitable expenditure, fund raising costs, etc.).

(e) When summarising, any form of grouping of receipts and payments is acceptable.

(f) The statement of assets and liabilities should be adequate to show the readers of the accounts what assets are controlled by the trustees. There is no need to list all individual assets but the list should be comprehensive in covering all classes of asset held by the charity trustees. No valuation of assets held is required, unless an evaluation is essential to a meaningful description of the asset, for example in the case of cash and other monetary assets, the cash value would be given. Trustees may add values if they wish and the valuation rules given earlier in relation to accruals accounts should be followed in this case.

355. Where receipts and payments accounts are subjected to external examination this will normally be done by an independent examiner. However the Charities Auditing Practice Note 11 (APN 11) does allow for the audit of receipts and payments accounts by a registered auditor (though a "true and fair" opinion cannot be given) and so an audit provision does not demand the production of accruals accounts. Occasionally, there is a requirement (*e.g.* by the governing document or by a donor) for both an audit by a registered auditor and for accruals accounts to be prepared.

356. The recommendations given above are minimum ones and charities should feel free to include more information if they think this will help readers understand the accounts.　　　　　　　　**3A–181**

Change in Accounting Basis

357. For each year in which the charity changes from accruals accounts to receipts and payments accounting or vice versa, the corresponding amounts for the previous financial year should be restated on the basis of the new accounting policy.　　　　　　　　**3A–182**

Charity Commission Publications

358. The Charity Commission has issued various publications which may be of help. They are all designed for non company charities below the audit threshold with no branches or investment assets and include proforma receipts and payments and accruals accounts. These publications are available from any of the Commission's offices but may be changed or replaced from time to time.　　**3A–183/4**

APPENDICES

APPENDIX 1

GLOSSARY

1. Branches

3A–185   "Branches" (which may also be known as supporters' groups, friends' groups, members' groups, communities or parishes which are part of a common trust etc) are entities or administrative bodies set up, for example, to conduct a particular aspect of the business of the reporting charity, or to conduct the business of the reporting charity in a particular geographical area. They may or may not be legal entities which are separate from the reporting charity. For the purpose of this SORP a "branch" is either:

(a)   simply part of the administrative machinery of the reporting charity; or

(b)   a separate legal entity which is administered by or on behalf of the reporting charity and whose funds are held for specific purposes which are within the general purposes of the reporting charity. "Legal entity" means a trust or unincorporated association or other body formed for a charitable purpose. The words "on behalf of" should be taken to mean that, under the constitution of the separate entity, a substantial degree of influence can be exerted by the reporting charity over the administration of its affairs; or,

(c)   in England and Wales, a separate legal entity not falling within (b) which the Charity Commission has united by a direction under section 96(5) or 96(6), Charities Act 1993 should be treated as linked to the reporting charity for accounting purposes.

This definition has been adopted to reflect the provisions of the Charities Act 1993 allocating responsibility for accounting in the case of multicellular charities.

Financial Reporting Standard 2 expressly disapplies its requirements where they are not consistent with a particular statutory accounting framework. Consequently, charitable bodies which are controlled by other charitable bodies will not normally be subject to the requirements of that standard as they will be treated as "special trusts" under the Charities Act 1993 or will be the subject of a direction as mentioned above in sub-paragraph (c)—see the definition of "subsidiary undertaking" below.

3A–186   Some of the characteristics of a branch are:

(i)   it uses the name of the reporting charity within its title;

(ii)   it exclusively raises funds for the reporting charity and/or for its own local activities;

(iii) it uses the reporting charity's registration number to receive tax relief on its activities;

(iv)   it is perceived by the public to be the reporting charity's local representative or its representative for a particular purpose;

(v)   it receives support from the reporting charity through advice, publicity materials, etc.

If the branch exists to carry out the primary objects of the charity, typically it will receive funds from the reporting charity for its work and may be staffed by employees of the reporting charity.

If the branch is not a separate legal entity, all funds held by a branch will be the legal property of the reporting charity, whether or not the branch has a separate bank account.

Organisations which are not branches

Some charities may be known as "branches" within a particular organisational or network structure, but if their level of administrative autonomy from the reporting charity—as determined by their constitutions—is such that legislation requires them to be treated as separate accounting entities, then they should not be regarded as "branches" for accounting purposes but should prepare separate accounts for submission to the appropriate regulatory authority.

3A–187

Other examples of organisations which are not "branches" for the purpose of these recommendations include groups of people who occasionally gather together to raise funds for one or a number of different charities and special interest groups who are affiliated to a particular charity, but do not themselves undertake charitable activities (including fundraising for the charity).

2. Capital

In the context of charity law "capital" means resources which become available to a charity and which the trustees are legally required to invest or retain and use for its purposes. "Capital" may be permanent endowment, where the trustees have no power to convert it into income and apply it as such, or expendable endowment, where they do have this power (see Appendix 3).

3A–188

Capital is also used in its various accounting meanings, such as the capital elements of fixed assets, working capital or share capital.

3. Charity

A "charity" is any institution established for purposes which are exclusively charitable. Where the institution is involved in more than one activity, operates more than one fund, or is not centralised into one unit of operation, the term is used in this statement to include all those activities, units and funds which fall within the scope of a either single governing instrument (or instruments supplemental to the main instrument) or for which the trustees are otherwise legally liable to account (*e.g.* branches, as defined in paragraph 1(b) above).

3A–189

4. Charity Trustees

"Charity trustees" has the same meaning as in s.97(1) of the Charities Act 1993, that is the persons having the general control and management of the administration of a charity regardless of what they are called. Custodian trustees are not within this definition.

3A–190

For instance, in the case of an unincorporated association the executive or management committee are its charity trustees, and in the case of a charitable company it is the directors who are the charity trustees.

Those concerned in any way with the administration of charities should note that the status of a charity trustee is defined in terms of the function to be performed, and not by reference to the title given to any office, or membership of any committee or committees.

5. "Connected Charities"

3A–191   "Connected charities" are those which have common, parallel or related objects and activities; and either:

(a) common control; or
(b) unity of administration.

Within this category may be charities which come together under one umbrella organisation.
Also see related parties.

6. Constructive Obligation

3A–192   An obligation that derives from an entity's actions where:

(a) by an established pattern of past practice, published policies or a sufficiently specific current statement, the entity has indicated to other parties that it will accept certain responsibilities; and
(b) as a result, the entity has created a valid expectation on the part of those other parties that it will discharge those responsibilities.

7. Contingent Asset

3A–193   A possible asset that arises from past events and whose existence will be confirmed only by the occurrence of one or more uncertain future events not wholly within the entitys' control.

8. Contingent Liability

3A–194   (a) A possible obligation that arises from past events and whose existence will be confirmed only by the occurrence of one or more uncertain future events not wholly within the entity's control; or
(b) a present obligation that arises from past events but is not recognised in the primary statements because:
(i) it is not probable that a transfer of economic benefits will be required to settle the obligation; or
(ii) the amount of the obligation cannot be measured with sufficient reliabilty.

9. Custodian Trustee

3A–195   "Custodian Trustee" includes for present purposes any other non-executive trustee in whose name property belonging to the charity is held.

10. Functional Classification

3A–196   A "functional classification" of costs is the aggregation of costs incurred in pursuit of a defined purpose (*e.g.* provision of services to elderly people or counselling), and is achieved by adding together all the costs (salaries, rents, depreciation etc) relating to that specific activity.
"Functional fixed assets" are those assets which are used for charitable purposes (*i.e.* within the functional activities).

11. Fundraising Costs

Fundraising costs comprise the costs actually incurred by a charity, or by an agent, in inducing others to make voluntary contributions to it. Such costs will include the costs of producing fundraising advertising, marketing and direct mail materials, as well as any remuneration payable to an agent. It will normally include publicity costs but not those used in an educational manner in furtherance of the charity's objects (see paragraphs 132–133).

3A–197

12. Funds

A "fund" is a pool of unexpended resources, held and maintained separately from other pools because of the circumstances in which the resources were originally received or the way in which they have subsequently been treated. At the broadest level a fund will be one of two kinds: a restricted fund or an unrestricted fund. (See also Appendix 3 for the legal position as regards the various funds of a charity).

3A–198

13. Grants

A grant is any voluntary payment (or other transfer of property) in favour of a person or institution, in furtherance of the objects of the grant-maker. The payment or transfer may be for the general purposes of the recipient, or for some specific purpose such as the supply of a particular service. It may be unconditional, or be subject to conditions which, if not satisfied by the recipient, may lead to the grant, or property acquired with the aid of the grant, or part of it, being reclaimed.

3A–199

14. Grants/Contract Income

A payment made to a charity for the purpose of providing goods or services may be by way of grant or contract. The main distinction is that grant payments are voluntary whereas contracts are normally legally binding between the payer and the charity. The payment is not then voluntary and is not a grant. The distinction is important because:

3A–200

(a)   a contractual payment will normally be unrestricted income of the charity, but a grant for the supply of specific services will normally be restricted income;

(b)   the nature of the payment may be relevant to its VAT treatment.

It is not always easy in practice to decide whether a particular arrangement is or is not intended by the parties to be a legally binding contract for the supply of services. If, under the arrangement, the payer, rather than the charity, has taken the lead in identifying the services to be provided, or if the arrangement provides for damages to be paid in the case of a breach of its terms, rather than, say, for total or partial refund of the payment, it is more probable that there is a contract for the supply of services. If there is no such contract, the rights and obligations of the parties will depend primarily on the law of trusts and conditional gifts, rather than on the law of contract.

15. Historic Asset

An asset of acknowledged historic, scientific (including environmental) or artistic importance, whether of former or present times, the continuing retention and use of which is in direct furtherance of the charity's objects as the primary reason for retaining it. Such assets are normally expected to be held for their lifetime and

3A–201

disposal should be a rare exception, while in the case of a "collection" (museums, galleries, etc) the proceeds of any individual items sold will normally be used only for their replacement in order to maintain the collection or in accordance with the terms of trust.

16. Inalienable Asset

3A–202 An asset which a charity is required by law to retain indefinitely for its own use/benefit and therefore cannot dispose of without external consent, whether prohibited by its governing document, the donor's wishes or in some other way. Normally the asset will belong to the charity's "permanent endowment" where it is held on trusts which contemplate its retention and continuing use but not its disposal. However, in the case of a gift-in-kind of a "wasting asset", such as a building, a long lease or a non-durable artefact, the terms of trust may not have provided for its maintenance in perpetuity or its replacement. In that case the endowment will be expended to the extent of the aggregate amount of its depreciation or amortisation properly provided for in the annual accounts (*i.e.* based on its currently anticipated useful life).

17. Incoming Resources and Gross Income

3A–203 Incoming resources means all resources which become available to a charity including contributions to endowment (capital) funds but excludes gains and losses on investment assets. Gross incoming resources includes all trading and investment income, legacies, donations, grants and gains from disposals of fixed assets for use by the charity.

This is to be distinguished from gross income which must be calculated in determining the thresholds made by regulation under the Charities Act 1993 for the requirement for an Independent Examination, the preparation of accruals accounts and to have an audit. Gross income does not include the gains from disposals of fixed assets and investments, and asset revaluation gains nor any resources being received into the endowment funds. It will however include funds released from endowments.

18. Investment Property

3A–204 "Investment Property" is an interest in land and/or buildings which is held primarily for the purpose of producing an income for the charity, any rental income being negotiated at arm's length. It does not include:

(a) land acquired primarily with a view to resale at a profit, whether or not after development; or

(b) property which is owned and mainly occupied by the charity for carrying out its purposes.

19. Liability

3A–205 A liability is an obligation of an entity to transfer economic benefits which:

(a) is expected to be settled by the entity parting with assets or in some way losing an economic benefit; and

(b) results from past transactions or events;

(c) embodies a present duty or responsibility to one or more other entities that entails settlement at a specified or determinable future date, on the occurrence of a specified event, or on demand; and

(d) results from a duty or responsibility which obligates the entity either legally, or practically (a constructive obligation), because it would be financially or otherwise operationally damaging to the entity not to discharge the duty or responsibility.

A moral obligation—such as results from the making of a non-contractual promise —does not create a liability unless it meets the definition above.

20. Market Value

"Market Value" is the price at which an asset could be, or could be expected to be, sold or acquired in a public market between a willing buyer and willing seller. For traded securities in which there is an established market, the market value basis that is to be used in the valuation for the balance sheet is defined as the midpoint of the quotation in the Stock Exchange Daily Official List or at a similar recognised market value. For other assets it is the trustees' or valuers' best estimate of such a value.   **3A–206**

21. Material

Materiality is the final test of what information should be given in a particular set of financial statements. An item of information is material to the financial statements if its misstatement or omission might reasonably be expected to influence the economic decisions of users of those financial statements, including their assessments of stewardship. Immaterial information will need to be excluded to avoid clutter which impairs the understandability of other information provided.   **3A–207**

Whether information is material will depend on the size and nature of the item in question judged in the particular circumstances of the case. Materiality is not capable of general mathematical definiton as it has both qualitative and quantitative aspects. The principal factors to be taken into account are set out below. It will usually be a combination of these factors, rather than any one in particular, that will determine materiality.

(a) The item's size is judged in the context both of financial statements as a whole and of the other information available to users that would affect their evaluation of the financial statements. This includes, for example, considering how the item affects the evaluation of trends and similar considerations.

(b) Consideration is given to the item's nature in relation to:
(i) the transactions or other events giving rise to it;
(ii) the legality, sensitivity, normality and potential consequences of the event or transaction;
(iii) the identity of the parties involved; and
(iv) the particular headings and disclosures that are affected.

If there are two or more similar items, the materiality of the items in aggregate as well as of the items individually needs to be considered.

Trustees are responsible for deciding whether an item is or is not material. In cases of doubt an item should be treated as material.   **3A–208**

22. Parent Undertaking and Subsidiary Undertaking

In relation to a charity an undertaking is the parent undertaking of another undertaking, a subsidiary undertaking, where the charity or its trustees hold or control the majority of the voting rights, or have the right to appoint or remove a majority of the board of directors or trustees of the subsidiary undertaking, or   **3A–209** have the right to exercise a dominant influence over the subsidiary undertaking. For a fuller definition, reference should be made to sections 258 and 259 Companies Act 1985.

Paragraphs 299 to 319 explain how to account for subsidiary undertakings within the consolidated accounts of a parent undertaking. This includes the exemptions from consolidation and the particular circumstances in which a charity can be considered to be a subsidiary undertaking of another charity.

23. Pension Schemes

3A–210   Money Purchase Scheme and Defined Benefit Scheme.

A "money purchase scheme" in relation to an employee, means a pension scheme under which all of the benefits that may become payable to or in respect of the employee are money purchase benefits. Such benefits are payable under a pension scheme the rate or amount of which is calculated by reference to payments made, or treated as made, by the employee or by any other person in respect of the employee and which are not average salary benefits.

A "defined benefit scheme" means a pension scheme which is not a money purchase scheme. This includes not only final salary schemes but any scheme which is not classified as a money purchase scheme.

24. Pooling Scheme Common Investment Funds (CIFs)

3A–211   A Pooling Scheme CIF fund is an arrangement for the pooling of investments belonging to two or more charities (which may be special trusts) which are administered by the same trustee body as the body managing the fund. Such schemes are referred to as Pool Charities and must be legally established by the Charity Commission or the Courts.

25. Provision

3A–212   A provision (as defined in FRS 12) is a liability of uncertain timing or amount. It is recognised when a charity has a present obligation (a legal or constructive obligation exists at the balance sheet date) as a result of a past event, it is probable that a transfer of economic benefits will be required to settle the obligation and the amount can be reliably estimated.

26. Related Parties

3A–213   Related parties include all of the following:

"Institution Connected with a Charity"

3A–214   An institution is connected with a charity if it is controlled by (in Scotland managed or controlled by), or if a participating interest in it is beneficially owned by, the charity.

"Related to the Charity"

3A–215   The following should be treated as related to the charity:

    (a)   any charity trustee and custodian trustee of the charity;
    (b)   any person or body with the power to appoint or remove a significant proportion of the charity trustees of the charity, or whose consent is

required to the exercise of any of the discretions of those trustees, or who is entitled to give directions to those trustees as to the exercise of any of those discretions. All or a majority of the trustees should always be treated as a "significant proportion". Fewer than 50% of the trustees may be a "significant proportion" if they collectively have a dominant influence on the operation of the charity, as, for example, is likely to be the case if one body has the power to appoint/remove 7 of a body of 15 trustees, and 8 other different bodies had the right to appoint/remove 1 each;

(c)   any institution connected with the charity, and any director of such an institution;

(d)   any other charity with which it is commonly controlled;

(e)   any pension fund for the benefit of the employees of the charity, and/or of any other person who is a related party of the charity;

(f)   any officer, agent or employee of the charity having authority or responsibility for directing or controlling the major activities or resources of the charity; and

(g)   any person connected to a person who is related to the charity.

"Connected with a charity trustee or to a person related to the charity"

The following should be treated as "connected with a charity trustee" or "connected to a person who is related to the charity":   **3A–216**

(a)   members of the same family or household of the charity trustee or related person who may be expected to influence, or be influenced by, that person in their dealings with the charity;

(b)   the trustees of any trust, not being a charity, the beneficiaries or potential beneficiaries of which include a charity trustee or related person or a person referred to in (a) as being connected with a charity trustee or to a related person, as the case may be;

(c)   any business partner of a charity trustee or related person, or of any person referred to in (a) or (b) as being connected with a charity trustee or to a related person, as the case may be;

(d)   any body corporate, not being a company which is controlled entirely by one or more charitable institutions, in which:

   (i)   the charity trustee has, or the charity trustee and any other charity trustee or trustees or person or persons referred to in (a), (b) or (c) above as being connected with a charity trustee, taken together, have a participating interest; or

   (ii)   the related person has, or the related person and any other related parties of the charity, taken together, have a participating interest.

(e)   Any person or body who makes available to the charity the services of any person or body as a charity trustee is connected with a charity trustee.

Common control exists if:

(i)   the same person, or persons have the right to appoint a majority of the charity trustees of both or all the charities; or

(ii)   the same person, or persons, hold a majority of the voting rights in the administration of both or all of the charities.

Persons who are related with each other through family or business relationships should be treated as the same person for the present purposes.

"Controlled" means that the charity is able to secure that the affairs of the institution are conducted in accordance with its wishes.   **3A–217**

"Participating interest" means that the charity:

(a)   is interested in shares comprised in the equity share capital of the body of a nominal value of more than one fifth of that share capital; or

(b)   is entitled to exercise or control the exercise of more than one-fifth of the voting power at any general meeting of that body.

27. Reserves

3A–218   The term "reserves" has a variety of technical and ordinary meanings, depending on the context in which it is used. In this SORP we use the term "reserves" (unless otherwise indicated) to describe that part of a charity's income funds that is freely available for its general purposes. "Reserves" are therefore the resources the charity has or can make available to spend for any or all of the charity's purposes once it has met its commitments and covered its other planned expenditure.

More specifically this defines reserves as income which becomes available to the charity and is to be spent at the trustees' discretion in furtherance of any of the charity's objects (sometimes referred to as "general purpose" income); but which is not yet spent, committed or designated (*i.e.* is "free").

This definition of reserves therefore excludes:

permanent endowment;
expendable endowment;
restricted funds;
designated funds; and
income funds which could only be realised by disposing of fixed assets held for charity use.

3A–219   There is an argument for saying that expendable endowment and designated income funds ought to be counted as reserves. The argument is that in each case the trustees are free to regard the funds, if they so choose, as available for general purpose expenditure. There are no legal restrictions preventing trustees treating those two types of funds as free, general purpose funds. But there are practical reasons, why the funds should not normally be regarded as free (though there are exceptions). A charity will not be justified in creating, or transferring resources to, a designated fund where the main purpose of doing this is to allow the charity to show a reduced level of reserves.

By contrast, restricted funds can never be regarded as general purpose funds. Restricted income funds do not fall within the scope of reserves as the term is used in this SORP. Nevertheless, the legal principles on the retention of income apply to restricted income funds, as do the principles of justifying and explaining any retention. For the purpose of applying the principles in this SORP it is suggested that trustees treat each restricted income fund as if it were a separate charity. Thus, each material restricted income fund could have its own "reserve", which should be justified and (if practicable) explained in its own right.

For further information see the Charity Commission's publication CC19 on Charities' Reserves.

28. Resources Expended and Expenditure

3A–220   Resources expended means all costs incurred in the course of expending or utilising the charity's funds. This includes all claims against the charity upon being recognised as liabilities by the trustees, as well as all accruals and payments made by the trustees of a charity, and all losses on the disposal of fixed assets (other than investments), together with all provisions for impairment of fixed assets.

This is to be distinguished from total expenditure which does not include losses on the disposal of fixed assets nor amounts paid for the acquisition of fixed assets nor any amounts paid out of endowment funds. Total expenditure is required to be calculated in the determination of whether a charity has crossed the thresholds for independent examination or audit set by regulations made under the Charities Act 1993 or The Charities Accounts (Scotland) Regulations 1992.

29. Support Costs

"Support costs" of charitable activities comprise costs incurred directly in sup- **3A–221** port of expenditure on the objects of the charity, and can therefore be considered as part of total expenditure directly relating to the objects of the charity. Such costs will include all services (either at headquarters or through a regional network) which are identifiable as wholly or mainly in support of the charity's project work or other charitable expenditure (excluding management and administration costs) if—but only if—they are an integral part of the cost of carrying out the direct charitable objectives of the charity.

30. Trading

In a strict legal sense trading activities are those carried out under contract **3A–222** whether at the point of sale or otherwise, where goods and services are provided in return for consideration for those goods or services. The Inland Revenue also has several criteria for determining when an activity can be regarded as trading for tax purposes, referred to as badges of trade. Normally trading activities are carried out on a regular basis with a view to making profits, though it is possible that some one-off activities could be regarded as trading.

However in an economic sense trading can be regarded as the provision of goods and services in return for a payment whether or not this payment is in fact under contract. Therefore restricted incoming grants which are in a legal sense donations, but which have specific terms attached to them such that a charity must spend the grant on the provision of specified goods or services, are in the context of this SORP regarded as trading income. This is because the charity has an obligation to provide the specific services or goods in the same way that it would have to provide them under contract. If it fails to provide the goods or services then if the funds are by way of grant this will be a breach of trust but if they are by way of contract this will be by way of breach of contract. The legal remedies of the funding body are different depending upon the circumstances.

Similarly the sale of donated goods is in a legal sense regarded as the realisation of a donation. However in the context of this SORP it is regarded as trading because it is so similar to the sale of bought in goods as to be indistinguishable in the actual processes involved except for the legal distinction.

31. Trustees

Has the same meaning as charity trustees. **3A–223**

APPENDIX 2

APPLICATION OF ACCOUNTING STANDARDS

3A–224   The following is a summary of the accounting standards and Urgent Issues Task Force abstracts extant at the date of issue of this SORP and their applicability to charities following this SORP. The standards should only be applied in so far as they are relevant to activities being carried out by an individual charity. Where this is the case the summaries below should not be relied upon as a substitute for reading the full text of the standard.

Statements of Standard Accounting Practice (SSAPs)

SSAPs which have been withdrawn

3A–225   SSAPs 1, 3, 6, 7, 8, 10, 11, 12, 14, 16, 18, 22, and 23.

SSAP 2 Disclosure of Accounting Policies
(Last Amended December 1998) (Revised for FRED 21)

3A–226   FRED 21 will replace SSAP 2, UITF 7 and UITF 14 when it is finalised. It promotes the adoption and review of accounting policies most appropriate to the particular circumstances of each entity for the purpose of giving a true and fair view and of sufficient disclosure for users to understand the policies adopted and how they have been applied. The FRED distinguishes between accounting policies which are the principles on which the accounts are prepared and estimation techniques which are the particular methods that an entity may choose to use in order to provide a monetary value for an asset, liability, gain or loss in accordance with the adopted principles in the chosen accounting policies.

The following two notions are emphasised as having a pervasive role in financial statements and hence in the selection of accounting policies:

(a) **The "going concern" assumption**: the enterprise will continue in operational existence for the foreseeable future.
(b) **The "accruals" concept**: the substance of transactions should be reflected in the accounts in the accounting period in which they occur rather than when any money or other form of consideration is received or paid in respect of the transactions.

The appropriateness of accounting policies and estimation techniques to each entity's particular circumstances should be judged against the objectives below balancing these against each other and against the cost of providing information with the likely benefit to the users of the accounts:

(a) **Relevance**: information is provided in a timely manner and has the ability to influence economic decisions of users of the accounts. It will have predictive or confirmatory value or both.
(b) **Reliability**: the information faithfully represents transactions being materially complete, free from bias and material error and have been prudently estimated when conditions are uncertain.
(c) **Comparability**: information can be compared from one period to another and against other entities. This can usually be achieved through a combination of consistency and disclosure. Industry practices in SORPs developed with public consultation will be particularly persuasive.
(d) **Understandability**: the information is capable of being understood by users with a reasonable knowledge of business and economic activities

and accounting and a willingness to study the information with reasonable diligence.

Equally applicable to charities as to other organisations but charities preparing receipts and payments accounts (see paragraphs 350 to 356) need only apply the objective of comparability usually by applying consistent policies.

SSAP 4 Accounting Treatment of Government Grants

SSAP 4 deals with the accounting treatment and disclosure of government grants and other forms of government assistance, including grants, equity finance, subsidised loans and advisory assistance. It is also indicative of best practice for accounting for grants and assistance from other sources. **3A–227**

This SORP provides the most appropriate interpretation of SSAP 4 for charities. In particular grants for fixed assets should not be deferred though normally they will have to be accounted for in a separate fund (see paragraphs 79 and 84).

SSAP 5 Accounting for Value Added Tax (VAT)

SSAP 5 follows the general principle that the treatment of VAT in the accounts should reflect an entity's role as a collector of the tax and VAT should not be included in income or in expenditure whether of a capital or revenue nature. However where the VAT is irrecoverable, it should be included in the cost of the items reported in the financial statements. **3A–228**

Many if not all charities will suffer irrecoverable VAT either because they are not registered or have a mixture of activities which are zero and standard rated, exempt and outside the scope of VAT. The irrecoverable tax should be included in the relevant cost headings on the face of the Statement of Financial Activities and not shown as a separate item though separate disclosure of the amount may be made in the notes to the accounts.

SSAP 9 Stocks and Long-term Contracts

SSAP 9 gives guidance on the values to be included in the balance sheet of stocks and long-term contracts and the criteria for recognition of income and expenditure on such items within the profit and loss account (Statement of Financial Activities for charities). **3A–229**

Equally applicable to charities as to other entities.

SSAP 13 Accounting for Research and Development

SSAP 13 provides guidance on three broad categories of activity, namely pure research, applied research and development. The standard defines these categories and specifies the accounting policies that may be followed for each. **3A–230**

SSAP 15 Accounting for Deferred Tax
(this is to be replaced upon the finalisation of FRED 19)

FRED 19 proposes that deferred tax timing differences should be provided for in full. **3A–231**

Not generally applicable to charities.

SSAP 17 Accounting for Post Balance Sheet Events

3A–232   SSAP 17 defines the period for post balance sheet events and describes the accounting treatment for adjusting and non adjusting events. Adjusting events are those which provide additional evidence of conditions existing at the balance sheet date. Non-adjusting events are those which concern conditions that did not exist at the balance sheet date.
Equally applicable to charities as to other entities.

SSAP 19 Accounting for Investment Purposes

3A–233   SSAP 19 requires investment properties to be included in the balance sheet at their open market value, but without charging depreciation.
Equally applicable to charities as to other entities.

SSAP 20 Foreign Currency Translation

3A–234   SSAP 20 generally requires, in individual financial statements, that each transaction should be translated into the entity's local currency using the exchange rate in operation at the date of the transaction. In consolidated accounts the standard allows two alternative methods of translation of a foreign entity's financial statements, depending on whether the enterprise is a separate quasi-independent entity, or a direct extension of the trade of the investing entity.
Generally applicable to charities entering directly into transactions overseas or with branches or subsidiaries overseas. Gains should be recorded as other income in the Statement of Financial Activities and losses as support costs or management and administration costs. Where the standard permits gains and losses to be taken to reserves these should be shown as a separate line in the Statement of Financial Activities after "net incoming/outgoing resources before revaluations and investment asset disposals".

SSAP 21 Accounting for Leases and Hire Purchase Contracts

3A–235   SSAP 21 describes how to identify and account for finance leases, operating leases and hire purchase contracts both for the lessee and the lessor.
Equally applicable to charities as to other entities.

SSAP 24 Accounting for Pension Costs
(currently subject to revision under FRED 20)

3A–236   SSAP 24 deals with the accounting for, and the disclosure of, pension costs and commitments in the financial statements of entities that have pension arrangements for their employees. It requires employers to recognise the expected cost of providing pensions on a systematic and rational basis over the period during which they derive benefit from the employees' services.
   FRED 20 Retirement Benefits will replace SSAP 24 when it is finalised as an FRS. It covers pensions and other retirement benefits such as medical care. The most significant proposals are that pension scheme assets would be measured at market value at the balance sheet date rather than at an actuarial value scheme liabilities would be discounted at the current rate of return on a long-term AA corporate bond rate actuarial gains and losses (variations from regular cost) would be recognised immediately in the statement of total recognised gains and losses rather than spread forward in the profit and loss account, resulting in the surplus (subject to a recoverability test) or deficit in the scheme being shown on the balance sheet.

Equally applicable to charities as to other entities with any references to the statement of total recognised gains and losses being the bottom part of the Statement of Financial Activities for charities. However the standard does not cover the provision of voluntary retirement benefits which are provided by some charities. It may be more appropriate to use designated funds to reflect such discretionary funding arrangements.

SSAP 25 Segmental Reporting

SSAP 25 requires the disclosure by class of business and by geographical segment of turnover, segment result and segment net assets. The turnover disclosure is required by all companies otherwise the disclosure is mandatory only for PLCs, banking and insurance companies and those over ten times the threshold for medium sized companies.   3A–237

This will only be applicable to the largest charities. The disclosure requirements in the SORP for details of activities by function meets the spirit of SSAP 25 for turnover by class of activity. The disclosure by geographical region and segment net assets would be additional.

Financial Reporting Standards (FRSs)

FRS 1 Cash Flow Statements (Revised 1996)

FRS 1 (Revised 1996) requires reporting entities within its scope (two of £2.8m gross turnover; £1.4m gross assets; 50 employees) to prepare a cash flow statement in the manner set out in the FRS. (Non company charities in Scotland are bound by the limits in the Scottish Regulations 1992 being £2m gross income and £975,000 gross assets.)   3A–238

Paragraphs 272 to 277 explain the applicability of FRS 1 to charities.

FRS 2 Accounting for Subsidiary Undertakings

FRS 2 sets out the conditions under which an entity qualifies as a parent undertaking which should prepare consolidated financial statements for its group, the parent and its subsidiaries. It also sets out the manner in which consolidated financial statements are to be prepared.   3A–239

Paragraphs 299 to 319 explain consolidation and the applicability of FRS 2 to charities.

FRS 3 Reporting Financial Performance

FRS 3 requires a layered format for the profit and loss (income and expenditure) account split between continuing, newly acquired and discontinued operations. It has effectively outlawed extraordinary items. The standard also requires a statement of total recognised gains and losses to be shown as a primary statement. A note of historical profits, which is a memorandum item, is also required as is the disclosure of earnings per share.   3A–240

The Statement of Financial Activities combines both the income and expenditure account and the statement of total recognised gains and losses and meets charity law. Exceptional items should be disclosed on a separate line within the activity to which they relate. The additional requirements for charitable companies are explained in paragraphs 331 to 343. Earnings per share is not relevant to charities.

FRS 4 Capital Instruments

3A–241   FRS 4 requires capital instruments to be presented in financial statements in a way that reflects the obligations of the issuer and the impact on shareholders equity.
Not generally applicable to charities following this SORP.

FRS 5 Reporting the Substance of Transactions

3A–242   FRS 5 requires that the substance of an entity's transactions is reported in its financial statements. This requires that the commercial effect of a transaction and any resulting assets, liabilities, gains and losses are shown and that the accounts do not merely report the legal form of a transaction.
Equally applicable to charities as to other entities.

FRS 6 Accounting for Acquisitions and Mergers

3A–243   FRS 6 sets out the circumstances in which the two methods of accounting for a business combination (acquisition accounting and merger accounting) are to be used. The FRS sets out five criteria that must be met for merger accounting to be used. If they are not met then acquisition accounting should be used.
The principles of merger accounting are applicable to charities where two or more charities merge. However where funds are merely transferred from one charity to another this may constitute a gift or in the case of a restricted fund simply the administrative transfer of the restricted fund from one set of trustees to another. Two of the five criteria apply to shareholders funds and so will not be applicable to charities. Charity's cannot merge with non charitable companies and so acquisition accounting will have to be used where such companies are acquired.

FRS 7 Fair Values in Acquisition Accounting

3A–244   FRS 7 sets out the principles of accounting for a business combination under the acquisition method of accounting. It explains what "identifiable assets and liabilities" means and how to determine their fair values. The difference between the sum of these fair values and the cost of acquisition is recognised as goodwill or negative goodwill.
Equally applicable to charities as to other entities where acquisition accounting is used.

FRS 8 Related Party Disclosures

3A–245   FRS 8 determines who and what are "related parties" and the disclosures necessary to draw attention to the possibility that the reported financial position and results may have been affected by the existence of related parties and by material transactions with them.
Paragraphs 157 to 169 explain the application of FRS 8 with respect to charities.

FRS 9 Associates and Joint Ventures

3A–246   FRS 9 sets out the definitions and accounting treatments for associates and joint ventures, two types of interests that a reporting entity may have in other entities. The FRS also deals with joint arrangements that are not entities.
Paragraphs 320 to 330 explain the applicability of FRS 9 to charities.

FRS 10 Goodwill and Intangible Fixed Assets

FRS 10 requires purchased goodwill and intangible fixed assets (where market-   **3A–247**
able) to be capitalised on the balance sheet and amortised over their life, normally
regarded as 20 years, subject to impairment reviews.

*FRS 10 covers common occurrences of goodwill and intangible assets. Where a
charity has an intangible asset which does not meet the criteria under the standard it
should not be included in the primary statements but details of the asset and its
financial effect must be disclosed in the notes to the accounts.*

FRS 11 Impairment of Tangible Fixed Assets

FRS 11 sets out the principles and methodology for accounting for impairments   **3A–248**
of fixed assets and goodwill. The carrying amount of an asset is compared with its
recoverable amount and, if the carrying amount is higher, the asset is written down.
Recoverable amount is defined as the higher of the amount that could be obtained
by selling the asset (net realisable value) and the amount that could be obtained
through using the asset (value in use). Impairment tests are only required when
there has been some indication that an impairment has occurred.

Paragraphs 224 to 230 explain the applicability of FRS 11 to charities.

FRS 12 Provisions, Contingent Liabilities and Contingent Assets

FRS 12 describes the circumstances in which a provision (a liability that is of   **3A–249**
uncertain timing or amount) may arise and how it should be measured and recognised in the financial statements. It also describes how to account for contingent
assets and liabilities.

*FRS 12 is generally applicable to charities. Paragraphs 119 to 130 and 250 to 269
describe some particular application points to charities.*

FRS 13 Derivatives and Other Financial Instruments

FRS 13 specifies the disclosure for financial instruments for entities which issue   **3A–250**
such instruments (such as swaps, forwards, caps and collars, and other derivatives)
by focusing on the way in which they are used by the reporting entity.

*It does not specifically apply to charities, but any charities which fall within the
standard should nevertheless report on their use of such instruments. Charities in
England and Wales without a power to use such instruments will need to seek authorisation from the Charity Commission to do so.*

FRS 14 Earnings Per Share

Not applicable to charities.   **3A–251**

FRS 15 Tangible Fixed Assets
(effective for accounting periods ending on or after 23 March 2000)

FRS 15 sets out the principles of accounting for tangible fixed assets, with the   **3A–252**
exception of investment properties. In principle all fixed assets must be capitalised
at cost or at revalued amount. However, where an enterprise chooses to adopt a
policy of revaluing some assets, all assets of the same class must be revalued and
the valuations kept up to date.

*The principles of FRS 15 are generally applicable to charities and are embodied in
the balance sheet section of this SORP. However, there are relaxed criteria for the*

valuations of charity assets and certain inalienable and historic assets need not be capitalised in certain circumstances as explained in paragraphs 208 to 217.

FRS 16 Current Tax

3A–253   *FRS 16 is generally not applicable to charities. However, the government are paying compensation payments to charities for 5 years from April 1999 for the removal of ACT credits on the payment of UK dividends. These payments should be included as part of the charities investment income.*

FRSSE Financial Reporting Standard for Smaller Entities

3A–254   The FRSSE brings together the relevant accounting requirements and disclosures from the other accounting standards and UITF abstracts, simplified and modified as appropriate for smaller entities. The FRSSE is an optional standard but entities adopting it are exempt from applying all the other accounting standards and UITF abstracts. Financial reporting is continually evolving and therefore the FRSSE needs to be updated, roughly on an annual basis, to reflect new or revised accounting standards and UITF abstracts.

Paragraphs 345 to 347 explain the applicability of the FRSSE to smaller charities. Whilst it can be followed there are certain principles and notes within this SORP which apply to all charities and must be included in the financial statements.

Urgent Issues Task Force (UITF) Abstracts

UITF Abstract 4 Presentation of Long-term Debtors in Current Assets

3A–255   Such items should be separately disclosed on the face of the balance sheet or in the notes to the accounts.

Equally applicable to charities as to other entities.

UITF Abstract 5 Transfers from Current Assets to Fixed Assets

3A–256   *Applicable in principle to charities but unlikely to arise in practice.*

UITF Abstract 6 Accounting for Post-retirement Benefits other than Pensions (to be replaced by FRED 20)

3A–257   Where such provisions exist they must be accounted for as liabilities in a similar manner to pension costs.

Applicable to any such financial provisions made by charities which are not considered to be ex-gratia payments.

UITF Abstract 7 True and Fair View Override Disclosures (to be replaced by FRED 21)

3A–258   *Equally applicable to charities as to other entities where such an override is used.*

UITF Abstract 9 Accounting for Operations in Hyper-inflationary Economies

3A–259   *Only applicable to charities which operate in countries where such conditions exist.*

UITF Abstract 10 Disclosure of Directors' Share Options

UITF Abstract 11 Capital Instruments: Issuer Call Options

Not generally applicable to charities. **3A–260**

UITF Abstract 12 Lessee Accounting for Reverse Premiums and Similar Incentives

Equally applicable to charities as to other entities. **3A–261**

UITF Abstract 13 Accounting for ESOP Trusts

Not generally applicable to charities. **3A–262**

UITF Abstract 14 Disclosure of Changes in Accounting Policy (to be replaced by FRED 21)

Where an accounting policy is changed disclosure should be made of the effect **3A–263** on the current year as well as the previous year's result.
Equally applicable to charities as to other entities.

UITF Abstract 15 Disclosure of Substantial Acquisitions

UITF Abstract 16 Income and Expenses Subject to Non-standard Rates of Tax

UITF Abstract 17 Employee Share Schemes

Not applicable to charities. **3A–264**

UITF Abstract 18 Pensions Costs Following the 1997 Tax Changes in Respect of Dividend Income (to be replaced by FRED 20)

The probable reduction in actuarial value as a result of pension schemes no **3A–265** longer being able to claim tax credits on dividends should be spread over the remaining service lives of current employees in line with SSAP 24.
Equally applicable to charities as to other entities.

UITF Abstract 19 Tax on Gains and Losses on Foreign Currency Borrowings that Hedge an Investment in a Foreign Enterprise

Not generally applicable to charities. **3A–266**

UITF Abstract 20 Year 2000 Issues: Accounting and Disclosures

Provides guidance on accounting for costs incurred in rendering existing soft- **3A–267** ware year 2000 compliant.
Generally applicable to charities but such costs should be regarded as expenditure on activities in furtherance of the charity's objects (including grants).

UITF Abstract 21 Accounting Issues Arising from the Proposed Introduction of the Euro

3A–268   *Generally applicable to charities though it will have limited impact unless the UK adopts the euro.*

UITF Abstract 22 The Acquisition of a Lloyd's Business

3A–269   *Not applicable to charities.*

UITF Abstract 23 Application of the transitional rules in FRS 15

3A–270   Provides transitional rules on the use of prior period adjustments where tangible fixed assets which were previously treated as a single asset are identified as having two or more major components with substantially different useful economic lives. *Equally applicable to charities as to other entities.*

APPENDIX 3

The Funds of a Charity

The purpose of this appendix is to explain the legal position as regards the various funds of a charity and the implications this has for the way in which the funds are accounted for.

3A–271

1. Unrestricted Funds (including designated funds)

Unrestricted funds are expendable at the discretion of the trustees in furtherance of the charity's objects. If part of an unrestricted fund is earmarked for a particular project it may be designated as a separate fund, but the designation has an administrative purpose only, and does not legally restrict the trustees' discretion to apply the fund. Some trustees have power to declare specific trust over unrestricted funds. If such a power is available and is exercised, the assets affected will form a restricted fund, and the trustees' discretion to apply the fund will be legally restricted.

3A–272

2. Restricted Funds

Restricted funds are funds subject to specific trusts, which may be declared by the donor(s) or with their authority (*e.g.* in a public appeal) or created through legal process, but still within the wider objects of the charity. Restricted funds may be restricted income funds, which are expendable at the discretion of the trustees in furtherance of some particular aspect(s) of the objects of the charity. Or they may be capital (*i.e.* endowment) funds, where the assets are required to be invested, or retained for actual use, rather than expended. Paragraph 116 explains some of the practical indicators as to whether a fund is restricted.

3A–273

Where funds are provided for fixed assets the treatment of the fixed assets acquired with those funds will depend on the basis on which they are held. The terms on which the funds were received may require that the fixed asset which is provided should be held by the charity on trust for a specific purpose. Alternatively if the charity's governing instrument allows them to do so, the trustees may choose to settle the fixed asset on trust for a specific purpose implied by the appeal (this will be legally binding as opposed to an administrative decision taken by the trustees to include assets in a designated fund). In either case the asset will form part of restricted funds, as will a fixed asset which has itself been given to the charity on trust for a specific purpose. There is however, no general rule and the treatment will depend upon the circumstances of each individual case.

3. Endowment Funds

An endowment fund where there is no power to convert the capital into income is known as a permanent endowment fund, which must generally be held indefinitely. This concept of "permanence" does not however necessarily mean that the assets held in the endowment fund cannot be exchanged (though in some cases the trusts will require the retention of a specific asset for the actual use *e.g.* a historic building), nor does it mean that they are incapable of depreciation or less. What it does mean is that the permanent endowment fund cannot be used as if it were income (*i.e.* to make payments or grants to others), however certain payments must be made out of the endowment, such as the payment of investment management fees where these relate to investments held within the endowment. Where assets held in a permanent endowment fund are exchanged, their place in the fund must be taken by the assets received in exchange. "Exchange" here may simply

3A–274

mean a change of investment, but it may also mean, for example, the application
of the proceeds of sale of freehold land and buildings in the purchase or improvement of freehold property.

Trustees may have the power to convert endowment funds into expendable
income; such funds are known as expendable endowments. (Expendable endowment is distinguishable from "income" by the absence of a positive duty on the
part of the trustees to apply it for the purposes of the charity, unless and until this
power to convert into "income" is actually exercised.) If such a power is exercised
the relevant funds become restricted or unrestricted income, depending upon
whether the trusts permit expenditure for any of the purposes of the charity, or
only for specific purposes.

4. Asset Gains and Losses

3A–275   If a gain is made on the disposal of an asset, the gain will form part of the fund
in which the asset was held. An unrealised gain on an asset will also form part of
the fund in which the asset is held. Similarly unrealised losses and provisions for
depreciation and impairment of an asset will reduce the fund in which the asset is
(or, in the case of a realised loss, was) held. In order to ensure that gains, losses and
provisions are added to or deducted from the correct fund it is therefore essential
to know which assets and liabilities are held in which fund.

5. Restricted Income and Expenditure

3A–276   The trustess of a charity will be in breach of trust if they expend restricted
income otherwise than in furtherance of that aspect or those aspects of the objects
of the charity to which expenditure is restricted. It is therefore essential that due
care is taken to spend out of a particular restricted income fund only where the
trusts so permit. Expenditure may be charged to a restricted fund which is not at
the time in credit, or not in sufficient credit, where there is a genuine anticipation
of receipts which can properly be credited to the fund in order to meet the expenditure (e.g. where a decision has been taken to invite donations for that fund). The
fund which is actually drawn upon to finance the expenditure should be held upon
trusts which are wide enough to permit the expenditure (in case the expected
receipts do not materialise). But if expenditure has been charged to an unrestricted
fund, it should not subsequently be recharged to restricted fund receipts simply in
order to increase the fund of unrestricted income.

6. Fund Assets and Liabilities

3A–277   It is also important for the trustees to ensure that the assets and liabilities held
in a fund are consistent with the fund type; if a fund which, because of donor
restrictions, must be applied in the short term is represented by assets which cannot
reasonably be expected to be realised in the short term, there is a real possibility
that the charity will not be able to apply the funds as directed.

7. Income Application

3A–278   Where restricted income has been invested prior to application for a suitable charitable purpose, any income/gains derived from the investment will be added to, and
form part of, the restricted income fund in question. Income derived from the investment of capital (endowment) funds may be applied for the general purposes of the
charity (unrestricted income), unless a specific purpose has been declared by the
donor for the application of the income from the capital fund in question. Such
income will be applicable for that purpose and will restricted income. Gains from the
realisation of investments in a capital (endowment) fund form part of the fund itself.

APPENDIX 4

A LIST OF DISCLOSURE PARAGRAPHS MARKED AS AA
(APPLICABLE TO ALL)

Requirment	Paragraph
Duty to Prepare Annual Report and Accounts	26–29
Legal and Administrative Information	30
Charity name	30(a)
Governing document	30(b)
Trustee details	30(c)(i)–(iv)
	(v) for companies
Address of principal office	30(d)
Addresses of others	30(e)
Investment powers	30(g)
Narrative Information	31
Objects	31(a)
Organisational Structure	31(b)
Connected Parties	31(c)
Review of activities	31(d)
Policies (reserves and others as applicable)	31(e)
Funds in deficit	31(f)
Internal controls	31(g)
Particulars of individual funds and notes to the accounts	
Assets and liabilities by fund	49(a)
Nature and purpose of each fund	49(b)
Funds in deficit	49(c)
Unusual movements and transfers	49(d)
Recognition of Liabilities	
Accounting policies recognising different liabilities	128/284(a)
Costs of Generating Funds	
Categories and major items of expenditure	135
Costs of Activities in Furtherance of the charity's objects and Support Costs	
Major items in support costs	150
Management and Administration	
Major items in management and administration	152
Allocations of Costs	
Accounting policies basis and principles	154/284(c)
Trustee Remuneration	
If there is remuneration	166(b) & (c)
If there is not remumeration	166(d)
Trustee Expenses	
If there are expenses	167 & 168
If there are not expenses	172
Staff Costs and Emoluments	
If there are higher paid staff	173 & 174
If there are not any higher paid staff	175

APPENDIX 5

THRESHOLDS

Companies Act 1985 Thresholds for small companies

The current thresholds in the Companies Act 1985 s.247(3) for qualification as a small company are as follows:
Any 2 of the following 3 conditions:

Annual turnover (gross income for charities) not exceeding – £2,800,000;
Balance sheet total not exceeding – £1,400,000;
Average number of employees not exceeding – 50.

For accounting periods which are shorter or longer than 12 months the thresholds should be adjusted in proportion to the accounting period.

Any charity which comes under these thresholds whether or not it is a company may be able to apply the Financial Reporting Standard For Small Entities (FRSSE) as described in paragraphs 345–347.

The size parameters are subject to periodic amendment. The latest change was in November 1992 under SI 1992/2452.

Charities Act 1993 Threshold for audit

As at 31 October 2000: Gross income above £250,000 (set by SI 1995: No 2696 The Charities Act 1993 (Substitution of Sums) Order 1995).

Charities Act 1993 Threshold for the preparation of accruals accounts

As at 31 October 2000: Gross income above £100,000 (set by SI 1995: No 2696 The Charities Act 1993 (Substitution of Sums) Order 1995).

Law Reform (Miscellaneous Provisions) (Scotland) Act 1990 Threshold for small charities.

Charities where gross receipts do not exceedc £5,000 can prepare receipts and payments accounts unless the founding deed says that the accounts should be audited (set by SI 1992: No 2165 (s.216) The Charities Accounts (Scotland) Regulations 1992).

APPENDIX 6

THE CHARITY ACCOUNTING REVIEW COMMITTEE (1999/2000)

Membership

Chairman

John Bonds

Members

Denis Cathcart	Andrew Dobson
James Dutton	Pesh Framjee
Vanessa Harris	Nicholas Jackson
David King	Roger Morris
David Nussbaum	Adrian Randall
Elwyn Roberts	Kate Sayer
Ian Smith	

Secretary

David Bogie

CC9—POLITICAL ACTIVITIES AND CAMPAIGNING BY CHARITIES

(Version – September 1999)

Preface

Charities in England and Wales have a long and distinguished history of contributing to social reform. They continue to make an invaluable contribution to issues central to the well-being of the community today. They do so by their practical work and by their example. They have a proud record of responding to new problems and developing new ways of tackling issues. They also do so by the informed contribution they make to public debate on how issues are best addressed. This can involve participation in issues that engage the political process. Charities cannot under our law be political bodies but this does not mean that they cannot contribute to the political process. The way in which they do so must take account of the constraints which the law places on political activity by charities.

3B–001

The law is clear that charities must not have political objects. There is, however, little direct guidance from the courts on the line to be drawn between activities by charities in a political context in pursuance of their objects which are permissible and those which encroach too far into the sphere of politics. Trustees need as clear an understanding of what is permissible as can be given. This publication seeks to provide revised and amplified guidance to charity trustees on the extent to which they may properly engage in political activities. It is principally designed to give helpful guidance:

- to assist trustees to ensure that any political activities they undertake are within the law;
- to indicate how the Commission would respond to allegations or evidence of undue political activities by a charity; and
- to afford some reassurance to trustees who follow this guidance that they are acting properly.

In this spirit, Sections 5 and 6 of this publication set out specific guidance on the basis of the principles set out on the previous pages on activities which charities may and may not undertake. Given the fact that the guidance is mostly derived from general principles rather than from specific judgements of the courts, it needs to be tested on the basis of practical examples. We will accordingly keep the guidelines under review, to ensure they are developed appropriately in the light of its experience of their impact upon the activities of charities.

The guidance was originally published in July 1995. This reprint clarifies some of the language used in the original publication. We have also responded to questions charities have asked us about their involvement in demonstrations and other forms of direct action by including a new section on that topic.

3B–002

Our view of the first 18 months has been that the guidance has had a positive reception, and we sense that it is beginning to establish itself as a clear and practicable framework for charities' political and political campaigning activities. We were fortified in that view by the report of the Commission on the Future of the Voluntary Sector (July 1996). That report attached especial importance to our continuing to apply the guidance with flexibility, and we reaffirm our commitment to doing so. Our task in that respect is made easier by charities who discuss with us beforehand any proposed activity over which they have doubts.

We expect to publish further revisions in future and particularly welcome comments on the practical implications of the guidelines as part of our continuing review of their impact. Comments should be sent to the Head of Publications at our Taunton office.

John Stoker
Chief Charity Commissioner September 1999

What is this publication about?

3B–003   1. This publication gives guidance on the degrees to which charities may engage in political activity. The guidance does not represent a view of what activities are acceptable as being social or moral worth, but seeks to describe what activities we consider charities can properly undertake under the existing law.

Meaning of expressions used in this publication

3B–004   2. In this publication:

Governing document means any document which sets out the charity's purposes and, usually, how it is to be administered. It may be a trust deed, constitution, memorandum and articles of association, will, conveyance, Royal Charter, or Scheme of the Commissioners.

Political activity means any activity which is directed at securing, or opposing, any change in the law or in the policy or decisions of central government or local authorities, whether in this country or abroad.

Political purpose means in essence any purpose direct at:

- furthering the interests of any political party; or
- securing, or opposing, any change in the law or in the policy or decisions of central government or local authorities, whether in this country or abroad.

3B–005   **Trustees** means charity trustee. Charity trustees are the people who are responsible for the general control and management of the administration of the charity. In the charity's governing document they may be called trustees, managing trustees, committee members, directors or governors, or they may be referred to by some other title.

Charitable purposes mean those which the law regards as charitable. These have been extended and developed by decisions of the Court and ourselves over the years by comparison with purposes originally held to be charitable. This development of law reflects changes in social conditions, and the process continues today. Charitable purposes are characterised by a desire to benefit others for the public good; this is known as public benefit. To be a charity, all purposes of an organisation must be exclusively charitable; a charity cannot have some purposes which are charitable as well as others which are not. A charity's charitable purposes are usually expressed as its objects.

SECTION 1: INTRODUCTION

3B–006   3. Charities operate for the public benefit and their contribution to public life is immense. It includes tackling new issues and developing new ways of dealing with problems. Charities have a wealth of knowledge and experience which they can contribute to the solution, as well as the treatment, of problems relating to their area of work. The nation would be impoverished if charities were cut off entirely from public debate and the opportunity to inform decision-makers.

4. Charities must not be political organisations. But they are not precluded from

all political activity. A distinction must be made between political **purposes** and political **activities**. The Courts have made it clear that a body whose stated purposes included the attainment of a political purpose cannot be charitable (Section 2 of this publication amplifies this). A body whose purposes **are** charitable (and therefore do not include a political purpose) **may** nevertheless engage in activities which are directed at securing, or opposing, changes in the law or in government policy or decisions, whether in this country or abroad (in this publication the expression "political activities" is used in this sense). But charities cannot engage in such political activities without restraint. In this there is a crucial difference between them and non-charitable voluntary bodies. Other voluntary bodies, unlike charities, having complete freedom within the law to support any cause they like. Charities on the other hand are restricted in the extent to which they can engage in political activities by the legal rules applying to them by virtue of their charitable status.

5. The degree to which charities may engage in political activity is the subject of this publication. The Guidance does not represent a view of what activities are acceptable as being of social or moral worth but seeks to describe what activities we consider charities can properly undertake under the existing law.

6. In any case where trustees remain uncertain as to the legality of proposed activities they should not hesitate to consult their legal advisers or to seek advice from us.

3B–007

Section 2: Charitable Status: Definition of a Political Purpose

7. What charities are allowed to do is determined by the "purposes", the objects for which they are established, as set out in their governing document. An institution whose stated purposes include the attainment of a political purpose cannot be a charity. This is clear from a number of cases decided by the Courts. The reason for this is that charities must be constituted for the public benefit. The Courts have made it clear that they will not determine whether a political purpose is or is not for the public benefit. Such questions are for political debate and Parliamentary dertermination.

3B–008

8. Briefly, the Courts have held that purposes designed to promote the interests of a political party (an expression which is used in this publication to mean any local, national or European political grouping) or to seek or oppose changes in the law or government policy or decisions, whether in this country or abroad, are political purposes and not, therefore, charitable. It is possible to derive from the decisions of the Courts certain basic principles about political purposes and these are set out in the Annex to this publication.

Section 3: Extent to Which Charities may Engage in Political Activities

9. Although an organisation established for political purposes can never be a charity, the trustees of a charity may do some things of a political nature as a means of achieving the purposes of the charity.

3B–009

10. This principle, although easy to state, is not always easy to apply in practice. In applying it charity trustees must take particular care, since the dividing line between proper debate in the public arena and improper political activity is a difficult one to judge. The guidance given in this publication, which is drawn from the principles established by the Courts, is designed to help trustees to determine that line in relation to a range of activities. Any political activity undertaken by trustees must be in furtherance of, and ancillary to, the charity's stated objects and within its powers.

11. To be ancillary, activities must serve and be subordinate to the charity's purposes. They cannot, therefore, be undertaken as an end in themselves and must not be allowed to dominate the activities which the charity undertakes to carry out its charitable purposes directly. The trustees must be able to show that there is a reasonable expectation that the activities will further the purposes of the charity, and so benefit its beneficiaries, to an extent justified by the resources devoted to those activities.

3B–010   12. Where these requirements are met, trustees of charities may properly enter into dialogue with government on matters relating to their purposes or the way in which the trustees carry out their work. They may publish the advice or views they express to Ministers. They may also seek to inform and educate the public on particular issues which are relevant to the charity and its purposes, including information about their experience of the needs met in their field of activities and the solutions they advocate. But they must do so on the basis of a reasoned case and their views must be expressed with a proper sense of proportion.

13. Trustees must not advocate policies, nor seek to inform and educate, on subjects and issues which do not bear on the purposes of their charity. Moreover, the manner and content of any support of, or opposition to, legislative or policy change must be consistent with these guidelines.

14. In summary, therefore, a charity can engage in political activity if:

- there is a reasonable expectation that the activity concerned will further the stated purposes of the charity, and so benefit its beneficiaries, to an extent justified by the resources devoted to the activity;
- the activity is within the powers which the trustees have to achieve those purposes;
- the activity is consistent with these guidelines; and
- the views expressed are based on a well-founded and reasoned case and are expressed in a responsible way.

3B–011   Section 5 of this publication gives more detailed guidance on the acceptability of particular kinds of political activity.

15. Because of the need to meet these requirements it is important that any charity undertaking political activities has adequate arrangements in place for the commissioning, control and evaluation of such activities by its trustees (who are, of course, ultimately responsible for ensuring that they are properly conducted).

SECTION 4: CAMPAIGNING

3B–012   16. Campaigning by charities to mobilise public opinion to influence government policy can arouse strong feelings. On the one hand, many people think that charities should be allowed, and indeed have a duty, to campaign freely to change public policy on any issue if it is relevant to their work and if they have direct experience to offer. On the other hand, some argue that such campaigning is a misuse of charity funds, a misdirection of effort by charities and a misue of the fiscal concessions from which charities benefit. This is particularly so if the charity appears to favour a particular political party or a policy of a political party.

17. By the very nature of their knowledge and social concern, however, some charities are well placed to play a part in public debate on important issues of the day and to make an important contribution to the development of public policy. Others will invariably be drawn into such debate. It would be wrong to think that this cannot and should not happen: it is open to charities to engage in campaigning activities, provided the requirements set out in Section 3 of this publication are satisfied.

18. Whether a charity can properly engage in campaigning will, therefore, depend upon the nature of its purposes, its powers and the way in which it contributes to public debate. Where charities wish to raise issues in a way which will

inform public debate and influence decisions of public bodies, great care must be taken to ensure that the issues concerned are relevant to their purposes and that the means by which they raise them are within their powers and consistent with these guidelines.

19. A charity should not seek to organise public opinion to support or oppose a political party which advocates a particular policy favoured or opposed by the charity. It is inevitable that sometimes a policy put forward by a charity coincides with that of a particular political party, or a political party decides to adopt such a policy. It does not follow that the charity is prevented from promoting its policy on the issue. However, it may influence how it does so. In such case the charity should take particular care—especially to ensure that the independence of its view is explained and understood.   **3B–013**

20. Where a charity can properly campaign, the information provided to the public in support of the campaign as a whole must be accurate and sufficiently full to support its position. In arguing its case a charity is not restricted to using print media alone. If it uses a communications medium the nature of which makes it impracticable to set out the full basis of the charity's position, without the need to set out the full factual basis and argument lying behind that position. It must be able to set out its full position, however, if called upon to do so.

21. Provided all other requirements are met, material produced in support of a campaign may have emotional content. Indeed, we accept that in the areas in which many charities work it is difficult to avoid engaging the emotions of the public. But it would be unacceptable (except where the nature of the medium makes it impracticable to set out the basis of the charity's position) for a charity to seek to persuade government or the public on the basis of material which was **merely** emotive.

SECTION 5: WHAT POLITICAL ACTIVITIES ARE ALLOWED?

22. A charity may undertake only those activities which further its purposes and which are authorised by its governing document. If the activity involves campaigning, then in all cases the manner in which it is conducted must be in accordance with the principles set out in Section 4 of this publication.   **3B–014**

23. Where this is the case, a charity may engage in activities of the kinds shown below. Examples of activities in which a charity must **not** engage are shown in *italics*.

Influencing government or public opinion

24. A charity may seek to influence government or public opinion through well-founded, reasoned argument based on research or direct experience on issues either relating directly to the achievement of the charity's own stated purposes or relevant to the well-being of the charitable sector.   **3B–015**

25. A charity may provide information to its supporters or the public on how individual Members of Parliament or parties have voted on an issue, provided they do so in way which will enable its supporters or the public to seek to persuade those Members or parties to change their position through well-founded, reasoned argument rather than **merely** through public pressure.

26. A charity may provide its supporters, or members of the public, with material to send to Members of Parliament or the government, provided that the material amounts to well-founded, reasoned argument.

27. A charity may organise and present a petition to either House of Parliament or to national or local government. It is advisable to ensure that the purpose of the petition is stated on each page.   **3B–016**

28. *A charity must not base any attempt to influence public opinion or to put pressure on the government, whether directly or indirectly through supporters or members*

of the public, to legislate or adopt a particular policy on data which it knows (or ought to know) is inaccurate or on a distorted selection of data in support of a preconceived position.

29. A charity must not participate in party political demonstrations.

3B–017   *30. A charity must not claim evidence of public support for its position on a political issue without adequate justification.*

31. Except where the nature of the medium being employed makes it impracticable to set out the basis of the charity's position, a charity must not seek to influence government or public opinion on the basis of material which is merely emotive.

32. A charity must not invite its supporters, or the public, to take action in support of its position without providing them with sufficient information to enable them to decide whether to give their support and to take the action requested. In particular, a charity must not invite its supporters or the public to write to their Members of Parliament or the government without providing them with sufficient information to enable them to advance a reasoned argument in favour of the charity's position.

3B–018   *33. A charity whose stated purposes include the advancement of education must not overstep the boundary between education and propaganda in promoting that purpose. The distinction is between providing balanced information designed to enable people to make up their own mind and providing one-sided information designed to promote a particular point of view.*

Responding to proposed legislation

3B–019   34. A charity may provide, and publish comments on possible or proposed changes in the law or government policy, whether contained in a Green or White Paper or otherwise.

35. A charity may, in response to a Parliamentary Bill, supply to Members of either House for use in debate such relevant information and reasoned arguments as can be reasonably be expected to assest the achievement of its charitable purposes.

Advocating and opposing changes in the law and public policy

3B–020   36. A charity may advocate a change in the law or public policy which can reasonably be expected to help it to achieve its charitable purposes and may oppose a change in the law or public policy which can reasonably be expected to hinder its ability to do so. In either case the charity can present government with a reasoned written argument in support of its position. It may well publish its views and may seek to influence public opinion in favour of its position by well-founded reasoned argument.

Supporting, opposing and promoting legislation

3B–021   37. A charity may support the passage of a Bill which can reasonably be expected to help it to achieve its charitable purposes and may oppose the passage of a Bill which can reasonably be expected to hinder its ability to do so.

38. A charity may spend its funds on the promotion of public general legislation provided it has the power to do so and the legislation can reasonably be expected to further its charitable purposes.

Commenting on public issues

3B–022   39. A charity may comment publicly on social, economic and political issues if these relate to its purpose or the way in which the charity is able to carry out its work.

Supporting political parties

40. A charity may advocate a particular solution if it can reasonably be expected   **3B–023**
to further the purposes of the charity, even though that solution is advocated by a
political party. If it does so it must make plain that its views are independent of the
political party.

41. *A charity must not support a political party.*

Acting with other bodies

42. A charity may affiliate to a campaigning alliance, even if the alliance   **3B–024**
includes non-charitable organisations, provided certain conditions are met. First,
the charity must carefully consider the alliance's activities, and the implications of
the charity's being associated with them, and should only affiliate if affiliation can
reasonably be expected to further the charity's own charitable purposes. Second,
since a charity may not undertake through an alliance, activities which it would be
improper for it to undertake directly. If the alliance engages in such activities the
charity must dissociate itself from them and take reasonable steps to ensure that
its name, and any funds it has contributed, are not used to support them.

Providing information

43. A charity may provide factual information to its members and those inter-   **3B–025**
ested in its work in seeking to inform their Members of Parliament and others on
matters related to the purposes of the charity.

44. A charity may employ Parliamentary staff to inform Members of
Parliament on matters relevant to its purposes.

45. *A charity must not provide information which it knows, or ought to know, to be
inaccurate, or which has been distorted by selection to support a preconceived position.*

46. *A charity must not provide supporters or members of the public with material*   **3B–026**
*specifically designed to underpin a party political campaign or for or against a
government or particular MPs.*

47. *A charity must not issue material which supports or opposes a particular
political party or the government.*

Forthcoming elections

48. A charity may respond to forthcoming elections, whether local, national or   **3B–027**
to the European Parliament, by analysis and commenting on the proposals of
political parties which relate to its purposes or the way in which it is able to carry
out its work, provided that it comments in a way which is consistent with these
guidelines and complies with all the relevant provisions of electoral law.

49. A charity may also bring to the attention of prospective candidates issues
relating to its purposes or the way in which it is able to carry out its work, and raise
public awareness about them generally, provided that the promotional material is
educational, informative, reasoned and well-founded.

50. *A charity must not seek to persuade members of the public to vote for or
against a candidate or for or against a political party.*

Conducting and publishing research

51. A charity which conducts research must ensure that it is properly conducted   **3B–028**
using a methodology appropriate to the subject. If the research is undertaken to
test a hypothesis arising from a charity's own experience or earlier research, it must
be undertaken objectively to test that hypothesis rather than merely to support a

preconceived position or objective. The aim in publishing the results of the research must be to inform and educate the public.

52. *A charity must not distort research, or the results of research, to support a preconceived position or objective.*

53. *A charity must not promote the results of research conducted by itself of others which it knows, or ought to know, to be flawed.*

3B–029
54. *A charity must not undertake research for another body where it is clear that body intends to use the research for party political propagandist purposes.*

55. We will be producing a further publication on charities and research, which will give more guidance in this area.

Seeking support for government grants

3B–030
56. A charity may seek the support of Members of Parliament where a question arises as to whether a government grant to the charity is to be made or continued.

SECTION 6: CHARITIES INVOLVEMENT IN DEMONSTRATIONS AND DIRECT ACTION

3B–031
57. Charities may wish, as part of a campaign, to organise, promote or participate in some kind of demonstration or direct action. If this involves nothing more than the provision of reasoned argument or information (such as the handing out of leaflets in a public place) the principles stated earlier in the publication will apply to it and no particular difficulties should normally arise, whether from the point of view of organising the event or of deciding whether it is one in which the charity can properly be involved.

58. Different considerations apply if an event moves beyond the mere provision of reasoned argument or information (as may be the case, for example, with marches, rallies, or peaceful picketing). This will be so even if elements of the event, such as the speeches made before a march, involve the provision of reasoned argument or information.

59. As in the case of other types of political activity, a charity can only organise, promote or take part in activity of this kind it if forms part of a well-founded and properly argued campaign which, seen as a whole, satisfies the requirements set out in Section 3. We will respond to any failure to meet this basic requirement in the same way as any other breach of these guidelines (see Section 7).

3B–032
60. There are other matters which must also be considered by charities proposing to engage in demonstrations or direct action.

61. Whilst events of this nature may be thought to offer significant opportunities in terms of publicising a charity's position or showing the extent of public support for it on the matter in question, they can also involve significant risks.

62. Precisely because they go beyond the merely educative or informative, some people will regard any involvement by a charity in activities of this kind as inappropriate. As a result, the participation of a charity in a demonstration or direct action may damage public support for it, or even for charities generally. The further the activity moves away from reasoned argument and debate, and the more it affects the rights of others, the more likely it is that this will happen.

3B–033
63. Additionally, events such as demonstrations and rallies can of course present real problems of control. Since the law relating to public order is complex and in parts unclear, there is considerable potential for the commission of an offence by the charity, its officers or those taking part.

64. The risks of incurring civil or criminal liability, and of adverse publicity, are of course increased significantly if an event is badly organised or if other groups who do not share the aims of the organisers become involved.

65. In our view, therefore, any charity considering taking part in demonstrations or direct action must consider the implications of doing so very carefully, from the

point of view of both the possible impact on public support and potential civil or criminal liability.

66. A charity should assess whether or not it needs to seek its own legal advice on the lawfulness of what it has in mind, with a view to satisfying itself that there is no significant risk of any civil or criminal proceedings being brought against it, its trustees or members or those taking part. The greater the risk of interference with the rights of others, the more important it is that such advice should be taken, and the less likely that the activity can be justified in terms of the charity trustees' duties not to expose the property of the charity to risk.   **3B–034**

67. If the charity decides to proceed, the duty imposed on all charity trustees to act prudently will require its charity trustees to take reasonable steps to ensure that the event in question:

- receives thorough and appropriate advance preparation (including, where necessary, liaison with the police and other authorities);
- is at all times fully under the control of the charity (or of the organisers of the event, where the charity is not solely responsible for organising it);
- is peaceful;
- does not take such a form, and is not conducted in such a way, as to give rise to a significant risk of civil or criminal proceedings being brought against the charity, its trustees or members or those participating in the event; and
- does not take such a form, and is not conducted in such a way, as to bring the charity, or charities generally, into disrepute (as a result, for example, of being intimidatory, provocative or excessively disruptive of the life of the community).

68. If the charity trustees fail to take such reasonable steps, and their charity incur financial loss as a result (*e.g.* by incurring a liability to a third party following a demonstration which gets out of control) the trustees may be exposed to a claim for want of prudence in their administration of the charity, which could result in financial claims against them personally.

69. We recommend that a charity consider carefully before requiring its staff to take part in a demonstration or other form of direct action. One important consideration is that it is an implied term of employment contracts than the employer must not require the employee to do an unlawful act. While no charity will deliberately require its staff to do something that the charity knows is unlawful, equally it must take care that any instructions it gives to its staff are capable of being fully carried out in a way which will not involve, or be likely to involve, the staff in any unlawful act.   **3B–035**

70. Finally, there can generally be no objection to members or officers of a charity participating in an individual capacity in demonstrations or direct action organised by others. Charities need to take reasonable steps, however, to ensure that if members or officers do take part **in an individual capacity**, there is no misunderstanding as to the basis of their participation. In particular, a charity should not do anything (such as supplying placards or badges for the purpose) which might suggest that participants are taking part as official representatives of the charity.

SECTION 7: WHAT PENALTIES ARE THERE FOR CARRYING OUT UNACCEPTABLE POLITICAL ACTIVITIES?

71. The pursuit of improper political activities by charities is a misuse of charity funds and can lead to the loss of tax relief on funds applied for that purpose. It may also be regarded as amounting to the use of a charity as a vehicle for the personal views of its trustees. It can therefore bring about a loss of support for the charity and damage the good name of charities generally.   **3B–036**

72. We therefore expect trustees to comply with these guidelines. Where it appears that they have failed to do so we will take the matter up with them to seek an explanation.

73. In the absence of a satisfactory explanation a range of possibilities arise, including simply giving advice to the trustees, taking proceedings against them for repayment of the funds applied on the activities in question (including any additional tax liability incurred as a result) and restricting future political activity.

3B–037   74. The action taken by us will depend upon all the circumstances of the case, including:

- the scale and nature of the activity in question;
- whether the charity has engaged in improper political activities before; and
- the attitude of the charity trustees.

75. Political activity by the trustees of a charity would not normally affect its charitable status and be a reason for removing it from the Register of Charities, as the issue would concern the propriety of the trustees management of the charity rather than the nature of the charity's purposes. If, however, the trustees could argue successfully that the express purposes of the institution were wide enough to cover impermissible political activities, then the question of whether the organisation was established for exclusively charitable purposes would arise, and could lead to its removal from the Register of Charities.

SECTION 8: CONCLUSION

3B–038   76. The extent to which charities are allowed to promote, support or take part in political activities has to be considered in each case in the light of all the relevant circumstances. It is not sufficient for the trustees simply to **believe** that their activities will effectively further the purposes of the charity; there must be a **reasonable expectation** that this is so. Trustees should not hesitate to consult their legal advisers, or to seek advice from us, before undertaking any activity which might be beyond the proper scope of the charity.

77. We are always willing to give advice on any specific problem a charity may have in this connection (on the distinction between education and propaganda, for example, or between an ancillary purpose and a main purpose) and to consider the draft of any publications such as advertisements, appeals, newsletters, etc on which trustees have doubts.

DISASTER APPEALS

ATTORNEY GENERAL'S GUIDELINES

(Version January 2002)

WHAT IS THIS PUBLICATION ABOUT?

1. This publication sets out the Attorney General's guidelines about disaster appeals. They were first printed in Appendix A of our Annual Report for 1981, and have been updated in line with current legislation. **3C–001**

2. Complementary guidance on the tax treatment of appeals funds has been produced jointly by Inland Revenue and HM Customs and Excise. This is available from the Inland Revenue Appeals Funds Helpdesk (telephone 0151 472 6061) or on their website at www.inlandrevenue. gov.uk/afg/index.htm

INTRODUCTION

3. Action to set up a public appeal following some tragic accident or disaster, or an occasion on which some special misfortune is brought to the public eye, is generally taken with little time to prepare the ground. The community may well feel an urgent need to give practical expression to its sorrow and respect, and the response may well exceed expectations. **3C–002**

4. In these circumstances it is not unnatural that questions should arise over the precise status of appeals after they have been set up; and events following past tragedies have shown how much unhappiness can be caused by these questions.

5. The Attorney General is anxious that doubts about the nature of appeals should be avoided if at all possible, and that those who answer an appeal should know that their generosity will have the results which they intend.

6. Accordingly, the Attorney General, after consultation, has prepared the following guidelines which might usefully be taken into account by those faced with the responsibility of making appeals in the future. **3C–003**

THE GUIDELINES

The making of the appeal

7. Those who use these guidelines must remember that no two appeals can ever be quite the same, and should do all that they can to ensure that their own appeal is appropriate to the particular circumstances of their case, and runs into no unforeseen difficulties, whether personal, administrative, or financial. **3C–004**

8. Amongst the most important and urgent decisions which must be made will be whether or not a charitable appeal is called for, and it may well be desirable to take advice on such questions before the appeal is issued. Generally speaking, the terms of the appeal will be all-important in deciding the status and ultimate application of the fund.

9. Once the terms are agreed, it will usually be desirable to publish the appeal as soon as possible, and as widely as appropriate in the circumstances.

10. Sometimes gifts may be sent before publication of the appeal. If there are **3C–005**

more than can be acknowledged individually, the published appeal should indicate that gifts already made will be added to the appeal fund unless the donors notify the organisers (say within ten days) that this is not their wish.

Pros and cons of the types of appeal

3C–006   11. **Charitable funds** attract generous tax relief; donations to them may also do so, especially through the Gift Aid scheme, details of which are available from your local tax office. In particular, donations will also for the most part be exempt from inheritance tax.

12. But charitable funds, being essentially public in their nature, cannot be used to give individuals benefits over and above those appropriate to their needs; and the operation of a charitable trust will be subject to our scrutiny.

13. **Non-charitable funds** attract no particular tax relief; donations to them are subject to no special tax treatment (and will have to be taken into account for inheritance tax purposes unless, as is likely to be the case for the bulk of donations, they are within the normal reliefs).

3C–007   14. But under a non-charitable trust there is no limit on the amount which can be paid to individual beneficiaries if none has been imposed by the appeal; and only the Court acting on behalf of the beneficiaries will have control over the trust, which will not be subject to scrutiny by us.

15. The terms of the non-charitable appeal must be prepared with particular care to ensure that there is no doubt who is to benefit, whether or not their benefit is to be at the discretion of the trustees, and whether or not the entire benefit is to go to the beneficiaries, and if not, for example because specific purposes are laid down and the funds may be more than is required for those purposes, or because the beneficiaries are only to take as much as the trustees think appropriate, what it is to happen to any surplus.

16. If specific purposes are laid down, and after they have been fulfilled a surplus remains for which no use has been specified, the surplus will belong to the donors, which may lead to expensive and wasteful problems of administration.

Forms of appeal

3C–008   17. If a **charitable** fund is intended then the appeal could take the following form:

"This appeal is to set up a charitable fund to relieve distress caused by the

accident/disaster

at

....

on

....

The purpose is to use the funds to relieve those who may be in need of help (whether now or in the future) as a result of this tragedy in accordance with charity law. Any surplus after their needs have been met will be used for charitable purposes in one or more of the following ways:

i.   To help those who suffer in similar tragedies.
ii.   To benefit charities with related purposes.
iii. To help the locality affected by the accident/disaster"

18. If a **non-charitable** fund is intended and those affected are to take the entirety of the fund in such shares as the trustees think fit the appeal could take the following form:

"This appeal is to set up a fund, the entire benefit of which will be used for those injured or bereaved in the accident/disaster

at

....

....

on

.... and their families and dependants as the trustees think fit. This fund will not be a charity".

19. A non-charitable fund in which the trustees would have the discretion to give as much as they think fit to those who have suffered with any surplus going to charity could be set up on the basis of the following form:

"This appeal is to set up a fund for those injured or bereaved in the accident/ disaster

at

.... on

....

and their families and dependants. The trustees will have a discretion how and to what extent to benefit individual claimants: the fund will not itself be a charity but any surplus as the trustees think most appropriate to commemorate those who died".

Appeals for individuals

20. It sometimes happens that publicity given to individuals suffering moves people to give. In such a case it is particularly desirable for those who make appeals to indicate whether or not the appeal is for a charitable fund.   **3C–009**

21. It is also desirable for those who give to say whether their gift is meant for the benefit of the individual, or for charitable purposes including helping the individual so far as that is charitable; if no such intention is stated, then the donation should be acknowledged with an indication how it will be used if the donor does not dissent.

22. Those who make appeals should bear in mind the possibility that generous response may produce more than is appropriate for the needs of the individual, and should be sure to ask themselves what should be done with any surplus.

23. Thus, if a child suffers from a disease, the alternatives are: **3C–010**

- to appeal for the benefit of the child; or
- to appeal for charitable purposes relating to the suffering of the child, such as may help them and others in the same misfortune, for example by helping to find a cure.

24. It may be that the child will not live long, in which case, that child may be able to enjoy the generosity shown to them as an individual; alternatively, the child may be intended to receive as much as possible, because they face a lifetime's suffering.

25. The pros and cons of setting up a charitable fund or a non-charitable fund should be considered before the appeal is made and the appeal should indicate which alternative is intended; once again, even if a non-charitable appeal is made, it may be thought right to make it on terms that any surplus can be used for charity.

Generally

3C–011   26. The terms of appeal suggested in this memorandum are only examples of forms which can be used; and before making an appeal it is always wise to seek advice on what form to use.

27. We will always be ready as a matter of urgency to advise on the terms of any intended charitable appeal, or to consider whether a proposed appeal is likely to be charitable, and if so to advise on the likely consequences.

28. In conclusion, the Attorney General would like to emphasise that those organising an appeal should do all they can to make sure that the purpose of the appeal is clear and that donors know how their gifts will be used.

3C–012   29. This will do much to reduce the risk of confusion and distress. It is considered undesirable to make a general appeal postponing until the size of the fund is known decisions whether the fund ought to be charitable and whether those affected should take the entire benefit; this can all too easily lead both donors and beneficiaries to form the view that the ultimate result is not what was intended, as well as giving rise to legal problems.

Appendix Four

WEB SITE ADDRESSES

Charity Commission—**www.charity-commission.gov.uk**

H.M. Customs and Excise—**www.hmce.gov.uk**

Inland Revenue—**www.inlandrevenue.gov.uk**

H.M. Land Registry—**www.landreg.gov.uk**

The Lord Chancellor's Department—for the Civil Procedure Rules—**www.lcd.gov.uk**

National Council for Voluntary Organisations—
www.ncvo-vol.org.uk

Wales Council for Voluntary Action—**www.wcva.org.uk**

Northern Ireland Council for Voluntary Action—
www.nicva.org

Association of Charitable Foundations—**www.acf.org.uk**

Charities Aid Foundation—**www.cafonline.org**

Institute of Fundraising—**www.institute-of-fundraising.org.uk**

Association of Fundraising Consultants—**www.afc.org.uk**

Independent Television Commission—**www.itc.org.uk**

Committee of Advertising Practice—**www.cap.org.uk**

Public Fundraising Regulatory Association—
www.pfra.org.uk

INDEX